The SAGE
Handbook *of*

Visual Research
Methods

SAGE has been part of the global academic community since 1965, supporting high quality research and learning that transforms society and our understanding of individuals, groups, and cultures. SAGE is the independent, innovative, natural home for authors, editors, and societies who share our commitment and passion for the social sciences.

Find out more at: **www.sagepublications.com**

The SAGE
Handbook *of*

Visual Research
Methods

Edited by
Eric Margolis
and
Luc Pauwels

Los Angeles | London | New Delhi
Singapore | Washington DC

First published 2011
Reprinted 2012

SAGE Publications Ltd
1 Oliver's Yard
55 City Road
London EC1Y 1SP

SAGE Publications Inc.
2455 Teller Road
Thousand Oaks, California 91320

SAGE Publications India Pvt Ltd
B 1/I 1 Mohan Cooperative Industrial Area
Mathura Road, Post Bag 7
New Delhi 110 044

SAGE Publications Asia-Pacific Pte Ltd
3 Church Street
#10-04 Samsung Hub
Singapore 049483

Library of Congress Control Number available

British Library Cataloguing in Publication data

A catalogue record for this book is available from the British Library

ISBN 978-1-84787-556-3

Typeset by Cenveo Publisher Services
Printed by MPG Books Group, Bodmin, Cornwall
Printed on paper from sustainable resources

MIX
Paper from
responsible sources
FSC® C018575

Contents

Color versions of the images used in the book are available on a companion website to the book which can be found at: www.sagepub.co.uk/margolis

About the Authors

Jan Baetens is professor of cultural studies at the Katholieke Universiteit Leuven (Belgium). He has published widely on word and image studies, mainly in the specific domain of so-called 'minor' genres (graphic novel, photonovella, novelization). He has also a special interest in the relationships between photography and poetry as well as in the field of constrained writing. His most recent book is *Pour le roman-photo* (2010).

Michael Ball is a senior lecturer in sociology and anthropology at Staffordshire University, UK. His work in the field of visual sociology includes *Analyzing Visual Data* (1992) and 'Technologies of Realism?' (in P.A. Atkinson et al., eds., *Handbook of Ethnography*, 2001), both written with Gregory Smith. Mike has research interests in ethnomethodology, interaction, police work, Buddhism and the philosophy of mind. He has published three edited collections that explore comparative methods of visual research. He has also published an edited collection of studies of Buddhist practice including visualization. He is currently working on books on Buddhism and visualization, and a text book on social theory.

Raewyn Bassett is an Assistant Professor (Sociology) with the Faculty of Health Professions, Dalhousie University, and qualitative methodologist with the Capital Health District Authority, Halifax, Nova Scotia, Canada. Her interests and research lie at the intersection of researcher, data analysis software programs, and qualitative methodologies and methods. She uses a range of data sources, including maps, drawings, diagrams, photographs, video, and audio. Raewyn provides workshops in a number of qualitative software programs, and seminars in qualitative research methodologies and methods and their use within qualitative software programs. Currently, she is developing and exploring novel qualitative research methods using new technologies; examining researchers' engagement with qualitative software; and investigating the influence of technologies such as qualitative software and digital tools including cellular phones and geographic positioning systems (GPS) on qualitative methodologies. She has published on methodological issues in peer review journals and reference books.

Annekatrin Bock is an Assistant Professor and doctoral candidate at the media research division of the Institute of Social Sciences at the Technical University Brunswick, Germany. She studied media and communication studies, business and social psychology and business studies at the University of Göttingen, Germany. For her dissertation she is concerned with the contexts in which production, distribution, and reception of contemporary US-American television prime time series take place. Her research foci are American television series, reception studies, film and television studies as well as online research.

Prasad Boradkar is Associate Professor and Coordinator of Industrial Design at Arizona State University in Tempe. He is the Director of InnovationSpace, a transdisciplinary laboratory at

Arizona State University where students and faculty partner with corporations to explore human-centered product concepts that improve society and the environment. His research activities focus on using cultural theory to understand the social significance of the designed environment. His publications include several articles and a book titled *Designing Things: A Critical Introduction to the Culture of Objects* (2010).

Richard Chalfen is Senior Scientist at the Center of Media and Child Health at Children's Hospital Boston/Harvard Medical School/Harvard School of Public Health. He is also Emeritus Professor of Anthropology at Temple University, former Chair of their Department of Anthropology and Director of the MA Program in Visual Anthropology. He is past president of the American Anthropological Association's Society of Visual Anthropology and recent recipient of their Lifetime Achievement Award. His research combines interests in cultural anthropology and visual communication, American Studies and, for the past 15 years, the visual culture of modern Japan. At the Center, he focuses on applying participant media research methods to studies of childhood chronic illness and to relationships of mobile telephonic media and young people. Publications include *Snapshot Version of Life* (1987), *Turning Leaves* (1997), and *Through Navajo Eyes* (co-author, 2001).

Elizabeth Chaplin calls herself 'a grandmother with a cameraphone.' She has kept a daily photo diary for 20 years. Before her retirement Elizabeth Chaplin was an associate lecturer for the Open University UK and a visiting lecturer in sociology at York University UK. She is the author of *Sociology and Visual Representation* (Routledge, 1994).

James Chapman is Professor of Film at the University of Leicester (UK). He has wide-ranging research interests in the history of British cinema, television, and popular culture. His books include: *The British at War: Cinema, State and Propaganda, 1939–1945* (1998), *Past and Present: National Identity and the British Historical Film* (2005), and *Licence To Thrill: A Cultural History of the James Bond Films* (second edition, 2007). He co-edited (with Sue Harper and Mark Glancy) *The New Film History: Sources, Methods, Approaches* (2007) and in 2011 became editor of the *Historical Journal of Film, Radio and Television*.

Andrew Clark is Lecturer in Sociology in the School of English, Sociology, Politics and Contemporary History at the University of Salford, UK. Previously, he worked as a research fellow for the Economic and Social Research Council funded National Centre for Research Methods: Real Life Methods Node at the University of Leeds, UK. His research focuses on the interplay between space, place, and everyday life, specifically in relation to neighborhoods and community, and inequalities and social exclusion. He also has a keen interest in methodological creativity and innovation. Recent publications have appeared in the journals *Arts and Health: An International Journal for Research, Policy and Practice*, *Journal of Youth Studies*, and the *International Journal of Social Research Methodology, Theory and Practice*.

Dan Collins joined the School of Art faculty at Arizona State University in 1989. He is founding Co-Director of the PRISM lab (a 3D modeling and prototyping facility) and coordinator of the foundation art program (artCore). Collins studied studio art and art history at the University of California, Davis, receiving a Bachelor of Arts degree in 1974. He holds a Master of Arts degree in Art Education from Stanford University (1975), a Master of Fine Arts (MFA) in 'New Forms' and Sculpture from UCLA (1984), and a PhD in Interdisciplinary Humanities from Arizona State University (2009). Collins's research investigates 'the gap between the body and technology—between the hand-made and the high-tech.' His recent publications and professional presentations explore 3D data capture, interactive educational media, and participatory mapping.

Roderick Coover is Associate Professor of Film and Media Arts at Temple University in Philadelphia, where he teaches media arts, visual research, and critical theory. An innovator in bridging the fields of visual research and interactive documentary production, Coover makes films such as *Verité to Virtual* (DER), *The Theory of Time Here* (Video Data Bank), and *The Language of Wine* (languageofwine.com) as well as interactive projects including *Cultures in Webs* (Eastgate Systems), *Outside/Inside* (American Philosophical Society Museum), and *Unknown Territories* (unknownterritories.org). Coover's essays are published in journals of film, anthropology, and digital culture, and he is the co-editor of the book, *Switching Codes: Thinking through Digital Technologies in the Humanities and Arts* (Chicago). His awards include USIS-Fulbright, the LEF Foundation, and the Mellon Foundation grants, among others.

Naydene de Lange holds the newly established HIV and AIDS Research Chair in the Faculty of Education at the Nelson Mandela Metropolitan University, Port Elizabeth, South Africa. Her research focuses on visual participatory methodologies in addressing gender and HIV&AIDS, particularly in rural communities. She publishes in international and national journals and is first editor of the book, *Putting People in the Picture: Visual Methodologies for Social Change* (2007) and co-author of the book, *Picturing Hope* (2009). She has headed up and collaborates in various funded research projects. She is also a National Research Foundation (South Africa) rated researcher.

Tirupalavanam G. Ganesh is Assistant Professor of Engineering Education at Arizona State University's Ira A. Fulton Schools of Engineering. He has bachelors and masters degrees in Computer Science and Engineering and a PhD in Curriculum and Instruction. His research interests include educational research methods, communication of research, and k-16+ engineering education. Ganesh's research is largely focused on studying k-12 curricula, and teaching-learning processes in both the formal and informal settings. He is principal investigator of the National Science Foundation sponsored project (2007–2011) Learning through Engineering Design and Practice aimed at designing, implementing, and systematically studying the impact an informal middle-school engineering education program.

John Grady is the William I. Cole Professor of Sociology at Wheaton College in Norton, Massachusetts. He is a past president of the International Visual Sociology Association (IVSA). He is currently the New Media Editor for *Visual Studies*. His research and teaching interests include the study of cities, technology, and social organization. He has written extensively on visual sociology in general and on the use of the visual mass media as evidence for social and cultural analysis. He has produced numerous documentary films including *Mission Hill and the Miracle of Boston* (1979) and *Water and the Dream of the Engineers* (1983).

Brian Gran is on the faculty of the Sociology Department and Law School of Case Western Reserve University. His research focuses on how law is used to designate public-private boundaries in social life. Gran is writing a book tentatively entitled, *Rarely Pure and Never Simple: Law and the Public-Private Dichotomy.*

Holger Isermann is an Assistant Professor and doctoral candidate at the media research division of the Institute of Social Sciences at the Technical University Brunswick. He studied media studies, mass communication, politics, film studies, and technical media at the University of Iceland, the Technical University Brunswick, and the Brunswick University of Art. Holger's primary research interests are journalism, science communication, and visual communication. He has also been working as a freelance journalist and photographer for several years.

Arvid Kappas has been Professor of Psychology at Jacobs University Bremen since 2003. He has been conducting research on emotions for over two decades in the USA, Canada, and in several European countries. Kappas is associate editor of *Emotion* and *Biological Psychology* and on the editorial boards of *Cognition and Emotion* and the *Journal of Nonverbal Behavior*. He is active in numerous scientific societies—at present he is a member of the executive board of *HUMAINE*. The focus of his research is on the causes and moderators of emotional behaviors, including what people feel and express as well as bodily reactions that can be assessed using psychophysiological methods. He is interested in intra- and interpersonal processes, specifically in direct or mediated communication including via the Internet. Kappas is on the steering committee of the research center, Visual Communication and Expertise (VisComX), at Jacobs University as well as on the scientific advisory committee of the Emotion Centre at the University of Portsmouth.

Mark Klett is a photographer interested in the intersection of cultures, landscapes, and time. His background includes working as a geologist before turning to photography. Klett has received fellowships from the Guggenheim Foundation, the National Endowment for the Arts, and the Japan/US Friendship Commission. Klett's work has been exhibited and published both in the USA and internationally for over 30 years, and his work is held in over 80 museum collections worldwide. He is the author of thirteen books including *Saguaros* (Radius Press and DAP, 2007), *After the Ruins* (University of California Press, 2006), *Yosemite in Time* (Trinity University Press, 2005), and *Third Views, Second Sights* (Museum of New Mexico Press, 2004), *Revealing Territory* (University of New Mexico Press, 1990), and *Second View, the Rephotographic Survey Project* (University of New Mexico Press, 1984). Klett lives in Tempe, Arizona where he is Regents' Professor of Art at Arizona State University.

Thomas Knieper his primary research interests are journalism, computer-mediated communication, methods, and visual communication. He studied mass communication, statistics, psychology, sociology, and philosophy of science. He received his diploma in statistics in 1989 on the topic of new methods in visualizing hierarchical cluster analysis. He received his doctoral degree in Mass Communication in 1995 on the topic of infographics. His postdoctoral thesis in 2001 was about editorial cartooning. From 2000 till 2004, together with Marion G. Müller, he co-chaired the Visual Communication Group in the German Association of Journalism and Mass Communication (DGPuK). In 2004, he became a full member of the Human Science Center (LMU Munich). Since 2008, he has been a full Professor of Mass Communication and Media at the Technical University Brunswick.

Hubert Knoblauch is Professor of General Sociology at the Technical University Berlin. His major interests include the sociology of knowledge, communication, and religion. Publications include: *Visual Analysis. New Developments in the Interpretative Analysis of Video and Photography Special Volume of Forum: Qualitative Social Research* (co-edited with Alejandro Baer, Eric Laurier, Sabine Petschke, and Bernt Schnettler, 2008); *Conocimento y sociedad. Ensayos sobre acción, religión y communicación* (co-edited with Bernt Schnettler and Jürgen Raab), *Video Analysis. Methodology and Methods. Qualitative Audiovisual Data Analysis in Sociology* (co-edited with Bernt Schnettler, Jürgen Raab, and Hans-Georg Soeffner, 2008), *Qualitative Methods in Europe: The Variety of Social Research Special Volume of Forum Qualitative Social Research* (co-edited with Uwe Flick and Christoph Maeder, 2005).

Francesco Lapenta is Associate Professor in Visual Culture and New Media at the Department of Communication, Business and Information Technologies, at the University of Roskilde. He is a member of the editorial board of the journal "Visual Studies", Taylor and Francis, Cambridge, and a member of the executive board of the Intentional Visual Sociology Association and currently a Visiting Professor at the Sociology Department of New York University. Lapenta's most recent work includes the special issue "Autonomy and Creative Labour" of the Journal for Cultural Research July 2010, and the article "Geomedia: on Location-Based Media, the Changing Status of Collective Image Production and the Emergence of Social Navigation Systems". He recently edited the special issue of Visual Studies,"Locative Media and the Digital Visualisation of Space, Place and Information " (March 2011).

David MacDougall is a documentary filmmaker and writer on cinema. He was educated at Harvard University and UCLA. His first feature-length film, *To Live With Herds*, won the Grand Prix Venezia Genti in 1972. Soon after this, he and his wife, Judith MacDougall, produced the *Turkana Conversations* trilogy of films in Kenya. He directed a number of films on indigenous communities in Australia; then in 1991 co-directed a film on photographic practices in an Indian hill town, and in 1993 made a film on goat herders of Sardinia. In 1997, he began a film study of the Doon School in India. His recent filming has been at a co-educational school in South India and a shelter for homeless children in New Delhi. MacDougall writes regularly on documentary and ethnographic cinema and is the author of *Transcultural Cinema* and *The Corporeal Image: Film, Ethnography, and the Senses*. He is presently a senior researcher at the Australian National University.

Eric Margolis is a sociologist and teaches in the Hugh Downs School of Human Communication at Arizona State University. He is the President of The International Visual Sociology Association. His visual ethnography of coal miners was broadcast as *Out of the Depth—The Miners' Story*, a segment of the PBS series *A Walk Through the 20th Century with Bill Moyers*. An article, 'Class Pictures: Representations of Race, Gender and Ability in a Century of School Photography,' (*Visual Sociology* Vol. 14, 1999) was reprinted in Education Policy Analysis Archives http://epaa.asu.edu/epaa/v8n31/ and received 'Honorable Mention' for Best Article in an Electronic Journal by the Communication of Research Special Interest Group of the American Educational Research Association. Forthcoming visual research includes: 'Architectural and Built Environment Discourses in an Educational Context: The Gottscho and Schleisner Collection' with Sheila Fram, *Visual Studies*, and School as Ceremony and Ritual: Photography Illuminates Moments of Ideological Transfer with Drew and Sharon Chappell (*Qualitative Inquiry* 2011).

Ray McDermott is a Professor of Education at Stanford University. For 40 years, he has used the tools of cultural analysis to critique how children learn, how schools work, and why Americans have invested so heavily in the institution of school failure. Recently, he has been working on the intellectual history of American ideas about learning, genius, and intelligence. He is the author (with Hervé Varenne) of *Successful Failure: The Schools America Builds* (1998).

Innisfree McKinnon is a PhD candidate in Geography at the University of Oregon. Her research interests include qualitative geographic information systems (GIS) and mixed methods research, the political ecology of industrial and post-industrial societies, social justice issues in relation to conservation and planning, and critical geographies of children and youth. Her dissertation examines the scale of government regulation in relation to land use, planning, and conservation. This research investigates a case study in Southern Oregon's Rogue Valley, where rapid urbanization is threatening rural livelihoods and lifestyles.

Claudia Mitchell is a James McGill Professor in the Faculty of Education of McGill University, Montreal, Canada. She is also an Honorary Professor in the School of Language, Literacies, Media and Drama Education at the University of KwaZulu-Natal in South Africa, where she is a co-founder of the Center for Visual Methodologies for Social Change. Her research looks at youth and sexuality in the age of AIDS, children's popular culture, rurality, girlhood, teacher identity, participatory visual and other arts-based methodologies, and strategic areas of gender and HIV&AIDS in social development contexts in South Africa, Rwanda, and Ethiopia. Her recent books include: *Making Connections: Self-study and Social Action* (co-edited with K. Pithouse and R. Moletsane) and *Teaching and HIV&AIDS* (with K. Pithouse). She is the co-founder and co-editor of *Girlhood Studies: An Interdisciplinary Journal*.

Marion G. Müller is Associate Professor of Mass Communication at Jacobs University Bremen, Germany. Her work is located at the intersection of visual communication, political science, and art history, applying iconology as a method of qualitative visual content analysis to questions arising in the social sciences. She has published extensively on the theory of visual communication, for example, the first textbook in German on *Grundlagen der visuellen Kommunikation* (Foundations of Visual Communication, 2003), and in 2008 edited a special issue of *Visual Studies* on the topic of *Visual Competence—A New Paradigm for Studying Visuals in the Social Sciences?* Her current interests are related to the role visuals play in war and conflict, particularly press photography and caricature. In 2000, she co-founded the Visual Communication Division of the German Communication Association (DGPuK), and since 2009 she has been Director of the Research Center, Visual Communication and Expertise (VisComX), at Jacobs University Bremen.

Darren Newbury is Professor of Photography at Birmingham Institute of Art and Design, Birmingham City University. He has a background in photography and cultural studies, and completed his PhD on photography and education in 1995. He has published widely on photography, photographic education, and visual research. His most recent research has focused on the development of photography in apartheid South Africa and the re-use of historical images as a form of memorialization in contemporary post-apartheid displays. His book on the subject, *Defiant Images: Photography and Apartheid South Africa*, was published by the University of South Africa (UNISA) Press in 2009. He has been editor of the international journal *Visual Studies* since 2003.

Winfried Nöth is Professor of Linguistics and Semiotics at the University of Kassel and Visiting Professor at the Catholic University of São Paulo. Nöth's 250 articles and 27 authored or edited books are on topics of English linguistics, semiotic aspects of language, literature, the image, maps, the media, systems theory, culture and evolution. His *Handbook of Semiotics* (translated into Bahasa and from its second revised German edition also into Croatian) was awarded the Choice Outstanding Academic Book prize. Among his other books are

Literatursemiotische Analysen—zu Lewis Carrolls Alice-Büchern, *Origins of Semiosis*, *Semiotics of the Media*, *Crisis of Representation* (with C. Ljungberg), *Imagen: Comunicación, semiótica y medios*, *Comunicação e semiótica* (both with L. Santaella), *Self-Reference in the Media* (with N. Bishara), *Mediale Selbstreferenz: Grundlagen und Fallstudien zu Werbung, Computerspiel und Comics* (with B. Bishara and B. Neitzel), and *Estratégias semióticas da publicidade* (with L. Santaella).

Dónal O'Donoghue is an Associate Professor in the Faculty of Education at the University of British Columbia (UBC), Vancouver, Canada, where he serves as Chair of Art Education. His research interests are in art education, arts-based visual research methodologies, curriculum theory, and masculinities. He has published widely in these areas and received the 2010 Manuel Barkan Memorial Award from the National Art Education Association (United States) for his scholarly writing. His current SSHRC funded research investigates place-cultures and place-making practices in private boys' schools. Prior to his appointment at UBC, he taught at the University of Limerick, Mary Immaculate College, Ireland. He serves as Editor of the Canadian Review of Art Education, a member of The NAEA Council for Policy Studies Art Education, The NAEA Higher Education Division Research Steering Committee, IVSA Executive Board and Studies in Art Education Editorial Board. Previously, he served as the Honorary Secretary of the Arts Based Educational Research SIG of AERA and the Educational Studies Association of Ireland. As an artist, he has exhibited his work in Europe and North America. He can be reached at: donalod@interchange.ubc.ca

Bettina Olk is Assistant Professor of Psychology at Jacobs University Bremen, Germany. Past and present research in Cognitive Psychology and Neuropsychology, which she has conducted at the University of Bristol (UK), the University of British Columbia (Vancouver, Canada), Rice University (Houston, USA), and is now carrying out at Jacobs University, focuses on the control of visual attention and eye movements. She employs methods such as eye tracking, transcranial magnetic stimulation and the assessment of patients with brain injury, to study the interaction between involuntary and voluntary attention/eye movements in the healthy and injured brain. Her work is published in international peer-reviewed journals. She is a member of the Research Center, Visual Communication and Expertise (VisComX), Cognitive Systems and Processes (COSYP) and Aging—Interaction of Processes (AGEACT) at Jacobs University. She is reviewer for more than fifteen international journals and a member of international societies, for example, the Psychonomic Society and the Vision Sciences Society.

Luc Pauwels is a Professor of Visual Culture at the University of Antwerp (Department of Communication Studies), Belgium. He is the director of the 'Visual Studies and Media Culture Research Group' and responsible for the Master program in 'Film Studies and Visual Culture' in Antwerp. Currently, Pauwels is the Chair of the Visual Communication Studies Division of the International Communication Association (ICA), and Vice-President of the International Visual Sociology Association (IVSA). As a visual sociologist and communication scientist, he has written extensively on visual research methodologies, visual ethics, family photography, website analysis, anthropological filmmaking, visual corporate culture, and scientific visualization in various international journals. Books include: *Visual Cultures of Science: Visual Representation and Expression in Scientific Knowledge Building and Science Communication* (2006), *Methodisch kijken: aspecten van onderzoek naar film- en beeldcultuur* (2007) and a forthcoming monograph with Cambridge University Press: *Reframing Visual Sociology*. Email: *luc.pauwels@ua.ac.be*

Sarah Pink is Professor of Social Sciences at Loughborough University. Her work, rooted in social anthropology, crosses social science, humanities, arts, design and engineering disciplines and makes connections between the agendas of academic, applied, and public scholarship. Her research covers everyday life practices and socialites in domestic and public environments, the senses, media, energy, sustainability and activism, and spatial and practice theories. Her methodological work develops principles for visual, digital, and sensory methods and media in research. Her recent books include: *The Future of Visual Anthropology* (2006), *Visual Interventions* (2007), *Doing Visual Ethnography* (2007), and *Doing Sensory Ethnography* (2009).

Jon Prosser is Director of the International Education Management program and a member of the Leeds Social Science Institute at Leeds University, UK. He was project leader for the Economic and Social Research Council's 'Building Capacity in Visual Methods' which was part of the UK Researcher Development Initiative. He was involved as a visual methodologist in the 'Real Life Methods' project based at Leeds and Manchester universities. Currently, he is contributing to the 'Realities' program based at the Morgan Centre, University of Manchester, and a study of Visual Ethics led by Rose Wiles, both funded by the National Centre for Research Methods. He is perhaps best known for editing *Image-based Research: A Sourcebook for Qualitative Researchers* (1998), which was the first book in the field to present visual research not as a 'stand-alone' strategy taking one particular form or perspective, but as a theoretically and methodologically varied approach that drew on other approaches to conducting research.

Jason Duque Raley is Lecturer SOE in the Gevirtz School of Education at the University of California, Santa Barbara. His current research explores the substance, conduct, and consequence of social relations in educational encounters, with a special focus on matters of trust and authority. While celebrating the ingenuity of children and adults improvising their way through everyday activities, his analyses aim to identify moments where such relations can be re-arranged. His work is oriented by the question of whether schools can be made to recover a democratic function. When not writing, teaching, or making video analyses, Raley grows avocadoes and citrus fruits in the Santa Clara River Valley in Ventura County, California.

Jon H. Rieger received his PhD at Michigan State University (MSU) in 1971 and is a Professor of Sociology at the University of Louisville. After years of engagement in longitudinal survey research, notably in a long-running MSU project in Ontonagon County in Michigan's Upper Peninsula, Professor Rieger became interested in visual approaches to sociological inquiry. As one of the founders of the visual sociology movement and a charter member of the IVSA, he served as secretary-treasurer of the organization for more than ten years. In his research in visual sociology, Dr. Rieger is best known for having pioneered the development of the visual method for studying social change that emphasizes various strategies of repeat photography. His 1996 article 'Photographing Social Change,' published in *Visual Sociology*, is widely considered a landmark of scholarship in this area.

Jeremy Rowe has collected, researched, and written about nineteenth and early twentieth century photographs for twenty-five years. He has written *Arizona Photographers 1850–1920: A History and Directory* and *Arizona Real Photo Postcards: A History and Portfolio*, and a number of articles on historic photographers of the Southwest. Rowe worked with the early development of the Library of Congress American Memory project, a digital historic photographic collection. Rowe has curated a number of photographic exhibitions, consults with collectors, museums and archives regarding historic photography, and manages http://vintage-photo.com. He was the Executive Director of the School of Computing and Informatics at Arizona State University, and is now research faculty. Dr. Rowe has been keynote speaker for the International Visual Literacy Association and Ephemera Society of America, and is on the board of the Daguerreian Society.

Gregory Smith is Professor of Sociology at the University of Salford. He has written *Analyzing Visual Data*, with Michael Ball and several articles in the field of visual sociology. He is a co-author of *Introducing Cultural Studies* (second edition, 2008). He has broad interests in the history and practice of interactionist sociology and has published three books on the sociology of Erving Goffman. Currently, he is working on a project about security in public places and an intellectual biography of Goffman.

Steven Surdiacourt has a Master Degree in German and Dutch literature and in Cultural Studies. He is currently a PhD fellow of Fonds Wetenschappelijk Onderzoek (FWO) Flanders at the Katholieke Universiteit Leuven (Belgium). His main interests lie in the field of visual studies, particularly in the relation between image and text. He wrote his Master's thesis about the representation of post-war German identity in René Burri's documentary work. His PhD research focuses on the narratology of the graphic novel, in a synchronic and a diachronic perspective. He is also interested in the pictorial representation of individual writers and in the consequences of Bruno Latour's thinking for media theory.

René Tuma is Research Assistant at the Technical University Berlin, Germany. His major interests include the sociology of knowledge, communication, and technology. Besides working with video analysis his current work focuses on the sociological study of the practices of video analysis. He is interested how video technology is used in a variety of fields.

Theo van Leeuwen is Professor of Media and Communication and Dean of the Faculty of Arts and Social Sciences at the University of Technology, Sydney. He has published widely in the area of visual communication, multimodality, and critical discourse analysis. He is a founding editor of the journal *Visual Communication*. His latest books include: *Global Media Discourse* (with David Machin, 2007) and *Discourse and Practice—New Tools for Critical Discourse Analysis* (2008). His new book, *The Language of Colour*, will be published in late 2010.

Jon Wagner is Professor Emeritus in the School of Education at the University of California, Davis. His research focuses on children's material culture, qualitative and visual research methods, school change, and the social and philosophical foundations of education. He is a past President of the International Visual Sociology Association and was the founding Image Editor of *Contexts*, the American Sociological Association's general interest publication. He authored *Misfits and Missionaries: A School for Black Dropouts* (1977), and also edited two volumes that focus on the intersection of visual studies and social research: *Images of Information: Still Photography in the Social Sciences* (1979) and *Visual Sociology 14(1 and 2): Seeing Kids, Worlds* (1999).

Rose Wiles is Co-Director and Principal Research Fellow at the National Centre for Research Methods (NCRM) Hub at the University of Southampton, UK. Her interests are in research ethics, qualitative research methods, innovation in research methods and medical sociology. Along with her colleagues, Sue Heath and Graham Crow, she conducted a study of informed consent as part of the Economic and Social Research Council's Research Methods Programme. In collaboration with colleagues from, and funded by the NCRM, she recently conducted a study of visual researchers' views and experiences of visual ethics. Recent publications have appeared in the journals *Arts and Health*; *Social Science and Medicine*; and the *International Journal of Social Research Methodology*.

Terence Wright is Professor of Visual Arts and Director of the Master of Fine Art Photography programme at the University of Ulster. For ten years, he worked for BBC Television News and Current Affairs and Independent Television News (ITN). He produced and directed *The Interactive Village* (2007): a digital ethnography for broadband delivery as part of 'NM2' (*New Millennium, New Media* European Union funded research project: www.ist-nm2.org) and *The River Boyne* (2009): mobile media guide funded by FUSION (a cross-border economic development initiative forming part of the Northern Ireland Peace Process). He is the author of *The Photography Handbook* (1999 and 2004) and *Visual Impact: Culture and the Meaning of Images* (2008). His current research focuses on the role of visualization in the representation of contested histories, identity and heritage, and their contemporary political ramifications.

Preface: Aims and Organization of this Handbook

Throughout the past several decades, visual research as a methodology and research on the visual as a topic of interest have produced an increasingly articulated set of paradigms and fields.

This handbook seeks to provide an accessible and coherent 'state-of-the-art' account of visual research across a growing number of disciplines and from a host of different perspectives.

It is intended as a guide for those new to the field, and interested in designing visual research projects, but also as a companion for seasoned visual researchers. We expect readers to come from across the academic spectrum: sociology, anthropology, psychology, communication, media studies, education, cultural studies, journalism, health, nursing, women's studies, ethnic studies, global studies, cultural geography, art and design, etc.

The handbook elucidates the theoretical currents and key controversies, but also different approaches to gathering, analyzing, and presenting visual data. It aims to present 'cutting-edge' as well as long-standing and recognized practices, exemplify both the best and most recent methods and techniques, and also present some emerging trends and debates.

Because visual research methods and interest in visual studies are global phenomena, we tried to include contributors, both leading authorities and new voices, from a wide geographical spread and from a variety of disciplinary backgrounds: sociology, anthropology, communication studies, geography, psychology, photography, the fine arts, history, film studies, education, semiotics, and legal studies, among others.

While a certain coherence is pursued in this handbook, it is not achieved by suppressing points of view or imposing an artificial uniformity based on just a few dominant theoretical perspectives. The contributions represent a wide range of epistemological positions and include methods and techniques as varied as eye tracking research, autoethnography, and arts-based approaches.

It was the deliberate choice of the handbook editors to reflect the empirical, theoretical, and methodological diversity typical for this burgeoning field of research. Authors were encouraged to present their views in substantiated ways, even if their views at times diverted or contradicted those of other contributors, including those of the editors. Thus, the handbook does not produce a consistent view or voice, but seeks to exemplify the diversity in methods and techniques as well as the sometimes conflicting views and assessments of the strengths and weaknesses of those approaches. This seemed to result in a more valid presentation of the field in its current diverse state of development.

The 37 chapters of this handbook have been arranged in seven parts that each highlight a key aspect or option of visual research in its present form of development. While this works well for most chapters, some have been difficult to classify because issues of collecting, producing, analyzing, and presenting visuals are typically intertwined in visual research. Moreover, many more threads tend to crosscut the seven sections, such as cross-disciplinary exchanges, for instance, between design and ethnography, or geography and sociology. Moreover, the very nature of the visual suggests the meeting and perhaps conflict of art and science.

Part One: Framing the Field of Visual Research provides a detailed view of the state of the field by discussing, theorizing, and conceptualizing the history, place, prospects, and broader context of visual methods and visual studies. It presents an integrated analytical framework that pinpoints key issues and options in visual research (Pauwels), offers a proposal to redirect visual culture studies to examine how one is looking, with or without camera technology, and how one is being seen or looked at (Chalfen), examines three manifestations of visual studies (as 'offshoot, branch, and root') including a systematic description of the material challenges of empirical enquiry (Wagner), and closes with a provocative exploration of the relationship between culture, materiality, and visibility (Wagner).

Part Two: Producing Visual Data and Insight consists of four chapters that elaborate on and discuss different ways to generate and process visual data. These 'researcher-generated production' methods cover both moving and still images, as well as computer-based and free-hand drawing techniques. This section covers a wide area ranging from anthropological filmmaking (MacDougall), the techniques and uses of repeat photography in both landscape research (Klett) and for documenting social change (Rieger), to the use of visualization methods in design practice (Boradkar).

Part Three: Participatory and Subject-centered Approaches similarly focuses on visual data production techniques, but particularly on those that explicitly seek to stimulate respondent participation in various forms, some of which challenge or interrogate the researcher—respondent or observer—subject divide. This section covers participatory video (Mitchell and De Lange), an integrated discussion of the many participatory techniques that enjoy an increasing popularity (Chalfen), photo-elicitation (Lapenta), subject-produced drawing (Ganesh), and concludes with a discussion and an example of the photo diary as auto-ethnography (Chaplin).

Part Four: Analytical Frameworks and Approaches presents the main theoretical frameworks and methodological tools for analyzing images ('found images' but also researcher produced ones): content analysis (Bock, Isermann, and Knieper), iconography (Müller), semiotics (Nöth), and rhetoric (Wright), as well as ethnomethodological (Ball and Smith) and micro-ethnographic accounts for producing and using images (McDermott and Raley; Knoblauch and Tuma). Special attention is paid to trying to make sense of historic images, both still (Margolis and Rowe) and moving images (Chapman).

Part Five: Visualization Technologies and Practices foregrounds rapidly emerging technologies for conducting and presenting visual research. It contains contributions about 'eye tracking' as a unique tool for examining how people literally are looking (Olk and Kappas), the emerging uses of cartography in social and cultural research (McKinnon), using Geographic Information Systems in a more participatory way (Collins), visualizing quantitative data (Grady), and using various software to analyze visual data (Bassett).

Recognizing both the expressive boundaries of the visual as well as its convoluted connections with other expressive systems and sensory experiences, *Part Six: Moving Beyond the Visual* first introduces the concept of 'multimodality' (van Leeuwen), to further include a multimodal tool for analyzing Internet phenomena (Pauwels), insights about image text relations (Baetens and Surdiacourt), and a call for research that also tries to include non-visual (auditory, olfactory, tactile) sensory experiences (Pink).

The final section of this collection, *Part Seven: Options and Issues for Using and Presenting Visual Research,* first addresses new multimedia opportunities (Coover), and arts-based research and presentation (O'Donoghue). Other chapters discuss: expressive (Newbury), ethical (Wiles, Clark, and Prosser) and legal (Rowe) issues of performing and publishing visual research. There is also an example of applying visual research methods to make a legal case (Gran).

While this collection colors outside the lines of traditional (visual) social science, and covers a broad spectrum of issues and uses, it cannot claim to cover the whole hybrid and dispersed universe of visual studies and visualization practices in the sciences, the social sciences, and the humanities. Moreover, the field is in rapid flux due to technological innovations, the adoption of visual research methods by traditional disciplines, and the rapidly developing transdisciplinary research groups. We strongly believe that the future of visual research will depend on the continued effort to cross disciplinary boundaries and engage in constructive dialogue with different schools of thought. The aim is to produce a more integrated knowledge base about the visual as a source, tool, and form of scholarly expression.

Eric Margolis and Luc Pauwels

Color versions of the images used in the book are available on a companion website to the book which can be found at: www.sagepub.co.uk/margolis

PART 1

Framing the Field
of Visual Research

An Integrated Conceptual Framework for Visual Social Research

Luc Pauwels

INTRODUCTION: TOWARD A MORE FIRM VISUAL METHODOLOGY

While visual methods in sociology and anthropology today may rejoice in a growing number of enthusiasts, along with a number of skeptics, most social scientists are completely unaware of their existence or potential. Visual sociology and visual anthropology are grounded in the idea that valid scientific insight in society can be acquired by observing, analyzing, and theorizing its visual manifestations: behavior of people and material products of culture.

The growing popularity of visual methods is expressed in a number of recently established or renewed scholarly journals: *Visual Studies* (formerly *Visual Sociology*), *Visual Anthropology*, *Visual Anthropology Review*, and the journals that gather their inspiration from a broader humanities base, such as *Visual Communication* and the *Journal of Visual Culture*. Equally significant is the steady stream of dedicated handbooks (Ball

and Smith, 1992; Chaplin, 1994; Pauwels, 1996b; Emmison and Smith, 2000; Banks, 2001, 2007; Pink, 2001) and readers (Prosser, 2000; Grimshaw and Ravetz, 2004; Hamilton, 2007; Stanczak, 2007), and a marked rise of membership in scholarly organizations devoted to the visual: for example, the 'International Visual Sociology Association' (IVSA), the 'ISA Visual Sociology Thematic Group,' the 'Visual Communication Studies Division of the International Communication Association' (ICA), and the 'International Visual Literacy Association' (IVLA).

Unfortunately, there is little integration with respect to the findings and practices of visual methods, especially between the social sciences and the humanities and behavioral sciences. Visual methods, therefore, seem to be reinvented over and over again without gaining much methodological depth and often without consideration of long-existing classics in the field (Mead and Bateson, [1942] 1985; Mead, 1963, [1975] 2003; Collier, [1967] 1986 with M. Collier;

Hockings [1975] 2003; Rouch, 1975; Heider [1976] 2006; Curry and Clarke, [1977] 1983; Wagner, 1979; Becker, 1986; Ruby, 1986, 2000; De Heusch, 1988; MacDougall and Taylor, 1998). Such ahistoric and highly dispersed efforts are detrimental to advancing a more mature methodology and developing a social and behavioral science that in its basic roots could easily become 'more visual' (that is, in its conceptualizing, capturing, and dissemination of knowledge about human society). Often more effort is expended in trying to 'appropriate' a field (through renaming it, by relabeling its techniques, and by imposing particular theoretical perspectives and themes) than in developing a more cumulative and integrative stance.

Even the above-mentioned classics of visual sociology and anthropology paid relatively little attention to the development of a more rigorous methodology for the collection, production, analysis, and communication of visual aspects and insights or an in-depth description of visual media's expressive capabilities. Often authors seem to hop from celebratory accounts of the iconic and indexical powers of the visual to the presentation of found or produced visual data, without paying much attention to sketching out the tedious path in between.

Given this current state of affairs, with the growing disparity of visual approaches and their ambiguous labeling, the lack of oversight and the methodological and conceptual vagueness, I present in this chapter a framework that seeks to bring some clarity to these matters in an integrated manner.

AN INTEGRATED FRAMEWORK FOR VISUAL SOCIAL RESEARCH

The 'Integrated Framework for Visual Social Research' (Pauwels, 2010) is an attempt to offer an integrated overview of the wide variety of interconnected options and opportunities researchers have when considering using visual input and/or output in the study of

society and culture. These options or choices are discussed systematically and are placed in perspective within the complete trajectory of a visual research project from its conception to the dissemination of the research findings or insights. The framework is grounded in the idea that a more refined analytical and synthesizing approach of the many issues and aspects of visual research may contribute significantly to the conceptual and methodological grounding of a 'more visual' social science (Henny, 1986).

Such an integrated conceptual framework for visual research is hitherto lacking. Most authors in the field limit themselves to discussing some existing modes or techniques (for example, photo-elicitation, native image making, systematic recording) or presentational formats (for example, film, visual essay), often without trying to explain the existing diversity, underlying claims or methodological caveats. While good examples and discussions of particular types of visual research do exist, few authors have ventured to provide an analytical and integrated approach to visual research as a whole.

The purpose of this framework is not just to provide a synthesis of existing methods and techniques. It deliberately does not follow customary distinctions and labels to address the essential elements of visual research in their most meaningful and basic components. It aims to offer better insight into current possibilities and approaches and to stimulate new and more refined approaches to visual research. It does not in any way seek to restrict the vast potential of enquiry to a number of standardized techniques and approaches.

The framework (as summarized in Figure 1.1) is built around three themes:

A. Origin and Nature of Visuals
B. Research Focus and Design
C. Format and Purpose

These themes correspond more or less with the interrelated aspects of the input, processing and output phases of a visual

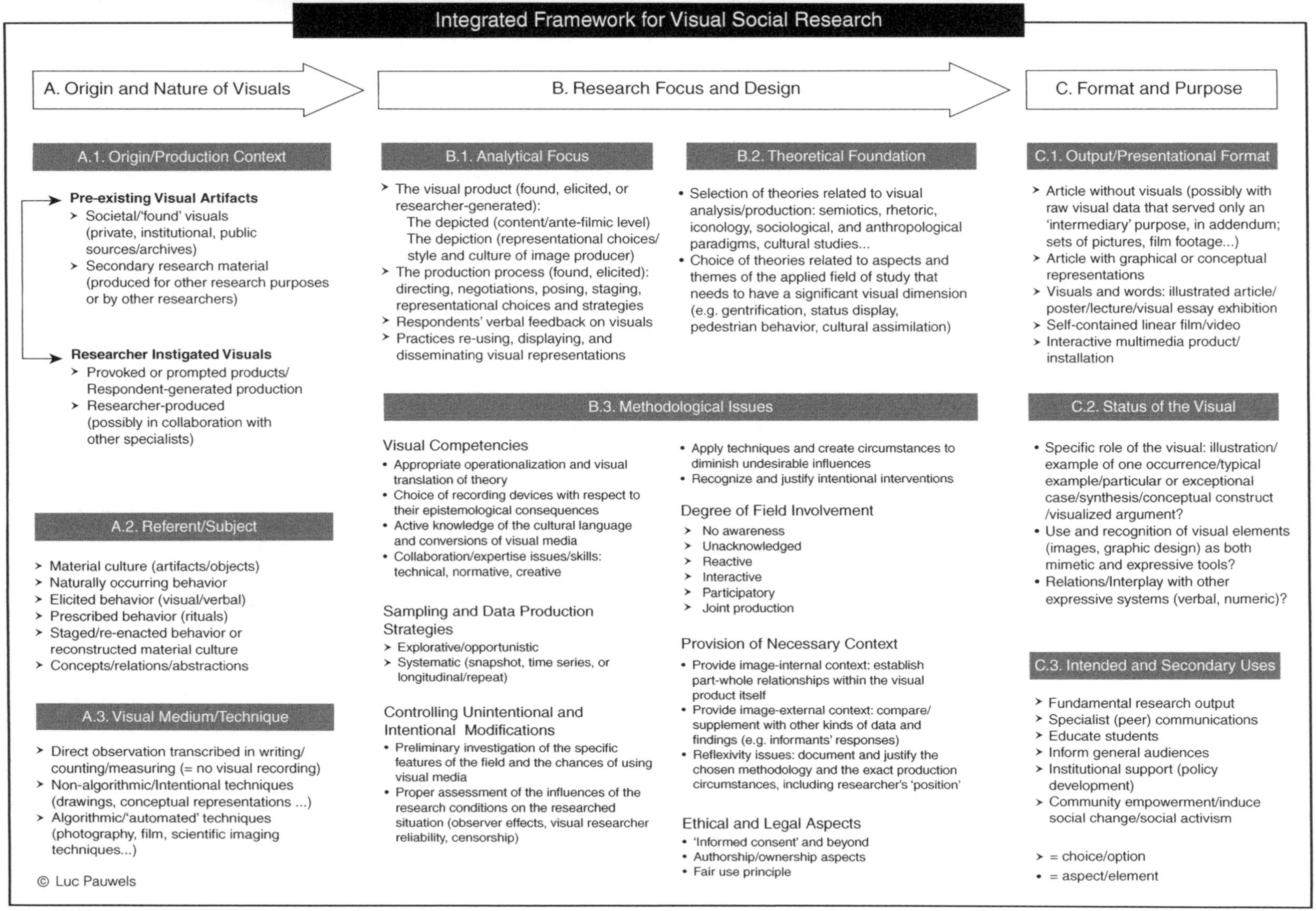

Integrated Framework for Visual Social Research

A. Origin and Nature of Visuals → B. Research Focus and Design → C. Format and Purpose

A. Origin and Nature of Visuals

A.1. Origin/Production Context

Pre-existing Visual Artifacts
➢ Societal/'found' visuals (private, institutional, public sources/archives)
➢ Secondary research material (produced for other research purposes or by other researchers)

Researcher Instigated Visuals
➢ Provoked or prompted products/Respondent-generated production
➢ Researcher-produced (possibly in collaboration with other specialists)

A.2. Referent/Subject

➢ Material culture (artifacts/objects)
➢ Naturally occurring behavior
➢ Elicited behavior (visual/verbal)
➢ Prescribed behavior (rituals)
➢ Staged/re-enacted behavior or reconstructed material culture
➢ Concepts/relations/abstractions

A.3. Visual Medium/Technique

➢ Direct observation transcribed in writing/counting/measuring (= no visual recording)
➢ Non-algorithmic/Intentional techniques (drawings, conceptual representations ...)
➢ Algorithmic/'automated' techniques (photography, film, scientific imaging techniques...)

© Luc Pauwels

B. Research Focus and Design

B.1. Analytical Focus

➢ The visual product (found, elicited, or researcher-generated):
  The depicted (content/ante-filmic level)
  The depiction (representational choices/style and culture of image producer)
➢ The production process (found, elicited): directing, negotiations, posing, staging, representational choices and strategies
➢ Respondents' verbal feedback on visuals
➢ Practices re-using, displaying, and disseminating visual representations

B.2. Theoretical Foundation

• Selection of theories related to visual analysis/production: semiotics, rhetoric, iconology, sociological, and anthropological paradigms, cultural studies...
• Choice of theories related to aspects and themes of the applied field of study that needs to have a significant visual dimension (e.g. gentrification, status display, pedestrian behavior, cultural assimilation)

B.3. Methodological Issues

Visual Competencies
• Appropriate operationalization and visual translation of theory
• Choice of recording devices with respect to their epistemological consequences
• Active knowledge of the cultural language and conversions of visual media
• Collaboration/expertise issues/skills: technical, normative, creative

Sampling and Data Production Strategies
➢ Explorative/opportunistic
➢ Systematic (snapshot, time series, or longitudinal/repeat)

Controlling Unintentional and Intentional Modifications
• Preliminary investigation of the specific features of the field and the chances of using visual media
• Proper assessment of the influences of the researched research conditions on the researched situation (observer effects, visual researcher reliability, censorship)

• Apply techniques and create circumstances to diminish undesirable influences
• Recognize and justify intentional interventions

Degree of Field Involvement
➢ No awareness
➢ Unacknowledged
➢ Reactive
➢ Interactive
➢ Participatory
➢ Joint production

Provision of Necessary Context
• Provide image-internal context: establish part-whole relationships within the visual product itself
• Provide image-external context: compare/supplement with other kinds of data and findings (e.g. informants' responses)
• Reflexivity issues: document and justify the chosen methodology and the exact production circumstances, including researcher's 'position'

Ethical and Legal Aspects
• 'Informed consent' and beyond
• Authorship/ownership aspects
• Fair use principle

C. Format and Purpose

C.1. Output/Presentational Format

➢ Article without visuals (possibly with raw visual data that served only an 'intermediary' purpose, in addendum; sets of pictures, film footage...)
➢ Article with graphical or conceptual representations
➢ Visuals and words: illustrated article/poster/lecture/visual essay exhibition
➢ Self-contained linear film/video
➢ Interactive multimedia product/installation

C.2. Status of the Visual

• Specific role of the visual: illustration/example of one occurrence/typical example/particular or exceptional case/synthesis/conceptual construct /visualized argument?
• Use and recognition of visual elements (images, graphic design) as both mimetic and expressive tools?
• Relations/Interplay with other expressive systems (verbal, numeric)?

C.3. Intended and Secondary Uses

➢ Fundamental research output
➢ Specialist (peer) communications
➢ Educate students
➢ Inform general audiences
➢ Institutional support (policy development)
➢ Community empowerment/induce social change/social activism

➢ = choice/option
• = aspect/element

Figure 1.1 An integrated framework for visual social research

research project. Within each of these themes different options and aspects are presented and discussed in the context of the broader research project.

A. Origin and nature of visuals

A.1. Origin / production context of visuals
One of the most essential choices or options in visual research is whether to use (or restrict oneself to using) existing visual material ('found' visuals) as primary data for research, or to initiate as a researcher first- hand observations or visual products. This choice has many consequences with respect to important aspects, such as (1) the nature and amount of control over different aspects of the production of the visual materials, (2) access to the field (less–more; direct–indirect), (3) knowledge of the broader ethnographic context, and (4) acceptable uses of the visual outcome and ethical issues.

A.1.1. Found materials as data source
First and foremost, social scientists should take advantage of the wide sweep of visual data sources available in society. Societal images and visual artifacts are ubiquitous, and produced on a daily basis without any researcher effort (for example, advertisements, newsreels, CCTV images, website content, artworks, cartoons, resulting in huge data repositories of actual, historic, and fictional(ized) worlds, which have become more accessible nowadays with network and database technologies. This huge offering of both contemporary and historic material has a highly divergent nature: it consists of naïve, utilitarian, mundane, or very professional types of visuals (family photography, advertising, fiction and non-fiction film, drawings, maps, diagrams, etc.) spanning many sectors of society (commercial, governmental, educational, entertainment, science, etc.) and thus offering access to a wide variety of public and private worlds.

Studying these materials, sociologists may acquire insight into the social functions of the cultural product itself (for example, family pictures or advertisements), but also gain access to broader and more profound aspects of society (the broader realm of values and norms of a given culture). Images often tend to offer a (not-unproblematic) window to the depicted world, but at the same time they invariably constitute cultural artifacts in themselves, and may offer a gateway to the culture of the producer and that of the implied audience.

On the down side, when using found materials, sociologists as 'image collectors' often lack sufficient background knowledge or contextual information with respect to the exact origin, the production circumstances, and the representative character of the acquired visual data set. This applies a fortiori to 'anonymous' visual artifacts (for example, family pictures found on a flea market) and to a varying degree to artifacts with known provenance. Researchers remain highly dependent on knowledgeable informants, to be able to contextualize the 'visual as presented' (the images or visual artifacts) through data from the past and/or outside their immediate frame of view.

Apart from a broad and specific cultural knowledge, researchers benefit from developing the expertise to analyze both content and form (style) of the visual product, which requires knowledge of both visual technologies and representational cultures over time and space. Moreover, researchers may encounter problems of quite another nature, such as copyright issues and censorship.

At present, many types of societal imagery (for example, family pictures, ads, postcards, paintings, newsreels, feature and documentary film, various picture archives, maps, and charts) have been used by social, cultural, and behavioral scientists to study a variety of subjects and issues: labor (Margolis, 1994); school culture (Margolis, 2004; Burke and Grosvenor, 2007); family dynamics (Musello, 1979; Chalfen, 1987; Pauwels, 2008a); traumatic experiences (McAllister, 2006; Gödel,

2007); youth culture (Larson, 1999); stereo-typing (Hagaman, 1993); migration (Wright, 2001); nature versus culture (Papson, 1991; Suonpää, 2000; Bousé, 2003); deviance (Lackey, 2001); race and ethnicity (Mellinger, 1992; Tomaselli and Shepperson, 2002; Grady, 2007); health (Bogdan and Marshal, 1997); gender and identity (Goffman, 1979; Edge, 1998); and globalization (Barndt, 1997). However, many areas of enquiry and many types of visual materials are still waiting to be explored.

A.1.2. Researcher-initiated production of visual data and meanings

With the collection of existing imagery from society, the emphasis of research lies on the decoding of a 'secondary' (mediated) visual reality, which is often no longer directly accessible. However, a number of key modes of visual research (including image production) begin with the primary reality from which the social scientist selects events and phenomena to be visually recorded and processed as an intermediate phase in a research project, or as a proper scientific end product. Researcher-generated production of visuals in general allows more control over the data-gathering procedures (and ideally more reflexivity) so that more highly contextualized material can be produced. In theory, this should provide better insight into the limitations of the produced material (external influences, sample characteristics, etc.).

Some typical strands of visual research based on researcher-produced imagery include a variety of topics and issues such as social change (Rieger, 1996, 2003; Page, 2001), urban processes (Suchar, 1988, 1992), education (Wagner, 1999; Prosser, 2007), corporate culture (Pauwels, 1996a), burial rituals (Synnott, 1985; Chalfen, 2003), gender construction (Harper and Faccioli, 2000; Brown, 2001), pedestrian behavior (Zube, 1979; McPhail and Wohlstein, 1982), youth culture (Hethorn and Kaiser, 1999; Wagner, 1999), social activism (Schwartz, 2002; David, 2007), and migration and ethnicity (Krase, 1997; Gold, 2007).

A.1.3. Secondary research uses and respondent-generated material

The origin or provenance of visual materials is one of the more solid and basic distinctions in visual research. A clear distinction can be made between 'found materials' of no known origin and researcher-generated visuals. But these types of material represent only the extremes of what can be thought of as a continuum that slides from 'anonymous artifacts,' 'collected artifacts with known provenance,' to 'other researcher's data,' 'respondent-generated data' and finally 'researcher-generated visuals.' Moreover, concrete examples of each of these categories may show a great deal of variation in terms of contextual background, production control, and expertise, thus really expressing the idea of a continuum.

A discussion of two specific categories in between the two extremes of the continuum 'found imagery' versus 'researcher-generated' may further illuminate the diverse nature visual materials may take and point out their implications for research.

First, I will address the case of 'secondary research material' or 'other researchers' visual data.' Researchers may indeed choose to use materials that have been produced by other researchers for similar or different research purposes. This material may be used for comparison with new data or (as a historic source) be revisited by a new researcher for the same purposes or to answer different research questions: for example, revisiting earlier anthropological and ethnographic pictures as cultural-specific visualizations of the 'Other' (see, for example, Edwards, 1990; Geary, 1990; Pinney, 1990; Hammond, 1998). This form of visual research combines features from both sides of the continuum: it uses pre-existing material that has been produced for research purposes. The central issue here is how much information is available regarding the exact context of production. Knowledge of the context is often better documented for research material than for other types of found material, but may still be insufficient. As availability of such information may vary considerably, this type of research may lie somewhere along the continuum. For the purpose of classification, I have positioned this visual material (in Figure 1.1) with 'Found' or 'Pre-existing material,' since it is not specifically produced with the current research purpose in mind, and thus lacks full control or freedom over several crucial aspects of production. Visual materials produced for research purposes are not the only highly contextualized data sources on the continuum. There are many more pre-existing visual materials, which have been produced in a more or less systematic and documented way: for example, private and state archives of all sorts, formal portraits and police photography.

A second distinctive instance along the line of the continuum is the now increasingly popular technique in the social sciences (and currently even in art practice and community development) called 'native image production' (Worth and Adair, 1975; Wagner, 1979: a term that cannot deny its anthropological roots), 'cultural self-portrayal' (Pauwels, 1996b), or the use of 'respondent-generated imagery' (probably the broadest and most descriptive term). These materials differ from pre-existing or 'societal' imagery or artifacts in that they are clearly produced within a research context, although not by the researchers or their collaborators, but on their request and following their basic instructions. These materials therefore belong to the broader category of researcher-initiated (or prompted) materials. The respondents or culture under study produce their own cultural data in a visual form. The researcher's control over the production process is therefore more limited than with researcher-generated visuals, but usually higher than with found visual data. It is important to note that the respondent-generated material, while offering a unique (insider) perspective, is never an end product, but just an intermediate step in the research. Researchers still need to analyze and make sense of the visual output generated by the respondents; their cultural self-portrayal or vision needs to be verbally or visually framed within the research output.

One of the most telling and reputed examples of the power of respondent-generated imagery is still the 'Through Navajo Eyes' project, whereby Worth and Adair (1975) taught the Navajo the very basics of handling a camera. The films produced by the Navajo were at first somewhat puzzling as they did not meet the (Western) expectations of the anthropologists. On closer inspection, this very quality established the films as extremely relevant expressions of Navajo culture. Cameras (both still and moving image) or paper and pencil have subsequently been handed out to many different groups of respondents, such as schoolchildren (Prosser, 2007), adolescents (Niesyto, 2000; Mizen, 2005), migrant children (Clark-Ibanez, 2007), and chronically ill patients (Rich and Chalfen, 1999) to depict aspects of their culture and experience for further scrutiny.

A.2. Referent /subject of research

Visual research in the social sciences predominantly has material culture and human behavior as its subject and—when visual representations are being produced—as its 'referent' (= that which is being depicted or visually referred to). Visual 'material culture' includes artifacts and objects (boardrooms, home settings, art objects) and larger visible structures (for example, urban areas, cemeteries) that may provide useful information about both the material and the immaterial traits in as much as they embody values and norms of a given society.

'Naturally occurring or spontaneous behavior' is another crucially important subject of visual social research. This type of behavior is often looked upon as one of the most valuable sources for visual data gathering. The main issue with this type of source is exactly its adjective, 'naturally occurring,' which seems to imply non-reactivity, a requirement that is hardly attainable when the researchers and their recording equipment are visible to the research subjects.

Moreover, researchers and their recording equipment being invisible is often questioned from an ethical viewpoint. It is therefore useful to assess the amount and nature of reactivity for each individual situation and the impact on what exactly we need to study. The same applies to relevant ethical aspects.

Of course not only naturally occurring or non-reactive behavior is a valid subject of research; 'elicited behavior of both a verbal or visual nature' may also yield valuable input for research. Researchers can prompt people to react (most often verbally) to visual stimuli (pictures, drawings, artifacts) and use these reactions as input or to correct their research (Collier, 1967; Wagner, 1979; Harper, 2002). Or researchers may even prompt people to produce their own imagery or visual representations as a response to a specific assignment (for example, 'depict a typical day of your life'). The first technique is known as 'photo or film elicitation' (the term 'visual elicitation' may be better, since it does not limit this technique to photographic media, but also includes drawing, for example). The latter technique whereby the respondents themselves produce imagery or visual representations about aspects of their culture for further use by the researcher is (as stated earlier) best described by the broad category of 'respondent-generated imagery.'

Though less common in social science than in psychological research, visual social scientists may also opt to record behavior resulting from an experimental situation, which has been constructed solely for the purpose: for example, an uncommon artifact is introduced or elements of a built-up environment are suddenly altered to study pedestrians' reactions. The recorded behavior in this situation is not (only) reactive to the research set-up, the camera, and the crew (which are often concealed), but also to the new and artificial situation (assumed to be real by the passers-by). The stimulus is not provided in an acknowledged research situation (different, for instance, to using

pictures in an interview). The behavior thus recorded is 'spontaneous' but not 'naturally occurring' in the sense that 'it would have occurred anyway' (for example, without a researcher intervention).

'Rituals and other highly prescribed activities' in a society offer very condensed information on important aspects of human organization. Depicting these processes may also benefit from a visual approach, because of its ability to capture the richness and complexity of the event, its capacity to cope with the semiotic hybridity (different types of signs and orders of signification) of the depicted including its cultural specificity, and development over time and space (especially when using continuous visual recording techniques: film or video).

Social scientists may even opt for 'staged or re-enacted behavior' as the referent for their visual research, not just for educational purposes (to show others how something has happened or could have been in the past) but also to generate new data in much the same way as a 'reconstruction' of a crime may generate new insights into what really happened. Crucial points in reconstruction are the number and nature of reconstructed aspects versus aspects that have remained unchanged over time; the knowledge, skills, and the exact briefing/ training of the participants, the sources that are being used to guide the reconstruction, such as memory, writings, oral accounts, visual materials, artifacts, etc. When re-enacting behavior from the past (for example, hunting or farming techniques), we often need to 'reconstruct accompanying aspects of material culture' (for example, tools such as bows, ploughs, and huts). It is important that the audience is kept informed of exactly how the information about the reconstruction was acquired and processed so that they know what they are looking at. This is important because whether behavioral and material reconstructions are based on memory, written accounts; or earlier visual representations, and whether an event is re-enacted by survivors or mere actors—both influence the outcome in numerous ways.

Finally, a more comprehensive and contemporary view on visual sociology and anthropology also includes the study and use of types of imagery and visual representations that don't necessarily have a (visual) referent in the material world, but rather embody relational and comparative constructs of 'non-visual data and conceptual representations of ideas' (see Tufte, 1983, 1990, 1997; Lynch, 1985; Grady, 2006; Pauwels, 2006b). Hitherto these aspects have been more prominently studied in the sociology of science, or by scholars from educational technology, visual communication, and science and technology studies (Latour and Woolgar, 1979; Cambrosio et al., 1993; Knor-Cetina, 1981; Lynch, 1985; Goodwin, 1995; Gordin and Pea, 1995). This expansion of non-visual data and conceptual representations of ideas, and the gradual interest arising, constitute a very important aspect of sociology becoming 'more visual.'

A.3. Visual medium/technique

Visual sociologists and anthropologists have primarily focused on camera-based imagery (both static and moving). The paramount importance of these kinds of imagery is beyond question, both because of their ubiquity in society, the ease with which they are produced and because of their specific iconic and indexical qualities (mostly understood as their high level of 'resemblance' and the 'natural' or even 'causal' relation to the depicted object). However, researchers may also take advantage of non-(technically) mediated or directly observed aspects of visual culture (signage, architecture) and of studying and using non-photographic representations (such as drawings, paintings, murals, graffiti, maps, charts). In many cases, 'fixing the shadows,' however, by producing a permanent (most often photographic) record is helpful or even necessary.

Any visual practice and its products embody a complex meeting of the cultures of the depicted and of the depicter, along with

the—again, culturally influenced—intricacies of the representational techniques or the medium. Visuals produced with 'non-algorithmic techniques' (techniques that require many 'intentional' choices by the maker, such as drawings: Mitchell, 1992) are readily used as existing data sources (for example, paintings, murals, graffiti, children's drawings). For 'researcher-generated' types of imagery, however, this category of imaging techniques is a far less obvious choice. Indeed, social scientists routinely turn to photography and film to record material cultural and human behavior in all of its complexity. Yet in some instances, non-algorithmic techniques (more intentional or less automated techniques) can be more suited or may even prove to be the only option (for example, to depict concepts or relational constructs as these 'entities' cannot be photographed since they have no visual material referent, or in cases where photography is not allowed). Intentional techniques, moreover, may be chosen because they allow simplification and abstraction; photos can be too detailed and particularistic. Intentional techniques also allow the simultaneous application of many different representational codes: for example, a map may combine many types of iconic and symbolic information, such as pictograms, arrows, colors, gradients, and text. The relation between a picture and its depicted content potentially becomes more problematic as more specialized (or non-canonic) techniques (special lenses, unusual vantage points, use of rays that are not visible to the naked eye) are used, or when the depicted cannot be observed directly and thus is only 'available' as a representation (Pauwels, 2006b).

B. Research focus and design

B.1. Analytical focus and fields of application

The analytical focus of a visual research project may be quite varied. Whereas we may primarily think of a detailed analysis of the visual product, it may also involve the processes of making (production) these visual artifacts or entail uses (consumption, reception) the visual representations are being put to, and the focal point of interest may even lie on the verbal reactions to visuals (verbal feedback).

The analytical focus will always be determined by the particular research questions being addressed. These research questions may cover a vast number of possible areas of research as long as the right visual angles to answer the questions are found.

B.1.1. Product: the depicted and the depiction

The content or that which is depicted is an important source of data, and for most researcher-generated visuals the focal point of analysis. Indeed, much research tries to produce images in a systematic way and thus relies explicitly or implicitly on the mimetic strengths of the camera image, thereby seeking to minimize the variations and expressive effects of style originating from dissimilar applications of filmic parameters (for example, camera distance, angle, position). Essentially, we then try to use images as 'windows' to the depicted world. This rather 'realist' approach is legitimate if we are primarily interested in the depicted matter for further scrutiny. However, researchers always need to be aware of the inevitable difference between the depicted (the referent) and the depiction (the visual representation), a difference that can seriously influence or even misinform their views on the depicted. This difference can also become a field of study in its own right: the study of style as a gateway to the norms and values and other immaterial traits of a culture.

Operationalizing research questions and foci from visually observable elements may involve deriving data from images in a fairly straightforward way (for example, number of people, distances, cultural inventory of objects) or may require more interpretative decoding (emotional states,

complex relations). Such operationalization may implicate the image or visual field as an integrated whole (the spatial organization of a town square, the global impression of a city as a cultural meeting place) or just small parts or aspects of it (clearly defined types of exchange between people, for example, such as a handshake, eye contact, or a nod).

Research of 'found' or pre-existing visuals (for example, advertising, family pictures) in general will also have a primary focus on the depicted (for example, changes in fashion, architecture, street art, events, poses and persons in a family snap or an ad). However, the researcher can also benefit from focusing on the depiction as a result of a representational practice (which involves cultural and technological normative systems) and thus scrutinize the ways in which particular objects or events are being represented visually by certain actors or institutions over time. Thus, the focus of attention moves to researching form and style, and so to the world of the image producers rather than that of the depicted (unless these worlds largely coincide as is often the case with family photography). Studies, for instance on the colonial gaze, have focused on how the 'Other' is represented (staged, selected, stereotyped, made docile). This research involves both looking at what is depicted and how it is depicted on a pro-filmic (mise-en-scène) and filmic level (framing, editing, post-production, etc.)

So an important focus of visual research is also the representational practices as cultural expressions in relation to what the visuals depict. The visual form is then problematized and the image no longer seen as an unproblematic window to the depicted world but (also) as mirroring the social and cultural world of the image producer. This focus of analysis requires sufficient knowledge of the medium and its culture (for example, the evolution of analog/digital camera techniques, the cultural codes of picture-making and the depicted culture in a broad sense).

B.1.2. Analyzing production processes and product uses

Analyzing the processes of image making and the subsequent uses and cultural practices surrounding the use of imagery and visual representations are not the most dominant foci in current visual research, but they too may yield very unique data. Indeed, in some cases the process may be more revealing than the end product. Anthropologists may, for instance, look at how a large sand painting is being created by members of a tribe. The process of negotiating the different choices, the forms of collaboration, the required skills that are being made and displayed make up a research interest in themselves. Next to studying the visual end products, family researchers can also take an interest in the dynamics just *before* and *during* the production of a family snap (the directing, posing, negotiations, the technical choices, and the implicit power relations) and the processes by which the snaps are *afterward* selected, manipulated, and combined with texts in an album or on a website; where, how, and which photos are displayed in the home or distributed among friends and acquaintances, for what reasons, etc. (Chalfen, 1987; Pauwels, 2008a). Psychotherapists may ask children of families under severe strain to make a drawing of the members of their family and study the order in which family members are drawn— for example, the mother before the father or vice versa—based on the belief that 'what is drawn' first may reveal what is most important for the drawer (Diem-Wille, 2001: 119). In a way, these examples, of course, involve (direct) observation of behavior (spontaneous, ritual, or instigated), yet the interesting link between the behavior and its immediate result in material culture, and the fact that it involves behavior related to image making and handling, make them an area of special relevance to the visual researcher.

B.1.3. Analysis of feedback

Some types of visual research (for example, visual interviewing or photo-elicitation) rely to a large part on the analysis of verbal reactions to visual stimuli (drawings, photos, film). Visual stimuli are provided by the researcher to gather factual information about the depicted cultural elements and—a very powerful and unique trait of the visual elicitation technique—to 'trigger' more projective information with the respondents (their deeper feelings, opinions). The method of 'respondent-generated images' also generates 'feedback,' but of a mainly visual nature, and thus this feedback needs to be analyzed both for its content and its form. It is to be considered as a research 'input' not an end product, even if it takes the form of a completed film or video. Through detailed analysis, the researcher will try to make sense of it and situate it within the larger framework of the discipline.

In a more general sense, visual researchers today are routinely using the reactions of their subjects to correct and improve their visual account and interpretations: for example, through regular screenings of the unfinished visual product in front of the culturally savvy audience.

In summary, the focus of analysis in visual research can lie on:

- the content of a visual representation (the depicted),
- its form and style (most often in conjunction with the depicted),
- the processes that are related with the production and use of visual representations,
- the verbal reactions to visual stimuli.

B.1.4. Fields of application

Possible fields and types of subject matter that can be studied with visual methods are virtually limitless so long as what is being researched has a significant visual dimension. Some questions about aspects and processes of the social world that have sizeable visual aspects—for example, status (display), social class and enculturation— may be more suited for visual research than others—for example, relative deprivation, fraudulent behavior—but it all comes down to finding the right visual entry points to disclose relevant aspects of social and cultural life. The inquisitive and visually literate mind may come up with many novel ways of looking at what (at first sight) might seem too abstract a subject.

Taking this into account, visual sociology is not really a specialized field of sociology in the same way as the sociology of law, or sociology of culture, but a cross-cutting field of inquiry, a way of doing and thinking that influences the whole process of researching (conceptualizing, gathering, and communicating). It is not only a 'sociology of the visual' (as subject) but also a method for sociology in general (whatever its field: law, religion, culture, etc.) and a way of thinking, conceptualizing and presenting ideas and findings.

B.2. Theoretical foundation

As in most types of research, theory usually guides visual data production and analysis. So whether looking at existing visual representations or producing new visual data, both approaches require a solid and fully motivated theoretical grounding. Without theory, our seeing is blind or tends to rest on unexplained views and expectations (implicit theory), which we may even be unaware of. It is fairly naïve to expect that the camera will automatically collect large quantities of relevant data. Theory is needed to give scientific research some direction. It can focus attention on issues which at first sight are not expected to have much significance, but which from a specific stance, hypothesis, or idea, can yield relevant scientific information.

Visual researchers can make use of several theoretical frameworks that have been adapted over the course of the years to visual analysis (Smith et al., 2005; Rose, 2006) for example, semiotics, socio-semiotics, rhetoric, several sociological paradigms, psychoanalysis, cultural studies, post-colonial theory, and feminist theory. Others, such as iconology, have been developed for that very purpose. Many embody already very particular interests in the image: from determining its subject and explaining its deeper meanings, to uncovering its signifying structure, revealing its power structure, gender biases, or racial prejudices. Some of these frameworks offer concrete methodological tools, while others don't seem to suggest any method of investigation and leave it to researchers to incorporate their views in a more or less systematic qualitative and/or quantitative type of content analysis. In fact, relatively few theories seem to offer handles for concrete in-depth analysis of both the depicted (or content) and the depiction (the stylistic choices at the level of the execution and the characteristics of the medium). Many visual studies, therefore, limit themselves to the analysis of the depicted, whereas the level of the depiction—which often proves much harder to investigate, since it falls outside the scope of expertise of most social scientists—may reveal particularly relevant data: for example, about the norms and values of the image makers or their commissioning institutions. Such data at the level of depiction may prove highly complementary with the content-related data.

However, the theoretical grounding of a project not only involves the visual analytical side (how to deal with the form and content of the visual products) but also includes the main subject matter or the thematic focus of the project. Researchers who, for instance, study gentrification processes or poverty issues start by selecting particular definitions and aspects of gentrification or poverty theories and research, and combine those in a solid framework that is compatible with the goals of the research and with the particular combination of research methods and techniques.

B.3. Methodological issues

B.3.1 Visual competencies: aspects and implementation options

Working toward a more visual scientific discourse implies the development of a particular sort of visual competence. When collecting pre-existing imagery ('societal imagery'), researchers preferably need at least a passive knowledge of the technical and expressive aspects of imagery and representational techniques, to be able to read and make use of them adequately. In analyzing such found imagery, most often special attention is paid to the historical and cultural context of production and consumption.

When researchers produce imagery themselves ('researcher-generated imagery') or are using visual elements in one or more stages of their research and scholarly communication, a more active visual knowledge and skill is required, since all technical or medium-related decisions have epistemological consequences. Thus, competent visual researchers not only have a sufficient degree of technical knowledge, allowing them to produce images or other types of visual representations with the required amount of visual detail (data richness), but also are aware of the cultural conventions regarding the medium they are using and, consequently, of the perceptual cultures of the academic or non-academic audience they intend to address.

Visual scientific competence thus implies a thorough insight into the specific characteristics of visual media along with the skill to translate scientific insights into verbo-visual constructs. Ultimately, visual scientific literacy manifests itself as a form of visual thinking and doing throughout the complete research process. This starts with the conception of a problem, and continues through the phase of data gathering or production of visual material, the phase of analysis or further preparation and handling, up to the presentation of the data and findings (Pauwels, 2006b).

B.3.2. Sampling and data production strategies

Different questions and research methods necessitate different sampling strategies and data collection/production (shooting) techniques. Hypothesis-testing visual research may require systematic recording techniques, random or stratified sampling (for example, every 10th house in a street), while more explorative research may benefit from more 'opportunistic sampling' (Sorenson and Jablonko, 1975). The latter is used for recording things which attract the researcher's attention or which can only be collected on an ad hoc—'when it occurs' or 'comes into view'—basis. Examples are the reactions of bystanders at the site of a car accident, illegal street sellers, and unanticipated or remarkable aspects of visual culture. As always, the sampling technique co-determines the inferences possible from the visual data in a later stage.

Standardized research designs often benefit from the use of 'shooting scripts' (Suchar, 1997) that detail the exact positions, subject matter and time, and enable comparison. A longitudinal variant of systematic observation, known as 'repeat photography,' is very much focused on keeping the recording parameters (angle of view, camera distance, framing) constant over time to record (social) change (Rieger, 1996).

Thus, a clearly theory driven or systematically conceptualized research project doesn't rule out more exploratory and intuitive approaches (Collier, 1967). These latter approaches may be particularly suited to get acquainted with a new field (a new city, settlement, culture, kind of behavior) and its products may stimulate thinking in a 'grounded theory' like fashion. Often it is very rewarding for research to remain open to the unexpected and the unanticipated events. Stochastic or, conversely, more exploratory and opportunistic approaches do therefore have a place in the process, as they can lead to new insights and sometimes even succeed in reaching the heart of the matter. Visual research in particular benefits from the continued fertilization between theory and practice, thinking and doing. Non-systematically acquired data can often serve as a test for more systematically acquired data.

B.3.3. Controlling intentional and unintentional influences and modifications

Visual researchers usually have a keen eye for unintended and uncontrolled influences on the researched situation, which could be attributed to their and/or their camera's presence (or to some other 'limiting' or 'disturbing' instances—for example, forms of censorship before, during, or after the shooting). It is their task then to evaluate how and to what extent these influences and instances affect what is considered 'normal,' or at least what could be considered acceptable within the context of their research. They are expected to be knowledgeable of techniques to reduce the occurrence of various forms of 'obtrusiveness' (Grimshaw, 1982) or other kinds of unintentional influence, or find ways to creatively take advantage of them (for example, by making them part of the focus of the research).

Undesired influences may be reduced first of all by a thorough investigation and preparation of the field of research ('prior ethnography': Corsaro, 1982), including a gradual introduction of both the set-up and the instrument of the research (the camera) and by providing information about the possible consequences for the people involved. 'Monitored' behavior (self-conscious reactions to being observed) often stems from an understandable fear on the part of the observed of being harmed by the way they are being represented visually (see 'Ethical and legal aspects' below).

Data are likely to be more representative when people have been given time to grow accustomed to the special situation and have sufficient information regarding the purpose of the research. Whether behavior is representative is also influenced by the varying degrees of freedom subjects have to respond to the camera (Becker, 1986). Recordings of rituals and other strictly prescribed activities are far less problematic in this regard than trying to record spontaneous behavior (for example, an informal conversation), where a certain degree of reactivity is unavoidable.

The relation and interaction between the researchers and the observed before, during and after the recording session may also prove to be important factors. In some cases interaction may be desirable, while in others keeping a distance is preferable to obtain valid data. Effects of 'monitoring' not only relate to behavior but also may occur when recording material aspects of culture. Thus, researchers could try to find out to what extent the setting has been modified (for example, what objects have been moved, removed or added) in anticipation of the recordings.

Sometimes 'reality' needs to be brought back to life via re-enactments or 'adapted' for technical or other reasons to be 'revealed' (for example, filming a sacred ritual, which is normally performed at night, during daylight). Obviously these rather radical types of interventions need to be well-thought-through, and above all, well motivated and explained so that the spectators know what they are looking at and what inferences can be made from the interplay of the depicted elements. The visual end product needs to be critically examined more than ever as a particular construction (a series of transformations and choices), not just as an unproblematic reflection of an unproblematic or pristine reality.

Next to reconstructing parts of the culture under study—for example, Asen Balikci's film on the life of the Netsilik before the introduction of the rifle in 1919 (Balickci, 1975)—social scientists may even go as far as to construct an experimental situation, which may never happen spontaneously in real life, but which may help to reveal some deeper aspects of a culture. For example, the anthropologist Rob Boonzaijer-Flaes once confronted Tibetan monks with Alpine horns to see how they responded to something alien to their culture.

B.3.4. Nature and degree of field involvement

Exploring society with visual media requires thorough preparation and consideration with regard to the field and the subjects treated. Involving the field of research (the subjects or otherwise related or concerned parties) in a more active, less passive ('object') role in the visual research set-up and execution (production, decoding, revising) may take many forms. Such involvement may be chosen for a variety of reasons, both for scientific (to acquire more in-depth knowledge from the 'inside') and for moral grounds (to pursue a more egalitarian relationship, with a willingness to share the benefits).

In a 'zero-state of involvement,' people may be 'totally unaware' of being the subject of research before, during, and after the research has been completed. This may be the case when using pre-existing material (for example, taken from archives) that is centrally stored and often relating to the past, or when hidden cameras are being used, or when fairly overt camera recording remains unnoticed due to the density of the public or the intensity of an event.

A further case may be that 'people are aware that they are being recorded' (for example, at tourist sites where almost everybody is running around with digital still and moving cameras) but don't know the particular purpose (and erroneously subsume it to be, for example, for private family pictures, or for journalistic purposes).

People may, however, react to being recorded whether or not they know its exact purpose: they may try to hide away, or to perform in front of the camera in less or more explicit ways. When people know they are being recorded they most often display a degree of reactivity. Looking into the camera is the most noticeable, but not necessarily the most significant reaction. This reactivity may even be, or become, the very subject matter of the research.

Many visual researchers have experienced the value of involving the field in a more active and encompassing way (not just during the recording, but before and afterward), which can lead to more 'participatory and joint forms of production' (Rouch, 1975). In fact, sometimes this participation of the community under study may be the main objective of the project, which then, rather than having a scientific purpose, seeks to promote community empowerment or activism. In this case, the researcher helps the community realize its goals rather than vice versa, which is normally the case.

B.3.5 Provision of the necessary (internal and external) context

It is important that visual researchers make every effort to situate the subject of their research, and their specific take on it, in its broader context, both visually and verbally. Researchers need to pay special attention to the scientific consequences of all the choices and decisions which have been made during research. Consequently, there must be a preparedness to make all these issues public: for example, to consider them as an integral part of the final research report. This is a particularly heavy and sizeable obligation, even more so than with other types of research. Limiting reporting to general descriptions of the steps taken is very seldom sufficient.

First of all, significant contextual information should, whenever possible, be part of the visual record or product itself (which may or may not consist of verbal and auditory types of information). To some extent 'part to whole' relationships are automatically provided by algorithmic visual recording devices such as a camera. Examples are an artifact pictured in its context of use, or moving images of an event as it chronologically unfolds itself. Hence, many ethnographers prefer using wide-angle lenses, although the issue is far more complex than this. Providing image-internal contexts requires a very active and careful effort on the part of the researcher; it is not something that is automatically—at least not in full—achieved by the camera, even though some cameras automatically record potentially useful information such as exposure data (aperture and shutter speed), date of exposure, and geographic coordinates (GPS).

Second, the relative meaning of the visual product (which may or may not contain verbal types of information) also needs to be related to, and contrasted against information obtained through other sources and techniques. Complex visual productions usually require an extensive verbal documentation that addresses the methodology followed, the choices made (technical, ethical, etc.), and the problems and uncertainties encountered from the concept to the end result. Also, some additional information should be provided about the broader context (cultural, historical) in which the visual product needs to be considered.

These basic requirements today form part and parcel of a broader call for *reflexivity* in science, which entails a clear recognition that all knowledge is 'work in progress,' incomplete, and perspectivistic (see also Rosaldo, 1989; Ruby, 2000; Pauwels, 2006c). With respect to visual research, reflexivity in particular involves giving a concrete shape to the idea that research is a complex 'meeting of cultures' (MacDougall, 1975: 119): to start with the cultures of the researchers (personal beliefs, preferences, experiences, characteristics, cultural backgrounds) and those of the researched, and at a later stage with the cultural stance of the viewers or users of the resulting visual product.

B.3.6. Ethical and legal aspects of visual research

The most important question here is how visual researchers can use visual media to collect data or communicate insights about human behavior and material culture in a way that will not harm subjects. The relatively irrefutable nature of (camera) images used in end reporting is likely to breach anonymity and thus raise rightful concerns with subjects. Both researchers and subjects are often unable to anticipate all the possible risks of being 'exposed' in such a way. Complex consideration of all contextual issues relevant to the particular research is required, including aspects such as how recognizable subjects are in images, the

acceptability of possible negative consequences, the conditions for access to the data, and the extent of participation on the part of those involved (Pauwels, 2008b).

While protection of subjects' rights is a paramount issue in visual research, issues such as authorship and copyright also require special attention. Image producers have the right to benefit from their creations and researchers should observe these rights when conducting visual research on the basis of pre-existing materials (for example, advertisements, documentary film, art). In particular, this includes using visual material from the Internet (Pauwels, 2006a). On the other hand, many visual researchers experience an urgent need for a more widely adopted and ratified 'fair use' policy. This would avoid being constantly slowed down (seeking permissions) or prevented (by pecuniary demands, absence of reactions, or negative responses) from using the materials for their study or from performing their customary 'intertextual' practice of citing and critiquing for strictly academic purposes.

C. Format and purpose of end product

C.1. Output/presentational format

The output or end result of visual social science can take different forms ranging from the standard article or research report (words only, or scant tables and graphs) to highly illustrated articles, added CD-ROMs, self-contained films, multimedia programs on DVD, or websites. Posters and exhibitions may also be used as a more temporary and space-bound outlet for visual research. The number of pictures or visualization elements (color, animation, design features) is not a valid indicator of the quality of research. The appropriate use of visuals and their interplay with other design elements is what counts most.

For some types of research it may be the right decision to limit the visuals to the bare minimum, to put them aside altogether, or to transform them into more manageable representations. This could be the solution for some forms of systematic camera recording whereby the significant data can easily be reduced to simpler types of data that still bear the essence: for example, numbers of people on a square at a given time, distances between actors, or vectors, etc. On the other hand, visual reporting approaches such as the 'visual essay' (Grady, 1991; Pauwels, 1993) rest to a large part on thoughtfully using most of the parameters of visual and verbal communication. Both the individual visuals and their interplay with the verbal may express insights that cannot be produced as effectively as in another, more traditional (at least for the sciences) form.

C.2. Status of the visual

The visual can take different roles in the end product. In principle, visuals should only be used in the end product if they fulfill a definite and unique role; they should not just be included as illustrations that have little or no added (informational or expressive) value. So it is conceivable that some visual research may have no visuals in the end product: for example, if the relevant aspects of photographs or direct observations can be transcribed into numbers or a verbal description for ease of use. But often the creation of a new visual representation (for example, a graphic representation of the summarized data) adds clarity to the insights conveyed.

While visuals can play just an intermediate role in the research process (often so with systematic and mimetic types of research), the collected or researcher-produced visuals more often play a very varied role in communicating what has come out of the study. Visuals can illustrate 'typical' settings, processes, give examples, or describe deviant or exceptional cases, and in doing so provide a 'holistic' account of elements in their often very meaningful spatial and relational surroundings.

As visuals may communicate a great variety of things and thus come to embody a

particularly varied 'status,' the problem is to adequately communicate this status. Users and audiences have a right to know what exactly they are looking at and to understand what current and potential purposes the depictions can serve.

C.3. Intended and secondary uses

Visual representations often have no 'intrinsic' or fixed value for research. Their research value is the combined result of a valid and representative data set for a given purpose, a particular research question and a sound process of going from visual facts or indications to a reasoned and substantiated set of inferences. As with any type of research, visual research is purpose driven and yields its particular design for a large part from this purpose. Purposes can be manifold and sometimes they can be combined. They not only determine the look of the end product but also determine the choices that should have been made in many of the previous steps. Images and visual representations to a large part derive their significance from the process and the context from which they emerge.

'Found images' by definition have not been produced with the researchers' particular purposes in mind. However, to the extent that they have been purposefully selected and insight has been acquired into the specific context from which they originate, they become capable of providing valid answers to particular research questions. The potential usefulness of a particular visual data set for particular purposes depends largely on the amount of contextual data which can be obtained.

The visual data or visual end product of visual research (for example, an anthropological film) or the intermediate visual data (systematic recordings of pedestrian activity on a square) may be used for new purposes: for example, as new input data or for other audiences (for example, lay audiences instead of students, or fieldworkers). Often, however, there will be at least some (minor or essential) reframing (or revisualization) and contextualization required for this to be successful. Some purposes are hard to combine (for example, highly specialized knowledge transfer with broad appeal) while others have much more leeway.

Sometimes the 'raw data' of a research product (for example, unedited film footage) can be packaged right away to suit various needs: for example, to produce a specialized visual report, to be included in a training module, to be edited into a product that can convince policymakers to try to remedy an unwanted situation, or help to empower a community in its struggle for a better life. But combining purposes or re-using materials for other purposes obviously always requires specific expertise and extra effort (time and money). Without proper care, the end result can easily become invalid, misleading or at least less effective.

CONCLUSION

Acknowledging the stark contrast between the current surge of interest in exploring visual aspects of society by scholars from the humanities and the social and behavioral sciences, and the relatively weak conceptual and methodical basis for realizing this interest in a more widely accepted manner, I have argued for a more integrated and analytical approach to visual research. This serves as a basis for the construction of more explicit, appropriate, and refined visual methodologies. Therefore, this chapter was devoted to the systematic presentation and clarification of a new 'integrated framework for visual social research' as represented in Figure 1.1. In addition to providing a synthesis of current research practices in an analytical manner, I sought to offer with this framework a broader and better understanding of the visual production, processing, and communication/dissemination stages of visual research and of the related methodological issues and research design concerns. As such, it may serve as a checklist for starting new research,

for assessing current research, or for offering insight into the many options in visual research, assumptions, and consequences.

So the framework is not just an analytical synthesis of existing options and issues, but also embodies a broader, future-directed program for a more visual sociology, aimed at inspiring further and more targeted methodological development. This framework—dense as it may already look—can be made even more detailed (for example, by linking specific ethical issues to specific approaches and techniques, and strategies to deal with these). However, this is exactly what is meant by the assertion that an overall framework may further feed and inspire more detailed and methodological expounding, focused on particular combinations of approaches, both visual and non-visual.

The use of the visual as a data source, or as a medium for capturing, processing, and expressing social scientific knowledge continues to challenge current scholarship as it is both a demanding and rewarding—but hitherto still rather uncommon (non-mainstream) and largely unchartered—territory. Both visual researchers and their diverse audiences should be prepared and educated to continue further along this road. More explicit and transparent methodologies and exemplary visual studies may help visual research to gradually enter the realm of widely accepted options in the study of society.

REFERENCES

Balikci, Asen (1975) 'Reconstructing cultures on film', in P. Hockings (ed.), *Principles of Visual Anthropology*. The Hague/Paris: Mouton Publishers. pp. 191–200.

Ball, Michael S. and Smith, Gregory W. H. (1992) *Analyzing Visual Data*. Newbury Park/London/New Delhi: Sage Publications.

Banks, Marcus (2001) *Visual Methods in Social Research*. London: Sage Publications.

Banks, Marcus (2007) *Using Visual Data in Qualitative Research*. Los Angeles, CA: Sage Publications.

Barndt, Deborah (1997) 'Zooming out/zooming in: Visualizing globalization', *Visual Sociology*, 12: 5–32.

Becker, Howard S. (1986) *Doing Things Together: Selected Papers*. Evanston, IL: Northwestern University Press.

Bogdan, Robert and Marshall, Ann (1997) 'Views of the asylum: Picture postcard depictions of institutions for people with mental disorders in the early 20th century', *Visual Sociology*, 12: 4–27.

Bousé, Derek (2003) 'False intimacy: Close-ups and viewer involvement in wildlife films', *Visual Studies*, 18: 123–132.

Brown, Brian J. (2001) 'Doing drag: A visual case study of gender performance and gay masculinities', *Visual Sociology*, 16: 37–54.

Burke, Caroline and Grosvenor, Ian (2007) 'The progressive image in the history of education: Stories of two schools', *Visual Studies*, 22: 155–168.

Cambrosio, Alberto, Jacobi, Daniel and Keating, Peter (1993) 'Ehrlich's "beautiful pictures" and the controversial beginnings of immunological imagery', *ISIS*, 84: 662–699.

Chalfen, Richard (1987) *Snapshot Versions of Life*. Bowling Green, OH: Bowling Green State University Popular Press.

Chalfen, Richard (2003) 'Celebrating life after death: The appearance of snapshots in Japanese pet gravesites', *Visual Studies*, 18: 144–156.

Chaplin, Elisabeth (1994) *Sociology and Visual Representation*. London: Routledge.

Clark-Ibanez, Marisol (2007) 'Inner-city children in sharper focus: Sociology of childhood and photo elicitation interviews', in G. Stanczak (ed.), *Visual Research Methods*. Thousand Oaks, CA: Sage Publications. pp. 167–198.

Collier, John (1967) *Visual Anthropology: Photography as a Research Method*. New York/London: Holt, Rinehart and Winston. Revised and expanded edition with Malcolm Collier (1986). Albuquerque, NM: University of New Mexico Press.

Corsaro, William (1982) 'Something old and something new. The importance of prior ethnography in the collection and analysis of audiovisual data', in A. Grimshaw (ed.), 'Special Issue on Sound–Image Records in Social Interaction Research', *Sociological Methods & Research*, 11: 145–166.

Curry, Timothy and Clarke, Alfred [1977] (1983) *Introducing Visual Sociology*, 2nd edn. Dubuque, IA: Kendall/Hunt.

David, Emmanuel A. (2007) 'Signs of resistance: marking public space through a renewed cultural activism', in G. Stanczak (ed.), *Visual Research Methods*. London/Thousand Oaks, CA/New Delhi: Sage Publications. pp. 225–254.

De Heusch, Luc (1988) 'The cinema and social science: A survey of ethnographic and sociological films', *Visual Anthropology*, 1: 99–156.

Diem-Wille, Gertrude (2001) 'A therapeutic perspective: The use of drawings in child psychoanalysis and social science', in T. van Leeuwen and C. Jewitt (eds.), *Handbook of Visual Analysis*. London/Thousand Oaks, CA/New Delhi: Sage Publications. pp. 157–182.

Edge, Sarah (1998) 'The power to fix the gaze: Gender and class in Victorian photographs of pit-brown women', *Visual Sociology*, 13: 37–56.

Edwards, Elizabeth (1990) 'Photographic "types": The pursuit of method', *Visual Anthropology*, 3: 235–258.

Emmison, Michael and Smith, Philip (2000) *Researching the Visual: Images, Objects, Contexts and Interactions in Social and Cultural Inquiry*. London/Thousand Oaks, CA/New Delhi: Sage Publications.

Geary, Christraud M. (1990) 'Impressions of the African past: Interpreting ethnographic photographs from Cameroon', *Visual Anthropology*, 3: 289–315.

Gödel, Margaret (2007), 'Images of stillbirth: Memory, mourning and memorial', *Visual Studies*, 22: 253–269.

Goffman, Erving (1979) *Gender Advertisements*. New York/London: Harper & Row.

Gold, Steven J. (2007) 'Using photography in studies of immigrant communities: Reflecting across projects and populations', in G. Stanczak (ed.), *Visual Research Methods*, London/Thousand Oaks, CA/New Delhi: Sage Publications. pp. 141–166.

Goodwin, Charles (1995) 'Seeing in depth', *Social Studies of Science*, 25: 237–274.

Gordin, Douglas N. and Pea, Roy D. (1995) 'Prospects for scientific visualization as an educational technology', *The Journal of the Learning Sciences*, 4: 249–279.

Grady, John (1991) 'The visual essay and sociology', *Visual Sociology*, 6: 23–38.

Grady, John (2006) 'Edward Tufte and the promise of a visual social science', in L. Pauwels (ed.), *Visual Cultures of Science: Rethinking Representational Practices in Knowledge Building and Science Communication*. Hannover and London: Dartmouth College Press—University Press of New England. pp. 222–265.

Grady, John (2007) 'Advertising images as social indicators: Depictions of blacks in LIFE magazine, 1936–2000', *Visual Studies*, 22: 211–239.

Grimshaw, Alan (ed.) (1982) 'Special issue on sound-image records in social interaction research', *Sociological Methods & Research*, 11: 115–255.

Grimshaw, Alan and Ravetz, A. (eds.) (2004) *Visualizing Anthropology: Experimenting with Image-Based Ethnography*. Bristol: Intellect Books.

Hagaman, Dianne (1993) 'The joy of victory, the agony of defeat: Stereotypes in newspaper sports feature photographs', *Visual Sociology*, 8: 48–66.

Hamilton, Peter (ed.) (2007) *Visual Research Methods*. London: Sage Publications.

Hammond, J.D. (1998) 'Photography and the "natives": Examining the hidden curriculum of photographs in introductory anthropology texts', *Visual Sociology*, 13(2): 57–73.

Harper, Douglas (2002) 'Talking about pictures: A case for photo elicitation', *Visual Studies*, 17: 13–26.

Harper, Douglas and Faccioli, Patricia (2000). 'Small, silly insults: Mutual seduction and misogyny: The interpretation of Italian advertising signs', *Visual Sociology*, 15: 23–49.

Heider, Karl G. [1976] (2006) *Ethnographic Film*, revised edition. Austin, TX: University of Texas Press.

Henny, Leonard (1986) 'Theory and practice of visual sociology', *Current Sociology*, 34(3): 1–76.

Hethorn, Janet and Kaiser, Susan (1999) 'Youth style: Articulating cultural anxiety', *Visual Sociology*, 14: 109–125.

Hockings, Paul (ed.) [1975] (2003) *Principles of Visual Anthropology*, 3rd edn. The Hague/Paris: Mouton de Gruyter.

Knor-Cetina, Karin (1981) *The Manufacture of Knowledge: An Essay on the Constructivist and Contextual Nature of Science*. New York: Pergamon.

Krase, Jerome (1997) 'Polish and Italian vernacular landscapes in Brooklyn', *Polish American Studies*, LIV: 9–31.

Lackey, Chad (2001) 'Visualizing white-collar crime: Generic imagery in popular film', *Visual Sociology*, 16: 75–94.

Larson, Heidi (1999) 'Voices of Pacific youth: Video research as a tool for youth expression', *Visual Sociology*, 14: 163–172.

Latour, Bruno and Woolgar, Steven (1979) *Laboratory Life: The Social Construction of Scientific Facts*. London: Sage Publications.

Lynch, Michael (1985) 'Discipline and the material form of images: An analysis of scientific visibility', *Social Studies of Science*, 15: 37–66.

McAllister, Kirsten (2006) 'Photographs of a Japanese Canadian internment camp: Mourning loss and invoking a future', *Visual Studies*, 21: 133–156.

MacDougall, David (1975) 'Beyond observational cinema', in P. Hockings (ed.), *Principles of Visual Anthropology*. The Hague/Paris: Mouton de Gruyter. pp.109–124.

MacDougall, David and Taylor, Lucien (eds.) (1998) *Transcultural Cinema*. Princeton, NJ: Princeton University Press.

McPhail, Clark and Wohlstein, Ronald T. (1982) 'Using film to analyze pedestrian behavior', *Sociological Methods & Research*, 10: 347–375.

Margolis, Eric (1994) 'Images in struggle: Photographs of Colorado coal camps', *Visual Sociology*, 9: 4–26.

Margolis, Eric (2004) 'Looking at discipline, looking at labor: Photographic representations of Indian boarding schools', *Visual Studies*, 19: 72–96.

Mead, Margaret (1963) 'Anthropology and the camera', in W. Morgan (ed.), *The Encyclopedia of Photography*. New York: Greystone Press. pp. 166–184.

Mead, Margaret [1975] 'Visual anthropology in a discipline of words', in P. Hockings (ed.), *Principles of Visual Anthropology*. The Hague/Paris: Mouton de Gruyter. pp. 3–10.

Mead, Margaret and Bateson, Gregory [1942] (1985) *Balinese Character: A Photographic Analysis*. New York: New York Academy of Sciences.

Mellinger, Wayne M. (1992) 'Representing blackness in the white imagination: Images of "happy darkeys" in popular culture, 1893–1917', *Visual Sociology*, 7: 3–21.

Mitchell, William J. (1992) *The Reconfigured Eye. Visual Truth in the Post-Photographic Era*. Cambridge, MA: MIT Press.

Mizen, Phil (2005) 'A little "light work"? Children's images of their labor', *Visual Studies*, 20: 124–158.

Musello, Christopher (1979). 'Family photography', in J. Wagner (ed.), *Images of Information*. Los Angeles, CA: Sage Publications. pp. 101–118.

Niesyto, Horst (2000) 'Youth research on video self-productions: Reflections on a social aesthetic approach', *Visual Sociology*, 15: 135–153.

Page, Edwin R. (2001) 'Social change at bike week', *Visual Sociology*, 16: 7–35.

Papson, Stephen (1991) 'Looking at Nature: the politics of landscape photography', *Visual Sociology*, 6: 4–12.

Pauwels, Luc (1993) 'The visual essay: Affinities and divergences between the social scientific and the social documentary modes', *Visual Anthropology*, 6: 199–210.

Pauwels, Luc (1996a) 'Managing impressions: On visually decoding the workplace as a symbolic environment', *Visual Sociology*, 11: 62–74.

Pauwels, Luc (1996b) *De Verbeelde Samenleving: Camera, Kennisverwerving en Communicatie*. Leuven/Apeldoorn: Garant.

Pauwels, Luc (2006a) 'Ethical issues of online (visual) research', *Visual Anthropology*, 19: 365–369.

Pauwels, Luc (2006b) 'A theoretical framework for assessing visual representational practices in knowledge building and science communications', in L. Pauwels (ed.), *Visual Cultures of Science: Rethinking Representational Practices in Knowledge Building and Science Communication*. Hanover and London: Dartmouth College Press—University Press of New England. pp. 1–25.

Pauwels, Luc (2006c) 'Representing moving cultures: Expression, multivocality and reflexivity in anthropological and sociological filmmaking', in L. Pauwels (ed.), *Visual Cultures of Science: Rethinking Representational Practices in Knowledge Building and Science Communication*. Hanover and London: Dartmouth College Press—University Press of New England. pp. 120–152.

Pauwels, Luc (2008a) 'A private visual practice going public? Social functions and sociological research opportunities of web-based family photography', *Visual Studies*, 23: 34–49.

Pauwels, Luc (2008b) 'Taking and using: Ethical issues of photographs for research purposes', *Visual Communication Quarterly*, 15: 243–257.

Pauwels, Luc (2010) 'Visual sociology reframed: An analytical synthesis and discussion of visual methods in social and cultural research', *Sociological Methods & Research*, 38(4): 545–581.

Pink, Sarah (2001) *Doing Visual Ethnography: Images, Media and Representation in Research*. London: Sage Publications.

Pinney, Christopher (1990) 'Classification and fantasy in the photographic construction of caste and tribe', *Visual Anthropology*, 3: 259–288.

Prosser, Jon (ed.) (2000) *Image-Based Research: A Sourcebook for Qualitative Researchers*. London: Routledge.

Prosser, Jon (2007) 'Visual methods and the visual culture of schools', *Visual Studies*, 22: 13–30.

Rich, Michael and Chalfen, Richard (1999) 'Showing and telling asthma: Children teaching physicians with visual narrative', *Visual Sociology*, 14: 51–71.

Rieger, Jon H. (1996) 'Photographing social change', *Visual Sociology*, 11: 5–49.

Rieger, Jon H. (2003) 'A retrospective visual study of social change: The pulp-logging industry in an Upper Peninsula Michigan County', *Visual Studies*, 18: 157–178.

Rosaldo, Renato (1989) 'Grief and the headhunter's rage', *Culture and Truth*, 1–21.

Rose, Gillian (2006) *Visual Methodologies: An Introduction to the Interpretation of Visual Methods*, 2nd edn. London: Sage Publications.

Rouch, Jean (1975) 'The camera and man', in P. Hockings (ed.), *Principles in Visual Anthropology*. Chicago, IL: Aldine. pp. 83–102.

Ruby, Jay (1986) 'The future of anthropological cinema—A modest polemic', *Visual Sociology Review*, 1: 9–13.

Ruby, Jay (2000) *Picturing Culture: Explorations of Film and Anthropology*. Chicago, IL: University of Chicago Press.

Schwartz, Donna (2002) 'Pictures at a demonstration', *Visual Studies*, 17: 27–36.

Smith, Ken L., Moriarty, Sandra, Barbatsis, Gretchen and Kenney, Keith (eds.) (2005) *Handbook of Visual Communication: Theory, Methods, and Media*. Mahwah, NJ: Lawrence Erlbaum Associates.

Sorenson, E. Richard and Jablonko, Allison (1975) 'Research filming of naturally occurring phenomena: Basic strategies' in P. Hockings (ed.), *Principles in Visual Anthropology*. Chicago, IL: Aldine. pp. 151–163.

Stanczak, Gregory C. (ed.) (2007) *Visual Research Methods: Image, Society and Representation*. Thousand Oaks, CA: Sage Publications.

Suchar, Charles (1988) 'Photographing the changing material culture of a gentrified community', *Visual Sociology Review*, 3: 17–22.

Suchar, Charles (1992) 'Icons and images of gentrification: The changed material culture of an urban community', in R. Hutchinson (ed.), *Gentrification and Urban Change: Research in Urban Sociology*. Greenwich, CT: JAI Press Inc. pp. 33–55.

Suchar, Charles (1997) 'Grounding visual sociology research in shooting scripts', *Qualitative Research*, 20: 33–55.

Suonpää, Juha (2000) 'Taming predators through photograph', *Visual Sociology*, 15: 51–64.

Synnott, Anthony (1985) 'Symbolic replica: A Sociology of cemetries', *International Journal of Visual Sociology*, 2: 46–56.

Tomaselli, Keyan G. and Shepperson, Arnold (2002) 'Where's Shaka Zulu?: Shaka Zulu as an intervention in contemporary political discourse', *Visual Studies*, 17: 129–140.

Tufte, Edward (1983) *The Visual Display of Quantitative Information*. Cheshire, CN: Graphics Press.

Tufte, Edward (1990) *Envisioning Information*. Cheshire, CN: Graphics Press.

Tufte, Edward (1997) *Visual Explanations*. Cheshire, CN: Graphics Press.

van Leeuwen, Theo and Jewitt, Carey (eds.) (2000) *The Handbook of Visual Analysis*. London: Sage Publications.

Wagner, Jon (ed.) (1979) *Images of Information: Still Photography in the Social Sciences*. Beverly Hills/London: Sage Publications.

Wagner, Jon (1999) 'Beyond the body in a box. Visualizing contexts of children's action', *Visual Sociology*, 14: 143–160.

Worth, Sol and Adair, John (1975) *Through Navajo Eyes, An Exploration in Film Communication and Anthropology*. Bloomington, IN: Indiana University Press.

Wright, Terrence (2001) 'Reflections on "The Looking Glass War": Photography, espionage and the Cold War', *Visual Sociology*, 16: 75–88.

Zube, Ervin (1979) 'Pedestrians and wind', in J. W. Wagner (ed.), *Images of Information: Still Photography in the Social Sciences*. Beverly Hills/London: Sage Publications. pp. 69–83.

2

Looking Two Ways: Mapping the Social Scientific Study of Visual Culture

Richard Chalfen

INTRODUCTION

Within the past two decades, we have seen a shift in primary preoccupation of the visual social sciences from the production of visual materials (social documentaries, photo essays, ethnographic films/videotapes, PowerPoint presentations, interactive websites), often for pedagogical purposes (illustration, classroom teaching) to a focus on explicating alternative ways of looking. Attention to the problematic nature of looking has occupied a number of scholars for a diversity of disciplines, notably Berger's now classic *Ways of Seeing* (1972) to his later book, *About Looking* (1980). These problematics also appear in popular and folk expressions and in the ambiguous significance of visual-oriented cultural materials.

In the following pages I treat 'looking' ('seeing' and 'being seen') as a culturally variable activity, one that is subject to ethnographic inquiry. This approach seems both timely and theoretically necessary. Within

visual anthropology, for example, when cameras have been involved, some have commented on a change 'from site to sight' (Banta and Hinsley, 1986),[1] redirecting our attention from 'objective' and 'realistically accurate' recording of 'what's there' to questions of how one is looking, watching, viewing and seeing, with or without camera technology (or some form of scopic technology).[2] In tandem, sociologist Michael Ball called our attention some years ago to the shift from the use of pictures to support ethnography to using a solid ethnographic approach to support pictures (Ball and Smith, 1992).

In my emphasis on 'looking' I have sought a way to avoid the frequently cited and reductive coincidence of visual social sciences with a myopic attention to camera-use and picture-making, most notably, the practice of ethnographic film for visual anthropology and documentary photography for visual sociology. But, if these activities are not central, where do they fit? Is there a convenient way to better integrate the non-verbal with the visual/pictorial realms of behavior? Is there a way of including the study of both 'site' and 'sight'? The answers to these questions suggest an important challenge: namely, to develop a way of organizing the field to be more inclusive, one based on culturally structured ways of looking and seeing, one grounded more on visual culture and less on camera technology, and one that provokes new questions and research opportunities.

Readers of the following pages will hopefully find a fresh model for organizing old information. Two comments from the social sciences offer an initial challenge. In 1995, Chris Jenks stated: 'The modern world is very much a "seen" phenomenon. Sociology, however, itself in many senses the emergent discourse of modernity, has been rather neglectful of addressing cultural ocular conventions and has subsequently become somewhat inarticulate in relation to the visual dimensions of social relations' (1995: 2).[3] Within anthropology, David MacDougall feels, 'Anthropology has had no lack of interest in the visual; its problem has always been what to do with it' (1997: 276). In the interests of organizing a practical perspective that afforded a priority to the visual in culture, I have tried to repackage standard and accepted topics of study along with classic references in this field of scholarship. My primary objective has been to offer a framework that incorporates the diverse subject matter of visual social sciences, focusing mostly on sociology and anthropology. Organization and convenience of use have been my primary objectives in conjunction with giving some sense of problem that is appropriate and relevant to this field of inquiry, and to understand what has counted as a problem or departure point for inquiry and program of original fieldwork. A related goal of this essay is to help students and newcomers perceive some sense of unity to the field. In these efforts, when someone asks: 'What is visual anthropology?' or 'What is visual sociology?' we might answer: 'A cultural approach to the study of *how people look* through time and space.'[4]

THE PLACE OF EYEGLASSES, CAMERAS, AND MEDIA

Sooner or later, most of us face the need for eyeglasses. We acknowledge the fact that glasses affect how we appear and how we see. Thus, we find a looking/appearing/seeing industry, one 'focused' on both sides of our looking/seeing framework. The natural deterioration of sight or imperfections of seeing is 'corrected' by applications of scientific knowledge. On the seeing side, we have eye examinations and the careful prescription of lens composition. On the appearance side, we find another kind of sensitivity—best heard when children are prescribed glasses. Glasses can produce an unwanted look (akin to teeth braces), often likened to 'four eyes' or the geek clique at school. Here the fashion industry plays a role as we also find ordinary people facing the choice of external frames or contact lenses (even tinted or clear). Other choices include shape and color of eyeglass lenses and frames—all interests of 'How I Look' in terms of both appearing and seeing.

Similar claims can be made for sunglasses. Within the suggested variety of meanings attributed to *how people look*, consider the simple decision to wear sunglasses and the range of reasons people might prefer to appear with their eyes covered. We know that some people want to enhance their appearance by wearing 'attractive shades' or ostentatiously expensive models, as a fashion statement, to enhance their overall attractive appearance or status, highlighted perhaps when we find people wearing sunglasses in darkened conditions. But motives may be quite different: namely, to conceal some feature of appearance such as hiding emotion or injury such as black eyes. But we must also consider matters central to acts of looking/seeing. Some may treat sunglasses as a form of protection for ocular health, preventing damage from sunrays, wind, and dust particles. Others want to increase their comfort while in sunny and bright light conditions, to ease difficulties in seeing, to reduce squinting. Still other individuals like the use of darkened lenses to prevent others from knowing what the wearer is observing. This act can be interpreted as imposing a political framework as the wearer can see others but others cannot see the wearer. Cross-culturally, one can imagine the range of potential meanings attached to wearing or not wearing sunglasses in interpersonal communication.

This theme of intervening lenses is extended to attention within visual studies; many believe that the visual social sciences always include some form of camera technology and camera use. This essay makes the point that the eyes and minds come before cameras and lenses.[5] We are reminded once again of anthropologist Paul Byers saying 'Cameras don't take pictures' (1966). Many now recognize that looking can be affected by a growing range of sight-aids from eyeglasses to telescopes and microscopes to cameras, most recently, embedded in cell phones.

The question, 'How Do People Look?' can be given and taken (asked, interpreted, and answered) in several ways. Importantly, the phrase *how people look* suggests at least two fundamental orientations, one active and one passive. Each orientation is tied to different lines of inquiry, which, in turn, lead to alternative content and questions. These two orientations can and frequently do overlap in the same phrase ('looking good' or 'good looks'), but they can be distinguished along the following lines.

Throughout, there is an important distinction between subjects/objects (that are seen) and subjects/actors (who are doing the seeing: see Table 2.1). Importantly, people can be subjects of inquiry in both columns; we also see that people/things serve as 'objects' in Column A, whereas people/things can be either 'subjects' and/or agents of inquiry in Column B.

Table 2.1 Two dimensions: comparing 'To Look/appear' and 'To Look/see'

Column (A) HOW PEOPLE APPEAR or 'to be seen'	Column (B) HOW PEOPLE SEE or 'to see'
Look meaning: To Appear	Look meaning: To See
LOOK as to be-looked-AT	LOOK as to look-AT
How to appear to self and to others	How to use eyes to look
'I wish to appear as…'	'It appears to me…'
Selective appearance	Selective perception
What people want seen…	What people see as…
To be seen	To do the seeing
'I'm lookin' jus' fine'	'I'm looking at myself'
About the OBSERVABLE	About the OBSERVER
Worth's 'about culture'	Worth's 'of culture'

Issues and problems with proposed paradigm

Readers will likely raise one important objection to this proposed focus on *how people look*. When referring to the validity of statements of appearance—the real question becomes: 'According to whom?' I would like to transform this potential liability into an asset by insisting on attention to agency—we must be careful to ask and ascertain who is making the observation, who is doing the seeing. Clearly members of a specific society and observers from outside that society will never see or interpret appearances in the 'same' way, though some social scientists may claim to be accomplishing this objective, or, at least, approaching this goal.

There will always be problems with any attempt to reduce complexity to a simple formulation such as *how people look*. Vision, looking, watching, sight, and seeing are proving to be more complex than most previously thought or currently think. In the first instance, there is a general understanding of differences between the meanings of 'look' and 'see,' not unlike distinctions of brain and mind, sex and gender, disease and illness, information and knowledge, among others, which might even extend to simple nature–culture relationships such as 'the raw and the cooked.' Referencing our other senses, we find parallel distinctions to hearing and listening.[6] Common to the proposed distinction, 'looking' is biologically and physiologically based—that is, as images that are formed on a retina, travel an optic nerve, and are processed by a brain. I want to retain a sense of minimal variation across cultures regarding the biological base of looking as mechanical, as a piece of human biology that is shared across the human condition, with minor variation, regardless of location in time and space.[7]

This sense of 'looking' might best be called natural. But seeing is not natural, mainly because, as defined, seeing is intimately attached to selective perception and interpretation. All interpretation, like all sensory experience, results from processes of construction. Making meaning from sensory input is a process guided by historic, social, and cultural context, open to change and variation across time and space (Classen, 1993). Following this thinking, there is infinitely more potential variation to 'How I see' than 'How I look.'

The important change I am suggesting hinges on our use of the word 'look.' I say this because I initially want to exaggerate a direct connection between 'looking' and 'appearing.' When we do this, we can emphasize that questions of *how people look,* as in 'how people appear,' are socially and culturally variable and thus amenable to ethnographic study. Clearly, there will be problems regarding look/appearance, especially when assuming some static existence. Importantly, there will always be situational and contextual complexity. People do not always appear/look the same under all personal and social circumstances. For instance, issues of clothing— what to wear (or not to wear) in different locations, at different events, and with different people—can be problematic and subject to a code-switching perspective (to be discussed shortly). Sub-cultural, generational, and age-grade variables always come into play, making it very important to carefully formulate specific questions or problems.

As a final introductory problem, using the verb 'look' to mean 'appear' and 'see' is not shared across all languages: while I have started with English, confusion may arise in other languages. In turn, some readers will undoubtedly dismiss the details of this proposed look–see distinction as playing with semantics, and, at times, as trying to be cute and little more. Semantics will always be a problem when trying to integrate vernacular and specialized uses of language. But little is to be gained in semantic confusion. My effort in these pages is to promote a clearly organized framework for clarification in an academic area that suffers from lack of a cohesive and articulated approach.

For the remainder of this chapter, I want to address the question of what subject matter is being organized and do so by accomplishing two tasks:

1 I want to present some indication of the kinds of specific questions and problems that naturally fall into each of these orientations in conjunction with the directions they take us. We will see that each of these two categorical orientations may contain sub-categories of content, topics, and paths of inquiry.
2 I will explore how this orientation works by referencing published studies and offering specific examples of questions and studies in science and society.

AMPLIFYING THE FIRST DIMENSION—APPEARANCE

In the Column A of Table 2.1, How People Look means 'How these people appear.' The appearance connotation of *how people look* can easily be heard in colloquial phrases, and we may speak of several clusters of 'look-related' comments, such as 'Ain't I lookin' jus' fine?' 'They looked sick after that cheap shrimp dinner!' among many others. Certain critical comments, that could be either positive or negative, are evoked here, including 'Did you see how she looked?' or 'Why did he want to look like that?' Or we might want to include common advertising mantras, from 'Change your looks in minutes!' to 'Look better—Lose 30 ugly pounds in 30 days!' I would speculate that aesthetic dimensions apply to appearance in all societies, meaning that all have preferences for good and bad looks.

I also acknowledge that appearances can include negative judgments. Looking can include questions about being morally and politically correct or incorrect that accompany questions of 'How will I/this look?' and 'How will I be seen/judged.' This dimension refers to controversial questions of 'witnessing' and becomes evident in such phrases as 'I don't want to be seen as someone who....' or not wanting to be judged for a flawed personal decision who decides to 'look the other way.'

Common household mirrors may play a large part in personal appearance, as when people monitor 'how they look' before leaving home (or, as discussed later, before having a picture 'taken') or, more generally, when appearing in front of others for impressions and potential comment ('first impressions count'... 'the look makes the man,' etc.). A woman's habit of carrying a compact mirror also serves this need. One is reminded here of Charles Cooley's classic and influential comments about a 'looking-glass':

> A social self ... might be called the reflected or looking-glass self.... A self-idea of this sort seems to have three principal elements: the imagination of our appearance to the other person; the imagination of his judgment of that appearance, and some sort of self-feeling, such as pride or mortification. (1922: 152)

Image consciousness is particularly important during adolescent years, when 'looking good' is a key social marker. Later in life, in the US, staying fit with the help of exercise machines and wall-sized mirrors is another familiar example. Issues and questions of 'presentation of self' (Goffman, 1959) and personal image management come to mind.

Anthropologists and sociologists have continually been drawn to the pictorial recording of people's appearances; results have served their ethnographic reports, and, in turn, their respective constructions of credibility. In his essay, 'The Visual in Anthropology,' David MacDougall reminds us of how some anthropologists at the turn of the century brought indigenous exotic-appearing peoples to museums and expositions, on lecture tours precisely to let people see what they looked like (1997: 276). Currently, we continue to see the public's interest in how indigenous people look; this is clearly evident in postcard photography when native people are photographed for popular consumption and sold at tourist locations.

Specific topics and applications

We have said that the first orientation (A), of *how people look* focuses on dimensions of 'how members of specific groups of people appear to themselves and to others.' In very fundamental ways, immediate and obvious attention is paid to factors of physical appearance, including body size, body shape, and skin color.[8] We must also ask: What do people do with (or to) themselves, their bodies or parts of their bodies, to appear in certain modified ways?

Central to questions of appearance is how people mediate questions of genetically structured or culturally favored *body size and shape*. Laura Miller (2006), drawing upon the work of Anthony Giddens, reminds us that 'modernity works a change from birth-determined identity to self-fashioned identity' (Miller, 2006: 11). Cultural preferences for body size become relevant alongside medically prescribed body weights, for example body mass index (BMI) .[9] Some are temporary, while others are meant to be permanent; some are medically designated as healthful, others become seen as harmful, even life-threatening. Manipulations include the assistance of multi-billion dollar industries devoted to a broad range of diets and special diet tablets, alongside the use of

Botox, collagen, fat injections or various implants and various forms of elective cosmetic surgery—liposuction procedures, breast enhancement and reduction, tummy tucks, and the like.

Observations of *body color*, both as given and changed, are relevant. As expected, we find considerable variation among any population, reinforcing the importance of refraining from simple generalizations.[10] In some contemporary societies, Japan for instance, many adult females continue to protect themselves and potential color change from sun exposure by using umbrellas in public settings. In comparison, we see a tendency for some of the younger population to seek a tanned or otherwise darkened skin complexion. In general, we find major industries devoted to offering clients a host of temporary 'skin' coloring adjustments, meaning a broad range of face and body cosmetics.

This large category of body alterations includes both permanent changes as well as more temporary changes. The topic of body aesthetics has been gaining scholarly interest, sometimes focused on modifying the appearance of body hair. Robinson's attention to 'Fashion in Shaving and the Trimming of the Beard' (1976) provides us with one example. We also include such topics as eyelid surgery, facial and body hair removal, and nipple bleaching (Miller, 2006). In this classification, permanent patterns of body alteration would include teeth-filings and patterned extractions. More common would be various customs of body-piercing and corporeal scarification. For example, studies of small and localized versus full-back or full-body tattoos would be appropriate, all of which produce immediate visual impressions. Schwartz's 2006 paper, 'Native American Tattoos: Identity and Spirituality in Contemporary America' helps us in this category.

Studies of *how people look* attract interest to details of facial and body habits, patterns of make-up, body painting, different hairstyles, including facial hair and pubic hair (crotch, venus-line shaping), hair coloration, eyebrow shaping, finger/toe-nail paintings and decoration as they might differ for young and old men and women. Needless to say, there is considerable cross-cultural variation; the diversity of cultural practices and systems of meaning accompanying such practices are amenable to ethnographic study.

Personal appearance often includes categories of what we might call '*add-ons*' and '*carry-ons*' or body adornments and attachments. For the former, most obvious would be sartorial choices and codes— articles of clothing that people elect to wear according to social norms, traditions, personal choices based on such variables as location, event, place, and time. We are reminded of such phrases as 'First appearances are the most important,' balanced by 'First appearances can be deceiving' as a version of 'Don't judge a book by its cover.'

The culturally variable notion of 'fashion' plays a major role in this context. One would also want to examine instances when items of clothing served as indicators of social and political rank. This would include the frequency of people wearing uniforms on an everyday basis, from blue collar support personnel to professional employees, including high fashion, costumes, work outfits, perhaps in settings such as sports fields, schools, the military, but also within contexts of the office, store personnel, hospital staff, various service sectors, and the like. Within a growing literature, anthropologist Fadwa El Guindi's 1999 study of veils offers a valuable contribution. We also see that as multiculturalism becomes the norm, contentious situations can emerge. I am reminded of ongoing struggles over Muslim schoolchildren wearing scarves or veils (or niquabs) in England[11] and women wearing burkas in France.

The absence of clothing should also be considered. Western and Victorian attitudes toward display of the naked human body. Cooley's (1922) 'mortification,' shame and decency, were certainly not dominant throughout the world. But in many contact situations, Westerners tried to alter some 'traditional' behavior by issuing ordinances about what could and could not be displayed and seen in public.

For the category of *carry-ons* (often called 'accessories'), we could include studies of the appearance and use of jewelry, amulets, fans, canes, handbags, and the like. Other artifacts that accompany on-body dress could also be net bags, tools, weapons, prayer beads among others. And for some in the US, water bottles, and in many cases, cell phones, may have replaced cigarettes.

In any consideration of 'look,' social variables become very important. Common reference points of looking/appearing a certain way are directly connected to the relevance of age grade, gender, marital status, social position, place, etc. To avoid any sense of rigidity or permanence, we must build in notions of situational *code-switching* and dimensions of change both across and within generations. In very simple and obvious terms, we do not always wear the same clothes in all social situations: for example, at home, parties, rituals, ceremonies, work/play and, in some cases, even at different times of the day. Who has not heard or said at some point in time: 'Go change your clothes—we're having company!' Outside the home, such activities as visiting friends, attending special events, and going to work have their own demands; some businesses in Japan, for instance, are now advocating a 'Casual Friday' tradition of dress (Sullivan and Jordan, 1995). Part of socialization includes learning 'when-to-wear-what' as in 'how to look' in different situations. It might be acceptable to dress one way in one setting and totally inappropriate in another (no shorts at the law firm, no swimsuits in the classroom or office, no jeans at the wedding). We are easily reminded of a parent's admonition: 'You're not going out of the house looking like that!'[12] Pattern analysis must always include the variation exhibited by humans to adapt to alternative social circumstances, states of contemporary fashion (Lowe and Lowe, 1982), as well as individual desires either to fit in or to standout.

In summary, the visibility of human appearance is tied to themes of 'wrapping the body,' as described by anthropologist Joy Hendry, as just one part of 'wrapping culture' (Hendry, 1993). All tie into culturally constructed nature of beauty ideals, the globalization of beauty technologies and standards, changes in beauty ideology.

Extending appearance: bodies in motion and space

How People Look incorporates other facets of appearance. Attention to appearance makes us consider *how people look* when using their bodies, body parts and limbs to pose, gesture, move, and even dance. We might hear: 'Stand up straight—don't slouch!' or 'You're walking like a baby' or 'Walk with conviction.' Examining patterns of body movements, including facial expressions and full-body gestures, fall into place. Anthropological studies of kinesics (Birdwhistell, 1970) and tacesics (or haptics) come into immediate relevance. Studies that relate posture, gesture, and body movement to work (Lomax, 1972) and to socialization fit well here (Bateson and Mead, 1942) as well as a broad literature on relations of dance movements, styles, and culture (Chakravorty, 2004; Adra, 2005).

Another large area of human appearance and interaction asks: 'How do people use their bodies to structure space as part of interpersonal relationships and communicative environment?' (Hall, 1966). An interesting relationship is found when connecting codes of body-part touching and the use of bodies in space: for example, hand-holding, hands around a partner's waist, what one touches during greeting or departing events. When people become crowded in public spaces—most notable, public transportation and elevators—when individuals often find themselves in body contact with strangers. Another set of situational code-shifts must take place to maintain a civil and acceptable atmosphere.

By extension: appearance through material culture

Ordinary people of all ages use material culture, their surroundings, belongings, and related possessions to extend their looks as reflections of personal appearance and identity. Frequently we have heard: 'Clean up the house ... we're having company!' 'A tidy [vs messy] desktop signals an organized [vs confused or creative] mind.' For example, the purposeful ordering of domestic space, including various means of shelter and housing, becomes relevant for study. Image-conscious young people, for instance, are fond of establishing an identity by the ways and means they decorate their rooms and zones of personal space. Image management includes looks of 'accessories,' both attached and, in this case, unattached from the human body. Peter Menzel et al.'s *Material World: A Global Family Portrait* (1995) and Adrienne Salinager's *In My Room: Teenagers in the Bedrooms* (1995) provide good examples.

In these ways, we see how extending space to studies of *design and decoration* (sometimes understood as extensions of self and identity) becomes important. Design and decoration of physical space in general can be added to what has been said about constructed appearances, appearances meant to be looked at and appreciated in culturally specific terms. Studies of graffiti and local murals find a place when we realize the image (tag, word, figure, statement, etc.) serves as an extension of self in both time and space, with ample attention to appearance (style, technique, size) and 'looking good.' Thus, various features of the built environment, especially architectural elements, are easily included in this formulation. We should keep in mind that placement of household walls and furniture can either encourage or restrict the ways that inhabitants can look at each other, how audio–verbal

interaction takes place, and how using movable panels (or sliding doors) as walls can effect change. Of visual interest, 'sight-lines' become important to Edward T. Hall's notion of proxemics and interpersonal communication (1966).

A modern and exceedingly popular way of extending appearance *through* space is facilitated by digital imaging and Internet communication. New opportunities for carefully considered construction of preferred appearance have been opened and given new life through Internet home pages and social network sites (SMS), perhaps best seen in Facebook or MySpace.[13] These audio-visual sites provide us with interesting parallels to the built environment, further extending an individual's or a group's symbolic environment, one that remains amenable to public observation and study.

In summary of How-People-Look in Column A, there are many ways that people may look/appear for others to know them, ways they extend appearance beyond the ways people 'wrap' their bodies through decorations and clothing. We can even add various means of transportation (most notably, a choice of car), but in other circumstances, we could add choice of bicycle, motorcycle, and other modern personal models of wheeled transportation (for example, self-balancing segues) in the future. These choices of extensions become visually significant markers, all of which contribute to a richly composed environment of visual communication.

Finally, I hasten to acknowledge that much of the work of archaeologists—from Paleolithic to historic sites—starts with searches for appearances. In conjunction with everyday living, we want to include a range of visual forms, from Paleolithic cave art and pottery design to contemporary examples of interior and exterior graffiti. What can be learned from the look of material culture (or even 'that which has been thrown away,' including contemporary references to 'garbology'[14]) that has survived for contemporary examination? But most archaeologists are not content to remain with this knowledge of appearances. From the appearance of material culture, they consistently work towards making sound inferences to understand better how a particular group of people lived their lives. Said differently, the primary interests lie in how a specific group of people saw, interpreted, and understood their surroundings and life. Thus, we find one of many connections between how people appear and our second dimension, how people see.

AMPLIFYING THE SECOND DIMENSION—LOOKING AT, SEEING, AND INTERPRETATION

Column B of the How-People-Look paradigm takes us into the second major collection of interests: namely, the category of 'How members of a specific group of people look at themselves and the world around them.' Following our earlier formulation, this is the area of how people SEE, which must include *both* 'vision' and 'visuality.' For our purposes, the former relates to the physical and biological apparatus operating on whatever it is that presents itself before the eye (in other words, the purely physiological side of seeing). In comparison, the latter attends to the culturally determined manner of looking at things, which defines 'what' we see and 'how' we see it, and includes how people make meanings and interpretations, attributions or inferences (Gross and Worth, 1974). We are asking how they understand their lives, their immediate environment, as well as the everyday lives of 'others,' the world around them and, in turn, how they are sometimes prompted to take action. These questions may only surface or become relevant when some form of threat or conflict occurs: for example, 'They just don't understand—they don't see it the same way we do!' Perhaps one by-product of education is an increased curiosity of both kinds of looking, coupled with increased sympathy for alternative ways of knowing. We shall see shortly

that epistemological and hermeneutic features, as related to questions of world view, play key roles in this orientation. Here we shift attention to the significance of interpreting and understanding appearances: namely, *how* and *what* one looks at.

A related and important domain of visual research attends to the ways and means that the physiology of perception can create optical illusions and 'mis-perceptions' of 'what's there' (Goodman, 1978). Studies here provide another reference point for understanding that things 'are not always what they appear to be.' In later pages, we will need to connect the physics of a camera's optical system to a human's physiology of perception to gain a better feeling for how, on occasion, 'pictures can lie' and when questions of 'camera truth' or the truth qualities of photographs come into serious contention. Complexities of camera-assisted visual communication become apparent when we acknowledge the integration of propensities and limitations of physiology, the visual options afforded by a camera's optical system all in conjunction with socio-cultural framing that directs images to predispositions, ongoing interests, curiosities, and concerns.

The duality of 'seeing' in conjunction with 'being seen' should come as no surprise to anthropologists and sociologists and represents no dramatic departure from familiar thinking. Anthropologists, as part of their fieldwork, have always sought to describe the people they study in conjunction with their surroundings—with and without photographic illustration. But equally important is the acknowledged intention to know how various peoples think about, interpret, make meaning, and understand their own lives and society—in short, their culture. This brief delineation is more complex than initially 'meets the eye,' so additional discussion is needed.[15]

On the level of the individual, we may be speaking of selective perception—what one attends to might be expressed in such comments as: 'You have to know what to look for!' or 'You were not picking up the right signs, but I know he likes you.' Or, in the context of interpersonal arguments, one might hear: 'You don't understand—you've got to look at it my way.' More to the point, we might even hear the admonishment, 'You may be looking, but you are *not* seeing!' Individuals and groups of people may be more used to looking for/at or attending to some features of a scene, event, or person than another group of people. Thus, the notion of selective perception—as a version of 'how I/we looked'—is very much a matter of scale.

Anthropologists have continually worked on the notion of understanding life and the world 'through the native's point of view,' gaining insights on world view and related metaphors. As in my previous references to the language-culture insights of Alan Dundes (1972), many ocular metaphors fit here quite well, including 'Seeing is believing' and 'Do you see what I mean?'[16] Other examples will be incorporated shortly.

General principles of ethnocentrism and cultural relativity speak to this issue: namely, that there are many ways of seeing the 'same' thing, none necessarily better or worse than others (an ethically corrupt notion according to some conservative thinking). The task has been to somehow discover and describe preferred ways of seeing and understanding the world. Indeed much of anthropological education and training has been so directed: that is, to allow for and appreciate alternative ways of seeing. The Whorfian hypothesis, efforts in ethno-science as well as cognition studies find a place here.

Finally, we must consider the ways people don't look—we need to add what people should not look at, should not see—to the previously mentioned ideas of how people should not appear in private or public. Erving Goffman cited examples of purposeful avoidance of looking as 'civil inattention' (Goffman, 1966), which, in turn, has connections with animal habits of direct and indirect gazes. Children are instructed not to look in the eyes of particular animals as a deterrent

to the animal sensing a harmful threat and reaction.

Patterns of appropriate seeing may also be guided by age-graded prohibitions on subject matter (no violent films/TV for children, no pornography for pre-teens) or age/gender-specific rules, such as when only the male elders of a specific society can view certain ritual or religiously significant artifacts. Questions of the sanctioning agency come into view: namely, the government, national film boards (responsible for feature film ratings), libraries, computer and server filters, and parental control among others.

Micro-categories of observation

It is convenient to divide relevant examples into micro- and macro-categories. Central to the former is a literal meaning of looking at: that is, the variety of normative ways that people use their eyes 'to look at' surroundings, people, and things. These interests may extend from someone saying, 'Keep your eyes open,' 'Just watch where you're going!,' to 'I just knew something was very wrong—Did you see the way he looked at me?,' to an admonition of 'Look at me when I am speaking to you!,' to the much more subtle senses of knowing when your conversational partner intends to interrupt your comment(s) or offer you a chance to speak.

Relevant research focuses on how patterns of looking, gazing, and staring are intimately related to linguistic activities, especially in studies of turn-taking as part of conversational analysis (Cook, 1977; Argyle, 1978). We find a significant niche for examinations of patterns of eye movement (Duchowski, 2003),[17] the culturally structured habits of 'eye behavior' or what to do with one's eyes (avoidances, aversions) in different situations and circumstances. Studies here include the uses of glances, winks (vs blinks or tics), glimpses, double-takes, stares, and all sorts of gazes (Seppanen, 2006). As a list of 'General Rules' for what is informally termed, 'the language of the eyes,' Hattersley (1971) offers the following intuitively derived list of recommendations:[18]

1 Never look at anyone more than absolutely necessary.
2 Be particularly careful to avoid looking at strangers.
3 When you are actually looking at someone, avoid thinking about it. Otherwise, he [sic] will become aware that he is being looked at by someone aware of doing it; and the relationship will become very strained.
4 When someone is telling you a lie, be very careful not to let your eyes inform him he is detected.
5 When two people are looking directly into each other's eyes, the more courteous one always breaks eye contact first.
6 If you have been looking at someone while listening to him, and suddenly find yourself looking through him, either bring your attention back to him or if he has noticed, apologize for momentarily being distracted from his conversation.
7 When you are looking at someone and he does something you think he would prefer were invisible—rubs his nose, blinks away a tear, twitches, etc.—allow the 'blind look' to come into your eyes as an indication that you respect his feelings by not seeing what he has done.
8 If you are telling someone a lie, and you know that he is aware it is a lie, do not look him directly in the eye, for that would make you a monstrous liar rather than an ordinary liar.
9 When looking at someone, take great care to omit the 'you are being judged' expression from your eyes. That is, always keep your expression neutral.
10 If you look into someone's eyes and discover that he is suffering from some kind of acute distress, do not allow your eyes to reveal your discovery to him (Hattersley, 1971: 84).

Hattersley also suggests that there are rules for women as well as men and different social relationships may take on their own special rules. He notes these rules can serve as a means of survival as well as one of the social graces. But less is said about the importance of cross-cultural variations. Goffman would have a different take on how these instances would relate to 'interaction ritual' (Goffman, 1982).

Patterns emerge when asking people to list the times when they have been told or they have said: 'Don't look!' and when people sense a need to avert their eyes to prevent looking. In one explicit example, one might find the admonition: 'For Your Eyes Only' written on private office folders. Selective looking becomes relevant and, again, includes examples of being aware of a scene and purposefully not looking; car drivers, for instance, may elect not to look at another driver competing for the same traffic lane, thus becoming 'non-accountable' for any altercation or even accident that might occur. Car drivers are also likely to be attracted to the tragedies of accidents: 'Everyone knows that what slows down highway traffic going past a horrendous car crash is not only curiosity. It is also, for many, the wish to see something gruesome' (Sontag, 1977: 95–96). Another example of selective seeing involves public men's rooms. In several countries, people can see vertical urinals in public settings, either unused or being used when passing by a men's room. But the norm is not to look in, not to purposefully seek out views of men using a urinal. Here we have a clear case of what can happen in comparison to what does happen.

Parents in the US will instruct their children not to stare at people's infirmities or at disabled people, or cover their eyes to scenes of overt sexuality or extreme violence. The subject of prohibited looking at people, things, or activities is not often discussed. But James Elkins cites certain patterns of avoidances in a chapter entitled 'Just Looking' (1996), where he states[19]: 'There is a provocative theory... proposed by surrealist Georges Bataille. He said that there are three things that cannot be seen, even though they might be right in front of our eyes: the sun, genitals, and death' (Elkins, 1996: 103). Elkins then proceeds to examine the reality and implications of this assertion.

In summary, it is probably the case that every society and culture has a latently realized set of norms for eye-use (how-to-look) for appropriate, preferred and, by contrast, incorrect ways of looking at people, things, and activities. It follows that we covertly recognize outsiders by slight variations of these norms—'Did you see the way they were looking at us?' 'That type of staring might be okay in New York but it's not here!' And after the fact, one might hear—'He just wouldn't stop staring at your boobs!' or 'I could tell there was something wrong just by the way he looked at us!'[20]

Macro-categories of observation

As stated earlier, our organization of *how people look* should include an array of macro-categories of looking/seeing. We may include the formal teaching of 'looking skills'— though that term or title will be unfamiliar. By 'looking skills' I call attention to efforts to teach which semiotic features 'should' be looked at, paid attention to, and appreciated in the effort to identify or learn something, to make the 'correct' reading or interpretation of a visual item or scene. In practical applications, we find education needed to develop skills for 'reading' an X-ray, a weather map, military reconnaissance images (even specialized graphs and charts), all of which are forms of 'visual literacy.'[21]

In the description of a recent book, entitled *Skilled Visions*, one that stresses ethnographic methods as a way to learn 'constructions of local knowledge,' we read: 'Most arguments for a rediscovery of the body and the senses hinge on a critique of "visualism" in our globalized, technified society. This approach has led to a lack of actual research on the processes of visual "enskillment"' (Grasseni, 2007: publisher's description). In addition, much of art appreciation falls into this category. At the heart of this interest is the tutored development (even management) of ways of looking, producing a 'critical viewing' of a visually mediated form, and a developed talent for seeing 'what's really there' or, even better, seeing as much as possible. Here we find purposeful and explicit training in developing the 'proper' way of

seeing an art piece on the way to making a competent interpretation. These tutored skills are easily extended to the larger context of the built environment, perhaps best illustrated by architectural efforts—another example of an expanded notion of visual literacy.[22]

This area now extends from fine arts to popular culture—to courses in critical viewing of mass media, including, but not limited to, ways 'to read' advertisements, feature films,[23] and television programming as well as to critical assessments of Internet information. We must also consider examples from non-media everyday life such as knowing to look for a green light while driving as well as going to an unfamiliar sports event for the first time (for example, the game of cricket for Americans), where we might hear such frustrations as, 'I just don't know what to look at yet!' Other selective ways of seeing include learning to interpret X-rays, MRI results, microscope slides, or aerial reconnaissance photographs, among other pictorial examples.[24]

Another macro-category focuses on *tourism*. Arguably, tourism is a visual phenomenon as we observe people using sight to see sites. Most travelers have a curiosity for 'how local people look,' how 'others' live, and what a particular location in the world looks like. Increasingly more attention is being given to relationships of tourism and visual culture in international conferences and publications.[25] Other scholars have documented the ways local residents have prepared themselves and their surroundings to be looked at by tourists, knowing that a 'good showing' will attract more interest and income. Dean MacCannell's (1976) look at 'staged authenticity' specifically his reformulation of Goffman's front and back stages for tourism are important contributions.

In tandem, and once again, we are increasingly drawn to questions of how local populations see their own lives. Thus, we would also want to include studies of how local people see outsiders and visitors, be they classified as missionaries, development specialists, art dealers, medical personnel, filmmakers or anthropologists, or as increasingly popular, tourists. Valene Smith's *Hosts and Guests* (1989) provides many relevant examples. Connections to behavior and material culture are again seen in carefully considered transformations for touristic visitation, including reorganizing art forms (including 'airport art'), dances, food, and clothing, among others. Nelson Graburn's book *Ethnic and Tourist Arts: Cultural Expressions from the Fourth World* (1976) is particularly useful for important examples.

Another macro-category of relevance appears in contemporary scholarship devoted to the broad area of media—'*reception studies.*' Here attention is directed towards what people look at and how they interpret what they see in various visually mediated forms, regardless of knowledge of the best or 'schooled' way of appreciating such information and communication. Researchers want to know what is 'actually' going on versus what 'should' be happening. For further clarification we need to move to the next layer of *how people look*: namely, when camera technology is involved, our next series of topics.

Finally, we would include the attention anthropologists have traditionally given to questions of world view and related metaphors for the diversity of ways that diverse peoples see and understand the world(s) they inhabit, including, of course, metaphysical aspects of before-and-after life. In this way, we find a comfortable way of integrating topics of religion and spirit domains, including problematic ghost-visibility, along with questions of ideology and inevitable connections to epistemology, revealed in such statements as 'Seeing is believing,' as mentioned earlier.

I have more than implied that issues of looking/seeing are at the heart of the How People Look model for organizing the visual social sciences. While this enterprise cannot be limited to the use of camera technology, it certainly cannot eliminate it either. Hence, attention now turns more comfortably to the incorporation of 'aids to looking,' including scopic technologies, in the interests of extending human looking and seeing.

ADDING CAMERAS TO ASSIST LOOKING/SEEING

The general thinking is that pictorial renditions of appearance serve as evidence of 'having been there,' as personal witness, a basis for backing a sound argument.[26] Thus, the use of cameras can make many valuable contributions—some certainly more critically sound than others. Sociologist Howard Becker offers a convenient way of linking two kinds of looking by suggesting we may want to ask different kinds of questions when thinking about photography. He describes this difference in the following way:

> The question we ask may be very simple and descriptive: What does Yosemite look like? What does the Republican candidate for President look like? How did our family and friends look in 1957? Sometimes the questions are historical or cultural: How did people take pictures in 1905? How do they take them in Yorubaland? (Becker, 1986: 293)

In short, we have the distinction between how people appear and how people see, but, now, with the addition of camera use. Thus, we can now continue this distinction by adding forms of technology such as eyeglasses and cameras.

Two anecdotes, focused on the theme of 'She didn't look herself,' introduce the problematic addition of cameras to learning more about *how people look*.

> It was Aunt Bea's 90th birthday party and lots of people brought food to help celebrate. They also brought cameras to take pictures—a natural thing to do I guess. But, you know, I had known her for almost 50 of her 90 years and something was wrong. We all knew Bea was losing her eyesight and she looked a little strange.... I just didn't want to take her photograph because she didn't look herself. (Anonymous, 2004)
>
> Last year, the funeral parlor director said we could take photographs of my grandmother in her

coffin, but only after official viewing hours. And my two cousins did just that. But I didn't feel like taking her picture because she didn't look herself. (Anonymous, 2005, personal communication)

These comments beg for a 're-focusing' or re-positioning of cameras in the How People Look framework. When previously considering the content of Column A (the appearance emphasis), I stressed versatility and change; however, no mention was made of changes in appearance that might be made when people explicitly know that their pictures are about to be taken. In professional contexts, we have the employment of make-up artists, costume specialists, and set designers, among others, for these purposes. But what corresponds to this luxury for ordinary people in everyday life, if anything? To demonstrate the reality of this question, I have frequently asked students to consider the following: 'When in the course of a life-time do people find themselves in front of an operating camera?' In other words, what does the 'on-camera presentation of life' look like? Does the anticipation of photography act as a change agent in *how people look* for the camera?[27] As a generalization, most people do something to or for themselves, again, 'to look good' in a family photograph. I will give an additional reference to home media shortly.

SOCIAL SCIENCE CAMERA USE FOR LOOKING AND SEEING

This proposed look/see paradigm can be understood as a means of de-centering ethnographic photography and film/video. Regardless, it is time to re-incorporate camera-related practices and images in general into the proposed perspective. One natural connection is to relate acts of seeing to models of showing (display and exhibition). As a logical extension of questions about 'looking at' we can add problematic issues surrounding the use of camera technology in the aid of looking, producing, and communicating pictorial data. Here we find a convenient home for all that has been discussed about ethnographic photography, film, and video. Even such non-technological methods of sketching, drawing, and painting should be included (though not discussed here: see Christova-Slavcheva, 1996, as just one example).[28]

Following our look/see designations and organization, cameras are used to help us see and later show what we (as observers) are looking at, or, better, the way things look to us. Justifications for camera use are many. Cameras extend sociological and anthropological looking at people, things, activities, and events in several important ways. These range from creating documents to bring visual renditions home from the field for additional study, to allowing us to see things that we cannot register as part of unaided everyday looking: for example, from telescopes and microscopes to telephoto and macro lenses and high-speed cameras. Early animal and human locomotion studies by Étienne-Jules Marey (1992) and Eadweard Muybridge (1979) and later by Ray Birdwhistell (1970), among others, amply demonstrated how cameras extend our abilities to see, show, and illustrate findings in a variety of exhibition contexts with different motivations in mind.

But the significance of cameras is not limited to pictures taken by social scientists. As expected there are many sub-divisions of visual/pictorial examples, some based initially on simple distinctions of who is using these cameras. How do we integrate the results of professional camera use, or images made by native/indigenous members of specific societies? In short, who is doing the observing, and who is looking at whom? (see Michaels, 1982; Pack, 2006).

Ethnographic (sociological and anthropological) filmmakers attempt to show what one society looks like to members of another society.[29] Traditionally, this has meant Western lenses looking at non-Western life, as something that 'we' do to 'others' (Banks and Morphy, 1997). Most will agree there is no one satisfactory definition of ethnographic photography or ethnographic film, and some have gone so far as to advise us that this is not even a productive question. Arguments continue regarding the most effective way(s) to use cameras to look at people—from observational, participatory, reflective/reflexive camera techniques to versions of 'cinéma realité' to the ethically challenged, hidden-camera model of recording 'real life.'[30]

Other authors, most notable, Howard Becker (1974, 1981) have made meaningful connections between sociological themes and the work of documentary and fine art photographers, sensing an overlap in ways of seeing and reporting appearances, and, in turn, asking what each might be offering or contributing to the other. Becker asks how some representatives of sociologists and photographers work towards similar goals through different means. In Japan, the work of George Hashiguchi (1988) has been interpreted as containing a visual sociological perspective (Chalfen, 2005) much as others have accorded August Sander for his portraits during the Weimar Republic. George Hashiguchi's work seems to give a fine example of 'when art which is aimed at exploring society ... might just as well be social science information' (Becker, 1981: 10–11).[31]

Simply put, using a camera is just one way to augment seeing and showing appearances discovered in the field. Camera-generated photographs and films answer important questions (problematically at times) for many observers at a distance. The visual recording of *how people look* has been the pictorial capital of such magazines as *National Geographic* (*NG*), as we all recognize, the very popular magazine used for the longest time by ordinary people for vicarious travel and 'accidental' ethnography. This is an important example; while *NG* photography has been abundantly admired, the use and interpretation of *NG* images has often been uncritical—a kind of what-you-see-is-what-you-get. But recently some authors have drawn scholarly attention to details of this 'camera-look' and the intentionally structured results of this way of looking and reporting human scenery (Lutz and Collins, 1991; O'Barr, 1994).

An important avenue of thinking here relies on the treatment of visual genres as cultural documents. The approach titled *The Study of Culture at a Distance* (Mead and Métraux, 1954) included the conceptualization of feature films as cultural documents (Weakland, 2003) and reported on the results of examining German, French, Italian, Chinese, and Indian feature films as well as the results of Hollywood productions (Powdermaker, 1950). Weakland's 'Themes in Chinese Communist Films' (1966) and Bateson's 'An Analysis of the Nazi Film Hitlerjunge Quex' (1954) are good examples. Similar questions of looking/seeing can be addressed to other popular, even daily, published photographs. For example, what are *visual journalists* (photo-journalists) doing as they report on and show us a highly selective (yet claimed to be objective) version of the world? How do cameras contribute to a belief system that allows people to believe they know how things look and how things might be changing? Related studies have examined the formulaic ways and organizational constraints used by visual journalists and their editors that predetermine how culturally different people will 'look' the same (Hagaman, 1993). Other research may investigate the versions of society and culture produced by professionals as seen in newspaper and magazine advertisements (Goffman, 1976; O'Barr, 1994; Grady, 2007), advertising campaigns based on posters, or a broad range of televisual communication such as everyday mass media.[32]

Recent introductions of new media via satellite communication systems make this all the more relevant as these mediated forms contribute a global perspective to local media. For instance, how are members of one society seeing and interpreting a film made by another society? The notions of multiple readings suggested by Stuart Hall (1973, 1997) and the important notion of 'unintended audiences' (Jhala, 1994) also become relevant, fostering notions of dominant, realist, negotiated, and aberrant readings. Examples of studies include interpretations made by different groups of people looking at the 'same' feature film or television program (Katz and Liebes, 1994).[33]

Studying the indigenous view as ways of seeing

We have seen a growing scholarly interest in 'indigenous media,' where people show how they are seeing themselves and their lives or what they are seeing with the aid of cameras (Ginsburg, 1991).[34] Four models predominate:

1 Instances when researchers have provided subjects with cameras and minimal technological instruction.
2 Cases when scholars have examined the process and results of people making various kinds of media on their own initiative.
3 Projects where image/photo elicitation interviewing is the key to gaining indigenous perspective, points of view, and ways of seeing.
4 Examples of people making their own films to express their wishes and needs for change based on how they see their own problematic life circumstances.

In the first model, several visual anthropologists and visual sociologists have introduced still or motion picture cameras to their subjects to learn how 'others' look at their own lives and see the world around them.[35] In turn, we have new information on how these people want to make images to show to themselves and to 'us' (Michaels, 1991; Turner, 1991). In the case of *Through Navajo Eyes* (and many similarly titled works), we see an attempt to learn if patterned ways of using cameras and constructing films are connected to other means of expression (folk tales, myths) and communicative codes (linguistics) (Chalfen, 1992; Worth et al., 1997).[36] The second approach to indigenous media directly demonstrates how the two *how-people-look* dimensions overlap.

Relevant cases include Michaels' paper, 'How to Look at Us Looking at the Yanomami Looking at Us' (1982), Sprague's 'Yoruba Photographers: How the Yoruba See the Themselves' (1978), and Pack's 'How They See Me vs How I See Them: The Ethnographic Self and the Personal Self' (2006). In the third model, subjects are interviewed as they look at images they make for their own purposes or in response to an investigator's questions and prompts. Research participants are asked to discuss their motives, expectations, and the meanings they attach to the pictures. Work in art therapy and 'phototherapy' (Furman, 1990; Weiser, 1993) and discussions of photo elicitation methodology and techniques (Harper, 2002) can be located here. The fourth model, which emphasizes another activist approach, includes multiple applications of Photovoice (Wang et al., 1996; Wang and Burris, 1997) for changing community health practices.

As a specialized interest in young people and youth media, a growing number of sociologists and anthropologists have sought a better understanding of how adolescents see and understand their own lives (Chalfen, 1981; Stokrocki, 1994; Cavin, 2000 among others). And most recently, we are seeing an applied direction, where, for instance, chronically ill patients are offered video cameras and asked: 'How do you see your own medical condition?' to teach their health personnel 'what it means to live with a particular illness' (Rich and Chalfen, 1999; Chalfen and Rich, 2004). Objectives focus on enhancing patient–doctor communication, having young patients take more charge of their own illnesses, and enabling physicians to improve treatment plans after studying such visual reports.

Home media

Finally, we find an interesting combination or convergence of the dualism underlying this essay: namely, 'seeing' and 'being seen' in what has been referred to as 'home media'

(Chalfen, 1987, 1991). In most parts of the world, though certainly not all, ordinary people have been making pictures of themselves as part of family photography and everyday life. When asked why so many ordinary people appreciate this model of photography, we are likely to hear: 'I like to make albums of our family photographs to see *how we looked*' or 'We wanted to remember *what we looked like*' or 'We wanted to see what they [parents, grandparents, distant relatives] *looked like* when they were young.' Here we find ideas and expressions directly in line with Column A of the How People Look paradigm. These pictures can be considered as extensions of appearance—that is, as pictorial statements of 'how they look.' As a result, patterns of 'preferred appearance' can be seen.

Two points become relevant. First, we can revert to earlier comments on extending personal choice of 'how to look' via appearance: for example, choices of surrounding artifacts including selection of clothing, car, home, decorations, and the like. The same can be said for the choice of our personal photographs and the ways we use them to decorate personal spaces, including different household rooms as well as work (business offices, cubicles) and recreation spaces (playrooms, lockers). Earlier comments on extensions into cyberspace via social network sites illustrate further the ways that private and public imagery are overlapping, when distinctions are becoming blurred. Here we accord a special attention to photographs of people, specifically because of the multidimensional qualities and meanings attached to appearance.

Second, family albums and collections of snapshots, slides, home movies, and home videos chronicle selective renditions of *how people looked* in the past. But these collections of pictures can be considered and valued in another way, when we jump to the second dimension (Column B): namely, how these people 'looked at' their lives with cameras; patterns of preferred ways of seeing can be found.[37] Thus, we find norms for

presenting a way of life to people who are using norms to look at that life with a camera. Hence, the notion of 'snapshot versions of life' (Chalfen, 1987, 1988) encourages us to ask:

- What kinds of stories are told by photograph albums?
- What defines these pictorial narratives?
- Can we find a way to understand how culture is wrapped in album covers and expressed on album pages?

Finally, paralleling previous comments on not-looking (as in 'Don't look!'), we find regulations for not looking-with-cameras as part of everyday picture-taking. Public signs indicating 'No Photography Allowed' are just one explicit indicator of such restrictions. However, given the new influx of digital camera and camera phones, there are many more instances that leave it up to 'good judgment' and 'common sense' as to what is allowed and forbidden, thus fostering change and ambiguity on how to look-with-cameras.[38]

CONCLUSIONS AND CLOSING THOUGHTS

Clearly, problems associated with the dualism of *how people look*, of 'being seen' and 'seeing,' of looking and seeing take center stage in the foregoing discussion. We easily find a growing scholarly attention to problematic domains of looking and being looked at (seen). From a talk given by Deirdre Mulligan in 2007, we read: 'Camera and video technology are changing who we watch, what we watch, when we are watched, and redefining the purposes for which we watch'[39] (Mulligan, 2007). In all parts of the world people are addressing panopticon problems and questioning what it means to be able to observe ('look at') people, scenes, events, activities with a camera and, in turn, what it means to be 'looked at' or seen with a camera. Just as social scientists have asked critical questions about 'the right to write,' so we have questions and even contentious debates about the rights, legalities, and ethics of both 'looking' and 'being looked at' or being an observer and being-observed by cameras in private or public spaces. Daily news in the US contains many problematic examples: we read of questionable uses of camera surveillance in banks, schools, on streets (including traffic violations), in newspaper stands, and in dressing rooms, among others. Camera-phone users are causing a parallel list of ethical and legal problems. There is every reason to believe that debate and argument about surveillance problems will increase. New attention to 'sousveillance'[40] adds significantly as the quantity and quality of camera phones increase. Again, context matters: Who is doing the photography, and under what conditions with what motivations, goals, outcomes in mind? More to the point, How will the images be used? How will they be 'shown and looked at' by others? In turn, is there adequate discussion and training in the social sciences to make meaningful contributions to this discourse?

The foregoing discussion suggests the usefulness of adopting a *how people look* framework. The visual social sciences are less about camera use and more about looking and seeing, watching, and being observed. At the heart of both kinds of looking—appearing (or 'being seen') and seeing—is the role of culture contributing to the patterns and dynamics of the kinds of visual communication that lie at the heart of this paradigm.

While avoiding a camera-centric position for understanding visual culture and visual studies, we should acknowledge the multi-layered value of photographs of people within the *how people look* framework. Pictures of people should be considered as a special category of artifact. The machine/mechanical qualities of camera apparatus have the ability to provide data for both sides of our looking divide—that is, to crystallize two kinds of record: namely, appearance and gaze. We may underestimate the cultural importance and value of how photographs provide us with two models of representation, both of which are highlighted in the dualism of 'being seen' and 'seeing.' 'Beyond commodification itself, there's something about the mimesis of a camera as a mechanical eye that is combined—in the production of a photograph—with a "record" or "representation" of both sides of "how we looked"' (Jon Wagner, personal communication, 2009).

At the same time, these statements offer many problems with visibility and visuality—especially with regard to the status of first-person looking, with or without cameras. In many ways, this proposed orientation suggests more questions than answers. The legal system is struggling more than ever with the notion and value of 'eye-witness accounts,' that different 'eyes' witnessing the 'same' event offer different, often conflicting, written or spoken accounts. Realizations now abound that something gets in the way of a consensus about the accurate verbal articulation of what was there to be seen. More credence is given to the statement: 'It all depends how you look at it.'

At the beginning of this essay, I stressed the need to integrate interests, activities, and studies within the visual social sciences. In promotion materials for a new book series, Series Editor Marguerite Helmers stated:

> The previously unquestioned hegemony of verbal text is being challenged by what W. J. T. Mitchell labels the "pictorial turn" (Picture Theory)—a recognition of the importance and ubiquity of images in the dissemination and reception of information, ideas, and opinions—processes that lie at the heart of all rhetorical practices, social movements, and cultural institutions. In the past decade, many scholars have called for collaborative ventures, in essence for disciplining of the study of visual information into a new field, variously labeled visual rhetoric, visual culture studies, or "image studies". This proposed new field would bring together the work currently being accomplished by scholars in a wide variety of disciplines, including art theory, anthropology, rhetoric, cultural studies, psychology, and media studies.[41] (Helmers, 2003)

One attempt to facilitate an organization of visual culture studies is the heart of this essay. A framework has been suggested to better understand complexity from simplicity, by using the phrase, *how people look*. Equal parts of attention are placed on the scholarly examination of *how* life appears, what appears, *what* is seen, and *how* life is seen. Future efforts will have to judge the merits and hopefully offer amendments.

ACKNOWLEDGMENTS

I am particularly grateful to the anonymous critical readers of earlier drafts of this paper. I was provided with many valuable insights that prodded me to think more about broader implications of this proposed framework.

NOTES

1 In an introductory essay for this edition, Margaret Blackman states: '"From Site to Sight" is about the "culture of imaging". Visually and in words it explores the changing patterns of belief and behavior brought to making, viewing and understanding photographic images within the context of anthropology' (Blackman, 1986: 11 in Banta and Hinsley, 1986).

2 This difference has a resemblance to how communication scholar Sol Worth (1981) identified visual recordings 'about culture' versus 'of culture.'

3 I am grateful to colleague Doug Harper (2000) for this observation, which appeared as an endnote for his paper.

4 It should be clear that this phrase is meant to be inclusive, allowing attention to: how they look, how we look, and how I look.

5 Perhaps the strongest statement regarding this revision comes from Australia in the form of an introductory textbook entitled, *Researching the Visual* (Emmison and Smith, 2000).

6 Parallel claims can be made for other senses, but we struggle for the appropriate vocabulary to express the differences. For example, 'how people feel' can be broken into how one feels (hot/cold, healthy/sickly, happy/sad) and one 'feels' in the sense of how one touches people or objects (eyes open/closed, with tongue, or finger, hand/foot, etc.).

Linguistic problems are particularly apparent when we want to discuss 'how people taste.'

7 This position is well aligned with the vision–visuality distinction made by Luc Pauwels who understands '…"visuality" or the culturally determined manner of looking at things, which defines "what" we see and "how" we see it. "Vision" differs from "visuality" in that it concerns a rather universal experience of looking on the basis of physical characteristics of the visual organ in relation to whatever it is that presents itself before the eye (in other words, the purely physiological side of seeing). Visuality, on the other hand, refers to the cultural codes that are applied in interpreting, and which thus turn the looking, the creating of images and their use or discussion, into a cultural activity' (2008: 82). Jon Wagner also offers a helpful clarification of such terms as 'visible,' 'visual', and 'visualized' (2006).

8 Many studies within the history of physical (or biological) anthropology become immediately relevant. Efforts to map the heterogeneity of the human form, changes through time, determining links with older forms as well as knowing connections between genotypes and phenotypes are well-established topics of study, I hasten to add a common fascination with controversial efforts to show us what early hominids and Paleolithic humans 'looked like.'

9 Body-lengthening or shortening practices are much less known, with the exception of several bone-extending experiments in Chinese surgery (see 'Chinese turn to bone stretching to get taller' [Online]. Available from: http://www.local6.com/news/4574140/detail.html [Accessed 20 November 2008]. Another example was 'Limb Lengthening' from the American Academy of Orthopedic Surgery [Online]. Available from: http://www.orthoinfo.org/fact/thr_report.cfm?Thread_ID=310&topcategory=General [No longer accessible].

10 For a good overview of what humans do to their skin, see Jablonski (2006): 'We expose it, cover it, paint it, tattoo it, scar it, and pierce it. Our intimate connection with the world, skin protects us while advertising our health, our identity, and our individuality (2006—book description (http://www.ucpress.edu/book.php?isbn=9780520256248)).' Skin is also treated 'as a canvas for self-expression, exploring our use of cosmetics, body paint, tattooing, and scarification' (2006—book description (http://www.ucpress.edu/book.php?isbn=9780520256248)).

11 The BBC (24 January 2007) reported: 'Parent fights over child's veil—Muslim woman wearing a niquab. The school allows Muslim girls to wear scarves but not niquabs. A parent in England has begun legal action against his daughter's school because it will not allow her to wear a veil which covers most of her face' [Online]. Available from: http://news.bbc.co.uk/2/hi/uk_news/education/6294225.stm [Accessed 20 November 2008].

12 Tragically, extreme consequences have been reported; in one note entitled: 'Makeup, un-Islamic dress bring death' we read: 'There came a bleak announcement Sunday from Basra's police chief: At least 40 women have been killed in Iraq's second largest city this year for "violating Islamic teachings". Sectarian gangs reportedly comb the streets, looking for women wearing nontraditional dress, and scrawl red graffiti warnings reading: "Your makeup and your decision to forgo the headscarf will bring you death"' [Online]. Available from: http://www.salon.com/mwt/broadsheet/2007/12/10/basra/index.html [Accessed 20 November 2008].

13 These two are the most popular choices in the USA; Facebook, for example, reports having 350 million active users. See 'Facebook Press Room, Statistics,' 2010 [Online]. Available from: http://www.facebook.com/press/info.php?statistics [Accessed 22 January 2010].

14 Garbology is the study of refuse and trash. It is an academic discipline and has a major outpost at the University of Arizona long directed by William Rathje. The project started in 1971, originating from an idea of two students for a class project. It is a major source of information on the nature and changing patterns in modern refuse. Industries wishing to demonstrate that discards originating with their products are (or are not) important in the trash stream are avid followers of this research, as are municipalities wishing to learn whether some parts of the trash they collect has any salable value. See 'Garbology' [Online]. Available from: http://en.wikipedia.org/wiki/Garbology [Accessed 20 November 2008].

15 Clearly, questions of *How-People-Look* are dramatically complicated, in both of these two orientations. Elkins would be the first to say this is atrociously simplistic, as he does with the phrases: 'The observer looks at an object' and 'just looking' (1996).

16 In comparison, statements like 'Are you blind?' suggest the opposite: that the person cannot recognize or see the obvious, and is therefore inadequate, dumb, and incompetent.

17 See Rolf Nelson's comments in his review (2005).

18 I was surprised to find this intuitively derived list in a book on photography, specifically about discovering yourself through photography.

19 It is important to distinguish between 'cannot look/see,' 'should not look/see,' and 'must not look/see.' Different sets of restriction lie behind each. Again, issues of what one can or cannot do come up against what one should/shouldn't do or what it is that people actually do or don't do as a variation on the ideal and the real.

20 New interest in looking is appearing in diverse locations; the 2nd Workshop on Research in Visual Culture, scheduled for March 2008, was devoted to 'Visual Attention,' which proposes to situate the aesthetic discussion on the activities of 'seeing' and 'being seen' in a broad cultural context that relocates seeing within an expanded perceptual layout of multiple histories (see: visualculturestudies@gmail.com).

21 One of the most important contributions made by James Elkins is the replacement of 'interpretation' and 'competence' for the problematic term, 'visual literacy.'

22 See Grasseni (2007) for a recent book that speaks directly to related issues of looking skills.

23 See Monaco (1977).

24 See Elkins (2003) for a chapter describing a series of problematic illustrations.

25 Examples include a 2007 conference entitled 'Gazing, Glancing, Glimpsing: Tourists and Tourism in a Visual World' and two references: Urry (2002) and Crouch and Lübbren (2003).

26 Clifford Geertz's book (1988) has several worthy discussions on just this point.

27 One example is provided for having a picture taken by the Registry of Motor Vehicles (Baker, 2008). But restricted behavior also counts. The 2004 guidelines issued by the US State Department permit people to smile for passport and visa pictures but frown on toothy smiles, which apparently are classified as unusual or unnatural expressions. 'The subject's expression should be neutral (non-smiling) with both eyes open, and mouth closed' (Anonymous, 2004). A smile with a closed jaw is allowed but is not preferred,' according to the guidelines. Mark Knapp, an immigration attorney with Reed Smith in Pittsburgh, said: 'You can't make this stuff up, honestly. What is interesting is the idea that you can't smile anymore and that they're rejecting photos. The idea that you can't smile is what most immigration lawyers find absurd.' (Anonymous, 2004) [Online]. Available from: http://www.usatoday.com/travel/news/2004-11-29-visa-smile_x.htm [Accessed 15 August 2010].

28 For just one example of looking at people in a politically charged way, see the controversy surrounding the 2006 publication of 12 Danish cartoons of the Prophet Mohammed. Also see Mitchell's 'Child-Centered? Thinking Critically about Children's Drawings as a Visual Research Method' (2006).

29 Classic references here include Heider (1976) and Loizos (1993), and some of the best thinking and writing about camera strategy is provided by David MacDougall (1997).

30 Several interesting and recent commentaries and analyses of how social scientists have used their cameras include Read (2005), Hammond (2003), Collier (2003), Lakoff (1996), and Ruby (1995) and, for a broader view, see *Navajo and Photography: A Critical History of the Representation of an American People* by James C. Faris (1996).

31 Many photography books have been endorsed and used in social science thinking and writing, including some of my favorites, *Material World* (Menzel et al., 1995), *Suburbia* (Owens, 1973), works by Barbara Norfleet, specifically *Wedding* (1979) and *City Families* by Roslyn Banish (1976), among many others. Norfleet, for instance, has emphasized exposing and exhibiting the ways events like weddings get looked at with cameras and seen in wedding pictures.

32 As an interesting contrast to Goffman's sense of gender advertisements, see 'Male and Female: Gender Performed in Photographs from the George Eastman House Collection' in which Alison Nordström, the Museum's Curator of Photographs and curator of the exhibition, explains, 'Many of the ways we identify and define gender are based on visual clues. They may be such secondary sexual characteristics as facial hair or its lack, or there may be culturally determined elements such as costume, stance, or activities.' [Online]. Available from: http://www. eastmanhouse.org/exhibits/container_78/index.php [Accessed 22 January 2010].

33 The book *Video Night at Kathmandu* by Pico Iyer provides a wonderful anecdotal example of different Asian cultures looking at the 'same' film: namely, *Rambo: First Blood* (1982) starring Sylvester Stallone.

34 'Indigenous' has become another controversial term. The emphasis here is on cameras used by members of local communities: people who have not necessarily been trained in the visual arts but have an interest in visual recording, for themselves or outsiders.

35 A comprehensive critical overview of this work written by the author appears in the Foreword and Afterword of the second edition of the 1972 *Through Navajo Eyes* (Worth et al., 1997).

36 A related effort appears in 'A Paradigm for Looking' (Bellman and Jules-Rosette, 1977).

37 The annual Christmas card photograph, either mailed or now e-mailed, provides an example for extending 'how we looked this year' to a social network of significant others. Reactions range from 'Look how the kids have grown up and changed' to 'What an ostentatious bunch they still are.'

38 Predictably, we find a website devoted to such proscriptions: On 'Strictly No Photography, Photos You Were Not Allowed To Take' posted by Scott Beale on Tuesday, 4 December 2007, we read: 'Strictly No Photography is a photo sharing service for photos that you were not allowed to take.' According to the site, their mission is 'To organize the world's forbidden visual information and make it universally accessible and useful.' [Online]. Available from: http://laughingsquid.com/ strictly-no-photography-photos-you-were-not-allowed-to-take/ [Accessed 22 January 2010].

39 [Online]. Available from: http://www.brighton. ac.uk/ssm/sympo2007/ [Accessed 20 November 2008].

40 This term is best understood as 'observation from below,' which means, in this context, the use of digital cameras, small camcorders, and now camera phones by ordinary citizens to report newsworthy activities, and in some cases transferring visual information to mass-mediated news agencies and/or police.

41 See the series [Online]. Available from: http:// www.parlorpress.com/visualrhetoric.html [Accessed 20 November 2008].

REFERENCES

Adra, Najwa (2005) 'Dance and glance: Visualizing tribal identity in Highland Yemen', *Visual Anthropology*, 11: 55–102.

Anonymous (2004) *Smiling frowned upon in visa photographs* [Online]. Available from: http://www. usatoday.com/travel/news/2004-11-29-visa-smile_x. htm [Accessed 15 August, 2010].

Anonymous (2005) Personal Communication.

Argyle, Michael (1978) 'The laws of looking.' *Human Nature*, (January).

Baker, Billy (2008) 'A license to look your best', *The Boston Globe*, December 13. [Online]. Available from: http://www.boston.com/news/local/massachusetts/ articles/2008/12/13/a_license_to_look_your_best/ [Accessed 21 January 2010].

Ball, Michael and Smith, Gregory (1992) *Analyzing Visual Data*. Newbury Park, CA: Sage Publications.

Banish, Roslyn (1976) *City Families: Chicago and London*. New York: Pantheon Books.

Banks, Marcus and Morphy, Howard (eds.) (1997) *Rethinking Visual Anthropology*. New Haven, CT: Yale University Press.

Banta, Melissa and Hinsley, Curtis M. (1986) *From Site to Sight: Anthropology, Photography, and the Power of Imagery*. Cambridge, MA: Peabody Museum Press.

Bateson, Gregory (1954) 'An Analysis of the Nazi film Hitlerjunge Quex', in Mead and M. Rhoda (eds.), *The Study of Culture at a Distance*. Chicago, IL: University of Chicago Press. pp. 331–347.

Bateson, Gregory and M. Mead, (1942) *Balinese Character, a Photographic Analysis*. New York: The New York Academy of Sciences.

Becker, Howard S. (1974) 'Photography and sociology', *Studies in the Anthropology of Visual Communication*, 1: 3–26.

Becker, Howard S. (1981) 'Introduction', in H. S. Becker (ed.) *Exploring Society Photographically*. Evanston, IL: Mary and Leigh Block Gallery, Northwestern University. pp. 8–11.

Becker, Howard S. (1986) 'Aesthetics and truth', in H. S. Becker (ed.) *Doing Things Together*. Evanston, IL: Northwestern University Press. pp. 293–301.

Bellman, Beryl L. and Jules-Rosette, Bennetta (1977) *Cross-Cultural Research with Visual Media*. Norwood, NJ: Ablex.

Berger, John (1972) *Ways of Seeing*. New York: Viking Press.

Berger, John (1980) *About Looking*. New York: Pantheon Books.

Birdwhistell, Ray L. (1970) *Kinesics and Context; Essays on Body Motion Communication*. Philadelphia, PA: University of Pennsylvania Press.

Blackman, Margaret L. (1986) 'Introduction' in Banta, Melissa and Hinsley, Curtis M. (eds.), *From Site to Sight: Anthropology, Photography, and the Power of Imagery*. Cambridge, MA: Peabody Museum Press. pp. 11–16.

Byers, Paul (1966) 'Cameras don't take pictures', *Columbia University Forum*, 9(1): 27–31. [Also Online]. Available from: http://varenne.tc.columbia.edu/byers/camera.html [Accessed 21 November 2008].

Cavin, Erica (2000) 'In search of the viewfinder: A study of a child's perspective [Photo essay]', *Visual Sociology*, 9(1): 27–41.

Chakravorty, Pallabi (2004) 'Dance, pleasure and Indian women as multisensorial subjects', *Visual Anthropology*, 17(1): 1–17.

Chalfen, Richard (1981) 'A sociovidistic approach to children's filmmaking: The Philadelphia project', *Studies in Visual Communication*, 7(1): 2–33.

Chalfen, Richard (1987) *Snapshot Versions of Life*. Bowling Green, OH: The Popular Press.

Chalfen, Richard (1988) 'Home video versions of life: Anything new?', *Society for Visual Anthropology Newsletter*, 4(1): 1–5.

Chalfen, Richard (1991) *Turning Leaves: The Photograph Collections of Two Japanese American Families*. Albuquerque, NM: University of New Mexico Press.

Chalfen, Richard (1992) 'Picturing culture through indigenous imagery: A telling story', in P. Crawford and D. Turton, (eds.), *Film as Ethnography*. Manchester: University of Manchester Press. pp. 222–241.

Chalfen, Richard (2005) 'Looking at Japanese society: Hashiguchi George as visual sociologist', *Visual Studies*, 20(2): 140–158.

Chalfen, Richard and Rich, Michael (2004) 'Applying visual research: Patients teaching physicians about asthma through visual illness narratives', *Visual Anthropology Review (VAR)*, 20(1): 17–30.

Christova-Slavcheva, Evdokia (1996) 'Drawing, the universal language: A cross-cultural analysis of children's drawings from Japan and Bulgaria', *Japan Foundation Newsletter*, 34(1), May.

Classen, Constance (1993) *Worlds of Sense: Exploring the Senses in History and Across Cultures*. London: Routledge.

Collier, Malcolm (2003) 'The Vicos photographs of John Collier Jr, and Mary E. T. Collier', *Visual Anthropology*, 16(2–3): 159–206.

Cook, Mark (1977) 'Gaze and mutual gaze in social encounters', *American Scientist*, 65 (May–June): 328–333.

Cooley, Charles H. (1922) *Human Nature and the Social Order*. New York: Scribner's.

Crouch, David and Lübbren, Nina (eds.) (2003) *Visual Culture and Tourism*. New York: Berg.

Duchowski, Andrew (2003) *Eye Tracking Methodology: Theory and Practice*. New York: Springer-Verlag.

Dundes, Alan (1972) 'Seeing is believing', *Natural History*, May.

El Guindi, Fadwa (1999) *Veil: Modesty, Privacy and Resistance*. Oxford: Berg.

Elkins, James (1996) "Just Looking" in *The Object Stares Back*, pp. 17–45. New York: Harcourt.

Elkins, James (2003) *Visual Studies: A Skeptical Introduction*. London: Routledge.

Emmison, Michael and Smith, Philip (2000) *Researching the Visual: Images, Objects, Contexts and Interactions in Social and Cultural Inquiry*. London: Sage Publications.

Faris, James C. (1996) *Navajo and Photography: A Critical History of the Representation of an American People*. Albuquerque, NM: University of New Mexico Press.

Furman, L. (1990) 'Video therapy: An alternative for the treatment of adolescents', Special issue: The creative arts therapy with adolescents, *Arts in Psychotherapy*, 17: 165–169.

Geertz, Clifford (1988) *Works and Lives: The Anthropologist as Author*. Stanford, CA: Stanford University Press.

Ginsburg, Faye (1991) 'Indigenous media: Faustian contract or global village?' *Cultural Anthropology*, 6(1): 92–112.

Goffman, Erving (1959) *The Presentation of Self in Everyday Life*. Garden City, NY: Doubleday.

Goffman, Erving (1966) *Behavior in Public Places: Notes on the Social Organization of Gatherings.* New York: Free Press.

Goffman, Erving (1976) 'Gender advertisements', *Studies in the Anthropology of Visual Communication*, 3: 69–154.

Goffman, Erving (1982) *Interaction Ritual—Essays on Face-to-Face Behavior.* New York: Pantheon Books.

Goodman, Nelson (1978) *Ways of Worldmaking.* Indiana, IN: Hackett Publishing Co. Inc.

Graburn, Nelson H. H. (ed.) (1976) *Ethnic and Tourist Arts: Cultural Expressions from the Fourth World.* Berkeley, CA: University of California Press.

Grady, John (2007) 'Advertising images as social indicators: Depictions of blacks In *LIFE Magazine* (1936–2000)', *Visual Studies*, 22(3): 211–239.

Grasseni, Cristina (ed.) (2007) *Skilled Visions: Between Apprenticeship and Standards.* Oxford, New York: Berghahn Books.

Gross, Larry and Worth, Sol (1974) 'Symbolic strategies', *Journal of Communication*, 24(4): 27–39.

Hagaman, Dianne (1993) 'The joy of victory, the agony of defeat: Stereotypes in newspaper sports feature photography', *Visual Sociology*, 8: 48–66.

Hall, Edward T. (1966) *The Hidden Dimension.* Garden City, NY: Doubleday.

Hall, Stuart (1973) *Encoding and Decoding in the Television Discourse.* Birmingham, UK: University of Birmingham, Centre for Contemporary Culture.

Hall, Stuart (1997) *Representation: Cultural Representations and Signifying Practices.* Thousand Oaks, CA: Sage Publications.

Hammond, Joyce (2003) 'Telling a tale: Margaret Mead's photographic portraits of Fa'amotu', *Visual Anthropology*, 16(4): 341–374.

Harper, Douglas (2000) 'Reimagining visual methods: Galileo to Neuromancer', in N. Denzin and Y. Lincoln, (eds.), *The Handbook of Qualitative Research*, 2nd edn. Thousand Oaks, CA: Sage Publications. pp. 717–732.

Harper, Douglas (2002) 'Talking about pictures: A case for photo elicitation', *Visual Studies*, 17(1): 13–26.

Hashiguchi, George (1988) *17's Map.* Japan: Bungeishunju.

Hattersley, Ralph (1971) *Discover Your Self Through Photography.* Dobbs Ferry, NY: Morgan & Morgan, Inc.

Heider, Karl G. (1976) *Ethnographic Film.* Austin, TX: University of Texas Press.

Hendry, Joy (1993) *Wrapping Culture: Politeness, Presentation and Power in Japan.* Oxford: Clarendon Press, 1993.

Iyer, Pico (1988) *Video Night in Kathmandu.* New York: Knopf.

Jablonski, Nina G. (2006) *Skin: A Natural History.* Berkeley, CA: University of California Press. [Also partially Online]. Available from: http://books. google.com/books?id=L6oMocBcaO0C [Accessed 20 November 2008].

Jenks, Chris (1995) 'The centrality of the eye in Western culture: An introduction', in C. Jenks (ed.), *Visual Culture.* London: Routledge. pp. 1–25. [Also Online]. Available from: http://books.google.com/books?hl= en&lr=&id=rlSOlpOYBQYC&oi=fnd&pg=PA1&dq= %22Jenks%22+%22THE+CENTRALITY+OF+THE+ EYE+IN+WESTERN+CULTURE%22+&ots=l7CeaUV 4DO&sig=WEa6ycSo610Uq1WqPVGlsqqzl2s#PPA2, M1 [Accessed 15 September 2008].

Jhala, Jayasinhji (1994) 'The Unintended Audience', in P. Crawford and B. H. Sigurjon (eds.), *The Construction of The Viewer: Media Ethnography and the Anthropology of Audiences.* Aarhus, Denmark: Intervention Press. pp. 207–228.

Katz, Elihu and Liebes, Tamar (1994) *The Export of Meaning: Cross-Cultural Readings of Dallas.* Cambridge: Polity Press.

Lakoff, Andrew (1996) 'Freezing time: Margaret Mead's diagnostic photography', *Visual Anthropology Review*, 12(1): 1–18.

Loizos, Peter (1993) *Innovation in Ethnographic Film: From Innocence to Self-consciousness, 1955–85.* Manchester, UK: Manchester University Press.

Lomax, Alan (1972) 'Brief progress report: Cantometrics-choreometrics projects', *Yearbook of the International Folk Music Council*, 4: 142–145.

Lowe, J. W. G. and Lowe, E. D. (1982) 'Cultural pattern and process: A study of stylistic change in women's dress', *American Anthropologist*, 84: 521–544.

Lutz, Catherine and Collins, Jane (1991) 'The photograph as an intersection of gazes: The example of *National Geographic*, *Visual Anthropology Review*, 7(3): 134–149.

MacCannell, Dean (1976) *The Tourist: A New Theory of the Leisure Class.* New York: Schocken Books.

MacDougall, David (1997) 'The visual in anthropology', in M. Banks and M. Howard (eds.), *Rethinking Visual Anthropology.* New Haven, CT: Yale University Press. pp. 276–295.

Marey, Étienne-Jules (1992) *Picturing Time: The Work of Etienne-Jules Marey.* Chicago, IL: University of Chicago Press.

Mead, Margaret and Métraux, Rhoda (eds.) (1954) *The Study of Culture at a Distance.* Chicago, IL: University of Chicago Press.

Menzel, Peter, Mann, Charles C. and Kennedy, Paul (1995) *Material World: A Global Family Portrait.* San Francisco, CA: Sierra Club Books.

Michaels, Eric (1982) 'How to look at us looking at the Yanomami looking at us', in J. Ruby (ed.), *A Crack in the Mirror*. Philadelphia, PA: University of Pennsylvania Press. pp. 133–146.

Michaels, Eric (1991) 'A primer of prescriptions on picture-taking in traditional areas of aboriginal Australia', *Visual Anthropology*, 4(3–4): 259–275.

Miller, Laura (2006) *Beauty Up: Exploring Contemporary Japanese Body Aesthetics*. Berkeley, CA: The University of California Press.

Mitchell, Lisa M. (2006) 'Child-centered? Thinking critically about children's drawings as a visual research method', *Visual Anthropology Review*, 22(1): 60–73.

Monaco, James (1977) *How to Read a Film: The Art, Technology, Language, History, and Theory of Film and Media*. New York: Oxford University Press.

Mulligan, Dierdre (2007) *In Defense of Public Places: New Perspectives on Visual Privacy in the 21st Century*. [Online]. Available from: http://www.trust-stc.org/wise/talks.html [Accessed 15 August 2010].

Muybridge, Eadweard (1979) *Muybridge's Complete Human and Animal Locomotion*. Mineola, NY: Dover Publications.

Nelson, Rolf (2005) 'Review of eye tracking methodology: Theory and practice by Andrew Duchowski', *Visual Studies*, 20(1): 91–93.

Norfleet, Barbara P. (1979) *Wedding*. New York: Simon and Schuster.

O'Barr, William M. (1994) 'Unexpected audiences: American and Japanese representations of one another' in *Culture and the Ad: Exploring Otherness in the World of Advertising*. Boulder, CO: Westview Press, pp. 157–198.

Owens, Bill (1973) *Suburbia*. New York: Straight Arrow Books.

Pack, Sam (2006) 'How they see me vs. How I see them: The ethnographic self and the personal self', *Anthropological Quarterly*, 79(1): 105–122.

Pauwels, Luc (2008) 'Visual literacy and visual culture: Reflections on developing more varied and explicit visual competencies', *The Open Communication Journal*, 2: 79–85.

Powdermaker, Hortense (1950) *Hollywood, the Dream Factory: An Anthropologist Studies the Movie Makers*. Boston: Little Brown & Co.

Read, Rosie (2005) 'Scopic regimes and the observational approach: Ethnographic filmmaking in a Czech institution', *Visual Anthropology*, 18(1): 47–64.

Rich, Michael and Chalfen, Richard (1999) 'Showing and telling asthma: Children teaching physicians with visual narrative', *Visual Sociology*, 14: 51–71.

Robinson, Dwight E. (1976) 'Fashion in shaving and the trimming of the beard: The men of the *Illustrated London News*, 1842–1972', *American Journal of Sociology*, 81(5): 1133–1141.

Ruby, Jay (1995) 'Out of sync: The cinema of Tim Asch', *Visual Anthropology Review*, 11(1): 19–35.

Salinager, Adrienne (1995) *In my Room: Teenagers in the Bedrooms*. San Francisco, CA: Chronicle Books.

Schwartz, Maureen Trudelle (2006) 'Native American tattoos: Identity and spirituality in contemporary America', *Visual Anthropology*, 19(3–4): 223–254.

Seppanen, Janne (2006) *The Power of the Gaze: An Introduction to Visual Literacy*. New York, NY: Peter Lang Publishing.

Smith, Valene L. (ed.) (1989) *Hosts and Guests: The Anthropology of Tourism*. Philadelphia, PA: University of Pennsylvania Press.

Sontag, Susan (1977) *On Photography*. New York: Farrar, Straus and Giroux.

Sprague, Steven (1978) 'Yoruba photographers: How the Yoruba see themselves', *African Arts*, Vol. XII(1): 52–59.

Stokrocki, Mary (1994) 'Through Navajo children's eyes: Cultural influences on representational abilities', *Visual Anthropology*, 7(1): 47–67.

Sullivan, Kevin and Jordan, Mary (1995) 'Japanese try on the "Casual Friday" look', *International Herald Tribune*, October 2.

Turner, Terence (1991) 'The social dynamics of video: Media in an indigenous society: The cultural meaning and the personal politics of video-making in Kayapo communities', *Visual Anthropology Review (VAR)*, 7(2): 68–76.

Urry, John (2002) *The Tourist Gaze (Theory, Culture & Society Series)*. London and Thousand Oaks, CA: Sage Publications.

Wagner, Jon (2006) 'Visible materials, visualized theory and images of social research', *Visual Studies*, 21(1): 55–69.

Wang, Caroline and Burris, Mary Ann (1997) 'Photovoice: Concept, methodology, and use for participatory needs assessment', *Health Education & Behavior*, 24(3): 369–387.

Wang, Caroline, Burris, Mary Ann and Ping, Xiang Yue (1996) 'Chinese village women as visual anthropologists: A participatory approach to reaching policymakers', *Social Science & Medicine*, 42(10): 1391–1400.

Weakland, John H. (2003) 'Feature films as cultural documents' in P. Hockings (ed.), *Principles of Visual Anthropology*, 3rd edn. Berlin, NY: Mouton de Gruyter. pp. 45–67.

Weakland, John H. (1966) 'Themes in Chinese Communist films', *American Anthropologist*, 68(2): 477–484.

Weiser, Judy (1993) *Photo Therapy Techniques: Exploring the Secrets of Personal Snapshots and Family Albums*. San Francisco, CA: Jossey-Bass.

Worth, Sol, Adair, John and Chalfen, Richard (1997) *Through Navajo Eyes: An Exploration in Film Communication and Anthropology*, revised edition. Albuquerque, NM: University of New Mexico Press.

Worth, Sol (1981) 'Margaret Mead and the shift from "visual anthropology" to an "anthropology of visual communication"', in L. Gross (ed.), *Studying Visual Communication*. Philadelphia, PA: University of Pennsylvania Press. pp. 185–199.

3

Visual Studies and Empirical Social Inquiry

Jon Wagner

INTRODUCTION

Framing visual studies as empirical social inquiry is not a simple matter. Only some visual study approaches support empirical inquiry, and only some of those focus on culture and social life. Beyond that, asking where these fit together is to pose three questions in one. There's the ideological or moral query about where visual studies *should* fit with social scientific inquiry, the analytical query of where such studies *could* fit, and the empirical query of where they *appear to fit*. It's the last question I want to explore here, for what it implies about visual studies and, by extension, other forms of empirical social inquiry.

The practice of visual studies and the landscape of empirical social inquiry are both evolving, so answers to this empirical question are evolving as well. But from the 1960s through the 1990s, the primary expression of visual studies appeared as an offshoot of other, more organized and well-established forms of scholarship—as a specialization within sociology or anthropology, for example, or an extension of work in art history,

design, or communication studies. Beginning in the mid- to late-1990s, some elements of these offshoots began coalescing around visual studies as a branch of empirical inquiry in its own right. Yet a third locus of visual studies attention emerged during that same period of time among the roots of empirical inquiry, not only in the social sciences and humanities but also in the physical and natural sciences and in the professions.

In this chapter I examine these three manifestations of visual studies and their implications for social inquiry. The framework and commentary I provide can hopefully clarify some contributions, promises, and challenges that characterize visual studies across all three contexts, but I will focus primarily on the second two—visual studies as a branch of social inquiry and as a root of empirical inquiry. A close look in this direction reveals the interface between visual studies, empirical inquiry, and contemporary folk life as a dynamic seam along which new knowledge of culture and social life is forming for both researchers and the general public. As a prelude to explicating that seam in more detail, let me comment briefly on empirical social inquiry from a visual studies point of view.

EMPIRICAL SOCIAL INQUIRY

For purposes of this chapter, I define empirical social inquiry as an effort to generate new knowledge of culture and social life through the systematic collection and analysis of sensory information and other forms of real-world evidence. This definition contrasts with the narrow view held by some social researchers that empirical studies are necessarily quantitative. It also contrasts with the idea that making photographs or video recordings in field settings is either necessary or sufficient to document culture and social life.

Consistent with this definition, work within individual social science disciplines may or may not take the form of empirical social inquiry, and that's true also for work in the arts or humanities. Some very thoughtful and systematic studies, for example, focus primarily on the internal coherence of theoretical arguments, semantic clarity of constructs and concepts, or the logical implications of different paradigms and experimental designs. These studies may reflect excellent scholarship, but they lack the kind of empirical warrant and complexities that I'm concerned with here. By the same token, other visual studies may be empirically sound—in the sense that they involve systematic collection and analysis of sensory evidence—but contribute little to our knowledge of culture and social life. Examples might include visual studies of printed circuit boards, freeway overpasses, or riparian ecosystems that lack attention to their social or cultural dimensions.

Of considerable significance to the visual studies issues examined in this chapter, a project or study could meet the criteria I've outlined for empirical social inquiry but be pursued or reported outside the boundaries of an academic discipline. Indeed, as both an offshoot of traditional disciplines and a branch of empirical inquiry, visual studies is rife with examples of this sort. These extra-disciplinary studies can involve individuals from one research community communicating about their work to another—for example, anthropologists presenting their work to film study buffs, medical educators reporting research results to visual anthropologists, or semioticians reporting theirs to medical researchers—but they can also involve substantial interplay between academic and folk communities. Cultural re-enactments, museum exhibitions and catalogs, theater performances, trade publications, feature films, and various forms of media-rich reportage can—and sometimes do—reflect substantive integration of empirical social inquiry, mass media production, and folk culture.

Interplay between academic disciplines, multi-disciplinary collaboration, interdisciplinary research, and folk culture constitutes an important secondary theme of the discussion that follows. This kind of back-and-forth shapes the contexts within which individuals pursue visual studies as a form of empirical *social* inquiry. Beneath the particulars of these efforts, the conduct of empirical inquiry *in general* is also nourished through an expanding constellation of visual studies considerations and skills.

DISCIPLINARY OFFSHOOTS

During the first half of the twentieth century, most social researchers interested in camera work, visual data, visual perception, visual culture, and visual tools of analysis and representation typically regarded and presented their work as a specialized strand of their home discipline. For Gregory Bateson and Margaret Mead (1942), visual explorations in the field were integral to the research practices of anthropologists and ethnographers, and that was also true for George Spindler (2008) and Louise Spindler. For Kenneth and

Mamie Clark, whose black-and-white doll experiments contributed to the case against racially segregated schools in the USA, image-based inquiries were one of several techniques for conducting experimental research in social psychology (Clark, 1963). While drawing on his own experience as a documentary photographer, John Collier Jr's (1967) seminal account of camera-assisted fieldwork was framed explicitly by Collier, and by the Spindlers, who edited the series in which this book appeared, as first and foremost a contribution to anthropology.

Despite the disciplinary contexts in which this work was pursued and reported, visual studies within anthropology and sociology developed a readership during the second half of the century that began to cross disciplines and professions. I first heard about Collier's, *Visual Anthropology*, for example, in a darkroom conversation with a photography student at Chicago's Columbia College. A few years later, Howard Becker's (1986) essay on photography and sociology appeared in an early issue of *Studies in the Anthropology of Visual Communication*, but it came to me shortly thereafter via my subscription to *Afterimage*, a publication of Nathan Lyons' Visual Studies Workshop that focused on photography and the media arts. A year or so later, an interview by Stuart Brand with Margaret Mead and Gregory Bateson (Mead and Bateson, 1976) about contrasting strategies for filming culture and social life went the other way: first published in *Co-Evolution Quarterly*, it was reprinted shortly thereafter in *Studies in the Anthropology of Visual Communication*. The annual Conferences on Visual Anthropology that Jay Ruby organized from 1968 to 1980 attracted not only anthropologists, filmmakers, and photographers, but also sociologists, folklorists, journalists, media activists, visual artists, schoolteachers, and musicologists.

Collier, Becker, and other sociologists and anthropologists such as Sol Worth, John Adair, Richard Chalfen, Jay Ruby, Paul Hockings, Karl Heider, and Deborah Barndt who were writing about visual inquiries in

the 1960s and 1970s, addressed members of their home disciplines as a primary audience, but their work attracted colleagues from other fields, some of whom became affiliated with visual anthropology or visual sociology. As these cross-disciplinary affiliations increased, they generated opportunities for examining visual studies as a focus of multidisciplinary inquiry—a perspective apparent in a 1979 collection I edited called *Images of Information* (Wagner, 1979). As this multidisciplinary perspective matured over the next few decades, it attracted other scholars and practitioners who extended both notions and questions about visual studies into a wide range of applications and settings.

Extra-disciplinary ways of thinking about visual studies developed in consort with the growth of scholarly communities defined as much by research method as by theoretical perspectives or objects of inquiry. In the 1950s, 1960s, and 1970s, this kind of methodological confluence occurred among social researchers working with numbers, surveys, and experiments. Item analysis, control groups, and multiple-regression analyses became topics that sociologists, anthropologists, psychologists, and political scientists could discuss within their own disciplines and also with each other. Beginning in the early 1980s, but accelerating thereafter, a similar kind of cross-disciplinary discourse emerged around the concept of 'qualitative research.' William J. Filstead (1970) edited a collection of essays under this title that was published in 1970, but the full force of this orienting term did not appear until the 1980s and 1990s. As it did, new journals, conferences, and associations were established, and some existing research forums broadened their focus and readership. The *Journal of Urban Ethnography* became *Contemporary Ethnography*. *Cultural Anthropology Methods* was reconstituted, with the same editor, as a new journal called *Field Methods*.

Broadened discourse about both quantitative and qualitative methods brought scholars from different disciplines to new insights, not only about methods but also about theory and reporting conventions. While the rhetoric of written sociology and anthropology had been critically examined throughout the disciplines' histories, these analyses rarely captured the attention of mainstream scholars. That changed in the 1980s, as sociologists, anthropologists, linguists, folklorists, cultural historians, and literary critics joined in common cause to look at issues of 'representation.' (*Representations* was the title of another new journal emerging at this time.) One by-product of this attention to written representations was an increasing understanding of the implicit theories that social scientists embedded in their writing, knowingly or not, through metaphor, synecdoche, and both literal and figurative imagery (Gusfield, 1981; Clifford and Marcus, 1986; Hunter, 1990; Van Maanen, 1995; Becker, 1998).

Cross-disciplinary attention to methods and representations grew hand-in-hand with emergent areas of interdisciplinary inquiry such as media and communication studies, gender studies, peace studies, ethnic studies, and religious studies. In each case, scholarship that may have first appeared as a disciplinary offshoot became something more substantial. When enough disciplines had related offshoots, the offshoots could form an interdisciplinary, intellectual enterprise of their own.

One turning point for thinking about visual studies in this way occurred in 1998 with the publication of *Image-Based Research*. Edited by Jon Prosser, this collection included several articles with a disciplinary focus that, taken together, provided a multi-disciplinary perspective. But Prosser's introduction and commentary went beyond that to locate image-based research as a separate strand of qualitative inquiry. This prefigured visual studies as an interdisciplinary field of inquiry in its own right and catalyzed both a broad readership for the volume itself and new rounds of scholarly work. Additional visual studies statements, research reports, and collections appeared that linked disciplinary

topics and concepts to interdisciplinary inquiry (Banks, 1998; Emmison and Smith, 2000; Pink, 2001; Rose, 2001). These were followed by others that framed visual studies as an approach to social research in general (Banks, 2001; Stanczak, 2007). As another move in the same direction, when *Visual Sociology*, the official journal of the International Visual Sociology Association, moved to a new publisher (Taylor and Francis) in 2002, the increasingly interdisciplinary Editorial Board approved a proposal to rename the journal *Visual Studies*.

The result of these developments is that while visual studies remains a special topic within some academic disciplines, it is widely recognized as a topic with multi-disciplinary dimensions and has also become, in some important respects, an interdisciplinary enterprise in its own right. This gives individual scholars ample opportunity to fret about whether a particular project should be considered visual studies or visual sociology, visual anthropology, journalism, or the fine arts. However, as the center of gravity has shifted to include interdisciplinary visual inquiries—and as new generations of scholars have pursued visual studies projects in concert with other interdisciplinary approaches—the vitality of visual studies has itself stimulated two new kinds of boundary issues. The first focuses less on the lines between visual studies and its parent social science disciplines than on distinctions between different strands of work *within* visual studies. The second focuses on connecting different fields of study with each other along their common interface with visual studies—the arts and sciences, for example, or social documentary work and the humanities, literacy and civic education, and so on.

The challenge of identifying different approaches *within* the enterprise of visual studies is the central focus of the following section. Before taking that up, however, let me comment briefly on this second set of boundary issues by noting that, in addition to emerging as a branch of empirical social inquiry—the focus of this chapter—visual studies also became a topic of considerable interest in the arts, humanities, education, and design. As a closely related matter, deliberations about the informational, expressive, aesthetic, and persuasive potential of visual media have framed 'visual literacy' as a focus of increasing pedagogic and research interest (Elkins, 2007). Over the past decade or so, this interest has moved visual literacy to an increasingly significant place in broad discussions of research, education, culture, and social policy. In some sense, these developments position visual studies as a research complement to visual literacy, and visual literacy as a pedagogic and critical thinking complement to visual studies.

Concerns about visual literacy have found considerable traction in discussions about reforming liberal arts and professional education and in discussions about science reporting and civic culture. These discussions posit a tension between contemporary folk culture on the one hand and the demands of scholarship and informed civic participation on the other. As a matter I explore later, this tension—within which visual study skills play a dual role—has significant implications for visual studies and empirical inquiry.

DIMENSIONS OF THE BRANCH ITSELF

As a branch of empirical social inquiry, precursors of which formed within several different disciplines, what does visual studies look like? What kind of work do people do who associate themselves with this line of inquiry? What questions do they ask? What evidence do they call on for answers? And what methods and skills do they value?

The most straightforward answer to these questions is that visual studies scholars do quite varied things. However, they also usually attend to one or more visual objects of inquiry, visual research methods, or visual studies skills. Indeed, variations in visual studies approaches appear to individual researchers as choices among different objects of inquiry, research methods, and visual study skills. Key dimensions of visual studies as a collective enterprise are consequently defined by the range of objects, methods, and skills that scholars choose between.

Objects of inquiry

Within visual studies as a branch of empirical social research, the most notable objects of inquiry include the following four areas.

Visually interesting materials and activities

The primary object of inquiry for many visual studies is a set of materials or activities that a scholar finds visually interesting. Some such phenomena are seen in primarily visual terms—for example, paintings, sculptures, and other works of art; diagrams, signs, and other elements of iconography (Mitchell, 1986); shop window mannequins (Schneider, 1996); or household altars (Salvo, 1997). Other phenomena of interest combine visual and other sensory dimensions more or less seamlessly (for example, television programming, vacation homes, motion pictures, food, clothing, human sexuality, automobiles, advertising, etc.). Studies that focus on material objects of inquiry—defined in this way—reflect a close correspondence between visual studies and studies of material culture (Banks, 1998). That's much less the case, however, for studies of visually interesting *activities*, or for studies in which visual materials are examined primarily for what they reveal about other dimensions of culture and social life.

How people see things

Another common visual studies focus is how people see things. This phrasing implicates an extremely important, but also complex, object of inquiry (Grady, 1996). The term 'seeing' can refer to the neurophysiologic process of vision, social-psychological dimensions of perception, sociological or anthropological takes on perspective and point of view, how people look at or think about environments and materials, or even their world view. It is difficult to consider this wide range of references as attributes of a single object of inquiry, but attention to how people see things is so fundamental to the concept of visual studies that many scholars draw darker lines around these different referents than between them.

The lives people live

A third cluster of visual studies work centers around core concerns of ethnography and ethnology to document and depict the lives of individuals or groups (Schwartz, 1989; Pink, 2001). These efforts diverge from the 'seeing things' approach in the same way that ethnography differs from oral history: subject perspectives and accounts are important in each approach, but ethnographic research typically extends to other dimensions of culture and social life, some of which only make sense to other researchers. Visual studies scholars working with an ethnographic intent are interested not only in how subjects themselves see things but also in etic points of view, or how their world looks to outsiders, including colleagues who fashion and follow social and cultural theory.

Visual representations

Yet a fourth visual study approach directs research attention to the content, form, production, and reception of visual representations themselves. As a methodological concern, many field researchers puzzle over the relationships their work instantiates between photographs, moving pictures, audio recording, and text. For other scholars, however, phenomena of visual representation are less a methodological or technical sidelight than a central intellectual focus. Studies of optical technologies, visual signs, and symbol systems, visual media and communication, the relationship of images to text and touch,

graphic design syntax, and art histories fall within this approach. The same is true for formal and semiotic studies of traffic signs and flags, visual literacy development (Messaris, 1994; Elkins, 2007), forensic evidence (Wakefield and Underwager, 1998), and the imagery of science and technology (Lynch, 1998; Lynch and Woolgar, 1990; Pauwels, 2006) and for empirical analyses of imagery appearing as journalism (Hagaman, 1993, 1996; Schwartz, 1999), advertising (Seiter, 1993; Grady, 2009), memorial photographs (Lesy, 1973; Ruby, 1995), and so on.

Methods of inquiry

In addition to choosing among objects of inquiry such as those noted above, visual studies scholars have tapped into a diverse array of research methods. These include elements that have made their way into visual studies from the wide beyond (for example, focus group protocols or documentary styles of work) as well as approaches imported in full from specific disciplines and professions (componential analysis, projective interviewing, or consumer satisfaction surveys). For purposes of this analysis, I'll focus on six meta-methods, one or more of which characterize most visual studies.

Artifact acquisition and analysis

For empirical research, perhaps the most long-standing strand of visual research is the observation, acquisition, collection, and analysis of material artifacts. Though frequently practiced alongside—or in conjunction with—various forms of conquest, imperialism, and subjugation, intellectual interest in materials from other cultures has a long, rich, and continuous history. Contemporary projects include not only archaeological excavations but also efforts to archive materials of potential historical interest and to preserve varied social and cultural documents (for example, family photographic albums, websites, presidential speeches and conversations, holiday ephemera, and so on).

Collections of 'native image-making' have a double life within this acquisition and analysis approach: as artifacts of a particular time and place and as representations of how the individuals who made them saw things.

Photo and video documentation

Visual documentation and image recording defines a second strand of visual studies methods. On the one hand, this is a direct extension of millennia-long traditions of artifact acquisition and analysis. It goes beyond that, however, in the potential of photo and video recording to create de nouveau artifacts of cultural practices and materials that are impossible to 'collect' in other ways. Good examples of the latter include photo inventories of arranged materials; panoramas of sites, settings, and environments; video recordings of formal and informal performances, including conversations, dance, and other rituals (Rhythms of Earth, 2009); handicraft production (Greenfield, 2004); and so on.

Both artifact acquisition and photo documentation have been insinuated so deeply into the ethos of contemporary cultures that they are frequently overlooked as tools and methods of empirical research. But taken-for-granted practices of 'collecting' and 'taking pictures' involve some of the same technical and representational processes that many researchers rely on to support empirical work in the physical and natural sciences, medicine, engineering, history, the social sciences, and some forms of the humanities.

Researcher-guided image-elicitation protocols

A third set of visual inquiry methods clusters around researcher-guided image-elicitation protocols that encourage subjects to disclose their perceptions, sentiments, and ideas. In some versions of this method, researchers invite (or instruct) subjects to make drawings, photographs, or videotape recordings that reveal how they think or feel about matters. In others, researchers present visual artifacts of this sort—made or acquired by researchers or subjects—as prompts for subject interviews and focus groups.

As noted by Collier (1967) in his presentation of the photo-elicitation interview, these methods extend earlier work in psychology with the Thematic Apperception and Rorschach tests to investigate culture and social life (Wagner, 2010). Artifacts, dramatizations, and other visible materials have also been used in much the same way (Hoskins, 1998; Wakefield and Underwager, 1998), but the convenience of using photographs or videotape recordings as 'records' of artifacts, activities, and environments has given elicitation approaches making use of these materials great contemporary vitality (Harper, 1987; Tobin et al., 1989; Clark, 1999; Clark-Ibanez, 2009).

Image-based ethnography

Ethnography constitutes yet a fourth approach to visual studies. Following Bateson and Mead's photographic study of Balinese culture (1942), other scholars have combined still images and text in preparing ethnographic accounts of culture and social life in a wide range of other settings. Notable book-length examples include works by Douglas Harper (1982, 1987, 2001), Douglas Harper and Patrizia Faccioli (2010), Dona Schwartz (1998), Cathy Greenblat (2004), Roby Page (2005), and Patricia Greenfield (2004). Similar approaches have been used to good effect in countless smaller-scale studies.

Still photography, video recording, artifact collection, audio recording, and text can be combined to good effect in conducting image-based ethnographies, but the different presentation formats required of each medium have stimulated somewhat separate genres of research reporting. This is less true for photographs and text, both of which can be accommodated by the printed page, than for text and motion pictures. These contrasts make ethnographic filmmaking a somewhat distinct form of social inquiry, with its own literature, lore, and craft (Heider, 1976; Biella, 1988; Rosenthal, 1988; Hocking,

1995; Ruby, 2000). Filmmakers and researchers taking this approach have produced extraordinary depictions of culture and social life in a wide range of circumstances. The balance between visual detail and interpretive commentary, however, is a world apart in film from what social researchers have come to expect in written ethnographies—even those replete with still photographs.

One consequence of their different presentation requirements is that moving pictures, photographic, audio, and text media used to collect data may or may not appear in research reports. This kind of asymmetry presents special challenges for ethnographic filmmaking. Audiences eager to immerse themselves in viewing other cultures may prefer presentations that conceal the circumstances in which films are made. From this point of view, a researcher's commentary disrupts the audience's viewing experience or, at worst, diminishes the culture and humanity of peoples depicted. On the other hand, scholars who care about the provenance of visual depictions may question the research value of films and photo sets that lack circumstantial and production details. These contrasting points of view implicate both the theory and practice of ethnographic filmmaking (Biella, 1988).

Neuropsychological measurements of visual perception

As a close companion to one version of 'how people see,' a fifth cluster of visual research meta-methods has been developed to examine the neurophysiology of human perception. Contemporary research of this sort includes magnetic resonance imaging (MRI) studies of brain activity linked to different perceptual and visual imaging tasks and eye-tracking studies (see Chapter 23) of how people decode text-on-screen, text-on-paper, photo and graphic imagery, or even complex natural world environments. These highly instrumented studies differ substantially from other approaches to investigating how people see things, including interviews or surveys of what people have to say about their surroundings (or photographs that depict them) and the analysis of native image-making.

Formal and semiotic analyses of visual representations

Visual studies aimed in this sixth direction have focused on the formal properties of signs and symbols (viewing size, apparent propinquity and sequence, etc.), relations between different signing systems, and the visual constraints and opportunities inherent in different media and presentation formats. One strand of this kind of work intersects with ethnographic projects by examining parallels between the formal structure of visual representations and the organization of cultural values and beliefs, an approach pursued to notable effect by anthropologists such as Franz Boas (1955) and Claude Levi-Strauss (1958). Visual studies scholars interested in how signs and symbols are developed and used by particular populations have worked along a similar seam between semiotics and ethnography. Beyond these hybrid approaches, however, a significant population of visual studies scholars approach signs and symbols as formal systems that can be examined independent of their origins and practical application.

Objects, methods, and skills

Some combinations of the objects and methods noted above have received much more attention than others, and the balance of potential and popular approaches reflects several additional considerations. One of these is that visual studies approaches may or may not emphasize visual phenomena that matter to research subjects, and studies that do may or may not employ visual research materials and methods.

In the first instance, many studies of visually interesting materials—including studies of films, paintings, architecture, clothing, cuisine, and product design—have framed these objects of inquiry within perspectives of history, economy, technology, personal taste, or prior scholarship that neglect or exclude the phenomenal world of people who make or use them. In the second instance, studies may focus on the visual dimensions of subject worlds but rely on text or speech as data instead of more explicitly visual research materials. Interviews, surveys, and conversations with residents about how they perceive (or receive) films, paintings, clothing, cuisine, or features of the communities in which they live, may or may not involve visual materials or methods of inquiry. Indeed, many studies of how individuals think about materials of this sort feature text-only (or telephone) survey questions and answers.

Asymmetries of this sort can also appear between visual methods and non-visual objects of inquiry. Interviews with residents that are videotaped or make use of photographs as interview prompts—or reflect other visual studies meta-methods—may focus on issues that have little or nothing to do with how subjects literally 'see things.' This is true historically for Thematic Apperception and Rorschach testing, both of which used visual imagery as a trigger for mapping a psychodynamic profile of individual subjects. It's also true for some forms of polling or market research in which videotaped subject responses are examined for clues about the upside or downside of a political or advertising campaign.

Some objects and methods noted above are pursued separately in practice (for example, within the ethos of one visual studies community or another) but are analytically or functionally interdependent. The term 'native imagery,' for example, usually refers to artifacts made by the subjects of a researcher's study, but it could refer—and has been pursued as such with studies in the sociology or history of science—to the native imagery of researchers themselves (Latour and Woolgar, 1986; Lynch, 1998; Pauwels, 2006; Wagner, 2006a). Similarly, image-elicitation studies of how people see things are typically tied to investigations in which researchers present photos, drawings, or video documents to subjects as part of an interview or focus group protocol. But the same elements—for example, subjects responding to visual stimuli and researchers observing and assessing their comments—can characterize reception studies of mass media events, studies of materials that are visually interesting in their own right, or, for that matter, studies of how scholars view visual research materials in their own field.

An important consideration in sorting out these variations in approach is that the conduct of visual studies also depends on the skills required to follow through with a chosen method and object of inquiry. Indeed, when visual studies scholars talk about their research and teaching, they frequently refer to skills that are both more general and more specific than the meta-methods described above. These skills are more general in their applicability to a wide range of situations and tasks, only some of which involve empirical social inquiry. Photographic or videographic skills, for example, might be valuable in conducting an ethnographic study of community life, but also could be useful in recording a friend's wedding or taking vacation pictures. As a reciprocal consideration, visual studies skills can be more specific than a method by focusing on particular kinds of materials—photographs taken by children, for example, the imagery of political cartoons published in a mass market magazine, or facades of nineteenth-century Canadian churches—each of which presents distinctive challenges for empirical inquiry.

Following these examples, a shortlist of the kind of skills noted by visual studies scholars in connection with their work would include the ability, technical expertise, and wherewithal to perform the following tasks, as these apply to particular images, visual representation, and other visible evidence required for a specific study:

- collecting and acquiring images and other visual representations
- creating or making images

- modifying or editing images
- reading and decoding images
- interpreting and analyzing images
- presenting and displaying images
- examining social and cultural contexts that shape the skills and tasks listed above.

Depending on the design of a specific study, the imagery associated with these tasks could take the form of physical artifacts and settings; photographs or video recordings; drawings, diagrams, or paintings; direct observation of activities and settings; visualizations inferred through observations of speech, gesture, and movement; visualizations manifest in other materials or reported directly through the comments of research subjects or other researchers; or other patterns of embodied culture and social life. Though this list is incomplete, reference to skills in working with one or more of these image forms is a defining dimension of most, if not all, visual studies projects.

Intersections of some of these skills and the objects and methods noted above correspond closely to boundaries of a relatively distinct research community. Connections between neurophysiologic objects of inquiry and neurophysiologic research methods, skills, and instruments, for example, are relatively well defined. That's much less the case for studies of visually interesting materials or for collecting artifacts (as I examine later in this handbook). In terms of backgrounds, skills, instrument sets, and career paths, individuals engaged in these pursuits are an extremely diverse lot. Only some of them are interested in empirical research, and those who are support a wide range of research networks, many of which have little or nothing to do with each other.

From within the context of visual studies as a branch of empirical inquiry, this kind of diversity increases intellectual vitality while simultaneously narrowing or diminishing the apparent strength of disciplinary ties (Wagner, 2001, 2002). Viewed from within an academic discipline or profession, however, the diversity of visual studies scholars and approaches can appear fragmented, theoretically undeveloped or undisciplined.

These contrasting perceptions of visual studies fuel continuing concerns about where the work of individual scholars fits, how it can best be assessed, and optimal trajectories for future research. Those concerns can displace attention to basic questions about where and how visual studies intersect with empirical inquiry. Understanding that intersection, however, requires inspection of not only the branches of empirical inquiry, among which visual studies may or may not hold its own, but also its roots.

VISUAL ROOTS

Many characterizations of empirical research refer, at least loosely, to three somewhat distinct activity sets: observation and data collection; data analysis and interpretation; and writing and reporting. There's nothing about this tripartite formulation that grants special distinctions to social or cultural studies that focus on visual objects of inquiry or make use of visual research methods or study skills. Distinctions of just that sort, however, appear if we unpack these three sets into the challenges they present to researchers in managing the material dimensions of their work.

Material challenges of empirical inquiry

For purposes of this analysis, I'll comment on five of these challenges, each defined by the need to convert one set of research materials into another. As displayed in Table 3.1, the material challenges for observation and data collection appear as researchers try to convert observations to records and records to artifacts. Data analysis and interpretation are linked to two other material transformations and challenges: converting artifacts to data sets and data sets

Table 3.1 Stages of empirical research: activity sets and material challenges

Stages/activity set	Material challenges		
	From	To	Generation removed (from phenomena)
1 Observation and data collection	Observations of phenomena	Records of individual observations (durable materials, one step removed from phenomena)	1
	Records of individual observations	Artifact collection (multiple records that include provenance information, meta-data, etc.)	2
2 Data analysis and interpretation	Artifact collection (records organized as collection)	Data set (i.e. artifact collection organized as evidence for examining specific research question)	3
	Data set (artifact collection organized as evidence)	Data-display patterns (data sets organized to make visible patterns of evidence salient to research questions)	4
3 Writing and reporting	Data-display patterns (data set organized to display patterns)	Lesson (data-display pattern organized to communicate with specific audience)	5+

to data-display patterns. Restated within the same typology, writing and reporting entails the challenge of converting data-display patterns to lessons for teaching research results to researchers, journalists, policymakers, the public, and so on.

Each activity set listed in the left column of Table 3.1 builds on the preceding, as does each material transformation listed on the right. Moving down the rows of Table 3.1 thus corresponds, on both sides, with a shift in attention from source phenomena and observation protocols to audience characteristics and reporting protocols. As noted in the far right column, research materials resulting from each transformation are one additional generation removed from the source phenomena.

The material transformations listed in Table 3.1 are distinctive to empirical research. Other forms of inquiry, such as speculation, spiritualism, meditation, projective expression, and fantasy, can generate insights and new ideas independent of material realities. Practitioners of these approaches have no need to wrestle with the challenges

of converting research evidence from one material form to another. Within empirical investigations, however, materiality—and, by extension, research materials—play an essential and somewhat inviolate role. Lacking material representations of phenomena and observations, investigations lack empirical warrant.

Recognizing that empirical research is grounded in various forms of material evidence has several implications. One of these is to define a common ground between the physical, natural, and social sciences—all of which value strategies and instruments that can read, measure, or otherwise sense the materiality of their focal phenomena. Another is to feature and foreground the logistics of managing research materials as a key element of research practice. Yet another is to represent the material culture of scientific inquiry as a key context shaping research conduct and new knowledge. The material culture of empirical inquiry thus links the material foundations of scientific theorizing with the material circumstances in which researchers exercise their craft.

Empirical researchers exercise the specifics of this craft when they convert transitory observations into durable records, when they manage those records as evidence, and when they communicate evidence patterns to others. In pragmatic terms, this kind of conversion, management, and communication requires researchers to link ideas and things.

Visual symbols, signs, cues, figures, representations, illustrations, and media can function as a kind of flux that broadens and deepens potential contacts between ideas and things. By attending to these visual props and properties, researchers can be more precise and complete in how they articulate research ideas with research things—for example, how they specify the significance of empirical evidence for challenging or supporting research propositions, concepts, and models. With this in mind, skills in working with visual props and properties can help researchers achieve what Ragin characterizes as the goal of empirical inquiry: 'to link the empirical and the theoretical—to use theory to make sense of evidence and to use evidence to sharpen and refine theory' (1992: 224–225). As a preface for examining what this assistance can entail for empirical *social* inquiry, let me describe how it works for empirical inquiry in general.

Converting materials step by step

A more complete picture of how skills in working with visual materials and representations—for example, 'visual study skills'—can help researchers move from empirical observation through analysis and research reporting appears as answers to questions about the material transformations listed in Table 3.1. What tools and strategies are valued by researchers in effecting each transformation? What potential problems and solutions do these entail for addressing material challenges farther down the line? And where might the crafts of making such transformations take a researcher closer to or farther away from initial objects of inquiry?

Observation to records

As a collective enterprise, the empirical sciences require evidence that is durable, stable, portable, and communicable. Memories of sensory observations—what I saw or heard, tasted or smelled a short or long moment ago—represent only a small step in the desired direction. Written notes and drawings go farther, as do audio or visual recordings and other instrumented record making. Research strategies that make use of these tools and technologies convert transitory *acts of observation* to the more durable materiality of *observation records*.

Visual study skills can play an important role in many conversions of this sort, and not just those that involve optical recording. It's through visual inspection that naturalists determine what specimens and samples are available and which of these are most feasible to collect. Visual representations on measuring devices and display screens are key in recording material specifications, including those that place specimens in contexts of time, space, and physical circumstances. Visual cues are also useful to social scientists in judging physical and social boundaries and tie-signs (for example, visual indications of what goes with what), tracking activities and conversations over time, noticing social and environmental change (Rieger, 2003), and reviewing research records in the field—on their own or in consultation with research subjects. As a visual study skill relevant to studying a wide range of phenomena, 'looking closely' is also valued in converting observations to records.

Above and beyond looking closely, other visual study skills can be put to good use in converting observations to records. These include documentary applications of visual recording media, the analysis of visual materials, and the production and analysis of visual representations. These skills are useful to studies of artifacts, activities, and symbolic cultural phenomena. For artifacts and activities, researchers can use photography and videography to create visual records of what they see in the field. For aspects of culture that cannot be observed directly, researchers can use visual materials to elicit or crystallize subject commentaries.

Scholars who investigate some forms of material culture can make the shift from observation to record by collecting the materials they are observing—the stock in trade of botanists, archaeologists, geologists, and so on. However, collecting is only feasible for materials small enough to transport and store and for those the researcher can legitimately acquire. For larger materials and those that have to stay put—by reason of law, ethics, scholarly integrity, or good sense—researchers must convert what they can see, hear, taste, or feel to notes and drawings, specifications (for example, measurements of volume, color, dimension, specific gravity, radioactivity, and so on), or analog depictions such as those created through evocative writing or audio or visual recordings. Visual study skills are essential to this process.

Record to artifact

Empirical researchers are expected to document and make explicit the circumstances in which phenomena are observed and observations recorded. Through this kind of documentation, individual records become artifacts wedded to the contextual information necessary to understand and appreciate them as evidence for empirical inquiries. For archaeological collections, this information, or meta-data, is used to classify materials by time, place, function, associated materials, collection/collector, and so on. Similar kinds of information are required to make good use of interview transcripts and field notes, survey responses, focus group interviews, code sheets, and audio-visual recordings.

Some materials are better than others in recording or preserving contextual information. Audio and video recordings, for example, can capture collateral information about the material surround that observers might leave out of notes and drawings. When records themselves lack contextual information, researchers have to obtain this from other sources—through additional observation or from commentary by subjects and other researchers about records already in hand. Records that can be retained and presented in the form of visual imagery are particularly well suited to this process.

A host of visual cues and icons are also available to researchers in attaching meta-data to records and marking conversion of records to artifacts. At the most mundane level these involve labels and tags for paper or digital folders, blank or populated boxes in database screen views, and other forms of materials processing.

Beyond the task of linking individual records and meta-data, the shift from record to artifact presents researchers with the challenge of visualizing relationships between the theoretical focus and boundaries of a study and the adequacy of their empirical evidence. Many researchers have found graphic organizers such as diagrams, charts, tables, and other figures to be extremely helpful in this process—see Miles and Huberman (1994) for a rich collection of examples. Knowing how to create visual representations of objects and ideas can be extremely useful in this regard, including skills in drawing figures, creating digital flow charts and animations, and displaying multiple images for comparative analysis. While some of these skills can be acquired through formal programs of study, many are also available through popular folk practices and consumer-level software applications.

Artifact to data set

Artifact collections include records organized by attribute, meta-data, and provenance, including information about where they came from and what they entail. A data set is composed of artifacts organized by their relevance to specific research questions and hypotheses. Data are always a set defined by the research questions for which the set might provide empirical answers. Lacking the organizing principle of a research question, records and artifacts remain just that.

In converting a collection of artifacts to a data set, researchers can use some of the same tools and strategies that work for converting records to artifacts. However, data sets also require researchers to explicate the focus of a study in terms that interest other researchers—not just documentarian or folk communities whose members care only about recording culture and social life, and for whom a project's final form may be an artifact collection.

New media and evolving computing resources have radically enriched the crafts through which social researchers can transform artifact collections into data sets in two key respects. First, the transition from artifact to data set can now be approached dynamically, as a real-time exploration of multi-dimensional records and artifacts. Though inductive approaches of this sort have characterized fieldwork for decades, the analytical tools for supporting them have increased significantly as databases developed a capacity to incorporate multi-dimensional and multi-media records. Second, and closely related to dynamic analysis tools, computing software and new media forms have expanded the potential for visual inspection and design of scientific data sets. An obvious resource in this regard is the kind of articulation now common between graphic display applications and quantitative and qualitative record keeping. With a few keystrokes, graphs and figures can be created from quantitative relationships. Current generation 'search and find' applications can just as easily create visual displays of text string frequencies and distributions. Computer software also makes it relatively easy to compare, scan, sort, cluster, and sequence a wide range of multi-media artifacts—including image and audio files—and to format the results to facilitate direct visual inspection.

Dynamic analyses of high bandwidth databases and tools that facilitate visual database inspection have had a substantial impact in the physical and social sciences and in the humanities. They also have special significance for researchers working with audio or visual materials. By incorporating and retaining multi-media records in their original form, these tools allow researchers to work directly with high-fidelity representations of social and cultural phenomena—and to do so from observation to record to artifact and data set, or even beyond. For investigations of source phenomena that are themselves audio or visual materials—family photographs, scientific diagrams, television or motion pictures, magazine advertisements, etc.—this eidetic correspondence can continue from the beginning to the end of the inquiry process.

Data set to data-display pattern

A data set links records of known provenance (artifacts) to research questions. Making these links explicit creates a kind of virtual laboratory within which researchers can use patterns of empirical evidence to frame, clarify, and answer research questions. However, while the patterns are inherent to the data set, they become visible only when the data set is organized and formatted to reveal them. Data-set design is thus a significant challenge for the conduct of empirical inquiry and the craft of creating, and managing different kinds of data sets is a resource of considerable value, within which visual study skills are a key ingredient.

Inspecting either source phenomena or a data set is a transitory act. To move beyond what the researcher *notices*, observations must also be *noted*. Conversions of this kind require researchers to create cognate representations that weld the idea of a data-display pattern to a particular material form.

Charts, graphs, figures, flowcharts, two- and three-dimensional models, tables and catalytic images, animations, texts and artifacts can all come into play as researchers try to convert observed data-display patterns to material form. So, too, can skills in editing such representations in different media and presentation formats. Some scholars have examined the form and syntax of this kind of data-display as natural phenomena in their own right, and some of those (Tukey, 1977; Tufte, 1983, 1990, 1997) have offered guidelines for how to use displays of this sort more effectively.

Depending on how artifacts and databases are constructed, converting patterns observed to durable displays can be managed within the database itself. A computer database can convert a table of frequencies to a printed pie chart or bar chart, for example, or find and display a video recording corresponding to a particular configuration of meta-data. But these features are limited to the kinds of records and artifacts they include. The frequency tables won't generate video output unless the video files have been incorporated earlier on, and a database of video artifacts won't generate frequencies unless meta-data for those artifacts are formatted so they can be counted and summed.

As a more general rule, the fidelity of data-display representations to source phenomena is a matter of continuing concern. Richly detailed and visually engaging displays can be a great resource in communicating about research to diverse audiences. However, they can also be generated through artifacts and data sets that differ profoundly from the source phenomena they are supposed to represent.

Dynamic, visually arresting and engaging displays of summative indicators are part and parcel of contemporary research presentations and policy discourse. When their attractions encourage misperceptions of source phenomena, however, they compromise empirical inquiry. The prevalence of high-impact data displays in contemporary journalism and policymaking is an important reminder that converting research materials from record to artifact to data set, and so on, shapes both research and public knowledge of culture and social life.

Data-display pattern to lesson

If a given data set is extremely well aligned with those used by other researchers, reporting a new pattern can challenge or support existing theories. The more common situation, however, is one in which a researcher must make the case that data patterns are significant for understanding a particular set of phenomena. The shorthand version of this challenge is the need to 'publish' research, but a more felicitous perspective is that researchers have to 'teach' their colleagues something significant for which their research data sets provide relevant, new information (Wagner, 1987). Publications can certainly work well for this kind of teaching, but so can presentation in other formats, including lectures, workshops, websites, and interactive DVDs (that allow other scholars to explore data and to discern, on their own, the same data-set patterns), handbooks, individual consultations, television programs, exhibits, and so on.

Considered within the full compass of their professional lives—writing research proposals and reports, preparing memos to request additional funding or personnel, evaluating programs, teaching and mentoring students, and so on—most academic researchers approach these broadly defined 'teaching' challenges with a variety of visual media and presentation tools. These require skills in creating and editing visual representations, using visual materials (including representations of this sort) to stimulate questions and comments from others, and examining how people are likely to 'see things' as a context in which new concepts and insights can be taught more or less effectively. Visual study skills become especially important when researchers try to teach public or lay audiences about their work, audiences that may have political, social, or personal concerns that overlap only in part with a researcher's disciplinary community.

As these comments hopefully illustrate, the skills researchers bring to bear as they construct, organize, analyze, and present evidence for projects of empirical inquiry insinuate significant visual dimensions into their research, even when their objects and methods of inquiry have nothing to do with visual studies. These visual dimensions derive from the emphasis empirical inquiry places on using material evidence to challenge or support concepts, theories, and models and from the value of visual study skills in helping researchers to link ideas and things.

Considered across the material transformations noted above, the visual study skills valuable to researchers correspond in important respects to the skills listed earlier as a defining dimension of visual studies as a branch of empirical social inquiry. This correspondence between roots and branch has critical and reflexive implications that are worth exploring further through visual studies of the practice of empirical inquiry and empirical studies of visual studies practice. As a small step in the second direction, it's worth considering whether some forms of material evidence present special challenges and opportunities for visual studies in supporting empirical *social* inquiry.

VISUAL MATERIALS AND SOCIAL INQUIRY

Compared with other resources for converting observations to records, artifacts, and data sets, visual media and materials have some distinctive strengths and weaknesses when standing in for evidence of culture and social life. Strengths include their analog fidelity to the visual, spatial, and (for videotape) temporal dimensions of source phenomena, a capacity to materialize perceptions of researchers and research subjects and to generate eidetic representation of other visual materials. As an extension of these special features, visual recording media are also well suited to elicit and capture collateral and contextual data.

The weaknesses of visual media and materials for purposes of empirical social inquiry include the potential for a kind of commodity fetishism (in which the *sui generis* attractions of visual materials displace attention to the phenomena they are intended to represent),

the power to generate more collateral and contextual data than researchers can analyze, and the technical demands of visual technologies appropriate to a given area of research activity. To clarify the scope of these strengths and weaknesses, and their significance for visual studies as both branch and root of empirical inquiry, let me comment on each in turn.

Phenomenal fidelity

Depending on the media through which they are materialized, some research records, artifacts, and data sets can be examined as an analog of their associated source phenomena while others cannot. Media formatted to record the passage of time, for example, such as audiotapes and videotapes, can reflect analog fidelity to how time passes within social and cultural processes. Media formatted to display spatial relationships (three-dimensional modeling, photographs, and maps) can provide analogous representations of the spatial organization of social and cultural activities. Media that support written or spoken language (text on paper or audio recordings) provide analog fidelity for different forms of spoken or written discourse that represent, in turn, an analog of how people think. Drawings, photographs, and videotapes can achieve something similar for how they see.

The potential for analogical analysis depends on the homology of research materials and source phenomena. In much the same way, the extent to which material transformations noted in Table 3.1 reduce fidelity depends on the homology of materials from one stage or generation to the next. For example, a researcher could take a video recording of an interview (a 'record' in the typology described in the preceding section) and convert it to an annotated written transcript (an 'artifact'). But the researcher could also effect the record-to-artifact transition by simply annotating the video recording. The first approach generates artifacts that lend themselves to text analysis tools and strategies, but forgoes nuances of the subject's gestures and voice and thereby reduces fidelity. By retaining voice and gesture, the second approach maintains greater fidelity to the source interview, but can leave the researcher with multi-media artifacts that are more complex than artifacts limited to text alone.

Trade-offs such as these reflect an abiding tension within empirical research between phenomenal fidelity and data reduction. Investigators who value phenomenal fidelity would like material transformations leading through a research project to subtract or add as little as possible to salient features of source phenomena. Preserving phenomenal fidelity at all costs, however, can leave researchers with multi-dimensional records, artifacts, and data sets that exceed the capacity of their most efficient analysis tools, quantitative tools in particular. Investigators intent on using these analysis tools must be willing to simplify and condense the complexity of research materials and live with the loss of empirical fidelity that entails.

Correspondence with source phenomena can be enhanced by creating data sets that *specify* relationships between different aspects, dimensions, and features of source phenomena or that *depict* source phenomena analogically. A continuous video recording of a wedding, assassination, or child development class, for example, will display activities in the same sequence and duration as they occurred in the event itself. Because they are linked mechanically to the materiality, time, and space occupied by the source phenomena, recordings exhibit a kind of homology (on these dimensions, at least) for which inspection of the data set can generate more detailed information about source phenomena themselves.

As a special case of phenomenal fidelity, visual (and audio) research materials can play a special role in studies of artifacts that are themselves visual (or audio) materials. Researchers who study family photographs, websites, Hollywood films, political buttons and posters, radio programs, fashion design, storytelling, or security camera videos can work routinely with extremely high-fidelity copies of their focal source phenomena. These copies allow both researchers and audiences to view (or hear) phenomena in the same material form—though not the same social contexts—as they could be apprehended in the field. This enables researchers to retain intimate contact with source phenomena throughout the inquiry process, or even to invite research colleagues and other audiences to examine directly the source phenomena at the center of their studies.

This special feature of multi-media recordings does not mean that scholarship about visual materials can only proceed as a series of visual studies projects. Nor does it mean that all photo- or videographic research records have the same epistemological status. Photo and video records that appear in social and cultural inquiry may or may not constitute source data. But when source phenomena are themselves audio-visual materials, they *can* be presented to other scholars (and lay audiences) in ways that are not possible for other elements of culture and social life.

The source phenomena observed by Erving Goffman for the analysis reported in *Asylums* (1963) or *The Presentation of Self in Everyday Life* (1959), for example, were recorded as field notes that very few people have ever seen. These differ in form and content from the mass media photographs Goffman examined in writing *Gender Advertisements* (1976). Within that publication, Goffman included a good sample of the image artifacts he collected. These do not just depict, but actually constitute source phenomena for his study. As such, they also define a class of imagery—representations of how producers and consumers visualized images of men, women, adults, and children in mid-twentieth century American culture—that many readers can access on their own.

The photographs in *Gender Advertisements* thus provide a different kind of empirical warrant from the photographs through which Margaret Mead and Gregory Bateson examined cultural practices (including gender display) in Balinese culture (1942). Bateson and Mead made photographs as records of other phenomena that interested them. Their images might do a good job of *depicting* culture and social life, but did not *constitute* the phenomena at the center of their interests—though the same photographs have constituted just that for subsequent examinations of Mead and Bateson's work (Sullivan, 1999).

Contextual and collateral evidence

In materializing observations, a key difference between a drawing or written note and a photograph or video recording is that the drawing or note will include only those details noticed and added by the observer. In contrast to this wholly deliberative process, the photograph or video record will quite likely include visible details that fell within the camera's field of view that, at the time, escaped the attention and interest of the photographer. This contrast makes machine records, such as photographs and audio or video recordings, extremely useful in collecting contextual evidence related to the focal phenomena of a study, the circumstances in which artifacts are found or collected, or otherwise acquired, and the terms by which researchers participated in a field setting.

The contributions of audio-visual recording in collecting contextual and collateral evidence include the opportunity such materials provide to stimulate the remembered experience of both researcher and research subjects. This can occur for researchers in reviewing and logging their recordings and for research subjects through various image-elicitation protocols. In both cases, the mix of focal and collateral information contained in machine-recorded artifacts can prompt discussions that help place focal phenomena within a context of broader social and cultural interchange.

If one upside of photographs, videotapes, and other machine recordings is their power to capture, represent, depict, or even constitute data that can contextualize focal phenomena, a downside is the cost in research time and attention of sorting through rivers of information when a small stream might suffice. These trade-offs, however, are neither inevitable nor straightforward. Most researchers have to keep at least one eye open for ways to finish projects, not just start them, and reducing the gross quantity of data that needs to be processed can be a valuable step in that direction. But avoiding, simplifying, and reducing multi-media data for convenience's sake alone is somewhat suspect, in part because convenience varies with both the researcher's experience and technical skill.

Tools, skills, and multi-media seductions

In trying to achieve both phenomenal fidelity and efficient data reduction, researchers can benefit greatly from strategies and tool-kits for working with complex, multi-dimensional records, artifacts, and data sets. As a loose corollary, a lack of either experience or tools has discouraged more than a few researchers from working with forms of data—including audio and video recordings—that seem inherently messy.

Relative to texts and numbers, multi-media research records and artifacts do present distinctive challenges. These warrant respect, but not fear or dread, for at least two reasons. First, multi-media records can be wrestled into shape by applying the same observation strategies researchers have used for decades to structure direct observations in the field—looking closely, taking good notes, and coding for key dimensions and variables. Second, beyond those traditional approaches, researchers can also call on a wide range of computer-assisted database, record keeping, logging, editing, and store-and-retrieve software.

In times past, tools needed to work with multi-media materials were expensive and the requisite skills considerable—and perhaps best acquired through advanced technical training. Increasingly, however, practical understanding of how to make, edit, and organize multi-media materials has become a routine feature of generalized computer literacy. Folk practices of photo and video documentation—including the collection, annotation, and organization of image, sound, and video files—have evolved in both technical and conceptual complexity; these currently represent a resource that researchers can draw upon to support their own empirical inquiries.

The downside of having these tools and skills readily available is that researchers may be tempted to use them even when they are inappropriate to a particular study or line of inquiry. Indeed, the potential for commodity fetishism, in which the aesthetic and symbolic attractions of particular tools and materials displace and override attention to the phenomena they are intended to represent, is a persistent concern among social researchers. Photographs, video recordings, three-color charts and graphs, pull quotes and catchy titles, correlation coefficients and confidence levels, evocative prose and detailed spreadsheets can all be invoked to make an empirical study seem more vital, thorough, or credible than it is. And, while good editing and presentation may depend on technical, as well as substantive, knowledge, scholars who oversell the significance of particular tools or materials court the suspicion and disdain of other researchers.

Within the social sciences, concerns about this kind of fetishism have fueled more challenges to photographs and video recordings than to other kinds of research materials. On the one hand, this is understandable. Many people make photographs and videos that celebrate the image as a commodity in its own right (for example, fine art photographs and feature films) or that advertise the attractions of specific products, perspectives, and ideas. Against the backdrop of this persuasion-oriented mediascape, it's worth considering how a particular photograph or video recording might or might not serve as evidence for social inquiry. But those questions are also worth asking about numbers and texts, as all three forms of representation can be manipulated, hijacked, or fetishized to diminish rather than increase our understanding of culture and social life. In general, looking for good data and determining how good the data look involves a delicate balance between phenomenal fidelity, data reduction, and what it takes to communicate findings to colleagues and other audiences: that's as true for visual materials as it is for numbers and texts, but not any more so.

FORMING NEW KNOWLEDGE

Visual studies scholars have no monopoly on developing new knowledge of culture and social life. Imagery is not the only game in town and perspectives that emphasize other dimensions are equally important to empirical social inquiry. However, familiarity with visual studies objects of inquiry, methods and skills can prepare researchers to make more rational and effective methodological choices. Whether or not scholars who develop this familiarity come to see their discipline or the world differently, there's a good chance they'll be more skilled in developing empirically sound accounts of what they notice and have to say.

This prospect is both enriched and complicated, however, by the linked growth of interdisciplinary work with computer literacy and skills in multi-media production. Taken together, these have fostered an increasingly vital relationship between the media and methods of empirical inquiry—defined by the material transformations described above—and contemporary folk life. New media tools that have made it much easier for researchers to create multi-media records of culture and social life have also increased exponentially the range of related folk materials that are now available to researchers. Whether or not researchers incorporate these materials into their own research, they point to folk practices that overlap in part with some visual study objects and methods of inquiry, particularly as these reflect interdisciplinary approaches. This kind of overlap may increase opportunities for researchers to share visual studies projects with students, subjects, and lay audiences, but they also heighten the challenge of distinguishing visual studies that warrant serious scholarly attention from those that don't.

Jay Ruby (1973) worried over this issue some decades ago as a concern that anthropologists' photographs were more likely to reflect the conventions of 'home mode' (Chalfen, 1987) family snapshots than the research tenets of their own discipline. This generalization may or may not have been true—and may be more or less true now than it was when Ruby first wrote about it. However, it rests on a notion of the home mode that is too simple to account for the visual documents of culture and social life that have been created in recent years by consumers with no obvious research background in the social sciences. In this respect, it may be less telling that some field researchers have a tendency to make images in the home mode than that some home-mode enthusiasts—including children, artists, and activists—have taken up audio and visual recording with imagination enough to support significant social and visual inquiries.

Along those lines, my own reviews of image-sharing websites such as *YouTube*®, *flickr*®, *vimeo*™, and *Facebook*® reveal a wealth of vernacular visual study projects that could enrich the collective enterprise of social scientific inquiry. Prominent among these are photo and video documents of social activities, cultural events and rituals, artifact collections and archives, 'think-aloud' accounts that range in focus from learning to use a new software program to shooting a wild turkey with a bow and arrow (and include pretty much everything in between) and projects to explicitly compare different elements of culture and social life (personal appearance, arrangements of household possessions, individual and group construction projects at different stages of development, urban or rural landscapes, changing family structures, and so on). Some of these folk materials have such strong expressive dimensions that they are best viewed as evidence about the vision and skills of the individuals who put them together—and not much more. But others seem to give a good account of the subjects in front of the camera, not just behind it, and mirror the kind of content and provenance that researchers look for in artifacts and records that can support empirical social inquiry (Wagner, 2007).

Most folk products that achieve this kind of evidentiary standard present photographs or video recordings without the kind of analysis we've come to expect from academic social research. In terms of the research materials' typology reviewed earlier, they are best described as collections of records and artifacts. In some cases, however, these collections achieve high levels of phenomenal fidelity and come with enough contextual or meta-data to support additional analysis. And a few folk projects include evidence and analysis that are both visually intriguing and significant (see, for example, the *oktrends* blog for the online dating site *OkCupid*: http://blog.okcupid.com/).

Within Ruby's reasoning about this matter, these online collections of visual folk documents might be of interest to social researchers, but they would fall short of constituting social scientific inquiry in their own right. I'm inclined to agree, but only up to a point. An increasing number of social scientists—and I include myself among them—have found these vernacular visual studies projects of value to disciplinary research and teaching: as illustrations, data sets, catalytic cases, evidence of natural variation, counter examples, existence proofs, and so on. And an increasing number of scholars, museums, galleries, and agencies have uploaded research and teaching materials of their own to some of the same sites that support vernacular image sharing. Searching on these sites for terms such as ritual, material culture, social reproduction, technology, or the name of a particular culture or social group can frequently bring up visual imagery (photographs, drawings, charts, and video recordings) from both folk producers and academics. This confluence does not equate folk projects of visual documentation with systematic social research, but the parallels are strong enough to consider the contributions of each to new knowledge of culture and social life—for both research communities and the public.

When viewed as an emerging interface between social scientific and folk inquiries, visual studies also seems to highlight a seam between what Marx regarded as the means and modes of production—in this case, the production of knowledge about culture and social life. As the technological means and tools of knowledge production change, they can become more or less at odds with existing modes of knowledge production, including relationships between those whose labor produces knowledge and those who control its valuation, exchange, and distribution. In terms of participation, visual referents and the ambiguity of material and virtual interchange, a shift of just this sort has increasingly challenged the dominant nodes and protocols of knowledge production, within which research universities and scientific disciplines have played a central role.

A growing rift between knowledge-production technologies and traditional modes of knowledge control is apparent in the increasingly unsettled role of universities, libraries, and media industries and in the conflict over state provisions for managing intellectual and cultural property. These developments may not be a revolution in the making, but they represent at least the possibility of continuing change and substantial dislocation within and around knowledge production and distribution. Within these dislocations, ideas about the ownership, control, distribution, attribution, and meaning of visual representations are highly contested, with significant consequences for scholarship, individual expression, and community life.

Because of its continuities with the fault line between means and modes of knowledge production, visual studies represents a site of considerable vitality and flux. As offshoot, branch, and root, it has framed significant empirical inquiries of culture and social life for a century or more now, some of which may well extend to the next century.

REFERENCES

Banks, Marcus (1998) 'Visual anthropology: Image, object and interpretation', in J. Prosser (ed.), *Image-Based Research*. London: Taylor and Francis. pp. 9–23.

Banks, Marcus (2001) *Visual Methods in Social Research*. Thousand Oaks, CA: Sage Publications.

Bateson, Gregory and Mead, Margaret (1942) *Balinese Character: A Photographic Analysis*. Vol. 2, *Special Publications of the New York Academy of Sciences*. New York: New York Academy of Sciences.

Becker, Howard (1986) 'Photography and sociology', in *Doing Things Together*. Evanston, IL: Northwestern University Press. pp. 221–272.

Becker, Howard (1998) *Tricks of the Trade*. Chicago, IL: University of Chicago.

Biella, Peter (1988) 'Against reductionism and idealist self-reflexivity: The Ilparakuyo Maasai Film Project', in J. R. Rollwagen (ed.), *Anthropological Filmmaking*. New York: Harwood. pp. 47–72.

Boas, Franz (1955) *Primitive Art*. New York: Dover.

Chalfen, Richard (1987) *Snapshot Versions of Life*. Bowling Green, OH: Bowling Green University Popular Press.

Clark, Cindy Dell (1999) 'The autodriven interview: A photographic viewfinder into children's experiences', *Visual Sociology*, 14(1): 39–50.

Clark, Kenneth (1963) *Prejudice and Your Child*. Boston, MA: Beacon Press.

Clark-Ibanez, Marisol (2009) 'Inner-city children in sharper focus: Sociology of childhood and photo-elicitation interviews', in G. C. Stanczak (ed.), *Visual Research Methods*. Newbury Park, CA: Sage Publications. pp. 167–196.

Clifford, James and Marcus, George E. (eds.) (1986) *Writing Culture*. Berkeley, CA: University of California.

Collier, John Jr (1967) *Visual Anthropology*. New York: Holt, Rinehart & Winston.

Elkins, James (ed.) (2007) *Visual Literacy*. New York: Routledge.

Emmison, Michael and Smith, Philip (2000) *Researching the Visual*. Thousand Oaks, CA: Sage Publications.

Filstead, William J. (1970) *Qualitative Methodology*. Chicago, IL: Rand McNally.

Goffman, Erving (1959) *The Presentation of Self in Everyday Life*. Garden City, NY: Doubleday Anchor Books.

Goffman, Erving (1963) *Asylums*. Garden City, NY: Anchor.

Goffman, Erving (1976) *Gender Advertisements*. New York: Harper and Row.

Grady, John (1996) 'The scope of visual sociology', *Visual Sociology*, 11(2): 10–24.

Grady, John (2009) 'Advertising images as social indicators: Depictions of blacks in *LIFE* magazine 1936–2000', *Visual Studies*, 22(3): 211–239.

Greenblat, Cathy Stein (2004) *Alive with Alzheimer's*. Chicago, IL: University of Chicago Press.

Greenfield, Patricia Marks (2004) *Weaving Generations Together*. Santa Fe, NM: School of American Research Press.

Gusfield, Joseph (1981) *The Culture of Public Problems*. Chicago, IL: University of Chicago Press.

Hagaman, Diane (1993) 'The joy of victory, the agony of defeat: Stereotypes in newspaper sports feature photographs', *Visual Sociology*, 6(2): 48–66.

Hagaman, Diane (1996) *How I Learned Not To Be a Photojournalist*. Louisville, KY: University Press of Kentucky.

Harper, Douglas (1982) *Good Company*. Chicago, IL: University of Chicago Press.

Harper, Douglas (1987) *Working Knowledge*. Chicago, IL: University of Chicago Press.

Harper, Douglas (2001) *Changing Works*. Chicago, IL: University of Chicago Press.

Harper, Douglas and Faccioli, Patrizia (2010) *The Italian Way*. Chicago, IL: University of Chicago Press.

Heider, Karl G. (1976) *Ethnographic Film*. Austin, TX: University of Texas.

Hocking, Paul (ed.) (1995) *Principles of Visual Anthropology*. New York: Mouton de Gruyter.

Hoskins, Janet (1998) *Biographical Objects*. New York: Routledge.

Hunter, Albert J. (ed.) (1990) *The Rhetoric of Social Research*. New Brunswick, NJ: Rutgers.

Latour, Bruno and Woolgar, Steve (1986) *Laboratory Life*. Princeton, NJ: Princeton University Press.

Lesy, Michael (1973) *Wisconsin Death Trip*. New York: Pantheon Books.

Levi-Strauss, Claude (1958) *Structural Anthropology*. London: Allen Lane, Penguin Press.

Lynch, Michael (1998) 'The production of scientific images: Vision and re-vision in the history, philosophy, and sociology of science', *Communication and Cognition*, 31(2/3): 213–228.

Lynch, Michael and Woolgar, Steve (eds.) (1990) *Representation in Scientific Practice*. Cambridge, MA: MIT Press.

Mead, Margaret and Bateson, Gregory (1976) 'For God's sake, Margaret', *Co-Evolution Quarterly*, 10: 32–44.

Messaris, Paul (1994) *Visual Literacy*. Boulder, CO: Westview Press.

Miles, M. B. and Huberman, A. M. (1994) *Qualitative Data Analysis*. Thousand Oaks, CA: Sage Publications.

Mitchell, W. J. T. (1986) *Iconology*. Chicago, IL: University of Chicago Press.

Page, Roby (2005) *Bike Week at Daytona Beach*. Jackson, MS: University Press of Mississippi.

Pauwels, Luc (ed.) (2006) *Visual Cultures of Science*. Hanover, NH: Dartmouth College Press.

Pink, Sarah (2001) *Doing Visual Ethnography*. London: Sage Publications.

Ragin, Charles C. (1992) '"Casing" and the process of social inquiry', in C. C. Ragin and H. S. Becker (eds.), *What Is a Case?* New York: Cambridge University Press. pp. 217–226.

Rhythms of Earth (2009) [DVD: Include all four choreometrics films by Alan Lomax and Forrestine Paulay, 150 minutes; 90 minutes of interviews with Lomax and Paley, and 177 pages of text] Portland, OR: Media-Generation.

Rieger, Jon H. (2003) 'A retrospective study of social change: The pulp-logging industry in an Upper Peninsula Michigan county', *Visual Studies*, 18(1): 156–177.

Rose, Gillian (2001) *Visual Methodologies*. London: Sage Publications.

Rosenthal, Alan (ed.) (1988) *New Challenges for Documentary*. Berkeley, CA: University of California.

Ruby, Jay (1973) 'Up the Zambezi with notebook and camera: Or, being anthropologist without doing anthropology... with pictures', *Program in Ethnographic Film Newsletter*, 4(3): 12–14.

Ruby, Jay (1995) *Secure the Shadow*. Cambridge, MA: MIT Press.

Ruby, Jay (2000) *Picturing Culture*. Chicago, IL: University of Chicago Press.

Salvo, Dana (1997) *Home Altars of Mexico*. London: Thames and Hudson.

Schneider, Sara K. (1996) *Vital Mummies*. New Haven, CT: Yale University Press.

Schwartz, Dona (1989) 'Visual ethnography: Using photography in qualitative research', *Qualitative Sociology,* 12(2): 119–154.

Schwartz, Dona (1998) *Contesting the Super Bowl.* New York: Routledge.

Schwartz, Dona (1999) 'Pictorial journalism: Photographs as facts', in B. Brennen and H. Hardt (eds.), *Pictures in the Public Sphere.* Champaign, IL: University of Illinois Press.

Seiter, Ellen (1993) *Sold Separately.* New Brunswick, NJ: Rutgers University.

Spindler, George (2008) 'Using visual stimuli in ethnography', *Anthropology & Education Quarterly,* 39(2): 127–140.

Stanczak, Gregory, (ed.) (2007) *Visual Research Methods.* Thousand Oaks, CA: Sage Publications.

Sullivan, Gerald (1999) *Margaret Mead, Gregory Bateson, and Highland Bali.* Chicago, IL: University of Chicago Press.

Tobin, Joseph J., Wu, Davis Y. H. and Davidson, Dana H. (1989) *Preschool in Three Cultures.* New Haven, CT: Yale University Press.

Tufte, Edward R. (1983) *The Visual Display of Quantitative Information.* Cheshire, CT: Graphics Press.

Tufte, Edward R. (1990) *Envisioning Information.* Cheshire, CT: Graphics Press.

Tufte, Edward R. (1997) *Visual Explanations.* Cheshire, CT: Graphics Press.

Tukey, John W. (1977) *Exploratory Data Analysis.* Reading, MA: Addison-Wesley.

Van Maanen, John (ed.) (1995) *Representation in Ethnography.* Thousand Oaks, CA: Sage Publications.

Wagner, Jon (ed.) (1979) *Images of Information.* Beverly Hills, CA: Sage Publications.

Wagner, Jon (1987) 'Teaching and research as student responsibilities', *Change,* 19: 26–35.

Wagner, Jon (2001) 'Does image-based field work have more to gain from extending or rejecting scientific realism?', *Visual Sociology,* 16(2): 7–21.

Wagner, Jon (2002) 'Contrasting images, complementary trajectories: Sociology, visual sociology and visual research', *Visual Studies* 17(2): 160–171.

Wagner, Jon (2006a) 'The visual substance of social research', in P. Hamilton (ed.), *Visual Research Methods.* Beverly Hills, CA: Sage Publications. pp. 401–424.

Wagner, Jon (2006b) 'Visible materials, visualized theory and images of social research', *Visual Studies,* 21(1): 55–69.

Wagner, Jon (2007). 'Observing culture and social life', in G. C. Stanczak (ed.), *Visual Research Methods.* Newbury Park, CA: Sage Publications. pp. 23–59.

Wagner, Jon (2010) 'Visual data in educational research', in P. Peterson, E. Baker and B. McGaw (eds.), *International Encyclopedia of Education.* Oxford: Elsevier. pp. 498–504.

Wakefield, Hollida and Underwager, Ralph (1998) 'The application of images in child abuse investigations', in J. Prosser (ed.), *Image-Based Research.* London: Taylor and Francis. pp. 176–194.

4

Seeing Things: Visual Research and Material Culture

Jon Wagner

INTRODUCTION

How we think about material culture goes hand in hand with how we think about culture, and it also shapes how we approach visual studies of culture and social life. As I will explore below, these definitional matters are also matters of theory. Propositions about the relationship of culture, materiality, and visibility implicate ideas about how people live, what they care about, who they are, what they see, and how they look.

Many sociologists, anthropologists, and lay communities think of material culture as the physical artifacts of a particular group of people. This 'world of things' includes foodstuffs, clothing, tools, family photographs, decorative beadwork or tattoos, religious regalia and relics, drugs, server farms, home and office furnishings—and the homes and offices themselves—dolls, toys, armaments, automobiles, and much more.

To the extent that they are material, bounded, and accessible, these manifestations of material culture can become interesting objects of visual inquiry. We can understand quite well, for example, the value of visual studies of the materials involved in food preparation and consumption (Pepin, 1976; Lifchez and Winslow, 1979), marriage or funeral practices (Norfleet, 1979; Secretan, 1995), dairy farming (Harper, 2001), timber harvesting (Rieger, 2003), electoral campaigns, or imprisonment (Lyon, 1971; Jackson, 1977).

As an implicit complement to the world of things, both scholars and lay audiences also affirm the significance of symbolic, non-material dimensions of culture and social life. Depending on discipline or disposition, these non-material elements can include how people think about their history, time and place, the universe, children and adults, work, play, life and death, family and community. Ideals for judging beauty, fairness, power, religiosity, and other such matters also fall within this non-material realm, as do typologies by which people sort out flora and fauna, kinship, political persuasions, what can and cannot be owned, and so on.

These forms of ideation cannot be observed directly, but they can be inferred from what people say, what they do, and the materials they work with. Through interactive image-making and interview strategies (Collier, 1967; Spindler, 1987; Hoskins, 1998; Clark, 1999; Clark-Ibanez, 2009), visual research methods can also play an important role in helping to construct such inferences from both researcher and subject points of view.

In the last few decades, the vitality of these complementary orientations has fueled an expanded appreciation of material culture and an enhanced role for visual studies in investigating culture and social life. In the remainder of this chapter, I will review some of these developments and implications. But one notable implication, to my way of thinking, is that the terms 'material culture' and 'visual studies' may not provide the best framework for guiding empirical research in this area, for at least three reasons:

First, the broad bifurcation of cultural studies into material and non-material domains has too often neglected how members of a culture act and behave, individually and in consort with others. Attending to what people actually do—as social, psychological and physical beings that embody cultural practices—blurs boundaries between things and ideas, the material and non-material, the visual and non-visual (Bronner, 1986). As a special instance of this ambiguity, the human body appears as a significant 'material' for the production and distribution of culture and corporeal behavior as an important, but frequently neglected, domain of material culture (Bell, 2009).

Second, by granting primacy to visual appearances, visual studies of material culture have often played a powerful role in disconnecting artifacts from the social and physical environments meaningful to their original makers and users. This disassociation both reflects and enables the commoditization of cultural materials for distribution and exchange within exogenous markets— markets in which even products and artifacts of social research can be appropriated for ulterior purposes. Recent controversies over legal attribution and control of cultural materials highlight the shortcomings of analyses that presume clear and stable divides between visual/material cultural forms and the social contexts of their origins and first use (Messenger, 1999; Lessig, 2004; Scafidi, 2005; Cuno, 2008; Lilley, 2008).

Third, new technologies of multi-media representation have generated a host of virtual locations, situations, transactions, relationships, and other culturally significant phenomena that are poorly accounted for by traditional perspectives on material culture and visual studies. Indeed, in their potential to link cultural ideas and things through visual inspection and touch-based interaction, virtual reality (VR) objects and environments have stimulated changes in how we talk about and see the world. References to being 'online' or 'off,' for example, or 'reading' audio books and podcasts, 'talking' with someone through online chat, 'going' to or 'visiting' websites, writing or reading on Facebook® 'walls,' and so on, stand some characteristic distinctions of material culture and visual study on their heads.

After reviewing several different orientations to material culture and their limitations in addressing these and other concerns, I will propose three propositions about culture, materiality, visibility, and methods of visual research that are hopefully more useful in guiding visual research in this area. While these propositions blur the commonsense distinction between ideas and things, understanding that distinction at face value is an important step toward assessing contributions of visual research to the study of material culture. With that in mind, things are by far the best place to begin.

ARTIFACTS AND OTHER CULTURAL MATERIALS

Compared with other noteworthy orientations, artifacts have been the stars of the material culture show. Both scholars and lay audiences are wowed by physical objects that people have fashioned or re-fashioned to support their culture and their lives. Museum collections and exhibitions, films and videotape documentaries, and photography-rich books lend a continuing vitality to this orientation toward material culture. It's part of what we appreciate in Franz Boas' analysis of primitive art (1955), the King Tut exhibition (Edwards, 1976) once again making the rounds of notable museums, Patricia Turner's (2009) thoughtful analysis of African-American Quilters and Errol Morris' (2009) blogs about fake photographs.

Artifact-oriented studies can play an important role in alerting scholars and lay audiences to information and materials they otherwise know little about—or misunderstand: Impressionist paintings, for example, or the houses architects live in (Plumb, 1977), product histories of automobiles, electrical virility devices (de la Pena, 2005), Boy Scout uniforms (Mechling, 2001), or Pez dispensers (Chertoff and Kahn, 2006). Of particular interest in this regard are studies that document artifacts associated with a particular time, people, and place, such as Tom Wolfe's (1965) impressionistic, but well-researched, essays about custom car culture in the mid-twentieth century and Lynn White's (1966) scholarly exegesis of the stirrup in fourteenth-century France. A convenience sample of artifact studies from my personal library might include the following:

- Erving Goffman's (1976) catalog and analysis of advertising photographs depicting male and female subjects.
- David Anthony's *The Lost World of Old Europe* (2010), a provocative history of early civilizations in the Balkans.
- Three volumes of *The Bowyer's Bible* (Hamm, 1992, 1993, 1994), an edited collection of illustrated essays about bows and arrows created and used by different peoples around the world.
- A narrative catalog of John Baeder's paintings of diners from various locales across the USA (1995).

- Volume 1 of the *1980 Scott's Standard Postage Stamp Catalogue* (Hatcher, 1979) that identifies all known stamps of the USA, United Nations, and British Commonwealth of Nations, by the year they were issued, face value and retail value in 1980.
- Dozens of illustrated cookbooks.
- Robert Coles' (1992) account of the drawings that children prepared during meetings with him as a therapist/interlocutor.
- Dana Salvo's (1997) photographs of home altars in Mexico.
- David Levinthal's photographic study of the 1950s children's playsets made by Louis Marx and T. Cohn (1996).
- An illustrated history of the Airstream trailer written by Burkhart and Hunt (2000).
- The *Isn't S/He a Doll?* catalog of an exhibition of African dolls at the Fowler Anthropology Museum, UCLA (Cameron, 1966).
- Peter Menzel's (1994) masterful photographic illustration of the contrasting life goods of families in 30 different countries: *Material World*.

The boundary between enthusiast and professional scholarship is unclear in many artifact studies, in part because of the broad aesthetic draw of the artifacts themselves. The same dynamic that brings both scholars and school children to museums can engage diverse audiences for other multi-media representations: movies and television programming, heritage villages and craft workshops, and cultural re-enactments. Within both scholarly and popular perspectives, there is also broad recognition of the artifact as a class of objects that reflects substantial value added to its constituent materials. This recognition recapitulates Levi-Strauss' attention to the moieties of 'raw' and 'cooked,' enshrines the cultural significance of the artifact over raw materials and acknowledges tensions between the two as a key signpost for reading a culture's particularities.

The significance of an artifact for social and cultural studies, however, may correspond only in part—or not at all—to its visual apprehension as a discrete, material object, for several reasons. First, boundaries between raw materials and fabricated objects may be more relative than absolute. Some of my own 'food' books, for example, include nothing but ingredients, others nothing but individual dishes, and others still menus for special dinners and festivals.

Second, the significance of objects, materials, and their origins varies both within and across cultures (see Figure 4.1). Artifacts can be regarded quite differently by community members and outsiders, and within the same group, materials may carry different meanings for people who produce artifacts and for those who only distribute or consume them (Becker, 1986). In general, the knowledge and skills that people bring to material objects make them more or less meaningful, not just for different cultural groups but even to the same person at different points in time (Kasten, 1987; Fisherkeller, 1997; McDonough, 1999).

As a third complication, material artifacts can be used for purposes other than those intended by their originators, makers, or designers (Goffman, 1961; Bronner, 1999). One person's high-quality skipping stone could be appropriated by someone else to mark a path, offer a prayer, scare away a pest, or cool a warm forehead. The cell phone used to call home by one person might be used by another to detonate an explosive device, or to surreptitiously acquire confidential information. The cookbook that one person consults for recipes can be used by another to complete a collection, to remember the family member from whom it was inherited, or to raise the seat of a chair high enough for a child to sit at the dinner table.

Many artifacts of material culture travel well and are photogenic enough to be referred to in exhibition advertisements as 'treasures,' 'wonders,' and 'exquisite,' examples of a

Figure 4.1 Artifacts associated with one culture can be appropriated by people from another and put to use in ways that have little if anything to do with their original significance—as in this black-and-white photograph purchased for $2.00 from a vendor's 'Ethnic/Culture' collection at an 'All Image Show' in Emeryville, California, April 2010. **Unknown photographer**

distinctive art, craft, or technological tradition. When compared with ideas alone, discrete objects of this sort can make culture more visible and, purportedly, more 'real.' Taken apart or looked at on their own, however, material objects have the potential to detach theorizing about culture and social life from actual cultures and social lives.

With these considerations in mind, the ideal of seeing an entire world through a handful of pottery shards—or a beaded vest, funerary figurine, stained glass window, map of the world, courtier's or campaign consultant's handbook, family photograph or Hollywood film—is not only ambitious, it's problematic. Shards, maps, books, photos, or films may prove rich subjects for visual study. Absent other kinds of evidence, however, the pictures they create of culture and social life are not only incomplete but also potentially misleading. Some of these shortcomings can be addressed by examining artifacts within contexts of significance that extend beyond their purely physical and visual attributes—contexts, for example, such as technology and social life.

TECHNOLOGY

Defined loosely as the constellation of resources, tools, techniques, and strategies necessary to accomplish something (Mumford, 1963; Ellul, 1964), technologies bring together some of the materials and ideas that characterize culture and social life and provide a functional context within which artifacts, other materials, and behavior are logically coordinated. While a plastered house may be an intriguing object of inquiry, so too are the social, material, and technical arrangements necessary to produce or repair it, some of which are visible for the New Mexico home pictured in Figure 4.2.

A technology orientation to material culture dims the brightness of artifact stars and directs more attention toward the material and social arrangements through which artifacts are produced. This blurs considerably the distinction—paramount in the artifact orientation—between materials that are found, cultivated, or fabricated. In doing so, it also blurs distinctions between materials, ideas, and behavior, in particular the manual dexterity, athleticism, and coordination that support craft, fabrication, and design (Bronner, 1986). Though some viewers may marvel at the intricate detail visible in a figurine, basket, dance step, computer program, or computer chip, others may direct their wonder at the technologies, physical skills, and social strategies that made those details possible.

Technology orientations to material culture are less common than examinations of artifacts on their own, but several intriguing studies point the way toward continued research value. Notable visual studies of food technology, for example, include Deborah Barndt's (1997) cross-national study of tomato production, Doug Harper's (2001) study of regional dairy farming and Harper and Patrizia Faccioli's (2010) study of Italian meals—all of which foreground photographs and analysis of artifacts within different, and quite varied, production contexts.

Another exemplar is provided by Patricia Greenfield's (2004) longitudinal study of Maya weaving in Chiapas Mexico. Through archival records, detailed observation, and photographic recording that span several decades, Greenfield documented how the means and significance of weaving production evolved from one generation of adolescent apprentices to the next. The photographs of woven fabrics that appear in the book based on this research are beautiful in their own right, but Greenfield's focus is less on their significance and aesthetic qualities as artifacts than on how visible differences in materials and artifacts correspond to changes in the social and cultural scheme of production and a shift from collective toward individual creativity.

Two other visual studies illustrate the extremely broad range of material phenomena that can be examined within a

Figure 4.2   Fabricating artifacts typically involves materials, tools, craft knowledge, bodies, and some form of social organization. Original caption: 'Spanish-American women replastering an adobe house. This is done once a year.' Chamisal, New Mexico. Photograph by Russell Lee. The US Farm Security Administration/Office of War Information

technology framework. In *Contesting the Super Bowl*, Dona Schwartz (1998) and her colleagues provide a visually rich account of the varied elements that contributed to the 1992 Super Bowl held in Minneapolis, Minnesota. Once again, many interesting materials are featured in photographs appearing in the book. Rather than celebrate, critique, or affirm these as individual artifacts, however, the author's commentary examines how different materials, arrangements, and imagery were articulated in constructing and memorializing a spectacle of local, national, and global dimensions.

Yet another intriguing application of the technology orientation to material culture is the 'Director's Cut' commentary that Michael Apted made in conjunction with his film, *42 Up*, one of seven films in the 'Up' series that documented the changing lives of a

dozen or so Britons. Apted examined the films themselves (and individual scenes within them) for what they portrayed, but he also commented on the films as a kind of raw material that became meaningful within the construction of his life and the lives of his subjects. In contrast to film scholars and historians who might consider the films as artifacts alone, Apted's exegesis is more attuned to the human and social contexts in which he and his subjects were collaborators in the technology of film production (Wagner, 2007).

All of these studies position artifacts within contexts of production, use, and appreciation by members of their culture of origin. In each case, visual questions about what an artifact 'looks like' are complemented with substantive questions about how artifacts are made and used. And, for the examples I've noted, at least some dimensions of the latter are examined by making or acquiring photographic or videographic records.

This notion of documenting technologies (and their attendant skills, craft, and materials) through visual recording has expanded rapidly with the growth of digital media and associated Internet distribution systems such as YouTube®, iTunes,[1] and Vimeo™. These increasingly visible folk practices strike some chords that echo the enduring research value of this approach (Mead and Bateson, 1977; Mead, 1995). If we want to know how Ishi used a bow and arrow, we can learn something from the photographs and motion pictures that Alfred and Theodora Kroeber had the foresight to make of him doing just that (Kroeber, 2002). In terms of the studies noted above, much the same can be said for milking cows, producing the Super Bowl, weaving, and making a film. As a result of a rapidly developing videographic folk culture, we can now also catch glimpses of countless other materials and technologies as they are recorded and posted online to broad public access.

As a context for understanding material artifacts—and as a framework for the analysis of material culture in general—technology directs attention to how design decisions, the social organization of effort and attention, craft and performance skills, and material resources are articulated with the processes of production. This articulation can help account for why a material object might take the form it does within a particular culture or local application.

While this emphasis on production and purpose can be helpful, it reflects three enduring challenges for visual studies of material culture. First, it requires some understanding of the multiple purposes and intentions that guide production cycles for different cultural groups. Second, it requires access and observations of the activities—including subtle handcrafts and social relations that are difficult enough to notice, let alone document—through which relatively raw materials become artifacts.

Third, with their emphasis on goal-directed and utilitarian behavior, technology accounts may neglect the expressive and playful qualities of both activities and arranged materials.

The first two challenges can be addressed somewhat through intimate familiarity and the exercise of expert observation and recording skills, but the third challenge questions whether technology is the most appropriate way to think about play, art, and other activities that include significant expressive and improvisational elements (Mumford, 1963; Bateson, 1972; Huizinga, 1976; Schechner, 1993). As Miller puts it, 'Play involves a relative autonomy of means. Ends are not obliterated, but they don't, as in some other modes of organization, determine the means' (1973: 92).

MATERIALS-THAT-MATTER

One way to move beyond the limitations of an artifact or technology emphasis is to explore material culture in terms of the 'materials-that-matter' to particular subject populations (see Figure 4.3). This is a promising approach, as even small steps in this direction encourage the recognition that materials may matter to different people for different reasons and in quite different ways (Bronner, 1986; Miller, 1998).

Visual studies that focus on artifacts or technologies can miss complexities of this sort and support distortions that keep them hidden. This potential shortcoming takes on added significance when the content of such studies crosses cultural boundaries. By tying images of things too closely to familiar categories, classes, and captions—dolls, for example, or child care, families, homes, celebrations, entertainment, religion, sports, natural disasters, terrorists, dying—visual studies can narrow, as well as broaden, our understanding of culture and social life.

Some visual field study strategies can play an iterative role in helping to reduce or

Figure 4.3 Figurines, toys, and stones are attached to this car in a folk culture remake of mass culture materials. While displays of this sort clearly reflect materials-that-matter, they can be difficult to account for fully within technology orientations to material culture.
© 2010 Jon Wagner

avoid these potential pitfalls and missteps. Visual researchers can make photographs or videotapes of materials and behavior, for example, and then invite subjects to propose their own categories or concepts for classification and analysis (Clark, 1999; Hethorn and Kaiser, 1999; Radley, 2009). They can also invite subjects to make photographs, videotapes, drawings, or other visual figures according to their own lights or in response to shooting scripts provided by the researcher (Chalfen, 1981; Rich and Chalfen, 1999; Luttrell, 2003; Salazar, 2008; Clark-Ibanez, 2009). Researchers can also examine photographs and video recordings that subjects make as evidence about how those subjects see their own world (Bellman and Jules-Rosett, 1977; Lesy, 1980; Chalfen, 1987; Halle, 1993; Koltyk, 1993; Ruby, 1995;

Lustig, 2004). All three approaches have proved valuable in collecting information from subjects about their surroundings, behavior, technologies, and concerns. Each can also be useful in eliciting information about materials-that-matter and their significance within the world view of an individual or group.

In general, sorting out how things matter to people is more complicated than determining if they matter at all, or if they matter more than other things to which they might be compared, but visual research methods can help refine this kind of significance as well. If data recording is limited to the choice itself, asking individuals to select photographs of things that might matter will not get the researcher very far. However, asking subjects to talk about their choices, or to sort and organize images of objects into arrays that reflect functional or symbolic relationships, can be more productive (Clark, 1999; Rich and Chalfen, 1999). If photos of a knife, food processor, stove, and countertop are clustered together by an informant, for example, we know something different than if they are sorted into two or three groups, one of which also includes photos of a freezer, community garden, supermarket, or best friend.

Some might argue that explicating subject accounts and categories—the emic, or insider, point of view—is the sine qua non of good fieldwork. But that position neglects the possibility that subjects could misrepresent their point of view (deliberately or not), be confused or forgetful, or have mixed priorities and sentiments. When someone reports that the most important implement in her or his kitchen is the stove, knife, or counter top, does this signify how the item functions within the technology of cooking, the status accorded to different household possessions, or the pleasures of associated social activities? Similar questions are worth asking about subject claims that other things matter: a pair of ear rings or a nose piercing, family photographs, a nearby pond or stream, proximity to a bus stop or delicatessen, the length of a lover's hair or employee's résumé, and so on.

Even if a researcher is lucky and persistent enough to get a good account of such complexities, 'the native point of view' may be necessary but not sufficient to answer important questions about culture and social life (Geertz, 1983). To keep in view those elements that subjects deny, ignore, are not in a position to see, or simply don't care about, researchers need to do something more than provide a good account of the subjects' world view, however valuable that may be.

MATERIAL CIRCUMSTANCES

One way of extending the 'materials-that-matter' orientation beyond dimensions of culture and social life that natives notice and care about is to include the researcher as an additional subject who is also a member of one or more non-native populations. For most researchers, one such population is constituted by an investigative profession or academic discipline. This conceit avoids arbitrary attributions of privilege and authority to the researcher in representing the 'outside' or etic point of view. It affirms instead the value of exploring two emic points of view: one representing the research subject or native point of view, and another that of the researcher and her or his colleagues.

This extension of the materials-that-matter orientation has both general and specific implications. One of the latter is that for communities of scholars who conduct empirical social research, the material circumstances of natural phenomena matter a great deal. This is the case not only for physical and natural scientists but also for social scientists, most of whom become uneasy when research reports stray too far from evidence—or at least illustrations—of particular people doing specific things in particular places. Among social researchers, these concerns about empirical evidence reflect an implicit but abiding interest in the materiality of culture and social life. Visual research methods can be of inestimable value in examining this kind of materiality and camerawork a key technical strategy in that regard.

As a special case of this potential, photographs and video recordings can be used to create a visibility baseline against which to plot and highlight what subjects and researcher actually notice (Collier, 1967; Menzel, 1994). A photograph or videotape of preparing or eating a meal, for example— or conducting a meeting, religious ritual, or athletic contest—can provide an account of everything visible that could matter to participants in that event. These material circumstances can be compared with specific features singled out by subjects for comment or special attention. They can also be compared with materials regarded by the researcher as important for their latent or manifest functions. The photographs thus provide an optically etic account of the meal, but also serve as a record of material circumstances of special interest to subjects and researchers within their different insider (emic) points of view.

In many respects, even the 'machine recording' of images owes much to the cultural perspective of the photographer or videographer who operates the machine. Cameras do not take pictures on their own, and photographs and videotape recordings are shaped by a multitude of operator decisions about where to point the camera, when to begin and end a recording, settings for focus and lighting, and so on. In another sense, however, the term is not that far off the mark, for cameras do not pick and choose among the details visible within their field of view. In that respect, these increasingly small machines enable people to create detailed visual records of natural phenomena— including features that camera operators may not be aware of at the time—that would be extremely difficult, if not impossible, to create in any other way.

As illustrated by Figure 4.4(a) and (b), the potential to articulate subject, researcher and visibly etic perspectives extends to social and cultural activities much larger in scale for both time and place: constructing or destroying a community, for example, or developing a service economy, mining diamonds or mechanizing farm work, waging a ground war or advertising campaign, reducing or increasing income inequality, and so on. These large-scale events, transitions, and developments also take place within a distinctive constellation of material circumstances. Some of these circumstances are more visible than others, and some of greater or lesser significance—symbolically or functionally— to different participants. Photographic and videographic studies have much to offer here as well, and in much the same way that they can help account for and explicate the material culture of small-scale events.

Explication and analysis of material circumstances in these broad terms reflect central concerns of social and human ecology. As outlined initially by sociologists Robert E. Park and Ernest W. Burgess (1921), and subsequently by Roderick McKenzie (Hawley, 1968) and Amos Hawley (1986), this perspective seeks to understand the obvious, but indeterminate interdependence of the physical, material environment with culture and social life. The origins of this approach during the early twentieth century were tied closely to urban sociology and the intellectual and political challenges of trying to manage city life and its environs. But social and human ecology has also found continuing and vital expressions within geography, ecology, and community development as well as in some strands of sociology and anthropology.

The materials that matter to researchers within this perspective go well beyond artifacts and technologies, narrowly defined, to include environmental features that facilitate or constrain culture and social life. A mountain ridge, broad plain, or dry stream bed may have both functional and symbolic significance in demarcating cultural boundaries, transportation routes, and meeting places. Good soil or bad may encourage the growth of good or bad grapes, housing developments, or mud play (deMarrais et al., 1992), but wine industries, housing developments, and children's recreational facilities can also enrich or degrade the soil or water, and do so in ways that those living and working around such facilities might not notice on their own. Visual studies of material culture, broadly defined, can help articulate these material and subjective realities within which culture and social life take shape.

IMAGERY AND OTHER FEATURES OF VISUAL STUDIES

Some parallels and contrasts between the orientations to material culture described

(a)

(b)

Figure 4.4   Berlin's Brandenburg Gate in 1984 (a) and the same view in 2001 (b). The comparison reveals that some key landmarks from a divided Berlin remain but the texture of their surroundings has been transformed, stimulating and reflecting changes in the social ecology of Berlin and the life of Berliners. Figure 4.4(a) © 1984 Jon Wagner and Figure 4.4(b) © 2001 Adrian Graham. Reproduced with permission

Table 4.1 Four orientations to material culture

Comparative dimensions	Orientations			
	Artifacts	Technology	Materials-that-matter	Materiality
Primary focus of inquiry	Products and tools of cultural practice	Cultural productions and associated materials, tools, strategies, and outcomes	Materials that subjects notice and regard as significant for whatever reason	Material foundations of culture and social life
Vernacular question	What are these things and what do they mean?	What materials and tools do these people use to accomplish x, y, or z?	What materials do these people care about and why?	What interaction effects characterize these people and their physical environment?
Primary contexts of analysis	Index objects to where they were found, acquired, used, and relative to other objects similar in form	Index objects within cycle or circuit of cultural production and relative to objects with related functions	Index objects to perceptual and symbolic world of subjects	Index objects to social/ physical ecology and relative to other populations and locales
Archetype disciplines	Archaeology and art history	Ethnography, bio-engineering	Ethnography, cultural studies, market research	Ethnology and human ecology

above are summarized in Table 4.1. The artifact approach has achieved its greatest intellectual refinement in connection with archaeology and art history. Technology, as a context for examining material culture, has been most fully developed within ethnographic work, ecology, history (Mumford, 1963; White, 1966), and in various specialized applications of kinesics and systems analysis. The materials-that-matter perspective is most likely to get its due in certain forms of ethnography, sociology, and market research (Seiter, 1993). The materiality orientation has a home among researchers who work as ethnologists, human/ social ecologists, and some geographers and historians.

Boundaries between these different perspectives are somewhat fluid and ill-defined. In designing and conducting a specific study, however, researchers face the challenge of aligning questions about the phenomena they are interested in with the most appropriate, productive, and feasible of potential research methods. It would be going too far to say that

the artifact, technology, and materiality orientations each go hand-in-hand with a distinctive research approach, but they typically lead researchers to somewhat different units of observation, data collection, and data analysis. Some of these differences carry over into how research is reported, distributed, and codified. Many reflect, support, or depend on different kinds of visual evidence, including products of different kinds of camerawork.

At least one thoughtful scholar (Banks, 1998) has argued that visual studies, visual anthropology in particular, is nothing more and nothing less than the visual study of material culture. This point is extremely well taken, but falls short of accounting for significant differences of history and trajectory. Material culture studies have been shaped profoundly by archaeological practice, artifact collections, and principles of organization that reflect an abiding distinction between material and non-material culture. This orientation emphasizes elements of culture that are materially durable enough to survive the passage of time—writing over speech, for example, or pottery over eating routines and costumes over dance steps.

Conversely, visual studies have been shaped by photographers, videographers, and artists attuned to what is visible and, beyond that, visually interesting. This emphasis can neglect elements of culture that are not visible or hidden from view—or that are visually uninteresting. However, it adds the prospect of making durable records, through photo of videographic recording, of activities and actions that material culture scholarship has typically neglected—for example, speech, eating routines, dance steps, gatherings, and other events.

These differences do not pit material culture scholars against visual studies scholars, but they do suggest that the two approaches overlap only in part. A more complete picture appears by examining specifically the objects and methods of inquiry linked most closely with visual studies, several of which are described elsewhere in this handbook. A shortlist of visual objects of inquiry, for example, would include at least the following:

- Visually interesting materials and activities.
- How people see the world.
- How people live, including ethnographic accounts of how the world looks to them and how they look to each other and to outsiders.
- Visual representations, including imagery, sign, and symbol systems.

As a complement and extension of these objects of inquiry, visual studies scholars have developed and practiced a variety of visual study methods. These are hardly doctrinaire, but key approaches would include at least the following, several of which are described more fully elsewhere in this handbook:

- Artifact acquisition and analysis
- Photo and video documentation
- Researcher-guided image-elicitation protocols
- Image-based ethnography
- Neuropsychological studies of visual perception

- Formal analyses of imagery and other visual representations.

Discrete elements of these visual studies methods may appear or disappear at any stage of a research process. Beyond that, self-defined visual studies approaches may or may not emphasize the visual phenomenal world of research subjects, and if they do, that may or may not involve the use of visual research materials and methods. Some of the methods listed above are also functionally interdependent—that is, independent variables associated with one can appear as dependent variables in another.

As a matter of some consequence for the development of both visual studies and material culture studies, several of the methods listed above correspond closely to folk practices that are widely distributed within and across contemporary cultures. This is very much the case for collecting and analyzing artifacts, making photo and video documents, and using visual imagery to ask people questions. While these approaches are critically important to material culture and visual studies scholarship, they are also part and parcel of how individuals, groups, and institutions go about creating, processing, and arranging elements of their own culture and social life. In conjunction with new media technologies and social networking resources, they also reflect an increasingly vital dimension of modern life.

As yet another consequential matter, these same three approaches also correspond closely to the skills by which many empirical researchers acquire and manage research materials—whether or not their studies have anything to do with visual studies and material cultural perspectives. The artifacts that researchers acquire and analyze are usually referred to as 'data.' Their photo and video documentation activities are shaped by scientific instrumentation and photocopying, and their use of 'researcher-guided image-elicitation strategies' is a familiar feature of research and teaching presentations that make use of PowerPoint® slides, charts and graphs, statistical tables, and so on. Though they hold special interest for visual studies scholars, the visual study skills associated with these three methods in particular—and those linked to formal analysis of visual representations as well—are integral to the conduct of scholarship in general.

These last two observations point to an implicit parallel between studies of material culture and visual studies: the boundaries of both orientations are blurred, on the one hand, by evolving folkways and technologies of cultural acquisition and production, and on the other, by the mechanics and evolving technologies of empirical research. This parallel suggests a kinship between visual studies and material culture that could support productive, collaborative research. However, it also raises questions about the value of visual studies and material culture as theoretical frameworks for guiding empirical inquiry. Are those terms necessary and informative or do they distract scholars from more productive ways of thinking about research related to culture, imagery, materials, and the visible? And, if material culture and visual studies do provide distractions of that sort, what other terms could guide researchers in their stead?

PROBLEMS, PROPOSITIONS, QUALIFICATIONS, AND PROSPECTS

The observations and commentaries above suggest that the terms 'material culture' and 'visual studies' serve as a kind of shorthand for a constellation of relationships between culture and social life, on the one hand, and an array of visual research questions, methods and reporting formats, on the other. This shorthand is useful in distinguishing approaches that acknowledge the cultural significance of materials, visual imagery, visual perception, and so on, from those that neglect or trivialize them. As a guide for the design and assessment of social scientific research, however, the same terms are somewhat problematic and encourage two key distortions.

The first distortion is to think of 'material' and 'non-material' culture as discrete phenomenal domains rather than the relative availability of empirical evidence. The material/non-material distinction may be useful to an archaeologist in characterizing surviving evidence of prior cultural activity, for example, but it does not follow that cultural representations for which evidence did not survive—gesture, dance, speech, or storytelling—are non-material. In effect, taking the separation of material and non-material culture at face value divides the phenomenon of culture itself along lines that have more to do with the availability or lack of empirical evidence than with the materiality of cultural representations.

It's worth noting, for example, that the kind of material evidence researchers care about varies not only with the questions they ask but also with evolving technologies of cultural production and distribution. Prior to the growth of visual recording media, for example, few empirical traces were available for some activities—including rituals, conversation, gatherings, and other forms of embodied expression and conduct—for which many are available now. It's also worth noting that the phenomenon of culture is constituted by the marriage of materials and ideas, not their divorce, even if the latter defines abiding challenges of empirical inquiry.

A more precise framework for guiding material culture studies would locate material dimensions of a culture relative to each other and in consort with their significance to both members and researchers. Within a framework of this sort, different constellations of meaning, technology, and history could be delimited by multiple subjects and researchers. Ideally, bodies and costumes, landscapes and paths, materials and materials in use, ideas and things would all get their due. Starting from the assumption of a material/non-material divide makes this unlikely at best.

Dividing culture into visible and non-visible forms supports parallel distortions. On the visible side, this clumps together all elements of culture and social life that might be visible—and useful to researchers conducting a study—with those elements that are visually meaningful and useful to members of the culture being studied. On the non-visible side, it simultaneously confounds what can't be seen with what has not yet been noticed—for lack of attention, access, or adequate theory.

A more precise framework for guiding visual studies would include at least three overlapping domains: all elements of a culture that are materially visible (whether or not subjects or researchers find them interesting); a subset of visible elements noticed and noted by researchers as significant for understanding the culture in question (whether or not they are regarded as such by members themselves); and another subset of elements noticed and noted by cultural members as significant to their phenomenal world. Yet a fourth dimension can exist when members of a culture 'see' things that are not visible to either the untrained eye of the researcher or her or his recording equipment.

In effect, starting with a division of cultural forms into visible and non-visible blurs distinctions between how the world looks, what researchers see and notice, and what members of a culture see, notice, and find meaningful. Everything we know about empirical social research suggests that confounding these orientations is a bad idea.

Guided by the two key divisions noted above, the interface between visual studies and material culture can appear as a relatively narrow field of inquiry centered on 'pictures of artifacts.' This narrow view is relatively widespread, but it is challenged by investigations noted earlier of technologies and social life, the material circumstances in which cultural forms emerge, and the diversity of materials—only some of which can be characterized as artifacts—that are meaningful to people. It is also challenged by the increasingly diverse objects of inquiry being examined through visual observation, recording, and elicitation strategies.

PROPOSITIONS

The research promise of the diverse studies noted in the preceding discussion and throughout this handbook is much greater than the promise of thinking only about 'pictures of artifacts.' Realizing that promise seems more likely if research were guided by a framework consistent with observed relationships between culture, materiality, visibility, inquiry, and meaning. Many distinctions that adhere to the terms 'material and non-material culture' or 'visual and non-visual studies' are at odds with these observed relationships, but these relationships are relatively consistent with the following three propositions:

Proposition #1: All cultural practices depend on material support and instantiation.

The principle underlying this proposition is relatively straightforward: communication requires materiality, and culture and social life depend on communication. Without the kind of interpersonal materiality necessary to hear, touch, see, taste, and so on, human organisms lack the medium they need to create and participate in culture. This frames the material circumstances and resources by which individuals make sounds, touch, see, hear, taste, and so on, as significant objects of cultural inquiry and an important ground against which to figure how people live their individual and collective lives.

With this kind of materiality in mind, even ideas, attitudes, or beliefs—or other cultural elements located in symbolic landscapes that subjects attach to ancestors, the cosmos, or to the Internet—depend for their existence and continuity on interactions between people and materials, interactions that take place in physical time and space. Games and kinship systems, language, religiosity, or law have all occurred to individuals or groups, caught our gaze, or invited consideration because they were made materially manifest in conversations, books, computer screens, a physical embrace, or harsh sound. Through interactions of this sort people learn about these 'non-material things,' pass them on to others, talk about them, create or remake them, or put them to rest. Though participants may overlook this fact, or even argue to the contrary, these interactions occur in specific, physical settings and require both time and material resources, without which they would not and could not take place.

Materiality, in this view, represents a somewhat mutable medium of constraints and opportunities within which culture, in quite varied forms, can be elaborated. All aspects of a culture are attached to this medium. The medium bears only an indirect and indeterminate relationship to specific cultural forms, but the attachments themselves reflect forms of materiality that have visual dimensions and can be examined as such.

Proposition #2: By definition, materials have physical properties that can be made visible, observed and recorded through the agency of human sight or other senses and a variety of optical–electrical–mechanical instruments.

This proposition draws on physics—not on anthropology, sociology, or cultural studies—but considered in consort with the first proposition, it has far-reaching implications for visual studies of culture and social life, the core of which appears in a third proposition.

Proposition #3: All cultural phenomena can be examined visually, either directly through the agency of human sight or through physical instruments and mediated representations that focus attention on attachments between cultural forms and the materiality on which they depend.

Taken together, these three propositions reflect a broad prospect for the visual study of culture and social life in general and the materiality of culture and social life in particular. To clarify the dimensions of this prospect, let me comment on some forms of cultural materiality that warrant, but have not yet received, the full attention of visual study scholars.

EXCEPTIONS AND QUALIFICATIONS

Few scholars will quibble about the value of visual studies in application to the familiar materiality of specific cultural forms—for example, clothing, food, architecture, dance, and so on. But what about cultural forms for which supporting materiality may be less clear—or even categorically denied? In practical applications, are some forms of culture and social life exempt from the three propositions noted above? Or does culture in any form truly depend on material dimensions that, by definition, can lend themselves to fruitful visual study?

To my way of thinking, no exemptions are called for, but the presumed boundaries of some cultural practices may be drawn too narrowly. This applies in some cases to material attachments that are obvious but so taken-for-granted that they go unnoticed. Unaided oral conversation, for example, is considered frequently as a kind of ephemeral performance that leaves no material or visible evidence in its wake. However, conversation depends on the material presence of relatively quiet air, the lack of which—in very noisy or turbulent environments, the vacuum of outer space, underwater, or over great distances—makes conversation impossible without some alternative mediating technology (telephones, texting, and so on).

While the material presence of good air is a constraint for conversation, it also makes possible material records (audio recordings) that can be converted mechanically or through various forms of coding, to a variety of visible and visual analogs—written transcripts, acoustic waveforms, audio clip databases, statistical tables, and so on. If we consider that some face-to-face conversations may also require enough light for people to see each other, we can add to situations that meet that requirement the prospect for other material evidence, including video recordings, that support even more complex forms of visual analysis. In both cases, the materiality upon which conversation depends also defines attachments between conversation and the material world that can be observed, recorded, and tracked for purposes of social and cultural analysis—including analyses that have explicit or implicit visual dimensions.

A similar reconsideration applies for how we think about the activity of reading. This is frequently regarded as a private and internal matter that cannot be observed or materialized. However, reading depends on the movement and concentration of optical attention, adequate lighting, and a materialized text. Take any of these away and reading, as we know it, is no longer possible (though something similar might be possible in another material form, such as books on tape). These requisite circumstances constrain the act of reading, but they also attach internal, private, cerebral processes of reading to material circumstances that can be recorded and examined. This may seem obvious for the 'materialized text'—though decades of reading scholarship have theorized about text comprehension without attending to the material form in which the text appeared to readers—but it's also true for the duration and direction of optical attention. Indeed, one of the more intriguing intersections between visual studies and material culture is the growth of instrumented 'eye-tracking' studies (see Chapter 23). These have become a resource for understanding not only how people move through words on a printed page but also for how they view and decode text and non-text features in a wide range of environments.

Beyond conversation and reading, similar prospects for material and visual analyses apply to a wide range of cultural forms that by definition or acclaim are considered to be 'non-material.' Thoughts, for example, and

feelings, beliefs, and attitudes are typically seen in just this way. However, a growing body of research suggests both the situation-specific dimensions of these supposedly internal states and processes and the salient materiality of the situations in which they occur—and, for that matter of their physiology, as revealed in magnetic resonance imaging (MRI) studies. Some of this research has focused on the particulars of how students learn or teachers teach (Dyson, 1989, 1993; Nespor, 1997; Wagner, 1999), while other studies have looked at the acquisition of knowledge and skills in non-school settings (Resnick, 1987; Lave, 1988). Cutting across perspectives of education, anthropology, sociology, and cultural studies, the gist of these studies is that the same kind of material transactions that make culture and communication both possible and likely also make possible and likely—or unlikely—a broad array of culturally appropriate activities of mind, including perspectives (Becker et al., 1961, 1995), beliefs (Best, 1990; Clark, 1995), emotions (Hochschild, 2003), and attitudes.

Examining the materiality attached to these expressions can be extremely useful in understanding how individual persons interact with specific social and physical environments, but it's also a key to understanding larger social processes. Indeed, not only conversations, reading, thinking, and feelings are attached to material media that have visual dimensions, so, are the collective phenomena of kinship, policymaking, morality, socializing, jurisprudence, and science, liberal arts, and vocational education—or as illustrated in Figure 4.5, thinking about school improvement. One need not argue that visual analyses of these phenomena can fully characterize or describe them to make the point that visible, material dimensions are among their essential constituents.

Of course, visual dimensions of cultural phenomena can be more or less salient than those accessed through other senses. And, as noted above, sensory perception is only one coefficient of social and cultural significance.

Figure 4.5 Materials brought together to help 22 fellow teachers think collectively about assessing and improving the mathematics achievement of their students. For both workshop leaders and participants, the thinking of participating teachers during this 2-day retreat depended on ready access to these materials and relative isolation from the familiar environment of their classrooms and school. © 2003 Jon Wagner

But determining the material and visual significance of phenomena for different subject populations is an empirical project, not something researchers can arbitrarily decide on their own. When and to whom does seeing the person we are talking to matter a lot or a little? What kinds of things can and do people look at to help them think? Which of these things are most noticeable to people who are good at thinking in certain ways? What kinds of materials are most meaningful to people in understanding their history? What do those materials look like, and where are they most likely to be found, lost, created, or destroyed? When people say they believe in something, what does that dispose them to see or not see?

PROSPECTS

The hypothetical questions posed above affirm an abiding connection between things and ideas and a broad agenda for visual studies and material culture. Attending to the propositions on which they rest could generate increased attention to several themes that have suffered relative neglect within the visual studies/material culture paradigm. Among these are the following themes.

Embodied cultural activity

Recognizing the role of human bodies in the production and distribution of culture could freshen and deepen understanding of the interface between social and physical contexts of culture and social life (see Figure 4.6 for a cross-culturally complex instance of this interface). Hopefully, this could extend visual studies of embodiment from the classic work by Bateson and Mead (1942) into a wide range of contemporary contexts—Lifchez and Winslow (1979), Harper (1987), Greenfield (2002), and Sudnow (2001) provide contrasting, but equally promising examples. Two useful questions to consider here, for any form of culture or social life, are: What is required of bodies for this cultural activity to thrive or die? And, how does that look to people whose bodies might be involved?

Commodified culture

The potential of multi-media recordings and artifact collections to commodify culture is poorly understood. At their worst, recordings and artifact collections can help transfer attribution and control of heritage materials from a culture of origin to outside entrepreneurs and investors (Kwak, 2005; Skrydstrup, 2006; Lilley, 2008). Policy frameworks that separate 'ideas' from their 'material form' make this unfortunate outcome more possible rather than less. These frameworks may be consistent with the narrow conception of material cultural noted above (and may have legal precedent within that), but they are also at

Figure 4.6 Visiting Bhutanese archers mix indigenous and exotic materials to demonstrate the construction of traditional bows and arrows at the Asian Art Museum of San Francisco. The archers used bamboo shoots from a particular region of Bhutan for the arrow shafts, but they borrowed a Swiss Army knife from an audience member to trim the feathers. Clear distinctions between material and non-material culture are challenged by the embodied integration of materials, knowledge, aesthetic ideals, and craft that characterize cultural activities of this sort. © 2003 Jon Wagner

odds with a diverse array of cultural practices (Hirsch, 2002; Scafidi, 2005). Advancing theory about the intersection of ideas, things, and imagery is key to sorting these matters out. An important orienting question for this line of inquiry is: What does it look like for different persons or groups to 'own' cultural forms that they care about?

Mediated communication

We know precious little about how mediated representations shape social interaction and common knowledge. Approaching this question from within a distinction between material and non-material culture seems cumbersome. In the same way that an understanding of food practices requires attention to the intersection of materials and ideas, so too does an understanding of multi-modal and mediated communication (Norris, 2004). In both cases, visual studies, questions, and methods represent a relatively untapped resource for guiding empirical work toward more sophisticated and robust theory. Interesting questions abound in this area, many of them attuned to some version of: What is it that people are interacting with when they interact with each other through different media?

Visualizing culture and social life

New media technologies frame perplexing questions about where culture and social life are located, created, and managed. However, they also bring researchers new tools for linking ideas and cultural things and for visualizing, teaching, and communicating about culture and social life. Applied within 'virtual reality' (VR) environments, some new media tools can create enriched representations of indigenous culture. They can also be configured as interactive environments that suspend culturally familiar perceptions of researchers, lay audiences,

and students or that simulate for VR participants a variety of hands-on experiences with features of the material world.

This dual potential for representation and simulation positions virtual reality technologies as an increasingly important feature of the human life space and a powerful resource for visualizing, teaching, and communicating about culture and social life. Some projects undertaken by my colleagues at the University of California, Davis to realize these potentials include: Milman Harrison's efforts to create a racially dynamic online environment in Second Life that his students can explore and examine as part of their undergraduate coursework; Peter Yellowlee's online simulations of schizophrenia as a teaching resource for medical students; and the Keck Caves interactive environment created at the W. M. Keck Center for Active Visualization in the Earth Sciences.

We don't know much about how any of these materials and environments work in purely educational terms, but that's true as well for the traditional modes and materials of teaching and learning—for example, books, lectures, courses of study—to which new media forms provide alternatives. In both a literal and figurative sense, we need to know how good versions of this kind of teaching and learning 'look'—to those who design and deliver it and to those who benefit from participating as students and audience members.

Documenting cultural production

We have much to learn about how different kinds of cultural materials come into being, are distributed and used, celebrated, or set aside. Visual studies of how and when material artifacts are fabricated represent a resource of continuing value in that regard, as do studies that examine the transposition and re-purposing of a wide range of materials (whether or not they appear as discrete artifacts). But important insights could also emerge from visual studies of social and cultural phenomena framed by the seam between materiality and ideation-social networks, for example, or regulatory texts; access points between doctors and patients, parents and children, politicians and those who vote for them (or don't); and evolving conceptions of location and direction, information and knowledge, narrative and news. How do such things look, not just now, but as they come into view for different individuals and groups? And what do different 'views' of these elements of the modern world imply for the worlds people are disposed to accept, reject, buy, sell or fight for?

It seems unlikely that these phenomena, concerns, and questions can get the attention and theorizing they deserve if scholars continue to think casually about material culture and visual studies. For better or worse, we live in a world in which bodies, materials, and ideas matter in consort; in which digital bits and bytes lead back and forth to real goods, services, opportunities, and scams; in which material and mediated cultural artifacts are alternately molded, melded, sanctified, trashed, and sold. For these reasons and more, seeing the things people live with, for, around, in spite of and through, while far from a simple matter, is well worth a close and continuing look.

NOTE

1 iTunes is a trademark of Apple Inc., registered in the USA and in other countries.

REFERENCES

Anthony, David W. (2010) *The Lost World of Old Europe: The Danube Valley, 5000–3500 BC*. Princeton, NJ: Princeton University Press.

Baeder, John (1995) *Diners*. New York: Harry N. Abrams.

Banks, Marcus (1998) 'Visual anthropology: Image, object and interpretation', in J. Prosser (ed.), *Image-Based Research*. London: Taylor and Francis. pp. 9–23.

Barndt, Deborah (1997) 'Zooming out/zooming in: Visualizing globalization', *Visual Sociology*, 12: 5–32.

Bateson, Gregory (1972) *Steps to an Ecology of Mind*. New York: Ballantine.

Bateson, Gregory and Mead, Margaret (1942) *Balinese Character: A Photographic Analysis*, Vol. 2. New York: New York Academy of Sciences.

Becker, Howard S. (1986) 'Telling about society', in H. S. Becker (ed.), *Doing Things Together*. Chicago, IL: Northwestern University Press. pp. 121–136.

Becker, Howard S., Geer, Blanche and Hughes, Everett C. (1995) *Making the Grade: The Academic Side of College Life*. New Brunswick, NJ: Transaction.

Becker, Howard S., Geer, Blanche, Hughes, Everett and Strauss, Anselm (1961) *Boys in white: Student culture in medical school*. Chicago, IL: University of Chicago Press.

Bell, Susan (2009) *DES Daughters: Embodied Knowledge and the Transformation of Women's Health*. Philadelphia, PA: Temple University Press.

Bellman, Beryl L. and Jules-Rosett, Benetta (1977) *A Paradigm for Looking: Cross-Cultural Research with Visual Media*. Norwood, NJ: Ablex.

Best, Joel (1990) *Threatened Children: Rhetoric and Concern about Child-Victims*. Chicago, IL: University of Chicago Press.

Boas, Franz (1955) *Primitive Art*. New York: Dover.

Bronner, Simon J. (1986) *Grasping Things: Folk Material Culture and Mass Society in America*. Lexington, KY: The University Press of Kentucky.

Bronner, Simon J. (1999) 'The material folk culture of children', in B. Sutton-Smith, J. Mechling, and F. McMahon (eds.), *Children's Folklore: A Source Book*. Logan, Utah T: Utah State University Press. pp. 251–271.

Burkhart, Bryan and Hunt, David (2000). *Airstream: The History of the Land Yacht*. San Francisco, CA: Chronicle Books.

Cameron, Elisabeth L. (1966) *Isn't S/He a Doll? Play and Ritual in African Sculpture*. Los Angeles, CA: UCLA Fowler Museum of Cultural History.

Chalfen, Richard (1981) 'A sociovidistic approach to children's filmmaking: The Philadelphia project', *Studies in Visual Communication*, 7: 2–33.

Chalfen, Richard (1987) *Snapshot Versions of Life*. Bowling Green, OH: Bowling Green University Popular Press.

Chertoff, Nina and Kahn, Susan (2006) *Celebrating Pez*. New York: Sterling.

Clark, Cindy Dell (1995) *Flights of Fancy, Leaps of Faith: Children's Myths in Contemporary America*. Chicago, IL: University of Chicago Press.

Clark, Cindy Dell (1999) 'The autodriven interview: A photographic viewfinder into children's experiences', *Visual Sociology*, 14: 39–50.

Clark-Ibanez, Marisol (2009) 'Inner-city children in sharper focus: Sociology of childhood and photo-elicitation interviews', in G. C. Stanczak (ed.), *Visual Research Methods: Image, Society, and Representation*. Newbury Park, CA: Sage Publications. pp. 167–196.

Coles, Robert (1992) *Their Eyes Meeting the World: The Drawings and Paintings of Cchildren*. New York: Houghton Mifflin.

Collier, John Jr. (1967) *Visual Anthropology: Photography as a Research Method*. New York: Holt, Rinehart & Winston.

Cuno, James (2008) *Who Owns Antiquity? Museums and the Battle over Our Ancient Heritage*. Princeton, NJ: Princeton University Press.

de la Pena, Carolyn Thomas (2005) *The Body Electric: How Strange Machines Built the Modern American*. New York: New York University Press.

deMarrais, Kathleen Bennett, Nelson, Patricia A. and Baker, Jill H. (1992) 'Meaning in Mud: Yup'ik Eskimo girls at play', *Anthropology & Education Quarterly*, 23: 120–144.

Dyson, Anne Haas (1989) *Multiple Worlds of Child Writers: Friends Learning to Write*. New York: Teachers College Press.

Dyson, Anne Haas (1993) *Social Worlds of Children Learning to Write in an Urban Primary School*. New York: Teachers College Press.

Edwards, I. E. S. (1976) *Tutankhamun, his Tomb and its Treasures*. New York: Metropolitan Museum of Art.

Ellul, Jacques (1964) *The Technological Society*. New York: Knopf.

Fisherkeller, JoEllen (1997) 'Everyday learning about identities among young adolescents in television culture', *Anthropology & Education Quarterly*, 28: 467–492.

Geertz, Clifford (1983) *Local Knowledge: Further Essays in Interpretive Anthropology*. New York: Basic Books.

Goffman, Erving (1961) 'The underlife of public institutions: A study of ways of making out in a mental hospital', in E. Goffman (ed.), *Asylums: Essays on the Social Situation of Mental Patients and Other Inmates*. Garden City, NY: Anchor Books. pp. 171–320.

Goffman, Erving (1976) *Gender Advertisements*. New York: Harper and Row.

Greenfield, Lauren (2002) *Girl Culture*. San Francisco, CA: Chronicle Books.

Greenfield, Patricia Marks (2004) *Weaving Generations Together: Evolving Creativity in the Maya of Chiapas*. Translated by P. B. L. Greenfield. Santa Fe, New Mexico: School of American Research Press.

Halle, David (1993) *Inside Things*. Chicago, IL: University of Chicago Press.

Hamm, Jim (1992) *The Traditional Bowyer's Bible Vol. 1*. Guilford, CT: Lyons Press.

Hamm, Jim (1993) *The Traditional Bowyer's Bible Vol. 2*. Guilford, CT: Lyons Press.

Hamm, Jim (1994) *The Traditional Bowyer's Bible. Vol. 3*. Guilford, CT: Lyons Press.

Harper, Douglas (1987) *Working Knowledge: Skill and Community in a Small Shop*. Chicago, IL: University of Chicago Press.

Harper, Douglas (2001) *Changing Works: Visions of a Lost Agriculture*. Chicago, IL: University of Chicago Press.

Harper, Douglas and Faccioli, Patrizia (2010) *The Italian Way: Food and Social Life*. Chicago, IL: University of Chicago Press.

Hatcher, James B. (ed.) (1979). *Scott 1980 Standard Postage Stamp Catalogue*: Volume 1. New York: Scott Publishing Co.

Hawley, Amos (ed.) (1968) Roderick D. McKenzie on human ecology, '*Heritage of Sociology Series*'. Chicago, IL: University of Chicago Press.

Hawley, Amos (1986) *Human Ecology: A Theoretical Essay*. Chicago, IL: University of Chicago Press.

Hethorn, Janet and Kaiser, Susan (1999) 'Youth style: Articulating cultural anxiety', *Visual Sociology*, 14: 107–124.

Hirsch, Eric (2002) 'Malinowski's intellectual property', *Anthropology Today*, 18: 1–2.

Hochschild, Arlie Russell (2003) *The Managed Heart: Commercialization of Human Feeling*, twentieth anniversary edition. Berkeley, CA: University of California Press.

Hoskins, Janet (1998). *Biographical Objects: How Things Tell the Stories of People's Lives*. New York: Routledge.

Huizinga, Johan (1976) 'Nature and significance of play as a cultural phenomenon', in R. Schechner and M. Schuman (eds.), *Ritual, Play and Performance*. New York: Seabury. pp. 46–66.

Jackson, Bruce (1977) *Killing Time: Life in the Arkansas Penitentiary*. Ithaca, NY: Cornell University.

Kasten, Wendy C. (1987) 'Medicine men, Bethlehem and Pacman: Writing in a cultural context', *Anthropology & Education Quarterly*, 18: 116–125.

Koltyk, Jo Ann (1993) 'Telling narratives through home videos: Hmong refugees and self-documentation of life in the old and new country', *The Journal of American Folklore*, 106: 435–449.

Kroeber, Theodora (2002) *Ishi in Two Worlds: A Biography of the Last Wild Indian in North America*. Berkeley, CA: University of California Press.

Kwak, Sun-Young (2005), 'World heritage rights versus national cultural property rights: The case of the Jikji', *Carnegie Council. Human Rights Dialogue*, 22: 3.

Lave, Jean (1988) *Cognition in Practice*. New York: Cambridge University Press.

Lessig, Lawrence (2004) *Free Culture: The Nature and Future of Creativity*. New York: Penguin Books.

Lesy, Michael (1980) *Time Frames: The Meaning of Family Pictures*. New York: Pantheon Books.

Levinthal, David (1996) *Small Wonder: Worlds in a Box*. Washington, DC: National Museum of American Art.

Lifchez, Raymond and Winslow, Barbara (1979) *Design for Independent Living: The Environment and Physically Disabled People*. New York: Whitney Library of Design.

Lilley, Spencer (2008) 'The last crusade: Maori culture and intellectual property rights'. Paper presented at the Traditional Cultural Expressions Conference: Cultural heritage and living culture: Defining the US library position on access and protection of traditional cultural expression, Washington, DC [Online]. Available from: http://wo.ala.org/tce/wp-content/uploads/2008/11/the-last-crusade-mark-2.pdf [Accessed 4 October 2010].

Lustig, Deborah Freedman (2004) 'Baby pictures: Family, consumerism and exchange among teen mothers in the USA', *Childhood*, 11: 175–192.

Luttrell, Wendy (2003) *Pregnant Bodies, Fertile Minds: Gender, Race and the Schooling of Pregnant Teens*. New York: Routledge.

Lyon, Danny (1971) *Conversations with the Dead*. New York: Holt, Rinehart & Winston.

McDonough, Y. Z. (1999) *The Barbie Chronicles: A Living Doll Turns Forty*. New York: Simon and Schuster, Touchstone.

Mead, Margaret (1995) 'Visual anthropology in a discipline of words', in P. Hockings (ed.), *Principles of Visual Anthropology*. New York: Mouton de Gruyter. pp. 3–10.

Mead, Margaret and Bateson, Gregory (1977) 'On the use of the camera in anthropology', *Studies in the Anthropology of Visual Communication*, 4: 78–80.

Mechling, Jay (2001) *On My Honor: Boy Scouts and the Making of American Youth*. Chicago, IL: University of Chicago Press.

Menzel, Peter (1994) *Material World: A Global Family Portrait*. San Francisco, CA: Sierra Club.

Messenger, Phyllis Mauch (1999) *The Ethics of Collecting Cultural Property: Whose Culture? Whose Property?* Albuquerque, NM: University of New Mexico Press.

Miller, Daniel (1998) *Material Cultures: Why Some Things Matter*. Chicago, IL: University of Chicago Press.

Miller, Stephen (1973) 'Ends, means and galumphing: Some leitmotifs of play', *American Anthropologist*, 75(1): 87–98.

Morris, Errol (2009). 'The case of the inappropriate alarm clock', *New York Times*, 18 October 2009.

Mumford, Lewis (1963) *Technics and Civilization*. New York: Harcourt, Brace and World.

Nespor, Jan (1997) *Tangled up in School: Politics, Space, Bodies and Signs in the Educational Process*. Mahwah, NJ: Lawrence Erlbaum.

Norfleet, Barbara (1979) *Wedding*. New York: Simon and Schuster (Fireside).

Norris, Sigrid (2004) *Analyzing Multimodal Interaction: A Methodological Framework*. New York: Routledge.

Park, Robert E. and Burgess, Ernest W. (1921) *Introduction to the Science of Sociology*. Chicago, IL: University of Chicago Press.

Pepin, Jacques (1976). *La Technique: The Fundamental Techniques of Cooking: An Illustrated Guide*. New York: New York Times Books.

Plumb, Barbara (1977) *Houses Architects live in*. New York: Viking.

Radley, Alan (2009) *Works of Illness: Narrative, Picturing and the Social Response to Serious Disease*. Ashby-de-la-Zouch, UK: InkerMen Press.

Resnick, Lauren B. (1987) 'The 1987 Presidential Address: Learning in school and out', *Educational Researcher*, 16: 13–20.

Rich, Michael and Chalfen, Richard (1999) 'Showing and telling asthma: Children teaching physicians with visual narrative', *Visual Sociology*, 14: 51–72.

Rieger, Jon H. (2003) 'A retrospective study of social change: The pulp-logging industry in an Upper Peninsula Michigan county', *Visual Studies*, 18: 156–177.

Ruby, Jay (1995) *Secure the Shadow: Death and Photography in America*. Cambridge, MA: MIT Press.

Salazar, Melissa (2008) 'Bodies in place, bodies in motion: Images of immigrant youth negotiating food, location and identity'. PhD Dissertation, University of California, Davis.

Salvo, Dana (1997) *Home Altars of Mexico*. London: Thames and Hudson.

Scafidi, Susan (2005) *Who Owns Culture? Appropriation and Authenticity in American Law*. New Brunswick, NJ: Rutgers University Press.

Schechner, Richard (1993) *The Future of Ritual: Writings on Culture and Performance*. New York: Routledge.

Schwartz, Dona (1998) *Contesting the Super Bowl*. New York: Routledge.

Secretan, Thierry (1995) *Going into Darkness: Fantastic Coffins from Africa*. London: Thames and Hudson.

Seiter, Ellen (1993) *Sold Separately: Parents and Children in Consumer Culture*. New Brunswick, NJ: Rutgers University.

Skrydstrup, Martin (2006) 'Toward intellectual property guidelines and best practices for recording and digitizing intangible cultural heritage: A survey of codes, conducts and challenges in North America', World Intellectual Property Organization (WIPO). [Online]. Available from the WIPO Electronic Bookshop: http://www.wipo.int/ebookshop [Accessed 4 October 2010].

Spindler, George (1987) 'Cultural dialogue and schooling in Schoenhausen and Roseville: A comparative analysis', *Anthropology and Education Quarterly*, 18: 3–16.

Sudnow, David (2001) *Ways of the Hand: A Rewritten Account*. Cambridge, MA: MIT Press.

Turner, Patricia (2009) *Crafted Lives: Stories and Studies of African American Quilters*. Jackson, MS: University Press of Mississippi.

Wagner, Jon (1999) 'The pragmatics of practitioner research: Linking new knowledge with power in an urban elementary school', *Elementary School Journal*, 100: 151–180.

Wagner, Jon (2007) 'Lives in transaction: An appreciation of Michael Apted's Up filmmaking project', *Visual Studies*, 22: 293–300.

White, Lynn (1966) *Medieval Technology and Social Change*. New York: Oxford University Press.

Wolfe, Tom (1965) *The Kandy-Kolored, Tangerine-Flake, Streamlined Baby*. New York: Farrar, Strauss & Giroux.

PART 2

Producing Visual Data and Insight

5

Anthropological Filmmaking: An Empirical Art

David MacDougall

THEORETICAL CONSIDERATIONS

Anthropological filmmaking is necessarily defined by what is considered anthropological at any particular time. But because there is no unanimity about anthropology, either today or historically, there are many different conceptions of what constitutes an anthropological film. These range from using film (or video) as a simple recording technology, to films being made according to specific rules or principles (designed to yield certain categories of knowledge), to audio-visual illustrations of written texts, to films combining these approaches with more interpretive accounts of social and cultural life. Anthropological films have also followed changes in what has been possible technically. Films from the silent era relied on images and inter-titles. Sound films added speech and natural sounds, with increasing flexibility as this became more feasible. The first anthropological sound films added soundtracks of commentary, natural sounds, and music to film footage previously shot, because recording image and sound simultaneously required massive and expensive equipment. When this became easier in the 1960s, anthropological films were able to incorporate spoken dialogue in the way fiction films had since the 1930s, although this still required manual synchronization in the editing room. With the advent of video, synchronous sound recording became essentially an integral part of the filming process, so that introducing non-synchronous sound actually became the greater challenge.

The ideas, subject matter, and methods of anthropology are always changing, and anthropological filmmaking has both influenced and reflected this process. Many of the recent concerns of anthropology—the agency of individuals, their subjective experience, social performance, built environments—are well served by the expressive potential of film, which was perhaps less well suited to the study of social structures and religious beliefs in an earlier anthropological era. Because of this, there has been a renewal of anthropological interest in the visual, reminiscent of the intense interest in visual knowledge among nineteenth-century anthropologists.

However, today's scientific interest in the visual (and audio-visual) has a markedly different character from that of the nineteenth century, when the technical and expressive range of film and photography was more limited and the focus was more strictly on material culture, technology, and human physiology. Anthropological filmmaking now is as much concerned with the non-visual as the visual. Audio-visual recording has evolved to become a means of exploring the full gamut of human social experience, including ideas, feelings, verbal and non-verbal expression, aesthetics, the role of the senses, and the formal and informal interactions of everyday life.

Visual anthropology and writing

It is important to understand that this has also created a tension between conventional ways of doing anthropology and the possibilities opened up by visual anthropology. Anthropology, as a discipline of words, developed specific methods of research and forms of discourse that were both challenged and complemented by anthropological filmmaking. As anthropology aspired to be a science, with systems of data collection equivalent to those of the laboratory sciences, it produced ways of summarizing and testing its knowledge that could in theory be reproduced by other researchers, even if this occurred rather rarely. Anthropological knowledge came to be understood as that which could be expressed in writing or in the schemata of diagrams and tables. Films, by comparison, do things in a very different way, and anthropological films, partly as a consequence of this, have often failed to live up to anthropological expectations. In considering the potential of filmmaking for anthropological research, we need to look more closely at the sorts of knowledge films can create and how they create it.

Much learning is visual, but in the processes of codification and communication it tends to become verbal. To a great extent films bypass this unless they are built around a verbal text, such as a spoken commentary or interviews with informants. The viewer of a film is exposed to scenes recorded by the camera, and these are organized in the editing to suggest a certain way of interpreting them. But there is always much more detail in the scenes than is governed by the interpretation, and viewers may derive knowledge from this material independently. Thus, despite the differences between human vision and photographic reproduction, and the many choices made in filming and editing, viewing a film is closer in character to the visual and auditory experience of the anthropologist in the field than to reading an anthropological text, where much of the detail must be reconstructed in the reader's imagination. This materialist basis of film stands in sharp contrast to the verbal codes of written anthropology.

Because film and writing are such different modes of communication, filmmaking is not just a way of communicating the same kinds of knowledge that can be conveyed by an anthropological text. It is a way of creating different knowledge. For many, this has been both its greatest drawback and greatest promise. The problem has been to identify what is anthropological in the knowledge that film uniquely makes possible, and to have this recognized by other scholars. The promise has been to introduce methods of research and publication that add to what anthropology has already achieved, and ultimately to expand the depth and range of the discipline. But to do so, anthropological filmmaking must make the best use of its specific properties, rather than attempt to copy anthropological writing. Anthropological filmmaking can thus be seen as a parallel stream of anthropology, with its own areas of interest and its own distinctive ways of creating meaning.

Filming and writing each have certain advantages and are subject to certain limitations in describing and interpreting human societies. Recognizing the limitations and utilizing the advantages of film are therefore important in deciding how to employ it. Anthropological film obviously has advantages in visual description. Every image is specific to a time and place, with all its particularities as well as its general features. But this is also a limitation in that it makes anthropological film an anthropology of the particular. Films can summarize by presenting a set of different cases for comparison, but they cannot make general statements and draw overall conclusions in the way writing can. This inability to state abstract propositions about society is however offset by the potential of film to explore the individual case in detail, not only visually but also in its temporal, physical, and emotional dimensions. Visual research using film is capable of investigating a wide range of elements, individually and in their combinations: movement, speech, the visual, the auditory, the material, the corporeal, and so on. There are thus certain areas of social research that are particularly accessible to filmmaking and in which it can make significant contributions, both as a method of enquiry and means of communicating knowledge to others. These areas include, at the very least, formal and informal interactions among people, their relationships with their physical environment, the social experience and agency of individuals, and the performative aspects of social life.

Anthropological filmmaking as a process

What also makes anthropological filmmaking deserving of special attention today is its relevance to many of the other current concerns of anthropology: globalization, migration, gender, emotion, individual and group identity, and visual culture. Yet it is important not to regard visual anthropology just as a method of reporting on these phenomena. Filmmaking is also a research process. Film has often been seen as a way of presenting knowledge previously gained by other means, a medium of publication and popularization. Conversely, it has also often been seen simply as a recording method, to extract data for later analysis. But the process of filming can be much more than this: it can be a means of interacting with a subject and exploring it in new ways. Filmmaking is a way of looking, sometimes motivated by intellectual objectives and sometimes anticipating thought. Often what is learned by filming is only an intermediate step toward quite different knowledge, or an indicator of what deserves closer attention. Thus, filming can become an integral part of the fieldwork process.

A major difference between anthropological filmmaking and most other modes of anthropological research is that it collapses the distance between enquiry and publication. The visual recording—that is, the research data—becomes the fabric of the finished work. What is filmed cannot be rewritten, although it can be edited and presented in different ways. This is in marked contrast to conventional anthropology, which is the result of gathering data, reflecting on it, and then presenting conclusions in a written form. This means that much of what the audience eventually sees, and how it sees it, will have been inalterably determined at the time of filming. The expressive strategies of an anthropological film must therefore be ever-present in the mind of the filmmaker as it is actually being shot.

Cinema and social science

Several recurring theoretical debates have bedeviled anthropological filmmaking since its origins, concerning the relation of the filmmaker to the work and the relation of cinematic art to science. In both cases the debate has become polarized, creating an impression of incompatible opposites when, in fact, more complex interrelationships are involved. In general, these debates run parallel to historical shifts in anthropological thought, although films, perhaps because they are judged to have more public influence, sometimes throw the issues into sharper relief.

Anthropological films take many forms and reflect different strategies for achieving an understanding of culture and society. One cause of anthropological disquiet over film has been the assumption by some of its advocates that anthropological filmmakers should adopt a single correct approach, and that approach only. Other approaches are dismissed as biased, naïve, or un-anthropological. A further suspicion surrounds the field as a whole, stemming from its uncomfortable position between cinema and social science. This is compounded by the different communicative systems of filming and writing, and by what they actually communicate. But knowledge of society is not independent of how it is pursued, and using the creative potential of cinema can be a legitimate way of enlarging previously unexamined subjects and increasing anthropological understanding. Art and science therefore need not be opposed if the art is in the service of more accurate description. Each filmmaker must decide at what point the means of expression employed begin to obscure rather than clarify the subject—in short, at what point aesthetic choices begin to undermine the creation of new knowledge. In the past, the development of clearly recognizable genres, and the specific contexts in which texts have been used (such as in teaching, or publication in journals), have provided the discipline with its guidelines as to what kinds of discourse are anthropological. But these genres and contexts remain less clearly defined for anthropological films.

Positioning, bias, and truth

Another source of uncertainty, fueling much debate, has been how anthropological filmmakers have positioned themselves in relation to their subjects and audiences. This positioning is crucial to understanding what any work represents; it provides a set of indicators on how to interpret it. Certain genres carry this information with them. We know, for example, that a Western will be a kind of morality play. In anthropological film, assumptions range from trusting that the work will explain itself, to believing that a meta-commentary outside the work is necessary. The points at issue are always how the author regards the subject and audience and how, in turn, the subject regards each of these. In films, these relationships are reflected in the camerawork, editing, and the content of the images. Do filmmakers stand aloof or record their interactions with the people in the film? Are the conditions of filming made evident? Is the filmic language familiar, relying on established conventions from fiction or documentary, or is it more personal, reflecting a particular sensibility? How much is assumed about what the audience already knows? Does the filmmaker expect the viewers to understand the situation or make explicit efforts to guide them? Each of these possibilities expresses an ideological position, a theory of knowledge, and expectations about how the film will be used.

One of the dominant debates in visual anthropology has centered on the reliability of the filmed record. Since their invention, photography and film have been regarded by many social scientists as ways of overcoming the inaccuracies of written description and the biases of the individual observer. It was thought that they might become a substitute for direct observation, allowing others to see accurately what the first observer had seen. To some extent this has proven true. Film has allowed anthropologists to inspect certain aspects of human behavior in minute detail, leading to a better understanding of facial expression, posture and gesture, technological processes, rituals, child-rearing practices, the social uses of space, and so on. But beyond questions of the accuracy of photographic reproduction lie more complex questions of scientific truth and interpretation.

Anthropological films should be distinguished from raw anthropological film footage: they are constructed works, making use of cinematic conventions and the selective potential of the camera and editing. Like written ethnographies they are authored works, influenced by the particular interests and circumstances of the anthropologist. This fact has run up against the ideal of a transparent work in which authorship is effectively erased or bracketed, whether by means of scientific rigor, self-restraint, or self-explanation. Thus, anthropological films are often expected to be both neutral and comprehensive, and are criticized when they are not. Perhaps more often than written works, they are accused of leaving things out or being misleading, as if they should include everything or avoid interpretation, even though neither is expected of writing. There is in this position what might be called a 'primitive' view of what an anthropological film can or should be.

The participant–observer

The problem has often come down to questioning the objectivity of the filmmaker, underpinned by the supposed neutrality of science. But anthropological filmmakers can never present reality as a single objective fact (assuming this even existed), just as they can never avoid the selectivity involved in filming from a specific camera position, or having certain interests, or being part of a particular historical and intellectual generation. What, for example, is the objective reality of a ritual? Is it the structure of the event, the symbolic meanings it encodes, or the thoughts and feelings of those performing it? It is all of these, but every film must choose which aspects to explore. Subjectivity and objectivity are not possible alternatives; they are elements to be balanced in the work, and each filmmaker will balance them differently.

This argument applies to whether, while filming, the filmmaker should stand apart from the people being filmed or interact with them. A stance apart is sometimes founded on the ideal of capturing an unmediated reality, but it may also simply reflect a strategy of learning through observation rather than employing more invasive means. Anthropological research typically utilizes a variety of methods: observation, participation in daily life, interviews with informants, statistical surveys, and so on. Filmmakers choose from similar possibilities. Malinowski's 'participant observation' was never meant to suggest opposed approaches, but rather the two combined: the participant as observer. Interaction with one's subjects is a quintessential part of fieldwork. The question facing anthropological filmmakers, therefore, becomes how much of this interaction to include in the film. We shall have more to say about this in relation to uses of the camera.

METHODOLOGICAL CONSIDERATIONS

Anthropological filmmaking involves both filming methods and research methods, although in practice the two are closely intertwined. When filming is itself a form of investigation, the two become almost synonymous. 'Visual research' may suggest the recording of images for later analysis, and it has meant this for many anthropologists; but it can also be a primary means of investigation. Research of the first kind views anthropological filmmaking primarily as a technology; research of the second kind as a practice, a way of actively exploring social phenomena.

Prospective uses

How one makes an anthropological film depends largely on how one hopes it will be seen. (There may also be an eye on posterity: creating a historical record for uses unknown today.) The prospective use is generally clear already, but it is well for the filmmaker to give it a second thought. This does not mean identifying a 'target audience,' as educators and television producers like to do, because a film may have several quite legitimate audiences. Rather, it means trying to imagine how it will be received, for without this it is unlikely to emerge as a coherent work. Will it be viewed as scientific data to be studied, or will it provide an experience from which viewers can gain insights into other people's lives? There are a range of possibilities in between. A filmmaker may want to illustrate a particular topic, create a case study, present a set of variations on a theme, or construct a narrative of events. Filming a craftsperson making an object, for example, could be (1) to show the technological process, (2) to show the craftsperson's knowledge and skill, (3) to make a point about labor, (4) to reveal the craftsperson's character, (5) to reflect a passage of time, (6) to recreate a sensory environment, (7) to describe a cultural function or artistic tradition, and so on. The context in which the material appears will direct different readings, and it will also influence the manner of filming.

What is filmed will also be determined by what it is possible to film. What is the best strategy for filming kinship? Should the anthropologist even try to use film for this? Clearly, a diagram is a better means of representing the abstract structural relations of kinship. But film may be better at expressing situations of dominance, affection, or such special relationships as avoidance or 'joking relationships.' How parents treat their children, and vice versa, can be described through written accounts and oral histories, but filming provides a further level of understanding by conveying postures, facial expressions, and records of actual incidents.

It was once thought by many anthropologists that film only offered anthropology a way of sketching in the background of anthropological study—the natural setting, the appearance of dwellings, how individuals exemplified certain social roles, and so on. Film was considered useful for illustration in teaching, but not intellectually important to anthropology. It is now increasingly believed that appearance is in fact a significant locus of meaning for anthropology. The physical body, material culture, the performance of social roles, the aesthetic systems of societies, and the agency of individuals—all these are now part of the mainstream of anthropological theory. This has provided new and productive opportunities for anthropological filmmakers.

Crews and collaborations

Approaching the task of filming in the field, the anthropologist will be faced with the question of whether to film alone or seek the help of one or more other persons. In the past, in order to film with 16mm and synchronous sound, a second person was usually essential to handle the tape recorder and microphone. Today, equipped with a video camera and smaller microphones, one person can achieve almost as much. But the choice also has important consequences for the resulting film material.

A film crew, even as small as two people, creates a quite different relationship of rapport with the people filmed than a single filmmaker. Two people form a social unit from which it is possible to feel excluded, whereas the anthropologist filming alone is always in a more exposed relationship with others. This can have benefits, in that people may be more likely to treat the filmmaker as a member of their social group, or as an intimate to whom information and feelings can be confided. The equipment carried by a single filmmaker is also less likely to appear threatening. Another difference, from the filmmaker's point of view, is that most decisions can be made immediately, without requiring consultation or pre-arrangement with an assistant or collaborator.

The advantages of working with another person are that the people being filmed may feel able to establish a more comfortable understanding about what will be filmed: that the whole process can in effect be more public and regulated. This may be particularly important when restricted knowledge is involved or the situation is politically sensitive. A crew of filmmakers may be seen as less likely to form allegiances with a particular faction. If the filmmaker's assistant is from the group being filmed, there may also be greater trust (but, it should be noted, sometimes quite the opposite). Two filmmakers may also have access to a wider range of events if they differ from one another: for example, if they are a married couple, or persons of different ages. Sometimes people will fully accept one of the two filmmakers, because of gender or ethnicity, and allow the other to be present in a supporting or honorary capacity. Working with another person also has the advantage of giving the filmmaker someone to talk to about the film, in ways not possible with the people being filmed. A second opinion can throw things into better perspective and contribute additional ideas.

Collaboration between a filmmaker and an anthropologist is often put forward as the ideal formula for successful anthropological filmmaking. Each, it is supposed, will complement the skills of the other, the assumption being that anthropologists are untrained in filmmaking and filmmakers are ignorant of anthropology. This may once have been true, but increasingly anthropologists are eager to add filmmaking to their traditional methods of note-taking and writing. In this, anthropologist-filmmakers like Jean Rouch have led the way. Filmmakers trained in anthropology are also more common, and indeed the separation of the two domains is beginning to look outdated. Younger anthropologists increasingly regard filming skills as a necessary part of their research repertoire.

In any case, collaboration of any kind can be difficult, and more so if the collaborators have different interests and ways of doing things. A common pitfall when an anthropologist and filmmaker collaborate is that the anthropologist wants the film to be all-inclusive, believing that anything left out will make the film misleading. The error here lies in assuming that a film must cover everything or avoid an interpretation, and that the viewer has no recourse to other sources of information. The anthropologist may therefore come armed with an encyclopedic list of topics and become upset when they cannot all be dealt with. A variant of this, also meant to guard against misinterpretation, is to load the film with a complex superstructure of verbal explanation, under which the film eventually sinks. Filmmakers, for their part, may be too eager to give the film a conventional dramatic structure, feeling that without this the audience will lose interest. They may become increasingly anxious if this doesn't emerge on its own and be tempted to interfere with events to make it happen. An obsessive fixation on 'story' is one of the weaknesses of many filmmakers.

Another kind of collaboration may be sought between filmmakers and their subjects, with the purpose of producing a film that includes a more interior perspective or gives a larger voice to the people filmed. A common problem here is that it becomes difficult to know whose view of a situation the film finally represents. Because of the different interests and objectives involved, the result may be a compromise that avoids exploring anything very deeply. Related to this is another potential problem. One of the underlying principles of an anthropological or cross-cultural perspective is that cultural specificities are best understood in relation to cultural difference. In theory, therefore, a cross-cultural collaboration should develop just such a comparative perspective. But if a film contains too many compromises between the collaborators, it tends to lose its cross-cultural edge. In recent years, a better alternative seems to have emerged: the simultaneous encouragement of both indigenous and cross-cultural filmmaking.

The cross-cultural perspective, in turn, can look in either direction.

Research relationships

This may be an appropriate point to introduce another problem often faced by filmmakers: resolving the tension between trying to present an honest analysis of a situation and avoiding giving offence to those who are part of it. Frequently, the very things that are most revealing of underlying social forces are precisely the things that people do not want shown or discussed. And yet to tailor one's analysis to what will not disturb anyone amounts to self-censorship. But this formulation perhaps represents a false dichotomy, for it suggests that people will always prefer silence to the truth, or will be intolerant of others' views, and that the filmmaker and subjects cannot work through such differences together. Often, too, with the passage of time, a film takes on a new ambiance. It begins to be viewed as a historical document, and even an object of nostalgia. Depending on the time taken between the filming and the film's completion, people's attitudes toward it may shift markedly. Thus, a situation that originally aroused controversy may later be regarded more dispassionately, and people may be quite happy for it to be shown.

However, sometimes this doesn't happen, and then the filmmaker must make a moral judgment about whether it is more important for the material to be seen or to protect people's sensibilities. And it is not only a matter of sensibilities, but of rights. The understanding under which the film was made is crucial to this decision. But rights are not always clear-cut, and the right course is not always obvious. Who has the right to speak for a community, or defend it? When there has been an injustice, does anyone have the right to prevent it being discussed? And there is the reverse situation in which the filmmaker realizes that even though people may allow something to be filmed, including it in

the film may cause distress or damage to some individual. In that case, the filmmaker might decide to leave it out. There are even cases in which someone's life may be endangered by a film. Ethics committees attempt to cover all the eventualities, but they cannot. There are some situations in which a legalistic interpretation of rights is useless, and filmmakers must ultimately be guided by their own consciences and understanding.

The relationship between a filmmaker and those filmed is clearly not a simple one, and it is important to realize that it evolves over time during the making of a film. For that reason, the understanding struck when the filming began will also change, for better or worse. Usually it is for the better, as filmmaker and subjects get to know each other, but tensions can also arise. Having a filmmaker around may look enjoyable at the beginning, but it can wear thin. Filmmakers must judge how not to overstay their welcome. Furthermore, the shift is not always in one direction; there will inevitably be ups and downs in the relationship. Both filmmaker and film subjects should feel they are deriving some benefit from the making of the film even if, as is usually the case, the reasons differ for each of them.

Fieldwork and filming

One question that frequently arises is how soon filming should begin. Is it better to conduct a period of research and familiarization before beginning to film, or to begin filming immediately? This is both a practical matter and a matter of principle. The conventional wisdom, based on the typical pattern of anthropological fieldwork, followed much later by publication, holds that filming should be introduced only after a period of preliminary research. How can one film what one does not know anything about? This is also the common formula for successful documentary filmmaking: that the research should precede the filming. For one thing it reassures the producers that they won't lose their money. But one consequence of this is that the filmmaker may film no more than what has already been established by the research, so that the filming simply becomes a way of illustrating it. In effect, the filming has contributed nothing in the way of new knowledge. One might well ask: If one makes a film based on what one already knows, what is the point of making it?

A different approach, based on the idea that filming is an integral part of the research process, is that it should begin quite soon, as the filmmaker begins to explore the subject. Often when this is done, the filmmaker realizes that the ideas that initially appeared so crucial are of less importance than the new ideas they lead to. In this case, the act of filming has served as a catalyst to understanding. But if the film is made according to a prefabricated script or treatment, it will tend to be frozen at that earlier stage. There are other reasons too for filming from the start. As first observations become more familiar, they are often taken for granted. They may become so familiar that the filmmaker loses sight of them altogether, only discovering the loss when it is too late. Filming when observations are fresh can cause one to film them more acutely.

Filming from the start can also be a matter of principle. If one introduces a camera after a long period of fieldwork, it tends to alter and even disrupt the nature of the relationships that one has built up, for the filming process necessarily introduces a different mode of behavior on the part of the filmmaker. One must focus more on one's job and may find it impossible to interact with people as before. Furthermore, filming inevitably means placing a piece of alien equipment between oneself and one's subjects. It may thus be thought preferable, from both a moral and practical point of view, to introduce the camera early, showing one's subjects straightforwardly what one is doing, and allowing the relationships to grow around that.

Filmmaking behavior

These relationships are also crucially affected by the methods and character of the filming. In the days when filming required massive equipment, and even later when it became somewhat less intrusive, the filming process tended to dominate any situation. No wonder documentary filmmakers had to direct people to play their parts. Today, with small video cameras, when technically excellent films can be made by even one person, the intrusion of the technology and the filmmaker need not be so great. But it is less the technology itself and more the approach of the filmmaker that makes the primary difference. If the filmmaker is constantly calling attention to the filming process, or constantly interfering in things for technical or other reasons, the camera will naturally remain the center of attention. But if the object is to make films about how people actually live, it is wise to learn how to work more unobtrusively.

How filmmakers comport themselves is the first consideration. A low-key approach to filming requires an ability to treat the camera not as a problem, but as a trusted companion. This means learning to operate it with a minimum of fuss. It is a little like mastering a musical instrument. Holding the camera steady, for example, is a skill that can be learned by almost anyone. The more experienced one becomes, the more one operates the controls without thinking, and the more the camera becomes an extension of one's way of looking at things and interacting with others. The more comfortable you are with the camera, the more open you can be to what is going on around you.

There are other factors involved in filming that affect how people respond to the camera and what the resulting film material looks like. This has partly to do with the filmmaker's individual personality and partly with larger matters of method and style. Is the filmmaker working alone or with others? Does the filmmaker work close to the people being filmed or stand farther back? Is the filming done with a tripod or a hand-held camera? Many of these factors are determined by the genre of the film, its anthropological objectives, or the culture from which the filmmaker comes. But they are also open to choice. For example, to film people's informal interactions and conversations may require staying close to them, hand-holding the camera in order to move easily with them, and using a wide-angle lens so that they don't constantly go out of frame. But this can also be a matter of personal stylistic choice, the filmmaker's own preferred way of seeing the world. Another approach, more interested in relations to space, or to the surrounding environment, might call for a camera on a tripod, framing the world in more formal ways. In both cases, it may be difficult to separate the subject matter from the aesthetics of representing it.

Camera modes

The choice of camera style is personal in another sense. It has to do with how the filmmaker relates to other people and what sort of relationship with them the film will ultimately express. This is an integral part of a larger strategy of how the film explores its subject. There are various ways of employing a camera, which could be described as responsive, interactive, and constructive. Each has its uses, and each represents not only a different mode of enquiry but also a different way of addressing the viewer. A responsive camera is largely reactive, responding to what is occurring in front of it. It looks, explores, but does not interfere, even though the filmmaker may be on intimate terms with the subjects. The viewer's perspective here resembles that of the filmmaker, who watches but does not otherwise enter into the event.

An interactive camera is quite the reverse. It does intervene, and records its own interaction with the subject. The filmmaker, even if not actually seen, is now pushed more into the forefront of the film, along with the subjects. Such interactions often take the form of conversations, or interviews. Clearly such events would not occur unless provoked or invited by the filmmaker. In a figurative sense the viewer is now situated farther outside the film, watching the filmmaker at work.

A constructive camera presents the viewer with an intervention of a different kind, focused this time on the film images themselves. Through the style of camerawork and editing, the images are reprocessed to produce an explicitly interpretive work, based on a concept of the subject or set of formal conventions. The manipulation of images by the filmmaker is made very obvious. This is a far cry from the realist mode of the other approaches, for here the filmmaker disassembles the subject and reassembles it according to some external logic. In effect, the filming is used not to report on an event but to report on the filmmaker's interpretation or impressions of it. The viewer's position is thus moved still farther outside the frame of the original event and closer to that of the filmmaker's own consciousness.

One of these modes of camera use may dominate a film, but often several modes are employed for different purposes, sometimes merging into one another. It may difficult, for example, to identify the point at which people who have previously been absorbed in their own affairs begin to involve the filmmaker in their conversations, or at which point the filmmaker starts introducing formal elements into the film that will become increasingly pronounced. It may also be difficult to distinguish between formal elements that are part of generic conventions and those that are idiosyncratically those of the filmmaker. For example, if one films always from a ground-level position, is this a cultural choice or a personal one? In the hands of a great filmmaker like Yasujiro Ozu, it is evidently both.

There is no good reason why several camera modes may not be used in a single film, provided they appear justified and are not sprung unexpectedly on the audience. For if this happens, the filmmaker will be judged to have lost control of the material or to be indulging personal whims at the expense of the viewer. Stylistic consistency has much to be said for it, as a guarantee of the coherence of the filmmaker's vision. If there are to be shifts of method, it is wise for the filmmaker to establish these possibilities early in the film. If film viewers do not know the ground rules of the film, they will have difficulty interpreting what they see.

Filming strategies

Anthropological filmmaking can center on an event such as a ritual, a social institution such as marriage, or even an abstraction such as identity or masculinity. It may look at the role of an individual or the experiences of a large group. In some cases, the structure of an event provides a framework for the film to follow. This can lend a degree of predictability to the filming, although sometimes even the people involved are unsure of what will happen next. It is not unusual to go to a place where something is supposed to happen only to be told that it is happening elsewhere, or happened last night. The best the filmmaker can do is get the most reliable information from knowledgeable people and be prepared for other possibilities. Patience and flexibility are both necessary assets in these situations. Filmmakers who are too rigid in their expectations are likely to face frustrations and resort to hasty decisions. All too often filmmakers refuse to film something because it doesn't fit into their plans, only to realize later that something of importance has happened right under their noses. Sometimes an unexpected scene contributes far more to the film than what the filmmaker originally had in mind.

There are a variety of strategies for anthropological filmmaking in the field. Some filmmakers will look for events or individuals to follow. Others will look for tensions or conflicts that appear to be moving toward some kind of crisis, reasoning that discovering what is at stake will reveal underlying forces at work. These social dramas, like more formalized events, have a certain predictability to them and, as Gregory Bateson, Victor Turner, and others have reasoned, reflect the ways in which communities reconcile fundamental structural divisions that threaten to disrupt them.

Still other filmmakers will try to explore social forces by concentrating on particular themes that express them, either symbolically or in everyday events. This theme-and-variations approach can be especially productive when the tensions never rise to the level of a crisis, but remain as undercurrents. It can be equally valuable in exploring less volatile aspects of culture, such as the transmission of knowledge from one group or generation to another, or the ways in which cultural traditions evolve and adapt to change.

One tactic in filming a set of related themes is to note down relevant material that may recur. These may be events one has witnessed, or other forms of expression. The filmmaker is then attuned to a specified range of possibilities and prepared to begin filming when something happens that fits one or another of the target items. As the film progresses, new items will be added and old ones removed, either because enough material about them has now been filmed or because they no longer appear relevant. Since the filmmaker is constantly learning more about the subject, it is quite normal for the priorities to change.

Visual anthropology also offers considerable scope for studying visual culture. We live increasingly in a world of visual images. Anthropological filmmaking can make an important contribution to the understanding of visual cultural forms, since it can show how visual images and visible objects are produced and consumed as well as their physical appearance. There is also a valuable differential perspective to be gained from using one visual medium to explore another, such as film or video to study still photography, religious iconography, or advertising. Here filming offers anthropology and cultural studies a 'language' particularly suited to its objects of research.

The cinematic triangle

Most anthropological films implicitly announce three separate relationships: (1) between the filmmaker and the viewers; (2) between the filmmaker and the subjects; and (3) between the subjects and the viewers. The last of these is often expressed in the way people in a film imagine the audience will see them, and how, through the film, they attempt to address them. The first is more like a pact between filmmaker and audience that is established by the genre of the film, but also by certain more direct signals from the filmmaker. The genre of the film—whether research filming, a television documentary, or a film for teaching—tells us partly what to expect. The filmmaker may then tell us more by establishing a particular style: for example, by introducing voice-over commentary, subtitles, inter-titles, or still images. A camera style will also be established. The filmmaker may prefer long takes or short ones, close shots or wide shots, movement or stillness, or a distinctive combination of these. The film may preserve a convention of omniscience or give the viewer an insight into the filmmaking process. The editing will also create a logic and rhythm. Does the filmmaker prefer smooth-flowing continuity or the use of juxtapositions? Do the images progress from the general to the specific, or vice versa? The point is not that one approach is necessarily better than another, but that viewers sense an intention and intelligence behind the work and feel they are in good hands.

It is also important for a film to establish the filmmaker's relationship to the people being filmed. This may evolve over the course of the film, but we get early evidence of it in people's behavior before the camera. Do they appear aware of the filmmaker's presence, and if so are they comfortable with it? Do they appear to have been directed? Is there interaction with the filmmaker? Does the filmmaker stay close to them or film from far away, as if from an observation post? The manner of filming embodies an attitude toward the subject.

It also embodies the filmmaker's attitude toward the viewer. Earlier styles of documentary encoded a theatrical convention of distance between the work and the audience. The film was a performance prepared for their consumption. How it was produced was a professional secret, and this mystery was part of its power. Like fiction films, most documentaries assumed an Olympian view of their subjects. Human beings were observed and recorded, but the eye observing them remained unacknowledged and unseen, both by the audience and apparently by the subjects as well. If someone noticed the camera, that shot was cut out. This was a far cry from the novel, in which authors frequently confided their thoughts and methods to the reader. Documentaries made since the 1960s, however, have begun to treat the camera more like a personal writing instrument, although this shift has yet to affect much of television production. In most films, but particularly in anthropological films, the acknowledgement within the film of the filmmaker's situation in the field becomes an important element in allowing us to interpret accurately what we see.

Modes of reflexivity

The disclosure of the filmmaking process, however, is not a single act but may be distributed through many aspects of the film. It need not take the form of overt self-reflexivity—in itself often unreliable, because it can never be wholly disinterested.

As filmmaking becomes a more personal and less industrial process, we can learn a great deal from the filmmaker's apparent behavior. A highly intrusive camera, creating signs of resentment, not only tells us about the insensitivity of the filmmaker but also that what we see is produced under a kind of duress. A camera that moves in certain ways and follows certain details tells us much about the particular interests of the film-maker. It has often been argued that anthropological films should be accompanied by written notes that describe the field situation and fill in much of the missing ethnographic detail. This may be valuable for teaching, but it should not become a crutch that the film depends upon. For in that case, anthropological filmmakers may take it as an invitation to produce inadequate work.

Reflexivity essentially means contextualizing the content of a film by revealing aspects of its production. Makers of anthropological films should distinguish between two kinds of reflexivity. One kind is explicit, making the conditions of filming more apparent. This may mean including footage of interactions between filmmaker and subjects, showing the subjects' acknowledgement of the filmmaking situation, providing a voice-over commentary, and so on. It also means providing a sufficiently rich context for the events shown to make them understandable in interpersonal and cultural terms. A more implicit kind of reflexivity also permeates most films, to which viewers should be sensitive. It is the stamp of the filmmaker's research interests and personal involvement. It can be read in a multitude of signs in how the film has been made, from the camerawork to the editing, to the responses of people on the screen. It is an expression of the filmmaker's living presence in the film.

The experiences of individuals

If the filmmaker's role is embodied in this way, what about that of the film's subjects and the viewer? The subjects are clearly embodied in a physical sense, because it is their existence that has generated the images on the screen. The camera also registers the outward expression of their emotions and, through their words, signs of their intellectual life. But these signs must be interpreted by the viewer and, in a sense, made their own. The viewer becomes a collaborator in the creation of a film's meaning. In anthropological films this can be complicated by cultural differences, since the signs (most obviously of language) may vary from one society to another. Filmmakers in such cases must often rely on the context to clarify these meanings, or provide explanations by other means. But one of the great assets of anthropological film, as opposed to writing, is its ability to reach across cultural boundaries through those aspects of life that are common to many societies. Viewers may not be able to understand another language, but they can recognize many situations in other people's lives and respond to them. The better the film contextualizes these situations, the better the viewer can interpret them in culturally appropriate ways.

Although films cannot get inside another person's mind or emotions, they can, by cinematic means, communicate aspects of their subjective experience. They do this partly by paying close attention to the expressions, movements, and responses of individuals and partly by following narratives in their lives. Viewers, through a process of identification, begin to make connections between the behavior on the screen and their own past experiences. Films rarely adopt the actual visual perspectives of individuals. Rather, figuratively and literally, they look over their shoulders, staying close to them through different events. Viewers come to understand others' feelings not by experiencing them directly, but by vicariously sharing their social interactions and physical surroundings.

In the creation of subjective identification, narrative has a central role. Because of this it has great potential for contributing to anthropological understanding, a potential more often employed in films than in anthropological writing. Narratives occur in every culture and provide an important mechanism for cross-cultural understanding. They have explanatory power, because they can demonstrate patterns of cause and effect. By observing how something happens, we can often come to understand why it happens. Perhaps more important, narratives of individual lives provide a way of leading us imaginatively through the experiences of others in societies different from our own. In the process, we encounter the complexity of social forces and the ways in which individuals are affected by them. Narratives of social interaction also provide a framework for observing how people inhabit their physical environment—how they use it, alter it, and experience it in sensory terms.

Lastly, the filmmaker needs to take account of how the people portrayed in an anthropological film see themselves, for they are by right its first audience. They are involved in it both personally and as preternaturally exposed representatives of their communities. Films can provoke a wide range of responses, many of them unpredictable. Like still photographs, they can elicit memories, emotions, and tacit cultural knowledge. People's responses to seeing themselves in films can tell us much about what we as filmmakers have got right and what we have got wrong, even if this does not always coincide with what they like or dislike. Their interpretations will also undoubtedly change over time. Many of the cultural and intellectual assumptions clinging to a film will drop away and it may well come to be valued less for these things than for the physical details it has captured. In a similar way, anthropologists can make use of old films in new ways. The films we make today become both sources of documentary evidence and evidence of the ideas, prejudices, and interests of their times.

A SELECTION OF FILMS AND PUBLICATIONS BY DAVID MACDOUGALL

Films

To Live With Herds (1972) [Film, 70 minutes]. Directed by David MacDougall. USA: University of California.

The Wedding Camels (1977) [Film, 108 minutes]. Directed by David MacDougall and Judith MacDougall. Australia: Fieldwork Films.

Lorang's Way (1979) [Film, 70 minutes]. Directed by David MacDougall and Judith MacDougall. Australia: Fieldwork Films.

Familiar Places (1980) [Film, 53 minutes]. Directed by David MacDougall. Australia: Australian Institute of Aboriginal Studies.

A Wife Among Wives (1981) [Film, 75 minutes]. Directed by David MacDougall and Judith MacDougall. Australia: Fieldwork Films.

Three Horsemen (1982) [Film, 54 minutes]. Directed by David MacDougall and Judith MacDougall. Australia: Australian Institute of Aboriginal Studies.

Photo Wallahs (1991) [Film, 60 minutes]. Directed by David MacDougall and Judith MacDougall. Fieldwork Films, Australian Film Commission, Australian Broadcasting Corporation and La Sept (France).

Tempus de Baristas (1993) [Film, 100 minutes] Directed by David MacDougall. Australia: Istituto Superiore Regional Etnografico/Fieldwork Films & BBC Television.

Doon School Chronicles (2000) [Film, 143 minutes]. Directed by David MacDougall. Australia: Centre for Cross-Cultural Research, Australian National University.

With Morning Hearts (2001) [Film, 110 minutes]. Directed by David MacDougall. Australia: Centre for Cross-Cultural Research, Australian National University.

The New Boys (2003) [Film, 100 minutes]. Directed by David MacDougall. Australia: Centre for Cross-Cultural Research, Australian National University.

The Age of Reason (2004) [Film, 87 minutes]. Directed by David MacDougall. Australia: Centre for Cross-Cultural Research, Australian National University.

SchoolScapes (2007) [Film, 77 minutes]. Directed by David MacDougall. Australia: Fieldwork Films & Centre for Cross-Cultural Research, Australian National University.

Gandhi's Children (2008) [Film, 185 minutes]. Directed by David MacDougall. Australia: Fieldwork Films, Prayas Institute of Juvenile Justice (India) & Centre for Cross-Cultural Research, Research School of Humanities, Australian National University.

Books

MacDougall, David (1998) *Transcultural Cinema*; edited and with an introduction by Lucien Taylor. Princeton, NJ: Princeton University Press.

MacDougall, David (2006) *The Corporeal Image: Film, Ethnography, and the Senses*. Princeton, NJ: Princeton University Press.

Articles and book sections

MacDougall, D. (1969) 'Prospects of the ethnographic film', *Film Quarterly*, 23(2): 16–30. Reprinted: in B. Nichols (ed.) (1976) *Movies and Methods*. Berkeley, CA: University of California Press. Vol. 1: pp. 135–150.

MacDougall, D. (1975) 'Beyond observational cinema', in P. Hockings (ed.), *Principles of Visual Anthropology*. The Hague/Paris: Mouton de Gruyter. pp. 109–24. Reprinted: in B. Nichols (ed.) (1985) *Movies and Methods*. Berkeley, CA: University of California Press. Vol. 2: pp. 274–287.

MacDougall, D. (1978) 'Ethnographic film: Failure and promise', in B. Siegel (ed.), *Annual Review of Anthropology*, 7: 405–425.

MacDougall, D. (1991) 'Whose story is it?', *Visual Anthropology Review*, 7(2): 2–10. Reprinted: in P. I. Crawford and J. K. Simonsen (eds.) (1992): *Ethnographic Film Aesthetics and Narrative Traditions*. Aarhus: Intervention Press. pp. 25–42. Reprinted: in L. Taylor (ed.) (1994) *Visualizing Theory*. New York: Routledge. pp. 27–36.

MacDougall, D. (1992) 'Complicities of style', in P. I. Crawford and D. Turton (eds.), *Film as Ethnography*. Manchester: Manchester University Press. pp. 90–99.

MacDougall, D. (1992) 'Photo Hierarchicus: Signs and mirrors in Indian photography', *Visual Anthropology*, 5(2): 103–129.

MacDougall, D. (1992) 'When less is less', *Film Quarterly*, 46(2): 36–45. Reprinted: in B. Henderson and A. Martin (eds.) (1999) *Film Quarterly: Forty Years—A Selection*. Berkeley, CA: University of California Press. pp. 290–306.

MacDougall, D. (1995) 'The subjective voice in ethnographic film', in L. Devereaux and R. Hillman (eds.), *Fields of Vision*. Berkeley, CA: University of California Press. pp. 217–256.

MacDougall, D. (1997) 'The visual in anthropology', in M. Banks and H. Morphy (eds.), *Rethinking Visual Anthropology*. New Haven and London: Yale University Press. pp. 276–295.

MacDougall, D. (1999) 'Social aesthetics and the Doon School', *Visual Anthropology Review*, 15(1): 3–20.

MacDougall, D. (2006) 'Ethnographic documentary film', in I. Aitken (ed.), *Encyclopedia of the Documentary Film*. New York and London: Routledge. Vol. I. pp. 353–360.

MacDougall, D. (2007) 'The experience of color', *The Senses & Society*, 2 (1): 5–26.

MacDougall, D. (2007) 'Gardner's bliss', in L. Barbash and L. Taylor (eds.), *The Cinema of Robert Gardner*. Oxford: Berg. pp. 153–173.

Interview

Barbash, L. and Taylor, L. (eds.) (2001) 'Radically empirical documentary: An interview with David and Judith MacDougall', *Film Quarterly*, 54(2): 2–14.

MacDougall, D. (2001) 'Renewing ethnographic film', *Anthropology Today. Royal Anthropological Institute*, 17(3): 15–21.

6

Repeat Photography in Landscape Research

Mark Klett

INTRODUCTION

A repeat photograph, or 'rephotograph' is a photograph specifically made to duplicate selected aspects of another, pre-existing photograph. The new image typically repeats the spatial location of the original, showing the viewer the same scene once again and inviting comparison. But other features of an existing photograph, the lighting, or the events depicted, may also be the subject of attempted duplication. The verb 'attempt' is appropriate in this effort, for a photograph made at one time can never be exactly replicated in another. And it is the differences between photographs that make them both compelling and informative when seen together. The result is a photographic diptych that spans an intervening period of time. The photographs act like bookends to the time in between, and the combination raises questions about what is not seen as well as what is seen in either photo. The ability of rephotographs to illustrate change as well as question assumptions about time insures their unique contribution to the medium of photography.

Rephotographs rely on a visual language that is almost universal. The ability to point out and compare differences between photographs spans a very wide range of viewer interests and levels of experience. However, the ability to interpret these differences is not universal; because when two photographs, an original and a rephotograph, are paired together the combination may illustrate change and the passage of time, but neither image can explain the events that led to that change.

Rephotographs have been used by researchers across many fields as tools, documents, and objects; how rephotographs are made varies among disciplines, just as what researchers expect from them ranges from documentation of data to poetic expression. Rephotographs can support both empirical and theoretical work; they may also become the subjects of research. From the natural sciences to the fine arts, rephotographs can help examine change and document the passage of time, most commonly in landscapes where the original subject of a photograph can be located and the space revisited.

For example, rephotographs have been used in such wide-reaching projects as studying changes in plant growth and population in the Arizona desert, revisiting the now famous photographs of a major city, exploring the route of a historic intercontinental highway, repeating a collection of vernacular snapshots as a departure point for conceptual art project, and rephotographing the collection of an automobile club as the pathway to a changing urban environment (Hastings and Turner, 1965; Vale and Vale, 1983; Rosier, 2004; Levere, 2005; Kinder and Roth, 2005). These studies span the natural and social sciences, the fine arts, urban planning and land management, to name only a few of the disciplines involved.

Intervening time spans between photographs may be short term, as in the record of plant growth over a few days, or long term, as in monitoring the creeping movement of a glacier (Fagre and McKeon, forthcoming). Common to many disciplines, there has been a need to visualize change, and the overall connection has been to gain a unique perspective on time related to place that is independent of discipline and challenges the observation of any single moment.

While there are common threads in the need for visualizing change, there have been two basic approaches to rephotography. I will describe each approach, based on my extensive experience in rephotography across a variety of projects, with examples of some of the ways rephotography can be used in visual research in a number of fields. I will focus, in particular, on *The Third View Project* (Third View), which attempted to repeat Western American survey photographs dating from the 1860s to 1870s along with a set of rephotographs made of these originals by the Rephotographic Survey Project (RSP). The RSP worked between 1977 and 1979 to precisely repeat the first photographs of the American West made by photographers such as Timothy O'Sullivan, William Henry Jackson, J. K. Hillers, and others

(Klett et al., 1984). The project is described on its website as follows:

> Third View revisits the sites of historic western American landscape photographs. The project makes new photographs, keeps a field diary of its travels, and collects materials useful in interpreting the scenes, change and the passage of time.
>
> The Third View project began in 1997 and completed fieldwork in the year 2000. Over the course of four years the project revisited 109 historic landscape sites, all subjects of nineteenth-century American western survey photographs. (*The Third View Project*, 2004: *Introduction*).

The first approach described in this chapter depends on finding the exact location where an original photograph was made, and accurately reoccupying the position and framing of the initial view. This technique is most useful to those wishing to make quantitative measurements from the photographic sets, and they are often used in the natural sciences. But the concepts are also important to those in other fields who wish to create convincing recreations of an original photograph. This is the most commonly used set of techniques and when used with care will deliver photographs that can be molded to a wide range of concerns.

The second approach also involves locating where an original photograph was made, but is less concerned with exact relocation of the original position or frame, and instead focuses on the context surrounding the photograph(s). This technique is useful when the researcher is interested in exploring stories associated with those images and locations: for instance, in noticing what is, or is not included in the photographic view. It is also a method for combining multiple photographs. This may be a better fit for the social sciences and the arts, but is often useful to other fields as well.

These two visual research methods have different purposes, and the techniques used have both virtues and limitations. However, the two approaches are not mutually exclusive since they share a common goal: finding where an existing photograph was made.

That 'place' becomes the basis for making new photographs.

VANTAGE POINT

One reason photographs are so useful is they originate from a real position in space. Unlike images made 'by hand,' such as drawings or paintings, photographs are subject to the laws of physics, chemistry, and optics, and it is therefore possible to repeat some of those physical processes in order to create a 'duplicate' image. In place-based photographs, or photographs that depict locations, landscapes, and other scenes that can be reoccupied over long periods of time, the photographer places a camera in a position that is accessible at a later date.

Photographs are formed by a lens projecting an image onto a light-sensitive medium; previously this was photographic film; however, now it is commonly a digital sensor. Thus, the relationship between the lens and the objects before it plays the biggest role in how an image is recorded: The optical properties of lenses resolve and represent the subject in a photograph, but it's where the photographer places the lens in space, or its 'vantage point,' that dictates the resulting composition.

Every photograph has a vantage point, and with the exception of stereo photographs there is only one vantage point per image. This point usually corresponds to a position at or near the diaphragm of the lens and controls how the lens records the objects before it. The vantage point is responsible for the way that three-dimensional space is translated into two dimensions. Thus, in a hypothetical landscape view, the way a rock in the foreground intersects a tree in the middle ground, and how that same tree lines up with a mountain peak in the distance, are all a function of the vantage point chosen by the photographer. If one chooses a different position to place the lens, these relationships will change, even by a small amount.

Experienced photographers go to great lengths to choose vantage points with care, and for good reason. Failure to consider the vantage point when making a photograph can result in unintended juxtapositions in space. Imagine the portrait of a loved one, taken from a poorly chosen camera position in front of the house, with the unfortunate visual impression of the chimney forever coming out of the subject's head.

There is only one position from which every photograph is made, and that position is dictated by the position of the vantage point. This should not to be confused with the focal length of a camera's lens; the choice of long focal length (telephoto) or short focal length (wide angle), affects how much of the scene will be included in the photograph. Long focal lengths record less of the scene but enlarge more in the distance; short focal lengths record wider views and describe areas closer to the camera.

APPROACH #1: EXACT RELOCATION OF A VANTAGE POINT

Whether for science or art, then, the job of the rephotographer is to find the vantage point of an original photograph as precisely as possible. And where the purpose is to achieve an accurate evaluation of physical change over time, there is a greater need to precisely duplicate this unique point in the rephotograph. Malde (1973) described how the camera can be used in the same way as a transit when measuring change directly from photographs; the camera is essentially used as an optical surveying instrument. But even studies that have little need for measuring change benefit from accurately repeating a prior vantage point, because the resulting photographs just *look* more alike as repeated images. Carefully relocated vantage points result in photographs that convince viewers they are made from the same place, and encourage greater participation in interpreting the image contents. By eliminating the variable of where two photographs were made in space, the viewer is free instead to contemplate other differences, such as visible changes between the two views (Klett et al., 1984).

Techniques used for locating vantage points depend on the camera format and materials employed, but the principle is independent of device or medium. Several publications describe methods for accurately reoccupying an existing vantage point (Malde, 1973; Harrison, 1974; Klett et al., 1984; Rogers et al., 1984). In practice, there are two stages to the work. First, the original photograph must be given a general, and then a more specific location: for example, a photograph taken in the Rocky Mountains in Colorado, and Mt Harvard in particular, and further, the photo shows the east side of the mountain, at a specific drainage, etc. This work is often done before rephotography fieldwork begins, and may require research into any titles or descriptions, in comparison to other known photographs, or consulting maps, field records, or other documents.

In recent years, some researchers have had success using web-based maps and aerial photographs to help locate the positions for landscape photographs. Google Maps, for example, used in combination with oblique views and lighting simulations can help narrow the choices when searching for where photographs were made. The information may provide both direction and approximate distances from known landforms. One recent rephotographic study used high-resolution satellite images not only to identify the landforms seen in an earlier photographic survey but also to make computer-based rephotographs of scenes inaccessible to fieldwork (Hanks et al., 2010).

In the next stage of the process the photograph's vantage point is relocated by taking a print of the original image into the field and locating the subject(s) that appeared in that image (and, for anyone who has made rephotographs, this is the exciting part of the work). Using the print as a guide, the observer moves through the space depicted in the photograph and finds points that are still identifiable from the earlier image. Then, usually through trial and error, the points identified in the view (for example, foreground and background objects) are lined up as in the original, and one quickly learns how moving in different directions affects the way the space looks in the photograph. It tends to be most efficient to locate the vantage points visually by maneuvering the view rather than the camera.

Once the camera has been placed at the chosen vantage point, the choice can be tested and refined. To locate a given vantage point in space, visualize this as movements along a three-point coordinate axis: the photographer may choose to move forward or backward, to the left or right, or up or down. After the vantage point is reoccupied as closely as possible without a camera, a lens is chosen to match the original photograph's angle of view and the camera is pointed in the direction to match the original's framing and camera inclination.

At this stage it is possible to quantitatively evaluate the choice of a vantage point more accurately by using measurements made on the surface of photographs (see Figure 6.1) (Harrison, 1974; Klett et al., 2004). There is a virtual demo of this at: *http://www.thirdview.org/3v/classroom/index.html;* by following the link to the Rephotography Simulation, a user can walk through the steps of recreating a vantage point and taking measurements between reference points, allowing the user to verify the accuracy of a chosen vantage point through those measurements (Figure 6.1).

Not long ago it was common to make these measurements in the field by using large-format cameras (4 inch × 5 inch negative size) exposing Polaroid Instant films. To do the work successfully, a 'copy-print' of the original photograph (this term will be used throughout) was carried into the field and measurements taken on the print surface to calculate numeric spatial relationships between objects in the scene. These measurements were then compared with the instant

Timothy O'Sullivan, 1867, Rock Formations, Pyramid Lake, NV.

Figure 6.1   A virtual demonstration from the book *Third Views Second Sights: A Rephotographic Survey of the American West* (DVD portion). The viewer interacts with the scene shown (Pyramid Lake, Nevada), attempting to emulate the original photograph shown to the left. A text describes how to align and make a test rephotograph, and the viewer moves the position of a virtual camera along three possible directions, left–right, up–down, forward–backward, to line up the scene until it matches the original image on the left. As the camera moves, the simulated view also changes. When a test shot is taken with a click of the computer mouse (shown here), the tutorial demonstrates how the choice of vantage point may be verified by comparing measurements between the original and the test print

test prints made at the selected vantage point and adjustments were made in the vantage point until the measurements lined up with the original. Large-format cameras (4 inch × 5 inch negative size) were the instruments of choice because they allowed for recreating any camera movements used by early photographers and most importantly because they provided large negatives with great clarity, and enabled the photographer to use the instant film for feedback while on site. Some variations of large-format instant films

remain, as of this writing, making this method viable, but their continued availability for fieldwork remains in jeopardy.

New techniques using digital cameras are replacing methods based on film, and while necessitating more equipment they also offer greater accuracy. The digital corollary to the method described above involves carrying a portable battery-operated printer into the field along with a digital camera. The photographs made with the digital camera are then printed on site, and the measurements described in the technique above are made as before on both the copy-print and digital print.

Another protocol for finding vantage points with precision involves taking a laptop into the field along with the digital camera. The laptop is pre-loaded with a digital copy of the original photograph. A new vantage point is chosen by eye and a trial photograph is made at the chosen vantage point using a camera on a tripod. The image file is downloaded to the laptop, and using image-editing software the new image is overlaid on the original, and made semi-transparent. The two images are scaled to the same size and features are compared. If the new vantage point matches the old, the identifiable features in both images will line up. If the overlap is not close enough, the tripod and camera is moved to a new position to correspond to movements needed to make the two photographs overlap more precisely. The principles of quantitative measurement are then used along with or instead of a trial-and-error method.

The trade-off when using digital technology for rephotographic work is that more equipment is required, costing more money and adding more weight. Power consumption can be a problem in remote locations and laptop screens are often hard to see in daylight. The skill level needed to work some image-editing software requires a steep learning curve. Furthermore, storage of digital image files can be a concern in both the short and long term. In spite of these drawbacks, finding a vantage point using digital techniques is more accurate than earlier techniques using film, and the option of using electronic media offers many new opportunities, some of which will be outlined below.

Regardless of equipment used, any attempt to relocate a pre-existing vantage point has limitations. The accuracy in matching two vantage points becomes greater when more information can be compared between the original and a rephotograph. This is especially true when the original image contains multiple objects at a variety of distances from the lens. Photographic vantage points that provide clearly identifiable objects or markers in the foreground, middle ground, and background of the photograph are the most accurately reoccupied. Foreground in this case can mean anything close enough to the camera for the photographer to touch, which is especially true when wide-angle lenses are used. Under these circumstances, when information at multiple distances from the camera is reliable, it is often possible to position the lens within centimeters of the original. But if the information is limited or the photographer can only rely on identifying similar distances from the camera, the degree of accuracy will be significantly reduced.

Lighting

Light plays an important role in defining the subject in an image, and another characteristic of photographs is that they are made at unique times of day. The lighting in the original image can be the most obvious indication of the photograph's moment in time, and can be an aid in identifying the vantage point, by matching both the time of day and time of year in which the photograph was made (Malde, 1973; Hoffman and Todd, 2010). Lighting defines how three-dimensional objects are rendered in a flat picture plane, and a change in lighting in the rephotograph will change the way a viewer interprets space in the scene.

Together with exact duplication of an earlier vantage point, replicating the lighting is an essential part of accurate rephotographic methods. In landscapes, the angle of the sun above the horizon will be determined by the season, and the lighting in any given location can theoretically be repeated twice a year, once on either side of the closest solstice. For example, the lighting in a photograph made in April, 2 months before the summer solstice can also be duplicated in August, 2 months after the summer solstice. But there may be seasonal differences that are important: for example, photographs made in October may look very different than those in February, even though the lighting matches. The direction of the light in the same landscape scene, east to west, will be determined by the time of day. Depending on the details in the photograph that is being repeated, both the time of day and the time of year may be critical to making a rephotograph.

In summary, accurate place-based rephotography is formulated on the principle that an earlier vantage point can be relocated with precision, regardless of camera type or output. Rephotographs made in this way can be the basis for making quantitative measurements from the photographs; they also convince viewers that the space has been matched. Replication of lighting is also an important part of this method; more than aesthetics, lighting provides viewers with clues to reading space. Together, careful replication of vantage point and lighting duplication provide the best visual evidence for monitoring changes over time through photographs and are an effective approach for projects, across disciplines. A viewer will depend on knowing that the places depicted are the same, and use that knowledge to

gauge how closely the pictures match. Thus, the level of accuracy achieved is an important conceptual as well as physical tool necessary to understanding how to read the photo pairs and in gauging the reliability of the photographic evidence. If the rephotographs are made with consistent quality, viewers will concentrate on interpreting the information the photos provide. If the methods vary in quality and approach, viewers will spend time assessing how the photos were made from different positions rather than interpreting other differences.

Pyramid Lake

An example of this method is shown in Figure 6.2, from the Third View (mentioned earlier). Again, from the Project website:

> The project's "rephotographs" were made from the originals' vantage points with as much precision as possible. Every attempt was also made to duplicate the original photographs' lighting conditions, both in time of day and year. (*The Third View Project*, 2004: *Introduction*)

The subject is Pyramid Lake, Nevada. In 1867, the original photographer, Timothy

Figure 6.2   An example of two rephotographs made using methods to accurately relocate the vantage point of an original photograph. The first photo was made in 1867 by Timothy O'Sullivan (Rock formations, Pyramid Lake, Nevada; collection of Massachusetts Institute of Technology). The second was made by Mark Klett for the Rephotographic Survey Project in 1979. The process involved photography with a large format camera (4 inch × 5 inch negative) and instant films. Measurements to verify the choice of vantage point were made comparing details that could be confirmed between photographs. The same process was used again in the second rephotograph made by Mark Klett and Byron Wolfe for Third View in 2000. The three photographs show changes in the water level of the lake, a fluctuation related to human interventions

O'Sullivan, placed his camera in an unusual and isolated position atop a 'tufa' knob, similar to those in the foreground of the photo. The closest subject was less than 10 feet away from his lens, and O'Sullivan's photograph is filled with details that can still be identified, making it an excellent candidate for accurate rephotography. The methods used are described in Klett et al. (1984) and illustrated by the interactive demonstration in *Third Views, Second Sights: A Rephotographic Survey of the American West (DVD)* (Klett et al., 2004; also available from: *www.thirdview.org*).

The rephotograph illustrates a drop of about 65 feet in the lake's water level when compared with the original, and the reasons are not explained by either image. The water coming in to the lake from the Truckee River was diverted, starting in the early twentieth century for irrigation, and the lake level was lowered as a result of water loss. The lake's Native American owners, the Pyramid Lake Indian Reservation, have litigated this loss in intervening years. The Third View photograph, *c.* 2000, shows the water partially restored to its earlier level.

APPROACH #2: WORKING WITH MULTIPLE PHOTOGRAPHS AND CREATING A CONTEXT FOR THE VIEW

As an accessible practice photography has only been around since the 1840s, making it a relative newcomer in the history of image representation. But it has also been a prolific provider of images and in the digital era their growing number bears significantly on our perspectives on the world. Given any location on earth, there is bound to be at least one photograph that covers the terrain, if even remotely, as in satellite imagery. In geographic areas hosting large populations the number of existing photographs made at ground level can be staggering. Questions regarding accessibility aside, social networking sites such as Flickr (*www.flickr.com*) and Facebook (*www.facebook.com*) provide examples of thousands of photographs made at the same locations or events and have already been the subject of testing by software makers seeking to develop engines that can sort through massive piles of visual data. Software, such as Microsoft Photosynth (see examples at *http://photosynth.net*) can sift through a large number of photographs, identify common subjects, recognize the spatial relationship of one photograph to another and piece together three-dimensional representations of the larger space based on hundreds and even tens of thousands of photographs (Agarwal et al., 2009).

The process that a software program uses to determine that one photograph is related to another is a form of rephotography done in an automated way; while it can be done by hand and eye as well, it may take much longer. Any individual photograph within a large group may be a candidate for traditional rephotography, but working with multiple photographs and sorting through large pools of images, rather than single pictures, opens up significant new possibilities. Groups of images empower relationships between photographs, invite questions about the context in which they were created, or enable a better examination of how a specific subject has been depicted through imagery. The ability to work with many photographs and edit them for specific reasons has become an important skill in an era when large numbers of photographs are becoming commonplace. The pictures may come from multiple users, commercial media, artists, or even surveillance cameras. But the specific choice of which images to use and how to put them together distinguishes the content of the work and its relevance to an audience. The next section will discuss only a few ideas related to the conventions of rephotography. But while developing technologies will undoubtedly open new possibilities for relating and combining existing photographs to the spaces they come from, it will always be the criteria used in selecting and editing these images that will matter.

Finding photographic resources

The same advances in technology that are changing how rephotographs are made in the field have also affected the way research is conducted with historic photographs. Major collections are being digitized and made accessible on the web, making thousands of pictures available to the public that were previously unknown, and enabling assessment across collections. This is especially significant when researching photographs made from a specific location. For example, many of the existing nineteenth-century survey photographs were spread out over collections nationwide. It wasn't known how many photographs were actually made of any given subject unless one traveled to these individual collections and compared detailed notes. Similar comparisons can now be made in a matter of hours at home by viewing photographs from several digital online collections at the same time. Furthermore, it's often possible to relate photographs to published reports and diaries that describe the photographer's experience or context for the view. One can also examine other photographs made by the same photographer at other locations to understand certain working techniques and personal idiosyncrasies of that photographer.

Most importantly, the availability of World Wide Web access to photographs means an important revision to the workflow linking research and fieldwork: it's now possible to download and bring more photographs into the field and compare these photos to the experience of place—that is, current geography, environment, location, and so on. Previously, this had to be done by visiting photo archives and making or ordering copy-prints of originals, work that was usually expensive and time consuming. The combination often limited the number of photographs taken into the field. By comparison, low-resolution downloads are typically free, and for an increasing number of 'important' photographs, sites like the US Library of Congress (*www.loc.gov/pictures/*) offer free downloads of high resolution (100+ mega-byte) files. And downloads can sometimes now be made on-site if a connection to the web is possible. Reviewing collections on-site may also reveal the locations of photographs that were previously unknown.

Working with multiple vantage points

Historically, some physical locations have generated more photographs than others. Places that attract photographers or cities with large populations have become focus points for disproportionately large numbers of photographs and are what might be called places of high image density. One example of an image-rich environment is Grand Canyon National Park in Arizona; with over 4 million visitors per year, it is the second most visited national park in the USA (Sullivan, 2007), and an internationally known landscape of the American West.

In the composite photograph shown in Figure 6.3, four photographs made by William Bell in 1872 appear embedded in a larger panorama of the scene near Toroweap Point on the North Rim of the Canyon. The historic photographs occupy their original positions and the contemporary view made at the same location shows the space around the photos. The combined image becomes what has been called a digital 'mashup,' a term that Wikipedia defines as 'a digital media file containing any or all of text, graphics, audio, video, and animation, which recombines and modifies existing digital works to create a derivative work ('Mashup,' 2010). We have similarly described this method as a photographic mash-up, or more formally as the 'embedded rephotograph' approach.

This method is made possible by digital image editing, whereby one photo can be placed over top of another, or made to slightly overlap the other, in a digital composite. What confirms that the photographs occupy the same space is the way the edges of one image merge with the details of the

Figure 6.3 Mark Klett and Byron Wolfe, 2008. At the Canyon's edge: from the foot of the Toroweap to the 'Devil's Anvil' overhang with an upstream view of the Colorado River. A 'nodal point' attachment was used on a tripod to create the underlying wide-angle panorama seen in the right-hand portion of this image of the Grand Canyon near Toroweap. From left to right are four 1872 photographs by William Bell made from the same tripod position and embedded into the underlying panorama (Canyon of Kanab Wash; Walls of the Grand Canyon Looking East, Colorado River; Looking South Across Grand Canyon, Colorado River; all Courtesy National Archives). The left-hand panel positions a fourth photograph made approximately 20 feet north of the others (William Bell, Canyon of Kanab Wash Looking North; Courtesy National Archives). The panel was created at an angle using photo-editing software to visually simulate its position relative to the larger panorama

other (similar to the 'stitch' feature now common on many point-and-shoot cameras). The technique is effective if the photo that is embedded seamlessly connects to the photo that appears to be 'beneath' it in space, and in order for this to happen the two must be made from at or near the same vantage point.

In this case, Bell made three of his four photographs from the same position, simply by rotating the camera on its tripod from southeast to northwest. Byron Wolfe and I were able to relocate his tripod position and recreate the three views using the standard rephotographic techniques described in the first section of this text. The vantage points for the three Bell photographs on the right and central part of the composite were nearly identical. The only difference between them was the distance the lens traveled when rotating around his tripod. It was apparent after studying the scene that the tripod itself had not been moved.

The underlying contemporary view was made by using special software to stitch

together 18 separate and detailed photographs of the scene into one large image. These photographs were made from one vantage point, which was judged the average position of Bell's three vantage points and was within inches of where he made his photographs. Unlike a simple rotation around a tripod, the stitched photographs were all made from one point using a 'nodal point' panorama attachment, a tool that attaches to the tripod and allows the camera and lens to rotate around the center of perspective for the lens. When the camera is rotated at this perspective point the resulting photographs can be stitched with great precision using software designed for the purpose. The advantage of using stitched photographs is that they allow extreme enlargement of the image while retaining exceptional detail and clarity. In the past, the only way to achieve similar quality was to use professional large-format equipment. Now, image files from any digital camera may be stitched together, though cameras and lenses using larger image sensors will produce better results.

The left-hand panel of this panorama bears mention. Bell's fourth photograph was not made from the same tripod location as the other three, and the vantage point was instead found approximately 30 feet to the north. In order to link this photograph virtually to the others, we rephotographed the view from its original vantage point, and then in the process of editing the composite placed the panel at what appears to be an angle to the main panorama, suggesting its relation in space to the other panels.

The role of rephotography in developing narrative

An example of an embedded rephotograph from Yosemite National Park, the third most visited national park in the USA with 3.7 million visitors in 2006 (Sullivan, 2007), will address another use of multiple photographs. We quickly found that while Yosemite is itself very large, the photographs that helped make the park famous tend to be clustered closely together (Klett et al., 2005). Historic photographers (discussed further below) were making views of the park's scenery and they often chose the same features as their subjects; as a result, vantage points were sometimes quite close to one another. If one were to plot the vantage points of the best-known scenic photographs on a map of Yosemite, there would be small clusters with great image densities in certain locations, and vast open areas without photographic representation throughout most of the park.

While searching for a vantage point used by one photographer, we sometimes found another vantage point nearby that was used by a second photographer from another era. Sometimes these separate photographers were photographing the same subjects, sometimes their focus was on slightly different subjects in different directions, but their framing of the views might overlap in space. Sometimes we could actually connect the views of different photographers by walking between the two vantage points. This discovery led to an adaptation of the embedded rephotograph technique and can be seen in the panorama of Lake Tenaya in Figure 6.4.

The panorama at Lake Tenaya connects three historic images to a wider panorama Byron Wolfe and I made at the scene. The large photograph on the left, made by Eadweard Muybridge in 1872, was perhaps the first photograph ever made of the lake. In the center of the panorama, an Ansel Adams photograph, *c.* 1942, of the rocks and dramatic clouds across the lake, was partially overlaid on an earlier view made by Edward Weston (1937). Each photographer, in separate trips to the lake, managed to choose vantage points that were within 20 feet of one another. Muybridge and Weston, photographing the lake some 65 years apart, were standing less than 2 feet from one another!

We were able to rephotograph each original using conventional techniques, but felt the most important thing to convey about this site was the overlapping nature of the historic photographs. We walked the distance between the three vantage points, but in the end chose one from which to base our own photographs, the widest view with the closest foreground, the vantage point used by Muybridge. Using instant film positives on a 4 inch × 5 inch view camera, we were able to plot the relationship of the three earlier photographs and create a larger panorama in which all views could be combined into a single image.

Two of the three photographs were displaced from the vantage point we chose (Muybridge's). But the act of laying the historic images on top of our contemporary view covered parts of the new image, making this position error less noticeable. The choice of embedding the historic photos also negated the capacity to compare details between first and second views. The final image composites photographs from all eras into one digital file. The methods used to make this panorama are based on the concept of

Figure 6.4 Mark Klett and Byron Wolfe, Four views from four times and one shoreline, Lake Tenaya, 2002. The left inset was taken by Eadweard Muybridge (1872); center top, Ansel Adams (*c.* 1942); inset center bottom, Edward Weston (1937). The three historical photographs were made within 20 feet of one another over a period of about 70 years. The panorama combines all photographs into one visual composite of time layers analogous to the lithographic layers of a stratigraphic rock. One way to approach rephotography of image-dense landscapes is to map the vantage points into real space. In the scene, photographer Byron Wolfe swats at the high country mosquitoes mentioned in Weston's historical account of the scene. (E. Muybridge, Mount Hoffman, Sierra Nevada Mountains. From Lake Tenaya. Number 48, courtesy of the Bancroft Library, University of California, Berkeley, California, USA; A. Adams, Tenaya Lake, Mount Conness, Yosemite National Park, courtesy of the Center for Creative Photography, Tucson, Arizona, USA; E. Weston, Lake Tenaya, courtesy of the Center for Creative Photography; M. Klett and B. Wolfe)

vantage point, but would not produce an acceptable result if quantitative information were desired when comparing the images. The composite panorama does not replace the usefulness of three more accurately made rephotographs from each original vantage point, but it does a better job of informing how the all the vantage points are related.

The composite loses some capacity for describing physical changes between photographs, but it may gain in other ways, such as an increased potential for narrative with this technique. Here, for example, a personal story accompanies the panorama, told to us by a man who was visiting the lake on the same day we made our rephotographs. Forty years earlier, he had camped with his wife in the wooded spot occupied by the trees in Muybridge's photograph. He was reliving that memory when we met him. He had returned, he said, with Park Service permission to spread her ashes there as she had died

of cancer earlier in the year. It was a poignant story of personal loss, and one that added a new layer to our mash-up of images by three famous photographers. In her essay in *Yosemite in Time: Ice Ages, Tree Clocks, Ghost Rivers* (2005), Rebecca Solnit wrote:

> Despite all those magnificent lumps of granite, this place is made out of memory, imagination, and desire, which are as tough, if not as slow to change. Scenic splendor must have brought the widower to camp in this place, but personal history is what brought him back, and it's on the return, over the long run, that meaning transforms a place into a ritual site or into home. (Klett et al., 2005)

Our desire for this project was to see Yosemite as a place that photographs had helped shape in the minds of viewers, whether they had been visitors or not, and to revisualize the Park's iconic imagery as a layered mix of time, cultural representation, and personal stories. This particular example also describes a multi-faceted history of photographic representation, bridging a historical divide between the era of exploration and the period of high Modernism. The addition of the widower's story alters this perspective by adding a personal layer to the record. It's a reminder that each time the lake is visited, a new layer may be added to its collective history. Our work also revealed the changes that have occurred to some of Yosemite's natural environments. So for our purposes, both methods of making rephotographs were useful, in combination, on this project, even though the expectations for the results were different for each type of rephotograph. Both involved accurate relocation of vantage points, but one technique was useful in visualizing physical changes; the other, by embedding historic photographs, had clear advantages for reaching the goal of revisualizing the Park's cultural history. The embedded technique opened the visual record to a broad range of interpretations and enabled the addition of different historical and personal narratives. The pictures became less about an exact description of place and change, and more about context for the views.

Summary: rephotography using multiple photographs and creating a context for the view

The second approach involves relocating the vantage point of an original photograph in a manner similar to the first method. Here, the purpose is not to duplicate the original precisely, but rather to expand the context surrounding the two views. Techniques for repeating the original image are less focused on duplicating the original's exact location than with placing either the earlier or newer works in relationship to other photographs and the larger space. Digital techniques allow smaller photographs to be embedded into a larger photograph at or near the same vantage point, with the effect of showing what surrounds the smaller view. A new panorama

made from that vantage point may show a wider angle of view, and may host an embedded original.

Variations include embedding a smaller second view into a larger original photograph, reversing the order of which image, old or new, is embedded; or placing a newly made photograph side-by-side or overlapped with an original photograph to form a continuous scene where the features of one image flow seamlessly into the next. In fact, the exact techniques used may be altered to meet the demands of the situation and not in response to a consistent framework. This approach will only work if the embedded photograph 'fits' seamlessly into the scene, something that requires the vantage points for the two photographs to be the same or nearly the same, and it relies upon digital technologies to edit the resulting composite.

Embedded photographs may connect separate photos from multiple vantage points into one scene or combine photographs made at different times into overlapping layers. It becomes a useful technique to convey narratives and/or stories related to or in support of the view. It is also useful for comparing and contrasting views across time periods.

NEW TECHNIQUES USEFUL FOR VISUALIZING REPHOTOGRAPHS: DIGITAL INTERACTIVE MEDIA AND THE THIRD VIEW PROJECT

The Third View project (1997–2000) attempted to repeat Western American survey photographs dating from the 1860s to 1870s along with a set of rephotographs made of these originals by the Rephotographic Survey Project (RSP). The RSP worked between 1977 and 1979 to precisely repeat the first photographs of the American West made by photographers such as Timothy O'Sullivan, William Henry Jackson, J. K. Hillers, and others (Klett et al., 1984). Essentially, the Third View project's job was to create a second set of rephotographs based on the original survey pictures, but also to reinterpret the ideas and methods developed by the first rephotographic project. The project began on the twentieth anniversary of the RSP and, by design, attempted to address questions raised by limitations of the first project's approaches. The new project field team explored technological advances that made it possible to collect new data in the field, as well as to solve to the problem of displaying multiple rephotographs.

Third View's methodology began with the conventional approach of precisely repeating vantage point and lighting; these were the same methods used to make the first set of rephotographs for the RSP. A view camera was used for the photography, and test shots were made onto instant film just as they were 20 years earlier for the RSP. Measurements were taken between copy-prints and the instant print and then compared to calculate the most accurate placement of the camera (Klett et al., 2004). In the case of discrepancies between first- and second-view vantage points, the Third View images were based on the vantage points of those made by the RSP. Departures from the earlier project and the introduction of new methods came after the precision rephotographs were made. New photographs of the landscape were taken to show the scene surrounding the original vantage point. Video footage recorded the journeys to the field locations and the team's experiences at those locations. Ambient sounds were recorded, and oral history interviews were conducted and recorded with people connected to those sites. Team members' personal photographs, made-for-computer animations and panoramas were added to show what was 'behind the camera' or outside of the picture frame. Contemporary artifacts (not of antique or archaeological value) were also collected at some locations. Each piece was chosen for its relation to the larger whole. The goal was to capture the experiences of the team at that site, and to provide context for how the rephotographs were made.

Third View was as much interested in the narrative of the journey as it was in adding to the documentation of the West. The project was conceived as an updated version of the traditional Western geographical survey, only rather than exploring unknown territory, the field team re-explored the once open spaces of the West, now transformed into home to millions of inhabitants. Besides physical changes, the project was equally concerned with the evolving perception of place and the shifting mythologies of the West of the imagination, as well as the evolving concerns of documentary photographic practice.

The fieldwork collected a large array of visual and aural documents. These could only be combined by editing the content into some form of an electronic presentation. The project launched the website with many of the less memory-intensive works, but it was not ideal for showing the large volume of content created. The fully edited materials were presented via an interactive DVD that was published and included with a hardbound book (Klett et al., 2004). Viewers of the DVD were given access to a full range of digital files, including video footage, text, interviews, and sound clips, with still images that connect places to events, people, and ideas.

In addition, there were several significant changes to the techniques used to view rephotographs themselves. Perhaps the most simple but effective technique used by Third View was a blended overlay of one image dissolving into the next. Photos at each time interval were sized and aligned using photo-editing software, and the images were then placed into a single window and made to dissolve into one another by clicking with the computer mouse. By constantly changing the view from one to the next and back, specific places in each photograph could be compared. This technique was a useful way to see three views together: rather than displaying the rephotographs side by side, this concept took up less space per page. (However, we also found that it required a greater degree of precision in making the rephotographs. If the new photographs were not remade exactly from the originals' vantage point, or if the lighting was significantly different between photos, the changes between the dissolves became immediately recognizable and distracting).

In addition to the simple dissolve between photographs, project programmer and designer Byron Wolfe created a novel way to compare and view selected parts of the rephotographic sets. By creating a mask that acts like a moveable window, the overlapped rephotographs also offer a 'Time Reveal' that places a view from one time period on top of

another (Figure 6.5). A viewer is able to choose the time period revealed in this moving window (from first, second, or third views) as well as that of the underlying photograph. The window appears to float on top of the photograph beneath it and is moved by grabbing and dragging it across the screen with the computer mouse. The Time Reveal window has proved the project's most dramatic way to visualize time.

Besides the Time Reveal tool, each rephotographic set offers other options for viewers, including a magnifying glass to enlarge details in each photo. The magnifier helps

Timothy O'Sullivan, 1872. Green River Buttes, Green River, Wyo. (United States Geological Survey)

First View   Second View   Third View

Close   Auto: OFF   Time Reveal   Magnify   Color: ON

Figure 6.5   The 'Time Reveal' window from the Third View project's interactive DVD. The information taken at one time period may be seen as through a window floating on top of the same location at a different time period. In this case, the window shows a house that is part of the rephotograph made in 1997 at Green River, Wyoming, as it appears in the window on top of the scene as originally photographed by Timothy O'Sullivan in 1872. Different time periods may be selected in either the reveal window or base photograph below

alleviate one problem with viewing photographs on computer screens: their relative coarseness and lack of fine detail. In order to enable the magnifying glass, we scanned images at twice the normal resolution for screen viewing, and then deployed the magnifier, which accesses the enlarged version of the photograph.

Each rephotograph is displayed in a window with additional controls at the bottom of the screen. One button allows viewers to turn color versions of the photographs on or off. The photos may be seen in monochrome or as full-color versions. Other buttons turn sound recordings on and off where available. The sound often recorded at sites ranged from ambient noise to recorded interviews.

Each site rephotographed by Third View included a panorama made at the original vantage point. The panoramas are basic versions of embedded rephotographs. The visibility of the historic photographs can be turned off and on using a mouse-controlled switch. The panorama can also be enlarged or reduced in scale, and navigation left or right is possible in the up/down and left/right screen.

Geography was used as the primary navigation interface for the project. A map of the Western states was used to display colored dots that indicate active locations (Figure 6.6).

When rolled over with the computer mouse, these sites reveal photographs that bring

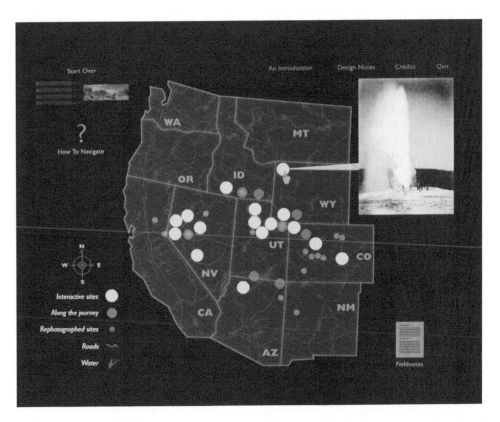

Figure 6.6   The map of the Western states used by the Third View DVD's 'Journey' section is a geographically based navigation device. Rolling over the enlarged colored dots triggers a photograph to appear, and clicking on the dot brings the user to that site location

viewers to those specific site locations. Some locations contain multiple rephotographs along with other materials. The site locations are displayed as photographs that act as 'hot' buttons to take viewers further into the program. The buttons are aligned in linear fashion, with a slider used as the navigation device to scroll through the choices.

The interface allows viewers access to all the materials the project offers as part of the 'Journey' section of the DVD, and also contains an 'Archive' feature. The database is a selection available upon first opening the disk on the computer. If viewers only wish to research the project's photographs, they can search based on location, title, keywords, photographer, and other parameters.

Taken together, the features of the Third View interactive disk represented a new approach to presenting rephotographs. In the meantime, although it wasn't possible to put the more memory-intensive material on a website originally, this has changed due to increases in processing and online access speeds; it is now possible to put most, if not all, of the project's content on the web. While publishing the photographs in this way does not replace the need for printed versions of the work, it significantly increases the exposure and accessibility of the work.

Since the Third View DVD was published in 2004, the software needed to combine media and make interactive programs has changed: that is the nature of digital media, and the actual software used to create the Third View disk is no longer available. New software will allow for improved interactivity between users and the material, but project results depend not upon specific software but on ideas enabled by any new technology. The purpose of Third View's DVD was to challenge the ways geographic change was visualized, and to provide a new context for the historic survey photographs and their sites. The content was meant to withstand the 'bells and whistles' of changing media over time, by emphasizing content and ideas over technology. To the degree that it succeeded, the content will remain pertinent even when the technology itself is dated.

THE FUTURE WILL BE DIFFERENT, AND THE SAME

Photography has always been a medium in transition and based on changing technologies. In recent years, the pace of change has quickened and it can be assumed that the materials and methods for making photographs in general and rephotographs in particular will continue to change along with the medium. But rephotography is based on the principles of how lenses describe and capture space, and these basics have not changed since camera systems were introduced well over a century ago. The fundamentals of choosing vantage points will not change and new technologies will not end the need to gather new information, visualize the world, or discover new perspectives from photographic images.

Content as diverse as text, sound, video, and still images can now also be combined, along with rephotographs, to create truly integrated presentations. Interactive approaches using digital technologies enable seemingly incompatible types and formats of data to be collected and used together. Organizing this material presents a new challenge that accentuates content over media type, and emphasizes the experience of the work as a way to discover the work's content. If done well the results can add layers of meaning and accessibility to photographs, extending their audience and reaching across disciplines. Then the old problem that photographs alone cannot explain their histories has found a new solution.

REFERENCES

Agarwal, S., Snavely, N., Simon, I., Seitz, S. and Szeliski, R. (2009) 'Building Rome in a day'.

Paper presented at the 2009 IEEE 12th International Conference on Computer Vision, Kyoto, Japan.

Fagre, D. B. and McKeon, L. A. (2010) 'Documenting disappearing glaciers: Repeat photography at Glacier National Park, Montana, USA', *Repeat Photography: Methods and Applications in the Natural Sciences*. Covelo, CA: Island Press.

Hanks, T. C., Blair, J. L. and Webb, R. (2010) 'Virtual repeat photography', *Repeat Photography: Methods and Applications in the Natural Sciences*. Covelo, CA: Island Press.

Harrison, A. E. (1974) 'Reoccupying unmarked camera stations for geological observations', *Geology*, 2: 469–471.

Hastings, R. H. and Turner, R. M. (1965) *The Changing Mile*. Tucson, AZ: University of Arizona Press.

Hoffman, T. M. and Todd, S. W. (2010) 'Using fixed-point photography, field surveys, and GIS to monitor environmental change in Riemvasmaak, South Africa. *Repeat Photography: Methods and Applications in the Natural Sciences*. Covelo, CA: Island Press.

Kinder, M. and Roth, M. (2005) (eds.) Labyrinth Project. *Cultivating Pasadena: From Roses to Redevelopment (DVD)*. CA: USC—Annenberg Center for Communications.

Klett, M., Manchester, E., Verburg, J., Bushaw, G., Dingus, R. and Berger, P. (1984) *Second View: The Rephotographic Survey Project*. Albuquerque, NM: University of New Mexico Press.

Klett, M., Bajakian, K., Fox, W. L., Marshall, M., Ueshina, T. and Wolfe, B. (2004) *Third Views, Second Sights: A Rephotographic Survey of the American West (with Interactive DVD)*. Santa Fe, NM: Museum of New Mexico Press.

Klett, M., Solnit, R. and Wolfe, B. G. (2005) *Yosemite in Time: Ice Ages, Tree Clocks, Ghost Rivers*. San Antonio, TX: Trinity University Press.

Levere, D. (2005) *New York Changing*. New York: Princeton Architectural Press.

Malde, H. E. (1973) 'Geologic bench marks by terrestrial photography', *Journal of Research of the U.S. Geological Survey*, 1: 193–206.

Mashup (digital). In *Wikipedia, The Free Encyclopedia*. [Online]. Available from: http://en.wikipedia.org/wiki/Mashup_(digital). [Accessed 29 September 2010].

Rogers, G. F., Malde, H. E. and Turner, R. M. (1984) *Bibliography of Repeat Photography for Evaluating Landscape Change*. Salt Lake City, UT: University of Utah Press.

Sullivan, J. (2007) *Top 10 Most Visited National Parks*, [Online] *National Parks Traveler* Available from: http://www.nationalparkstraveler.com/2007/07/top-10-most-visited-national-parks. [Accessed 29 September 2010].

Rosier, B. (2004) *Un état des lieux, ou la mémoire des parallèles*. Lyon: Lieux Dits.

The Third View Project (2004) *Introduction* [Online]. Available from: http://www.thirdview.org/3v/home/index.html [Accessed 28 September 2010].

Vale, T. R. and Vale, G. R. (1983) *US 40 Today, Thirty Years of Landscape Change in America*. Madison, WI: University of Wisconsin Press.

7

Rephotography for Documenting Social Change[1]

Jon H. Rieger

INTRODUCTION

The employment of temporally ordered photographs to show change has been a common practice for many years. Sociologists have long been interested in studying change—in particular, *social change*—but have not until recently developed methods for harnessing photographs to study it. In this chapter, I describe several ways in which photographs may be used in documenting social change and in fostering the development of insights about the meaning and significance of that change.

PHOTOGRAPHS AS SOCIOLOGICAL EVIDENCE

Research on a complex phenomenon such as social change almost inevitably requires the use of *indicators*. We gauge social change by examining a variety of things, such as changes in population, employment, and other statistics; in attitudes, opinions, and social practices; and in the physical size, character, layout, and condition of the built landscape.

These material and non-material variables fit together in a form that we recognize as the social structure. The interconnections between the variables mean that changes in one facet of the structure typically lead to changes in others. Many elements of social structure are literally on display. They include physical and behavioral markers accessible to the eye, and therefore to the camera. My challenge as a visual sociologist has been to find the visual indicators of change. From this standpoint, a visual approach differs from other approaches only in that I am using *visual* indicators (in addition, usually, to other, more common ones) to help form a basis for analysis and interpretation (Rieger, 1996).

As I have suggested above, the usefulness of visual evidence depends on drawing information from the images that can form the basis of interpretations about what is happening socially. We have to examine every part of the image, not only the nominal subject of the photograph but also the details in the background and near the edges of the picture for clues pertinent to our analysis.

THE USE OF REPEAT PHOTOGRAPHY

Perhaps the most reliable way we can use photography to study social change is through the systematic visual measurement technique of 'repeat photography' or, simply, 'rephotography.' These terms refer to a process by which we create a temporally ordered, that is, *longitudinal*, photographic record of a particular place, social group, or other phenomenon. We then review the photographs for evidence of change. Here we confront the same issues of evaluation and interpretation that are encountered in reviewing other kinds of evidence, such as statistical data. A numerical change may reach the level of 'statistical significance,' but that does not necessarily determine its substantive significance. Likewise, photographs may reveal some change that may or may not be substantively significant. In interpreting either visual or quantitative data, we must ascertain their meaning and importance in terms of their consistency with other evidence and its bearing on the theory guiding our research.

REPEAT PHOTOGRAPHY AS A METHODOLOGY

As I have shown above, the logic of repeat photography is similar to more conventional approaches to the study of change. Measurements—in this case, photographs—are taken at successive points in time, which we designate *Time 1* and *Time 2*. We compare the content of the photographs, looking for evidence of change in a manner similar to survey data in panel studies. The change, or lack of change, that the photographs reveal we then interpret in accordance with our theoretical expectations.

Repeat photographs may be used in both quantitative and qualitative studies. We can employ photographs in quantitative measurement, for example, as William Whyte did to gauge the changing size of crowds in small urban spaces (Whyte, 1980). Whyte's procedure was to set up automatic equipment in a strategic location—say, an upper story window—to photograph in time-lapse fashion a particular location, such as a street corner, a plaza, mini-park, a market, or even a bus stop. The photographs provided an ongoing census of those locations, showing the rhythm of their use and pattern of occupancy. More frequently, though, we are likely to use repeat photographs to study change in a qualitative way. We will be looking for obvious or subtle clues about the changing character of social life.

To make meaningful comparisons possible, we have to maintain some element of *continuity*. Continuity may reside in the fact that the photographs were of the same scene, or because they trace the experience of the same or similar participants, or because they follow the development of a particular function, activity, or process over time.

While a pair of temporally ordered photographs (at Time 1 and Time 2) would generally be the minimum we would need in using this method, we can take photographs at additional points (Time 3, Time 4, and so on), producing a more extensive record of change. If we take a series of photographs that is continuous or nearly so, as in 'time-lapse' photography, we may actually record change as it takes place.

REPHOTOGRAPHING PLACES

The most basic strategy we can use in studying social change visually is to rephotograph sites or things that we (or others) have previously documented. In my study of social change in Ontonagon County, a rural area in the western part of Michigan's Upper Peninsula, my approach was to systematically document the 'built environment.' In 1970, I took a series of baseline (Time 1) photos that showed the main streets, businesses, schools, and residences in the small communities in the study area. In 1985, I completed the first set of repeat photographs of these places, and took new pictures of some additional places in the area. Although the time gap in my pictures was just 15 years, the change that had occurred in Ontonagon County was profound. The area had visibly shifted from an expansionary mode to one of decline. The following pair of photographs (Figures 7.1 and 7.2) show change that is emblematic of the type I saw in many places around Ontonagon County. This study of social change in Ontonagon County has continued to the present with repeat visual surveys every 5 years.

REPHOTOGRAPHING PARTICIPANTS

A second strategy of rephotography exploits the continuity provided, not by a specific site of a photograph, but by the experience of the human participants in the social change process. In this approach, our objective is to track the witnesses. The participants' biographies and experiences become the linkage between temporally ordered contexts and events.

My implementation of this kind of approach came in my attempts to reconstruct the history of growth and decline of a small community named Trout Creek in a remote portion of southeastern Ontonagon County. This community had been a robust lumber milling town through the early and middle parts of the twentieth century, but had declined to a remnant of its former self by the 1970s. When I began my inquiries, I discovered that the residents had made or preserved very few records that would afford an insight into life as it had been in Trout Creek. Most of the community's facilities had decayed or disappeared entirely. By the 1980s, only a bar and a small general store

Figure 7.1   Rockland, Michigan, 1970. This small community had a small business district and its own post office, township government, and school system in the late 1960s. Although Rockland had no commercial lodging facilities, it did have two grocery stores, two saloons, a restaurant, and a gas station. © 1970 Jon H. Rieger

Figure 7.2   Rockland, Michigan, 1985. By 1985, Rockland had lost four of its six businesses, its school was closing, and at least a portion of its population had left. It had really lost its 'center of gravity' and was now more nearly a residential subdivision of Ontonagon, about 12 miles to the northwest. © 1985 Jon H. Rieger

remained of what had once been a fairly complete complement of main street businesses and services. The railroad through the town had been abandoned and even the state highway that ran through the center of town had been rerouted around its periphery. The school had been closed and the few school-age children were bussed to Ewen, about 20 miles to the west. Eventually, even the bar burned down and the small store remained only intermittently in business.

It was my good fortune to acquire a copy of a photograph (Figure 7.3) of a local family made by Farm Security Administration (FSA) photographer John Vachon in 1941 as he passed through Trout Creek en route from the Keweenaw to an assignment in Minnesota. I was able to learn the identity of the family in the nearly 60-year-old picture and to connect with surviving members of that family, the Carlisles.

This family had resided in Trout Creek since around 1911, fairly early in the community's history. It had been a large family, with nine children. Some of the seven surviving children at the time of the Vachon photograph were already adults with children of their own. The Carlisles' family home shown in the Vachon photograph was located in 'Milltown,' a neighborhood where the poorest workers resided.

From interviews with local residents, I learned that the Carlisles were one of the 'core' families in Trout Creek, not because of their wealth or prominent standing, but because they were a big family that gained a reputation as solid, reliable, hard-working, and respectable people. The Carlisles apparently participated in nearly every aspect of village life and were well-known by people of the town. The centrality of the Carlisle family made its members apt informants

Figure 7.3   Residents of Trout Creek, Michigan, 1941 (John Vachon). This photograph was taken in August 1941 by FSA photographer John Vachon, who drove through town on a Sunday afternoon on the unpaved Mill Road and stopped when he saw this family lounging outside their house. Source: Library of Congress

about the dynamics of the town's growth and decline (Rieger, 2004).

In addition to the Vachon photograph, I found other key historical photographs in local family picture albums: a picture of the mill work force from around 1952 (which included four men from the Carlisle family who were employees); another photograph that showed the inaugural members of the Trout Creek Volunteer Fire Department (including a Carlisle son); and a picture taken of a military honor guard at the local cemetery (not surprisingly, including a Carlisle as a participant, one of several Carlisles who had served in the military). Multiple school yearbooks also turned up. Even a recent snapshot of the community's centennial reunion organizing committee (that contained no fewer than four members of the extended Carlisle family as participants) helped form a

visual documentary foundation for reconstructing the community's history.

These and other photos, including pictures I myself had made over the period since 1970, along with various artifacts, became the basis for extensive photo-elicitation interviews with the Carlisles and other members of the community. While I cannot be sure, I believe that with the collection of photographs and artifacts serving as anchor points—in effect a *de facto* community archive—I was able to reconstruct the saga of growth and decline in Trout Creek about as well as any that could be produced under the prevailing circumstances (Rieger, 2006). I took new photographs of the Carlisles and others in their present contexts: one of the Carlisles who was in the Vachon photograph was still living in the ancestral house (Figure 7.4).

Figure 7.4   Carlisle family home with Gilda and Everett, 1999. Gilda (Carlisle) Russell and Everett Carlisle pose next to the family home originally photographed by John Vachon in 1941. Everett still lives in this house, in which he grew up. The house has obviously undergone much remodeling over the years. © 1999 Jon H. Rieger

REPHOTOGRAPHING ACTIVITIES, PROCESSES, OR FUNCTIONS

Sometimes the link between successive points in time lies not in a specific site or object, nor in the lives of individuals, but in some particular *process*, *activity*, or *function*. We might want to track an institutional process, such as education, or trace people's changing levels of living, as shown, for example, in the kinds of houses they live in. Or we might follow the evolution of a group's leisure activities. Such phenomena are quite basic in social life, and photography offers a means for documenting both their persistence and their changing incarnations over time. Here the camera is an especially powerful tool of measurement.

An example of using photography in studying changes in a process came in a study

I did of the pulp wood industry in Ontonagon County (Rieger, 2003). Cutting pulp wood for the local brown paper mill has been an important secondary industry in the Ontonagon area for many decades, but the technology and organization of woods work changed radically after World War II. In investigating the way woods work was done, I discovered that change came to every aspect of the process—from which trees were cut, how they were cut, gathered, hauled out of the woods, prepared for transport to the mill or, more recently, processed into chips on site. Photographic documentation of the changing procedures and equipment became an essential strategy in tracing the evolution of the woods work process in this setting. Photographs were not only essential in recording how the work was done and how it changed but also in reporting the research

Figures 7.5 and 7.6　Harvesting trees in Ontonagon County, 1986–90. At left, a logger cuts a notch on the side toward which he wants the tree to fall, after which he will slice through from the opposite side. At right, a feller-buncher moves on a large, heavy crawler base only partially visible in the deep snow, harvesting trees literally by the bunch. The machine can shear a tree off in 8 seconds and hold up to a half-a-dozen trees in the fixture before the operator deposits them in a pile for later pick-up. © 1986–90 Jon H. Rieger

findings in a comprehensible way. A pair of photographs (Figures 7.5 and 7.6) show the change in how trees were cut ('harvested') for the manufacture of pulp for paper-making.

These two photographs trace the change in just one facet of the woods industry in Northwest Michigan. Many people might at least have some idea of how a chain saw works and how a tree can be taken down with one, but very few who are not familiar with this industry have ever seen a massive feller-buncher in action or could imagine the power and speed with which such machinery can harvest trees. The transformation in this industry had big consequences for those employed in it. At the same time that it was

greatly adding to the volume of material delivered to the mill, mechanization was steadily reducing the number of workers needed to produce it.

An example of tracking an activity or function comes from my study of community change in Ontonagon County. In this case, I was attempting to document a 'teenage hangout' in Ontonagon Village. In 1970, I had photographed 'Cue and Cushion,' the then popular place in town for teenagers to hang around and kill time (Figure 7.7), located on the main street at the southeast end of the business district.

In the first follow-up documentation in 1985, I noticed that the building housing the

Figure 7.7   Cue and Cushion, River Street, Ontonagon, Michigan, 1970. This popular place for teenagers to 'hang out' offered pool tables and an assortment of soft drinks and some food items. © 1970 Jon H. Rieger

original hangout had been converted into an insurance office. Since I thought that the motivation among teenagers to find or cultivate some place to gather was probably pretty irrepressible, the challenge was simply to find the replacement for Cue and Cushion. What new form would it take? I eventually discovered that the new hangout was at the opposite end of the main street, at something called 'Sip and Snack' (Figure 7.8).

This location was noticeably less accommodating than Cue and Cushion had been. Furthermore, it was functional only during the summer when the ice cream shop was in operation, and certainly inconvenient when it rained. But it was all the teenagers had for the time being. Eventually, the owner of the ice cream shop made some concessions to the young people and others who hung around by placing sitting benches up and down the sidewalk adjacent to the little shop.

This example traces the persistence of a community activity or function and the various incarnations of that phenomenon that arise. Sip and Snack was eventually replaced as a teenage hangout by a new sandwich shop which opened almost directly across the street from the original location of Cue and Cushion. That sandwich shop, which at least offered indoor respite from the elements, has very recently closed and been replaced by a video store in the same space. The prospect is that this location will continue to serve the need of teenagers for a place to gather.

ALTERNATIVE STRATEGIES

Studying social change visually is a challenge under even the best of conditions, where the researcher has the opportunity to

Figure 7.8   Sip and Snack, River Street, Ontonagon, Michigan, 1985. This little business had not really attracted teenagers as a place to gather until Cue and Cushion closed. Sip and Snack was open only seasonally, it offered no shelter from the weather and, at the start, no convenient seating. © 1985 Jon H. Rieger

track change as it unfolds—to observe the process, interview participants, produce images, and collect other evidence essential to a sound understanding of the nature and significance of the change. The ideal way— and the strictest, methodologically—to study social change visually is *prospectively*; that is, where we can begin our study at Time 1. Using that approach, we choose what we want to study and proceed to make our initial visual measurements (Time 1), after which we wait for some period of time and then make our Time 2 measurements. We can continue by repeating the measurements at Time 3, and so on. But sometimes the change we want to study may have already occurred, or it is presently underway and we cannot wait until it has reached a state of finality. In those situations it is sometimes possible, by making certain compromises in procedure, to

study change in such a way as to approximate the results that could be gained from using a stricter regimen.

RETROSPECTIVE STUDIES

If we want to study change retrospectively, that is, where Time 1 has already passed, it is sometimes possible to reconstruct the conditions that existed at Time 1 by finding photographs that were taken in the past and which might serve as a proxy for Time 1 measurements. We use that earlier documentation as a baseline and make the new Time 2 photos, thus approximating the procedure outlined above for prospective research. While the two approaches are not logically different, the practical difficulties of studying visual change retrospectively can be quite daunting. This strategy depends on the quality of surviving images and other evidence which is not under our control.

Certain factors make studying social change retrospectively attractive. In the first place, nowadays there are many repositories, both public and private, that have collected vast quantities of historical photographs, many of which may appear to be amenable for use in a study like that we might want to undertake. Second, studying social change prospectively involves a potentially long, hard-to-predict wait for things to change, and with the typical cycle of our work in the social sciences, the prospect of such delays in getting 'results' tends to make such research unappealing.

Despite the serious potential problems of depending on salvaged photographs, it is often feasible to make retrospective studies work. I confronted this challenge in doing my study of the transformation of the pulp wood industry around Ontonagon County. By the time I noticed that the industry was undergoing a conversion to mechanization— with all the implications that this change had for the people who had long toiled in the woods—the change was already largely complete. Time 1 was long past. Photo-documenting the equipment and procedures in the woods at Time 2 (the present) took me less than a month of fieldwork, but nearly 7 years elapsed while I tried to reconstruct and understand the industry's past. And my attempts to find photographs that showed all of the details of how woods work was done in the industry in earlier times were not completely successful.

In spite of years of searching, I was never able to turn up a historical photograph of the 'peeling' process or the particular tool used to do this work. Since this was an integral part of woods procedure for more than two generations, and because the tool used, known as a 'spud,' was typically an item that was not manufactured, but homemade, it demanded documentation. Here I engaged in a methodological innovation: a semi-retired logger took me out into the woods, cut down a tree, and demonstrated peeling the bark off the log with a spud while I took photographs (Figures 7.9 and 7.10).

To what degree may such a strategy—a re-enactment of the process studied—suffice in lieu of contemporaneous documentation? In the present case, the re-enactment exhibited certain limitations. It took place in the summer rather than in the spring when the work photographed would normally have taken place. In a real-woods operation, other members of the crew besides the sawyer would have been present, providing an opportunity to capture the woods craft as the dynamic social process that it was. Notwithstanding these shortcomings, in this instance the re-enactment photographs provided useful and essential information. In some situations a re-enactment may not be possible, if there is no one still around who can authentically carry out such a demonstration.

CROSS-SECTIONAL STUDIES

Where we want to study ongoing change but are restricted to collecting data at a single time, we may employ another common methodological compromise, a cross-sectional design. In this approach, we photograph many individual instances of the broader social change we are documenting, each at a different stage in that process. By collecting the examples into a group and, perhaps, putting them in an appropriate sequence, we construct a facsimile of the larger social change process, and ask the reader to accept it as an approximation of what longitudinal evidence would show. As with other applications of the cross-sectional method, this procedure is not without difficulties, prominent among which is the lack of a firm determination of what the 'final' stage of the social change process might look like and when it might be reached.

I used such a strategy in a study of the changing structure of rural residence

Figures 7.9 and 7.10   Debarking a felled pulp tree in Ontonagon County, 1990. Using a 'peeling spud,' a logger demonstrates debarking a tree. With a chain saw cut along the length, he can insert the tool under the bark and pry it off, first from one side, then the other. This demonstration was done in July: peeling is easier in the spring when the sap is flowing amply—the bark will separate readily and often pop off in a single piece, like a stiff wrapper. © 1990 Jon H. Rieger

(Rieger, 1982). The growth of the rural non-farm population and the relative decline of the farm population in rural America have been very gradual, but this change has progressed to the point that the farm segment is now actually a relatively small minority of the total US rural population. Nevertheless, the popular perception of rural residents as mostly farmers continues. I wanted to document this important but little-noticed demographic and structural change in the rural Midwest.

I visited rural areas in eight states (Iowa, Missouri, Wisconsin, Illinois, Michigan, Indiana, Kentucky, and Ohio), interviewing residents to get a better understanding of the ongoing demographic transformation and to determine which residences were occupied by farm or non-farm people. I recorded key details of the histories of these sites and also photographed them. Eventually, I accumulated more than 300 cases, spread throughout the eight states, and was able to get some insight into the pattern of social change.

The non-farm residents in the rural population are spread out through the landscape. They are hidden in plain sight. They live in small towns and in older houses in the open country, in new houses and rural subdivisions, in roadside businesses, converted former farmhouses, converted barns, old schoolhouses, and even former gas stations. A good number live in house trailers, either in solo locations or in mobile home parks.

Figure 7.11 *Little Sport* service station, Hancock County, Kentucky, 1981. This station, built around 1969, sits next to a large farm. The owner and his family live in the mobile home behind the station. © 1981 Jon H. Rieger

My collection of photographs is a kaleidoscope of the many forms that this change has taken, much of it still ongoing. The images are like frames in a moving picture of what is happening in rural areas of the US Midwest. Figure 7.11 is an example from this study.

PHOTOGRAPHS AS PART OF A COMPREHENSIVE APPROACH

In implementing the visual approach, our objective must be to build up a comprehensive photographic record, buttressed by interviews and field notes. Pictures alone, like other indices, are hazardous to interpret without the contextual reinforcement of other information gathered in the field situation. Furthermore, sociologists who use photographs in the presentation of their research generally combine them with written commentary, just as they do when they use statistical forms of evidence, such as tables or graphs. The photographs are not expected to stand alone, without interpretation or explanation, any more than are graphs or tables. The words and pictures reinforce each other in communicating our insights and discoveries.

In the foregoing discussion, I have attempted to show how photography can be effectively brought to bear on the study of social change. I described several approaches to using photographs in illuminating the social process and revealing the direction and character of social change. When used in conjunction with other sociological investigative methods, photographs can strengthen our research. Photographs are valuable both as a tool of discovery and in the presentation of our findings. But their utility is not without limits, and even pitfalls. In the next section, I will review the strengths and weaknesses of investigating social change with photographs.

THE STRENGTHS OF THE VISUAL APPROACH

In studying social change, recording the present state of things provides us with a baseline for repeat inventories in the future. These make possible the comparisons that will help us determine the extent of any changes that have occurred. Photography is well-suited to this process because of its capacity to record a scene with far greater speed and completeness than could ever be accomplished by a human observer taking notes. Visual changes can be very subtle or so complex that they are virtually impossible to document adequately without the use of a camera, which permits 'freezing' a scene in extraordinary detail. Furthermore, photography can often be used in a relatively expeditious manner compared with more conventional approaches, with little practical limitation on the number of photographs that can be made of the scene or phenomenon we are studying. Digital technology has made photography especially cheap, convenient, and effective, with its capacity for 'field editing' of the pictures, and its exceptional facility in securing usable images under marginal lighting conditions. With photography we can make a more complete, reliable, and comprehensive record of the change process than we could without it.

One of the most felicitous advantages brought to social research by the use of photographs is in facilitating interviewing as a data-gathering method. My success in reconstructing the rise and fall of Trout Creek depended heavily on the effectiveness of my photo-elicitation interviews (Collier and Collier, 1986) with my informants. The photographs fostered the flow of information from my subjects in a relatively non-threatening way. Because the scrutiny and discussion soon shifted to the images, my interviewees became guides to understanding and interpreting the pictorial record. The pictures stimulated revelations that might not otherwise have occurred and the interviews were less stressful and fatiguing for

my interview subjects. The photographs I used in such interviews varied from snapshots in family albums to those that I or my subjects had themselves taken. Pictures used for photo-elicitation do not even need to be 'good' photographs in an aesthetic sense.

LIMITATIONS AND PITFALLS IN THE VISUAL APPROACH

Notwithstanding the great value of photographs in social research, and specifically in the study of social change, they also exhibit limitations and their use can involve some significant pitfalls. We know that visual change and social change are generally related, and we can often draw useful insights about what is happening within the social structure from a careful analysis of visual evidence. Likewise, we may be able to predict visual changes from prior knowledge of social structural dynamics. But the connection between visual change and social change is not simple and linear: visual and social phenomena do not co-vary in a uniform way. Visual change can actually precede social change, as when a natural catastrophe—a tornado or flood—strikes a community. Photographs of such events show the great physical impact of natural forces. The social changes triggered include not only immediate behavioral reactions but also other, longer-term social structural adaptations. Visual change can also lag behind social change. When a community has just suffered a major plant closing, the only immediate visual effect of the event may be the idleness of the plant itself and its former workers. Only with the passage of time might the full consequence of the closing become evident visually—in the general decline of the community.

The strength of the relationship between visual and social change also varies: some visual changes seem to have little social significance, and there are social changes that may not have very obvious or prominent visual manifestations. All of these limitations must be kept in mind when attempting to use photographic images in the study of social change.

Another limitation bearing on the use of photographs in studying social change actually pervades all of our research, and that is the serious lack of predictive power of our sociological theories. More than 100 years of sociological research has not yielded theories that can reliably predict the future. In my work in Ontonagon County, the gradual realization of this shortcoming had a practical consequence: I could not afford to concentrate my photographic documentation just on those particular aspects of community life, or those specific locations in the county, where I thought change would occur. In the early years, I had thought that documenting a sampling of sites around the county would provide an adequate 'baseline' for gauging later change. With the inadequacy of that approach becoming clearer, I increased the number of sites recorded in my visual surveys from about 110 to more 500. Since I couldn't be sure where or what kind of change might occur (or even if any change would occur at all), the only feasible strategy was, essentially, to photograph *everything*. In the Ontonagon project this meant that the quintennial survey now takes me nearly 6 weeks, even with the help of an assistant. The importance of comprehensive documentation applies to many kinds of sociological research, especially where the focus is on a complex process, such as social change, in which many variables may be in play and the effects we are looking for can be quite broad.

In any series of discrete measurements separated in time there is a risk that certain changes which occur between those measurements may be missed. Consider the example of community growth and decline. Suppose we visit and photographically document a particular town at Time 1 and then return 20 years later (Time 2) and repeat the documentation. If at Time 2 things seem to be the same, we may conclude that there has

been no change. What if significant growth had occurred during the interim but the community had declined again by the time chosen as Time 2? In this situation, change that was *curvilinear* would have been missed. Complex changes of many sorts can be unobserved during the period between measurements. Where we depend on such repeated measurements, visual studies are comparable in their strengths and limitations to panel studies (repeat surveys) and other similar types of longitudinal research. Additional, more frequent documentation is the obvious strategy for dealing with this contingency. We must always keep the risk of erroneous interpretation in mind. If the time between observations is long, a careful researcher will look for indications of unobserved change. In addition to possible tell-tale visual signs, one can draw upon witness reports and, perhaps, available statistical sources to confirm its occurrence. In some circumstances, researchers studying social change may be able to maintain a schedule of fairly steady surveillance and make frequent observations of the phenomenon they are studying, and will thus be in a position to avoid the pitfalls of the simple linear assumption about social change.

Visual evidence may not always be 'consistent.' In quantitative studies, exceptions of this type—often unexplained—which run counter to the overall trends in the data, are not uncommon and are dismissed as 'statistical anomalies.' Similar things can happen in studies of visual change: not everything changes at the same rate nor, necessarily, in the same direction, and sometimes there are visual flukes in the change process.

An example of this occurred in the Ontonagon study in the small community of Ewen. In 1970, I had photographed the Soo Line railroad that passed through the center of town. Ewen was a loading point for rail service in the central part of the county and the location of shift change for the railroad crews, which provided Ewen with some steady restaurant and lodging trade. But the

Figure 7.12   Former railroad station, Ewen, Michigan, 1990. This building had been abandoned, but in 1990 it looked like it was being revived. This turned out to be a good example of a 'visual anomaly.' © 1990 Jon H. Rieger

railroad had ceased operations by 1985, and by 1990 the tracks were actually being torn up and the ties retrieved (Figure 7.12).

In rephotographing the scene in 1990, I noticed that the former train station looked noticeably better than it had in the previous survey. Its window frames had been freshly painted and a large planter containing a tree had been placed nearby. I had heard rumors about its possible revival as an activity center for senior citizens. In this community, where the dominant impression was one of gradual decline, could this be a small exception? I subsequently learned that the 'improvements' were merely cosmetic and intended simply to disguise a deteriorating building during an important community event. The fix-up of the Ewen station in 1990 was clearly a 'visual anomaly.' The building was later torn down.

Problems sometimes encountered in photographing social change are that important sites can disappear or become inaccessible to visual documentation, witnesses can die,

move away, or refuse to cooperate, and processes and activities can be curtailed or terminated. When this happens in panel studies or similar longitudinal research, it's called 'subject mortality.' In Ontonagon County, which has experienced a long, relentless decline, I have seen a number of cases of subject mortality: for example, the closure of the Ontonagon Valley Creamery; the abandonment of the Soo Line railroad line through the area; and the closure of half the schools. Those schools are effectively dropouts, although the buildings still exist (albeit in deteriorated condition), but the creamery has been torn down completely and the railroad bed survives only as a recreational trail. These developments are emblematic of the change taking place in the area. In evaluating subject mortality, it is important to consider the extent to which a dropout may be, in itself, significant in the analysis of the change being studied.

Sometimes a repeat photograph can't be taken because the original vantage point has disappeared, or because trees or bushes have grown up and obscured the view from the original vantage point. Where I encounter such situations, I try to find a different, more workable vantage point, if possible, and change lenses as needed to secure the documentation. Exact repetition, while ideal, is not as absolutely essential in sociological research as it may be in some other situations. Our objective is to visually document the scene well enough to permit an analysis of social change. When I repeat pictures, or attempt to, I make notes about the cause of any adjustments that have to be made or why the photograph cannot effectively be repeated.

POTENTIAL APPLICATIONS OF THE VISUAL METHOD

The visual method outlined above should be amenable for use in studying social change in a variety of contexts. The choice may be determined by the theory guiding the research, although you may start out without any theory at all and select an object of study on the basis of its sheer interest. Sometimes you develop a study focus over a period of observation in a field setting. Community growth and decline is the kind of social change I first fixed on in developing the photographic method described here. In such studies, one is concentrating primarily on the built environment as the indicator. The built environment does not usually change very rapidly. So selecting this type of subject for research may require considerable patience and persistence.

Besides growth and decline, many other changes in a community can profoundly affect the character of social life, including alterations in patterns of community settlement, business, and industrial ecology, the establishment or disestablishment of any large enterprise, such as a military base, or the building of a reservoir or park, or devastation by pollution, flooding, or forest fires.

Communities dominated by extractive industries whose vitality is sensitive to fluctuating commodity prices, weather and rainfall issues, or environmental regulation, are likely to show visible effects of those kinds of factors.

Another potentially fruitful area where a visual approach could be used is in the changes induced by technology, which can have a profound impact on social organization, as I found in the case of the woods industry in Western Upper Michigan. Technology can change the size, character, and organization of the work force, eliminate some occupations, skills, or practices while creating new ones. Alternatively, our object of study might be just a neighborhood or even the activity at a particular street corner. It could be a store, a park, a school athletic program, a gang, or a family.

The potential for employing a visual approach may become evident only over time, perhaps after a research study is already underway. In such situations it may be possible to add a visual component to the research. In some situations, gathering and analyzing visual data can be an ancillary component or part of a battery of indicators that may be employed. Photography might be useful at either the macro- or the micro-level or both. Researchers should be alert to potential photographic applications in sociological research so that they are prepared to make good use of the strengths that such an approach can bring to it.

UTILIZING THE VISUAL METHOD

As indicated above, the visual study of social change involves a number of basic steps:

1 Selecting a subject that will become the focus of the research and developing a theoretical framework that suggests what changes might be expected.
2 Determining and identifying visual indicators to be recorded.

3 Finding existing documentation or creating such documentation for the initial (Time 1) measurement.
4 Carrying out the follow-up (Time 2) documentation when appropriate.
5 Analyzing the accumulated evidence.

In embarking on research with photography you will be using film and/or digital technology and deciding whether to do the work in black and white or color. While the traditional medium in documentary research has been black and white, contemporary practitioners often work in color. (Digital technology easily permits the documentation to be carried out in color and later converted to black and white if needed or desired.)

Some study settings are amenable to documentation with fairly simple photographic equipment such as a small film or digital camera with a zoom lens. Other projects may require a more elaborate approach using larger or more specialized equipment, including cameras with multiple lenses, filters, flash, tripod exposures, etc. In the Ontonagon project, for example, where the 500+ sites to be documented are spread around the third largest county in Michigan, my movement from site to site is necessarily by auto, which is equipped with a tray locked into the right front passenger seat (Figure 7.13) to accommodate the needed equipment and records. When documenting a study site, the careful researcher will make an accurate record of each picture taken, including the location, the time, and any other relevant circumstantial or technical information. Those records will be of vital importance in the later repetition of the photos.

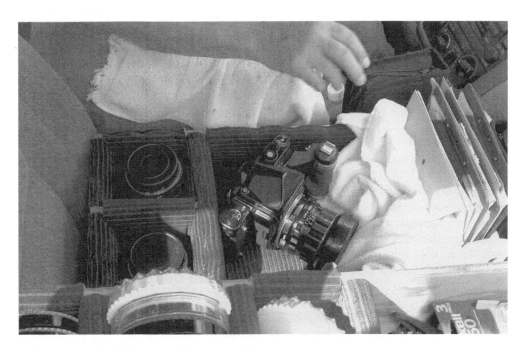

Figure 7.13 Car equipment tray, 2005. This photograph, shot through the passenger window, looks down over the filters shelved in the foreground to the tray nestled in the front seat beside the armrest. It has padded pockets for the camera and lenses and separate slots for clipboards containing previous photographs and record forms, etc. Towels are kept handy for protection from the sun between sites. This device greatly speeds up the work and ensures better safety and accessibility for the equipment and records. © 2005 Dave Bishop. Reproduced with permission

NOTE

1 Some of the content of this chapter is excerpted, condensed, or elaborated from my previously published and unpublished work in the study of social change and from an unfinished monograph on the subject.

REFERENCES

Collier, John, Jr and Collier, Malcolm (1986) *Visual Anthropology: Photography as a Research Method.* Albuquerque, NM: University of New Mexico Press.

Rieger, Jon H. (1982) 'Rural nonfarm residence in the Midwest', *The Rural Sociologist*, 2(4): 215–232.

Rieger, Jon H. (1996) 'Photographing social change', *Visual Sociology*, 11(1): 5–49.

Rieger, Jon H. (2003) 'A retrospective visual study of social change: The pulp-logging industry in an Upper Peninsula Michigan County', *Visual Studies*, 18(2): 157–178.

Rieger, Jon H. (2004) 'Witnesses to social change: The experience of the Carlisle family, Trout Creek, Michigan'. Paper presented at the Annual Meeting of the International Visual Sociology Association, San Francisco, California.

Rieger, Jon H. (2006) 'Family documents as community archive: Reconstructing social change in a small rural community'. Paper presented at the Annual Meeting of the Rural Sociological Society, Louisville, Kentucky.

Whyte, William (1980) *The Social Life of Small Urban Spaces*. Washington, DC: The Conservation Foundation.

8

Visual Research Methods in the Design Process

Prasad Boradkar

INTRODUCTION

Design, like the arts, is often regarded as a visual discipline. The design disciplines have, throughout their histories, actively engaged visual methods of problem-solving. Architecture, industrial design, graphic design, and interior design—some of the core design disciplines—clearly employ a variety of visual techniques in their standard praxis. The creation of aesthetically appealing artifacts is often described as one of design's primary goals and, therefore, the research that is conducted in the design disciplines includes several visual methods. These typically include photography, videography, sketching, diagramming, storyboarding, model-making, prototyping, and so on. A variety of visual practices exist as a central component of all phases of design methodology, from the early research in understanding user needs and leading up to the final implementation or manufacturing. In fact, one may say that design as a discipline has been obsessed with the visual ever since its inception. However, the growing use of ethnography in design (mostly observations, interviews, surveys, etc.) might, in some ways, signal somewhat of a turn away from the visual. In the world of product design, a project that focuses primarily on designing an object's shape or form is often referred to as 'styling,' and some designers are offended to be referred to as stylists. They believe that their work extends beyond the visual. Designers are embracing the notion that their task is to solve people's real needs, not merely create beautiful artifacts. Therefore, while there may be a growing recognition and acceptance of visual research methods in the social sciences, design research, over the past few years, seems to be trying to get beyond the visual.

Understanding design

What is design? This question is continually asked by scholars within the design community, and the answers vary widely, in part due to the relative youth of the design disciplines. In addition, as it evolves, design takes on new meanings, adopts new methodologies, addresses a broader range of

Scholar	Definition
Herbert A. Simon	Devising courses of action aimed at changing existing situations into preferred ones
J. Christopher Jones	Initiating change in manmade things
L. Bruce Archer	Collected experience of the material culture, and the collected body of experience, skill, and understanding embodied in the arts of planning, inventing, making, and doing
Christopher Alexander	The process of inventing physical things which display new physical order, organization, form, in response to function
Horst Rittel	Structuring argumentation to solve 'wicked' problems
Donald Schon	A reflective conversation with the materials of a design situation
Pelle Ehn	A democratic and participatory process
Jens Rasmussen/Kim Vicente	Creating complex sociotechnical systems that help workers adapt to the changing and uncertain demands of their job
Richard Buchanan	The conception and planning of the artificial
Gui Bonsiepe	Design is concrete invention to develop and produce artifacts

Figure 8.1   Diversity in definitions of design, an updated version of the diagram from Atwood et al. (2002)

problems, and redefines its scope, making it challenging to find a singular definition. A comparative study by Atwood et al. (2002) demonstrates some of the semantic diversity that exists in the various definitions of design (Figure 8.1).

The authors explain that this list is by no means exhaustive; the individual definitions represent a small sample extracted from seminal definitions that scholars have formulated over time. Some common threads do emerge from this diversity. It is clear, for instance, that all design is a form of problem-solving and planning for the future. The employment of such terms as 'action,' 'change,' 'inventing,' and 'creating' in these definitions establishes design as a generative process of transformation that leads to tangible outcomes. If the goal of design, as Max Bill of the Hochschule für Gestaltung in Ulm

once explained, is 'to participate in the making of a new culture—from spoon to city' (Lindinger, 1991: 10), its scope is vast and the diversity in definitions is only to be expected.

DESIGN'S (SUB)DISCIPLINES

The wide variety of (sub)disciplines, such as architecture, industrial design, graphic design, interior design, fashion design, interaction design, and so on, included under the label of design, only complicates the task of creating singular definitions. The divisions among the various forms of design practice serve a critical role. The design and manufacturing of products present challenges that are far different from those faced by an architect who is called on to oversee the design and construction of a building. The designs of objects, graphics, websites, buildings, etc., require a related yet distinct set of skills and tools, and therefore each of these disciplines defines its task on its own terms. The Industrial Designers Society of America (IDSA), for instance, defines industrial design as 'the professional service of creating and developing concepts and specifications that optimize the function, value, and appearance of products and systems for the mutual benefit of both user and manufacturer' (IDSA.org, 2009). The American Institute of Graphic Arts (AIGA) defines graphic design as 'a creative process that combines art and technology to communicate ideas. The designer works with a variety of communication tools in order to convey a message from a client to a particular audience. The main tools are image and typography' (AIGA.org, 2010). And, according to the American Institute of Architects, 'architecture is the imaginative blend of art and science in the design of environments for people' (AIA.org, 2010). While there are clear differences among the disciplines of industrial design, graphic design, and architecture, the inclusion of such terms as 'appearance' and 'art' in their definitions make it clear that the visual plays an important role in all forms of design. And, therefore, visual methods of research play an equally critical role. This chapter focuses on some of the visual research methods used in industrial design in the development of new products.

DESIGN AS ART AND/OR SCIENCE

The fundamental goal of the design of a product, room, poster or building is the creation of a tangible artifact for a client and/or a consumer. In this process, design has to engage the professions of engineering and business, as the goods produced have to be manufactured and they have to be sold. In addition, they have to be appealing to the buyer. This form of appeal includes beauty, utility, safety, accessibility, affordability, sustainability, durability, identity, brand recognition, emotional connection, symbolic meaning, etc. Of all these qualities, beauty and utility have garnered the most attention through design's history; *form* and *function* are regarded as the two primary concerns of the designer. Things have to look good and they have to work well. If designers are expected to create artifacts that are beautiful and functional, they have to be trained artistically and they need to understand the principles of engineering. It is therefore no surprise that design has been described at times as a form of art and at times as science. However, both these characterizations have been rejected by design scholars. 'The concept that design is closely related to the world of art is deep-rooted. But opposing this widely shared opinion is the fact that design is design and not art' (Bonsiepe and Cullars, 1991: 20). Further along in the same essay, Bonsiepe and Cullars note that 'there can be a scientific component to design discourse, but design by its very constitution is not science' (21). There is recognition that design is both, and cannot be strictly defined as one or the other. 'It is misleading to divide human actions into "art", "science", or "technology", for the artist has something of the scientist in him, and the engineer of both, and the very meaning of these terms varies with time so that analysis can easily degenerate into semantics' (Smith, 1970: 493). Design is inherently interdisciplinary; it is the discipline which straddles craft and science, creativity and commerce, the humanities and the social sciences, art and engineering. Design is generative and analytical; it demands creative thinking and critical problem solving. If such is the task of design, its practice necessitates the designer to draw upon the type of knowledge that resides in disparate disciplines, and requires a type of thinking that is flexible enough to fluctuate between divergent and convergent modes—divergent thinking for the creative and brainstorming tasks, convergent thinking for the analytical tasks.

DESIGN'S RELATIONSHIP TO THE VISUAL

Designers working within corporations or as consultants are often called upon to update the appearance of products through manipulation of form, color, material, and textures. While design practice includes much more, projects that involve mostly aesthetic modification of products are not unusual. And while designers take the task of beautification as an important responsibility, pure styling is also sometimes perceived as superficial ornamentation and therefore has negative connotative meanings. 'Designers of all stripes regularly lament that they are seen by the rest of the world as stylists—pseudo-professionals brought in to smooth the edges, improve the palette and make the medicine go down more easily' (Lunenfeld, 2003: 11). The industrial design profession often bristles at this word and is unhappy when its work is described as mere modification of product form for market differentiation and increased profits. In design practice today, there is increasing attention being given to ethnographic research, human-centered methods and sustainability. This testifies to the gradual shift in design's image—within and outside the profession—from a style-driven occupation to an empathic, problem-solving practice.

Design's relationship to the visual is evident in common language too—the word design is often used to refer to style. Design, in noun form, can mean spatial arrangement, compositional layout or pattern (as in the design of a room or quilt or other material artifact). In addition, articles about design in the popular press often tend to emphasize the visual, stylistic, and sensual qualities of products. After all, the most visible aspect of all design work is appearance. Over the last decade, however, there has been a perceptible shift in how design is 'read' and therefore written about by journalists, critics, and business writers. Design has been steadily gaining recognition as a key activity in processes of innovation, and offers tangible and intangible benefits to all stakeholders, including users, manufacturers, society, and the environment.

DESIGN RESEARCH

The classical definition of design research is traced to Bruce Archer, who presented it at a conference of the Design Research Society in 1980. According to Archer, 'design research is systematic inquiry whose goal is knowledge of, or in, the embodiment of configuration, composition, structure, purpose, value, and meaning in man-made things and systems' (Bayazit, 2004: 16). This definition is expansive enough to sweep up a broad range of investigations surrounding design's process and its end product. Since Archer, a variety of scholars have produced articles and books on design research (Downton, 2003; Laurel, 2003; Cross, 2007; Ralf, 2007), several design research conferences have been organized, and in 1966, the professional organization called the Design Research Society was formed. Bayazit lists five major concerns of design research as they apply to design methodology and design science:

1 Design research is concerned with the physical embodiment of man-made things, how these things perform their jobs, and how they work.
2 Design research is concerned with construction as a human activity, how designers work, how they think, and how they carry out design activity.
3 Design research is concerned with what is achieved at the end of a purposeful design

activity, how an artificial thing appears, and what it means.

4 Design research is concerned with the embodiment of configurations.
5 Design research is a systematic search and acquisition of knowledge related to design and design activity (Bayazit, 2004: 16).

It is clear from the list above that design research deals primarily with the analysis of human-made artifacts and the process of doing design. And there are several reasons why visual methods play a critical role in design research:

1 The artifacts of human design have a visible presence in the world, and designers pay careful attention to the visual quality of things. In other words, designing aesthetic appeal into things is an important component of the design process, and therefore visual techniques are central to design activity.
2 Giving shape to things involves the processes of sketching, computer visualization, illustration, model-making, etc., and all these methods are

forms of doing research. All of them involve the use of images.

3 The utilization of ethnographic methods to discover consumer needs and to document how consumers use products is now standard practice in design. The use of photography and videography is central to this practice.

Figure 8.2 shows the research methodology for a product development project that includes primary research for understanding user needs and secondary research for technology and market research. Such visual tools are often used in planning research projects in design.

FORMS OF VISUAL RESEARCH IN THE DESIGN PROCESS

Throughout the process of new product development, designers use a variety of visual and tactile means of doing research.

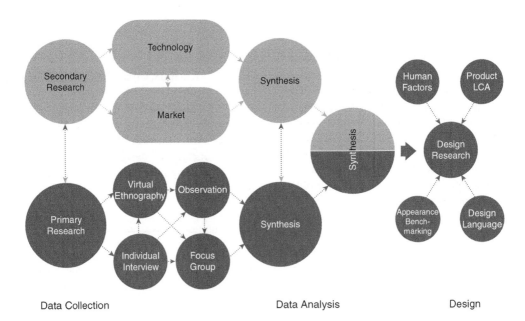

Figure 8.2   Research methodology for a product development project known as the In-Class Communicator, a product that assists students with low vision in the activity of note-taking in the classroom (illustration by Liqing Zhou)

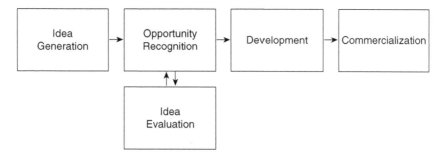

Figure 8.3 'The Innovation Process' by Luecke, R. (2003), from the Harvard Business Essentials book *Managing Creativity and Innovation*, pp. xi

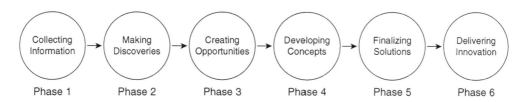

Figure 8.4 The process of new product design and development

Figure 8.3 is a generic process of innovation as explained in the Harvard Business Essentials book *Managing Creativity and Innovation* (Luecke, 2003). With some variation, all processes of innovation and new product development include the phases of research, analysis, ideation, idea selection, and implementation.

Corporations involved in new product development routinely customize this process to suit the unique characteristics of their institution. The *PDMA Handbook of New Product Development* (Kahn, 2005) lists a number of these industry-specific variations. The process illustrated in Figure 8.4 is one variation that is employed by transdisciplinary new product development teams of design, business, and engineering students at Arizona State University, in a program called InnovationSpace. Students in this program learn how to develop new product-service systems that address significant social problems while minimizing impacts on the environment. Examples include medication management devices for older adults, reading aids for people who are blind and visually impaired, renewable energy systems for people living off the electrical grid, and so on. The process involves a series of steps that include research, analysis, ideation, development, refinement, and delivery (Boradkar, 2010). Each phase calls for a set of visual methods of research and problem-solving. For instance, the earlier phases involve primary and secondary data collection as well as analysis, and therefore photography, videography, and diagramming are the key visual tools used. During the ideation and development phase, designers tend to use the visual skills of drawing, sketching, and digital renderings as well as computer modeling. And, finally, in the refinement, and delivery phases, prototyping and presentations play a key role. The following explanations of the phases of new product development include descriptions of some of the visual research tools used.

Phase 1—Collecting information

The process of design starts with collecting information about consumers, the market, potential technologies, related social issues, and environmental conditions. The goal of Phase 1 is to understand the needs and desires of the people for whom the product is being designed, the constraints and possibilities presented by technology and engineering, competition in the marketplace with other industries, social trends that will affect and be affected by the new design, and environmental conditions that have to be considered to make the product sustainable. The activities include comprehensive primary and secondary research such as literature reviews, interviews with experts and users, as well as ethnographic observations.

As designers and design researchers collect information in Phase 1, they typically use photography as well as videography to document users' behaviors, lifestyles, and daily activities. In situations where the project involves the redesign of an existing product, the goal is to capture visual data about how people operate existing products and discover means by which to make them better. Design researchers routinely conduct observations and interviews with users and collect images and audio to serve as raw data to be analyzed in Phase 2 of the design process. The other information collected at this stage may include images of competitors' products, market research reports, and technology briefs that help map the context within which the new designs are meant to operate.

Figure 8.5   Photograph of a low-income neighborhood in Phoenix, Arizona (photograph by Studio 1:1)

The complexity of the project often determines the type of data collected and the methods used. For instance, large urban design projects might require a team of researchers, several citizen participants, and a wide range of tools. Figure 8.5 is a photograph of a low-income neighborhood in Phoenix, Arizona, where a team of graduate students in architecture and industrial design—called Studio 1:1—used interviews, observations, and other ethnographic methods in order to understand the context and develop solutions that appropriately addressed the needs of the community. Several such photographs served as initial data in mapping the neighborhood visually.

Phase 2—Making discoveries

The objective of Phase 2 of the design process is to analyze the data gathered in Phase 1 with the hope of discovering unique insights that can help the designers in fashioning the new product or service. A variety of analysis tools are typically deployed to derive insights about the context within which the new product will exist. A comprehensive research report typically emerges at the end of this phase that catalogs key research insights concerning the user, market, technology, society, and the environment. At this stage, quantitative and qualitative data are represented through such visual means as bi-axial diagrams, illustrations, charts, timelines, etc. The visuals serve to convert complex textual or statistical data into more accessible information.

For instance, Figure 8.6 shows consumer preference for transportation in urban environments in the form of a three-dimensional diagram. Similarly, Figure 8.7 shows a hierarchy of transportation needs of the key stakeholders (commuters, businesses, the municipality, and society at large) in an urban environment. These diagrams illustrate that visual information can help in not only representation of data but also in its comprehension.

Figure 8.8 is an illustration of some of the data gathered by the team members of Studio 1:1 regarding automobile traffic, aircraft flight patterns, noise levels, and the routine, everyday activities of the people living in Memorial Towers, a non-assisted senior apartment living complex in Phoenix, Arizona. The researchers discovered that many of the older adults living there had redesigned their environments and repurposed the facilities to suit their needs. For instance, many had placed potted plants so

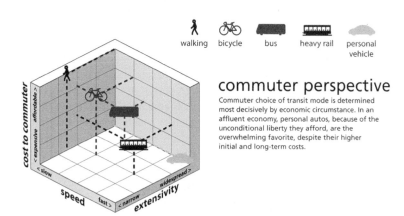

Figure 8.6 Transportation needs assessment diagram for multiple stakeholders (illustration by Katherine Randall and Luke Morey)

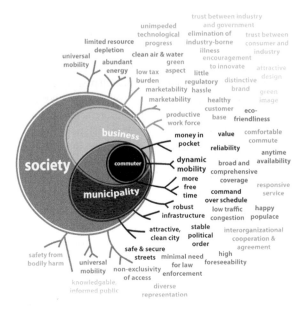

Figure 8.7   Transportation needs assessment diagram for multiple stakeholders (illustration by Katherine Randall and Luke Morey)

they had visual access to greenery, many were using the large open parking space for exercise and using underutilized spaces as gardens. The illustration shows view angles, walking/exercise paths, and the gardens. Such visual representations are critical in bringing research insights to life for the design team.

Similar illustrations are often created for market and engineering analyses as well. Figure 8.9 shows an example of product benchmarking—a visual tool that is often used to map industry competitors. In this case, the benchmarking shows a variety of devices that use display and software-based technologies to assist people who are blind. The diagram presents the unique insight that there might be a market opportunity for portable display-related technologies, as there are very few competitors in that space.

Phase 3—Creating opportunities

During Phase 3, the product development team starts generating ideas for how the problems identified during research can be tackled through the design of new products, brands, and services. Also referred to as ideation, this phase involves brainstorming and other creative problem-solving exercises aimed at generating as many ideas as possible. These solutions are typically visualized through product sketches, digital renderings, and quick models. Figure 8.10 and 8.11 are examples of sketches developed for a product that assists students who are partially blind with the process of taking notes during a lecture in a classroom. These sketches provide information about the form, shape, color, texture, and materials that could be used in the design of the new assistive device.

Figure 8.12 illustrates the visual and tactile rough models that are constructed during Phase 3 as a means to develop a three-dimensional understanding of the product's form, scale, size, shape, and feel. While the two-dimensional sketches provide an early visualization of what the product might look like, the three-dimensional models provide a higher level of fidelity and tactile representation of form.

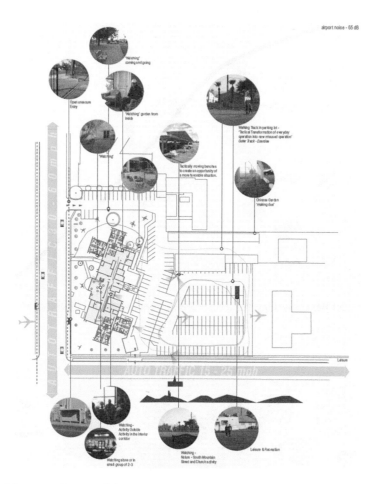

Figure 8.8 Diagram of Memorial Towers, a senior apartment complex showing patterns of use and behavior (illustration by Studio 1:1)

Phase 4—Developing concepts

The aim of Phase 4, the process of developing a single concept in further detail, is to start making critical decisions to resolve all issues relating to the proposed product design concept. The activities in this phase include making strategic decisions about how this product can be designed, branded, engineered and sold. The visual materials developed in Phase 3 are developed further and additional sketches, and models are created to start the process of finalizing the design. During this phase, many of the decisions about the aesthetic development are made and the final product starts taking form. The sketches created in Phase 3 are embellished with further detail and rapid prototyping machines are often utilized to build three-dimensional models.

One of the fundamental goals of design research is to inspire designers and make them truly understand the lives of the people for whom they are creating design solutions. Research has to inspire empathy. Studio environments where creative design work often happens are visually active spaces replete with photographs, diagrams, sketches, and models to serve as inspirations. The visual energy plays a critical in helping

Product Benchmarking

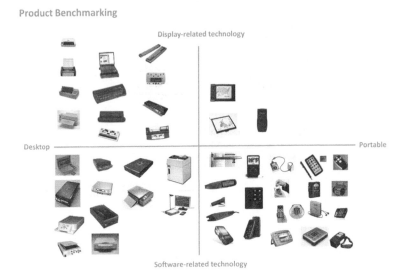

Figure 8.9   **Product benchmarking for a new Braille reading device (illustration by Qian Yang)**

Figure 8.10   **Product sketches for the In-Class Communicator, a product that assists students with low vision in the activity of note-taking in the classroom (sketches by Liqing Zhou)**

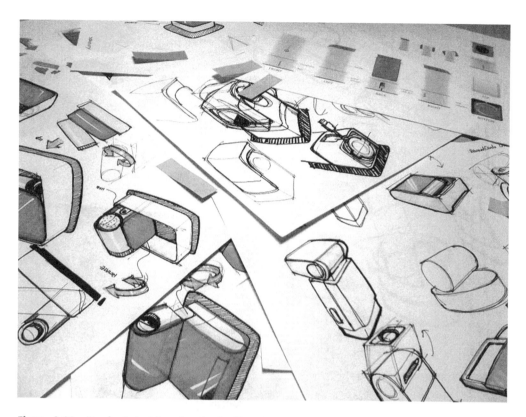

Figure 8.11   Product sketches for the In-Class Communicator, a product that assists students with low vision in the activity of note-taking in the classroom (sketches by Liqing Zhou)

designers translate research insights into tangible solutions. Figure 8.13 shows one such example of a research and design environment.

Figure 8.14 shows an illustration of the development of a design language. A design language (also referred to as the aesthetic language) helps the designers define the kinds of forms, colors, shapes, and details that will best suit the context and the needs of the consumers. For instance, in Figure 8.14, for the design of a Braille reading device, the designer has identified 'simplified, rounded, organic, and smooth' forms as appropriate for the user group, which in this case is people who are totally blind. Similarly, 'obvious contour lines' have been included in the design language as critical

for the users to be able to maneuver the product and find the buttons through tactile means.

Phase 5—Finalizing solutions

The purpose of Phase 5 is to finalize the design and engineering for the product, along with the graphic language and marketing materials. In this phase, designers create final digital illustrations (also referred to as renderings) and appearance models that demonstrate the product appearance. In addition to design drawings, at this stage, detailed and accurate engineering drawings and functional prototypes are also prepared to finalize the solution.

Figure 8.12   Rough conceptual models of the In-Class Communicator, a product that assists students with low vision in the activity of note-taking in the classroom (photographs and models by Liqing Zhou)

Figure 8.13   The Studio 1:1 creative environment (photograph by Studio 1:1)

Design Language

FORM

simplified, integrated, rounded, organic, asymmetric, smooth, portable, minimal

DETAILS

two distinct interfaces, one button activated, scattered buttons, obvious contour lines,

COLOR

primary color: white or grey
accent color: light green, warm yellow

Figure 8.14   Design language for a new Braille reading device (illustration by Qian Yang)

During this phase, storyboards outlining the process of installation, use, and repair are also generated.

Phase 6—Delivering innovation

The goal of this phase is to demonstrate the final product solution through appropriate materials to clients, investors, or other experts. The activities include the development of text-based, visual and presentational media to communicate and promote the project to the audience.

The visual research tools used in the six phases of the new product design and development process outlined above are but some of the tools used by designers; new methods are routinely developed and tested.

CONCLUSION

The application of critical research methods in the disciplines of design is relatively new. Often accused of focusing too much

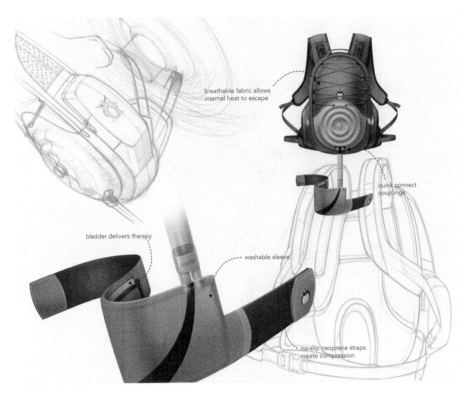

Figure 8.15   Final product rendering for a therapeutic backpack with hot–cold therapy (illustration by Matt Storey and Shelby Sandler; project sponsored by Dow Corning Corporation)

breathable fabric allows
internal heat to escape

quick connect
couplings

bladder delivers therapy

washable sleeve

no-slip neoprene straps
create compression

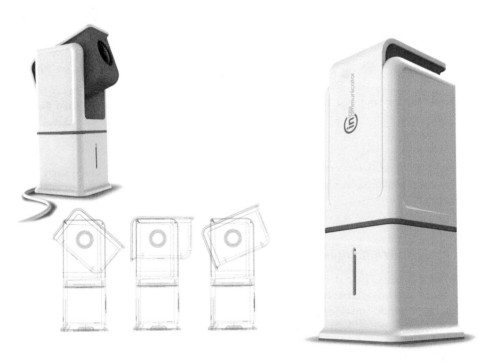

Figure 8.16   Final digital renderings of the In-Class Communicator, a product that assists students with low vision in the activity of note-taking in the classroom (illustration by Liqing Zhou)

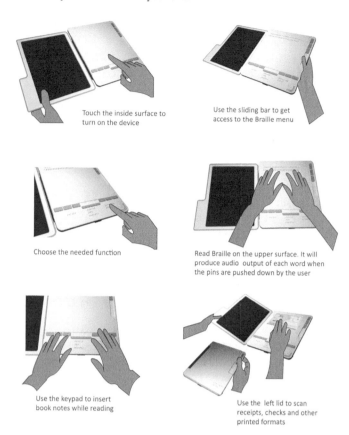

Touch the inside surface to
turn on the device

Use the sliding bar to get
access to the Braille menu

Choose the needed function

Read Braille on the upper surface. It will
produce audio output of each word when
the pins are pushed down by the user

Use the keypad to insert
book notes while reading

Use the left lid to scan
receipts, checks and other
printed formats

**Figure 8.17   User experience storyboard for a new Braille reading device (illustration
by Qian Yang)**

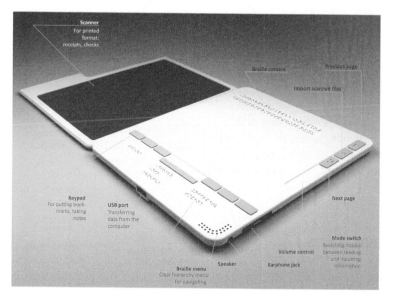

**Figure 8.18   Final digital rendering for a new Braille reading device (illustration by
Qian Yang)**

attention on the visual aspects of artifacts, designers have adopted a variety of research methods into their profession to ensure that the solutions are truly human-centered. The growing recognition of design research and the widespread use of rapid ethnography in design are indicators of this shift. And while the visual continues to play a central role in all design praxis, tactile forms of research are equally important too. Whereas photographs, videos, sketches, and renderings are valid forms of visual research, prototyping and model-making step beyond the visual into the tactile realm. It is also important to note a key distinction between the visual data used in design research and that used in social science and humanities research. While the photography and videography employed in the early stages of design attempt to capture the world as accurately as it appears, many of the visual and tactile methods used in design rely on image creation rather than image capture. The sketches and renderings developed by designers are not representations of the world outside but visualizations of ideas that are yet to take physical form. 'Design research is inherently paradoxical: it is both imaginative and empirical' (Johnson, 2007: 39). Visual research changes roles gradually through the design process. Photographs and videos of users that are taken early in the design process represent the empirical nature of visual research, while the sketches and models that are created later emerge from the imagination. Visual research in design can therefore serve two roles—it can help us in making sense of the material world in which we live and also help us in understanding the creative process of design thinking.

ACKNOWLEDGMENTS

Some of the text of this chapter about design research is modified but based upon Boradkar, P. (2010) 'Design as problem-solving' in R. Frodeman, J. Thompson Klein and C. Mitcham, *The Oxford Handbook of Interdisciplinarity*. Oxford: Oxford University Press. A special thanks to all the excellent undergraduate and graduate students who provided images for this article: Matt Krise, Katherine Randall, Matt Storey, Qian Yang and Liqing Zhou.

REFERENCES

AIA.org (2010) *What is Architecture?* [Online]. Available from: http://www.archcareers.org/archoverview.html [Accessed 12 May 2010].

AIGA.org (2010) *What is Graphic Design* [Online]. Available from: http://www.aiga.org/content.cfm/guide-whatisgraphicdesign [Accessed 12 January 2010].

Atwood, M., McCain, K. and Williams, J. (2002). 'How does the design community think about design?' in *Designing Interactive Systems: Proceedings of the 4th Conference on Designing Interactive Systems— Processes, Practices, Methods, and Techniques.* pp. 125–132.

Bayazit, N. (2004) 'Investigating design: A review of forty years of design research', *Design Issues*, 20(1): 16–29.

Bonsiepe, G. and Cullars, J. (1991) 'Designing the future: Perspectives on industrial and graphic design in Latin America', *Design Issues*, 7(2): 17–24.

Boradkar, P. (2010) 'Transdisciplinary design and innovation in the classroom', in T. Porter O'Grady and K. Malloch (eds.), *Innovation Leadership: Creating the Landscape of Healthcare.* Sudbury, MA: Jones and Bartlett Publishers, pp. 109–134.

Cross, N. (2007) *Designerly Ways of Knowing.* Berlin: Birkhäuser Verlag AG.

Downton, P. (2003) *Design Research.* Melbourne: RMIT University Press.

IDSA.org (2009) *What is ID?* [Online]. Available from: http://idsa.org/absolutenm/templates/?a=89 [Accessed 29 March 2010].

Johnson, B. (2007) 'The paradox of design research: The role of informance', in B. Laurel (ed.), *Design Research: Methods and Perspectives.* Cambridge, MA: MIT Press. pp. 39–40.

Kahn, K. (2005) *PDMA Handbook of New Product Development,* 2nd edn. John Wiley & Sons. [Online]. Available from: http://knovel.com.ezproxy1.lib.asu.

edu/web/portal/browse/display?_EXT_KNOVEL_ DISPLAY_bookid=1416&VerticalID=0

Laurel, B. (2003) *Design Research: Methods and Perspectives.* Cambridge, MA: MIT Press.

Lindinger, H. (1991) *Ulm Design: The Morality of Objects.* Tr. D. Britt, Cambridge, MA: MIT Press.

Luecke, R. (2003) *Managing Creativity and Innovation,* Boston, MA: Harvard Business School Publishing.

Lunenfeld, P. (2003) 'The design cluster', in B. Laurel (ed.), *Design Research: Methods and Perspectives.* Cambridge, MA: MIT Press.

Ralf, M. (2007) *Design Research Now: Essays and Selected Projects.* Berlin: Birkhäuser Verlag AG.

Smith, C. (1970) 'Art, technology, and science: Notes on their historical interaction', *Technology and Culture,* 11(4): 493–549.

PART 3

Participatory and Subject-Centered Approaches

9

Community-Based Participatory Video and Social Action in Rural South Africa

Claudia Mitchell and Naydene de Lange

INTRODUCTION

The essence of community-based participatory video can be found, we believe, in the words of a member of a rural community who, upon viewing a video created by other members of the community, commented: '…it is easy to understand a thing if it means you sit with him/her and talk about the matter… rather than standing in front of them.' This equaling of power relations creates a space for dynamic interaction around topics that have often been kept silent in rural southern African communities ravaged by HIV and AIDS, where communication at various levels, as well as between generations, has often been difficult.

Video in participatory research has been used in a number of ways in social science research, usually under the umbrella of such terms as collaborative video, community video, and participatory video. Marcus Banks (2001), Sarah Pink (2001), and others refer to *collaborative video* as a process where

the researcher or community worker works with a group of participants to create a video production, whereas in *participatory video* the process involves a group of participants primarily constructing their own video texts with only minimal assistance from the research team. The approaches are not entirely different from one another; even within the community project we describe here, degrees of participation and collaboration can vary.

Following the work of Mak (2006), Nair and White (2003) and Goldfarb (2002), 'participatory' refers not only to the ways in which community members are involved with creating the video narrative but also to the ways in which the video text itself can function as a catalyst or trigger in post-screening discussions. Thus, for example, in some of our previous video-making work with young people from Khayelitsha and Atlantis, two townships near Cape Town, where we produced the HIV and AIDS-focused video documentary, *Fire + Hope*, it was not the technology side of the production process that served as a catalyst to critical reflection, but rather the participation of youth as informants/interviewees in the video itself, and as co-directors in determining the key themes to be addressed (Walsh and Mitchell, 2006; Mitchell et al., 2007). In a related video-making project involving many of the same participants, Walsh worked with a group of young black filmmakers from township schools whose project was to turn the camera on white youth from more privileged schools. The resulting video, *Facing the Truth*, was highly participatory in its conceptualization, though the final product also involved the editing skills of Walsh as a filmmaker (Walsh, 2007). In the production of another series of community-based videos also focusing on HIV and AIDS (see Mak et al., 2004: *Our Photos, Our Videos, Our Stories*), participants engaged in all aspects of the video-making process, including mastering the technical side of editing, using Adobe® Premier®.

At the same time, the notion of community-based participatory video also refers to the engagement with a particular community and the relationships that are built up over time and as such contribute, we believe, to social change (Shratz and Walker, 1995).

The community-based video-making we describe here comes out of 4 or 5 years of working with the same schools and local clinic and is part of a series of visual participatory activities carried out with community members. The process is based on what we have termed a No Editing Required (NER)[1] approach to the technicalities of video-making. Our decision to develop (and indeed fine tune) an NER approach for first-time filmmakers meant that it was possible for participants to see the full production process in 1 day, and actually have a 3-minute video to show for their work. And while we describe this in detail in this chapter, what we must highlight from the beginning is the way community-based video-making for us is more than simply a 'once off' activity. Rather, it is part of a more extensive process of community engagement in working with the videos over time, and involving the social actors beyond those who made the video. Thus, we emphasize dialogue and ultimately the possibilities for social action, particularly in the context of such burning social issues as poverty and gender-based violence that are so prevalent in the rural South African context. The chapter is divided into four sections. In the first section, we provide a theoretical framework for community-based participatory video work. In the second section, we offer a case study of the production and use of *Izindaba Yethu* (*Our Stories*) within a district in a rural community in KwaZulu-Natal, a province of South Africa. In the third section, we consider some of the challenges of community-based participatory video. In the final section, we pose the question 'What difference does this make?' to consider some of the ways in which research and community video link to social action.

A SENSE OF COMMUNITY

An understanding of community processes is a critical element for framing community-based participatory video. According to Visser, community can 'refer to people in a specific geographical area and time; it can refer to a social system; to the construction of a way of life or to a sociopolitical organization' (Visser, 2007: 5–6, 7). Community is also a 'complex system of interactions between cultural, social, political, psychological and ecological elements' (Visser, 2007: 5–6, 7). We view the rural community in which our work takes place as a complex interplay of these elements. Furthermore, our work takes place within a community where addressing the complexities of HIV and AIDS is critical. Our entry-point to the rural community was facilitated by the Centre for the AIDS Programme of Research in South Africa (CAPRISA). With CAPRISA's assistance we gained access to a healthcare clinic and two senior secondary schools. Realizing that social change is a slow, complex process, we intentionally chose to work *deeper* and not *wider* over several years with the goal of intensification of effort over time. For example, teachers and community healthcare workers working in this community noted a few years ago that, 'the main thing that we have in common is death' (Mak et al., 2004). They meant that every day they encounter painful situations—the death of patients and friends, children heading up households, absenteeism of students and teachers from school, and so on. The instance of a petrol station doubling as a funeral parlor demonstrates how death has become commonplace. Our use of video, along with other participatory methods such as drawing and photovoice,[2] has been about exploring with the community members themselves, ways of coping, and taking action.

Three key areas underpin our *community-based participatory video*:

1   The values and goals of community psychology.
2   The 'externalizing' of the story.
3   Reflexivity through collectivity.

The values and goals of community psychology

Community psychology focuses on the interaction between the individual and her/his social context; it draws on psychological knowledge and skills to better people's well-being. In *Contextualizing Community Psychology*, Visser argues that 'personhood can be located in the collective' (2007: 4). The values of community psychology underpinned our research, while its goals informed the specific aims as an intervention particular to the context. According to Visser (2007), the most important values and goals are the promotion of not only individual but also interpersonal and communal health and well-being (Prilleltensky, 2006). This includes: caring and compassion in the sense of cultivating an emotional connectedness within the community; self-determination and participation; creating a sense of agency; respect

for diversity and human dignity; creating opportunities for all voices to be valued and heard (Prilleltensky and Nelson, 1997); and, finally, social justice. These values are particularly important in communities 'in the age of AIDS,' where infection, affectedness, stigma, and poverty exacerbate difficulties and the overall quality of life. Furthermore, Visser accentuated 'a democratic style of collaboration and partnership with community members in research and intervention' (2007: 13). Collaboration and partnership are foregrounded in the use of visual participatory methodologies like community-based video where the research is not the goal in itself, but is rather aimed at 'assist[ing] the community in improving its functioning, and enhancing its quality of life and social equity' (Visser, 2007: 13). Therefore, it is a valuable means of 'understanding and addressing the psychosocial problems disrupting the lives of people' (Visser, 2007: 4). In our work, the 'psychosocial problems' referred to are those affecting the fabric of a community and its people in the context of HIV and AIDS.

'Externalizing the story'

White, a narrative therapist, wrote that 'stories don't mirror life, they shape it' (2007: n.p.). His approach relies on 'externalizing the problems' and then 'challenging fixed and pessimistic versions of events' in order to imagine 'new and more optimistic stories' to bring about change. Such narratives bring community members together around particular shared experiences, creating opportunities for reciprocal support. In some communities, it is culturally unacceptable to make use of individual counseling, and hence collective methodologies are more appropriate. In others, such as the one we describe here, community members are likely to have little access to counseling services in any case. We then contend that, in instances like this, community-based participatory video work is both culturally acceptable and necessary, as it opens up the space and opportunity for the community to 'externalize its problems,' to engage collaboratively with them, and significantly, to envisage solutions.

Reflexivity through collective work

Working with video production as a group process (from initial concept through to storyboarding, planning shots, shooting, initial screening, and post-screening discussion) offers participants access to a type of socially constructed knowledge that is particularly significant to addressing themes which have often been taboo—the unspeakable. As we have argued elsewhere (Weber and Mitchell, 2007), video production offers participants an opportunity to engage actively in the 'social construction' of knowledge. The group chooses the themes, decides on the images, and 'constructs' the staging, and so on. In the case of video (vs live performance), there is a whole array of techniques that expand the possibilities for 'constructedness'—from shot angles, to dialogue, to theme music. Participants can stop the process, view, and re-view the work—and indeed, they are even able to see themselves in action. Each frame is considered and reconsidered. Nothing is accidental.

Visual anthropologist Jay Ruby (2000) discussed how reflexivity, autobiography, and self-awareness can all figure prominently when working with the film texts. This is important when working with young people and video, for example, on issues like gender violence—an issue where the dominant images of sexism and power inequalities need to be challenged. The types of follow-up interventions that draw on reflexivity are extensive. How, for example, could a group of young people 're-vision' their video as a text explicitly contesting traditional power dimensions—and how does video lend itself to this kind of critical awareness? How might other students (a group of girls, for example) respond differently and how could this audience component contribute to the reflexivity of the original filmmakers? How would

teachers, other adults, and education officials respond to the video? (see also Mitchell et al., 2007). Like the work of Barnes et al. (1997), who used collaborative video to work with HIV-positive mothers, the participants were able to 'reproduce and understand their world as opposed to the dominant representations in the mass media' (cited in Pink, 2001: 86).

Schratz and Walker (1995: 172) argued that a critical feature of various interventions that lend themselves to social change is that they are in fact social in nature in the first place. They involve the group and cannot be managed 'individually and in isolation.' As they wrote: 'It [motivation] requires a collaborative effort and a reassessment of the nature of self in relation to social context, not a submerging of the individual within the collective, but a recognition that the person only exists in the light of significant others' (Schratz and Walker, 1995: 172). Highly participatory video production can create a strong sense of the collective response that includes all participants—producers, viewers, directors, actors, and technicians. While it is possible that individual responses may sometimes be overshadowed by the activities of the collective, we found that in issues of violence, sexual abuse, and HIV and AIDS, which are social in nature and multi-layered in meaning, the collective response is vital.

IZINDABA YETHU—OUR STORIES

In this section, we describe the community-based participatory video project that began with a 1-day video making workshop and continued with follow-up viewings, small group discussions, and community screenings over several months. This section is presented in five parts: first, describing the video-making process; second, the engagement of the participants in viewing their own short videos; third, compiling a composite edited video[3] (our own creative endeavor) *Izindaba Yethu*; fourth, taking the composite video back to the participants for viewing and analysis; and finally, taking the composite video to a broader audience for viewing and engagement within the rural community.

Stage one: video-making

The initial 1-day video-making workshop came out of planning with the community: arranging place, time, and the number and nature of the participants. We were encouraged by the turnout: 19 senior secondary school students, 3 teachers, 3 community healthcare workers, and several parents. After a brief introduction explaining the purpose of the day and its envisaged outcomes for them and for us, we set up groups: a boys-only group; a girls-only group; a mixed boy and girl group; a group of teachers; and a group consisting of community healthcare workers and parents. The first activity began with a simple prompt: 'What are the key issues affecting your daily lives in your community?' Each group was facilitated by a member

of the research team and the responses were written on a large sheet of paper. The issues identified included poverty, disease, HIV and AIDS, child abuse, rape, crime, murder and robbery, joblessness, gangs, school safety, youth pregnancy, substance abuse, and lack of recreational facilities.

The participants in each group were asked to identify the most pressing issue through a 'voting' process (see Figure 9.1). Participants stuck a colored dot next to the three issues they thought to be the most critical in their lives. The theme to be pursued in the video, then, was based on which topic had the most votes, for the goal of the exercise was democratic engagement and decision making. It is important to note that, independently of each other, the three youth (student) groups identified rape and gender violence as the key issues, whereas the two adult groups independently identified poverty as the most pressing issue.

After identifying a focus for their video, each group created a simple storyboard consisting of 10 scenes (shots), each of which

Figure 9.1   Participants 'voting' to identify the key issue they want to address in their video. © de Lange 2010

was between 10 and 30 seconds in length. A template was provided to allow participants to construct the storyline and title, identify key issues, write a rough script for each scene, and select the actors. Creating the storyboards allowed for a deeper discussion of the chosen topic. Furthermore, production roles such as director and camera person were negotiated. Participants took on and changed roles as required.

Since none of the participants had ever used a video camera before, a brief training session on the use of the video camera was given to the whole group before they set out to do the shoot. Camera operation was demonstrated, along with simple ideas on framing, panning and zooming. In the training session we emphasized the NER approach, and especially the idea of 'no turning back' in the actual filming. Doing such work in a rural community with health concerns,

despite lacking a reliable electrical source and computers, accentuates the possibilities for digital technology to be transformative under less than ideal conditions (see section Practical Guidelines).

Each group, accompanied by a facilitator, set of with a video camera and tripod. The groups had about an hour 'on location' for shooting a 3–5-minute video (see Figure 9.2).

The titles of the short videos they made were very provocative themselves, especially considering the context of HIV and AIDS: *Rape at school: Trust no one*; *How raping got me HIV&AIDS*; *Rape*; *Effect of poverty in school*; and *It all began with poverty*. Each of the five videos produced in this workshop, along with the videos that had been produced in similar workshops in neighboring schools, were remarkably sophisticated in relation to the genres that were chosen: public service advertisements, talk show interviews,

Figure 9.2   Participants using a video camera to film the story they created to visually present their selected issue. © de Lange 2010

and melodramas. And despite being short, the videos were successful in bringing the different messages across to the audiences. For example, in *Rape at school: Trust no one*, a student plays the main character—a teacher who rapes a girl after luring her to his classroom by promising extra tuition. In this video, the camera lingers on a closed door with the audience left to imagine what is happening while hearing the girl protesting and crying. It ends with the teacher leaving the classroom, turning to the girl and saying in a threatening voice: *'You tell ... you're dead.'*

The groups all assembled together in one large group to view each others' videos. This was something that we felt was very important because it allowed each group to see their production 'on the big screen' and it also allowed them to showcase their video to the other filmmakers in the larger group. After the screening they discussed each others' work. This raised the level of reflection and engagement among the community of participants.

Stage two: participants working with their own videos

After the first workshop the small groups reviewed and re-engaged with their own video. In viewing their video again, the participants reflected on their work using the following open-ended questions:

- What did you like about the video?
- What are some of the images that stay in your mind?
- If you had a copy of the video, who would you want to show it to and why?
- How do you think it could help address gender-based violence?
- What would help you in the school and community to address the main issue in this video? (In the case of most of the videos produced by the students this was the issue of gender-based violence.)

This stage is a critical one as it means that the producers themselves have an opportunity to

consider the issues from other angles. It also stimulates them to think about the target audience and distribution. Community-based participatory video is after all not just about a 1-day production process.

Stage three: creating the composite video Izindaba Yethu—Our Stories

One of the limitations of the NER and one-day video-making activity is the general rough-cut quality of the productions. As a research team, we therefore reflected on how the individual 3-minute videos could be used to continue the engagement. While we did not want to tamper with the actual video productions, which in themselves say a great deal—and indeed exist as research data—we felt that in their raw (and very short) state they might have very limited use beyond the day of production. At the same time, the issue of gender violence was so dramatically (and urgently) presented in the videos by the young people that we felt an obligation to develop a strategy or tool for taking the videos further, and so we came up with the idea of developing a composite video.

Ruby (2000), Pink (2001), and others have highlighted in discussions of ethnographic video that composite videos create their own interpretive framework. Moreover, as with the work of Holland et al. (1992) with transcript analysis, the research team itself engaged in a type of reflexivity about 'What matters in the overall workshop program?' Working collaboratively with the research team, a videographer compiled a 17-minute rough-cut video, *Izindaba Yethu (Our Stories)*. It was complete with a musical soundtrack, text boxes containing statistics on gender violence, footage of the workshop itself, English subtitles of the short videos in the composite video and even credits. Not only is it a reflexive tool for the research team but also it is an opportunity, as we discovered, to engage community members more fully in the process. Ultimately, this composite video is ideal as a reflective tool, a teaching tool and tool, for stimulating engagement beyond the workshop.

Stage four: taking Izindaba Yethu back to the participants

The rough-cut of *Izindaba Yethu* was taken back to the participating school a month or so after the video-making workshop and initial screening for viewing and discussion. After the screening, the participants were asked to reflect on the same open-ended questions, with an additional question: 'We haven't finished editing the video, what would you like changed or added?'

The participants clearly highlighted the importance and the need for their own engagement in the process. They felt that the video work opened up opportunities to engage with issues that are seldom talked about, but also to envisage how the composite video could be used as a tool to inform and encourage further debate. The following responses to the first question regarding what the participants liked about the video, demonstrates this: '*acting about what is hidden beyond the school walls,*' '*that it teach[es] and show[s] us what is happening to our community,*' '*What I like most is that it was made by us,*' '*We were together and sharing our ideas,*' '*Learners were participating actively,*' '*an opportunity to talk about how you feel,*' '*that we as learners we should not trust teachers that much.*' The above quotations confirm the agency of the participants in bringing out into the open 'what is hidden' in their schools and community and what is not talked about or addressed. However, it also affirms the possibility of meaningful participation.

Reflecting on images that linger in the mind underscores the impact that gender violence has on the community, particularly on young people and on women, as the following responses show: '*the door, what was happening behind the door,*' '*it's the part where the teacher rape[s] the child,*' '*when the learner was crying [after the rape]...*

looking so sad,' '*women and female learners are vulnerable,*' and '*all young people.*' These comments have an immediate quality in relation to the effects of gender-based violence on the victims as well as on the witnesses, and there is a sense of urgency, of doing something, because '*all young people are vulnerable.*'

Taking up the issue of extending the debate around gender-based violence in the context of HIV and AIDS to other audiences, the groups referred to the school, family, friends, church, community, the department of education, and the government. The responses to the 'Why' question confirmed the urgency of addressing the issues: '*they must help,*' '*to stop ... abuse in this community.*' It also raised the issue of the vulnerability of the students in spaces traditionally seen as safe: '*to show them how easily a child can be raped in the school,*' '*to teach about abuse that is taking place in homes, schools, even in the workplace and churches.*' The participants did not only think of their own vulnerability, but of the vulnerability of youth in a collective way: '*I want them to see ...that our generation is in a situation,*' and '*I want them to know how dangerous [it is] to go alone ... if you are a boy or a girl.*'

Turning to the key issue of addressing gender violence, and how the composite video could help, responses of participants foregrounded the need for information and communication, as '*understanding violence because it can teach other people,*' '*many people they know nothing about it,*' and '*the community would inform police about the stories and not to take law into their hands.*' In asking what would help to address gender-based violence in schools and in the community, viewers stressed information, support, a sound value system, and punishment for the criminals. Teachers felt the need for it to '*be explained in subjects, different media should be used ... to teach respect to women and men.*'

Finally, once again drawing on the participants' own understanding, when asked what they would like added to the video, the response of one participant included a thought-provoking comment: 'How is life after rape?' Clearly, the people in the community think deeply about these issues and have definite views on the impact that such an act of crime would have on the life of a victim.

Stage five: screenings in the community

...artists ... aim to disturb, to interrogate personal and cultural assumptions that have come to be taken for granted; to do so, they employ design elements that are appropriate for their intent. These elements (which vary according to art form) are important for their usefulness in recasting the contents of experience into forms with the potential for challenging (sometimes deeply held) beliefs and values. (Barone, 2001: 26)

One of the key purpose of community-based participatory video in our work is to engage the community in exploring and 'making visible' the issues about which people are silent—those issues which are 'hidden' and around which community action is required. The very process of stepping outside of everyday life to produce the videos can create feelings of uneasiness and vulnerability to some participants. We were encouraged by comments from the participants to take the video to a wider audience for viewing and to create an opportunity for engagement. Our data in this section refer to *Our Photos, Our Videos, Our Stories* (Mak et al., 2004), another composite video produced within the same community and around similar issues of gender and HIV and AIDS. The responses of community members demonstrate the richness of post-screening discussions and similar levels of engagement, as highlighted by Goldfarb (2002), Mak (2006), and Levine (2009). At the district community clinic, we brought together various community members, including a community activist, an *induna* (an advisor to one of the chiefs of the district), respected elderly women, teachers, and community healthcare workers. We first

explained the origin of the video, screened it, and then created an opportunity for their engagement through focus group discussions. Because it is a rural district with many members of the audience only being able to communicate in their mother tongue, isiZulu, much of the discussion occurred through the medium of isiZulu, with some code-switching to English. The discussions were recorded, transcribed, and translated into English to allow wider access to the richness of the text. Here we refer to a number of key issues arising from the focus group discussions and related to the theoretical framing of community-based participatory video work.

First, the audience highlighted their sense of being a community (Visser, 2007). They reiterated the idea that people in the community respond better when messages, in this case addressing HIV and AIDS, originate from the community, are created by the community and do not come from somebody outside of the community, as highlighted by Ford et al. (2003). The comments of the participants emphasized this aspect of community-based participatory video work: 'The person from the location [township] has to speak to people of the location [township] and the one from the rural areas speak to those of the rural areas,' 'We saw our places in the rural areas and how many things happen there,' and 'I like the way that you acknowledge everybody that participated because in most cases you see [only] the project coordinators ... I think that was a wonderful idea.'

The role of community healthcare workers, and how much they are valued, is closely linked to this sense of community, as the participants described above: 'It is a surprise because we do not take things in rural areas seriously because we do not have much knowledge. It is like being a health worker: we from the rural areas did not get them soon enough. Their movement into the rural areas is good because many women now know the purpose of clinics through the health workers because there are health workers. We don't quickly get many things and we don't know about them.'

The audience commented that people from within the community could improve the quality of their own lives, through drawing on their individual and collective assets: '*A person gets a chance to do things that are relevant to the environment that you are in,*' '*because I think it's good that if a person has found a better future ... share it with others in the community so that the community may benefit. We are grateful because most of the time when people get educated they flee... they have developed our rural area because... we realize that the future is bright in our area.*' Kretzmann and McKnight (1993) concur that the strengths within a community are rich assets from which individuals can draw strength, even when the community seems under-resourced.

The participants' commitment to their community was deepened by their use of community-based participatory video to stimulate dialogue and action around the issue of HIV and AIDS, especially concerning the community's health and well-being (Visser, 2007). It was clear that they appreciated this aspect of the exercise: '*I think it would encourage the community, if it was to be seen by the community,*' '*In my opinion there should be groups that are there, that go around visiting families, teaching them about this thing,*' even '*the owner of the tavern ...[can] show the cassette in order for the community to listen intently about this thing that is here.*'

Another important issue that was raised relates to the difficulties of communication between and among different generations, as we see in the following responses: '*It is easy for us young people to speak when we are on our own ...,*' '*If they assemble together, it is good for them to hear the grownups ... why don't they allow the youth and adults to assemble with them in order for us to beat the virus that is here...,*' '*It is easy for an old person to understand a thing if it means you sit with him/her and talk about the matter. He/she understands better that way, rather than standing in front of them.*'

Messages of teaching and preaching are deemed less useful, whereas collaborative

video equals out power relations. It was interesting to note that the HIV and AIDS epidemic was conceptualized by the audience as not only affecting adolescents and adults, as one member of the audience saw the importance of including '*small children like those in crèche since they are also important ... I don't know, adapting to small children in order to entice them to understand better.*'

Finally, for us the importance of getting the story out (White, 2007)—to look at it and reflect upon it—is critical, as is demonstrated in the following response, '*What I like the most is that... eh... this is now being spoken about. It even appears on video and yet it was not spoken about. It was hidden. If you spoke about it you would close everything you were doing.*' Opening up the story allows for engagement and healing, and improving the well-being of the individual and community. The importance of video work resides in allowing the hidden issues to be discussed and to be viewed from different perspectives, in allowing communities to open up to the possibilities of addressing HIV and AIDS, and to shift toward taking action. One participant expressed this in the following way: '*If we hide it ... it doesn't exist, when it actually does.*'

PRACTICAL GUIDELINES

The simple guidelines in Table 9.1 could be used as pointers for planning NER video work.

CHALLENGES

As the responses of the producers (participants), as well as those of the audience show, community-based participatory video can offer the possibility for rich and textured discussions. At the same time, the strengths of community video also pose a number of challenges, as we demonstrate below.

Table 9.1 Practical guidelines for 'No Editing Required' video work

What to do	Check
Train how to use user-friendly video cameras	

Setting up tripod
Attaching camera to tripod
Switching on the camera
Opening the viewer and interpreting the information on it
Using the recording, forward, rewind buttons
Zooming in and out
Panning

Allow participants opportunity to practice using the equipment

Explain 'No Editing Required'
Each scene/shot videotaped only once
First shot taken is the 'title of the video'
Ensure that the record button is pressed before the actors read from the script and press the stop record button only after the actor has finished his sentence
Raise awareness that actors should

- be near the microphone of the camera so as to ensure audibility
- face the camera when talking

Consider interference of surrounding noise levels (and wind) if recording outside
Encourage participants to practice each scene before shooting (and to keep to the 10–30 seconds per scene)
Final shot taken is that of the 'credits' at the end

Allow participants 45–60 minutes to shoot their video

Showing and viewing the videos
Data projector and screen required and set-up
Play videos through the video camera

Ethical issues

As with any research undertaken from within a university faculty, we applied for ethical clearance from the University Ethics Committee (UEC). Drawing on a fairly new methodology—not always understood by the UEC—required us to spell out how we intended to do the most good and the least harm. The issue of doing the least harm, as is taken up elsewhere (Moletsane et al., 2008), was complex. Despite efforts to maintain ethical protocol, the unexpected is inevitable. For example, we were concerned when one group of students staged their narrative of three boys raping a girl at school in a way which might be construed as reinforcing gender stereotyping and gender-based violence. To counter our concern, we developed a booklet to accompany the video, and conducted workshops with the teachers and students on ways of using the composite video and booklet on gender-based violence in a sensitive way.

Visual anthropologists and ethnographers such as Banks (2001), Ruby (2000), and Pink (2001) all draw attention to some of the common issues of working with communities, such as: 'How is informed consent understood by the participants?' 'Who owns the images?' and 'Where/when can the videos be screened?' Much of this work is in the context of issues that are not necessarily life-threatening. In our work, we have had to think about the safety and security of participants, particularly the students. The students, for example, who produced *Rape at school: Trust no one,* clearly had a scenario in mind how teachers abuse girls. The question was did they run the risk of being the victims of retaliation? Incest was a topic that was quickly thrown back to the research team through the production of a video called *Vikela Abantwana* or *Protect the Children* (a story about incest) in one of the neighboring schools. How do we ensure that the themes raised in the videos do not simply remain as unexplored issues? At the same time, we also began to see that video might in some ways circumvent some of the ethical issues that arise in photovoice; because the episodes are so clearly acted or staged, issues of ethical concern are reduced. No one would mistake the resulting production as being 'real' (as in the case of a photograph). Indeed, its 'staged quality' gives it its potency.

Working within a community-based participatory framework, we are sensitive to the issue of ownership and we explored with the participants how they might use the video and with whom. We then provided them with copies of the video. We had arranged that each school would receive a data projector and laptop, thus enabling them to screen their videos as required. We did not encounter any participant who was resistant to 'acting' in the video, or who did not want to have the video shown publicly. This was possibly due to the production being based on an issue that was decided on democratically and the fact that it was relevant to their lives, with 'local' and real persons performing the production. Similarly, we considered to what extent the participants would understand informed consent. How might we engage the participants so that they clearly understood what they could do with the video, but also what we as researchers intended doing with it. In trying to address this concern, one of our postgraduate students designed an informed consent form which visually unpacked the notion of informed consent.

Technical concerns

Unlike drawing, performance, or even photovoice, which are visual tools that are relatively inexpensive, filmmaking requires video cameras and, sometimes access to editing equipment and of course requires training in the use of editing equipment. In addressing some of the complexities, our NER approach only required the participants to have an introduction to the video camera equipment, and some idea of basic shots and storyboarding. Experienced facilitators worked with each of the small groups to assist with the planning and execution of the shoots. Technical concerns also include access to electricity—a key consideration for the screenings. Typically, we have conducted our workshops in rural schools as 'hubs' within the community. One of the schools where we worked only had electricity in the principal's office and so our screenings for the 30 or more participants took place in a small room just outside the principal's office, using the wall as the screen. A practical solution, as we have discovered from our colleagues in Rwanda,[4] is to invest in a generator, although if the community is to take ownership of the resulting productions, there is a serious limitation if they themselves cannot screen the videos (in the absence of a projector or video player).

Another issue, potentially adding to cost, is compensation for the participants. In this instance, we invited students, teachers, parents, and community healthcare workers to a Saturday workshop. Saturday is a day when most people in the rural district do not go to work, and therefore they would not lose out on their wages. However, we reimbursed them for their travel expenses (minibus taxi fares) if they had to travel to the venue, and also provided them with refreshments during the day.

WHAT DIFFERENCE DOES THIS MAKE? COMMUNITY VIDEO AND SOCIAL ACTION

Visual anthropology provides critical debates about what constitutes ethnographic film (Rouch, 1974), critiques of indigenous media (Ginsburg, 1995), and concise methodological applications of visual media for fieldwork (Collier and Collier, 1986). However, there is perhaps less attention paid to the ways that visual media can help to shift consciousness and behavioral practices, and how these mechanisms can be used to stem the tide of discrimination and stigma that surrounds HIV and AIDS (Levine, 2009).

Central to our work with community video is a recognition both of the significance of community and community processes (as we note in the first section), but also a consideration of the contribution of interventions like this to social action and the kinds of shifts in consciousness to which Levine (2009) alluded. We think of social action in two ways: social action within the particular rural communities and social action within academic communities. Clearly, the producers themselves saw potential audiences for their work. The community screenings had an impact on the audiences, so it is possible to see ways in which the composite video, focusing on gender violence, played a role in the follow-up work in the community. It is worth noting that the school itself has chosen to embark on further work with the research team in this area.

Furthermore, we noted that the idea of social action within academic communities is also critical. What is the responsibility of the research team regarding the mobilization of funds and its response to the day-to-day needs of the participating schools and communities? As Islam (2008) argued, if community projects (including those using community video) are to be successful, there must be recognition of the differing needs of all partners. Speaking specifically of community video, Banks observed:

> ...community video projects work best when the researcher has had an extensive engagement with the community prior to the video project, when she has a thorough understanding of processes of decision making within the community, and most of all when she is prepared to relinquish control. (2001: 127)

Arguing compellingly for the idea of an applied visual anthropology, Sarah Pink looks at the ways in which applied visual anthropology (which includes community video) can be regarded as social intervention 'practiced across private, public and NGO sectors, as well as in serendipitous situations, in contexts that are shaped by global, national, transnational, institutional, local and individual agencies' (Pink, 2007: 11). Social intervention is best configured as a set of relations over time and not some sort of 'in and out' type of activity.

CONCLUSION

In this chapter, we have argued that community-based participatory video can play a critical role in raising awareness of key social issues, and at the same time engaging communities in exploring solutions. We see the potential of this work to be transformative even in settings that might be regarded as being on the 'wrong side' of the digital divide. Our own reflection as researchers, on engagement with the participants in the community around a sensitive issue such as HIV and AIDS, leaves us convinced that there is much to be gained from taking a visual participatory approach to community-based research. Our treatment of community-based video work here is both critical and celebratory. On the critical side, we have highlighted some of the ethical issues and in particular the challenges of community dynamics in community-based work, and we would hesitate to recommend that researchers take on visual participatory work around sensitive issues such as HIV and AIDS and gender-based violence without committing to a long-term engagement with the community. But on the celebratory side, it is difficult to overlook the significance of what can take place in a rural setting, or to ignore the comments of participants who have made videos for the first time (and their enthusiasm for continuing with participatory video), or the responses of local audiences who have viewed the videos, made right in their own community, and produced by their friends, neighbors, relatives, and even their own children. As one of the community participants commented: *'That's what I like about the video. It did not end here.'*

ACKNOWLEDGMENTS

We gratefully acknowledge both the community participants and members of the research team who have been involved in the community video project: Jean Stuart, Myra Taylor, Relebohile Moletsane, Thabisile Buthelezi, and Fikile Mazibuko as members of the Learning Together research team; Shannon Walsh, Sally Giles, and Ruan Henning for photographing, video-taping, and providing technical assistance during the workshops; and the workshop facilitators Lucky Dubazane, Brenda-Lee Ndlovu, Zolile Mamba-Ndlovu, Kathleen Pithouse, Jackie Simmons, and Nancy Lesko. We would also like to thank all of the young people, teachers, parents, community healthworkers, and community members who enthusiastically gave their time to participate in the video-making workshops and post-screening discussions. We are particularly grateful to Dr Janet Frolich of CAPRISA at the Mafakatini Clinic.

We also acknowledge the financial support of the National Research Foundation (South Africa) and the Social Sciences and Humanities Research Council (Canada).

NOTES

1 Monica Mak and Claudia Mitchell first worked with the No Editing Required (NER) Approach in the Visual Methodologies for Social Change course, McGill University, May–June, 2005.

2 Photovoice is a research strategy that uses photography as a tool for social change. It is a process that gives people the opportunity to record, reflect, and critique personal and community issues in a creative way. In the Learning Together Project (2004–2006), community healthcare workers and teachers used photovoice to explore challenges and solutions in addressing HIV and AIDS in their rural community. A collection of over 500 photographs emanated from this work.

3 The production of composite videos coming out of community-based video work has been replicated in several of our projects and with various participants, and along the way we have come to refine the composite video genre. The biggest change (from the production of *Izindaba Yethu*) has been to ensure that all of the short video productions, from any one project, are included in a single video/DVD. This helps to maximize the use of the resulting composite video as a teaching tool in various communities, as well as to ensure the equal representation of the work of all participants.

4 Here we acknowledge the work of Cineduc, a community-based organization in Rwanda which takes films to communities for the purpose of facilitating dialogue around culture and ethnicity. In order to do this, the organizers temporarily provide the communities with a generator, since so few of them have electricity.

REFERENCES

Banks, M. (2001) *Visual Methods in Social Research*. Thousand Oaks, CA: Sage Publications.

Barnes, D. B., Taylor-Brown, S. and Weinder, L. (1997) '"I didn't leave y'all on purpose': HIV-infected mothers videotaped legacies for their children', *Qualitative Sociology*, 20 (1): 7–322.

Barone, T. (2001) 'Science, art and the predisposition of educational researchers', *Educational Researcher*, 30 (7): 24–29.

Collier, J. and Collier, M. (eds.) (1986) *Visual Anthropology: Photography as a Research Method*. Albuquerque, NM: University of New Mexico Press.

Ford, N., Odallo, D. and Chorlton, R. (2003) 'Communications from a human rights perspective: Responding to the HIV/AIDS pandemic in eastern and southern Africa'. *Journal of Health Communication*, 8: 519–612.

Ginsburg, F. (1995) 'Mediating culture: Indigenous media, ethnographic film and the production of identity', in L. Devereaux and R. Hillman (eds.), *Field of vision: Essays in film studies, visual anthropology and photography*. Berkely, CA: University of California Press.

Goldfarb, B. (2002) *Visual Pedagogy: Media Cultures in and beyond the Classroom*. Durham and London: Duke University Press.

Holland, J., Ramazanoglu, C., Sharpe, S. and Thomson, R. (1992) 'Pleasure, pressure and power: Some contradictions of gendered sexuality', *The Sociological Review*, 40: 645–674.

Islam, F. (2008) *Dispelling the Myths: A Partnership in Support of Preservice Teacher Education in Rural KwaZulu-Natal*. Centre for Visual Methodologies for Social Change, Unpublished manuscript.

Kretzmann, J. P. and McKnight, J. L (1993) *Building Communities from the Inside Out*. Chicago, IL: Acta Publications.

Levine, S. (2009) 'Steps for the future: HIV/AIDS, media activism and applied visual anthropology in Southern Africa', in S. Pink (ed.), *Visual Interventions: Applied Visual Anthropology*. New York and Oxford: Berghahn. pp. 71–89.

Mak, M. (2006) 'Unwanted images: Tackling gender-based violence in South African school through youth artwork', in F. Leach and C. Mitchell (eds.), *Combating Gender Violence in and around Schools*. London: Trentham Books. pp. 113–123.

Mak, M., Mitchell, C. and Stuart, J. (2004) *Our Photos, Our Videos, Our Stories*. Video documentary. Montreal: Taffeta Productions.

Mitchell, C., Walsh, S. and Weber, S. (2007) 'Behind the lens: Reflexivity and video documentary', in G. Knowles and A. Cole (eds.), *The Art of Visual Inquiry*. Halifax: Backalong Press. pp. 97–108.

Moletsane, R., Mitchell, C., Smith, A. and Chisholm, L. (2008) *Methodologies for Mapping a Southern African Girlhood*. Rotterdam: Sense Publishers.

Nair, K. and White, S. (2003) 'Trapped: Women take control of video storytelling', in S. White (ed.), *Participatory Video: Images that Transform and Empower*. New Delhi/Thousand Oaks, CA/London: Sage Publications.

Pink, S. (2001) *Doing Visual Ethnography*. Thousand Oaks, CA: Sage Publications.

Pink, S. (ed.) (2007) *Visual Interventions: Applied Visual Anthropology*. Oxford: Berghahn.

Prilleltensky, I. (2006) 'Psychopolitical validity: Working with power to promote justice and well-being'. Paper presented at the First International Conference on Community Psychology, San Juan, Puerto Rico.

Prilleltensky, I. and Nelson, G. (1997) 'Community psychology: Reclaiming social justice', in D. Fox and I. Prilleltensky (eds.), *Critical Psychology: An Introduction*. London: Sage Publications. pp. 166–184.

Rouch, J. (1974) 'The camera and the man', *Studies in the Anthropology of Visual Communication*, 1(1): 37–44.

Ruby, J. (2000) *Picturing Culture: Explorations of Film and Anthropology*. Chicago, IL and London: University of Chicago Press.

Schratz, M. and Walker, R. (1995) *Research as Social Change: New Opportunities for Qualitative Research*. London: Routledge.

Visser, M. (ed.) (2007) *Contextualizing Community Psychology in South Africa*. Pretoria: Van Schaik.

Walsh, S. (2007) 'Power, race and agency: "Facing the truth" through visual methodology', in N. de Lange, C. Mitchell and J. Stuart (eds.), *Putting People in the Picture, Visual Methodologies for Social Change*. Amsterdam: Sense Publishers. pp. 241–255.

Walsh, S. and Mitchell, C. (2006) '"I'm too young to die" Danger, desire and masculinity in the neighbourhood', *Gender and Development*, 14(1): 57–68.

Weber, S. and Mitchell, C. (2007) 'Imaging, keyboarding, and posting identities: Young people and new media technologies', in D. Buckingham (ed.), *Youth, Identity, and Digital Media*. Cambridge, MA: MIT Press. pp. 25–48.

White, M. (2007) *Maps of Narrative Practice*. New York: W.W. Norton & Co.

10

Differentiating Practices of Participatory Visual Media Production

Richard Chalfen

INTRODUCTION

Over the past few decades and across the world, a range of 'participatory visual methods' has caught the imagination of people seeking to investigate social conditions, lived experience, subjective viewpoints and, in some cases, interventions for social action. By using the term 'participatory visual methods,' attention is drawn to collaborations of participants (sometimes research 'subjects') and researchers in the production of pictorial expression of personal thoughts and life circumstances. Though seldom defined or codified, the process often brings together an unfamiliar 'outside' person(s) and an individual or group of 'inside' people to explore a phenomenon by collaborating on the production of visual (often audio-visual) documentation. The design of these collaborations between 'ordinary people' and 'outsiders' (for example, researchers, educators, artists, professional photographers) may vary widely. However, there is a general sense that ordinary

people will welcome the opportunity to express themselves by collaborating in the production of visual data for exhibition, new observation and comment, or academic study. The current diversity found in professional and non-professional approaches is both impressive and worthy of some clarification.

The majority of accounts in this domain of research methods refer to people using camera technology for the first time, but other relevant examples center on non-camera means of pictorial representation such as drawing, sketching, or otherwise illustrating their ideas.[1] This review will favor the former: namely, when some form of camera technology has been used to generate data. I stress the inclusion of projects motivated by a simple (sometimes naïve) sense of curiosity ('How does the world look to X group of young people?' or 'How does this person, so unlike us, see the same things we do?') as well as formally organized, IRB (Institutional Review Board)-sanctioned research projects.[2] Research is broadly conceptualized as fieldwork undertaken in domestic and international venues, in home, neighborhood, and community.

One frequently heard justification for offering cameras to individuals and groups is to 'give them a voice.'[3] Motivations and intentions can include providing a new channel of expression, seeing, and acknowledging another's point of view, learning what others see as part of everyday life and providing an artistic context for personal expression, among others. Authors frequently cite the need to work with under-represented, disenfranchised sectors of the population. Metaphorically and literally, this represents an intellectual project as well as a humanistic and even noble calling, when the objective is 'to reduce discrimination, marginalization, and inequality and increase empowerment' (personal communication, Jon Prosser, 2002). But we will see that projects have different end points, and that results are valued in different ways. This chapter offers an overview of this domain of visual methods research. The term 'participant visual methods' covers a lot of ground and requires some insight into how various sub-categories of activity are related to one another.

REFERENCE POINT: BIO-DOCUMENTARY NARRATIVES

One principal objective of participatory media research is to eliminate the conceptual and practical filters (literally and metaphorically) that professional filmmakers put in place when gaining access to the lives of certain groups of people and to certain activities. The need arises to 'see through' these filters and lenses in an effort to gain access to more authentic views—fully realizing that complete 'unobstructed views' are impossible. However, the filters that naïve imagemakers put in place are amenable to scrutiny and study.

Within this objective, one convenient reference point for the following collection of work is the notion of 'bio-documentary filmmaking'

introduced and developed by communication scholar Sol Worth (1922–1977).[4] The relevance of this term is seen in the following definition:

A Bio-Documentary film is a film made by a person to show how he [sic] feels about himself [sic] and his [sic] world. It is a subjective way of showing what the objective world that a person sees is "really" like. In part, this kind of film bears the same relation of a documentary film that a self-portrait has to a portrait or a [biography to an] autobiography. In addition, because of the specific way that this kind of film is made, it often captures feelings and reveals values, attitudes, and concerns that lie beyond conscious control of the maker. (Worth and Adair, 1972: 25)[5]

For purposes of this chapter, I am enlarging this cover term and general category to include other media: namely, still photography ('bio-documentary photography')[6] and videotape ('bio-documentary video'). Creating a more inclusive category reduces attention to the specific medium and enhances consideration of personal visual communication.

I am not claiming that all projects under review conform to all of Worth's criteria; important variables associated with this practice and process are outlined below and discussed more thoroughly later in the chapter. However, I am drawing on a general principle suggested by Worth and others that results of camera use by non-professionals, ordinary people untrained in the visual arts, can inform interested observers and contribute a source of information and knowledge not obtainable in any other way. For instance, I am not insisting that members of subject groups remain naïve in photographic techniques or, by contrast, become skilled photographers, while using their cameras. This becomes an interesting independent variable; we will see that many projects include the participation of professional photographers and artists. However, the fact that ordinary people themselves are doing the camerawork, using cameras, and producing their own images remains paramount.

What is left most open is how the results of these projects are treated: that is, displayed, described, studied, analyzed, written about, or otherwise valued. This diversity may, in fact, be most responsible for an observed lack of cross-referencing or continuity across the full range of these projects, inhibiting any comprehensive sense of accumulated knowledge and tradition. This chapter is, in part, one attempt to redirect this trend and counteract this unproductive trajectory.

BACKGROUND

I find that distinctions between 'collaborative media' and 'participant media' are quite instructive. Agreeing with Mitchell and de Lange:

> Video has been used in various ways in social science research, and a distinction between collaborative video overlapping with participatory video, is necessary. Marcus Banks (2001), Sarah Pink (2001) and others refer to *collaborative video* as a process where the researcher or community worker works with a group of participants to create a video production, while in *participatory video*, the process involves a group of participants primarily constructing their own video texts with only minimal assistance from the research team. (Mitchell and de Lange, Chapter 9; my italics)

Most examples of collaborative media center on the ways that interested parties enter into a cooperative scheme in the image-making process and how different tasks are shared to produce a series of photographs, a film, or a videotape. A visiting researcher, social activist, or filmmaker can request cooperation in different ways—these may include:

- Asking for help from local people by having them appear on-camera for a pre-planned theme, storyline, etc. (see Film: Flaherty, 1922).
- Asking different members of the community to say what they want included and why they want certain subject matter filmed; more often than not, community members propose a selection of subject matter for purposes of local improvement in physical, social, or political conditions (Kennedy, 1971, 1982; Elder, 1995).
- Asking for local people to collaborate in editing or otherwise organizing a film; this may also entail asking for preferred meanings of particular

visual sequences and overall meaning of a film (Asch et al., 1991; MacDougall, 1992).

Importantly, these categories are not mutually exclusive as any one may include several forms of cooperation (Chalfen, 1997).

SUB-CATEGORIES AND INDIVIDUAL VARIATIONS

Another fundamental distinction within participant media and related counterparts lies in stipulating who is actually using the camera. This dramatic difference in model of cooperation occurs when a researcher or filmmaker makes a selection of local people living in a particular community to make their own films. Variations of participant media include: autophotographic method (Ziller, 1990), hermeneutic photography (Hagedorn, 1994, 1996), visual narratives (Rich and Chalfen, 1999; Rich et al., 2005), visual/digital storytelling (Lambert, 2009), pictorial diaries (Meth, 2003; Holliday, 2004), bio-documentary film (Worth, 1966), socio-documentary film (Chalfen and Haley, 1971; Chalfen, 1981, 1992), 'participative video' (Prosser and Loxley, 2008), 'auto-driving' (Clark, 1999), and photo/video therapy (Furman, 1990; Weiser, 1999) among others. These efforts are occasionally referred to as subject-generated images or as one form of 'indigenous media' and may be developed as applied work (Pink, 2007) or 'participatory action research' (PAR).

All participatory models are not aimed at just *what* members of a local community simply want to show in audio-visual formats, but the frame of inquiry also includes *how* they want to construct their ideas in mediated forms. Thus, a central aim of the participatory visual media process is to create pictorial narratives that convey what respondents want to communicate in the manner they wish to communicate. The common denominator centers on an individual or small group of people using borrowed cameras to produce their own visual texts following their own incentives, ideas, concerns and objectives, and local conditions.

SUGGESTED ORGANIZATION—TWO STRANDS OF WORK

I suggest a broad division of work in participatory media production based on two streams of activity and contribution, each of which can be instructive to the other. The first strand has attracted human interest commentary, and is made visible to the public in diverse forms of mass media, including articles in newspapers, well-illustrated books, clips on television, and now spots appearing on websites, blogs, YouTube, and the like. One example even drew Academy Award attention (the feature documentary film *Born into Brothels* (2004), see: http://www.kids-with-cameras.org/bornintobrothels/ Accessed 5 August 2010). Many projects in this strand spring from local problems and are organized by individual initiatives on behalf of caring and concerned individuals. These are often local efforts, supported with local funds or domestic private organizations or, on rare occasions, international grants. Picture-making projects mentioned in these reports have been directed by a diverse set of practitioners, including artists, social workers, photography instructors, and community workers, among others.

Informal projects in the first strand have taken some inspiration and guidelines from the academic examples in conjunction with the successful and immensely popular emergence of consumer models of still and motion picture cameras. While we recognize that recent developments in digitalization have played a large role, we must also acknowledge that popular use of pre-digital instamatics, instant cameras (for example, Polaroids), and disposable (one-use or throw-away) cameras were also significant in this democratization process. As just one example, we find a range of projects directed toward

knowing more about the lives of children and young people. These include *Fotokids,* started by Nancy McGirr in 1991; *Kids with Cameras,* founded by Zana Briski in 2002; *Shooting Back*, created by Jim Hubbard in 1989; *Visible Voice* projects, started by Vincent O'Brien, 2002–06; the *Eye-to-Eye Project/Save the Children* (UK), and *Literacy and Photography,* established by Wendy Ewald (1985), among others.

The second strand is characterized more by formal models of research that are undertaken in academic contexts of fieldwork and publication. Thus, results are much less known to the public. This strand features results and findings that are published in professional journals and offer other perspectives from the more prevalent human-interest documentation. Work here is derived from institutional settings, grounded in academic interests and motivations, and rewards. These efforts are characterized by formal research proposals with sections devoted to background literature, hypothesis, or set of expected outcomes, research protocols, and detailed division of labor, and are aimed at funding from government agencies and foundations, sanctioned by an IRB submission and approval to safeguard ethical concerns, privacy issues and human protection, and the like.

Work in the second strand has a rich history found in many international examples of fieldwork done by visual anthropologists and visual sociologists, in projects that have asked members of different social groups to create their own images for research questions. Early and frequently cited examples include the 1966 project with the Navajo (Worth and Adair, 1972), the Inuit (Kennedy, 1982), as well as groups living in East Africa (Bellman and Jules-Rosette, 1977), Australia (Michaels, 1985), South America (Carelli, 1988; Asch et al., 1991; Turner, 1991), and Aibel's follow-up with the Navajo working with their own video equipment (Aibel, 1976).

These two stands of work can also be thought of as *projects* and *studies*. This characteristic difference focuses on different values of respective 'end points' as well as the status and meaning of 'results' and 'findings.' Briefly, the 'project strand' is likely to privilege the visual products of image production as 'the results' and to celebrate them in exhibitions, screenings, award-giving contests, and the like. Work that comprise the second 'studies strand' treats the photographic/video results as a 'mid-point' in the knowledge-production process; these resultant images become the focus of description and analysis to produce a set of findings that then serve as 'end points.' The significance of this difference will become clearer in the following pages.

KINDS OF QUESTIONS BEING ASKED

The many examples of projects and studies in participatory media research reviewed for this chapter are united by certain kinds of curiosity, questions, problems, and solutions. General and specific questions that span the two strands of work cited above include the following:

1   'What does life look like as…' or 'What is it like to live as…'

- a person living in slum or street conditions (Mizen, 2005), a shelter, as a gang member
- someone at the 'bottom of the pyramid,' such as homeless people (Radley et al., 2005; Packard, 2008);
- a member of a persecuted political party or religious group and possibly compared with members of other competing groups (Lykes, 2001);
- a person living with a chronic or terminal illness (Rich and Chalfen, 1999; Buchbinder et al., 2005; Lopez et al., 2005), with HIV (Dobnik, 2005; Elber, 2008), as an alcoholic or drug-addicted person (Evans et al., 1979), as someone confined to a wheelchair (Berland, 2007);
- a survivor of a harmful medical episode, for example, a stroke or related brain trauma and damage (Lorenz, 2006); and
- a survivor of a human-made or natural disaster (Varoli, 2005).

2   How does the structure of a visual sequence, a visual narrative in film or video correspond to structures found in written or spoken expression, as in storytelling, myths, fables, and related models of linguistic expression? (Worth and Adair, 1972).

3   How can these models of indigenous photography become a stimulus to memory (Radley and Taylor, 2003) or other modes of expression and/or channels of communication: for example, literacy, writing, and public speaking?

4   How does the structure of the process, the making of a visual narrative, reflect, or reveal the social structure or social organization of its producers? (Chalfen, 1981).

5   How successful is a visual narrative at revealing information that cannot be reported in any other mode of expression—How are naïve views and perspectives revealed through participatory visual methods?

6   How can first-time camerawork serve political ends: for example, to reveal and begin to change harmful antisocial conditions or even subversive activities? (Wang et al., 1996; Wang and Burris, 1997).

These questions are indicative of common interests, but they are not offered as an exhaustive inventory from a rapidly growing literature featuring participatory research methods.

FORMAL AND INFORMAL MODELS OF INQUIRY

Methodological decisions about research design and picture-making protocols depend largely on particular questions being asked, questions that motivate each project in conjunction with who is being asked to use cameras. Participatory visual methods encompass a range of 'projects' accompanied by different means of observation that ask people to show interested observers how and what they see as important aspects of their lives. In different models, the outside agent takes on the role of a project director (PD) usually for informal projects, or principal investigator (PI) for more academic formal ones. Again we can locate some variation; both models contain variants based on different ways the PD or PI may elect to intervene. Three categories of independent variables are most common, comprising:

- The PD/PI may want to offer varying amounts of *technological and/or aesthetic instruction for camera use* (shooting strategy, camera technique) or editing (shot juxtaposition, sequencing) following different cinematic traditions.
- In other cases, the PD/PI may want *to question the filmmakers at different points* in the image-making process, gaining additional perspective on objectives, strategy and anticipated outcomes.
- In yet other examples, the PD/PI may want *to feed back* the visual results to community members to elicit additional information by learning more about locally realized meanings, interpretations, and results.

Variations and additional complexity will be reviewed shortly.

DESIGN AND METHODOLOGICAL VARIATION

When surveying the accumulation of participatory media projects and studies, we clearly find a broad diversity of social and physical contexts, a range of work based on differing objectives, subjects, motives, and intended outcomes going in several directions. Some projects are grounded in contexts of experimentation and research, some emphasizing quantitative measures, others, qualitative ones, and with varying degrees of rigor or academic discipline. Many reports have proved to be very vague on these latter variables. In conjunction, incentives and rewards have varied, the breadth of participants has broadened, and results have been valued in different ways and advertised in alternative formats and venues. The general method is very versatile but, due to these varying contexts, comparing results of these projects is difficult and, indeed, problematic. Significant variables in participatory media research, all

bordering on methodology, include the following:

1. *Sponsorship varies*; the range of financial support extends from popular forms of individual and community-sponsored projects to more ambitious projects that require some form of private foundation and/or government funding.[7]

2. As suggested above, *different kinds of equipment* have been introduced—from 8 mm, Super-8, and even 16 mm technology, to instant cameras, for example, Polaroids, to 'point-and-shoot' cameras, to one-use or disposable cameras, to videocams, to newer digital technologies, in both still and motion picture formats. In turn, we can predict the development of camera-phone projects.

3. Projects have been conducted with considerable *pedagogical variation* and protocols. This variation has ranged from a heavy hands-on approach, when projects included aesthetic information from professional photographers and some artists to enhance 'good' pictures; in these cases, participation included a professional photojournalist, fine artist, commercial photographer, or documentary filmmaker or feature film producer.[8] As just one example: '[T]he 14 students ages 10 to 16, … We talked them through the photo shoot and about composition and then gave them a camera...' (Gonser, 2005). By contrast, other projects have remained closer to the bio-documentary preference for minimal instruction, by teaching just technology, avoiding any preferred choice of content or style, technique, and the like, purposefully refraining from any aesthetic instruction beyond basic camera mechanics.[9] In one project with Nepali women, we read: 'She gave each subject a camera, showed them how to use the viewfinder and the flash. She then asked them to photograph things that were important to them and things that they thought Americans did not understand about their lives' (Anonymous, n.d.).[10]

4. The range of assignments to research subjects varied in important ways. In order to understand the results of these projects, it is

important to have some information on first, how the student-subjects received their training and how they were introduced to photography and, second, on what they were asked to do. Differences were found in the degree of direction and assigned picture-taking. There was always some form of assignment; asking the student 'to take whatever they wanted' still counts as a form of assignment. But the other extreme would be the actual assignment of specific topics and perspectives. In one example, for a project with both Palestinian and Israeli children, the instructor made several recommendations: 'Not dramas, just little documentaries about who they are and what they believe in, who their parents are, where they go to school, what they had to eat, what movies they watch, what CDs they listen to' (Anonymous, 2005b).

5. Variation was also found when research participants were given *freedom to select their own image content*. The majority of projects professed a strong interest in learning what different people saw, admitting a bio-documentary curiosity. One approach was to encourage freedom of choice—freedom to select content, topics, settings for their pictures. Of course, this premise raises interesting questions—Is it ever possible to photograph anything and/or everything? A revealing example came from Iraq: 'In Herat, Rerras's students—mostly 14–18 years old—were restricted to taking pictures at the girls' school they attended, or at home, although some ventured out with their cameras while wearing burkas. In Kabul, the girls could wander a bit farther, searching for subjects for their photos' (Barisic, 2004). In another example, dealing with abused Canadian immigrant women: 'Mehta gave the children the cameras and the freedom to ask their parents tough questions because she wanted to show that kids suffer almost as much as the abused spouse' (MacDonald, 2005). At the other extreme, we approach more of the strategy suggested by Worth's bio-documentary model, asking young people to decide, without collusion or coercion by personnel, as

part of a desire to learn what and how a specific group of people decide for themselves, what and how they prefer to look and see with their cameras. Interestingly, this ideal is never reached (Eckholm, 2005).

6. Many projects stressed the importance of incorporating some form or *subject feedback and photo-elicitation* as a methodological component (Collier and Collier, 1986; Harper, 2002). Both visual anthropologists and visual sociologists have gained important information by using participant-made images to ask for comments, insights, and even questions in narratives that were obtained from subjects who had been given cameras to record their lives (Venkateswar, 2005). In these ways, we find a kind of double bio-documentary function, as they stimulate additional thought and comment from the same subject group. In one project involving the Israeli/Palestinian conflict, we read: 'Twelve children from each side of the conflict took pictures of the Old City and offered their perspective on the ongoing conflict. After all the photos were taken they met to discuss their work and points of view. The hope being a lasting understanding of one another' (Sommer, 2007).

7. *Methods of study and analysis* varied greatly. These ranged from anecdotal comments and observations of participants' photographs to systematic gathering of pictures as data, to using an orderly and explicit analytical approach to visual results, requiring an explicit model of orderly annotation, logging, and coding, content analysis, and sometimes, the use of qualitative analysis software (Rich and Patashnick, 2002). In many cases, however, reports never describe how the pictures are actually looked at or how certain observations were made about the results, leaving it to the viewer, suggesting the problematic stance of 'pictures-speak-for-themselves.'

8. Parallel to the variation noted for project 'inputs,' we need to consider potential *variation in 'output.'* We are thus drawn to ask about the uses of tangible results and who might be the benefactors of such results.

What happened after the pictures were successfully taken—in addition to learning how they were treated, for example, examined, studied, and analyzed—we are asking about if and how they were exhibited, sold, given back to original photographers, and used for new projects, among many other possibilities.

The two strands of participatory media research differed in process, meaning that different emphases were put on 'front ends' versus 'back ends' of the process. Projects emphasized the making and display of images; in comparison, studies attended to post-production, post-display components of the overall process, including description, analysis, and reporting results and findings. In the former, I found more variation, including local display and/or public exhibition, often associated with raising funds for additional projects. In the latter and at the other extreme, pictorial results of the research process were treated as private research data, as personal documents, and not for public viewing. Such results become part of academia, as published reports, articles, and even books.

Clearly, the most commonly reported results in the project strand mentioned the development of *some kind of public exhibition*, some way of displaying the project's pictures, but also in formats that were not limited to gallery walls, including films, CDs, slide shows, photo-essays, among other photographic products such as catalogs and a 'Through My Eyes' Calendar' (Ziu, 2005). On occasion, the function of an exhibition is linked to art therapy, as mentioned above, when the photography workshop for the children of Beslan 'turned into an extraordinary period of rehabilitation and rejuvenation... . It was at this point that it ceased to be simply a photography workshop and became a profound form of therapy' (Varoli, 2005).

9. The two strands are also differentiated by what is first considered, and second done, with *'results'* and *'findings.'* In the majority of 'projects,' the visual/pictorial results are thought to stand on their own; they are meant

to be appreciated for themselves as achievements of people expressing themselves through visual media. In short, the results are not treated as findings. However, there are rare and interesting exceptions. One such example was provided in a report on Wendy Ewald's work[11]: Ewald found that, 'Mexican children were most interested in photographing dream images that were very playful [and they rarely photographed their families]. But in South Africa, the children didn't want to make photos of their dreams. They preferred family portraits and taking pictures of their daily lives' (Hayes and Rader, 2006). Another rare example was provided by Meikle and Whalen (2005), when one student stated: 'Doing the project has made me much more confident about having my photo taken.' The project directors reported: 'Girls were more interested in the project than boys, perhaps because teenage girls are a lot more image-conscious than boys at that age... . In the process, their self-esteem and confidence have improved dramatically' (Meikle and Whalen, 2005).

Virtually by definition, academic studies comprising the second strand were required to go beyond pictorial results into interpretations and statements of findings. The scientific discourse that validates work in the studies strand is not accomplished in pictures; the medium of communication is writing, as we see that written texts are supported by visual ones. The inverse is true of most work in the projects strand—the images are supported with words when they are requested, as when the project is reported upon by interested writers.

10. Finally, there is considerable variation regarding any sense of intended *application of results*. For instance, who benefits from such picture-taking—people doing the photography or people looking at the results, neither or, more likely, both? The range is indeed quite impressive but seldom acknowledged or summarized. Many projects implied beneficial change (social improvements,

improved health care and/or education, a more balanced political control, human rights, among others) for participants (often, children and young people), community members, neighborhoods, and the like.

Examples included gaining financial support for worthy causes such as improved healthcare facilities, better recreational services or public understanding of a social problem, or what professionals are dealing with on an everyday basis. In one medically related project that asked 'medically fragile children' to photographically illustrate their lives, project director Jennifer Swanberg said she hoped the pictures would help medical professionals remember that the children have lives and needs outside of those tied to their conditions (Meehan, 2005). In the context of medically related studies, results and findings are being incorporated into medical school curricula (Chalfen and Rich, in press a).

However, knowledge of successful or unsuccessful application of results is uneven and differs across projects and studies. In the former, reports seldom indicate if and how applications of project results have been made successfully. Since this information often relies on news accounts, readers are more likely to hear of problems than successes: for example, people running off with funds meant for young people. The opposite appears to be true with the reporting of studies. Here we find a 'celebratory' tendency when the success of research efforts is given most attention.

ETHICAL CONCERNS

Increased camera activity on a worldwide scale, largely facilitated by greater availability of electronics and digital technology, may be contributing to a growing suspicion of both the use of cameras and of pictures. The potential for deception and malicious surveillance are reaching the knowledge of ordinary people, who may more readily ask: 'What's going to happen to these pictures?' 'Who said you could take my picture here?' In short, there is a greater awareness of the politics underlying photographic practices, including the uses of cameras and pictures, of both taking pictures, and 'being taken' in pictures. There is a growing cry for regulations to be put in place to reduce harm, deception, and misrepresentation. This applies as well to police surveillance, photojournalism, and visual research, among others.

In turn, ethical dimensions of the participatory media research landscape are often problematic (Prosser, 2000; Wang and Redwood-Jones, 2001; Cannella and Lincoln, 2007; Nakamura, 2008; McDonnell, 2009). Ethical questions arise at all stages of research projects—from planning stages, before the research actually starts, to long after its completion. We do not yet have ethical codes of conduct or sets of guidelines for what constitutes 'good practice in different contexts and different socio-political environments' (Prosser and Loxley, 2008: 48). Much of the problem lies in the fact that existing ethics statements were originally directed toward word-based researchers, but they remain of limited use to visual researchers.

The maxim of 'do no harm' still holds an exalted priority of ethical concern, especially when children are involved. However, with the multi-faceted process of media production and, perhaps more importantly, within media exhibition, display, and even unanticipated distribution, there are many unknown variables, unanticipated reactions and results accompanied by points of possible danger and harm. The representational characteristics or features of photographic images pose questions and problems that eclipse the written word.

Two important examples stand out, both focusing on questions of identity, privacy, and personal security. The first is the issue of *anonymity*. Researchers, parent institutions, and sponsoring agencies generally agree that details of their research participants' identities should be protected; their privacy should be respected. In written contexts of reporting, anonymity can be assured by the use of pseudonyms; visual research presents other obstacles and challenges. This applies to 'found images' already in existence as well as those produced as part of a current research project (Jon Prosser, personal communication, 2002).

An interesting twist is added when comparing what we have been referencing as either 'projects' or 'studies.' In the former, participants may want to be shown and seen. However, in studies, legal safeguards may prescribe that people should *not* be seen or identified without explicit permissions.

A second issue is *'informed consent.'* Whereas this safeguard was once an answer to potential problems in using ordinary people in professional productions, this concept has come under considerable scrutiny given basic questions about shared understandings of what 'informed' means when so many uninformed and unforeseen possibilities are a reality. In addition, there is the complicated question of how 'informed consent' will be translated and understood by different subject groups and even ability levels of those with different disabilities? One can ask: 'Consent but who for and what for?' (Prosser and Loxley, 2008). One response has been to institute a progressive or sequential consent format whereby participants are asked to sign informed consent agreements at different times in any given study and agree to specific uses of their materials, for example, showing photographs or videotapes in academic publications, as part of professional presentations or Internet websites (Chalfen and Rich, in press b).

All institution-based research programs are subject to intense review and IRB approval. Primary attention is given to their concerns for research with human subjects; they insist that research proposals contain specific details for requiring informed consent/release forms, interview constraints, dissemination plans, and the like. Often cited as a means of legal and hence financial protection for a sponsoring institution, ethical concerns are increasingly important, in societies with varying degrees of enthusiasm for litigation.

By contrast, reports of community projects seldom mention these two points. Funding has not been reliant on ethical safeguards; my feeling is that PDs and participants feel the benefits of such work assets may well outweigh any potential detrimental effects or harmful results. Thus, again, we find differences in the relevancy of specific ethical issues between informal projects and academic studies. With regard to anonymity, many participants in projects want to be shown and seen as clearly identifiable individuals rather than concealed or renamed. In comparison, in academic studies, legal safeguards may dictate that people should not be recognized or identified without adequate adult consent.

Participatory visual researchers must be aware of the potential for trouble spots. Consider the following:

- It is very hard to predict interpersonal and political conflicts that might develop in the picture-taking process.
- There may be a chance of putting young participants at physical risk because they are carrying cameras.
- People have uneven feelings about the identification and identity of participants, especially when medical disabilities and related problems are involved.
- Confidentiality questions may arise regarding people who just happen to be in pictures taken in public places (passing or loitering individuals or crowds in a public space) about keeping the identity of subjects/participants confidential.
- Legal responsibilities may arise when PDs or PIs gain knowledge of unacceptable or illegal acts and behavior.
- The ease of image dissemination can pose additional trouble; people can (and certainly do) post project or program pictures to image-sharing websites with great ease.
- Research may involve different respondents—for example, parents, teachers, children, and disabled people—each with different understandings of the project, different sensitivities, and different expectations and needs.

DISCUSSION AND CONCLUDING THOUGHTS

Practitioners of both projects and studies, PDs and PIs, have demonstrated and illustrated a great potential for the visual and audio-visual versions of participatory research methods. As more work is done, we gain a better idea of both advantages and disadvantages, of assets and liabilities.

Perhaps as a characteristic of a new subdiscipline, work in visual studies too often ignores the past; practitioners will not do sufficient homework and fail to account for previous efforts, mistakes, and advances. There seems to be a divide between the excitement of getting on with the picture-making and, for many, the less-exciting need of doing background research in any attempt to learn from our predecessors and, in some cases, ancestors. In short, an accumulation of experience and knowledge would benefit future efforts.

One of biggest stumbling blocks remains with the 'back end' of projects and studies. For example, additional attention should be given to what happens after images are made, and, furthermore, what and how viewers learn from photographic results within these variations of bio-documentary narratives. If these pictures are said to serve as metaphorical voices, let us listen more and commit to discourse our interpretations of what is being shown, of what is being expressed by research participants. Whenever possible, we should take advantage of photo-elicitation to aid both 'speaking' and 'listening,' to gain valuable insights from feedback, to ask the picture-makers what *they* see in their own visual expression, and to neutralize any bias we bring to our observations and conclusions. In turn, this commentary allows us to incorporate their ideas into our communicative framework. Here we might have a chance to make genuine progress in gaining a greater understanding of the power of these modified bio-documentary methods.

The formal or informal analysis components of participatory media research remain as a weak point in the process; analysis of photographic content is more often than not left undone. In too many cases, putting pictures on an exhibition wall appears to be the crowning achievement, accompanied by the justification, 'Let the pictures speak for themselves.' But some would argue that pictures never speak for themselves—viewers have to do the work in terms of looking, seeing, thinking, and speaking (Chalfen, 2002). Much of this criticism reduces to the question: 'When is showing the same thing as saying?' (Rich, 2003) To chase the metaphor, practitioners, scholars, and observers need to offer mindful ears to hear these liberated voices. We are seeing a need for more discussion of photographic results in the context of analytical models that we have at our disposal. But herein lies an important problem: the popular and scholarly literature on participatory media offers little in the way of analytical models to serve these needs. In short, great opportunities are lost for more informative, substantial conclusions.

In this spirit, the foregoing overview can provide new initiatives and projects with background and knowledge of previous efforts. Directors of new projects can exploit this report for a better view of alternatives—choices that can be applied to different contexts and circumstances. This variety of motivations, objectives, methods, and outcomes alongside techniques and models of instruction contributes to understanding better that any innovation of communication can take many shapes and forms. One goal of this comparative overview has been to seek improvements in theory and practice underlying the general theme of applying visual research methods and participatory media to understand better the diversity of human visual culture.

NOTES

1 Jon Prosser suggests the inclusion of other examples such as drawn or painted self-portraits or related illustrations, personal timelines or life maps, concept maps, pictorial diaries on paper, or related

medium (personal communication, 2002). However, these forms will not be discussed here.

2 Lyn Yates (2010) introduces the distinction of participant visual media offering 'windows on the world' versus 'windows on the self' while admitting that some projects can do both.

3 An entire Special Issue of the journal *Visual Studies* (2010) has been recently devoted to issues of 'visual voice' and clarifying this ambiguous phrase.

4 By way of a reflexive footnote, I was a student of Worth, while in the doctoral curriculum at the Annenberg School of Communication at the University of Pennsylvania in the mid-1960s. I was fortunate to serve as a research assistant for John Adair and Worth on the Navajo Film Themselves Project (Worth et al., 1997), and later worked with him alongside Dell Hymes and Erving Goffman to develop notions of socio-documentary filmmaking and 'sociovidistics' (Chalfen, 1981).

5 Just as one example, in a documentary film about the Navajo, one would expect to find an outsider's 'objective' representation of how Navajo live: but a bio-documentary would be made by a Navajo, and viewers would gain access to a filmic version of how a Navajo sees and structures his own life and the world around him.

6 The meaning of this term is not the same as 'bio-photography' described as: '... Barron exploring the intersection of science and biology with disorienting close-in views. Barron evokes a future in which, as his artist statement reads, "... we stand poised to gain direct control of our own evolution"' (see Libby, 2006).

7 Grants, fellowships, gifts, and private donations have been means of support. Specific sources have included United Nations funds: for example, UN children's agency UNICEF, Government-sponsored Neighborhood Renewal Fund, the Ford Foundation, the Abbott Fund, Johnson & Johnson, Big Brothers Big Sisters, university funding sources, just to mention a few. Finally, we see that some projects are more directly affiliated with art projects and picture-making—for example, the Amateur Photographers and Cinematographers Association, Arts and Culture Council, and the Society for Arts in Health Care—but most projects much less so.

8 An example is described in the following quotation:

An Indian film producer taught the children how to use cameras and basic filming techniques. He hopes this documentary will give the children a chance to express what is on their minds so that adults can better heal their psychological wounds. ... four children—despite never having seen a video camera before—have made a film, documenting their lives before and after the Tsunami. The boys, Sobarnath and Arivazhagan, and the girls, Padma Sivaraman, Manisha, Roja Ramani, and Pakya, took 10 days to make the 20-minute documentary under guidance from renowned Bollywood filmmaker Govind Nihalani (Anonymous, 2005a).

9 One might argue that professionals get in the way of 'natural' expression by prematurely structuring results; on the other hand, others would claim that this instructional model is a good thing, to let the young people take their photographic efforts further, to facilitate some form of later employment and potential financial gain.

10 In yet another collection of projects, we find the instructions included some form of verbal communication, such as when students were asked to keep a written journal alongside their photography (Nilsen, 2005). In one project, 'The children's [photographic] narratives were extended by asking them also to write and illustrate any aspect of their lives by providing them with notebooks, pencils, erasers, and color pencils. The research methodology proved extremely successful in terms of the children's involvement in it, the use of photography as a means for children to both compose and reflect on aspects of interest to them in their daily lives, as well as generating richly detailed narratives (Venkateswar, 2005).

11 Wendy Ewald was trained as a professional art photographer and admitted to being consistently drawn to the expression of young people as she addressed conceptual, formal, and narrative concerns. Ewald asked different groups of children 'to take photos of everything from their friends and homes to themselves'. As they got to know each other better, she asked them to use their imaginations more, and their photographs became more complex' (Hayes and Rader, 2006).

REFERENCES

Aibel, R. (1976) 'Communication, cognitive maps and interpretive strategies: Filmmakers and anthropologists interpret films made by Navajo and Anglos'. Master's Thesis. Annenberg School for Communications, University of Pennsylvania.

Anonymous (2005a) *Tsunami-Hit Children Reel out Real Life Experience*, Rediff.COM. [Online]. Available from: http://in.rediff.com/news/2005/sep/26tsunami.htm [Accessed 26 September 2005].

Anonymous (2005b) *Spielberg Plans Peace Project*, Virgin.net. [Online]. Available from: http://movienews.virgin.net/Virgin/Lifestyle/Movies/virginMoviesNewsDetail/0,15384,888089_movies,00.html [Accessed 30 October 2005].

Anonymous (n.d.) *Nepali Women by Nepali Women*. [Online]. Available from: http://www.nepalitimes.com/issue209/nation_2.htm [No longer available].

Asch, T., Cardozo, J. I., Cabellero, H. and Bortoli, (1991) 'The story we now want to hear is not ours to tell: Relinquishing control over representation: Toward sharing visual communication skills with the Yanomami', *Visual Anthropology Review*, 7(2): 102–106.

Banks, M. (2001) *Visual Methods in Social Research*. London: Sage Publications.

Barisic, S. (2004) *Va. Woman Teaches Afghan Girls Photography*. [Online]. Available from: http://www.kansascity.com/mld/kansascity/news/world/10490975.htm?1c [Accessed 24 December 2005].

Bellman, B. and Jules-Rosette, B. (1977) *A Paradigm for Looking: Cross-Cultural Research with Visual Media*. Norwood, NJ: Ablex.

Berland, G. (2007) 'The view from the other side—patients, doctors, and the power of a camera', *New England Journal of Medicine*, 357(25): 2533, 2535–2536.

Buchbinder, M. H., Detzer, M. J., Welsch, R. L., Christiano, A. S., Patashnick, J. L. and Rich, M. (2005) 'Assessing adolescents with insulin-dependent diabetes mellitus: A multiple perspective pilot study using visual illness narratives and interviews', *Journal of Adolescent Health*, 36(1): 71.e9–71.e13.

Cannella, G. S. and Lincoln Y. S. (2007) 'Predatory vs. dialogic ethics. Constructing an illusion or ethical practice as the core of research methods', *Qualitative Inquiry*, 13(3): 315–335.

Carelli, V. (1988) 'Video in the villages: Utilization of videotapes as an instrument of ethnic affirmation among Brazilian Indian groups', *CVA Newsletter*, May: 10–15 (see also [Online]. Available from: http://www.nativenetworks.si.edu/Eng/blue/vai_08_dc.htm [Accessed 11 June 2010].

Chalfen, R. (1981) 'A sociovidistic approach to children's filmmaking: The Philadelphia Project', *Studies in Visual Communication*, 7(1): 2–33.

Chalfen, R. (1992) 'Picturing culture through indigenous imagery: A telling story', in P. Crawford and D. Turton (eds.), *Film As Ethnography*. Manchester: University of Manchester Press. pp. 222–241.

Chalfen, R. (1997) 'Foreword and afterword', in S. Worth, J. Adair and R. Chalfen (eds.), *Through Navajo Eyes: An Exploration in Anthropology and Film Communication*, revised 2nd edn. Albuquerque, NM: University of New Mexico Press.

Chalfen, R. (2002) 'Commentary: Hearing what is shown and seeing what is said', *Narrative Inquiry*, 12(2): 397–404.

Chalfen R. and Haley, J. (1971) 'Reaction to socio-documentary film research in a mental health clinic' (with Jay Haley), *American Journal of Orthopsychiatry*, 41(1): 91–100.

Chalfen, R. and Rich, M. (in press a) 'Sharing information about the pain: Patient–doctor collaboration in therapy and research', in J. Foster (ed.), *Collaborative Information Behavior: User Engagement and Communication*. Hershey, PA: IGI Global.

Chalfen, R. and Rich, M. (in press b) 'Studying research capabilities of youth media: Analyzing children's audiovisual expressions about health', in J. E. Fisherkeller (ed.), *International Perspectives on Youth Media: Cultures of Production & Education*. New York: Peter Lang Publishers, Inc.

Clark, D. C. (1999) 'The autodriven interview: A photographic viewfinder into children's experience', *Visual Sociology*, 14(1): 39–50.

Collier, J. and Collier, M. (eds.) (1986) *Visual Anthropology: Photography as a Research Method*. Albuquerque, NM: University of New Mexico Press.

Dobnik, V. (2005) *Young People's Photographs Document the Ravages of AIDS* [Online]. Available from: http://www.journalnow.com/servlet/Satellite?pagename=WSJ%2FMGArticle%2FWSJ_RelishArticle&c=MGArticle&cid=1128768492526 [Accessed 4 December 2006].

Eckholm, E. (2005) 'Native eyes on a land south of the clouds', *The New York Times*, November 7.

Elber, L. (2008) *Photo Project Lets Africa AIDS Victims Show Their Own Story* [Online]. Available from: http://www.huffingtonpost.com/2008/06/10/photo-project-lets-africa_n_106386.html [Accessed 26 October 2008].

Elder, S. (1995) 'Collaborative filmmaking: An open space for making meaning, a moral ground for ethnographic film', *Visual Anthropology Review*, 11(2): 94–101.

Evans, G. B., Steer, R. A. and Fine, E. W. (1979) 'Alcohol, value clarification in sixth graders: A film-making project', *Journal of Alcohol and Drug Education*, 24(2): 1–10.

Ewald, W. (1985) *Portraits and Dreams: Photographs and Stories by Children of the Appalachians*. UK: Writers and Readers Publishing Inc.

Furman, L. (1990) 'Video therapy: An alternative for the treatment of adolescents', *Special Issue: The Creative Arts Therapies with Adolescents. Arts in Psychotherapy*, 17: 165–169.

Gonser, J. (2005) *Children's Lives Come into Focus*, HonoluluAdvertiser.com. [Online]. Available from: http://www.honoluluadvertiser.com/apps/pbcs.dll/article?AID=/20050812/NEWS01/508120351/1190/NEWS [Accessed 12 August 2006].

Hagedorn, M. I. E. (1994) 'Hermeneutic photography: An innovative aesthetic technique for generating data in nursing research', *Advances in Nursing Science*, 17(1): 46–50.

Hagedorn, M. I. E. (1996) 'Photography: An aesthetic technique for nursing enquiry', *Issues in Mental Health Nursing*, 17: 517–527.

Harper, D. (2002) 'Talking about pictures: A case for photo elicitation', *Visual Studies*, 17(1): 13–26.

Hayes, I. and Rader, A. (2006) 'Photography empowers kids with cameras—Wendy Ewald has devoted 30 years to encouraging kids to photograph the world', *The Indianapolis Star*, February 5. [Online]. Available from: http://www.indystar.com/apps/pbcs.dll/article?AID=/20060205/LIVING/602050348 [Accessed 8 February 2006].

Holliday, R. (2004) 'Filming "The Closet"—The role of video diaries in researching sexualities', *American Behavioral Scientist*, 47(12): 1597–1616.

Kennedy, T. (1971) 'The Skyriver Project: The story of a process', *Access National Film Board of Canada Challenge for Change Program*, 12: 3–21.

Kennedy, T. (1982) 'Beyond advocacy: A facilitative approach to public participation', *Journal of the University Film and Video Association*, 34(3): 33–46.

Lambert, J. (2009) *Digital Storytelling: Capturing Lives, Creating Community (3E)*. Berkeley, CA: Center for Digital Storytelling.

Libby, Brian (2006) 'Bio-photography and artifice', *The Oregonian*. [Online]. Available from: http://www.danielbarron.com/brian%20libby%20review.pdf [Accessed 5 August 2010].

Lopez, Ellen S., Eng, Eugenia, Randall-David, Elizabeth and Robinson, Naomi (2005) 'Quality-of-life concerns of African American breast survivors within rural North Carolina: Blending the techniques of photovoice and grounded theory', *Qualitative Health Research*, 15(1): 99–115.

Lorenz, L. S. (2006) Living without connections: Using narrative analysis of photographs and interview text to understand living with traumatic brain injury and facilitators and barriers to recovery from the patient's perspective'. Paper presented at the European Sociological Association, Mid-term Conference, Cardiff, Wales.

Lykes, M. B. (2001) 'Creative arts and photography in participatory action research in Guatemala', in P. Reason and H. Bradbury (eds.), *Handbook of Action Research*. Thousand Oaks, CA: Sage Publications. pp. 363–371.

McDonnell, B. (2009) 'Ethical considerations in collaborative visual work: Developing the Somali Lenses Photo Exhibition', *The Anthropology Newsletter*, April.

MacDonald, G. (2005) 'Alone in Canada, "They don't call 911"—Deepa Mehta produces a searing documentary on abuse in immigrant families', *globeandmail.com*. [Online]. Available from: http://www.theglobeandmail.com/servlet/ArticleNews/TPStory/LAC/20051022/DEEPA22/TPEntertainment/TopStories [Accessed 22 October 2006].

MacDougall, D. (1992) 'Whose story is it?' in P. I. Crawford and J. K. Siminsen (eds.), *Ethnographic Film Aesthetics and Narrative Traditions*. Arhaus, Denmark: Intervention Press. pp. 25–42.

Meehan, M. (2005) 'The images of typical kids—Medically fragile children illustrate their lives', *Lexington Herald* Leader [Online]. Available from: http://www.kentucky.com/mld/kentucky/12251632.htm [Accessed 29 July 2005].

Meikle, S. and Whalen, R. (2005) 'Photography: Image is everything', *YoungPeopleNowMagazione.com*. [Online]. Available from: http://www.ypnmagazine.com/news/index.cfm?fuseaction=full_news&ID=5849 [Accessed 17 December 2005].

Meth, P. (2003) 'Entries and omissions: Using solicited diaries in geographical research', *Area*, 35(2): 195–205.

Michaels, E. (1985) 'How video has helped a group of Aborigines in Australia', *Media Development*, 1: 16–18.

Mizen, P. (2005) 'A little light work? Children's images of their labor', *Visual Studies*, 20(2): 124–139.

Nakamura, K. (2008) 'A case against giving informants cameras and coming back weeks later', *Anthropology News*, 20.

Nilsen, L. (2005) 'Cameras capture creativity—Photo programs geared to students', *Sun-Sentinal.com*. [Online]. Available from: http://www.sun-sentinel.com/news/local/palmbeach/sflbc17pictures-jul17,0,6982834.story?coll=sfl-news-palmcomm [Accessed 17 July 2006].

Packard, J. (2008) '"I'm gonna show you what it's really like out here": the power and limitations of participatory visual media', *Visual Studies*, 23(1): 63–77.

Pink, S. (2001) *Doing Visual Ethnography*. London: Sage Publications.

Pink, S. (ed.) (2007) *Visual Interventions: Applied Visual Anthropology*. Oxford: Berghahn.

Prosser, J. (2000) 'The moral maze of visual ethics', in H. Simons and R. Usher (eds.), *Situated Ethics in Educational Research*. London: RoutledgeFalmer.

Prosser, J. and Loxley, A. (2008) 'Introducing visual methods', An ESRC National Centre for Research Methods Review Paper. National Centre for Research Methods, NCRM Review Papers, No. NCRM/010.

Radley, A. and Taylor, D. (2003) 'Remembering one's stay in hospital: a study in photography, recovery and forgetting', *Health: An Interdisciplinary Journal for the Social Study of Health, Illness and Medicine*, 7(2): 129–159.

Radley, A., Hodgetts, D. and Cullen, A. (2005) 'Visualizing homelessness: A study of photography and estrangement', *Journal of Community and Applied Social Psychology*, 15: 273–295.

Rich, M. (2003) 'Show is tell', *Narrative Inquiry*, 14(3): 691–715.

Rich, M. and Chalfen, R. (1999) 'Showing and telling asthma: Children teaching physicians with visual narrative', *Visual Sociology*, 14: 51–71.

Rich, M. and Patashnick J. L. (2002) 'Narrative research with audiovisual data: Video Intervention/Prevention Assessment (VIA) and NVivo', *International Journal of Social Research Methodology*, 5(3): 245–261.

Rich, M., Polvinen, J. and Patashnick, J. (2005) 'Visual narratives of the pediatric illness experience: Children communicating with clinicians through video', *Child and Adolescent Psychiatric Clinics of North America*, 14(3): 571–587.

Sommer, S. (2007) 'Eyes Wide Open photography project focuses on the Wright properties'. [Online]. Available from: http://www.springfieldnewssun.com/hp/content/oh/story/news/local/2007/09/29/sns093007eyeswideopen.html [Accessed 26 October 2008].

Turner, T. (1991) 'The social dynamics of video media in an indigenous society: The cultural meaning and personal politics of video-making in Kayapo communities', *Visual Anthropology Review*, 7(2): 6–76.

Varoli, J. (2005) 'Beslan children's photos show their view of town', *The St. Petersburg Times* [Online]. Available from: http://www.sptimes.ru/story/15458 [Accessed 6 September 2006].

Venkateswar, S. (2005) 'The lives of child workers in Nepal: Research methodology', *Their World—Their Eyes*, Asia Source. [Online]. Available from: http://www.asiasource.org/asip/sita/sita_references.htm [Accessed 17 August 2006].

Wang, C. and Burris, M. A. (1997) 'Photovoice: concept, methodology, and use for participatory needs assessment', *Health Education & Behavior*, 24(3): 369–387.

Wang, C., Burris, M. A. and Ping, X. Y. (1996) 'Chinese village women as visual anthropologists: A participatory approach to reaching policymakers', *Social Science & Medicine*, 42(10): 1391–1400.

Wang, C. C. and Redwood-Jones, Y. A. (2001) 'Photovoice ethics: Perspectives from Flint photovoice', *Health Education & Behavior*, 28(5): 560–572.

Weiser, J. (1999) *Phototherapy Techniques: Exploring the Secrets of Personal Snapshots and Family Albums*. Vancouver, BC: PhotoTherapy Center Press.

Worth, S. (1966) 'Film as non-art: An approach to the study of film', *The American Scholar*, 35(2): 322–334.

Worth, S. and Adair, J. (1972) *Through Navajo Eyes—An Exploration in Film Communication and Anthropology*. Bloomington, IN: Indiana University Press.

Worth, S., Adair, J. and Chalfen, R. (1997) *Through Navajo Eyes—An Exploration in Film Communication and Anthropology*, revised 2nd edn. Albuquerque, NM: University of New Mexico Press.

Yates, L. (2010) 'The story they want to tell, and the visual story as evidence: Young people, research authority and research purposes in the education and health domains'. Unpublished manuscript; files of the author.

Ziller, R. C. (1990) *Photographing the Self: Methods for Observing Personal Orientations*. Newbury Park, CA: Sage Publications.

Ziu, D. (2005) 'Through my eyes calendar presented', *Oneworld.net*. [Online]. Available from: http://see.oneworld.net/article/view/124419/1/3260?Prin—Version=enabled [Accessed 24 December 2005].

FILMS

Nanook of the North (1922) [Film, Criterion Collection Spine #33, black and white, 35 mm, silent, 75 minutes, 1525 meters]. Directed by R. J. Flaherty. New York: Révillon Frères.

11

Some Theoretical and Methodological Views on Photo-Elicitation

Francesco Lapenta

INTRODUCTION—A CASE FOR PHOTO-ELICITATION[1]

Photo-elicitation, the use of photographs during the interview process, was first described in a paper published by John Collier, Jr (1957), 'Photography in Anthropology: a Report on Two Experiments.' The method, which Collier called 'photo interviewing,' was later described in greater detail in the chapter 'Interviewing with Photographs,' in the book *Visual Anthropology: Photography as a Research Method* (Collier and Collier, 1986: 99–125), in which the authors offer a systematic survey of the visual techniques utilized in anthropology at the time. In this context, photo-elicitation was, for the first time, described as a variation on open-ended interviewing (Harper, 1994: 410), a non-directive method that favored collaboration between researcher and respondent. This approach emerged from theoretical and methodological debates that questioned the tenets of classic structured interviews/surveys, the nature of the researcher–respondent relationship, and any knowledge that this interaction was supposed to produce.

Open-ended methods see an interview as an exchange that, although initiated and guided by the interviewer, aims to grant to an interviewee greater space for personal interpretations and responses. In the photo-elicitation interview, this exchange is stimulated and guided by images. Typically, these are images that the researcher has made of the subjects' world (Harper, 1987; Harper and Faccioli, 2000), or they are photographs that have been selected by the researcher because they are assumed to be meaningful to the interviewee (Lapenta, 2004; Epstein et al., 2006). The pictures, however, might also have been taken by the researcher, while accompanied by one or more informants who might suggest what to photograph and/or how (Pink, 2006). They can also be images that interviewees themselves have taken or selected for the specific aims of the interview, in an approach that has been referred to as 'reflexive photography' or 'autodriven photo elicitation' (Harper, 1987; Clark, 1999).

A number of authors have described this approach theoretically (Grant and Fine, 1992; Banks, 2001; van Leeuwen and Jewitt, 2001; Harper, 2002) and it has been included among other established research methods and methodologies used in sociology (Wagner, 1979; Schwartz, 1989), anthropology (Rose, 2001; Pink, 2006), and cultural studies. The general consensus in this literature is that the use of images and/or film in the interview process elicits 'deep and interesting talk' (Harper, 2002: 23) on subjects otherwise too complex to explore (Rose, 2001; Pink, 2006). Photographs can convey contents that words can only approximately represent, and can represent subjects that might be invisible to the researcher but visible to the interviewee, triggering unforeseen meanings and interpretations (Schwartz, 1989). The nature of the method is also described as intrinsically collaborative (Banks, 2001; Pink, 2006). As originally noted by the Collier and Collier (1986), and later by others (Banks, 2001; Harper, 2002; Lapenta, 2004; Pink, 2006), interpreting the meanings of images can be explored in a conversation between the researcher and the respondent. Images can also be the response to a conversation, as when respondents are asked to photograph or film their own lives (Levy, 1991; Clark, 1999; Chalfen and Rich, 2004; Pink, 2006) to discuss their subjects and meanings later.[2] It is in these contexts that images can be hypothesized (Lapenta, 2004), using Gadamer's concept, as a path to a 'fusion of horizons' or broadening, of one's own horizon or knowledge. This is achieved through the opening up the interview to the content and communicative potential of images and the subjectively and linguistically negotiated interpretations, descriptions, and meanings they invoke (Lapenta, 2004: 50).[3]

Although it remains fairly marginal to mainstream research, photo-elicitation has recently gained broader recognition for its heuristic and collaborative potential. Indeed, it is becoming an established element in the methodological toolbox of the visual anthropologist or sociologist and is increasingly popular in a range of interdisciplinary research studies. Photo-elicitation has been used in a widening range of research designs and anthropological subjects such as studies of social class or organization, family, community and historical ethnography, or identity and cultural studies (Collier and Collier, 1986; Harper, 2002). For example, photo-elicitation has been used to study ethnic identification (Gold, 1986), farming communities (Schwartz, 1989), change in a town (Chiozzi, 1989), gentrification (Suchar and Rotenberg, 1994), memories of a steel town (Modell and Brodsky, 1994), and children's experience of place (Smith and Barker, 2000; Rasmussen, 2004). Photo-elicitation has also increasingly expanded to other disciplines (Hurworth, 2003; Epstein et al., 2006), such as in healthcare as a tool for nursing, medical, or gerontological research (Hagedorn, 1996; Riley and Manias, 2003), in individual and family therapy (Entin, 1979; Wessels, 1985) and to enhance memory retrieval (Aschermann et al., 1998), in social work (Weinger, 1998), child psychology (Salmon, 2001), and in education as a way to teach students (Killion, 2001) or talk about abstract concepts (Bender et al., 2001).

This variety of research areas, applications, and topics has remained strongly grounded in the interpretations and theoretical tenets described in 1986 by Collier and Collier (herein referred to as 'the Colliers'). In what follows I will describe, and then depart from, their accounts of photo-elicitation and elaborate on more contemporary interpretations and applications.

PHOTO-ELICITATION: THE COLLIERS' (1986) FOUNDING THEORETICAL TENETS

In this section, I will describe the Colliers' original analyses of the photo-interviewing process. They described a number of direct experiences with photo-elicited interviewing in the chapter 'Interviewing with Photographs' (Collier and Collier, 1986: 99–115), and then went on to discuss psychological implications that can be available to the researcher using photographs in projective interviewing (117–132). While describing the contexts and subjects of their research, they developed a case for photo-elicitation as a method that seemed to meet, almost 'spontaneously,' the aims of a qualitatively informed open-ended interview. Collaboration between interviewer and interviewee, non-directivity of the discourse, and a higher level of engagement by interviewees with the themes and subjects of the interview emerged as the recurring qualities described by authors that have used or described the method since then (Schwartz, 1989; Banks, 2001; Harper, 2002; Pink, 2006).

The Colliers discussed the *why* and *how* of the use of photographs in interviews. How are these communicative elements used? How do they affect the interaction and discourse structure? Do they achieve the greater collaboration between the researcher and the interviewee promised? They described photographs as tools, useful for obtaining knowledge 'above and beyond' what might be obtained by the analysis of the photographs themselves. As they wrote:

> When native eyes interpret and enlarge upon the photographic content, through interviewing with photographs, the potential range of data enlarges beyond that contained in the photographs themselves.... [becoming] communication bridges between strangers... [and] pathways into unfamiliar, unforeseen environments and subjects. (Collier and Collier, 1986: 99)

What is now termed the 'polysemic quality' (Harper, 2002: 15; Margolis, 2008) of images creates the possibility for different observers to interpret their contents according to their identity of views, native knowledge and ethos, and to actively discuss and exchange the personal values and meanings that these subjects might have for them (Collier and Collier, 1986: 103–108). Photographs, in their interpretation, have two relevant informational values for the researcher: The first,

or encyclopedic value, is produced by the photograph's immediate character of realistic reconstruction, which is best defined as the potential for survey offered to the researchers by the photographs' capacity to visually record objects, persons, and physical and social circumstances. The second, or projective interviewing, goes beyond this mere capacity to record objects, persons, and situations. When eliciting individual interpretations and responses, images can acquire multiple and unpredictable meanings. The Colliers explain that, below their 'surface content,' strongly descriptive photographs can become charged with highly subjective meanings and values that can ultimately be opened up only through *'the projective interpretation by the native'* [italics in original] (Collier and Collier, 1986: 108).

The combination of these two informational characteristics of the image constitute the *intrinsic potential* of the photo-elicited interview as a tool to pursue the researchers' aims to gain an enriched knowledge of other people's lives, opinions, knowledge, and behaviors. The Colliers found that photographs not only operated as a projective tool to constitute a communicative path into the lives and worlds of the observers, but also created a new communicative situation in which the report between subjects was reshaped and refocused. Images, they explained, 'invited people to take the lead in the inquiry, making full use of their expertise,' and they readily 'invited open expression while maintaining concrete and explicit reference points' (Collier and Collier, 1986: 105) in a way that verbal interviewing could not. Photographs may offer an opportunity for developing a sense of self-expression for respondents who are identifying and explaining the image's contents by 'tell[ing] their own stories,' and allowing for joint discovery of the 'realities of the photographs... [by] exploring the photographs together' with the researcher (Collier and Collier, 1986:105).

For the Colliers, these uses of photographs were helpful in building a level of trust that would allow for the interactional dynamics of the interview and provide increased access to information. Rapport and trust, they reminded us, remain 'a major focus of concern' for the researcher who 'struggles to define a genuine functional relationship' (Collier and Collier, 1986: 105) with respondents. 'Psychologically, the photographs performed as a third party in the interview session (Collier and Collier, 1986: 105), since, in their experience, '(t)he use of photographs tempered many of these difficulties' (Collier and Collier, 1986: 105) encountered while forming such relationships:

> We are asking questions of the photographs, and the informants became our assistants in discovering the answers in the realities of the photographs. (Collier and Collier, 1986: 105)

Schwartz also noted that interviewees respond to photographs without hesitation (Schwartz, 1989: 151–152). By providing informants with a task similar to viewing a family album, the strangeness of the interview situation was averted. In the Colliers' experiences, as related throughout these chapters, this effect is a direct outcome of the specific communicative qualities of photographs. While questions asked during strictly verbal exchanges bear meaning in themselves, photographs represent the possibility for the researcher to acquire a specific meaning through participant interpretation and verbal description. The understanding of this interpretation is that participants, through the confrontation of their respective interpretations and points of view, use words to define a photograph's meaning in the interview. Both participant and researcher have to collaborate to focus their interpretative attempt (Collier and Collier, 1986: 99–132).

The approach and theoretical support described by the Colliers and adopted by most researchers following their approach has some theoretical limits which I discussed in detail (Lapenta, 2004). Yet their contribution has been fruitful in describing ways of recasting traditional open-ended interviews. The Colliers' descriptions delineated a communicative interaction characterized by a changing in the relationships between the interviewer, the interviewee, and the stimuli (the photograph), and they described what were, at that time, novel possibilities for the social dynamics of interviewing. An initial implication of such uses of photographs during the interview process was to break down the unidimensional linguistic structure of the interview discourse by adding a second, relevant, communicative element. This shift in the nature of the stimuli has two associated effects. First, the use of photographs supplements the dialogue with new visual informational elements and symbols that verbal communication cannot deliver (Collier and Collier, 1986: 105). Second, the introduction of a non-verbal element in the interaction transforms the question-and-answer dynamics of the verbal interaction between the interviewer and the interviewee (Lapenta, 2004). This is no small achievement for an interaction whose primary purpose is to elicit a rich exchange of information.

FOUR APPROACHES TO PHOTO-ELICITATION

At a very basic level, researchers who decide to use photo-elicitation must make key decisions that will affect the research structure and the actual application of the method. These key decisions can be synthesized, according to Epstein et al. (2006), into three basic questions:

- Who is going to make or select the images to be used in the interviews?
- What is the content of the images going to be?
- Where are the images going to be used, and how?

It is methodologically significant who makes or selects certain images over others from the pool used in the interview process. Images used in photo-elicitation can generally be categorized into one of three sources: researcher-produced images that they have taken or acquired, for example from historical archives or from collectors; participant-produced images taken for the purpose of the research or 'found,' as in family albums[4]; and images co-produced during the study by the researcher and the research participants.

As noted by Epstein et al. (2006), photo-elicitation, faithful to its original description and applications, has mainly been adopted in interviews as an 'ice breaker' activity to create a comfortable space for discussion, and as a tool to 'invoke comments, memory, and discussion in the course of a semi-structured interview' (Banks, 2001: 87, as cited by Epstein et al., 2006). And, despite the diversity of fields and applications (for example, see Chapters 9 and 12), photo-elicitation has, until recently, often involved the use of pictures taken and/or selected by the researcher. This decision, however, is characterized by different levels of feasibility and organizational complexity, and, more importantly, each approach entails different methodological strengths and weaknesses. Sometimes it might be not possible for the researcher to directly take appropriate photographs, or it might be impossible for the researcher to ask respondents to make or select their own pictures. These circumstances will shape practical applications of photo-elicitation in a given research context.

Perhaps more importantly, as discussed in the existing literature, each practical method is also associated with specific methodological tenets. For example, scholars interested in exploring social spaces and contexts, or exploring theoretical concepts, have tended to use photographs selected by the researcher in order to map spaces, objects, or subjects of interest, and to focus respondents' attention on these researcher-selected themes and subjects (Harper, 1982, 1984; Schwartz, 1989; Weinger, 1998). An advantage of this approach is that it allows a set of selected photographs to function as a consistent and structured, yet flexibly organized, tableau of images. These can be used to assess respondents' differing levels of understanding and perception given the same pictures and subjects. The approach can be used to test specific research hypotheses with a large sample of respondents, and to compare research results and interpretations against other interviews or studies that may have used the same or similar images. Researcher-produced sets of photographs can generate descriptions and meanings that may illuminate subjects initially invisible to the researcher but visible to interviewees (Schwartz, 1989), thus enabling the researcher to develop new hypotheses and interpretations. If necessary, additional images can be acquired to further the analysis. Such image collections can also help to 'break the frame' by showing familiar things in unfamiliar ways to respondents who may critically and reflexively observe their own lives (Harper, 2002: 20).

The epistemological quandary of this classic approach to photo-elicitation arises from questions surrounding *whose* knowledge did selected pictures actually represent? For whom were those pictures really made? Whose subjects of interest, discourses, and aesthetics do they represent?

As a consequence of the theoretical questions generated by the use of researcher-produced images, a range of alternative approaches have been developed that employ respondents' self- or collaboratively produced images, or a mix of both. The main alternatives to 'classic' photo-elicitation have been categorized by Hurworth (2003) as: 'Autodriving,' 'Reflexive Photography,' and 'Photo Voice (or Photo Novella),' and they reflect methodological differences in the researchers' use of photographs.[5]

Considering the use of images made collaboratively, that is, those selected or made by the respondents themselves or those produced by the researcher in collaboration with respondents, addresses pivotal theoretical distinctions between images of different origins. Each collaborative approach typically involves asking respondents to photograph places and subjects that are meaningful to them in some way (Clark, 1999; Clark-Ibanez, 2004; Epstein et al., 2006), or to take photographs together with the researcher while participating in private or social events and environments (Pink, 2007). These alternative approaches aim to empower respondents by allowing them to show to researchers the respondents' worlds from their own point of view. In the following sections, I will describe these different approaches and their methodological tenets in greater detail.

REFLEXIVE PHOTOGRAPHY: RESPONDENT-GENERATED IMAGE PRODUCTION

The idea of reflexive photography was originally introduced by Harper (1988b), who hypothesized that:

> in the reflexive photographic method, the subject shares in the definition of the meaning; thus, the definitions are said to 'reflect back' from the subject. (Harper, 1988a: 64–65)

In common with other forms of photo-elicitation, this method uses photos to enhance informants' engagement in the interview; however, respondents are not presented with photos taken by the researcher but, rather, are encouraged to elaborate on the content and meaning of photographs they produce themselves. Termed 'Autodriving' by Heisley and Levy (1991) in marketing research, the informant's responses to research questions would be driven by stimuli drawn directly from photographs taken by respondents. An advantage of this approach is its capacity to reduce the researcher bias embedded in the selection of specific images, subjects, and themes used in the interviews. In this form of photo-elicitation, 'the interview is "driven" by informants who are seeing their own behavior' through the process of selection, observation, and interpretation of their own photos (Heisley and Levy, 1991: 261). This not only allows researcher and informants to negotiate interpretations of the photographs but also provides a means for informants to

have increased voice and authority in interpreting their own lives, social contexts, and a 'perspective of action' that helps make their life-views and social systems meaningful to outsiders (Gould, 1974: 25). Photographs allow people to 'view' themselves from a distance, outside their everyday lives. This distance can help informants to interpret the selected photographs and perhaps 'see familiar data in unfamiliar ways' (Heisley and Levy, 1991: 257). This motivation can be used to enhance informants' involvement and elicit a qualitatively enriched body of information concerning events as informants perceived them (Heisley and Levy, 1991).

Another advantage of respondent-based collections of images resides in the fact that the image sample can also be employed as a tool 'to reinforce and elaborate on findings typically revealed through standard quantitative approaches such as... surveys' (Heisley and Levy, 1991: 257). Or they can be deployed as part of other modes of qualitative inquiry, such as focus groups. One example of research based on the use of reflexive photography is the study conducted by Harrington and Schibik (2003) of the freshman year experience (FYE). In their project, students were asked to take pictures during their first 6 weeks on campus. Students were asked to '(t)ake pictures that will illustrate your impression of the university or that will help you describe your impressions' (Harrington and Schibik, 2003: 30). The aim was to capture early impressions of college life in order to gain an understanding of different issues affecting student perceptions of their FYE. They were also asked to record their thoughts and feelings about ways that each photograph was illustrative of those early college experiences. Students were then interviewed, first in individual photo-elicitation interviews, and later in focus-group interviews in which they could discuss the photographs, as a group, in light of their experiences and common perceptions and themes. The research approach helped to reveal themes that included 'perceptions about the university's physical environment,... interactions with faculty, interactions with other students, student support services, and career counseling' (Harrington and Schibik, 2003: 25). It provided insight into students' 'impressions of the institution,' their perceptions of the relative importance of certain collegiate experiences and expectations, and descriptions of what 'expectations were unreal or unreasonable' (15). The use of reflexive photography provided specific and concrete examples of freshman experiences on campus that were not highlighted by other, more general, survey instruments, by capturing both by students' words and their pictures (Harrington and Schibik, 2003).

PHOTOVOICE: COMMUNITY-BASED IMAGE PRODUCTION

Further enriching the spectrum of image-based interviewing methods, *Photovoice* adds additional potentials for respondent-based image production and analysis. Originally described as 'photo novella' by Wang and Burris (1994), the method is now largely referred to as 'photovoice' (Wang and Burris, 1997; Wang, 1999, 2001, 2005). As Hurworth (2003) described the process, photovoice is a participatory action research approach that asks interviewees to take photographs that they feel portray their daily routines, common events or community life. They subsequently talk about the significance and meaning of these images with other members of the community, and the researcher.

Photovoice, as initially conceived, had three main goals:

1 To enable people to record and reflect their community's strengths and concerns.
2 To promote critical dialogue and knowledge about personal and community issues through large- and small-group discussion of their photographs.
3 To reach policymakers (Wang, 1997: 370).

Wang presented different stages involved in the process that moves from a general conceptualization, to the definition of broader goals and objectives, the devising of the

initial themes for taking pictures, and the final critical evaluation and group discussions of the photographs. She described important stages of this process (Wang, 1997), four of which are as follows:

> Photovoice training begins with a discussion of cameras, ethics, and power; ways of seeing photographs; and a philosophy of giving photographs back to community members to express appreciation, respect, or camaraderie. It may also engage with the description of mechanical aspects of camera use. (Wang, 1997: 378)

These considerations are by no means unique to photovoice; other authors, including Pink, Harper and Heisley and Levy, similarly describe an ethically informed research practice that interprets the use of photographs as both an opportunity to empower respondents and voice their interpretations and by that create an opportunity to give back to the research participants. Photovoice is unique in that following a similarly participatory approach engages all the 'members of the community [to] select those photographs that most accurately reflect their concerns and assets. These might include those they consider most significant, or simply like best' (Wang, 1997: 380).

> The participatory approach then generates a second stage of contextualizing or storytelling. This occurs in the process of group discussion, suggested by the acronym VOICE, Voicing Our Individual and Collective Experience. [...] People describe the meaning of their images in small and large group discussions. (Wang, 1997: 381)

This approach distinctly separates photovoice from other methods in that it conceives the photographs as catalysts of participatory 'stories' that emerge from the composed 'voices,' meanings and interpretations elaborated by the members of a small or large group, thus framing the fourth participatory stage of the method: 'codifying':

> Here participants may identify three dimensions that arise from the dialogue process: issues, themes, or theories. They codify issues when the concerns targeted for action are pragmatic, immediate, and tangible. This is the most direct

application of the analysis. They may also codify themes and patterns, or develop theories that are grounded in data that have been systematically gathered and analyzed in collective discussion. (Wang, 1997: 381)

A key component of photovoice is then characterized by its aim to elicit dialogue among participants through the use of photographs taken by the participants and employed in an open discussion about their broader significance and meaning. This grounding of the images in a shared interpretation of the real and personal experience of the members of the group has the potential to be a valuable tool to empower marginalized groups to articulate and 'voice' their opinions to researchers or policymakers. Of course, it also has the potential to be harnessed in consumer research, as we have seen with 'auto-driving.' Photo- elicitation-based interaction not only enables the researcher to observe and participate in the discussion but also may provide a useful collective photographic representation drawn from the participants' consensus regarding photos that depict how they view their own lives and community. As Wang pointed out:

Such an approach avoids the distortion of fitting data into a predetermined paradigm; through it we hear and understand how people make meaning themselves, or construct what matters to them. (Wang, 1997: 382)

COLLABORATIVE OR PARTICIPATORY IMAGE PRODUCTION

Another participatory approach involves images generated by the researcher 'together' with respondents as 'collaborative representation,' which serves to remove barriers between the observer and the observed (Banks, 1995). Banks later argued that, to some degree, all research efforts are collaborative (Banks, 2001: 119), concluding that the researcher's very presence when using a camera among a group of people is necessarily (by today's ethical standards) the result of a series of earlier contacts and negotiations. In collaborative research, then, negotiations with respondents emerge as a methodological dilemma: the researcher has to decide how much information to share with respondents about the research agenda.

While the approach to these negotiations and disclosure practices, and their resolution, differs between projects, in some cases the very process of negotiation becomes fundamental to the research methodology. In her description of reflexive ethnographic visual research, for example, Pink (2006) described how negotiations around the use of a camera can become a process through which informants and researchers negotiate and select what they would and would not like the images to show, and how they would like to be represented (Pink, 2006: 102). The process of informant selection and guidance offer opportunities for the researcher to learn about existing conventions and local visual cultures. The experience of photographing or filming together provides opportunities to discuss how the researcher sees, what s/he photographs, and how informants interpret the researcher's photographs. These interactions can bring researchers closer 'to understanding their visual knowledge' and provide 'criteria for evaluating' what researchers and respondents see differently (Pink, 2006: 102). This reflexive process can be used 'as part of the process of learning to see as others do, in a directed way.' By 'collaboratively representing everyday experiences,' researchers empower respondents to produce 'shared understandings of their past experiences and current practices' (Pink, 2006: 107) and the images and audio-visual materials provide data 'that informants can... comment on to produce a further layer of knowledge.' Parker (2009), who followed Pink's and Banks' methods, concluded that:

collaboration with interviewees in producing photographs (or videos) entails the interviewees recognizing both aspects of the research study that they wish to highlight and discuss, as well as their interpretation of what may be relevant and useful to the researcher. (Parker, 2009: 8)

She then explained how collaborative image production offers a number of opportunities:

> It can reveal how interviewees "see" their world and their past, as well as how they wish themselves and their own roles to be visually represented, perceived and understood. (Parker, 2009: 8)

It can also empower interviewees by granting them a role in the selection and framing of images, thereby uncovering their experiences, perspectives, and histories.

ETHICAL CONSIDERATIONS AND 'BEST PRACTICE'

While reflections on ethics inform all areas and methods of social research, these considerations acquire an extra layer of significance when dealing with image-based approaches. For visual researchers, Prosser et al. (2008) argued:

> general ethics guidelines and codes of practice cover important principles. [But being] "visual" in orientation... brings its own set of methodological practices and its own distinct set of ethical conundrums that require resolving. (Prosser et al., 2008: 28)[6]

The main ethical problems for photo elicitation-based research are twofold. First, interviews often may include images of other identifiable persons. Second, once photographs are removed from the original context of the interview in which they were discussed and used (for instance in publication or display), they may be understood in ways that misrepresent their subjects. Moreover, the problem with images produced by respondents for a sociological interview resides in their diversity of origin, and the complex social networks they may be embedded in.

Although most researchers are aware of ethical and legal issues such as copyright, informed consent, agreed conditions of publication, or status of confidentiality or anonymity, this is probably not the case with respondents. The diverse origins of the pictures, and the different relations between the author/s of the images, the subjects depicted and the researcher, may mean it is not always possible to know when images selected by informants for discussion in interviews comply with ethical and legal considerations.[7] Even when respondents have been trained, researchers should remain particularly vigilant to ensure that no visual representations made for the research are made public (accidentally, or by a participant's own exuberance to 'go public') without appropriate consent. A particularly telling example can be found in Darren Newbury's chapter (Chapter 34), where he comments on Joanou's decision not to publish photographs from her photovoice project.

In her discussion of ethics on the Photovoice website, Wang described a set of 'best practice' guidelines, both for the researchers and the respondents (Photovoice, 2005). These guidelines are not a checklist, guaranteed to solve ethical problems involved in research; rather, they should be interpreted as possible areas of discussion and evaluation when initiating research. While initially designed for the development of photovoice projects, these guidelines have also proved useful for other applications of participatory methods. Wang regarded general safety of the participants as primary:

> Be aware of, and execute ways to minimize, participants' risks, including physical harm and loss of privacy to themselves or their community. Put another way, participants' safety and well-being are paramount. (Photovoice, 2005)

She described the job of facilitators, as addressing the following:

- describe during group discussions the participants' responsibilities when they carry a camera to respect the privacy and rights of others;
- facilitate critical dialogue that yields specific suggestions and ways to respect others' privacy and rights; and
- emphasize that no picture is worth taking if it begets the photographer harm or ill will (Photovoice, 2005).

Wang suggested that researchers and respondents should discuss the responsibilities of the photographer to respect the privacy and rights of others. She highlighted the need for written consent, including the importance of requiring participants to obtain written consent from people they themselves photograph, including, in the case of minors, those of parents or guardians. Wang noted:

> This has some drawbacks—it sometimes yields stiff, less spontaneous pictures—but experience has shown that the drawbacks are outweighed by the advantages: preventing misunderstanding and building trust by giving participants an opportunity to describe the project and solicit the subjects' own insights about a community issue; establishing the possibility of a long-term relationship that may allow for future photographs and exchange of knowledge; and acquiring written consent to use the photographs to promote community wellness. (Photovoice, 2005)

Wang concluded with a list of 'shared questions' that may be used to elicit discussion of these issues among the participants. The questions included:

- What is an acceptable way to approach someone to take their picture?
- Should someone take pictures of other people without their knowledge?
- What kind of responsibility does carrying a camera confer?
- What would you not want to be photographed doing?
- To whom might you wish to give photographs, and what might be the implications (Photovoice, 2005)?

CONSIDERATIONS FOR USE OF PHOTO-INTERVIEWING

Photo-elicitation does not eliminate all power relationships or sequential rules of discourse from research interviews. Images may lend themselves to different probing and communicative techniques, but they can obviously be manipulated by the researcher during discussions to imply themes or emphasize elements of their content: for example, in ordering or arrangement of the images chosen. Like all research methods, photo-elicitation techniques remain valuable as a participatory technique when one keeps these methodological challenges in mind.

Hurworth provided a useful summary of the research potential of photo-elicitation in terms of its methodological strengths. Photo-elicitation can:

- be used at any stage of the research
- provide a means of 'getting inside' a program and its context
- bridge psychological and physical realities
- allow the combination of visual and verbal language
- assist with building trust and rapport
- produce unpredictable information
- promote longer, more detailed interviews in comparison with verbal interviews
- provide a component of multi-methods triangulation
- form a core technique to enhance collaborative/participatory research and needs assessments
- be preferable to conventional interviews for many participants (Hurworth, 2003: n.p.).

Bringing together verbal and visual communication systems creates variations within the typical discourse structure of a research interview that proves methodological meaningful.[8] The 'classic' verbal semi-structured interview is organized around an unbalanced 'question–answer' discourse structure. This turn-taking system is said to either create or reinforce an epistemological and social asymmetry between the interactants. Schegloff and Sacks (1973), and Drew and Heritage (1992) described this discursive asymmetry as a typical feature of many well-defined social identities, practices, and institutional discourses (for example, doctor–patient–hospital; judge–defendant–court, etc.) that are characterized by established power relations. While these epistemological asymmetries may be unproblematic, or even necessary, in many social contexts they raise crucial methodological issues for sociological inquiry. In the context of an interview, questions and answers, if not equally distributed among interactants, create unequal power relations and representation

(Fairclough, 1989). Questions and answers, unlike many other forms of utterances, are 'sequential objects' (Schegloff and Sacks, 1973), one leading to the other.[9]

The problem is that, in a discourse structured around an unbalanced Q and A turn-taking, the questioner has the authority to manage the discourse, imposed through choices of questions asked, in terms of the topics, subjects, and themes of those questions, and in terms of interpretations drawn from participants' responses (Drew and Heritage, 1992), thereby removing participants from true partnership with the researcher. This poses the question: 'Who's knowledge does the interview's topics, themes, and interpretations really represent?'

It is from this perspective that the use of photographs in the research interview can be a tool to break the directive nature of verbal questioning. Unlike verbally delivered questions, images are not generally part of an established turn-taking system (and they do not represent a question per se). Importantly, images remain ambiguous (or polysemic) in their communicative function until embedded into the conversation. Moreover, they are not bound by the same criteria characteristic of established discourse genres (Bakhtin, 1986), and may remain available to negotiation and definition by interactants. Unlike verbal interaction, images do not necessarily follow a linear path. Since images can be rearranged, shown individually, or viewed as a group, they may not directly probe an interviewee in the same way that a verbal question does.

As Hurworth (2003) summarized, advantages of photo-elicitation are based on the method's ability to:

...challenge participants, provide nuances, trigger memories, lead to new perspectives and explanations, and help to avoid researcher misinterpretation (Hurworth, 2003: n.p.).

Images, when used in a participatory approach between researcher and participants, can simultaneously allow a researcher to maintain a prespecified interview agenda and structure, while still leaving respondents to prioritize what is selected and interpreted, leading to new insights and knowledge.

NOTES

1 This chapter refers exclusively to interview elicitation processes with still photographs. The possibilities of other kinds of 'image' elicitation and participation are discussed elsewhere in this volume: see Chapters 9 and 25.

2 See Chapter 9.

3 Language, in this theoretical framework, remains the means, in the sense of 'dimension' of this encounter, and the images become the 'tools' used to achieve a new synthesis of knowledge.

4 So called 'reflexive photographs' (Harper, 1987: 64–65).

5 One could add a fourth, 'Collaborative' or 'Participatory' Video (Pink, 2006), also referred to as collaborative image production, in which images or videos are taken by the researcher in collaboration with respondents who will later analyze and discuss them. Collaborative video is outside the discussion of this chapter (see Note 1).

6 See Chapter 36.

7 These issues are also discussed in Chapters 34 and 37.

8 What I call verbal–visual interdiscursive hybridity (Lapenta, 2004).

9 In this volume, Knoblauch and Tuma (Chapter 22) provide ways of looking at visual and verbal sequences recorded on video and closely examined. One of their examples, an auction, demonstrates the question–answer format discussed here.

REFERENCES

Aschermann, E., Dannenberg, U. and Schulz, A. (1998) 'Photographs as retrieval cues for children', *Applied Cognitive Psychology*, 12(1): 55–66.

Banks, M. (1995) 'Visual research methods', *Social Research Update*, 11(3).

Banks, M. (2001) *Visual Methods in Social Research*. London/Thousand Oaks, CA: Sage Publications.

Bakhtin, M. (1986) *Speech Genres and Other Late Essays*. Trans. by V. McGee. Austin, TX: University of Texas Press.

Bender, D., Harbour, C., Thorp, J. and Morris, P. (2001) 'Tell me what you mean by 'Si': Perceptions of quality of prenatal care among immigrant Latina women', *Qualitative Health Research*, 11(6): 780–794.

Brown R., Peterson, C. and Sanstead, M. (1980) 'Photographic evaluation: The use of the camera as an evaluation tool for student affairs', *Journal of College Student Personnel*, 558–563.

Chalfen, R. and Rich, M. (2004) 'Applying visual research: Patients teaching physicians about asthma through visual illness narratives', *Visual Anthropology Review*, 20(1): 17–30.

Chiozzi, P. (1989) 'Photography and anthropological research: Three case studies', in F. Boonzajer (ed.), *Eyes Across the Water*. Amsterdam: Het Spinhuis. pp. 43–50.

Clark, C. D. (1999) 'The autodriven interview: A photographic viewfinder into children's experiences', *Visual Sociology*, 14(1): 39–50.

Clark-Ibanez, M. (2004) 'Framing the social world with photo elicitation interviews', *American Behavioral Scientist*, 47(12): 1507–1527.

Collier, J. (1957) 'Photography in anthropology: A report on two experiments', *American Anthropologist*, 59: 843–859.

Collier, J. and Collier, M. (1986) *Visual Anthropology*. Albuquerque, NM: University of New Mexico Press.

Drew, P. and Heritage, J. (1992) *Talk at Work: Interaction in Institutional Settings*. New York: Cambridge University Press.

Entin, A. (1979) 'Reflection of families', *Photo Therapy Quarterly*, 2(2): 19–21.

Epstein, I., Stevens, B., McKeever, P. and Baruchel, S. (2006) 'Photo elicitation interview (PEI): Using photos to elicit children's perspectives', *International Journal of Qualitative Methods*, 5(3).

Fairclough, N. (1989) *Language and Power*, New York: Longman.

Gadamer, H.G. (1976) *Hegel's Dialectic: Five Hermeneutical Studies*. New Haven, CT: Yale University Press.

Gold, S. (1986) 'Ethnic boundaries and ethnic entrepreneurship: A photo elicitation study', *Visual Sociology*, 6(2): 9–22.

Gould, C., Walker A., Lansing E. and Lidz, C. (1974) *Connections: Notes from the Heroin World*. New Haven, CT: Yale University Press.

Grant, L. and Fine, G. A. (1992) 'Sociology unleashed: Creative directions in classical ethnography', in M. D. LeCompte, W. L. Millroy and J. Preissle (eds.), *The Handbook of Qualitative Research in Education*. New York: Academic Press. pp. 405–446.

Hagedorn, M. I. E. (1996) 'Photography: An aesthetic technique for nursing inquiry', *Issues in Mental Health Nursing*, 17: 517–527.

Hareven, T. and Langenbach, R. (1978) *Amoskeag: Life and Work in an American Factory City*. New York: Pantheon Press.

Harper, D. (1982) *Good Company*. Chicago, IL: University of Chicago Press.

Harper, D. (1984) 'Meaning and work: A study in photo elicitation', *International Journal of Visual Sociology*, 2(1): 20–43.

Harper, D. (1987) *Working Knowledge*. Chicago, IL: University of Chicago Press.

Harper, D. (1988a) 'Visual sociology: Expanding sociological vision', *American Sociologist*, 19(1): 54–70.

Harper, D. (1988b) 'The visual ethnographic narrative', *Visual Anthropology*, 1(1): 1–19.

Harper, D. (1989) 'Interpretive ethnography: From "Authentic Voice" to "Interpretive Eye"', *Visual Sociology*, 4(2): 33–43.

Harper, D. (1994) 'On the authority of the image: Visual methods at the crossroads', in N. K. Denzin and Y. S. Lincoln (eds.), *Handbook of Qualitative Research*. Thousand Oaks, CA: Sage Publications. pp. 403–412.

Harper, D., (2002) 'Talking about pictures: A case for photo elicitation', *Visual Studies*, 17: 13–26.

Harper, D. and Faccioli, P. (2000) 'Small, silly insults, mutual seduction and misogyny: The interpretation of Italian advertising signs', *Visual Sociology*, 15(1): 23–49.

Harrington, C. and Schibik, T. (2003) 'Reflexive photography as an alternative method for the study of the freshman year experience', *NASPA Journal*, 41(1): 23–40.

Heisley, D. and Levy, S. (1991) 'Autodriving: A photo-elicitation technique', *Journal of Consumer Research*, 18(3): 257–272.

Hurworth, R. (2003) 'Photo-interviewing for research', *Social Research Update*, (40). [Online]. Retrieved from http://sru.soc.surrey.ac.uk/SRU40.pdf. [Accessed 20 October 2010].

Killion, C. (2001) 'Understanding cultural aspects of health through photography', *Nursing Outlook*, 49(1): 50–54.

Lapenta, F. (2004) 'The image as a form of sociological data: A methodological approach to the analysis of photo elicited interviews'. PhD dissertation, University of London (available online).

Linell, P. and Luckmann, T. (1991) 'Asymmetries in dialogue: Some conceptual preliminaries', in I. Marková and K. Foppa (eds.), *Asymmetries in Dialogue*. Hemel Hempstead: Harvester Wheatsheaf. pp. 1–20.

Margolis, E. (2008) 'Through a lens darkly', *Bifurcaciones*, 4. [Online]. Available from: http://dialnet.unirioja.es/servlet/articulo?codigo=2912845 [Accessed 19 October 2010].

Modell, J. and Brodsky, C. (1994) *Envisioning Homestead: Using Photographs in Interviewing in Interactive Oral History Interviewing*. Hillsdale, NJ: Erlbaum.

Parker, L. D. (2009) 'Photo elicitation: An ethno-historical accounting and management research prospect', *Accounting, Auditing and Accountability Journal*, 22(7): 1111–1129.

Photovoice (2005) 'Social change through photography. Ethics. [Online]. Available from: http://web.archive.org/web/20070626232822/http://www.photovoice.com/method/ethics.html [Accessed 21 October 2010].

Pink, S. (2006) *Doing Visual Ethnography*. London: Sage Publications.

Prosser, J., Clark, A. and Wiles, R. (2008) 'Visual research ethics at the crossroads', *NCRM Working Paper*. Manchester, UK: Realities.

Rasmussen, K. (2004) 'Places for children—Children's places', *Childhood*, 11(2): 155–173.

Riley, R. and Manias, E. (2003) 'Snap-shots of live theatre: The use of photography to research governance in operating room nursing', *Nursing Inquiry*, 10(2): 81–90.

Rose, G. (2001) *Visual Methodologies: An Introduction to the Interpretation of Visual Materials*. London: Sage Publications.

Salmon, K. (2001) 'Remembering and reporting by children: The influence of cues and props', *Clinical Psychology Review*, 21(2): 267–300.

Schegloff, E. and Sacks, H. (1973) 'Opening up closings', *Semiotica*, 4(8): 289–327.

Schwartz, D. (1989) 'Visual ethnography: Using photography in qualitative research', *Qualitative Sociology*, 12(2): 119–154.

Smith, F. and Barker, J. (2000) 'Contested spaces: Children's experiences of out of school care in England Wales', *Childhood*, 7(3): 315–333.

Suchar, C. S. and Rotenberg, R. (1994) 'Judging the adequacy of shelter—A case from Lincoln Park', *Journal of Architectural and Planning Research*, 11(2): 149–165.

van Leeuwen, T. and Jewitt, C. (eds.) (2001) *A Handbook of Visual Analysis*. London: Sage Publications.

Wagner, J. (ed.) (1979) *Images of Information*. Beverly Hills, CA: Sage Publications.

Wang, C. (1999) 'Photovoice: A participatory action research strategy applied to women's health', *Journal of Women's Health*, 8(2): 185–192.

Wang, C. C. (2001) 'Photovoice Ethics, *Health Education and Behaviour*', 28(5), 560–572.

Wang C. (2005) Photovoice, HYPERLINK "http://web.archive.org/web/20070626232939/www.photovoice.com/index.html"http://web.archive.org/web/20070626232939/www.photovoice.com/index.html accessed December 2009.

Wang C. (2006) 'Youth participation in photovoice as a strategy for community change', in B. Checkoway and L. Gutiérrez (eds.), *Youth Participation and Community Change*. Philadelphia, PA: Haworth Press, pp. 147–161.

Wang, C. and Burris, M. (1994) 'Empowerment through photovoice: Portraits of participation', *Health Education Quarterly*, 21(2): 171–186.

Wang, C. and Burris, M. (1997) 'Photovoice; concept, methodology and use for participatory needs assessment', *Health and Behaviour*, 24(3): 369–387.

Wang, C. and Redwood-Jones, Y. A. (2001) 'Photovoice Ethics', *Health Education and Behaviour*, 28(5): 560–572.

Weinger, S. (1998) 'Children living in poverty: Their perception of career opportunities', *Families in Society: The Journal of Contemporary Human Services*, 79(3): 320–330.

Wessels, D. T. Jr (1985) 'Using family photographs in the treatment of eating disorders', *Psychotherapy in Private Practice*, 3: 95–105.

12

Children-Produced Drawings: An Interpretive and Analytic Tool for Researchers

Tirupalavanam G. Ganesh

A BRIEF HISTORY OF THE USE OF SUBJECT-PRODUCED DRAWINGS OF THE HUMAN FIGURE

Charles Darwin's 1877 publication 'A biographical sketch of an infant' represented growing interest in child study. In his report, Darwin described long-term observations of his own son from birth, examining the child's expression in response to actions. Interest began with systematic observations of children's behaviors and eventually included the collection and examination of drawings produced by children. The notion that young children's unprompted drawings could shed light on the psychology of child development evolved over time, from interest in what was then termed children's artwork (Cooke, 1885; Ricci, 1887) to scientific studies of children's drawings prompted by standard directions (Partridge, 1902; Schuyten, 1904; Lamprecht, 1906; Claparede, 1907; Ivanoff, 1909; Rouma, 1913). The scientific interest manifested itself as exploring and understanding relationships between children's intellectual ability, as measured by school work through teacher ratings for example, and children's ability to draw, as measured by a scoring system on a scale, or rating system.

John French (1956) included examples of children's drawings from Ricci's *L'Arte dei Bambini* (as translated by Maitland, 1894). Ricci had collected over 1250 drawings from elementary school children and observed:

> ... children at first do not artistically represent an object, but describe it according as the memory of it is more or less complete, and suggests to them while drawing the different parts of the object. Art, as art, is to them unknown. (1887: 306)

Ricci compared children's art to adult art and concluded that children represent the figure of man 'in his literal completeness and not according to the visual impression' (304).

In the USA, Barnes (1892) and Burgess (1895) collected and analyzed children's drawings. Barnes collected 6393 drawings from children aged 6–16, in California and the eastern USA. He asked children to illustrate a poem with the idea that it would allow for comparison of the collected drawings and some large generalizations (455–456). Barnes concluded from his analysis of these drawings that:

> Pictures are for a young child simply a language. He makes pictures not to exactly imitate something, nor to produce an aesthetic feeling, but to convey an idea. Picture making is picture writing. (1892: 460)

Barnes (1892), like Ricci (1887), concluded that children needed to be taught to make art and that this teaching should keep pace with the child's development.

A review of these early studies indicates the challenges with the idea of subject-produced drawings: What should the child be asked to draw? Could the child draw anything of her or his choice? How then might one score drawings that did not have any standards? At that point in time, scientific interest was focused on developing objective measurement scales. Attention was given to assessing cognitive development through the characteristics and subject (content) of the drawings.

Partridge (1902) collected drawings of the human figure from children aged 4 through 10, and then associated age and development with the details of the drawings. Schuyten (1904) attempted to devise an objective system for rating children's drawings and established a standard of excellence for each age. Rouma (1913) used children's drawings of the human figure to suggest that there was a sequence of stages in children's human figure drawings.

Standardizing the prompt from a drawing 'in general' to that of 'a human figure' made it possible to hypothesize, study, and propose a general pattern of child development that is visible in children's drawings. Concerns that women's and children's clothing offered greater variety than men's clothing, using 'a man' for the human figure drawing test was settled upon. The uniformity of men's clothing was a factor considered important in providing a standardized prompt to elicit subject-produced human figure drawings. Prompts that could potentially offer too many varieties from a child's perspective would be counterproductive when it came to developing a standardized scoring process.

Thus, in Florence Goodenough's (1926) *Draw-a-Man Test*, she developed standardized procedures and used a large sample in her study. The *Draw-a-Man Test* comprised the following: a child was asked to draw a picture of a man. The ensuing drawing was then examined for a relationship between concept development and general intelligence as visible in the quality of the drawing. The test had 51 scoring items. The fundamental assumption of the analysis was that the accuracy and the number of details in the drawing was an indicator of the child's intellectual maturity. This became the foundation for subsequent techniques that attempted to quantify qualities in the drawing by counting the number of details.

Children's human figure drawings as a measure of intelligence

The Goodenough *Draw-a-Man Test* was later modified by Dale Harris (1963) to be known as the Goodenough–Harris *Draw-a-Person Test*. This test included three drawings: 'draw a man,' 'draw a woman,' and 'draw yourself.' The scoring system included 73 items for the drawing of a man, 71 items for the drawing of a woman, and a 12-point quality scale. A scoring system for the drawing of the self was never fully developed.

Nevertheless, this revision represented an interesting change from 'draw a man' to 'draw a person,' by attempting to extend the original test to include the figure of a woman and the child's self-portrait. An important distinction here was the provision of alternates to drawing 'a man,' since the drawing of 'the self' personalized the test. This personalization fundamentally altered the original test by offering the potential to extend the test as a perhaps more valid projective technique which could be used to study the respondent's affect and interests. The idea of a projective test is that, through the process of projection, subjects reveal their private worlds and personality processes by reacting to stimuli presented. The subject-produced drawings were then used as a medium for interpreting symbols and observing expressions in the drawings. This personalization, via the inclusion of a projective prompt, opened up the possibility of studying emotional indicators, such as that offered by Koppitz (1968, 1983), who designed a scoring system for the *Draw-a-Person Test*.

Naglieri (1988) modified the test further to develop the *Draw-a-Person: A Quantitative Scoring System (DAP)*. Here the scoring system was designed with the idea that human figure drawings—of the woman, the man, and the self—could be scored with criteria where the subjects' language, verbal skills, and cultural differences would not become confounding factors (Naglieri and Bardos, 1987).

The idea that the technique of eliciting subject-produced human figure drawings was relatively culture-free was fundamental to its employment as a means to collect information about human cognitive abilities. A common use for this technique was to assess intelligence and academic readiness of young children, especially children who were nonreaders, hyperactive, developmentally delayed, etc. This assumption about relative freedom from subjects' cultural difference would prove to be problematic when subject-produced drawings as a form of assessment were extended to other contexts and purposes (Chapman and Chapman, 1971; Koppitz, 1983; Golomb, 1992; Smith and Dumont, 1995; Dumont and Smith, 1996).

With increased interest in the *Draw-a-Person (DAP) Test* as a measure of intelligence, Neisworth and Butler (1990) began to carefully study the theoretical underpinnings of the test, its validity, reliability, and use across cultures. Construct validity and concurrent validity were specifically circumspect as researchers began to examine the usage of the *DAP Test* as an intelligence test. The Naglieri *DAP Test*'s validity was based on evidence of *concurrent validity:* how strongly does the *DAP Test* correlate with its earlier predecessor such as the Goodenough–Harris *Draw-a-Person Test*? With the availability of other forms of comprehensive intelligence tests, such as versions of the *Wechsler Intelligence Scale for Children (WISC)*, concurrent validity of the *DAP* with the WISC was found to be weak (Motta et al., 1993; Smith and Dumont, 1995; Abell et al., 2001). There is considerable controversy about the use of children's human figure drawing as a measure of ability or intelligence; thus, authentic decisions about intellectual functioning based solely on subject-produced drawings is considered entirely unwarranted. The early challenges, related to the development of the prompts used to elicit subject-produced drawings, the subsequent development of methods such as scoring systems to make sense of the drawings, and the quality of interpretations drawn from such data continue to persist today, albeit to varying degrees, especially as we situate research with subject-produced drawings in socio-cultural contexts.

Psychological tests and Brown v. Board of Education (1954)

Kenneth and Mamie Clark (1950) conducted studies that challenged the notion that there were differences in the mental abilities of Black and White children and the results of their studies played a significant role in the desegregation of American public schools. They were the first African-American man and woman to earn psychology doctorates from Columbia University, NY. By 1950, they and other scholars had already conducted studies (Horowitz, 1939; Clark and Clark, 1939a; Clark and Clark, 1939b) showing that Black children of ages 3–7 years:

had a well developed knowledge of the concept of racial difference between 'White' and 'Colored' as indicated by the characteristic of skin color—and that this knowledge develops more definitely from year to year to the point of absolute stability at the age of seven. (Clark and Clark, 1950: 341)

The colored doll test involved showing groups of Black and White children two black and two white dolls and asked them to choose the doll that was 'nice,' 'pretty,' or 'bad.' The test results showed that both groups of children associated the white dolls with commendable characteristics. They then devised a technique to further investigate the development of racial identification and preference in Black children using the *Coloring Test* and spontaneous remarks of the children as they responded to other techniques, including the colored doll test.

The *Coloring Test* (Clark and Clark, 1950: 342) in Figure 12.1 was used to establish the use of color and its relationship to specific objects, specifically skin color of the respondent to self-image and preference for skin color, thereby linking skin color to racial preference. The test comprised a sheet of paper with outline drawings of a leaf, an apple, an orange, a mouse, a boy, and a girl. A set of crayons that included the customary colors and brown, black, white, and tan was given to each subject. The study had 160 children aged 5–7 years old, whose responses

Figure 12.1 *Coloring Test*, developed by Clark and Clark (1950). Source: Box 45, Kenneth Bancroft Papers, Manuscript Division, Library of Congress, Washington, D.C.

on the coloring test were stable enough to analyze.

The first portion of the test was to determine whether subjects had a 'stable concept of the relationship of color to object' by coloring the objects and the mouse. Each child who passed this screening portion of the test was then given the prompt to color a human (child's) figure that represented the subject: 'Color this little boy (or girl) the color that you are. This is _____ (child's name), color him (or her) the color you are' (342). Once this portion of the test was completed, the child was given a human figure outline of the opposite sex to that of the subject, along with the second prompt: 'Now this is a little girl, (or boy). Color her (or him) the color you like little boys (or girls) to be' (342).

The data from the *Coloring Test* were categorized, based on their age; the region in which they lived (Southern or Northern USA); and skin color (Light, Medium, and Dark), as 'Reality,' 'Phantasy,' [sic] and 'Irrelevant' or 'Escape' responses. These categories and their definitions were based on the colors used as well as qualitative observations of the responses as the subjects worked on their drawings. For instance, a response was categorized as a 'Reality' response when the coloring of the outline drawing of the child was reasonably close to the subject's own skin color. The Clarks reported that the qualitative observations indicated that subjects colored figure drawings that represented themselves with 'painstaking care' (343) when compared with the 'matter-of-fact' manner in which they colored the objects and the mouse. Through qualitative observations, they noted a difference in cases where the responses were classified as 'Escape' responses. In these cases, the subjects had been observed to make random scribbles when asked to color the outline drawing that represented the subject. And finally, the Clarks noted that, in addition to the color used in coloring an outline drawing of themselves, and this color's relationship to the subject's own skin color, they observed how

much 'pressure' the subjects applied when coloring.

In order to further develop the results of the coloring test, the Clarks recorded the subject's spontaneous remarks and explanations of their responses to the *Colored Doll Test, Preference Series*. This served as a form of concurrent validity. They then categorized subjects' responses for preference as *color*: 'Black–White'; as *beauty*: 'Ugly–Pretty'; as *purity*: 'Dirty–Clean'; and identified some explanations as 'Evasive' as well as the use of the epithet 'Nigger,' and tallied according to where the children lived: 'North' or 'South' (347). In their analysis, they found that Southern children had three times as many spontaneous explanations as the Northern children. In explaining this result they noted, 'This might be considered as being indicative of the greater preoccupation of these Southern children with racial matters, or a greater spontaneity on their part in reference to this subject, or an attempt...' (347). This kind of analysis required deep knowledge of the social context in which the subjects lived and the relation of the subject's skin color to the subject's perceived place in the social hierarchy where the subject lived. Location assumed significance with the traditions of the South versus North as they related to segregation and the Civil Rights movement. This was further enhanced by the fact that the Clarks were cultural insiders—they themselves were Black and had seen and experienced at first hand the effects of segregation. Ultimately, the Clarks found that Black children, by age 7, had internalized racism caused by the discrimination and stigmatization resulting from racial segregation (349–350).

On 17 May 1954, the Supreme Court issued a decision in Brown v. Board of Education declaring that, 'separate educational facilities are inherently unequal.' This decision specifically cited Kenneth B. Clark's work titled, *The Effects of Prejudice and Discrimination on Personality Development* (K. B. Clark, 1950). I have highlighted the Clarks' use of qualitative observations of children's responses to the *Coloring Test* and

Colored Doll Test, their collection of verbal responses as explanations from participants, their identification of emergent categories of those responses, and the interpretation of the responses as a whole. In my view, the meaning-making process was firmly situated within the socio-cultural context of the research study, at a time when American society was legally segregated based on racial differences. The Clarks' roles, as African-American psychologists and researchers who were active in the American Civil Rights Movement, influenced their motivations for engaging with the type of research that had the potential to influence social policies. This is a powerful example of ways that results from visual research on child development, which involved subject-produced coloring of outline drawings of children, have had a lasting impact on public education policy.

Subject-produced drawings as contemporaneous responses to society and culture

Margaret Mead used subject-produced drawings as contemporary responses by the public to events that represented rapid technological change after the World War II. She had been deeply affected by the 1945 bombing of Hiroshima, and was concerned with the idea that everyone on earth was interconnected. The launch of the Sputnik satellite by Soviet Russia in 1957 produced fear and perceptions of loss of prestige in American science and engineering. In the 1950s, Mead and her colleague Rhoda Métraux, who had been studying contemporary culture after World War II, began a study of American students' 'Image of the Scientist,' in which they collected essays and drawings from children and college students about their perceptions of a scientist (Mead and Métraux, 1957). After Sputnik, Mead and Métraux collected essays and drawings from children about the satellite. They presented an analysis of 35,000 high school students' essays in which the subjects described their image of a scientist.

They found that the typical American high school student had a stereotypical notion of what a scientist looks like and does at work. They described this shared image from the national sample as:

> The scientist is a man who wears a white coat and works in a laboratory. He is elderly or middle aged and wears glasses. He is small, sometimes small and stout, or tall and thin. He may be bald. He may wear a beard, may be unshaven and unkempt.... He is surrounded by equipment: test tubes, Bunsen burners, flasks, and bottles....He spends his days doing experiments.... He experiments with plants and animals, cutting them apart, injecting serum into animals. He writes neatly in black notebooks. (1957: 386–387)

Thanks to Mead's use of subject-produced drawings, the study has a place in the study of human culture, specifically in traditions that have their origins in cultural anthropology.

Chambers (1983) developed the *Draw-a-Scientist Test*, where subjects were simply asked to 'draw a scientist' as a means to identify when elementary school children develop the stereotypic image of the scientist described by Mead and Métraux (1957). Between 1966 and 1977, Chambers (1983) collected and studied over 4800 drawings-of-a-scientist made by elementary school children. He patterned the *Draw-a-Scientist Test* after the Goodenough *Draw-a-Man Test*. He selected the following characteristics to analyze the drawings: lab coat, eyeglasses, facial hair (for example, beard, mustache, long sideburns), symbols of research (for example, scientific instruments, laboratory equipment), symbols of knowledge (for example, books and filing cabinets), technology (as products of science), and relevant captions (for example, formulae, taxonomic classifications, 'Eureka!'). He found that this standard image of a scientist begins to emerge around second grade (Chambers, 1983: 258).

Fort and Varney (1989) similarly analyzed drawings of scientists made by 1600 students in grades 2–12. They also asked students to write about their drawing. They found that, of the 1600 drawings, only 20 depicted minority (non-White) scientists, and only 165 depicted females as scientists. In their analysis of the subject-produced drawings, they and other researchers began to note and count the presence of features such as the size of a scientific instrument in relation to the scientist; evidence of danger; the presence of light bulbs; the sex, race, or ethnicity of the scientist; and figures that represented eccentricity ('mad scientists' like *Frankenstein*). This quantification of indicators allowed researchers to record and provide evidence of the existence and prevalence of the stereotypical image of a scientist.

Researchers next began to conduct cross-cultural studies in various countries to understand students' perceptions of the scientist; studies were conducted in China (Chambers, 1983); India (Rampal, 1992), and Australia (Schibeci and Sorensen, 1993). Researchers also paid attention to gender, race, and ethnicity of the scientists depicted in the drawing (Sumrall, 1995; Finson, 2002). Sumrall (1995), for example, interviewed students to access their reasons for drawing a scientist of a particular race and gender. Thus, instruments that used subject-produced drawings were supplemented with verbal data collected via interviews or descriptive written responses about the drawing in mixed-method research approaches.

Validity and reliability of subject-produced drawings

As researchers began to use subject-produced drawings, attempts to demonstrate validity and reliability of the instrument began to emerge. Techniques to ensure validity focused on ensuring that the instrument was designed to measure what it was supposed to measure: Did the students' drawings of a scientist depict specific characteristics that are stereotypical of a scientist's image? To increase the validity of the subject-produced drawings, researchers developed coding schemes that attempted to standardize the identification of stereotypical characteristics in the drawings. Codification schemes allow for human 'raters' or 'coders' to be trained, and

the use of inter-rater reliability measures among raters allowed researchers to either modify the coding scheme or retrain the raters. Humans as 'raters' are fallible; therefore, the use of a score or statistical measure of homogeneity among raters was important.

Finson (2001) conducted a study to validate the *Draw a Scientist Test* for populations other than the population of White middle class students for which the original instrument was validated. He used quantitative analysis and statistical techniques to describe relationships between variables such as the subject's gender and race/ethnicity, with each of the observed characteristics of the scientist depicted in their drawings.

Another attempt to improve the validity of subject-produced drawings as a measurement tool was to extend its use from that of a merely descriptive tool to that of an analytical tool. The studies described thus far in this chapter largely used subject-produced drawings to 'describe' what specific populations knew about some culturally relevant idea. These could be generally classified as descriptive studies that either used qualitative, quantitative, or mixed methods. Researchers began to use subject-produced drawings as pre- and post-assessments to measure the impact of an intervention. The post-drawings could then be compared with the pre-drawings, allowing for a form of analysis using each individual respondent's own initial response as a benchmark.

Flick (1990) reported using the *Draw a Scientist Test* before and after an intervention that included scientists (three female and one male), who visited two fifth-grade classrooms for an hour each week for 3 weeks to share their enthusiasm for science. The 47 fifth-grade students also visited the scientists' laboratories. Flick found that more males were depicted before the female scientists visited the classes, but more females were drawn after the intervention. A number of additional studies have focused on attempts to change students' perceptions of scientists (Mason et al., 1991; Finson et al., 1995; Huber and Burton, 1995; Bodzin and Gehringer, 2001; Bohrmann and Akerson, 2001). Impacts of the interventions were studied using quantitative surveys that measured perceptions of science and attitudes toward science and science careers, as well as using qualitative measures such as the *Draw a Scientist Test*. In these cases, the subject-produced drawings were not used by themselves; they were typically combined with other measures such as questionnaires, open-ended written responses, and interviews. Over time, the sole use of drawings became less common, especially with the assessment of students' perceptions of a scientist.

Margaret Mead's work using subject-produced drawings as a means of accessing contemporary cultural knowledge not only influenced the study of students' perceptions of scientists but also extended to other professions (teaching, engineering, statistics) and addressed other areas, such as the impact of media (TV, computer, Internet) on participants' perceptions. For instance, Barba and Mason (1994) and Mercier et al. (2006) examined age and gender differences in the drawings of computer and technology users.

Other examples of subject-produced drawings: Education studies

Weber and Mitchell (1995) reported on the enduring image of schooling among students via student-produced drawings of teachers. They used a variety of prompts to elicit students' conceptions of teachers that led to an examination of the dialectical relationship between schooling and the popular culture of everyday life. Fischman (2000) examined teacher education and the role of gender in education using drawings made by teachers-in-training. Kolb and Fishman (2006) elicited preservice teachers' beliefs about technology integration using drawings and a survey. All of these studies, however, used drawings as a part of a larger data collection strategy that included interviews and embedded the data analysis in qualitative research traditions. Wheelock et al. (2000) used drawings from students in Massachusetts in a study of

student's feelings about high-stakes testing. Haney et al. (2004) described the use of subject-produced drawings to show how they could be used as a tool to examine teacher behavior and the impact of education reform.

THE *DRAW-AN-ENGINEER TEST* TO ASSESS MIDDLE SCHOOL STUDENTS PERCEPTIONS OF ENGINEERS

Just as subject-produced drawings have been used to study children's attitudes toward professions in science, researchers have used the *Draw-an-Engineer Test*, an adaptation of the *Draw-a-Scientist Test*, as a tool to examine children's attitudes and knowledge of engineers and engineering (Cunningham and Knight, 2004; Cunningham et al., 2005). Similarly, I used the *Draw-an-Engineer Test* in a longitudinal study of middle school children engaged in an after-school engineering education program over 2 years. The drawings collected pre-program were initially used as a type of formative assessment of the engineering education program. These assessments were used to help design and implement specific learning experiences by addressing students' conceptions and misconceptions about engineering. The use of drawings collected from participants over time—before, during, and after their program experience—allowed me to investigate, using a formative-summative evaluation strategy (Scriven, 1972), whether the engineering education intervention helped influence students' identities as engineers, and in what ways.

Context for the study

The publication of the report *Rising Above the Gathering Storm*, by the National Academy of Sciences (NAS) (Augustine, 2005), highlighted political and popular concerns in the USA that the globalization of knowledge and increased use of low-cost labor had led to the erosion of the USA as a leader in science, technology, and engineering. The report also argued that the federal government needed to act to ensure the country's continued success in this area. As with the Sputnik 'crisis' nearly a half century earlier, these concerns were manifest as a call to increase the number of American-born students entering science, technology, and engineering careers. In 2006–07, I responded to a call for proposals from the National Science Foundation's (NSF) *Division for Research on Learning in Formal and Informal Settings* for a program known as the *Innovative Technology Experiences for Students and Teachers*. My proposal, *Learning through Engineering Design and Practice*, intended to provide middle school students with in-depth experiences with engineering-related and project-based challenges.

A total of 116 seventh and eighth grade students from four different middle schools took part in the project during the 2007–10 school years. Each student participated in the after-school program from the start of seventh grade through the end of eighth grade. Participants' gender and race/ethnicity are noted in Tables 12.1 and 12.2. Female participants and populations, traditionally underrepresented in the engineering fields, were over-sampled at high rates per NSF program guidelines.

One of the project's goals was to help middle school students to confront their own misconceptions about engineers and engineering (NAE, 2008). I wanted to examine changes in students' development of their own identity of engineers. I used the *Draw-an-Engineer* assessment, along with written descriptions and interviews, to assess what middle school students know about engineers. I collected students' drawings of an engineer from participants at different points during their 2-year involvement in the project, and they offered an interesting and useful glimpse of how students depicted their understanding of engineers.

Table 12.1   Per cent project participants by gender and year

	Number of students		Combined sample	Per cent by gender
	2007–08	2008–09		
Female	32	35	67	58
Male	16	33	49	42
Total	48	68	116	

Table 12.2   Per cent project participants by race/ethnicity and year

	Number of students		Combined sample	Per cent by race/ethnicity
	2007–08	2008–09		
American Indian	4	1	5	4
Asian	2	0	2	2
Black	5	0	5	4
Hispanic	25	46	71	61
White	12	21	33	28
Total	48	68	116	

Assessment protocol

Students were given 20–30 minutes to draw an engineer and answer three questions related to what they had drawn. Assessment directions and question prompts were as follows:

> Close your eyes and imagine an engineer at work… Open your eyes. On the attached sheet of paper, draw what you imagined. Once you have completed your drawing, please respond to the following prompts:
>
> 1. Describe what the engineer is doing in the picture. Write at least two sentences.
> 2. List at least three words/phrases that come to mind when you think of this engineer.
> 3. What kinds of things do you think this engineer does on a typical day? List at least three things.

Project coordinators were instructed to be careful not to talk about engineers or engineering during the first day of the project or during the administration of the *Draw-an-Engineer* assessment. During assessment administration, project coordinators offered help to clarify directions and question prompts, but were again careful not to offer any ideas or assistance that would influence the students' own conceptions of engineers or engineering. Semi-formal interviews were conducted—one-on-one discussions with students to understand their drawings and responses and to also elicit their thinking behind the drawings. This form of image elicitation was an integral part of our data analysis process.

Pre-program drawings

With the pre-program *Draw-an-Engineer* assessments, the intent was to examine the 'drawings' (by which I mean students' drawings and accompanying written responses to the questions) to see what participants knew about engineers. With the assistance of a graduate research assistant in education with a bachelor's degree in engineering and experience teaching high school mathematics, and an undergraduate engineering student who worked as a student data-analyst, we reviewed the drawings to identify elements that we felt were helpful in developing a description of what seventh-grade students depicted about engineers. It is important to note that I have also earned bachelor's and master's degrees in engineering, and bring my own background and experience to this project.

To make sense of the drawings, we engaged in what Strauss and Corbin (1998) termed *open coding* and *axial coding*. We began *open coding* (101–121) with three broad theoretical categories:

- *Gender of the engineer.* Participants were 58% female and 42% male. We were interested in observing whether female participants depicted engineers as male in their drawings and whether those representations would change to a female engineer over time. Similarly, we were interested in observing whether male students made drawings of female engineers and if those changed.
- *Engineers in action.* The drawing prompt asked students to draw an engineer at work. Therefore, we felt strongly that this category was important to focus on understanding what students perceived engineers did at work.
- *Engineers use tools.* The objects that students believe engineers use when at work are related to understanding what the engineer could potentially do with those objects. Therefore, we felt it was important to attend to the types of objects the engineer held or were around the engineer in the drawing.

We labeled the drawings with likely concepts suggested by the context in which the drawing was located, including the accompanying written responses describing the drawing. We prepared memos describing our thoughts about key elements we identified in the drawings. We reviewed the entire data corpus in this manner.

Once this process was completed, we compared the drawings, our labels, and memos to search for cross-cutting concepts. This process is what Strauss and Corbin termed *axial coding* (123–142). Our analysis of the pre-program drawings yielded three conceptual categories that represent our interpretations of students' initial conceptions of what engineers do at work: *engineers* work with engines, *engineers build*, and *engineers repair* technical devices. These concepts represented our interpretation of students' representations of engineers at work. We also used *image elicitation interviews* to confirm our interpretations of the students' drawings. The image elicitation helped us access the 'why' and/or 'how' students thought about engineers at work. Many of them made the quite logical English language connection between 'engines' and 'engineers'; similarly, probably influenced by television and movies, they recognized that 'engineer' is also the name of one who drives a train—even though many of them have probably never ridden a train themselves.

In the following sections, I have illustrated our process of conceptualization with examples. Codes are in bold print. Not all instances of a concept are coded and others may use different labels or identify altogether different concepts.

Engineers work with engines

Written response (Figure 12.2):

The engineer has just finished fixing the train ['**engineers fix trains**']. He ['**engineers are male**'] is also smiling. He really likes his job ['**engineers are male**']. He is very happy that he fixed the train ['**engineers fix trains**']. I think he drives the train ['**engineers drive trains**'], he fixes the train ['**engineers fix trains**'], and he puts coal into the train's engine ['**engineers work with train engines**'] so it can go.

We identified specific elements in the drawings that represented our theoretical categories. The specific elements we noted in Figure 12.2 included:

1. the engineer is described as male represented *gender of the engineer;*
2. the engineer is standing by a train represented *engineers in action;* and
3. the engineer in the drawing has an object that looks like a wrench represented our theoretical category *engineers use tools.*

Figure 12.2 'My engineer has just finished fixing the train.' Author: 12-year-old, seventh-grade, White, female

We labeled the drawings 'engineers work with train engines.' As we encountered more drawings that included an engineer as fixing a car, truck, or a train or driving a car, truck, or a train, we recorded a short memo describing possible concepts and general thoughts about those drawings:

> **Memo**. It will be useful to explore the relationship between engineers and cars, trucks, and trains. What is common among these objects? They are all vehicles. They have engines. Maybe students think that because the word engineer has the word 'engine' in it, they believe that *engineers work with engines*. This is a much broader interpretation, a concept that encompasses the specific labels of engineers fix trains, engineers fix cars, and engineers fix trucks. We should probe this idea when we interview the students.

In the drawing in Figure 12.2, the student described that the engineer 'puts coal into the train's engine so it can go,' indicating the student's belief that the engineer has to do something to or with the engine (for example, drive the train, fix the train, put coal in the train's engine). We examined what operations the engineer was described as doing with the car, truck, or train with our theoretical category *engineers in action*. The engineer was described as either fixing the vehicle or driving it—these operations or dimensions represented the sub-categories *engineers fixing* or *engineers driving* vehicles.

Written response (Figure 12.3):

> The engineer is fixing a broken car ['**engineers fix cars'**]. The man ['**engineers are male'**] is laying on a board to fix the car. He installs things on the car. An engineer fixes broken engines ['**engineers fix engines'**]. He fixes leaks in the car ['**engineers fix cars'**].

Similar to this student, a number students depicted engineers as mechanics: people who worked on cars and fixed cars. This was by far the most popular initial conception of engineers at work. The specific elements we noted in Figure 12.3 included:

1 the engineer is described as male represented *gender of the engineer;*

2 the engineer is under a car represented *engineers in action;* and

3 the engineer in the drawing has an object that looks like a wrench and that the car was raised from the floor with a car jack represented our theoretical category *engineers use tools.*

We labeled the drawing, 'engineers work with car engines.'

As we engaged in axial coding, we reviewed the key elements and memos and searched for categories that linked with each other (Strauss and Corbin, 1998: 123–142). For instance, we wanted to explore why students believed that engineers work with cars, trucks, and trains. We began to group the notions that engineers fixing or driving a car, truck, or train were all related to each other. The common property among these vehicles was that the car, truck, and train each had an engine and the common dimension was that the engineer drove or fixed the car, truck, or train engine. Figures 12.2 and 12.3, and other drawings with similar concepts, were now conceptualized as *engineers work with engines*. This concept emerged from our data analysis. By constantly comparing drawings that had similar elements, we attempted to validate our interpretation that some participants believed that *engineers work with engines*. I found that member checking was also important; we talked with participants about their drawings to make sure that our interpretation was recognized by them. In this process of image elicitation, participants provided insights about their drawings and thinking about engineers that were not always found in the accompanying written responses. For instance, to understand why middle school students made drawings of people working on cars or driving a train as representative of engineers, I provide this brief excerpt of an interview with the author who made the drawing in Figure 12.3:

> Interviewer: I see that you made this drawing where a person is working on a car. Can you tell me why you made this drawing?
> Student: The car has an engine and it breaks down. He is fixing it. ['**engineers fix cars'**]

Figure 12.3 'My engineer is fixing a broken car.' Author: 13-year-old, seventh-grade, Hispanic, female

Interviewer: Do you know of anyone who fixes cars?
Student: Yes, my older brother does. And... there are people like mechanics who work on cars.
Interviewer: Are these people engineers?
Student: They work on engines. [*'engineers work with engines'*]
Interviewer: Hmm...
Student: I guess 'engineer' has 'engine' in it. [*'the word 'engineer' has the word 'engine' in it'*]

Our concept *engineers work with engines* represents the phenomenon that some middle school students believe that engineers work with engines. We made memos that allowed us to further conceptualize and probe students' thinking about engineers.

Memo. This student said that the word 'engineer' has the word 'engine' in it. Perhaps students don't know for sure what an engineer does. Some students are making sense of what the word could mean by examining the word itself. For instance 'teacher' has the word 'teach' in it, and 'teachers teach.' This is something familiar. The students who don't know anything about engineers may think that they could find meaning in the word itself. Because the word 'engineer' has the word 'engine' in it, students believe that engineers have to be people who work on engines. Do they know anything that has engines? Do they know anyone that works on those objects that have engines? We should explore this idea further when we interview the students. Students will need to feel comfortable with us, before they are likely to share how and why they made sense of the word engineer by examining the word.

The process of conceptualization was essentially also a process of abstraction. We reconceptualized the drawings based on coding key elements and categories as sharing common properties and dimensions. We iteratively reviewed all of the drawings in the pre-program data corpus and arrived at the following additional conceptualizations about what some seventh-grade students thought engineers do at work.

Engineers build

Engineers build is a phenomenon that encompasses participant's ideas such as *engineers assemble things in a factory*, *engineers build buildings*, and *engineers build bridges*. I have provided examples of students' drawings to illustrate each sub-category. It is important to note that this concept primarily includes the dimension of assembly-line labor involved in working in a factory and the physical labor of constructing buildings and bridges. We confirmed our interpretations of the drawings we categorized as *engineers build* with students by member checking during image-elicitation interviews.

Written response (Figure 12.4):

> The engineer is putting things together with a hammer ['**engineers assemble things**'] ['**engineers use tools like a hammer**']. His ['**engineers are male**'] job is to put things together properly and not let things go without putting them together ['**engineers do assembly line work**']. He works 8-10 hours a day, but not on weekends. He takes two 15-minute breaks and a lunch break during his workday ['**engineers work in a factory**']. He does not mess around and does a good job. His favorite tool is the hammer.

The participant who made the drawing in Figure 12.4 lived in a neighborhood with largely Spanish-speaking people, sometimes referred to as the 'barrio.' When interviewed about his drawing, he said that he thought, 'Engineers assemble things and work in a factory. They build things that are made in factories.' This is an example of the sub-category *engineers assemble things in a factory*.

Written response (Figure 12.5):

> The engineer is building a house ['**engineers build houses**']. He wears a hard hat. He ['**engineers are male**'] uses a crane, hammer, nail gun, drill, and tools like that ['**engineers use tools**']. He puts the house together and there are other workers also. They all build the house. He works hard. Today, he is lifting beams using the crane onto the house ['**engineers do construction work**'].

The participant who made the drawing in Figure 12.5 also lived in a barrio. When interviewed about his drawing, he said:

> I made this drawing to show that engineers work to build houses, offices, and schools ['**engineers build buildings**']. They do the work to actually construct the house itself like hammering nails into

Figure 12.4 'My engineer assembles things in a factory.' Author: 12-year-old, seventh-grade, Hispanic, male

Figure 12.5 'My engineer is building a house.' Author: 13-year-old, seventh-grade, Hispanic, male

beams, stuffing insulation, wiring a house, and things like that ['**engineers do construction work**'].

This is an example of the sub-category *engineers build buildings*. This conceptualization encompasses the dimension of physical labor involved in constructing a house.

Written response (Figure 12.6):

> This engineer is digging to build a bridge ['**engineers build bridges**']. He ['**engineers are male**'] is holding a shovel ['**engineers use tools**'] to dig the hole in the ground where the bridge is going to be built ['**engineers do manual labor at the construction site**']. There are others workers also who build the bridge.

This is an example of the sub-category *engineers build bridges*. This conceptualization encompasses the dimension of physical labor involved in constructing a bridge (Figure 12.6).

Engineers repair technical devices

Engineers repair technical devices is a phenomenon that encompasses participants ideas such as *engineers fix computers* (Figure 12.7), *engineers fix clocks and watches*, and *engineers fix televisions, microwaves*.

Written response (Figure 12.7):

> The engineer is working to fix a broken computer hard drive. He also knows how to fix televisions, microwaves, etc., but this particular engineer is a computer repair specialist. He works for Dell, Macintosh, or any other technology business. On a typical day, this engineer goes to work at the Macintosh headquarters. His job is to fix any computers that have defects. He loves his job. His motto is, 'Choose a job you like and you'll never have to work a day in your life.'

Other drawings in this category included representations of engineers as repairing microwaves, televisions, refrigerators, and watches.

Figure 12.6 'My engineer is digging. He is working to build a bridge.' Author: 13-year-old, seventh-grade, White, female

Drawings not categorized

In some cases we did not assign the drawings a specific label. There were a few drawings that we felt did not clearly indicate any specific conception of engineers. Interview data were used to access students' reasons for their drawing of an engineer.

Figure 12.8 is an illustration of such a drawing. This drawing was made by Nancy, a Hispanic female who started the program as a 12-year-old, seventh-grade student. The school she attended in 2007–08 was 66% Hispanic, 10% American Indian, 7% African-American, 2% Asian, and 16% White; 80% of these students were enrolled in the free and reduced-price lunch program, a measure of poverty established by government standards. Her school was near a barrio, in an older neighborhood, where Spanish-speaking families had lived since World War II. One of the program goals was to provide students traditionally under-represented in the science, technology, engineering, and mathematics (STEM) fields with in-depth experiences to explore those subjects. Nancy explained that her motivation for volunteering to attend the after-school program (which met twice a week for 90 minutes during the school year from September to May, and included summer programming in June and July) was, 'I wanted to join this program because I could be with others and have fun, go on field trips.'

Nancy illustrates how the use of subject-produced drawings and image elicitation during the 2-year after-school program helped me follow Nancy's development of a self-identity as a potential engineer. In an interview, Nancy revealed that she did not

Figure 12.7 'My engineer is working to fix a broken computer hard drive.' 12-year-old, seventh-grade, White, female

know what engineers did, but she wanted to make a drawing:

Written response (Figure 12.8):

> The engineer guy builds a tower of Legos. He is trying to put the last Lego piece on the top of the tower. He looks very stressed out. He does not want to fall.

In summary, our analyses of the pre-program data as represented within our theoretical frames indicated the following early conceptions:

- *Gender of the engineer*. A majority of the participants depicted engineers as male. Only two showed engineers as female. One drawing by a female student depicted the engineer as a female who fixed cars. Another drawing by a male student depicted the engineer as one of the female project coordinators and he labeled her by name.

- *Engineers in action*. Students depicted engineers as mechanics who repaired and drove cars, trucks, or trains; as people who assemble products in factories; as people who build buildings, roads, and bridges; and as people who repaired technical or electronic devices such as computers, microwaves, televisions, and watches.
- *Engineers use tools*. Students believed that engineers use tools. Tools depicted were largely used in construction (for example, shovel, crane, hammer, wrench, nail gun, drill) or repair work (for example, screwdriver).

Participants' pre-program conceptions of what engineers do at work encompassed *engineers work with engines, engineers build*, and *engineers repair technical devices*. The National Academy of Engineering (2008) in a report titled 'Changing the conversation: Messages for improving public understanding of engineering' recommended that four specific messages be adopted by the

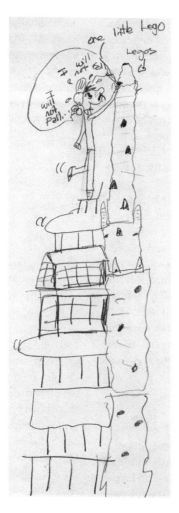

Figure 12.8 'The engineer guy built a tower of Legos.' Author: 12-year-old, seventh-grade, Hispanic, female

engineering and engineering education community: 'Engineers make a world of difference,' 'Engineers are creative problem solvers,' 'Engineers help shape the future,' and 'Engineering is essential to our health, happiness, and safety' (12). These abstract ideas about what engineers do were not in evidence in students' pre-program conceptions.

The *Learning through Engineering Design and Practice* program introduced participants to engineers who worked in the information technology and engineering industries and also to undergraduate engineering students. There were two female and three male undergraduate engineering students who worked side-by-side with the participants on program activities throughout the year-round engineering education program. There were three female and four male professional engineers who volunteered their time to work with the participants 8–10 times a year during the after-school program. In addition, two female middle school educators in participant schools who helped facilitate the after-school program were former engineers with industry experience. One was an aeronautics design engineer who worked as a middle school math teacher and another was a chemical engineer who worked as a middle school science teacher.

Print resources (ASEE, 2007) that had visual images and descriptions of engineers and undergraduate students in engineering degree programs, and images and descriptions of engineering products, were introduced to participants. In addition, the program introduced participants to video resources (*PBS Design Squad*: http://pbskids.org/designsquad/profiles; *Engineer Girl*: http://www.engineergirl.org/) that profiled engineers and their work.

I wanted to access program participants' developing understandings of what engineers *do* throughout the program. I used the *Draw-an-Engineer* assessment and accompanying image elicitation interviews to access participants' conceptions of engineers during the program and at the end of the 2-year after-school program. Image-elicitation interviews, along with analysis of written responses that accompanied the *Draw-an-Engineer* assessment were used to confirm our interpretations of students' representations.

Post-program drawings

Data analysis followed the same iterative pattern described in the pre-program data analysis section with open coding and axial coding (Strauss and Corbin, 1998) until saturation occurred when the data analysis team felt that we had exhausted identification of all categories, elements, properties, and dimensions. Open coding and axial coding occurred simultaneously at times, and were not necessarily sequential in nature. As we reviewed the data, we not only assigned labels representing categories but also began to link data elements to others in the data corpus that we had encountered earlier. Our memos helped us articulate our thoughts about categories, speculate about concepts, and specifically explore the why and how of students' thinking through image elicitation.

Emerging conceptions of engineers at work

I concluded that participants' emerging conceptions of engineers were literal understandings of adult descriptions of engineers at work. Through image-elicitation interviews we confirmed this interpretation of the *Draw-an-Engineer* assessments. As before, I have provided a few examples of students' representations of engineers at work that were collected post-program.

Written response (Figure 12.9):

> The engineer is working on a damaged F-35. He does his work of repairing it and the F-35 turns on. I think he makes designs for building F-35s. He makes things he was trained to do. He makes things he studied in college [**'engineers go to college'**].

The student who made the drawing (Figure 12.9) attended the engineering education after-school program where one of the after-school program teachers was a former aeronautical engineer. This teacher, Ms S, had said that she had an engineering degree and had worked for the US military as a design engineer working on a team that developed designs for a Stealth bomber. In this drawing, the participant made a literal representation of his understanding of what Ms S did as a design engineer. Interestingly, the student described the engineer in his drawing as a male. I wanted to understand why the student made this drawing. The image-elicitation interview with the student illustrates how the student thought about engineers and the influence he attributed to his understanding of engineers:

> Interviewer: What was your reason for making this drawing of an engineer at work?
> Student: I thought it was cool that Ms S had worked on a Stealth bomber.
> Interviewer: Hmm...
> Student: I think engineers like her [**'engineers are female'**] work on F-35s, fixing them. That is what I think!
> Interviewer: I don't remember what Ms S said about what she used to do as an engineer... Do you?
> Student: I think she said that she made designs for a bomber [**'engineers design things'**].
> Interviewer: What does 'making designs for a bomber...' mean?
> Student: Hmm... I don't know. She also said that she worked on a Stealth bomber...

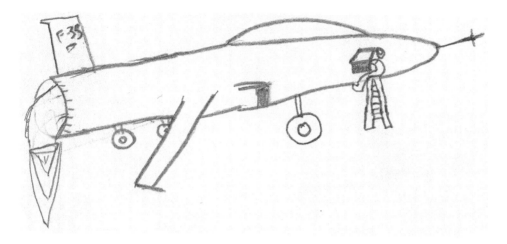

Figure 12.9 'He is working on a damaged F-35.' Author: 14-year-old, eighth-grade, Hispanic, male

Interviewer: OK. Let us get back to your drawing. What did you draw?
Student: I made a drawing of a man ['**engineers are male**'], an engineer who does things like Ms S did. He learned how to design an F-35 or parts for an F-35 in college. ['**engineers attend college**']

Although the student said he made his drawing of an engineer to represent the type of work Ms S said she had done as an aeronautical design engineer, the engineer in his drawing was male. As he did not know exactly what 'designing a bomber' meant, he drew the engineer literally fixing the F-35 which he equated to a bomber aircraft.

Written response (Figure 12.10):

The engineer is checking the steel. He is a man ['**engineers are male**']. He is smart. He inspects stuff. He is checking what material this structure is made with.

In Figure 12.10, a male participant represented his understanding of what a materials science engineer does at work. The participant had depicted his understanding of what Mr D, then a graduating senior from the Materials Science and Engineering bachelors' program, had said he is studying. The participant depicted this engineer as a person who literally examines the quality of construction materials.

The emerging understanding of what materials science engineers do was a representation that these types of engineers are concerned about materials and their uses. Mr D had interacted with participants at this after-school program for a year. In the image-elicitation interview the student traced his representation of an engineer to his interactions with Mr D during the after-school program.

Student: I made a drawing of Mr D ['**engineers are like the undergraduate engineer student interns in the program**']. He is a materials engineer who looks at the quality of materials like steel ['**materials engineers are interested in studying materials**'].
Interviewer: What kinds of things does this engineer do at work?
Student: I think that engineers are interested in making new materials that are strong and powerful than what we have now ['**materials engineers invent new materials**'].
Interviewer: OK...Hmm...and?
Student: Engineers like Mr D make sure that the materials in a nuclear power plant like we have here in Phoenix are safe ['**engineers ensure our safety**'] and that the nuclear waste doesn't harm us and the environment.

In this particular case, although the participant's drawing doesn't fully represent what he shared with the interviewer, it shows his emerging understanding of a specific aspect of what materials science engineers do. In his

Figure 12.10 'The engineer is checking the steel.' Author: 14-year-old, eighth-grade, Hispanic, male

interview, the participant literally described what Mr D had shared with the group about the type of job he intended to do when he graduated at the end of the year. Mr D had talked about his future job working for the United States Nuclear Regulatory Commission and the type of work he hopes to do in his new job. It is clear that the role models we introduced to the after-school program were represented in participants' understandings of engineers, and they incorporated emerging ideas that approached conceptions of what engineers do at work that were prevalent in the engineering education community.

Engineers go to college

When I examined individual participants' *Draw-an-Engineer* responses over a 2-year period I was able to trace the participant's developing understanding of what an engineer did. While not all participants' drawings indicated a change in their thinking about engineers in action, some middle school participants demonstrated significant changes—developing an identity as future engineers. The *Draw-an-Engineer* also began to include a projective element. By the fourth observation point, approximately 22 months into a 2-year program, some students identified themselves as the engineer in their drawing. (See Figure 12.8 for Nancy's pre-program conception of an engineer.) At the end of Year 1, Nancy represented a female engineer (see Figure 12.11) who worked at Microchip, a semiconductor company in Phoenix, Arizona, and had graduated from an engineering degree program.

Written response (Figure 12.11):

A 21-year-old female engineer ['**engineers are female**'] who graduated from Arizona State University ['**engineers go to college**'] is working on a microchip. She ['**engineers are female**'] needs to be very careful, so she doesn't damage the whole microchip. She works on computers and uses technology and software ['**engineers use tools**'] to design microchips.

Figure 12.11 'A 21-year-old female engineer who graduated from Arizona State University is working on a microchip.' Author: 12-year-old, seventh-grade, Hispanic female

And interview responses:

Nancy: I made my engineer look a little like Ms M, because she is an engineer [**'engineers are female'**]! And she works at Microchip.
Interviewer: Yes...
Nancy: She [**'engineers are female'**] went to college at Arizona State University (ASU) and got a degree in electrical, electronics engineering? [**'engineers go to college'**]. I want to go to college like her [**'participant projected personal education-career pathway goal'**].
Interviewer: OK.
Nancy: Like we went on a field trip to ASU and saw that lab where they made microchips [**'participant linked attending college to preparation for work as an engineer'**]. I want to work in a place like that.
Interviewer: OK... [Pauses]...What is the engineer in your drawing doing?
Nancy: Like Ms M, she is making, she is designing a microchip [**'engineers design things'**]. She showed us the kinds of things she designs.

They are like the electronic circuits that go in our cell phones [**'participant identified real life use for products made by engineers'**].

Ms M's influence on Nancy was represented in the drawing and Nancy's verbal description of her drawing of an engineer at work. In addition, Nancy had connected her own visit to Arizona State University, where she observed a micro-fabrication clean room facility in the Center for Solid State Electronics Research, with what she had learned from Ms M about Ms M's degree program and job at Microchip.

At Nancy's school, at the end of the first year during a family engineering night, a female Hispanic undergraduate chemical engineering student named Ms G discussed her engineering program and the type of work she wanted to do when she graduated. Ms G said:

> I want to work in a pharmaceutical company, that is a company where medicines are made. I want to help make new medicines that will help people who have a medical illness.

Ms G had visited the program site only once. Nancy made the drawing (Figure 12.12) 5 months after Ms G had visited the after-school program, at the start of the second year. The influence of these program experiences appeared in the drawings that Nancy made. At the start of the second year, Nancy had begun to develop a self-identity as an engineer, although she did not directly label her drawing of an engineer as depicting herself.

Written response (Figure 12.12):

> The female engineer tries to figure out a cure for cancer ['**engineers help people**']. She works with chemicals and designs new medicines ['**engineers design things**'] ['**engineers make new products**']. She is always thinking. She makes notes based on what she finds from her experiments. She then uses it to redesign the drug ['**engineers follow a process**'] and make changes to the medicine she is designing to cure cancer.

Participants were introduced to the engineering design as a process that engineers follow to generate the best possible solution(s) to any given problem (Ertas and Jones, 1996). They were encouraged to use the engineering design process in all of the project-based challenges they experienced throughout the program. Students were aware that the engineering design process is iterative and included identifying the challenge, gathering information, imagining or brainstorming solutions, planning, designing, building, testing, and redesigning a product based on information gathered from the previous iteration.

Figure 12.12 'The female engineer is attempting to figure out a cure for cancer.' Author: 13-year-old, eighth-grade, Hispanic, female

In the related image-elicitation interview, Nancy also referred to the engineering design process that she would follow in designing new medicines to cure cancer.

Interviewer: Tell us about your drawing.
Nancy: I have an aunt who has cancer. I want to do something that will help people who have cancer. [**'engineers help people'**].
Interviewer: Hmm...
Nancy: I want to help find a cure for cancer [**'engineers help people'**]... . I want to be like Ms G. I want to make a cure and make it better for people.
Interviewer: OK.
Nancy: I can help people then. I can design medicines that will help people. I want to go to college [**'engineers go to college'**] so I can learn about this [**'college prepares engineers for their job'**].
Interviewer: OK.
Nancy: When I grow up, I will be that engineer, who works with others who study people with illness like cancer and find a cure for people like that [**'engineers help people'**].
Interviewer: Hmm...
Nancy: We will use the process to understand the challenge. What cancer is like and what we need to cure it. What they do now. Then we will come up with new ideas. Find ways to make new medicines. Design new medicines to cure cancer. Test it. Collect data to see if it worked. Then redesign it [**'engineers follow a process'**]. It will be hard work. But I want to do it so I can help people like my aunt.

Nancy's fourth drawing of an engineer, at the end of the 2-year program, extended her belief that *engineers go to college* to include the idea that *engineers work in a team*.

Written response (Figure 12.13):

In my drawing, it shows two people. I am the chemical engineer [**'self as engineer'**]. I am designing a cure for cancer. I work with a research team on an experiment. We use chemicals and equipment like beakers, test tubes in our experiments. We also use computers, record different data from our experiments and study them. We discover new medicines to help people [**'engineers help people'**].

In Figure 12.13, Nancy specifically indicated herself as the female chemical engineer. She was sure that she would go to college and become an engineer: 'I will go to college.

I want to help people and make medicine that can cure people who have, like cancer.'

The longitudinal analysis of students' drawings of engineers at work is a useful example of how subject-produced drawings may be used in understanding the impact of educational interventions. Nancy's case illustrates how the *Draw-an-Engineer* process, along with image-elicitation interviews, were used to trace her development of her self-identification as an engineer. Over the 2-year period, Nancy moved from an early conception of the 'engineer as a guy who builds a tower of Legos' to 'I am a chemical engineer who designs medicine for illnesses like cancer.'

Analysis of post-program drawings indicated a shift from students' early understandings that included representations of concepts such as *engineers work with engines, engineers build*, and *engineers repair technical devices* to emerging understandings that included representations of concepts such as *engineers go to college, engineers use the engineering design process, engineers design products we need, engineers invent new devices to help people, engineers find ways to improve things we use every day*, and *engineers can be female and engineers can be male*. My intent with this chapter was to provide a glimpse into the process we followed for data analysis. I also demonstrated how broad conceptualizations were arrived at by analyzing subject-produced drawings, and illustrated ways that related data collected from image-elicitation interviews were broken down into key elements, properties and dimensions, and conceptualized the image as a whole.

CONCLUSION

Subject-produced drawings have the potential, when used with care and rigor, to serve as useful descriptive and analytical tools. As a descriptive tool, subject-produced drawings can be used to elicit individuals' understandings of a specific idea or construct. As an analytical tool, subject-produced drawings

Figure 12.13 'I am a chemical engineer working with a medical research team to design a cure for cancer. I am working on an experiment.' Author: 13-year-old, eighth-grade, Hispanic female

can be used to compare an individual's changes over time. While the subject-produced drawings offer rich descriptive data, the related issues with construct validity will persist, as data collected using drawings will be interpreted through the human perceptions of the researcher. It is not fully possible to discern the author's intent without speaking with the author of the drawing. When drawings are considered as visual data and are analyzed in context, along with other sources of data such as author descriptions of the drawing or image-elicitation interviews, the validity of the inferences that one can make from such data is enhanced, as the inferences will not rely solely on the researchers' interpretations. Ultimately, what matters is whether one has the evidence to warrant claims made. Subject-produced drawings offer an important tool for visual

researchers, as they have the following qualities: they can be projective; they permit expression of feeling and imagery; they allow for defining and redefining shared attitudes held by society; and they can be analyzed using psychological, sociological, and cultural lenses with attention to the phenomena or concepts under study.

ACKNOWLEDGMENT

This material is based upon work supported by the National Science Foundation under Innovative Technology Experiences for Students and Teachers (ITEST) Youth-based Project, Award# 0737616, Division of Research on Learning in Formal and Informal Settings, National Science Foundation.

Opinions, findings, conclusions, or recommendations expressed in this material are those of the author and do not necessarily reflect the views of the National Science Foundation (NSF).

REFERENCES

Abell, S. C., Wood, W. and Liebman, S. J. (2001) 'Children's human figure drawings as measures of intelligence: The comparative validity of three scoring systems', *Journal of Psychoeducational Assessment*, 19(3): 204–215.

American Society for Engineering Education (ASEE) (2007) *Engineering Go For It!: Make a Difference, Change the World*. Washington, DC: Author.

Augustine, N. (Chair) (2005) *Rising Above the Gathering Storm: Energizing and Employing America for a Brighter Economic Future*, National Academies Committee on Prospering in The Global Economy of the 21st Century. Washington, DC: National Academies Press.

Barba, R. H. and Mason, C. L. (1994) 'The emergence of the "nerd": An assessment of children's attitudes towards computer technologies', *Journal of Research on Computing in Education*, 26: 382–390.

Barnes, E. (1892) A study of children's drawings. Vol. 2, *The Pedagogical Seminary*. Worcester, MA: J. H. Orpha. pp. 455–463.

Bodzin, A. and Gehringer, M. (2001) 'Breaking science stereotypes', *Science and Children*, 39(1): 36–41.

Bohrmann, M. L. and Akerson, V. L. (2001) 'A teacher's reflections on her actions to improve her female students' self-efficacy toward science', *Journal of Elementary Science Education*, 13(2): 41–55.

Brown v. Board of Education (1954) 347 U.S. 483.

Burgess, G. (1895) 'Some phases of primitive art', *The Lark, Book I*: 1–16.

Chambers, D. W. (1983) 'Stereotypic images of the scientist: The *Draw-a-Scientist Test*', *Science Education*, 67: 255–265.

Chapman, L. J. and Chapman, J. (1971) 'Test results are what you think they are', *Psychology Today*, 18(22): 106–110.

Claparede, E. (1907) 'Plan d'experiences collectives sur le dessin des enfants', *Archives de Psychologie*, 6: 276–278.

Clark, K. B. (1950 [2004]) 'The effects of prejudice and discrimination on personality development', in W. Klein (ed.), *Toward Humanity and Justice: The Writings of Kenneth B. Clark*. New York: Greenwood Press (the White House Conference report originally published in 1950). pp. 206–210.

Clark, K. B. and Clark, M. P. (1939a) 'Segregation as a factor in the racial identification of Negro preschool children: A preliminary report', *Journal of Experimental Education*, 11: 161–163.

Clark, K. B. and Clark, M. P. (1939b) 'The development of consciousness of self and the emergence of racial identification in Negro Preschool Children', *Journal of Social Psychology*, 10: 591–599.

Clark, K. B. and Clark, M. P. (1950) 'Emotional factors in racial identification and preference in Negro children', *The Journal of Negro Education*, 19(3): 341–350.

Cooke, E. (1885) 'Art teaching and child nature', *London Journal of Education*, 7(197): 462–465.

Cunningham, C. and Knight, M. (2004) '*Draw an Engineer Test*: Development of a tool to investigate students' ideas about engineers and engineering', *Proceedings of the 2004 American Society for Engineering Education Annual Conference and Exposition*. Salt Lake City, UT, June 20–23. Washington, DC: ASEE.

Cunningham, C., Lachapelle, C. and Lindgren-Streicher, A. (2005) 'Assessing elementary school students conceptions of engineering and technology'. Paper presented at the *Proceedings of the 2005 American Society for Engineering Education Annual Conference and Exposition*, Portland, OR, June 12–15. Washington, DC: ASEE.

Darwin, C. (1877) 'A biographical sketch of an infant', *Mind*, 2(7): 285–294.

Dumont, F. and Smith, D. (1996) 'Projectives and their infirm research base', *Professional Psychology: Research and Practice*, 27: 419–420.

Ertas, A. and Jones, J. C. (1996) *The Engineering Design Process*, 2nd edn. New York: John Wiley and Sons.

Finson, K. D. (2002) 'Drawing a scientist: What we do and do not know after fifty years of drawings', *School Science and Mathematics*, 102(7): 335–345.

Finson, K., Beaver, J. and Cramond, B. (1995) 'Development and field test of a checklist for the Draw-a-Scientist test', *School Science and Mathematics*, 95(4): 195–205.

Finson, K. D. (2001) 'Applicability of the DAST-C to the images of scientists drawn by students of different racial groups'. Paper presented at the annual regional meeting of the North Central Region Association for the Education of Teachers of Science, Madison, WI.

Fischman, G. (2000) *Imagining Teachers: Rethinking Gender Dynamics in Teacher Education*. Lanham, MD: Rowman and Littlefield.

Flick, L. (1990) 'Scientist in residence program improving children's image of science and scientists', *School Science and Mathematics*, 90(3): 204–214.

Fort, D. and Varney, H. (1989) 'How students see scientists: Mostly male, mostly white and mostly benevolent', *Science and Children*, 26: 8–13.

French, J. (1956) 'Victorian responses to children's art', *College Art Journal*, 15(4): 327–333.

Golomb, C. (1992) *The Child's Creation of a Pictorial World*. Berkeley, CA: University of California Press.

Goodenough, F. L. (1926) *Measurement of Intelligence by Drawings*. New York: Harcourt Brace.

Haney, W., Russell, M. and Bebell, D. (2004) 'Drawing on education: Using drawings to document schooling and support change', *Harvard Educational Review*, 74(3): 241–271.

Harris, D. B. (1963) *Children's Drawings as Measures of Intellectual Maturity: A Revision and Extension of the Goodenough Draw-A-Man Test*. New York: Harcourt Brace Jovanovich.

Horowitz, R. E. (1939) 'Racial aspects of self-identification in nursery school children', *Journal Psychology*, 8: 91–99.

Huber, R. and Burton, G. (1995) 'What do students think scientists look like?', *School Science and Mathematics*, 95(7): 371–376.

Ivanoff, E. (1909) 'Recherches experimentales sur le dessin des ecoliers de la Suisse Romande: Correlation entre inaptitude au dessin et les autres aptitudes', *Archives de Psychologie*, 8: 97–156.

Kolb, L. and Fishman, B. (2006) 'Using drawings and interviews to diagram entering preservice teachers' preconceived beliefs about technology integration', in S. Barab, K. Hay and D. Hickey (eds.), *The Proceedings of the International Conference of the Learning Sciences*. Mahwah, NJ: Erlbaum. pp. 328–334.

Koppitz, E. M. (1968) *Psychological Evaluation of Children's Human Figure Drawings*. New York: Grune and Stratton.

Koppitz, E. M. (1983) *Psychological Evaluation of Human Figure Drawings by Middle School Pupils*. New York: Grune and Stratton.

Lamprecht, K. (1906) 'Les dessins d'enfants comme source historique', *Bulletin l'Academie Royale de Belgique: Classe des Lettre*, 9–10: 457–469.

Maitland, L. (1894) 'The art of little children, a translation of Ricci's *L'Arte dei Bambini*', *Pedagogical Seminary*, 3: 302–307.

Mason, C. L., Kahle, J. B. and Gardner, A. L. (1991) '*Draw-a-Scientist Test*: Future implications', *School Science and Mathematics*, 91(5): 193–198.

Mead, M. and Métraux, R. (1957) 'Image of the scientist among high-school students', *Science*, 126: 384–390.

Mercier, E. M., Barron, B. and O'Conner, K. M. (2006) 'Images of self and others as computer users: The role of gender and experience', *Journal of Computer Assisted Learning*, 22: 335–348.

Motta, R., Little, S. and Tobin, M. (1993) 'The use and abuse of human figure drawings', *School Psychology Quarterly*, 8: 162–169.

Naglieri, J. A. (1988) *Draw-a-Person: A quantitative scoring system*. San Antonio, TX: The Psychological Corporation.

Naglieri, J. A. and Bardos, A. N. (1987) '*Draw-a-Person* and Matrix Analogies Test's cross-culture validity'. Paper presented at the annual meeting of the National Association of School Psychologists, New Orleans.

National Academy of Engineering (NAE) (2008) *Changing the Conversation: Messages for Improving Public Understanding of Engineering*. Committee on Public Understanding of Engineering Messages. Washington, DC: The National Academies Press.

Neisworth, J. T. and Butler, R. J. (1990) 'Review of the *Draw a Person*: A quantitative scoring system', *Journal of Psychoeducational Assessment*, 8: 190–194.

Partridge, L. (1902) 'Children's drawings of men and women', *Studies in Education*, 2: 163–179.

Rampal, A. (1992) 'Images of science and scientists: A study of school teachers views and characteristics of scientists', *International Science Education*, 76(4): 415–436.

Ricci, C. (1887) *L'Arte dei Bambini*. Bologna, Italy: Nicola Zanichelli.

Rouma, G. (1913) *Le Langage Graphique de l'Enfant*. Paris: Alcan.

Schibeci, R. A. and Sorensen, I. (1993) 'Elementary school children's perceptions of scientists', *School Science and Mathematics*, 83(1): 14–19.

Schuyten, M. C. (1904) 'De oorspronkelijke 'ventjes' der Antwerpsche schoolkindern', *Paedologisch Jaarboek*, 5: 1–87.

Scriven, M. (1972 [1967]) 'The methodology of evaluation', in R. W. Tyler, R. M. Gagné and M. Scriven (eds.), Vol 1, *Perspectives of Curriculum Evaluation*. Chicago, IL: Rand McNally. pp. 28–48.

Smith, D. and Dumont, F. (1995) 'A cautionary study: Unwarranted interpretations of the *Draw-a-Person-Test*', *Professional Psychology: Research and Practice*, 26(3): 298–303.

Strauss, A. and Corbin, J. (1998) *Basics of Qualitative Research*, 2nd edn. Thousand Oaks, CA: Sage Publications.

Sumrall, W. J. (1995) 'Reasons for the perceived images of scientists by race and gender of students in grades 1–7', *School Science and Mathematics*, 95(2): 83–90.

Weber, S. and Mitchell, C. (1995) *That's Funny, You Don't Look Like a Teacher*. Washington, DC: Falmer Press.

Wheelock, A., Bebell, D. and Haney, W. (2000) *What Can Student Drawings Tell Us about High-Stakes Testing in Massachusetts?* [Online]. Available from: http://www.tcrecord.org/Content.asp?ContentID=10634 [Retrieved 15 December 2000].

13

The Photo Diary as an Autoethnographic Method

Elizabeth Chaplin

INTRODUCTION

In the past, visual diaries were mostly personal—collections of drawings or watercolors, or snapshots combined with text—and were often the province of artists, such as those by Ian Breakwell, Stephen Chaplin, Wendy Ewald, and Jamie Livingston.[1] But the Internet has made visual diary-keeping much simpler, opening it up to a wider range of participants. For the social scientist, keeping a visual diary is a good way of collecting and amassing field notes. But this poses the problem of how to work this raw material up into 'proper social science.'[2] Autoethnography, which has also been gaining recognition in recent years, can go a step further, by adding the personal experiences of the author to the fieldwork.

In common with the diary, the autoethnographic text tells the author's story in the author's own voice (*JCE*, 2006). Visual 'field notes' and autoethnography have become closely linked; the method of observing and writing through personal observations is well established in a variety of disciplines such as human communications, ethnography, anthropology, and narrative research (Ellis and Bochner, 2006; Goodall, 2000, 2008; Barone, 2001a, 2001b; Bochner, 2001).

My aim in this chapter is to explore this closeness, and to see how visual sociology, and especially the visual diary, can contribute to autoethnography. Accordingly, I will turn to my own daily photographic diary, which I came to see was akin to autoethnography and fueled my interest in the practice as a way of knowing. But first, I offer a short general account of autoethnography, starting with an examination of its roots. For it seems to me worth asking how, during my 30 years as a sociologist, the social scientific text has managed to move so far away from positivism and the third-person passive.

PART 1. AUTOETHNOGRAPHY EXPLAINED

Some historical roots of autoethnography

Relativism
Karl Marx's (1844) *Economic and Philosophical Manuscripts* relativized economics, and

contextualized politics. The first English translation from the German did not appear until 1959. Three years later, Thomas Kuhn's (1962) *The Structure of Scientific Revolutions* began the process of relativizing natural science knowledge. And, following either the Marxist 'critical' tradition or the Kuhnian 'empirical' approach, many branches of social science eventually adopted relativist methodologies to some degree (this is discussed further below). That is to say, positivism, with its essentialist claims to objectivity and neutrality, was increasingly rejected. In *Search for a Method*, Sartre (1963) summarized the relativist position:

We are not only knowers, in the triumph of intellectual self consciousness, we appear as the known (9). The only theory of knowledge which can be valid today is one which is founded on that truth of microphysics: the experimenter is a part of the experimental system (32n). [Thus] research is a living relation between men [sic.] (72).

Yet post-positivism lingers on in various guises; for example, in the status given to picture captions, and in the scholarly article format. Guba and Lincoln (1998) posed important arguments intended to challenge the primacy of this approach to analysis and reporting of social research.

Feminism

In the early 1960s, a new generation of feminists began to percolate through university student life and study. The first UK Open University social science courses, such as *Understanding Society*, were studied by thousands of students in the late 1960s, yet they made no mention of gender. But by 1975, feminists were arguing that then-current theories of inequality did not account satisfactorily for women's position in society (see Steedman, 1986: 7, for an interesting discussion; also Bowles and Klein, 1983: Ch. 11; also Smith, 1977). As female graduate students in the sociology department at York University, we were women in a man's world. We were just beginning to regard formal social science texts as lacking neutrality and objectivity; they seemed to reflect heavily the male tendencies to separate 'work' from 'home.' We maintained that home *was* work, and that the personal was political.

To encourage new social research, the British government, via its Social Science Research Council (SSRC), provided what they termed 'New Blood' money at some point during my second year as a postgraduate. As a 'mature' student, however, I was too old to qualify for it. I remembered thinking that the expression 'New Blood' was unfortunate—it smacked of horse racing and aggressive young men jostling for pole position. Carolyn Ellis, in her work discussing feminist ways of knowing, explored ways that women's experiences such as these, and women's interest in introspection, could be integrated with social science field work (Ellis, 1991; Bochner and Ellis, 1992).

Postmodernism and visual representation

Friedrich Nietzsche prefigured postmodernism. He wrote in 1888 that *'die "wahre Welt" endlich zür Fabel wurde'* ('The "true world" finally became a fable'). Nearly 100 years later, J. F. Lyotard (1979) echoed these words in *The Postmodern Condition*, when he argued that there is no objective truth, only narratives about truth. Lyotard used the term 'figural' to refer to the visual in the narrative: images, typography, and page layout each exert a degree of autonomy.

Many others at that time explored taking the photograph itself into postmodern theory, as they were beginning to take more interest in the relationship between images and words (Berger, Barthes, Mitchell, Danto). Cindy Sherman, in her photographic self-portraits, *Untitled Film Stills (1977–80)*, blurred distinctions between author, sitter, and stereotype. She explored ways that the image that meets the eye was clearly not a record of some 'found' reality; showing instead how its subject matter had been meticulously contrived. Sherman figurally expounded postmodern theory—each created scene is itself an art version of reality.

Thus, by 1980, the photograph had been theoretically and visually released from its conventional roles, whether in science as documentary record, or in art as substitute painting. And, with the arrival of the digital age came *technological* release: photographic images became cheaper to make, and easier to adjust, store, and send. Photography now touched everyone. The postmodern theorist faced a situation in which images fairly jostled for attention with words.

Autoethnography

Each of these historical roots helped dislodge positivist and other assumptions about the status and character of social science. Each strand, interwoven with the others, helped bring the personal into the social scientific. Autoethnography is arguably—from a theoretical point of view—another stage in this process, for now the researcher leaves her shadowy position in or 'behind' the narrative, and steps out to become the principal *subject* of the research project. (And, as the first-time autoethnographer discovers for herself, she is now really exposed—see Part 2 of this chapter). Thus, in autoethnography two different meanings of the term *subject* come together: the researcher is the *subject* of the research, and also the *subjective voice* in the narration. So the narrative starts with the self, and proceeds in the first-person singular; the author takes the reader on a journey—mental and physical, real and metaphorical—into and through her own social world. The journey, and the telling of it, constitute the research project. Embedded in the narrative, and clearly an integral part of it, are the author's reflections on the project, since it is centered on herself. This means that the important topic of reflexivity—and as some of the aforementioned authors have argued, social science is not a special case, since the researcher *is* an integral part of the research project and *does* influence its outcome—now seems curiously hard to keep in focus as a topic in its own right. It has, in effect, folded right into, and become part and parcel of, the autoethnographic approach.

Underlying this distinctive methodological approach is the conviction that a narrative that closely documents the researcher's personal thoughts, feelings, and actions and relates them to the wider social world will give the reader a richer and more intimate experience of that world than they would get from the generalized results of a conventional social scientific research project. It's hardly surprising, then, that abstract explanations are treated with suspicion by autoethnographers and, in turn, are not made lightly. For if the self is the focus, and all selves differ, then generalizing might seem to be a strategy for concealing a lack of evidence or blurring pieces of evidence that don't quite fit together. Ellis and Bochner (2006: 429) went further, when they championed the position of Tim O'Brien, a novelist[3] and veteran of the Vietnam War. O'Brien maintained that the author's story, with its close-up sights, smells, and 'rawness,' can convey a 'story truth' to the reader which is more present than even a 'happening truth' (2006, 429).

An autoethnographic project—in its early stages at least—often hopes to bring aspects of the research process into the open that, in a more conventional project, would remain hidden: for example, personal opinion, informal asides, doubts and worries, or confessions. When I photographed everyone in my street outside their front doors as a way of marking the millennium, I used a conventional qualitative approach and I found myself rejecting some of the most interesting material because it seemed too personal (Chaplin, 2002). In fact, I felt obliged to delete so much from the file that I sometimes felt as though the whole project was slipping away. An autoethnographical approach (had I known about it at the time) would have helped 'solve' this kind of problem. In its later stages, however, an autoethnography sometimes shifts direction. Because of its unusual character compared with most social science projects, researchers are likely to become involved in discussions with peer reviewers about publication. The reviewers' comments, and the author's responses, become part of the research product (Holt, 2003).

So how can this personal research journey, this narrative, be effectively communicated? Autoethnography takes on the textual form that best conveys the author's story to the reader. Using the third-person passive within a conventionally laid-out academic article is a relic of positivism and a habit that seems to die hard. But now that positivism and its special relationship to science have been relativized, the field is open—in theory at least—and an autoethnographic account might take many forms: for example, a play, a descriptive report, a photographic display, even a performance.

I vividly remember a book from my student days called *The Private Worlds of Dying Children* (Bluebond-Langner, 1978), because one of the chapters is written in the form of a play. The children, the author, their parents, nurses, and other participants speak to one another, as they presumably did during the period of research; and we learn, 'as though at first-hand,' how a dying child, in a hospital environment, makes sense of what is happening around her or him. This creative approach, sandwiched between chapters of conventional textual form, raised the question: 'How far can an author push the boundaries of academic convention?' A social science text that takes the form of a play, for example, will evoke comparisons with dramatic reading as a literary experience, and perhaps also with the social experience of visiting the theater. Indeed, in autoethnography, the boundary between social science and art can become blurred (Wall, 2006: 10). As the practice of autoethnography has matured, however, these concerns about boundaries and roles have been hashed out and autoethnography firmly established as a qualitative approach (Barone, 2001a, 2001b; Denzin, 2006; Goodall, 2008).

Visual sociologists have also found themselves up against this boundary. First, from a purely practical point of view, they need to know how many photographs they can include in an academic article, what size the images will be, whether color reproduction (or 'just black and white') is available, and how each page will be laid out.[4] Thought will be given to the relationships between image and words. Images may appeal to the reader's emotions

and judgments, and text may leave readers pondering meaning and relevance of a sequence of words.[5]

National Geographic, for example, is a magazine that prides itself on its balanced presentation of arguments as well as on its high-quality photographs, but may not always achieve the desired balance. In Mark Jacobson's 'Dharavi—India's Shadow City' (2008), the arguments for and against slum clearance in a district of Mumbai are indeed carefully balanced. The written text was overshadowed by the aesthetic force of the photographs, leaving readers with the impression that Dharavi was an extraordinary and colorful place. Dharvari is in fact Asia's largest slum.[6] On the other hand, consider the writings and images of W. G. Sebald (1993, 1995, 1997, 2001). The black-and-white photographs were not captioned, but were placed on the page between passages of written text that refer to the scene depicted in the photograph. The images did not illustrate the words; the words did not caption/capture the image. The balance of image to text was deliberately kept fluid, each remaining semi-autonomous, yet clearly accessible to the reader to be interpreted 'in itself' and in the light of its relationship to the others.

Visual autoethnography

Narrowing the focus now to 'visual autoethnography,' the relationship between image and words, between aesthetic force and written argument, becomes even more important. This is because the author wants the reader 'to feel what I felt' (O'Brien, 1991; in Ellis and Bochner, 2006: 429) and what better way to achieve this than with images that can make an immediate aesthetic impact on the viewer's feelings? Images can be a formidable tool of the autoethnographer; yet because we are operating within the discourse of social science rather than art, that aesthetic force cannot be allowed to overwhelm the social argument.

So, as many others in this volume have pointed out, visual sociology brings an awareness of how images can be made to work with written text in research, and autoethnography benefits in much the same ways. In addition, autoethnography helps reinforce visual sociology's case for unconventional textual formats. In Part 2, I'll refer again to the balance between words and image, in relation to my own visual diary. Next, though, I turn to critiques of autoethnography.

What the critics say

In the past, critics questioned whether autoethnography was 'proper research.' Holt (2003), whose own autoethnographic account was finally published after being examined by seven different reviewers and four journal editors, noted that the emphasis on the personal might be seen as narcissistic; the showing of emotion was considered shocking. Certainly, a first-person account is a violation of positivist ideology, and autoethnography was, for some, a travesty of social science methodology.[7] But the situation is changing: postmodern culture has loosened boundaries between disciplines such as social science, documentary filmmaking, and creative writing. Autoethnography is now discussed and taught in some university departments, where student assignments include writing first-person narratives.[8]

Some critics also wonder how such an approach can produce *theory*—long assumed to be a basic aim of science, whether natural or social.[9] Autoethnographers may be divided on the degree to which they support certain goals in theory development. 'Analytic' autoethnographers (Anderson, 2006a) see autoethnography as rooted in ethnography itself, and want it to be 'committed to developing theoretical understandings of broader social phenomena' (373). But 'evocative' autoethnographers (Ellis and Bochner, 2006) completely reject the idea of producing theory, even in the long term. A special issue of *The Journal of Contemporary Ethnography (JCE)* (2006) was largely devoted to a debate between these two camps. Analytic autoethnographers argued that autoethnography is quite compatible with more traditional

ethnographic practices, as indeed its name would seem to imply; and these traditional practices provide a base from which theory can be developed and into which it can be linked. The more experimental and evocative autoethnographers said that linking autoethnography into mainstream social science in this way would be to 'tear its heart out': an autoethnographic account tells a 'unique' story (to a unique reader), whereas social science theory has had generalization as its end goal.

The point is that the systematic approach an autoethnographer takes toward developing an evocative account reflects the 'signature' features of social science. Source referencing, the crafting and character of arguments, and the general sense of carefulness and accuracy are characteristics that all good researchers attend to. Add to this a narrative that, in many cases, pursues reflexive awareness and a sense of spontaneity and freshness.

Context is also a key factor in defining what counts as autoethnography, and what doesn't. In the case of an academic journal article, the journal itself provides authentication for an autoethnographic account—hence the importance of earlier discussions with peer reviewers, editors, publishers. So, although the autoethnographic text speaks in its author's voice, this professed openness should not blind us to the fact that there are yet more voices lurking behind the autoethnographic text. The voices of editors and publishers, and—further behind still—the 'voices' of those with the power (for example, 'class' power) to uphold unacknowledged conventions, ultimately form the boundaries between what counts as social science and what doesn't.

PART 2. IN WHICH I TURN 18 DAYS OF MY VISUAL DIARY INTO AUTOETHNOGRAPHY

Introduction

When I was first asked to write this chapter I was reminded of Molière's *Bourgeois*

Gentilhomme who was tremendously bucked to be told he was speaking prose—and had been all along. I'd been keeping a visual diary for 20 years without knowing that autoethnography could be an approach to making sense of what I'd collected. I began to read all about the struggles authors had gone through in order to publish their work and to gain acceptance by colleagues. My situation has been the other way round, attempting to produce an autoethnography from 'data' I'd collected without an awareness of those arguments, values, and approaches, and I've struggled to do so.

To start with, I should explain how I came to keep a visual diary at all. I am married to an artist, who has always kept a diary/sketchbook in which he draws on a daily basis, and, as he says, 'writes round each drawing.' As a mature graduate student of sociology in the 1970s, I was intrigued by the idea of building a bridge between our two worlds. Then, while researching some constructivist artists in the 1980s, and wanting the experience of producing visual work like they did, I thought of keeping a daily image-plus-words diary because it would also be field notes, *and* it connected up with the earlier idea of bridge-building. My first daily entry was on 7 February 1988. It showed my mother and my husband in the Lake District of Northern England, and was accompanied by a short piece of writing. Eighteen years later, the diary went online and became a blog, an ideal forum for my visual diary. The verbal comments, added sometime later in the day, were meant to lightly contextualize the image, yet leaving it semi-autonomous (in the manner of W. G. Sebald). By presenting readers with a particular 'image and words' combination, readers can construct a connection between what they see and other stuff in my mind that they don't see. That's the idea. It doesn't always happen, like if I'm pressed for time, which is quite often.

My diary has the following elements: It is *longitudinal*. It is *visual*, though, importantly, each image has a short accompanying written comment—not necessarily a description of

what's in the photograph. My diary records incidents in *my day-to-day life*. In the short term it is *non-theoretical*. Lurking somewhere behind all this is *feminism*. These elements all link up. But—and this is now the point—how can these links form up into autoethnography? What, if anything, do the diary and autoethnography have in common—apart from the intriguing coincidence (Anderson, 2006a: 378–380; Charmaz, 2006: 398) that, round about the time of my first diary entry, autoethnography was emerging as a distinct academic field?

I wanted to use my photographs to make theory, but I found them unyielding, intractable, resistant, in a way that Goffman might have described (1979: 20), for each one recorded an utterly unique instance. And this failure to wring theory out of my images meant that the visual diary just ticked over in the background of my life as a sociologist for at least 15 years. It was field notes (Anderson 2006a: 384).[10] It was an ideas bank and a leaping-off point to other projects. I felt vaguely apologetic about it—and when I'm with conventional sociologists, I still do (Burnier, 2006: 412). But when I read evocative autoethnographers Carolyn Ellis and Arthur Bochner's pronouncement that 'the narrative text refuses to abstract and explain' (Ellis and Bochner, 2000: 744), I got a kind of mental electric shock, a sense of relief, of something I could connect to. Furthermore, a text dominated by images cannot ignore aesthetic considerations.[11] Aesthetics is an important concept in its own right for autoethnographers, because it's about conveying feeling. Here again, I found myself close to autoethnography, in contrast to conventional sociology, which is inclined to dismantle the concept of aesthetics, or to treat it as synonymous with 'art.'

Diaries give a longitudinal view. Meanings *emerge* from diaries, and this establishes another link to autoethnography. Ellis and Bochner (2006) quoted Hannah Arendt's conception of storytelling as an activity that 'reveals meaning without committing the error of defining it' (438). This is very much what my visual diary hopes to do in the long term. For example, *Nella Last's War: The Second World War Diaries of Housewife, 49* (Last, 2006) does this, yet her diary doesn't just reveal meaning. By the time you've read two-thirds of her book, generalizations begin to hover in your mind, and eventually they just won't go away.[12] Isn't this a step toward theorizing? While Ellis and Bochner (2006) have taken issue with the systematic search for generalizable theory, I (in common with analytical and some evocative autoethnographers) do not reject the idea of theory per se. What I'm uneasy about is forcing the theoretical pace: 'generating' theory from data, and privileging theory over knowledge.

My visual diary clearly exhibits certain 'autoethnographic features.' It has also shown that it is adaptable: technologically, it has moved from chemical photography to cameraphones and blogging, and theoretically it has been influenced by trends over the past 20 years in sociology, anthropology, and art practice. Even at low points, when I thought I was 'just keeping going for the sake of it,' my words and images have been showing the patterns, and changes in patterns, of my daily life. But now the diary is about to embark on *another* change: it and the concept of autoethnography come up side by side, like railway lines that run in parallel before merging at a points.[13]

What follows next is my diary itself: the daily entries of image and text as they were created then. I start with March 10, 2008 as the time when my first awareness of the autoethnographic nature of this work was being explored.

My visual diary goes autoethnographic

In my quest to turn the diary into autoethnography, I certainly made changes to it. But it was already approaching the form of autoethnography, if not the substance. You'll have seen that the diary mode itself gets me 'speaking' personally, naturally, and 'familiarly,' as on March 21 (Figure 13.16): 'Shink

Poos' is what the children call my pink shoes. That little literary nugget wouldn't see the light of day in many writing situations. I'm also making quick pictures, adopting a fairly casual approach to photography because I'm doing it every day. And with the diary now a blog, I'm at the center of a project which throws out links to other Internet users. It does this on a daily basis. And the *dailyness* of the diary allows detail to be recorded and preserved.

By the same token, those Easter eggs on March 22 (Figure 13.18) aren't quite in focus and the image doesn't give off much information; nor does 'Shink Poos' from the day before. You wouldn't see them in a more selective show of images like an art exhibition, yet sequentially, and in conjunction with the words, a daily structure is provided for the

10 March 2008

Figure 13.1 **We have been warned that a big storm is on its way. This picture shows one of S's two barometers, both of which show that today's barometric pressure is the lowest ever recorded**

11 March 2008

Figure 13.2 We changed round the drawings in the long frame at the top this morning. I don't know how S got it down by himself. I helped him get it back, and we nearly didn't manage it. The frame is appallingly heavy

autoethnographic project. A rather thin description of a routine event may acquire more meaning—even potential theoretical significance—as part of a sequence or cluster of entries. And some aspects of my story, with a relation to the wider world, are better expressed in images than by words, particularly those concerning location, atmosphere, or emotion: for example, those of March 14(b), 15, and 27 (Figures 13.7, 13.8, and 13.23).

So, now, what 'changes' did I make to the visual diary in order to turn it into autoethnography? There is more to say about the images and their contribution to the autoethnographic project. I have often felt as though I am photographing something just slightly out of the ordinary: see, for example, the entries on March 10, 11, and 20 (Figures 13.1, 13.2, and 13.15). But this is complicated by the fact that, online, my blog images are in color, whereas here they are reproduced in black and white: March 21 (Figure 13.16) now makes no sense; March 26 (Figure 13.22) doesn't make a lot of sense either.

It worries me that in my own experience of images, contextualizing words very often threaten to dominate them. The entry for March 14 works because the words are subsumed into the image. But some daily entries are turning into a discussion about how to proceed (March 13, 14, 26, 27). By March 25, I am resigned to showing only a short run of small black-and-white images plus written comment. So has autoethnography really 'kicked in'? I think so, since almost all the other features discussed earlier are also recognizable. These are—in list form: *author is subject*, *narrative documents author's thoughts and actions* (these two items become far more noticeable after the first 3 days); *aspects of research usually hidden are brought out* (March 13, 15, 17, 19, 25, etc.); *referencing* (March 14, 23, 27); *systematic approach* (wasn't that already built in?); *insertion into 'the field'* (March 14, 27); *crafting* (I certainly tried); *aesthetics not paramount but important* (March 20 and 22 veer toward aesthetic dominance, perhaps).

12 March 2008

Figures 13.3 and 13.4   After the Goethe lesson, I turned right up Exhibition Road, into Hyde Park. Saw a Derek Jarman exhibition at the Serpentine, and took these two pictures. This is water disturbed where a heron has just taken off, frightened by a dog

So now that it looks like we've got a stretch of autoethnography, what use is it to the reader/viewer? Well, in the e-mail pictured on March 14 (and with a social science training evidently weighing heavily on my shoulders!) I see I said that I hoped respondents would learn 'something about the everyday life of a middle-class English woman, living in London and semi-retired from being a social scientist.'[14] So how much would they get from this short stretch of images-and-words? There are lots of clues to my *middle-classness*: friends (March 15); class distinctions (March 19); taste in music (March 25). But is it clear that I am *female*? There are no photos of me. I hardly ever

13 March 2008

Figure 13.5   I went to see the film 'No Country For Old Men'—really because I have reached a stumbling block in how to actually proceed with my autoethnography project. The film has affected much that I see at the moment. I took this picture as soon as I got home, and I took it and look at it through the film's eyes. The drops of water hanging from the seat seem to portend disaster. (Is this the first day my diary becomes autoethnography? Not sure)

14 March 2008 (a)

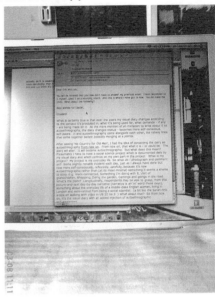

Figure 13.6   Here's the e-mail I sent Eric and Luc continuing the discussion about the project, and making some suggestions. From now on, the diary will become autoethnographic. But what does this mean? I have to have a social science project which is documented daily by my visual diary and which centres on my own part in the project What is my project? As the e-mail says, my project is my everyday life. So what do I photograph and comment on? Some slightly notable incident each day, just as I always have done but now more self-consciously, carefully, in relation to other ethnographic projects, because it's now autoethnographic rather than (at its most minimal) something it seems a shame to stop. Slightly notable incidents could be work-connected, something I'm doing with S, visit of grandchildren, shopping, doing the garden, comings and goings in the road. What's the point? Longitudinally, respondents may be able to grasp, from this picture-and-text narrative something about the everyday life of a middle-class English woman, living in London and semi-retired from being a social scientist: cf. Pink on 'Walking with video' (Pink, 2007). So from now on, it's the visual diary injected with autoethnographic awareness and self-awareness

photograph myself, and the daily photo is rarely taken by someone else[15]—but maybe March 10, 11, and 18c give enough information. March 20 and 27 give clues to the *locality*. March 17 actually gives the name of our road. March 23 shows local suburban architecture. *Englishness*? (I see I've written 'English' rather than 'British'). The written text is in English, though that doesn't clinch it. March 24 is a nice example of a conventional stereotype! The play-on-words in March 21 might be regarded as a British trait. March 23 talks about 'our English grandchildren' and 'our German ones.'

14 March 2008 (b)

15 March 2008

Figure 13.7 Patricia is over from New York. She used to live in our street and we have remained really good friends. Forgot to photograph her when she came to tea, so chased after her in the street (wouldn't have bothered before the diary went autoethnographic)

**Figure 13.8 Nicky and her mother at the Farmers' Market. Nicky runs it. She's become a good friend. I told them it was for an article on autoethnography. 'What on earth's that?' said Mrs Hartopp.
I tried to explain. Nicky said 'You've given me a reason for living.' This is becoming very self-conscious. I thought about photographing Jeremy's car, which won't go, and Xionane has had to get the train to take her class, but thought it would be intruding**

Semi-retired? March 17 talks about relying on commercial help with computer technology, which suggests that I am not regularly 'on-site' at work. March 13 and 14 show that I have time for 'hobbies,' and that I get up to central London for German lessons. The size of the grandchildren may suggest my age. And what am I doing in Wimbledon Village on a weekday afternoon, discovering horses? *Social scientist*? Well, that is probably clear every time I refer to the autoethnography project; it's also mentioned on March 17 and 19.

So the entries of the 10–27 March don't exactly lack information about me, and I hope that information is conveyed to the reader more fully and vividly by words *and* images than it would have been by words alone. For my part, there are occasions when words do not represent my feelings— for example, on March 27, as I gaze at Chester, and he gazes at me from his stable behind Wimbledon High Street. Yet what strikes me on returning to these entries is how wordy they are compared with entries made before and after the 'turn'; and how self-consciously self-centered they seem. But isn't that what we might have expected, given the sense of occasion attaching to this stretch of the diary, the additional 'layer' of social science? Yes. But theater critic Michael Billington's review of Alan Bennett's play *Enjoy*—published while I was writing this

16 March 2008

Figure 13.9   Sidney's bed is all made up in my work room. They arrive tomorrow, and getting ready in this small house has been like a military exercise

17 March 2008

Figure 13.10   'Olympia Computers' at the end of our road. I couldn't carry on as a visual sociologist without the technological expertise and help which Jeff gives me—less than a minute from our house. I never planned to live near a Mac shop, but it's turned out to be a providential coincidence. This morning he gave me a second-hand Toshiba laptop on approval. There are a few things my Mac won't do... .Visual sociologists tend to underplay the technological aspect of their texts

18 March 2008 (a)

Figure 13.11   S said: 'take this.' They arrived in the night. Here is the evidence. But we haven't seen them yet

18 March 2008 (b)

Figure 13.12   Now they're up. Sidney is very proud of his new tracksuit. He said: 'It cost 60 euros. Take it'

piece—spells out a methodological concern, which is actually hinted at in both my entries for March 14:

> Alan Bennett's rich and wondrous play is, among many other things, about the way we assume a false identity when under observation [by a sociologist].... Bennett is clearly attacking the self-consciousness of closely scrutinized behaviour. (Billington, 2008)

False identity? Would that apply to me too? Even when I'm being scrutinized by (admittedly) another version of myself? (March 26) (So which is the 'real' me, autoethnography or the visual diary as 'itself' (as I think of it (March 27)? You could say there are two versions of the 'real me.' Autoethnography is the 'working me,' and the diary as itself is the 'off-duty me.' It's strange: autoethnography—particularly the evocative sort—distinguishes itself sharply from 'conventional social science,' as we saw in Part 1. Yet when I attempted to turn my visual diary autoethnographic, it was *the social science* element still present in autoethnography that made the difference, that presented me with

14 March 2008 (c)

19 March 2008

Figure 13.13   Miranda said: 'take this. It'll be one in a million.' S playing tennis
It's notable how often other people suggest what I take. It's not so much because they know about the autoethnography project, but because they have known for ages that I take a photo each day

Figure 13.14   The builders next door have almost finished doing stuff on our side of the fence. This morning they rendered the bottom part of the wall. It is still wet. It's sad I have to be careful about photographing while they still are around, because they could see this as criticism of their work (and in the back of my mind looms the nightmare spectre of a court case...). In fact, we're not critical of their work at all. And we like them a lot. I just want to record that the rendering was done today. And it's been done well. But try telling them what's behind taking the photo, and there you come abruptly up against the difference between working- and middle-class cultures. I've been that way before. The look of incredulity. The struggle to bridge the gap

a different identity—not exactly a false one, but one which was changed by the autoethnographic project itself.

When I started, I thought autoethnography was so honest (you can still perhaps see traces of this in parts of the article). And in the sense that it exposes conventional sociology's suppression of the author's feelings, it is. But in comparison with run-of-the-mill blogging or diary-keeping, the autoethnographic text requires considerable crafting—I would say more than your average piece of social science (it's taken me a year to write this). And that is partly because in professing and apparently displaying more authorial honesty than conventional social scientific texts display, autoethnography inevitably amplifies the significance of what it does conceal: underlying structural elements such as academic

craftwork, methodological 'distortions,' editing demands, personal secrets; all of which lurk in the shadows.

Shouldn't these too be brought out in the open—rather as my old Amstrad computer used to offer to 'reveal codes'—in line with the reflexive character of autoethnography itself? It would of course be impossible to

20 March 2008

Figure 13.15   Christopher on the new climbing frame in Wimbledon Park. Not a lot of children can get up there

21 March 2008 (a)

Figure 13.16   Shink Pues—only the point is lost in black and white

21 March 2008 (b)

Figure 13.17   A photo-opportunity with 'John McEnroe' at the Tennis Museum

22 March 2008

Figure 13.18   The spoils from the Easter eggs hunt

23 March 2008

Figure 13.19 Easter Sunday morning, and it's snowing. There's been discussion in the press about the disadvantages of keeping Easter as a movable feast. This year it's very early, and some schools don't break up for another fortnight—including our English grandchildren. Our German ones have already been on holiday 5 days here (went back yesterday)

24 March 2008

Figure 13.20 A tea party for S's cousin Louise: cucumber sandwiches and a cake from the market. They are upstairs looking at photos of the family. The china is from my side of the family, and I made the tablecloth

25 March 2008

Figure 13.21   This evening we went to a concert at the Cadogan Hall (converted from a Christian Science church in 2004), off Sloane Square. Joanna MacGregor played Messiaen's 'Vingt Regards sur l'Enfant-Jesus.' An absolute tour de force. I've now done March 10–25 (21 images in all), and I'm beginning to wonder how long I should keep this up, what with my allowance of only 8500 words in all, and subtracting 210 words for each half-page image. These daily images aren't even quarter-page at present—perhaps an eighth. So one image = 26 words; 21 images = 546 words. If the images were half-page or better still whole page, they would change the meaning of this chapter a lot, because they would show detail which is hidden at present, and also have a bigger impact, possibly even dominate over the words, which I would like to push to the edge (When does sociology stop being sociology and start being a sequence of captioned images?) Another problem. Eric said: 'Continuing your research while paying attention to the growing field of autoethnography should yield interesting insights.' That's fine, except that the field of autoethnography grows more slowly than my daily visual diary. I shall keep this up for long enough to be able to pay attention to the growing field of autoethnography, but the number of pages of diary I shall have ready even by the date fixed for handing in the final draft will be colossal—way over my word limit—whereas by that time autoethnography might perhaps have yielded half-a-dozen new articles at most(?). So, 4416 words up to here + 546 = 4962. I suppose I might just get a month's diary within the word limit if I cut down on the commentary. Richardson (1995) remarked that how researchers are expected to write influences what they can write about.

   Nevertheless, I must carry on with words just for a moment to record here how much my visual diary has been influenced, not by other autoethnographies (though these do give me the confidence to feel that what I am doing bears formal scrutiny), but by the novels of W. G. Sebald, who intersperses uncaptioned photographs with text in a seemingly simple manner which is helpful to the reader. The implications of this simple, original move are anything but simple (Chaplin, 2006). Sebald removed the conventions concerning the relationship of image to text

26 March 2008

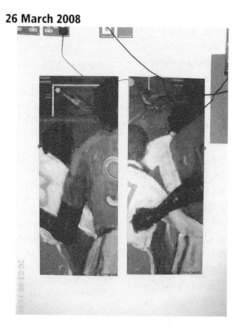

Figure 13.22 Today I went to Moorfields Eye Hospital Outpatients, at St. George's, for my regular checkup. This pair of paintings is in the waiting room and is surely a bit of a teaser for those with severe eye problems

27 March 2008

Figure 13.23 Chester in the Wimbledon Village stables. We only discovered these extensive stables running behind the High Street this afternoon, after 15 years of living in the area

bring them all out; human society doesn't much resemble the workings of a computer. Nevertheless, it seems to me that autoethnography has struggled with a meta-problem: how to explain concealing what you do conceal. This nagged at me a lot of the time while working on this piece.

A more positive preoccupation has been the place of *images* in autoethnography. The analysis of the autoethnographic diary excerpt indicated that images can say things that words can't, and that a combination of images and words can suggest a great deal of 'information.' I also noted in Part 1 that the novels of W. G. Sebald contain photographs, but none is captioned: each image's meaning is only loosely tied down by the verbal text surrounding it. The work of fine-tuning the interpretation is left to the respondent who, in turn, wants to resolve the uncertainty. (And, as I write alongside my daily image, I do remind myself periodically that captioning—so easy to slip into—is a cultural convention). Now to have the reader/viewer working emotionally alongside the author is surely just what the autoethnographer wants. Yet this has to be weighed against the fact that in social science, verbal text (argument, description) still takes precedence over images. So the *balance* in autoethnography between image and writing would seem to be more acutely in focus, more delicately at issue, than in many other discursive formations.

NOTES

1 Much of this discussion is built on my 30 years as a sociologist. The underlying theoretical positions about social scientific research are covered in detail by many of the authors in this volume and will not be cited extensively here. In addition, readers may want to consult my book *Sociology and Visual Representation* (Chaplin, 1994), which:

provides a selective historical survey of tests whose authors have contributed to the development of the social analysis of visual representation. It focuses, especially, on those recent texts

which have changed the relationship of analysis to topic by incorporating visual representation "into the analysis itself" (at *http://books.google. com/books?id=ax7AvdJPOIIC andsource=gbs_ navlinks_s*. [Accessed 5 October 2010]).

2 In 'Visual Studies and Empirical Social Enquiry' (Chapter 3 of this handbook), Wagner does an excellent job explaining how raw visual images can be converted into data sets for analysis.

3 O'Brien, T. (1990) *The Things they Carried*. New York: Broadway Books, Random. See also Barone (2001a, 2001b) and Polkinghorne (1995).

4 See 'Making Arguments with Images: Visual Scholarship and Academic Publishing', by Darren Newbury (Chapter 34, this volume).

5 The Rupert Bear comic strip, for example, *Rupert, Daily Express Annual (1960)*, provides a fascinating example of written text, picture sequence, and rhyming sequence all proceeding together, telling the same story. See also discussion on IVSA listserv e-mails, December 2008 to January 2009.

6 From reports of the terrorist attacks on Mumbai of 27 November 2008 we learn that Dharvari was an illegal settlement, without clean water, sewage, or schools, where undernourished children work without pause scrubbing clothes or cutting rubber from the inner tubes of bicycle tyres.

7 Holt (2003) laid out and dissected various objections by social scientists.

8 For example, at Indiana University of Pennsylvania, USA <http://kaytlingeorgia.wordpress. com/final-autoethnography-the-end/>. Also in the Communication Department at Arizona State University.

9 However, Eric Margolis notes that ethnography can be happy with 'accurate' description of social life and cultural productions' (personal communication).

10 Cf. 'salvage ethnography,' as described in Chau (2008: 204).

11 The term 'aesthetic,' as I use it in a social science context, refers to cathectic as opposed to cognitive communication, and therefore tends to be used in relation to the visual (images, layout) rather than the verbal (description, argument).

12 For example, pertaining to the attitude to homosexuality in the 1940s in Britain.

13 Diary entries before March 10 and after March 27 can be viewed online at http://www. wimbledonpark.blogspot.com. The first few entries show how wobbly I become when I actually embark on the project rather than just talk about it.

14 I feel almost ashamed to say—Why?—the project sometimes seems to smack of comfort, privilege—but then most of what counts as

knowledge is middle-class knowledge: come to think of it, neither upper *nor* lower class folks—in my experience—tend to see the point of all this knowledge-making.

15 Though, see April 9 and 14 on the website.

REFERENCES

Anderson, L. (2006a) 'Analytic autoethnography', *Journal of Contemporary Ethnography*, 35(4): 372–395.

Anderson, L. (2006b) 'On apples, oranges, and autopsies: A response to commentators', *Journal of Contemporary Ethnography*, 35(4): 450–465.

Anon (1960) *Rupert, the Daily Express Annual.* London: Beaverbrook Newspapers, Ltd.

Barone, T. (2001a) 'Researching, writing, and reading narrative studies: Issues of epistemology and method', in *Touching Eternity: The Enduring Outcomes of Teaching.* New York: Teachers College Press. pp. 131–180.

Barone, T. (2001b) *Touching Eternity: The Enduring Outcomes of Teaching.* New York: Teachers College Press.

Bluebond-Langner, M. (1978) *The Private Worlds of Dying Children.* Princeton, NJ: Princeton University Press.

Bochner, A. P. (2001) 'Narrative's virtues', *Qualitative Inquiry,* 7(2): 131–157.

Bochner, A. P. and Ellis, C. (1992) 'Personal narrative as a social approach to interpersonal communication', *Communication Theory,* 2: 165–172.

Bowles, G. and Klein, R. (eds.) (1983) *Theories of Women's Studies.* London and New York: Routledge and Kegan Paul.

Burnier, D. (2006) 'Encounters with the self in social science research: A political scientist looks at Autoethnography', *Journal of Contemporary Ethnography*, 35(40): 410–418.

Chaplin, E. (2002) 'Photographs in social research: The residents of South London Road', *Everyday Cultures Working Papers No 2.* Open University, Pavis Center for Social and Cultural Research. [Online]. Available from: http://www.open.ac.uk/socialsciences/includes/__cms/download.php?file=65itbcdvooip4xfgwz.pdf andname=necp_working_paper_no.2.pdf [Accessed 22 September 2010].

Chaplin, E. (2006) 'The convention of captioning: W.G. Sebald and the release of the captive image', *Visual Studies*, 21(1): 42–54.

Charmaz, K. (2006) 'The power of names', *Journal of Contemporary Ethnography*, 35(4): 396–399.

Chau, A. Y. (2008) 'An awful mark: Symbolic violence and urban renewal in reform-era China', *Visual Studies*, 23(3): 195–210.

Denzin, N. (2006) 'Analytic autoethnography, or déjà vu all over again', *Journal of Contemporary Ethnography*, 35(4): 419–428.

Ellis, C. (1991) 'Sociological introspection and emotional experience', *Social Interaction*, 14(1): 23–50.

Ellis, C. S. and Bochner, A. P. (2000) 'Autoethnography, personal narrative, reflexivity: Researcher as subject', in N. Denzin and Y. Lincoln (eds.), *The Handbook of Qualitative Research*, 2nd edn. Thousand Oaks, CA: Sage Publications. pp. 733–768.

Ellis, C. S. and Bochner, A. P. (2006) 'Analyzing analytic autoethnography: An autopsy', *Journal of Contemporary Ethnography*, 35(4): 429–429.

Goffman, E. (1979) *Gender Advertisements.* London and Basingstoke: Macmillan.

Goodall, H. L. (2000) *Writing the New Ethnography.* Lanham, MD: Alta Mira Press.

Goodall, H. L. (2008) *Writing Qualitative Inquiry: Self, Stories, and Academic Life.* Walnut Creek, CA: Left Coast Press.

Guba, E. G. and Lincoln, Y. S. (1998) 'Competing paradigms in qualitative research', in N. K. Denzin and Y. S. Lincoln (eds.), *The Landscape of Qualitative Research: Theories and Issues.* Newbury Park, CA: Sage Publications.

Holt, N. L. (2003) 'Representation, legitimation, and autoethnography: An autoethnographic writing story', *International Journal of Qualitative Methods*, 2(1). [Online]. Available from: http://www.ualberta.ca/iiqm/backissues/2_1final/html/holt.html [Accessed 1 January 2008].

Jacobson, M. (2007) 'Dharavi—India's shadow city', *National Geographic*, 211(5): 68–93

Journal of Contemporary Ethnography (JCE) (2006) Special Issue, 35(4).

Kuhn, T. (1962) *The Structure of Scientific Revolutions.* Chicago, IL: University of Chicago Press.

Last, N. ([1981] 2006) *Nella Last's War. The Second World War Diaries of 'Housewife 49'.* London: Profile Books.

Lyotard, J. F. ([1979] 1986) *The Postmodern Condition: A Report on Knowledge.* Manchester: University of Manchester Press.

Marx, K. ([1844] 1959) *Economic and Philosophical Manuscripts.* Moscow: Progress Publishers.

Molière [J. B. Poquelin] (1670). *Le Bourgeois Getilhomme*. (ballet/comedy). Chambord, France.

Nietzsche, F. (1889) *Götzen-Dämmerung*. Leipzig: C.G. Naumann.

O'Brien, T. (1991) *The Things they Carried*. New York: Penguin

Pink, S. (2007) 'Walking with video', *Visual Studies*, *22*(3): 240–252.

Polkinghorne, D. F. (1995) 'Narrative configuration in qualitative analysis', in J. Hatch and R. Wisniewski (eds.), *Life History and Narrative*. London: Falmer Press. pp. 5–25.

Richardson, L. (1995) 'Writing-stories: Co-authoring "The sea monster", a writing story', *Qualitative Inquiry*, 1: 189–203.

Sartre, J. (1963) *Search for a Method*. Tr. H. Barnes (1968). New York: Vintage Books.

Sebald, W. G. (1993) *Die Ausgewanderten (The Emigrants)*. Tr. M. Hulse (1996). London: The Harvill Press.

Sebald, W. G. (1995) *Die Ringe des Saturn (The Rings of Saturn)*. Tr. M. Hulse (1998). London: Harvill Press.

Sebald, W. G. (1997) *On the Natural History of Destruction*. Tr. A. Bell (1999). London: Hamish Hamilton.

Sebald, W. G. (2001) *Austerlitz*. Tr. A. Bell. Munich, Vienna: Hanser.

Sherman, C. (1995) *Untitled Film Stills (1977–1980)*. New York: Museum of Modern Art.

Smith, D. E. (1977) *Feminism and Marxism: A Place to Begin, A Way to Go*. Vancouver: New Star Books.

Steedman, C. (1986) *Landscape for a Good Woman*. London: Virago.

Wall, S. (2006) 'An autoethnography on learning about autoethnography', *International Journal of Qualitative Methods*, 5(2). [Online]. Available from: http://www.ualberta.ca/~iiqm/backissues/5_2/pdf/wall [Accessed 8 November 2007].

PART 4

Analytical Frameworks and Approaches

14

Quantitative Content Analysis of the Visual

Annekatrin Bock, Holger Isermann
and Thomas Knieper

INTRODUCTION

In this chapter we describe visual content analysis of journalistic images. In order to answer more complex questions than commonly addressed with visual content analysis, we have developed a coding strategy addressing specific phases of Knieper's (2003) scheme for the process of image communication.

We will first provide a brief overview of quantitative content analysis, its strengths, issues, and limitations. We then describe how Knieper's (2003) scheme of the process of image communication can help to focus visual content analysis appropriately. After this backdrop of the image communication process, we then develop strategies for systematic coding of images, demonstrating the use of these strategies on images sourced from the G8 summit in Heiligendamm, 6–8 June 2007.

OVERVIEW OF QUANTITATIVE CONTENT ANALYSIS

Quantitative content analysis is an empirical method for the systematic analysis of well-defined, audio, textual, visual, and/or audio-visual media content (Krippendorf, 2004; Rössler, 2005; Früh, 2007). It is a non-reactive method, which requires deciding whether to analyze all available content or only a representative sample, defining the sample period, sample material, sample unit and unit of analysis, and compiling a code book. Recruiting and coaching coders is also important, as well as fixing interpretation rules and procedures, and evaluating possible costs for the entire project. Methodologically, quantitative content analysis must comply with the scientific criteria of objectivity, reliability, and validity. Commonly, the quantitative analysis of media content is concerned with a large quantity of media messages which are surveyed to produce generalizable predictions. Such research aims to show trends in the content of media messages rather than gain a profound understanding of a single (media) message (Rössler, 2005: 16). Quantitative content analysis of visual content presents particular challenges, which we discuss below.

By 'visual content' we refer to graphic images such as photographs, moving images, paintings, drawings, and sculptures (Mitchell, 1987: 7–46; Knieper, 2003; Müller, 2003: 18–31). Even though immaterial mental images (for example, Knieper, 2003; Müller, 2003) and materialized pictures play an important role in the process of image communication, only the latter are appropriate for visual content analysis; their objectification, even in non-material, electronic form, provides a basis for a scientific observation. In this chapter, we focus especially on pictures in a journalistic context, touching only marginally on moving pictures and audio-visual media. Many insights from the content analysis of pictures are transferable to moving pictures and audio-visual media, but the analysis of moving-picture sequences adds several challenges outside the scope of this chapter.

Strengths

As long as the research hypotheses refer to manifest, unambiguous and clearly defined attributes, the content analysis of pictures is a relatively uncomplicated method.

> [V]isual content analysis is a systematic, observational method used for testing hypotheses about the ways in which the media represent people, events, situations, and so on. It allows the quantification of samples of observable content classified into distinct categories. (Bell, 2001: 14)

Visual content analysis can answer the questions of who or what is represented by the media and count the number of appearances of actors or themes using frequency analysis. By concentrating simply on certain aspects

of the (visual) media messages, this method can be used to reduce the complexity of media content. Common research questions relating to the priority/salience of media content, bias, or historical changes in modes of representation can also be answered quantitatively (Bell, 2001: 14).

Quantitative content analysis is a highly standardized method which claims to provide 'objective' or intersubjective replicable and valid results. Another strength of this method is its ability to reduce the visual material to a small number of codes, which can be counted and analyzed mathematically/statistically. This method (in contrast to qualitative content analysis) can thus be used to deal with a large amount of visual data, which allows generalizable predictions to be deduced from the research material.

Issues in the research phases

In general, a quantitative content analysis consists of five phases. First, the main unit (basic population) needs to be defined. In this phase, the researcher also decides whether to take a sample unit or to examine the whole research material and selects the unit of analysis (full pages, articles, pictures, infographs, and so forth). Second, the researcher compiles a code book, which contains the categories to be used to code the research material. This is followed by encoding in the third step and later the data analysis. Finally, the results are summarized and published. In the following section, we direct explicit attention to the issues of visual content analysis, which may occur in the first four phases.

Defining the main unit, sample unit, and unit of analysis

The main question in this first phase is to ask what kind of visual material needs to be examined. What will the main unit of analysis be? The answer to this question depends on the research question. Quantitative content analysis usually demands a definite research question with a clear focus (Früh, 2007: 78). The main unit could consist of all articles concerning a specific media event in the last decade, or refer to all pages of an online magazine published in the last 3 months. To overcome this issue it is necessary to explicitly define what is to be understood as 'visual content.'

Additionally, quantity does not always mean relevance. This is especially true for visual data. It might be the case that there is just one picture of an important event. Because of its uniqueness it could be more expressive or immersive than 1000 photographs of a regular happening that all look alike. The more precisely the researcher formulates the research interest, the more accurately the main unit can be identified and the more reliable the results will be.

It is then only possible to take a representative *sample unit* if all elements of the main unit have an equal chance of selection for analysis. Visual content makes the sampling difficult, for example, if there are different pictures of the same event. To determine the size of the sample unit depends on the variation in the visual content. 'If there is a whole range of extreme variations, the sample size must be large enough to contain examples of those extremes' (Rose, 2001: 59). Additionally, visual media content is usually integrated in a newspaper page or online homepage; photographs are also contextualized by headlines, text, and captions. It is therefore necessary to archive the picture with the entire context that surrounds it.

Having determined the main unit and sample unit, the next question to answer is what the unit of analysis will be. Concerning visual context in general, it is possible to code photographs, illustrations, infographics, caricatures, etc. If one is also taking into account online content, pop-up windows, animations, audio-visual media, advertising spots, and so on can also be examined. Regarding the identified research question, the researcher must now decide whether to simply concentrate on photographs, or to also analyze other visual content.

Compiling a code book and defining categories

Categories should be relevant to the research question, which means they should be useful to deduce answers related to whatever the interest of the study might be. Is the code book suitable for operationalization? This question asks whether it is possible to transfer theoretical constructs into variables, which can later be counted and correlated. Categories of a quantitative content analysis must at least be exhaustive and discreet (exclusive) (Rössler, 2005: 93). 'Exhaustive' means 'every aspect of the images with which the research is concerned must be covered by a category' (Rose, 2001: 60). 'Exclusive' defines that categories should not overlap.

A quantitative content analysis usually starts with examination of formal categories such as picture size, picture position in the newspaper text, the amount of space allocated relative to the presented text, and so on. Whether a photograph is presented at an exclusive angle to the paper side might also be relevant. This information might support conclusions regarding salience/priority of visual content. Furthermore, counting pictures of the same event in different media (newspapers, online journals, magazines, and the like) provides data on the (absolute and relative) frequency of visual media content.

After determining these more 'objective' categories, the coding may then also include more 'subjective' categories concerning the content of the visual data. Analysis of the content of a photograph could start with questions about the people shown. Who is portrayed? How many people are presented? What is their position in the picture? Is there something specific to say about their gesture or mimic? Second, the representation of the place shown should be examined. Where was the photograph taken? At what time and in which context was it taken? In addition, production factors can be coded such as light source, choice of camera, focal length and exposure time, contrast, image sharpness, etc. These categories are problematic, however, in that they are not always easy to identify by simply 'looking at' the visual material. We will show later in this chapter how this can be overcome by taking into account the complex process of image communication.

Encoding the research material and data analysis

Even though the coding of formal categories (for example, image size, position) is a relatively uncomplicated procedure, it is especially problematic to code categories concerning the content of photographs. This is the case because the recipient usually attributes meanings to a picture in fractions of seconds (see Todorov et al., 2005). It is therefore necessary to train coders in order to overcome their subjectivity and to gain intercoder reliability. The research material needs to be presented randomly to several coders. Their coding can then be compared; if there is a high level of agreement between the results from different coders, the method is assumed to be reliable.

Another issue of content analysis of the visual is the handling of large sets of visual data. While there are several, more or less useful, software programs to code text material; there is still no well-proven, reliable method to code photographs or other visual content.

In the fourth step of content analysis the coded data are analyzed. Pictures are polysemic and therefore can have several meanings depending on the context in which they are presented. This ambiguity makes it difficult to validate the results of an analysis of visual content. To overcome this issue, data interpretation must be explicitly fixed before analysis of the visual material starts.

PRACTICAL APPLICATION— QUANTITATIVE ANALYSIS OF VISUAL JOURNALISTIC CONTENT

Having introduced the main steps of quantitative content analysis, we will now give example strategies for the coding of images sourced from the G8 summit in Heiligendamm, 6–8 June 2007. The research process starts with a theory-driven study of the research subject. It is necessary to name a research hypothesis (which claims a correlation between at least two variables) or at least a specific research question. For our example, possible research questions include: Which photographs of the G8 summit were shown by the German media? What topics were visually reported on? Did the media prefer to refer to the summit of international politicians itself, or to concentrate on protests by Greenpeace or other interest groups, and so forth. Did reporting change between the first and last report on the event? The main unit for such a study would include all media content (print, television, radio, and online content) published and distributed in Germany. As all newspapers have an online presence, it would also be useful to integrate the (visual) content of online pages. Because handling such an enormous amount of material is not practical, one might reduce it by concentrating on a specific medium (for example, the Internet), and compare only two magazines, or take into account just one specific online newspaper (for example, *Die Welt*).

The G8 summit took place 6–8 July 2007. However, it is likely that an online newspaper would report on the summit during a period longer than these 3 days alone, so that it would be rational to analyze the reporting several weeks before and after the actual event. In this way, one could demonstrate a possible change in the topics presented. To concentrate on the 'visual reporting' of the G8 summit in the online version of the German newspaper *Die Welt*, for example, our main unit could be every online edition of this newspaper published from 15 June 2007 to 29 July 2007, excluding audio-visual content and hyperlinks which possibly lead to other pages and other photographs.

It may be difficult with visual content (as it can sometimes be with textual content too) for researchers to collect all of the relevant pictures. For example, depending on how well funded the research is, it might be too expensive to buy the rights for certain photographs or to pay the costs for online archives.

Having compiled the main unit, the next step is to decide whether or not to take a sample unit. If the number of photographs contained in the main unit is manageable, then sampling is not necessary. Otherwise, one can, for instance, randomize the pictures, by selecting a significant number of images to analyze in lottery style (Rose, 2001: 57). Our example research question asks whether there was a development in the 'visual reporting' (such as, for example, the media centering on the protesters early on, the politicians and their decisions during the summit, and the costs of the summit after the event), which requires a stratified sample. This requires dividing the material into data sets for the weeks before, during and after the summit, and then taking a systematic sample (for example, every third or fifth of the numbered photographs). Each photograph retrieved for the sample is then a unit of analysis.

Figures 14.1–14.6 show some of the pictures of the G8 summit that were presented online by *Die Welt* (2007). Figures 14.1–14.3 show the attendant politicians in several situations. Figures 14.4–14.6 present the demonstrators who protested against the summit.

A code book for our research needs to contain categories that are able to answer the research question. Operationalization means transferring specific aspects of the research question into concrete instructions for the coder. We are searching for a change in the reporting on the G8 summit. Our code book therefore needs to include categories related to this question. For our example, we will need formal ('objective') categories such as the 'publishing facts,' with variables like *publishing date* of the photograph (before, during, and after the summit), *picture size* (small, medium, large), *position on the page* (top, centre, or end of the page), and so forth. When searching for change in reporting and the topics represented visually, it is also necessary to name (subjective) categories related to the content of the photographs. An example category is 'people in the picture.' The following variables might belong to this category: *gender*, with the value 'male,' 'female,' and 'unknown'; *profession/function* (politician, police officer, other officials, protester, other civilians, unknown); *clothes, gesture, mimic*; and so on. Every coder is also a recipient, with their own socially constructed perspective, so that researchers need to be aware of this variation in perspective during coding. To avoid individuals impacting the results and to guarantee inter-subjective replicability or inter-coder reliability, coders require explicit instructions for coding parameters in a 'media picture.'

Later, when the data are being analyzed, variables such as *publishing date* and *profession/function* can be considered in relation to each other. A possible result might be that more pictures of protesters and police officers were reported before, than during, the summit, and that during the summit most pictures showed politicians.

Overcoming limitations of quantitative content analysis

Quantitative visual content analysis is, however, problematic when predictions about relevance or meanings of visual representation need to be made, because pictures are ambiguous and polysemic; their potential impact on the recipient is hardly predictable.

Coding photographs by simply looking at the picture and counting what is shown is almost impossible. To understand the meaning of visual content, and therefore be able to code and count it, it is essential to compile

Figure 14.1–14.3 Pictures of the attendant politicians at the G8 summit at Heiligendamm, 7 June 2007 presented by *Die Welt* (2007). Reproduced with permission: © 2007 ddp images GmbH

Figures 14.4–14.6 Pictures of the demonstrators at the G8 summit at Heiligendamm, 7 June 2007 presented by *Die Welt* (2007). Reproduced with permission: © 2007 Agence France Press GmbH

contextual information from the photograph. Analysis of visual content is almost impossible without taking into account the context in which the visual was produced and finally received. We therefore suggest in this chapter that visual content analysis should additionally integrate the complex and multilevel process of image communication.

THE PROCESS OF IMAGE COMMUNICATION

The process of image communication is characterized by a high degree of influence by the involved agents, who may be advisors/consultants, the depicted actors, the originator of the picture, media production companies, and/or the recipient. In visual content analysis, all the agent groups need to be considered because each selects, interprets, reduces, and constructs media content within a particular context; by doing so they decisively affect the meaning and impact of pictures, which ultimately form the basis for the sample unit to be examined by the researcher. In addition, individual characteristics of the agents subconsciously affect the production and reception process of pictures. These include individual experiences, different socialization processes, opinions, cultural background, and so on. This concept of acting agents, with individual impact as well as social structures and contexts playing an important role, leans toward the 'Theory of Structuration' (Giddens, 1988).

Giddens (1988) argued that structure can be conceptualized as rules and resources that actors mobilize in interactions that extend across space and over time. By using these rules and resources, actors sustain or reproduce structures in space and time. Rules are generalizable procedures that actors understand and use in various circumstances. Giddens posits that a rule is a method or technique, which actors know about, often only subconsciously, and which provides a relevant formula for action. From a sociological

perspective, the most important rules are those that agents use in the reproduction of social relations over significant lengths of time and across space (Turner, 1998: 492).

The unconscious and informal rules that determine human behavior in interaction with others require special consideration for the content analysis of pictures. The close relation between acting agents and social structures representing contexts in which they act is also significant for the process of image communication.

Figure 14.7 shows the process of image communication with the various contexts, picture stages, and actors. In general, only contextualized, media-published pictures are available for content analysis. The process of image communication is therefore researched backward or forward from the concrete 'media picture' (see Figure 14.7), depending on whether the research hypothesis requires predictions about the communicator or recipient. Beginning with the concrete 'media picture' allows conclusions to be drawn about the 'concept picture' or the 'transfer picture.' Particular processes of selection, interpretation, reduction, and construction in the encoding process may be revealed. In this way, the intentions of agents and agencies (advisors, spin doctors, originators, and the like) to produce a particular impact on the recipient through their editing of the 'media picture' become more obvious. It is also possible—although much more difficult—to project future effects on the recipient based on the 'media picture.'

Trying to predict or describe 'pictures in mind' or 'cognition pictures' of recipients can only be successful, however, if content analysis results are strengthened with insights from other disciplines, such as media impact studies, cognitive psychology, sociology, etc. Nonetheless, regardless of whether the process of image communication is focused backward or forward (concentrating on the communicator or the recipient, respectively), content analysis is usually an appropriate basis and useful start for answering several research questions. The kind of question to

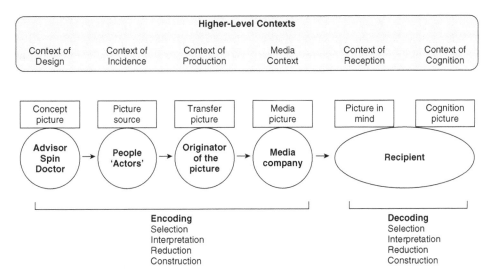

Figure 14.7   The process of image communication: © 2010 Bock, Isermann and Knieper

be answered determines which of the named contexts in Figure 14.7 should be examined, and which contexts might provide further insights. The scheme of the image communication process (Knieper, 2003, 2006) thus helps to concretely locate where answers need to be derived for different research questions.

The 'concept picture' (see Figure 14.7) originates if, for example, a public policy organization is staging a certain event (Knieper, 2006: 29–39; Forster and Knieper, 2008: 434–441). This staging of so-called pseudo events (Boorstin, 1961; Kepplinger, 1996: 13) may continue to the extent that an event is exclusively organized for media representatives and, without their appearance, would not take place or would be reduced to absurdity. Such an agency might comprise public relation consultants, election campaign leaders, or consulting agencies, who mostly intend to influence the recipient in some way, or produce a certain reaction. Content analysis in the '*context of design*' conveys findings with limitations. A close examination and evaluation of the degree of staging in pictures demands much time to gather data about who is part of the brain trust that staged the media event, and what

the intentions were for doing so. The research effort and complexity of information to be studied invite qualitative methods such as iconology (Panofsky, 1984) or iconological context analysis (Knieper, 2003; Forster and Knieper, 2008). However, basic assumptions about potential impacts of pictures and their construction can also be determined from quantitative content analysis in the '*context of design*.'

In the '*context of incidence*' (see Figure 14.7), the actual visible agents appear (for example, politicians) as the people who are later shown in the 'media picture.' This second level of the process of image communication concerns the actual event that is transferred into the image content by the 'originator of the picture.' For content analysis to simply compile data about how often a person is depicted is easily operationalizable. However, research questions requiring a closer, more intensive study of the representation of a person and possible appeal of the picture are more demanding. This is especially the case because the influence of visible elements such as positioning, shown body details, size of the face, face or hair attributes, facial displays, direction of view, head posture, physique, clothes, body poise, gestures, moves and dynamics, acting, touch and interaction with people and things, etc., are as yet insufficiently researched (Kinnebrock and Knieper, 2008).

Recipients allocate meanings from pictures in fractions of a second (Todorov et al., 2005) and—at least for representation of people—in a relatively stable way across cultures (Curran et al., 2001). The recipient spontaneously attributes several characteristics, including competence, attractiveness, health, youthfulness, or assertiveness, to the person depicted in the picture. Cunningham (1986), for instance, demonstrated that recipients suppose attractive persons to be more intelligent and self-confident significantly more often than less attractive persons. These phenomena can be explained by the model of visual stereotyping. For this reason, the perception of stimuli in democratic election campaigns, for instance, may influence attribution processes of recipients, making them prefer a certain political agent. This process of attribution by the recipient as a result of spontaneous visual perception happens involuntarily, and is influenced by personal experiences, learned previous knowledge, and the individual's construction of reality. What is still missing, however, is a systematic cataloguing of attribution processes on the basis of pictures and their elements. The fact that recipient interpretations of single elements in a picture can change reciprocally with specific combinations of picture details, strengthening or weakening attributions, adds further complexity to the problem. Petersen (2001, 2003), therefore, demands a systematic and long-term research program for iteratively exploring the meaning of pictures or picture details.

In the '*context of production*' (see Figure 14.7) and within image restrictions, the photographer, camera person, designer, or painter transfers an actual event into the 'transfer picture' (Knieper, 2003: 193–212). This is the first of three important acts of selection within the process. In this case, the selection is made by the 'originator of the picture' as the communicator. Subsequent selections are made by the 'media company'—also a communicator—and by the viewer of the picture, the recipient. During the '*context of production*,' the photographer only maps part of the whole scenery, which was presented during the (pseudo) media event and also decides which parts not to photograph. By doing so, he or she makes a first preselection of media content, which the recipient sees later. Again, at this point in the process, individual characteristics, abilities and skills of the originator of the picture influence the picture production together with the '*context of production*.' The producer of the picture makes many different decisions within the '*context of production*' (Müller, 2003: 47–48; Knieper, 2005a: 56–70, 2005b: 85–86). These decisions include the choice of camera (digital or analog), focal length and exposure time (depth of focus, dynamic), perspective (worm's eye view, normal, bird's eye view), light source (flash or available light), field sizes (detail, long shot, medium shot, etc.), format (height, horizontal format), picture composition (golden ratio, etc.), and also technical parameters (monochrome or color, ISO-norm, resolution, etc.). These parameters have a broad influence on the picture and its impact on the recipient. By giving precise instructions for content analysis coding, such parameters can be operationalized relatively easily. Again, combinations of parameters may change the meaning of a picture, so that it is not only important to record the parameters precisely but also to formulate explicit interpretation rules for combinations of parameters.

The contextualizing and editing of the 'transfer picture' by the media company in the '*media context*' (see Figure 14.7) leads to the final 'media picture,' which is distributed as a print, television, film, or online product. Depending on the medium in which the 'media picture' is published, it may appear with audio or textual elements. The context in which the media picture is finally represented also influences how the recipient perceives a picture, so that for content analysis, questions of weighting need to be decided on. Do recipients decode pictures and audio-visual media content together? Do context-integrated pictures have the same meaning as stand-alone pictures? Is it reasonable to assume in general the equal impact of pictures, moving pictures, caricatures, etc.? Whether, for instance, a picture is more meaningful than the associated headline of an article has still not been answered definitively. Reception and media impact studies present arguments about the unequal influence of different media, even though reciprocity or correlation between different types of media and the recipient's patterns of reception has not yet been adequately researched or understood. The Poynter Institute for Media Studies has conducted several eye-tracking studies to answer such questions. While previous studies suggested that recipients pay more attention to textual elements, the Poynter research shows that the mental weighting processes of media content is much more complex (Poynter Institute, 2000). Pictures or headlines can be eye-catchers depending on the layout of newspaper or online pages. Alternative design elements such as information graphics, charts, etc., similarly aim to attract attention to specific content (Bucher and Schumacher, 2007; Poynter Institute, 2007).

The perception or decoding by the viewer is the last step of the process of image communication. In these contexts, the *'context of reception'* and *'context of cognition'* (see Figure 14.7), the recipient decodes the media picture, which becomes a 'picture in mind' and later a 'cognition picture' (see Figure 14.7). This decoding and interpretation process is highly complex and again influenced by individual characteristics of the recipient, such as individual experiences and schemata, cultural or social symbols and the entire reception context as well as framing effects. On the basis of several sign stimuli, the recipient activates cognitive schemata for systematizing and interpreting visual information (for example, Fiske and Taylor, 1991). A skinhead, combat boots, or specific symbols in a picture of a demonstration might, for example, be the sign stimulus for a recipient to

classify the picture as radical right wing. The received media picture becomes an immaterial mental image or 'picture in mind' and through physiological and cognitive processes a 'cognition picture' in the head of the recipient. 'Cognition picture' in this context should be understood as an illusion of a mental image that originates from neuronal activities in the head of a thinking individual. In general, this 'cognition picture' does not correspond to the immaterial 'concept picture' planned by the picture producer, because the complex, interconnected process of image communication—which is characterized and influenced by several social structures and contexts as well as the involved individuals—evokes a range of encoding–decoding differences that impede (for example, through existing connotations) a distinct allocation of meaning. Moreover, the saved 'cognition picture' is modified by other visual impressions in the brain of the recipient between the actual event and reception of the 'media picture.'

QUANTITATIVE CONTENT ANALYSIS OF THE VISUAL AND THE PROCESS OF IMAGE COMMUNICATION

We will now explain how the process of image communication can be used as a basis for practical implementation of quantitative analysis of visual content, and how it may help to overcome some of the issues and limitations of quantitative content analysis. Using Knieper's (2003) scheme of the image communication process described above, we give here example strategies for the systematic coding of images, demonstrating their use on images sourced from the G8 summit.

Context of design

Content analysis may aim, for example, to determine how authentically (realistically) a media event was represented in the media, or how intensively the visual representation in the 'media picture' was manipulated. The first question might be whether a preceding planning authority was responsible for the media event. Genuine, mediated, and staged events need to be distinguished (Kepplinger, 1996: 13) and this is mostly possible without extensive research by simply studying the available 'media picture.' For example, probable hints for the staging of events are the presence of media representatives, a speaker's desk, podium or stage, and the appearance of prominent persons or politicians, etc. From these aspects, corresponding categories for the content analysis can be derived, as shown and explained in the following example. Figure 14.8 was taken at the G8 summit in Heiligendamm in 2007 and shows the heads of government of the eight largest national economies of the world. The apparent spontaneity mediated by the picture easily hides the fact that the event was planned and the scene arranged well in advance.

One category might be 'staging.' A question for the coder would be whether there is a speaker's desk, a tribune, or a similar platform in the picture (variable a: speaker's desk/tribune/platform; with values: yes, no, unknown). A second question might be whether the shown actors are staged in a specific way (variable b: actors; with values: staged, not staged, other). The third question might then be whether there are media representatives/journalists represented in the photograph (variable c: media representatives/journalists; with values: present, absent). With the answers for the three questions: 'no tribune,' 'specific staging,' and 'absent journalists,' it becomes obvious that the picture of the G8 summit in Heiligendamm was staged to a high degree. Additional research would reveal further insights. The oversized roofed wicker beach chair in which the politicians are positioned implies an enormous organizational effort in the run-up to the summit and photo-shooting. The chair had to be exclusively manufactured by the beach chair company Korb GmbH on the Isle of Usedom. This idea was suggested by the Schwerin project group Landesmarketing, as the beach chair is a typical German product, which celebrated its 125th anniversary in 2007, and would thus serve well to advertise the region. Additionally, a beach chair provokes the association of a holiday, a sense of togetherness and privacy. Thus, the delegates of the G8 summit presented themselves (or were presented) as a large peaceful family.

The arrangement of the agents corresponds with the protocol of G8 summits: the representative of the host country, Germany, is

Figure 14.8   G8 summit at Heiligendamm, 7 June 2007. Reproduced with permission: © 2007 ddp images GmbH

seated centrally, framed by the heads of government of the USA and Russia. Delegates from France and the UK are then seated to the left and right, with representatives from Italy and Canada, Japan and the United Nations on the outside. This background information would not be necessary for a quantitative content analysis, but enriches the insight into the research topic.

The absence of media representatives in this picture is also a sign of a high degree of staging, because the accredited journalists are purposely positioned opposite the scene (see Figure 14.9), so that the private atmosphere in the picture is not disturbed by media self-reference. For example, a photographer shown in the later 'media picture' might remind the recipient that the photo was taken at a press conference.

If the photographers are only allowed to take pictures from a fixed camera position, almost identical pictures of the same media event emerge, only distinguished from each other by a slight horizontal shift of the camera angle and a temporary phase shift (depending on when photographers pressed the shutter release button). This example shows how it is possible—at least according to camera perspective and camera position—to manipulate probable media impact of the 'concept pictures' (and later 'transfer pictures' as well as 'media pictures') by allocation of space for positioning the camera and staging the media event.

We can usually assume that staged events covered in detail by the media are sophisticatedly prepared and that details such as location, setting, clothes, gestures, and facial expression of the acting agents are not chosen coincidentally, but are consciously used to provoke a certain impact, for example, on the recipient of the later 'media picture.' It is

Figure 14.9   Photographers at the G8 summit at Heiligendamm, 7 June 2007 presented by *Die Welt* **(2007). Reproduced with permission: © 2007 dpa Picture Alliance GmbH**

also useful to examine the acting agents in the '*context of design*' for information on the possible impact of a picture. The kind of event taking place also influences what kind of media representatives attend. At a staged press conference, it is likely that professional photographers and journalists are present, while at a genuine event probably only amateur photographers are present, producing snapshots, which do not conform to regular quality standards.

Context of incidence

In the '*context of incidence*' (see Figure 14.7) agents appear who are later represented in the picture. This context is therefore especially important in frequency analysis to determine how often specific agents are portrayed in the media. Answers to more profound research questions (such as 'What action was the depicted person performing?' and 'What was the impact?') can be interpreted from the '*context of incidence*,' although this is a more complex task. The more complex or multilayered a research question is, the more important it becomes to examine in detail the other five contexts and agents in the process of image communication. For frequency analysis of agents in media pictures, the category construction is simple, reduced to a dichotomous variable— namely, appearance and non-appearance of an agent in a picture.

Accurate identification of a person in a 'media picture' corresponds to the occurrence of a name in a textual frequency analysis. However, it is also possible to analyze the weighting of an agent, for example whether he or she dominates the event or is a minor character, is presented as sympathetic or not, etc. In this case the picture size, the context in which it is presented in a newspaper or the length of the newspaper text, etc., need to be considered as well.

The categorizing in general (regardless of the level of complexity of the quantitative content analysis) should first address occurrence

for frequency analysis and then move on to weighting and valence evaluation.

The entire impact a picture of a person may have on the recipient can only be fully analyzed if the whole process of image communication is taken into consideration. To make an assertion about the complex and multilayered impact of persons represented in images, it is necessary to enrich the proposed categories and research questions with results from examining other aspects such as the contexts of production, media contextualizing, and reception.

Context of production

The 'originator of the picture' makes many decisions during the production process. Besides the first motivation for the production, there are many technical and creative decisions. For example, if it is interesting to see how a politician is represented in the media, then it is useful to examine the '*context of production*' closely. Decisions made by the 'originator of the picture' over how to take the picture and what to include are influenced by his or her individual preferences and technical skills. They are also influenced by media socialization, which again is shaped by viewing patterns and visual standards, which are already established and which contribute to meaning potential as well as sales potential. Again, if the research question underpinning a quantitative content analysis is to determine the degree of staging of a media event by studying the published 'media picture,' then the quality of these pictures in terms of their professional production hints that professional media representatives took part in the planning and documenting of the media event. Assuming that in current journalistic contexts, professional pictures (with high definition, correct lightning, etc.) are fundamental benchmarks for professional photographers, the absence of such professional pictures could indicate that the picture recorded a genuine event, rather than a mediatized or staged one. Content analysis can verify this by examining the named parameters, such as resolution (high or low), image noise, definition (high or low), over- or underexposure. The main category here could be 'production factors' or 'technical parameters.' Instructions for the coder would be to ask if there is a recognizable image sharpness (variable a: image sharpness; with values: yes, no, unknown). Another question might be whether the picture was correctly exposed (variable b: exposure; with values: overexposed, correctly exposed, underexposed, unknown). A picture might be coded as recognizably sharp, correctly exposed (no high lights or 'flooded shadows'), with homogenous tonal value, optimal contrast and high resolution. This might then be a hint for the researcher that the picture was produced by a professional photographer or an image agency.

Media context

How the 'media picture' itself as a part of a sample unit/unit of analysis can be coded with a strictly quantitative content analysis has been demonstrated above. We now address how research questions in communication studies can be answered by examining the 'media context.'

Stock photo agencies provide the media with the 'transfer picture,' which is further edited and contextualized by the 'media company.' For many research questions, examining how pictures are contextualized (for example, in a newspaper page) is of major importance, because the appearance of a picture in specific media (Internet, paper, television, etc.) arouses certain expectations. The way a recipient decodes ambiguous pictures is influenced by the context in which the 'media picture' is published (caption, or other related text elements such as headlines and sub-lines and article text). It has become less important for the media to answer all of the 'Who?' 'What?' 'When?' and 'Where?' questions, etc., in a picture caption (Beifuß et al., 1984: 193). Increased de-contextualizing

of 'media pictures' is driven by changes in journalistic handling of pictures and the increasing tendency to visualize everything. For example, if no appropriate picture is available, an editorial team may choose a picture from the archives and fail to clarify in the caption whether the picture derives from the current event or from a completely different context. Quantitative content analysis of the visual therefore has to deal with the fact that pictures in a journalistic context might be 'recycled' from other media events. The researcher has to identify them and to specify how to handle those pictures, whether they are excluded from the analysis or not.

Context of reception/context of cognition

Research questions addressing the impact of pictures and the allocation of meaning require analysis of the 'context of reception' and 'context of cognition.' Most of the decisions which influence the media impact, however, have already been made in earlier contexts. We have discussed above how content analysis of 'media pictures' provides hints about their probable impact on the recipient. To complement such content analysis findings for deeper insights into the recipients' decoding of 'media pictures,' we need to complete user surveys or experimental setups.

For example, to answer whether recipients regard a 'media picture' as authentic, content analysis of picture content and technical and functional parameters can be interpreted to derive the potential impact on recipients. However, this is where quantitative content analysis reaches its limits, because it tries to assume the (unknown) cognitions of a recipient. Most recipients may not have the skills to critically analyze pictures or media, or be sufficiently self-reflexive. A picture interpreted from content analysis as 'professionally taken' may be interpreted as perfectly 'authentic' by a recipient. An unskilled viewer of the beach chair picture (Figure 14.8) might interpret the scene as private and familial and also harmonious, because of the polite interaction of the referents and might therefore assume the picture to be very authentic. A professional and highly staged picture could very well convey high authenticity and the illusion of a spontaneously taken snapshot. The results from quantitative content analysis in relation to the impact of pictures are therefore only partly satisfactory. Such results need to be complemented using methods appropriate to media impact studies.

CONCLUSION

The process of consolidating visual communication studies is ongoing (Emmison and Smith, 2000; Knieper and Müller, 2001, 2003, 2004; van Leeuwen and Jewitt, 2001; Müller, 2003; Petersen and Schwender, 2009). Research findings that explicitly explain the impact of pictures and interdependencies between pictures and other media are still missing. Logically, such findings should be the theoretical basis for quantitative content analysis from which research questions are deduced and to which the research design and methodology are adapted. Currently, several disciplines contribute insights to answer questions of semantization or allocation of meaning to visual content: for example, sociology (especially context aspects such as thematic contexts, contexts of acting or figures, functions of figures, etc.), communication studies (especially aspects of representation, such as camera angle or field sizes, perspectives, later on also aspects of figure) or (social) psychology (aspects of figure, such as positioning, shown details of the body, face size, parameters of face and hair style, facial displays, direction of view, physiques, etc. (Bock et al., 2009). For a first overview on combining results from different disciplines, see for example Fleissner (2002) or Kinnebrock and Knieper (2008). Productively combining the findings from these disciplines will overcome current

methodological weaknesses by creating a solid theoretical foundation for content analysis of the visual.

The systematization of visual communication within the above-introduced process of image communication might be a first important step in this direction. It helps to usefully locate concrete research questions, with the associated contexts and agents. Furthermore, the theoretical findings which already exist for several contexts of the process of image communication (for example, of production, reception, etc.) can now systematically be linked with future research questions.

REFERENCES

Beifuß, Hartmut, Blume, Jochen and Rauch, Friedrich (1984) *Bildjournalismus. Ein Handbuch für Ausbildung und Praxis*. München: List.

Bell, Philip, (2001) 'Content analysis of visual images', in T. van Leeuwen and C. Jewitt (eds.), *Handbook of Visual Analysis*. London: Sage Publications. pp. 10–34.

Bock, Annekatrin, Isermann, Holger and Knieper, Thomas (2009) 'Herausforderungen bei der quantitativen (visuellen) Inhaltsanalyse von Online-Inhalten', in C. Wünsch and M. Welker (eds.), *Die Online-Inhaltsanalyse: Forschungsobjekt Internet*. Köln: Herbert von Halem. pp. 224–239.

Boorstin, Daniel J. (1961) *The Image: or What Happened to the American Dream*. New York: Ateneum.

Bucher, Hans-Jürgen and Schumacher, Peter (2007) 'Tabloid versus broadsheet: Wie Zeitungsformate gelesen werden', *Media Perspektiven* 10: 514–528.

Cunningham, Michael R. (1986) 'Measuring the physical in physical attractiveness: Quasi-experiments on the sociobiology of female face beauty', *Journal of Personality and Social Psychology*, 50: 925–935.

Curran, Margaret Ann, Kamps, Klaus and Schubert, James N. (2001) 'What you see is what you get? Physische Einschätzung von politischen Kandidaten— eine interkulturelle Perspektive', in T. Knieper and M.G. Müller (eds.), *Kommunikation visuell: Das Bild als Forschungsgegenstand—Grundlagen und Perspektiven*. Köln: Herbert von Halem. pp. 131–143.

Die Welt (2007) Pictures of the G8 summit at Heiligendamm, 7 June 2007. [Online]. Available from: http://www.welt.de/politik/article926882/ http://www.welt.de/politik/article926882/G_8_ Gipfel_Tag_2.html [Accessed 2 July 2009].

Emmison, Michael and Smith, Philip (2000) *Researching the Visual: Images, Objects, Contexts and Interactions in Social and Cultural Inquiry*. London: Sage Publications.

Fiske, Susan and Taylor, Shelley (1991) *Social Cognition*, 2nd edn. New York: McGraw-Hill.

Fleissner, Karin (2002) 'Vor der Kür ist nach der Kür? Bundestagswahl 2002: Die Kandidatendebatte der Union im Spiegel der Pressefotografie', in T. Knieper and M. G. Müller (eds.), *Visuelle Wahlkampfkommunikation*. Köln: Herbert von Halem. pp. 129–147.

Forster, Klaus and Knieper, Thomas (2008) 'Das Blutbad von München: Terrorismus im Fernsehzeitalter', in P. Gerhard (ed.), *Das Jahrhundert der Bilder. Band II: 1949 bis heute*. Göttingen:Verlag Vandenhoeck & Ruprecht/Bonn: Bundeszentrale für politische Bildung. pp. 434–441.

Früh, Werner (2007) *Inhaltsanalyse: Theorie und Praxis*. Konstanz: UVK.

Giddens, Anthony (1988) *The Constitution of Society: Outline of the Theory of Structuration*. Berkley, CA: University of California Press.

Kepplinger, Hans Mathias (1996) 'Inszenierte Wirklichkeiten', *Medien + Erziehung* (40)1: 12–19.

Kinnebrock, Susanne and Knieper, Thomas (2008) 'Männliche Angie und weiblicher Gerd? Visuelle Geschlechter- und Machtkonstruktionen auf Titelseiten von politischen Nachrichtenmagazinen', in C. Holtz-Bacha (ed.), *Frauen, Politik und Medien*. Wiesbaden: VS Verlag für Sozialwissenschaften. pp. 83–103.

Knieper, Thomas (2003) 'Die ikonologische Analyse von Medienbildern und deren Beitrag zur Bildkompetenz', in T. Knieper and M. G. Müller (eds.), *Authentizität und Inszenierung von Bilderwelten*. Köln: Herbert von Halem. pp. 193–212.

Knieper, Thomas (2005a) 'Kommunikationswissenschaftliche Beiträge zu einer interdisziplinären Bildwissenschaft', in K. Sachs-Hombach (ed.), *Bildwissenschaft zwischen Reflexion und Anwendung*. Köln: Herbert von Halem. pp. 56–70.

Knieper, Thomas (2005b) 'Professioneller Bildjournalismus und Medienkompetenz', in C. Fasel (ed.), *Qualität und Erfolg im Journalismus. Festschrift zum 60. Geburtstag von Michael Haller*. Konstanz: UVK. pp. 83–92.

Knieper, Thomas (2006) 'Geschichtsvermittlung durch Ikonen der Pressefotografie', in J. Kirschenmann and E. Wagner (eds.), *Bilder, die die Welt bedeuten: 'Ikonen' des Bildgedächtnisses und ihre Vermittlung über Datenbanken*. München: Kopaed. pp. 29–39.

Knieper, Thomas and Müller, Marion G. (eds.) (2001) *Kommunikation visuell: Das Bild als Forschungsgegenstand—Grundlagen und Perspektiven*. Köln: Herbert von Halem.

Knieper, Thomas and Müller, Marion G. (eds.) (2003) *Authentizität und Inszenierung von Bilderwelten*. Köln: Herbert von Halem.

Knieper, Thomas and Müller, Marion G. (eds.) (2004) *Visuelle Wahlkampfkommunikation*. Köln: Herbert von Halem.

Krippendorf, Klaus (2004) *Content Analysis: An Introduction to Its Methodology*. London, Thousand Oaks, CA, New Delhi: Sage Publications.

Mitchell, William J. Thomas (1987) *Iconology. Image, Text, Ideology*. Chicago, IL: University of Chicago Press.

Müller, Marion G. (2003) *Grundlagen der visuellen Kommunikation*. Konstanz: UVK.

Panofsky, Erwin (1984) 'Ikonographie und Ikonologie', in E. Kaemmerling (ed.), *Ikonographie und Ikonologie: Theorien—Entwicklung—Probleme. Bildende Kunst als Zeichensystem*. Köln: du Mont. pp. 207–225.

Petersen, Thomas (2001) 'Der Test von Bildsignalen in Repräsentativumfragen: Vorschlag für ein Forschungsprogramm', in T. Knieper and M. G. Müller (eds.), *Kommunikation visuell: Das Bild als Forschungsgegenstand—Grundlagen und Perspektiven*. Köln: Herbert von Halem. pp. 159–175.

Petersen, Thomas (2003) 'Der Test von Bildsignalen in Repräsentativumfragen: Erste Ergebnisse', in T. Knieper and M. G. Müller (eds.), *Authentizität und Inszenierung von Bilderwelten*. Köln: Herbert von Halem. pp. 102–122.

Petersen, Thomas and Schwender, Clemens (2009) *Visuelle Stereotype*. Köln: Herbert von Halem.

Poynter Institute (2000) *Front Page Entry Points* [Online]. Available from: http://www.poynter.org/ eyetrack2000/ [Accessed 21 August 2010].

Poynter Institute (2007) *The Poynter Institute Eyetrack 2007. Study for Print and Online News*. [Online]. Available from: http://www.poynter.org [Accessed 21 August 2010].

Rose, Gillian (2001) *Visual Methodologies. An Introduction to the Interpretation of Visual Materials*. London: Sage Publications.

Rössler, Patrick (2005) *Inhaltsanalyse*. Konstanz: UVK.

Todorov, Alexander, Mandisodza, Anesu N., Goren, Amir and Hall, Crystal C. (2005) 'Inferences of competence from faces predict election outcomes', *Science*, 308(5728): 1623–1626.

Turner, Jonathan H (1998) *The Structure of Sociological Theory*. Belmont, CA: Wadsworth Publ.

van Leeuwen, Theo and Jewitt, Carey (eds.) (2001) *Handbook of Visual Analysis*. London: Sage Publications.

15

Iconography and Iconology as a Visual Method and Approach

Marion G. Müller

INTRODUCTION

Iconography is both a method and an approach to studying the content and meanings of visuals. Originally devised in the context of sixteenth-century art collecting to categorize the particular visual motifs of paintings, iconography was first modernized by the art and cultural historian Aby M. Warburg (1866–1929) at the beginning of the twentieth century (Schmidt, 1993; Diers, 1995; Forster, 1999; Rampley, 2001; Woodfield, 2001). It was further refined by art historian Erwin Panofsky (1892–1968), who popularized this method of visual interpretation in the USA during the 1950s and 1960s.

Warburg used the term 'iconography' in his early research, but in 1908 replaced this term with 'iconology,' describing a particular method of visual interpretation (Schmidt, 1993: 24). Panofsky, a colleague of Warburg, published a seminal article (Panofsky, 1982) in 1932, introducing a three-step method of visual interpretation first labeled 'iconography' and later termed 'iconology.' Panofsky himself did not give credit to his iconological predecessor (Schmidt, 1993: 12), leading subsequent scholars to link the iconological method only with Panofsky's name.

ORIGINS AND KEY READINGS

Before its modernization as a method in art and cultural history at the beginning of the twentieth century, iconography had been applied in the realm of art collecting, and was particularly inspired by the encompassing work of Cesare Ripa. Ripa's book 'Iconologia' first published in Italian in 1593, had nine editions; the second, published in 1603, was the first illustrated version (Eberlein, 2008: 184). The book had been translated into many languages; the first English edition was published in 1709, on the assumption that this visual handbook of emblems and their meanings had an international impact during the seventeenth century.

However, as late as 1876, iconology was still confined to the role of an ancillary tool to art history and art collecting (Warnke, 1980: 55). A popular German encyclopedia of the late nineteenth century, *Meyers Konversations-Lexikon*, defined iconology in the following way:

> Iconology, previously, according to etymology, the reference, listing and history of portraits of famous personalities in antiquity...currently is understood as the knowledge about attributes, emblems and symbols, with which gods, heroes and mythological objects of antiquity, and particularly Christian saints and idioms, are typically depicted. (Quoted in Warnke, 1980: 55; my translation)

Iconology in its modern, more encompassing function as an analytical method of visual content analysis was first mentioned publicly by Aby Warburg in his pivotal lecture on 'Italian Art and International Astrology in the Palazzo Schifanoia, Ferrara' in October 1912. He uses the term three times, and always in connection with 'analysis,' thus turning 'iconological analysis' into the keywords of his presentation (Heckscher, 1967/1994: 114). Both the Schifanoia lecture (Warburg, 1912) and his article on 'Pagan-Antique Prophecy in Words and Images in the Age of Luther,' published 8 years later (Warburg, 1920), figure among the key readings on iconography and iconology (Warburg, 1999). Further key readings in iconology are the study by Erwin Panofsky and Fritz Saxl on Dürer's etching *Melencolia I* (Panofsky and Saxl, 1923), which was later edited in a larger volume (Klibansky et al., 1964). This applied example of iconological methodology traces the motif of *Melecolia I*—a female figure seated with her head resting on her right hand—through various cultural, religious, and historical contexts, and applying a variety of different theories to explaining the 'travels' of both the motif and its meaning through time and space. In a similar vein, using iconology not as a method, but as a general approach, the historian Emile Mâle (1862–1954) has been credited for popularizing the term 'iconology' as early as 1927 (see Mâle, 1932; Heckscher, 1967/1994: 140). And the Dutch art historian, G. J. Hoogewerff (1884–1963), at the time oblivious to Mâle's usage of the term, gave a lecture in Oslo in 1928 with the title 'L'Iconologie

et son Importance pour l'Etude systématique de l'Art Chrétien.' Among the key readings, should be mentioned two works of historians who did not apply iconology as a method but used an iconological approach to study political and social history: the co-founder of the influential French school of historians—*Annales*—Marc Bloch (1886–1944) and his germinal book *Les Rois Thaumaturges* (1924), and Ernst H. Kantorowicz's (1895–1963) 'classic' study on *The King's Two Bodies* (1957).

As remote as some of these topics might appear to an audience of the twenty-first century, Warburg's topic of image propaganda during the reformation period was a reflection on his contemporary obsession with the visual propaganda of the First World War. This proximity between problems of contemporary reality, 'disguised' in the costume of scholarly findings on a previous period, is characteristic for iconographic–iconological research. The founding father of modern iconology was mainly interested in image transfers, visual migration, or, more poignantly, the mobility of visuals ('die Mobilität der Bilder,' Warnke, 1980: 75) across time and space. Despite being grounded in history as a discipline, iconology's *problem orientation* (Warnke, 1993: 29) leads to a close link between the historic topic studied and problems in the contemporary reality of the scholar using the iconological method. This intrinsic connection between problems in the past and problems in the present makes this method highly attractive for social scientists dedicated to analyzing social and political reality. In addition, Warburg conceived iconology as a 'critical' method (Warnke, 1980: 58). This critical approach is also befitting the social scientific research agenda.

The origins of iconography and iconology as well as their developmental path can only be understood if the transdisciplinary atmosphere of the early twentieth century in Europe is taken into account. Scholarly history since then has seen a long period of disciplinary specialization and professionalization, which is still pervasive today. However, in the early days of modern iconology Warburg and his contemporaries crossed disciplines easily, Warburg himself being fiercely opposed to any form of disciplinary boundary keeping ('*Grenzwächtertum*' or '*grenzpolizeiliche Befangenheit*'). Thus, influences on Warburg's iconology are manifold (Gombrich, 1970; Syamken, 1980), ranging from the works of the Swiss cultural historian Jacob Burckhardt (1818–97), to the historian Karl Lamprecht (1856–1915), who introduced a psychological approach to the field, and the philologist Hermann Usener (1834–1905), who introduced Warburg to the field of comparative religious studies, as well as the German classical philologist Franz Boll (1867–1924), who familiarized Warburg with the history of astrology. Other influences on Warburg's iconology were coming from the natural sciences and psychology, including Charles Darwin's (1809–82) biological approach to explaining human emotions. For Erwin Panofsky, the sociology of knowledge, conceived by the Hungarian-born Karl Mannheim (1893–1947) was an inspiration in further developing the iconographic–iconological method (see Mannheim, 1952). In turn, Warburg and Panofsky influenced many prominent scholars in their time. To name just a few, the German philosopher Ernst Cassirer (1874–1945), who actually wrote parts of his most prominent book on the *Philosophy of Symbolic Forms* in Warburg's library (Kulturwissenschaftliche Bibliothek Warburg), the German literary scholar Ernst Robert Curtius (1886–1956) built his topological research on Warburg's pathos formula, and the sociologist Pierre Bourdieu (1930–2002) was influenced by Panofsky's findings in developing the sociological category of '*habitus*.' Another scholar should be mentioned here: the German film sociologist Siegfried Kracauer (1889–1966), who extended the application of iconology to moving images. His exceptional study *From Caligari to Hitler: A Psychological History of the German Film* (1947) demonstrated how iconography can be fused with sociological analysis, reaching tentative explanations of the Nazi regime's ideological foundations. Panofsky, who was in regular contact with Kracauer after both had emigrated to the USA, was highly interested in iconological film analysis. His 1937 study on *Style and Medium in the Motion Pictures,* published in the volume *Three Essays on Style* (Panofsky, 1997) can be considered the first iconological contribution to film analysis.

However, these disciplinary crossovers were interrupted and remain difficult to trace from the vantage point of the twenty-first century. They deserve much closer scrutiny than can be applied in the context of this contribution. For both students, and scholars who want to dig deeper into iconographic–iconological methodology, the compilation of key articles on the issue in German, edited by Ekkehard Kaemmerling (1987/1994), is a prerequisite for understanding the origins and intricacies of iconology as a method. The legacy of the iconographic–iconological founders is to apply iconology as a critical, analytical, and transdisciplinary method with a bifocal perspective—focusing on the visual aspects of contemporary problems in politics, society, and culture, reflected in the lens of thorough historical comparison.

ICONOGRAPHY AS A METHOD

Iconography can best be described as a qualitative method of visual content analysis and interpretation, influenced by cultural traditions and guided by research interests originating both in the humanities and the social sciences. In its *Warburgian sense*, iconography/iconology is therefore an interdisciplinary comparative method, focused on the 'visual interval' (Rampley, 2001), both temporal and spatial. Iconography/iconology is based on the critical analysis of visual and textual sources, and their original contexts (Grittmann, 2007: 134; see also Woodfield, 2001).

At heart, iconology is a forensic method. Iconology at its best can take on the form of a detective story, in which various threads are woven together to gain a full picture of a given period and its visual reproduction (see Baxandall, 1972; Warnke, 1984, 2007; Bredekamp, 1990, 1999, 2007). The visual material is treated as evidence supporting a particular hypothesis on the meanings that the visuals elicited in their original context. Visuals are treated as historic sources on culture, politics, society, life at a given time in the past. As historic material they also bear witness to visual forms of expression in the present, and can thus illuminate both past and present communication processes.

Panofsky (1982: 40–41) distinguishes between the first step, pre-iconographical description, the second step, iconographical analysis, and the third step, iconological interpretation. This differentiation is only a theoretical model. For the scholar applying iconography/iconology, the method is an integrated process with no distinct stages (Eberlein, 2008: 179); it has the holistic goal of achieving an encompassing interpretation of the meanings of the analyzed visuals.

To this day, Panofsky's three steps constitute the core of iconology as a method. These three steps form the 'Act of Interpretation.' Each of the three acts has a different 'Object of Interpretation,' each needs different 'Equipment for Interpretation' and follows a different 'Corrective Principle of Interpretation.'

Pre-iconographical description focuses on the primary or natural subject matter, which is usually the 'world of artistic motifs.' Iconographical analysis is concerned with 'conventional subject matter'—culturally shared visual signs and connotations—and thus 'the world of images, stories, and allegories.' Iconological interpretation aims at unraveling the 'Intrinsic meaning or content constituting the world of "symbolical" values' (Panofsky, 1982: 40).

The 'Equipment for Interpretation' changes from (1) mere practical experience and familiarity with depicted objects to (2) knowledge of literary sources to finally (3) 'Synthetic intuition,' 'conditioned by personal psychology and "Weltanschauung".'

Panofsky's (1982: 41) reference to the German term *Weltanschauung* not only hints at his personal root but also reveals a primary influence on his thinking—fellow emigrant and eminent sociologist Karl Mannheim. In 1923, Mannheim published an article in German on 'The Interpretation of "Weltanschauung"' in which he not only defines *Weltanschauung* as the 'global outlook of an epoch' (Mannheim, 1952: 33) but also hints at an interpretation method involving three levels of meaning ('objective,' 'expressive,' and 'documentary') as well as 'objective correctives' of interpretation. Panofsky adapted Mannheim's sociological method of interpretation to suit the needs of art history. Both sociology and art history are interested in understanding and unraveling how individuals as well as groups of people make sense of cultural artifacts and how, in turn, the visuals shape cultural belief systems at a given time.

To phrase the actual steps in iconography/iconology more practically: iconographic research uses an inductive and subjective sampling strategy. The intuition of the respective researcher is part of the method. She or he uses her or his particular fascination and interest in certain motif types to get an overview of similar motifs, both in contemporary and past visual production, often transgressing different types of media. The most prominent iconologists each created their own visual archive, collecting, combining, and constantly assessing and tagging the collected visuals: from Warburg's '*Zettelkästen*' (postcards with notes and visuals attached to them, sorted according to categories he designed and relabeled according to his changing research interests) to Warnke's impressive Political Iconographic Archive, or William S. Heckscher's filing cabinet with all kinds of clippings (see Schoell-Glass and Sears, 2008). Tagging, indexing, and archiving are essential parts of the iconological research process. Scholars collect visuals and categorize them, thereby constantly sharpening their analytical understanding of the studied visual topic. In the ideal typical research process, scholars, through collecting, retrieving, and comparing relevant sources, gain both expertise and an overview of the studied visual material. The early collecting stage of Panofsky's three-level analysis began with the so-called pre-iconographic description. This is the attempt to describe each visual in a most neutral way, avoiding too early attributions of meaning. After most of the selected visuals have been described in this way, simultaneously paying attention to details by comparing the visuals to each other, the next step—iconographical analysis—is reached. Note that in a real research situation these two steps would go hand in hand. Being in the field, or in the archive, scholars would collect all available visual, textual, and maybe even oral sources thought to be relevant for unraveling the meaning(s) of the visuals they are interested in. The visuals are then analyzed in the light of all available sources, attributing meanings to the analyzed visuals related to their original temporal and spatial context. Both pre-iconographical description and iconographical analysis require deep immersion in the visual material, related sources, and contexts. But the 'crowning' step is the last one in Panofsky's scheme—iconological interpretation, which usually requires several years of scholarly immersion and research. Only very few studies fulfill these high expectations. More often the outcome of a hurried iconographical analysis is just an assembly of pictures with similar motifs. However, if practiced in a sound and thorough fashion, the method gives access to processes of meaning construction and meaning attribution of particular groups and motifs of pictures. Methodologically, Panofsky's method has been further improved and adapted to suit mass-mediated visuals. The most far-reaching methodological contribution originates in media pedagogy, transferring the mass aspect of the topic studied to the method itself: Pilarczyk and Mietzner (2005) call their method 'serial-iconographic photo-analysis.' They devised this method with a particular view toward research questions arising in the social sciences and in pedagogy. Following a sociological approach, photography is considered to be a 'social practice' (Pilarczyk and Mietzner, 2005: 81). Accordingly, research fields to which serial-iconographic photo-analysis is applied focus on interactive behavior and social roles as, for example, in researching the 'habitus' of teachers in school or the 'mise en scène' of gender in photography.

Although systematic, iconography as a method is also highly subjective, raising questions about the validity of the interpretation of results.

ICONOGRAPHY AND ICONOLOGY

Many researchers use both terms interchangeably. But in Warburg's and Panofsky's understanding, iconology as a method went beyond iconography. While the iconographical analysis only constitutes the second of three steps in the interpretation process, iconology is the ultimate goal. Panofsky (1982: 31–32) pointed to the difference between the two, hinting at the etymological origin of both terms. Iconography's suffix 'graphy' is derived from Greek '*graphein*,' meaning to write, thus stipulating that this is a merely descriptive method, aimed at an objective and neutral description and classification of depicted motifs. Iconology, on the other hand, relates etymologically to the more encompassing concept of '*logos*.' Thus, Panofsky concludes, 'Iconology... is a method of interpretation which arises from synthesis rather than analysis' (1982: 32). The 'synthetic intuition' that is necessary according to Panofsky's method is the crowning of the analytic process. While iconography has few prerequisites and is associated with the first, descriptive step, iconology comes last as the third step, and is based on thorough research of visual and textual sources and their verbal condensation in the form of a contextualized interpretation.

While iconography contends itself with identifying types of visual motifs and attributing particular meanings to them, iconology uses the visual objects not simply for the sake of gaining more information about the visuals themselves; the visuals are treated as sources and evidence for wider social, political, and cultural analysis of the time in which the visuals were produced and used.

ICONOGRAPHY AS AN APPROACH

Iconography in the Warburg tradition operates with complex concepts and understandings of the visual. Warburg himself enlarged the scope of art history by including 'any visual image,' regardless of its artistic quality. This meant that press photographs and other forms of mass-mediated imagery could be considered appropriate objects of study for art history. The concept of iconography is closely linked to the German language. The key term of the German iconographic tradition—*Bild* (image, picture, visual)— cannot be fully translated into English (for more details on image etymology see Müller, 2007). For every material image there are mental images corresponding to the material image. But not every mental image takes on a material form (see Table 15.1). Warburg was only interested in those visuals that have both dimensions, leading to the hypothesis that the material images can be used as sources to learn about the mental images of times past.

In the second half of the twentieth century, iconology became the foremost art historical method, particularly in the Anglophone countries. This almost dogmatic position of the method elicited criticism mainly directed at its elitist attitude that only the 'initiated' scholars with a humanistic education could be using this method and approach properly (Eberlein, 2008: 185). The popularity of Panofsky's method redirected the focus of the applied iconological method away from the originally more encompassing definition of Warburg. Instead, the method stayed within the realms of art history, confined to the expert analysis of artwork.

Scholars outside of art history have appropriated the terms iconography and iconology to denote not a method, but an approach. The most influential work in this respect is Mitchell's *Iconology. Image, Text, Ideology.* He takes the word 'iconology' literally, aiming at 'a study of the "logos" (the words, ideas, discourse, or "science") of "icons" (images, pictures, or likenesses)' (Mitchell, 1987: 1). van Leeuwen (2000) connects Panofsky's approach with semiotics in the tradition of Roland Barthes. Other works limit themselves to Christian and Pagan iconography: that is, the classification and analysis of figures, poses, gestures, garments, colors, objects, and symbols that denote religious stories and theological concepts in European art and antiquity (Kopp-Schmidt, 2004; Büttner and Gottdang, 2006). This strand of art historical research focuses exclusively on artwork and limits its findings to the merely descriptive, iconographic level. Another strand of art history follows a more encompassing approach under the umbrella of the Warburg-based *Bildwissenschaften* (Bredekamp, 2003), reconnecting to Warburg's original practice of extending iconology to any kind of visual, and not just 'high art.' Political iconography fills the gap created by the dissolution of a general visual covenant at the beginning of the twentieth century. Secularization and individuation as well as an increase in individual freedoms of visual expression have turned modern and contemporary art into a system of its own with no intention to relate to problems of general importance. This gap, from the perspective of political iconography, is filled by visual mass media that bear witness to contemporary social, political, and cultural processes. Art history is still a valid source for the visual patterns, but political iconography extends its scope also to mass-mediated visuals like cartoons and press photographs.

POLITICAL ICONOGRAPHY

Largely unnoticed by the non-German-speaking academic community, a 'New Warburg School' emerged in the early 1990s. The driving force behind this 'Warburg revival' is the German art historian Martin Warnke, who, together with his Hamburg collaborators, initiated the renovation of the still-existing original Warburg—Haus that hosted the famous research center established by Aby Warburg—the Kulturwissenschaftliche Bibliothek Warburg (K.B.W.). Warnke, inspired by Warburg's image collection, recalibrated the iconological method to the topic of politics in its widest sense, creating an approach of his own labeled 'Politische Ikonographie'—'Political Iconography' (Warnke, 1994). Warnke's work is based on his collection of approximately 500,000 image cards, which are archived and accessible for researchers in the reopened Warburg-Haus in Hamburg. Due to the lack of translation, the international impact of this 'New Warburg School' has been limited.

A selection of political iconographic studies will be presented below to illustrate the scope and potential of this method. Applications of political iconography can be found in different disciplinary contexts, ranging from art history to communication science, from anthropology to history.

Martin Warnke's Gerda Henkel lecture (Warnke, 2007) illustrates the uses of political iconography in scrutinizing the question of political leaders' zeal for creating something new. Bereft of an artistic way of expressing their ideas, they force their 'visions' on a whole political system which they want to form according to their own creative, or—more often—destructive impulses. Warnke analyzes the opposing stereotypes of statesmen and artists. He gives an array of examples of more or less haphazard attempts of rulers and politicians from the seventeenth century to US President Bill Clinton, who immersed themselves in artistic activities. The clumsy drawing of French King Louis XIII (Warnke, 2007: 48) is an example for the long-standing tradition of drawing and painting in the education of European royals. In this context, another pivotal study by the historian Peter Burke (1992) has to be mentioned—*The Fabrication of Louis XIV*—analyzing the public image-making of the French king and the role visualization played in the power politics of his time. Warnke concludes his lecture with several sketches by Adolf Hitler, who, before his rise to politician, dictator, and mass-murderer, had unsuccessfully attempted to become an artist. Warnke's iconological brilliance is in the far-reaching consequences of his analysis that good political practice and the quest for artistic genius are an ominous connection.

The connection between artistic creativity, and here it is the capacity to draw, and scientific genius is explored in Horst Bredekamp's groundbreaking study on *Galilei the Artist* (2007). Coining the term of 'the drawing intelligence' ('*zeichnerische Intelligenz*' Bredekamp, 2007: 6), Bredekamp suggests that Galilei achieved his revolutionary insights only because of his early developed capacity and practice of drawing. The study is the third part of a trilogy of previous books on the philosophers Thomas Hobbes (Bredekamp, 1999), and Gottfried Wilhelm Leibniz (Bredekamp, 2004). Galilei's early drawings inspired him to question the papal dogma. What the scientist could see and depict himself was not a static flat moon, but three-dimensional and changing. Galilei's capacity to visualize his own impressions were tantamount in convincing him that he was right, and the Church was wrong, even risking his own life by sticking to his findings. Bredekamp's study of all the original drawings of Galileo and his in-depth research of all accessible textual and visual sources is a good example of an iconological study that took years to complete, but that opened a completely new aspect on the contingency of visual production shaping intellectual and popular knowledge. This inner connection between political thought and its visualization was the topic of Bredekamp's previous study (1999) on Thomas Hobbes' *Leviathan*. An icon of political thought, the frontispiece of Hobbes' book, prepared by Abraham Bosse, published in 1651, is analyzed in detail, including all further copies. It is the link between this material epitome of the state and its absolutist ideology—the relationship between the *Abbild* and the *Denkbild*, material and mental image—that intrigues Bredekamp, and which, in turn, makes this iconological study intriguing to read.

From a practical point of view, any corpus of mass-mediated images can serve as a field for applying a political iconographic approach. The US presidential campaigns, for example, show a long-standing tradition of political visualizations. In conducting an iconological project, the first step is to define the most relevant visual expressions in a current campaign. This can be political commercials on online websites, the press photographs of political magazines like *Time* or *Newsweek*, or the footage of the televised presidential debates. Once the type of visuals that are at the center of the study are identified, all available visuals in the relevant time period have to be sampled: for example, all online commercials of all candidates in the primary elections; all issues of *Time* magazine in the main campaign; or all televised presidential debates. Once the material is secured, these visual sources need to be properly referenced and assessed, including the time and place of publication, the name of the photographer or image designer, the format of the debate, etc. The research question needs to be implemented into an iconological research design. Depending on the thrust of the question, particular visual motifs will be selected from the full sample. If the research question tries to position the 2008 presidential contest in the historic context of visual campaign strategies, the typology developed in a previous study (Müller, 1997) would be applied to the new sample, looking for the way in which the candidates were portrayed in the respective medium. Were the main contestants in the primary campaign—Barack Obama, Hillary Clinton, and John McCain—portrayed as common people or rather as heroes? Which political ancestors were invoked by the different candidates? What kind of visual symbolism was alluded to? The first stratum of Panofsky's three-step method—the pre-iconographic description—sharpens the attention to visual detail. All images in the sample need to be described as neutrally as possible. A result of these in-depth descriptions is the growing expertise of the researchers, who immerse themselves in the visual data and become alert to subtle similarities and differences. This visual expertise is then carrying the analysis to the next stage—the second stratum in Panofsky's method design—the iconographical analysis, including now contextual information in order to create a typological set of categories that characterizes the various images in the sample. These typological descriptions enable the scholar to compare the various images and find similarities and differences among them, which will, in the third step—the iconological interpretation—be synthesized and reflected on in the larger socio-political and cultural context in which the campaign is taking place. Ideally, the iconological method will enhance the understanding of the subtle messages and ideas conveyed through the visual presentations of the candidates, and thus implicitly allow identification of the expectations raised by the winning candidate on which his or her presidency will be tested.

Similar research into campaigns in Russia could build on existing literature on Soviet iconography: the political poster in pre-revolutionary Russia and the Soviet Union is the topic of a study that uses an iconographical approach, though not iconology as a method. The historian Frank Kämpfer (1985) first explored the theory of political posters, developing a classification scheme of his own (Kämpfer, 1985: 131) that is more informed by semiology than by iconology. In his case study on Russian and Soviet image language he is able to decipher the complex messages and intricate principles that made political posters highly successful propagandistic communication tools. The 'fate' of

Kämpfer's relevant book, shared by most of the aforementioned German-language publications, was that it has gone unnoticed by international academia. The excellent study by Victoria E. Bonnell (1997) on the same topic, *Iconography of Power: Soviet Political Posters under Lenin and Stalin*, is oblivious to Kämpfer's earlier categorizations, which would certainly have been helpful to her endeavor.

Five more German scholars and their publications shall be mentioned: Rudolf Herz (1994) used political iconology as a method to research the public image of Hitler created in his time. He researched the production background, finding that the key to the success of Hitler's image was a strict limitation to one personal photographer—Heinrich Hoffmann—who controlled every single photograph of his employer that was shot and published. Not the visual motifs or the impressiveness of Hitler's personality, but the complete and total image control exercised are behind the *Führer-myth* created by the Nazis. Herz succinctly co-edited a volume comparing the Hitler image with images of contemporary leaders, Stalin, Mussolini, and Roosevelt (Loiperdinger et al., 1995). Ines Kampe (1998) analyzed the images of Germans in the period following the Second World War, applying the iconographic method to photographs. In a similar attempt, aimed at an explanation for the transformed image of Germans in France, Ulrich Hägele (1998) scrutinized the national image from an anthropological point of view.

One of the most promising studies in the field of political iconography is a complex qualitative–quantitative method developed and devised by Elke Grittmann (2007) in her communication-oriented study of photojournalism and press photography (see also Grittmann and Ammann, 2009; Ammann et al., 2010). Methodologically, she combined qualitative political iconography with quantitative visual content analysis, coming to a complex evaluation both of the visual types of press photographs and their contextual production and selection structures.

From the vantage point of visual history, Gerhard Paul (2008) has edited two volumes on iconic images from 1900 to 2007. The individual contributions are written by prominent scholars in their respective fields. They cover the iconographic history of each motif and explain the meanings these (photo) graphic icons have taken on in various contexts. In this respect the two volumes are a treasure trove of iconological research. Paul's edition demonstrated that at the beginning of the twenty-first century the combination of visual interpretation as a method and political pictures as a topic appeared to see a revival, reflecting the need for explanation of visual phenomena like the terrorist instrumentalization of visuals, the publication of torture images at the Abu Ghraib prison in Iraq (Eisenman, 2007), or the controversy about the publication of Muhammad cartoons (Müller and Özcan, 2007; Müller et al., 2009). In these studies, the most neutral description technique proved to be particularly fruitful when applied to a group of participants coming from very different cultural backgrounds. Participants with a Muslim background already described the images in a different way to Western participants. Little details like the depiction of sandals on one Muhammad portrait invoked negative meaning attributions to the image which were absent in the descriptions by participants from a Western background. Particularly for one Turkish participant, the visual verbal association with the term 'sandal' was relevant, since the term 'sandal' in Turkish is used in a derogatory way to insult a person as an uneducated and backward-oriented Muslim. Political iconography as a method appears to be particularly promising if applied in a way to test intercultural differences in visual meaning attribution.

While being thoroughly grounded in Western European research traditions, recent research demonstrates an increased interest in non-Western applications. Although many of the publications apply iconology without any deeper knowledge of its theoretical and methodological roots—while some (Bonnell,

1997; Grant, 2007) reference Panofsky, none of the authors seems to be aware of the Warburg tradition—these are valuable contributions to both the applied field of iconological research and, particularly, to the interdisciplinary appeal of iconography and iconology as visual methods (Boeckl, 2000; Didi-Huberman, 2002, 2003; Grant, 2007: O'Kane, 2007).

ICONOLOGICAL CONTEXT ANALYSIS

Influenced by communication science, a further methodological development of iconology—Iconological Context Analysis—has been suggested, adding the context dimension to the historic analysis of the motif (Müller, 2003: 22; Kappas and Müller 2006: see Table 15.1).

Three types of visual contexts can be distinguished: (1) the form, motif, or 'gestalt' of the visual; (2) the production context; and (3) the reception context. Visuals analyzed with Iconological Context Analysis can take

on diverse forms, ranging from architecture, sculpture to graphic art (for example, caricatures), photography, film, television, video and electronic images. On the first context level—the 'form' or 'gestalt' level—iconology in the Warburg–Panofsky tradition can then be applied, helping to unravel the historical development of the depicted motifs. For the second level of context analysis, communication research traditions are helpful, particularly when the scrutinized visuals originated in a journalistic production context. Six ideal types of production contexts can be distinguished: the artistic (for example, paintings); commercial (for example, advertising); journalistic (for example, press photography); scientific (for example, brain scans); political (for example, campaign advertising); and private (for example, wedding photos).

Each of the six production contexts follows a different logic and has a different structure. Both inner logic and structure influence the form and the meaning of the visual product. Artistic production usually focuses on a single producer—the artist. It is

Table 15.1 Context analysis in visual communication research

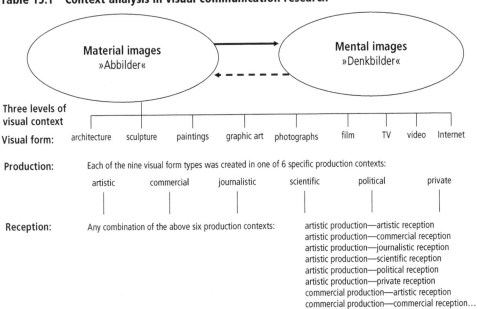

her or his professional experience, skill, and ultimately the individual's satisfaction with the final product that is relevant for both the form and content of the artwork.

In a commercial production context, on the contrary, the client who commissioned, for example, a poster advertising sportswear, plays an important role in shaping the end product. If the client is not satisfied with the visual drafts for the poster, a team of advertising experts and visual designers will try to accommodate their wishes. Also, both the client and the ad agency have to take the consumer into account when creating the visual. On top of client and consumers, commercial visual producers also have to keep their competitors in mind. Thus, the influences on the shape and the message of the commercially produced visual are manifold.

The journalistic production context is also a team context characterized by a high degree of labor division. Press photographers, press agencies, cartoonists, editors, writers, publishers, and readers play a role in the selection and production process of visual journalistic products. For press photographers, the major question will be which photo sells to the newspaper or newsmagazine? They do also have their competing colleagues and their respective visual styles in mind, when shooting on location, but the major goal is to sell the image. Of course, journalistic routines, expertise as well as journalistic ethics, also play a role in the journalistic production context.

The scientific production context resembles the artistic more than journalistic context, since, at its heart, there is the freedom of the scientist to decide on the publication or non-publication of the visual. Typically, scientific visuals have the goal to visualize invisible phenomena like, for example, ultrasounds, X-rays, or magnetic resonance images. In addition, charts and maps visualizing a certain process or theory can be considered as scientific visuals.

The political and the private production contexts seem, at first, to follow a different logic, and in fact in many cases these contexts overlap with one or more of the other contexts. Still, political campaign visualization, despite its commercial implications, has a different goal than maximizing profit. Political posters and TV commercials aim at getting parties and politicians elected. They communicate on a different level to the ordinary commercial product and pursue a specific strategic goal, usually limiting the visual message to the election deadline, while commercial visualization, and branding in particular, has to pay attention also to the long-term effects. The private production context has seen a steep increase since the mass impact of digitization. In contrast to the huge future potential of this production context, academically speaking this steadily growing realm of image production is still under-researched. Just imagine your own private photos on your hard disk, but also pictures of catastrophes where an amateur happened to shoot pictures that later appear on the front page of a yellow press newspaper. The omnipresence of picture-creating technology will increase the availability of privately, non-professionally produced visuals. Here, the production history of the Abu-Ghraib torture images has to be mentioned. These photos, shot with a digital camera, were originally meant as 'trophy shots' for private consumption, very much like a sick variant of pornography to document the 'great time' that the torturers had while humiliating their victims. Only when this private production context is taken into consideration can be explained the insane smile of one of the female police officers, who is depicted beside two corpses showing signs of having been tortured to death. Both for analyzing the intended and the later attributed meanings of visuals, knowledge about their production and reception contexts are crucial.

The first stratum of visual context analysis focuses on compositional traditions across different types of media and different types of contexts. The second stratum—production context analysis—pays particular attention to the constraints and production routines in the six different contexts. For example, the influence of the client on the actual form and style of the picture is much stronger in the commercial production context than in the artistic, where, since the twentieth century at least, a client typically only comes in after the artwork has been completed. This is different in authoritarian and totalitarian regimes or in commissioned artwork for public display, where the political and ideological demands already come into play during the production process.

At the reception level, context analysis becomes even more complex, since, in theory, a mixture of all six ideal contexts is possible. When aiming to analyze the reception context, iconology as a method reaches its limit. Experimental designs, informed by psychology and communication science, have to be integrated in order to test the actual reactions of different groups of people toward the visuals at stake.

The intention of iconological context analysis as a method is to unravel the meanings of mass-mediated visuals and contexts, both in terms of the history of the material motifs and their immaterial associations and elicited emotions.

- Base your research on a problem-oriented research question which you refine and improve throughout the research process.
- Once you have an overview of the visuals, begin to classify them into different types. Create your own categories, labels, and tags and reference each visual and textual source properly.
- Describe prototypes of visuals that appear to be important for your research in a most neutral way, paying particular attention to details and differences in form and style. Document your descriptions and compare them with one another.
- In the iconographic analysis, bring together visual and verbal sources, attributing meaning or clusters of meaning to individual pictures or to whole picture categories, thereby developing your hypothesis.
- Read and write about the visual production context, its structure and function, as well as potential changes. How does the production context influence the form and the intended meanings of the studied visuals?
- Which meanings do or did the visuals have in their particular reception context?
- Lastly, and most importantly for an iconological interpretation: What information do the studied visuals convey about the social, political, and cultural context in which they were produced and perceived?

SUMMARY AND GUIDELINES

Iconology is a qualitative method aimed at the interpretation of visual content. Rooted both in art history and sociology, the method has the potential to better understand and explain the meanings of contemporary mass-mediated visuals. As a method, iconology is inductive, subjective, critical, analytic, and transdisciplinary in its thrust. The holistic approach, intrinsic subjectivity, and cultural focus on Western traditions are both iconology's strengths and shortcomings.

Some guidelines for applying iconography/iconology as a visual research method:

- Begin by researching and collecting the visual material you are interested in.

REFERENCES

Ammann, Ilona, Krämer, Benjamin and Engesser, Sven (2010) 'Bildhafte Themen und kuriose Typen. Die Bedeutung der Fotos der Bild-Leserreporter' [Visual topics and curious types. The relevance of amateur photography in the German tabloid BILD]', *Medien & Kommunikationswissenschaft*, 58(1): 83–101.

Baxandall, Michael (1972) *Painting and Experience in Fifteenth Century Italy: A Primer in the Social History of Pictorial Style*. Oxford: Clarendon Press.

Bloch, Marc (1924) *Les Rois Thaumaturges: Étude sur le charactere surnaturel attribué à la puissance royale particulièrement en France et en Angleterre* [*The Royal Touch: Sacred Monarchy and Scrofula in England and France*]. Strasbourg: Librairie Istra.

Boeckl, Christine M. (2000) *Images of Plague and Pestilence. Iconography and Iconology.* [Sixteenth Century Essays & Studies, Volume LIII]. Ann Arbor, MI: Truman State University Press.

Bonnell, Victoria E. (1997) *Iconography of Power. Soviet Political Posters under Lenin and Stalin.* Berkeley, CA: University of California Press.

Bredekamp, Horst (1990) *Sandro Botticelli. La Primavera. Florenz als Garten der Venus* [*Sandro Botticelli. La Primavera. Florence as Garden of Venus*]. Frankfurt am Main: Fischer.

Bredekamp, Horst (1999) *Thomas Hobbes Visuelle Strategien. Der Leviathan: Das Urbild des modernen Staates. Werkillustrationen und Portraits* [*Thomas Hobbes Visual Strategies: The Leviathan: The Archimage of the Modern State*]. Berlin: Akademie Verlag.

Bredekamp, Horst (2003) 'A neglected tradition? Art history as Bildwissenschaft', *Critical Inquiry*, 29: 418–428.

Bredekamp, Horst (2004) *Die Fenster der Monade. Gottfried Wilhelm Leibniz' Theater der Kunst und der Natur.* Berlin: Akademie Verlag.

Bredekamp, Horst (2007) *Galilei der Künstler. Der Mond. Die Sonne. Die Hand* [*Galilei the Artist. The Moon. The Sun. The Hand*]. Berlin: Akademie-Verlag.

Büttner, F. and Gottdang, A. (2006) *Einführung in die Ikonographie: Wege zur Deutung von Bildinhalten* [*Introduction to Iconography: Paths to Interpreting the Content of Images*]. München: C.H. Beck.

Burke, Peter (1992) *The Fabrication of Louis XIV.* New Haven, CT: Yale University Press.

Didi-Huberman, G. (2002) *L'Image survivante. Histoire de l'Art et Temps des Fantômes selon Aby Warburg* [*The Surviving Image. History of Art and the Age of Phantoms According to Aby Warburg*]. Paris: Les Éditions de Minuit.

Didi-Huberman, George (2003) *Invention of Hysteria. Charcot and the Photographic Iconography of the Salpêtrière.* Cambridge, MA: MIT Press.

Diers, Michael (1995) 'Warburg and the Warburgian tradition of cultural history', *New German Critique*, 22: 59–73.

Eberlein, Johann Konrad (2008) 'Inhalt und Gehalt: Die ikonografisch-ikonologische Methode' [Content and substance: The iconographic-iconological method], in H. Belting, H. Dilly, W. Kemp, W. Sauerländer and M. Warnke (eds.), *Kunstgeschichte. Eine Einführung* [*Art History. An Introduction*], 7th edn, Berlin: Dietrich Reimer Verlag. pp. 175–197.

Eisenman, Stephen F. (2007) *The Abu Ghraib Effect.* London: Reaktion Books.

Forster, Kurt W. (1999) 'Introduction', in A. Warburg, *The Renewal of Pagan Antiquity: Contributions to the Cultural History of the European Renaissance.* Los Angeles, CA: The Getty Research Institute for the History of Art and the Humanities. pp. 1–76.

Gombrich, E. H. (1970) *Aby Warburg. An Intellectual Biography.* London: The Warburg Institute.

Grant, Barry Keith (2007) *Film Genre. From Iconography to Ideology.* London, New York: Wallflower.

Grittmann, Elke and Ammann, Ilona (2009) 'Die Methode der qualitativen Bildtypenanalyse. Zur Routinisierung der Bildberichterstattung am Beispiel von 9/11 in der journalistischen Erinnerungskultur' [The method of qualitative image-type analysis. On the regularities of visual coverage about 9/11 and journalistic memory], in T. Petersen and C. Schwender (eds.), *Visuelle Stereotype* [*Visual Stereotypes*]. Köln: von Halem Verlag. pp.141–158.

Grittmann, Elke (2007) *Das politische Bild. Fotojournalismus und Pressefotografie in Theorie und Empirie* [*The Political Picture. Photojournalism and Press Photography in Theory and Empirical Research*]. Köln: von Halem Verlag.

Hägele, Ulrich (1998) *Fotodeutsche. Zur Ikonographie einer Nation in französischen Illustrierten 1930–1940* [*Photogermans. On the Iconography of a Nation in French Illustrated Magazines, 1930–1940*]. Tübingen: Tübinger Verein für Volkskunde.

Heckscher, William (1967/1994) 'The genesis of iconology', in *Stil und Überlieferung in der Kunst des Abendlandes (= Akten des 21. Internationalen Kongresses für Kunstgeschichte in Bonn 1964), Bd. 3 (= Theorien und Probleme).* Berlin: Gebr. Mann Verlag, pp. 239–262. Reprint in German translation, 'Die Genesis der Ikonologie', in E. Kaemmerling (ed.) (1994) *Ikonographie und Ikonologie. Theorien, Entwicklung, Probleme* [*Iconography and Iconology. Theories, Development, Problems*]. [Bildende Kunst als Zeichensystem 1], 6th edn. Köln: Dumont. pp. 112–164.

Herz, Rudolf (1994) *Hoffmann & Hitler. Fotografie als Medium des Führer-Mythos* [*Hoffmann & Hitler: Photography as Medium of the Führer Myth*]. München: Klinkhardt & Biermann.

Kaemmerling, Ekkehard (ed.) (1987) *Ikonographie und Ikonologie. Theorien, Entwicklung, Probleme.* [*Iconography and Iconology. Theories, Development, Problems*]. [Bildende Kunst als Zeichensystem 1], 6th edn. Köln: Dumont.

Kämpfer, Frank (1985) '*Der Rote Keil'. Das politische Plakat: Theorie und Geschichte* ['*The Red Wedge'. The Political Poster: Theory and History*]. Berlin: Gebr. Mann Verlag.

Kampe, Ines (1998) 'Vom "Faceless Fritz" zum "Ottonormalverbraucher". Zur Imagebildung der Deutschen in fotografischen Werken nach 1945',

[From "Faceless Fritz" to "Ottonormalverbraucher". On image construction of Germans in photography after 1945], in A. Koestler and E. Seidl (eds.), *Bildnis und Image. Das Portrait zwischen Intention und Rezeption*. Köln: Böhlau. pp. 309–325.

Kantorowicz, Ernst H. (1957) *The King's Two Bodies. A Study in Mediaeval Political Theology*. Princeton, NJ: Princeton University Press.

Kappas, Arvid and Müller, Marion G. (2006) 'Bild und Emotion—ein neues Forschungsfeld', [Image and Emotion—a new field of research]. *Publizistik*, 1: 3–23.

Klibansky, Raymond, Panofsky, Erwin and Saxl, Fritz (1964) *Saturn and Melancholy*. London: Nelson.

Kopp-Schmidt, Gabriele (2004) *Ikonographie und Ikonologie. Eine Einführung*. Köln: Deubner Verlag.

Kracauer, Siegfried (1947) *From Caligari to Hitler. A Psychological History of the German Film*. Princeton, NJ: Princeton University Press.

Loiperdinger, Martin, Herz, Rudolf and Pohlmann, Ulrich (eds.) (1995), *Führerbilder. Hitler, Mussolini, Roosevelt, Stalin in Fotografie und Film* [*Leaders' Images. Hitler, Mussolini, Roosevelt, Stalin in Photography and Film*]. München: Piper.

Mâle, Emile [1925] (1932) *L'art religieux de la fin du XVIe siècle du XVIIe siècle, étude sur l'iconographie après le Concile de Trente, Italie-France-Espagne-Flandres* [Religious Art of the Turn of the 16th to the 17th Century. A Study on the Iconography after the Trent Consilium, Italy, France, Spain, Flanders]. Reprint, Paris: Collin.

Mannheim, Karl (1952) 'On the interpretation of "weltanschauung"', in K. Mannheim, *Essays on the Sociology of Knowledge*. London: Routledge & Kegan Paul. pp. 33–83.

Mitchell, W. J. T. (1987) *Iconology: Image, Text, Ideology*. Chicago, IL: University of Chicago Press.

Müller, Marion G. (2007) 'What is visual communication? Past and future of an emerging field of communication research', *Studies in Communication Sciences*, 7(2): 7–34.

Müller, Marion G. (2003) *Grundlagen der visuellen Kommunikation. Theorieansätze und Analysemethoden* [*Foundations of Visual Communication, Theoretical Approaches and Methods of Analysis*]. Konstanz: UVK, utb.

Müller, Marion G. (1997) *Politische Bildstrategien im amerikanischen Präsidentschaftswahlkampf, 1828–1996* [*Political Image Strategies in US presidential campaigns, 1828–1996*]. Berlin: Akademie Verlag.

Müller, Marion G. and Özcan, Esra (2007) 'The political iconography of Muhammad cartoons: Understanding cultural conflict and political action', *Political Science & Politics*, Vol. XL, 2: 287–292.

Müller, Marion G., Özcan, Esra and Seizov, Ognyan (2009) 'Dangerous depictions. A visual case-study of contemporary cartoon controversies', in S. Lockyer and F. Attwood (eds.), *Popular Communication Special Issue 'Controversial Images'*, 1: 28–39.

O'Kane, Bernard (2007) *The Iconography of Islamic Art. Studies in Honour of Robert Hillenbrand*. Edinburgh: Edinburgh University Press.

Panofsky, Erwin (1997) 'Style and medium in the motion pictures', in I. Lavin (ed.), *Three Essays on Style*. Cambridge, MA: MIT Press.

Panofsky, Erwin [1955](1982) 'Iconography and iconology: An introduction to the study of Renaissance art', in E. Panofsky (ed.), *Meaning in the Visual Arts*. Chicago, IL: University of Chicago Press. pp. 26–54.

Panofsky, Erwin and Saxl, Fritz (1923) 'Dürers Kupferstich Melencolia I: Eine quellen- und typengeschichtliche Untersuchung', in *Studien der Bibliothek Warburg*, vol. 2. Leipzig: Teubner.

Paul, Gerhard (2008) *Das Jahrhundert der Bilder* [*The Century of Images*], *Vol. 1: 1900–1949, Vol. 2: 1949–heute* [today]. Göttingen: Vandenhoek & Ruprecht.

Pilarczyk, Ulrike and Mietzner, Ulrike (2005) *Das reflektierte Bild. Die seriell-ikonografische Fotoanalyse in den Erziehungs- und Sozialwissenschaften* [*The reflected image. The serial-iconographic photo-analysis in pedagogy and the social sciences*]. Bad Heilbrunn: Verlag Julius Klinkhardt.

Rampley, Matthew (2001) 'Iconology of the interval: Aby Warburg's legacy', *Word & Image*, 17(4): 303–324.

Ripa, Cesare (1709) *Iconologia*. London: B. Motte.

Schmidt, Peter (1993) *Aby M. Warburg und die Ikonologie* [*Aby M. Warburg and Iconology*]. Wiesbaden: Harrassowitz.

Schoell-Glass, Charlotte and Sears, Elizabeth (2008) *Verzetteln als Methode. Der humanistische Ikonologe William S. Heckscher 1904–1999* [Tagging as Method. The Humanistic Iconologist William S. Heckscher, 1904–1999]. Berlin: Akademie Verlag.

Syamken, Georg (1980) 'Aby Warburg—Ideen und Initiativen' [*Aby Warburg—Ideas and initiatives*], in W. Hofmann, G. Syamken and M. Warnke (eds.), *Die Menschenrechte des Auges. Über Aby Warburg.* [*The Human Rights of the Eye. On Aby Warburg*]. Frankfurt am Main: Europäische Verlagsanstalt. pp. 11–51.

van Leeuwen, Theo (2000) 'Semiotics and iconography', in T. van Leeuwen and C. Jewitt (eds.),

Handbook of Visual Analysis. London: Sage Publications. pp. 92–118.

Warburg, Aby [1932 in German] (1999) *The Renewal of Pagan Antiquity. Contributions to the Cultural History of the European Renaissance*. Los Angeles, CA: The Getty Research Institute for the History of Art and the Humanities.

Warburg, Aby (1912) 'Italian art and international astrology in the Palazzo Schifanoia, Ferrara', in Aby Warburg (1999) *The Renewal of Pagan Antiquity. Contributions to the Cultural History of the European Renaissance*. Los Angeles, CA: The Getty Research Institute for the History of Art and the Humanities. pp. 732–757.

Warburg, Aby (1920) 'Pagan-antique prophecy in words and images in the age of Luther' in Aby Warburg (1999) *The Renewal of Pagan Antiquity. Contributions to the Cultural History of the European Renaissance*. Los Angeles, CA: The Getty Research Institute for the History of Art and the Humanities. pp. 760–774.

Warnke, Martin (2007) 'Könige als Künstler' [Kings as artists]. Lecture on the occasion of the Gerda Henkel Award 2006. Münster: RHEMA. pp. 45–75.

Warnke, Martin (1994) 'Politische Ikonographie. Hinweise auf eine sichtbare Politik' [Political iconography. Hints at visible politics], in C. Leggewie (ed.), *Wozu Politikwissenschaft? Über das Neue in der Politik*. Darmstadt: Wissenschaftliche Buchgesellschaft.

Warnke, Martin (1993) 'Die Bibliothek Warburg und ihr Forschungsprogramm' [The Warburg Library and its research program], in M. Diers (ed.), *Porträt aus Büchern*. Bibliothek Warburg & Warburg Institute. Hamburg: Dölling & Galitz Verlag, pp. 29–34.

Warnke, Martin (1984) *Cranachs Luther. Entwürfe für ein Image* [*Cranach's Luther. Drafts for an Image*]. Frankfurt am Main: Fischer.

Warnke, Martin (1980) 'Vier Stichworte. Ikonologie—Pathosformel—Polarität und Ausgleich—Schlagbilder und Bilderfahrzeuge' [Four keywords. Iconology—pathosformulae—polarity and balance—key visuals and visual vehicles], in W. Hofmann, G. Syamken and M. Warnke (eds.), *Die Menschenrechte des Auges. Über Aby Warburg*. Frankfurt am Main: Europäische Verlagsanstalt. pp. 53–83.

Woodfield, Richard (2001) 'Warburg's "Method"', in R. Woodfield (ed.), *Art History as Cultural History. Warburg's Projects*. Australia: G+B Arts. pp. 259–293.

16

Visual Semiotics: Key Features and an Application to Picture Ads

Winfried Nöth

INTRODUCTION: SEMIOTICS AND VISUAL SEMIOTICS

Semiotics (from Greek, *sēmeion*, 'sign') is the study of signs. Mainly in its French tradition, *semiology* can be found as a synonym. The study of signs has a tradition beginning in Greek antiquity. Today, semiotics is a transdisciplinary field of research of relevance to a wide spectrum of disciplines such as biology (animal and cellular communication), cultural studies (cultures as sign systems), media studies (verbal and visual communication), consumer research (goods as signs), linguistics, logic, aesthetics, musicology (signs of/in music), architectural theory (buildings and urban design as signs), cartography (the signs of/in maps), religion (rites and religious myths as signs), or social psychology (non-verbal communication).

General Semiotics is the study of signs, sign systems, and communicative processes in general, whereas Applied Semiotics studies specific contexts of sign use. Some branches of Applied Semiotics have established themselves as sub-disciplines of semiotics under names of their own: for example, medical, musical, or film semiotics. Visual semiotics is one of the domains of Applied Semiotics. *The International Association for Visual Semiotics* organizes studies in this field.

The term 'visual semiotics' is not synonymous with 'the study of visually communicated signs.' Pictures (Santaella and Nöth, 1998), drawings, paintings, photographs, colors (Thürlemann, 1984; Eco, 1985), print ads (Santaella and Nöth, 2010), posters, design (Ashwin, 1984; Nadin, 1990), films (cf. Nöth, 2000), diagrams (Stjernfelt, 2007), logograms, traffic signs (Krampen, 1983), and maps (Nöth, 2007b) are topics of visual semiotics, but other visually communicated signs are not usually considered sub-domains of visual semiotics: for example, geometry, writing, or non-verbal communication (gestures, eye contact, 'body language').

Without pretending to define the field of visual semiotics as such, the present chapter is mostly restricted to the semiotics of still images, such as paintings, photographs, and pictures from the print media.

TRENDS, SCHOOLS, AND TOPICS OF VISUAL SEMIOTICS

General surveys can be found in Calabrese (1980), Nadin (1985), Sonesson (1989, 1993), Sebeok and Umiker-Sebeok (1995), and Nöth (2000, 2005b, 2009a). Visual semiotics was founded in the 1960s by structural linguists endeavoring to extend their scope of analysis from the study of language and literature to the visual contexts of language in the media. Roland Barthes (1964) was the first to speak of a 'rhetoric of the image' and to postulate a visual semiotics based on the semiology of Ferdinand de Saussure (1857–1913) and Louis Hjelmslev (1899–1965). Barthes's books on the semiotics of fashion, photography, and pictures from the print media are milestones in the history of visual semiotics (Barthes, 1967, 1977, 1980).

There are several schools and trends of research in visual semiotics, among them the ones of visual rhetoric and of the Paris School. Visual rhetoric, outlined by the Liège Group μ in their *Treatise of the Visual Sign* (Edeline et al., 1992), postulates that paintings and other pictures can be studied in analogy to figurative language as deviations from 'normal' pictures constituting a generic 'degree zero' of visual communication. The visual semiotics of the Paris School is founded on the assumption of essential analogies between pictures and verbal language. Like language, pictures are studied at the levels of expression (color, forms, etc.) and content (things, plants, animals, men and women, etc.). Pictures are segmented into minimal units, which are structured in oppositions such as colored/colorless, black/white,

round/angular, living/non-living, culture/nature. More complex thematic and figurative meanings appear at higher levels of analysis. Exemplary studies of paintings and pictures from the print media are Floch (1985, 1990), Thürlemann (1990), and Fontanille (1995).

Other approaches to the semiotics of pictures can be found in the frameworks of M. A. K. Halliday's sociosemiotics (Kress and van Leeuwen, 1996), and Charles S. Peirce's semiotics (Deledalle, 1979: 115–129; Iversen, 1986; Santaella and Nöth, 1998, 2010; Nöth and Santaella, 2000; Halawa, 2008). Some authors have adopted implicitly semiotic approaches to pictorial analysis. Although based on semiotic premises, they do not use any specifically semiotic terminology. Arnheim's theses that visual patterns are 'forms associated with contents' and 'all shape is the form of some content' (1954: 65) are implicitly semiotic, since they amount to saying that pictures are signs. The most elaborate implicitly semiotic approach to art is Nelson Goodman's *Languages of Art* (1968).

THE SEMIOTIC POTENTIAL OF PICTURES

Pictures and words differ in their semiotic potential and communicative efficiency. The former require a two-dimensional visible space, whereas the latter (like music) are produced and perceived in a linear sequence. Written language is a hybrid medium: although writing requires space, the processing of language in writing and reading is still largely linear.

Nevertheless, verbal communication is rarely restricted to the linearity of time, as are telephone conversations and radio programs. In face-to-face communication, language is transmitted in an acoustic space and embedded in the visual context of non-verbal communication. Pictures are not restricted to their visual space either: rarely can they be found without any verbal context. Paintings have names (titles), or at least the painter's name is associated with them. A passport photo needs a name, too; it does not only document how the passport owner looks like but also needs to identify his or her name.

The semiotic potential of language is superior when temporal as well as causal relationships have to be represented. Stories develop in time and are best told in language. Pictures, by contrast, are superior to verbal communication when spatial configurations have to be represented. An architectural plan, for example, cannot be very well translated into words, and it is difficult to convey the appearance of an unknown person by means of words only. The difference between the linearity of verbal language and the two-dimensionality of pictures also involves a difference in information processing. In a given span of time, we can process more visual than verbal data. The proverbial saying that 'a picture is worth a thousand words,' even though it may not be true in all respects, conveys this insight. Nevertheless, in some respects, language is not merely linear, and pictures are not only spatial media either. Syntactic tree diagrams show that language is also hierarchically structured and words also evoke mental images, which are spatial configurations. Visual perception, in turn, is not only a holistic process; to see and to understand a picture also takes time.

shown, even abstract logical and mathematical relations are not intelligible without the aid of verbal, geometrical, or graphic diagrams, which are icons and not symbols.

It has been argued that the meaning of a picture *depends* on its verbal comments, whereas words do not need pictures to be understood. Roland Barthes, for example, argues that our reading of a press photo depends on its legend:

> Images… can signify…, but never autonomously; every semiological system has its verbal admixture. Where there is a visual substance, for example, the meaning is confirmed by being duplicated in a linguistic message… so that at least a span of the iconic message is… either redundant or taken up by the linguistic system. (Barthes, 1964: 10)

Although it is true that words contribute to the interpretation of pictures and thereby make their meaning more specific, Barthes's argument is too logocentric. It ignores that words in face-to-face communication also have a visual context which contributes to the meaning of the verbal utterance. Furthermore, pictures such as paintings and photos often have no verbal context whatsoever, and even when they have one, it tends to be trivial in its meaning or redundant. Finally, it must also be recognized that verbal texts in strictly or mainly verbal media, such as conversations, books, letters, telegrams, or e-mails, evoke *mental* images by means of words.

COMPLEMENTARITY OF PICTORIAL AND VERBAL COMMUNICATION

Language and pictures are complementary in their semiotic potential; both are needed in efficient media communication (cf. Nöth, 2004). The superiority of pictures as a medium for the representation of the visible and imaginable world is counterbalanced by the superiority of language for representing the invisible world of sounds, smells, tastes, temperature, or logical relations. However, as Peirce has

PICTURES AS SIGNS

Pictorial semiotics presupposes that pictures are signs (cf. Nöth, 2005a). Whether they are or not is both a terminological question and one which depends on how signs are defined. Pictures (*imagines*) and paintings (*picturae*) were first defined as signs in Rogers Bacon's treatise *De Signis* of 1267 (cf. Meier-Oeser, 1997: 54). According to Bacon, pictures function as signs 'by their own nature,' due to a 'natural correspondence' with what they depict. Not only natural pictures such as mirror reflections but also handmade pictures are natural signs according to this definition. It is not the painter's intention which makes a painting a sign but its natural similarity with the object it represents: 'Whether the artist wants it or not, the picture always represents what it represents because it is similar to it' (*De Signis* I, 15; cf. Meier-Oeser, 1997: 58–59). Today, although the iconicity of pictures is still a topic, paintings are usually no longer defined as natural signs.

The concept of sign has also been defined in ways which exclude pictures. Some authors distinguish between signs and symbols, restricting the concept of *sign* to *natural signs* (or *signals*), while defining all products of culture, including pictures and words, as *symbols* (cf. Nöth, 2000: 40–41). This is not the terminology of visual semiotics.

Pictures are not only signs when they depict the visible reality of things. To assume the contrary characterizes the naive conception of the picture as a depiction criticized by Boehm as follows: 'It is the idea that pictures *mirror a presupposed* reality (in whatever stylistic distortion). What we know and what we are acquainted with meets us once more under exonerating visual circumstances. At any rate, the nature of depiction consists in a doubling' (1994: 327). However, no sign is a mere double of reality, and no sign system is restricted to representing singular objects only. In language, for example, only proper names represent singular objects. Not even words representing really existing things depict singular objects. Nouns such as 'apple,' 'house,' or 'fish' represent classes of things in general, and this generality makes them vague.

Although the notion that pictures represent objects in a mirror-like fashion is naive, there are pictures which typically do so, namely mirror images (cf. Eco, 1984) and photographs. Other pictures, for example, international pictograms, are rather similar to the verbal signs into which they can be translated (see later section: Iconic, Indexical, and Symbolic Pictures).

THE TRIADIC MODEL OF THE PICTORIAL SIGN

According to a medieval definition, a sign is something (*aliquid*) that stands for (*stat pro*) something else (*aliquo*): *aliquid stat pro aliquo*. This formula conveys the useful insight that the sign is not the object to which it refers; the picture must not be confounded with what it depicts. However, insofar as it suggests that the sign can be essentially reduced to a dyad of sign vehicle and its object of reference, or a signifier and a signified, the formula is misleading. Three correlates have to be considered: the sign (vehicle), its referential object, and its meaning. In many terminological variants, the three correlates (sign, object, and meaning) constitute the triadic model of the sign, often represented in the form of a triangle (cf. Nöth, 1990, 2000). A classic of semiotics who has given a triadic account of the nature of the sign is Charles Sanders Peirce (1839–1914). (Throughout the rest of this chapter, I refer to his work with 'CP' followed by volume and paragraph numbers.) One of his definitions of the sign is the following:

> A sign, or representamen, is something which stands to somebody for something in some respect or capacity. It addresses somebody, that is, creates in the mind of that person an equivalent sign, or perhaps a more developed sign. That sign which it creates I call the interpretant of the first sign. The sign stands for something, its object. It stands for that object, not in all respects, but in reference to a sort of idea. (CP 2.228, c. 1897)

In the context of visual semiotic, that which 'stands to somebody for something in some respect' is the picture. It is not necessary that the sign should have a material form. A sign, according to Peirce, can also be an idea, a mere thought. Hence, a mental image can also be a sign. The visual sign refers back to previously seen visual perceptions (its object) and it causes an interpretation, a reaction, a new thought, or mental image as its interpretant. Thus defined, signs occur in semiotic processes. The sign (word, picture, or mental image) is a semiotic 'first.' It is associated with something else (a 'second'), which is the object represented by the sign. The object of the visual sign is something once seen, experienced, or imagined. A sign associated with its object leads to a 'third,' its interpretant, which is the mental or behavioral interpretation of the sign.

The object for which the pictorial sign stands can be a thing depicted by the picture, but it can also be the memory of something once seen, and even something purely imaginary, a mental image. The triadic model of the sign does not postulate the existence of the object. Peirce even goes so far as to speculate that 'perhaps the Object is altogether fictive' (CP 8.314, 1909). A picture of a unicorn is not a sign without an object because unicorns do not exist in reality. The object of this picture consists of the pictures, sculptures, and stories which have once formed our mental image of what a unicorn is.

The interpretant of a pictorial sign is the mental image, the idea, the thought, the action, or reaction evoked by it. Since ideas are (mental) signs, the interpretant of a sign which is a mental image is itself a sign. In Peirce's semiotics, the distinction between the object and the interpretant is not one between something material and something mental. All three correlates of the pictorial sign can be mental as well as material. An example of a material interpretant of a famous painting is the copy painted of it by an amateur or artist. The difference between a mental picture as a sign, an object, and an interpretant is a matter of the sequence in the semiotic process. When the mental image is the object of a sign, it precedes the sign as something that is evoked by the sign. When it is the interpretant, it is the effect that the sign has created in a mind. When the sign itself is a mental image we are considering the point of departure of a semiotic process; for example, a process in which a present mental image (sign) evokes memories of the past (its object), which are then interpreted in a new light (as its interpretant). While the object of the sign relates to the past, and the

sign is a matter of what comes first in perception, the interpretant as its interpretation follows the sign.

ICONIC, INDEXICAL, AND SYMBOLIC PICTURES

Pictures are typically iconic signs. According to Peirce, an icon is a sign which is similar to its object; it shares qualities with its object and is neither a sign because of a convention nor because it is the natural effect of an object which is its cause. A picture of a yellow banana is yellow like the object which it represents; the picture of a triangle is itself triangular. The words for these objects evince no such similarities with what they represent. Based on conventions, which differ from language to language, words are symbols. The association between a symbol and its object is arbitrary, conventional, and it must be learned.

The term 'iconic' is not a synonym of the term 'visual.' Although most pictures are iconic signs, there are also acoustic icons: for example, the sounds in a radio play or a film. Words can be icons, too. Sound symbolic words are verbal icons.

The degree to which an icon is similar to its object is called *iconicity*. The concepts of similarity and iconicity have been criticized for their vagueness, in particular by Eco (1968, 1976). Eco and other critics have argued that everything is somehow similar to everything, but although a banana and the moon, for example, are similar in color, this does not make the banana a sign of the moon. Similarity is indeed not an objectively measurable quality, but it could not even be so since the object of a sign can also be a mental picture, and mental pictures cannot easily be compared with visual pictures. Nevertheless, similarity is a cognitive reality. We make judgments of similarity in everyday life, and these judgments can be described and evaluated, and tests can reveal to which degree people find things similar.

A picture is an index in addition to being an icon when it refers to, and can serve to identify, a singular object. Passport photos are indexical signs; they serve to identify their owners. In fact, all photos are indices, because one of the characteristics of some indices is that they are connected with their objects by a natural cause or a spatial or temporal contiguity. Photographs, despite their similarity with their objects, are indexical signs for two reasons: first, they are produced by the physical cause of a light ray projection on a film; second, they serve to identify the object which they depict. The indexicality of the photo does not exclude or contradict its iconicity; the latter is included in the former. Paintings, too, evince elements of indexicality. The style of a painting is an index of its painter and the time in which it was painted. The perspective in which a picture is drawn is an index which allows us to infer from which point in space the draftsman produced the drawing, and a portrait in oil that allows us to identify the portrayed person as an individual is as much an index of the person as his or her passport photo.

According to Peirce, the object of a sign cannot be identified as such from its iconic representation despite the similarity between them. An icon is a sign 'by virtue of a character which it possesses in itself, and would possess just the same though its object did not exist,' explains Peirce, giving the example of the iconic statue of a centaur, which represents a centaur 'by virtue of its shape,' which 'it will have, just as much, whether there be a centaur or not' (CP 5.73, 1903). Icons do not necessarily refer to real objects. When, and insofar as they do, they are indices. The object of an icon can be a mere possibility; this is why pictures can depict objects which do not exist.

One of the characteristics of indexical signs is 'that they direct the attention to their objects by blind compulsion' (CP 2.306, 1902). A child who cries to attract his or her mother's attention communicates by means of a genuine index. To some degree, the blindly compulsive attraction which Peirce mentions as a characteristic of some indices is also a characteristic of pictures, especially in the media. It is well known that pictures attract more attention than mere words. The tabloid press makes use of this effect by ceding space to photos on their front pages. To the degree that pictures have such an appellative (or 'conative,' as Roman Jakobson calls it) power, they are indexical signs. Some pictures are more indexical than others in this respect. Pictures with 'loud' colors or the photos of pin-up girls attract more attention. Posters and outdoor ads make use of this indexicality to attract the attention of the masses.

Pictures can also be symbols. Words are typical symbols. The logographic traffic sign for cyclists, an abstract picture of a bicycle, is a symbol but because of its similarity to real bicycles it is at the same time an icon. Logograms are symbols insofar as they have a general meaning, just like the words into which they can be translated. When it is used to orient cyclists in traffic, the traffic sign serves as an index, informing the road users that '*this* path *(here)*' is for cyclists only.

Thus, Peirce's trichotomy of the icon, the index, and the symbol is a system of inclusion. Symbols include indexical signs since no general idea can be formed without 'existent instances of what the Symbol denotes': that is, without indices of the symbol (CP 2.249, 1903). Indices include icons, for, 'in so far as the Index is affected by the Object, it necessarily has some Quality in common with the Object' (CP 2.248, 1903). The word *bicycle* evokes the mental image (and thus an icon) of the vehicle it designates, but it also directs our mind to specific vehicles which we have known in reality (index). Indices include icons, as the example of the photo has shown. Only the icon does not include any other types of sign. Since icons evince qualities of their objects, Peirce concludes that 'a great distinguishing property of the icon is that by the direct observation of it other truths concerning its object can be discovered than those which suffice to determine its construction' (CP 2.279). Icons are hence the only kind of sign from which we can derive new insights concerning the nature of their objects. This is particularly true of the diagram, which Peirce defines as an icon which, without any 'sensuous resemblance' with its object, shows an 'analogy between the relations of its parts' with the structure of its object (CP 2.279, c. 1895). A city map, which is a diagrammatic icon, not only represents the streets of the city but also allows the map user to discover how to get from one address to another.

The iconicity of pictures explains their global utility and efficiency in the media. What they refer to can be recognized from its forms and colors; the information conveyed by a press photo needs no translator. This does not preclude that pictures may not also be determined by cultures and styles and need to be contextualized. Furthermore, what pictures depict is very often already a symbolic sign whose interpretation requires cultural knowledge. The picture of a totem pole can only be properly understood by one who has some collateral knowledge of the cultures which produce totem poles as symbols of clans. The degree to which icons mix with indices and symbols allows the distinction between pictorial styles. Realist paintings, for example, are more indexical than iconic ones. Paintings whose interpretation requires the knowledge of an iconographic code, by contrast, are symbols to the degree that cultural knowledge of conventions is required to interpret them.

WHY NON-FIGURATIVE (ABSTRACT) PICTURES ARE SIGNS

The sign nature of figurative pictures is mostly not in question, since it is acknowledged that they are signs of whatever they represent. By contrast, with the argument that nothing can be a sign that does not represent or refer to objects of 'real' or at least to possible worlds, non-representational pictures have been described as works of art which are not signs (cf. Nöth, 2005a); however, visual semiotics sees this differently, and therefore abstract paintings are not excluded from its field of research.

The Paris and Liège Schools of visual semiotics distinguish between figurative (or iconic) and abstract (or plastic) signs in pictures. Figurative signs are those which can be recognized as representing the things of our visual world, such as the sun, a tree, a table, a cat, a boy, or a girl. These are evidently the signs we find in representational paintings. Abstract signs consisting of patterns of color and form such as colors, triangles, circles, etc., can be found both in figurative and in non-figurative pictures. Structured in minimal units called abstract elements, these signs are described in pairs of binary oppositions. At the abstract level, *chromatic* patterns (of color) are distinguished from *eidetic* patterns (of form). Chromatic patterns are structured in contrasts of colors, such as 'red' versus 'green' or 'saturated' versus 'unsaturated.' Eidetic patterns are structured in so-called *categories*, consisting of binary opposites of form, such as 'angular versus round' or 'convex versus concave.' In a next step of the analysis of abstract paintings, the configurations found in the analysis of the chromatic and eidetic patterns are interpreted in terms of semantic categories, such as 'nature versus culture,' 'life versus death' (cf. Thürlemann, 1990: 25–31; Edeline et al., 1992). This final step of analysis of this semiotic approach to abstract paintings thus consists in rendering the non-figurative structures of the abstract picture as figuratively meaningful.

A different way of accounting for the sign nature of abstract pictures is to postulate the category of the self-referential aesthetic sign, a sign that refers to nothing but itself (Nöth and Santaella, 2000; Nöth, 2003, 2007a, 2007c). A key term of this approach is Peirce's concept of the pure icon. Pure icons 'can represent nothing but Forms and Feelings' (CP 4.544, 1905). Without being just similar to (and hence, in a way, also different from) its object, the pure icon is a sign only by virtue of qualities of its own. Without drawing 'any distinction between itself and its object, it represents whatever it may represent, and whatever it is like… . It is an affair of suchness only' (CP 5.74, 1903). In the context in which Peirce develops the theory of pure iconicity, he draws a distinction between (pure) icons and *hypoicons*. A pure icon, as described above, functions as a sign by its own quality, irrespective of any other object of reference, whereas the hypoicon functions as a sign because of its similarity to its object (CP 2.276, 1903). Elsewhere (and also in the previous paragraph of this chapter), the term icon is simply a synonym of hypoicon.

Pure icons 'are so completely substituted for their objects as hardly to be distinguished from them… . The distinction of the real and the copy disappears, and it is for the moment a pure dream—not any particular existence, and yet not general' (CP 3.362, 1885). Once a picture is contemplated in such a total disregard of any referent, it is no longer a sign by similarity to its object. Being indistinguishable from its object, the pure icon is a self-referential sign of its own pure forms. This way of looking at a picture as a pure form is the one which classical aesthetics has described as the defining characteristic of aesthetic perception. The work of art is perceived 'for its own sake,' according to the doctrine of classical aesthetics (cf. Nöth, 2000: 426–427). When the icon does no longer refer to an object differing from itself, representing nothing but pure forms and feelings, it is a mere constellation of colors and forms.

The classical distinctive feature of aesthetic perception, namely self-referentiality, the fact that aesthetic pictures begin to be perceived in their suchness, only with respect of their iconic qualities, was only radicalized by the aesthetic revolution that took place in abstract art. Once the art work was liberated from its bonds with its objects of reference, its viewers no longer needed to abstract from its figurative signs to perceive it as an autonomous aesthetic sign representing colors and pure forms.

The avant-gardes of the twentieth century adopted various semiotic strategies to liberate their works of art from their bonds of reference. All of them can be described as different strategies of approaching the ideal of aesthetic self-reference. Pure iconicity is in fact only an ideal, a borderline case of iconicity, reachable only by asymptotic approximation. No real picture can be an absolutely pure icon, since each picture is a singular object and in this sense not an 'ideal' form. The work of art is always also the product of an individual artist and in this respect an index of the artist's style. Furthermore, insofar as it participates in and exemplifies a specific aesthetic trend (such as 'abstract art'), it is the result of aesthetic conventions, and in this respect a symbol. No work of art can fully embody the ideal of pure form, but there are degrees of approximation to pure iconicity.

Three such degrees of approximation to pure iconicity can be derived from Peirce's classification of signs into qualisigns, sinsigns, and legisigns outlined in his theory of the 10 classes of signs (CP 2.254-264, 1903): first, as an icon because of its own qualities, the iconic qualisign is the one that comes closest to the ideal of the pure icon; second, comes the iconic sinsign, which is characterized by its singularity; and third, comes the iconic legisign, which is an icon embodying 'a general law of type' (CP 2.258).

Iconic qualisigns

The prototype of abstract painting coming closest to an iconic qualisign is the monochrome painting. Yves Klein's *Proposition monochromes* of 1956 consist of a series of pictures in pure orange, yellow, red, pink, and blue. These minimalist pictures probably negate the referential object of the pictorial sign most radically. Any reference to the world of objects is eliminated in a picture reduced to pure color and referring to nothing but itself. And yet, despite their approximation to the category of qualisign, these monochromes cannot be pure qualisigns, 'since quality is a mere logical possibility'

(CP 2.255), whereas a painting is a real object of experience. As such, Klein's paintings are also sinsigns, signs whose singularity is important, although this is not what distinguishes them from other works of art. Furthermore, as works of art, they also belong to the category of the iconic legisign, since they are instances of the class of artworks, which are cultural signs determined by aesthetic conventions. Despite their radical attempt of breaking with the traditions of art history, even the most revolutionary work of art still wants to belong to the class of artworks: that is, to a category of signs determined by cultural conventions. The legisign character of Klein's *Proposition monochromes* is also evident in its title. If these monochromes are *propositions*, they are pictures which propose a general idea about the nature of painting: that is, they are metapaintings.

Iconic sinsigns

Among the works of twentieth century avantgarde in which the aspect of singularity is predominant and which therefore function primarily as iconic sinsigns are those which have demonstrated the unrepeatability, absolute uniqueness, and in this sense utter singularity of experiencing them. The absolute unrepeatability of the aesthetic experience of a work of art was the ideal of the performances, happenings, events, and installations in the art of the late 1960s and early 1970s (Nöth, 1972). No work of art can be more singular than an unrepeatable happening, the performance of which is programmatically unique.

A different kind of radicalization of the ideal of aesthetic singularity is exemplified by works in the tradition of the Dadaist *found objects*. The singularity of an *objet trouvé* is not the one of its aesthetic experience, which is in fact repeatable; it is the uniqueness of the selection of the objects as an object of art. Of course, works of art, as creations of individual artists, have always been products of unique selections. However, in contrast to the

traditional kind of creative uniqueness, *found objects* are not materially created at all; they are only selected by the artist from an easily available general repertoire of mass products and made singular by the mere act of their presentation in an art exhibition. Among the things selected by Marcel Duchamp as objects of art were: a comb, a bottle rack, and a urinal. It was the artist's unique gesture of selection that transformed these ordinary objects of everyday life into singular works of art, aesthetic sinsigns. The objects which Duchamp had 'found' in, and selected from, the repertoire of everyday life objects had been signs before they were selected, but signs of a different kind. As members of a class of objects serving a practical purpose, they were replicas of legisigns, the mass products serving those everyday life purposes which made them culturally meaningful (cf. Nöth, 1998). Duchamp's selection of these mass products deprived them of their reference to their practical utility and modes of use and transformed them into singular works of art, self-referential iconic sinsigns.

Iconic legisigns

Iconic legisigns are the third class of iconic sign of relevance to the semiotics of nonrepresentational art. Legisigns are signs due to a general law that makes them a sign. In painting, such laws can be styles or conventions, but also symmetry, balance, polarity, tension, contrast, opposition, invariance, geometrical form, or chromatic complementarity. Prototypically, laws of the latter kind determine the compositional principles of Constructivism and Suprematism. Piet Mondrian's *Composition in Red, Black, Yellow and Gray* (1920), for example, is composed according to the geometrical laws by which rectangular forms are constructed; it is radically reduced to colored squares and rectangles separated by black lines. A square forms the visual center around which rectangles are displayed in quasi-symmetrical arrangements, and the colors are chosen to create a harmonious balance. The forms and colors are neither presented as pure forms nor as the artist's spontaneous and singular intuition, but by a chromatic and geometrical morphology and syntax that make the picture an iconic legisign.

VISUAL SYNTAX AND THE QUESTION OF DOUBLE ARTICULATION

A major topic of the early semiotics of the image of the 1960s and 1970s was whether the metaphor of the 'language of pictures' can be taken literally: that is, whether pictures are structured in analogy to the levels of the phoneme, the word, and the sentence of the verbal language. Among the semioticians who participated in the search for analogies between the grammar of language and the structure of pictures are Zemsz (1967), Metz (1968), Eco (1968, 1976), Schefer (1969), Marin (1971), Paris (1975), Lindekens (1976), Carter (1972, 1976), and Saint-Martin (1990). A much discussed topic of this period of visual semiotics was whether pictures are signs with a so-called double articulation: that is, with a level consisting of elements with meaning (analogous to the words of language) and a level consisting of elements without meaning (like the phonemes or letters of language). Undoubtedly, visual images have meanings, but in contrast to words, pictures are not composed of a finite set of recurrent minimal elements, which are themselves without meaning (cf. Benveniste, 1969: 237, 242).

Although there is now a general agreement that pictures are sign systems without a second articulation similar to the one of language, the French and Belgian traditions of visual semiotics postulate a double articulation of pictures of a different kind. The two levels of structure of a visual image are the ones of the figurative and the abstract signs of pictures. (See above section on non-figurative [abstract] pictures and the last section on pictures as semi-symbolic systems.)

Although there is no grammar to compose syntactically well-formed pictures by means of a finite number of elements and rules, it is nevertheless possible to recognize a pictorial syntax in a different sense. Pictures are certainly composed of figures whose spatial arrangement obeys certain principles of order. Unlike the syntax of language, which consists of largely arbitrary rules varying from language to language, figurative pictures have an *iconic syntax* whose rules are determined by the order in which the things in the world represented by them are structured. For example, the sun is up, the ground is down, and a butterfly has wings to the right and the left of its body, etc. It is by means of such iconic orders of representation corresponding to the order of the things of the visual world as we know it that pictures can be read as representing the things they depict. The grammar of figurative pictures is iconic of the order of things.

Abstract pictures have no such grammar, since they negate any reference to them. Insofar as each abstract painting has its own chromatic and formal order of colors and forms, one can either conclude that each abstract painting has its own syntax or that non-figurative paintings are pictures without a syntactic structure. Traditional principles of aesthetic order (harmony, balance, symmetry, colors that combine or not) are examples of the non-figurative pictorial syntax by which a large class of pictures has been and continues to be generated.

In contrast to the syntax of verbal language of linear surface structures with hierarchical deep structures, the grammar of pictures generates more complex two-dimensional surface structures. Nevertheless, there are also structures below the surface of a picture which testify to a kind of visual deep structure: for example, foreground–background or center–periphery configurations marking the greater or lesser importance of pictorial elements. Visual salience of a figure, its foregrounding, or its position in the center, correspond to the importance in pictorial meaning.

The iconic syntax of pictures is thus an iconic syntax of recognition, reflecting the patterns of visual cognition. One of the syntactic orders underlying our cognition both of pictures and of the visual world which has no counterpart in verbal syntax is meronymic order. A meronymy describes the part–whole order of things. An example is the human body: its parts are the trunk, the arms, legs, and the head. Each of these parts is structured in further parts: for example, the arm into upper arm, forearm, and hand, etc., each of these parts having an order of its two-dimensional representation, right, left, up, or down in the visual configuration. The knowledge of such part–whole relations is one of the elements of pictorial syntax. A syntactically well-formed picture of a human head must show hair, eyes, nose, mouth, chin, etc., each in its syntactically (or meronymically) correct place. The rules of the projection of the three-dimensional space onto the two-dimensional plane of the surface of a picture are a sub-domain of pictorial syntax.

VISUAL SEMANTICS

The semantics of figurative pictures is equally derived from our knowledge of the objects of the visual world. Whatever meaning we associate with an object (a rock, a dog, the sky, etc.), a figure, or a color, the same meaning will be recognized as a meaning of its pictorial representation. To the degree that pictures represent the visual world more accurately than verbal language, the semantics of pictures is more differentiated than the semantics of language. The small number of color words in contrast to the large number of colors available to a graphic artist may suffice as an example of the superiority of visual to verbal semantics. In other respects, pictorial semantics can also be inferior in its semiotic potential in comparison with verbal semantics. Some of the respects in which pictures cannot express meanings which words can express are negation and exclusive disjunctions, causality, modalization, meta-reference, self-reference, and deixis.

Negation and exclusive disjunction

Pictures cannot say *no*, nor can they express *either-or-but-not-both* relationships. 'Bicycle' is certainly a meaning which can be represented in a picture, but the meaning 'no bicycle' cannot. Negative meanings can inferentially be derived from pictures, or are expressed by symbolic means. The concept 'no bicycle' can be inferred from a picture without bicycles, but since the number of judgments about the invisible derivable from the visible is always unlimited (the number of things not in picture being uncountable), it is uncertain whether the picture will lead to this judgment or not. A crossed-out picture of a bicycle uses a symbolic device to negate the concept of 'bicycle.' A picture cannot express the concept of the exclusive *or*. For example, it cannot represent the meaning 'either a cyclist or a pedestrian.'

Causality

Can pictures visualize the causes of the effects they represent? A photo of a fire and the smoke caused by it represents a cause–effect relationship, but the causality must be inferred by the viewer of the photo; there is no pictorial device which expresses it. An X-ray picture seems to visualize the cause of a disease, but it is only the iconic (and indexical) representation of a malformation which is itself the symptom of the disease that is its cause. A photo shows a man shooting a woman, but did she really die, or were the two only the actors of a film? To the degree that pictures cannot affirm what they show, they cannot represent causality. Sequences of pictures and films are more likely to represent cause–effect relations. A film of a man lighting a match and setting fire to a barn shows a cause–effect sequence.

Modality

Pictures cannot modalize what they show. They cannot express the ideas of possibility, necessity, obligation, or volition. The picture of a running girl does not tell us whether she wants to, must, or can run or is only pretending to run.

Metareference and self-reference

Pictures and language also differ with respect to their metareferential and self-referential potential (Nöth, 2007c, 2009b). They have no metasigns corresponding to words referring to words, their elements, and functions, such as *vowel, consonant, word*, or *sentence*. Only language can self-referentially be used to describe words. For example, it is possible to say: 'I mean *eye—e, y, e*, and not *I*, the personal pronoun.' Furthermore, language can also be used to speak about pictures, but pictures hardly describe language, although they may be used to illustrate texts. No pictorial form can express the idea of a 'form,' no triangle the idea of a 'triangle,' and no color the idea of a 'color' without being itself the color in question. Pictures can only show their own qualities: they cannot explicitly 'speak' about them, nor can they generalize. A picture can only show a triangle or a color but cannot show without being itself triangular or having the color it represents. Although pictures have no signs to refer to pictures and their elements, metapictures become possible by way of inference. A picture about another picture is interpreted as a metapicture by the inference of an interpreter in whose mind the present picture evokes the other picture (which it quotes or comments on) as a mental picture.

Deixis and indexicality

Pictures cannot point from *here* to *there*. There are no internal means of referring from one locus within the picture to another; there is nothing that can express the meaning of *here, there, this*, or *that* (but for the way in which pictures can be indices of what they represent, see above).

VISUAL PRAGMATICS

Like all signs, pictures also have a pragmatic dimension, in which they are studied in relation to their modes and effects of use. Visual pragmatics deals with the way pictures are used and the effects which they have on their viewers. That pictures attract more immediate attention than words, as discussed above, pertains to their pragmatic dimension. Other topics of visual pragmatics include: In which way do pictures exert their effect on their viewers and which purposes do they serve? A semiotic way of examining this question is to compare the pragmatics of language with the use and the effects of communication by means of pictures.

An important method of linguistic pragmatics is speech act theory (cf. Nöth, 2010), which studies the diverse modes language uses as acts of 'doing things' by means of language (cf. Austin, 1962). Examples of speech acts are promising, threatening, asking, ordering, congratulating, taking an oath, etc. An important distinction is the one between direct and indirect speech acts. Direct speech acts are marked as such by speech act verbs (so-called performative verbs) or syntactic forms that characterize the utterance as the speech act for which it is used. For example, the speech act or ordering is direct if the speaker says *I order you to be quiet* or uses the imperative form (*Be quiet!*). Indirect speech acts omit performative verbs or syntactic forms that signalize the speech act which it is. A speaker may give an order in the form of a (more polite) question or as a mere statement.

Pictures are also used for diverse purposes: for example, in advertising, to make customers buy products or in public places to orient the masses. Is a theory of pictorial acts in analogy to speech acts possible? Performative verbs are verbal metasigns. If I say *I ask you the following question…* or *I tell you…*, these utterances are metalinguistic comments on the ensuing questions or orders. Since pictures have no explicit metasigns, as shown above, it must be concluded that there can be no direct pictorial acts analogous to direct speech acts. A picture cannot express explicitly whether it is used to ask a question, to give an order, to threaten, to make a promise, or to congratulate. Hence, a theory of pictorial acts can only be a theory of indirect pictorial acts. If a picture addresses its readers with the purpose of asking a question or warning against a danger, the pictorial question or warning can only be an indirect one. Of course, the purpose for which the picture serves can be expressed directly by means of verbal speech acts.

Pictures cannot affirm what they show because to affirm requires a metasign of the truth of what is affirmed (cf. Nöth 2009b). A spokesman who affirms that his company has dismissed its chairman claims implicitly that the proposition *We have dismissed our chairman* is true; to say that something is true is to make a metastatement. Pictures, by contrast, have no such metasigns. They can only show what they represent, but since they have no iconic metasigns, they can neither affirm what they represent nor lie about it. Nevertheless, pictures can give indexical evidence of facts, especially as photographs. As indexical signs, photos come close to pictures that express the truth and in the sense in which photos are acceptable as documents of facts, they can be said to affirm what they represent. However, the photo cannot be made to affirm what it shows nor can it tell whether it was manipulated or not. We need additional evidence about the circumstances under which it was taken, revealed, or digitally processed. This is why even photos can neither affirm nor lie explicitly but can only be used to lie. The circumstances under which pictures are used for certain purposes are either expressed verbally or by means of indirect pictorial acts.

The photographer who sells a manipulated photo as a representation of a real scene either does so by means of the speech act of a lie or by concealing the truth in a non-verbal way: for example, by profiting from his professional credibility. The non-verbal way of deceiving the clients is an indirect pictorial act.

In their pragmatic dimension, pictures are essentially open messages, more so than in their semantic dimension. A picture of a violin can hardly be interpreted to mean anything other than a violin, but it can be used for many purposes: for example, to inform about the kind of instrument a violin is, to teach how it is built, to illustrate an invitation to a concert, to advertise, to exemplify the idea of symmetry, etc. This is another parallelism between pictures and language: just like a picture can be used for many purposes, one and the same verbal utterance can be used in many direct and indirect ways to perform the most diverse speech acts.

THE SEMIOTICS OF VISUAL IMAGES IN PRINT ADS: TWO CASE STUDIES

Two semiotic approaches to the study of visual images will be presented here with due shortenings, some additions, and necessary modifications. Both are studies of print ads from news magazines. The first exemplifies the Paris School approach; the second exemplifies the approach based on Peirce's semiotics. The Paris School method of visual semiotics is exemplified by means of a summary of the main ideas of a study by J. M. Floch (1985: 139–169, 1989, 1990. 85–89) of some print ads from an advertising campaign of 1980 launched to introduce the cigarette brand 'News' in France (Figure 16.1).

In the tradition of semiotic structuralism, Floch characterizes the verbo-visual text of Figure 16.1 as a system of opposites at several levels of which the dichotomy of expression versus content is the most fundamental.

Figure 16.1   A French ad of 1980 (Floch, 1989: 56) for the cigarette brand 'News'

Figure 16.2   A gin ad of 1974 (Santaella and Nöth, 2010: 148) for the brand 'Beefeater,' produced by the company James Burrough Limited

At the *expression plane*, which is the level of the graphic and typographic forms as well as chromatic and achromatic nuances and contrasts, the opposition 'straight' versus 'oblique' is most striking. The upper and lower text typographic zones are arranged in straight and horizontally parallel fields (or bands), whereas the typographic middle field contains obliquely arranged rectangular forms within a rectangular frame whose margins go parallel to the ones of the whole page. The arrangement implies oppositions such as symmetry (in the upper and lower bands) versus asymmetry (in the middle field) or regularity versus irregularity. This set of fundamental opposites goes parallel (is 'coupled') with other oppositions at the expression plane: language (in the upper and lower bands) versus photography (in the middle field); colored (above and below) versus black and white (the photos in the middle); 'broad' with several lines versus 'narrow' with one line only (upper and lower bands). Opposites structuring the middle field are: foreground (the pack of cigarettes) with colors versus background in black and white (the photos), overlapping (arrangement of the photos) versus superimposed (the pack of cigarettes on top of the photos), 'framing' (the upper and lower band frame the middle field) versus 'framed' (the cigarette pack is framed by the photos around it), and finally 'oblique with descending parallel lines' versus 'oblique with ascending parallel lines' from left to right (of the photos in the background versus the pack of cigarettes in the foreground). Among the colors, there is the opposition between 'chromatic' (above and below and on the cigarette pack) versus 'achromatic' (the photos) and between 'primary color' (of the red broad bar below the upper band and on the cigarette pack) versus 'secondary color' (the color of the filter tips is ochre).

At the *content plane*, the visual elements found at the expression plane are now interpreted as meaningful. They are considered as signifiers (expressions) associated with signifieds (contents). The resulting semantization of the expression plane of an image according to this method can be illustrated by the 'foreground' versus 'background' opposition: in general, the meaning of what is in the foreground is more important than what is in the background, and indeed, it is the cigarette pack, for which the campaign is launched, that is in the foreground of this ad. A further semantization of this kind: descending lines have negative, and ascending ones have positive connotations. Indeed, it is only the image of the cigarette pack whose edges have ascending lines in their oblique representation, whereas the photos of the 'restless' life of photojournalists have an oblique orientation descending from left to right.

After reducing the various pairs of opposites at the expression plane to the one fundamental common denominator of 'discontinuity' versus 'continuity,' Floch arrives at the conclusion that this opposition characteristic of the ad's layout is coupled with the fundamental semantic opposition of 'identity' versus 'alterity.' Identity is the common denominator of the continuity and regularity with which daily newspapers are published, the cigarettes' 'full flavor' remaining available for ever, and also of the consumers' freedom to take a break while the others continue in their restless professional lifestyle. The latter symbolizes the 'alterity' of all those who do not participate in taking a break (and do not consume this brand product). The fundamental distinction between 'identity' and 'alterity' is coupled with other opposites: 'permanence' (and continuity in the publication of a daily newspaper) versus 'change' (of the issues reported from day to day), photos (the daily raw material of any press photographer) versus the (ever-changing) 'events' they depict. In sum: 'What the "News" advertisement proposes… is a lifestyle… that it displays two contrary states: participation in the hectic life of society…

[vs] attainment of a personal style imprinted upon the former' (Floch 1989: 57).

The system of correlations between elements of expression and content, thus established, exemplifies that pictures are semi-symbolic languages and how they are structured in semi-symbolic systems. Unlike symbolic languages, which evince a one-to-one correspondence between their units of expression and content (example: the system of traffic lights), pictures are semi-symbolic languages because the elements of their expression plane evince only loose correspondences to certain categories of content, as illustrated above.

Whereas the Paris School approach aims at revealing fundamental, but hidden, meanings inherent in the deep structure of an image, the approach based on principles of Peirce's semiotics adopted by Santaella and Nöth (2010) starts from different premises. Reading pictures is a semiotic process (a process of semiosis). Images are signs that do not only *have* meanings but also *create* meanings. The meanings they have are related to the *objects* of the visual signs; the meaning they create to their *interpretants*.

Consider the example of Figure 16.2. The ad itself (image and text) is a complex *sign* consisting of two pictures in juxtaposition with a few verbal text elements associated with them. The object of this sign does not only consist of the two things we see and the meanings of the words we read. That which we must know in order to interpret the sign (that is, the object) comprises all cultural knowledge necessary to interpret the sign. This knowledge is not restricted to visible knowledge. For example, we know that the crown is itself a sign, a symbol of the British monarchy. The bottle, too, is a sign, since it represents a brand and not only one particular bottle. The knowledge we have of the objects represented in this ad may be vague, but the verbal text, consisting of signs with objects of their own, informs about further details. The *interpretant* created by this complex sign (the ad) not only consists of meanings in the sense of information, ideas, concepts, or mental images but also of the beliefs, desires, and habits which the complex sign creates in its readers. The ultimate interpretant, which is the real aim of all advertisements, is the consumers' habits of consuming the product presented in this ad.

The two juxtaposed objects shown in the gin ad of Figure 16.2 are *iconic* signs since they are similar to the objects they represent. At first sight, the two objects seem completely unrelated: we know that the crown is unique and of incalculable value, whereas a single bottle of gin is an ordinary mass product. However, for a mass product, the verbal claim printed in the top line 'There is only one'—vague as it may be—cannot be true. To make more sense of this juxtaposition of crown and bottle, the reader is obliged to look for a better interpretation. The two objects are evidently signs of different types. The object of the first icon 'crown,' in its singularity, is a *sinsign*; the picture of the bottle does not represent a sinsign (evidently, the company does not only want to sell a single bottle), but a *legisign*, that is, a sign type, based on a law. All brands are *legisigns*; they are literally protected by laws. As a legisign, the bottle not only stands for itself but also for a brand. With this in mind, the juxtaposition makes more sense: a brand image is certainly something that has a high value. There are brand images which sell for more than the financial value of the Imperial Crown.

However, if a single bottle serves as a sign of a whole brand, it can only be an indexical legisign. The sign is an index (in addition to being a legisign), since it represents its object in a *pars pro toto* relationship: one bottle serves to represent all bottles of the brand. This more detailed analysis reveals one more inequality in the semiotics of the juxtaposition: although the two objects 'crown' and 'bottle' are both legisigns, only the latter is an *indexical legisign*, whereas the former is a *symbolic legisign*. In addition to being a legisign (protected by the laws of England),

the Imperial Crown is a symbol, a sign related to its object by cultural habits and conventions.

The semiotic purpose of the juxtaposition of the two unequal objects is evidently to achieve the effect of a transfer of those meanings associated with the object of culturally higher value (the crown) to the sign representing the object of a culturally lower value (the brand of gin). Culturally highly esteemed qualities, such as 'precious,' 'royal,' 'traditional,' 'ancient,' or 'worth to be guarded,' all inherent in the cultural image of the Imperial Crown, but in addition once more explicitly addressed in the verbal comments below, are meant to be transferred to the brand image of the beverage.

The device of meaning transfer apparent in these ads is one of semiotic parasitism. The ad's purpose is to enhance the image of the brand at the cost of the higher symbolic values associated with the crown in a process of *parasitical semiosis*. The strategy operates mainly by means of indices, which naturally attract the reader's attention and only then point to the less interesting product represented in juxtaposition with them. Such indices can be found in several places of this ad. In the juxtaposition of crown and bottle, the crown serves as an index pointing by its high attention value (and uniqueness) to the bottle next to it; the bottle *participates* ('is part of') the fame irradiating from the picture of the crown. The product name, 'Beefeater,' is itself an index of the product it designates (all proper names are indices), but it is also an index in many other respects. Homonymous with the name of the guardians of the royal treasures kept in the Tower of London, traditionally also called 'Beefeaters,' this brand name not only parasitically participates by its own name in the fame of the guardians of the Tower but also profits from their fine reputation indexically insofar as these guardians are in professional contiguity with the royal treasures they guard. The label, an index of the product to which it is attached (as all labels are), contains in its graphic design further indices associating the product with the values of the Royal treasures by the principle of contiguity. On it, we see iconic representations of medals won in '1823, 1911, 1924,' which serve as indices of the quality of the product. There is the place name 'London' (a verbal index of the capital of England), a picture of the crown (an icon, which in relation to the bottle marks it indexically as a 'royal' product), an icon of the Tower of London, which is an index in relation to the treasures kept there, and, of course, the icon of the Beefeater guarding all this.

In the end, the ad suggests so many similarities between the product and the crown that the uncritical reader may be led to believe that there is also an iconic relationship between the gin contained in the bottle and the treasures kept in the Tower of London. What seemed to be related only indexically, at first sight, now seems to be similar and hence iconically related, too: the name of the product is not only similar to, but is even a *copy* of, the guardians' name. Both the crown and the gin are 'guarded' by valiant guardians placed in front of the place in which they are kept. It is true that the Beefeater guarding the gin is only a picture of a Beefeater (on the label of the bottle). The iconic sign of the guardian thus turns out to be a visual metaphor. Whereas the crown is literally guarded by the traditional Beefeaters, the gin is only metaphorically guarded by them: by the picture of the guardian in the center of its label. This set of similarities makes the product, which has so many similarities with the treasures of England, a metaphorical icon of these 'treasures.' Metaphorically, we are led to conclude that not only the Tower of London but also the bottle of Beefeater Gin contains a treasure. This parasitic iconicity is coupled with the claim made by the ambiguous and vague top line that 'There is only one,' which we are led to read as 'There are really two unique treasures to be discovered here.' Read literally, the referent of the pronoun 'one' can only be the crown, since only the crown is unique, whereas the 'treasure' contained in the bottle is not literally a precious treasure. Metaphorically, the top line,

which claims 'uniqueness,' is also meant to refer to the branded product. Uniqueness, according to this claim, is the main quality shared by both objects in juxtaposition. If all these implicit and explicit claims become firmly rooted in the consumer's minds and if it becomes a belief and habit that this product is as unique as the Imperial Crown, the brand has the chance of becoming a true symbolic legisign, a symbol of values rooted in laws and habits. However, in the language of consumer goods, symbols tend to change with consumers' preferences and habits. Symbols live, but they can die, too. The efforts of advertisers are efforts to prevent their brand images from disappearing from the consumers' attention and memory.

REFERENCES

Arnheim, R. (1954) *Art and Visual Perception*. Berkeley, CA: University of California Press.

Ashwin, C. (1984) 'Drawing, design and semiotics', in V. Margolin (ed.), *Design Discourse*. Chicago, IL: University of Chicago Press. pp. 199–209.

Austin, J. L. (1962) *How to Do Things with Words*. Oxford: Oxford University Press.

Barthes, R. (1964) 'Rhétorique de l'image', *Communications*, 4: 40–51.

Barthes, R. (1967) *Système de la Mode*. Paris: Seuil.

Barthes, R. (1977) *Image—Music—Text*. New York: Hill & Wang.

Barthes, R. (1980) *La chambre claire: Note sur la photographie*. Paris: Cahiers du Cinéma.

Benveniste, E. (1969) 'Sémiologie de la langue', *Semiotica*, 1: 1–12, 127–135.

Boehm, G. (1994) 'Die Bilderfrage', in G. Boehm (ed.), *Was ist ein Bild?* München: Fink. pp. 325–343.

Calabrese, O. (1980) 'From the semiotics of painting to the semiotics of pictorial text', *Versus*, 25: 3–27.

Carter, C. L. (1972) 'Syntax in language and painting', *The Structurist*, 12: 45–50.

Carter, C. L. (1976) 'Painting and language', *Leonardo*, 9: 111–118.

Deledalle, G. (1979) *Théorie et pratique du signe*. Paris: Payot.

Eco, U. (1968) *La struttura assente*. Milano: Bompiani. German translation (1972) *Einführung in die Semiotik*. München: Fink.

Eco, U. (1976) *A Theory of Semiotics*. Bloomington, IN: Indiana University Press.

Eco, U. (1984) *Semiotics and the Philosophy of Language*. Bloomington, IN: Indiana University Press.

Eco, U. (1985) 'How culture conditions the colors we see', in M. Blonsky (ed.), *On Signs*. Baltimore, MD: Johns Hopkins University Press. pp. 157–175.

Edeline, F., Klinkenberg, J.-M. and Minguet, P. (Groupe µ). (1992) *Traité du signe visuel*. Paris: Seuil.

Floch, J. M. (1985) *Petites mythologies de l'oeil et de l'esprit: Pour une sémiotique plastique*. Paris–Amsterdam: Hadès-Benjamins.

Floch, J. M. (1989) 'The semiotics of the plastic arts and the language of advertising', in P. Perron and F. Collins (eds.), *Paris School Semiotics II: Practice*. Amsterdam: Benjamins. pp. 55–77.

Floch, J. M. (1990) *Sémiotique, marketing et communication: Sous les signes, les stratégies*. Paris: Presses University de France. Translated by Orr-Bodkin, R. (2001) *Semiotics, Marketing and Communication: Beneath the Signs, the Strategies*. Houndmills: Palgrave Macmillan.

Fontanille, J. (1995) *Sémiotique du visible*. Paris: Presses University de France.

Goodman, N. (1968) *Languages of Art*. Indianapolis, IN: Bobbs-Merrill.

Halawa, M. A. (2008) *Wie sind Bilder Möglich? Argumente für eine Semiotische Fundierung des Bildbegriffes*. Köln: Halem.

Iversen, M. (1986) 'Saussure vs Peirce: Models for a semiotics of visual art', in A. L. Rees and F. Borzello (eds.), *The New Art History*. London: Camden. pp. 82–94.

Krampen, M. (1983) *Icons of the Road* (=*Semiotica*, 44[1–2]). Berlin: Mouton de Gruyter.

Kress, G. and van Leeuwen, T. (1996) *Reading Images: The Grammar of Visual Design*. London: Routledge.

Lindekens, R. (1976) *Essai de sémiotique visuelle*. Paris: Klincksieck.

Marin, L. (1971) 'Eléments pour une sémiologie picturale', in L. Marin (ed.), *Etudes sémiologiques*. Paris: Klincksieck. pp. 17–43.

Meier-Oeser, S. (1997) *Die Spur des Zeichens*. Berlin: Mouton de Gruyter.

Metz, C. (1968) *Essais sur la signification au cinéma I*. Paris: Klincksieck.

Nadin, M. (ed.) (1985) *The Meaning of the Visual: On Defining the Field* (=*Semiotica*, 52[3–4]). Berlin: Mouton de Gruyter.

Nadin, M. (1990) 'Design and semiotics', in W. A. Koch (ed.), *Semiotics in the Individual Sciences*. Bochum: Brockmeyer. pp. 418–436.

Nöth, W. (1972) *Strukturen des Happenings*. Hildesheim, New York: Olms.

Nöth, W. (1990) *Handbook of Semiotics*. Bloomington, IN: Indiana University Press.

Nöth, W. (1998) 'The language of commodities', *International Journal of Research in Marketing*, 4: 173–186.

Nöth, W. (2000) *Handbuch der Semiotik*, 2nd edn. Stuttgart: Metzler.

Nöth, W. (2003) 'Photography between reference and self-reference', in R. Horak (ed.), *Rethinking Photography I+II: Narration and New Reduction in Photography*. Salzburg: Fotohof Edition. pp. 22–39.

Nöth, W. (2004) 'Zur Komplementarität von Sprache und Bild aus semiotischer Sicht', *Mitteilungen des Deutschen Germanistenverbandes*, 51(1): 8–22.

Nöth, W. (2005a) 'Warum Bilder Zeichen sind: Bild- und Zeichenwissenschaft', in S. Majetschak (ed.), *Bild-Zeichen: Perspektiven einer Wissenschaft vom Bild*. München: Fink. pp. 49–61.

Nöth, W. (2005b) 'Zeichentheoretische Grundlagen der Bildwissenschaft', in K. Sachs-Hombach (ed.), *Bildwissenschaft zwischen Reflexion und Anwendung*. Köln: Halem. pp. 33-44.

Nöth, W. (2007a) 'The death of photography in self-reference', in W. Nöth and N. Bishara (eds.), *Self-Reference in the Media*. Berlin: Mouton de Gruyter. pp. 95–106.

Nöth, W. (2007b) 'Die Karte und ihre Territorien in der Geschichte der Kartographie', in J. Glauser and C. Kiening (eds.), *Text—Bild—Karte. Kartographien der Vormoderne*. Freiburg: Rombach. pp. 39–68.

Nöth, W. (2007c) 'Metapictures and self-referential pictures', in W. Nöth and N. Bishara (eds.), *Self-Reference in the Media*. Berlin: Mouton de Gruyter. pp. 61–78.

Nöth, W. (2009a) 'Bildsemiotik', in K. Sachs-Hombach (ed.), *Bildtheorien: Anthropologische und kulturelle Grundlagen des Visualistic Turn*. Frankfurt/Main: Suhrkamp. pp. 235–254.

Nöth, W. (2009b) 'Metareference from a semiotic perspective', in W. Wolf (ed.), *Metareference across Media: Theory and Case studies*. Amsterdam: Rodopi. pp. 89–134.

Nöth, W. (2010) 'Semiotic foundations of pragmatics', in W. Bublitz and N. Norrick (eds.), *Handbook of Pragmatics*. Berlin: Mouton de Gruyter.

Nöth, W. and Santaella, L. (2000) 'Bild, Malerei und Photographie aus der Sicht der peirceschen Semiotik'. in U. Wirth (ed.), *Die Welt als Zeichen und Hypothese*. Frankfurt/Main: Suhrkamp. pp. 354–374.

Paris, J. (1975) *Painting and Linguistics*. Pittsburgh, PA: Carnegie-Mellon University.

Peirce, C. S. (1931–1958) *Collected Papers, Vols 1–6*, C. Hartshorne and P. Weiss (eds.); *Vols 7–8*, A. W. Burks (ed.). Cambridge, MA: Harvard University Press. [Cited as CP. References are to volumes and paragraphs.]

Saint-Martin, F. (1990) *Semiotics of Visual Language*. Bloomington, IN: Indiana University Press.

Santaella, L. and Nöth, W. (1998) *Imagem: Cognição, Semiótica, Mídia*. São Paulo: Iluminuras.

Santaella, L. and Nöth, W. (2010) *Estratégias Semióticas da Publicidade*. São Paulo: Cengage

Schefer, J. L. (1969) *Scénographie d'un tableau*. Paris: Seuil.

Sebeok, T. A. and Umiker-Sebeok, J. (eds.) (1995) *Advances in Visual Semiotics*. Berlin: Mouton de Gruyter.

Sonesson, G. (1989) *Pictorial Concepts*. Lund: Lund University Press.

Sonesson, G. (1993) 'Die Semiotik des Bildes: Zum Forschungsstand am Anfang der 90er Jahre', *Zeitschrift für Semiotik*, 15: 127–160.

Stjernfelt, F. (2007) *Diagrammatology: An Investigation on the Borderlines of Phenomenology, Ontology, and Semiotics*. Berlin: Springer.

Thürlemann, F. (1984) 'Die Farbe in der Malerei', in T. Borbé (ed.), *Semiotics Unfolding*. Berlin: Mouton de Gruyter. pp. 1389–1396.

Thürlemann, F. (1990) *Vom Bild zum Raum: Beiträge zu einer semiotischen Kunstwissenschaft*. Köln: DuMont.

Zemsz, A. (1967) 'Les optiques cohérentes (La peinture est-elle langage?)', *Revue d'esthétique*, 2: 40–73.

17

Press Photography and Visual Rhetoric[1]

Terence Wright

INTRODUCTION

It used to be common practice for fish and chip shops to wrap their produce in old newspaper, thus giving rise to a derogatory description of the print media as 'tomorrow's fish-and-chip wrapping.'[2] The rock singer Elvis Costello even used this metaphor in his song 'Fish 'n' Chip paper' to refer to the superficiality and short life span of news stories. Similar to pop music, news is subject to fashion, triviality, and chance factors. Just as songs make their way up the music charts, so news stories enter the running orders of news organizations. Situated in a highly competitive climate, they vie with each other to attain prime headline position. And while stories may come and go (from old favorites to one-hit wonders), the overall structure of the news remains intact. For instance, irrespective of the amount or relevance of possible news items, the *Ten O'Clock News* always lasts half-an-hour. Whatever might be the number or magnitude of the daily events happening in the world, there will always be 30 minutes of television news.[3] This means

that, depending on competition (that is, the other stories running that day), an item high on the agenda one day might appear at the end of the running order on another, or perhaps be unlucky enough not to feature at all. News photographs also fall into this strange pattern of luck and judgment. They can result from the opportune moment of a photographer being in the right place at the right time, or they can be highly contrived with little or no actual news content in order to amuse the reader. Nonetheless, the presence or absence of visual images has the power to make or break the worthiness of any news story.

Visual rhetoric is concerned with understanding how images communicate, how they function in a social and cultural environment, and how they embody meaning. In the press context, photographs might be seen primarily as conveyors of information about important events in the world—but as we shall see—the structure of the news media and the expectations of readers somewhat complicate the matter. We have to regard press photographs as part of a complex network of cultural phenomena. Rhetoric is normally considered to be a persuasive skill, classically to convince us of a point of view; in the modern age, to encourage us to purchase goods. However, we can also consider it has a role in the formation of community identity and reinforcing our beliefs. Readers also look to photographs to convey something of the emotion of the event, or they can seek visual information that will amuse or entertain—and the news media are only too happy to comply.

THOUSANDS DEAD

In 1999, the journalist and television foreign-correspondent Michael Nicholson wrote an article for London's *Evening Standard* newspaper titled, 'Thousands dead in India—not many interested.' Critical of the workings of his own profession, Nicholson provided some important insights into what he called 'the chemistry of the news agenda.' His particular focus was the reporting of humanitarian disasters. Written during the week following the Orissa cyclone, when more than 10,000 died and 2 million people were left homeless, he asked some pertinent if rhetorical questions:

> How do you decide which calamities to cover and which to ignore, which tragedy will make the lead story and which will be consigned to a less conspicuous space?... Does the reader and viewer wonder at the decision that places the deaths of 217 EgyptAir passengers and crew above those of many, many thousands of drowned Indians?... Throughout this week, India's worst natural calamity this century has not appeared on the front page of any of our national newspapers and you have to ask, why? (Nicholson, 1999: 13)

Nicholson concluded that the Orissa disaster did not make the headlines because there were no pictures that could match the first eyewitness accounts. Even in instances when pictures do finally arrive, 'we filter out the worst under the banner of "good taste" and "decency," parameters set by editors determined not to cause offence' (Nicholson,

1999: 13). Most frequently the editor 'opts for caution at the expense of reality,' selecting one image to epitomize the story, and thus arises one of the essential problems of visual imagery: To what extent can a single picture be representative of the wider situation? According to Nicholson, 'To convey the deaths of thousands you will be shown the body of one ... at a distance, on the long lens' (1999: 13), in order not to cause viewers to turn away. How does this affect the impact of the item?

As a subject for academic research (particularly in the context of the social sciences), press photographs are especially problematic. As readers of newspapers we do look to the photograph to provide a visual identity for a story. The anthropologist Marcus Banks has remarked that this illustrative use of the newspaper photograph serves 'as a visual clue to allow readers to follow the story over the days as it unfold[s]' (Banks, 2001: 16). Often this clue puts a 'face' to the story, personalizing the words we read or hear. Our need to identify a story's face may be simply an instinctive response: when someone at the back of the audience asks a question, few present can resist turning round to get a view of the questioner. This is a basic psychological response whereby 'The visual system *hunts* for comprehension and clarity' (Gibson, 1979: 219).[4] Sensationalist newspapers tend to capitalize on this tendency, demanding that press photographers obtain mug shots of current news celebrities to capture the attention of readers. These shots do not just illustrate the story: their inclusion implies that seeing a person's picture enables us 'to take the measure' of them (Highfield et al., 2009). According to Elias (1991: 121), the human face has evolved as a 'signaling board':

> Its unique characteristics can serve as a reminder of the singularity of human beings... . The face is one of the chief instruments for indicating their feelings with which human beings are endowed by nature, that is, as a result of an evolutionary process. (Elias, 1991: 120)

So the desire to scrutinize the photograph of someone in the news, whether a politician or a mass murderer, may not necessarily stem from a ghoulish, voyeuristic desire, but from a natural reflex response closely related to our usual strategy for obtaining information about the world. Seeing someone's face can provide clues to their character and motivation.

> The face in Western culture … is central to building a picture of who someone is, and it is through expressive features of the face that we gain access to a perception of who someone "really" is. (Howson, 2004: 29)

But photography involves an additional factor in the process of information transfer: people tend to present themselves to the camera as they wish to be perceived, so that the photograph already carries a deliberate implicit message. Such signals can also be culturally determined. When sitting for a portrait photograph, 'The sitter addresses to the viewer an act of reverence, of courtesy, according to conventional rules' (Bourdieu, 1990: 82). These rules vary from culture to culture. While Sprague (1978) describes how photographic poses in West Africa conform to cultural conventions, this chapter later addresses the way choice of attire—the leather jacket for example—can carry iconic connotations and thus add layers to visual messages. It is no coincidence that the teenage killers who perpetrated the Columbine High School massacre of 1999 wore long trench coats similar to those worn by the merciless gunmen in the opening scenes of Sergio Leone's film *Once Upon a Time in the West* (1968) or the characters in Larry and Andy Wachowski's futuristic dystopian film *The Matrix* (1999) (see Ogle et al., 2003; Frymer, 2009). So when we read the report of a gruesome murder and ask 'What kind of person could do such a thing?' in publishing a mug shot of the perpetrator, newspapers are, in effect, replying, 'This sort of person.' A photograph is not, however, a person: whether static artificial displays of photographs in newspapers really deliver the information we seek as part of 'everyday' perception, in order to make good judgments, is a matter for contention.

AN UNEMPLOYED MAN

In his analysis of the way visual images can illustrate abstract concepts, Banks (2001) describes how newspapers use photographs like visual figures of speech: *metaphor* and *metonym*. While 'Visual metaphor can also involve a function of "transference", transferring certain qualities from one sign to another… *metonymy* is a function which involves using one signified to stand for another signified which is *directly related* to it or *closely associated* with it in some way' (Chandler, 1994).[5] Banks provides two hypothetical, yet quite commonplace and easily recognizable examples. First, for 'metaphor,' he suggests 'an unemployed man can be photographed in a bleak urban wasteland, the empty building plots and boarded up windows standing as metaphors for the emptiness of his life and the closure of opportunity' (Banks, 2001: 18). Second, for 'metonym,' 'a photograph of a single African child, stomach bulging due to malnutrition, stands for all starving people in that society' (Banks, 2001: 18).[6] As expressed by McQuire, such metonymic use of the image of the starving victim 'loses specificity and becomes emblematic, contributing to a media environment in which all images slide towards radical interchangeability. All peoples affected by famine can be made into the same archetypal victim… ' (1998: 59).

Of course, we are all familiar with these kinds of images, but how aware are we of the way this calculated use of visual metaphor and metonymy affects us in practice? If we take a specific example—Banks' unemployed man is a good one—to show photographically someone *not* doing something (that is not working), presents a considerable challenge. In January 1939, this assignment was allocated to photographer Kurt Hutton. He was commissioned by the weekly UK journal *Picture Post* to photograph the day-to-day life of an unemployed man living in Peckham, South London. Hutton's assignment, working with journalist Sidney Jacobson, resulted in a published photo-story consisting of 17 photographs. Taken on the eve of the outbreak of World War II (1 September 1939) in the heyday of the photo-illustrated magazine, the images capture a world about to disappear forever, but highlight the problem of unemployment that stubbornly remains with us today. The distinction between metaphor and metonym is blurred.

Through the series of photographs, Alfred Smith is shown standing in the dole queue inside the Labour Exchange, his wife and children waiting outside. We follow Smith in his quest for a job, then his return home, unsuccessful. The settings for all these images are certainly 'bleak' (see Figure 17.1). However, the last lines of Jacobson's copy firmly place the unemployed man in Banks' metonymic category—that of the individual standing for all of those in the same state in a society. The copy reads: '... he is beginning to feel that perhaps there is no longer a place for him in our scheme of things, that he must change it or perish.

Figure 17.1 *Alfred Smith*. **1939. Photograph by Kurt Hutton / Hulton Archive / Getty Images. Reproduced with permission**

He wants work, he cannot find it. And Alfred Smith is only one of 2 million' (Jacobson, 1970: 53). This metonymic dénouement, in which the circumstances of the individual are extended to embrace the wider group, evidently all anxious, like Alfred, to change the scheme of things or perish, implies a barely concealed revolutionary threat. Three years later, maintaining its campaigning standpoint, *Picture Post* returned to the issue of unemployment.[7] This time, concluding a sequence of nine photographs, a picture of Alfred Smith reappears from the 1939 *Unemployed* article. The earlier version had been captioned 'The Picture of Our Time: Alone, Walking for Miles, Trying to Find a Job' accompanied by a text that personalizes the article as Alfred Smith's story—but the 4 January 1941 article *Social Security* does not mention him by name. The photograph of Smith with a dog, simply captioned 'The Unwanted Worker,' performs the function of the dénouement. In this context, while still maintaining its *metaphoric* function, the photograph has moved much closer to a *metonymic* role—standing for all unemployed workers in the industrial environment, like Banks' 'single African child... stand[ing] for all starving people in that society' (2001: 18). Metaphor and metonym are conflated in a single image with high impact.

In 1978, *Picture Post* editor Tom Hopkinson told me, in conversation, that the dog actually had no connection with Alfred Smith whatsoever. The stray had just wandered into the picture. While Smith has his back to us walking into the mist—Banks' metaphor signifying 'the emptiness of his life and the closure of opportunity'—we automatically connect him with the animal. The dog looks straight towards the camera, fixing the viewer with its gaze and, despite its accidental appearance in the photograph, it is the dog's *metaphoric* role that completes the picture. Does it matter that Smith is not a dog owner? So long as this is a feature article with a wider reference, not a specific news story purporting to record factual actuality, not really: the purpose of the dog is rhetorical. It acts as a kind of narrator. While Smith walks away, hands in pockets with despondent demeanor, it is the dog that takes command of the situation.[8] Its eye contact challenges the reader as if to say 'Look! He's walking into an uncertain future. He's tried everything. What can *you* do about it?' thus reinforcing the campaigning standpoint of the article.

Azoulay takes a highly ethical standpoint, claiming that: 'It is very rare to come across a photographer who has intentionally created the situation [he or] she has photographed,' offering as evidence that 'the public scandal erupting around a few such events is a testimony to their occurrence being rare and exceptional' (2008: 156). The instance of Smith's dog shows that random factors and chance occurrences can actually contribute to the creation of pictorial elements which are essentially fictional, but which add impact to a journalistic image and are therefore used to express and communicate—some would say interpret—facts. Azoulay's claim does not stand up to scrutiny: ethics can be flexible in journalism, as anyone who has worked in the news media knows. Many press photographs are designed and constructed from the outset to create a specific effect, particularly in the field of 'human interest' stories.

HUMAN INTEREST STORIES

> … the press photograph is an object that has been worked on, chosen, composed, constructed, treated according to professional or ideological norms. (Barthes, 1977: 19)

Editors' ideas of 'good taste' referred to by Nicholson (see above) are not the only determinants of the way news pictures may be standardized. Many are posed to grab attention through sensationalism, 'hooking' readers' interest to sell the paper. Usually, these photographs fall under the category of 'human interest' stories, which can take the form of premeditated manufactured observations designed to amuse the reader. For example, in his *Pictures on a Page* (1978: 44–46), newspaper editor Harold Evans provides an example of a constructed Easter story, describing how a photographer took a newborn chick to London Zoo in order to photograph it on an elephant's trunk. I myself once heard of a photographer who hired an actor, dressed him as a London city gent— pin-striped suit, bowler hat, and rolled umbrella—set him astride a 'space hopper,' and instructed him to hop across Westminster Bridge. With Big Ben and the Houses of Parliament in the background, the crossing was photographed and captioned 'London businessmen find a new way to get to work'. The photographer had staged the photograph to include all the ingredients needed to appeal to the paper's readership. An image had been created by collating symbolic elements and effective clichés that comprise an internationally recognized stereotype— businessman, London. Then, by including the space hopper, a child's toy purporting to be a viable mode of transport, not only is the metonymic stereotype challenged but also the image teases the viewer, demanding investigation. The curious reader is impelled to seek further information as to how this bizarre situation had arisen, and this stimulus is effective, even if we immediately suspect that the image may be set up, pulling us in with a trivial trick. It is the high degree of artifice employed in the construction of press photographs—from Nicholson's editors who impose 'taste' to constructed images manufactured for purposes of mild entertainment— that raises a question as to their value for the serious academic study of their subject matter.

Items such as space hoppers provide ready-made props for frivolous news stories. Easily categorized as 'normal' if pictured as a simple child's toy, when they move into the adult world, they may not be so innocent. Newspapers can, it seems, just as easily imbue them with 'whacky' and dubious sexual connotations. Under the headline 'Hollyoaks hotties strip off,' *The Sun* journalist Nadia

Mendoza proclaimed: 'The girls paired their saucy smalls with killer heels as they unleashed their bouncing bosoms while bopping along on space hoppers' (2 June 2008). This 'news' story concerned a photo-shoot for a pin-up calendar featuring six of the female stars of Channel 4's *Hollyoaks* soap opera.[9] The news value is minimal; the entertainment value is questionable. Here the editors have not exercised much of their power to avoid offence. If there is to be any academic value, or factual information, to be extracted from a story of this kind, it is to be obtained by reading between the lines and examining the motivation behind the pictures. While the immediate intention may be to titillate readers with pictures of pneumatic-breasted actresses spreading their legs around pneumatic toys, the creation of this rather desperate photo-opportunity can also be seen as indicating a response to dwindling audiences for the soap. Indeed, it transpires that while, according to BARB (Broadcasters' Audience Research Board), in the year 2000 *Hollyoaks* enjoyed viewing figures of over 3.5 million, by 2007 these had dropped to 1.2 million.[10] Desperate times, it seems, call for desperate measures—3 months after the story appeared in the papers, the *Hollyoaks* soap opera launched its own range of perfumes! Notwithstanding such commercial impetus, according to Keeble, many of the newspapers' titillatory stories may also have a subversive humorous function:

A lot of their contrived stories are based on down-right lies. But in a complex way, people want to be lied to, seduced into a fantasy world while at the same time seeing through the lies. (1994: 164)

This commentary might certainly apply to the businessman on Westminster Bridge, but it would be even more apposite, in Keeble's terms, to the *Hollyoak* bouncers. Such stories, he suggests, may be 'built on the smutty, cheeky humor associated with holiday postcards and bare bottoms. It's guaranteed to provoke a giggle' (1994: 165). It would be easy to write off the *Hollyoaks* article as

simple sexploitation, but Keeble's notion of the 'fantasy world' suggests a Rabelaisian impulse on the part of newspaper editors preoccupied with sexual innuendo where 'the elements associated with the bottom part of the body ... are given comic privilege over the spirit and the head' (White, 1985: 105). Perhaps its promoters were anxious for viewers to perceive the series as comedy—even lighter entertainment than soap. And indeed there are strong elements of the carnivalesque 'world turned upside down' in the space-hopping businessman.

However frivolous or contrived, Keeble believes that as journalism, the human interest story 'stresses the importance of human sources as opposed to abstract ideas' (1994: 158–159); for readers it feeds 'a curiosity people have about others' (159), reinforcing the suggestion already made in the observations on human facial expression above. This function, as visual reflections of cultural phenomena, places such stories well within the domain of anthropology. At the same time, it is ironic that often the *Hollyoaks* story's brand of trivia and titillation is found in columns adjacent to reports of death and disaster in such tabloids as the *Sun* (as discussed by Nicholson above). From the editor's point of view, juxtaposing trivial sensation with serious world news is not necessarily adhering to a double standard. Eamonn McCabe, picture editor of the *Guardian* from 1988 to 2001, writes (about another 1930s photograph by Kurt Hutton):

Although *Picture Post* set the standard for serious photojournalism, lighter material was also regularly included—you can't sell newspapers and magazines on news and politics alone; then as now, readers want to be entertained. (2005: 48)

At first glance, this rationale seems unproblematic—classically paralleled by Shakespeare's deployment of the gravedigger's macabre humor in *Hamlet*, to counterpoint and leaven the tragedy of events at Elsinore. However, some apparently innocent examples not only indicate a blurring of the divisions between news and entertainment but also between objectivity and narrativity:

> News and entertainment have never been absolutely separate, and there is no reason why they should be. The best journalists have always been good story-tellers. Story-telling is essential to journalism because it generates popular interest... . [N]ews has never been only about providing information in the narrow sense, but also a contribution to dialogue about values and collective identity, and that kind of dialogue is carried on largely through narrative. (Hallin, 2000: 229)

The simplistic explanation is not always adequate. Campaigning groups routinely exploit the newspapers' propensity for the trivial and frivolous. For example, tempting the news media with their own constructed event—as aware of the international metaphoric value of Big Ben as the photographer of the space-hopping businessmen—on Monday 11 June 1984, Greenpeace activists climbed the Clock Tower, to unfurl a banner bearing the words 'Time to stop nuclear testing' (see Figure 17.2). On this occasion, the news media were eager to report the story, even though it had been purposefully staged by the protestors.

In the process of the stunt, an iconic picture—a single photographic image—was created, which captures the central message of the story. Some photographs are able, in this way, to transcend their immediate news context and themselves become international symbols.

STREET FIGHTING MAN

The Rolling Stones' 1968 song *Street Fighting Man* is an appropriate symbol of its era. Social unrest and street battles were taking

Figure 17.2 *Greenpeace Protest*, **London 1984. Photograph by Terence Wright /BBC Television News. Reproduced with permission**

place in numerous European cities ignited by a range of causes: the Prague Spring, American Civil Rights protests, 'Valle Giulia' student protest in Rome, protests against US involvement in the Vietnam War across the USA and in London's Grosvenor Square; the May demonstrations in Paris; a student demonstration turned massacre in Mexico City; the so-called 'Rodney Riots' in Kingston, Jamaica; and civil rights demonstrations in Derry, marking the beginning of Northern Ireland's 'Troubles.'

The second line of the Stones' song refers to summer and fighting in the street, and is a deliberate rephrasing of the seemingly innocent Motown hit *Dancing in the Street,* released 4 years earlier by Martha and the Vandellas (1964)—written by William 'Mickey' Stevenson, Marvin Gaye, and Ivy Jo

Hunter (Smith, 2001). Stevenson's inspiration for the song was the sight of people in Detroit cooling off in the jets of water from street fire hydrants.[11] To him, it looked as if they were dancing in the water: an image which was already something of a photographic cliché. Often used by newspapers to indicate the intensity of a heat wave, it is a theme that appears in the repertoire of many famous US photographers, for example, Weegee's (Arthur Fellig) *Cooling Down* of the 1940s and Bruce Davidson's (see Figure 17.3) *East 100th Street, Spanish Harlem, USA, 1966.*[12]

Cooling off in the jet of a fire hydrant can be seen as a minor act of civil disobedience, though especially pertinent as fire hoses were used to combat the US Civil Rights demonstrators. As an endorsement of his successful representation of the era, Davidson's photographs

Figure 17.3 *East 100th Street, Spanish Harlem, USA,* **1966. Photograph by Bruce Davidson / Magnum Photos. Reproduced with permission**

of demonstrators struggling against jets of water appeared in the *Road to Freedom* exhibition in Atlanta, 2008.

> ... his emphasis on the desperate attempt of these youths to continue to brandish their handwritten placards in the face of a brutal onslaught adds a distinct layer of emotional power to these pictures. (Cox, 2008: 38)

However, it was unfortunate that in July 1967, while Martha and the Vandellas were on the stage of the Fox Theatre, Detroit, launching into their greatest hit 'Dancing in the Street,' an outbreak of rioting and arson should break out in the city. Two years later, when their tour reached England:

> The British press aggravated [Martha] Reeves when someone put a microphone in her face and asked her if she was a militant leader. The British journalist wanted to know if Reeves agreed, as many people had claimed, that "Dancing in the Street" was a call to riot. To Reeves, the query was patently absurd. "My Lord, it was a *party* song", she remarked in retrospect. (Smith, 2001: 2)

While Jagger and Richards had been prepared to rewrite the second line of the song (changing 'dancing in the street' to 'fighting in the street'), making quite explicit the seditious interpretation of the lyrics, the US Civil Rights campaign had already adopted the original, with its newly acquired political connotation, as something of an anthem.[13] While this demonstrates the impact on popular music of the changing social, cultural, and political environments, photographs, too, have the ability to attain an iconic status which epitomizes periods of civil unrest. In 1968, partly inspired by its US counterpart, in Northern Ireland the Civil Rights demonstrations and the counter-reactions to these protests marked the beginning of 'The Troubles.' One of the lasting images from this conflict is Clive Limpkin's photograph of a boy wearing a gas mask (Figure 17.4).

As a press photo, arising from a chance encounter, Limpkin's image contains as many significant ingredients and contradictory metaphors as the constructed photograph of the space-hopping businessman. While the

Figure 17.4   *Boy Petrol Bomber,* Londonderry. 1969. Photograph by Clive Limpkin. Reproduced with permission

primed petrol-bomb bottle suggests a lethally aggressive intent, and despite the subject's features being almost obscured by the mask, we are left in little doubt that this is the image of a child. The mask ostensibly acts as a means of protection, perhaps from the intended explosion; but a need for protection also implies a sense of vulnerability. From a practical point of view, the type of gas mask the boy is wearing would have been unlikely to offer any protection against the type of CS gas used by the Royal Ulster Constabulary (RUC) or British Army in 1969. Survivors of an earlier era, the filters in these masks deteriorate with age. However in addition, they contain blue asbestos, which presents a significant hazard to the wearer and would militate against their being used under modern conditions.[14] The reflection on the mask makes the precise direction of the boy's gaze indeterminate, but there is a clue to the location of the event: the badge on his leather jacket displays a map of a divided Ireland. The leather jacket itself can be seen in popular culture as a metaphor of youthful rebellion, as instigated by the character Johnny Strabler (played by Marlon Brando) in László Benedek's film *The Wild One* (1953).[15] The jazz singer and film and TV critic George Melly (not particularly renowned for his studies of Sigmund Freud) aptly described the Brando character's simultaneous potency and threat to conventional society as 'a black leather phallus whom it was necessary for society to castrate in its own interests' (1972: 33). Melly continued by pointing out the trans-Atlantic influence of this image on the UK's youth culture of the 1950s and 1960s: '[Brando] was the link between the dangerous motor-biking nomads of America and their British working-class imitators' (33). While activating the ethos of *The Wild One*, Limpkin's photograph is also representative of its own era, epitomizing and providing a metonymic image of the worldwide protest movements that characterized the last years of the 1960s.

Limpkin, photographing for the *Daily Sketch*—a national UK tabloid that was to fold 2 years later[16]—was not too impressed by the subject of his photograph, but recognized its potential for iconic status.

> If ever we photographers needed a symbol of the fighting, this was it. Wearing an over-sized gas-mask; a petrol bomb permanently in his hand, so it seemed; and a map of the whole problem on his jacket.
>   For hours he taunted the police and troops, ignoring the cameras. He was about eight. God knows what he's advanced to now.[17] (Limpkin, 1972: 121)

Referencing an earlier period of conflict, the significance of a photograph of a child wearing a gas mask was noted by the photographer August Sander in 1931. Although the petrol bomber is not exactly an infant, Sander's remarks shed an interesting light on Limpkin's more recent juxtaposition, emphasizing the connotation of the replacement of secure nurturing with destruction and violence:

> The newspapers are now preparing the populace for a coming bestial war in which poison gas will be used; they recommend gas masks to protect the lives of the civilian population. To photograph an infant wearing a gas mask, instead of being at its mother's breast, and to label the photograph as being from the Twentieth Century would be sufficient. It would express the whole brutal, inhuman spirit of the time in universally comprehensible form. (Sander, 1980: 30)[18]

Eleven years later, the war that Sander had predicted in 1931 was well underway. And in the year following the Japanese attack on Pearl Harbor, in 1942 an image was created more terrifying than Sander could anticipate: *The Mickey Mouse Gas Mask*, 'designed for small children in a valiant attempt to give them something that would work and still be fun' (Walk, 2010). War, toys, and children: resonant subjects with connotations that recur in different contexts, juxtapositions, and combinations throughout this survey.

Returning to the Derry *Petrol Bomber*, technically speaking, the wide aperture of Limpkin's lens has thrown the background out of focus—apart from the two blurred figures which frame the bomber, there is nothing to indicate the precise context of the boy. Does Limpkin's approach therefore merit criticism? The issue is controversial. The use of *differential focus* as a personal aesthetic to isolate the *figure* of the photographer's interest from the *ground* of the location is embraced by some photographers, abhorred by others. In the newspaper context, as long as it produces the desired results, either strategy is fair game. The basic ingredients of the photograph may have contradictory connotations (as implied by Sander) but the photograph as a whole might well have the effect of capturing viewers' interest, leading them to seek out further information—the crucial requirement of the front page or cover photograph. In some senses, Limpkin's photograph has given a human identity to civil unrest—even though, ironically, the boy's face remains obscured. Like the metonymic photo of Alfred Smith, it can be said to go some way to satisfying the public's need for news imagery—but at the same time it communicates and expresses more than the individual circumstances of its capture.

Despite its virtues and high visual impact, as the visual component of a news story, the photograph of the boy in the gas mask would normally have a relatively short life, and could soon have been used to wrap fish and chips. But as news turns into history, some images are re-contextualized. Although the photograph shows us one individual, what does it contribute to the general picture of the events that took place? How effectively does it move viewers? While historian Ludmilla Jordanova questions the documentary value of Walker Evans's photographs of the American Depression of the 1930s, she admires them for their emotional iconic value: 'so much so that "the depression" and some kinds of documentary photography have become virtually synonymous' (Jordanova, 2006: 93).

In the case of Limpkin's photograph, we can view the boy from a number of perspectives: for example, as a local hero representing the outcome of the repression of an entire community; or (as Limpkin's caption would suggest), a young delinquent already set on the road to ruin. Given the appropriate contexts, the photograph could support the conflicting viewpoints of the British Army, Republicans or Loyalists as the three key players in the Northern Ireland Troubles. To confirm its iconic status, 25 years after the *Battle of the Bogside*, the boy in the photograph was 'canonized' through its renewed appearance. On a gable-end wall in the area known as Free Derry Corner in Northern Ireland, there is now a large painting of the boy, known locally as *The Petrol Bomber* mural, standing over 8.5 m (28 ft) in height, executed in the mediums of emulsion and acrylic paint. The 'Bogside Artists,' William and Tom Kelly, and Kevin Hasson, titled their work 'The Battle of The Bogside' (1994), as a commemoration of the 25th anniversary of The Battle of August 1969.[19] While the artists openly acknowledge their indebtedness to Limpkin, they felt it necessary to resite the bomber, and took the liberty

of adding the Rossville flats to the picture's background in an Adobe® Photoshop®-style montage. The flats (which were demolished in the 1980s as unfit for human habitation) formed the backdrop for the 'Battle' and the events of 'Bloody Sunday.'[20] The artists have also added clouds of CS gas and a couple of RUC policemen standing next to a burning building. While the muralists' (somewhat grandiose) interpretation of the *Petrol Bomber* is very different from that of Clive Limpkin, it does amount to significant praise for the photographer who first produced the image:

> Of all our murals, it is the one that appears to have the most appeal. Just as Michelangelo's Statue of David ushered in the new Republic and demonstrated Florentine "virtus" and self-reliance, so also does the *Petrol Bomber* mural put a face on the struggle for civil rights and gives voice to the resolve of oppressed peoples everywhere. Its popularity is owed to that. (The Bogside Artists, 2009: no page reference)

The internally uncontextualized original image is here appropriated to a particular cause (refocused from metonym to metaphor) by setting it in a very concrete background in time and place (see Figure 17.5).

Meanwhile, on the other side of the River Foyle, the petrol bomber makes yet another appearance, this time on a Loyalist mural (typical of the tit-for-tat exchange between rival political groups in the Province). In this context (appearing in a mural influenced by the CD cover of Iron Maiden's *The Trooper*), the interpretation is less generous, but all the same constitutes a back-handed recognition of the importance of Limpkin's photograph, providing further endorsement of the image's iconic status, particularly as the image has by now been adopted (but partly obscured by a seventeenth-century cannon) by the opposition (see Figure 17.6).

Limpkin himself recognizes that the position of the photographer is not a neutral one to start with. 'The covering journalist not only runs the risk of being "used" in propaganda exercises, but also in creating and prolonging rioting by his very presence' (1972: 149). This sentiment is further extended by Carruthers: 'Not infrequently, journalists and photographers return from war with the confession that they ceased to be mere observers and became "participants"' (2000: 273). The photographer's observation may not be neutral; but neither is it under his or her control: 'The photographer's intentions do not determine the meaning of the photograph, which will have its own career, blown by the whims and loyalties of the diverse communities that have use for it' (Sontag, 2003: 39).[21]

The rule of usefulness (to readers and/or editors) applies to the photographers themselves: 'We... would be sent out [to Northern Ireland] whenever trouble threatened... and brought back after a couple of weeks when the readers "grew tired" of Ulster' (Limpkin, personal communication, 4 March 2010). As far as Limpkin can remember, the *Petrol Bomber* never made it to the chippie,[22] and was never published in the newspapers—it appeared in print in his own book, *The Battle of the Bogside* (1972). Nonetheless, the image evidently captured the imagination of those who saw it, and has stood the test of time, to emerge as a national icon. Meanwhile, for the photographer himself, ruminating on the impact of his professional output, the position and longevity of serious journalism versus titillation provides a provocative full stop to this section:

Figure 17.5 *The Battle of The Bogside*, **Derry. 1994. The Bogside Artists. Photograph © 2009 Terence Wright**

> In 1972, my book, *The Battle of Bogside*, ... showing three years of fighting in Northern Ireland won the Robert Capa Gold Medal from Life magazine "for superlative photography requiring exceptional courage and enterprise abroad". (My photograph of the first topless girl to appear in *The Sun*, however, has failed to receive any official recognition). (Limpkin, 2009)

Figure 17.6 *Loyalist Mural with Petrol Bomber Detail* **(enlarged to the right). Artist/date unknown. Photograph © 2009 Terence Wright**

OUT OF AFRICA

In January 2008, reporter Lucy Adams and photographer Simon Murphy traveled to Northern Uganda to cover a story that had dropped out of the media spotlight: the abduction of children by the rebel group 'The Lord's Resistance Army' (LRA). A shaky ceasefire provided a window of opportunity for the journalists to see how people were coping with everyday life. Now that the children were returning to their villages, how would the issue of reconciliation be addressed? The outcome of the trip was an article titled 'A History of Violence' with 12 accompanying photographs. It appeared in Glasgow's *Herald Magazine* on Saturday 2 February 2008 (Figure 17.7). The cover photograph is of Dennis Oyeto, who had been abducted at the age of eight and forced to become a rebel soldier. At the time of writing, he was 18; but the photograph shows him holding a home-made toy gun that appears to have been tied together from old pieces of scrap metal, cloth, corks, and banana leaves. As in the image of the Derry bomber, the subject's overall appearance is one of ambiguity—adults kill to protect children: but … is this a child, killing? This world is upside-down indeed. But unlike the Derry *Petrol Bomber*, Oyeto's age is difficult to determine, as we pick up mixed messages from his serious and mature expression. Certainly not one of childlike innocence—contrasted with the childish 'weapon' he is carrying. Oyeto's attire is part tribal, part worse-for-wear, disheveled Western—perhaps typical for the African degraded rather than uplifted by contact with Europe. These visual connotations are reminiscent of another Marlon Brando character: the insane Colonel Walter Kurtz, who has 'gone native.' Dennis would not look out of place in Kurtz's jungle-based renegade army unit operating during the Vietnam War, in Francis Ford Coppola's film *Apocalypse Now* (1979).

However, unnervingly, there are closer affinities between the young tribesman and the old madman. The copy text reveals that young Oyeto is unable to remember how many people he has killed during his time as a soldier. Over a period of 7 years, he was forced to perform atrocious acts of cruelty, until he was finally able to escape and return home. Now he says he is a changed man. On the next page of the article, the photograph of Jenneth Oyella (Figure 17.8) is less obviously militaristic in appearance, but once again the copy reveals that her innocent, cheerful and friendly appearance belies her violent background. This is not a normal young woman.

Stories of abduction, enslavement, mutilation, murder, and rape are not normally considered to be popular subjects, particularly for a local paper's Saturday readership. Their publication in this case is impelled by individual journalists championing a cause; that it is a 'cause' which does not form part of the current news landscape makes the task especially worthwhile.[23] Indeed, the story fulfills many of the recommendations made by the International Broadcasting Trust's report on global news coverage, *Screening the World*. African stories are almost always complex, but are all too often represented using simplistic tribal stereotypes delivered to audiences unaware of the overall context, which reduce them to banality. To counteract this lack of local knowledge, 'Covering off-the-agenda stories [is] a vital way of providing a context, alternative perspectives and variety that audiences say they want' (Scott, 2008: 27).[24]

In some respects, the *Glasgow Herald* journalist and photographer featuring the human cost of internecine war, emphasizing the personal in traditional style, were swimming against the retreating tide of foreign news reporting of the 'developing world,' which has been subject to dramatic cutbacks by news agencies in recent years (as detailed by Scott 2008 and 2009, for example). They did include a local interest element, however, which linked the report directly with the concerns of readers (rather than devoting itself to issues with general, rather than neighborhood, impact): they interviewed a Glaswegian

**Figure 17.7   *Dennis Oyeto*. 2008. Photograph by Simon Murphy / the *Glasgow Herald*.
Reproduced with permission**

Figure 17.8 *Jenneth Oyella.* 2008. Photograph by Simon Murphy / the *Glasgow Herald*. Reproduced with permission

priest, who runs a radio station in Uganda for the Scottish Catholic International Aid Fund (SCIAF), with the aim of 'promoting the peaceful reintegration of former child soldiers in communities' (Adams, 2008: 9). Adams' six-page feature concludes with a call for action from readers, who are invited to donate money to SCIAF.

In 2008, the article won the local media section of the One World Media Awards. The virtues of such reporting are that both photography and text personalize the tragic and horrific situations in which some children and young people can find themselves. At the same time, the magazine has been generous in allocating enough space to allow the publication of a series of photographs to tell the story in some depth. Rather than dwelling on the sensationalist aspects, the article attempts to explain the wider context and circumstances of the subjects' plight. And in the UK environment, where television promotes holiday programs 'mostly about what tourists

could obtain cheaply from the developing world' (Department for International Development, 2000: 3), the article offers the reader a route of positive action that they themselves can take to help relieve the situation. This is engaged, not trivialized, photojournalism. It captures attention not through sensationalism, sexy bouncing, or quirky staging, but by offering an informed and thoughtful view of an issue considered by reporters, editors and readers to be of importance to us all. It does not offend the sensibilities of its viewers with overblown and numbing images of violence, but takes an approach where the metaphorical and metonymic properties of the image are juxtaposed to provide context and interpretation.

CONCLUSION

Despite the fact that photographers and journalists have long stipulated that the referential force matters in news photographs, it is the photo-graph's symbolic or connotative force ... that facilitates the durability and the memorability of the news image. (Zelizer, 2004: 130)

The standardization, and endless reproduc-tion and echoing, of press photography means that in order to assess its value as a legitimate subject for study, we have to consider the wider social, cultural, and political aspects of visual representation. Our understanding of the news is based upon 'assumptions about narrative, story-telling, human interest, and the conventions of photographic and linguistic presentation in news production' (Schudson, 2000: 192).

During the 1930s, it was the photo-illus-trated magazine with the picture essay that constituted a central means of communicat-ing in-depth news, social conditions (and tit-illation) to a broad readership. Nowadays, with few exceptions, newspapers and maga-zine features rely on one key photograph—but, in the best case, are unlikely to contain more than half-a-dozen images. A number of reasons have been cited for the demise of the photo magazine. Primary among them seems to be the proliferation of television journal-ism, which rapidly took over the role of sat-isfying the public's hunger for pictorial stimulation. This apparently does not apply to the current popularity of 'gossip' maga-zines such as *Hello* and *OK* where color photo-stories can run as many images as their antecedents:[25] perhaps this is because the celebrities who constitute the pabulum of these TV-based magazines exist for the public as narrated images in their onscreen life, so the photoplay aspects of the journalism are a medium-specific phenomenon.

Another contributing factor may be that photography itself had changed. The advent of the 35mm camera, which brought about a more fluid relationship between photographer and subject, resulting in Cartier-Bresson's notion of 'the decisive moment' (not unlike Eisenstaedt's 'story-telling moment'), set the standard for a new style of photojournalism. This emphasis on the evocative nature of the single photograph is not easy to replicate or replace in the time- and moving-image-based medium of television, where frame necessar-ily succeeds frame to form a sequence. In traditional print journalism, rather than spell out the story over a series of images, empha-sis was placed on the single picture that could partly describe and partly intrigue. The photograph's metaphoric and metonymic functions were critical to this end, and the art and craft of the photographer and editor largely depended on identifying and commu-nicating them.

Bearing this in mind, we should certainly be wary of a naive use of newspaper photo-graphs as evidence either of history or of sociological conditions, yet nor should we simply dismiss them as irrelevant representa-tions of society. The best newspaper stories are based on meticulous research—and unlike academic histories—they chronicle not only events but also the interest these events have for human beings: subjects, read-ers/viewers, and reporters. Their task is a delicate one. As Gjelten puts it:

...journalists are storytellers, not social scientists or historians or criminal investigators. ...When people are in anguish, or when they are elated, it is our unique professional responsibility to convey what they *feel* and not just the facts. ...Too often, news coverage of tragedies dehumanizes the victims, and when their suffering is gruesome, the report-ing can border on pornography. Stories that pander to emotion and offer no insight or analysis titillate but do not explain and may even distort what has happened. To manage emotion and to balance it properly with dispassionate observation is one of the greatest professional challenges... (1998: 26)

Addressing the issue of the academic value of studying the news, Burke suggests that the 'evidence' provided by journalists should always be examined in the context of its pro-duction, re-emphasizing that 'the historian cannot afford to forget the pressures of news-paper editors and television stations, con-cerned with "human interest" stories' (Burke, 2001: 151). In other words, the news media have to be treated as an anthropological phenomenon in their own right. As this chapter has attempted to show, the content of news media is constrained by tight principles of organization and well-defined expectations of what the public wants/is able to take.

Finally, the rationale behind the flirtation with the lyrics of songs is to offer pop music as a metaphor for press photography. The music and lyrics of popular singers present a heart-felt rhetorical response to situations, unashamedly arousing equally intense feelings in hearers. Their effect is not dissimilar to the emotional impact of photographs of the American Depression of the 1930s, to follow out Jordanova's analysis (see above). News photographs are much more than mere 'mirrors' of society: they offer a description of states of affairs in the world and an evocation of context: certainly acting as signs of their times. As such, they offer a uniquely valuable source for the study of human history and cultural anthropology—always provided that they are approached with an informed understanding of the art, craft, and constraints of their production.

NOTES

1 With thanks to Lucy Adams, Tom Kelly, Clive Limpkin, Simon Murphy, Maureen Thomas, and the *Glasgow Herald* for their valuable help, cooperation, and comments in the writing of this chapter.

2 In the 1980s, this form of food packaging was banned as unhygienic—fears of toxins in newsprint. Recently, feeding the nostalgia market, some outlets have returned to this tradition, though it is rumoured that fish and chips are now wrapped in specially printed fake newspaper (see *Edinburgh Evening News*, 2009).

3 Only on very rare occasions (usually of disasters of a national or international scale, for example, The World Trade Center attacks of 2001), will the news be extended beyond its allotted time slot.

4 The psychologist James Gibson refers to 'non-modal' forms of perception, 'cutting across the perceptual systems and transcending the "senses". Touching and listening accompany looking' (1979: 208).

5 Chandler provides a valuable discussion of the origins and use of these terms (Chandler, 1994:

http://www.aber.ac.uk/media/Documents/S4B/sem07.html). Nonetheless, at the best of times, the exact definition of these terms in everyday language can become quite complex (see Geeraerts, 2002).

6 Elsewhere (Wright, 2008: 77), I discuss how a photograph by Dorothea Lange came to stand for the American Depression of the 1930s and then moved on to become a universal symbol of motherhood.

7 *Picture Post*'s campaigning approach helped to pave the way for the post-World War II Labour government.

8 This instance of using an animal to accentuate the human condition is neither unique nor confined to photography. For example, Roberto Rossellini, in his 1948 film *Una voce umana* (A Human Voice) included the dog belonging to the actress Anna Magnani in her role as central character to accentuate her sense of loneliness, despite conventional expectations that a dog would offer companionship. As Brunette put it, 'Curiously, the presence of a dog serves to heighten the woman's isolation even more, rather than relieve it' (1996: 87). In the Italian context, it seems that dogs have a habit of getting into the picture. When Rossellini was filming *Roma, città aperta* (Rome, Open City), during a short sequence of a partisan attack on a German armoured column filmed on the outskirts of Rome, a dog runs towards the vehicles and then turns and makes a hasty retreat out of the frame. It would be quite in keeping with the tenets of Neorealism not to shoot the scene again as a dog could easily have done the same in 'real life.'

9 Not averse to sexual stereotyping, two *Hollyoaks* calendars are produced each year: 'Hollyoaks Babes,' featuring female cast, and 'Hollyoaks Hunks,' featuring the males.

10 Sourced from the Broadcasters' Audience Research Board [Online]. Available from: www.barb.co.uk [Accessed 8 February 2010].

11 Sourced from *Songfacts* [Online]. Available from: http://www.songfacts.com/detail.php?id=3313 [Accessed 5 September 2010].

12 In the movie context, Spike Lee's (1989) *Do the Right Thing* contains a scene which may have been inspired by these images and their connotations.

13 In 1984, Mick Jagger returned to the original and, with David Bowie, provided a 'camped-up' version with a video filmed in London's Docklands.

14 See Acheson et al. (1982). According to local artist Tom Kelly (in conversation) at the time of the *Battle of the Bogside* about 100 World War II gas masks had been found in an old army hut in the vicinity. They had proved quite popular with the children, though the CS gas crept into the masks from the back, making them useless from any practical point of view.

15 Truman Capote described *The Wild One* as 'the strange film in which [Brando] was presented as the Führer of a tribe of Fascist-like delinquents' (2008: 201).

16 Sourced from *On This Day* [Online]. Available from: http://news.bbc.co.uk/onthisday/low/dates/stories/may/11/newsid_2860000/2860297.stm [Accessed 5 September 2010].

17 The boy petrol bomber, is now a man in his 50s. He still lives in Derry and works as a driving instructor.

18 Quoted from Kramer, Robert, 'Historical Commentary' in Sander (1980).

19 *The Bogside Artists* [Online]. Available from: http://www.bogsideartists.com [Accessed 5 September 2010]. (See also Bogside Artists, 2009 and Kelly, 2001.)

20 'Most of those shot dead on "Bloody Sunday" were killed in four main areas: the car park (courtyard) of Rossville Flats; the forecourt of Rossville Flats (between the Flats and Joseph Place); at the rubble and wire barricade on Rossville Street (between Rossville Flats and Glenfada Park); and in the area around Glenfada Park (between Glenfada Park and Abbey Park)' (Melaugh 1996–2010).

21 And this is a common problem for both movie and still photographs:

> By some viewers, images of war are read in a straight-forwardly anti-war fashion, as necessary testimony to war's inhumanity. But others will regard war footage as evidence of the enemy's barbarity and affirmation of the necessity of fighting the good fight... (Carruthers, 2000: 71).

22 'Chippie' is a UK colloquialism for the local fish and chip shop.

23 Another example is Matt Frei's television coverage of the Afghan Refugee crisis of February 2001 (Wright, 2008: 113).

24 The paper provides further contextualization in the form of a running chronology printed at the bottom of the pages outlining the key events in Uganda's history that led up to the story.

25 For example, a 1995 *Hello* article explaining why Princess Diana chose to speak out on television used 16 photos to tell the story (Wade, 1995) though admittedly parasitic on the other media form.

REFERENCES

Acheson, E. D., Gardner, M. J., Pippard, E. C. and Grime, L. P. (1982) 'Mortality of two groups of women who manufactured gas masks from chrysotile and crocidolite asbestos: A 40-year follow-up', *British Journal of Independent Medicine*, 39(4): 344–348.

Adams, Lucy (2008) 'A history of violence', in the *Herald Magazine*. Glasgow: Herald. pp. 8–13.

Azoulay, Ariella (2008) *The Civil Contract of Photography*. New York: Zone Books.

Banks, Marcus (2001) *Visual Methods in Social Research*. London: Sage Publications.

Barthes, Roland (1977): *Image-Music-Text*. London: Fontana.

Bogside Artists (2009) *The People's Gallery*. Derry: Bogside Artists.

Bourdieu, Pierre (1990) *Photography: A Middle-brow Art*. Cambridge: Polity.

Brunette, Peter (1996) *Roberto Rossellini*. Berkeley, CA: University of California Press.

Burke, Peter (2001) *Eyewitnessing: The Uses of Images as Historical Evidence*. London: Reaktion Books.

Capote T. (2008) 'The duke in his domain', in T. Capote (ed.), *Portraits and Observations: The Essays of Truman Capote*. New York: Modern Library Classics. pp. 179–211.

Carruthers, Susan L. (2000) *The Media at War: Communication and Conflict in the Twentieth Century*. Basingstoke: Palgrave Macmillan.

Chandler, Daniel (1994) *Semiotics for Beginners* [Online]. Available from: http://www.aber.ac.uk/media/Documents/S4B [Accessed 1 March 2010].

Cox, Julian (2008) *Road to Freedom: Photographs of the Civil Rights Movement, 1956–1968*. High Museum of Art. p. 38.

Department for International Development (DFID) (2000) *Viewing the World: A Study of British Television Coverage of Developing Countries*. London: Department for International Development.

Edinburgh Evening News (27 August 2009) *Fish and Chips Back on the Menu* [Online]. Available from: http://edinburghnews.scotsman.com/edinburgh/Fish-and-chips-in-newspaper.5593299.jp [Accessed 5 September 2010].

Elias, Norbert (1991) 'Human beings and their emotions: A process-sociological essay', in M. Featherstone, M. Hepworth and B. S. Turner (eds.), *The Body: Social Process and Cultural Theory*. London: Sage Publications. pp. 103–125.

Evans, Harold (1978) *Pictures on a Page*. London: Heinemann.

Frymer, Benjamin (2009) 'The media spectacle of Columbine: Alienated youth as an object of fear', *American Behavioral Scientist*, 52(10): 1387–1404.

Geeraerts, Dirk (2002) 'The interaction of metaphor and metonymy in composite expressions', in

R. Dirven and R. Pörings (eds.), *Metaphor and Metonymy in Comparison and Contrast*. Berlin: Mouton de Gruyter. pp. 435–465.

Gibson, James J. (1979) *The Ecological Approach to Visual Perception*. Boston, MA: Houghton Mifflin.

Gjelten, Tom (1998) *Professionalism in War Reporting: A Correspondent's View. Report to the Carnegie Commission on Preventing Deadly Conflict*. New York: Carnegie Corporation.

Hallin, Daniel C., (2000) 'Commercialism and professionalism in the American news media', in J. Curran and M. Gurevitch (eds.), *Mass Media and Society*, 3rd edn. London: Edward Arnold. pp. 218–237.

Highfield, Roger, Wiseman, Richard and Jenkins, Rob (2009) 'How your looks betray your personality', *New Scientist*, 11 February.

Howson, Alexandra (2004) *The Body in Society: An Introduction*. Cambridge: Polity.

Jacobson, Sidney (1970) 'Unemployed', in T. Hopkinson (ed.), *Picture Post 1938–1950*. Harmondsworth: Penguin pp. 45–53.

Jordanova, Ludmilla (2006) *History in Practice*, 2nd edn. London: Hodder Arnold.

Keeble, Richard (1994) *The Newspapers Handbook*. London: Routledge.

Kelly, William (with contributions from Tom Kelly and Kevin Hasson) (2001) *Murals: The Bogside Artists*. Derry: Guildhall Press.

Limpkin, Clive (1972) *The Battle of the Bogside*. London: Penguin.

Limpkin, Clive (2009) *Profile* [Online]. Available from: http://clivelimpkin.com/profile/ [Accessed 5 September 2010].

McCabe, Eamonn (2005) *The Making of Great Photographs: Approaches and Techniques of the Masters*. Newton Abbot: David & Charles.

McQuire, Scott (1998) *Visions of Modernity: Representations, Memory, Time and Space in the Age of the Camera*. London: Sage Publications.

Melaugh, Martin (1996–2010) *'Bloody Sunday', Derry 30 January 1972 —Circumstances in Which People were Killed* [Online]. Available from: http://cain.ulst.ac.uk/events/bsunday/circum.htm [Accessed 5 September 2010].

Melly, George (1972) *Revolt into Style: Pop Arts in Britain*. London: Penguin.

Mendoza, Nadia (2008) 'Hollyoaks hotties strip off', *The Sun*, 2 June 2008 [Online]. Available from: http://www.thesun.co.uk/sol/homepage/showbiz/tv/1237329/Hollyoaks-girls-Roxanne-McKee-Loui-Batley-and-Carley-Stenson-strip-off-for-a-new-calendar.html#ixzz0ex5AUYg4 [Accessed 2 September 2010].

Nicholson, Michael (1999) 'Thousands dead in India—not many interested', *Evening Standard*, Friday 5 November. p. 13.

Ogle, Jennifer Paff, Eckman, Molly and Leslie, Catherine Amoroso (2003) 'Appearance cues and the shootings at Columbine High: Construction of a social problem in the print media', *Sociological Inquiry*, 73(1): 1–27.

Sander, A. (1980) *Photographs of an Epoch 1904–1959*. New York: Aperture. pp. 11–38.

Schudson, Michael (2000) 'The sociology of news production revisited (again)', in J. Curran and M. Gurevitch (eds.), *Mass Media and Society*, 3rd edn. London: Edward Arnold. pp. 175–200.

Scott, Martin (2009) 'Marginalized, negative or trivial? Coverage of Africa in the UK press', *Media Culture Society*, 31: 533–557.

Scott, Martin (2008) *Screening the World, How UK Broadcasters Portrayed the Wider World in 2007–8*. London: International Broadcasting Trust.

Smith, Suzanne E. (2001) *Dancing in the Street*. Cambridge, MA: Harvard University Press.

Sontag, Susan (2003) *Regarding the Pain of Others*. New York: Farrar, Straus and Giroux.

Sprague, S. (1978) 'Yoruba photography: How the Yoruba see themselves', *African Arts*, 12(1): 52–59.

Wade, Judy (1995) 'Why did she speak? The reasons behind the Princess of Wales' decision to appear on television', *Hello*, 383: 50–56.

Walk, R. D. (2010) *The Mickey Mouse Mask* [Online]. Available from: http://www.gasmasklexikon.com/Page/USA-Mil-Mikey.htm [Accessed 21 January 2010].

White, Allon (1985) 'Hysteria and the end of carnival: Festivity and bourgeois neurosis', *Semiotica*, 54(1/2): 97–111.

Wright, Terence (2008) *Visual Impact: Culture and the Meaning of Images*. Oxford: Berg.

Zelizer, Barbie (2004) 'When war is reduced to a photograph', in S. Allan and B. Zelizer (eds.), *Reporting War: Journalism in Wartime*. London: Routledge. pp. 115–135.

DISCOGRAPHY

Elvis Costello (1981) 'Fish 'N Chip Paper', *Trust* [CD]. London: F-Beat.

Iron Maiden (1983) 'The Trooper' [CD single]. London: EMI.

Martha and the Vandellas (1964) 'Dancing in the Street' [7-inch Vinyl]. Hitsville, USA: Gordy.

The Rolling Stones (1968) 'Street Fighting Man', *Beggars Banquet* [CD]. London: Decca.

FILMOGRAPHY

Apocalypse Now (1979) [Film, 153 minutes, color, feature]. Directed by Francis Ford Coppola. USA: Zoetrope Studios.

Do the Right Thing (1989) [Film, 120 minutes, color, feature]. Directed by Spike Lee. USA: 40 Acres & A Mule Filmworks.

Once Upon a Time in the West (1968) [Film, 165 minutes, color, feature]. Directed by Sergio Leone. Italy/USA: Finanza San Marco/Paramount Pictures.

Roma, città aperta (Rome, Open City) (1945) [Film, 103 minutes, black and white, feature]. Directed by Roberto Rossellini. Italy: Excelsa Film.

The Matrix (1999) [Film, 136 minutes, color, feature]. Directed by Andy Wachowski and Larry Wachowski. USA: Groucho II Film Partnership.

The Wild One (1953) [Film, 79 minutes, black and white, feature]. Directed by László Benedek. USA: Stanley Kramer Productions.

Una voce umana (A Human Voice) (1948) [Film, 35 minutes, black and white, feature]. Directed by Roberto Rossellini. Italy: Tevere Film.

18

Methodological Approaches to Disclosing Historic Photographs

Eric Margolis and Jeremy Rowe

NOTES ON HISTORIC PHOTOGRAPHS

Our research draws from the genre often called 'historic.' In a real sense all photographs are historical; they are two-dimensional representation of scenes captured with lenses, and frozen in a fraction of a second. From the instant of exposure, the photograph recedes into the distance of time. However, for the purpose of analysis and discussion, this chapter uses a conventional historians' definition of 'historic' photographs as being 50 years or older.

Like the photographs in Barrett's descriptive and explanatory categories discussed below, people tend to accept historical photographs at 'face value,' as accurate, indexical reflections of reality. Historic images have been concentrated in libraries, museums, and archives, and have become increasingly popular for illustrating books and used in 'documentary' motion pictures. There are also less visible, but very active markets for sale and private collection of historic images. Some historic photographs come with extensive provenance: they were made by known or important photographers; they are accompanied by collateral information, such as written documentation; or they are well-known and have been studied by generations of scholars. Other photographs are drawn from the much larger category of 'vernacular' photographs. Such images come from more obscure sources and usually offer little documentary information to provide a 'warrantable' understanding of the photograph, other than that provided by the image itself. We may be provided with only observable information such as the size, format, and subjective description. Collateral information such as date, location, photographer's name, subject, or reason for being made have been lost or are unavailable to the researcher.

The vernacular genre, as popularly described, includes indigenous or 'native' photographs, typically made by unknown or amateur photographers that tend to depict common subjects, objects, family, and events of daily life. There are literally millions of these vernacular historical photographs, which are becoming more accessible and widely available to researchers. Access to vernacular historic photographs previously required time-consuming and costly trips to archives. Increasing numbers of large-scale digitization projects, the resulting online access to these collections, and social media and sharing sites like Flickr, Photobucket, and Picasa are making millions of vernacular images readily available to researchers.

Many sites have also begun to solicit and share input about the images that can assist in identification and interpretation. Additionally, traffic in buying and selling photos has moved from swap meets and estate sales into regional trade shows and conferences like the National Stereoscopic Association, the Daguerreian Society, and Papermania, and to large-scale online auction sites like eBay and Delcampe. These images, and where still extant, the associated data concerning their provenance, constitute a significant resource for the human and cultural sciences with tremendous untapped potential for researchers. In what follows we explore ways to investigate the meanings of historic photographs.

INTRODUCTION: TO GLIMPSE A WORLD THAT WAS

Clifford Geertz saw the strength of ethnography as its ability to 'put us in touch with the lives of strangers' and to 'see things from the other's perspective' (Geertz, 1983). In confronting our own history we similarly try to fathom the lives of strangers. Traditionally, historic research primarily incorporated document analysis and oral history. But as culture has become more visually literate, photographs, graphics, and other images offer the historian/ethnographer an additional window on the 'webs of significance' that Geertz (following Max Weber) said comprised culture (Geertz, 1973: 5). Some researchers have adopted and use cameras as recording mechanisms to provide their own images for analysis. Others, the authors included, emphasize 'found object'

photographs originally made for reasons other than research. In either case, by themselves photographs provide only 'thin' descriptions, but this information can prove helpful in constructing our own 'thick' descriptions (Geertz, 1973). Erving Goffman emphasized the human ability to make categorical inferences about the glimpsed world in 'real life' and the glimpses provided by photographs:

> To glimpse a world ... is to employ a set of categories more or less distinctive to glimpsing and often entirely adequate for the job they are designed to do.[1] (1976: 22)

In the essays that introduce Goffman's study of the portrayal of gender in advertising images, he makes the point that photographs—posed or candid—are of the same nature as a glimpse of 'real life.'

> We are all in our society trained to employ a somewhat common idiom of posture, position, and glances, wordlessly choreographing ourselves relative to others in social situations with the effect that interpretability of scenes is possible. ... however posed and "artificial" a picture is, it is likely to contain elements that record instances of real things. (1976: 21)

Visual ethnography has an academic interest in analyzing historical photographs to learn as much as possible about the way the world was. The study of historic photographs builds upon the same foundational issues as other visual research techniques. There are also different analytic approaches, such as the 'postpositivist' and 'hermeneutic' paradigm communities (Kuhn, 1970). Berger and Mohr noted the connection of photography both to the modernist project of positivism and to the discipline of sociology:

> The camera was invented in 1839. August Comte was just finishing his *Cours De Philosophie Positive*. Positivism and the camera and sociology grew up together. What sustained them all as practices was the belief that observable quantifiable facts, recorded by scientists and experts, would one day offer man such a total knowledge about nature and society that he would be able to order them both. (1982: 99)

This chapter presents two approaches to photographic research, each presented in the voice of one co-author. In general, we believe that potential synergies exist in approaching photographic research from perspectives of both postpositivist evidence from indexical and iconic sources, and interpretivist/hermeneutical approaches that draw on symbolic dimensions that are essential in the examination of photographs. Each brings tools and lenses for viewing and analysis of photographs that are neither mutually exclusive nor individually exhaustive.

While Margolis leans toward theoretical hermeneutic approaches, Rowe applies a postpositivist evidentiary process that he terms *photographic forensics*. In a previous co-authored piece about an album of Arizona Indian school photographs, the co-authors found that each technique added value to the analysis: the whole was clearly more than the sum of the two parts (Margolis and Rowe, 2002). This chapter continues the dialogue between and about the two approaches to photographic analyses, providing general background to each approach, and brief examples that catalyze the discussion.

Today, there is a growing awareness of the limitations of the strict positivist position that considers photographs as merely a 'mirror with a memory' (as daguerreotypes were labeled soon after their introduction in 1839). Similarly, few argue that cameras function merely as 'pencils of nature,' a popular implication in the nineteenth century. Englishman William Henry Fox Talbot produced the first book illustrated with photographs in 1844. Talbot laid the foundation for this interpretation with his introduction: '...the plates of this work have been obtained by the mere action of light upon sensitive paper. They have been formed by optical and chemical means alone, and without the aid of any one acquainted with the art of drawing....' (Fox Talbot, 1844 [1989] Book No. 1, n.p.). W. J. T. Mitchell contended that:

It is getting increasingly hard to find anyone who will defend the view (variously labeled "positivist", "naturalistic", or "superstitious and naïve") that photographs have a special causal and structural relationship with the reality that they represent. (1994: 282)

We don't necessarily agree with Mitchell's concern that positivist beliefs in images have been killed by postmodernists like Victor Burgin. As discussed later, Errol Morris, among others, maintains a firm distinction between words and photographic images in his analysis, and argues that photographs do have a 'special' relationship with what stood before the lens.

Currently, there are two vibrant metaphysical conceptions of photographs. The first we'll term 'postpositivist' in that, while confident in the indexical relationship between a photograph and the material world in front of the lens, assertions about photographic meaning have two limitations:

1 These assertions are statistically probable, not certain.
2 They must be subject to rigorous testing and must be in principal falsifiable if they are to be considered scientific (Philips and Burbules, 2000).

The photographic researcher/critic makes 'warranted' statements backed by evidence— but the warrants can be extended or even overturned at any time by new evidence.

The second conception emphasizes 'interpretivist' views. In contrast to the postpositivist perspective that considers photographs as documents that convey descriptive or explanatory representations, merely reflecting reality, or even representing 'the thing in itself,' John Tagg (1988), following Foucault, emphasized photography in terms of associated power relationships: 'Photography as such has no identity. Its status as technology varies with the power relations that invest it. Its nature as a practice depends on the institutions and agents which define it and set it to work' (63). Hermeneutic perspectives emphasize photographs as texts, demanding semantic and semiotic interpretation to determine meaning.

Postpositivist approaches to researching historical photographs

Postpositivism emphasizes that photographs represent 'things in the world.' It recognizes that cameras are not simply mechanical transcription devices, and acknowledges that photographs result from photographers infusing their own perspectives and interpretations of subjects through decisions about framing and composition, by manipulating depth of field and exposure time, choosing when to release the shutter, etc. Oliver Wendell Holmes commented in 1859: 'The photograph has completed the triumph, by making a sheet of paper reflect images like a mirror and hold them as a picture ... the mirror with a memory.'[2] An anonymous quotation plays on this by inserting the importance of the human element: 'The camera is a mirror with a memory, but it can not think.' Nonetheless, traces of the old positivist belief in 'observable facts,' recorded mechanically, analyzed, or quantified by 'objective' scientists and experts lurks close to the surface of what Martin Jay termed 'the dominant scopic regime' (Jay, 1994). For postpositivists the most important quality of a photograph is its indexical connection to things in the world. As Edward Steichen described the relationship between optical/chemical machinery and operator:

> The camera is a witness of objects, places, and events. A photograph of an object is, in a sense, a portrait. But the camera with its glass eye, the lens, and its memory, the film, can in itself produce little more than mirrored verisimilitudes. A good photograph requires more than that. .... The technical process simply serves as a vehicle of transcription and not as the art.
> The photographer, unlike the painter and regardless of his subjective feelings, is forced by the very nature of his medium to concentrate on the object, on what Goethe referred to as "Das Ding an sich" in a portrait: on the person, or the meadow, the mountain, the flowers, or the horse being photographed. (Steichen, 1984: Chapter 10, facing plate 164)

Art educator Terry Barrett (1986), created a taxonomic system for art historians that categorized photographs as descriptive, explanatory, interpretive, ethically evaluative, aesthetically evaluative, and theoretical. Much of Barrett's conceptualization can be applied equally well within our framework for researching historical photographs. The first two categories, for example, are useful when discussing how historical photographs emphasize a postpositivist approach to research. As Barrett explained, 'The photographs are falsifiable in that potentially they could be empirically demonstrated to be true or false, accurate or inaccurate' (Barrett, 1986: 56). Barrett defined these photographs as:

- **Descriptive:** photographs such as crime scene photos, X-rays, portraits, and photographic reproductions of art.
- **Explanatory:** includes photographs made by visual sociologists and anthropologists and photographs like Andrew Davidhazy's stop motion shots.[3]

In addition, Barrett's typology is also useful for considering photographs with more interpretive/hermeneutic characteristics. Our intention, here, is to move away from having two hard and fast approaches, as in the old paradigm wars. Our emphasis is rather on the interpenetration of postpositive and hermeneutic approaches to researching historical photographs, without de-emphasizing their differences. As such, Barrett's second two categories work to emphasize interpretivist views of research on historical photographs, which regard photographs as texts to be interpreted:

- **Ethically evaluative images** include much of what has been termed 'liberal documentary' (Rosler, 1990). Barrett includes the works of Riis and Hine in the category that uses photography to force moral judgments in the viewer.
- **Aesthetically evaluative images** seek a response from the viewer as well. They 'function as notifications that the photographic presentation of people, places, objects, or events is worthy of aesthetic apprehension, (Barrett, 1986: 57).

Interpretivist approaches to researching historical photographs.

Hermeneutic perspectives emphasize photographs as texts demanding semantic and semiotic interpretation to determine meaning. Allan Sekula termed assumptions that a photograph can 'transmit truths'; 'reflect reality'; or be an 'historical document' as *fallacy*. 'The very term document entails a notion of legal or official truth, as well as a notion of proximity to and verification of an original event' (Sekula, 1983: 195). Sekula also asked with regard to exploring and understanding power relations: 'How is historical and social memory preserved, transformed, restricted, and obliterated by photographs?' (Sekula, 1983: 193). The iconic and symbolic life of photographs is the basis that the hermeneutic approach insists on for meaning—photographs are defined by their social and cultural contexts and, as a result, can never be either ethically or aesthetically neutral.

POSTPOSITIVIST APPROACHES

Postpositivist photographic researchers hypothesize that the image and its contextual information contain data such as where, how, by whom, when, and why the images were produced; and use this information to attempt to infer embedded representations within the images. Ultimately, the goal is to use this information, and knowledge of photography, culture, and context, to reach a warranted comprehension of the image. Jeremy Rowe devised a three-part strategy for photo research:

1 **Evidence—objective, factual, documentary information provided by the photograph or its context.** This is its provenance, or context (for example, format, content within the photograph, attribution to photographic studio based on imprint or printed identification from the period, etc.); the focus is on primary source information.
2 **Interpretation—where we have little documentation and must rely on deductions built on circumstantial evidence and context that can be clearly verified to and by others.**

Interpretation builds on the factual evidence with explanatory or derived information that can be clearly verified to and by others (for example, dating from format or image content, contextual comparisons with companion or other known images, verified period or more recent written identification, etc.); includes secondary source material.
3 **Speculation—subjective inferences not necessarily based on evidence provided by the photograph.** It is the information that can augment the factual information that may range from attribution by later generations based on family legends, to hearsay or creative interpretation to 'leaps of faith' based on desire to fit the image into a specific hypothesis or intellectual framework without sufficient factual basis (Rowe, 2002).

The first two of Rowe's strategies stand firmly in the postpositivist tradition. They draw on what Roland Barthes *termed*: 'studium'— informed by education. Studium is the socially prescribed, statistically 'average' meaning of the historian, the social scientist—interested in describing what the image depicts: date, location, event, caption, and so on (Barthes, 1981: 22–26). Valuable research methods include standard historical research into the photographer and the events depicted, content analysis of the image itself, which can be used for hypothesis testing and for a more inductive process of hypothesis generation, and close analysis of the photograph itself.

Many visual ethnographers recognize the importance of understanding the relationship between the researcher and the subject, yet these same researchers rarely address the importance of understanding the relationship between the photographer that created the image and the image itself, or exploring the context in which the images were originally created. The evolution from reliance on text alone, to incorporating images as sources for researchers, requires new methods and analytic techniques. Though many researchers reference the link between image and subject, photographer, and ethnographer, few have taken the next step to examine the information embedded in the image (format, media, imprint, notes, etc.) or of incorporating knowledge of the larger body of work created by a photographer, or of comparisons with work by other photographers who may have made additional images of an area or event. If such images can be located, they can provide a foundation for inferences such as the prominence of the subject at the time, and permit triangulation of style and context across the work by each individual photographer.

Recently, aided by copyright policy and emerging current practice, many library and archival collections, commercial sources, and some collectors have been successful in demanding source credits when images from their collections are published. However, providing credit to the photographer, when known, in popular press publication captions (other than to a few well-known fine art and journalistic photographers), has been rare. When information about the photographer, format, and other contextual information is presented at all, it is usually separated from the image and appears in end credits or on a photo source page at the end of the publication.

The interaction between the photographer and viewer extends to the size, format, presentation style, and labeling or captioning of the images that are produced. Changes in the presentation of the photograph in print or online publication, for example. cropping or extraction of detail within a photograph, can have significant implications on the viewer's interpretation and understanding of the image. Such changes are rarely noted as photographs are reproduced. For example, images are routinely cropped to fit layouts, and image information such as format, mount type or style, and photo credits are regularly removed. Historic images such as *cartes de visite* and cabinet cards are typically cropped and printed without mount information that can often identify location, and provide assistance in verifying date. Photographer's imprints are rarely included unless a notable photographer produced the image. Stereographs are routinely reproduced without noting the original format, and using only one of the stereo pairs instead of presenting the overall image. Even simple information about the original format of the photograph can be potentially valuable, but is rarely noted in publications.

Identification of the photographer can provide valuable context about related work from which researchers can infer information about style, approach (as in documentary versus staged or posed), ability to interact with the subject, use of props, etc. For example, studying photographer-produced stereographs in the late nineteenth century can provide insight regarding the entrepreneurial nature of the photographer, interest in location work in addition to studio portraits, etc. (Rowe, 1991, 2008). Knowledge that the photographer or photographic publisher produced primarily prints from original negatives, as opposed to marketing copy photographs of the work of that of others, can offer additional insights.

Changes in mount colors or styles of imprints, when combined with knowledge about the photographer and changing presentation styles, can provide collateral information that can provide a range of dates when the image may have been produced (Rowe, 1997: 116–118; 2007: 75–88). Imprints identifying the photographer open the door to researching photographic business records and directories of photographers that can provide additional data for analysis.

The technology to scan, enlarge, crop, and enhance photographs has dramatically improved the ability of researchers to explore images for embedded clues. Examination of information embedded within the image, such as artwork, calendars, or signage, can provide temporal cues about when the image was originally made. Software provides researchers with capabilities for comparison of images that were previously extremely difficult if not impossible using traditional magnification and photographic techniques. Included are techniques such as: overlaying images; scaling; transformations to match perspectives, contrast, and sharpness enhancement; and automated comparison tools that can identify and compare elements within the images.[4] Rowe coined the term *Photographic Forensics* to describe the full spectrum of photographic analysis from: examining image content using these techniques to identify embedded clues; mount and format data; contextual information about the photographer (when known) and related images by other photographers; and the contextual information associated with single photographs or collection of images (Rowe, 2002).

Often, the date the photograph was taken can add substantial information about the subject through an understanding of the style and symbolism of the era. For example, a woman wearing a black veil and clothing may indicate mourning. Dark clothing with black gloves covering the palm but with bare fingers can symbolize a progression of the mourning process over time. Arrangement and relationship of multiple individuals within the frame, or placement of hands or contact between subjects; each had its own Victorian symbolism.

Information on the approximate cost and resulting economic impact of the photographs on the subject when it was made can also be valuable. Knowing that a large daguerreotype was a significant expense in the 1840s, as much as $150, can be an indicator of the wealth of the subject. Knowing that smaller 1/6-plate-sized images cost about $30 in the 1840s, with the price dropping to $7.50 for two portraits by the late 1850s, provides additional insight to the subjects of these images (all prices adjusted to approximate current dollars).

The social context of *cartes de visite*, which were exchanged in the 1860s, and knowledge that images of notable authors, performers, and politicians were collected and included in family albums provides valuable understanding of collections of family photographs of the era. The dates that tax stamps appear on the reverse, or changes in mount style and borders occurred, also provide useful information in dating photographs and discovering locations. Recognizing photographic copies versus originals, particularly when copies were made of much earlier images, such as the common practice of making *cartes de visite* copies of daguerreotypes or ambrotypes, can similarly improve the accuracy of dating and attributions.

Another potential source of contextual information is knowledge about the photographer. For example, was she or he the sole operator in a small town, or one of a number of studios in a city? Did she cater to upper or working class clientele? Were the images known outside of the region? Was the photographer recognized for their artistic or documentary styles-? Is the photograph in question typical of the photographer's work, or is it unusual in terms of pose, interaction with the photographer, or inclusion of props?

Learning about the nature of the equipment and photographic process frequently contributes useful information. Was the process used common or more unique when the image was made? Did the process produce a single copy of the image, like the daguerreotype, ambrotype, or tintype, or a negative capable of producing many prints? Was the camera mounted on a tripod or studio stand, or hand-held? Was lighting manipulated, or was flash or auxiliary lighting added? Was the equipment high-level professional or lower-cost amateur gear? Does the image fit into the aesthetic style of the time, or is it retrospective or groundbreaking?

In addition to examining clues within the image, researchers can explore available contextual or documentary information that may be associated with the photograph. In comprehending meaning, provenance and the history of the photograph and the collection, archive, or source can provide additional clues about why and how the photograph was made and why it was valued and preserved. Examining contextual information, such as companion images in an album or collection, proof sheets, or other images made by the photographer, can reveal information about the photographer's intent, as can journals, daybooks, assignments, or other collateral references (cf. Margolis and Rowe, 2002).

There may also be captions and other descriptive information about the image and subject. If available, studying both the negative and original print can be meaningful.

As noted, images change their meaning as they are cropped or reprinted (cf. Margolis, 1988). Some photographers use cropping to provide editorial control and to shape the meaning that the image conveys. Christopher Lyman's study of the Edward Curtis collection, for example, revealed how Curtis himself altered the images of Native Americans to eliminate traces of modern life as he composed shots and printed his negatives (Lyman, 1982).

Original owners can often provide substantial information about the images in their personal collections. But most historical photographs have been completely torn from their original contexts. In most cases, it is only a matter of luck when the collateral information remains paired with the photographs. Unfortunately, only a single gap in provenance can break the tenuous connection to virtually all of this collateral information associated with an image. In the growing image marketplace, individual photographs are often separated from collections or removed from albums with their associated captions and context to sell the images individually in an attempt to increase revenue. In other cases quirks of history and custody, much of which is desirable documentation, is simply missing. But, as we shall see, this lack of context does not make these images meaningless.

Confounding the impact of missing information is the impact of dissemination of incorrect information about a photograph. Unfortunately, once incorrect information becomes widely available it takes on a life of its own through references and citations, making it extremely difficult to rein in misinformation or correct errors. Rowe developed a research strategy to determine the accuracy of the attribution of an image published with the label 'Kaloma,' that was claimed to be Josephine Earp by author Glenn Boyer (1998 [1976]). Soon after the publication of

Boyer's book, *I Married Wyatt Earp*, debate arose about the real subject of the image labeled 'Kaloma.' The image of Kaloma took on a life of its own through Boyer's book cover and the trail of auction catalog descriptions that built upon his attribution. Since no provenance has yet surfaced definitively to identify this image, it provides an exemplar of the process of analyzing clues that are associated with the image to demonstrate a postpositivist approach to photographic research.[5]

Photographic research is based on obtaining as much information as possible about an image, then building a logical context for a possible identification of the image. As new information is located, it is compared, and the interpretations checked for 'fit,' given the new data. This embedded contextual information can be structured into three categories of increasing confidence as noted above: evidence, interpretation, and speculation.

Each level of analysis can provide a valuable source of information that can be evaluated, verified, and weighted as part of the research process. For example, evidence such as photographer's imprints can usually provide valuable insight about the image. But for copy photographs the mount imprint may not accurately identify the original photographer. For example, the well-known images of Geronimo by Irwin, Randall, and Wittick, and C. S. Fly were frequently copied, and today examples of these images exist with imprints of dozens of other photographers.

Interpretation based on the format of the photograph or information within the image, such as building signs, can help verify or refute written identification that may have been added to the mount.

All written information associated with an image should be confirmed, particularly if it was added after the image was originally produced. Well-intentioned family members, collectors, and museum staff often add attributions to the photographs that pass through their hands. Their impressions or knowledge, and the accuracy of the written information, should be verified before it is assumed to be correct.

Speculation may be based on interpretation of available evidence, on emotional reaction to a photograph, or desire to 'trim' a piece of the puzzle of history to make it fit a particular research hypothesis or philosophy. Speculation can also be benign or unintentional, based on little knowledge or on incorrect information. Personal desire or a potentially escalating value for a given photograph can also drive speculative interpretations. For example, images of young Abraham Lincoln are rare, likely due to both his economic circumstances and frontier location. As a result, extremely high values are placed on any new image of Lincoln that might surface. Several well-intentioned individuals have found vintage photographs that they feel appear similar to known Lincoln portraits. Without specific evidence or provenance linking the images to Lincoln, attempts to generate such connections range from trying to convince experts to authenticate based on the apparent physical similarity, to computerized morphing of the image to the known Lincoln portraits.

Each photographic identification is only as accurate as the weakest link in the chain of information about the image that is available at a given time. Anecdotes and speculation can make great stories, but without evidence to support the assumptions, provide merely weak links in the process of accurately identifying a photograph.

Rowe examined the image labeled 'Kaloma' and the attributions based on evidence, interpretation of that evidence, and speculation about the image and its impact on the perception of the image and market value (Rowe, 2002). Based on evidence available to date, the trail of information about the image of 'Kaloma' begins in 1914, when the vignetted image of a beautiful young woman boldly posed for the camera in a sheer gauze peignoir became popular (Figure 18.1). Titled 'Kaloma,' it was originally produced as a photogravure. These high-quality reproductions from photographs

Figure 18.1 Kaloma, the vignetted image of a beautiful young woman boldly posed for the camera in a sheer gauze peignoir. Collection of Jeremy Rowe vintage photography, vintagephoto.com

were produced from engraving plates on a printing press, and were much less costly for publication runs than actual photographs. Photogravures were often printed with title and publication data below the image and were commonly used to create many copies of high-quality illustrations for books, postcards, and art magazines. Though photogravures had been used since the 1850s; their surge in popularity was between 1890 and 1920.

Many of the prints of Kaloma bear a credit to either the ABC Novelty Company in New York or to the Pastime Novelty Company at 1313 Broadway, New York. Labels on the back of commercially framed prints indicate that it was widely popular. Prints of 'Kaloma' have surfaced with framing shop labels from Hawaii and states throughout the USA and into Canada.

The risqué image was popular and sold well as both photogravure and silver print. Also in 1914, the image appeared on the cover of 'Kaloma, Valse Hesitante (Hesitation Waltz)' composed by Gire Goulineaux, and published by the Cosmopolitan Music Publishing Company, 1367–69 Broadway, New York. Kaloma's popularity continued as she became a pin-up during World War I, and appeared after the war on postcards. After discrete airbrushing darkened her peignoir, Kaloma also appeared in other popular advertising during that era.

The relatively benign history of Kaloma changed significantly in 1976 when Glenn Boyer used an airbrushed version of Kaloma as the cover illustration for *I Married Wyatt Earp*. Gradually, interest in the image began to shift from risqué nostalgia. Kaloma became an icon of the mania for Western collecting that grew through the 1980s and escalated dramatically in the 1990s. Almost entirely as a result of the book cover attribution, copies of the Kaloma image began to sell for hundreds, then thousands of dollars as portraits of Josephine Marcus Earp.

Questions about the historical accuracy of Boyer's book and the attribution of the cover photograph of Kaloma arose in the mid-1990s. The debate about the cover image escalated, reaching the popular press in the late 1990s. Donald Ackerman wrote to the *Maine Antique Digest (M.A.D.)* in June 1997, requesting assistance in verifying the attribution of the Kaloma image as Josie Earp. Ackerman noted the similarity to the early silent film publicity stills that he was familiar with and questioned the attribution to the 1880s and the strength of the purported link to Josie Earp. He further noted that recent auction sale prices would likely draw more copies into the marketplace, and that additional copies of the Kaloma image were being offered by H.C.A. Auctions in their 27 April 1997 sale and an auction house in

Kingston, New York on 28 May of that same year (Ackerman, 1997).

The following month, *M.A.D.* published a response to the Ackerman letter by Bob Raynor of H.C.A. Auctions. Mr. Raynor acknowledged that H.C.A. represented the Kaloma image as that of Josie Earp after researching the image, and argued 'Both Sotheby's and Swann Galleries identified and sold the photo image in 1996, both auctions prior to the December H.C.A auction.' Raynor stated:

> Please note that the image was used as a dust cover of the book *I Married Wyatt Earp*, published by University of Arizona Press, 1976. Additionally, the image was used in another book, Wyatt Earp's *Tombstone Vendetta*, published by Talei, and also in *Pioneer Jews*, Houghton Mifflin, 1984. In all instances the image was identified as Josephine Earp. (Raynor, 1997)[6]

Though this level of research is credible, it is interesting to note that all of the references hinge on, and post date, the attribution of Boyer's book cover.

As prices rose, so did the number of auction sales of the 'Kaloma' image. Sotheby's 8 April 1998 sale included a photograph labeled an anonymous picture, taken in 1914 and titled 'Kaloma,' of a siren-like figure dressed in a sheer gown with a plunging neckline. Described in the catalog as a hand-tinted photograph of Josephine Marcus Earp, the one-time wife of lawman Wyatt Earp, the photograph was estimated at $3000–4000 and sold for $2875. The Sotheby's catalog saw broad distribution and afterward was frequently cited as the source used to 'identify' Kaloma images as Josie Earp in many subsequent auction and dealer sales.

As the perceived value and notoriety of the image of 'Kaloma' rose, so did the stories that surrounded her:

- Josephine Earp was born in 1861 and would have been 53 in 1914. After this fact became an issue, Kaloma conveniently began to be described as a later print of an image of Josie taken in Tombstone, Arizona in 1881, when she would have been 19 or 20—roughly the same age as the subject of Kaloma.

- At some point purported ties to C. S. Fly began to surface as the original photographer of a drunken Josie coerced into posing for the portrait.
- Legends of attribution prospered. Quotes from many sources have been touted as the definitive word on the history of the image. Unsupported tales of bar owners or those in attendance when the image was supposedly made have been used to rationalize the Kaloma image as a portrait of Josie Earp.
- Similarities with other, better-attributed images of Josie Earp have been cited but little provenance has been given that could definitively connect any of the Kaloma images to Josie Earp.
- As an example of the market incentive, many copies of the 'Kaloma' image surfaced and citations in auction catalogs and from dealer sales, all after the 1976 publication of *I Married Wyatt Earp* were regularly used to 'verify' that Kaloma is Josie Earp and establish a high potential value.

Unfortunately, little concrete evidence has been found to help settle the controversy. Rowe (2002) published an analysis of the evidence and speculation that revolved around the 'Kaloma' image that looked at a number of context and dating clues in the photograph as a starting point for his analysis. Several significant questions were posed. Why has no evidence of the tie between 'Kaloma' and Josephine Earp surfaced that predates publication of Boyer's book in 1976? Also, where are the primary source citations from the period between Josie's time in Tombstone, and the emergence of Kaloma in 1914 that link the image to the personality? What do we actually know about the image titled 'Kaloma' from the available evidence?

If one examines the image to see what evidence is presented, certain inferences and interpretations can be derived. Photographic styles changed regularly every few years as photographers sought to justify new portrait business, and as lenses, formats, and emulsions continually evolved. By looking at large numbers of images it is possible to get a feel for the photographic style of a given era. Images that don't fit the norm do exist,

and are often highly valued by collectors as precursors of future styles and trends. However, most images generally fit the stylistic trends of their era.

The Kaloma image exhibits three strong stylistic elements that can be used to try to assign a range of dates to the original photographic image:

1 The sultry interaction between the subject in Kaloma and the photographer is very direct. This aesthetic style is more common and representative of risqué images and nude studies from the postcard era (1905–1920) and appears rarely in earlier nineteenth-century images.
2 The full-figure vignetting of the image is also stylistically more common during the postcard era. However, earlier images were reprinted in current formats years after they were originally taken. It is possible that the central image of Kaloma could have printed from an older negative and vignetted to update its appearance.
3 The use of narrow depth of field (the range of sharp focus in the photograph) was popularized by art photographers in England and Europe beginning in the late 1880s, and became popular in America around the turn of the century. Aesthetically, the Kaloma image shares much more with post-1900 images than it does with earlier images such as the cabinet cards that were popular during the early 1880s, when the image had to have been taken if Josephine Earp was in fact the subject.

Risqué photographs like the Kaloma image have been made and sold since the 1840s. The subjects of such 'art' photographs were not usually identified. It is highly unlikely that even if the subject of Kaloma had been identified at some point, such documentation by photographer or publisher would still exist. However, given the heated levels of discussion about the current attributions, and possible liability given Kaloma's high sales prices based on its attribution to Josephine Earp, it is not likely that even if such information is available, that publishers or distributors would actively take sides in this matter. Obviously, locating any original documentation of the sitter of the Kaloma image would be key to unraveling the controversy about this image.

Copyright notifications have been printed on photograph mounts and occasionally in the image area since the 1850s. Notices were occasionally printed or etched in the negative, or later added to the mount or print with a rubber stamp. Though copying and piracy were common, pirates rarely included previous notices when illegally reproduced. The Kaloma images seen to date have all been associated with copyright notices dating after 1914. The 'Kaloma' photograph on the sheet music is unattributed, though the music is copyrighted to Cosmopolitan Publishing Company.

The number and format of extant copies of the image also provide some clues. If in fact the image were of Josephine Earp one would assume that it would have been popular and many copies would have been made and marketed soon after it had been taken. If it had been originally taken in the 1880s, most of the extant copies would likely be in the cabinet card format. This would hold true even if it were merely an unidentified nude image made during that era. Virtually all of the copies of the Kaloma images identified to date are printed paper photographs or postcards that date after the 1914 date indicated in the copyright notice. Rowe is not aware of any copies of this image that have surfaced in original nineteenth-century cabinet card mounts.

The purported attribution to the C. S. Fly studio in Tombstone can also be evaluated. In addition to his entrepreneurial personality, Fly was known for the aggressive marketing and promotion of his photographs, particularly of his Geronimo series. Thousands of copies of images made during the surrender of Geronimo in 1885 were printed and sold, each prominently identifying Fly as photographer and most carrying his copyright notice. Similarly, portraits of personalities visiting Tombstone, and photographs of local events like the hanging of John Heath, were also broadly distributed. If as speculated, Fly took a salable image of Josie Earp, it is highly unlikely that he would not have sought to capitalize on the opportunity to sell copies.

To date, no copies of the Kaloma image have been located on C. S. Fly studio mounts.

Looking at the purported attribution of the subject as Josie Earp provides a bit of additional insight. During much of their lives, the Earps were popular, widely known, public personalities. Though few commercial portraits of the Earps exist today, if images of the Earps had been available at the time it is likely that they would have had a large and ready market. Individual cabinet card portraits were relatively affordable, costing about $1.25 per dozen, with group portraits slightly more expensive at about $1.50 per dozen. It is also highly likely that period documentation and references to such images would have been produced, providing additional evidence for such attributions. The lack of such evidence is telling.

Looking at the evidence provided by the image and trying to read the story that it tells logically leads to it being an early twentieth-century photograph of a beautiful young woman, likely made after about 1910, which was taken about the time that it first burst on the scene in 1914. No clues clearly indicate this image was copied from an earlier image of Josie Earp or another as-yet unidentified young woman. Given the broad exposure that the image of Kaloma has had since the publication of the Boyer book, and strong interest in the legends of Tombstone and the West, the search for compelling evidence to link this image with Josie Earp will likely continue. In short, at this point there is little evidence, some *interpretation* loosely based on that *evidence*, and much *speculation* about the subject of the image known as Kaloma.

Content analysis

An important postpositivist approach is content analysis, a technique developed in the field of media studies. It is a taxonomic and counting strategy for determining the relative frequency of certain representations within groups of images. Philip Bell gave an excellent review of the technical procedures but concluded:

> It is also of limited value in many research contexts, and might best be thought of as a necessary but not sufficient methodology for answering questions about what the media depicts or represents. Content analysis alone is seldom able to support statements about the significance, effects, or interpreted meaning of a domain of representation. (2001: 13)

The technical procedures, in Bell's account, are a form of hypothesis testing. Content analysis requires defining explicit categories that are exhaustive and mutually exclusive, and employing checks like inter-coder reliability. These techniques are most applicable to comparisons between two discrete sample populations that can be considered comprehensive representations of the sample population. Content analysis is most applicable to research where a collection of images defines the sample population than with less comprehensive collections that only are representative of the populations being analyzed. A hypothetical example to illustrate Bell's method involves an analysis of magazine covers.

One of Bell's examples involved two subjects using explicitly defined categories to code and compare the portrayal of subjects and social contexts expressed in images of women appearing on the cover of *Cleo Magazine* during two periods, 1972–4 and 1996–7. Points of comparison included observables such as hair color (number of blonds and brunettes), age (older and younger models), and social distance (involved or distant). For example, values coded for social distance were: 'intimate, close personal, far personal, close social, far social, and public' (Bell, 2001: 29).

The two coders were naive in the sense that they were blind to the hypotheses being tested. Each was trained to 'classify images according to the specified definitions' (31). The coding was then compared to establish statistical reliability. The magazine covers were presented randomly, and technical procedures were used to determine if there was a statistically significant difference in the points of comparison for the representations of the observables between the early and later periods. Bell noted that not only could coders be trained to recognize easy observables, for example, blond or brunette, but also they could accurately discriminate between more semiotic categories, for example 'social distance,' which he operationally defined as 'how much of the (human) participant's body is represented in the frame' (29).

Similar procedures can be applied to sample populations of historic photographs. For example, one might examine representative collections of studio portraits from two periods, the 1880s and the 1910s. Social distance could define one axis of comparison and one might hypothesize that social distance decreased as photographers and subjects became more comfortable with the camera's presence, or as exposure times decreased and head clamps became unnecessary, reducing the discomfort of posing for portraits.[7] Similarly, one might test the oft-noted increase in smiling faces over time. The same sample of portraits could be coded with a set of values for facial expression: frown, deadpan, slightly upturned lips, teeth visible, mouth open in a toothy grin. Once again, naive coders could be asked to discriminate randomly presented images, then their judgments compared until high values for agreement were achieved, and ultimately the hypothesis that smiling increased could be tested.

There are two weaknesses of content analysis as a tool for analyzing historic photographs. The accuracy of this technique depends on the ability of the sample to represent the total population, and is extremely sensitive to misinterpretation because of sample bias due to the inability to identify or have access to the entire population, and the likelihood that some images are more likely to be chosen than others. Although it is relatively easy to assemble collections of historic photographs, in many cases it is difficult to create a representative sample that is realistic, comprehensive, and unbiased, and that can be used to provide accurate inferences about the sample population.

Also, as Bell noted, even when representative samples can be identified, the entire approach is under-theorized and cannot speak to whether the hypotheses would have been 'meaningful to those who habitually "read" or "use" the images' (25). 'In short, content analysis cannot be used as though it reflects un-problematically or a-theoretically the social or ideological world...' (24). This is especially true in the case of historic photographs. In most cases, it is virtually impossible for modern coders and content analysts to know how the content was perceived at the time the images were originally made.

Still, content analysis has been used to test hypotheses in historic photograph collections. For example, in his 1993 book *How Teacher's Taught*, Larry Cuban employed, as data, Frances Benjamin Johnston's famous set of more than 700 photographs made in Washington, DC schools in 1900 (Cuban, 1993). Cuban counted whether desks were bolted down or movable and also compared classroom activities to determine whether progressive or traditional classroom techniques were employed. In his analysis, he found that traditional techniques of schooling were overwhelmingly depicted:

> Out of almost 300 prints of elementary school classrooms, nearly 30 show groups of students working with large relief maps in geography, preserved rabbits and squirrels being used for a lesson, students watching a teacher carve into a cow's heart to show the parts of the organ, and classes taking a trip to the zoo. The remaining 90% of the prints show students sitting in rows at their desks doing uniform tasks at the teacher's direction. (Cuban, 1993: 26)[8]

Close inspection

Where content analysis tries to tease meaning from large collections of images, one can also study single historical photographs in particular detail. 'Photographs do not translate from appearances. They quote from them' (Berger and Mohr, 1982: 96). Thus, the optical/chemical apparatus may record things the photographer did not see, and much can be learned by closely and systematically examining photographs. As noted above, one can frequently find clues: clocks recorded the time of day; calendars show month and year; and license plates, newspaper headlines, and flags similarly help date images. Postmarks, notations, and dedications, provenance and collateral contextual information can also expand the understanding of the image and its subjects.

In Margolis' research on classrooms, what might be incidentally written on blackboards provides clues to curriculum. Small details provide insights. The social and technological history of the medium provides useful information.

Tintypes, daguerreotypes, panoramics, Kodak snapshots, and digital files each had their day and produced certain social reactions to image-making technology. Each technique has its own representative vocabulary of process evidence. Examples include: quality of surface preparation and sharpness of focus and tonality of daguerreotypes; consistency of collodion flow and contrast in tintypes; size and evenness of exposure and focus for panoramics; image size and processing or mounting artifacts for snapshots (such as the representative circular images produced by the first string-set Kodak cameras); and file format, bit depth, and resolution for digital images. In addition, other contextual information or comparisons with other similar images to infer studio quality or importance to the subject provide additional clues. Other information, such as estimating how long an exposure might have taken, or how rapidly a series of subsequent images could be made using a given technology, may also be useful (cf. Newhall, 1964; Leggat, 1995).

Probably one of the most thorough and provocative postpositivist approaches to discovering the meaning of photographs was undertaken by filmmaker Errol Morris, who writes the blog *Zoom*, for the *New York Times*. Morris wrote three long pieces comparing two Crimean War photographs made by one of the first war photographers, Roger Fenton, in 1855. Morris initially seemed ready to defend the 'pencil of nature view,' asserting 'Photographs provide a "window" into history.' The implication was that the comment applied to the history of a specific moment, and specific place 'as if we have reached into the past and created a tiny peephole' (Morris, 2007b). But Morris had no patience with interpretive or hermeneutic accounts. His obsession with Fenton's two images of the 'Valley of the Shadow of Death' began in reaction to Susan Sontag, whom he cited from *Regarding the Pain of Others*:

Not surprisingly many of the canonical images of early war photography turn out to have been staged, or to have had their subjects tampered with. ... Fenton made two exposures from the same tripod position: in the first version of the celebrated photo he was to call "The Valley of the Shadow of Death" ... the cannonballs are thick on the ground to the left of the road, but before taking the second picture—the one that is always reproduced—he oversaw the scattering of the cannonballs on the road itself. (Sontag, 2003 quoted in Morris, 2007b)

The two photos were taken from the same position: one showed a valley and road covered with cannonballs, which Morris christened 'on'; the other showed the same view with no cannonballs present, which Morris named 'off.' Morris did not believe Sontag (and others discussed) could warrant their conclusions about 'faked' photographs based merely on cursory views of the photographs, or on other primary source data about Fenton's work in the Crimea. He consulted five 'esteemed curators,' experts on Fenton familiar with his letters, photographs, and documentary material on the Crimean War, and received contrasting interpretations: two supported Sontag's argument, arguing that 'off' came first; two suggested the opposite, arguing that the balls were removed so the road could be used or that the cannonballs had been 'harvested' by British soldiers so they could be recycled and fired back at the

Russians. One expert was ambivalent. Morris (2007b) wondered:

Would it be possible to order these photographs not based on anything that Fenton said (which might be unreliable)—but based on evidence in the photographs themselves? This idea appealed to me because it did not require me to imagine something about Fenton's intentions, that is, about his internal mental state.

The answer was provided by Morris' friend Dennis Purcell, who focused on small changes in the images. 'We were scrutinizing individual rocks in the Fenton photographs:

When the rocks are uphill, and you look at the road, you see that the balls are off the road... . Then, you look at the rocks after they have been dislodged—rocks that were kicked and then tumbled downhill—the balls are on the road... . In short, the first shot had to be taken when the balls were uphill. (Morris, 2007c)

Morris concluded: 'The one thing that we know about the rocks ... is that they were not posed. No one noticed them, let alone posed them. But together they helped unlock the secret of how to order the Fenton photographs.

I tried hard to prove that Keller and Sontag were wrong.... I failed. I can't deny it. But I did prove that they were right for the wrong reasons. It is not their assessment of Fenton's character or lack of character that establishes the order of the pictures.[9] (Morris, 2007c)

Of course, as Morris noted, both photographs were posed, if only by being framed by the photographer. The real dispute between Morris and the ghost of Susan Sontag is actually a paradigm difference between the postpositivist focus on photographs as indexical signs that are causally related to the objects that they reflect, and the hermeneutic view that the use and understanding of photographs is governed by socially established symbolic codes. While recognizing that photographs cannot be 'true' or 'false,' Morris insisted on *photographic* proof of which image came first, while the semiotician/hermeneutician insists that the meaning of photographs, as perceived things in the world, are created by interactions between photographer, image, and viewer.[10] Sontag's point was not an attack on Fenton's character, it was the political argument that 'early war photography turn(s) out to have been staged, or to have had their subjects tampered with' (Sontag, 2003; quoted in Morris, 2007b) and nothing in Morris's dissertation on cannonballs, especially the conclusion that she was right for the wrong reasons, disproves her argument. Hermeneutic and postpositivist paradigms rely on different approaches and standards of 'proof' to warrant their assertions.

INTERPRETIVE/HERMENEUTIC ANALYSES

In keeping with the Sekula and Tagg view of photography as a technology of power and a mechanism for creating 'texts' which must be 'read' to make sense, interpretative approaches seek photographic meaning in quite different ways from the postpositivists. This is not to argue that hermeneutic approaches may not take advantage of the techniques discussed above, just that hermeneutic approaches may go further and in different directions from the postpositivist approaches. In essence, there are two semiotic approaches to analyzing photographs, both discussed in other chapters in this volume:

1 Structural semiotics, which assumes there are certain signs that can be read and understood by everyone or nearly everyone in a culture.[11]
2 Social semiotics/iconology, which argues that different people and different social groups have

differing understandings of the meanings of texts—including photographs.[12]

Oral history, using photographs to solicit comments and analysis about the image and its original context, can be very helpful but is limited to the life span of potential interviewees. If human sources are not available, researchers must seek to understand the meanings of embedded information, such as Victorian hand gestures, dress, flowers, and group poses, by identifying and studying other resources.

A grounded theory approach to content analysis

Content analysis is not restricted to postpositivist hypothesis testing; it can also be employed more iteratively and inductively. Systematic approaches associated with grounded theory have been found to work effectively when applied to content analysis (Glaser, 1978; Glaser and Strauss, 1967; Strauss, 1987). Margolis collected and coded photographs of schools in the Farm Security Administration-Office of War Information Archives (FSA-OWI) into emergent categories using a three-phase process (Margolis, 2005).

As a first step, Margolis counted the number of school photos in these collections by year and discovered that they increased steadily (as shown in Table 18.1)

The second phase applied 'open' coding categories that were neither mutually exclusive nor exhaustive. Using a 'constant comparative' approach, the photographs were examined sequentially and provisional judgments were made about appropriate category coding for each image. For example,

Table 18.1 School photos in collections, by year

Date	1935	1936	1937	1938	1939	1940	1941	1942	1943	Total
School photos	42	79	74	177	292	436	351	1305	1711	4467

FSA-OWI images were coded using categories such as 'connotation' date, location, photographer, race of teachers and students, as well as 'denotative' or semiotic categories describing the image: social distance, perceived age of children, and whether the schools appeared to be 'healthy happy places' or impoverished and unhealthy. The categories Margolis used were not mutually exclusive; each photograph could be coded into more than one category if appropriate.

The third phase examined similarities and differences, and each category was reconsidered for applicability using axial coding. As new codes were identified, they were added. The categories were collapsed or expanded when appropriate as the process continued. The process was both inductive in reaching for hypotheses, and deductive in testing theories as they emerged (Charmaz and Mitchell, 2001). In the FSA-OWI project, Margolis concluded that the number of images coded 'schools as social problems' declined, and the number of schools depicted as 'healthy American schools' increased. Moreover, schools in the social problem category disappeared entirely when the sponsorship of the documentary process shifted from the Farm Security Administration's mission of the 1930s to the Office of War Information project of the 1940s. A theoretical hunch led to adding the code 'patriotic.' As a result, he found only a single image of saluting the flag before 1942, while in 1942–3 alone, 18 shots of pledging allegiance to the flag were taken (Margolis, 2005: 111).[13]

Theoretical coding offers another potential benefit: the ability to identify and recode for categories that were noted as absent, or null. Margolis repeated analysis of the collection, adding the codes 'Black schools' and White schools.' He discovered that these categories were mutually exclusive within the collection. Additional research of photographs from other sources from the 1930s and 1940s found a number of Black and White children in the same class; however, such images were not found in the FSA-OWI collection.[14]

While grounded theory avoids some issues related to the conclusion that postpositivist content analysis is un- or under-theorized, this approach cannot solve problems related to adequacy of the research sample in representing overall population, nor does it address Bell's question: Does the analysis yield statements that are meaningful to those who habitually 'read' or 'use' the images (Bell, 2001: 25)? Both forms of content analysis remain at the epistemological level of structuralist semiotics; the investigators define the categories as if these 'resources' were available to everyone (Jewitt and Omori, 2001).

INTENTIONALLY CREATED PHOTOGRAPHIC SYMBOLS

In *Camera Lucida*, Barthes coined the term 'punctum' to characterize the personal/ emotional effect some photographs have on the viewer (Barthes, 1981: 22–26). Many photographers seek to create images that function at this level, and such images virtually cry out for semiotic/symbolic examination.[15] As Rowe noted previously, above and beyond the 'truth' of the image there is a 'sultry interaction' between the photograph of Kaloma and viewers. The 'risqué' symbolism is an integral component of the image and cannot simply be ignored. Similarly, the *cabinet card* (Figure 18.2) is a complex image with carefully constructed symbolic elements on many levels. The tableau is carefully created and posed in a photographer's studio to show 'Professor Lutz' being teased by his students.[16] Analysis can begin with an inventory of iconic qualities. The professor is male; all the future teachers are women. The image blatantly parodies the 'normal school' class for future teachers.

Each woman poses, or was posed, to represent specific types of resistant student behavior. Two appear to engage, and potentially distract, the instructor while the rest of

Figure 18.2 An original cabinet card group photograph, *c.* late 1890s or early 1900s, by a portrait photographer at Blodgett's Studio in Hicksville, Ohio. Collection of Eric Margolis

the class acts out a range of misbehaviors. None of the other students attend to the lesson. Two pass a note; one pokes her classmate with a pencil, while another feigns sleep. The woman on the right appears to be tickling the student with her hands raised. While the professor concentrates on his lesson with the two students, another reaches to take the pencil from behind his ear.

Other meanings about the image and its intent can be deduced. The body is of course the site of desire, as are classrooms full of bodies. This image can be seen to speak to intentionally or desublimated sexuality. Despite a death grip on his pointer, the male body of Professor Lutz (or Lust?) struggles to maintain rigidity and decorum while surrounded by teasing young women. Underlying sexual tensions are revealed in images of school classrooms composed of all female students with a male professor. The arch gaze of the spectators contributes to the power,

sexuality, and repressed desire that saturate this image. Sex, of course, is an often unspoken text of schooling—and photography. Semiotic/iconographical approaches, though, cannot ultimately tell us the meaning the image had to its subjects and participants. All the women signed the back of the card, so perhaps it was made as an end of term gift. Alternately, the image could be a play or tableau, or even a photo to be used as a lesson about teaching. On the other hand, it is hard to miss Barthes' 'punctum' as it was constructed by both photographer and subjects.

CONCLUDING REMARKS

The role of historic photographs in research, and their use by historians, sociologists, ethnographers, geographers, and others is still being defined. When Margolis began studying coal miners in the mid-1970s historical societies and libraries gave essentially unrestricted access to the copying and use of their photographs. Rowe used to peruse boxes of unaccessioned material while curating exhibits and researching early photographers of the American Southwest.[17] Discoveries of new materials and relationships between images didn't depend on cataloging and 'finding aids' alone; luck and proximity were valuable collaborators. The rules of discovery have changed, though, as archives have begun to realize the value of their collections and the fragility of photographic materials and have emphasized preservation over convenience. As we noted above, the digitization of vast collections and their availability on the Internet has made images available as never before. 'Accidents of discovery' that used to only come from scanning Hollinger boxes now also come online. Increasing access to enormous online public collections like the California Digital Library and 'American Memory,' which incorporated hundreds of smaller collections, or commercial archives like Alinari, Corbis, and Getty continue to grow. Online sharing of images through Facebook and Flickr and other sites permits individuals, and increasingly museums, to post images, creating huge visual resources with research potential. These formal and informal resources and online access appear to approach Oliver Wendell Holmes' dream, in 1859, of an 'Imperial, National, or City Stereographic Library' where people could visit to see 'any object, natural or artificial' (Trachtenberg, 1989:16).

Historians and social scientists are just beginning to come to grips with the fact that photographs are much more than illustrations. Photographs are finally being recognized as valuable data sources that should be examined, using a variety of rigorous approaches and techniques, to explore the depth of information that they contain. Also, we agree with Barthes that photographs are intricate texts that must be responded to with the emotions, as well as with analytical reason.

This chapter does not propose a single methodology for the studying and analyzing of historic photographs. Images are complex, and as the value of the information that they contain is recognized, the palette of approaches to analyze and explore them will also be expanded and refined. Our intent is to share approaches that have proven valuable, to catalyze discussion, and to exchange ideas for continuing the evolution of approaches to photographic research.

NOTES

1 McDermott and Raley (Chapter 20) begin from a similar epistemological presupposition in their chapter, 'Looking closely: toward a natural history of human ingenuity,' tracing all visual social science to the rapid processing of symbolic interactions done by all people.

2 Holmes, Oliver Wendell (1859) 'The stereoscope and the stereograph,' *Atlantic Monthly*, 3(20): 738–748.

3 http://people.rit.edu/andpph/exhibit-3.html

4 See Mark Klett's contribution (Chapter 6), 'Repeat photography in landscape research,' for an excellent discussion of the digital technologies he uses to make rephotographs of historic images.

5 Some of the content of the present essay is excerpted, condensed, or elaborated from my previously published work in the study of historic photographs and especially the Kaloma image. For example, see: http://vintagephoto.com/reference/kaloma/1-02JosieKaloma%20article.htm

6 See: Rochlin, H. (1984) *Pioneer Jews—A New Life in the Far West*. Boston, MA: Houghton Mifflin.

7 Clamps and stands were used to hold subject's heads still during long exposures, such as in a studio. Improvements in the plates in use by the mid-1880s allowed for shorter exposures, and the clamps were eventually unnecessary.

8 Many of Frances Benjamin Johnston's photographs can be examined online. Several hundred of images of school classes can be found in her collection at the Library of Congress (keyword: 'school'). Available from: http://lcweb2.loc.gov/pp/fbjquery.html

9 Morris's postpositivism is most visible in his Popperian assertion of falsifiability (in the Postscript to his three-part series):

I spoke with Dennis Purcell recently and asked, 'Do you think these essays will put this issue—the issue of which came first—finally to rest.' Dennis replied, 'No. I don't think so. There could be some guy who reads your essays, writes in, and says: 'You know, there aren't just two photographs. I found another. There are actually three' (Morris, 2007b).

10 In an earlier *New York Times* blog, Morris also recognized that social knowledge was essential:

> Without a caption, without a context, without some idea about what the picture is a picture of, I can't answer. I simply cannot talk about the photograph as being true or false independently of beliefs about the picture. A caption less photograph, stripped of all context, is virtually meaningless. I need to know more (Morris, 2007a).

(In this he follows Gombrich (1961), who argued back in the 1960s that only captions or labels [as statements or propositions] can be true or false, not pictures.) But unless one is discussing formal logical propositions, this conclusion seems to defy common sense since if I look at a painting, say Jackson Pollock's 'Number 5,' I don't need a caption to tell me the meaning of what I am seeing, I just make it up. As John Berger wrote, 'In every act of looking there is an expectation of meaning' (Berger and Mohr, 1982: 117). Morris is right in that 'truth' is not a quality of photographs, but as Berger makes clear, meaning is. In the case of vernacular photographs torn from their context, we also create meaning in viewing them, but, as I will argue, we make the meanings using socially established and learned clues.

11 See Winfried Nöth's contribution (Chapter 16), 'Visual semiotics,' for a detailed discussion.

12 Marion Müller's contribution (Chapter 15) in this volume provides an excellent introduction to a long German literature on iconography and iconology, which has been little noticed outside Germany. Social semiotics/iconology lends itself to use of techniques, like audience studies, in communication and photo-elicitation research. These techniques are also addressed in Francesco Lapenta's contribution (Chapter 11) in this volume.

13 It might be possible to discover in the FSA-OWI written archives whether the decision to make 'patriotic' photographs was made by Roy Stryker who directed the project, or by individual photographers. The images and their sparse captions do not provide that information.

14 Margolis speculated that integrated classrooms would have angered the Southern 'Dixiecrats' who were an important part of the Roosevelt administration. Testing this hypothesis, as with the 'patriotic' images, however, would require analysis of many additional sources beyond the sample collection assembled by Margolis for his research.

15 In an earlier article, Margolis and Rowe conducted a detailed hermeneutic analysis of a photograph from the Phoenix Indian School with the title 'Good Night' (see Margolis and Rowe, 2002).

16 This is an original cabinet card group photograph, c. late 1890s or early 1900s, by a portrait photographer at Blodgett's Studio in Hicksville, Ohio.

17 Archives frequently went unguarded. Researchers brought briefcases gear including cameras, lights, and copy stands and were left alone. On a more positive note, while reviewing a collection for an exhibition, Rowe was able to identify and reassemble a missing album (Number 2 in a three-album series documenting construction of the Phoenix, Prescott, and Santa Fe railroad, c. 1891 by J. C. Burge), by identifying mount and captions information that appeared on photographs that had been disbound and distributed throughout the collection by individual image topic.

REFERENCES

Ackerman, D. (1997) *Mrs. Earp?* [Letters to the editor: June]. [Online]. *Maine Antiques Digest*. Available from: http://maineantiquedigest.com/articles_archive/articles/lett0697.htm [Accessed 2001].

Barrett, T. (1986) 'A theoretical construct for interpreting photographs', *Studies in Art Education*, 27(2): 52–60.

Barthes, R. (1981) *Camera Lucida: Reflections on Photography*. Tr. R. Howard. New York: Hill and Wang.

Bell, P. (2001) 'Content analysis of visual images', in T. van Leeuwen and C. Jewitt (eds.), *Handbook of Visual Analysis*. London: Sage Publications. pp. 10–34.

Berger, J. and Mohr, J. (1982) *Another Way of Telling*. New York: Pantheon.

Boyer, G. G. (1998 [1976]) *I Married Wyatt Earp. The Recollections of Josephine Sarah Marcus Earp*. Tucson, AZ: University of Arizona Press.

Charmaz, K. and Mitchell, R. (2001) 'Grounded theory in ethnography', in P. Atkinson, A. Coffey, S. Delamont, J. Lofland and L. Lofland (eds.), *Handbook of Ethnography*. London: Sage Publications. pp. 160–174.

Cuban, L. (1993) *How Teachers Taught: Consistency and Change in American Classrooms 1890–1990*, 2nd edn. New York and London: Teachers College Press.

Fox Talbot, W. H. (1844 [1989]) *The Pencil of Nature* (Facsimile ed). New York: Hans P. Kraus, Jr.

Geertz, C. (1973) 'Thick description: Toward an interpretative theory of culture', in C. Geertz (ed.), *The Interpretation of Cultures; Selected Essays.* New York: Basic Books. pp. 3–30.

Geertz, C. (1983) 'From the "Native's Point of View": On the nature of anthropological understanding', in *Local Knowledge: Further Essays in Interpretative Anthropology.* New York: Basic Books. pp. 55–70.

Glaser, B. (1978) *Advances in the Methodology of Grounded Theory: Theoretical Sensitivity.* Mill Valley, CA: The Sociology Press.

Glaser, B. and Strauss, A. (1967) *The Discovery of Grounded Theory: Strategies for Qualitative Research.* Chicago, IL: Aldine.

Goffman, E. (1976) *Gender Advertisements.* New York: Harper Colophon Books.

Gombrich, E. H. (1961) *Art and Illusion.* New York: Bollingen Foundation.

Jay, M. (1994) *Downcast Eyes: The Denigration of Vision in Twentieth-century French Thought.* Berkeley and Los Angeles, CA: University of California Press.

Jewitt, C. and Omori, R. (2001) 'Visual meaning: A social semiotic approach', in T. van Leeuwen and C. Jewitt (eds.), *Handbook of Visual Analysis.* London: Sage Publications. pp. 134–156.

Kuhn, T. (1970) *The Structure of Scientific Revolutions,* 2nd edn. Chicago, IL: University of Chicago Press.

Leggat, R. (1995) *A History of Photography from Its Beginnings Till the 1920s.* [Online]. Available from: http://www.rleggat.com/photohistory/

Lyman, C. M. (1982) *The Vanishing Race and Other Illusions: Photographs of Indians by Edward S. Curtis.* Washington, DC: Smithsonian Institution Press.

Margolis, E. (1988) 'Mining photographs: Unearthing the meaning of historical photos', *Radical History Review,* 40(January): 32–48.

Margolis, E. (2005) 'Liberal documentary goes to school: Farm Security Administration photographs of students, teachers and schools', in D. Holloway and J. Beck (eds.), *American Visual Cultures.* London and New York: Continuum.

Margolis, E. and Rowe, J. (2002) *Manufacturing Assimilation: Photographs of Indian Schools in Arizona.* [Online]. Available from: http://courses.ed. asu.edu/margolis/paper/paper.htm [Accessed 1 October 2002].

Mitchell, W. J. T. (1994) *Picture Theory: Essays on Verbal and Visual Representation.* Chicago, IL: University of Chicago Press.

Morris, E. (2007a) *Liar, Liar, Pants on Fire.* [Online]. Available from: http://opinionator.blogs.nytimes. com/2007/07/10/pictures-are-supposed-to-be-worth-a-thousand-words/ [Accessed 10 July 2007].

Morris, E. (2007b) *Which Came First, the Chicken or the Egg? (Part One).* [Online]. Available from: http:// opinionator.blogs.nytimes.com/2007/09/25/which-came-first-the-chicken-or-the-egg-part-one/ [Accessed 25 September 2007].

Morris, E. (2007c) *Which Came First? (Part Three): Can George, Lionel and Marmaduke Help Us Order the Fenton Photographs?* [Online]. Available from: http://opinionator.blogs.nytimes.com/2007/10/23/ which-came-first-part-three-can-george-lionel-and-marmaduke-help-us-order-the-fenton-photographs/ [Accessed 23 October 2007].

Newhall, B. (1964) *The History of Photography: 1839 to the Present Day.* New York: Museum of Modern Art.

Philips, D. C. and Burbules, N. (2000) 'What is post-positivism', in D. C. Philips and N. Burbules (eds.), *Postpositivism and Educational Research.* Lanham, MD: Rowman and Littlefield Publishers.

Raynor, B. (1997) *Re: Mr. Ackerman's Letter as Recently Published by Maine Antique Digest* [Letters to the editor: July]. [Online]. *Maine Antiques Digest.* Available from: http://maineantiquedigest.com/ articles_archive/articles/lett797.htm [Accessed 2001].

Rosler, M. (1990) 'In, around, and afterthoughts (on documentary photography)', in R. Bolton (ed.), *The Contest of Meaning: Critical Histories of Photography.* Cambridge, MA: MIT Press. pp. 304–341.

Rowe, J. (1991), 'Dudley P. Flanders stereoscopic views of a trip to Arizona', *Stereoworld, National Stereoscopic Association,* 18(5): 28–33.

Rowe, J. (1997) *Photographers in Arizona 1850–1920: A History and Directory.* Nevada City, CA: Carl Mautz Publishing.

Rowe, J. (2002) *Evidence, Interpretation, and Speculation: Thoughts on Kaloma, the Purported Photograph of Josie Earp.* [Online]. Available from: http://www.maineantiquedigest.com/articles/oct02/ josi1002.htm [Accessed 2 March 2003].

Rowe, J. (2007) *Real Photographic Postcards: A History and Portfolio.* Nevada City, CA: Carl Mautz Publishing.

Rowe, J. (2008) 'Arizona pioneer photographer George H. Rothrock', *Journal of Arizona History,* 49(Winter): 355–392.

Sekula, A. (1983) 'Photography between labor and capital', in B. H. D. Buchloh and R. Wilkie (eds.), *Mining Photographs and Other Pictures, 1848–1968.* Halifax, NS: Nova Scotia Press.

Steichen, E. (1984) *A Life in Photography.* New York: Bonanza Books and the Museum of Modern Art.

Strauss, A. (1987) *Qualitative Analysis for Social Scientists.* New York: The Press Syndicate of the University of Cambridge.

Tagg, J. (1988) *The Burden of Representation.* Amherst, MA: The University of Massachusetts Press.

Trachtenberg, A. (1989) *Reading American Photographs: Images as History.* New York: Hill and Wang.

19

Researching Film and History: Sources, Methods, Approaches

James Chapman

INTRODUCTION

Film has been the pre-eminent modern mass medium and, as such, offers a valuable source for the historian. That it is also a highly problematic source, however, is evident from the fact that relatively few historians seem willing or able to engage with the medium. Partly this may reflect an entrenched cultural resistance toward what is often regarded as an ephemeral and low-brow medium of popular entertainment. But it may also arise from an uncertainty within the historical profession over the nature of film both as a source and as a form of historical communication. The US academic Professor Robert A. Rosenstone has suggested that 'the topic of history and film... still must be seen as a field (or a sub-field or a sub-sub-field) in search of a methodology' (Rosenstone, 2006: 165). Rosenstone's assertion makes a provocative starting point for a historiographical discussion of history and film. This chapter will provide a short summary of the emergence of film history as an academic discipline; it will consider the nature and value of

film as a historical source; it will demonstrate how we can interpret film from a historical perspective as both a social document and a cultural artifact; and it will evaluate the possibilities and limitations of film as a medium of historical communication. What I hope to demonstrate is that, far from being a 'field in search of a methodology,' film history is a distinctive area of historical inquiry that has reached a state of methodological sophistication that belies Rosenstone's claim.

A SHORT HISTORY OF FILM HISTORY

While the history of film dates back to the invention of the medium in the 1890s—the first public film shows occurred in 1895 when the Skladanowsky brothers projected their Bioskop in Berlin and the Lumière brothers unveiled their Cinématographe in Paris—the academic study of film is a much more recent development. The first histories of film were written in the late 1920s, such as

Terry Ramsaye's *A Million and One Nights* (1926) and Paul Rotha's *The Film Till Now* (1930), and tended to privilege an aesthetic history that argued for film as an art form and therefore focused on a relatively narrow selection of important films from the major film-producing countries (the USA, France, Germany, Russia, and Britain). It was not until the 1960s, however, that film was being taught as a subject in American and British universities—often, in those days, as an adjunct to English literature—and that the first academic journals appeared in the form of the historically oriented *Journal of the University Film Association* and the more theoretically inclined *Screen Education*. The arrival of film on the university curriculum prompted the establishment of professional associations for film researchers, such as the Society for Education in Film and Television (Britain), the Society for Cinema Studies (USA), and the International Association for Media and History.

The key period for the emergence of film history was during the 1960s and 1970s. This period saw the publication of important scholarly texts that did much to shape the nature of the discipline. Robin Wood's *Hitchcock's Films* (1965) was the first English-language text to adopt the French '*politique des auteurs*' and apply it to the study of a popular filmmaker.[1] Jim Kitses's *Horizons West* (1969) and Colin McArthur's *Underworld USA* (1971) laid the foundations of genre criticism in their studies of the American Western and gangster film. Raymond Durgnat's *A Mirror for England* (1970), Jeffrey Richards's *Visions of Yesterday* (1973), and Robert Sklar's *Movie-Made America* (1975) were social histories of film arguing that popular films could be understood as reflections of the cultural and ideological currents prevailing in the societies in which they were made. Richard Taylor's *Film Propaganda* (1979) was the first comparative analysis of how the state-controlled film industries of the Soviet Union and Nazi Germany embraced cinema as an instrument of mass persuasion. And Marc Ferro's *Cinema and History* (1977) and Pierre

Sorlin's *The Film in History* (1980) represented the first attempts to theorize the nature of historical representation in film.

The entry of film into the academic curriculum led, perhaps inevitably, certainly regrettably, to a schism within the field that divided on methodological and ideological lines. On the one hand, emerging principally from an English literature background, was a tradition of high theory that adopted linguistic methods of semiotics and structuralism and applied them to the textual analysis of film. '*Screen* theory' (as it became known after the journal in which much of this research appeared) attempted to move beyond the aesthetic criticism and quality judgments that informed conventional film criticism (especially the '*auteur* theory') and to understand cinema as an ideological apparatus. To this end it drew upon a range of theoretical perspectives from Althussarian Marxism to Lacanian psychoanalysis. *Screen* theory might be seen as an attempt to construct a totalizing theory of cinema, but it was criticized for its tendency to homogenize films in a way that did not allow for differences between texts and to see the cinema spectator as a theoretical construct rather than as groups of historical individuals. On the other hand, emerging principally from social and cultural history, another approach privileged context rather than text, exploring the historical conditions under which films were made and documenting their production and reception through the available primary sources. Film historians understand the meaning of films to arise not from the decoding of films by a theoretical spectator but rather from the relationship between films and the societies in which they were produced and consumed. This approach has been criticized, in turn, for reading films as a crude 'reflection' or 'mirror' of society and for not paying due attention to their status as cultural artifacts. The institutionalization of the intellectual differences between the two schools was exemplified in the direction of the two leading film journals. While *Screen* has been at the vanguard of theoretical developments in the field (including psychoanalysis in the 1970s, gender studies in the 1980s, and reception theory in the 1990s), the *Historical Journal of Film, Radio and Television* is the leading forum for those seeking to locate films in their social, political, and economic contexts.

Since the mid-1980s, however, the ideological cold war between the film theory and film history schools has thawed and their proponents have become less trenchant in their criticisms of the other. The emergence of what has been called 'New Film History' has seen a more holistic and inclusive approach that combines both textual and contextual analysis.[2] The most influential publication in this regard was David Bordwell, Janet Staiger, and Kristin Thompson's *The Classical Hollywood Cinema* (1985), a *magnum opus* that looked at the US film industry between the late 1910s and *c.* 1960 as a 'mode of film practice' in which the institutionalization of an industrial method of filmmaking (the studio system) was intimately connected to the ascendancy of a particular style of film (the 'classical' feature film). The authors use both films and other primary sources, such as scripts, technical manuals, and trade journals, to demonstrate how 'style and industry came to be so closely synchronized' in the Hollywood studios (Bordwell et al., 1985: 9).

New Film History has three particular characteristics. The first is its greater level of methodological sophistication. It understands films neither as a straightforward reflection of social trends nor as 'texts' waiting to be decoded through the application of theory, but rather as complex cultural artifacts whose content and style is determined by a range of historical processes (including, but not limited to, industrial practices, economic constraints, relations with external bodies, the interventions of producers and censors, and the role of individual creative agency within the filmmaking process). It also recognizes that the production and reception of films are historically specific and seeks out evidence of actual responses rather than assuming a homogeneous audience. This relates to the second element of New Film History: the

central importance of primary sources. These include both the films themselves and non-filmic sources such as company records, personal papers, scripts, diaries, letters, publicity materials, reviews, and box-office receipts. The third characteristic of New Film History is its cultural competence in reading films through both their narrative content and their visual style. One of the criticisms leveled against the work of some film historians is the tendency to read films solely as narratives, as if they were novels, without any acknowledgement that films also create meaning through their *mise-en-scène*—a term that refers to the formal and visual properties of film, including set design, art direction, lighting, costumes, and editing. Film style is historically and culturally specific—movements such as the German expressionist cinema of the early 1920s or the American *film noir* cycle between the mid-1940s and mid-1950s arose from particular conditions and circumstances—and the film historian must be alert to changes in fashion and popular taste in order to understand the history of film style.

A note on film preservation and archiving

All history is determined, in the first instance, by the nature and extent of the sources that are available. In this sense film historical research faces the same challenges as other areas of history: often it is based on an archival record that is fragmentary and incomplete. For such a modern medium, it may seem surprising that there are so many gaps in the archival materials. This is particularly true of the period before the 1930s. It has been estimated that up to three-quarters of 'early cinema' (*c.* 1895–1905) no longer survives. Our knowledge of this formative period in the history of the medium is, therefore, based on a sample of films that may not be entirely representative. Early works by important filmmakers such as John Ford and F. W. Murnau remain 'lost,' and other films survive only in fragments. Even some of the great 'classics,' such as Fritz Lang's *Metropolis* (1926) and Abel Gance's *Napoléon* (1927), exist today only in versions that have been restored through the painstaking efforts of archivists and historians but which may be different from the films as they were originally screened. This calls into question the idea of there being a 'definitive' version of the film. It may never be possible to see these important films in the form in which they were originally released.

Why has so much of our film heritage been lost? There are two principal reasons. For one thing film is a highly perishable medium: celluloid film stock decays more rapidly than paper.[3] Today, many films are transferred onto digital media—some are even created digitally—but the long-term stability of these media is still uncertain. Film also tends to be seen as an ephemeral medium. For early distributors and exhibitors, especially, films were a commodity that would be screened for a few days and then forgotten when the next batch arrived. It was not until the 1930s that any serious attention was given to film preservation when archives such as the Museum of Modern Art in New York, the National Film Library in London and the Cinémathèque Française in Paris began collecting prints of films for posterity. Even then the film preservation movement has struggled against the ingrained attitude that film was and is foremost a commodity rather than a historical source or an art form. As Ernest Lindgren, curator of the National Film Library, observed in 1948: 'The word "archive" rings with a deathly sound in the world of cinema, which is so young, vital and dynamic, eager for the future and impatient of the past' (Lindgren, 1947: 47).

The nature of film as a historical source

All films comprise moving images recorded through a technical process of photomechanical reproduction and most films consist of multiple images edited together in sequence. The unique formal property of film is its photographic representation of external reality: for this reason film has been claimed as the most realistic of all media. The influential French critic André Bazin, for example, averred that film represented 'an integral realism, a recreation of the world in its own image, an image unburdened by the freedom of interpretation of the artist or the irreversibility of time' (Bazin, 1967: 21). Perhaps the nearest that the medium has ever come to this ideal was in the early '*actualités*' of the Lumière brothers: simple films of everyday events such as workers leaving the factory gate or of a train arriving in a station.

Early cinematographers, certainly, made great claims for their medium as a historical document. In 1898, for example, the Polish cinematographer Boleslas Matuszewski, whose films included records of the Coronation of Tsar Nicholas II and the Diamond Jubilee of Queen Victoria, gave a lecture in Paris where he described film as 'a new source of history' and expressed his belief that 'animated photography could become a singularly efficacious teaching process' (Matuszewski, 1995: 322). Matuszewski held that cinematography, even more so than still photography, had a unique quality of authenticity or 'truth':

> Perhaps the cinematograph does not give history in its entirety, but what it does deliver is incontestable and of an absolute truth. Ordinary photography admits of *retouching*, to the point of transformation. But try to retouch, in an identical way for each figure, these thousand or twelve hundred, almost microscopic negatives!... One could say that animated photography has a character of authenticity, accuracy and precision that belongs to it alone. It is the ocular evidence that is truthful and infallible *par excellence*. (Matuszewski, 1995: 323)

Much of the appeal of early cinema was its ability to present images of people and places to its patrons. Two of the earliest film genres were 'topicals' (records of newsworthy events) and 'scenics' (travelogues of foreign places and landscapes). The films of the Delhi Durbars of 1903 and 1911—great

Orientalist spectacles welcoming first Edward VII and then George V as Emperor of India—could be included in both these categories.

Matuszewski's belief in the 'absolute truth' of the cinematograph, however, does not stand up to scrutiny. Indeed, never has there been a more misleading dictum than 'the camera never lies.' Early cinematographers were not averse to reconstructing events for the camera if they were unable to capture the original event. The French pioneer Georges Méliès produced films of the sinking of the battleship *USS Maine* (1898) and the Coronation of Edward VII (1901) that were entirely recreated in the studio: the latter film was actually shot before the event itself! To be fair to the early pioneers, their intention was not necessarily to deceive the audience and such films were often acknowledged as studio reconstructions. British pioneer R. W. Paul, for example, produced a series of topicals entitled *Reproductions of Incidents of the Boer War* 'arranged under the supervision of an experienced military officer from the front.' As far as evidence of the reception of these films is available, it would suggest that early cinema patrons did not distinguish between real and reconstructed films.

The question of actuality versus reconstruction is best exemplified by the case of the first long (feature-length) documentary film: *The Battle of the Somme* (1916). *The Battle of the Somme* was a compilation of footage shot at the front by two British War Office cinematographers, Geoffrey Malins and J. B. McDowell, on the first day of the major British offensive against the German positions (1 July 1916). Malins and McDowell shot film of the opening artillery bombardment, the explosion of a giant mine under Hawthorn Ridge, British troops on the way to the front, scenes at a first aid station showing wounded British and captured German troops, and captured German trenches. When the rushes of this material were shown to the Topical Committee for War Films in London—an organization set up to supervise films about the front for public consumption—it was decided they should be edited into a full-length feature film. *The Battle of the Somme* was first shown in London on 21 August 1916 and a general release across the country followed a week later *The Battle of the Somme*, 2010.

The reception of *The Battle of the Somme* has been well documented: it evidently had an enormous impact on the British public and there are reports of hundreds of thousands of people flocking to see it (Badsey, 1983; Reeves, 1997). Reviews in both the national press and the trade papers were much impressed by its vivid and authentic pictures of the front. One sequence in particular was much commented upon: where a platoon of soldiers goes 'over the top' and two fall dead. Among those who saw the film was the author Sir Henry Rider Haggard, who recorded in his diary that the film:

> ...does give a wonderful idea of the fighting. "The most impressive [shot] to my mind," is that of a regiment scrambling out of a trench to charge and of the one man who slides back shot dead. There is something appalling about the instantaneous change from fierce activity to supine death. (Badsey, 1983: 84)

As film archivist Roger Smither has conclusively demonstrated, however, these shots that created such an impact were staged for the camera behind the lines. There are numerous visual clues. The trench is too shallow for the front line and there is no barbed wire on the parapet; the troops themselves are lightly equipped and are not wearing field backpacks; the position of the camera is too exposed for this to have been taken under enemy fire; and the clinching detail is that one of the 'dead' soldiers who falls forward onto barbed wire can then be seen crossing his legs. How far does this compromise *The Battle of the Somme* as an authentic historical record? Smither points out that 'the proportion of such film to the whole work is actually quite small' and that the vast majority of *The Battle of the Somme* is indeed the real thing (Smither, 1988: 160). The inclusion of a small amount of 'faked' film in *The Battle of the Somme* does not detract from its value as a historical source.

Regardless of whether a film image is indeed what it purports to be, or whether it has been reconstructed for the camera after the event, no film can ever claim to be an unmediated reproduction of reality. Films are highly mediated texts: choices have been made about what to film, where to place the camera, which shots to select, and the sequence in which they are edited together. This is true even of the most straightforward '*actualité*' films. The Lumières' films *Workers Leaving the Factory Gate* and *Arrival of a Train at La Ciotat* (1895) both consist of one shot under a minute in length. In both films the camera is placed in a position that approximates the point of view of a spectator watching the event, but whereas the first film is shot in a side-on tableau frame, the second is shot at an angle that makes it seem that the locomotive is heading toward the camera. This accounts for the reaction of audiences, who reportedly moved out of the way as the train approached. In the sense that the train in the film is not a real train, but rather a visual image of a train, then the film medium should be understood not as a *reproduction* of reality but rather as a *representation* of it.

The notion that film represents the external world through its own formal codes and conventions underlies what has been called the 'formative' tradition in film theory. The early film theorist Rudolf Arnheim, for example, recognized that filmmakers soon started to explore the formal possibilities of the medium:

> What had hitherto been merely the urge to record certain events now became the aim to represent objects by means exclusive to film. These means obtrude themselves, show themselves able to do more than simply reproduce the required object; they sharpen it, impose a style upon it, point out special features, make it vivid and decorative. Art begins where mechanical reproduction leaves off, where the conditions of representation serve in some way to mould the object. (Arnheim, 1958: 55)

Arnheim goes on to list the ways in which film could be made to differ from external reality, including the framing of the image, optical effects such as fades and dissolves, and the use of editing (or montage) to disrupt the continuities of space and time.

One of the unique properties of film, and one that problematizes its status as a historical source, is its ability to create an impression of reality through artifice. A good recent example of this is *Saving Private Ryan* (dir. Steven Spielberg, 1998), which is widely held to have set new standards of realism and authenticity in the representation of combat in a fiction film. Its sequence of the American D-Day landings on Omaha Beach, Normandy (France), on 6 June 1944, was described by critics as 'Hollywood's most grimly realistic and historically accurate depiction of a World II battlefield' and 'as graphic as any war footage I've ever seen' (Chapman, 2008: 21). Further evidence of the film's impact is to be found in the responses of Normandy veterans who spoke of 'powerful memories being reawakened.' Even military historians such as John Keegan and Stephen E. Ambrose averred that it exhibited 'historical truth' and was 'the most accurate and realistic depiction of war on screen that I have ever seen' (Chapman, 2008: 22–23).

Yet this 'most realistic' of combat movies is, of course, entirely fictitious (contrary to some accounts it is not based on a true story) and its 'graphic' war footage is the work of a master filmmaker with all the technical expertise and resources of Hollywood behind him. The publicity material around the film emphasized the lengths to which the filmmakers had gone to achieve the impression of realism. *Saving Private Ryan* is unusual even in this genre for its attention to visual and aural authenticity. Thus, in order to simulate the noise of bullets ripping into bodies the sound editor recorded rounds being fired into meat carcasses wrapped in cloth, while Spielberg and cinematographer Janusz Kaminski used desaturated color and deliberately out-of-focus shots to replicate the 'look' of authentic combat footage. Archivist Toby Haggith has shown that, in fact, Spielberg over-egged the pudding, creating effects that would have been impossible for a camera-man to achieve under combat conditions. For example, the shot of the first fatalities, machine-gunned as the ramp of their landing craft is lowered, is taken from outside the landing craft looking back toward it. Haggith concedes that 'the Spielberg version of D-Day is a more impressive account of the event' than the existing actuality footage of the landings, but nevertheless points out 'the artificial and manipulative technique with which the battle has been recreated' (Haggith, 2002: 348).

ANALYZING FILM AS A HISTORICAL SOURCE

The historian may be interested in films as records of the past (actuality and documentary films), films as cultural artifacts (the historical analysis of film form, style, and aesthetics), or films as social documents (the idea that films reflect the values, attitudes, and assumptions of the societies in which they were produced and consumed). In using film the historian must ask the same questions as of any source: What was its provenance? Who made it and who saw it? Under what circumstances was it made, and with what intention? How widely was it disseminated, and what effects or consequences might it have had? Rarely, if at all, will the answers to these questions be evident solely from the film itself, and therefore film historical research must be supplemented by other sources such as company records, personal papers, scripts, diaries, letters, publicity materials, reviews, and box-office receipts. The availability of such material varies between countries and periods: the classical Hollywood film industry is well documented, as the archives of the major film studios have been deposited in research libraries, but elsewhere, particularly in the developing world, the archival record is patchy.

The term 'film' covers a wide range of forms, ranging from short 'actuality' scenes to the fictional feature film, but as historical sources films tend to fall into two broad categories. On the one hand, there are films where the empirical content has value as a historical source: these tend to be non-fiction films—actuality, newsreels, and documentaries—that represent a particular event or subject. This is true no matter how heavily mediated the source is. Thus, for example, a newsreel of the liberation of Belsen provides a record of that event and also has some value as historical evidence for the extent of the Nazi extermination program and the physical condition of the survivors. And a documentary such as *Nanook of the North* (dir. Robert Flaherty, 1922), for all that we know that Flaherty staged scenes for the camera, nevertheless still acts as an ethnographic record of the daily life of an Eskimo and his family. On the other hand, there is the fictional feature film where the film's value as a historical source is detached from its empirical content. For example, neither *The Birth of a Nation* (dir. D. W. Griffith, 1915) nor *Gone with the Wind* (dir. Victor Fleming, 1939) would ever be used as sources for the American Civil War and its aftermath, any more than *Gladiator* (dir. Ridley Scott, 2000) tells us anything about the architecture of the Colosseum or the nature of Roman politics *c.* AD 180. What these films do reveal, however, is evidence of American attitudes toward race and gender in the 1910s and 1930s, while *Gladiator* has been interpreted as 'a critique of Clintonian America' (Richards, 2008: 176).

It will be clear that the different types of film will provide different sorts of historical evidence. For the historian interested in, for example, social conditions or leisure activities, the most useful type of film is likely to be unedited actuality film. This will often have been taken by local cameramen and may range from semi-professional to 'home movie' footage. Amateur filmmaking was a popular pastime between the 1920s and 1960s, though it tended to be more prosperous families who could afford cine-cameras (usually using 8 mm or 9.5 mm film) and so the available material is weighted disproportionately in favor of the middle classes. The most famous 'home movie' footage is surely that shot by Eva Braun, which shows Adolf Hitler relaxing in his mountain retreat at Berchtesgaden. While it provides a fascinating insight into the 'home life' of the Führer, however, it is of little value in understanding the historical conditions of the Third Reich as it is, by its nature, restricted to an elite group around Hitler. But there is sufficient amateur footage from the period to suggest that a large proportion of the German people seemed happy and prosperous under the Third Reich: at the very least there was clearly ample time for leisure and sport.

Perhaps the type of film used most by the social historian is the edited non-fiction film. This provides visual evidence of material conditions, working practices, social customs and behavior, though it has gone through an extra layer of mediation than unedited footage. The most extensive collection of this sort of material in the world is believed to be that of the Lancashire filmmakers Sagar Mitchell and James Kenyon, which comprises over 800 non-fiction subjects shot between the late 1890s and 1913 (Toulin et al., 2005). The Mitchell and Kenyon films were mostly actuality films of particular events that were shown in local cinemas under the banner: 'See yourself as others see you.' The interest of Mitchell and Kenyon's films lies in their representation of commonplace events, from football matches to days at the fairground. A type of film known as a 'phantom ride'—where a camera was attached to a moving tram—was popular around the turn of the century. These films are useful sources for urban and architectural historians as records of the modern city *c.* 1900.

These early 'topicals' can be seen as the precursors of the newsreel film. The first regular weekly newsreels were introduced *c.* 1910 and thereafter became institutionalized with the emergence of major newsreel companies such as Pathé, Gaumont, and Movietone. The chief value of the newsreels is in documenting what topical events were

reported to the public and how those events were represented. The newsreel is even more heavily mediated than the edited non-fiction film: editorial choices have been made about what to report; the film has been edited into a sequence; and, from the late 1920s, music and commentary have been added as an additional layer of exposition. The content of the newsreels was also subject to a range of institutional and political determinants. Anthony Aldgate's study of the British newsreels during the 1930s, for example, demonstrates that the newsreels promoted a consensual view of the major topical issues of the day and effectively endorsed the National Government's policies on rearmament and appeasement. Aldgate concludes that the newsreel companies 'knew that film was a medium which could easily be manipulated, and they knew how to manipulate the medium to best advantage' (Aldgate, 1979: 193).

One example must suffice to illustrate how the newsreels manipulated public opinion. British Movietone's *Epic of Dunkirk* (6 June 1940) is far from being an objective account of the withdrawal of the British Expeditionary Force. It clearly sets out to place a positive 'spin' on events through its up-tempo music and jaunty commentary. The evacuation is presented as an unqualified success: commentary refers to 'the success of this amazing military exploit' and asserts that 'the story of that epic withdrawal will live in history both as a glorious example of discipline and as a monument to sea power.' There is no mention of casualties, and all the shots of British and French troops show them smiling and in good spirits. It can be seen as nothing less than an attempt to position Dunkirk as a victory rather than a defeat. And it makes clear where the blame lies: the 'gallant British and French troops [were] betrayed by the desertion of the Belgian king.' This is not to say that *Epic of Dunkirk* has no value as a historical source: merely, that that we must be alert that it is a highly mediated source.

The same is true of documentary films. Again, one example must suffice to illustrate a general point. *Triumph of the Will* (dir. Leni

Riefenstahl, 1935) was a film of the 1934 Nazi Party rally in Nuremberg: it was compiled from 61 hours of film shot by 16 cameramen. On one level, of course, *Triumph of the Will* acts as a historical record of the rally, showing Hitler's arrival in Nuremberg and his speech to the party faithful. (The audience includes, ironically, Ernst Rohm and other members of the *Sturm Abteilung* who would be assassinated on Hitler's orders in the 'Night of the Long Knives' after the film was shot but before it was released.) On another level, however, *Triumph of the Will* is clearly a highly crafted piece of propaganda that uses film technique (editing, lighting, camera angles) to promote the idea of *Führerprinzip* (leadership) and create an impression of mass support for the regime. *Triumph of the Will* has been described as 'the most powerful propaganda film ever made' (Katz, 1996: 1151). To this extent the historical evidence it contains is largely of the sort that Arthur Marwick appropriately described as 'witting testimony' (Marwick, 1989: 216).

By contrast, the fictional feature film— which has been by far the dominant mode of filmmaking—is largely of value for the 'unwitting testimony' it contains. The feature film has been seen as 'a reflection of certain ideas and preoccupations' (Richards, 1973: xv) and as 'a primary source of information about society and human behavior for large masses of people' (Sklar, 1975: 316). This idea can be traced to the work of the German sociologist Siegfried Kracauer, whose book *From Caligari to Hitler* (1947) argued that the cinema of Weimar Germany provided a unique insight into the psychological state of the German people in the aftermath of the First World War. Kracauer maintained that films reflect society more directly than other cultural practices because film is a collective medium that has to satisfy the desires of a mass audience. 'What films reflect,' he claimed, 'are not so much explicit credos as psychological dispositions—those deep layers of mentality which extend more or less below the dimension of consciousness'

(Kracauer, 1947: 6). In particular, the distorted imagery of expressionist films such as *The Cabinet of Dr Caligari* (dir. Robert Wiene, 1919) and *Dr Mabuse, the Gambler* (dir. Fritz Lang, 1922) was seen as reflecting the social dislocation and political instability of postwar Germany. This notion has since been much criticized and is no longer accepted uncritically. In particular, Kracauer's suggestion that these films revealed the unconscious inclination of the German people toward dictatorship, and thus anticipated the rise of Nazism, has been criticized for 'mixing weak history with flimsy psychology' and for reading 'too much out of the films through hindsight' (Monaco, 1976: 160). Most film historians, however, accept that—sometimes in general ways, other times in highly specific ways—feature films respond to and are informed by the cultural, social, and political contexts in which they are produced and consumed.

FILM AS A MEDIUM OF HISTORICAL COMMUNICATION

From the outset, film has been used to tell historical stories. Among the early kinetoscope films were *Joan of Arc* and *The Execution of Mary, Queen of Scots*. Early narrative films such as *The Great Train Robbery* (dir. Edwin S. Porter, 1903) and *The Story of the Kelly Gang* (dirs. John and Nevin Tait, 1906) were based on 'true' stories of notorious criminals. The first historical epics were produced in Italy before the First World War: *Quo Vadis?* (dir. Enrico Guazzoni, 1913) and *Cabiria* (dir. Giovanni Pastrone, 1914). These in turn influenced D. W. Griffith's *Judith of Bethulia* (1913), *The Birth of a Nation* (1915) and *Intolerance* (1916). The historical feature film, in one form or another, has been a staple of most national cinemas. Films such as the British *Scott of the Antarctic* (dir. Charles Frend, 1948) and the Australian *Gallipoli* (dir. Peter Weir, 1981) demonstrate the special relationship between the historical film and the representation of national identity in cinema.

Most professional historians tend to be highly skeptical about the feature film as a medium of historical communication. They will typically focus on its historical inaccuracies, especially in arcane points of detail. A good example is the expert on arms and heraldry who took great delight in listing the many historical infelicities of *The Private Life of Henry VIII* (dir. Alexander Korda, 1933). These included the Gentlemen of the Court wearing swords within the palace precincts, the king's shoe buckles being on the inside of his feet rather than the outside ('Mr Laughton wears his spurs like a cowboy'), the Earl of Essex not wearing his Lesser George Garter 'as he was bound to by the Statutes of the Order,' and the executioner of Anne Boleyn using a German fighting sword of 1580 (Beard, 1934: 124). While this level of criticism may seem absurdly pedantic, it is not unusual for historical films to provoke such nit-picking responses from historical experts.

A more general criticism of the historical film is its tendency to take liberties with recorded history for dramatic or ideological effect. A few examples will suffice to make this point. While there is no evidence to suggest that Charles I and Oliver Cromwell ever met, the film *Cromwell* (dir. Ken Hughes, 1970) contrives no fewer than three face-to-face meetings. *Mary, Queen of Scots* (dir. Charles Jarrott, 1971) also included two entirely fictitious meetings between Mary Stuart and Elizabeth I. The producers defended these invented incidents on the grounds of dramatic necessity: the films required them to provide 'big' moments of drama. This exemplifies the tendency of the historical feature film to represent history as biography rather than as social process. Sometimes, however, filmmakers are seen as taking too great a liberty. The *Daily Telegraph* was so outraged by *Elizabeth* (dir. Shekhar Kapur, 1998) that it published a leading article describing the film as 'a blackguardly slur upon a good Christian woman' for its

suggestion that the 'Virgin Queen' enjoyed a passionate sexual affair with the Earl of Leicester (Chapman, 2005: 6). *Braveheart* (dir. Mel Gibson, 1995) similarly provoked controversy by suggesting that William Wallace fathered the future Edward III by Princess Isabelle of Wales. And British critics were outraged when *U-571* (dir. Jonathan Mostow, 2001) showed the US Navy rather than the Royal Navy capturing the Enigma machine.

Have there been any historical films that met with the approval of historians? It would be fair to say that examples have been rare. Christopher Hill, the Master of Balliol College, Oxford, and renowned social historian of the seventeenth century, was sufficiently impressed by *Winstanley* (dirs Kevin Brownlow and Andrew Mollo, 1975) that he gave the film his scholarly endorsement in the prestigious journal *Past and Present*:

> Good historical films are sufficiently rare for it to be worth drawing attention to *Winstanley* ... . Although made on a shoe-string budget, the film's detail is meticulously accurate, down to the shoes which the Diggers wear, the agricultural implements they use, the breed of animals they farm ... . But more important than this convincing background is the imaginative reconstruction of the world in which the Diggers lived—still torn by social conflict, but one in which fundamental reform still seemed possible. The film can tell us more about ordinary people in seventeenth-century England than a score of textbooks. (Hill, 1975: 132)

Winstanley, however, was a very different kind of historical film from most. It was independently produced for the British Film Institute rather than for a commercial producer and was filmed using a cast of mostly non-professional actors—a technique that some filmmakers employ to elicit performances that seem more like 'real' people than recognizable actors.

Winstanley exemplifies what Rosenstone has termed 'the New History film.' This is a film that 'finds the space to *contest* history, to interrogate either the meta-narratives that structure historical knowledge, or smaller historical truths, received notions, conventional images' (Rosenstone, 1995: 8). Other examples of this type include *Hiroshima, mon amour* (dir. Alain Resnais, 1959), *Hitler: A Film from Germany* (dir. Hans-Jürgen Syderberg, 1977), and *Walker* (dir. Alex Cox, 1987). These films tend to be on the margins of commercial film culture and are often the work of directors with a highly self-conscious and formalist style.

There has always been a tradition of alternative historical filmmaking. This emerged first in the Soviet avant-garde of the 1920s where a cycle of 'Jubilee' films, including *Strike* (dir. Sergei Eisenstein, 1925), *Battleship Potemkin* (dir. Sergei Eisenstein, 1925), *The End of St Petersburg* (dir. Vsevolod Pudovkin, 1927), *The Fall of the Romanov Dynasty* (dir. Esther Shub, 1927), and *October* (dir. Sergei Eisenstein, 1928), were commissioned to commemorate landmarks in the revolutionary struggle. These films are recognized as some of the most technically innovative in the history of cinema, especially for their use of montage—a form of rhythmic editing that saw the individual shot as a building block in the creation of meaning. They are also notable for their focus on the mass rather than the individual, thus representing history as a process rather than a personalized narrative. Yet they also took dramatic license in their representation of history. This is exemplified by the famous 'Odessa steps' sequence of *Battleship Potemkin* where Eisenstein employs montage to brilliant effect in depicting the massacre of demonstrators by Tsarist troops. Yet, as Richard Taylor reminds us, this not only lays claim to being 'the most famous sequence of images in the history of world cinema' but 'also provides a classic example of poetic license: a filmic creation of a historical event that in itself never happened but that encapsulates in *microcosm* the *macrocosmic* drama of the more general historical process' (Taylor, 2000: 35).

Rosenstone sees *Battleship Potemkin* and *October* as 'innovative historicals' that are more than works of propaganda. *October*, he claims, 'is also a work of history that can stand beside written interpretations of the same topic' (Rosenstone, 2006: 51). He argues against the orthodox historical critique of film that focuses on its factual inaccuracies and asserts that the historical film is simply another form of historical communication that is different from, not inferior to, the written word. Rosenstone draws upon the work of poststructuralist critics such as Hayden White and Frank Ankersmit for intellectual ballast. The poststructuralist critique of history calls into question the idea of historical 'fact' and sees works of history as 'texts' or 'discourses.' Film, in this argument, is another text or discourse. Rosenstone argues that 'filmmakers can be and already are historians (some of them), but *of necessity the rules of engagement of their works with the stuff of the past are and must be different from those that govern written history*' (Rosenstone, 2006: 8).

It seems to me that Rosenstone is correct only insofar as historians who attack films for their departures from the historical record have generally failed to understand the nature of film as a medium of representation and (let it be said) entertainment. To suggest, however, that a historical film has the same status as a piece of historical scholarship is utterly absurd. All forms of historical communication are not equal: if they were we would have to attach equal weight to a student essay as to a scholarly monograph! The historical film is at best a popular form of history in the manner of the historical novel. Its purpose is to entertain rather than to educate us about the past. *The Private Life of Henry VIII* succeeded because it was a period 'romp' rather than a history lesson. Even *October*, which clearly has a highly didactic intent, is a spectacle first and a historical narrative second.

The real value of film as a historical source is what it tells us about the time in which it was made rather than the period in which it is set. Sometimes, as in *October*, the historical distance from the subject may be relatively short (a decade), but even so the chief ideological import of *October* is what it reveals about the nature of Soviet politics in the late 1920s (particularly the emerging cult of Stalin and the elimination of Trotsky from the official history). *Gone with the Wind* is of interest not for what it says about the causes of the American Civil War, but rather as an example of the retrospective cultural and ideological contest over the meaning of the war. *Saving Private Ryan* may not be an authentic account of the landings on Omaha Beach, but it is a rich source for understanding the popular memory of the Second World War. *The Private Life of Henry VIII* may have got its spurs in a muddle, but it tells us a great deal about British social attitudes of the 1930s. Even *Winstanley*, a rare example of a feature film that met the rigorous standards of authenticity demanded by the historical community, was at least partly conditioned by the counter-cultural movements of the 1960s: its account of the failure of a revolutionary movement is told from the perspective of post-1968 ideological disillusionment. Ultimately, film, like all historical sources, speaks of and for its time.

NOTES

1 *'La politiques des auteurs'*—translated into English as 'the *auteur* theory'—maintains that despite the collective nature of filmmaking, the creative agency resides with the director, who is best regarded as the 'author' of the finished film.

2 The phrase was first used in a review article by Thomas Elsaesser (1985) 'The New Film History', *Sight & Sound*, 55(4): 246–251.

3 The base material of most film stock until the early 1950s was cellulose nitrate, which is highly unstable and usually decomposes within 50 years. It is also highly inflammable.

REFERENCES

Aldgate, Anthony (1979) *Cinema and History: British Newsreels and the Spanish Civil War*. London: Scolar Press.

Arnheim, Rudolf (1958) *Film as Art*, trans. L. M. Sieveking and Ian F. D. Morrow. London: Faber and Faber.

Badsey, S. D. (1983) '*Battle of the Somme*: British war-propaganda', *Historical Journal of Film, Radio and Television*, 3(2): 99–115.

Bazin, André (1967) *What Is Cinema? Volume I*, ed. and trans. Hugh Gray. Berkeley, CA: University of California Press.

Beard, Charles (1934) 'Why get it wrong?', *Sight and Sound*, 2(8): 124.

Bordwell, David, Staiger, Janet and Thompson, Kristin (1985) *The Classical Hollywood Cinema: Film Style and Mode of Production to 1960*. London: Routledge.

Chapman, James (2005) *Past and Present: National Identity and the British Historical Film*. London: I. B. Tauris.

Chapman, James (2008) *War and Film*. London: Reaktion.

Durgnat, Raymond (1970) *A Mirror for England: British Movies from Austerity to Affluence*. London: Faber and Faber.

Ferro, Marc (1988) *Cinema and History* [1977]. Trans. Naomi Greene. Detroit, MI: Wayne State University Press.

Haggith, Toby (2002) 'D-Day filming—for real: A comparison of "Truth" and "Reality" in *Saving Private Ryan* and combat film by the British Army Film and Photographic Unit', *Film History*, 14(3–4): 332–353.

Hill, Christopher (1975) 'Notes and comments', *Past and Present*, 68: 132.

Katz, Ephraim (1996) *The Macmillan International Film Encyclopedia*. London, Macmillan.

Kracauer, Siegfried (1947) *From Caligari to Hitler: A Psychological Study of the German Film*. Princeton, NJ: Princeton University Press.

Lindgren, Ernest (1947) 'The importance of film archives', *The Penguin Film Review*, 5: 47–52.

Marwick, Arthur (1989) *The Nature of History*, 3rd edn. Houndmills: Macmillan.

Matuszewski, Boleslas (1995) 'A new source of history' [1898], *Film and History*, 7(3): 322–324.

Monaco, Paul (1976) *Cinema and Society: France and Germany during the Twenties*. New York: Elsevier.

Reeves, Nicholas (1997) 'Cinema, spectatorship and propaganda: *Battle of the Somme* (1916) and its contemporary reception', *Historical Journal of Film, Radio and Television*, 13(2): 181–201.

Richards, Jeffrey (1973) *Visions of Yesterday*. London: Routledge & Kegan Paul.

Richards, Jeffrey (2008) *Hollywood's Ancient Worlds*. London: Continuum.

Rosenstone, Robert (ed.) (1995) *Revisioning History: Film and the Construction of a New Past*. Princeton, NJ: Princeton University Press.

Rosenstone, Robert A. (2006) *History on Film/Film on History*. Harlow: Pearson Education.

Sklar, Robert (1975) *Movie-Made America: A Social History of American Movies*. New York: Random House.

Smither, Roger (1988) '"A wonderful idea of the fighting": The question of fakes in *The Battle of the Somme*', *Imperial War Museum Review*, 3: 4–16.

Sorlin, Pierre (1980) *The Film in History: Restaging the Past*. Oxford: Basil Blackwell.

Taylor, Richard (1979) *Film Propaganda: Soviet Russia and Nazi Germany*. London: Croom Helm.

Taylor, Richard (2000) *The Battleship Potemkin: Film Companion*. London: I. B. Tauris.

Toulin, Vanessa, Popple, Simon and Russell, Patrick (eds.) (2005) *The Lost World of Mitchell and Kenyon: Edwardian Britain on Film*. London: British Film Institute.

Wood, Robin (1965) *Hitchcock's Films*. London: Tantivy Press.

FURTHER READING

Allen, Robert C. and Gomery, Douglas (1985) *Film and History: Theory and Practice*. New York: McGraw-Hill.

Barta, Tony (ed.) (1998) *Screening the Past: Film and the Representation of History*. Westport: Praeger.

Cameron, Kenneth M. (1997) *America on Film: Hollywood and American History*. New York: Continuum.

Chapman, James, Glancy, Mark and Harper, Sue (eds.) (2007) *The New Film History: Sources, Methods, Approaches*. Houndmills: Palgrave Macmillan.

Ellwood, David M. (ed.) (2000) *The Movies as History: Visions of the Twentieth Century*. Stroud: Sutton.

Engelen, Leen and Vande Winkel, Roel (eds.) (2007) *Perspectives on European Film and History*. Gent: Academia Press.

Harper, Sue (1994) *Picturing the Past: The Rise and Fall of the British Costume Film*. London: British Film Institute.

Hughes-Warrington, Marnie (2007) *History Goes to the Movies*. London: Routledge.

Kitses, Jim (1969) *Horizons West: Studies of Authorship within the Western*. London: Secker & Warburg in association with the British Film Institute.

Landy, Marcia (1996) *Cinematic Uses of the Past*. Minneapolis, MN: University of Minnesota Press.

Landy, Marcia (ed.) (2001) *The Historical Film: History and Memory in Media*. London: Athlone Press.

McArthur, Colin (1972) *Underworld USA*. London: Secker & Warburg in association with the British Film Institute.

O'Connor, John E. (ed.) (1990) *Image as Artifact: The Historical Analysis of Film and Television*. Malabar, FL: Robert E. Krieger Publishing.

Ramsaye, Terry (1926) *A Million and One Nights: A History of the Motion Picture*. New York: Simon & Schuster.

Roberts, Graham and Taylor, Philip M. (eds.) (2001) *The Historian, Television and Television History*. Luton: University of Luton Press.

Rollins, Peter C. (ed.) (1983) *Hollywood as Historian: American Film in a Cultural Context*. Lexington, KY: University Press of Kentucky.

Rotha, Paul (1930) *The Film Till Now: A Survey of World Cinema*. London: Secker & Warburg.

Short, K. R. M. (ed.) (1981) *Feature Films as History*. London: Croom Helm.

Smith, Paul (ed.) (1976) *The Historian and Film*. Cambridge, UK: Cambridge University Press.

Sobchack, Vivian (ed.) (1996) *The Persistence of History: Cinema, Television and the Modern Event*. London: Routledge.

Toplin, Robert Brent (1996) *History by Hollywood: The Use and Abuse of the American Past*. Urbana, IL: University of Illinois Press.

Wyke, Maria (1997) *Projecting the Past: Ancient Rome, Cinema and History*. London: Routledge.

20

Looking Closely: Toward a Natural History of Human Ingenuity

Ray McDermott and Jason Raley

INTRODUCTION

Traditional social thought and recent decades of social interaction analysis agree that no matter how difficult it can be to navigate or describe, the social world is always well organized. Participants in the social world constantly struggle to figure out what to do next, and they use their ongoing contact with others to guide them to usually regular outcomes. People figuring out what to do next are a boon for researchers. In the work people do to make their versions of the world available to each other, researchers can find the ordering principles of social life.

Even surprising outcomes are systematic. If the social world seems driven by an invisible hand, as if people were stars in the sky, this is a result of what people have done and are doing with each other—with their eyes and ears open[1] (Adam Smith, 1776).

Even if the underlying dynamics of the social world are obscured, this condition, too, is a systematic result of people distorting their vision and repressing their interpretations of each other under difficult circumstances (Karl Marx, 1867/1976).

Even if unaware of the full implications of their activities, people are usually ingenious, both locally in their most personal circumstances and collectively in their most distributed consequences. In coordinating with each other, people show themselves, to those who would look carefully, to be orderly, knowledgeable, and precise. Given the demands of necessity, they do well what has to be done even if under limiting, or worse, pathological conditions (Gregory Bateson, 1936/1958). We agree (McDermott and Raley, 2009; McDermott, 2010).

Analytic attention to the visual has had its moments. This chapter highlights visible behavior because looking carefully at the world has not been nurtured by current articulations of knowledge and expertise. We do not mean that looking is more important than listening, smelling, or touching. That the visible is a good source for inquiry should not obscure the larger point that the world is more available to all our senses than received categories can allow. W. J. T. Mitchell has identified historical periods when inquiries into the world have run more through a people's eyes than the other senses: 'the invention of artificial perspective, the arrival of easel painting, and the invention of photography were all greeted as "pictorial turns"' (2008: 16). While this makes the twentieth century—driven by cinema, television, and views from outer space—fundamentally visual, one must wonder how the same century's social sciences have insisted on learning about the world mostly with their eyes closed. Strangely, in the name of objectivity, the visual has not fared well in accounts of contemporary production, consumption, social structure, politics, religion, and education. Even personal developments and events—even desire—get described and managed as if intelligible to a cold and calculating eye that looks on activities not as they are performed, but by their symptoms—their droppings—lined up in patterns only after they have run their course.

Proxies, measures, factors, variables, and controlled results—all honored too easily by the word data—are treated as available for the asking, as if on our own terms, strewn conveniently across our conceptual grounds and needing only to be picked up, put in order, and correlated with other debris.

To make the visual even more endangered, when social analysts do look at what people are doing, they privilege what is heard over what can be seen, touched, smelled, tasted, or otherwise sensed (for exceptions, see Howes, 1991). Even speech is often understood as nothing more than what people say, and treated as just discourse, as culturally mandated and prescribed talk intelligible to anyone who might listen in without regard to all else that people are doing with each other.

This chapter tells of a small, but alternative visual tradition that has developed on the edges of mainstream social sciences. The tradition has no single name, but for the last half-century, it has drawn heavily from ethnography, interaction and conversation analysis, sociolinguistics, and kinesics. To describe the approach, we call on (and impose) the term: natural history. Now thousands of years old and still mostly respectable, and even enlightened,[2] the term is usually associated with what can be found in Museums of Natural History: the 'exhaustive catalogue of nature' tradition (Healy, 1991: xii). From Pliny the Elder in 79 CE, to the many volumes of Buffon (starting in 1744) almost 1700 years later, we acknowledge this dustbin of mystery—what seventeenth-century collectors of tidbits from around the world used to call their 'fardle of façions' (Hodgen, 1964)—but we also claim (briefly, without adequate justification) more recent traditions of natural history inquiry that focus directly on the production of organism/environment relations in human cultures. As we use it, *a natural history analysis examines organisms and environments interwoven in real time in situations consequential to their participants and beyond*. A natural history of human ingenuity studies the ways people create environments for each other. Situation is conceived as neither a variable, nor an environment, but as a playground for adaptation, rearrangement, and ingenuity.

The work we cite represents a natural history approach by either self- or other-attribution. We include examples to the extent they clear a ground for looking carefully at human behavior as ingenuity at work, for better and for worse, on the specifics of emerging environments, but our enthusiasm could be shared with a diverse lot of authors. Take, for example, the American poster-boy for inarticulate wisdom, Yogi Berra, 'You can observe a lot by watching'; or better, the master sleuth, Sherlock Holmes, 'It is, of course, a trifle, but there is nothing so important as trifles' (Doyle, 2009: 116); or best, Franz Kafka, 'Now the world is known, however, to be uncommonly various, which can be verified at any time by taking a handful of world and looking at it closely' (Kafka, 1935/1961: 41).[3] We rely primarily on two traditions: one more visionary and one more precise.

For visionary, we point to a rich background (much ignored by social theory) of almost two centuries of American naturalism, starting with Ralph Waldo Emerson's call for a 'Natural History of Intellect' (1894; 1833–1835), and later developed by William James, John Dewey, G. H. Mead, and Arthur Bentley.[4] The tradition has been relentless in its appreciation of how people continually construct their most immediate conditions with and for each other. It is a 'half-way empiricism,' said James (1912/1976), that collects facts as if there were only one world just waiting to be described, the one world allowed by received categories 'with which all experience has got to square.' James recommended instead 'a more radical empiricism' that seeks things in the full variety of their connections in experience (1897/1956: viii). Bentley used the same point to address social relations, where it is 'not the point of view of one toward the other' that we seek, but 'the very processing itself of the ones-with-others' (1926, 457). A natural history documents how people together create their worlds with each other in real time. People enact and enforce the contexts in which and by which they reflexively organize their next behavior.

For precision, we celebrate and foreground about 70 years of cross-disciplinary detailed analyses of visual records of social—including conversational—interaction.[5] And, because the words *detailed, slow,* and *careful* are easy to misuse, we offer arbitrary but approximately realistic measures. An initial *detailed* transcript of people interacting with each other should take a minimum of 1 hour of analysis for every second of behavior transcribed. The best work has been done more *slowly*—months on a few seconds of transcript—although we should not exclude work that achieved a suggestive empirical focus without transcripts (like the first of the two examples we present in this chapter). A *carefully* developed transcript should display all the noisy movements participants make with their oral cavity—utterances and mutterances: 'uhhm,' 'nyem,' coughs, sniffs, teethsucks, laughs, and so on—as well as more

visible movements performed outside the mouth (we are struggling to avoid the misnomer, non-verbal, that allows communication to be divided into two autonomous channels—verbal and non-verbal—even though people in interaction are rarely allowed the simplification). Such a transcript marks the onsets and endings of all units of behavior at whatever level of duration they can be discerned.

We proceed in four sections. The first distinguishes what we are doing from mainstream social science. The second unpacks a telling moment, from the late 1930s, in the analysis of gesture as a tie between race and intelligence. The third presents a more recent moment in which children and their teacher establish (and disrupt) a tie between the labor of learning to read and the ritual display of intelligence demanded by a kindergarten. In the conclusion, we return to why it is politically, as well as methodologically, important to square the results of social science inquiries with what happens in front of our eyes.

LOOK BEFORE ASKING

To fashion a natural history approach, we state a *problem*, make a *claim*, and *promise* a better way to proceed.

The *problem* is that the world is not easily available for the asking. The categories by which we inquire into the world are reflexively and relentlessly part of the problems that have caught our attention. Our categories have been shaped by others, to their ends, not ours. Laurence Sterne said that 'A man cannot dress but his ideas get clothed at the same time' (1759–67/1996: 502).[6] He thought the world hidden away, dressed in old clothes. To fit ideas to new ends, to appropriate them for new tasks, is hard work. Good research begins when people change their easy categories into the very stuff, or focus, of new inquiry.

The *claim* adds good news to the bad: that the world is more available—more intelligible and more malleable—for the looking, listening, and doing, than for the asking. 'We lie in the lap of a great intelligence,' said Emerson[7] (1842/2000: 141), but it takes vigilance and sacrifice to gain access to that intelligence and hard work to articulate it (see Dewey, 1927). There is great know-how in the world we get paid to ignore. Think, for example, of employers underestimating workers, men ruling over women, teachers degrading students, and politicians manipulating the facts of public life. Inattention to the intelligence of the people is so institutionalized that it now takes hard work to uncover it. No great lap of intelligence can be found in responses to standard, and standardized, questions. No immense intelligence can be found in response, that is, to the questions imposed by those in a position to profit from not looking more carefully.

The *promise* hinges on looking slowly and carefully at people's activities. If we can stop overriding each other with privileged categories, we might instead see accomplishments, critiques, and frustrations where others have seen only disorder and stupidity. The complexities of the world are more available—not easily available, but more so—to those willing to look again and again at the varied ways people put their lives together. Assembled by human ingenuity, and drawing on an immense intelligence, the social world is there to be seen, operated on, and reassembled. To proceed with preset ideas—that is, to ask before looking, to insist that current categories are prescient enough to identify what must be changed, to probe with interviews and questionnaires before knowing what and how to ask, and all that without identifying grounds for appreciating answers—may be exactly the wrong order.[8] Visibility and consequentiality should set the approximate order of available categories ahead of any vocabulary-driven diagnosis and explanation.

The distorting lens of scientific research done from a distance has been perhaps most invidious in the attribution of intelligence. Americans in particular push themselves around by calling each other smart and dumb; they even have tests for measuring and quiz shows for highlighting its importance. In this chapter, we use examples of intelligence politics to illustrate how people at varying levels of analysis, perform, ignore, degrade, and, when pressed, rediscover the intelligence and wisdom in human affairs. We deliver two cases—one of whole groups of people in interaction, the other of a few children in school with their teacher. Both scenes turn on the accusation of a seeming scarcity of intelligence despite the complexity of what the participants are doing.

Both examples play out in the context of tensions between named racial/ethnic groups, in competition under conditions where looking smart might turn out to be useful and not looking smart, or being accused of not looking smart, can turn out to be disastrous. We use a narrow lens to make our point, that small events are the playhouse for large-scale social forces. *Ab uno disce omnes*: from one thing, everything can be said—and must be said. Ludwig Wittgenstein (1980) noted that 'a curious analogy could be based on the fact that even the hugest telescope has to have an eye-piece no larger than the eye' (17). Everything must be accounted for in terms of what the lens (both eyepiece and I-piece) makes available and obscures. The *promise* in this position: that even if not on their own terms, even if not under conditions of their own making,[9] people build their world with great regularity and ingenuity that can be observed, studied, recorded, and reorganized for the better.

RACE, GESTURE, AND INTELLIGENCE

David Efron did the world a great favor in 1941. He published a detailed study of gestures among Italian and Jewish conversationalists in New York City. Efron was a student of the anthropologist Franz Boas.[10] Both were driven by two passions: first to show the foolishness in racial stereotypes; second, to demonstrate a cultural organization and intelligence in people's behavior. The first was particularly of the moment: Nazi scientists and other pro-Aryan commentators had been making claims about the ties between a people's gestural range and their intelligence and capacity for civility and civilization.[11] Eastern European Jews and Southern Italians came off badly in the comparisons. They talk with their hands, went the story, and the reason was that they could not think without resorting to manual gestures. The narrow gestural range of the English or Germans was taken as a sign of intelligence and deep culture (for an early example, see Addison, 1712/1970). The pseudo-science and racism in the German texts are startling. One from the 1930s claimed that a hereditary disposition is 'common to all Jewish groups' and that in ' "half-Jews" whose bodily traits, as a result of racial miscegenation, appear to us as "non-Jewish," their Jewishness…. is recognizable in their gestures' (Efron, 1972: 22). Another text (from decades before, but moved forward as legitimate) argued that

the ideas of the Graeco-Latins are "simple and unencumbered by a multitude of side thoughts" which makes them flow over easily into words and movements. In contrast to this, the Teutonic is "habitually filled with a multitude of opposing impulses and thoughts…thought translates itself into motor results but slowly…Germanic taciturnity is due to wealth and complexity of thought." (31).

The arguments devolve quickly from biological types, to gestural types, and on to personality types, including each group's capacity for rational thought.

Efron made three moves of his own.

First, he showed how the fascist texts were corrupt: that the 'scientific' descriptions relied more on stereotype than behavior and reveal more about the racism of their authors than about gestural patterns. Efron's case was convincing.

Second, he showed a variability over centuries in how high-profile gestures for preaching and oratory were performed and interpreted. He documented how, in England and France, styles of high- and low-emotional display and gesticulation could

follow on each other—on the same pulpit or soapbox—with a rapidity that might mark fashion shifts in clothing or political rhetoric. Three versions of French relations between gesture, culture, and politics tell Efron's story:

(a) the French courtiers before the arrival of Catherine de Medici, gesturing little and considering gesticulation a vulgar form of demeanor, but soon viewing it as a token of high civility when the Florentine nobility brings it to France, (b) the "honnête gens" (those French Victorians of the first half of the 17th century), showing considerable restraint in their expressive bodily motions, and (c) the "âmes sensibles" of the restoration indulging rather freely in gesticulation.[12] (Efron, 1972: 59–60)

From many examples like this, Efron was able to move easily against any theory that would tie race to an inherent style of gesticulation, or either of these to intelligence. Even better, he used the materials to question the very category of race as just so much selective inattention to detail: 'The common observation of outstanding morphological differences between certain so-called racial groups is likely to make us disregard the existence of marked differences within each of the chosen groups' (39).[13]

Third, and this took detailed empirical analysis, Efron used drawings, movies, and interviews to document the gestural habits of Eastern European Jews and Southern Italian immigrants around New York City. The drawings are central to the analysis.[14] Efron found both extensive regularities within each group and considerable differences across the two groups. More importantly, he found a striking variability by generation and even by situation. We present the regularities in the two immigrant groups, and then the variability that develops with continued assimilation to life in New York. Both are necessary to his conclusion that assimilated Jewish and Italian young men moved more like each other, and more like long-term New Yorkers, than they moved like their parent's generation.[15]

The regularities are easy to see (actors isolate them willy-nilly for imitation). Efron went deeper. His first contribution was to show the gestures as a detailed system of nuanced differences and similarities in the hand, arm, and head movements that are likely consequential to ongoing communication. Table 20.1 lists the salient details, but with the proviso that every item listed has only a variable status and that, as with any list of communicative devices (alphabets, dictionaries, phonemic charts), how the characteristic elements are woven into social interaction is always more lively and complex than a list can reveal.

Efron also showed a variability in gestural performance by generation and situation. As young Jewish and Italian men adjusted to the communicative demands of their new situation, they reigned in their gestures to fit more closely the form and tempo of the mainstream groups around them. Of particular interest were what Efron called the hybrid gestures that inhabited a space between immigrant and assimilated inventories. The hybrid styles were called on in mix-and-match ways by situations. Efron's portrait of then NYC Mayor Laguardia showed a high-style combination of Italian (his father), Jewish (his mother), and American (early schooling in Arizona) gestures. The Mayor's

major constituencies were embodied in his behavioral routines (Figure 20.5).

Other examples showed assimilated Jewish and Italian men devoid of gesture.

The well-structured variability in gestural style across and within kinds of people in Efron's data left no room for tying gestural inventories to either racial groups or imagined measures of intelligence. Words for races or psychological complexities like intelligence promise more coherence than a careful look at the facts can deliver. Whether in 1941 or in 2010, Efron's dual message remains relevant: that racism is a way of not looking carefully at others and that, as Kafka promised, it can be confronted 'by taking a handful of world and looking at it closely.'[16]

LEARNING AND INTELLIGENCE

Jump ahead 70 years from Boas and Efron's New York to today's California, and the intelligence wars are still on, but in a different format. The single measure IQ tests that dominated the lives of schoolchildren in the first half of the twentieth century have been

Table 20.1 Gesticulation styles

	Traditional Eastern European Jewish	Traditional Southern Italian
Movement from:	The elbow (upper arms to the side) (Figure 20.1)	The shoulder (Figure 20.2)
Direction:	Frontal, in 'the immediate area of his chest and face' (p. 68) and 'towards the interlocutor' (p. 89)	Off to both sides of the body and up and down the vertical plane
Touch:	Frequent to constant, but 'rarely comes into contact with his own body' (p. 90)	Rare, but a speaker 'manipulates quite frequently … the other parts of his own physique' (p. 90)
Spacing:	Crowded, close enough for touching	Enough room for a wide gestural range for each speaker
Head movement:	Frequent	Rare
Tempo:	Choppy, with the three parts of the arm used independently; staccato	Smooth, with a 'synergy in the use of the three parts of his arm' (p. 81)
Symmetry:	One hand or arm at time	Both hands and/or arms used together
Gesture form:	Ideographic, 'tracing a line of thought' (p. 107); logico-pictorial (Figure 20.3)	Physiographic, 'illustrating the very things referred to by the accompanying words' (p. 122); emblematic (Figure 20.4)

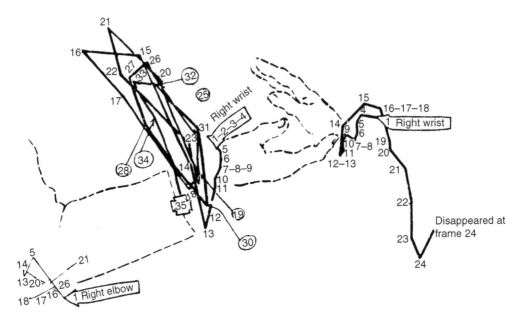

Figure 20.1   Traditional Jewish: 'confined gestural radius, movement from elbow'
(Efron, 1941, Fig. 8)

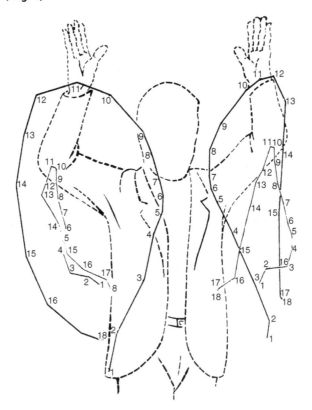

Figure 20.2   Traditional Italian: 'wide gestural radius, movement from shoulder' (Efron,
1941, Fig. 37)

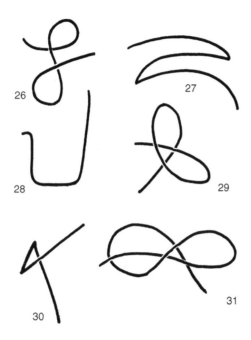

Figure 20.3 Traditional Jewish: 'logico-topographical gestures (gestures = syllogisms)' (Efron, 1941, Fig. 26)

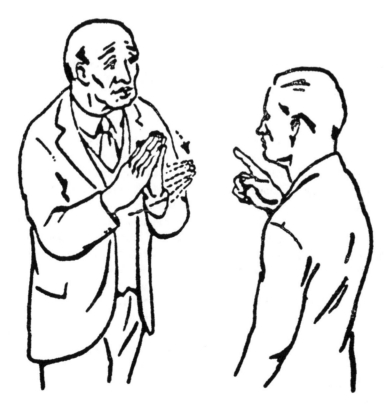

Figure 20.4 Traditional Italian: 'the placing of the hands together' (Efron, 1941, Fig. 65)

Figure 20.5   Mayor Laguardia: '(1) Entirely Italian in form … ; (2a)…Italian type of gesture, chiefly because of tempo, and (2b)…typical American gesture…; (3)…a rejective type gesture, typical of both Italian and Jew, made fleetingly; (4)…there is some Italian in this gesture' (Efron, 1972, Fig. 77)

on the run, and high stereotype characterizations of the intelligence of various groups now sound more like hate crimes than science. To that good news—make that mostly good news, as the stereotypes still make public appearances and have a rich life-in-waiting and baiting under the surface—we can add the bad news that schools are active in carving children at ever-earlier ages into ability piles. The language is softer and kinder, a language of disability and disadvantage over a language of stupidity and race, but the results are amazingly the same. Race and class biases operate convincingly under the new linguistic constraints (McDermott and Raley, 2009; McDermott et al., 2009).

It is easy to make assumptions about how children from the bottom of the social structure wind up at the bottom of their class, but most everyone who has looked carefully, that is slowly, and in detail, at classrooms comes away with stories more about what children can do than about what they cannot do. Gradually a new story, with new assumptions, has been taking shape. Classrooms—even kindergarten classrooms—are the places where American social structure stages try-outs for success and failure based on intelligence measures with a preset number of winner and losers. The key is that the games often have no relation—no more than daytime quiz shows and nighttime survivor specials on television—to what the children can do eventually or what they might have to do in life beyond the classroom. As long as there are winners and losers, or at least as long as the American dream that winning is possibly within everyone's hardworking reach is at play, everyone goes home happy, or if not happy, then at least knowing where they stand. From the child's point of view, the day is spent arranging to not get caught not knowing something and/or getting caught knowing something at just the right time. From the teacher's point of view, the day is spent finding failure while, at the same time, preaching the availability of success for all and trying not to degrade those who look less able. No child is left behind, goes the cant, but if some are—and some always are—the rule seems to be that everyone must not feel terrible about it. While this system of games beats handing out rewards on the basis of race, national origin, or gestural habits, it makes little sense as a way to set apart 4 and 5 year olds learning how to read. Let's take a careful look at how it works on the ground, and wonder if we can imagine how to change it.

The findings are presented below in three versions—three perspectives on an ever-emerging reality. First, we offer a narrative description of a few minutes of life in kindergarten that produces a celebration of a young girl's success at reading. Neither the Spanish-language-dominant girl nor her classroom group is known for easy reading. Second, we offer a close analysis of a few seconds within that episode, and notice that the episode seems to be actively organized for displays of who can or cannot read and celebrations about being able to read. Finally, we present an argument for a different celebration and a new set of worries.

The narrative

Five kindergartners sit at a kidney-shaped table, coloring outlined illustrations of objects on a photocopied half-page they will later add to a stapled, illustrated book on parts of speech. The camera focuses on one half of the table. Three children are in the visible frame, talking to each other as they work: Jared is nearest the table's left end; Alexis is

sitting at the midpoint of the table's curve; and Giordano is between them. The teacher enters from behind the students and reaches over them to put something on the table. As the teacher withdraws her hand and begins to turn away, Alexis, facing away from the camera, leans across Giordano and points to something posted on a bulletin board. As she does, she announces, 'Mrs. Pomeroy, I have one of those.'

The object is nearly within reach. Jared, closest, and Giordano, at Jared's left, leave their coloring aside to consider the object more closely. It is a list of kindergartners in the other language arts group, all native speakers of English. Working together to decode the names, Jared and Giordano quickly focus on what the list, with some names crossed out and others not, can tell them. In particular, they worry about who finished the last assignment. They also consider what it might mean for those students who did not finish, particularly about how they might feel sad.

Alexis meanwhile explains that she got her own copy of the list out of the trashcan. Mrs. Pomeroy offers 'a clean one,' an offer Alexis enthusiastically accepts. The teacher's aide, Miss Sonia, enters the scene. Mrs. Pomeroy explains to Miss Sonia that she gave Alexis the list because Alexis 'took one from the trash and it was dirty.'

Miss Sonia turns to Alexis and asks, 'You wanted a list from the English group?' 'Yes,' Alexis says, and then, 'I can read it!' Miss Sonia replies with a question, 'You wanna read it?' Alexis leans back, holds the paper away from her, and begins to read. Three minutes later, as she finishes sounding out the last name on the list, Miss Sonia stands, applauds, and celebrates, 'Yeah! Very good, Alexis!' Alexis smiles, puts the paper down, and resumes coloring. End of story.

Well, maybe the end, but not quite the whole story, even in this narrative version. Interesting things happen between 'I can read it!' and 'Yeah! Very good, Alexis!' Most of the time, Alexis is not able to decode the names, at least not by herself. Giordano points, leans in, leans over, corrects, and proceeds where Alexis pauses. He does variations of this more than once, but at least once does so while reading the name in reverse through the back of the paper. Jared stops reading the posted list and announces that he, too, can read. Again, and again, but no one pays him much attention. About midway, and in the face of it all, in the face of them all, Alexis waves her hand in the air and declares, 'I can do it myself!' All the while, Miss Sonia prods and praises. At one point, she turns to Mrs. Pomeroy, who is now engaged in other things, and declares, 'She's reading the names!'

Interesting things happen after Miss Sonia leaves, too. Without looking up and in a voice almost a whisper, Giordano tells Alexis (in Spanish) that he helped her with (at least) one of the names, although he does not say anything about reading backward and through the paper. Alexis insists: 'Lo hice so*lita*' (I did it my*self*). Just after this exchange, Jared recruits Giordano and Alexis as witnesses to his attempts at reading. Giordano turns, but Alexis challenges: 'A ver?' (Let's see!). Despite his earlier successes, Jared stumbles. And finally, just before recess and just visible in the background of the recording, Alexis waves the list in front of Giordano and Jared. At best, she's sharing her joy. More likely, she's flaunting her victory, the clean list of names her trophy.

The detail

It takes visible work for participants to take each other from 'You want a list?' through 'I can read it!' to 'Yeah! Very good, Alexis!' In the 22 seconds that follow Alexis' receipt of the list, we can see a version of the story that will get replayed over the next 2.5 minutes, and likely over the next 12 or more years of schooling. For Alexis to 'read it' means that she must do it alone and in a way that the teacher—any teacher—can see it. This is the achievement, if not the aim of the work. It takes arranging bodies and materials

and talk to keep people in their respective positions. It does not require being able to read. The funny thing here is that successfully arranging for Alexis to 'read it' involves Alexis first declaring, 'I can read it,' and then, at the right time, *not* actually reading it. Giordano does plenty of the reading, backward and forward, but his 'successful' decoding is effectively erased by not being included in the arrangement for Alexis' reading (Figures 20.6–20.9).

On this day, 'I can read it' gives the children and their adults something to work on. It recruits their bodies and words to do the work. This may be the easiest part. Between Alexis saying, 'I can read it,' and Miss Sonia's applauding, laughing, 'Yeah! Very good, Alexis!' Alexis keeps the right people doing the right things at the right times. The most effective strategy seems to be the one most likely to undermine her initial claim of being able to read. She reads wrongly, hesitatingly, mistakenly. Ironically, she achieves Miss Sonia's praise by requiring her assistance. For Alexis, being seen being able to read at the end means being unable to read at just the right times along the way. Risky, but in this case, with a nice payoff.

And the story retold

Who 'can read it' might be the question of moment for these people over these several minutes. Or not! Alexis 'can read it' might not be what is going on any more than that Jared can read with less guidance or that Giordano seems to be able to read in two directions and through paper. Focusing on race, Efron warned, is dangerous because it narrows the field of vision and leaves no trace of what else might be going on: so, too, is a focus on reading, ability, or linguistic competence. The first revelation of a natural history approach is that 'can read it' is much less a property of individual minds—it's not personal property at all—and more the systematic product of real people pointing at, gathering around, interrupting, and tugging

Jared and Giordano decode a list of names posted to the right of their worktable.

Ms. Sonia puts her left hand on Alexis' left shoulder. Alexis begins to lift her right hand from the sheet of paper she is coloring. Alexis holds a copy of the list of student names under her chin. Walking behind the table, Danielle turns her head to the right and directs her gaze downward toward Alexis' hand or paper.

1:44:02.10

```
49   Jared    //Kelly's sa:d    Ms.Sonia              [you wanted
                                 a list//from the-
                                 for the English group] Alexis?
50                                                     (1.0)
51   Jared    //(Alec is) sa:d  Alexis    yes //[I ¡can read it]
52                               Mrs.Pom        [( )] want the list
                                 from the (English group)
53                               Ms.Sonia  you wanna read it?
                                 okay go ahead mi'ja
```

Jared and Giordano continue decoding the list of names to determine which students have not completed an assignment.

Alexis leans back, holds the list with both hands, moves this list away from her body, declaring, "I can read it!" Ms. Sonia removes her hand from Alexis' shoulder. Danielle's gaze moves up to the list.

1:44:04.03

Figure 20.6 'I can read it!'

Jared reads the list aloud. **Mrs. Pomeroy** has just moved behind Jared and pointed to the list **Jared** is reading. **Mrs. Pomeroy's** body faces the room. Though not visible, her head and arm appear to be in slight torque.

Alexis inclines her head toward **Ms. Sonia** and indicates a spot on the list with her left hand. With her talk, it appears to be a request for assistance. **Danielle** begins to sound out a name on the list. **Carolina** stands behind **Alexis**. **Giordano** directs his gaze to the paper in **Alexis'** hands.

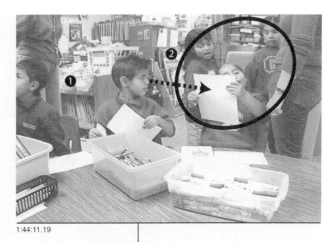

1:44:11.19

```
53                              Ms.Sonia   you wanna read it?
                                           okay go ahead mi'ja
54   Jared      //Kh- eh- l      Alexis    //I don know this name
56   Mrs.Pom    [(what?)]
57   Jared      [Kel//↑ly        Ms.Sonia  //read it-
58                               Danielle   [[(that's candy class)]
59                               Ms.Sonia   [oh that's a spanish name]
60   (?)        see:                        (0.8)
61                               Ms.Sonia   name in Spani- ah:
62                               Danielle   ah- eh- ah-
63   Mrs.Pom    you read (all) the
                name?
64   Mrs.Pom    //yeh good ↑job!  Giordano  Gabri↑//e: [:  l:
65                               Ms.Sonia             [°mira°
66   Mrs.Pom    //m: : :[a: y-    Alexis    //Ga-
```

Jared leans toward the posted list as **Mrs. Pomeroy** praises his reading.

Giordano begins to point to the back of the paper with his left hand as he reads from the right-hand column of names on the paper in **Alexis'** hands. The name is only visible in reverse, through the back of the paper. **Giordano** starts to move his body out of torque. At the same time, **Ms. Sonia** begins to move her hand toward the paper.

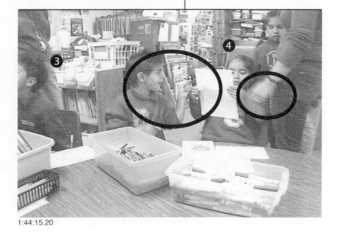

1:44:15.20

Figure 20.7   'You wanna read it?'

Giordano completes the rotation of his body out of torque to face the paper in **Alexis'** hands. He moves his left hand down and reaches toward the back of the paper with his right index finger. He continues to read the name "Gabriel." He stretches the name and reads in an animated voice.

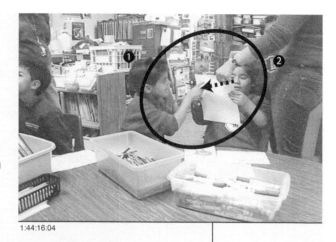

Alexis shifts her gaze to the right, toward the column of names that Giordano is reading (through the back of the paper). **Ms. Sonia** grasps the top of the paper and says (in Spanish), *"mira"* ("look").

1:44:16:04

```
63  Mrs.Pom   you read (all) the name?
64  Mrs.Pom   //yeh good ↑job!
65
66  Mrs.Pom   //m: : :[a: y-
67
68
69  Jared              [Ma//ya
70  Mrs.Pom   yes:
71
72            (2.8)
73
74  Jared     Mi//guel,
75  Mrs.Pom   ye:s,
76            (3.2)
77  Jared     Charl:
78
```

```
Giordano   Gabri://e: [: l:
Ms.Sonia              [°mira°
Alexis     //Ga-
Ms.Sonia   °mira°
           (0.2)
Ms.Sonia   //a:h:?
           (1.8)
Ms.Sonia   deh-
           (0.2)
Ms.Sonia   dri:?
Ms.Sonia   //ahdri:?
           (0.2)
Alexis     ahn. (0.2) Adrian? Alec.

Giordano   ira. °(Chris didn fin-)°
           look
```

Ms. Sonia pulls the paper slightly away from **Alexis** with her left hand, points to a place on the paper with her right hand, and begins to bend down toward **Alexis**. **Ms. Sonia's** body opens slightly toward the paper.

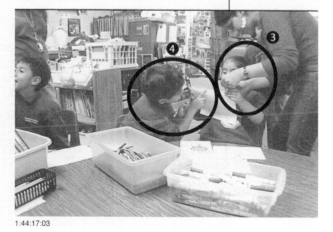

Giordano moves his face closer to the back of the paper and angles his head to follow the paper's now slightly angled position. He continues to sound out the name "Gabriel."

1:44:17:03

Figure 20.8 Decoding, in reverse and through the paper

Jared continues decoding the posted list of student names. **Mrs. Pomeroy** stands behind and to the right of **Jared**.

Ms. Sonia holds the upper corner of the paper with her left hand and points to the first name on the list with her right hand. She sounds out the name one syllable at a time. **Alexis** puts her own right hand on or near the same word. **Carolina** stands to the right of **Alexis**, looking at the paper. Just visible between **Alexis** and **Ms. Sonia**, **Iliana** gazes at the paper. She is smiling.

Giordano leans away from the paper and appears to be looking at the spot indicated by **Alexis** and **Ms. Sonia**. He brings his left hand to his mouth; his right hand is suspended.

1:44:21:19

```
63  Mrs.Pom   you read (all) the name?
64  Mrs.Pom   //yeh good ↑job!
65
66  Mrs.Pom   //m: : :[a: y-
67
68
69  Jared               [Ma//ya
70  Mrs.Pom   yes:
71
72            (2.8)
73
74  Jared     Mi//guel,
75  Mrs.Pom   ye:s,
76            (3.2)
77  Jared     Charl:
78
```

```
Giordano   Gabri↑//e: [:  l:
Ms.Sonia              [°mira°
Alexis     //Ga-
Ms.Sonia   °mira°
           (0.2)
Ms.Sonia   //a:h:?
           (1.8)
Ms.Sonia   deh▪
           (0.2)
Ms.Sonia   dri:?
Ms.Sonia   //ahdri:?
           (0.2)
Alexis     ahn. (0.2) Adrian? Alec.
Giordano   ira. °(Chris didn fin-)°
           look
```

Giordano sits erect. The fingers of his left hand are poised in front of his mouth; his right hand remains suspended. His eyes are directed up, toward **Ms. Sonia**, in slight torque relative to his body and face.

Alexis successfuly decodes the name "Adrian." She smiles. **Carolina** and **Iliana** remain looking at the paper. **Ms. Sonia** removes her hands from the paper and begins to straighten her torso.

1:44:24:29

Figure 20.9   Reading (with others)

on other real people and real objects in real time—sometimes with and sometimes without regard for who really can or cannot read. It's all in the sometimes and in the work of the people who put them together. The first revelation disrupts our thinking, revealing both our subjects' and our own habits in a new light (or for the first time).

A second revelation follows: that the obsession—*our* obsession—with figuring out who can read and what (and especially compared with whom) is likewise a product of our collusion. We are not dopes, but the best proof is that we can sometimes find ourselves duped.

Taken together, the analyses reveal what is routinely proclaimed but too rarely held up for contemplation or argument.

First, children in school are knowledgeable, curious, imaginative, and resourceful. They are more ingenious than their adults seem to notice, even when they are taking pictures of them (see Margolis and Fram, 2007).

Second, ingenuity is a distributed phenomenon, less the property of individual persons than a way to express our aesthetic appreciation for what a person does inside, across, and along unfolding environments of materials and other persons. We consider the children's performance to be a kind of jazz (Klemp et al., 2008). A performance can be called 'swinging' or described as 'got swing,' and a jazz musician can be described as someone who 'can swing.' What makes us call a given act—or a given person—ingenious? Given the materials and persons and moments at hand, what a person does is 'ingenious' if it transforms those materials into something interesting, fun, or new.

Third, official school environments either make ingenuity appear scarce, make ingenuity a refugee phenomenon, or bend the purposes of ingenuity toward the pursuit of being seen being able. It takes ingenuity to make reading what it must be for it to count in school: it has to be precisely timed; used to recruit others; and made available to be seen, noticed, and commented on, as an example of what individuals can do, by

virtue of their inherent ability and intelligence.

A natural history of ingenuity reveals ingenuity, but also the systematic narrowing of what ingenuity means. In the present case, everyone is visibly ingenious, but Alexis' ingenuity matters the most for everyone. Her announcement 'I can read it,' said at the right time, in the right way, with the right materials, recruits people into a new arrangement where what she cannot do well by herself gets turned into something she *can* do with a little adult help and a lot of adult noticing. Together the children and their adults put on a play: *The Precise Timing of Ability in School*. Whether she intends her announcement to rearrange the environment is not important. That the environment is arranged, and rearranged—now *this* is important.

ASKING BETTER QUESTIONS

With two examples in hand, we return now to the *problem, claim*, and *promise* that urged us to look before asking. Now that we have seen gestures in New York in the 1930s and children learning how to read in California in 2005, can we ask better questions of the situations?

The *problem* we identified is that language is a great invention for helping people to recreate yesterday's world today, but a biased resource for making today and tomorrow different from yesterday. Ordinary language delivers Jews and Italians, Learning Disabled and English Language Learners (LD and ELL, respectively) children, intelligence, and illiteracy, all as if they were simply and only what they are called. Artists, writers, and an eyes-open social science each mount assaults on the common lexicon in favor of a more evocative and precise language. Careful looking turns all these apparent things into contingent events. Jewish and Italian gestures are not determined, nor do they determine next events; they are better seen as resources sequenced with, and fitted into, the behavior of others as circumstances invite and make relevant. LD and ELL children are not brain types as much as they are students spotlighted in a system of negative categories built for the purpose, and often disguised as helping the needy, of sorting out and putting down children who are not doing as well as other children (Varenne and McDermott, 1998; McDermott and Raley, 2009). 'Intelligent' and 'literate' become words applicable to systems of people doing things rather than names for kinds of persons.

The *claim* we made is that the social world is built by people working together, and by their work we can know them. The world may be easier to see and perform than it is to describe, and the best way to study it is on its own terms: that is, with an eye to how it is organized. After looking at how gesturing immigrants and kids make sense, we can seek new procedures of analysis. For the dozens of terms available for describing what is wrong with individual schoolchildren (or migrating adults, why not) there is a literature that counts, correlates, and explains them—more than it helps anyone to examine the role of our institutions in organizing their problems, the same institutions that have us in the cushy position of explaining them. The misfit between the simplistic terms of diagnosis, and the complex terms of productive engagements in situations not dominated by mini-max intelligence games, demands that we ask who is being served by a system of labeling and disabling children, unguided by careful observation and self-examination. Our new effort is to imagine solutions better fitted to their experiences with the constraints we place on their lives.

And then we *promised* that reform is more possible if we approach problems where they are organized, on the ground, as they come at and get enacted by people mixing and matching the constraints and possibilities of the systems in which they, and the people profiting from the problems, are immersed. Mainstream social and psychological research has generally studied received problems

with analytic distance and without careful observation, and each research community has looked away when their descriptions of communicative gestures in one political nexus, or of children learning to read in another, have made things worse. Immigrant Jews and Italians used their full intelligence to pass the 'gesture tests' of New York and take their place in the middle class. In a system designed to make them look bad, children's attempts at intellectual growth run into roadblocks of injustices and eyes-closed research that describes them without a serious look at what they can do in the classroom. The last point is perhaps the most pressing. The cumulative effect of research into social problems continues to be negative, in phrasing and consequence, for those studied. Run for your lives! The social scientists are coming, and things are about to get worse. Beware becoming a named social problem! Keep your eyes open.

ACKNOWLEDGMENTS

In 2007, we attended a weekend seminar celebrating *The Natural History of the Interview* at the Center for Advanced Study in the Behavioral Sciences. Fred Erickson organized that seminar. For this and other kindnesses, we thank him.

NOTES

1 W. J. T. Mitchell warns that 'the first lesson in any course in visual culture should be to dispel it-"visual media" are mixed or hybrid formations, combining sound and sight, text and image; they are often more attached to anxiety than to insight and lead more to idolatry than to clarity' (2008: 16–17; see also Ungar, 2003).

2 Since the eighteenth century, natural history has been associated with an 'egalitarian ideology' (Drouin and Bensuade-Vincent, 1996: 408; Secord, 1996). We exclude the effort of Louis Agassiz, the influential nineteenth-century Harvard biologist,

to commandeer the term for the study of the differential development and potential of human races (see Irmscher, 1999).

3   Kafka's line appeared as the last footnote in an early paper by Harvey Sacks (1963).

4   For Emerson, see his early essay on 'The uses of natural history' (1833–1835/2005; for more on which, see Brown, 1992) as well as the posthumously published lectures of 1870–181 (1894, on which, see Bosco, 1997). James' sense of activity is methodologically central to a natural history approach: 'an activity-series is defined by its whence and whither... each activity-situation is a segment in a longer experience-chain...' (1905: 255; see also Siegfried, 1992). Dewey called for a psychology as 'the natural history of the various attitudes and structures through which experiencing passes, as an account of the conditions under which this or that attitude emerges' (1916/2007: 95). Mead's (1938) situated, temporal and perspectival approach to thoughts and things also resonates with a natural history of organism–environment relations: 'The reflective experience, the world, and the things within it exist in the form of situations.... The peculiarities of the different situations are not those of appearances or phenomena which inadequately reflect an absolute reality. These situations are the reality' (215). To complete the circle, there is now a *Natural History of Pragmatism* (Richardson, 2007).

5   Some self-ascribe to natural history or encourage reading those who do. See Birdwhistell (1970); Goffman (1971, 1976); McQuown (1971); Bateson (1972); Scheflen (1973); Smith (1977); Kendon (1990, 2004); for a summary of the best-known set of efforts, see Leeds-Hurwitz (1987); from history, see Bremmer and Roodenburg (1992); from literature, a paper by Burke (1964) is remarkably on point. For other-ascription, conversation analysis is most relevant: See Sacks (1990); Schegloff (2007); Goodwin (1994, in press); Goodwin (2006). And for a visual strain in conversation analysis, see Goodwin (1981) and Schegloff (1984, 1996). How these traditions have stayed disconnected from American pragmatism is an ongoing mystery.

6   Goethe and Marx were fans of Sterne, and we should not be surprised to find Goethe's claim in *Faust* quoted approximately in Marx, 'When thoughts are absent, words are brought in as convenient replacements' (1867/1976: 161).

7   So too John Dewey: 'We lie, as Emerson said, in the lap of an immense intelligence. But that intelligence is dormant and its communications are broken, inarticulate and faint until it possesses the local community as its medium' (1927: 219).

8   Questions are essential to ethnographic inquiry, but not without an appreciation of how questions build on observation and participation. On mid-century definitions of ethnography as the search for right questions asked in right ways at right times, see Goodenough (1956), Radin (1957), and Frake (1964).

9   Marx: 'Men make their own history, but they do not make it just as they please in circumstances they choose for themselves; rather they make it in present circumstances given and inherited. Tradition from all the dead generations weighs like a nightmare on the brain of the living' (1852/2002: 19).

10   Boas (1940); on Boas and natural history, see Smith (1959).

11   The stereotypes were everywhere. When McDermott attended school in Brooklyn in the 1960s, the gestural range of Italian students was an occasion for repression by teachers, humor among kids, and conflict for crowded subway riders.

12   There are three English language editions of Efron's work. The dissertation of 1940 is the most extensive; the published edition of 1941 is least so; the Mouton edition of 1972 (with a new title) restores 14 figures mostly showing hybrid gestures and a 'Dictionary' of 151 gestures Southern Italians can use to communicate without words. We have not seen the Spanish language edition of 1970. On the drama of etiquette and gesture in the corporal politics of European court society, see Elias (1969/1983).

13   This was Boas' (1940; also see Stocking, 1993) point, across 40 years of research measuring variation in the body parts of immigrant and Native American populations: that there is always more physical variability within a population, however defined, than across to a next category, and that racial groupings are held together primarily by the interests and biases of the observers.

14   Comments by Efron's artist and collaborator, Stuyvesant Van Veen, are particularly insightful. Drawings are not the same as analysis, but they train one's eye for analysis.

15   That Efron's use of 'ghetto' sounds negative now does not mean he was using it pejoratively. The term has an interesting history: from the Italian word for 'foundry,' it referred to the quarters for ironworks where Jews and, ironically, Germans were sequestered by Venetian authorities in 1516. A contemporary back-translation of ghettoblaster into Italian as 'maxistereo portatile' shows new tendencies, with neither an ironworks nor an Iron Cross in sight.

16   Two more reasons for recovering Efron: first, gesture studies have come of age with Adam Kendon's (2004) foundational volume; and second, also due to Kendon, Efron forms a midpoint in a long history of studies of Italian gesture—from De Jorio's (1832/2000) account of gesture in both the potsherds of ancient Naples and the living nineteenth-century city, through Efron a century later, to Kendon's restudy (2000, 2004). Italian gesture stands out for its comparative elaborateness, in contrast to,

say, Japanese gesture, remarkable for its subtlety (Befu, 1974). The contrast works well, but should not imply that Italian gesture is not subtle, nor that Japanese gesture, even in Noh drama, is not elaborate (Bethe and Brazell, 1978).

REFERENCES

Addison, J. (1712/1970) 'Speaking gestures', in R. Halsband (ed.), *The Spectator*. London: Curwen Press. pp. 174–176.

Bateson, G. (1936/1958) *Naven*. Stanford, CT: Stanford University Press.

Bateson, G. (1972) *Steps to an Ecology of Mind*. New York: Aronson.

Befu, H. (1974) 'An ethnography of dinner entertainment in Japan', *Artic Anthropology*. 11(supplement): 196–203.

Bentley, A. (1926) 'Remarks on method in the study of society', *American Journal of Sociology*, 32, 456–460.

Bethe, M. and Brazell, K. (1978) *Noh as Performance: An Analysis of the Kuse Scene of Yamamba*. Cornell University East Asia Papers, No. 15. Ithaca, NY: China–Japan Program, Cornell University.

Birdwhistell, R. (1970) *Kinesics and Context*. Philadelphia, PA: University of Pennsylvania Press.

Boas, F. (1940) *Race, Language, and Culture*. New York: Free Press.

Bosco, R. (1997) 'His lectures were poetry, his teaching the music of the spheres', *Harvard Library Bulletin*, n.s., 8: 5–79

Bremmer, J. and Roodenburg, H. (eds.) (1992) *A Cultural History of Gesture*. Ithaca, NY: Cornell University Press.

Brown, L. R. (1992) 'The Emerson museum', *Representations*, 40: 57–80.

Burke, K. (1964) 'Fact, inference, and proof in the analysis of literary symbolism', in S. E. Hyman (ed.), *Terms for Order*. Bloomington, IN: Indiana University Press. pp. 145–172.

De Jorio, A. (1832/2000) *Gesture in Naples and Gesture in Classical Antiquity*. A. Kendon (ed.), Bloomington, IN: Indiana University Press.

Dewey, J. (1916/2007) *Essays in Experimental Logic*. Carbondale, IL: Southern Illinois University Press.

Dewey, J. (1927) *The Public and its Problems*. New York: Henry Holt.

Doyle, A. C. (2009) 'The adventure of the man with the twisted lip', in *The Adventures and Memoirs of Sherlock Holmes*. New York: Vintage. pp. 103–124.

Drouin, J. M. and Bensuade-Vincent, B. (1996) 'Nature for the people', in N. Jardine, J. Secord, and E. Spary (eds.), *Cultures of Nature History*. Cambridge, UK: Cambridge University Press. pp. 408–425.

Efron, D. (1941) *Gesture and Environment*. New York: King's Crown Press.

Efron, D. (1972) *Gesture, Race, and Culture*. The Hague: Mouton.

Elias, N. (1969/1983) *The Court Society*. New York: Pantheon.

Emerson, R. W. (1833–1835/2005) 'The uses of natural history', in R. Bosco and J. Meyerson (eds.), *The Selected Lectures of Ralph Waldo Emerson*. Athens, GA: University of Georgia Press. pp. 1–17.

Emerson, R. W. (1842/2000) 'Self-reliance', in R. Richardson (ed.), *Ralph Waldo Emerson: Selected Essays, Lectures and Poems*. New York: Bantam. pp. 141–171.

Emerson, R. W. (1894) *Natural History of Intellect and Other Essays*. Boston, MA: Houghton, Mifflin, and Co.

Frake, C. O. (1964) 'Notes on queries in ethnography', *American Anthropologist*, 58(2, part 2): 132–145.

Goffman, E. (1971) *Relations in Public*. New York: Harper.

Goffman, E. (1976) 'Gender advertisements', *Studies in the Anthropology of Visual Communication*, 3: 69–154.

Goodenough, W. (1956) 'Residence rules', *American Anthropologist*, 58: 22–37.

Goodwin, C. (1981) *Conversational Organization*. New York: Academic Press.

Goodwin, C. (1994) 'Professional vision', *American Anthropologist,* 96: 606–633.

Goodwin, C. (in press) 'Building action in public environments with diverse semiotic resources', *The External Mind* (a special issue of *Versus: Quaderni di studi semiotici*).

Goodwin, M. H. (2006) *The Secret Life of Girls*. Cambridge, UK: Cambridge University Press.

Healy, J. F. (1991) '*Introduction*' In Gaius Plinius Secundus *(Pliny the Elder), Natural History: A Selection* . New York: Penguin. pp. ix–xi.

Hodgen, M. T. (1964) *Early Anthropology in the Sixteenth and Seventeenth Centuries*. Philadelphia, PA: University of Pennsylvania Press.

Howes, D. (ed.) (1991) *The Varieties of Sensory Experience*. Toronto: University of Toronto Press.

Irmscher, C. (1999) *The Poetics of Natural History: From John Bartrum to William James*. New Brunswick, NJ: Rutgers University Press.

James, W. (1897/1956) *The Will to Believe and Other Essays*. New York: Dover.

James, W. (1905) 'The experience of activity', *Psychological Bulletin*, 2: 39–40.

James, W. (1912/1976) *Essays in Radical Empiricism*. Cambridge, MA: Harvard University Press.

Kafka, F. (1935/1961) *Parable and Paradoxes*. Berlin: Schocken Verlag.

Kendon, A. (1990) *Conducting Interaction*. Cambridge, UK: Cambridge University Press.

Kendon, A. (2000) 'Andrea de Jorio and his work on gesture', in A. de Jorio (ed.), *Gesture in Naples and Gesture in Classical Antiquity*. Bloomington, IN: Indiana University Press. pp. xix–cvii

Kendon, A. (2004) *Gesture: Visible Action as Utterance*. Cambridge, UK: Cambridge University Press.

Klemp, N., McDermott, R., Raley, J., Thibeault, M., Powell, K. and Levitin, D. (2008) 'Plans, takes, mis-takes'. *Critical Social Studies*, 10(1): 4–21.

Leeds-Hurwitz, W. (1987) 'The social history of *The natural history of an interview:* A multi-disciplinary investigation of social communication', *Research on Language and Social Communication*, 2: 1–51.

McDermott, R. P. (2010) 'The passions of learning in tight circumstances: Toward a political economy of the mind', *National Society for the Study of Education Yearbook*, 109: 144–159.

McDermott, R. P. and Raley, J. (2009) 'The tell-tale body: The constitution of disability in schools', in W. Ayers, T. Quinn, and D. Stoval (eds.), *Handbook of Social Justice in Education*. Mahwah, NJ: LEA. pp. 431–445.

McDermott, R. P., Raley, J. and Seyer-Ochi, I. (2009) 'Race and class in a culture of risk', *Review of Research in Education*, 33: 101–116.

McQuown, N. A. (ed.) (1971) *The natural history of an interview*. Microfilm Collection, Manuscripts on Cultural Anthropology, Series 15: Nos. 95–8. Chicago, IL: University of Chicago Manuscripts.

Margolis, E. and Fram, S. (2007) 'Caught napping: Images of surveillance, discipline and punishment on the body of the schoolchild', *History of Education*, 36: 191–211.

Marx, K. (1852/2002) 'The Eighteenth Brumaire of Louis Bonaparte', in M. Cowling and J. Martin (eds.), *Marx's 'Eighteenth Brumaire': (Post)modern interpretations*. London: Pluto Press. pp. 19–109.

Marx, K. (1867/1976) *Capital, Vol I*. New York: Penguin.

Mead, G. H. (1938) *The Philosophy of the Act*. Chicago, IL: University of Chicago Press.

Mitchell, W. J. T. (2008) 'Four fundamental concepts of image science', in D. Birnbaum and I. Graw (eds.), *Under Pressure: Pictures, Subjects, and the New Spirit of Capitalism*. New York: Sternberg Press. pp. 14–24.

Radin, P. (1957) 'Method of approach', in P. Radin (ed.), *Primitive Man as Philosopher*. New York: Dover. pp. xxi–xli

Richardson, J. (2007) *The Natural History of Pragmatism*. Cambridge, UK: Cambridge University Press.

Sacks, H. (1963) 'Sociological description', *Berkeley Journal of Sociology*, 8: 1–16.

Sacks, H. (1990) *Lectures on Conversation*. London: Blackwell.

Scheflen, A. E. (1973) *Communicational Structure*. Bloomington, IN: Indiana University Press.

Schegloff, E. (1984) 'On some gestures' relation to talk', in J. Atkinson and J. Heritage (eds.), *Structures of Social Action*. Cambridge, UK: Cambridge University Press. pp. 266–296.

Schegloff, E. (1996) 'Body torque', *Social Research*, 65: 535–596.

Schegloff, E. (2007) *Sequence Organization in Interaction*. Cambridge, UK: Cambridge University Press.

Secord, A. (1996) 'Artisan botany', N. Jardine, J. Secord, and E. Spary (eds), *Cultures of Natural History*. Cambridge, UK: Cambridge University Press. pp. 378–393.

Siegfried, C. H. (1992) 'James's natural history methodology', in R. W. Burch and H. J. Saatkamp (eds.), *Frontiers in American Philosophy*. College Station, TX: Texas A&M Press. pp. 230–239.

Smith, A. (1776/1988) *An Inquiry into the Nature and Causes of the Wealth of Nations*. New York: Modern Library.

Smith, M. (1959) 'Boas's 'natural history' approach to field method', *American Anthropologist*, 61(5: part 2): 46–60.

Smith, W. J. (1977) *The Behavior of Communicating: An Ethological Approach*. Cambridge, MA: Harvard University Press.

Sterne, L. (1759–1767/2003) *Tristram Shandy*. London: Penguin.

Stocking, G. (1993) 'The turn-of-the-century concept of race', *Modernism/Modernity*, 1: 4–16.

Ungar, S. (2003) 'Visuality', in J. Wolfreys (ed.), *Glossalalia*. New York: Routledge. pp. 309–323.

Varenne, H. and McDermott, R. (1998) *Successful Failure*. Boulder, CO: Westview.

Wittgenstein, L. (1980) *Culture and Value*. Chicago, IL: University of Chicago Press.

21

Ethnomethodology and the Visual: Practices of Looking, Visualization, and Embodied Action

Michael Ball and Gregory Smith

INTRODUCTION

Ethnomethodology (hereafter EM) occupies a unique position in contemporary sociology. It has developed within academic sociology but is at odds with many, if not most, of sociology's methods, approaches, and presuppositions. Yet it retains enough of an emphasis on the fundamental sociality of action and cognition to be frequently described as a species of micro-sociology. Ethnomethodologists often prefer to regard EM as an 'alternative sociology'—a radically different way of doing sociological investigation (Lynch and Sharrock, 2003).

At the heart of this alternative sociology is a sustained commitment to study empirically the characteristics of actual social practices. The social world that sociologists study is full of people doing things that seem ordinary to them such as standing in line, having a conversation, giving directions, and figuring out a math problem. Such ordinary social actions or practices are the 'stuff' of social life. What sets EM apart from most other sociological approaches is its determination to observe and analyze ordinary social practices as they *actually* occur. EM is critical of 'typical' or 'idealized' or 'representative' or 'imagined' renderings of practices. This preoccupation with analyzing actual social practices and their components is evident in the studies reviewed in this chapter. Topics covered include queues, glances, directional maps and signs, mammograms, astronomical discoveries, courtroom testimony, and the teaching of new surgical procedures. EM casts fresh light on how the visual properties of these and many other everyday practices are socially organized. In this endeavor to capture and analyze the actualities of social practices, photographic and video technologies have proved invaluable in providing recordings of the details of actions that EM considers so central.

Since its inception, EM has maintained an abiding concern with the visual dimension of everyday social life—what its founder, Harold Garfinkel (1917–2011) termed the looks of things.[1] An appreciation of the importance of how the world looks to its members, of how the orderliness and intelligibility of ordinary human action critically depends upon its appearance, has led ethnomethodologists to accord the visual dimension an important role in their analyses. In addition, ethnomethodology's openness to the deployment of new technologies to collect data and facilitate analysis has ensured that the visual has always been accorded significance within this perspective.

Garfinkel has long acknowledged both the significance of the visual dimension in social life and the issues of representation posed by sociological investigation. Garfinkel's early (1948) manuscript published under the title, *Seeing Sociologically* (Garfinkel, 2006), stressed the primordial character of ordinary acts of looking and hearing. His major statement (Garfinkel, 1967) included such standard graphical forms as tables and tree diagrams. It also included a novel textual format to attempt to represent the background understandings informing ordinary conversations (see Garfinkel, 1967: 25–26, 38–39). Our discussion first turns to a review of visuality in Garfinkel's work.

GARFINKEL AND THE LOOKS OF THINGS, CONCEIVED ETHNOMETHODOLOGICALLY

Since its emergence in the 1960s, EM has made distinctive contributions to visual studies. To understand this contribution, it is necessary to consider some of the theoretical and methodological emphases that have made EM a unique sociological perspective. Garfinkel's now classic work, *Studies in Ethnomethodology* (Garfinkel, 1967; see also Garfinkel, 2002, 2006), established a project that was developed by a group of similarly minded scholars who recognized the conceptually and methodologically radical character of the venture that he initiated. Although often misunderstood and, in many respects, still in process of being worked out, EM's concerns and a number of its characteristic ideas have attracted a multi-disciplinary audience. The close analytic attention given to all forms of practical action that EM recommends has found ready audiences beyond academic sociology wherein EM originated. EM has inspired empirical research and scholarship in a variety of domains, including studies of work, organizational practices, practical reasoning, conversation analysis, phenomenological investigations, and studies of visual analysis and visual competencies.

EM's distinctive approach to social actions can be understood as a radical re-specification of Durkheim's famous aphorism that can be summarized in the statement: 'the objective reality of social facts is sociology's most fundamental phenomenon' (Rawls, 2002: 20). Garfinkel (1967, 2002) draws upon a neglected theme in Durkheim's thought: namely, social facts are constructed out of the specific and concrete details of social actions. The constant attention to what actually transpires in specific situations distinguishes EM from those many kinds of social science that are content to proceed on the basis of generalized descriptions of social practices and ideal-typical models of what it is believed motivates persons' actions. Garfinkel maintained that the orderliness of social action arises from the orderliness of the specific details of the action on any actual occasion. These details of social actions were orderly because they were socially organized, and thus could be studied sociologically. EM sought to investigate the methodical or orderly character of ordinary social actions. It especially focused upon the procedural bases of social activities: how, exactly, were actions built up out of their constituent details? It empirically investigated the methodical ways in which, for example, jurors make decisions, conversationalists produce and respond to an interruption, astronomers make discoveries in the course of a night's work in the observatory. One feature of the construction of activities is that they are 'reflexively accountable': that is, they are assembled so as to display their recognizability for whatever they are. In the details of their construction, a reasonably founded juror's decision, an interrupted turn at talk, a new astronomical object discovered, can each be recognized by competent members of society (jurors, conversationalists, astronomers) for what they are. Members of society unavoidably do the production and *recognition* of ordinary actions locally, *in situ*. Actions are 'indexical' in that their specific sense on any actual occasion is tied to a multitude of features of the local social context. These contextual features include identities and relationships acknowledged, resources mobilized, and aims pursued. In other words, the recognition and production of ordinary social actions is a practical, everyday accomplishment of society members. Producing and making sense is a demand facing all members of society—as Garfinkel notes, there is 'no time out ... no possibility of evasion' (1988: 103) from this ineluctable demand. At the heart of EM's empirical investigations is the study of the methods of how members make sense of and put together those actions—how they are recognized and produced.

Garfinkel captured this concern with the essential observability of the details of daily life as follows:

> The idea is this: worldly objects, as of the cogency and the cohesion of details, are available in the looks of organizational *Things*. If not, then where else in the world are you going to find them? Ethnomethodologically, they are available in an instructably observable arrangement, of apparent details—of details in and as their coherence producedly provided for. (2002: 211)

In contrast to many traditions in sociology, the visual dimension within EM studies is integral to the enterprise. As Baccus (1986) argued, 'That visibility is a "criterion" for the real-worldliness of social objects is to say that social objects, the objects of analytic social theorizing are constituted so as to provide for their visibility via some means' (1986: 6). For normally sighted persons numerous courses of embodied action involve a powerful and inescapable visual dimension.

In a later study, Garfinkel employed a collection of photographic images to show how instructions and instructed actions function in everyday contexts. One example features a photograph of the layout and visual appearance of things in Helen's kitchen (see Exhibit 3 in Garfinkel, 2002: 213). Helen is a sight-impaired person. It was consequently important that within her kitchen there was a visual order and clear spatial relationship between relevant things, so that they were readily locatable for her to work in her kitchen. So, for example, several cooking implements are hung from hooks on the wall behind the oven. The range of cooking implements displayed a visual spatial pattern or organization with which Helen was familiar, for very good practical reasons. Her sight impairment required much scanning on her part to locate implements and ingredients when preparing a meal. Even with sight impairment, Helen was able to locate what she needed efficiently. Constructing a spatial layout for tools, implements and materials that is visually clear is a common practice in many workshops, garages, offices, and the like. In the case of people with sight impairment, such organization takes on a greater practical significance, revealing aspects of the 'endogenously produced coherent appearances of Things' (Garfinkel, 2002: 211).

SITUATING ETHNOMETHODOLOGY

The distinct analytic orientation of EM can be better understood if it is compared with some other leading approaches in visual studies (see Table 21.1). Very briefly: compared

Table 21.1 Comparison of ethnomethodology with other perspectives in visual studies

	Ethnomethodology	Content analysis	Semiotics	Psychoanalysis	Symbolic interactionism
Key questions	What are the methods that people use to produce and recognize the practices of ordinary social life?	What are the significant categories and themes predominant in any communication?	What do signs mean within socio-cultural contexts?	How are spectators and visual images mutually constituted? How are 'repressed' instincts allowed licensed expression?	How are meanings created and sustained in social interaction?
Aim of analysis	Elucidation of people's methods for producing and recognizing features of social practices. Analysis shows how social practices are made 'accountable'; i.e. observable and reportable	Identification of patterns of messages. Manifest and latent contents of communication	Discovery of how signs work to convey socio-cultural meaning	Exploration of how unconscious motives, usually linked to sexual desire, manifest themselves in acts of looking by audiences	Analytic description; concept generation and development
Exemplars	Sacks (1972); Mondada (2003)	Robinson (1976); Lutz and Collins (1993)	Barthes (1977); Williamson (1978)	Mulvey (1975); Doane (1991)	Goffman (1979); Chalfen (1987)
Units and topics of analysis	Social practices and specifically socially situated talk and visually available behavior	Texts that contain messages communicated from a source to a receiving audience	Signifiers and their signifieds and referents; relations between signs (syntagmatic and paradigmatic)	Films and film genres	Symbols, their interactional currency and significance
Attention to visual data	Observations and recordings of visual aspects of talk and activity.	Drawings, images, photographs, and paintings that can be collected and coded into predetermined categories	Photographic images, advertising images analyzed by semiotic conceptual terminology	The filmic text as a vehicle to explore a range of unconscious fantasies and desires such as scopophilia	Participant and direct observation to examine interactional uses of images and pictorial forms (e.g. advertisements, snapshot photography)
Conception of the research subject's human nature	A skilled social agent constantly making sense of everyday situations and ordinary actions	An absorber of messages. Meaning of message for the receiver assumed to be identical to that of the sender	Persons placed in subject positions by semiotic codes	Emotional states such as dreams and fantasies, often repressed by the unconscious, are the key to human subjectivity	A skilled social agent at home with specific cultural repertoires
Conception of the social world premised by analysis	An emphasis on the constructed character of social practices and the particularities of their contexts	A web of messages exchanged by senders and receivers	A multiplicity of codes. Certain codes become dominant ideologies	Civilization represses instincts to enforce social conformity via law, taboo, etc.	A vast network of interactants

with *content analysis*, EM is a qualitative not quantitative approach; compared with *semiotics*, EM sees meaning as more contextual and less a matter of sign relationships; compared with *psychoanalysis*, it is much more focused on people's conduct—what they say and do—rather than their conscious and unconscious mental life; and compared with *symbolic interactionism* (to which it stands closest), EM is likewise much concerned with the participant's point of view but is more attentive to the contextual particulars of talk and action as a source of the understandings and orientations that guide participants' actions (Ball and Smith, 1992). We hope that similarities and differences between EM and these other popular approaches in visual studies will become clearer as the chapter's review of studies proceeds.

The chapter examines how researchers working in the tradition of EM have addressed the visual dimension in their research studies. Its orientation is broadly historical and methodological. As an organizing device, we have stressed the role of technological developments in recording devices. A summary statement is given in Table 21.2, 'Ethnomethodology, visuality, and its technological assists.' In speaking of technological assists, we want to highlight the opportunities new technologies have lent EM inquiries. We hope that it goes without saying that we disavow any suggestion that determinism is involved in accounting for the development of the field of visual EM studies in this way. It remains, we stress, nothing more than an organizing device designed to highlight the various ways in which visual data have been gathered for EM analysis. That said, it is notable that at the low-technology end of EM research, EM- inspired ethnographic research shares much in common with well-known classics of ethnographic research. However at the high-technology end of our schema, researcher- generated audio-video recordings of indigenous uses of images, there is a degree of technological sophistication that lies far beyond the imagination of even a Malinowski or a Park.

This shift toward more technologically sophisticated methods of data collection has helped to shape the broad direction taken by more than four decades of visual EM research. Earlier studies tended to concentrate on the 'practices of looking' used by individuals in varying capacities, while more recent studies increasingly focus on 'practices of visualization.' What do we mean by this distinction?

Our contention is that Garfinkel's appreciation of visuality in ethnomethodological inquiry was taken forward by ethnographic studies of public, formal organizational, and occupational settings. The visual orientations of early EM concentrated on aspects of, in the phrase popularized by Goffman (1963), 'behavior in public places'—studies of using directional signs to find one's way about, glancing, urban walking, making inferences based on appearances about the moral character of passers-by, queuing, and the like. These studies are investigations of 'practices of looking' within the natural attitude of everyday life. The aim was to articulate those visual features of public places that members of society noticed and used as a basis for their action. Some of this research drew upon still photographic images, film, or video data. The visual dimension also figured in conversation analysis (CA), the first significant methodological development to emerge out of EM (Francis and Hester, 2004). This may seem paradoxical since CA concentrates on what can be heard rather than seen. However, CA was significant for its principled dependence on recorded audio materials to facilitate the close analytical scrutiny of conversation, or what Schegloff (1987) more accurately came to refer to as 'talk-in-interaction.' The relevance of CA was to show how the analytical sensitivities of EM could address a variety of practices, in which the visualization of an object, course of action or scene was central. The concern with 'practices of visualization' has generated a rich research program that has included forms of pedagogy and instructed action, scientific investigation and workplace studies, in a range of organizational and occupational

Table 21.2 Ethnomethodology, visuality, and its technological assists

Source of data	Approach	Representative studies
Ethnographic research	EM-inspired studies of social (and especially work) practices that include visual arrangements, using data collected by conventional ethnographic observational and interviewing techniques	Bittner (1967) on policing on skid row Cicourel (1968) on juvenile justice Sudnow (1978, 2001) on jazz improvisation Sudnow (1972) on the timing of glances
Found images and documents	Analysis of found images and records— and how people use these objects in courses of action	Psathas (1979) on directional maps Garfinkel (1967) on psychiatric clinic records Slack et al. (2007) on reading mammograms
Audiotaped recordings	Canonical CA: talk as social-action-based transcribed data of naturally occurring conversations. Visuality is incidental to the treatment of talk	Sacks (1972) on conversational data Schegloff (1972) on place formulations Garfinkel et al. (1981) on scientific discoveries
Researcher-generated photographic images	Photographs for analytic as against illustrative use. Here the visual is a silent analytical domain and appearances are rendered as still images	Sharrock and Anderson (1979) on directional hospital signs Ball and Smith (1986) on queuing
Researcher-generated real-time video recordings	Video data produced by the researcher, lacking a soundtrack, analyzed for analytical purposes	Ryave and Schenkein (1974) on walking
Researcher-generated real-time audio-video recordings.	Moving images with natural sound.	Goodwin (1994) on professional vision Heath (1986) and West (1984) on medical consultations
Researcher-generated audio-video recordings of indigenous uses of images and video	Real-time researcher-generated audio-visual data of how professionals use images and video as part of their work	Mondada (2003) on how surgeons teach using video of their surgery Hindmarsh and Heath (1998) on how video can be used for the analysis of objects in action

contexts where practitioners are faced with the task of working with visual images. This research has exploited the potential of video technology as a method of data collection in order to study the working practices of those who themselves work with images, in locations such as security camera surveillance centers, operating theaters, or control rooms.

Our chapter concentrates on six of the categories identified in Table 21.2, beginning with studies adopting ethnographic techniques, where a good eye (and ear!) and memory matters more than an effective recording device, to the high-technology end of the spectrum, where visual methods are used to study the activities of those who are themselves reliant upon visual technologies to carry out their working practices. The chapter concludes with a summary of issues and projected future directions for EM-inspired research into the visual.

ETHNOGRAPHIC RESEARCH

Many early studies in EM used the established methods of ethnographic observation and interviewing. In some of these studies, the visual dimension was submerged in a broader notion of appearances that formed the basis for inferences and action. Bittner's (1967) study of how the police keep the peace in skid row suggested that they make on-the-spot judgments about the likelihood of a situation getting out of hand. Cicourel's (1968) study of juvenile justice procedures noted the importance of offenders possessing an appropriately well-demeaned appearance when their cases came up for disposal by the courts. Attention to the visual has always formed a component within EM studies, evident in studies of such diverse phenomena as the visual dimension involved in learning to play jazz piano (Sudnow, 1978, 2001), and working with the visual features of numbers in mathematics (Livingston, 1986).

As Garfinkel's consideration (above) of the case of Helen's practices of scanning her immediate environment demonstrates, there is a form of interpretive work that the normally sighted largely take for granted. In the course of our ordinary affairs we routinely glance at the looks of things we encounter. Especially in public places, glancing is a routinely employed practice of looking. Sudnow reminds us of the range of visual glancing work that members routinely engage in for gleaning relevant information about social contexts while carrying out courses of practical action, such as:

> in the co-ordination of automobile or sidewalk pedestrian traffic where single-glanced monitoring of others' actions is an often required procedure, or, in other situations chiefly ceremonial and social, as in the numerous activities where the immediate spontaneous, glance-based recognition of another's moves, categorical status, gestures, etc. is strongly sanctioned and violations sometimes harshly noticed (for example "Hey I was in line here", "Why are you staring" etc.). (1972: 260)

Sudnow's treatment of the glance starts from the premise that the glance is a member's device and not an analytic unit. By so doing, he draws our attention to the practical relevance of time and space for understanding contexts of non-verbal social behavior.

For Sudnow, a single glance in public spaces is often fully adequate to the task of categorizing persons and features of settings while engaging in courses of practical action. He writes: 'for many activities, the glance is the maximally appropriate unit of interpersonal observation' (1972: 260). Sudnow emphasizes the temporal dimension of glances, which can be consequential and accountable in terms of the information acquired and the interactional context. As Sudnow notes:

> That the timing of a glance might be consequential for its informational adequacy may be suspected in the light of the fact that many of the aspects of scenes whose glanced-at "observability" and 'interpretation' seem regularly achieved are aspects that may be regarded as organized as "courses of action", having spatially and temporally extended dimensions. (1972: 261)

Sudnow further explores the informational potential of the glance by comparing it with the still photographic image. Glancing might be thought of as a kind of mobile, embodied camera work, a form of mechanical glancing. But Sudnow insists that this is not a fair analogy. In contrast to glances, still photographic images are records of the 'decisive moment' (Cartier-Bresson's [1952] memorable phrase) in which the image is made, and aided by subjects who may 'pose' for the camera.

EM's concern to analyze the specifics of situated conduct focused on how the looks of things are used by skilled embodied agents working in a material world. One compelling examination of how attention to the looks of things connects looking with subsequent sociological preoccupations with embodiment and materiality is Sudnow's treatment of learning to play improvised jazz piano (Sudnow, 1978, 2001). This is an early EM example of what has come to be known as autoethnography. The technique involves the researcher turning ethnographic techniques toward their own actions and experiences.

Learning to play the piano is a practical embodied achievement. It involves acquiring the competence and dexterity to produce recognizable patterns of sound from the work of fingers on the keyboard. Learning to play improvised jazz piano calls for a further competence. As Sudnow put it, 'My hands have come to develop an intimate knowledge of the piano keyboard, ways of exploratory engagement with routings through its spaces, modalities of reaching and articulating, and now I choose places to go in the course of moving from place to place as a handful choosing' (Sudnow, 1978: xiii). Sudnow's analysis of how he learned to play improvised jazz emphasizes learned embodied skills. It was very much a matter of developing particular musical skills in his hands (hence the book's title, *Ways of the Hand*). The acquisition of these skills often involved scrutinizing the keyboard for solutions to the problem of where the hands are to go next:

> ...my looking, an appeal to the keyboard for answers, was party to a theoretic in-course analysis I did over the keyboard's sights, trying to keep the terrain under regard to aid large leaps and get from one path to another, a looking that was altogether frantic, like searching for a parking place in a big hurry. (Sudnow, 2001: 35)

Sudnow takes the reader through the intricacies of notes, chords, timings, pulsings, repetitions, runs, returns, and so forth. These courses of practical action made up the work of playing improvised jazz piano. He used photographs of hand positions on the keyboard and diagrams alongside linguistic descriptions to convey the difficulties and challenges his hands encountered in his efforts to learn to play improvised jazz piano. These images give specific material sense to the written description of the text, showing that which is linguistically described.

In an early paper originally prepared for his class with Goffman at Berkeley, Harvey Sacks (1972) explores aspects of the practical work of the patrolling police officer. Sacks drew upon his ethnographic observations as well as documentary sources such as police training manuals for data. Sacks treated the police as an occupational group licensed to engage in the detailed glancing or observation of people in public spaces. How do the police assess the moral character of persons in public spaces, based only on the looks of things (Sacks, 1972: 280)? The solution 'begins with the fact that persons within society are trained to naively present and naively employ presented appearances as the grounds of treatment of the persons they encounter in public places' (Sacks, 1972: 283). In this paper, Sacks considered how the police on patrol learn to operate with a collection of background relevancies and expectancies for making sense of the behavior of those they routinely encounter. He showed how the police learned to see the appearances of persons and their presented behaviors, when nothing out of the ordinary seemed to be transpiring, as collections of normal appearances. As Sacks informs us about the training of novice police officers:

> As he walks through his beat with a mature officer, persons who to him appear legit are cast in terms of the illicit activities in which the latter knows they are engaged. The novice is shown how to see the streets as, so to speak, scenes from pornographic films. (1972: 285)

The novice is thus taught to look for people who 'don't look like they belong round here,' vehicles parked in places and times that seem 'unusual,' or activities that do not seem to be transpiring in quite the expected pattern. Such sense-making involves what Sacks refers to as an 'incongruity procedure.' It depends upon the acquisition of occupationally specific cultural knowledge by police officers that sets a baseline set of understandings about the normal appearances of persons, districts, activities, and so on. The situated and localized inferential work of the incongruity procedure is not just looking but is thoroughly cultured looking enacted in specific social contexts.

FOUND IMAGES AND DOCUMENTS

One of EM's interests in images resides in how they are used as documents to facilitate the carrying-out ('accomplishment') of a particular social practice. In this section, we shall consider two studies that focus on the role of existing (or 'found') images in the social practices of (1) finding one's way to a specific destination and (2) reading a mammogram for evidence of possible pathology.

George Psathas (1979) studied the directional maps people draw by hand in order to help guide other persons to a location (usually their home or some other meeting place). Often these maps are sent out with party invitations and are intended to be self-explanatory. Sometimes, however, these maps can be sketched on the spot in the presence of another person to whom directions are being given. Psathas calls these 'occasioned maps' because they are talked about while being drawn, often with questions, answers, and explanations being provided in the course of drawing. Occasioned maps address the co-present person and their particular journey. The analysis provided by Psathas is one example of an ethnomethodological study of a visual object.

Unlike the maps that cartographers draw, the directional map is not a descriptive, objective, all-inclusive map of an area. Rather, it is a map constructed with the very specific purpose of 'showing a way to a particular place.' It is just intended to show someone how to get to a specific destination. Only those roads and landmarks that are 'on the map' are deemed relevant for getting to the destination. Psathas reviewed a number of directional maps and elaborated their features. He showed how streets can be located in sequential terms 'as *between, across from, before* and *after, over* and *under*' (Psathas, 1979: 222) other streets and landmarks. The orderly properties of sense-making were established by a careful scrutiny of a sample of directional maps as visual objects used by people in the practical matter of finding their destination.

Found images and documents were the principal source of data for an EM study of the reading of mammograms by radiologists and other medical staff (Slack et al., 2007).

The researchers suggested that reading mammograms was best understood as a cultural practice rather than an individual cognitive act. The work of creating mammograms and interpreting them for evidence of pathologies is highly skilled. Slack et al. focused on the 'lived work' involved in reaching an adequate interpretation of what the mammogram set shows about the condition of a woman's breasts. The lived work included practices such as the comparison of a current mammogram set with earlier sets for the same patient, and various techniques to distinguish the artifactual from the actual in the mammogram. In focusing on the mammogram as a central diagnostic document for a community of users, Slack and co-workers drew upon their own observations of how radiologists made decisions. They also interviewed staff about their working practices. By using these methods in combination, they were able to highlight how the mammograms were used and thus show the social dimensions of the looking that led to an appropriate decision by the radiologist.

RESEARCHER-GENERATED PHOTOGRAPHY

Our next category considers some EM studies that draw upon photographic images as data in order to highlight how features of local social settings are visually conveyed to persons: here, photographs are used to supplement observational research. As 'aids to a sluggish imagination' (Spiegelberg's phrase, quoted by Garfinkel, 1967: 38), photographs provide the researcher with a documentary record of appearances that can be repeatedly viewed and scrutinized for features that may escape the unaided ethnographic eye. This section concentrates on queues and finding one's way using directional signs.

Queues and queuing arrangements are routine features of daily life in many cultures across the world. For ethnomethodology, the queue is but one example of 'the witnessed and produced orderliness of practical action' (Livingston, 1987: 13). Queues arise when a desired service or facility is temporarily available to an agent or item requiring access to the service or facility. They are an organizational arrangement for allocating access to the facility or service. Queues frequently occur in public spaces among unacquainted persons. They tend to be relatively short-lived units of social organization that are visually available to viewers who readily recognize what they see. For queues to work as successful social arrangements, members must possess the interpretive capacity to recognize them as visual behavioral patterns.[2]

In a study of a set of still photographic data, we (Ball and Smith, 1986) formulated a typology of queuing arrangements as a preliminary to the analysis of the 'properties of the order of service in queues.' We distinguished 'incarnate' queues that included people and vehicles from queues of 'items,' such as books waiting to be returned to stacks by librarians, exam scripts and essays waiting to be marked by an examiner, and factory products awaiting the next stage of the manufacturing process (Ball and Smith, 1986: 29). The distinguishing characteristic of item queues was that they have no potential for self-organization or regulation. They are ordered and organized by external human agency either directly or indirectly. Incarnate queues—people at bus stops and milk floats at a dairy—were the principal concern of our analysis. As we suggested:

Visual information about persons and objects in the immediate environment plays a major role in all unfocused interaction and queuing is no exception. In this paper we wish to propose a further refinement of this idea. We suggest that the orderliness of queues is primarily dependent upon the interpretive work undertaken by queuers, interpretive work that centers upon the reflexive monitoring of visual information. This feature we shall refer to as the "visual availability" (Sharrock and Anderson, 1979) of queuing's local organization, for queues possess a social organization the elements of which are transparent and available to participants and passers-by alike. In this paper we

attempt to specify some of the elements figuring in the queuer's practical reasoning. (1986: 27–28)

We drew attention to the visual dimensions of queuing in part by sharing our data, still photographic images, with the reader (see Figure 21.1). Queues are particularly photogenic social phenomena, as Garfinkel and Livingston also noted: queuers are 'incessantly engaged with the work of producing the order of service, embodied audio-visual details are their central, substantive, content-specific congregationally relevant business at hand' (2003: 22). In keeping with these emphases, we examined the queue as a unit of social organization. We approached the queue from the vantage of the members who assemble it—'doing queuing'—and also from the more abstract analytic level of the queue as a social system constructed from people's practical actions. The study took into account aspects of queue ecology, the basic and evident visual parameters of queues, such as the practical significance of the height, width, length of queues, and the 'natural boundaries' (Ryave and Schenkein, 1974) of the environment in which the queue was located.

In most everyday examples of queuing arrangements, their practical assembly is informed by the turn-taking system of 'first come, first served' (FCFS). As an organizational principle, FCFS is also of relevance in other instances of social organization such as turn-taking in conversations (Sacks et al., 1974; ten Have, 1999; Francis and Hester, 2004). However, the turn-taking system of queues was visually available to other people in the situation. As Garfinkel and Livingston suggested, 'parties to a queue characteristically want the queue to be evident with conveniently assessed displays of its statistics' (2003: 21). Similarly, as Ball and Smith pointed out:

Queues are ... not just visible social phenomena; they display their turn organization in their linear appearance. It is the orderliness of FCFS which the linear appearance of the queue reveals. Ordinal position and thus turn are available to co-present persons in the setting "at a glance." (1986: 35)

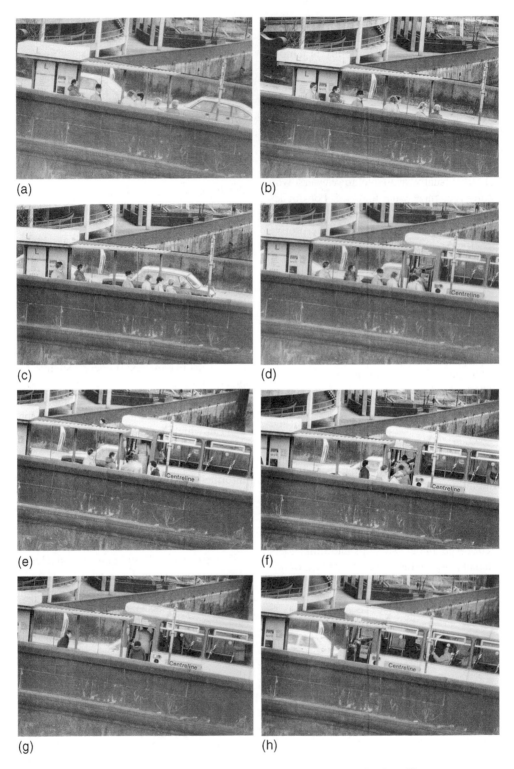

Figure 21.1 (a)–(h) The visual availability of a queue's local organization: 'first come, first served' in action. © 1986 Ball and Smith, reproduced with permission from *Communication and Cognition*, **19(1)**.

Using a series of strategically made still photographs as data, our research developed an account of the social process of queuing, showing how queues emerge and dissipate and how movement through queues occurs. The methodological significance of our research lies in how our photographic images demonstrate the visual availability of the orderliness of queuing in a manner that can be subjected to scrutiny by analyst and reader alike.

Our queuing study built upon the methodologically innovative work of Sharrock and Anderson (1979), which also used a small collection of still photographs in an investigation of hospital directional signs. In large organizations such as hospitals, finding one's way is assisted by the placement of directional signs within the hospital environment. The patient's general competence with and commonsense practical use of such a system of signs to find their way around is taken for granted. Sharrock and Anderson began by asking, 'Why should two sociologists be interested in some hospital signs, more precisely in five photographs of a dozen or so such signs?' (81). Their answer was:

> In our case, the collection is, first, a collection of photographs, of signs, made because we thought that signs were natural things to choose in the context of enquiring into the visual availability of social scenes, for signs are to be looked at. (1979: 83)

Plainly, this returns us to our consideration of the methodological bases of EM research into the visual, and the analytic uses of still photography. For Sharrock and Anderson, systems of directional signs serve the practical purposes of people finding their way within the hospital. But more generally, pictorial and written signs are there for a purpose, and comprise a visually available feature of public and semi-public spaces. Directional signs can be seen individually at a particular site or they can be treated as part of a broader system of related signs. Directional signs in hospital environments are read in ways shaped by practical purposes. People will encounter the signs one at a time and at their normal walking pace. The signs will be sufficiently brief that people will not usually need to pause to read them before continuing on their way. Thus, the signs are read *in situ* and the reading is governed by a thoroughly practical motive ('How can I get to...?'). In hospitals, directional signs are designed to furnish information and are frequently organized sequentially, so that a sign to 'Physiotherapy' will be followed by further so-named signs until the follower of the sign has arrived at the Physiotherapy Department. In this respect, they share common characteristics with other forms of directional signs such as road signs that provide directions and the road number: for example, M1, London, The South (Ball, 2005). As Sharrock and Anderson put the matter:

> When we think of people using signs it becomes obvious that the use they make of them is practical. They are not interested in the meaning of the sign but are interested in using the sign for some purpose. They are not interested in what signs in general mean, but in the use they can make of *This* sign, *Here* and *Now*. Their reasoning is not theoretical and general but practical, particularized and in context. (1979: 81)

But these readings of directional signs were not haphazard or idiosyncratic. Rather, readers of these signs (and those who design signage for hospitals, road networks and the like) employed methodical practices of sense-making that carefully distinguish the location, juxtaposition, and sequencing of signs.

RESEARCHER-GENERATED REAL-TIME VIDEO

Early ethnomethodology also used videotaped data to investigate further features of the orderliness of actions in public places. In this section we commence with a review of a classic study on the 'art' of walking by A. Lincoln Ryave and James N. Schenkein (1974). What is methodologically significant about this paper is that it is based upon two

8-minute segments of videotape of a public pavement mainly used by students. The researchers 'filmed at a time when students are routinely negotiating their way from class to class' (Ryave and Schenkein, 1974: 265). As the video lacked a soundtrack, it isolated the visual component of behaving as a pedestrian in public settings (Ryave and Schenkein, 1974; also see Lee and Watson, 1992).

The videotaped students were characterized as 'doing walking,' the verb employed in order to emphasize the active, produced feature of this routine and mundane activity. The commonplace action of walking was analyzed as an ongoing situated accomplishment in terms of its production and recognition. Walkers navigated their way through environments that are shaped and structured by 'natural boundaries,' such as walls, curbs, parked vehicles, posts, and other items of street furniture (Ryave and Schenkein, 1974: 266). Ryave and Schenkein explored aspects of how people move their way through public spaces, while encountering what they refer to as a 'navigational problem': how to avoid collision with others. Once again, they addressed aspects of the production and recognition of normal everyday orderly behavior in public spaces by considering how individuals and collections of people can come to be seen as moving obstacles. They distinguished between people walking together as a group, which Goffman (1963) has referred to as a 'with,' from people walking alone, who were careful not to 'walk through' people walking together.

It may be instructive to compare Ryave and Schenkein's study with a more recent EM treatment of walking in public spaces. Hester and Francis (2003) explored aspects of the visual order of walking by in part becoming what Sacks had referred to as a self-commenting machine. Here the researcher, when walking to a supermarket, narrates into an audio recording machine a description of their actions, for all practical 'analytic' purposes. One consequence of this methodological strategy is that the visual is transformed into the verbal, a common device

in a 'discipline of words' (Mead, 1975; Signorelli, 1984).

The development of the visual analysis of methodical practices of sense-making in public places has been furthered by Watson's (2005) adaptation of membership categorization analysis to the phenomenon of 'flow files.' Using naturalistic observation as well as videotaped data, Watson identified one form of locomotion through public space: the flow file. This form of locomotion is found where a group of pedestrians make their way toward a destination, one following the next, at a regular pace. There is a moral order to the flow file. The first pedestrian assumes the 'leader' category, forging a path through the sometimes-crowded public spaces. The leader has category-bound obligations about the direction and pace of the file, ensuring it travels at a rate that all file members can maintain. Flow files, Watson concludes, 'are at once locally situated, sequential-categorial phenomena' (Watson, 2005: 221). He further suggests that 'A huge variety of membership categories can be seen to be in play in urban public spaces. In this sense, it is misleading to see those spaces as a "world of strangers"' (Watson, 2005: 222).

A conspicuous methodological advantage of the use of videotaped data is that it offers the analyst the permanent possibility of reviewing the particulars of the conduct it records. Re-inspection and re-analysis of the visual data is facilitated by the playback opportunities allowed by the technology. In addition, recorded visual data has the potential to be shared with the reader/viewer in an open manner that lays bare the processes of interpretation that are so often simply taken on trust in standard forms of ethnographic research. This methodological strategy was inspired by the use by conversation analysts of audiotaped data.[3] However, inspection of the publication of both Ryave and Schenkein's study and Watson's study shows that no extracts from their visual data were presented to readers. In this respect, their research resembles the observation-based work of Sudnow and Sacks with the attendant concerns about ethnographic validity (the empirical foundation of the analysis was not presented). However, this difficulty might be better regarded as a presentational and publishing issue than as a methodological or analytical one. Often, simply the economics of academic publishing create the constraint.

RESEARCHER-GENERATED REAL-TIME AUDIO AND VIDEO

We commence this section with a study by Garfinkel et al. (1981) that properly speaking belongs under a different heading, that of audiotaped recordings. Our decision to stretch our headings is motivated by the importance of the approaches that follow from this study. Garfinkel et al. has been an important source in the area of science studies and has contributed to further development of the study of 'lived work' in various other areas of EM research.

Although specialized bodies of knowledge and highly technical procedures are implicated in scientific investigation and discovery, from EM's perspective the same orders of practical reasoning and communicative skills are found as are involved in walking together or finding one's way through hospital corridors. EM's emphasis on science as a form of situated social activity was not intended to downgrade or undermine scientific work. Rather, EM studies of science sought to preserve and analyze the actual practices of scientific work, while also noting how these practices depended upon broader forms of commonsense cultural knowledge and competence in conjunction with the more obvious esoteric forms of knowledge and practice conventionally associated with science as an activity.

Some of these emphases can be found in the analysis of the practical work of discovery in science reported in Harold Garfinkel, Michael Lynch, and Eric Livingston's 1981 study of astronomical discovery. Garfinkel et al.

were given access to a recording of a group of scientists who taped their talk as they worked at the Steward Observatory when discovering an optical pulsar on the night of 16 January 1969. Garfinkel et al. used the data recorded on the tape to find significant insights into the practical organization of the work of discovery, including the visual analysis of scientific data. They sought to understand the nature of scientific discovery as a form of situated social action that preserves the 'local historicity' of the discovery: that is, the scientists, when they reported for work at the Steward Observatory on the 16 January, did not know at the outset that they would be discovering the first optical pulsar. So, Garfinkel et al. paid close attention to parts of the talk such as the following:

Disney: (we've got a little bit of shape now). (0.4)
McCallister: We::ll, (1.0)
McCallister: (it's) about like I saw in that sky: over there, t'tell you the truth. (0.5)
McCallister: The's a nice di(hh)p on the (hh) si(hh) de of that sky. (0.5)
McCallister: I'm gonna turn this thing down. (2.5) ((machine sound—probably gain switch))
Disney: We've got a bleeding pulse here (2.0)
Cocke: He::y! (4.5)
Cocke: Wo:::w! (1.2)
Cocke: You don't suppose that's reyally it, do you? (2.0)
Cocke: Ca::n't be:.
Disney: It's right bang in the middle of the period. (look), I mean right bang in the middle of the (sca::le). (0.8)
Disney: It reyally looks something (from here) at the moment. (to me) (0.8)
Cocke: Hmm:! (3.0)
Disney: (an') its growing too. (hey) (1.0)
Disney: It's growing up the side a bit too. (Garfinkel et al., 1981: 149).

Much of the practice of scientific work reported here was concerned with rendering visible the invisible. In the instance above, the scientists worked with images in the form of electronic data displays. Their talk concerned their practices as astronomers as they worked with and reacted to data that came in live from a radio telescope, working in real time, moment by moment, and discovering that the data revealed evidence of an optical pulsar. This was the work of scientific discovery: phenomena that are invisible with the naked eye were transformed into visible traces.

Even a cursory examination of this corpus of data showed that the work of science, in common with many other practical activities for normally sighted people, was embedded in the visual domain. Scientists have been characterized as engaged in a process of 'seeing the physics' (Lynch and Edgerton, 1988: 213). This involved digital image techniques that used pictorial and graphical electronic displays to show abstract measures in a more palpable, visual format. The use of an observational terminology was reflected in the talk of the scientists as they worked. Visual matters were oriented to in and through talk. Within the 15 units of talk between Disney, McCallister, and Cocke, mention was made of: visual 'shapes,' seeing things ('I saw in that sky over there'), turning down a machine to obtain a better image, the initial recognition of a 'pulse' and the description of its observed growth. The talk progressed from Disney's utterance, 'we've got a little bit of shape now'—a comment referring to an emerging image of an astronomical phenomenon—to Disney's comment, 'It's growing up the side a bit too.' All this talk was derived from just one 'observational run' of a number carried out that night. Successive subsequent runs were new and different from previous ones but were designed to furnish further evidence of the presence of the optical pulsar. Of course, all this work depended upon knowledge of the scientific specialism shared by the scientists working that night in the observatory. The idea that shared specialist knowledge provides the basis for specialized ways of looking takes us toward Charles Goodwin's (1994) influential concept of 'professional vision.'

The notion of 'professional vision' was designed to show how all occupational specialists work within the accepted ways of seeing licensed by their professional domain (Goodwin, 1994). Goodwin examined how

field archaeologists and lawyers draw upon occupationally specific ways of seeing in order to accomplish their professional work. Goodwin notes how:

> Discursive practices are used by members of a profession to shape events in the domains subject to their professional scrutiny. The shaping process creates the objects of knowledge that become the insignia of a profession's craft: the theories, artifacts, and bodies of expertise that distinguish it from other professions. (1994: 606)

He examines how a profession's craft is embodied in its routine practices with especial reference to the visual dimensions of that work. To investigate the professional vision of archaeologists and lawyers, Goodwin principally drew upon videotaped data of archaeological field schools in Argentina and the USA, and videotapes of the first Rodney King trial. Videotape preserved both participants' talk and body movements, rendering them amenable to repeated, detailed scrutiny. Recorded talk in particular was amenable to transcription (CA systems of notation have become standard in EM). Goodwin's analysis focused upon three practices in each of his two settings: (1) the 'coding schemes' used to transform features of a setting into objects of profession-relevant discourse; (2) the 'highlighting' practices used to mark as significant certain specific phenomena in the setting; and (3) the production and articulation of graphic representations.

In the case of archaeological fieldwork, Goodwin shows how students are taught to use Munsell color charts as coding schemes to systematically identify the color of the dirt they are digging through. Highlighting in the field is often done by the trowel work of archaeologists, who use their trowels to mark lines in the ground to identify features of interest such as molds of posts that may once have supported a house. Archaeologists also produce sketches, maps, and diagrams that are graphic material representations of features of archaeological relevance. Their production is a collaborative and sometimes contested endeavor.

The element of contestation was much more pronounced in lawyers' work. The novel move Goodwin then made was to suggest that the same framework of coding, highlighting, and graphic representation can be used to illuminate the trial of Rodney King, the African-American motorist filmed by an amateur photographer being violently beaten by four Los Angeles police officers in 1991. Goodwin provided a detailed analysis of how King's conduct was coded by the officers' defense lawyers as aggressive, his body movements minutely highlighted and pointed to as indicative of incipient violence, so that the amateur video of the beating came to be seen as a representation of 'police craftwork' in dealing with an 'aggressive offender.' In this way three of the officers were acquitted of wrongdoing at the first trial.[4]

Goodwin developed his analysis of professional vision with close attention to stills and videos of archaeological fieldwork and the trial as shown on TV. He made the now-standard EM observation that the use of videotaped data renders his analysis open to ready checking and challenge by other researchers. In conclusion, Goodwin (1994: 628) emphasized that professional vision is not merely a frame of mind or mental set. Professional vision is made manifest through people's embodied, situated practices,[5] and it is through these practices that something as apparently subjective as ways of seeing can be accessed for analysis. The practices themselves require processes of learning, whether in archaeology field school or the courtroom. He also suggested that professional vision could be seen as part of the workings of professional power, especially if power was understood in the Foucauldian sense of discourses that articulated the conditions of rationality in a society and the kinds of talk that can and cannot be heard. In this way, Goodwin points to some ways in which EM can deepen the understandings provided by other social scientific perspectives.

Technological developments have simplified the making of audio and video recordings of ordinary human actions.

Ethnomethodologists have long been aware of the potential of these developments for their explorations of the production and recognition of ordinary actions. One early significant contribution was Christian Heath's (1986) study of medical consultations in general practice in the UK. Drawing upon a substantial corpus of videotaped data, Heath (1986: 3) was especially interested in the visual aspects of conduct during the consultation and their relation to the vocal stream. While vocal elements of the consultation could be graphically rendered by normal CA transcription conventions, visual elements proved more difficult to transcribe (an oft-noted difficulty that Heath informs us first attracted comment in 1806). Heath devised a system of notation to represent aspects of actions such as gaze direction, turning away from a participant, turning toward another participant, and raising of the hands. While these symbols could be integrated into standard CA-type transcripts, the system seemed not quite as robust as CA's orthography. Heath often needed to make supplemental notations in the form of his brief written descriptions of the activities occurring.[6]

Conversation analysts have shown the many ways in which talk is responsive to its sequential organization. How turns at talking are taken is one of the fundamental ways in which conversation is organized. CA has identified the organization and workings of adjacency pair structures, structures of repair and closing and the like. Heath proposed that visual actions are also structured on a step-by-step basis that is locally organized and sensitive to the immediate situation:

> ...in exploring the action(s) a movement accomplishes, it is helpful to examine how it is dealt with both during and following its production and to consider "why this now": How does the person's conduct assist with or deal with the circumstances at hand? Certain components of a body movement may implicate action by others whilst forming part of an overall activity accomplished with talk. (1986: 17)

These analytic and methodological considerations equipped Heath to analyze key aspects of the medical consultation: how looking is used to initiate the consultation; how vocal and visual actions are coordinated to maintain involvement in the consultation; the various forms of participation possible in the consultation; the management of the physical examination; and the organization of leave-taking at the end of the consultation.[7]

RESEARCHER-GENERATED AUDIO-VIDEO RECORDINGS OF INDIGENOUS USES OF IMAGES AND VIDEO

Heath's work served as a model for subsequent researchers to develop. Notable in this regard is Lorenza Mondada's (2003) study of the use of video technologies in medical contexts. Mondada's research was particularly striking because of its central focus upon a range of visual practices. She examined a surgical procedure in which endoscopic cameras were introduced into the patient's body (along with other instruments) by a minimally invasive surgical technique (laparoscopy). The endoscope facilitated an internal view that enabled the surgeons to see their work site within the patient's body on a nearby visual monitor in the operating theater. It was a form of surgery by 'remote control.' The surgeon operated by reference to endoscopic images of locations within the patient's body that were displayed on a visual monitor.

As Mondada informs us:

Surgeons operate on patients not by looking at the patient's body but by viewing video monitors where the images produced by an endoscopic camera navigating into the body are displayed. This technique foregrounds the visual skill of the surgeon. It involves work site specific ways of seeing and producing new images of the body, characterized by small-scale details, two-dimensional anatomical space and magnified particularities made available by particular optical devices. (2003: 58)

As if this visual environment were not complex enough, there was another layer of

intricacy to Mondada's data. The surgical operation was simultaneously a site of pedagogic activity. While the surgical team carried out the complex tasks of surgery via laparoscopic technology, their surgical activities were recorded simultaneously on video and relayed in real time for an audience of trainee surgeons who were outside the operating theater. Also simultaneously, the surgery was 'broadcast' via a video conference connection to an external expert on another continent who offered advice online. So there were three categories of participant in the event: the operating team, the trainees, and the external expert. Each category reflected the three kinds of activity that were going on simultaneously—an operation; a demonstration of a surgical technique; and an occasion for expert counseling and learning about that technique. Mondada's analysis showed how the participants orient to their respective participation statuses in this 'telemedical event,' and provided an examination of the workings of professional vision in action.

In the published paper, Mondada presented the reader with three types of images: (1) from inside the patient's body, generated by the endoscopic camera and shown on the operating theater's visual monitor (the endoscopic view); (2) images of the surgical team working on the surface of the patient's abdomen with their hands when inserting and extracting surgical implements (the external view); and finally (3) an image of the surgical team who are making reference to the visual monitor (the researcher's view). Mondada's analysis of the practices of visualization employed on this occasion concentrated on the details of switching between endoscopic to external views; the discussion of the endoscope's optics; and the various, fundamentally collaborative, practices of looking, pointing, and showing in the course of operation. With reference to transcribed data and still images drawn from the video materials, Mondada explicated how 'Surgeons display their attention toward the ways in which their action is being recorded and viewed online by the audience.

They accomplish their action in such a way that it is recipient designed, visible and accountable for both the audience and the expert' (Mondada, 2003: 58).

Mondada's analyses, like many others in the tradition now known as 'workplace studies' (Heath et al., 2000; Heath and Button 2002; Luff et al., 2000), 'consider the ways in which the visual, the vocal, and the material, feature with talk, in the production and coordination of organizational conduct' (Heath et al., 2000: 314). While the technology made it possible to repeatedly scrutinize the details of social practices investigated by this research tradition, it is clear that without ethnomethodology there would not have been either the analytical motivation or the theoretical justification for the initiation of such studies.

CONCLUSION

Our discussion in this chapter has been constructed so as to show the increasingly analytic uses of visual data employed by EM. It introduced Garfinkel's classic formulations of EM and traced their translation into a program for research that accords significance to the visual dimension of social life. While we have resisted offering a presentist history of EM's interest in the visual, we have provided grounds for reading history that shows some evidence of methodological development and cumulation.

We can trace a development in EM from a broad ethnographic observation-based interest in the visual in the 1960s giving way to the analysis of still images in the 1970s and beyond, before leading to current interests in a range of visualization practices routinely employed in workplace activities. It would be easy to introduce an element of technological determinism into our account. Before the advent of portable video in the 1980s, filmmaking equipment could be bulky, intrusive, and require extensive specialist training for its use.[8] EM studies, like the social

sciences more broadly, have benefited from advances in digital technologies that have made the recording and analysis of visual data more straightforward technically, less obtrusive, and less costly than was known by previous generations of film and video users. In our view, these technological developments simply supplied a resource that served to articulate EM's existing analytical and methodological concerns—the technology has not been a driver in any stronger sense.

This is not to deny the very real practical challenges and opportunities for EM analysis afforded by the use of new technologies. Heath and Hindmarsh (2002) have provided a helpful introduction to the mechanics of data collection and analysis for EM studies of situated conduct. A more detailed guidebook to the practical, theoretical and methodological issues of working in this tradition can be found in Heath et al. (2010). Discussions of the many opportunities offered to students by EM ways of approaching visual data are offered in Emmison and Smith (2000) and ten Have (2003). These publications offer accessible introductions that may help to build a bridge to the interests of mainstream practitioners of visual studies.

Issues of representation characteristic of visual studies more broadly also figure in EM studies. Every camera angle implies others not taken. Some of these issues are practical. For example, Hindmarsh and Pilnick's (2007) study of the work of surgical anesthesia described how the camera was positioned so as to capture the surgical procedure in a manner that did not require frequent altering of the position or focus of the camera during filming. The researchers were present during the filming, and their presence was often commented upon (then to be ignored as the procedure commenced). Clearly, different settings will require different decisions of this order. Overall, the primary aim has to be to secure a good record of the actions in question. Other issues of representation have taken a more political character. As Goodwin pointed out, 'any camera position constitutes a theory about what is relevant within a scene, one that will have enormous consequences for what can be seen in it later, and what forms of subsequent analysis are possible' (1994: 607).

In addition, presentational concerns need to be noted. As we know from watching and listening to seminar talks, Mondada's research can be more effectively conveyed in a face-to-face setting using a presentational program (such as PowerPoint®) than by reading the printed page and looking at the images contained in a journal article. For example, Mondada's seminar presentations used split-screen techniques that allowed viewers to see simultaneously what was captured by the surgeons' and researcher's video cameras in real time. Such presentational issues remind us of Margaret Mead's (1975) famous query about the role of images in disciplines of words. They highlight the logocentric character of the traditional academic format of the book and the article. New digital technologies offer opportunities to present academic work in durable form beyond the printed page.

Questions of image ethics also arise. The special ethical difficulties faced by visual researchers center upon data anonymization. Ethnomethodological researchers continue to be committed to recording and analyzing the details of human conduct 'naturalistically': that is, as it naturally occurs in actual social settings. This creates some obvious difficulties. The storing of images of identifiable individuals held electronically for research purposes is subject to legal restrictions, such as the Data Protection Act (1998) in the UK. In addition, in sociology and neighboring disciplines there are codes of professional conduct that demand that researchers respect the anonymity and privacy of research participants. Frequently, in the images and recordings used in EM research, participants may be readily identifiable by their physical appearance, dress, and voice.

One early solution addressing these ethical sensitivities was Heath's (1986: xiv) use of drawings of medical consultations based on stills made from the video, rather than reproducing the stills themselves. Additionally, Heath (1986: 178, note 22) suggested that the drawings on occasion could offer a clearer representation of phenomena of interest than do photographs. Interestingly, line drawing can now be generated automatically (see Heath et al., 2010:126). Another solution is to blur the person's face in the image by use of a pixelation technique (see, for example, its use by Hindmarsh and Pilnick, 2007). The pixilation technique can also be used on video images. While this technique can lend a certain strangeness to the resulting images, it is effective in reducing the general identifiability of a person's face, though of course pixilation is not entirely successful at disguising the individual from those who may be able to pick up on other visual clues to personal identity, such as the location of the research. Whether EM analysis requires such 'blanket anonymization' practices in every case is a question that can only be addressed when wider methodological and substantive issues called for by the research design are taken into account (see Clark, 2006; Wiles et al., Chapter 36 in this volume).

Photography has long been lauded in social scientific circles for its capacity to record the concrete and the particular. EM has long sought to reorient sociology away from generalized or ideal-typical versions of social life toward the study of actual instances in real settings. There is an elective affinity between EM and photography's unique capacity to record the particulars of appearances. The vast impetus given to visual studies and visual sociology by digital technologies is likely to continue. These technologies have functioned as an important methodological resource for EM inquiry, allowing researchers access to analyze the intricacies of human conduct. However, these same digital technologies, insofar as they involve image work and practices of visualization, are increasingly a part of social life and especially occupational life, as the workplace studies tradition attests. Here the analytic focus is directed toward 'working practice, part of which involves those observed, rather than the researchers, using images' (Banks, 2007: 49)[9]—using images to monitor air traffic in a control room, scrutinize public space on a CCTV screen, interpret videotaped evidence in court, read and act upon financial news displays in a trader's office, and the like.

These studies are consistent with contemporary social theory's preoccupations with materiality and embodiment and indicate areas where EM continues to make a distinctive contribution (see Goodwin, 2001). Workplace studies offer a close empirical approach to how people use and interact with objects and technologies in their daily lives. At the same time, the focus on actual instances of embodied skill suggests a fruitful way of developing empirical studies of Mauss's (1973; original 1934) key concept of body techniques. Visually oriented EM studies look set to continue to illuminate the intricacies of situated conduct in a material world.

NOTES

1   Recalling his many discussions with Garfinkel, David Sudnow remembered how 'he pushed me at every point to go for the detailed looks of things' (Sudnow, 1978: viii).

2   Sharrock and Coulter (2003) present a philosophically detailed account of some fundamentals of pattern recognition within visual systems in daily life through their examination of the 'projection problem.'

3   Some of the early transcripts worked on by Sacks and his collaborators were in fact abstracted from video recordings (Mondada, 2008: 2). Similarly, Goodwin's (1981) early attempt to extend conversation analysis to include gaze was based on audio-visual recordings.

4   At the later Federal trial two officers were found guilty.

5   Goodwin (1995) extends his analysis to the biologists, geochemists, and physical oceanographers working on a research ship investigating the composition of water around the mouth of the Amazon. Goodwin examined the multiple professional visions at work on board the ship, while also acknowledging the role of 'seeing in common' (Goodwin, 1995: 262–264).

6   There seems to be a trade-off between the comprehensiveness of a transcription and its ready intelligibility. Schegloff (2000) refers to this as the issue of 'granularity'—How much detail is required in a specific transcript?

7   Later work by Heath and his colleagues has adopted this same approach to the ways in which talk and conduct feature in everyday work contexts. The tradition of 'workplace studies' (Heath et al., 2000; see also Heath and Button, 2002) has examined the situated use of new technologies in settings such as control centers, financial institutions, operating theaters, the construction industry, and the mass media.

8   In anthropology a tradition of ethnographic film developed throughout the course of the second half of the twentieth century (Ball and Smith, 2001). It often involved collaboration between a filmmaker and an anthropologist.

9   Of course images are also used by the researcher. Banks draws our attention to the increasingly characteristic EM concern with practices of visualization.

REFERENCES

Baccus, Melinda (1986) 'Sociological indication and the visibility criterion of real world social theorizing', in H. Garfinkel (ed.), *Ethnomethodological Studies of Work*. London: Routledge and Kegan Paul.

Ball, Michael S. (2005) 'Working with images in daily life and police practice: An assessment of the documentary tradition', *Qualitative Research*, 5(4): 499–521.

Ball, Michael S. and Smith, Gregory W. H. (1986) 'The visual availability of queueing's local organization', *Communication and Cognition*, 19(1): 27–58.

Ball, Michael S. and Smith, Gregory W. H. (1992) *Analyzing Visual Data*. Newbury Park, CA: Sage Publications.

Ball, Michael S. and Smith, Gregory W. H. (2001) 'Technologies of realism? Ethnographic uses of photography and film', in P. A. Atkinson, A. Coffey, S. Delamont, L. H. Lofland and J. Lofland (eds.), *Handbook of Ethnography*. London: Sage Publications. pp. 302–319.

Banks, Marcus (2007) *Using Visual Data in Qualitative Research*. London: Sage Publications.

Barthes, Roland (1977) *Image-Music-Text*. Glasgow: Fontana.

Bittner, Egon (1967) 'The police on skid-row: A study of peace keeping', *American Sociological Review*, 32(5): 699–715.

Cartier-Bresson, Henri (1952) *The Decisive Moment.* New York: Simon and Schuster.

Chalfen, Richard (1987) *Snapshot Versions of Life.* Bowling Green, OH: Bowling Green State University Popular Press.

Cicourel, Aaron V. (1968) *The Social Organization of Juvenile Justice.* New York: Wiley.

Clark, Andrew (2006) *Anonymising Research Data.* ESRC National Centre for Research Methods Working Paper 07/06. [Online]. Available from: http://www.ncrm.ac.uk/research/outputs/publications/Working-Papers/2006/0706_anonymising_research_data.pdf [Accessed 20 September 2010].

Doane, Mary Anne (1991) *Femme Fatales: Feminism, Film Theory, Psychoanalysis.* London: Routledge.

Emmison, Michael and Smith, Philip (2000) *Researching the Visual.* London: Sage Publications.

Francis, David and Hester, Stephen (2004) *An Invitation to Ethnomethodology.* London: Sage Publications.

Garfinkel, Harold (1967) *Studies in Ethnomethodology.* Englewood Cliffs, NJ: Prentice Hall.

Garfinkel, Harold (1988) 'Evidence for locally produced, naturally accountable phenomena of order*, logic, reason, meaning, method, etc. in and as of the essential quiddity of immortal ordinary society (I of IV): An announcement of studies', *Sociological Theory*, 6(1): 103–109.

Garfinkel, Harold (2002) *Ethnomethodology's Program: Working Out Durkheim's Aphorism*, edited and introduced by A. W. Rawls. Lanham, MD: Rowman and Littlefield.

Garfinkel, Harold (2006) *Seeing Sociologically: The Routine Grounds of Social Action*, edited and introduced by A. W. Rawls. Boulder, CO: Paradigm.

Garfinkel, Harold and Livingston, Eric (2003) 'Phenomenal field properties of order in formatted queues and their neglected standing in the current situation of enquiry', *Visual Studies*, 18(1): 21–28.

Garfinkel, Harold, Lynch, Michael and Livingston, Eric (1981) 'The work of a discovering science construed with materials from the optically discovered pulsar', *Philosophy of the Social Sciences*, 11: 131–158.

Goffman, Erving (1963) *Behavior in Public Places: Notes on the Social Organization of Gatherings.* New York: The Free Press.

Goffman, Erving (1979) *Gender Advertisements.* New York: Harper and Row.

Goodwin, Charles (1981) *Conversational Organization: Interaction between Hearers and Speakers.* New York: Academic Press.

Goodwin, Charles (1994) 'Professional vision', *American Anthropologist*, 96(3): 606–633.

Goodwin, Charles (1995) 'Seeing in depth', *Social Studies of Science*, 25: 237–274.

Goodwin, Charles (2001) 'Practices of seeing visual analysis: An ethnomethodological approach', in T. van Leeuwen and C. Jewitt (eds.), *Handbook of Visual Analysis*. London: Sage Publications. pp. 157–182.

Heath, Christian (1986) *Body Movement and Speech in Medical Interaction.* Cambridge, UK: Cambridge University Press.

Heath, Christian and Button, Graeme (2002) 'Editorial introduction: Special issue on workplace studies' *British Journal of Sociology*, 52(2):157–161.

Heath, Christian and Hindmarsh, Jon (2002) 'Analyzing interaction: Video, ethnography and situated conduct', in T. May (ed.), *Qualitative Research in Action.* London: Sage Publications.

Heath, Christian, Knoblauch, Hubert and Luff, Paul (2000) 'Technology and social interaction: The emergence of "workplace studies"', *British Journal of Sociology*, 51(2): 299–320.

Heath, Christian, Hindmarsh, Jon and Luff, Paul (2010) *Video in Qualitative Research: Analysing Social Interaction in Everyday Life.* London: Sage Publications.

Hester, Stephen and Francis, David (2003) 'Analysing visually available mundane order: A walk to the supermarket', *Visual Studies*, 18(1): 36–46.

Hindmarsh Jon and Heath, Christian (1998) 'Video and the analysis of objects in action', *Communication & Cognition*, 31(2/3): 111–130.

Hindmarsh, Jon and Pilnick, Alison (2007) 'Knowing bodies at work: Embodiment and ephemeral teamwork in anesthesia', *Organization Studies*, 28(09): 1395–1416.

Lee, J. R. E. and Watson, D. R. (1992) *Interaction in Urban Public Space.* Final Report, Paris: Plan Urbain, unpublished.

Livingston, Eric (1986) *The Ethnomethodological Foundations of Mathematics.* London: Routledge and Kegan Paul.

Livingston, Eric (1987) *Making Sense of Ethnomethodology.* London: Routledge and Kegan Paul.

Luff, Paul, Hindmarsh, Jon and Heath, Christian (eds.) (2000) *Workplace Studies: Recovering Work Practice and Informing Systems Design.* Cambridge, UK: Cambridge University Press.

Lutz, Catherine A. and Collins, Jane L. (1993) *Reading National Geographic.* Chicago, IL: University of Chicago Press.

Lynch, Michael and Edgerton, Samuel Y. (1988) 'Aesthetics and digital image processing: Representational craft in contemporary astronomy', in G. Fyfe and J. Law (eds.), *Picturing Power: Visual Depiction and Social Relations, Sociological Review*

Monograph No. 35. London: Routledge and Kegan Paul. pp. 184–220.

Lynch, Michael and Sharrock, Wes (2003) 'Editors' Introduction', in M. Lynch and W. Sharrock (eds.), *Harold Garfinkel*. Sage Masters of Modern Social Thought, four volumes. London: Sage Publications. pp. vii–xlvi.

Mauss, Marcel (1973) 'Techniques of the body', *Economy and Society* 2(1): 70–88.

Mead, Margaret (1975) 'Visual anthropology in a discipline of words', in P. Hockings (ed.), *Principles of Visual Anthropology*. The Hague: Mouton.

Mondada, Lorenza (2003) 'Working with video: How surgeons produce video records of their actions', *Visual Studies*, 18(1): 58–72.

Mondada, Lorenza (2008) 'Using video for a sequential and multimodal analysis of social interaction: Videotaping institutional phone calls', *Forum Qualitative Sozialforschung/Forum: Qualitative Social Research*, 9(3), Art. 39. [Online]. Available from http://www.qualitative-research.net/fqs [Accessed 20 September 2010].

Mulvey, Laura (1975) 'Visual pleasure and narrative cinema', *Screen* 16(3): 6–18.

Psathas, George (1979) 'Some organizational features of direction maps', in G. Psathas (ed.), *Everyday Language: Studies in Ethnomethodology*. New York: Irvington. pp. 203–225.

Rawls, Anne (2002) 'Editor's introduction', in H. Garfinkel (ed.), *Ethnomethodology's Program: Working Out Durkheim's Aphorism*, edited and introduced by A. W. Rawls. Lanham, MD: Rowman and Littlefield.

Robinson, Dwight E. (1976) 'Fashions in shaving and trimming of the beard: The men of the *Illustrated London News*, 1842–1972', *American Journal of Sociology,* 81(5): 1133–1141.

Ryave, A. Lincoln and Schenkein, James N. (1974) 'Notes on the art of walking', in R. Turner (ed.), *Ethnomethodology*. Harmondsworth: Penguin. pp. 265–274.

Sacks, Harvey (1972) 'Notes on police assessment of moral character', in D. Sudnow (ed.), *Studies in Social Interaction*. New York: Free Press. pp. 280–293.

Sacks, Harvey, Schegloff, Emanuel A. and Jefferson, Gail (1974) 'A simplest systematics for the organization of turn-taking in conversation', *Language* 50(4): 696–735.

Schegloff, Emanuel A. (1972) 'Notes on a conversational practice: Formulating place', in D. Sudnow (ed.), *Studies in Social Interaction*. New York: Free Press.

Schegloff, Emanuel A. (1987) 'Description in the social sciences I: Talk-in-interaction', *Papers in Pragmatics*, 2: 1–24.

Schegloff, Emanuel A. (2000) 'On granularity', *Annual Review of Sociology*, 26: 715–720.

Sharrock, Wesley W. and Anderson, Digby C. (1979) 'Directional hospital signs as sociological data', *Informational Design Journal*, 1(2): 81–94.

Sharrock, Wesley W. and Coulter, Jeff (2003) 'Dissolving the "projection problem"', *Visual Studies*, 18(1): 73–82.

Signorelli, Vito (1984) 'Capitulating to the captions: The verbal transformation of visual images', *Human Studies*, 10: 281–310.

Slack, Roger, Hartswood, Mark, Procter, Rob and Rouncefield, Mark (2007) 'Cultures of reading: On professional vision and the lived work of mammography', in S. Hester and D. Francis (eds.), *Orders of Ordinary Action: Respecifying Sociological Knowledge*. Aldershot: Ashgate. pp. 175–193.

Sudnow, David (1972) 'Temporal parameters of interpersonal observation', in D. Sudnow (ed.), *Studies in Social Interaction*. New York: Free Press.

Sudnow, David (1978) *Ways of the Hand*. London: Routledge and Kegan Paul.

Sudnow, David (2001) *Ways of the Hand: A Rewritten Account*. Cambridge, MA: MIT Press.

ten Have, Paul (1999) *Doing Conversation Analysis*. London: Sage Publications.

ten Have, Paul (2003) 'Teaching students observational methods: Visual studies and visual analysis', *Visual Studies*, 18(1): 29–35.

Watson, Rodney (2005) 'The visibility arrangements of public space: Conceptual resources and methodological issues in analyzing pedestrian movements', *Communication and Cognition*, 38(3/4): 201–228.

West, Candace (1984) *Routine Complications: Troubles with Talk between Doctors and Patients*. Bloomington, IN: Indiana University Press.

Williamson, Judith (1978) *Decoding Advertisements*. London: Marion Boyars.

22

Videography: An Interpretative Approach to Video-Recorded Micro-Social Interaction

Hubert Knoblauch and René Tuma

INTRODUCTION

Video technology offers expanded possibilities for looking at interaction and communication in various 'natural' settings: for example, workplaces and situations of informal communication or educational interaction. In the last decades international groups of scholars have developed a prominent approach to sequentially analyze visual data from social interaction. In addition to standardized ways of looking at video-recorded interaction, this approach is interpretive. After a short overview of earlier research, we will briefly discuss the relevance of interpretation to video analysis. Before we describe how to sequentially analyze video-recorded social interaction, we sketch the role of data collection, coding, and sampling. Because these processes are part of a focused ethnography, we use the shorthand 'videography' rather than video interaction analysis. 'Sequentiality' is a central category in fine-grained analyzes of video-recorded interaction that supports empirically based interpretations of actions. This will be illustrated through three empirical examples, which also highlight the interrelatedness between textural and visual elements. Finally, we will discuss the relation between sequential analysis of video-recorded interaction and the wider ethnographic and social context, which is essential to videography.

BACKGROUND

During the past decades, video, that is, audio-visual records on analogue as well as on digital technical media, not only has replaced film as a medium for private and most scientific recording but also has triggered forms of usage unknown to users of older film media. The technical feasibility of slow motion at any point, of zooming and inserting pictures as well as the digital examination of picture frames have changed the ways of studying visual interaction. This has led to an explosive diffusion of privately produced videos using the Internet as a favorite medium of distribution. It has also opened new ways for the social sciences to produce and present data. Before the advent of the video, social scientists had been using films in quite innovative ways. In fact, the analysis of conduct was one of the first uses.[1] Throughout the twentieth century, researchers have developed ingenious ways to use film for the analysis of social conduct. Whereas these uses were restricted to an avant-garde of a few researchers, often in experimental settings, the dissemination of video as a technology has now allowed many more social scientists to use it, because it is not only relatively cheap, reliable, and available but—due to its widespread private use—video has become less and less obtrusive.

To the degree that video is establishing itself in the social sciences as a technical medium for producing data, the question of how to analyze video has become an urgent topic of social scientific methodology. This chapter addresses the question of how to use video as data in the social sciences. We will examine what one may call the dominant approach in the interpretive analysis of video data. When discussing interpretive video analysis, we adopt a basic phenomenological and methodological assumption of any interpretive social science: actions cannot merely be observed; rather, actions are guided by meanings. Therefore, observers must try to account for meaning not only as a general principle but also in each empirical instance (Schütz, 1971; Weber, [1921] 1984). On this background (to be elaborated later), we can distinguish interpretive video analysis from standardized video analysis. Standardized video analysis derives its categories from interpreting the audiovisually recorded on the basis of theoretical assumptions. The empirical instances are then subsumed to these categories by coding, so that, for example, certain stretches of conduct are coded as 'supportive' or 'non-supportive,' 'aggressive' or 'non-aggressive behavior' (Mittenecker,

1987). Note that the reasons for subsuming instances to codes, while theoretically based, are not explicated, so that the process of interpretation remains implicit. Indeed the code may be habitualized (tested by way of 'intercoder reliability') or even automated. In fields such as computer supported work or human–computer interaction, there are more than 40 software programs for such standardized analysis available, most of them based on predefined categories (Koch and Zumbach, 2002). Standardized methods are not restricted to experimental and quantitative studies of audio-visual conduct, but are also to be found in the so-called 'qualitative method' field. Thus, Dinkelaker and Herrle (2009) suggest subdividing video recorded interactions according to predefined 'segments' and 'configurations.'[2]

As useful as standardized procedures may be for certain purposes, they differ from interpretive video analyses. For example, Heath and Luff (2007) have demonstrated that even the most standardized forms of action and interaction, such as auctions in England with their rigid pattern of bidding, exhibit interpretive elements defining the very courses of these actions. Thus, interpretation is an essential part of any video analysis that assumes conduct to carry meaning and subjects to exhibit some form of agency or subjectivity.

SUBJECTIVITY, ETHNOGRAPHY, AND THE FOCUS

Starting from the assumption that actions can only be explained if we understand their meanings, Schutz (1962) suggests distinguishing between the meanings actors themselves link with their actions, 'constructs of the first order,' and the ways that outside observers conceive of these meanings, that is 'constructs of the second order.' With his notion of double hermeneutics, Giddens (1984: 284) added the idea that the scientific constructs themselves are not separated from the first-order constructs, but interact with them. This interaction, however, must not be considered merely as a problem, but constitutes a resource for understanding the subject matter under investigation. Social scientific analysis, thus, rests on the assumption that the analysts themselves participate in the knowledge of a certain culture under investigation, knowledge that can be explicated in the hermeneutic circle (Soeffner, 1997). In interpreting the 'object,' we are also simultaneously explicating the observer's knowledge. In this sense, the observer's and interpreter's subjectivity (based on their own competence as actors) is always involved in the process of understanding the meanings of other subject's actions.

In addition to the observer's general competence in understanding actions of others, video analysis presupposes another kind of knowledge, generally termed 'ethnographic.' Since the structure of knowledge in modern society is highly specialized and fragmented into many different settings, situations, and institutions,[3] social scientists are often not familiar with many aspects of the social situations to be observed and recorded on videotape. The various methods of acquiring the situative knowledge relevant to the actors for them to be competent actors, and for the observers in order to know what is going on, is frequently referred to as ethnographic. Ethnographic methods typically include observation, some form of participation in the field, interviewing, eliciting and collecting field documents. These methods allow researchers to gather subjective knowledge of the field under investigation. Typically, it is only by doing ethnography prior to video analysis[4] that we can understand other actors in the field. As Heath and Hindmarsh stress, for the analysis of video recordings of naturally occurring activities, 'it is critical that the researcher undertakes more conventional fieldwork' (2002: 107). For routine research practices, this implies that it is extremely useful if the researchers doing the video analysis are the same as those who do the ethnography.

One should note that definitions of ethnography differ significantly across disciplines. The type of ethnography to which we refer, focused ethnography, does not aim at encompassing large, locally distributed social structures, such as tribes, villages or cities. As opposed to such encompassing 'conventional' ethnographies (as we will call them for the sake of brevity), these ethnographies may be said to be focused in several ways.[5]

Conventional and focused ethnographies differ, first, with respect to their demands on time. The former are time extensive since they require a long, continuous period of data collection, as a rule for most students about a year. As opposed to this kind of experience-based ethnography, focused ethnographies are short term and data intensive. Even if they linger on for months and years, field contacts and recordings are rather discontinuous and selective, and fields are visited at various intervals. The standard argument against this short-ranged character is that this kind of ethnography may favor 'superficial' or 'quick and dirty' research (Hughes et al., 1994). However, this critique ignores the fact that the shorter time periods of the field contacts are compensated for by immense data intensity. As opposed to classical ethnography, which frequently reduces rich personal experiences into a restricted number of field notes and documents, focused ethnography is data intensive, collecting huge amounts of data on short stretches of actions by means of mechanical data collection devices, including audio, video, and photographic recordings.

We consider videography to be a specific form of focused ethnography since the use of video has important consequences for the focusing process. First, the video as a technology entails a focus on its own. By virtue of, for example, its optical focus, the selection of a frame and the transformation into two dimensionality, data collection by video is not only 'recording' but also a sociotechnical construction of data. Although important to keep these constructive aspects of technology in mind, they have been broadly discussed elsewhere by Heath et al. (2010), who also provide an introduction to data collection; our aim here is to address the essential role of ethnography for video analysis. For it is only by means of ethnography that situations and actions relevant to the setting or to the basic research question are identified. Preliminary ethnography allows researchers to identify the focus of observations, and it serves to collect information and data on this focus and its context. To be more specific, ethnography helps to determine exactly where, when, and who is to be recorded on video.[6]

In addition to the focus on a particular situation, the use of video exhibits a particular bias. As Erickson noted, video recordings 'focus on the particular': that is, the 'particulars of situated interaction as it occurs naturally in everyday social situations' (1988: 1083). The focus on action and interaction is linked to the specific advantages of video as a technical medium. For video is mimetic; it mimics ongoing actions to such a degree that any actor easily identifies his or her action in the medium. Moreover, video is a temporal medium. As opposed to photography, it allows the researcher to record and identify processes taking place in time. Since what are to be recorded are processes in time, there is a strong tendency to record interactions and audio-visual conduct.[7]

Video is a technology for recording as well as for the permanent re-use of audiovisual data for the sake of validation and comparison. This re-use is facilitated by a range of technical options: playing, repeating, slow motion, and zooming are among the most important techniques from which researchers profit with video analysis. These techniques allow actions to be observed in a detail not even accessible to the actors themselves. For this reason, video has also been rightly compared with a 'microscope.'

The comparison with the microscope raises a third most important question which is directly related to the technical focus of the video camera: What is being focused on by the technology? Why and how is this being done?

The questions of focus are, of course, dependent on the research questions asked by the particular study, informed by theory, the area of research and the discipline. Thus, linguistics may once have emphasized the audio channel in interaction. In recent years, however, linguistics has closely examined aspects of what are termed 'modalities': next to lexical choices, codes, and prosody, gestures, mimic behavior, or body posture are now subject to the analysis of 'multimodality,' strongly influenced either by structural linguistics or by more recent pragmatic cross-fertilizations between linguistics and neighboring disciplines (Kendon, 2004; Mondada, 2006).

In the social sciences, social actions and interactions have long been a major interest. The paradigmatic case for social scientific video analysis is what Goffman (1961) called 'focused interaction,' which is the form of interaction in which the participants share a common focus of attention. In the simplest case, the interaction's focus is constituted by two actors, but focused interactions may also extend to large social occasions, such as meetings, staged events, and demonstrations. The interactive focus in such situations can also be established by material items and spatial structures (such as microphones or stages), and other technological mediations of social interaction: for instance, interactivity with computer and other technologies (Rammert and Schulz-Schaeffer, 2002), computer-mediated communication in underground control rooms (Heath and Luff, 1996, 2000), or the social actions performed by medical professionals in an operating room (Schubert, 2006).

It goes without saying that the focus of the camera follows the focus of the study[8]; on more or less static social occasions the camera itself may be static. For example, in recording PowerPoint presentations on video in various settings (to which we will refer below), the authors used fixed cameras since audiences were fixed, as were the presenters. The fact that audience and speakers were facing one another required two cameras: one directed to the audience and the other to the speaker. If the activity is itself moving, the camera is supposed to follow the movements: for instance, during work in the operating room, when the hands of the operator are the core activity in the setting and are moving into the patient (Schubert, 2006). Under some circumstances it may therefore be useful for the camera to pan, tilt, or zoom to follow the gaze of the participating observer (Mohn, 2007).

DATA COLLECTION AND CODING

The specific demands for how to produce the video recordings are revealed through the ethnographic work preceding it. This ethnographic work is not restricted to the interactions as the primary subject of the video analysis; it also takes into account the situational and institutional context and the subjective knowledge of the actors (and of the researchers studying it). What will then be recorded depends first on what activities can be observed and, importantly, are accessible in the field. On the other hand, the production of audio-visual data depends on the distinct research question derived, the research context, and one's discipline, all of which affect which actions and sequences will be considered relevant to the study. Thus, both the scientific context, as well as the field (as a frame of the research), provide the frame of the research question.

Let us summarize the steps of the research process in more detail. After the first explorative visits in the field, researchers determine which situations to focus on. One of the principal goals of this phase of preliminary scouting is also to identify common features of social situations (such as work interactions, encounters, events) to start the collection of video data. As part of a videography, data collection should not be restricted to one situation or even one type of situation. Thus, when video recording PowerPoint presentations (for example, Knoblauch, 2008), one

may want to compare them with, for example, blackboard or flip chart presentations. This ethnographic search for situations and fields can be called ethnographic sampling.

After the first hours of video data have been collected, the internal video data sampling starts: that is, the selection of relevant sequences in the data corpus. The basic activity here consists of coding. By coding, we do not mean the application of certain fixed, theoretically deduced categories of analysis to the video data, as practiced with standardized video analysis. Rather, initial codes are developed from the 'bottom up' (as suggested by grounded theory).[9] The first codes are informed by both ethnographic and everyday knowledge about the field, before they are verified by fine-grained sequential analysis. These codes are entered into a content log or an index describing the temporal unfolding of the interaction by reference to the video time code, so that the video fragments referred to can be found easily.[10] Let us repeat that the various steps in the analysis are neither linear nor separated, but rather intertwined and iterative, as depicted in Figure 22.1.

This iterative character of the research process also holds for the codes and the logbook, which are continuously changed and corrected in the light of sequential analyses and ethnographic fieldwork. Nevertheless, it is helpful to start internal sampling with preliminary codes. As soon as initial ethnographic understanding of the situation has been achieved and some types of interactions have been established by fine-grained sequential analysis, codes start to be corroborated, and researchers should select relevant situations for further scrutiny: that is, for further internal or ethnographic sampling. Depending on the type of situation under study, the activities and events to be coded vary in type and data extension. For example, when studying auctions, it is easy to find meaningful units: for example, bidding for a specific item will typically be marked by openings and closings.[11] To assign codes to certain sequences in the data, it is necessary to

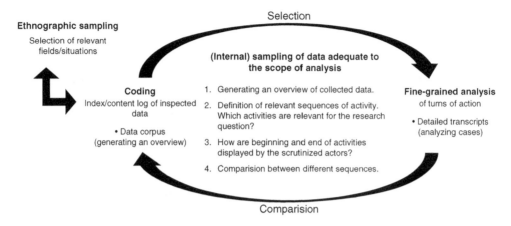

Figure 22.1   Process of analysis: © Knoblauch and Tuma (2010).

analyze sequentially: for example, to determine where and how actors mark beginnings and ends. For this purpose one has to carefully re-examine the data, scrutinizing the order of sequence (this step will be elaborated below), and comparing different situations in which these sequences occur.

When analyzing single sequences in the data, one should pay particular attention to the variation of any found pattern in the observed data corpus. This is typically accomplished by comparison. Comparison helps to identify similar and dissimilar cases according to features that are identified by coding and sequential analysis. Comparisons are associative, looking for similarities, or differentiating, looking for minimal and maximal contrasts. Both ways, the analysis will attempt to determine patterns in the sequences, varying either in terms of their internal structures, in their situative occurrence, or with respect to aspects of the setting in terms of ethnography.

INTERPRETATION AND ANALYSIS

As mentioned at the beginning, the fine-grained sequential analysis starts with interpretation. The necessity of interpretation indicates that video analysis is basically a hermeneutic activity: interpreting not only means describing and explaining non-verbal and/or verbal behavior but also determining the knowledge that one needs to understand what is going on in a situation and identifying the visible conduct that constitutes the situation (Heath, 1997). Understanding is already involved in the basic production of data: words and sentences must be understood for transcriptions to be produced, and the description of visual processes requires seeing the directions of gazes in the recordings and knowing what people are referring to, so that all essential parts (sentence, word, movement) of a sequence make sense for observers. It is on this basic level of the everyday understanding of first-order constructs that ethnographic knowledge is indispensable. At the same time, professional, second-order constructs—that is, theoretical, disciplinary—come into play.

Interpretation in everyday terms is the essential basis for analysis. It is involved when approaching the data, which is the tapes and transcripts; it is required for the everyday understanding of what is seen and heard, and it is needed for sequential analysis. Nevertheless, we can distinguish it from analysis. Although both processes are intertwined in practice, the latter is characterized by following certain analytical assumptions.[12] The first assumption lies in the meaningfulness of communication, reflected in the necessity to interpret (and understand). Since meaning cannot be directly observed, the second assumption is the objectivity of what is to be understood; this objectivity is reflected in the video technology, which can by definition only record objectivated aspects of verbal and physical behavior. Methodologically, objectivity means that only those interpretations are accepted which refer to what is expressed in audio-visual conduct. Interpretations should not be based on general theoretical assumptions, or invisible factors of actors (like 'motives,' 'subconscious desires,' or 'attitudes'), but only on what can be observed (on the basis of understanding).

The third assumption lies in the reflexivity of communicative actions. By reflexivity, we do not mean that actions are reflected consciously, as Giddens (1984) seems to suggest. To the contrary, most video analyses address practices: that is, the habitualized knowledge implicit in social action. The notion of reflexivity also refers to this kind of habitualized knowledge, including the ways in which actors 'indicate,' 'frame,' or 'contextualize' their actions.[13] When asking a question, for example, not only do we ask the question concerning some content but also we demonstrate that we are asking a question: that is, we are performing an action. It is because of this reflexivity that co-actors can understand what is meant by an action. The assumption of reflexivity is reflected in the order exhibited by the objectified actions, which allows the action to be understood. In this sense, a joke or a PowerPoint presentation is not considered as something taken for granted, but as something exhibiting an order that allows participants to identify it as a joke or a Powerpoint presentation. In order to identify this order, the focus of observations lies in how the actions are being performed. By investigating the methodological resources used by participants themselves in the production of social actions and activities (Heath, 1997: 184), reflexivity is, therefore, a crucial resource for interpretation.

Sequentiality is the fourth assumption exploited in video analysis. Sequentiality is due to the basic temporality of action and interaction—a feature that is maintained if not intensified by the technological medium of video. Like film, video is defined by the temporal sequence of frames (pictures). As a result of their temporality, pictures are watched in sequence, and sequentiality is therefore characteristic for video analysis. It is the feature of sequentiality which causes the particular focus of many video analyses—actions, reactions, and interactions—since this medium preserves the time structure of these processes in a way unprecedented by earlier media (except film).

Video analysis is related to other forms of analysis based on sequentiality, including conversation analysis and hermeneutics (Soeffner, 1997; Raab and Tänzler, 2006).[14] These forms share in common their consideration of sequentiality as the very structure by which social action and, thus, social order, are accomplished. For this reason, sequential analysis starts with sequences of actions or interactions as the primary subject matter. However, as opposed to structural or objective hermeneutics, the 'unit' of sequences is not defined in advance or by the technical medium as, for example, one 'frame' of the 24 frames shown on film) or one word (which in spoken language may not be the most relevant unit). Based on the notion of reflexivity, the very task of the video sequence analysis is, rather, to identify on the basis of the data what actors consider as a 'unit': that is, anything rendered distinct by the actors, which is preceded by something else and followed by something different.

SEQUENTIAL ANALYSIS

The activities focused by sequential analysis with video are identified as sequences of social action, interaction, and communication. Therefore, sequential analysis forms the core of videography, the fine-grained video analysis. In order to get a sense of this kind of analysis, we will illustrate the procedure with some data. The notion of sequentiality may be best understood with respect to a classical empirical example from conversation analysis in which Schegloff (1968) analyzed openings of telephone calls to a 'disaster center.' After his first analysis of the acoustic data, Schegloff had assumed that there must be a 'distribution rule of first utterances,' that is, the answerer speaks first. Then, however, he confronted what is called a 'deviant case' to this rule as follows:

#9 (Police makes call)
Receiver is lifted, and there is a one second pause

Police: Hello.
Other: American Red Cross
Police: Hello, this is Police Headquarters... er, Officer Stratton

(Schegloff, 1968: 1079)

As Schegloff found, the rule does not hold because of the one-second pause.

The fact that the caller is talking is not really a violation of the rule; rather, the pause left by the person called is taken as a kind of answer to which the 'Hello' in the second turn replies. (Moreover, this 'Hello' is not only a greeting but also takes into account the lack of response.) The general insight is that actions are rendered meaningful in the context of other actions, and that this context is constituted by the sequence of this action.

The most interesting aspect for us in Schegloff's example is that the 'turn' is not actually constituted by a 'speech act.' In fact, it is not even direct human action but rather a technologically mediated action—the ringing of the phone. Thus, the 'unit' to be considered can be a non-linguistic event if it triggers another action.

That telephone rings fulfill this function is not surprising, since acoustically coordinated action depends on the temporal ordering of sound. But how, we have to ask, can audio-visual conduct be analyzed sequentially? In order to answer this question, we discuss an audio-visual example from our own research.[15] The following still is taken from an auction at a point where an auctioneer is offering a new item to the audience. The offer is interesting because the auctioneer does not reveal what it contains, but describes it as a 'surprise.' He starts by identifying its number in the catalogue, as indicated in Table 22.1.

The auctioneer (S.) starts (1–2 in Table 22.1) with a number that, for the moment, seems to be opaque, and also his description of a 'surprise' object (3 in Table 22.1) remains opaque if we look only at the text. If we turn our attention to his visual conduct, we can tell that he is looking at the desk during (2 in Table 22.1)—which can easily be understood as 'reading.' Since, as ethnographic knowledge of the situation tells us, there is one common document available in the auction—the catalogue which includes all objects on sale—actors and observers may infer that his glance is for the catalogue. In fact, we can identify a number of actors in the audience looking at a copy of the document

Table 22.1 Audio-visual example, using Gesprächsanalytisches Transkriptionssystem (GAT) transcription conventions

Sequence	Original German	Translation in English
1	S:D:ie w:o<u>sechs</u>ndsiebzich*	S: number tw:o<u>seventy</u>six*
2	(0.6s)	(0.6s)
3	<u>EIN</u> Überraschungsposten	<u>a</u> surprise item
4	(.)	(.)
5	Reisetasche <u>mit</u> Inhalt;	a travel bag <u>with</u> ((unknown)) content
6	(0.9s)	(0.9s)
7	Fünf <u>sind</u> geboten; zehn sin´	Five <u>are</u> offered; ten are
8	geboten <u>Fünf</u>zehn sin´ geboten	offered <u>fif</u>teen are offered

Source: Selting et al. (1998) and Degenhardt (2010).

lying on their knees (see Figure 22.2). In this case, the visual conduct is not only accompanying turn-taking (1 in Table 22.1); it helps to specify what the speaker is referring to while speaking—a specification that is made visible by his glance and the pause (2 in Table 22.1). The verbal interaction consists of a dual unit separated by a short pause (3–5 in Table 22.1). The first part is pronounced upward—announcing the 'surprise,' whereas the second part prosodically turns down so as to finish the turn and open the floor for the next turn. In conversation analysis, this would be called a transition relevance place (Sacks et al., 1974). Again, our analysis does not need to depend on prosodic knowledge of how the speaker inflects his voice, for the interpretation is supported sequentially: the speaker (while pronouncing 'a surprise item') raises his head and looks at the audience. What appears as a pause in the verbal transcript is

full of action, if we look at the video. The audience camera shows that immediately after the transition point a number of audience members raise their hands. As with the telephone ring, the raising of the auctioneer's head can be understood as him opening the floor for the audience. The 'reaction' (raising of hands) of the audience, on the other hand, can be considered as a reflexive interpretation of the action by the speaker. This interpretation, again, is ratified in the next turn, for the speaker hints with his arm (as shown in Figure 22.2) toward certain actors in the audience who are raising their hands (not visible in still, highlighted with text). In the next turn, he 'interprets' their action by identifying it with a number—'Five are offered'— in response to an understanding that raising the hand is an offer. We do not want to indulge into more intricate questions, such as to how prices are fixed and negotiated in

Figure 22.2   Split screen (auctioneer/audience) taken from auction sequence corresponding to Line 7 in the transcript reported in Table 22.1. Sourced from a video by Degenhardt (2010).

such settings.[16] Rather, we point out that the turn following the speaker's initiation is a purely visual 'unit' of action (looking up, raising the hand), and that this visual 'unit' is produced as such by the next turn of the speaker identifying it as a bid verbally and hinting in a certain direction. The visuality of these turns is emphasized if we acknowledge that none of these sequences could have been discovered from an audio recording or transcript alone. Careful study of the video not only allows the researcher to become familiar with the transcript and the spoken words but also is the concrete basis for visual observations of the structure of the sequences. Moreover, the production of the visual transcript makes understanding the speech acts easier. Familiarity with the words spoken makes it easier to identify the sequence of events and 'locate' the visual events with respect to the text.

The video sequence must be watched repeatedly to discover the order of acoustic and visual events and to identify when things are done or said.

One may argue that this could be accomplished without the transcript, but experience proves that the written transcript is very helpful as a location device when identifying the sequences. (If there are no verbal utterances, other temporal actions, such as gazing, may be transcribed into more detail.) The study of sequences thus moves from the transcribed (written) to include the visual. Hence, the visual is not treated only as an addendum to the spoken. Rather, in watching the video recordings, one frequently discovers additional sequences which allow the researcher to make sense of prior turns or sequences.

The previous example demonstrates the sequential function of 'visual conduct' since the audience only 'reacts' in a visual way (which is relevant to both the observer as well as to the speaker). One may take the 'raising' of the hand as a pure sign out of a more or less systematic sign system that is extra-situational.[17] But then again, raising the hand is neither purely a reaction nor a 'sign,' but is rather synchronized with the speaker's

action to make sense: the hands are only raised when the speaker turns to the audience. The audience 'reads' the speaker's body, particularly his face direction, as an indication of his focus of attention. Moreover, the indication by the speaker functions both as recognition and as a legally binding identification of the person bidding; it also opens the floor to other bidders and suggests where they are sitting. One could say that the speaker's body works as a 'mirror' to the audience, since he not only talks and turns to the audience but also indicates to the members of the audience if there are other persons acting and where they are.

Visual conduct cannot be considered as one 'mode' alongside others; the meaning of an act is constituted by visual conduct in addition to verbal utterances. In the next example, we compare actions in which the visual is considered to be meaningful on its own. It is not by accident that we turn at this point to the example of PowerPoint presentations. Although there is debate concerning how much 'information' the slides of PowerPoint presentations should contain, there is no doubt that text and diagrams of the slides projected to a live audience carry meaning on the grounds of their visual features. PowerPoint presentations with speakers showing slides to an audience are, therefore, a useful example for analyzing how the visual enters social interaction. In the following fragment, which forms part of a more extended study of PowerPoint presentations,[18] the speaker confronts an audience with an elaborate diagrammatic structure on his slides. While he shows the slides, he speaks the words presented in Table 22.2 (to about 50 persons in a high-profile scientific event):

The speaker starts by turning to the screen and by leaving a pause (1 in Table 22.2)—as he did quite frequently before in his speech. The new slide he refers to in this fragment opens a new topic, which is identified by the pseudonym 'lakedemons' (our pseudonym used here for a biochemical structure analyzed by his research group). As the video

Table 22.2   Visual example. Underlines indicate the time of pointing to the slides. The Gesprächsanalytisches Transkriptionssystem (GAT) transcription conventions are used

Sequence	Original German	Translation in English
1	(1.0) die Auswanderung von Lakedämonen aus dem Gefäß in das Gewebe	*(1.0) The migration of lakedemons out of the vessels into the texture*
2	ist=relativ=gut=untersucht, man weiß die Flakomeuten brauchen=zuerst n	*has=been=studied=quite well, one knows that the flamokeuts first=need 'n*
3	initialen Kontakt, (hat ä / geringe affine) Anlagerung;	*initial contact, (has a reduced affine) adaption;*
4	des Rollen verstärkt dann den Kreisbewegung Kontakt=diese=feste=Anlagerung	*rolling motions then support the circular movements contact=this=fixed*
5	wandert dann raus; und wird sehr viel über die Moleküle in	*then migrates; and then via the molecules it will*
6	Interaktion von Lakedämonen mit Europolzellen steuern	*control the interaction of lakedemons the flacocyte cells*

Source: Selting et al. (1998) and Knoblauch (2008).

demonstrates, he does not simply show the slide; he also relates to the slides by pointing to them with a laser pointer. Also, his introduction of the new topic is accompanied by discursive gestures illustrating the direction of movements of the 'lakedemons' ('aus' or 'out,' 'in' or 'in,' line 1 in Table 22.2) by two hand gestures turning outward and turning inward. In addition, he uses the laser pointer as a way to direct attention to features on the slide. This use of the laser pointer not only complements the structure of the talk (the time of pointing is shown by underlines in the transcript in Table 22.2); by moving the laser pointer in various ways, he also transforms the meaning of the diagram. Let us have a look at the ways in which he moves the laser pointer[19] (see Figure 22.3).

As the reconstruction of the laser pointer's movements demonstrate, the speaker does not merely point at the 'lakedemons'; the movements are represented by little circles on the slide. Rather, he moves the pointer in different ways on the surface of the slides. In relating these movements to what he is speaking about, it becomes quite clear that these pointing movements and their differences are quite meaningful: the 'initial contact' (line 3 in Table 22.2) of the biochemical structures mentioned with the 'Europol-cells'

(pseudonym) are underlined by a wave-like movement, their 'rolling' by a circular movement (line 4), their 'migration' by sudden straight movements (line 5) and their interaction by loop-shaped movements (line 5f). The movements of the laser pointer seem to mimic the movements of the microscopic objects talked about. In doing so, the moving laser pointer 'illustrates' what is being said or shown. The difference between these movements corresponds to different parts of the talk ('first,' 'then,' 'will then').

This has serious consequences. Keeping in mind that we are talking about one slide which stays the same during these sequences, the laser pointer movements contribute to transforming the static slide into a dynamic movement. What appears as a fixed structure on the slide's diagram is thus turned into a temporal sequence of processes characterized by the movements. Of course, this meaning is accomplished by the interplay of spoken words, graphics and gestures.[20] It results from the speaker's sequentially fine-grained coordination, timing, ways of pointing at the slide diagram, and utterances. Nonetheless, the sequence of different movements of the laser pointer takes the form of different units and thus contributes to the construction of a particular sequence for what is being talked about.

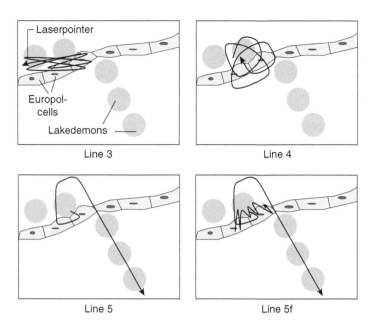

Figure 22.3 Reconstruction of the movement of the laser pointer: © Knoblauch (2008).

As this example shows, sequentiality does not only constitute a resource for the interpretation of interaction. It may also be regarded as a criterion to validate an interpretation. Or, following Schegloff (1992), what is of relevance for the analyst must be shown to be of relevance to the actors. Methodologically, it is the sequential embedding in prior and later turns that can be considered as a decisive indication of the relevance for certain visual aspects of an interactive turn.[21] For the validation of interpretations, it is therefore critically relevant to answer detailed questions like: Do actors look at the screen before they push a button? Does a phone ring before person A walks away? Does person B point at the slide after she said X or when she says Y? Video analysis thus makes it possible to examine the sequential organization of social and human technological interactions (Heath, 1997: 184). Or, as Goodwin suggests:

Rather than wandering onto field sites as disinterested observers, attempting the impossible task of trying to catalog everything in the setting, we can use the visible orientation of the participants as a spotlight to show us just those features of context that we have to come to terms with if we are to adequately describe the organization of their action. (2000: 1508f)

THE VISUAL, THE SITUATION, AND ETHNOGRAPHY

Sequentiality provides an essential resource for the interpretation of interaction, but it is not the only resource. Within a situation and during the time span recorded, there may just be nothing happening. Even during a series of actions happening sequentially one after another (or diachronically), there are always visual elements, such as desks, doors, or projectors, which do not change at all. This may also hold for parts of the decorum of actors (such as clothing, glasses, or hairstyle). These synchronic elements appear permanent on the visual representation, but it would be an error to consider them as mere 'background.'

On the contrary, as the examples in this chapter have shown, single slide representations or the location of persons in an audience may become relevant in certain situations. Goffman has suggested a helpful distinction that allows us to grasp these two aspects. Following his suggestion we can use the term situated for anything that occurs within the situation and 'could not occur outside the situation' (Goffman, 1961: 22): that is, the situative character of social action (Suchman, 1987).[22] Situational, on the other hand, are those elements of the situation that can also be present in other situations. In this sense, what is coordinated sequentially in the situation may be considered as essentially situated, whereas those aspects that can occur in other situations are situational. The distinction between situative and situational allows us to turn to the question how video may help address the synchronic aspects of the visual and situational elements.

One way to approach these synchronic aspects of the situational in video analysis has been suggested by Goodwin (2000). He assumed that semiotics might help comprehend these visual features. Thus, talk is embedded in multiple sign systems (such as graphic codes, gestures, and other features of the environment). To Goodwin, actors orient to what he called 'semiotic fields,' including different kinds of signs and their expressions in different kinds of media. In accordance with the principle of relevance mentioned above, these semiotic fields may be of local relevance in that the actors demonstrably orient toward them in the situation of action. Goodwin (2000) calls this 'contextual configuration.'

There is no doubt that the concept of 'semiotic field' is very useful in those cases where actors use well-developed sign systems (such as the alphabet, professional knowledge systems, or even the sign elements of children playing hopscotch). We doubt, however, that semiotics remedies the problem of visuality in general, since structural semiotics presupposes that the signs visible are organized in a more or less

systematic way.[23] Even if one admits that words form part of a system, one may doubt that gestures can be considered as forming a sign system, let alone other visual elements (such as expressions, clothing, furniture, the order of things in space, etc.[24]). On top of this, the meanings of visual elements are often not fixed in such a way as to be shared by any individual. Even the specialized knowledge of professionals is mostly fixed in a de-contextualized way and needs re-contextualization by 'situated action' (Suchman, 1987).

In order to grasp specialized and situated visual knowledge, ethnography again provides a useful set of methods. In order to clarify the meaning and signification of visual elements of the recorded data, one may, for example, use elicitation procedures. Showing the videos to the persons who have been acting in the setting and interviewing them simultaneously can retrieve their intentions, their understandings and their knowledge.[25] Also 'autoconfrontation,' 'autoethnography,' (of the participant observer) or 'video-based interviewing' can be useful methods to uncover various situational aspects of objects and events (Bayart et al., 1997).[26] For example, Schubert (2009) exposed medical personnel he had been video recording to recordings of their work in operating rooms, asking them to clarify actions they were involved in. These methods help researchers to reconstruct actors' perceptions and orientations in the situations at hand. Since actors may also be able to explicate the functioning and significance of other items visible in the scene, the methods also contribute to the interpretation of the actions observed.

The importance of background knowledge elucidating visual aspects of the recordings recapitulates the importance of ethnography for video analysis referred to in the introduction. For it is by way of observation, interviews, expert interviews, etc., that researchers become familiar with the settings which are recorded by video. One must acquire local knowledge in order to understand the audio-visual sequences: that is, the series of actions, reactions, and interactions, (which, in many cases, involves intricate technologies). In this way, videography still incorporates the actor's perspective, yet in a specific material sense: we examine visible situations, activities, and actions. This does not mean that one needs to reconstruct the whole stock of knowledge necessary to comprehend the whole field. Rather, the task of the researcher is to acquire those elements of (partly embodied) knowledge relevant to the activity on which the study is focusing. In studying technological activities, for example, only those elements of knowledge need be considered which are relevant to understanding practices involved in handling the technology under scrutiny.

As an essential part of videography, ethnography not only serves to clarify the details of interaction; by uncovering relevant knowledge, ethnography also opens the way to relate these interactions to wider social contexts and more conventional sociological concerns. Indeed, contexts such as social welfare agencies, underground stations, or management offices have always been the subject of ethnography. Videography—the interpretive video analysis of social interaction—contributes to these concerns not only because it provides empirically the most reliable and 'hard' data for analysis but also because it allows reconstruction of the social construction of these contexts.

NOTES

1 Muybridge is famous for his early photographic studies of animal and human movement (Muybridge, 1901); in anthropology, Bateson and Mead (1942) used visual media for their study on the 'Balinese Character' before Birdwhistell (1952) analyzed everyday movements like smoking with the help of film. See also the film-based studies by Gregory Bateson, Frieda Fromm-Reichmann, Paul Watzlawick et al. (Bateson, 1958) at Palo Alto and the studies by Ekman and Friesen (1969ab) and Scheflen (1965) for the development of film in the social sciences.

2 The authors only analyze one type of institution (education) with wide yet not universal institutionalized standards of interaction.

3 For the general notions of knowledge, institutions, and the structure of the stock of knowledge, see Berger and Luckmann (Berger and Luckmann, [1966]1991; Goodwin, 2000: 1508f).

4 For this reason, in the 1980s Corsaro (1981) proposed that there should be no video recording and analysis without completing prior ethnography—a procedure Albrecht (1985: 328f) already called 'scouting.' Also Cicourel (1992) has stressed that this focusing process presupposes prior knowledge of and prior familiarity with the field and, therefore, prior ethnography.

5 At this point, the first author draws on papers on focused ethnography, first published in German (Knoblauch, 2001b) and in English (Knoblauch, 2005).

6 Ethnography also has to clarify to what degree the use of video is 'participatory,' proactive, contributing to the actions observed (Suchman and Trigg, 1991; Laurier and Philo, 2006) or 'reactive,' which refers to affecting and manipulating the situation being taped. Although the technology may be obtrusive and even obstructive to the situation, there are situations in which video recording may be less distorting than the presence of an (overt or covert) observer (see, for example, vom Lehn and Heath, 2006). The use of video technology, however, may also relieve the researcher from other tasks and allow for ethnographical observations, questions, and reflections while making the video records. Since the data collection is supported technically, researchers have more time to observe specific features or to enquire into aspects of the already-focused field.

7 By audio-visual conduct, we do not mean to refer to a specific sort of datum constructed by the technical medium of video recording.

8 See Heath et al. (2010: 37–60) for a very useful introduction on how to collect data in the field.

9 Cf. the methodology of the refined version of grounded theory (Glaser and Strauss, 1967; Strauss and Corbin, 1998)

10 Sophisticated software (such as Dartfish©) increasingly allows one to create visual code books with video samples and to simply insert drawings and highlight relevant movements directly in the video. NVivo™, ATLAS.ti™, HyperRESEARCH™, and Transana© allow one to code video 'on the fly.' See Chapter 27 by Raewyn Bassett in this handbook.

11 In conversation analysis, this feature of communication has been studied by Schegloff and Sacks (Schegloff, 1968; Schegloff and Sacks, 1973).

12 For a more detailed account of these theoretical assumptions, see Knoblauch (2001a).

13 This notion of reflexivity differs from notions of reflexivity that address the presentation of research (cf. Ruby, 2000).

14 Structural hermeneutics is one way to tackle the indefiniteness of synchronous visual references.

Basically it starts from the assumption that audio-visual data encompasses meaning patterns that reflect the meaning of the situations represented. It proceeds by producing as many competing interpretations of single frames as possible (in interpretation groups), which are reduced by the interpretations triggered by consecutive frames. Structural hermeneutics assumes that these meanings are reduced step by step to what becomes the 'objective meaning' (cf. Soeffner, 1997).

15 We would like to thank Felix Degenhardt (2010) for contributing this data fragment and detailed transcription. The Gesprächsanalytisches Transkriptionssystem (GAT) transcription conventions were used (Selting et al., 1998).

16 Heath and Luff (2007).

17 In fact, even the kinds of signs audience members use at auctions differ substantially, ranging from very subtle nods, short waves of the hand, to the raising of numbered signs or phone calls—the differences are not only dependent on the size of the audience but also on the 'milieu' of the auction and its formality.

18 For a more detailed analysis and transcription conventions, see Knoblauch (2008).

19 We would like to thank Marion Mackert and Sabine Petschke for the detailed reconstruction of those movements.

20 Schnettler (2006: 157) compares this interplay to 'orchestration.'

21 As seen, the turn may be observed only visually.

22 Of course video data are reducing the situated again to some aspects of the situation, but which should however cover the relevant aspects of it.

23 See Chapter 16 by Winfried Nöth on visual semiotics in this handbook.

24 Hodge and Kress (1988).

25 See Chapter 11 by Francesco Lapenta on photo-elicitation in this handbook.

26 The method dates back, of course, to Jean Rouch (Jackson, 2004).

REFERENCES

Albrecht, G. L. (1985) 'Videotape safaris: Entering the field with the camera', *Qualitative Sociology*, 8(4): 325–344.

Bateson, G. (1958) 'Language and psychotherapy: Frieda Fromm-Reichmann's last project', *Psychiatry*, 21(21): 96–100.

Bateson, G. and Mead, M. (1942) *Balinese Character. A Photographic Analysis*. New York: New York Academy of Sciences.

Bayart, D., Borzeix, A. and Lacoste, M. (1997) 'Les traversées de la gare: Filmer des activités itinerantes', *Champs Visuels*, 6: 75–90.

Berger, P. L. and Luckmann, T. [1966] (1991) *The Social Construction of Reality. A Treatise in the Sociology of Knowledge*. New York: Penguin.

Birdwhistell, R. L. (1952) *Introduction to Kinesics. An Annotation System for the Analysis of Body Motion and Gesture*. Louisville, KY: University of Louisville.

Cicourel, A. V. (1992) 'The interpretation of communicative contexts: Examples from medical encounters', in A. Duranti and C. Goodwin (eds.), *Rethinking Context: Language as an Interactive Phenomenon*. Cambridge, UK: Cambridge University Press. pp. 291–310.

Corsaro, W. A. (1981) 'Something old and something new. The importance of prior ethnography in the collection and analysis of audiovisual data', *Sociological Methods and Research*, 11(2): 145–166.

Degenhardt, F. (2010) 'Auktion, Akteurskonstellation und Struktur'. Unpublished manuscript, Technical University Berlin.

Dinkelaker, J. and Herrle, M. (2009) *Erziehungswissenschaftliche Videographie*. Wiesbaden: VS Verlag für Sozialwissenschaften.

Ekman, P. and Friesen, W. (1969a) 'The repertoire of nonverbal behavior: Categories, origins, usage and coding', *Semiotica*, 1: 63–68.

Ekman, P. and Friesen, W. (1969b) 'A tool for the analysis of motion picture film or videotapes', *American Psychologist*, 24(3): 240–243.

Erickson, F. (1988) 'Ethnographic description', in U. Ammon (ed.), *Sociolinguistics. An International Handbook of the Science of Language and Society*. Berlin, New York: de Gruyter. pp. 1081–1095.

Giddens, A. (1984) *The Constitution of Society: Outline of the Theory of Structuration*. Cambridge: Polity.

Glaser, B. G. and Strauss, A. (1967) *The Discovery of Grounded Theory: Strategies for Qualitative Research*. New York: Aldine.

Goffman, E. (1961) 'Behavior in public places. Notes on the social organization of gatherings'. Unpublished manuscript, New York.

Goodwin, C. (2000) 'Action and embodiment within situated human interaction', *Journal of Pragmatics*, 32: 1489–1522.

Heath, C. (1997) 'The analysis of activities in face to face interaction using video', in D. Silverman (ed.), *Qualitative Research. Theory, Method, and Practice*. London: Sage Publications. pp. 183–200.

Heath, C. and Hindmarsh, J. (2002) 'Analysing interaction: Video, ethnography and situated conduct', in M. Tim (ed.), *Qualitative Research in Action*. London: Sage Publications. pp. 99–121.

Heath, C. and Luff, P. (1996) 'Convergent activities: Line control and passenger information on the London Underground', in Y. Engeström and D. Middleton (eds.), *Cognition and Communication at Work*. Cambridge, UK: Cambridge University Press. pp. 96–129.

Heath, C. and Luff, P. (2000) *Technology in Action*. Cambridge, UK: Cambridge University Press.

Heath, C. and Luff, P. (2007) 'Ordering competition: The interactional accomplishment of the sale of art and antiques at auction', *British Journal of Sociology*, 58(1): 63–85.

Heath, C., Hindmarsh, J. and Luff, P. (2010) *Video in Qualitative Research: Analysing Social Interaction in Everyday Life*. London: Sage Publications.

Hodge, R. and Kress, G. (1988) *Social Semiotics*. Ithaca, New York: Cornell University Press.

Hughes, J. A., King, V., Rodden, T. and Anderson, H. (1994) 'Moving out of the control room: Ethnography in system design', in R. Futura and C. Neuwirth (eds.), *Transcending Boundaries. Proceedings of the ACM Conference on Computer Supported Cooperative Work*. Chapel Hill, North Carolina. pp. 429–439.

Jackson, J. (2004) 'An ethnographic Filmflam: Giving gifts, doing research, and videotaping the native subject/object', *American Anthropologist*, 106(1): 32–42.

Kendon, A. (2004) *Gesture. Visible Action as Utterance*. Cambridge, UK: Cambridge University Press.

Knoblauch, H. (2001a) 'Communication, contexts and culture. A communicative constructivist approach to intercultural communication', in A. di Luzio, S. Günthner and F. Orletti (eds.), *Culture in Communication. Analyses of Intercultural Situations*. Amsterdam, Philadelphia: John Benjamins. pp. 3–33.

Knoblauch, H. (2001b) 'Fokussierte Ethnographie', *sozialer sinn*, (1): 123–141.

Knoblauch, H. (2005) 'Focused ethnography', *Forum Qualitative Sozialforschung / Forum: Qualitative Social Research*, 6(3). [Online]. Available from: http://nbn-resolving.de/urn:nbn:de:0114-fqs0503440 [Accessed 10 October 2010].

Knoblauch, H. (2008) 'The performance of knowledge: Pointing and knowledge in PowerPoint presentations', *Cultural Sociology*, 2(1): 75–97.

Koch, S. C. and Zumbach, J. (2002) 'The use of video analysis software in behavior observation research: Interaction patterns of task-oriented small groups', *Forum Qualitative Sozialforschung/Forum: Qualitative Social Research*, 3(2). [Online]. Available from: http://nbn-resolving.de/urn:nbn:de:0114-fqs0202187 [Accessed 10 October 2010].

Laurier, E. and Philo, C. (2006) 'Natural problems of naturalistic video data', in H. Knoblauch, B. Schnettler, J. Raab and H. -G. Soeffner (eds.), *Video Analysis. Methodology and Methods. Qualitative Audiovisual Analysis in Sociology*. Frankfurt am Main, New York: Lang. pp. 183–192.

Mittenecker, E. (1987) *Video in der Psychologie. Methoden und Anwendungsbeispiele in Forschung und Praxis*. Bern: Huber.

Mohn, E. (2007) 'Kamera-Ethnografie: Vom Blickentwurf zur Denkbewegung', in G. Brandstetter and G. Klein (eds.), *Methoden der Tanzwissenschaft. Modellanalysen zu Pina Bauschs 'Sacre du Printemps'*. Bielefeld: Transcript. pp. 173–194.

Mondada, L. (2006) 'Video recording as the reflexive preservation and configuration of phenomenal features for analysis', in H. Knoblauch, B. Schnettler, J. Raab and H. -G. Soeffner (eds.), *Video Analysis. Methodology and Methods. Qualitative Audiovisual Analysis in Sociology*. Frankfurt am Main, New York: Lang. pp. 51–67.

Muybridge, E. (1901) *The Human Figure in Motion: An Electro Photographic Investigation of Consecutive Phases in Muscular Actions*. London: Chapman and Hall.

Raab, J. and Tänzler, D. (2006) 'Video-Hermeneutics', in H. Knoblauch, B. Schnettler, J. Raab and H. -G. Soeffner (eds.), *Video Analysis. Methodology and Methods. Qualitative Audiovisual Analysis in Sociology*. Frankfurt am Main, New York: Lang. pp. 85–97.

Rammert, W. and Schulz-Schaeffer, I. (2002) 'Technik und Handeln. Wenn soziales Handeln sich auf menschliches Verhalten und technische Abläufe verteilt', in W. Rammert and I. Schulz-Schaeffer (eds.), *Können Maschinen denken? Soziologische Beiträge zum Verhältnis von Mensch und Technik*. Frankfurt am Main: Campus. pp. 11–64.

Ruby, J. (2000) *Picturing Culture: Explorations of Film and Anthropology*. Chicago, IL: UCP.

Sacks, H., Schegloff, E. A. and Jefferson, G. (1974) 'A simplest systematics for the organization of turn-taking for conversation', *Language*, 50(4): 696–735.

Scheflen, A. E. (1965) 'The significance of posture in communication systems', *Psychiatry*, 27: 316–331.

Schegloff, E. (1968) 'Sequencing in conversational openings', *American Anthropologist*, 70: 1075–1095.

Schegloff, E. (1992) 'On talk and its institutional occasions', in P. Drew and J. Heritage (eds.), *Talk at Work. Interaction in Institutional Settings.* Cambridge, UK: Cambridge University Press. pp. 101–136.

Schegloff, E. and Sacks, H. (1973) 'Opening up closings', *Semiotica* (8): 289–327.

Schnettler, B. (2006) 'Orchestrating bullet lists and commentaries. A video performance analysis of computer supported presentations', in H. Knoblauch, B. Schnettler, J. Raab and H. -G. Soeffner (eds.), *Video Analysis. Methodology and Methods. Qualitative Audiovisual Data Analysis in Sociology.* Frankfurt am Main, New York: Lang. pp. 155–168.

Schubert, C. (2006) 'Video-analysis of practice and the practice of video-analysis', in H. Knoblauch, B. Schnettler, J. Raab and H. -G. Soeffner (eds.), *Video Analysis. Methodology and Methods. Qualitative Audiovisual Analysis in Sociology.* Frankfurt am Main, New York: Lang. pp. 115–126.

Schubert, C. (2009) 'Videographic elicitation interviews. Studying technologies, Practices and narratives in organisations', in U. T. Kissmann (ed.), *Video Interaction Analysis.* Berlin, New York: Lang. pp. 199–220.

Schutz, A. (1962) 'Common sense and scientific interpretation of human action', in M. Natanson (ed.), *Collected Papers I: The Problem of Social Reality.* The Hague: Nijhoff. pp. 3–47.

Schütz, A. (1971) *Gesammelte Aufsätze I. Das Problem der Sozialen Wirklichkeit.* Den Haag: Nijhoff.

Selting, M., Auer, P., Barden, B., Bergmann, J., et al. (1998) 'Gesprächsanalytisches Transkriptionssystem, (GAT)', *Linguistische Berichte,* (173): 91–122.

Soeffner, H. -G. (1997) *The Order of Rituals. The Interpretation of Everyday Life.* New Brunswick: Transaction.

Strauss, A. and Corbin, J. (1998) *Basics of Qualitative Research: Techniques and Procedures for Developing Grounded Theory,* 2nd edn. London: Sage Publications.

Suchman, L. (1987) *Plans and Situated Actions. The Problem of Human–Machine Communication.* Cambridge, UK: Cambridge University Press.

Suchman, L. and Trigg, R. H. (1991) 'Understanding practice: Video as a medium for reflection and design', in J. Greenbaum and M. Kyng (eds.), *Design at Work. Cooperative Design of Computer Systems.* Hillsdale, NJ: Lawrence Erlbaum. pp. 65–89.

vom Lehn, D. and Heath, C. (2006) 'Discovering exhibits: Video-based studies of interaction in museums and science centres', in H. Knoblauch, B. Schnettler, J. Raab and H. -G. Soeffner (eds.), *Video Analysis. Methodology and Methods. Qualitative Audiovisual Analysis in Sociology.* Frankfurt am Main, New York: Lang. pp. 101–113.

Weber, M. [1921] (1984) *Soziologische Grundbegriffe.* Tübingen: Mohr.

PART 5

Visualization Technologies and Practices

23

Eye Tracking as a Tool for Visual Research

Bettina Olk and Arvid Kappas

INTRODUCTION

All of us are doing it about 170,000 times each day, about three times per second, but we rarely think about it: moving our eyes. A closer look at our eye movement patterns reveals that our eyes tend to fixate only very briefly—typically fractions of a second—on objects or locations in space before they move on. The movements that we make with our eyes, the jumps from fixation point to fixation point, are called *saccades*. Saccades are important because moving our eyes allows us to represent samples of our visual environment on the fovea, the part of our retina, where visual acuity and color sensitivity are highest because here the density of photoreceptors is greatest (for example, Sparks, 2002; Duchowski, 2007). Saccades permit us to obtain samples of the visual world in high spatial resolution. Obviously, we are also able to perceive stimuli that fall outside the fovea. In fact, our peripheral vision provides us with much important information. For example, when we are looking at a page of text, we are aware of the entire text, but reading it requires fixation on its parts, the words and letters. Thus, in order to represent the different parts of the text on the fovea we move our eyes. Figure 23.1 shows a typical scanpath of a person while reading. The person started at the top left-hand side and with each saccade moved further toward the right, the end of the line, before beginning with a new line. Apart from providing us with information regarding the normal reading process, data such as these are also very helpful in understanding why some individuals may have difficulties reading. For example, proficient readers are able to jump back and forth, anticipating features of sentence structures, whereas non-proficient readers are more glued to the sequence of words as they unfold (see Kutas et al., 2000).

Because we can only fixate a small area at a time and then move our eyes in only one direction at a time, our brain needs to decide where the eyes should be moved to and for how long they should dwell on a given area. Eye movement research is concerned with identifying the factors that influence and

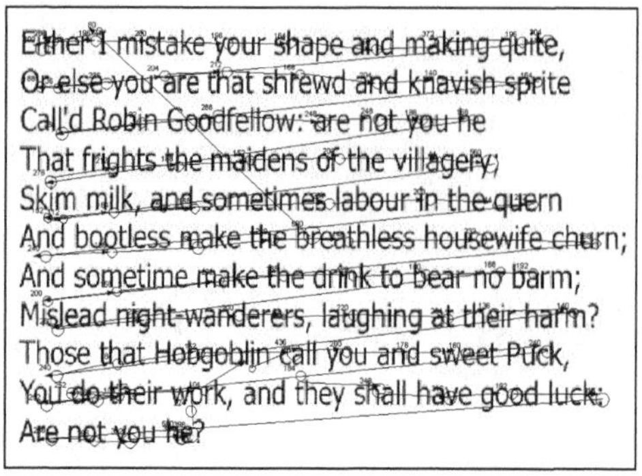

Either I mistake your shape and making quite,
Or else you are that shrewd and knavish sprite
Call'd Robin Goodfellow: are not you he
That frights the maidens of the villagery;
Skim milk, and sometimes labour in the quern
And bootless make the breathless housewife churn;
And sometime make the drink to bear no barm;
Mislead night-wanderers, laughing at their harm?
Those that Hobgoblin call you and sweet Puck,
You do their work, and they shall have good luck:
Are not you he?

Figure 23.1 Example of a scanpath during reading. The arrows represent saccadic eye movements, the circles fixations, the numbers fixation duration in milliseconds. The option to show numbers referring to the order of saccades was deselected for this example. © 2010 Arvid Kappas and Bettina Olk

determine the outcome of this decision process. For instance, it is established knowledge that eye movements and attention are closely related (Hoffman and Subramaniam, 1995; Deubel and Schneider, 1996; Corbetta, 1998). Hence, eye movement patterns are informative about where attention is directed. Further, emotional content affects eye movements. People tend to look at emotional pictures first and for longer than at neutral pictures (Nummenmaa et al., 2006; Alpers, 2008; Kissler and Keil, 2008). In addition, eye movements are guided by the goals of observers (Yarbus, 1967). To provide a full review of the factors that have been identified and the models that have been created by researchers to describe and explain the processes involved in directing eye movements would be well beyond the scope of this chapter. Also, given the available space, an in-depth introduction into the more technical aspects is not possible. We thus refer the reader to review articles and books (for example, Duchowski, 2007; Land and Tatler, 2009). The purpose of the present chapter is to give an overview and thus we will provide examples of representative work. We will also point to possible applications of eye

movement research in different areas of visual research.

Measuring eye movements has become a tool for drawing inferences regarding underlying psychological processes, such as interest in certain contents, motivations, and the like (Duchowski, 2007). The problem is, of course, as in many other areas where behavioral or physiological measures are used to draw inferences regarding mental processes, that frequently, there are multiple determinants leading to a particular behavioral or physiological change (see Cacioppo and Tassinary, 1990). Without knowing more about the underlying processes one is bound to draw false conclusions as to the meaning of eye movements. Thus, even if the reader's interest is primarily in the applications of eye movement research, learning about the underlying processes is crucial for data interpretation (Coren et al., 1999; Hyönä et al., 2003; Duchowski, 2007; Goldstein, 2007).

WHICH FACTORS MODULATE EYE MOVEMENT PATTERNS?

In a typical experiment in the laboratory, the rapid sequences of saccades and fixations are recorded under different experimental conditions. Experiments have shown that where we look is influenced by several factors (see Henderson and Hollingworth, 1999 and Henderson, 2003 for reviews). Our attention and our eyes are attracted by suddenly appearing, visually salient, and new stimuli and we may at times not be aware of this. Such behavior is for instance demonstrated in studies using the 'oculomotor capture paradigm' (for example, Theeuwes et al., 1998). In the experiment by Theeuwes et al. (1998), participants started each trial of the experiment by looking at six gray circles (dashed lines), each containing a small gray '8' (see Figure 23.2). These stimuli were equally spaced around an imaginary circle around a small asterisk in the center of

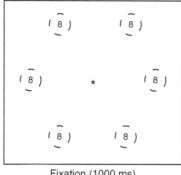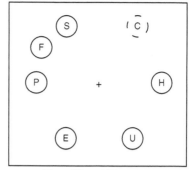

Fixation (1000 ms) Target/Onset Distractor

Figure 23.2 Graphic illustration of the displays and the temporal sequence of an experimental trial (from left to right). The target is defined simultaneously with the appearance of the onset distracter. The gray circles are indicated by the dashed lines. The red circles are indicated by the solid lines. Reproduced with kind permission from Jan Theeuwes from Theeuwes et al. (1998): © 1998 SAGE

the screen. At the beginning participants looked at the asterisk. After 1000 ms all but one circle changed their color to red (solid lines) and at the same time each small '8' changed to a different letter. The task of the participants was to look directly from the center toward the odd one out—the circle that remained gray—and to determine whether the letter inside it was a 'C' or a reverse 'C.' Importantly, participants did not know which one of the circles would be the odd one out in a given trial because its location changed randomly from trial to trial. In half of the trials an additional red circle was presented at one of four locations among the other red circles simultaneously with the color change. Although this additional stimulus was irrelevant for the task, participants tended to look at it first in about half of the trials, despite their instruction to look directly toward the gray circle. This finding demonstrates that participants' eyes were 'captured' by the additional stimulus. That they had understood the task was confirmed by the trials in which no additional red circle was shown. In those trials, participants tended to look at the gray circle right away. And most interestingly, when asked after the experiment whether they were aware that the

appearance of the new circle affected their saccades, they denied an influence of the additional circle, even though their eye movement data proved that they had looked at it. This work demonstrates that where we look at is not always under our control and that suddenly appearing stimuli capture our attention and our eyes.

Studies in which participants were shown different pictures indicate that characteristics such as contrast, color, texture, luminance, and shape of the visual information affect which areas are fixated. For example, areas of higher contrast, where contrast can be calculated as the local measure of the variability of image intensity, are fixated more (Reinagel and Zador, 1999; Parkhurst and Niebur, 2003).

Importantly, we are also able to direct our attention and eyes in a controlled, goal-directed manner to relevant information. Knowledge about types of scenes guides our eyes. For instance, when looking for your cat in the garden, you are more likely to find it sitting on the grass or in a tree than flying through the sky. Furthermore, the famous study by Yarbus (1967) illustrates the impact of goals. He recorded eye movements while observers looked at a print of the painting 'They Did Not Expect Him' by Repin. The painting depicts a living room scene with a family and a person entering the room. Participants either engaged in free viewing or they were, for example, asked to estimate the social status of the persons, their age, to memorize the clothing of the persons, or to estimate for how long the person entering the room had been away. The crucial finding was that the fixation patterns differed depending on the task that the participants had to complete. For instance, when they were asked about the economic standing of the persons, they looked predominantly at the clothes of the person in the foreground and on the furniture in the room and when asked to estimate for how long the person entering the room had been away, their gaze moved frequently back and forth between the faces of the persons. These results show that the distribution of fixations and saccades was influenced by the type of information required and illustrates that participants viewed scenes in an active manner, looking for pieces of information that were relevant for the task they had to complete. Recently, we replicated the findings by Yarbus with a different type of material: namely, press photographs (Olk et al., 2007). We presented participants with online press photographs that depicted a current event but were unknown to the participants. Photographs were a mixture of different camera angles, showed emotional situations that expressed a certain tension and anxiety and depicted motifs that were ambivalent in their interpretation outside their actual news context. In the experimental condition, participants viewed all photographs several times, each time with a different instruction. For instance, for the first viewing, participants were asked to simply look at each picture, and for the second viewing to describe what the people depicted felt. To analyze the eye movement patterns, 'areas of interest' were defined, and it was calculated how often and for how long those areas were fixated. This tested whether the fixation patterns changed with the

instructions, as would be expected according to Yarbus (1967). We found a clear effect of instructions on eye movements. When participants described what the people depicted felt, they clearly looked more at the persons in a photograph, which are the most informative components for this purpose, than at other parts of the images, such as objects. These data demonstrate that the observers' goals guided their attention and eyes.

THE NEUROPHYSIOLOGY OF EYE MOVEMENTS

Eye movement research also addresses the question of which brain areas are involved in the decision where eyes should be moved to, and what role these brain areas play in the decision process. Before we move our eyes, the information that is received on the retina has to undergo several stages of processing, which already begin on the retina itself. From the retina, the visual information is passed on via the visual pathways to those brain areas that deal further with the processing of location, shape, color, size, brightness, and texture of the seen stimuli and eventually detect at which objects or people we are looking (see Duchowski, 2007). In order to determine and understand what we are looking at, the visual information has to be combined with our knowledge. For example, if we see something round with objects of different color, shape, and texture on it, only the combination of the seen visuals with our knowledge will tell us that this is a plate of food in front of us. Visual perception is thus clearly more than the projection of the outside visual world onto the retina of the eye and the transfer of information to visual areas in the brain (see Bear et al., 2007). The features of the stimuli we see and their meaning both influence where we look.

Neurophysiological and neuropsychological studies have contributed much knowledge about the network of brain areas involved in the generation of eye movements and how these brain areas work. The network of brain areas consists of structures lying under the cortex (subcortical) such as the basal ganglia, the brainstem, and the superior colliculi. In the superior colliculi, for instance, cells have been identified that are active when we fixate and cells that are active when we move our eyes. These types of cells are rarely active at the same time and are involved in mutual inhibition (for example, Coren et al., 1999: 68). The size and direction of each saccade is determined by where the superior colliculi are stimulated. For example, stimulation of the front part results in small saccades while stimulation more toward the back produces large eye movements (Schiller, 1984). Signals from the superior colliculi are passed on to the brainstem, where omnipause neurons fire tonically when we fixate and stop when we make a saccade. Burst neurons are active before and during saccades. This information is further sent to the six extraocular muscles that move each eye (Schiller, 1984; Sparks, 2002). Cortical areas that are involved in eye movement generation and control are for example the frontal eye field, the supplementary eye field, and the dorsolateral prefrontal cortex in the front of the brain, as well as the parietal eye field, which is located more toward the back of the brain (Schiller, 1984; Guitton et al., 1985; Henik et al., 1994; Schlag-Rey et al., 1997; Everling and Fischer, 1998; Gaymard et al., 1998; Connolly et al., 2000; Rafal et al., 2000; Olk et al., 2006). Frontal cortical areas have, among other functions, been associated with the control of eye movements, such as the inhibition of unwanted saccades toward irrelevant stimuli. Understanding the exact role of such areas as part of the network and their connections, as well as which rules and mechanisms underlie their processing and communication between each other, is one of the major fascinating challenges of eye movement research.

TECHNOLOGY FOR THE RECORDING OF EYE MOVEMENTS

Modern technology allows us to track eye movements in and outside the laboratory. Eye trackers allow the non-invasive registration of eye movements with a great spatial and temporal accuracy. Some eye trackers are able to record the fixation location of the eyes up to twice every millisecond. There are different types of eye tracking devices on the market, produced and sold by different companies. Some eye trackers consist of headsets with small cameras attached to them that are placed on the head of the participants (see Figure 23.3a). The headsets can be adjusted to the dimensions of a person's head in order to be comfortable. However, when designing an eye movement study, researchers should take into consideration that participants may find such headsets heavy after a while, although this may vary from person to person. We have found that, typically, experiments of a length of half an hour to an hour are very feasible. The tolerance of the headset can be greatly enhanced by including short breaks. Remote eye trackers are positioned on the table about 40–70 cm away from the eyes of the participant, while the participant views visual stimuli on a computer monitor (see Figure 23.3b). These eye trackers are especially useful if the participant to be tested might feel uncomfortable wearing a headset, or if the participant's head needs to remain free of a headset so that further measurements are possible. For example, the activation of facial muscles can be measured with small electrodes applied to the participant's face (see below). Apart from eye trackers that are used in the laboratory, mobile systems allow the participant to move around, usually wearing an eye camera and a camera that records the environment on their head, and carrying further necessary equipment in a small bag (see Figure 23.3c). Mobile eye trackers can be used to study eye movement patterns while participants engage in everyday life tasks, such as making tea and

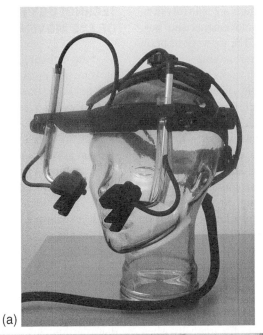

(a)

(b)

Figure 23.3 **The figure shows three different eye trackers (EyeLink® and Applied Science Laboratories). It should be noted explicitly that this is only a selection and many other excellent systems are on the market. (a) The 'EyeLink II' eye tracker (www.sr-research.com) consists of two eye cameras for binocular tracking. A head-tracking camera is integrated into the headband and allows accurate tracking of the participant's point of gaze while allowing head motion and speech. (b) The EyeLink 1000 Desktop System is a remote eye tracker. (c) The 'Mobile Eye' eye tracker (www.asleyetracking.com/Site/) is an example of a mobile eye tracker. © 2010 Bettina Olk**

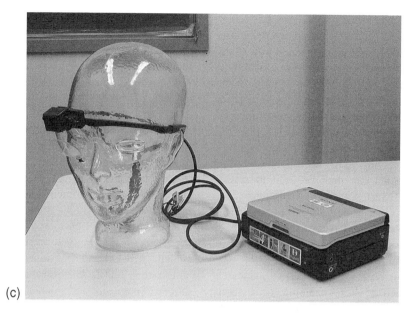

(c)

Figure 23.3   Cont'd

driving (Land and Lee, 1994; Land et al., 1999). Further eye tracking devices are described by Duchowski (2007).

SETTING UP AND CONDUCTING AN EYE TRACKING EXPERIMENT

Before an experiment in the laboratory can begin, a computer program needs to be written for displaying the visual stimuli and specifying the parameters of the experiment, such as for how long and at which position a stimulus or a sequence of stimuli should be shown. The program can further specify which variables are recorded. Such programs are frequently written in programming languages such as C, C++, or MATLAB® and require specialized programming training, but depending on the eye tracking device other languages may also be used and some companies sell special software for the development of experiments (see also Duchowski, 2007).

Before the actual data collection can start, a calibration procedure needs to be completed to determine the correspondence between pupil position in the eye-camera image and the gaze position on the display shown to participants. Experience has shown that this procedure is not too cumbersome and even particular participant populations, such as children or clinical populations, can easily be calibrated. During calibration, fixations on target stimuli are recorded. A typical calibration procedure may require the participant to look at a simple dot that appears randomly at different locations on the screen, while the system records where on the screen the person is looking, and normally only takes a few minutes. At times, it may take longer to calibrate participants who wear glasses as the surface may produce reflections, which interfere with the detection of the pupil by the system. The calibration procedure should be repeated for validation. If the calibration and validation are satisfactory, the experiment can begin. The visuals are presented on screen and the participant completes an assigned task. A wealth of information is recorded, including spatial data such as each fixation location and start and end position of each saccade. Each location on the screen can be described in x and y coordinates. For example, if the screen resolution is 800×600 pixels, then a data point with the x value 400 and the y value 300 would indicate a gaze position in the center of the screen. Further, temporal data are recorded, such as the beginning and end time of fixations and saccades. This is possible through time-stamping of each recording in milliseconds. The recorded objective measurements can then be used to reconstruct the exact scanpath (see Figures 23.1 and 23.4a). It can be inferred where, when, and for how long a participant looked at a certain location, where the exploration started, and how it continued.

Data analysis depends on the research question at hand. If, for example, the research question is similar to Yarbus (1967), whether participants look at a picture differently, depending on which question they need to answer about it, one may choose to define '*areas of interest*,' using special software. Based on those defined areas, the researcher can obtain data reports that inform about how much time a participant spent looking at a given area of interest, how many fixations were made and in which area of interest a saccade started and ended. Figure 23.4a shows the scanpath of a participant who was asked how the depicted people felt.

The analysis reveals that the participant fixated the faces of the man and the woman 30 times, for 6628 ms, which amounts to 77 per cent of the total fixation time. In comparison, the body and the arms of the man were fixated for 1088 ms with seven fixations, which constitutes 12 per cent of the total fixation time. Only 1 per cent of the time was spent on the rowing machine. The percentages are shown as the dark bars in Figure 23.4b. The light bars in the same figure indicate the outcome of the analysis when the same person was asked what was happening in the picture. Only 23 per cent of the total fixation time was then spent looking at the faces, but 32 percent on the body and arms of the man and 27 per cent on the rowing machine. Clearly, modern eye

tracking technology allows and supports statistical analyses that were not possible in the late 1960s when Yarbus conducted his seminal study.

The reconstruction of a scanpath and defining areas of interest is one way of analyzing the data. Other research questions may need to determine the time between the onset of a stimulus to when the eyes start to move. This time is termed saccadic latency or saccadic reaction time and is one of the main dependent variables used in experiments such as the oculomotor capture study mentioned above (Theeuwes et al., 1998) or the antisaccade paradigm described below (for example, Hallett, 1978; Olk and Kingstone, 2003; Godijn and Kramer, 2006). Other research may require the use of pupil size or the duration, amplitude, and velocity of saccades as dependent variables (see also Duchowski, 2007).

THE COMBINATION OF EYE TRACKING TECHNOLOGY WITH OTHER ONGOING MEASUREMENTS

Depending on the research question at hand, the recording of eye movements is motivated by the wish to draw specific inferences as to the cause of the eye movements. In other words, the eye movements are seen as a privileged pathway to obtain knowledge about a mental process that is typically hidden, or about which participants cannot or do not want to provide explicit reports: for instance, which details are of particular interest to participants or are emotionally arousing and hence receive attention. Instead of just relying on the information provided by where people look and for how long, there is also the possibility to combine the analysis of eye movements with other dependent variables that are relevant for a diagnosis of underlying processes, such as emotional responses. For example, if somebody is looking repeatedly and for long periods of time at a particular feature of a car—is this because this feature is interesting and positive, or is it

(a)

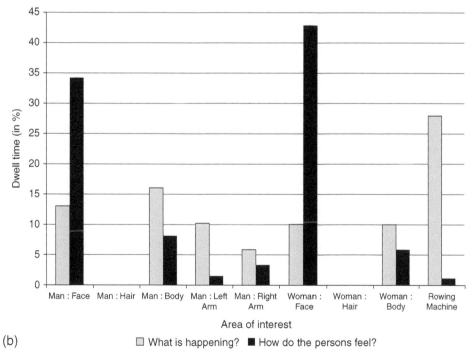

(b) □ What is happening? ■ How do the persons feel?

Figure 23.4   (a) Example of a scanpath while looking at a photograph. © 2008 Jacobs University. **(b) Behavioral data for a single participant looking at the photograph in two different conditions—describing what happened and describing what the two people feel. The bars indicate dwell times on regions of the image that were previously defined as areas of interest.** © 2010 Arvid Kappas and Bettina Olk

because it is perceived as being ugly and disappointing? If we know that a particular spot is relevant—because it is being repeatedly regarded—and it is associated with indications/reports of pleasure or liking, then we have learned more about the underlying mental process when exploring the visual stimulus at hand.

When discussing multi-method approaches one has to distinguish sequential from concurrent paradigms. In a sequential paradigm the same material is tested more than once, allowing the assessment of eye movements at one point, and self-report, behavioral, or physiological measures at another point in time. The problem is, of course, that the second time around an object or an image is processed in a different way. The alternative, thus, is a concurrent approach where other measures are taken simultaneously, while the participant explores a target stimulus.

The easiest concurrent measurement is self-report, more specifically the think-aloud procedure. Participants are asked to comment on what they are seeing, or what they like, while their eye movements are recorded. Later, the content can be coded and related to fixations or dwell times on particular aspects (for example, in the case of a preference task between several products). However, it is clear that the think-aloud task, despite being used in different areas of psychology, interferes with ongoing processing. It shapes and biases interaction with the visual material and it is, depending on the material under study, subject to pressures associated with the social context. In other words, having to comment aloud might shift a spontaneous exploration into an analytical exercise. In the case of dynamic stimuli, such as a movie or a television spot, speaking also interferes with the participant's understanding of the sound track. Clearly, a participant commenting aloud while their eye movements are being assessed is frequently not what the researcher or practitioner wants. Furthermore, we have already stated that on average there are three fixations per second; it is thus very difficult to link specific verbal

content to a subset of an image currently being observed.

The alternative is using behavioral or physiological measures that can be taken at the same time and with a temporal resolution that is comparable with the recording of the eye movement. There are many reasons why such an approach is desirable—for example, using multiple dependent measures, the ambiguity as to the origin of a particular behavioral or physiological response can be reduced (see Cacioppo and Tassinary, 1990). The problem is, of course, that some measures relate to processes that take a certain time between the perception of a stimulus, or stimulus feature, and the presence of the bodily correlate. For example, in principle it is highly desirable to combine the analysis of eye movements with an analysis of electrodermal activity, a classical measure in psychophysiology associated with a sweat reaction linked to the activation of the sympathetic branch of the autonomous nervous system and frequently used as an indicator of psychological arousal. The salt in the sweat makes skin thus more electrically conductive. Psychologically, skin conductance changes as a function of several factors, particularly personal relevance of a stimulus (see Dawson et al., 2000; Pecchinenda, 2001). However, the problem is that there is a latency of about 2000 ms between the perception of a relevant stimulus and the response in electrical conductivity. This means that linking specific physiological reactions to observing specific contents on a computer screen still might require complex procedures to account for the time shift. Nevertheless, there have been published attempts for example to link changes in skin conductance and heart rate with an analysis of eye movements (for example, Wieser et al., 2009).

Ever since Charles Darwin's publication of *The Expression of the Emotions in Man and Animals* (1872), there has been a considerable number of empirical studies investigating the relationship between how someone feels and the muscular activity on their face.

While facial behavior is in no way a simple readout of emotion (Kappas, 2003), there is, under certain circumstances, a link between feeling and muscular activation in the face, moderated by the social situation (see also Kappas and Descôteaux, 2003). While the results of empirical studies concerning facial activity during specific emotional states, such as anger, fear, or disgust, do not recommend using muscular activity as a diagnostic of underlying emotional state (see Russell and Fernández-Dols, 1997; also Russell et al., 2003), the situation is more straightforward when it comes to the more general notion of valence: that is, to what degree something is evaluated positively or negatively (see also Cacioppo et al., 1986; Larsen et al., 2003). Thus, if a person frowns while looking at something, chances are that the object in visual focus is associated with a blocking of important goals (see Smith, 1989; Smith and Scott, 1997), or more generally, negative affect. Hence, measuring the contraction of the brows, associated with the activation of the corrugator supercilii muscle, is a frequently used measure in emotion research. Inversely, activity at the two muscle sites involved in smiling, zygomaticus major (pulls the corners of the mouth back and up) and orbicularis oculi (muscle around the eyes, produces the 'crow's feet wrinkles'; see also Niedenthal et al., 2009) is frequently measured for positive emotions. However, while these measurements are quite reliable at a moderate level of affect, the contraction of the brows is a better measure than activity related to smiling when very negative material is being investigated. As Larsen et al. (2003) reported, there is smiling-related muscle activity when looking at very negative images—likely, a grimace rather than a typical smile (also Kappas and Pecchinenda, 1998). However, without a qualitative assessment of the facial actions using methods such as Ekman and Friesen's Facial Action Coding System (FACS, 1978) these expressions cannot be differentiated. Yet, a FACS analysis is costly in terms of time and money.

The advantage of using facial activity as a correlate of affective processes is the short latency between the perception of an emotional stimulus and the response. Unlike electrodermal activity, mentioned above, changes in facial activity occur in the range of several hundred milliseconds after stimulus onset. We are currently evaluating the concurrent use of electromyography (EMG) (Fridlund and Cacioppo, 1986; Tassinary and Cacioppo, 2000) and eye tracking in our laboratories to assess affective responses to complex press photography of conflict (also Olk et al., 2007).

While emotional responses are obviously associated with changes in bodily activation, many researchers are increasingly interested in measuring these directly in the brain. However, functional magnetic resonance imaging (fMRI), currently the most popular means of assessing in vivo brain activity, relies on a change in blood oxygenation level that has a latency of seconds (Cacioppo and Berntson, 2005). Thus, fMRI is clearly slower than the measures discussed above, particularly facial EMG. This means that 'peripheral' bodily reactions such as facial responses will remain relevant in the foreseeable future as dependent variables for understanding visual perception. Nevertheless, there is some promising progress being made linking simultaneous measurement of brain activity while eye movements are recorded (see Van Reekum et al., 2007).

EYE MOVEMENTS—EXPERIMENTAL PROCEDURES AND INFERENCE

It should be kept in mind that interpreting eye tracking data requires more than employing a particular technical apparatus. Depending on the particular research question or applied purpose, specific control material must be found and included in the experimental session. For example, to scale the affective reactions to press photography material that we are currently studying (for example, Olk et al., 2007) all participants are also reacting to positive, negative, and neutral samples of the International Affective Picture System (IAPS; Lang et al., 2005). These images have been used in psychological research in many different countries and have well-known properties as regards their valence and the arousal they elicit (Bradley and Lang, 2007). They show, for example, babies, cuddly animals, food, exciting sports, household objects, bodily injuries, or threatening images, such as guns pointed at the camera. Using this standardized material allows us to scale the affective responses to the new material we investigate.

A study that illustrates the importance of proper control stimuli from a different research context was conducted by Turati (2004). It is apparent that faces are very important stimuli in everyday life. Many researchers assume that faces are biologically potent stimuli and, thus, already relevant for babies from birth (see Kappas, 2003). To test the assumption that faces are 'special,' several classical studies showed pictures of faces to infants or, as control stimuli, outlines of faces where features such as the eyes, nose, and mouth were shuffled around, so that the resulting image held little resemblance to a face, but contained all of its elements. In this case, babies looked longer at the real faces— a pattern of behavior interpreted as them preferring the real faces. But can it really be concluded that infants always prefer realistic stimuli—only based on the comparison of real and scrambled faces? In fact, Turati (2004) presented face-like stimuli (see Figure 23.5) and other controls. She showed that the critical factor appears to be that babies are attracted to a particular distribution of features in a bounded shape—more high-contrast elements in the upper part. In the natural environment, real human faces do correspond to such a distribution. However, Turati demonstrated (see also Turati, 2004) that infants even preferred stimuli which looked less like faces but contained more features in the upper part of the oval shape,

than the more face-like stimuli (see Figure 23.5). Thus, the conclusion that it was specifically face-likeness that attracted infants was incorrect. Earlier conclusions were based on an analysis of eye movements using the 'wrong' control stimuli. Examples such as these highlight the importance of procedural details that are often disguised by the high-tech aspect of eye movement recording. Measuring and interpreting eye movements is only in part a technological challenge. Engineering problems can and will be solved—it is the experimental tasks that are used and the conditions under which the data are recorded that are the biggest challenges to drawing firm and accurate conclusions.

There is no doubt that in the next few years complex multi-modal measurement of eye movements and other variables targeted at information processing and affective responses will become more and more established. While some of these methods require multi-million dollar equipment (such as magnetic resonance imaging), others will be more affordable and hence trickle down from piloting and basic research to concrete applications in a variety of fields.

THE APPLICATION OF EYE TRACKING

Eye tracking technology can be applied in a vast number of research fields, ranging from studies that investigate the fundamental mechanisms underlying eye movements, such as the programming of saccades, and that aim at devising and improving models to explain eye movement patterns, to studies in advertising and marketing that seek to characterize consumer preferences or human factors, for example to optimize the interfaces between humans and machines (see Duchowski, 2007 for an overview). In the following sections, we will provide examples of the application of eye tracking in the fields of research dealing with eye movement control and clinical applications.

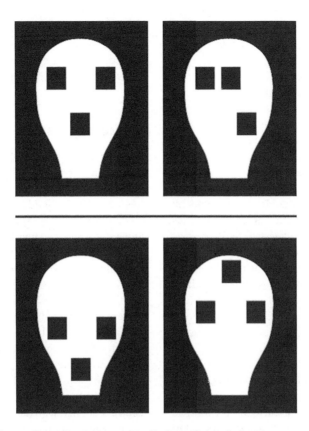

Figure 23.5 Both panels on the top are equally long fixated, despite one resembling a face more than the other. At the bottom panel it is the right stimulus that is more regarded, despite the fact that the left panel is more face-like. In particular, this example is consistent with the hypothesis of Turati that faces are interesting because they have a particular preference for non-specific image features. Reproduced with kind permission from Chiara Turati; from Turati (2004): © 2004 SAGE Publications

Eye movement control

How well are we able to ignore distractions and to attend and look toward information in accordance with the goals that we wish to achieve? An effective interaction with our complex visual world necessitates that we are able to direct our eyes to relevant pieces of information and to suppress gaze toward distractions. In some situations, involuntary shifts of our gaze may be rather disrupting and in conflict with our goals: for example, if a colorful, salient advertisement at the side of the road distracts us and we look there, instead of looking at the road ahead.

This situation requires controlled, voluntary guidance of our eye movements in line with our goals. Studying oculomotor control is important because it contributes significantly to our knowledge about the mechanisms underlying eye movement behavior and also because it allows us to discover and characterize differences in performance under different conditions of a task—for instance, differences in difficulty of tasks or differences in performance between persons. For example, research in this area has shown that the ability to control our eye movements may decline as we age. This has been demonstrated using different experimental paradigms, one being the 'pro- and antisaccade task.' In this task, participants are typically presented with a stimulus, such as a simple dot, in the center of the screen, and are asked to fixate on it. After about 1 second, a further simple dot appears on the left or on the right side of the screen. On 'prosaccade' trials participants are instructed to look at the peripheral dot as quickly and accurately as possible. These trials do not require much oculomotor control as participants can simply allow their eyes to be guided by the suddenly appearing stimulus. On 'antisaccade' trials, however, they are requested to look *away* from the peripheral dot in the opposite direction, without first looking at it. Antisaccade trials require control because it is essential to suppress the tendency to look at the visual stimulus and to select the saccadic response in the direction opposite to the stimulus (Reuter et al., 2006; Olk and Kingstone, 2009). This task may seem easy, but in fact participants look erroneously toward the stimulus in a certain percentage of antisaccade trials, and they are also slower to make an antisaccade than a prosaccade (Olk and Kingstone, 2003; Godijn and Kramer, 2006). When comparing younger and older participants, it is typically found that elderly participants have longer saccadic reaction times and a higher rate of erroneous saccades to the dot when saccades away from it are required than younger participants (Olincy et al., 1997; Klein et al., 2000; Sweeney et al., 2001; Bojko et al., 2004; Eenshuistra et al., 2004; Abel and Douglas, 2007). Furthermore, the difference between age groups becomes especially apparent when the demands for control increase (Olk and Kingstone, 2009). Such a decline in oculomotor control is commonly attributed to a decline in the ability to inhibit the prepotent saccade to the visual stimulus (for example, Hasher et al., 1999; Butler and Zacks, 2006) or to the failure to select the less potent antisaccade response away from the stimulus in a situation when two opposing saccade programs compete (Olk and Kingstone, 2009). One implication of such

findings is that in certain conditions aging may be related to being more easily distracted, and such knowledge can be used to devise tailored training programs.

Clinical applications

Eye movement studies with clinical populations such as patients with brain injuries can help to characterize the impact of brain injuries and thereby guide the way to efficient rehabilitation. They also contribute to our understanding of which brain areas mediate visual exploration. Brain injuries can, for example, lead to a syndrome referred to as visuospatial neglect. Patients with this syndrome do not respond or orient to stimuli presented to the side opposite a brain lesion or can be very slow to respond to such stimuli, thus exploring the visual world differently than healthy persons (Heilman et al., 1987; Mark et al., 1988; Làdavas et al., 1993; Rusconi et al., 2002; Olk and Harvey, 2006). Patients with an injury to the right brain hemisphere may thus not orient toward stimuli presented on their left side. Eye tracking studies have shown that patients exhibit a strong deviation of exploratory gaze toward one side of space—for example, the right side of space after an injury to the right brain hemisphere—although in principle being able to move their eyes toward the other, left side (Karnath and Fetter, 1995; Karnath et al., 1998; Olk et al., 2002). The registration of eye movements has also proven to be a very sensitive method to demonstrate where patients allocate attention, to reveal deficits that may not be apparent on standard neuropsychological tests and to illustrate differences in performance between patients (Harvey et al., 2002).

A good example of how measuring eye movements can considerably affect understanding the neural bases of mental processes is the discussion concerning the role of the amygdala in the processing of fear-relevant data. It is widely assumed that the amygdala, a particular brain structure, part of the so-called limbic system, is critical for processing emotions, specifically fear and anxiety. LeDoux (1996) asserted in studies on rats the importance of the amygdala for emotional processes. However, while it is possible to experiment on rats—for example, destroying a particular brain region—as LeDoux has done, such research is not possible on humans. This means that it is not always clear to what degree animal research can be translated to understanding human psychological processes. It was thus with particular interest that the scientific community learned in an article in the well-esteemed journal *Nature*, that the research group of Antonio Damasio in Iowa had tested a patient, S.M., regarding her capacity to recognize emotions in photos of faces. S.M. suffers from an exceedingly rare condition in which the amygdalae on both sides of the brain have been destroyed (Adolphs et al., 1994). Using standardized pictures, developed by Ekman and Friesen (1976), Adolphs and his colleagues described a specific deficit of S.M. to identify fearful expressions. Independent of the question of how specific the deficits were for fearful faces (there had been the notion that the pattern of data could also support a more general pattern of recognition deficits—S.M. might have difficulties recognizing negative expressions in general, but more pronouncedly so for fear), a recent study by the authors of the original study (Adolphs et al., 2005) changed the interpretation of the original data completely and dramatically. In the context of investigating a different question, the authors had recorded eye movements and noticed that S.M. would not look at the upper part of faces spontaneously. However, in particular, the eye region provides important cues to the identification of fear expressions. Thus, it is not that the damage to a brain region caused a failure to interpret a particular facial configuration in a particular way, but instead the damage influenced the visual exploration—a consequence then was a deficit in identifying fear expression. Causing the patient to look at the upper part of the picture either by explicitly telling her or by pulling the image of the faces down to the lower part of her visual field led to a normal performance in the identification of fear. Thus, measuring eye movements can have a dramatic impact on interpretation of certain behaviors.

CONCLUDING REMARKS

Modern eye tracking technology provides user- and participant-friendly as well as affordable eye trackers and it allows us to investigate a wealth of research questions inside and outside the laboratory—basic or applied—with great spatial and temporal accuracy. There are thus many reasons why eye tracking could be of interest to researchers from different disciplines. The questions that are investigated stem from many different areas such as understanding eye movement control, reading, scene perception, neuropsychology, brain mechanisms, advertising, or human factors. Eye movement patterns provide information on where persons are attending. So taking research on advertising as an example, information about dwell times on an advertisement or areas of an advertisement will provide information about how much attention it attracts. Surely, this information is useful for design purposes and the evaluation of advertising campaigns. To what degree visual attention to details of an advertisement translates into consumer behavior is an open question. Here one of the problems is that much of the applied research done by commercial enterprises is not available for scientific scrutiny, but remains proprietary.

The set-up of specific studies does require programming and technical expertise, knowledge with respect to the planning of research studies, and the analysis of the obtained data sets. However, a number of vendors sell very powerful systems, some of which are completely integrated into large monitors and include user-friendly software for the design and analysis of experiments. Clearly, these methods are getting more and more accessible. Detailed information on the different devices is available from manufacturers of eye trackers (see also Duchowski, 2007), helping those interested in adding the study of eye movements to their methodological toolbox. A potential drawback could be that only one person can be tested at a time and some types of analysis might be time-consuming. However, this is also true for other types of measures and does not constitute a unique issue for eye tracking. The combination of eye tracking technology with other current methodologies such as electromyography opens new, exciting ways of studying the processes that underlie our exploration of the visual world.

REFERENCES

Abel, L. A. and Douglas, J. (2007) 'Effects of age on latency and error generation in internally mediated saccades', *Neurobiology of Aging*, 28(4): 627–637.

Adolphs, R., Gosselin, F., Buchanan, T., Tranel, D., Schyns, P. and Damasio, A. (2005) 'A mechanism for impaired fear recognition after amygdala damage', *Nature*, 433(7021): 68–72.

Adolphs, R., Tranel, D., Damasio, H. and Damasio, A. (1994) 'Impaired recognition of emotion in facial expressions following bilateral damage to the human amygdala', *Nature*, 372(6507): 669–672.

Alpers, G. W. (2008) 'Eye-catching: Right hemisphere attentional bias for emotional pictures', *Laterality*, 13(2): 158–178.

Bear, M. F., Connors, B. W. and Paradiso, M. A. (2007) *Neuroscience: Exploring the Brain*. Philadelphia, PA: Lippincott Williams & Wilkins.

Bojko, A., Kramer, A. F. and Peterson, M. S. (2004) 'Age equivalence in switch costs for prosaccade and antisaccade tasks', *Psychology and Aging*, 19(1): 226–234.

Bradley, Margaret, M. and Lang, Peter J. (2007) 'The International Affective Picture System (IAPS) in the study of emotion and attention', in J. A. Coan and J. J. B. Allen (eds.), *Handbook of Emotion Elicitation and Assessment*. Oxford: Oxford University Press. pp. 29–46.

Butler, K. M. and Zacks, R. T. (2006) 'Age deficits in the control of prepotent responses: Evidence for an

inhibitory decline', *Psychology and Aging*, 21(3): 638–643.

Cacioppo, John T. and Berntson, Gary G. (2005) 'Analyses of the social brain through the lens of human brain imaging', in J. T. Cacioppo and G. G. Berntson (eds.), *Social Neuroscience*. New York: Psychology Press. pp. 1–17.

Cacioppo, John T. and Tassinary, Louis G. (1990) 'Psychophysiology and psychophysiological inference', in J. T. Cacioppo and L. G. Tassinary (eds.), *Principles of Psychophysiology: Physical, Social, and Inferential Elements*. New York: Cambridge University Press. pp. 3–33.

Cacioppo, J. T., Petty, R. E., Losch, M. E. and Kim, H. S. (1986) 'Electromyographic activity over facial muscle regions can differentiate the valence and intensity of affective reactions', *Journal of Personality and Social Psychology*, 50(2): 260–268.

Connolly, J. D., Goodale, M. A., DeSouza, J. F. X., Menon, R. S. and Vilis, T. (2000) 'A comparison of frontoparietal fMRI activation during anti-saccades and anti-pointing', *Journal of Neurophysiology*, 84(3): 1645–1655.

Corbetta, M. (1998) 'Frontoparietal cortical networks for directing attention and the eye to visual locations: Identical, independent, or overlapping neural systems?', *Proceedings of the National Academy of Sciences of the United States of America*, 95(3): 831–838.

Coren, S., Ward, L. M. and Enns, J. T. (1999) *Sensation and Perception*. New York: Harcourt Brace.

Darwin, C. (1872) *The Expression of the Emotions in Man and Animals*. London: Murray.

Dawson, Michael E., Schell, Anne M. and Filion, Diane L. (2000) 'The electrodermal system', in J. T. Cacioppo and L. G. Tassinary (eds.), *Principles of Psychophysiology: Physical, Social, and Inferential Elements*. Cambridge, UK: Cambridge University Press. pp. 200–223.

Deubel, H. and Schneider, W. X. (1996) 'Saccade target selection and object recognition: Evidence for a common attentional mechanism', *Vision Research*, 36(12): 1827–1837.

Duchowski, A. T. (2007) *Eye Tracking Methodology: Theory and Practice*. London: Springer Verlag.

Eenshuistra, R. M., Ridderinkhof, K. R. and van der Molen, M. W. (2004) 'Age-related changes in antisaccade task performance: Inhibitory control or working-memory engagement?', *Brain and Cognition*, 56(2): 177–188.

Ekman, P. and Friesen, W. V. (1976) *Pictures of facial affect*. Palo Alto, CA: Consulting Psychologists Press.

Ekman, P. and Friesen, W. V. (1978) *Facial Action Coding System*. Palo Alto, CA: Consulting Psychologists Press.

Everling, S. and Fischer, B. (1998) 'The antisaccade: A review of basic research and clinical studies', *Neuropsychologia*, 36(9): 885–899.

Fridlund, A. J. and Cacioppo, J. T. (1986) 'Guidelines for human electromyographic research', *Psychophysiology*, 23(5): 567–589.

Gaymard, B., Ploner, C. J., Rivaud, S., Vermersch, A. I. and Pierrot-Deseilligny, C. (1998) 'Cortical control of saccades', *Experimental Brain Research*, 123(1–2): 159–163.

Godijn, R. and Kramer A. F. (2006) 'Prosaccades and antisaccades to onsets and color singletons: Evidence that erroneous prosaccades are not reflexive', *Experimental Brain Research*, 172(4): 439–448.

Goldstein, E. B. (2007) *Sensation and Perception*. Belmont, CA: Thomson Wadsworth.

Guitton, D., Buchtel, H. A. and Douglas, R. M. (1985) 'Frontal lobe lesions in man cause difficulties in suppressing reflexive glances and in generating goal-directed saccades', *Experimental Brain Research*, 58(3): 455–472.

Hallett, P. E. (1978) 'Primary and secondary saccades to goals defined by instructions', *Vision Research*, 18(10): 1279–1296.

Harvey, M., Olk, B., Muir, K. and Gilchrist, I. D. (2002) 'Manual responses and saccades in chronic and recovered hemispatial neglect: A study using visual search', *Neuropsychologia*, 40(7): 705–717.

Hasher, L., Zacks, R. T. and May, C. P. (1999) 'Inhibitory control, circadian arousal, and age', *Attention and Performance XVII*, 17: 653–675.

Heilman, Kenneth M., Bowers Dawn, Valenstein, Edward and Watson, Robert T. (1987) 'Hemispace and hemispatial neglect', in M. Jeannerod (ed.), *Neurophysiological and Neuropsychological Aspects of Spatial Neglect*. Amsterdam: Elsevier. pp. 115–150.

Henderson, J. M. 2003. 'Human gaze control during real-world scene perception', *Trends in Cognitive Sciences* 7(11): 498–504.

Henderson, J. M. and Hollingworth, A. (1999) 'High-level scene perception', *Annual Review of Psychology*, 50(1): 243–271.

Henik, A., Rafal, R. and Rhode, D. (1994) 'Endogenously generated and visually guided saccades after lesions of the human frontal eye fields', *Journal of Cognitive Neuroscience*, 6(4): 400–411.

Hoffman, J. E. and Subramaniam, B. (1995) 'The role of visual attention in saccadic eye movements', *Perception & Psychophysics*, 57(6): 787–795.

Hyönä, J., Radach, R. and Deubel, H. (eds.) (2003) *The Mind's Eye: Cognitive and Applied Aspects of Eye Movement Research*. Amsterdam; Boston, MA: North-Holland.

Kappas, A. (2003) 'What facial activity can and cannot tell us about emotions', in M. Katsikitis (ed.), *The Human Face: Measurement and Meaning*. Dordrecht: Kluwer Academic Publishers. pp. 215–234.

Kappas, A. and Descôteaux, J. (2003) 'Of butterflies and roaring thunder: Nonverbal communication in interaction and regulation of emotion', in P. Philippot, R. S. Feldman and E. J. Coats (eds.), *Nonverbal Behavior in Clinical Settings*. New York: Oxford University Press. pp. 45–74.

Kappas, A. and Pecchinenda, A. (1998) 'Zygomaticus major activity is not a selective indicator of positive affective state in ongoing interactive tasks', *Psychophysiology*, 35: S44.

Karnath, H. -O. and Fetter, M. (1995) 'Ocular space exploration in the dark and its relationship to subjective and objective body orientation in neglect patients with parietal lesions', *Neuropsychologia*, 33(3): 371–377.

Karnath, H. -O., Niemeier, M. and Dichgans, J. (1998) 'Space exploration in neglect', *Brain*, 121(12): 2357–2367.

Kissler, J. and Keil, A. (2008) 'Look—don't look! How emotional pictures affect pro- and anti-saccades', *Experimental Brain Research*, 188(2): 215–222.

Klein, C., Fischer, B., Hartnegg, K., Heiss, W. H. and Roth, M. (2000) 'Optomotor and neuropsychological performance in old age', *Experimental Brain Research*, 135(2): 141–154.

Kutas, Marta, Federmeier, Kara D., Coulson, Seana, King, Jonathan W. and Münte, Thomas F. (2000) 'Language', in J. T. Cacioppo, L. G. Tassinary and G. G. Berntson (eds.), *Handbook of Psychophysiology*. Cambridge, UK: Cambridge University Press. pp. 576–601.

Làdavas, E., Umiltà, C., Ziani, P., Brogi, A. and Minarini, M. (1993) 'The role of right side objects in left side neglect: A dissociation between perceptual and directional motor neglect', *Neuropsychologia*, 31(8): 761–773.

Land, M. F. and Lee, D. N. (1994) 'Where we look when we steer', *Nature*, 369(6483): 742–744.

Land, M. F. and Tatler, B. W. (2009) *Looking and Acting: Vision in Natural Behaviour*. Oxford: Oxford University Press.

Land, M. F., Mennie, N. and Rusted, J. (1999) 'The roles of vision and eye movements in the control of activities of daily living', *Perception*, 28(11): 1311–1328.

Lang, P. J., Bradley, M. M. and Cuthbert, B. N. (2005) 'International affective picture system (IAPS): Affective ratings of pictures and instruction manual'. Technical Report A-6. Gainesville, FL: University of Florida.

Larsen, J. T., Norris, C. J. and Cacioppo, J. T. (2003) 'Effects of positive and negative affect on electromyographic activity over the zygomaticus major and corrugator supercilii', *Psychophysiology*, 40(5): 776–785.

LeDoux, J. (1996) *The Emotional Brain*. New York: Simon & Schuster.

Mark, V. W., Kooistra, C. A. and Heilman, K. M. (1988) 'Hemispatial neglect affected by non-neglected stimuli', *Neurology*, 38(8): 1207–1211.

Niedenthal, P. M., Winkielman, P. Mondillon, L. and Vermeulen, N. (2009) 'Embodiment of emotional concepts: Evidence from EMG measures', *Journal of Personality and Social Psychology*, 96(6): 1120–1136.

Nummenmaa, L., Hyönä, J. and Calvo, M. G. (2006) 'Eye movement assessment of selective attentional capture by emotional pictures', *Emotion*, 6(2): 257–268.

Olincy, A., Ross, R. G., Young, D. A. and Freedman, R. (1997) 'Age diminishes performance on an antisaccade eye movement task', *Neurobiology of Aging*, 18(5): 483–489.

Olk, B. and Harvey, M. (2006) 'Characterizing exploration behaviour in spatial neglect: Omissions and repetitive search', *Brain Research*, 1118(1): 106–115.

Olk, B. and Kingstone, A. (2003) 'Why are antisaccades slower than prosaccades? A novel finding using a new paradigm', *NeuroReport*, 14(1): 151–155.

Olk, B. and Kingstone, A. (2009) 'A new look at aging and performance in the antisaccade task: The impact of response selection', *European Journal of Cognitive Psychology. Special Issue 'Ageing, Cognition, and Neuroscience'*, 21(2&3): 406–427.

Olk, B., Harvey, M. and Gilchrist, I. D. (2002) 'First saccades reveal biases in recovered neglect', *Neurocase*, 8(4): 306–313.

Olk, B., Chang, E., Kingstone, A. and Ro, T. (2006) 'Modulation of antisaccades by transcranial magnetic stimulation over the human frontal eye field', *Cerebral Cortex*, 16(1): 76–82.

Olk, Bettina, Kappas, Arvid and Müller, Marion, G. (2007) 'Perceiving press photography. Who sees what, when, how?' Paper presented at the Visual Competence Symposium—Facets of a Paradigm Shift, Bremen, Germany.

Parkhurst, D. J. and Niebur, E. (2003) 'Scene content selected by active vision', *Spatial Vision*, 16(2): 125–154.

Pecchinenda, A. (2001) 'The psychophysiology of appraisals', in K. R. Scherer, A. Schorr and T. Johnstone (eds.), *Appraisal Processes in Emotion: Theory, Methods, Research*. New York: Oxford University Press. pp. 301–318.

Rafal, Robert D., Machado, Liana, Ro, Tony and Ingle, Harris. (2000) 'Looking forward to looking: Saccade preparation and the control of midbrain visuomotor reflexes', in S. Monsell and J. Driver (eds.), *Attention & Performance XVIII*. Cambridge, MA: MIT Press. pp. 155–174.

Reinagel, P. and Zador, A. M. (1999) 'Natural scene statistics at the centre of gaze', *Network-Computation in Neural Systems*, 10(4): 341–350.

Reuter, B., Philipp, A. M., Koch, I. and Kathmann, N. (2006) 'Effects of switching between leftward and rightward pro- and antisaccades', *Biological Psychology*, 72(11): 88–95.

Rusconi, M. L., Maravita, A., Bottini, G. and Vallar, G. (2002) 'Is the intact side really intact? Perseverative responses in patients with unilateral neglect: A productive manifestation', *Neuropsychologia*, 40(6): 594–604.

Russell, James A. and Fernández-Dols, José-Miguel (1997) 'What does a facial expression mean?', in J. A. Russell and J. M. Fernández-Dols (eds.), *The Psychology of Facial Expression*. Cambridge, UK: Cambridge University Press. pp. 3–30.

Russell, J. A., Bachorowski, J. A. and Fernández-Dols, J. M. (2003) 'Facial and vocal expressions of emotion', *Annual Review of Psychology*, 54: 329–349.

Schiller, Peter H. (1984) 'The neural control of visually guided eye movements', in J. Richards (ed.), *Cognitive Neuroscience of Attention*. Mahwah, NJ: Lawrence Erlbaum Associates. pp. 3–50.

Schlag-Rey, M., Amador, N., Sanchez, H. and Schlag, J. (1997) 'Antisaccade performance predicted by neuronal activity in the supplementary eye field', *Nature*, 390(6658): 398–401.

Smith, C. A. (1989) 'Dimensions of appraisal and physiological response in emotion', *Journal of Personality and Social Psychology*, 56(3): 339–353.

Smith, Craig A. and Scott, Heather S. (1997) 'A componential approach to the meaning of facial expressions', in J. A. Russell and J. M. Fernández-Dols (eds.), *The Psychology of Facial Expression*. Cambridge, UK: Cambridge University Press. pp. 229–254.

Sparks, D. L. (2002) 'The brainstem control of saccadic eye movements', *Nature Reviews Neuroscience*, 3(12): 952–964.

Sweeney, J. A., Rosano, C., Berman, R. A. and Luna, B. (2001) 'Inhibitory control of attention declines more than working memory during normal aging', *Neurobiology of Aging*, 22(1): 39–47.

Tassinary, Louis G. and Cacioppo, John T. (2000) 'The skeletomuscular system: Surface electromyography', in J. T. Cacioppo, L. G. Tassinary, and G. G. Berntson (eds.), *Handbook of Psychophysiology*. New York: Cambridge University Press. pp. 163–199.

Theeuwes, J., Kramer, A. F., Hahn, S. and Irwin, D. E. (1998) 'Our eyes do not always go where we want them to go: Capture of the eyes by new objects', *Psychological Science*, 9(5): 379–385.

Turati, C. (2004) 'Why faces are not special to newborns: An alternative account of the face preference', *Current Directions in Psychological Science*, 13(1): 5–8.

Van Reekum, C. M., Urry, H. L., Johnstone, T., et al. (2007) 'Individual differences in amygdala and ventromedial prefrontal cortex activity are associated with evaluation speed and psychological well-being', *Journal of Cognitive Neuroscience*, 19(2): 237–248.

Wieser, M. J., Pauli, P., Alpers, G. W. and Mühlberger, A. (2009) 'Is eye to eye contact really threatening and avoided in social anxiety? An eye-tracking and psychophysiology study', *Journal of Anxiety Disorders*, 23(1): 93–103.

Yarbus, Alfred L. (1967) *Eye Movements and Vision*. New York: Plenum Press.

24

Expanding Cartographic Practices in the Social Sciences

Innisfree McKinnon

INTRODUCTION

We live in the age of mapping. More maps exist today than any other time in history, and this mapping explosion just continues to expand as digital technologies allow new maps to proliferate. The advent of micro-computing and the creation of web-based geographic information systems such as Google Earth™ and Yahoo® Maps has transformed the laborious process of creating paper maps, so that Internet users can query and transform online maps for their own purposes, creating new maps with the click of a few buttons. Accompanying this explosion in neocartography has been a related expansion in the use of geographic visualizations by researchers in a variety of fields. Computing now allows for the storage and manipulation of huge volumes of geographic data.

While these innovations have been noted, and their implications for the field of cartography considered, the focus on the mechanics of these changes has, in some ways, hidden a fundamental transformation that has begun in the way maps are made and used. The opening of the mapping process to non-experts, in combination with evolving epistemologies, has also created an opportunity for innovators within and outside academia to reconsider the authority and power of maps, and in the process develop new ways of creating and using maps. While these new mapping forms do not make up the majority of maps being created or used today, there is a new air of experimentation and cross-disciplinary collaboration that invites the consideration of maps across the social sciences and humanities.

Twenty years ago, many intellectuals would have considered maps only as a part of their efforts to critique or deconstruct the hegemonic aspects of such representations (Monmonier and de Blij, 1996; Harley, 2002). Maps have long been implicated in the controlling impulses of empire. While maps existed before the rise of empires, some have argued that mapping began to proliferate as part of the Enlightenment project of the scientific cataloging of the world in order to render it governable (Scott, 1999), a significant part of what Foucault (1976) termed 'governmentality.'

Critiques of the role of mapping in the fixing of territory, and the control of the populace have been widespread within geography and related disciplines (Schuurman, 2000). One response to these critiques has been numerous attempts to transform the practice of mapping, efforts that attempt to reclaim the power of the map, giving rise to a proliferation of new mapping practices such as counter-mapping (Harris and Hazen, 2006), critical geographic information systems (GIS), radical cartography (Mogel and Bhagat, 2007), and participatory GIS (Hallisey, 2005; Dunn, 2007).

In considering how maps and mapping relate to other sorts of visual research, it would be easy to focus primarily on the transformation of mapping practices by the new digital mapping techniques, namely the invention of GIS and the more recent combination of GIS and web-based software applications. This combination has created ubiquitous web mapping technologies such as Google Maps™ and mobile phones equipped with global positioning system (GPS) capabilities, allowing users to map and be mapped. Certainly these changes in how maps are created and consumed dominate both the economics of mapping and how maps intrude into the popular imagination. In fact, the rise of interactive web mapping has produced a significant amount of discussion among academics and activists about the possibilities of what has been called 'neocartography' to separate map making from its long association with the power of the state and projects of empire building (Crampton, 2009). However, to focus solely on these technical changes would be a mistake. Such a position would overlook the breadth of critique and theoretical innovation that has come from both activist neocartographers and researchers in a wide variety of disciplines such as political ecology, development

studies, history, women's studies, planning, and the arts.

These theoretical innovations have sought not only to advance technologically but to open mapping practices epistemologically to post-positivist methods of researching culture and society. In this chapter, we will consider both the possibilities created by new mapping technologies, and those created by new ways of thinking about what mapping is and what maps do, so that visual researchers might consider the variety of ways that maps and mapping fit into their own methods and epistemologies.

WHAT IS A MAP?

Before we can consider the uses of maps in visual research, it is important to consider what we mean when we use the term. One simple and broad definition might be that a map is a visual representation of spatial data. However, this definition would allow us to categorize a large number of visual representations as maps that are not commonly included in the category. Virtually any visual representation includes spatial data of one sort or another. A diagram of an atom communicates important spatial information, as does an image of a brain created by an MRI (magnetic resonance imaging) scan, but these would not commonly be thought of as maps. The frequent usage of the terms 'map' and 'mapping' as spatial metaphors makes a clear division difficult, since a wide variety of diagrams of social connections or virtual spaces are now frequently called maps.

Traditional maps attempt to show spatial relationships while minimizing distortions in spatial attributes—shape, area, direction, and distance. Some mapping techniques such as cartograms, however, rely on distortion to visualize something other than spatial relationships.[1] Other forms of geographic visualization may communicate spatial information, but rather than focusing on the allocentric perspective used in traditional paper maps, create an immersive first-person view (Wyeld and Allan, 2006). Some visualizations, now frequently called maps, display not Cartesian spatial relationships between objects or people, but rather the flow of materials or information through networks (Abrams and Hall, 2006).[2] These relational maps show topological connections rather than fixed spatial relationships. Examples of this type of topological map can be seen in attempts to diagram global economic flows. A similar form of topological map or diagram can be found in situational analysis (a form of grounded theory) developed by Adele Clarke (2005), which uses a process of diagramming to understand relationships between the huge numbers of codes created through grounded theory methodologies.

Another potential source of confusion in our attempts to define maps are the techniques used in aerial photography and remote sensing, which create photographic images, since traditionally maps were drawn representations of geographic relationships in which the cartographer selected out particular features to represent. In fact, John Kirtland Wright in his 1944 essay on the subjective nature of map making, asserts that we have thought of maps too readily as the equivalent of a photograph, 'the object before the camera draws its own image through the operation of optical and chemical processes. The image on a map is drawn by human hands, controlled by operations in the human mind' (Wright, 1942: 582).

Visual researchers are keenly aware of the dangers of relying on the mechanical nature of photography to bolster claims of objectivity. Wright himself goes on to explore the objective and subjective natures of both mapping and photography. Yet in the intervening 60-some years since the publication of his essay, the line between mapping and photography has been significantly blurred. Images that are first created with satellites and cameras or airplanes and lasers can be transformed through the digital technologies of GIS into something greatly resembling a hand-drawn map. Even remote sensing

images, which could nominally be considered photographs, are taken from an allocentric point of view, thus fitting most with our conceptions of maps, which can be linked to Haraway's critique of 'the god-trick of seeing everything from nowhere'(1988: 678).

It is challenging to come to a precise definition of a map under these conditions. An alternative definition of a map from Harley is 'a social construction of the world expressed through the medium of cartography' (2002: 35). However, this definition does not truly answer the question since it leaves us with the task of defining the medium of cartography. For the purposes of this chapter, we will consider a wide variety of visualizations with ties to traditional cartographic practice, including three-dimensional (3-D) maps, immersive visualizations, animated maps, and the works of radical cartographers. While many traditional cartographers might argue with this treatment, it will allow an overview of innovations in cartographic practice and consideration of the many ways that researchers use maps and mapping in their praxis.

MAPPING ACROSS DISCIPLINES

Visual researchers know that we are increasingly surrounded by an immense proliferation of visual images, including maps (Jay, 1994; Virilio 1994; Mirzoeff, 1999). Increasingly, the traditional divisions between maps and other images are blurred. This is largely the result of the convergence of various types of image-making practices that now principally take place through the use of digital technologies and the growing number of ways that maps are made and used.

The advent of the personal computer has opened up image making, including map making, to millions of computer users. New maps are created through the interactions of the map user with the vast database of geographic data stored on faraway servers, allowing map users to become map makers in ways never before possible. In fact, the 'mashup' of mapping technologies with social media sites has led to almost real-time creation of hazard and resource maps by groups of users. For example, during a rash of wildfires in Southern California in 2007, local news outlets, the *Los Angeles Times,* and radio station KPBS in the San Diego area, communicated with those impacted by the fires through the social networking site Twitter, constructing a map using the Google Maps interface along with reports from officials and also the stream of tweets produced by those on the ground (Figure 24.1) (Liu and Palen, 2010).

Increasingly, people's locations can be mapped through digital phones that include GPS locators. These technologies allow map users to become map makers as they inscribe their location and movements onto virtual maps. A large-scale example of this is the Open Street Map project (http://www.open-streetmap.org/), which seeks to create freely available street maps of the entire globe. These collaborative maps are created through a combination of existing free data from government sources, GPS traces, and local user knowledge.

Academia has experienced a similar flowering of map usage and map making across a broad range of disciplines in the humanities and social sciences (Craglia and Onsrud, 1998; Okabe, 2005; Conolly and Lake, 2006; Knowles and Hillier, 2008; Amoroso, 2010; Harmon and Clemans, 2010). Mapping is pervasive not only in the natural sciences (ecology and geology for example) but also in planning and design (Lejano, 2008). These fields have long had connections to cartography, and in fact the

Figure 24.1 Twitter-Google Maps Mashup, created by Virender Ajmani [Online]. Available from: http://blog.mibazaar.com/ [Accessed 23 September 2010]. Reproduced with permission

development of GIS technologies was largely fueled by innovators from these landscape management fields. However, the 'spatial turn' in the humanities and social sciences in recent decades has also led to increased awareness of the importance of spatial factors in cultural and social life across a wide variety of disciplines.

This, spatial turn, emerged from a wide variety of critiques that universalize narratives common to modernist discourses (Foucault, 1982; Soja, 1989; Lefebvre, 1991; Cox, 1997; Rose, 1997; Harvey, 1998). Feminist calls for situated knowledges and post positivist conceptions of science have also led to an increased interest in how 'things' (that is, people, cultures, and practices) vary spatially (Haraway, 1988; Harding, 1991; Katz, 1994; Rose, 1997). The spatial turn:

> involves a reworking of the very notion and significance of spatiality to offer a perspective in which space is every bit as important as time in the unfolding of human affairs, a view in which geography is not relegated to an afterthought of social relations, but is intimately involved in their construction. Geography matters, not for the simplistic and overly used reason that everything happens in space, but because where things happen is critical to knowing *how* and *why* they happen. (Warf and Arias, 2008: 1)

On a superficial level, this has led to an increase in the use of spatial metaphors in disciplines from cultural studies to history and sociology. Words like 'space,' 'place,' and 'mapping' are in common use across a wide range of disciplines. However, the wide acknowledgement of the significance of the spatial did not lead to an immediate, or wholehearted embrace of the actual, rather than metaphorical, practice of mapping among researchers concerned with contingent understandings of the world. In fact, for many associated with this spatial turn, the act of mapping was still linked with universalist and positivist conceptions of the world that were highly suspect (Cobarrubias and Pickles, 2008). When the links between cartography and projects of government control—both current and historical—were added to these misgivings, it is not surprising that many were deeply suspicious of the cartographic impulse. The drawing of a line on a map erased the flowing nature of existence and 'fixed' reality, creating one single, official version of reality.[3] Certainly, this is one way that maps have been used by states to fix their borders, and control their populaces.

However, this is not the only way to use or think about maps and mapping, and in recent years researchers from a broad spectrum of epistemological stances and disciplines have begun experimenting with using and creating maps to open up traditional cartographic practices to experiential and contingent visions, rather than fixing the world in one static representation (Jones and Evans, n.d.; Rocheleau, 1995; Cieri, 2003; Dennis, 2006; Duncan, 2006; Barnes, 2007; Kwan 2007; Middleton, 2010). These new cartographies are not limited to the work of academics. Artists and activists have also increasingly been swept up by the cartographic impulse, often subverting cartographic conventions or the authority of cartography.[4] A recent exhibit in London, titled 'Whose Map is it?' (Figure 24.2), featured the work of artists seeking to 'subvert the socio-political structures and cultural hierarchies that traditionally inform mapmaking' (Iniva, 2010).

This sort of mapping work often combines the impulses of academic research, art, and activism to produce new sorts of knowledge and commentary. The rest of this chapter will consider the breadth of these new cartographic practices in relation to academic research and the possibilities being developed through these practices. This will include a review of the types of maps being produced and an examination of research applications for maps.

USE OF MAPS IN RESEARCH

The use of maps and mapping in visual research can be divided into three

Figure 24.2 *River of Blood*. © 2010 Artist Susan Stockwell, is 8 meters wide and made from laser cut vinyl attached to the window. This work was exhibited at 'Whose Map is it? new mapping by artists,' Iniva (Institute of International Visual Arts), Installation view at Rivington Place. Photo: Thierry Bal. Reproduced with permission

basic groupings: the use of maps in collecting data; the use of maps in exploring data; and the use of maps in displaying data. These three basic divisions could be used to think about ways of using other mediums in visual research. The question then becomes: When might researchers consider using maps as part of their research plan? Many researchers in the social sciences and humanities use maps as part of the presentation of their data without much thought beyond the simple display of their research site or sites. These maps are usually called 'reference maps' and serve to help readers orient themselves to the study area. However, as visual researchers, we seek to take visuals, including maps, more seriously within the research process. So, beyond the rather simple task fulfilled by reference maps, what work can maps do in research?

The answer is usually that maps help us to understand geographic data. So, researchers who are asking research questions that include a significant geographic component may find themselves considering using a map to collect, explore, or display their data. This is why, despite serious epistemological misgivings, some researchers involved in the spatial turn have in fact found themselves turning to maps.

The spatial turn, at its most basic level, involves a rejection of some of the grand narratives of the twentieth century and the recognition of the ways that the social worlds we live in are impacted by spatial differences. For example, what David Harvey has called the spatial unevenness of global capitalism produces not a single path through time in which each state or each region passes, as through the developmental stages of growth from child to adult, but rather uneven development, in which some locations become sources of raw materials or cheap labor while others develop post-industrial service-oriented economies (Harvey, 2006). In asking geographic questions, we are not only considering where things occur, but also why and how they occur in one place and not another.

Almost any data we might collect would have some geographic component that could be recorded and mapped. If we conduct interviews or surveys responses, they could be mapped and organized geographically. If we follow the influence of global economic trends, their impact on local people and cultures could be mapped to show the rates of mortgage defaults in a particular state or city. If we conduct ethnographic research about the daily use of space by members of a community, this also could be mapped.

Cartographers commonly consider geographic data to have three components— space, time, and attribute. So while practically any data would have these components, depending on the design of our research, a map may or may not be a useful way to investigate or display your data. Asking geographic questions involves considering how things (attributes) vary, not only over time or because of other variables but also in space.

Even some studies that take seriously the impact of the spatial may not be best served by mapping. Studies that focus on place might focus on a particular location (a place is often defined by geographers as a space imbued with meaning by its users) and focus on the meaning of this place to people in it or how they use or create this place. For example, a researcher might study people in their homes or children in their classrooms. In such a study, the researcher is essentially limiting the scope of his data collection to one particular space in order to better understand how attributes of that space change over time, or are different from other places. Data from such a study might be better collected as written observations, drawings, photos, or videos of activities, rather than maps. Now activities within these spaces could be mapped, but the meaningfulness of such maps depends entirely on

the conceptualization of the study by the researcher.

Using maps in data collection

One obvious use of maps and mapping in the research process is in data collection. There are several methods that one might use to gather geographic data from research participants. These include soliciting spatial information from research participants, as well as the direct collection of geographic data by the researcher (for example, using GPS). During the 1960s interest in how people's internal conceptions of space varied from the Cartesian view we commonly see on maps led to a line of research on mental maps (Gould and White, 1986). Such studies often asked participants to draw a map of some space, such as their hometown or route to school. These maps were then analyzed both for their similarities and differences to Cartesian maps, but also to look for similarities among them with an eye to understanding more about how the human brain conceptualizes space.

While this type of mental mapping research has become less frequent, since behavioral geographers now focus on controlled experimental methods to understand mental processes, the drawing of mental maps continues to be a method used by some researchers (Müllauer-Seichter, 2003; Gieseking, 2007), particularly in relation to participatory research with youth (Al-Zoabi and Riyadh, 2002). Such mental maps are drawn, and then either collected and analyzed by the researcher, or discussed by the participants in order to identify places of common significance.

Base maps can also be used to solicit geographic information from research participants (Travlou, 2007). For example, Travlou et al. (2008) used street maps of two cities to solicit spatial information from teenagers. This type of data can be collected through the use of a paper map or digitally with the help of a handheld GPS. For example, the researchers at University College London, as part of the Children's Activities, Perceptions and Behaviour in the Local Environment (CAPABLE) project, ask the participants to carry a GPS unit with them as they travel (Figure 24.3). In similar projects, researcher and participant could visit a location together and record the coordinates during their visit. Using a paper or digital map to collect information from study participants has the advantage of avoiding a large investment of research funds in buying GPS units for participants to use. However, it assumes that participants are comfortable reading maps, and understand map conventions, and relies on their ability to accurately match their memories or perceptions of places with locations on the map.

Using maps for data analysis

As visual researchers, we know that images allow us to 'see' or understand our data in new ways. Visual representations do more than merely displaying what we already know; they are themselves a type of data and so produce new understandings. A major component of GIS is, in fact, not the visual display of research results, but rather the ability of GIS software to allow researchers to explore the spatial relationships of data from a variety of sources. The bringing together of disparate data sets can produce new insights and reveal relationships that otherwise might remain hidden.

In GIS analysis, data from disparate sources are brought together through the use of GIS software. GIS software differs from other types of graphical software in that data representations are given fixed geographic coordinates within a global reference system, allowing the software to compute spatial relationships between pieces of data. Within a GIS, a database with spatial coordinates for each piece of data is linked to a map, which displays these pieces of data. This has meant that GIS has a long history of association with quantitative spatial science (Goodchild, 1991; Openshaw, 1991; Pickles, 1994;

Lupton and Mather, 1997; Schuurman, 2000)—GIS software allows for the quick production of large numerical data sets detailing spatial relationships such as distances, areas, and densities. However, as Pavlovskaya (2009) points out, much of what GIS software produces is not quantitative but rather qualitative. One form of qualitative data produced by GIS is new visualizations—that is, maps.

In the 1990s, a surge of interest in using GIS to explore data and formulate hypotheses began. Exploratory spatial data analysis and geovisualization emphasize the use of GIS and other computerized visualizations as a way of data exploration and hypothesis building (Dodge et al., 2008). In these methods, rather than creating maps to visually display the results of research, digital tools are used by researchers to explore spatial relationships in the data. In this process, the researcher uses the software to create and explore numerous map iterations, displaying them immediately and interactively. Through this process new spatial relationships may be hypothesized. Then, if desired, statistical analysis can be performed to quantitatively verify the statistical likelihood of the relationship.

Researchers working with qualitative, and specifically visual, methods may be less interested in using these quantitative and statistical methods. However, some working with qualitative methodologies have begun to incorporate the use of GIS as a complimentary tool, rather than seeing GIS as inherently quantitative (Al-Kodmany, 2002; Jiang, 2003; Matthews et al., 2005; Kwan and Knigge, 2006; Cope and Elwood, 2009).

Academics working with ethnographic or mixed methods, for example, have found a variety of ways to incorporate mapping and GIS databases into their research. Rather than creating a map in order to tell one story, the multiple stories created through ethnographic research can be introduced into a GIS database along with quantitative data from official sources such as census or crime data (Pain et al., 2006; also see Collins

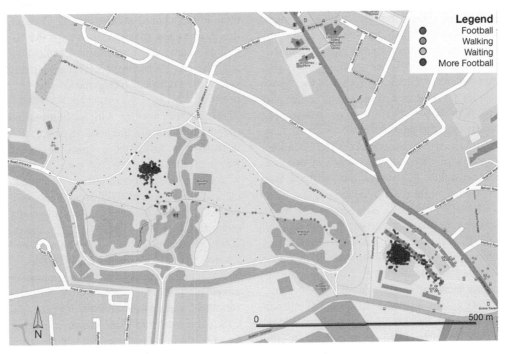

Figure 24.3 (a) Student with a GPS unit. Photograph by James Paskins, the EPSRC (Engineering and Physical Sciences Research Council)-funded project CAPABLE (Children's Activities Perceptions and Behaviour in the Local Environment). Reproduced with permission. (b) Resulting map of a child's activities created by James Paskins using OpenStreetMap map images (© OpenStreetMap contributors, CC-BY-SA). Reproduced with permission

(Chapter 25) in this handbook). Through the meeting of disparate data types, disjunctions and discontinuities may be revealed.

Rather than viewing these disjunctions as problematic, mixed methods researchers find that including multiple data types that are not always in agreement may produce new questions and push the research project in new directions (Knigge and Cope, 2006). As Knigge and Cope point out, rather than qualitative research simply pointing to opportunities for the eventual mapping of quantitative data for the purposes of data display, exploratory mapping of quantitative data can inform the researcher and provide background for further in-depth ethnographic research. They term this combination of ethnographic research and iterative visualization of spatial data 'grounded visualization.' An example of this type of research has been completed by Hurley et al. (2008). They examined the impacts of urbanization and gentrification on access to sweetgrass in South Carolina among African-American basket makers. By using a combination of historical data on land use, botanical literature, and the reports of basket makers, they were able to map access in a way that would not otherwise have been possible given limited research funding. By working with a combination of quantitative and ethnographic research they found that the changes caused by the development of residences with driveways and gates ('gated subdivisions') was surprisingly uneven, reducing sweetgrass habitat and access in some areas while in others sweetgrass was being conserved and access permitted.

Another common method of using maps and spatial representations in qualitative research is through participatory research with local communities (Al-Kodmany, 1999; Bojorquez-Tapia et al., 2001; McCall and Minang, 2005; Elwood, 2006; Stewart et al., 2008; Shearer and Xiang, 2009). Participatory methods invite the use of maps at all stages of the research process. As discussed above, maps may be used or created during data collection. Clearly, these maps may be presented

(perhaps in distilled or edited forms) to the community or in academic publications as part of the culmination of the research. However, a more extensively participatory project would likely involve the local community in the analysis process as well. In this case, community members could be involved in the iterative process of data visualization and exploration.

It should be pointed out that this type of data exploration is not limited to conventional GIS software, but rather may involve a wide variety of digital tools that produce visualizations. For example, several research groups have begun developing what Hudson-Smith (2008) terms 'the visual city': in other words, a visual representation of the built environment. The Centre for Advanced Spatial Analysis (CASA) has created a model of London using a variety of tools, including the 3-D capabilities of GIS software and the online visualization capabilities of Google SketchUp™ and Google Earth™ (Figure 24.4). A number of such digital spaces, or virtual models of cities, have been both created and used in research, primarily related to urban planning[5] (Howard and Gaborit, 2007; Thomas and Hollander, 2010).

Other researcher teams are working on creating large-scale immersive visualizations using stereoscopic projectors and goggles, large screens, and in some cases gloves or control wands to allow the researcher to interact with the visualization[6] (Shepherd, 2008). Currently, such visualizations require large sums of money and so their use has been limited to fields such as the earth sciences. However, as these technologies develop and costs are lowered there is no reason to think that they won't allow for similar exploration of cultural spaces.

Data display

Displaying geographic data can be considered the traditional role of maps.

Researchers who use cartography as part of their research practice, either through data

Figure 24.4   A 3-D model of London, created by the Centre for Advanced Spatial Analysis (CASA), University College London

collection or data analysis, still need to decide whether to include maps as part of their research output. If maps are to be included as one product of the project, then design decisions proliferate. The revolution in cartographic technology over the last 50 years has meant that technology has often outpaced cartographic theory, resulting in the proliferation of new types of maps before their effectiveness as visualizations has been assessed. The format and design of the map should be carefully considered in order to most effectively display the research findings.

Before examining various choices to be made by a researcher wishing to use cartography to display research findings, it is vital to point out that researchers who use cartography in their research process may choose

not to display or publish some or all of their maps. Recording spatial information about vulnerable people or social groups may provide valuable insights into their lives. However, as Packard (2008) argues in relation to participatory photographic methods, such research practices may also present limitations and ethical quandaries for researchers. Photography can be an intrusive act, and research participants could be put at risk by attempting to photograph dangerous situations or illegal activities. The collection of spatial data could similarly expose private or community-based knowledge to outsiders. This dilemma is common to researchers working with traditional communities for documenting a community's claims to traditional land rights. Documenting community members' use of resources is essential to legitimizing their legal rights to traditional lands. Resource use may, however, involve practices that have been made illegal by the enclosure of lands. Researchers working with homeless or other marginalized groups in urban settings may find themselves facing similar dilemmas. In some cases, researchers may choose not to publish maps with their research findings, or in some way limit the precision of their representations in order to protect community knowledge or sensitive personal information (VanWey, 2005; Wieland et al., 2008).

In making the decision to act as cartographer, the researcher takes on new dilemmas, both practical and ethical. Each cartographic choice—what to include or exclude and how to symbolize the material world—involves the practical limitations of the medium, but also carries with it political implications. If we take seriously McLuhan's proposal that 'the medium is the message,' then a map carries with it a particular set of implications (McLuhan and Lapham, 1994). Maps tend to be read as scientific and accurate, despite cartographers' understandings of the limitations and distortions of the medium.

The advent of GIS and the move of cartography into the world of computing has led some to minimize the role of art in cartography, but historically cartography was considered both a science and an art. Cartographic historian J. B. Harley encourages us not to think of maps as mirrors of the world but rather texts, which 'redescribe the world—like any other document—in terms of relations of power and of cultural practices, preferences, and priorities' (Harley, 2002: 35). In recent decades, some artists and academics concerned with spatial representation have taken on the role of cartographer to subvert the authority of the map, highlighting the art in cartography and frequently flouting mapping conventions (Thompson, 2009; Harmon and Clemans, 2010). For example, in her exhibit 'Macropus eugenii (tammar wallaby)'[7] Australian artist Perdita Phillips displaces wildlife mapping by placing the radio trackings of two tammar wallabies in an art gallery, questioning the divisions between the practices of art and those of science.

Even conventional cartographers acknowledge the dialectical tension inherent in map reading and interpretation. Behavioral geographers, and psychologists seeking to understand how people read and use maps, recognize that much of how people use maps is shaped by limitations in visual perception and cognition (Lobben, 2004). In other words, certain mapping conventions are the result of these limitations and likely to be universal across cultures. However, geographers also frequently lament the inability of the general public to understand many basic mapping conventions—the map illiteracy of their students. So clearly, many of the symbolic choices we make in order to make maps readable are, in fact, culturally specific—for example, symbolizing water with the color blue and danger with the color red.

In the following section, we will consider some of the strengths and limitations of various mapping mediums, with a focus on the desire of the cartographer to communicate something, some story about the world, through the map. This leads us to a discussion of what experiments have discovered, so far, about the limits of visual perception and cognition. This does not mean that we should ignore the cultural or textual aspects of map reading, but rather that both biological and cultural factors need to be considered. While some artists and radical cartographers (Mogel and Bhagat, 2007) seek to make maps that include confusion or fuzziness, to understand the impacts of such maps on their readers it is essential to first understand what evidence we have about how people read and understand maps. The emphasis in this chapter is on academic publications, but visual researchers may also generate research products that are displayed through non-traditional means such as personal websites and exhibits.

Although researchers in a number of fields are beginning to experiment with digital mapping mediums, most academic papers are still limited by the requirements of academic publishers to print maps, frequently in black and white. Paper maps, as many critical scholars have pointed out, simplify the world and fix objects in space, favoring representation of static landmarks over dynamic temporal processes. On a paper map, it is necessary to remove extraneous details in order to clearly symbolize a small number of variables. This limits what can be represented, but also offers an opportunity for the cartographer to focus the reader's attention.

Mapping conventions focus on eliminating anything that introduces misperceptions, or leads the reader to make erroneous conclusions, in relation to the information the map is seeking to communicate. For example, color ramps used in choropleth maps to shade areas in proportion to the variable being displayed are usually limited to five to seven shades because it has been found that map readers have trouble distinguishing more than seven shades (Krygier and Wood, 2005). Similarly, the introduction of many color variations, or strong contrast, may serve to distract or confuse the reader. Edward Tufte (1997), in his writings on visualizing data, calls this phenomenon the 'smallest effective difference,' meaning that visual displays should use subtle difference in tone, and thickness of lines, in order to avoid exaggerating distinctions in the data. As Tufte points out, often simpler is better in terms of communicating clearly.

Beyond the consideration of basic cartographic conventions, it is also important to consider the publication medium. As academic publishing has moved online, there has been an increase in the creation of digital maps in research. Although many of the maps now published online are dynamic or interactive in some way, static digital maps should be considered as well, since digital displays differ significantly from what is possible on paper.

Print maps are limited by the size of the printed page and resolution of the printer. However, print maps are frequently created in large scales—in the case of wall maps and many art maps, or at least in the case of atlases, in large-sized books. Print maps are often produced using the best-quality printing technology and the cartographer can control the details of the map's production.

Digital maps face additional, or perhaps different, limitations. Computer screens have until recently been limited in resolution to 72 pixels per inch although some screens now display up to 100 pixels and digital phones up to 160, whereas print media can accomplish 200 or more pixels per inch. This limits the clarity and precision of the map being displayed on the screen. High-quality print maps are often printed using offset printing, which avoids the issue of pixels altogether. Additionally, computer screens differ in their sizes and display specification and different Internet browser softwares introduce additional variations in the way that a map is finally presented. A full discussion of the issues involved in displaying and printing maps is not within the scope of this chapter, but researchers can consult general texts on cartography (for example, Brewer, 2005; Krygier and Wood, 2005; Peterson, 2009).

Cartographers working with digital maps must also learn the conventions of web designers: for example, learning to examine their maps through a variety of browsers and differing screen types and sizes. The popularization of web browsing through handheld devices such as cell phones further complicates questions of presentation. Map reading to a large degree relies on the ability of the reader to examine different portions of the map in relation to each other and so the tendency of small screens of handheld devices to show only portions of the map renders common map-reading tasks challenging (MacEachren, 2004).

Putting maps online, presents the opportunity to create interactive and animated maps. Although these maps are relatively common now and familiar to many users, the implications of these technologies in terms of legibility of maps is still being explored.

Well-known sites such as Google Maps™ and MapQuest™ provide users with the opportunity to manipulate maps as well as add their own content to online repositories. There are also a growing number of academic projects that attempt to make paper map archives available to larger numbers of researchers by creating interactive atlases or in other ways share spatial data with the public through interactive map interfaces. For example, the Center for Neighborhood Knowledge created and hosted by the University of California, Los Angeles, allows users to access and manipulate geographic data on California from a variety of sources (http://www.api.ucla.edu/). Such interfaces allow the user to manipulate various layers of data in a manner similar to conventional GIS software, although in a more limited fashion. This interactivity allows for the inclusion of many more layers of data and hands over some power to the user. Users are able to examine the map at varying scales and select variables to compare.

Historians have been increasingly involved in projects that work to place historical maps within a GIS system, georeferencing known points on these maps, allowing for temporal comparisons to be made (Knowles, 2002; Gregory and Ell, 2007; Knowles and Hillier, 2008). Often such projects include initiatives that make historical data available online such as the National Historical Geographic Information System (www.nhgis.org) or develop interactive online historical atlases, such as the China Historical GIS (www.fas. harvard.edu/~chigis/). Recent experiments with historical GIS even allow users to examine spaces through time by manipulating a temporal scale interface, often a slider-style button with a timeline.

These innovations provide many opportunities, but also complicate the ability of the cartographer to focus the user's attention on particular aspects of the data. Additionally, the cartographer must either use available software platforms with their conventions in terms of user interfaces, or take on the formidable task of either modifying existing software, or programming an interface specific to their application. Since existing software by and large has not emerged from academic applications, it may not be ideal for use in academic projects. On the other hand, using online interfaces could make research findings widely available beyond the limited audience of academic journals.

Another innovation available to the cartographer—similar to interactive maps, but with its own set of challenges—is the creation of animated maps. Numerous projects in recent years have worked on representing the passage of time in maps (Weber and Kwan, 2002; Miller and Bridwell, 2009; Lei and Church, 2010). One obvious method is through animation of the map. While not all map animations are temporal, this is the most common use of animation in mapping. Although map animations may seem an obvious choice for historians or other researchers wishing to represent changes in the use of space over time, there are still some questions about the best way to use animation in mapping. In general, research on the effectiveness of map animation has shown mixed results (Harrower and Fabrikant, 2008).

Map animations may reveal previously unknown spatio-temporal patterns, for example, or allow users to see general trends that would otherwise be difficult to grasp (Dorling and Openshaw, 1992). However, some research has shown that individual changes are likely to be more difficult to grasp in animated maps (Slocum et al., 2004). One way to deal with this issue is to allow users to pause and step slowly through each frame of the animation. This, though, means that mostly what users are experiencing is not an animated map, but rather a series of static maps, which may actually reduce the benefits of the animation. In such a case, users might learn more from the opportunity to examine each frame side by side, in what Tufte (1997) calls 'small multiples.'

Another step beyond the limitations of traditional two-dimensional maps—assisted by rapidly developing software—is the 3-D map, which in fact is most often a 2.5-D map. These representations use the principles of perspective to construct a map that appears three-dimensional while being viewed on a flat page or a flat computer screen. Many of these maps have the additional benefit of being interactive, allowing the user to rotate and change the position of their view. This is an interesting feature on Google Earth™, which allows the user to view the earth not only as a smooth marble but also with satellite imagery draped over topography and with 3-D models of buildings in many major cities.

Some cartographic researchers have noted that representing a three-dimensional world in 2.5-D may actually provide readers with more familiar visuals, thus making map reading easier (Robertson, 1990). While this may be true for some maps, many maps that use the 3-D capabilities of GIS software make use of the third dimension not to realistically model space, but rather to increase the number of variables that can be displayed on the map. For example, work by Mei-Po Kwan (2002) uses the third dimension to visualize the daily activities of African-American women in Portland, Oregon as they move through the city (available online[8]). This research showed that African-American women were spatially restricted in comparison to women of other ethnicities. These maps show the path an individual woman traveled, with a line gradually climbing off the flat page as time passes. Other visualizations create poles from points, walls from lines, and prisms from flat polygons in order to display additional variables. However, 3-D maps may introduce unintentional distortions. Comparing sizes and distances within such 3-D maps is considerably more challenging and care should be taken to minimize distortions (Shepherd, 2008).

INNOVATION AND PRACTICAL CONSIDERATIONS

While the combination of new technology and new epistemological perspectives has led to a small renaissance in mapping both within academia and among artists and activists, there are a number of limitations facing those of us attempting to use maps as a form of visual research. First, while technology provides an opportunity, becoming fluent with the rather complex software used in cartography can be a challenge for some academics. Although many visual researchers are relatively technologically savvy with photo- or video-editing software, learning to use GIS software can take a significant investment of time. Additionally, the most commonly used software, ArcGIS™ technology from ESRI, might be cost-prohibitive if a researcher does not have access through a university-wide license. There are low- or no-cost open-source software alternatives available, but they tend to have limited tools available or require additional technical skills to use. Certainly in the USA many private companies and government agencies currently use ESRI software, and most colleges and universities train students to use it, so it may be easier to find technical help and research assistants familiar with the ArcGIS® product. This leaves researchers with difficult choices in terms of affordability and accessibility versus ease of use and availability of technical support. Hopefully, as open-source options become more widely used, the functionality of these packages will expand, providing expanded access.

For those working with participatory methods the challenges of the digital divide can present additional roadblocks. Researchers collecting spatial information from local communities are often faced with difficult gaps in both technical knowledge and access that put the researcher in the role of cartographer and spatial 'translator.' In such situations, the researcher transforms local forms of knowledge into visualizations for the community (Roth, 2007; Collins (Chapter 25) in this handbook). The alternative, providing access and training to locals, might be considered the ideal in terms of a participatory methodology, but may not be practical given limited time and money. Additionally, local politics and institutions have a strong impact, either positive or negative, on the outcomes and impacts of participatory mapping projects (Elwood and Ghose, 2001; Ghose and Elwood, 2003).

Using mapping as a method of visual research is additionally challenging because theoretical concepts have tended to lag behind technological innovations. New visualization methods are driven largely by the commercial market and the work of neocartographers. Social scientists need to consider in a deeper way the implications of new visualization technologies for their research practices.

For example, the question of how to visualize uncertainty is an issue that researchers have sought to solve through new techniques. On a basic level, the problem is how to visualize an object on a map if there is uncertainty about the accuracy of the data in terms of locations or instances of the phenomenon being studied. On a traditional paper map, something either occurs or does not occur; there is no easy way to show an object or characteristic that cannot be directly and precisely measured. Placing a symbol on the map implies a level of certainty that may not be warranted. However, this provides an opportunity for researchers to develop new visualization methods and combine mapping with other research methods. Some research teams have created secondary maps that accompany their primary visualization, indicating the level of certainty in the data at different points on the map (Deitrick and Edsall, 2008).

Other researchers have suggested that another way to visualize uncertainty and disrupt the perception of certainty in maps is through subverting official representations using artistic practices (Kwan, 2007). Researchers working in qualitative GIS maintain that the value in such methodologies is in the tension produced by the differing perspectives engendered by differing methodologies (Cope and Elwood, 2009). Thus, by including maps with conflicting information on them, the certainty of any one map is brought into question.

The tension in such works is produced in part at least by the interdisciplinary nature of such research, requiring researchers to either learn the research traditions and techniques of more than one discipline, or adapt to working in interdisciplinary teams with others who may have very different epistemological standpoints. Another danger of the renaissance in map making is that it is difficult to keep up with new developments and innovative work in multiple disciplines. As a result there is a tendency to reinvent the wheel in terms of the development of effective cartographic techniques.

However, this interdisciplinarity is also an opportunity for disciplinary cross-fertilization, which produces beautiful and innovative new work. In practical terms, it may be more productive for researchers interested in working with cartography to enlist the assistance of experienced map makers than to start from scratch in developing their cartographic skills. However, such collaborations require comfort with differing perspectives not only in research subjects but also among members of the research team.

CONCLUSIONS

Mapping is, in some ways, a natural addition to other visual research techniques, particularly with the recognition by many researchers of the influence of the specifics of space and place, thanks to the spatial turn. However, maps have traditionally had more in common with drawing than photography or videography. Yet GIS, and related digital technologies, have pushed innovations in geographic visualization into the realm of computer and information science.

Taking on mapping as part of one's research practice involves a new set of technical skills, and requires careful negotiation of cartography's difficult history. Cartography's long association with science and empire has obscured its potential for productive alliance with visual research. Recent work in a variety of disciplines, spurred on by the spatial turn and new epistemologies of qualitative research, has produced new forms of research using mapping. Researchers across a variety of disciplines have been drawn to experimentation with these new cartographic techniques and epistemologies. While maps have traditionally been used to display spatial data, social science researchers also use maps to collect and analyze data. New visualization techniques such as animated and 3-D maps present opportunities for social scientists to innovate in terms of what can be represented via a map.

However, there is still much work to be done before these new beginnings produce a full revolution in the way that we think about and create maps. Digital map making technologies may require significant investments of time and money. Social scientists must also carefully consider the politics of representation; increasing numbers are choosing to wade into participatory methodologies or volunteered geographic information created by neocartographers in order to disrupt power differentials between cartographers and map users. Because of the complexity of new visualization technologies, in order to develop the full potential for mapping as a social science research tool, it will be necessary to develop new interdisciplinary connections between scholars from a variety of fields.

Now is a great time to incorporate cartography into your research. New cartographic technologies and epistemological developments have opened the possibilities of mapping as a research technique. More than ever before, social scientists are recognizing the value in thinking spatially and asking spatial questions. Using and making maps is a vital part of this spatial turn. Researchers who choose to experiment with mapping will find themselves in excellent company.

NOTES

1 One of the most compelling examples of this type of visualization can be found at www.

worldmapper.org. For a discussion of the creation of these cartograms, see Barford and Dorling (2008).

2 Also see the work of the Counter-Cartographies Collective on the flows of knowledge economies of the University of North Carolina: http://www.countercartographies.org.

3 For a discussion of conceptions of space and time in relation to this tendency, see Massey (2005).

4 Examples of this type of art work with mapping can be seen at the following websites: http://www.nienschwarz.com/; http://www.perditaphillips.com/; http://www.johnwolseley.net/; http://www.land2.uwe.ac.uk/; and http://aporee.org/maps/work/projects.php?project=jgrzinich.

5 Additional examples of the use of 3-D models in urban planning can be viewed at the Environmental Simulation Center website: http://www.simcenter.org/.

6 See also the W. M. Keck Cave for Active Visualization in the Earth Sciences at the University of California Davis: http://keckcaves.org/.

7 See Perdita Phillips' online gallery at www.perditaphillips.com and follow the path: archive > by theme > to map > *Macropus eugenii* (tammar wallaby).

8 This visualization of space-time paths of a sample of African-American women in Portland, Oregon (Kwan, 2002) can be viewed online at: http://www.geography.osu.edu/faculty/mkwan/Figures/Annals_links.htm.

REFERENCES

Abrams, Janet and Hall, Peter (eds.) (2006) *Else/Where: Mapping—New Cartographies of Networks and Territories*. Minneapolis, MN: University of Minnesota Design Institute.

Al-Kodmany, K. (1999) 'Using visualization techniques for enhancing public participation in planning and design: Process, implementation, and evaluation', *Landscape and Urban Planning*, 45(1): 37–45.

Al-Kodmany, Kheir (2002) 'GIS and the artist: Shaping the image of a neighborhood through participatory environmental design', in W. J. Craig, T. M. Harris and D. Weiner (eds.), *Community Participation and Geographical Information Systems*. London: Taylor & Francis. pp. 320–329.

Al-Zoabi, A. Y. and Riyadh, S. A. (2002) 'Children's "mental maps" and neighborhood design of Abu Nuseir, Jordan'. Paper presented at the Children and the City Conference, Amman, Jordan.

Amoroso, Nadia (2010) *The Exposed City: Mapping the Urban Invisibles*. London: Routledge.

Barford, Anna and Dorling, Danny (2008) 'Telling an old story with new maps', in M. Dodge, M. McDerby and M. Turner (eds.), *Geographic Visualization: Concepts, Tools and Applications*. Chichester: Wiley. pp. 67–107.

Barnes, A. (2007) 'Geo/graphic mapping', *Cultural Geographies,* 14(1): 139–147.

Bojorquez-Tapia, L. A., Diaz-Mondragon, S. and Ezcurra, E. (2001) 'GIS-based approach for participatory decision making and land suitability assessment', *International Journal of Geographical Information Science*, 15(2): 129–151.

Brewer, Cynthia A. (2005) *Designing Better Maps: A Guide for GIS Users*. Redlands, CA: ESRI Press.

Cieri, M. (2003) 'Between being and looking: Queer tourism promotion and lesbian social space in Greater Philadelphia', *ACME: An International E-Journal of Critical Geographies*, 2(2): 147–166.

Clarke, Adele E. (2005) *Situational Analysis: Grounded Theory after the Postmodern Turn*. Thousand Oaks, CA: Sage Publications.

Cobarrubias, Sebastian and Pickles, John (2008) 'Spacing movements: The turn to cartographies and mapping practices in contemporary social movements', in B. Warf and S. Arias (eds.), *The Spatial Turn: Interdisciplinary Perspectives*. Thousand Oaks, CA: Routledge. pp. 36–58.

Conolly, James and Lake, Mark (2006) *Geographical Information Systems in Archaeology*. Cambridge, UK: Cambridge University Press.

Cope, Meghan S. and Elwood, Sarah (2009) *Qualitative GIS: A Mixed Methods Approach*. Thousand Oaks, CA: Sage Publications.

Cox, Kevin R. (1997) *Spaces of Globalization: Reasserting the Power of the Local*. New York: The Guilford Press.

Craglia, M. and Onsrud, H. (1998) *Geographic Information Research: Transatlantic Perspectives*. London: Taylor & Francis.

Crampton, Jeremy W. (2009) 'Cartography: Maps 2.0', *Progress in Human Geography*, 33(1): 91–100.

Deitrick, Stephanie and Edsall, Robert (2008) 'Making uncertainty usable: Approaches for visualizing uncertainty information', in M. Dodge, M. McDerby and M. Turner (eds.), *Geographic Visualization: Concepts, Tools and Applications*. Chichester: Wiley. pp. 277–292.

Dennis, S. F. Jr (2006) 'Prospects for qualitative GIS at the intersection of youth development and participatory urban planning', *Environment and Planning A,* 38(11): 2039–2054.

Dodge, Martin, McDerby, Mary and Turner, Martin (eds.) (2008) *Geographic Visualization: Concepts, Tools and Applications*. Chichester: Wiley.

Dorling, D. and Openshaw, S. (1992) 'Using computer animation to visualize space-time patterns', *Environment and Planning B: Planning and Design* 19(6): 639–650.

Duncan, Sally L. (2006) 'Mapping whose reality? Geographic information systems (GIS) and "wild science"', *Public Understanding of Science,* 15(4): 411–434.

Dunn, Christine E. (2007) 'Participatory GIS—A people's GIS?', *Progress in Human Geography*, 31(5): 616–637.

Elwood, S. (2006) 'Beyond cooptation or resistance: Urban spatial politics, community organizations, and GIS-based spatial narratives', *Annals of the Associat-ion of American Geographers,* 96(2): 323–341.

Elwood, Sarah and Ghose, Rina (2001) 'PPGIS in community development planning: Framing the organizational context', *Cartographica: The International Journal for Geographic Information and Geovisualization* 38(3): 19–33.

Foucault, Michel (1976) *The Archaeology of Knowledge*. New York: Harper & Row.

Ghose, Rina and Elwood, Sarah (2003) 'Public participation GIS and local political context: Propositions and research directions', *URISA Journal* 15(2): 17–24.

Gieseking, J. (2007) '(Re)constructing women: Scaled portrayals of privilege and gender norms on campus', *Area*, 39(3): 278–286.

Goodchild, Michael F. (1991) 'Just the facts', *Political Geography Quarterly*, 10(4): 335–337.

Gould, Peter and White, Rodney (1986) *Mental Maps*. Harmondsworth: Penguin.

Gregory, Ian and Ell, Paul S. (2007) *Historical GIS: Technologies, Methodologies and Scholarship*. Cambridge, UK: Cambridge University Press.

Hallisey, Elaine J. (2005) 'Cartographic visualization: An assessment and epistemological review', *The Professional Geographer,* 57(3): 350–364.

Haraway, Donna (1988) 'Situated knowledges: The science question in feminism as a site of discourse on the privilege of partial perspective', *Feminist Studies,* 14(3): 575–599.

Harding, Sandra (1991) *Whose Science? Whose Knowledge?: Thinking from Women's Lives*. Ithaca, NY: Cornell University Press.

Harley, J. B. (2002) *The New Nature of Maps: Essays in the History of Cartography*. Baltimore, MD: Johns Hopkins University Press.

Harmon, Katharine and Clemans, Gayle (2010) *The Map as Art: Contemporary Artists Explore Cartography*. New York: Princeton Architectural Press.

Harris, L. and Hazen, H. D. (2006) 'Power of maps: (Counter)-mapping for conservation', *ACME: An International E-Journal of Critical Geographies*, 4(1): 99–130.

Harrower, Mark and Fabrikant, Sara (2008) 'The role of map animation for geographic visualization', in M. Dodge, M. McDerby and M. Turner (eds.), *Geographic Visualization: Concepts, Tools and Applications*. Hoboken, NJ: Wiley. pp. 49–66.

Harvey, David (1998) *Social Justice and the City*. Oxford: Blackwell.

Harvey, David (2006) *Spaces of Global Capitalism: A Theory of Uneven Geographical Development*. New York: Verso.

Howard, T. L. J. and Gaborit, N. (2007) 'Using virtual environment technology to improve public participation in urban planning process', *Journal of Urban Planning and Development—ASCE*, 133(4): 233–241.

Hudson-Smith, Andy (2008) 'The visual city', in M. Dodge, M. McDerby, and M. Turner (eds.), *Geographic Visualization: Concepts, Tools and Applications*. Chichester: Wiley. pp. 183–198.

Hurley, Patrick T., Halfacre, Angela C., Levine, Norm S. and Burke Marianne K. (2008) 'Finding a "disappearing" nontimber forest resource: Using grounded visualization to explore urbanization impacts on sweetgrass basketmaking in Greater Mt. Pleasant, South Carolina', *The Professional Geographer*, 60(4): 556.

Iniva: Institute of International Visual Arts (2010) *Whose Map Is It? New Mapping by Artists* [Online]. Available from: http://www.iniva.org/exhibitions_projects/2010/whose_map_is_it [Accessed 24 September 2010].

Jay, Martin (1994) *Downcast Eyes: The Denigration of Vision in Twentieth-Century French Thought*. Berkeley, CA: University of California Press.

Jiang, Hong (2003) 'Stories remote sensing images can tell: Integrating remote sensing analysis with ethnographic research in the study of cultural landscapes', *Human Ecology* 31(2): 215–232.

Jones, Phil and Evans, James (n.d.) *Rescue Geography* [Online]. Available from: http://www.rescuegeography.org.uk/ [Accessed 24 September 2010].

Katz, Cindi (1994) 'Playing the field: Questions of fieldwork in geography', *The Professional Geographer*, 46(1): 67–72.

Knigge, LaDona and Cope, Meghan (2006) 'Grounded visualization: Integrating the analysis of qualitative and quantitative data through grounded theory and visualization', *Environment and Planning A*, 38(11): 2021–2037.

Knowles, Anne Kelly (2002) *Past Time, Past Place: GIS for History*. Redlands, CA: ESRI, Inc.

Knowles, Anne Kelly and Hillier, Amy (2008) *Placing History: How Maps, Spatial Data, and GIS Are Changing Historical Scholarship*. Redlands, CA: ESRI, Inc.

Krygier, John and Wood, Denis (2005) *Making Maps: A Visual Guide to Map Design for GIS*. New York: Guilford Press.

Kwan, Mei-Po (2002) 'Feminist visualization: Re-envisioning GIS as a method in feminist geographic research', *Annals of the Association of American Geographers*, 92(4): 645–661.

Kwan, Mei-Po (2007) 'Affecting geospatial technologies: Toward a feminist politics of emotion', *The Professional Geographer*, 59(1): 22.

Kwan, Mei-Po and Knigge, LaDona (2006) 'Doing qualitative research using GIS: An oxymoronic endeavor?', *Environment and Planning A*, 38(11): 1999–2002.

Lefebvre, Henri (1991) *The Production of Space*. Cambridge, MA: Blackwell.

Lei, T. L. and Church, R. L. (2010) 'Mapping transit-based access: Integrating GIS, routes and schedules', *International Journal of Geographical Information Science*, 24(2): 283–304.

Lejano, Raul P. (2008) 'Technology and institutions', *Science, Technology & Human Values* 33(5): 653–678.

Liu, Sophia B. and Palen, Leysia (2010) 'The new cartographers: Crisis map mashups and the emergence of neogeographic practice. (Report)', *Cartography and Geographic Information Science*, 37(1): 69–91.

Lobben, Amy (2004) 'Tasks, strategies and cognitive processes associated with navigational map reading: A review perspective', *The Professional Geographer*, 56(2): 270–281.

Lupton, M. and Mather, C. (1997) '"The anti-politics machine": GIS and the reconstruction of the Johannesburg local state', *Political Geography* 16(7): 565–580.

McCall, M. K. and Minang, P. A. (2005) 'Assessing participatory GIS for community-based natural resource management: Claiming community forests in Cameroon', *Geographical Journal*, 171 (4): 340–356.

MacEachren, Alan M. (2004). *How Maps Work: Representation, Visualization, and Design*. New York: Guilford Press.

McLuhan, Marshall and Lapham, Lewis H. (1994) *Understanding Media: The Extensions of Man*. Cambridge: MIT Press.

Massey, Doreen B. (2005) *For Space*. London: Sage Publications.

Matthews, Stephen A., Detwiler, James E. and Burton, Linda M. (2005) 'Geo-ethnography: Coupling geographic information analysis techniques with ethnographic methods in urban research', *Cartographica: The International Journal for Geographic Information and Geovisualization,* 40(4): 75–90.

Middleton, Elisabeth Rose (2010) 'Seeking spatial representation: Reflections on participatory ethnohistorical GIS mapping of Maidu allotment lands', *Ethnohistory,* 57(3): 363–387.

Miller, H. J. and Bridwell, S. A. (2009) 'A field-based theory for time geography', *Annals of the Association of American Geographers,* 99(1): 49–75.

Mirzoeff, Nicholas (1999) *An Introduction to Visual Culture*. London: Routledge.

Mogel, Lize and Bhagat, Alexis (eds.) (2007) *An Atlas of Radical Cartography*. Los Angeles, CA: Journal of Aesthetics & Protest Press.

Monmonier, M. and de Blij, H. J. (1996) *How to Lie with Maps*, 2nd edn. Chicago, IL: University Of Chicago Press.

Müllauer-Seichter, Traude (2003) 'Rendimiento y utilidad de técnicas prestadas de la gergrafía humana: trabajando la percepción individual', *Revista de dialectología y tradiciones populares* 58(1): 47–70.

Okabe, Atsuyuki (2005) *GIS-Based Studies in the Humanities and Social Sciences*. Boca Raton, FL: CRC Press.

Openshaw, S. (1991) *'Commentary:* A view on the GIS crisis in geography, or, using GIS to put Humpty-Dumpty back together again', *Environment and Planning A,* 23(5): 621–628.

Packard, Josh (2008) '"I'm gonna show you what it's really like out here": The power and limitation of participatory visual methods', *Visual Studies,* 23(1): 63–77.

Pain, R., MacFarlane R. and Turner, K. (2006) 'When, where, if, and but: Qualifying GIS and the effect of streetlighting on crime and fear', *Environment and Planning A,* 38(11): 2055–2074.

Pavlovskaya, Marianna (2009) 'Non-quantitative GIS', in M. S. Cope and S. Elwood (eds.), *Qualitative GIS: A Mixed Methods Approach*. Thousand Oaks, CA: Sage Publications. pp. 13–37.

Peterson, Gretchen N. (2009) *GIS Cartography: A Guide to Effective Map Design*. Boca Raton, FL: CRC Press.

Pickles, John (1994) *Ground Truth: The Social Implications of Geographic Information Systems*. New York: Guilford Press.

Robertson, Philip K. (1990) 'A methodology for scientific data visualisation: choosing representations based on a natural scene paradigm', in *Proceedings of the 1st Conference on Visualization '90*. San Francisco, CA: IEEE Computer Society Press. pp. 114–123.

Rocheleau, Dianne (1995) 'Maps, numbers, text, and context: Mixing methods in feminist political ecology', *The Professional Geographer,* 47(4): 458–466.

Rose, Gillian (1997) 'Situating knowledges: Positionality, reflexivities and other tactics', *Progress in Human Geography,* 21(3): 305–320.

Roth, Robin. (2007) 'Two-dimensional maps in multi-dimensional worlds: A case of community-based mapping in Northern Thailand', *Geoforum* 38(1): 49–59.

Schuurman, Nadine (2000) 'Trouble in the heartland: GIS and its critics in the 1990s', *Progress in Human Geography,* 24(4): 569–590.

Scott, James C. (1999) *Seeing Like a State: How Certain Schemes to Improve the Human Condition Have Failed*. New Haven, CT: Yale University Press.

Shearer, K. S. and Xiang, W. N. (2009) 'Representing multiple voices in landscape planning: A land suitability assessment study for a park land-banking program in Concord, North Carolina, USA', *Landscape and Urban Planning,* 93(2): 111–122.

Shepherd, Ifan (2008) 'Travails in the third dimension: A critical evaluation of three-dimensional geographical visualization', in M. Dodge, M. McDerby and M. Turner (eds.), *Geographic Visualization: Concepts, Tools and Applications*. Chichester: Wiley. pp. 199–222.

Slocum, Terry, Sluter, Robert, Kessler, Fritz and Yoder, Stephen (2004) 'A qualitative evaluation of MapTime, a program for exploring spatiotemporal point data', *Cartographica: The International Journal for Geographic Information and Geovisualization,* (39)3: 43–68.

Soja, Edward W. (1989) *Postmodern Geographies: The Reassertion of Space in Critical Social Theory*. London: Verso.

Stewart, E. J., Jacobson, D. and Draper, D. (2008) 'Public participation geographic information systems (PPGIS): Challenges of implementation in Churchill, Manitoba', *Canadian Geographer—Geographe Canadien*, 52(3): 351–366.

Thomas, D. and Hollander, J. B. (2010) 'The city at play: Second Life and the virtual urban planning studio', *Learning, Media and Technology*, 35(2): 227–242.

Thompson, Nato and Independent Curators International (2009) *Experimental Geography: Radical Approaches to Landscape, Cartography, and Urbanism*. Brooklyn, NY: Melville House.

Travlou, Penny (2007) 'Mapping youth spaces in the public realm: Identity, space and social exclusion', in C. W. Thompson and P. Travlou (eds.), *Open Space: People Space*. London: Taylor & Francis. pp. 71–82.

Travlou, Penny, Eubanks Owens, Patsy, Ward Thompson, Catharine and Maxwell, Lorraine (2008), 'Place mapping with teenagers: Locating their territories and documenting their experience of the public realm', *Children's Geographies*, 6(3): 309–326.

Tufte, Edward R. (1997) *Visual Explanations: Images and Quantities, Evidence and Narrative*. Cheshire, CT: Graphics Press.

VanWey, Leah K., Rindfuss, Ronald R., Gutmann, Myron P., Entwisle, Barbara and Balk, Deborah L. (2005) 'Confidentiality and spatially explicit data: Concerns and challenges', *Proceedings of the National Academy of Sciences of the United States of America*, 102(43): 15337–15342.

Virilio, Paul (1994) *The Vision Machine*. Bloomington, IN: Indiana University Press.

Warf, Barney and Arias, Santa (2008) *The Spatial Turn: Interdisciplinary Perspectives*. New York: Routledge.

Weber, J. and Kwan. M. P. (2002) 'Bringing time back in: A study on the influence of travel time variations and facility opening hours on individual accessibility', *The Professional Geographer*, 54(2): 226–240.

Wieland, S. C., Cassa, C. A., Mandl, K. D. and Berger, B. (2008) 'Revealing the spatial distribution of a disease while preserving privacy', *Proceedings of the National Academy of Sciences of the United States*, 105(46): 17608–17613.

Wright, John K. (1942) 'Map makers are human: Comments on the subjective in maps', *Geographical Review*, 32(4): 527–544.

Wyeld, Theodor G. and Allan, Andrew (2006) 'The virtual city: Perspectives on the dystopic cybercity', *Journal of Architecture*, 11(5): 613–620.

WEBSITES AND BLOGS RELATED TO CARTOGRAPHY

This list includes just a few of the many websites and blogs related to neo-cartography, critical cartography, and participatory mapping. These sites are offered as potential starting points for researchers interested in exploring the potentials of such practices. This list is by no means exhaustive, but it will give the reader some idea of the range of work being done at the intersection of art, activism, and academia.

Barnes, Alison (2010) *St Bride's Library: Graffiti: Overground Archaeology or Environmental Crime?* [Online]. Available from: http://stbride.org/friends/conference/temporarytype/overgroundarchaeology [Accessed 4 October 2010].

Carr, Garrett (2010) *New Maps of Ulster: Making Maps...Looking at Maps: Mapping Blog*. [Online]. Available from: http://newmapsofulster.blogspot.com/ [Accessed 4 October 2010].

Coolidge, Matthew (2010) *The Center for Land Use Interpretation* [Online]. Available from: http://www.clui.org/ [Accessed 29 September 2010].

Counter-Cartographies Collective (2010) *3Cs: Counter-Cartographies Collective* [Online]. Available from: http://www.countercartographies.org/ [Accessed 29 September 2010].

Crowe, Jonathan (2010) *The Map Room: A Weblog About Maps* [Online]. Available from: http://www.mcwetboy.net/maproom/ [Accessed 4 October 2010].

de Soto, Pablo and Pello, David (2010) *Mapeando Asturias* [Online]. Available from: http://mapeandoasturias.info/ [Accessed: 29 September 2010].

del Río San José, Jorge (2010) *El mundo de los mapas* [Online]. Available from: http://www.orbemapa.com/ [Accessed 4 October 2010].

German Federal Cultural Foundation, Pro Helvetia, Arts Council of Switzerland and the Aargauer Kuratorium (2010) *MigMap: A Virtual Carography of European Migration Policies* [Online]. Available from: http://www.transitmigration.org/migmap/ [Accessed 12 October 2010].

Gorman, Sean (2006) *Off the Map* [Online]. Available from: http://blog.fortiusone.com/ [Accessed 4 October 2010].

Hessler, John (2010) *Warping History: Analytical Methods in Historical Cartography* [Online]. Available from: http://warpinghistory.blogspot.com/ [Accessed 4 October 2010].

Independent Curators International (2010) *Experimental Geography Exhibit* [Online]. Available from: http://www.ici-exhibitions.org/index.php/exhibitions/experimental_geography/ [Accessed 12 October 2010].

Jégou, Laurent (2010) *Le petit blog cartographique* [Online]. Available from: http://www.geotests.net/blog/ [Accessed 4 October 2010].

Light, Claire (2010) *atlas(t): mapping, landscapes, and you* [Online]. Available from: http://clairelight.typepad.com/atlast/ [Accessed 4 October 2010].

MapeándoNos (2010) *MapeándoNos: Patrimonio 2.0 y Cartografía Colaborativa* Available from: http://mapeandonos.net/ [Accessed 29 September 2010].

Nold, Christian (2005–6) *Greenwich emotion map* [Online]. Available from: http://www.emotionmap.net/ [Accessed 29 September 2010].

The Center for Urban Pedagogy (2010) *The Center for Urban Pedagogy* [Online]. Available from: http://www.anothercupdevelopment.org/ [Accessed 12 October 2010].

Participatory Geographic Information Systems (PGIS) in Visual Research

Daniel Collins

INTRODUCTION

In the digital age, interactive maps have become ubiquitous parts of our phones, automobiles, cameras, and hiking gear. Whereas maps were once the result of highly specialized and privileged procedures implemented by professional cartographers, and were instruments which wielded control and power (see also Innisfree McKinnon (Chapter 24), in this volume), they are now available to anyone with a computer hooked to the Internet. But with the increased use of digital mapping programs, new questions are being raised about access and interpretation. As visual researchers, we wonder how the widespread availability of tools that link data with maps that visually display information contribute to visual research?

One of the most compelling features of digital mapping tools is their potential to correlate and display text, images, and numbers within visually accessible data displays linked to physical space. In addition, digital maps may be scaled, altered, and shared. They have potential as tools that help visual researchers build a spatial context around what might otherwise appear to be unrelated or disparate localized data.

The attraction of digital mapping instruments for visual research is tied to the fusing of two key elements: spatial representation of a range of data and robust computerized databases, which may include numeric, text, audio, visual, or other types of digital data. A web-mapping application, such as the 'Map,' 'Satellite,' and 'Earth' views provided by Google Maps (see http://maps.google.com), gives every point on a digital map the potential to be linked to varieties of additional data. Images and other kinds of digital data may be bound together in scalable structures that encourage connections, correlations, and broad distribution.

Geographic information systems (GIS) help manage all this data. While we commonly think of these as sophisticated digital systems, approaches to collecting and managing geographical data have long been in use, and there are a number of companies producing such systems today. ESRI, for example, accounts for a large share of the GIS software market worldwide. ESRI defines GIS as:

A geographic information system (GIS) integrates hardware, software, and data for capturing, managing, analyzing, and displaying all forms of geographically referenced information.

GIS allows us to view, understand, question, interpret, and visualize data in many ways that reveal relationships, patterns, and trends in the form of maps, globes, reports, and charts.

A GIS helps you answer questions and solve problems by looking at your data in a way that is quickly understood and easily shared. (2010)

Computerized mapping tools can give a GIS visual power: maps can be drawn from the database, or alternately, data can be referenced from maps. When a database is updated, an associated map can be updated as well. Still, even a sophisticated GIS is only as good as the data it contains. While there is no denying the potential power of a GIS for integrating many kinds of data into a coherent visual system, a promising alternative to systems designed for the use of specialists is the evolution of participatory methods known generally as public participation GIS (PPGIS) or participatory GIS (PGIS in this chapter). PGIS projects are meant to promote community self-advocacy and local control, as well as to encourage knowledge production and access for community members by providing access to data and tools once considered unavailable to local organizations (Al-Kodmany, 2002; Knigge and Cope, 2006; Sieber, 2006).

In the following sections, I briefly review GIS and mapping in general and introduce a number of strategies for using maps in the humanities and social sciences. I also describe developments in participatory GIS, and discuss benefits of incorporating PGIS approaches in social research projects, where community members are given access to planning processes as well as to emerging and powerful mapping tools; I then present examples of PGIS projects developed for a variety of purposes. These summaries are intended to introduce readers to projects involving PGIS to demonstrate the broad potential for increasing community participation in data management and decision making.

As a deeper illustration of the power of PGIS, I share a case study describing my own work on the development of a PGIS system which employed a cultural studies approach to supplement the planning needs of the San Miguel watershed in southwest Colorado (Collins, 2009); I added to the conversation by layering local cultural practices on existing maps. The project strategy was designed to utilize the very instruments that reside at the core of many local planning processes—in this case, county GIS maps— to engage local residents in mapping the culture of that geolocated place. Using county maps as a base layer, I created additional layers tied to the underlying geographic locations of artifacts, including historic photographs, photographs and art work by local residents, as well as oral history and interviews with members of the community. Rather than excluding the local, personalized, and subjective aspects of the experiences of individuals and communities, the use of a GIS in participatory decision making and land-use planning processes was supplemented by the addition of visual techniques to highlight important cultural practices.

VIEWS OF MAPS AND MAPPING PROCESSES

We go about our daily business, as individuals and as members of various communities, in the spaces that are the raw material for maps. And, we may transform those geolocated *spaces*, through our own actions and interactions, into *places* of community. Cartography can represent space by literally reflecting 'the lay of the land.' Until recently, most significant mapping efforts were directed by dominant institutions and groups that defined, researched, and/or managed spatial contexts, and their outputs became expressions of institutional power and control of knowledge (Harley, 1989; Crampton, 2001; Kitchen and Dodge, 2007). Consider, for example, the development of the 'grid' system typically used in many US cities in the planning process. This system, the Public Land Survey System (PLSS), was originally conceived by Thomas Jefferson:

> ... shortly after the Revolutionary War, when the Federal government became responsible for large areas west of the thirteen original colonies. The government wished both to distribute land to Revolutionary War soldiers in reward for their service, as well as to sell land as a way of raising money for the nation. Before this could happen, the land needed to be surveyed.
>
> The Land Ordinance of 1785 which provided for the systematic survey and monumentation of public domain lands, and the Northwest Ordinance of 1787 which established a rectangular survey system designed to facilitate the transfer of Federal lands to private citizens, were the beginning of the PLSS. (NationalAtlas.gov, 2010)

This system is still in use today and has been applied to purposes far beyond its original design: for example, in planning, land management, or energy policy. These data are also available for public download (see http://www.blm.gov/wo/st/en/prog/more/gcdb.html).

Modern maps that are considered authoritative documents—especially those used for planning, navigation, resource allocation, etc.—are typically the result of huge amounts of processed data such as this, derived from large-scale data-gathering instruments and procedures including satellite-born cameras, political polling, voter registration, tax records, census data, property values, environmental assessment reports, crime statistics, and the like (Dorling et al., 2006). Data collected in this way are stored in large databases, and tied to physical spaces as geographically referenced datapoints. Referred to as 'geocoding,' this process matches up the attribute data to a 'basemap,' which

allows it to be displayed in visual form (Jardine and Teodorescu, 2003). As GIS data have been increasingly linked to sophisticated but readily available mapping software, much of the analysis is output directly in the form of maps and map-layers. This allows users to visualize patterns and relationships from the beginning of the research process; it has also led to a blurring of the distinction of a GIS as solely the underlying raw data, and many now use the terms 'GIS' and 'computer mapping' interchangeably (Jardine and Teodorescu, 2003: 6).

Large GIS's are often managed by a variety of agencies, both public and private, for an increasing number of applications in government, education, and industry, and increasingly in public/private partnerships (Ghose, 2007: 1961). Other well-known and publicly-available examples (to name but a few) are:

- the *US Census* (http://factfinder.census.gov/home/saff/main.html?_lang=en)
- the *CIA Factbook* (https://www.cia.gov/library/publications/the-world-factbook/index.html)
- the *UN Environment Programme* (UNEP, see http://geodata.grid.unep.ch/).

In commercial use, the Multiple Listing Service (MLS) in the USA now links geographic information to real estate sales information and public records, to provide agents, buyers, sellers, and financiers with a full picture of property history and transaction information (DeLorme, 2010). More commonly, anyone can 'Google' a street address and discover satellite photos, topographic features, or directions for walkers, bicyclists, drivers, or those taking public transport.

The use of GIS applications by government agencies to map social (or anti-social) behaviors continues to be a largely centralized enterprise, and conclusions based on such data sources are often guided by post-positivist and reductionist views on the nature of what constitutes reality. For example, historical data on burglaries committed in an area may also be tagged with data such as day, time, location, frequency, and even weather, and used to generate predictions on

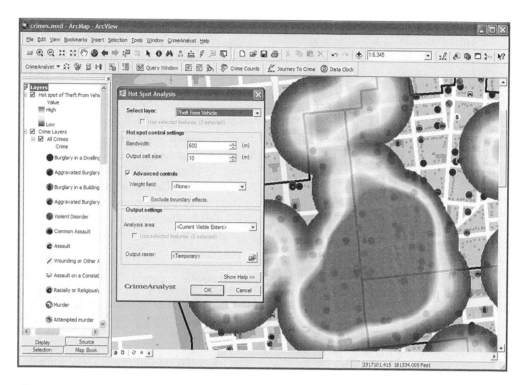

Figure 25.1   Fear of crime. Using so-called 'hot spot mapping,' this GIS software helps to identify and analyze high-risk areas

Source: http://www.geo-comm.com/geolynx_crimeanalyst.html

the probability of future burglaries in a neighborhood, and public safety resources allocated accordingly (Steinberg and Steinberg, 2006).

In addition to its use in localized planning and decision making, a GIS can be a useful tool for qualitative research and inductive theory building. Knigge and Cope made the case for creating locally-*grounded* explanations that aid theory building, by combining 'everyday experiences and actions' with 'data about the social world.' They commented:

> Displaying quantitative spatial data in a variety of ways may reveal patterns, and statistical analysis may reveal correlations, but it is often the case that explanation (and thus theory building) is grounded in the experiences of real people living through specific conditions and they are in many ways the "experts", even if their explanations

seem to be at odds with other sources of data. (2006: 2028)

Articulating alternatives to traditional centralized approaches, Steinberg and Steinberg argued that spatial information provided by GIS can also be employed in more inductive approaches to research. Patterns visible in spatial data can be powerful aids in developing theory when exploring emergent themes drawn from existing social data (78–94). They outlined strategies for integrating spatial concepts into social science research and pointed out that GIS provides a wide range of opportunities for examining relationships in space, often by focusing on information not traditionally considered:

> Because a GIS can integrate data from a variety of sources, it allows the researcher to develop a holis-

tic view of the many different contextual variables that may be important in addressing a particular social issue or research question. (2006: 37)

In the case of mapping incidents of crime (mentioned earlier), for example, a map-making process that integrates multiple vectors—demographic data, *income*, environmental factors, education, *and* crime statistics—may be more useful in long-term efforts to eradicate crime. If the goal is to actually improve the conditions on the ground, map-making efforts should not simply be a catalog of spatial/temporal incidents. Armed with a range of 'contextual variables,' it may be possible to identify root causes rather than to simply visualize symptoms (Steinberg and Steinberg, 2006).

Maps are also increasingly being seen to represent socially constructed views of *place* (Crampton, 2001; Kwan, 2002). In his seminal essay (Crampton, 2001: 240) on critical mapping, Harley (1989) pointed out that, whatever else they are, maps are never value neutral; they are active agents that can help to preserve the status quo or catalyze change (14). In a book review in the *Annals of the Association of American Geographers*, Aberley and Herlihy noted:

As most geographers today are quick to acknowledge, "map power" has long been controlled by the dominant societies of the world who portray and interpret cartographic information in terms of their own privileged perspectives, often for their own economic gain. Geographers are equally aware that indigenous peoples' oral, action-based knowledge of the environment is seldom represented in these dominant forms of mapping. (1994: n.p.)

A number of theorists have discussed embedded ideologies inherent in maps, or as Harley referred to them, the 'second text within the map' (1989: 9), and have shown how maps may misrepresent, distort, or even deliberately skew representations of reality through decisions made and techniques used by map makers (Wood, 1992; Dodge and

Kitchin, 2000: n.p.; Kwan, 2002; Pickles, 2004; Dorling et al., 2006). For example, the choice of method used to produce a flattened representation of three-dimensional (3-D) space, known as a map projection, will result in certain predictable visual distortions. The projection of a global map that most of us are familiar with is the Mercator projection of longitude and latitude; the resulting representation displays India as a much smaller land mass than Greenland, while in physical reality, it is seven times larger (Dorling, 2007: 0013). Dorling pointed out that, when applied to analysis of global disease:

The world distribution of malaria shown on a conventional map gives the impression that the global distribution of clinical episodes of Plasmodium falciparum malaria is confined to a much smaller proportion of the earth's surface than is actually the case.

And users, too, will filter messages portrayed by a map and draw conclusions based on their own frames of reference (Becker, 2007: 93–94). 'The power of maps is diffuse, reliant on actors embedded in contexts to mobilise their potential effects' (7); in increasingly pluralist societies, geographic information and mapping can help communities coalesce by delivering useful and usable data, informing both human and spatial relations (Craig and Elwood, 1998; Al-Kodmany, 2002). Mapping this data and visualizing these relations can also add form to individual and collective realities, and stimulate interest in further investigation (Aberley, 1993). Indeed, geosocial visualizations can incorporate diverse cultural, political, ideological, class, or gender views that may act as counter-narratives to those produced by centralized and powerful political or scientific organizations (Kwan, 2002). Approached as place-based technologies with a strong participatory component, digital maps may be used to foster a shared sense of place among people, improving programs and outcomes by encouraging cooperative problem-solving.

PARTICIPATORY GIS (PGIS)

Encouraging public participation by providing access to localized data and encouraging cooperative planning processes have not been actively pursued until recently:

Increasingly, urban planning activities in the United States are undertaken through a local governance model in which public/private collaborative partnerships are prioritized and the rhetoric of citizen participation is strongly echoed.... [T]o facilitate this... a range of "public participation GIS" (PPGIS) initiatives have taken place, providing grassroots, inner-city neighborhood-based citizen groups (hence forth called "community organisations") with equitable access to spatial data and GIS-based analysis. (Ghose, 2007: 1961)

There are compelling reasons to consider PGIS approaches as alternatives to traditional institutional planning based on depersonalized and summarized data leading to generalized conclusions. Feminist GIS researchers, for example, have taken issue with positivist approaches that ignore subjective differences related to culture or gender, stripped of locally situated experience (Kwan, 2002: 646–648). Kwan also noted:

the representational possibilities of GIS can be used for enacting creative discursive tactics that disrupt the dualist understanding of geographical methods where visual images, words, and numbers are used together to compose contextualized cartographic narratives in geographical discourse. (2002b: 272, as cited in Knigge and Cope, 2006: 2023)

PGIS methods can provide various opportunities for engaging communities in decision making. Among the benefits provided by a PGIS project are:

1 Incorporating community-based knowledge as data.
2 Integrating and contextualizing complex local spatial information.
3 Allowing participants to dynamically interact with input, and to analyze alternatives.
4 Empowering individuals and groups to pursue joint knowledge production and improve community access.

A key objective of PGIS approaches is the empowerment and inclusion of marginalized populations—those with little voice in the public arena (Sieber, 2006; Ghose, 2007). At Oregon State University, Professor Dawn Wright directed a group of graduate students in an advanced GIS program to create a community-focused PGIS website in the fall of 2007 (see http://kilumijimforest.wordpress.com/about-us/ for more on this project). The focus was to provide a platform for collaborative efforts directed toward forest conservation of an important bird habitat in Cameroon, bringing together the local community and conservation groups. Through this work, the *Public Participatory GIS for The Kilum-Ijim Community Forest Project (Kilum-Ijim Forest Project)*, they found that when given the opportunity, community members could be directly involved in many aspects of the PGIS process, including the production of sketch maps, physical models, digital maps, databases, and other spatial and visual tools. Their focus was to promote networking with existing programs and agencies who could provide access to pertinent available data, technical skills, and financial or educational resources. The project successfully led to the development of a sophisticated PGIS user community who could help foster awareness of available technical resources previously unknown (Kilum-Ijim Forest Project, 2007).

PGIS researchers can rely on spatial data that they collect or create themselves, or they may use publicly accessible data or some combination of the two. The last two decades have led to a significant increase in the availability of public data, including those mentioned earlier, as well as more at local levels, through clearinghouses and web-based services, a process Tulloch (2007) described as *Democratization*. In this way, a PGIS has the potential to encompass a vast range of visual, qualitative, and quantitative data available to build foundations of knowledge for bridging gaps and misunderstandings between social scientists and the individuals and communities with which they work.

Whereas some PGIS developers seek to empower individuals, others may be managed by groups intending to shift power in their favor (Sieber, 2006; Tulloch, 2007). Ghose discussed issues relating to the need for effective network formation to address issues of imbalances in scales of power:

> Network formation at multiple scales, with powerful actors located in public and private sectors, is crucial for grassroots community organizations in their urban revitalization activities, as they occupy a subordinate position in terms of political and economic hierarchies.... [because] scalar politics can enable one to control material resources and can legitimize one's own viewpoint and agenda over that of others. (2007: 1962; citing Kurtz, 2002)

PGIS, then, is not so easy to pin down; rather, the methods, tools, and intentions of a project, including the nature and degree of actual community involvement, will depend on a project's context, the project goals, resource availability, degree of cultural acceptance at the local level, etc. The conversation around attempts to define what PGIS is or isn't 'is being mutually constituted, locally and philosophically' (Sieber, 2006: 492–494).

EXAMPLES OF PGIS

In the paragraphs that follow I present brief, suggestive but not exhaustive, examples of PGIS programs. They range from a slightly less conventional 'pin in the map' way to convert crime data into a visual/spatial representation, to more innovative collaborations between artists and policymakers. No technological development is, by itself, empowering. Clearly, all PGIS projects are not 'bottom-up' ways of empowering individuals or communities; some may be simply sophisticated manipulations 'buying' compliance. On the other hand, there are interesting examples of public involvement in decision making in which map making is a helpful and perhaps necessary step.

There are also object lessons where the best laid plans of researchers and communities are simply overridden by policymakers with agendas of their own. Another developing model is 'hybrid' PGIS in which participatory elements in a public planning process are integrated into a more traditional and authoritative presentation 'owned' by bureaucratic institutions. These brief examples were influential in my own project design process.

City of Bradford, UK: fear of crime

A group of urban geographers at the University of Leeds set about to map the *fuzziness* associated with the *fear of crime* (see Figure 25.2). By 'fuzziness' the authors were referring to what they called 'vernacular geography,' which they defined as having some or all of the following characteristics:

1 Continuousness: when boundaries are difficult to define because the measurements of an entity produce a gradient (the start of a mountain, for example).
2 Aggregation in the categorization of variables: where discrete boundaries actually represent the average location of a geographically varying set of continuous or discrete variables that are binned together for descriptive convenience (soil types, for example).
3 Averaging: where discrete boundaries are actually an average of time or scale, varying geographical boundaries (the definition of a col, the boundary of a river, etc.).
4 Ambiguity: where boundaries are tied to linguistic factors (for example, 'high' crime areas) (Waters and Evans, 2003: n.p.).

Using maps to track something as intangible as fear required some innovative techniques. Areas associated with crime are not necessarily bounded by identifiable landscape, but they are usually diffuse and have different levels of intensity depending on the individual. The researchers settled upon the metaphor of the *spray can* as an appropriate tool to *tag* those areas in the neighborhoods that individuals associated with high levels of crime (Waters and Evans, 2003). Local users in the City of Bradford, UK were asked to 'spray' a map to indicate areas where they felt there was a 'fear of crime.' This input was translated into a series of 'density maps' that were correlated with particular neighborhoods and actual crimes (Waters and Evans, 2005: slide 20).

South Africa: post-apartheid land reform

David Weiner and Trevor Harris (2003) collaborated with a rural South African community to capture local knowledge of perceived landscape boundaries in GIS format. They examined the role that GIS played in how

people viewed, exploited, and managed their physical resource base. The research included not only PGIS techniques but also implementation of a community-integrated GIS. Weiner and Harris emphasized non-hegemonic ways of knowing and provided conceptual and methodological guidance for integrating local community knowledge with geospatial technologies. While their work provided a useful roadmap to others interested in applying PGIS techniques, they highlighted the point that impacting local policy was difficult to sustain, in their experience, because of personnel changes and shifting national policies in post-apartheid South Africa. To be blunt, the good wishes and research processes of social scientists and community members may be overridden by policymakers—no

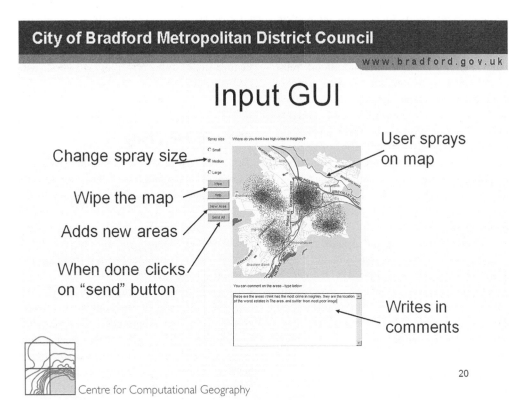

Figure 25.2   Fear of crime. In this graphical user interface (GUI), local users in the City of Bradford, UK 'spray' a map to indicate areas where there is a 'fear of crime.' This input is translated into a series of 'density maps' that can be correlated with particular neighborhoods and actual crimes (Waters and Evans, 2005, slide 20)

matter what technologies are employed (Weiner and Harris, 2003).

Chicago, Illinois: neighborhood planning and the arts

In his study, 'GIS and the artist: Shaping the image of a neighborhood in participatory environmental design,' Kheir Al-Kodmany (2002) used geospatial technology, in conjunction with a graphic artist, to help a local Chicago neighborhood group to work cooperatively with public officials to improve neighborhood safety. Al-Kodmany reported on ways that a GIS and an artist played interdependent roles in a community planning process. The GIS provided community leaders, planners, architects, and designers with an interactive visual representation of the neighborhood as a *space*, and helped to create sample design prototypes in relation to their geographic context. The artist, on the other hand, translated neighborhood residents' ideas of the neighborhood as a *place*, with ascribed social meanings, into quick sketches, merging their ideas and thoughts into a shared neighborhood vision. Together, the GIS and the artist provided ways for residents to visualize past, present, and future neighborhood conditions, and enabled them to express a greater voice in the design of their neighborhood. Al-Kodmany defined public participation as a key component of environmental planning and design. He also pointed out, however, that planners and designers may not be equipped with tools or techniques needed to achieve meaningful public collaboration. The study reinforced the view that being able to visualize architectural and social change is a key component in public participation.

Neighborhood revitalization

Sarah Elwood and Helga Leitner (2003) critically examined the role of geographic information systems used by neighborhood organizations in planning and revitalization efforts in US inner cities. They argued that the use of GIS is related to marked changes in the roles and responsibilities of neighborhood organizations and is part of a neoliberal policy agenda that expects them to play an increasing role in neighborhood revitalization. Drawing upon research about neighborhood organizations in Milwaukee, Minneapolis, and St. Paul, the team showed how the spatial knowledge and revitalization strategies produced by these organizations frequently reflect and reinforce those promoted by the state. In other words, they also caution that all so-called 'bottom-up' strategies are not necessarily empowering but may instead be ways of producing compliance. At the same time, they observed that some neighborhood organizations construct alternative knowledge through their use of GIS and employed alternative visions of neighborhood revitalization as they navigated the tensions between community visions and state priorities (Elwood and Leitner, 2003).

Aboriginal mapping

'First Nations' in British Columbia (BC) and elsewhere in Canada have been using GIS to manage land and resources and other traditional perspectives on *place*. Two 'First Nations' tribes, the Squamish and the Lil'wat, based north of Vancouver, BC, have utilized GIS for their tribal needs and applications. During a conference focusing on Native American traditions and GIS mapping, Chrystal Nahanee of the Squamish Nation provided details on the process they followed for adopting GIS to meet tribal needs, and she discussed projects to develop comprehensive parcel maps, emergency planning, and resource maps with up-to-date land cover data. Tracy Howlett of the Lil'wat Nation described participatory mapping exercises for developing traditional lands inventory and parcel maps. Both speakers emphasized the importance of *growing* the technology from within the tribes, without the use of external consultants; for example, Howlett described ways that using 3-D maps helped achieve visual understanding of digital data by community members. Another tribal representative described the Aboriginal Mapping Network (AMN, 2009), a website that provided the ability to network indigenous communities that are otherwise professionally and geographically isolated. Using the website, participants were able to share best practices, leading to development of an interactive online GIS toolkit (Laituri, 2006: n.p.).

HYBRID FORMS OF GIS/PGIS

Though the history of GIS is still in process, with the development of new user-friendly applications for PGIS, improvements in communications technology, and the near-universal accessibility of the Internet (through public institutions if not at home), it is now reasonable to assume that a significant population of users can participate in studies seeking *community-grounded* data for GIS mapping projects. In many recent mapping projects a hybrid approach has been used. Large-scale (macro-level) data are combined with fine-grain (local-level) data collected via participatory processes. For example, the US Bureau of Land Management (BLM) in Southwestern Colorado (Montrose Office) has worked on including social and economic information into their GIS mapping strategies when evaluating the biophysical processes on a landscape. By soliciting input from local citizens, the BLM planned to build maps that would provide a deeper understanding of how the general public interacts with public lands.

Rather than following a participatory model, however, the data from this participatory GIS mapping exercise are expected to 'be integrated into a more "top-down" mapping model (SIMPPLLE) developed by the US Forest Service (Maggie McCaffey,

Montrose Interagency Fire Education Specialist, personal communication).'[1]

Another example of a hybrid GIS mapping project that combined 'top-down' and 'bottom-up' approaches is a 2005 study by Richardson and Peyser (2006). The researchers used a multi-layered GIS mapping system to develop a 12-part conservation strategy for the lesser prairie chicken. In the course of their study they proposed three key principles:

- First, the trustworthiness of the data—e.g. layers of land classifications, land ownership, grazing leases, and oil and gas development information that the stakeholders believed to be true.
- Secondly, the transparency of the system—the graphic images were easy to read, the ways the data were combined and manipulated were understandable.
- Thirdly, the accessibility of the system—participants could debate and adjust key parameters, including habitat quality boundaries and land classifications.

The authors emphasized the importance of including 'non-science perspectives' and 'on-the-ground knowledge':

Early on, stakeholders expressed different perspectives about the causes of the decline in the habitat and the species. These perspectives were particularly related to the Prairie-chicken habitat characteristics, impacts from oil and gas development, and the natural and human caused reasons for decline in good habitat (e.g. drought vs. Development and human encroachment). Some felt it particularly important to incorporate 'on-the-ground' knowledge and cutting edge research, while others felt strongly that decision-making should include only the best scientific information already published. It was challenging to include non-science perspectives and to convince technical experts to value local perceptions in the decision-making process. The participants all agreed that the process should not rely on the generation of new scientific information already published. In cases where participants questioned data or their use, the negotiating process was sufficiently flexible to allow for joint fact-finding and the verification of on-the-ground effects of different conservations strategies. Further, the system was designed to protect confidential information about bird nesting and lek2 locations on private land (Richardson and Peyser, 2005: 22–26).

RECENT DEVELOPMENTS IN GIS AND PGIS

Professional mapping products like ArcGIS and open-source products such as GRASS GIS—used by professional geographers, urban planners, and cartographers—are rapidly being supplemented and even displaced by an explosion of tools made available through the Internet and personal computing devices. Global positioning systems (GPS) are now widely available on personal cell phones, digital cameras, and automobile navigation systems. Individuals who have no interest in mastering the technical features of GIS may simply use an inexpensive digital camera that has GPS built in. Many of the newer 'point and shoot' cameras can provide GPS coordinates and time stamps that simplify the process of geocoding and organizing photographs. Coupled with social networking applications, participants can upload their own photos to a preconfigured website. PGIS researcher Andrew Clark solicited participants for a study involving individuals with disabilities, and the aging. By using geotagged data collected through cell phones, he invited people to submit photographs they had taken. The indexed tags are consistent with broader government data sets in Australia, so Clark and his team could link individual photographic data with 'official' data, where it was mapped and sorted again. 'Essentially,' wrote Clark (2009), 'the site organizes information spatially, thematically, and temporally [sic].'

New approaches that combine the power of social networking with digital mapping are being explored. The practice of geocoding images (in particular) and uploading them to websites has exploded in the past 2 years. While photo archiving sites such as Flickr, Picasa, and Photobucket are well known, we are seeing increasing numbers of application programming interface (API)-driven[3] sites that enable other features such as image processing, extensive annotation, geocoding, and map-based display. For example, www.Panoramio.com, an image archiving site, has a very clever interface for geolocating images. The company was acquired by Google Inc. in 2007, and the application features a seamless process that takes a user from the uploading of photos, to a tagged photo archive, to their linkage and display on Google Earth (available for download at http://www.google.com/earth). While these applications are not in themselves 'research,' they may provide a range of visual data of interest to researchers.

CASE STUDY

My family has lived in the mountains, high mesas, towns, plateaus, and riverbanks of the San Miguel River watershed in Southwestern Colorado for well over a century. The area, to quote local author and eco-educator Pam Zoline, 'has its head in the clouds and its feet in the desert.' In its journey from far above the tree line, the San Miguel River plummets through forests of subalpine fir, blue spruce, and quaking aspen, traverses broad plateaus of pinyon pine and Utah Juniper, and cuts deep canyons into the red rock of the Colorado Plateau.

I used GIS mapping, as a component of visual, place-based research, to capture the personal histories and cultural practices of the current inhabitants of the watershed (Collins, 2009). Utilizing inductive *participatory* methods, my study focused upon the subjective perceptions and qualitative understandings of individuals, and the cultural life of the communities that dot the watershed. The goal of the *Interactive Watershed* project has been to integrate the typical day-to-day planning needs of the region with the desire for a broader conversation about the culture of place. The research methodology employed was a mixed-methods approach following the specific principles of *participatory action research* (PAR) (Hult and Lennung, 1980; Reason and Bradbury, 2001; Dick, 2002; McNiff, 2002). Their approaches to action research involves systematic cyclical method of planning, taking action, observing, evaluating (including self-evaluation), and critical reflection in a series of generative research cycles (O'Brien, 2001; McNiff, 2002). It is closely related to the notion of formative summative evaluation developed by Michael Scriven (1967).

The study proceeded from the assumption that to understand a given phenomenon I needed to become even more fully embedded in the community—and the natural environment of which it is a part. I was, by definition, a full participant in the process—not a neutral observer. In contrast to more positivist approaches, it was crucial that I maintained flexibility in interacting with (other) participants and remained sensitive to the overarching effects of the environmental and social context.

A test of the PAR methodology is the degree to which there is an improvement of the *performance quality* of the community or an area of concern (Hult and Lennung, 1980; Reason and Bradbury, 2001; Dick, 2002; McNiff, 2002). The PAR approach has a goal of addressing an identified problem in a workplace or community—for example, reducing the illiteracy of students through use of new strategies (Quigley, 2000). In my study, I sought to identify and raise awareness of hidden or suppressed aspects of community knowledge about *place*. I used PAR and PGIS as collaborative and complementary methods to demonstrate new ideas and implement action for change involving direct participation in a dynamic research process; at the same time I monitored and evaluated the effects of the investigator's actions with the express aim of improving practice (Hult and Lennung, 1980; Checkland and Holwell, 1998; Dick, 2002). At its core, PAR methods are a way to increase understanding of how change in one's actions or practices

can mutually benefit a community of practitioners (Carr and Kremmis 1986; Masters, 1995; Wadsworth, 1998; McNiff, 2002; Reason and Bradbury, 2001).

Participatory research is designed to address specific issues identified by local people, and the results are directly applied to problems at hand. The process is not about a researcher investigating her or his own practices, but is rather a dynamic circle of co-researchers, mostly non-academic, sharing a commitment to social change in a particular situation. The circle is dynamic partly because members of the project choose their own level of involvement. In this sort of *participatory* action research, all participants are considered equal, whether they are formally trained researchers or members of the community (Andrews, 2003). There is a collapse in the usual distinction between *subject* (the researcher and her research) and the *object* (the study participants). The subject/object of the work is generated and guided by the participants using visual, audio, and textual materials produced by and communicated to each other.

Maps for community action

While PAR provided a methodology for community involvement and commitment, PGIS provided the framework for mapping and redistributing the information assembled by the group. While public input is routinely solicited for planning processes in places like the San Miguel River watershed, one problem is the lack of scope of the discussion. Among policymakers and planners, there may be acknowledgement of the *cultural* dimension—that is, the importance of artifacts, personal expressions, historic and current events—that gives character and meaning to place. But culture is impossible to quantify and difficult to present and thus remains on the periphery, separate, or more or less irrelevant to the conversation that drives typical day-to-day planning—for example, zoning, infrastructure, environmental impact, and budgetary concerns. From a practical stand-point, this is completely understandable. But when the fabric of place is defined by subtle cultural practices, approaches are incomplete that do not account for the presence and importance of culture at par with environ-mental, economic, and social concerns.

Once County Commissioner approvals were secured, I began investigating the online GIS hosted by the San Miguel County Planning Department as a publically acces-sible portal and objective inventory docu-menting the culture of the place. I sought to demonstrate that the creative capacity and cultural history of the region could be repre-sented by a new *cultural* layer that exists simultaneously with the more typical layers currently maintained by the GIS office in the County Planning Office: for example, water quality, grazing units, or zoning. My assump-tion was that priorities of the planning proc-ess were driven largely by the visual representations of the official mapping docu-ments residing in the County Planning Office and in the County Courthouse; changing those views had the potential to change the planning process.

As a 'participant observer,' my roles have included, variously, that of sounding board, collaborator, and technical advisor. It soon became clear that I needed to develop user-friendly protocols to ensure participation and follow-through by the participants. However, early in the project I decided that the proto-cols of the Internet and standard hypertext markup language would be useful intermedi-ary tools for storing and sharing cultural artifacts and personal projects behind the mapping efforts. But I also determined that this level of technical prowess would make direct individual or community participation essentially impossible. As an alternative I created a 'wiki' or co-authored website. Participants in the Interactive Watershed project had the choice of either uploading their own information to the private wiki, or to simply to send text, images, or other media to me as e-mail attachments. One advantage of the wiki was that all the relevant documents associated with the study were available to participants as they were posted. This obviated the need to send separate attachments for each of the several docu-ments that were required for participation (for example, cover letter, questionnaire, IRB approvals). All members could upload their own data, add to the discussion, and down-load documents. If enlisted to help with management of the site, participants could also edit existing content on the wiki. The content of the wiki was, in turn, translated into a working website that reflected the scope of the project as a whole.

While the participants in the current project have not been able to directly input their cultural artifacts and practices into the County's GIS, they have generated meaning-ful and expressive forms using digital media that I was able to subsequently translate into the necessary protocols for the development of a shared cultural layer on the GIS. In future iterations of the Interactive Watershed, it will be possible for an individual to upload their data automatically with a user-friendly API. This, in turn, would be moderated by a group comprised of the researcher, individual citizens, and representatives of San Miguel County.

In private conversations and public meet-ings participants were invited to develop original projects that explored creative, expressive, and/or personal perspectives on life in the San Miguel River watershed. There were few rules regarding the structure or media employed for this project; however, projects needed to be able to be represented in some way on the Interactive Watershed website.

The path from initial presentation by the investigator to concrete contribution by par-ticipants on the web-based GIS took several steps. Participants were asked to complete a questionnaire regarding their background, comfort with computer-based applications, and views on regional watershed issues and the environment. They also participated in structured face-to-face interviews with me that employed local maps in an image elicitation process. These interviews were conducted under a variety of circumstances. Whenever possible, they were videotaped; in other cases, an audio recorder was used. In still others, written notes taken during the course of the interview were the only documentation employed.

Participants were asked to focus upon their daily experiences in the watershed and consider a range of possible ways to construct a creative response for the Interactive Watershed project. Through an elucidative process of sharing maps, photographs, and personal experiences, participants began to develop ideas about possible subject matter and creative approaches. This in turn provided the basis for a brainstorming exercise in which different media or topics were discussed.

In many cases, a key task for me was to assist the participant in eliciting *conscious* memories of place. Once a memory or set of associations was made explicit, a variety of self-documentation exercises were employed—such as generating lists of key words or descriptive phrases, creating diaries, making scrapbooks, maps, diagrams, or recordings of personal stories.

One particularly productive elicitation strategy employed various maps of the area; participants were asked to trace with their finger a pathway or place on a regional map that represented a favorite hike or destination. Both physical and online maps were helpful in targeting the site or sites to be used in their projects. For example, a favorite destination or hike could be located on the map. I would then encourage the participant to consider what was special about that place. While not universally applied, some participants found that the creation of collages, bubble diagrams, or 'mental maps' of the processes or features of place were helpful as intermediate steps between conscious identification of place and the development of a specific creative project that reflected that place.

After locating the participant's chosen area within the watershed and providing a few intermediary tools, they began to create

solutions that communicated their subjective experience of place. Participants chose multiple and sometimes unexpected pathways. One woman proposed a series of watercolor paintings of various 'put-in-points' along the San Miguel River that reflected her rafting experiences. Pen and ink served another artist for her Tree Portraits—a series of highly representational hand-drawn studies of ancient trees in the watershed (see Figure 25.5). Two participants focused on their ongoing work as poets, but gave special attention to the specifics of place expressed in their work. Still others chose photography to document place. In a number of cases, there was a juxtaposition made between historical and contemporary photos using the kind of 'rephotography' explored by documentary landscape photographers such as Mark Klett (see Chapter 6 in this volume).

As long-term residents of the area, a number of participants had preconceived notions of what they wanted to express. One woman began reflecting on the possibility of visualizing the geomorphology of the region, but then shifted gears and settled upon a topic nearer to her heart—the sacred ground of the Ute Indians that inhabited the Valley Floor just west of Telluride. Another participant, a novelist, had used the Telluride region as the setting for her fictional narratives dealing with relationships and general life experiences. Instead of generating new work, we agreed that her stories already provided a compelling perspective on place.

In addition to their individual projects, participants collaborated on the creation of the Interactive Watershed website itself. I helped develop a web-based method for capturing subjective responses to specific sites in the watershed. For instance, a fifth-grade teacher conducted a summer camp for kids at a site known as the Norwood Bridge on the San Miguel River. She documented children's responses to the river both qualitatively (for example, drawings, poetry, etc.) and quantitatively (measurements of water velocity, temperature, etc.) using digital photography and video. I then worked with her in formatting and uploading the documentation of her summer camp experience to her own personal watershed website which was then linked to the Interactive Watershed URL.

One of the serendipitous outcomes was the emergence of common themes among several of the participants' websites. A few examples: the high altitude gardening guide created by a local landscape architect shares a common interest in indigenous flora with the Bridal Veil Falls living classroom; the *venerable* trees documented by the former County assessor resonates nicely with the tree portraits created by the landscape painter; and the downtown history tour of the Town of Telluride finds further detail in the maps and discussion of the early 'Galloping Goose' rail service. These common themes became part of the basis for coding the documents. While these connections were 'discovered' during the actual research process, the resulting data, information, and artifacts were thoroughly and rigorously coded and analyzed to find patterns and themes (Gage and Kalari, 2002).

Different individuals dedicated varying amounts of time on my project: in general, minimum of 12 hours was expected of each participant on project-related activities, although many invested far more time. The number of hours per participant required includes the following:

- completion of online survey questionnaire (30 minutes);
- initial face-to-face interview (1–2 hours);
- contribution to wiki and development of Watershed website (6 hours);
- follow-up interview (1–2 hours); and

- group meetings involving all participants (pre and post; 3–4 hours).

Technical details: Building the GIS

The mapping of participant contributions to geocoordinates within a true GIS requires more than a passing acquaintance with the software. In my case, the authoring environment of choice was the ESRI product, ArcView 9.3.

My first step was to use ArcView to develop a georeferenced database of users' projects. As the database associated with the GIS version of the map evolved, types and sub-types were identified for more targeted searches. I employed the native row-and-column organization of GIS ArtCatalog (dBASE) instead of the branching categories typically found in social science coding processes (for example, categories, types, classes, etc.). While all project types in the Interactive Watershed GIS are *cultural*, I established a schema in which further detail is captured using the attributes of 'SUB_TYPE,' 'SUB_TYPE2,' etc.—the column headers commonly used in ArcCatalog. For example, a work of fiction is listed first as 'CULTURAL' (TYPE), second as a work of 'LITERATURE' (SUBTYPE), and third as 'FICTION' (SUB_TYPE2). In order to achieve a seamless integration with San Miguel County's GIS, I mimicked the organizational structure of their database (Figure 25.3). I added the additional columns for cultural subtypes and URLs (Internet addresses) associated with each cultural site.

The goal of generating a cultural knowledge base was well-served by this

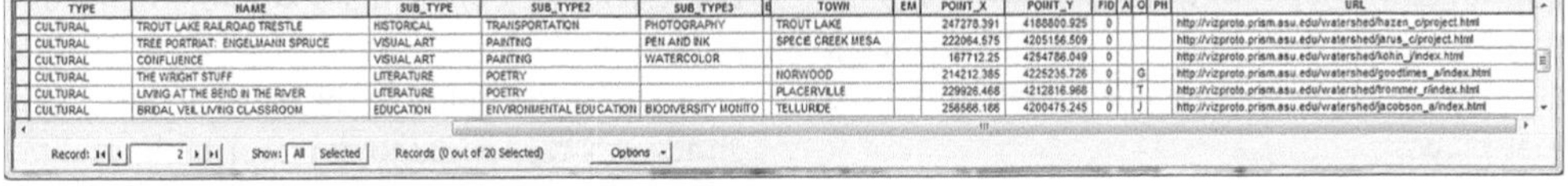

	TYPE	NAME	SUB_TYPE	SUB_TYPE2	SUB_TYPE3		TOWN	EM	POINT_X	POINT_Y	FID	A	G	PH	URL
	CULTURAL	TROUT LAKE RAILROAD TRESTLE	HISTORICAL	TRANSPORTATION	PHOTOGRAPHY		TROUT LAKE		247278.391	4188800.925	0				http://vizproto.prism.asu.edu/watershed/hazen_c/project.html
	CULTURAL	TREE PORTRAIT: ENGELMANN SPRUCE	VISUAL ART	PAINTING	PEN AND INK		SPECIE CREEK MESA		222064.575	4205156.509	0				http://vizproto.prism.asu.edu/watershed/arus_c/project.html
	CULTURAL	CONFLUENCE	VISUAL ART	PAINTING	WATERCOLOR				167712.25	4294786.049	0				http://vizproto.prism.asu.edu/watershed/kohin_i/index.htm
	CULTURAL	THE WRIGHT STUFF	LITERATURE	POETRY			NORWOOD		214212.385	4225236.726	0		G		http://vizproto.prism.asu.edu/watershed/goodlines_a/index.html
	CULTURAL	LIVING AT THE BEND IN THE RIVER	LITERATURE	POETRY			PLACERVILLE		229920.468	4212016.968	0		T		http://vizproto.prism.asu.edu/watershed/frommer_r/index.html
	CULTURAL	BRIDAL VEIL LIVING CLASSROOM	EDUCATION	ENVIRONMENTAL EDUCATION	BIODIVERSITY MONITO		TELLURIDE		256566.168	4200475.245	0		J		http://vizproto.prism.asu.edu/watershed/jacobson_a/index.html

Figure 25.3 Detail of GIS database developed by the author for the new cultural layer of the San Miguel County GIS

process. Moving from raw documents to participant-described projects featured on the web (a distillation process of its own), through coded types, and directly into the ArcGIS database was efficient and made sense with respect to the development of the final GIS product.

As indicated earlier, the proposal to include a cultural layer in the extant County GIS was approved by the San Miguel County commissioners. This, in effect, placed cultural practices on par with other regional features deemed worthy of mapping. From the beginning, I envisioned populating the cultural layer with many more entries. Ideally, this process will eventually be automated using API. The goal of allowing users to

upload their own data to a true 'participatory GIS' is now feasible technically—but there is a transition cost of between $4000 and $5000. Nevertheless, with the working prototype already embedded in the official GIS, I see raising these funds from the greater Telluride area as achievable.

OUTCOMES

At the conclusion of the project, I conducted summative interviews with participants using the website itself and other support materials as image elicitation tools. Participants and other community members were also

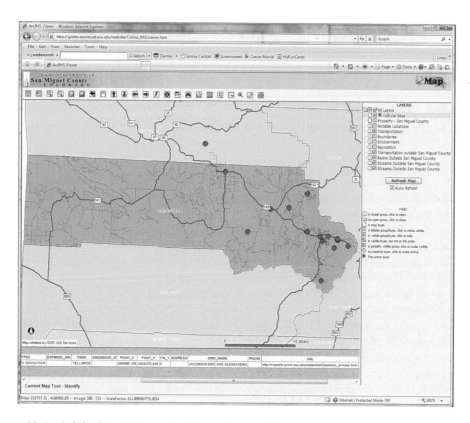

Figure 25.4 Original ArcIMS map by the author detailing the new cultural layer (shown by gray dots). This online version of the uses database protocols and map design appropriated from the San Miguel County GIS. An official enhanced version of this map will be published on the San Miguel County GIS in 2011

Figure 25.5   'Tree Portrait' by Christine Jarus. Watercolor and ink on paper

Source: http://vizproto.prism.asu.edu/watershed/jarus_c/project.html

invited to a community meeting. Using the documentation of the issues and themes gathered during the preliminary phases of the project, a final focus group discussion identified key ideas emerging from the study. Recommendations of the group were video-recorded and included an action list for further work in the area of watershed education and conservation.

While space doesn't permit a full description of the work of all 20 participants, suffice it to say that a wonderful array of artworks and creative projects were produced. The reader can find all of the artworks and related maps linked to the *Interactive Watershed* website.[4] One example, Chris Jarus's *Tree Portraits* (Figure 25.5), speaks to the deep *sense of place* that goes to the heart of the project.

IMPLICATIONS FOR VISUAL RESEARCH AND PLACE-BASED CULTURAL STUDIES

The use of PGIS in decision making or land-use planning could benefit greatly from an infusion of visual techniques and other cultural practices, including photo documentation, site-specific paintings, poems about place, and storytelling and narrative elements that would anchor the map representation within the lived experience of place.

Revealing hidden cultural practices via PGIS and the accompanying dialogue contributes to a close analysis of a region's cultural practices and reveals working intentions, shared experiences, lived realities, and understandings within particular cultural domains. As the recent literature suggests, a *participatory* GIS, with its mix of *hard* and *soft* data, provides a richer portrait of place—one that not only provides an accurate description of the physical location and its many features but also offers evidence of lived experience, creative interactions with the land, and public concerns. Rich descriptions of place come as no surprise to environmental writers, poets, visual ethnographers, and others who have always understood that it is the people who give form and substance to the contours of a place. Taken collectively, these approaches help to make manifest one's *sense of place* and provide a set of tools for helping to create, describe, and maintain a local culture.

NOTES

1   Personal e-mail correspondence, 5 March 2007.
2   A lek is a gathering of males, of certain animal species, for the purposes of competitive mating display.
3   An application programming interface (API) is an interface that a software program implements in order to allow other software to interact with it, much in the same way that software might implement a user interface in order to allow humans to use it.
4   Available from: http://vizproto.prism.asu.edu/watershed.

REFERENCES

Aberley, D. (1993) *Boundaries of Home: Mapping for Local Empowerment*. Gabriola Island, BC: New Society Publishers.

Aberley, D. and Herlihy, P. (1994) *Annals of the Association of American Geographers*, 84(4): 777–779. [Online]. Available from: http://www.jstor.org/view/00045608/di010513/01p0034l/0 [Accessed 9 February 2008].

Aboriginal Mapping Network (AMN) (2009) [Online]. Available from: http://www.nativemaps.org [Accessed 30 September 2009].

Al-Kodmany, K. (2002) 'GIS and the artist: Shaping the image of a neighborhood through participatory environmental design', in W. J. Craig, T. M. Harris and D. Weiner (eds.), *Community Participation and Geographic Information Systems*. London: Taylor & Francis. pp. 320–329.

Andrews, S. (2003) 'Examining participation and home-based technology integration with a high risk population'. PhD dissertation, Arizona State University, Tempe.

Becker, H. S. (2007) *Telling about Society*. Chicago, IL: University of Chicago Press.

Carr, W. and Kremmis, S. (1986) *Becoming Critical: Education, Knowledge, and Action Research*. London: Falmer Press.

Checkland, P. and Holwell, S. (1998) 'Action research: Its nature and validity', *Systemic Practice and Action Research*, 11(1): 9–21.

City of Memory (n.d.). *City of Memory: A Story Map of New York*. [Online]. http://www.cityofmemory.org/map/index.php [Accessed 9 February 2008].

Clark, A. (24 January 2009) *Looking for Strategic Advice*. [Online]. Message posted to *The Open Forum on Participatory Geographic Information Systems and Technologies*. Forum can be accessed at: http://dgroups.org/Discussions.aspx?c=98db21ba-861e-47bc-8491-ff972bb0b66d.

Collins, D. (2009) 'The interactive watershed: Mapping place-based cultural practices using geographic information tools'. PhD dissertation. Arizona State University, Tempe.

Cooke, L. (2009) *7000 Oaks*. New York: Dia Foundation. [Online]. Available from: http://www.diaart.org/ltproj/7000/essay.html [Accessed 4 May 2009].

Craig, W. and Elwood, S. (1998) 'How and why community groups use maps and geographic information', *Cartography and Geographic Information Systems*, 25(2): 95–104.

Crampton, J. W. (2001) 'Maps as social constructions: power, communication and visualization', *Progress in Human Geography*, 25(2): 235.

DeLorme (2010) *Advanced Mapping and GIS for Real Estate*, [Online]. Available from: http://www.delorme.com/byIndustry/realestate/default.aspx [Accessed 9 September 2010].

Dick, B. (2002) *Action Research: Action and Research*. [Online]. Available from: http://www.scu.edu.au/schools/gcm/ar/arp/aandr.html [Accessed 3 February 2007].

Dodge, M. and Kitchin, R. (2001) *Mapping Cyberspace*. London: Routledge. [Online]. Available from: http://www.UCM.eblib.com/EBLWeb/patron?target=patronandextendedid=P_170550_0and. [Accessed 6 October 2010].

Dorling, D., Barford, A. and Newman, M. (2006) 'Worldmapper: The world as you've never seen it before', *IEEE Transactions on Visualization and Computer Graphics*, 12(5): 757–764. [Downloaded: 11 June 2009].

Elwood, S. and Leitner, H. (2003) 'GIS and spatial knowledge production for neighborhood revitalization: Negotiating state priorities and neighborhood visions', *Journal of Urban Affairs*, 25(2): 139–157.

ESRI (2010) *What is GIS: Geographic Information Systems?* [Online]. Available from: http://www.esri.com/what-is-gis/index.html [Accessed 6 September 2010].

Evans, A. (2006) 'Fuzzy GIS and the fear of crime', in I. Heywood, S. Cornelius, and S. Carver (eds.), *An Introduction to Geographical Information Systems*, 3rd edn. Englewood Cliffs, NJ: Prentice Hall.

Evans, A. J. and Waters, T. (2007) 'Mapping vernacular geography: Web-based GIS tools for capturing "fuzzy" or "vague" entities', *International Journal of Technology, Policy and Management*, 7(2): 134–150.

Gage, M. and Kalari, P. (2002) *Making Emotional Connections through Participatory Design*. [Online]. Available from: http://www.boxesandarrows.com/view/making_emotional_connections_through_participatory_design. [Accessed 2 January 2009].

Ghose, R. (2007) 'Politics of scale and networks of association in public participation GIS', *Environment and Planning A*, 39(8): 1961–1980.

GIS Lounge (2001) *Crime Mapping: GIS Goes Mainstream*. [Online]. Available from: http://gislounge.com/crime-mapping-gis-goes-mainstream/[Accessed 17 August 2008].

Harley, J. B. (1989) 'Deconstructing the map', *Cartographica*, 26: 1–20.

Hult, M. and Lennung, S. (1980) 'Towards a definition of action research: A note and bibliography', *Journal of Management Studies*, 17(2): 242–250.

Jardine, D. and Teodorescu, D. (2003) 'An introduction to GIS: Concepts, tools, data sources, and types of analysis', *New Directions for Institutional Research*, 120(Winter): 5–13.

Kitchin, R. and Dodge, M. (2007) 'Rethinking maps', *Progress in Human Geography*, 31(3): 331–344.

Knigge, L. and Cope, M. (2006) 'Grounded visualization: Integrating the analysis of qualitative and quantitative data through grounded theory and visualization', *Environment and Planning A*, 38: 2028.

Kilum-Ijim Forest Project (2007) *Public Participatory GIS for The Kilum-Ijim Community Forest Project*. [Online]. Available from: http://kilumijimforest.wordpress.com/ppgis/ [Accessed 16 August 2008].

Kwan, M. P. (2002) 'Feminist visualization: Re-envisioning GIS as a method in feminist geographic research', *Annals of the Association of American Geographers*, 92(4): 645–661.

Laituri, M. (2006) 'Indigenous issues: Engagement and empowerment track'. *Summary of Conference: PPGIS 6th Annual Conference*, Vancouver, BC, Canada. [Online]. Available from: http://www.urisa.org/conferences/publicparticipation [Accessed October 2 2009].

McNiff, J. (2002) *Action Research for Professional Development*. [Online]. Available from: http://www.jeanmcniff.com/booklet1.html [Accessed 2 February 2007].

Margolis, E. (1994) 'Video ethnography', *Jump Cut*, 39: 122–131; Retreived as: *Video ethnography: Toward a Reflexive Paradigm for Documentary* from: http://courses.ed.asu.edu/margolis/videth2001.html [Accessed 11 January 2009].

Masters, J. (1995) 'The history of action research', in I. Hughes (ed.), *Action Research Electronic Reader*. The University of Sydney. Available from: http://www.scu.edu.au/schools/gcm/ar/arr/arow/rmasters.html [Accessed 2 February 2007].

NationalAtlas.gov (2010) *The Public Land Survey System (PLSS)*. [Online]. Available from: http://www.nationalatlas.gov/articles/boundaries/a_plss.html [Accessed 9 September 2010].

Nyerges, T. (2005) *Public Participation GIS Support for Transportation Improvement Decision Making in the Age of Instant Access*. [Online]. Available from: http://depts.washington.edu/pgist/doc/Nyerges_societies_cities_draft.pdf [Accessed 16 August 2008].

O'Brien, R. (2001) 'An overview of the methodological approach of action research', in R. Richardson (ed.), *Theory and Practice of Action Research*. João Pessoa, Brazil: Universidade Federal da Paraíba. [Online]. English version available from: http://www.web.ca/~robrien/papers/arfinal.html [Accessed 21 June 2008].

Participatory Design (6 May 2009). In *Wikipedia, the Free Encyclopedia*. Retrieved from: http://en.wikipedia.org/wiki/ Participatory_design.

Pickles, J. (2004) *A History of Spaces: Cartographic Reason, Mapping, and the Geo-coded World*. London: Routledge.

Quigley, B. (2000) 'The practitioner-researcher: A research revolution in literacy?', *Adult Learning*, 11(3): 6–8.

Reason, P. and Bradbury, H. (eds.) (2001) *Handbook of Action Research: Participative Inquiry and Practice*. London: Sage Publications.

Richardson, R. and Peyser, J. (2006) 'Collaborative approaches to using geographic information systems in science intensive resource management planning: Implications for practice from the lesser prairie-chicken working group'. Unpublished paper presented at the ACSP Conference, Ft. Worth. [Online], Available from: http://web.mit.edu/dusp/epp/music/pdf/richardson.pdf [Accessed 16 August 2008].

Salling, M. (2005) 'The 2005 PPGIS Conference: Raising questions on the interaction of GIS and the public'. Lecture presented at the PPGIS Conference, British Columbia. [Online]. Available from: http://www.urisa.org/conferences/publicparticipation [Accessed 28 December 2008].

Scriven, M. (1972 [1967]) 'The methodology of evaluation', in R. W. Tyler, R. M. Gagné and M. Scriven (eds.), *Perspectives of Curriculum Evaluation, Vol.1.* Chicago, IL: Rand McNally. p. 102.

Sieber, R. (2006) 'Public participation geographic information systems: A literature review and framework', *Annals of the Association of American Geographers.* 96(3): 491–507.

Steinberg, S. and Steinberg, S. (2006): *Geographic Information Systems for the Social Sciences: Investigating Space and Place.* Thousand Oaks, CA: Sage Publications.

Tulloch, D. (2007) 'Many, many maps: Empowerment and online participatory mapping', *First Monday,* 12(2). Available from: http://firstmonday.org/issues/issue12_2/tulloch/index.html [Accessed 16 August 2008].

Wadsworth, Y. (1998) 'What is participatory action research?', *Action Research International* (Paper 2). [Online]. Available from: http://www.scu.edu.au/schools/gcm/ar/ari/p-ywadsworth98.html [Accessed 21 June 2008].

Waters, T. and Evans, A. J. (2003) 'Tools for web-based GIS mapping of a "fuzzy" vernacular geography'. [Online] Available from: http://www.geocomputation.org/2003/Papers/Waters_Paper.pdf [Accessed 2 October 2009].

Waters, T. and Evans, A. J. (2005) 'Mapping the fear of crime: Web-based GIS solution to capturing 'fuzzy' geography'. [Online]. Available from: http://gislearn.org/presentations/05-1/05-1.ppt [Accessed 2 October 2009].

Weiner, D. and Harris, T. (2003) 'Community-integrated GIS for land reform in South Africa', *URISA Journal,* 15: (APA II). [Online]. Available from: http://www.urisa.org/Journal/protect/APANo2/Weiner.pdf [Accessed 9 April 2009].

Wood, D. (1992) *The Power of Maps.* New York: The Guilford Press.

26

Numbers into Pictures: Visualization in Social Analysis[1]

John Grady

INTRODUCTION

Howard Wainer in *Picturing the Uncertain World* uses Figure 26.1, 'Confidence in Institutions,' to illustrate a fine point of graph design. The chart, which appeared in the *New York Times*, nicely resolves the problem of the 'distracting legend':

> In 1973 Jacques Bertin, the maître de graphique moderne, explained that when one produces a graph it is best to label each of the elements in the graph directly. He proposed this as the preferred alternative to appending some sort of legend that defines each element. His point was that when the two are connected you can comprehend the graph in a single moment of perception as opposed to having first to look at the lines, then read the legend, and then match the legend to the lines. (Wainer, 2009: 96)

The designer Ben Schott achieves this goal, as Bertin advises, by labeling each of the lines in the chart. Even better—because this is a trend line with lots of data points where

the lines cross—the author labels the lines twice, on each side of the chart. Wainer does not tell us where the data in the chart comes from, nor does he comment on the pattern it suggests: a general decline in confidence in four of the five institutions and an upward, albeit volatile, trend in only one, the military. There is no need, however, to fault him for giving the data short shrift. After all, his focus is on how to chart information, not the information itself.

Nevertheless, American sociologists will readily recognize that the data comes from the General Social Survey (GSS),[2] and might then be drawn to the stories that could be told with the graph, which is why it appeared in the *New York Times* in the first place. The responses to the questions about confidence charted in Figure 26.1 refer to only five of the 13 major institutions that the GSS includes in its, now, every other year survey.[3] When combined with additional information derived from the GSS and other sources, these

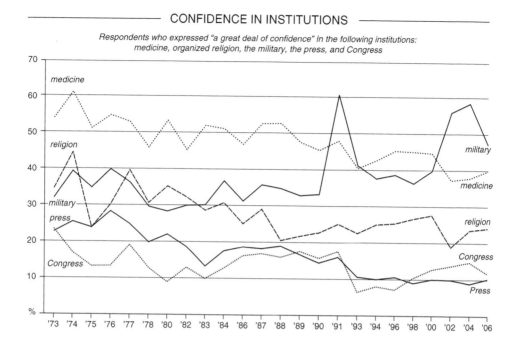

Figure 26.1   A graph taken from the 'News of the Week in Review' section of the 25 February 2007 issue of the *New York Times*. Designed by Ben Schott

Data source: General Social Survey (GSS), USA. Reproduced with permission.

responses suggest a steady and startling erosion of American public life over the last 35 years. This conclusion is not new and echoes both pundits of the left and right but, unlike their opinions, the data from the GSS is more reliable and less susceptible to transitory shifts in political enthusiasm. *To tell this story adequately, however, we must understand the data; and understanding data requires that we first see it, visualizing it in ways that reveal its patterns.*

In this chapter, I demonstrate that making good and imaginative choices in visualizing evidence enables us to see what these questions, concerning confidence in 13 of America's most important institutions, the responses to them, and the array of numbers they generate, portend about the directions that the lives of Americans may be taking. While surveys like the GSS do provide evidence that social bonds might be fraying, a closer look at this data by sociologists yields a more modulated view. These GSS researchers, however, have not identified any

specific factors that are consistently associated with an overall decline in institutional confidence, with the possible exception of generational change. Nor have they pinpointed a social process that could explain why confidence should vary from one generation to the next. This chapter will conclude by identifying just such a mechanism and thereby demonstrate that the craft of visualizing data is essential for social analysis. Enlisting the cognitive competency of the eye in this manner leads us to make a surprising discovery that is obscured by more conventional statistical analysis.

In any event, the major goal of this chapter is to show how ubiquitous graphic design software—to wit the 'chart wizard' function in Microsoft Excel®—can be used to construct many, if not most, of the graphs needed to analyze and display simple descriptive statistics like those in Figure 26.1. The charts that I have created for this chapter will show what different types of charts are good for, when they should be used, and how

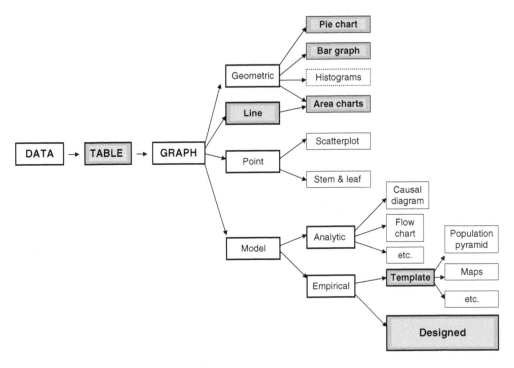

Figure 26.2   Typology of non-animated ('still') visual displays of information

they should be constructed. Figure 26.2 is a typology of some of the graphs that social scientists are able to deploy for analysis and communication. This chapter will focus specifically on those types that are shaded, beginning with elementary forms and progressing to the construction of idiosyncratic designs, which are often especially useful for making sense of complex analytic puzzles. Nevertheless, variants of the more elementary forms will reappear throughout as the story unfolds. The chapter's takeaway story is that sociologists should pay as much attention to the analytic and visual manipulation of descriptive statistics as they do to developing increasingly powerful algorithms.

This chapter will exemplify how to use good visualization techniques as analytic tools to resolve a specific sociological puzzle: Why has Americans' confidence in their institutions changed? Therefore, it will introduce the reader to visualization in sociology by modeling how to use visual display as an

analytic tool. This form of exposition is less common in the social sciences, which tend to prefer presenting general principles that are then selectively illustrated. Unfortunately, articulating the relationship between abstract concepts and concrete applications in this fashion is usually so formal and idealized that it rarely addresses the challenges faced in most empirical research, which are best served by exemplifying the kind of thinking—and pragmatic moves—useful for social analysis. Howard Becker refers to this process as deploying a 'trick of the trade,' which he defines as:

A specific operation that shows a way around some common difficulty; and suggests a procedure that solves relatively easily what would otherwise seem an intractable and persistent problem. (1998: 4)

In other words, this chapter will explore the ways that visual methods can be of help in 'how to think about your research while you're doing it' as Becker puts it in the sub-title on the cover of his book, *Tricks of the Trade.* Reading this chapter will be most rewarding if readers actively imagine how 'tricks' like those discussed below—as well as many others designed by visualization specialists like Stephen Few, Edward Tufte, and Howard Wainer who are referenced throughout—could be applied, modified, or even invented to deal with the challenges they encounter in their own research.

PRODUCING YOUR OWN CHARTS

One of the most important lessons of Edward Tufte's[4] path-breaking work on thinking visually with graphs and charts is to avoid the allure of the egregiously distorted and eye-popping designs that so littered the pages of even the very best newspapers when he first prepared and published *The Visual Display of Quantitative Information* in 1983.[5] Tufte's critique of 'chartjunk'—where visual attraction is inversely related to information value—has influenced newspapers like the *New York Times,* which now produce and disseminate visual displays that are as thoughtfully informative as they are excellent graphically. As more social scientists appreciate the breathtaking intelligence and imagination of these new graphics, they will be prompted to improve their own charts. Currently, however, the software required to design complex visualizations and animations has a steep learning curve that few working social scientists have time to master. While trends in digital technology suggest that the future will undoubtedly deliver more user-friendly products for various kinds of data analysis and graph design, that future is not imminent. Fortunately, most of our work-aday challenges are relatively simple, and Excel's chart functions are fairly easy to use and provide an array of chart types diverse enough for displaying most descriptive statistics. There are also manuals like John Walkenbach's *Excel 2007 Charts*

(2007), which are invaluable for making the most of Excel.

Successfully visualizing information requires being attentive to three matters: first, identifying the purpose of the display; second, addressing the conceptual issues it raises; and, third, making choices between various display formats. Generally speaking, data are visualized for one of three purposes: laying out information for simple inspection in order to identify patterns; displaying data in order to analyze both variation as well as pattern; and, finally, as a way of formally presenting data either to summarize, or provide evidence for, an argument. Similarly, visualizing information invariably entails addressing several concerns. These include: issues of substance, which are posed both by the topic and provenance of the data (What is the data about?); formal issues that are posed by the numerical properties of the data (What form does the data take?); and logical and aesthetic questions posed by the story-telling possibilities of the display. Finally, the display choices for most descriptive statistics fall into one of the following categories: single-variable displays, correlations, and comparisons of two or more variables. These matters will be addressed as each of the major chart types is discussed.

Pie charts

A pie chart consists of a circle divided into wedge-shaped segments. The area of each segment... is the same per cent of the total circle as the data elements it represents is of the sum of all the data elements in its data set. (Harris, 1999: 281)

Figure 26.3, for example, represents the number of Americans in 2008 that believe in other people's 'fairness.' A pie chart like this one is one of the most ubiquitous graphs for showing proportions, or 'the relative sizes of components to one another and to the whole' (Harris, 1999: 281). There are two major reasons for its popularity as a graphic choice; it is invariably dramatic and, as it is loaded on any software program (like Excel)

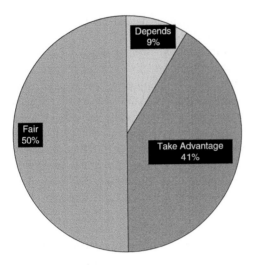

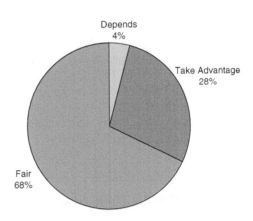

Figure 26.3 'Do you think most people would try to take advantage of you if they got a chance, or would they try to be fair?' Text of question asked since 1972 for variable FAIR by the General Social Survey (GSS), USA

Figure 26.4 'Do you think most people would try to take advantage of you if they got a chance, or would they try to be fair?' Text of question asked by the American National Election Survey (ANES) between 1964 and 2004

that has a charting function, it is easy to render.

Figure 26.3 was drawn with Excel and follows the guidelines of the cognitive neuroscientist Stephen Kosslyn (1994) for constructing this type of chart.[6] It does not use an exploding wedge; the wedges are arranged in a simple clockwise progression, beginning with the smallest at the top; readily visible labels obviate the need for a legend and are placed within each wedge. Finally, the text in the chart is made legible by using either a serif or sans serif font[7] (106–109).

But how useful is this display, either to lay out data for simple visual inspection or for analysis, and does it have any communicative value to warrant its creation? Might this chart actually distract the analyst from searching for language to convey what these proportions mean? One-half of Americans expect others to be fair, while just over two out of five report that others would take advantage. Do we need a graph to make that point? And does the chart encourage us to interrogate the data? Does the fact that only one out of two

Americans expects others to be fair guarantee stability in a society where a great many, if not most, encounters are with strangers? Absent a theory that identifies acceptable thresholds for wariness, it is always a useful move to compare trends over time and see if anything has changed.

Figure 26.4 represents the answer to essentially the same question when asked in 1964 by a survey with greater time depth than the GSS. Placing the two pie charts side by side, we see that over the course of 44 years, Americans are 18 per centage points less likely to attribute a proclivity for fairness to others, dropping from over two-thirds of the population to just one-half. We follow the same display rules for the pie chart, which were suggested by Kosslyn, except that now we place the labels outside the pie and immediately adjacent to their respective wedges because we can't fit one of the labels within a very narrow wedge.[8] It is pretty evident that the decline of confidence in selected institutions, which was suggested by Figure 26.1, is complemented by one measure of a decline in confidence in people generally, which suggests that the social glue holding Americans together might be quite frayed indeed. Nevertheless, the question remains whether the charts add much to the story. Why wouldn't a simple table suffice?

Tables

The table, or art of tabling, is so neglected in the literature on visualization that it is often considered little more than drudgery, a first—albeit necessary—step to real visualization. This is a mistake, as even a humble table like Table 26.1 has some properties that make it an indispensable tool for displaying data. Robert Harris advises:

> Sometimes referred to as a matrix. Tables are charts with information arranged in rows and columns in some meaningful way. The following list summarizes some of the major reasons for using tables.

- They are one of the best ways to convey exact numerical values.
- They present data more compactly than in sentence form.
- They assist the viewer in making comparisons, determining how things are organized, noting relationships between various sets of data, etc.
- They are one of the most convenient ways of storing data for rapid reference.
- They are an excellent vehicle for recording and communicating repetitive information (forms).
- They organize information for which graphing would be inappropriate (Harris, 1999: 387).

Table 26.1 Believing in fairness: Change between 1964 and 2008

Year	Per cent of US population reporting if others will be fair or take advantage		
	Be fair	Take advantage	It depends
1964 (ANES)	67	28	4
2008 (GSS)	50	41	9

Data source: American National Election Survey (ANES) 1964) and General Social Survey, USA (GSS 2008).

Tables are so commonplace that we overlook how often we turn to them as a way of organizing information. These applications include schedules, checklists, and calendars and constitute the graphic template for constructing trellis displays, or small multiples, which are invaluable in making comparisons (Tufte, 1990: 67–80; 1997: 105–119; Harris, 1999: 388, 397; Few, 2009: 98–104). Harris (1999) and Stephen Few (2004: 47–54, 127–161) provide very useful introductions to the art of tabling. For our purposes I will focus on three aspects of table design that make them particularly valuable for social scientists. First, the table is capable of containing more information—or data points—in a display than most other charts. Second, it can be used simultaneously for reference as well as analysis. Third, a table's simplicity does not prevent it from being designed to highlight information in an elegant manner. I will discuss these three aspects of tabling and then explore how to most effectively extract the stories that a table may contain.

Figure 26.1 shows a steady decline of Americans' confidence in a number of their institutions. The military is an exception and exhibits a more volatile, yet generally, upward, trend. Table 26.2 recodes the data for three of these measures into decades. The value of the table for reference is that it invites the reader to evaluate the adequacy of how well the data in the table supports

Table 26.2 Comparison of confidence levels between 1972 and 2008

	Per cent of US population reporting a great deal of confidence in those who run selected institutions			
	1970s	1980s	1990s	2000s
Medicine (CONMEDIC)	54	50	45	41
Military (CONARMY)	37	33	41	49
Press (CONPRESS)	25	18	11	10

Data source: General Social Survey, USA.

the argument. Such an assessment should include not only the explicit claims in the argument—let's say, the decline in confidence for two of the institutions—but also a consideration of evidence that might modify the argument, which the author may not have chosen to discuss. For example, whereas the average per centage point decline for the three institutions between the 1970s and 1990s is **6.3** in Table 26.2, it actually increases by **0.6** from the 1990s to the 2000s, suggesting that the drop in confidence may be leveling off, and our awareness of it is a common—although perhaps misplaced—expression of anxiety that occurs once the worst part of a bad time is over.

Using a table in this way, therefore, probably would be even more valuable if it included the same information for the remaining 10 institutions. Thus, even if a table doesn't dramatize a pattern, it may contain a large number of cells (and numbers), which are easily referenced by a reader, and might encourage a deeper engagement with the argument. Finally, resizing, **bolding**, *italicizing* or coloring[9] the numerical information that the author wishes to underscore—for whatever reasons—means that the reader's attention is readily drawn to that portion of the evidence that supports the argument, while preserving access to other figures they may want to consult.

One of the most important skills for a social scientist to learn is how to extract a story from a table. This involves many of the same practices that those in visual studies deploy when they inspect an image. In a nutshell, the visual analysis of an image entails identifying each element in the composition of a picture, ascertaining how it relates to other elements and defining what each contributes to the effect of the composition as a whole.[10] In a table, the story elements are found in each cell's values and its composition is encoded in the proportional relationships between these different values. The dynamics of the stories that can be drawn from a table, therefore, are primarily expressed by differing rates and ratios

between the numbers in the cells, as well as evaluative judgments about the significance of certain numbers. Story development of this sort is a three-stage process.

First, the analyst should carefully look at each row and describe its pattern. In row 1 of Table 26.2 we witness a steady *decline* in confidence in medicine that goes from slightly above one-half of the population (**54** per cent) to just over two out of five (**41** per cent) for a drop of 13 per centage points, or **24** per cent (13 divided by 54) between the 1970s and 2000s. Row 2, or confidence in the military, however, is almost the mirror image of this trend, showing an *increase* in confidence from under two out of five Americans (**37** per cent) to almost one-half (**49** per cent) for a jump of 12 per centage points or **32** per cent (12 divided by 37). The analyst would certainly note that this increase was not steady but happened after an initial decline in the 1980s of four per centage points. Finally, an inspection of row 3 in Table 26.2 reveals that confidence in the press during this period has dramatically declined from one-quarter of the population (**25** per cent) to just one out of 10 (**10** per cent), a drop of 15 per centage points or **60** per cent (15 divided by 25).

The preceding paragraph is not something an analyst would want to publish; it is more of a scratch sheet, summarizing patterns. I have put it in a narrative form for the sake of exposition, but on my desktop it would appear as an enumeration of bullet points. Nevertheless, because we haven't completed deconstructing the table, there is still space to exemplify bulleting.

The second step in reading a table, therefore, would be to look at each column and summarize the patterns that can be discerned in them:

- In the 1970s, the range of variation between the three variables was 29 per centage points.
- In the 1970s, the institution with the most confidence was more than twice that of the lowest.
- In the 2000s, the range of variation between the three variables had widened to 39 per centage points.

- In the 2000s, the institution inspiring the most confidence was still only supported by around one-half the population, whereas that with the least by only one-fifth of this value.
- And so on.

After similarly inspecting Figure 26.1 and Table 26.1, we might summarize our findings in a way that is certainly consistent with the image of a 'frayed' America:

> Americans have generally lost confidence in most of their institutions, except the military. They show a steady deterioration in confidence of anywhere from 10 to 15 per centage points. Nevertheless, among those institutions with declining confidence levels, there seems to be three patterns: characterized by small, moderate, or large decreases in a 'great deal of confidence'. Additionally, the higher the initial vote of confidence, the slower its rate of decline over time. Medicine has shown the smallest decrease, from the sixth to the fifth decile. Religion is next, from the fourth to the third decile. Finally, Congress and the press bring up the rear, dropping from the third to the cusp of the first and second deciles. Data for the military may represent a very different pattern or just be an anomaly. Finally, a

measure of confidence in personal relationships in general—fairness—also shows a marked decline over much of the same time period. Losing confidence in other people's fairness occurs at roughly the same rate (25 per cent) as those institutions with only small decreases.

Line charts

After preparing a table, perhaps the most useful visualization technique for analyzing descriptive statistics is to compose a *trend line*, which is a simple line chart that includes the entire range of relevant values in a variable. The point is to deploy the spatial competence of the eye to ascertain the direction and shape of a trend. Caitlin Amos (2009) has used the chart wizard in Excel to create a *time series*—a trend line that covers a period of time—for a question from the GSS that measures confidence in banks and financial institutions (CONFINAN). The chart (Figure 26.5) is exemplary in many ways. It maximizes the size of the frame within which the data are displayed, although

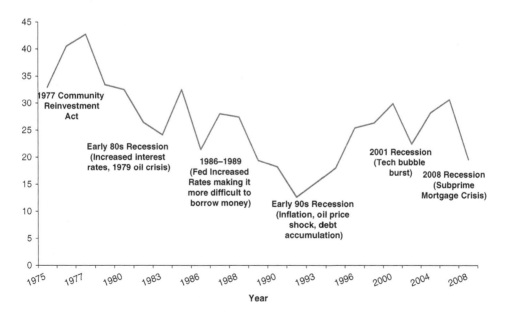

Figure 26.5   Trend line for Americans expressing confidence in banks and financial institutions
Data source: General Social Survey (GSS), USA. Chart prepared by Caitlin Amos (2009). Reproduced with permission.

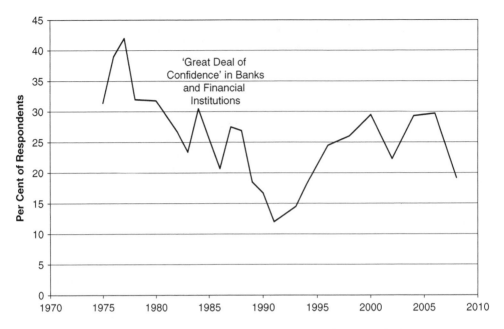

Figure 26.6   Revised version of Figure 26.5, charted as an XY (or scatter) plot

the unnecessary labeling of the *x*-axis does eat up space. Wisely, the chart does not include a legend. The line for the time series is clearly visible and the lines delineating the vertical axes are rendered with a muted gray-scale, which, while legible, doesn't draw attention away from the trend line, which carries the burden of the argument.

There is one flaw in Amos' chart that is found throughout the literature using GSS data, including Figure 26.1. Ideally, in a time series, the spaces between years should be equivalent. Thus, the spacing between 2-year intervals should be twice the length of those that separate succeeding years. In Figure 26.5, however, the spaces between adjacent values in some cases represent 1 year, while in others, 2 years. The result is that, even though the mid-point of the survey is just before its lowest point in 1993, the values for subsequent years are compressed, perhaps exaggerating their rate of change.[11] The most effective way of eliminating this distortion is to chart the data as an XY (or scatter) plot using the option provided by

Excel under 'chart types' (see Figure 26.6). All subsequent line charts in this chapter, which display GSS data over time, will be constructed with the scatter plot option.

The reader will note that the graph for confidence in banks and financial institutions charted in Figures 26.5 and 26.6 exhibits a different pattern from those we have discussed previously. Confidence in banks and financial institutions declines over time, like most of the institutions we have already examined, but it also exhibits the volatility found with confidence in the military. Volatility of this sort often reflects a *period effect*, which suggests that the survey is responding to the influence of historical events rather than more fundamental changes rooted in a population's demography and social organization.

To exemplify her argument, Amos labels each of the temporary declines in the trend line with a brief summary of the economic or financial events that correlate with responses to the survey. Attitudes about financial institutions appear to be strongly influenced by recessions and other down-turns in the economy. Revisiting Figure 26.1, we notice that the two dramatic upturns in confidence in the military coincide with the Persian Gulf and the Iraq/Afghanistan wars. Using a chart to identify period effects in this fashion is usually only effective with one variable. Nevertheless, it is possible to do so for several variables if they trend in a similar direction.

Recently, Pamela Paxton (2005) has reasoned that a close look at some of these trends suggests a more optimistic reading of the state of trust in American society. She focuses on three trends in particular: the question of fairness in Table 26.1, confidence in banks and financial institutions (CONFINAN) in Figure 26.5, and confidence in the military (CONARMY), which is charted in Figure 26.1, and concludes that although there is a steady decline in peo-ple's willingness to attribute 'fairness'—and, ple's willingness to attribute 'fairness'—and,

by extension, 'trustworthiness'—to others, the very volatility of CONFINAN and CONARMY suggests a resilience in institu-tional life 'that is our best hope of restoring trust in individuals' (Paxton, 2005: 45). In this view, while we may despair of our fellow human beings in general, we can still quickly regain faith in them as part of a team that—when working together—is effective in accomplishing objectives. Over the long run, a positive institutional experience not only may compensate for our 'misanthropy'[12] but also may nurture a sunnier view of others. This is a plausible thesis, but how does it fare when we examine not only two other ques-tions about human nature—whether people are helpful and can be trusted—but also include all 13 institutions considered by the GSS in our investigation?

Figure 26.7 is a line chart, which—as we have already established—is useful for com-paring trends over time. This chart follows

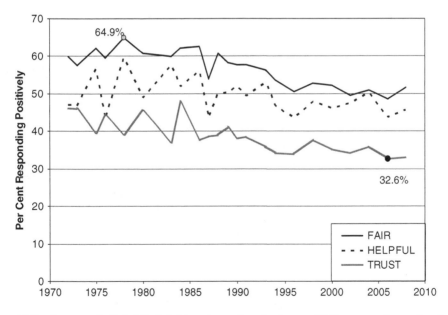

Figure 26.7 Are people 'fair,' 'helpful,' and can they be 'trusted'? For text of question for FAIR see Figure 26.3. TRUST: Generally speaking, would you say that most people can be trusted or that you can't be too careful in life? HELPFUL: Would you say that most of the time people try to be helpful, or that they are mostly just looking out for themselves?
Data source: General Social Survey (GSS), USA.

Stephen Kosslyn's guidelines for constructing such charts. The chart ensures that the three series, or lines, are distinguishable and the direction of the trend legible. This is often easier to accomplish if we color the lines appropriately. Unfortunately, we are often limited to grayscale and don't have that option. Figure 26.7 adapts to this limitation and uses three different black lines of the same size. They vary in being bold, dotted or hatched. Only two data points, with labels showing their values, are displayed—the very highest and lowest value within the frame—because adding more points and numbers is unnecessary and would clutter the frame with extraneous information. If the exact values of each, or most, of the data points are important to an argument, they should then, as a matter of course, be put into a table rather than crammed into a chart. The data point markers in Figure 26.7 are configured to be at least twice the size of the line. In addition, the chart has a legend because the trend lines are too close together to follow Bertin's recommendation to position labels next to the line. The legend, however, is placed on the right of the chart's body as close as possible to the lines it identifies (Kosslyn, 1994: 140–151).

A quick glance at Figure 26.7 makes it clear that there has been a parallel decline in positive responses to all three variables and that judging others to be 'fair' tends to be espoused more often than designating them as 'trustworthy' by 15–20 per centage points since 1972. Respondents to the GSS invariably also identify others as 'helpful' less often than 'fair' and more often than 'trustworthy.' It should be stressed, however, that these variables are not merely three versions of the same question.

Trustworthiness implies that another person can be relied upon to protect your interests. Someone is helpful, however, when they go out of their way to facilitate another person achieving a goal. Finally, to be fair usually refers to a person modifying their behavior to abide by a situationally sensitive interpretation of a moral code. Trustworthiness

is important in relationships with intimates and friends, but may not be advisable with those that you don't know well. Helpfulness is valuable with neighbors and those who are encountered in a person's daily round and is usually taken for granted with intimates. Finally, fairness is an expectation that should apply to those we don't know as well as those we do. Therefore, it shouldn't surprise us that the responses to these three questions not only diverge from each other in the way they do but also vary consistently over time.

Paxton is certainly correct to choose 'fairness' as most closely connected to the demands of institutional life. Nevertheless, a drop of 13 per centage points in Americans' evaluation of their fellow citizens 'trustworthiness'—to just under one out of three (**33** per cent)—is troubling and must be accounted for in any assessment of the role of institutions in organized life. At the very least—as Robert Putnam's *Bowling Alone* (2000) suggests—the decline in TRUST indicates a turning inward from others that may seriously inhibit a population's willingness to engage in civic affairs.

Tom Smith (2008), who has extensively analyzed confidence trends in the entire gamut of institutions surveyed by the GSS, is less sanguine than Paxton, and detects a far more nuanced story in the data. Figure 26.8 charts the proportion of the population with a 'great deal of confidence' in all 13 institutions between 1972 and 2008. Trying to include 13 variables on a single line chart almost invariably results in a confused jumble of lines, so it is advisable to begin by creating separate charts for each variable. Generally speaking, the charts should share a common template and be closely juxtaposed to invite an unhurried visual inspection of the assemblage as a whole.[13] An analyst should then print each chart and inspect them for story in much the same fashion as was done above for tables. The order for viewing the assemblage might be organized by various typologies. In this case, an obvious one would include the following five institutional spheres: Governmental

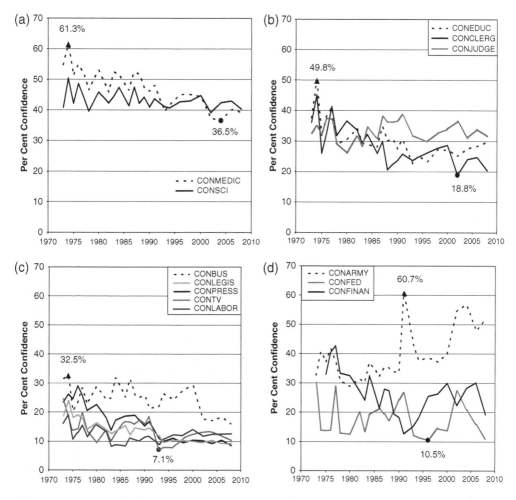

Figure 26.8   Per cent of Americans with a 'great deal of confidence' in the leadership of 13 institutions—Medicine (CONMEDIC), Science (CONSCI), Education (CONEDUC), Religion (COMCLERG), Supreme Court (CONJUDGE), Congress (CONLEGIS), Press (CONPRESS), Television (CONTV), Unions (CONLABOR), Corporations (CONBUS), Military (CONARMY), Executive Branch of Federal Government (CONFED), Banks and Financial Institutions (CONFINAN)—from 1972 to 2008, organized into four charts, showing those institutions with the most confidence (a), those with moderate confidence (b), those with least (c), and those with the most volatile levels of support (d)

Data source: General Social Survey (GSS), USA.

(CONFED, CONLEGIS, CONJUDGE, and CONARMY); Economic (CONBUS, CONFINAN, and CONLABOR); Knowledge/ Ideology (CONEDUC and CONSCI); Media (CONTV and CONPRESS), and Professional Services (CONMEDIC and CONCLERG). Other arrangements are possible and would depend on the theoretical goals of the researcher. In any event, one alternative that visual displays not only make possible, and which should *always* be considered, is to arrange the 13 charts by their visual similarity, and examine this ordering as a basis for identifying macro patterns, a way of letting your eyes help you do the thinking (Bertin, 1977: 7).

Figure 26.8 is the product of just such an ordering and arranges the variables into four small multiples: Most, Moderate, Least, and Volatile Confidence. Those in the Most Confidence group (CONMEDIC and CONSCI) trend consistently from the sixth to the fifth decile over the course of 35 years. The Moderate Confidence group (CONEDUC, CONCLERG, and CONJUDGE) moves from the fourth to the third decile, while the Least Confidence group (CONBUS, CONLEGIS, CONPRESS, CONTV, and CONLABOR) descends from third to the second decile. Finally, the most Volatile Confidence group (CONARMY, CONFED, and CONFINAN) has, as one might expect, the widest range of variation in their approval rates during these years (over 50 per centage points).

Area and bar charts

Those who are surveyed by the GSS are prompted to answer the 'confidence in institutions' questions with one of three responses: Does the respondent have 'a great deal of confidence,' 'only some,' or 'hardly any?' Most commentators focus on the value expressing the most confidence, because it appears to be extremely sensitive to changes in opinion. 'Hardly any' tends to inversely mirror 'a great deal,' and 'only some' is an intermediate category that might express indifference as much as it does moderation. Even so, it is important not to neglect the other values and what they reveal about the weight of opinion. One way of doing this is to use area charts and bar graphs and to construct indices to recode the information that the GSS makes available.

Figure 26.9 is an important chart variant—a shaded area chart—which enables the viewer to assess the direction of a trend over time—the strength of the line chart—as well as what each value's proportion of the whole may be, which is often measured, as we shall soon see, in bar graphs. The great advantage of Figure 26.9 is that it permits us to assess the confidence that Americans have

in each of these institutions in several ways. First, we can ascertain the weight of the three different responses that were available to those surveyed. Second, we can combine them for viewing in any manner we find suitable. Thus, a 'great deal' and 'only some' can be combined as a measure of, say, 'general confidence.' Finally, we can get a rough sense of the difference between any two of the values. In this case—and for other questions like it—it is often useful to compare the extreme values: here, a 'great deal of confidence' and 'hardly any.' In this last instance we note that there are anywhere from 2–10 times more people who express a 'great deal of confidence' than those who have 'hardly any confidence.' Conversely, the number of those who have 'hardly any confidence' in Congress goes from less than parity to almost seven times more than the number of those who express a 'great deal of confidence.'[14]

Constructing a shaded area chart in Excel permits the designer to choose the order in which the values are displayed. One option is to display them according to their semantic weight, which in this case would suggest beginning at the bottom with either 'hardly any' or 'a great deal,' and putting 'only some' in the middle, or vice versa. Another common recommendation is to insert the value that varies the least at the bottom because 'you can make it easier for the reader to compare the degree of change in specific segments' (Kosslyn, 1994: 152). In this case, we have put 'only some' at the bottom for three reasons. First, it tends to be the one that changes the least and is also the largest, which makes it easier to visualize how the other two, more extreme, responses vary. Second, we are able to put 'a great deal' above it, which makes it possible to imagine the combined value of these two as a measure of 'general confidence.' Moreover, designing the chart so that 'hardly any' is just above 'a great deal' creates a semantic tension that encourages the viewer to assess the respective weights of these extreme values. This is particularly apparent when—as in

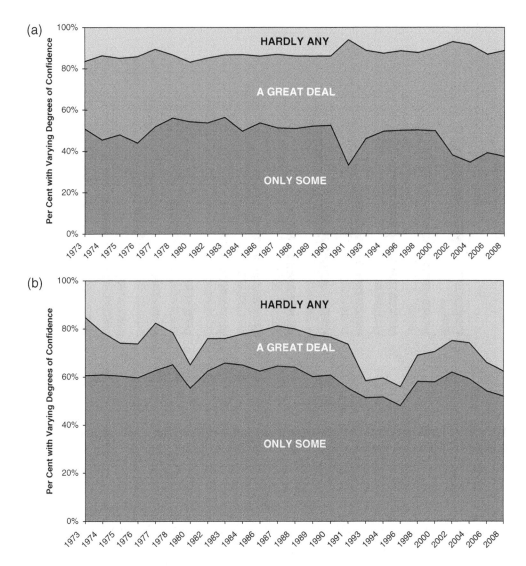

Figure 26.9   Shaded area chart measuring confidence in the Military (a) and Congress (b)
Data source: General Social Survey (GSS), USA.

Figure 26.9—graphs with contrasting levels of confidence, like CONARMY and CONLEGIS, are juxtaposed.

It is often advisable when constructing graphs and charts to devise ways to aggregate the data as a tool for determining whether a more general pattern can be discovered in the evidence. In this case, one such move might be to chart how all the institutions compare with each other when we contrast the cumulative averages of the three possible responses to the confidence query for each institution. The decision to aggregate data should be made cautiously because overall averages tend to obscure variation within the values even as they facilitate comparison between them. Nevertheless, so long as the analyst has been attentive to designing other charts that reveal as much variation as possible, and remembers to account for this variation, then this pitfall can often be avoided.

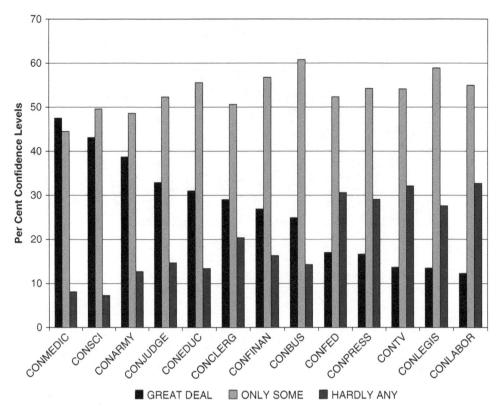

Figure 26.10 Vertical bar (or column) graph comparing the average responses for 'confidence' during the period 1973–2008

Data source: General Social Survey (GSS), USA.

Figure 26.10 is a vertical bar, or column, graph based on the cumulative average of the responses to the GSS on these 13 questions since 1973. It reveals four interesting findings:

1 It confirms the pattern in Figure 26.9 that 'a great deal of confidence' and 'hardly any' covary inversely or, in other words, that those institutions, which Americans report as meriting a 'great deal of confidence' over time, tend to have lower 'hardly any' responses.

2 As we might expect, there is a marked tendency for the cumulative averages to mirror the patterns found in the line charts in Figure 26.8. Those institutions with the highest initial level of a 'great deal of confidence' tend to be those with the highest cumulative average over the course of the survey period. The exceptions to the

second observation are the institutions labeled 'Most Volatile' in Figure 26.8.

3 We see from Figure 26.10, that the level of confidence averaged over time generally reflects the categories we chose for Figure 26.8, but that the institutions labeled 'Volatile' in Figure 26.8 are spread across quite a large range in Figure 26.10. Using the ranking in Figure 26.10, we will reallocate the institutions into three categories—those with Most Confidence, Moderate Confidence, and Least Confidence, typified as follows in Table 26.3. Figure 26.10 provides the new insight that institutions in the 'Least' category in Table 26.3 have two to three times more respondents answering 'hardly any' confidence compared to those answering 'a great deal.'

4 It is important to note that those Americans who have 'only some' confidence in their institutions constitute a plurality in all but one of the institutions (CONMEDIC) and less than a majority in

Table 26.3   Confidence levels of 13 institutions by strength of ratio between those expressing 'a great deal' and 'hardly any confidence,' based on cumulative average 1973–2008

Confidence level	Institution	Ratio: 'great deal' to 'hardly any'
Most Confidence	CONMEDIC	5.9
	CONSCI	5.9
Moderate	CONARMY	3.0
Confidence	CONEDUC	2.3
	CONJUDGE	2.2
	CONFINAN	1.7
	CONBUS	1.7
	CONCLERG	1.4
Least	CONPRESS	0.6
Confidence	CONFED	0.6
	CONLEGIS	0.5
	CONTV	0.4
	CONLABOR	0.4

Data source: General Social Survey, USA.

only three (CONMEDIC, CONSCI, and CONARMY). Needless to say, these three institutions have the highest number of respondents answering that they have 'a great deal of confidence' since 1973. When we add 'only some' and 'a great deal of confidence' together and recode the sum as a new measure entitled 'general confidence,' we note than no institution has less than two out of three responses (**67.3** per cent) in this new category (Figure 26.11). Nevertheless, there does appear to be a marked ratcheting down of confidence when we arrive at those in the 'least confidence' category. This should not surprise, as these are the only five institutions where more people respond with 'hardly any' confidence than report a 'great deal.'

Figure 26.11 is a horizontal bar graph that displays the recoded variable, 'general confidence.' As Kosslyn tells us, bars graphs are particularly appropriate for comparing

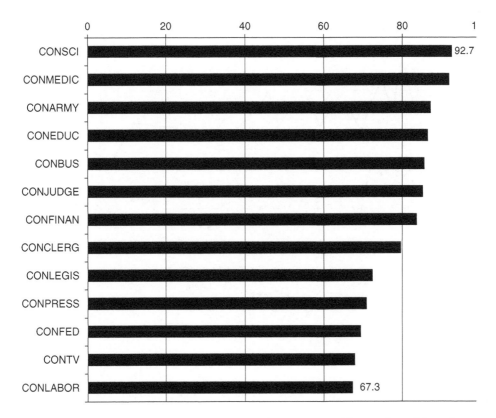

Figure 26.11   Horizontal bar graph of the cumulative average of 'general confidence' in 13 American institutions, 1973–2008

Data source: General Social Survey (GSS), USA.

precise measurements and nominal values such as discrete entities rather than ordinal values such as sequential numbers or years (Kosslyn, 1994: 37–38). It is generally advisable to use vertical bar graphs, but in a case like Figure 26.11 it makes more sense to display the data horizontally. For one, there are too many labels in the chart and they would be harder to read if they were displayed at a diagonal as in Figure 26.10. Figure 26.10 charts three values for each variable and while it could have been displayed horizontally, the overall pattern would not have been as visible as it is when displayed vertically. No such disadvantage accompanies Figure 26.11. Also, putting the numbers that label the *x*-axis along the top border of the chart makes it easier to follow the trend in the data points from one institution to the other as we descend from higher rankings at the top.

Custom-designed charts

Figure 26.12 is a revised and summary version of Figure 26.8. It aggregates the averages for each of the institutions into the three new categories defined by Table 26.3, and provides us with an overview of institutional trends, which—when viewed with the other charts and tables above—can be provisionally summarized as follows:

A closer look at Figure 26.12 and the data describing Americans' attitudes about their institutions suggests that their confidence has not been eroded as much as some commentators have suggested.

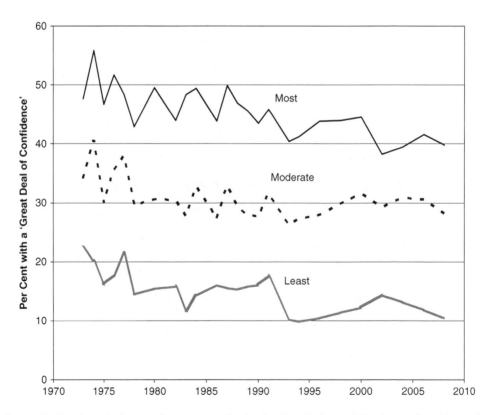

Figure 26.12 Cumulative yearly averages for institutions in 'Most,' 'Moderate,' and 'Least' confidence levels. See Table 26.3

Data source: General Social Survey (GSS), USA.

Figure 26.11 shows that, over the last 35 years, each of these 13 institutions earned a 'general confidence' response from at least two-thirds of Americans. Some institutions held the general confidence of over 90 per cent of the population. As might be expected, they correspond to the three categories in Table 26.3: those with Most Confidence ('general confidence' scores of 90 per cent or above); those with Moderate Confidence ('general confidence' scores of just about 80 per cent to somewhat under 90 per cent), and those with Least Confidence ('general confidence' scores of from 67 per cent to just over 70 per cent). The Least Confidence category differs from the others because more people responded that they have 'hardly any' rather than 'a great deal' of confidence in these institutions (see Figure 26.10). Whether or not we conclude that the level of Americans' confidence in these institutions indicates a weakening of social ties, it is important to note the steady decline in confidence in all institutions between 1973 and 2008 (Figure 26.12). Scores for the institutions in the Most and Moderate Confidence categories have dropped by one-sixth, whereas for the Least Confidence category, the drop has been precipitous; scores for these institutions dropped by more than one-half (57 per cent).

While this pattern seems to be clear enough, determining what factors might be shaping it is not so evident. Demographic and social factors—like gender, race, class, and education—as well as political ideology show no consistent correlation, if any, with responses to these questions as Smith (2008) has established and as just a few minutes running cross-tabs on the GSS confirm. The only strong association for 10 out of the 13 institutions that surface with multiple regressions[15] is with cohort, or birth year, and age (Figure 26.13). This association, however, is quite puzzling as it lumps together people from earlier cohorts—who tend to be older in the GSS sample—and younger respondents. This pattern of weak, or no, associations has led many commentators, like Paxton and Smith, to search for ad hoc explanations that emphasize independent period effects—particular historical events—for each institution. Idiosyncratic accounts like these invariably appear plausible in most

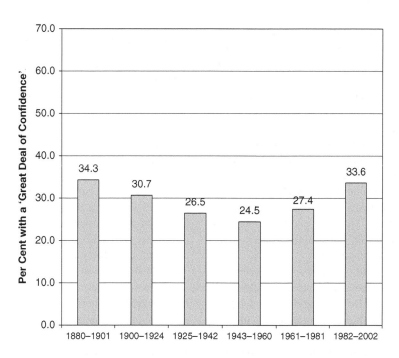

Figure 26.13   Confidence for average of all institutions by year of birth (COHORT), 1973–2008
Source: General Social Survey, USA.

cases, as is Caitlin Amos' thoughtful identification of the role of economic downturns in the changing fortunes of financial institutions in Figure 26.5. Very often, however, these accounts seem a bit like 'just-so' stories made to fit the facts. Tom Smith, for example, in his account of confidence in science (CONSCI) asserts that:

> There is some evidence that ratings are responsive to events such as the Challenger disaster. The Challenger spacecraft exploded on launch on January 28, 1986 and the proportion with a great deal of confidence dropped from **44.5** per cent in 1984 to the post disaster **39.5** per cent in 1986. It then rebounded to **45.1** per cent in 1987. The Columbia spacecraft was destroyed on re-entry on February 1, 2003. But with no post-disaster reading until over a year after the event, there was no evidence of a drop with **37.2** per cent having a great deal of confidence in 2002 and **41.8** per cent in 2004. (2008: 6; my **bold** emphasis)

Smith's comments are judicious. If there had been a GSS survey in 2003, it is quite possible that it might have shown the same decline and rebound effect after the Columbia tragedy, which has been attributed to the Challenger disaster. But, then again, it might not.[16] Generally, the clearest, and most compelling, evidence for the effects of specific historical events are those that entail dramatic and prolonged impacts on the functioning of an institution; but these events occur less often than we imagine. The most notable exception that we have encountered so far in this chapter is the increased confidence in the military (CONARMY) since the terrorist attack on the World Trade Center in New York. Usually, period effects—if they can even be pinpointed properly—are episodic and transitory.[17]

If, for the sake of argument, however, it is conceded that no general causal factors are discernable in declining institutional confidence, and if each institution appears to have its own unique history, we are still left with the problem of accounting for the patterns that we *do see* in Figures 26.11 and 26.12, and Table 26.3. Smith suggests that devising

more sophisticated algorithms might solve the answer: 'Once the role of specific events on specific institutions are modeled, the impact of more general societal trends may be identified and a fuller understanding of confidence trends achieved' (2008: 17). There are, nevertheless, some visual techniques that can be devised to display simpler statistical operations, which we might want to turn to first, and which often provide more enlightenment than more complex measures do.

One of the most useful aspects of Excel—and spreadsheets in general—is that it's matrix design can be modified to display data in unconventional, and illuminating, ways. Cells can be resized, outlined, and filled with various colors and/or grayscale shades to reveal patterns that otherwise might not be apparent. Manipulating 'graphical matrices' to organize, analyze, and display data was developed by Jacques Bertin in the 1960s to enlist the eye's design for pattern recognition as a tool for quantitative analysis.[18] The central purpose of Bertin's method is to *simplify* data:

> The aim of simplification is to make the relationships appear, that is, to *display* sought after information. In problems involving more than three components, simplification is achieved by the transformation of the image. Visual permutations are based on the eye's ability to perceive spatial entities. The eye perceives sets and can thus compare and bring together two similar rows by disregarding meaningless distances. Modern equipment, often very simple, makes these permutations possible for nearly everyone. (1977: 20)

Table 26.4 is composed of two charts. Table 26.4(a) is for reference purposes only. When originally constructed, the rows in this table were arranged quite differently, more or less randomly. The current order emerged as Table 26.4(b) was designed. In its final form, Table 26.4(b) explicitly follows Bertin's recommendations. Therefore, instead of looking at each institution separately, they are all gathered into a single graphic matrix. Put simply, an average of all the values in a variable—in this case confidence in an institution spanning 1973–2008—is calculated and

Table 26.4 (a) Per Cent with 'a great deal of confidence' in institution

	1973	1974	1975	1976	1977	1978	1980	1982	1983	1984	1986	1987	1988	1989	1990	1991	1993	1994	1996	1998	2000	2002	2004	2006	2008
CONEDUC	37.5	49.8	31.5	38.2	41	28.9	30.5	34.2	29.2	28.8	28	34.8	30	30.8	27.4	30.6	22.6	25.2	23.2	27.2	27.1	25.1	27.5	28.3	29.5
CONPRESS	23.4	26.2	24.5	29	25.7	20.5	22.6	18.1	13.7	17.3	18.6	18.8	18.9	17.1	15.2	16.7	11	9.9	11	9.5	10.4	10.2	9.2	10.3	8.6
CONMEDIC	54.6	61.3	51.3	54.8	52.1	46.4	53.1	45.7	52.3	51.5	46.5	52.4	51.7	47	46.1	48.1	39.6	41.8	45.1	45	44.4	37.2	36.5	40.1	39.2
CONLEGIS	24.1	17.6	13.7	14.1	19.7	13.3	9.7	13.5	10.2	12.9	16.7	16.7	15.9	17.4	15.8	18.3	7.1	7.9	7.9	10.9	12.6	13.1	13.3	11.9	10.5
CONTV	18.8	23.7	18.3	19.1	17.7	14	16.3	14.2	12.7	13.4	15.2	12	14.4	14.3	13.9	14.5	11.7	9.6	10.4	10.4	10	9.6	10.3	9.1	9.3
CONCLERG	36.1	45.2	26	32.7	41.4	31.9	36.7	33.7	29.4	32.2	26	30	20.6	22.4	23.7	25.9	23.6	24.8	26.3	27.8	28.7	18.8	24.1	24.7	20.4
CONBUS	31.4	32.5	20.4	23.2	28.3	22.7	28.8	24.5	24.8	31.8	25	31.5	25.8	25.1	25.8	21.2	21.8	26.3	24.2	27.5	29.1	17.7	17	18.3	16
CONSCI	40.8	50.4	42.2	48.6	44.5	39.5	45.9	42.3	44.4	47.4	41.3	47.5	42.1	44.2	40.9	43.7	41.1	40.6	42.7	43	44.8	39.2	42.5	43	40.4
CONFED	29.9	13.9	13.7	13.9	28.8	12.9	12.5	19.9	13.3	19	21.2	19.3	17.1	20.5	24.2	26.6	12.2	11.5	10.5	14.4	13.8	27.3	20.8	16	10.9
CONJUDGE	32.6	34.8	32.2	37.5	37.2	29.4	26.1	31.4	28.3	34.5	30.9	38	36.3	36.2	36.6	38.6	31.9	31.2	29.8	32.7	33.9	36.5	31	33.9	31.6
CONFINAN	(n.d.)	(n.d.)	32.9	40.5	42.7	33.4	32.5	27.2	24.1	32.5	21.4	27.9	27.4	19.4	18.2	12.6	15.3	18	25.4	26.3	29.9	22.4	28.2	30.1	19.2
CONLABOR	16.2	18.8	10.8	12.6	15.4	11.6	15.9	13.1	8.3	8.8	8.4	11	10.5	10	11.3	11.8	8.9	10.5	12.2	12	14.1	11.7	12.4	12.4	12.7
CONARMY	32.6	40.7	37	41.7	37.5	30.6	28.8	31.3	30.2	37.1	32.3	35.6	35.1	33.8	33.6	60.7	42.6	37.7	38.5	37.2	40	54.8	56.8	47.8	51.9

Continued

Table 26.4 Cont'd—(b) Same table where all columns with above average scores are shaded

	1973	1974	1975	1976	1977	1978	1980	1982	1983	1984	1986	1987	1988	1989	1990	1991	1993	1994	1996	1998	2000	2002	2004	2006	2008	Ave.
CONEDUC	37.5	49.8	31.5	38.2	41.0	28.9	30.5	34.2	29.2	28.8	28	34.8	30.0	30.8	27.4	30.6	22.6	25.2	23.2	27.2	27.1	25.1	27.5	28.3	29.5	30.7
CONPRESS	23.4	26.2	24.5	29.0	25.7	20.5	22.6	18.1	13.7	17.3	18.6	18.8	18.9	17.1	15.2	16.7	11.0	9.9	11.0	9.5	10.4	10.2	9.2	10.3	8.6	16.7
CONMEDIC	54.6	61.3	51.3	54.8	52.1	46.4	53.1	45.7	52.3	51.5	46.5	52.4	51.7	47.0	46.1	48.1	39.6	41.8	45.1	45.0	44.4	37.2	36.5	40.1	39.2	47.4
CONLEGIS	24.1	17.6	13.7	14.1	19.7	13.3	9.7	13.5	10.2	12.9	16.7	16.7	15.9	17.4	15.8	18.3	7.1	7.9	7.9	10.9	12.6	13.1	13.3	11.9	10.5	13.8
CONTV	18.8	23.7	18.3	19.1	17.7	14.0	16.3	14.2	12.7	13.4	15.2	12.0	14.4	14.3	13.9	14.5	11.7	9.6	10.4	10.4	10.0	9.6	10.3	9.1	9.3	13.7
CONCLERG	36.1	45.2	26.0	32.7	41.4	31.9	36.7	33.7	29.4	32.2	26.0	30.0	20.6	22.4	23.7	25.9	23.6	24.8	26.3	27.8	28.7	18.8	24.1	24.7	20.4	28.5
CONBUS	31.4	32.5	20.4	23.2	28.3	22.7	28.8	24.5	24.8	31.8	25.0	31.5	25.8	25.1	25.8	21.2	21.8	26.3	24.2	27.5	29.1	17.7	17.0	18.3	16.0	24.8
CONSCI	40.8	50.4	42.2	48.6	44.5	39.5	45.9	42.3	44.4	47.4	41.3	47.5	42.1	44.2	40.9	43.7	41.1	40.6	42.7	43.0	44.8	39.2	42.5	43.0	40.4	43.3
CONFED	29.9	13.9	13.7	13.9	28.8	12.9	12.5	19.9	13.3	19.0	21.2	19.3	17.1	20.5	24.2	26.6	12.2	11.5	10.5	14.4	13.8	27.3	20.8	16.0	10.9	17.8
CONJUDGE	32.6	34.8	32.2	37.5	37.2	29.4	26.1	31.4	28.3	34.5	30.9	38.0	36.3	36.2	36.6	38.6	31.9	31.2	29.8	32.7	33.9	36.5	31.0	33.9	31.6	33.3
CONFINAN	(n.d.)	(n.d.)	32.9	40.5	42.7	33.4	32.5	27.2	24.1	32.5	21.4	27.9	27.4	19.4	18.2	12.6	15.3	18.0	25.4	26.3	29.9	22.4	28.2	30.1	19.2	26.4
CONLABOR	16.2	18.8	10.8	12.6	15.4	11.6	15.9	13.1	8.3	8.8	8.4	11.0	10.5	10.0	11.3	11.8	8.9	10.5	12.2	12.0	14.1	11.7	12.4	12.4	12.7	12.1
CONARMY	32.6	40.7	37.0	41.7	37.5	30.6	28.8	31.3	30.2	37.1	32.3	35.6	35.1	33.8	33.6	60.7	42.6	37.7	38.5	37.2	40.0	54.8	56.8	47.8	51.9	39.4
Ave.	31.5	34.6	27.3	31.2	33.2	25.8	27.6	26.9	24.7	28.2	25.5	28.9	26.6	26.0	25.6	28.4	22.3	22.7	23.6	24.9	26.1	24.9	25.4	25.1	23.1	26.8

Data source: General Social Survey, USA.

those values that are determined to be above the overall mean of the row are shaded. In most cases this operation yields a patchwork quilt of black and white cells. The task of the analyst then is to arrange the rows by essentially cutting and pasting them into a pattern with a meaningful visual order, resulting in more or less discrete blocks of shaded cells. In this particular case, the final order was produced by beginning at the top with those rows whose scores dropped below the mean for the row at an earlier point in time, and descending to those that drop below the mean in later years.[19] Thus, the table begins with CONEDUC and CONPRESS at the top—both of which drop below the mean in 1989—to CONLABOR and CONARMY, which still had above-average scores in 2008.

Next, an average for each of the columns measuring the mean for the sum of the institutions by year was compiled and those values that were above average on the last row were shaded in a 25 per cent grayscale. Viewed in this format, the following pattern is visible in Table 26.4(b):

- a big drop in confidence in 1975 with a quick rebound to previous levels;
- a big drop in 1978 from the low fourth decile to the high third decile;
- a small drop in 1983 and a quick rebound; and
- a big drop in 1993 from the high third decile to the low third decile.

When summarized, the general pattern shows a more or less steady overall decline of **8.2** per centage points from 1973 to 2008, which takes place in two big drops: 1978 and 1993. For emphasis, I have bolded the values for these 2 years in the bottom row of Table 26.4(b).

These two drops are separated by 15 years and hint at the influence of generational change, which was suggested by our multiple regressions and clearly noted by Smith in his survey of the confidence in institutions data:

For most institutions cohort has a curvilinear relationship with confidence…. [C]onfidence declines

from the pre-1923 generations to a nadir in the 1943–1952 cohort. Confidence then rises to a high point for the cohort born in 1983 and later. Confidence among the newest cohort exceeds that of all earlier cohorts. The individual trends [for each cohort] all agree to a greater or lesser extent with this summary pattern, but differ considerably in details…. But since relatively optimistic new cohorts have been largely replacing positive early generations, this has generally not driven up confidence. But as the most pessimistic middle cohorts begin to edge out, cohort turnover should become an engine for rising confidence. (2008: 9–10)

If Smith is correct, this curvilinear pattern explains why more confidence in institutions correlates both with earlier generations (in the past) and younger people (in the present). Nevertheless, Smith does not pay as much attention to the role of generational cohorts in changing public attitudes as he might, because his concern with detail has obscured attending to the big picture that Table 26.4(b) suggests and Figure 26.12 provides.

Figure 26.13 is a bar graph of the number of people in each birth cohort, or generation, who express a 'great deal of confidence' in all 13 institutions. The cohorts are dated somewhat differently than Smith's, and are based on the years that Strauss and Howe (1991 and 1997) in their widely cited work on generational theory use to demarcate American generations. The GSS covers six of these generations and in a decade or so will begin to include a seventh in its sample. These generational cohorts, to use Strauss and Howe's nomenclature, comprise:

- 1883–1900 'The Lost Generation'
- 1901–1924 'The GI Generation'
- 1925–1942 'The Silent Generation'
- 1943–1960 'The Baby Boom Generation'
- 1961–1981 'Generation X'
- 1982–2002 'The Millennial Generation'

Figure 26.13 shows a clear curvilinear pattern, bottoming out with the Baby Boomers. Care must be shown, however, when comparing generational responses over time because the age composition of each cohort in this survey period may vary.

For example, everyone in the Lost Generation surveyed by the GSS was above 65 years old at the time, and, as of 2008, the oldest members in the Millennial Generation were only 26 years old.

One way to avoid comparing what might turn out to be apples and oranges is to control generation for age. Table 26.5 uses the 'Draw Table' function of Word to create a template that graphs how attitudes vary at defined stages of the life cycle over six succeeding generations. The numbers represent the per centage in each age group with a 'great deal of confidence' in either the Congress (CONLEGIS) or the Military (CONARMY). Reading from top left to right

in Table 26.5(a), we see that 18–24 year olds in the Baby Boomer Generation were the first age group of younger people interviewed by the GSS at its inception in 1973. The first oldest age group (75–89) the GSS followed was composed of people in the Lost Generation, and so on. The blank cells with the diagonal stripe on the left of the chart will never be filled with information from this database because the survey wasn't administered before 1973 when earlier generations would have been younger. In time, all of the empty cells to the right will be filled in, so long as the GSS continues to be administered. The numbers in italics represent those cells with less than 75 respondents and, thus,

Table 26.5 Per Cent of population with a 'great deal of confidence' by age (AGE) and generation (COHORT). (a) Contains responses for Congress (CONLEGIS). (b) Contains responses for the Military (CONARMY)

(a) CONLEGIS

	1881–1900 Lost	1901–1924 GI	1925–1942 Silent	1943–1960 Boomer	1961–1981 Gen-X	1982–2002 Millennial
18–24				14	19	25
25–34			17	12	13	14
35–44			15	11	10	
45–54		21	15	9	9	
55–64		17	11	7		
65–74	29	16	9	9		
75–89	19	13	11			

(b) CONARMY

	1881–1900 Lost	1901–1924 GI	1925–1942 Silent	1943–1960 Boomer	1961–1981 Gen-X	1982–2002 Millennial
18–24				35	44	62
25–34			37	29	43	55
35–44			35	33	48	
45–54		40	35	40	46	
55–64		41	43	45		
65–74	47	42	51	55		
75–89	41	47	59			

Data source: General Social Survey, USA.

possess less statistical significance. With each succeeding survey, the numbers in these italicized cells on the right side of the frame will become more robust. Finally, the numbers are sized larger for that cohort with the lowest confidence to make the patterns more legible.

Reading Table 26.5 for story reveals the following patterns:

- Both tables show that the lowest scores are found either in the Baby Boomer Generation (CONLEGIS) or in a complex pattern that descends from the very oldest group of the Lost Generation through the GI Generation and Silent Generation and bottoms out with the Baby Boomer Generation for those 44 or under (CONARMY).
- Confidence in the Military increases as a cohort ages while confidence in Congress decreases over the life course.
- Both institutions show a slight (CONLEGIS) or dramatic (CONARMY) rebound effect beginning with Gen-X and continuing through the Millennial Generation.
- Utilizing the same template to examine the remaining 11 institutions reveals that confidence in all of them—with the single exception of the Military—either stays level or declines over the life course.
- In terms of generational change the institutions fall into one of two patterns displayed in Table 26.6. First, the 'Weak Confidence' group shows little, or no, evidence of a rebound in confidence among more recent cohorts, which includes all of the institutions in the *Least Confidence* category in Table 26.3 with the addition of organized religion (CONCLERG) and big business (CONBUS). Second, the 'Strong Confidence' group is composed of the rest of those in Table 26.3 with *Moderate Confidence* and also includes the scientific community (CONSCI). Most of these institutions evidence a rebound in more recent cohorts. Organized medicine (CONMEDIC), which has the highest overall support over the course of the GSS, continues to decline although it shows signs of leveling off in the Millennial Generation. All in all, 9 of the 13 institutions plummet to their lowest confidence levels with the Baby Boomer Generation (1943–1960).[20]

It is important to recognize that, while we have controlled for age in Table 26.5, each

Table 26.6　Confidence levels for institutions (Table 26.3 revised)

Confidence level	Institutions
Weak and level confidence	CONLABOR
	CONTV
	CONLEGIS
	CONFED
	CONPRESS
	CONCLERG
	CONBUS
Strong and often growing confidence*	CONFINAN
	CONJUDGE
	CONEDUC
	CONARMY
	CONSCI
	CONMEDIC

*The two exceptions are CONSCI, where the proportion of those having a 'great deal of confidence' remains level, and CONMEDIC, which has had a 15 per centage point drop. Nevertheless, almost two out of five (39 per cent) Americans expressed 'a great deal of confidence' in Medicine.

cell may encompass as much as 20 calendar years or so. Because this way of defining a generational age group tends to be chronologically diffused, it is generally advisable, then, to also construct a line graph for each institution, charting how different generations—no matter how much their members' ages vary—respond in any given year.

Figure 26.14 charts confidence in education by cohort and year. It is representative of the nine institutions where confidence levels bottom out with the Baby Boomer Generation, and generally reflects the patterns of the remaining four. Figure 26.14(a) includes the three earliest cohorts, while Figure 26.14(b) includes the latest two. The Baby Boomer Generation is placed in both charts to facilitate comparison. Visual inspection reveals the following:

- Each succeeding generation tends to have lower confidence scores than the one before until it levels off with the Baby Boomer Generation, and then increases with each subsequent generation.
- Generally, all of the generational cohorts' scores move in tandem and reflect the two big drops in 1978 and 1993.

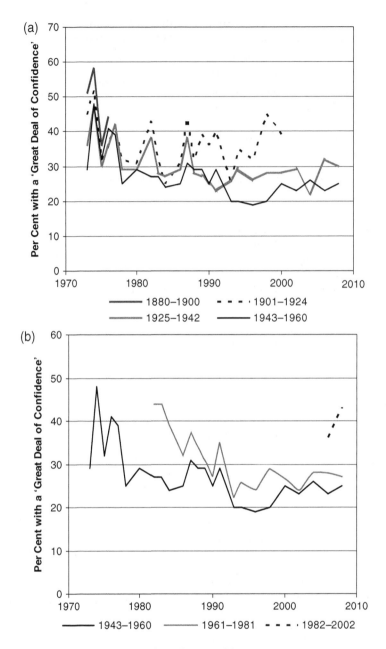

Figure 26.14   Confidence in education by cohort and by year

Data source: General Social Survey (GSS), USA.

These patterns suggest that if there is an increase in overall confidence in coming years, it will most likely be gradual because the 'cohort replacement effect' of rising Gen-Xers (1961–1981) and Millennials (1982–2002) will first push out a more confident generation—the Silent Generation (1925–1942)—before they replace the least confident Baby Boomers (1943–1960), as Smith (2008: 10) has indicated.

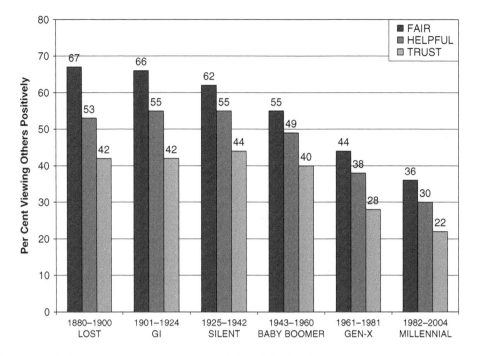

Figure 26.15   Per cent viewing others as 'Fair,' 'Helpful,' and 'Trustworthy' by cohort
Data source: General Social Survey (GSS), USA.

There is one final puzzle that must be addressed before we assess what this visual excursion has revealed about Americans' confidence in their institutions. Figure 26.15 shows that the steady decline in confidence in other people that was charted as a 'Misanthropy Scale' in Figure 26.7 reflects generational differences, which remain more or less stable in the Lost, GI, and Silent generations and then decline precipitously through each succeeding cohort. The Millennial Generation, which has evidenced increased confidence in institutions, here occupies rock bottom. Barely more than a third of those in this generation believe that others will treat you fairly (**36** per cent) and less than one out of four find others to be 'trustworthy' (**22** per cent).[21] In other words, the two most recent generations, which are gaining confidence in their institutions, are also the ones whose faith in their fellows is plummeting toward all-time lows.

One way of resolving this paradox is Pamela Paxton's view that Gen-Xers and Millennials compensate for uncertainly in social relationships by putting their faith in institutions, not people (Paxton, 2005). But what accounts for this growing misanthropy, and just how might it translate into increased support for institutions? Figures 26.16 and 26.17 and Tables 26.6 through 26.8, address this conundrum, and suggest another explanation that—while it doesn't contradict Paxton—more clearly illuminates both the historic context and social dynamics of the rebound in institutional confidence among more recent generations.

Table 26.6 establishes that trends in the confidence data sort institutions into two groups. 'Strong' institutions are those with higher overall levels of a 'great deal of confidence' that generally show evidence of a rebound since 1994. 'Weak' institutions have lower confidence levels and, generally, no

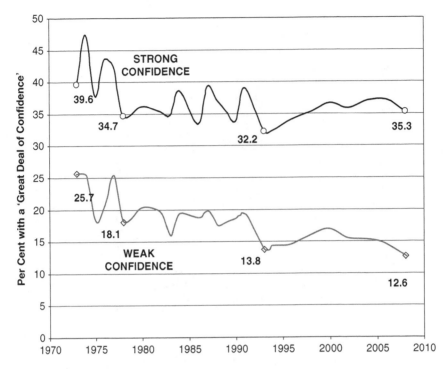

Figure 26.16   Per cent of population with a 'great deal of confidence' in institutions in the 'strong' and 'weak' confidence groupings 1973–2008

Data source: General Social Survey (GSS), USA.

rebound. Reading Figure 26.16 for story suggests the following:

- For the most part, the two institutional confidence levels trend in a similar direction, although the gap between them widens significantly, from **13.9** to **22.7** per centage points.
- The 'Strong' institutions drop a total of **4.3** per centage points, or almost **11** per cent between 1973 and 2008. There is, however, clear evidence of a rebound since 1994.
- During the same period, the 'Weak' institutions decline by a total of **13.1** per centage points, which is over **51** per cent, with no rebound.

Also, very important are differences in the organizational characteristics of the two groups listed in Table 26.6. 'Strong' institutions tend to be led by professionals who manage organizational cultures with clear missions and clearly articulated, if not rigorous, standards. 'Weak' institutions,

however, are more dependent on public approval or support. Their high officials are either elected (congress or the presidency); respond, if not pander, to popular concerns and desires (television, the press), or they address and channel mass aspirations for a better world (organized religion and the labor movement).

In other words, the rebound in confidence is not distributed across all institutions. The professionally dominated 'Strong' institutions not only have evidenced a small decline in confidence over the years but also appear to be rebounding, while those institutions where either the electorate, consumer or member is king have witnessed a startling decline in confidence and no evidence of a rebound. In addition, Table 26.7 demonstrates that Gen-Xers—and especially Millennials—are more apt to have confidence in the 'strong' institutions than are

Table 26.7 Confidence in institutions by cohort and age group (18–26)

	STRONG CONFIDENCE		
	1943–1960 Baby Boomer	1961–1981 Gen-X	1982–2002 Millennial
CONFINAN	26.8	30.3	41.9
CONARMY	32.5	43.2	58.0
CONEDUC	33.9	34.6	39.7
CONMEDIC	61.1	57.1	55.4
CONSIC	45.6	48.2	49.4
CONJUDGE	34.6	42.3	38.9
Average	39.1	42.6	47.2

	WEAK CONFIDENCE		
	1943–1960 Baby Boomer	1961–1981 Gen-X	1982–2002 Millennial
CONLEGIS	13.5	19.0	23.5
CONLABOR	15.1	17.1	21.1
CONFED	15.6	19.8	19.4
CONTV	21.0	17.5	13.2
CONBUS	19.8	27.3	23.8
CONPRESS	24.6	18.2	13.0
CONCLERG	30.3	26.5	28.0
Average	20.0	20.8	20.3

Data Source: General Social Survey, USA.

their Baby Boomer elders, even though their more negative evaluation of the 'Weak' institutions is virtually the same as the Baby Boomers. In short, it appears that only the 'Strong' institutions inspire the confidence that can, perhaps, compensate for what people cannot count on from others. But why should these institutions inspire increased confidence among more recent cohorts?

A "generation" can be defined as "a cohort-group whose length approximates the span of a phase of life [roughly twenty years or so]... [has] a common age location [in historic time], common beliefs and behavior, and perceived membership in a common generation [however inchoate]" (assembled from Strauss and Howe, 1991: 60–64).

While it is generally acknowledged that important dimensions of a generation's beliefs are formed in childhood, it is certainly true that they are codified when people become adults where—both as values and norms—they are used to regulate their own children's lives. This process, however, is quite dynamic and children incessantly test the strictures, with which they are inculcated, in the cauldron of experience and history for consistency and efficacy. Parents often pass on to their children what they believe is an improved version not only of what they themselves received from their parents but also what they imagine they would have told themselves as children had they been their own parents. This dynamic tends to produce forms of cultural exaggeration that often overemphasize the value of certain strictures and virtues more than others, and under-appreciate the importance of what has not been stressed, either through neglect or outright rejection.

A close examination of Table 26.8 and Figure 26.17 suggests that one reason why more recent cohorts have regained faith in the 'strong' institutions is that these institutions may address needs that were not satisfied by their parents' patterns of child rearing. This claim for the effect of child-rearing ideology is based on data generated by two series of questions in the GSS. Between 1973 and 1983, the GSS asked people to name their three most desirable traits in children out of a list of 13. The line of questioning was changed in 1986 to a five-trait scale and has been administered ever since.

Table 26.8 represents how often each of the 13 traits was identified as one of the 'three most desirable qualities in children' by members of different generations. They are ranked from those most often (#1), to least often (#13), mentioned within each cohort. There are five different patterns: 'level' (HONEST and ROLE); 'secular decrease' (CONTROL and STUDIOUS); 'secular increase' (SUCCESS and INTEREST); 'curvilinear "∪" shaped' (MANNERS, OBEYS, CLEAN, and AMICABLE); 'curvilinear "∩" shaped' (JUDGMENT, CONSIDERATE, and RESPONSIBLE). While the 'level' pattern appears to represent persisting cultural values,

Table 26.8 Desirable qualities in children by cohort. 'Which three qualities… would you say are desirable for a child to have: be honest (HONEST); good manners (MANNERS), obeys parents well (OBEYS), gets along well with other children (AMICABLE), good sense and sound judgment (JUDGMENT), self-control (CONTROL), neat and clean (CLEAN), a good student (STUDIOUS), tries hard to succeed (SUCCESS), interest in how and why things happen (INTEREST), acts like a boy or girl (ROLE), considerate of others (CONSIDERATE), responsible (RESPONSIBLE).' Ranked in order from most to least often mentioned

	Lost 1881–1900	GI 1901–1924	Silent 1925–1942	Baby Boomer 1943–1960	Gen-X 1961–1980
1	HONEST	HONEST	HONEST	HONEST	HONEST
2	MANNERS	MANNERS	RESPONSIBLE	RESPONSIBLE	MANNERS
3	OBEYS	RESPONSIBLE	CONSIDERATE	CONSIDERATE	SUCCESS
4	AMICABLE	OBEYS	JUDGMENT	JUDGMENT	OBEYS
5	JUDGMENT	CONSIDERATE	MANNERS	MANNERS	RESPONSIBLE
6	CONSIDERATE	JUDGMENT	OBEYS	INTEREST	CONSIDERATE
7	CONTROL	CONTROL	CONTROL	OBEYS	INTEREST
8	RESPONSIBLE	AMICABLE	INTEREST	CONTROL	JUDGMENT
9	CLEAN	INTEREST	SUCCESS	SUCCESS	AMICABLE
10	STUDIOUS	SUCCESS	AMICABLE	AMICABLE	CLEAN
11	SUCCESS	CLEAN	CLEAN	CLEAN	CONTROL
12	INTEREST	STUDIOUS	STUDIOUS	STUDIOUS	STUDIOUS
13	ROLE	ROLE	ROLE	ROLE	ROLE

Data source: General Social Survey, USA.

the 'secular decrease' and 'secular increase' represent century-long trends. For our purposes, I will focus on the contrast between the two curvilinear patterns, which suggest a pattern of cyclical change.

Put simply, the 'curvilinear "∩" shaped' (JUDGMENT, CONSIDERATE, and RESPONSIBLE) emphasize the child as a 'rule definer,' one who is expected to decide what is proper in a given situation or course of action. The 'curvilinear "∪" shaped' (MANNERS, OBEYS, CLEAN, and AMICABLE), however, imagines a child as one who is 'rule attentive,' or concerned with aligning their behavior to well-established rules and conventions. The Baby Boomer Generation envisioned a future for their children wherein they would make their own way in life, showing judgment, exercising

responsibility for their actions, and, of course, being considerate of those with whom you had to manage these new social contracts, perhaps because the Baby Boomers found the 'role attentiveness' of their own parents' strictures to be overly constraining in the rapid social mobility of post-World War II America when they grew up.

The five-trait scale represented in Figure 26.17 also reflects the same curvilinear patterns. Thinking for oneself (THINKSELF) is just another way of eliciting a commitment to 'rule defining,' while valuing hard work (WORKHARD) only makes sense in a social environment that predictably rewards such effort. OBEY in Figure 26.17 does not follow the same pattern as OBEYS in Table 26.8, probably because it is about obedience in general and

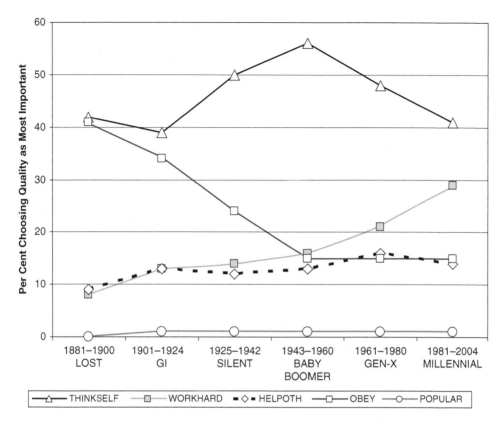

Figure 26.17   Desirable qualities in children by cohort. If you had to choose, which thing on this list would you pick as the most important for a child to learn to prepare him or her for life: to obey (OBEY); to think for himself or herself (THINKSELF); to work hard (WORKHARD); to help others when they need help (HELPOTH); to be well liked or popular (POPULAR).

Data source: General Social Survey (GSS), USA.

not just obedience to one's parents. I've included Figure 26.17 because the later line of questioning has the time depth to include Millennials.

This shift in child-rearing ideology suggests that Gen-Xers and Millennials, who were expected to take responsibility to think for themselves, may have found themselves wanting more structure in their lives to provide a latticework of rules and stable expectations, which would reward working hard toward the goals that they had been encouraged to set. Such a generation, presumably, might arrive at not only an increased wariness of others in a world where rules and contracts were expected to be constantly

negotiable but also develop more of an appreciation of the value of reasonably well-functioning institutions than their parents had. An inter-generational socialization dynamic of this sort, therefore, is consistent with a pattern of both increased misanthropy and also growing support for institutions that possess an organizational culture not unlike that which characterizes the 'Strong' institutions in Table 26.6: professional leaders, clear missions, and rigorous standards.

In sum, there are reasons to be sanguine that Americans' confidence in some of their institutions is growing. The inter-generational dynamic that is producing more confident recent cohorts is one that might also encourage a positive feedback loop. Being able to look at the bright side encourages people to invest their energies in what they value, which can lead, in this case, to 'Strong' institutions being able to recruit more highly motivated employees.

The future, however, does not appear to be that bright for the group of 'Weak' institutions. 'We have seen the enemy, and he is us!', Pogo announces in Walt Kelly's cartoon of the same name. When we elect our leaders, select our media, and choose our associations, we have, in a sense, no one to blame but ourselves when they lack sufficiency in our eyes. The value system of the Gen-Xers and Millennials may not be designed to readily enlist their loyalties and energies for institutions with no clear sense of purpose and direction. While it is possible for trends like these to change, it usually takes a perceived sense of crisis spurring a broad cultural and moral reawakening to create the political realignment necessary to re-energize popular energies and institutional commitments (Fogel, 2000). It is beyond the scope of this paper to consider the likelihood of such an eventuality. However, the current prospects for confidence in those institutions that are most sensitive to the popular will appear to justify those who worry about cultural malaise and the 'fraying' of America.[22]

CONCLUSION

This chapter, which began with a concern about general institutional decline in the contemporary Unites States, has become a sort of sociologist's *Tale of Two Cities*. On the one hand, Americans have generally retained their confidence in professionally dominated institutions, which only promises to increase in the long run because support for them is growing among more recent cohorts. On the other hand, those institutions that are most responsive to public demand and popular control appear to be in somewhat of a free

fall in confidence with no rebound in sight among these same generations. My concluding remarks, however, will shift back to the animating purpose of this chapter and reiterate the important role that visualizing data has played in the analysis, and draw some lessons from this.

Getting an audience to consider the topics and issues that have been raised about the visual display of information encounters two obstacles: on the one hand, the visual tends to be dismissed because it is too accessible; on the other hand, however, viewers don't attend to images because they are exasperating and often demand too much effort to decipher. We like to look at pictures, including charts and diagrams, but because anyone can do it—one line of reasoning suggests— therefore it mustn't be either that important or significant. Stanley Lieberson compares this contemporary academic scenario with the old Jewish joke that expresses dismay at how demeaning it is to join a club, which would accept you as a member:

> Empirical data can tell us what is happening far more readily than they can tell us why it is happening. "What happens" can include all of the cross-tabulations, interactions, controls, modeling, and the like, that one might desire. There is nothing wrong with contemporary social science research in that regard... . [T]he use of social research to describe or examine a set of events is perfectly appropriate. The social sciences are better equipped to do such work, and it is tragic to look down on these skills and the desirable function of describing the state of society. (1985: 219)

This chapter has argued that because the basic tasks of social description and analysis are at the core of sociology's mission, using visualization to improve our performance in this regard should be regarded as a priority for social scientists, and visual sociologists in particular. But, as this chapter has demonstrated, designing charts is demanding work. It requires care and attention to choose the most illuminating forms of display, and some effort to make the final published display as legible as possible. There is a craft both to visualization and how it is deployed in analysis and discovery, which social scientists need to develop. This is all the more important when designing more unconventional ways of displaying information.

Howard Becker states:

> Someone once told me that "word people" and "picture people" are two different breeds, but I don't believe it. The people whose studies I've discussed here made both words and pictures work for them. The combination produces, I'm convinced, increased understanding. But it is uncommon. Like [John] Tukey's statistical innovations—box-and-whisker diagrams, for instance—they require users to work a little harder. Data don't appear in simple formulaic patterns that users can inspect quickly. Users have to put some effort into extracting the meaning. (2007: 185)

For social scientists the hard nut at the core of their craft is that they cannot avoid the challenge of how numbers, words, and pictures intersect in their minds and in their communications. This is a work of logic, craft, intuition, and the imagination. Social scientists tell true stories with data. No less than literary journalists, they have to write about what they discover, even if it is based on nothing more than reams of numbers generated by a computer. They have to find ways to discern meaning in their data and ways to communicate that clearly to their audiences. Enlisting the visual is indispensable to achieve this goal, as is learning the craft of visual display and analysis, and how to commit what is envisioned to paper.

Read from top to bottom, Figure 26.18 represents the sequence in which the visual displays appear in this chapter's narrative. It identifies five different threads of evidence, which have been woven into a story about contemporary American attitudes ('misanthropy'; 'great deal of confidence in institutions'; 'three confidence values and general confidence'; 'cohorts'; and 'desirable qualities in children'). It also shows that on four occasions, deciding whether a chart should be included in the narrative required that the same chart should first be created for each of

the institutions, and then analyzed in depth. Note that each of those analytic moments is linked to revisions in the typology of institutions. Thus, the progression from a four-fold categorization of institutions—'More,' 'Moderate,' 'Least,' and 'Volatile'—to the final typology of 'Strong' and 'Weak' institutions is driven by a visual analysis of various kinds of displays created for that purpose. Also note that, apart from Figure 26.1, which functions as a 'grabber,' the story is developed in stages from threads that begin with 'Misanthropy' and culminate with 'Qualities.' If all the text in this chapter suddenly disappeared, the argument could be reconstructed from the sequence of illustrations alone. But this is only because both the diagrams and the argument are two modes of thinking whose relationship makes analysis possible.

It requires just as much effort to look at a chart as it does a photograph or painting. This is especially true, as Becker points out, when the chart is an innovation (2007: 71–91). One way of encouraging readers to look at these charts carefully is to construct them thoughtfully, and then discuss their contents at some length. The writing should be limpid and use the power of language to capture and enliven the patterns in the chart. If the charts are the skeleton of an argument, then the written word is its flesh and blood. The more that the craft of turning numbers into pictures and then into words is valued, the more comfortable people will become reading them. Graphs in sociology, therefore, should function as paintings and photographs do in art history, and the art of constructing and interpreting them should be an integral part of the discipline's curriculum.

Some of the charts designed for idiosyncratic purposes—like Minard's famous graph of Napoleon's march to Moscow (see Wainer, 1997: 63–65)—may rarely, if ever, be replicated. But this is not so with Tables 26.4, 26.5, and 26.8, which could easily serve as templates to construct, variously, the types of graphic matrices that Jacques Bertin recommends, visualizing, as they do, the life course over time and comparing rankings.

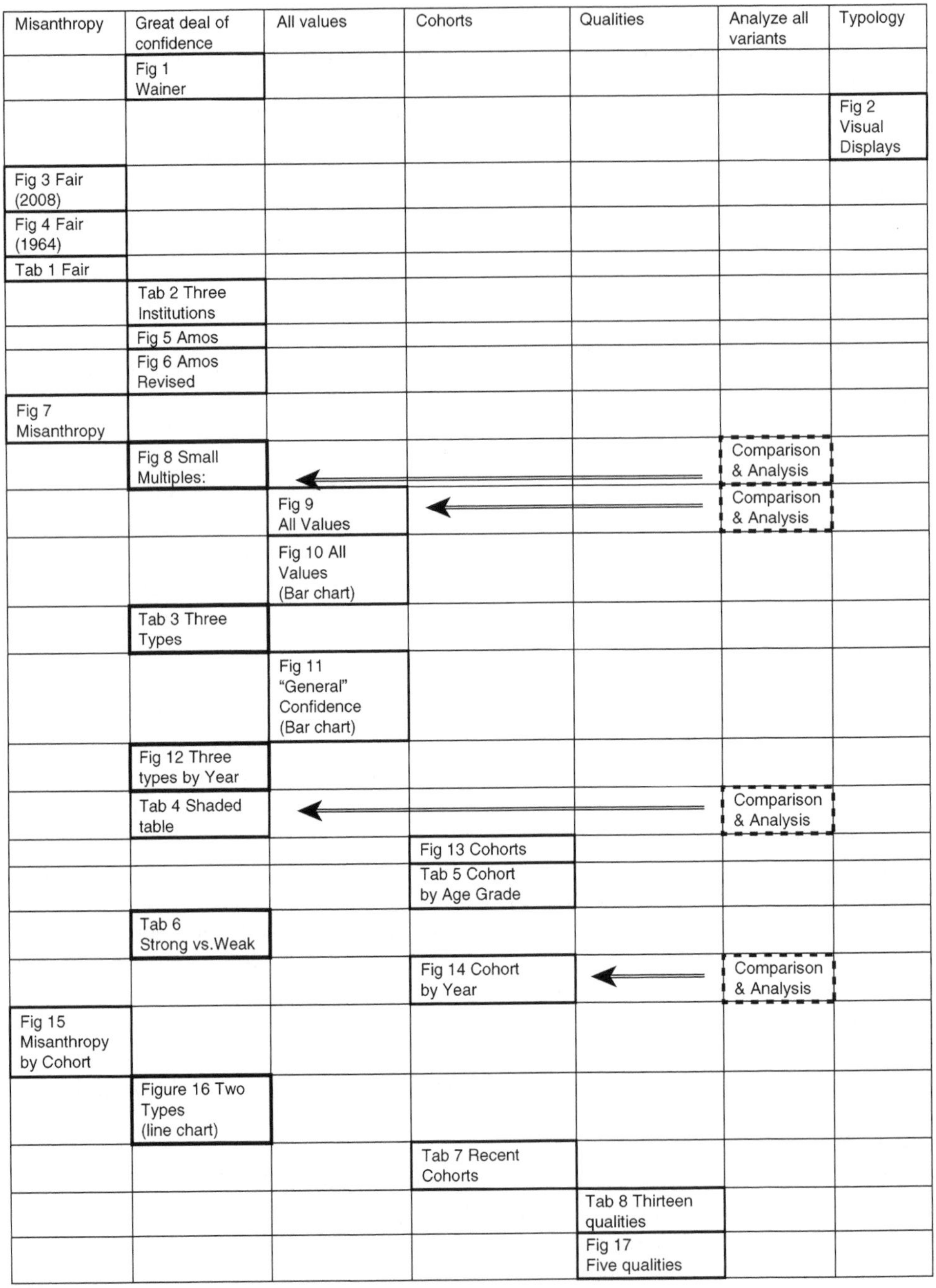

Misanthropy	Great deal of confidence	All values	Cohorts	Qualities	Analyze all variants	Typology
	Fig 1 Wainer					
						Fig 2 Visual Displays
Fig 3 Fair (2008)						
Fig 4 Fair (1964)						
Tab 1 Fair						
	Tab 2 Three Institutions					
	Fig 5 Amos					
	Fig 6 Amos Revised					
Fig 7 Misanthropy						
	Fig 8 Small Multiples:	←			Comparison & Analysis	
		Fig 9 All Values	←		Comparison & Analysis	
		Fig 10 All Values (Bar chart)				
	Tab 3 Three Types					
		Fig 11 "General" Confidence (Bar chart)				
	Fig 12 Three types by Year					
	Tab 4 Shaded table	←			Comparison & Analysis	
			Fig 13 Cohorts			
			Tab 5 Cohort by Age Grade			
	Tab 6 Strong vs.Weak					
			Fig 14 Cohort by Year	←	Comparison & Analysis	
Fig 15 Misanthropy by Cohort						
	Figure 16 Two Types (line chart)					
			Tab 7 Recent Cohorts			
				Tab 8 Thirteen qualities		
				Fig 17 Five qualities		

Figure 26.18   Tables and figures as threads of story in this chapter

It is often the case that the best solution for a particular puzzle can also be applied to similar problems.

Finally, Table 26.8 shows us how a graph can help transform numbers into words. Table 26.8 charts a total of 15 variables: the 13 desirable qualities, generation, and rank order. Once the qualities are arranged in the appropriate rank order, the numbers are no longer necessary, and how the concepts cluster almost dictates what will be written about them. The same is true for Table 26.6, where the GSS' marvelous mnemonics suggest the organizational characteristics of the two institutional groups. Transforming numbers into words on our charts, whenever possible, can also suggest associations that lead to further discoveries.[23]

We live in an era where we are awash in information that is growing geometrically. In order to avoid information overload, we need to find ways of simplifying data without losing sight of its variety and complexity. Statisticians provide us with increasingly complex algorithms, which enable us to manipulate vast amounts of information in ways that are as productive as they are interesting. Very often, the output from these statistical manipulations leaves us at some remove from the evidence itself. The danger in this situation is that it reduces our analysis to a formula, which hinders our ability to switch our analytic perspective from the big picture to seeing how it plays itself out in the details. Visualization of data into images for analytic purposes complements these more sophisticated statistical approaches by enabling us to shift our vision from the large scale to the medium range to the micro level (Grady, 2008). The result is pictures of various sorts—whether photographs, renderings, or, as in our case, standardized charts and creative graphic designs—that can be interpreted, compared and analyzed. A sociology that incorporates a visual sensibility and the craft of image production and display not only will be more fully grounded in its evidence but also will produce accounts and explanations that are more supple than those that do not avail themselves of these modes of seeing and thinking.

NOTES

1 Jon Prosser, Arnie Lieber, Jenni Lund, and Howard Wainer provided very useful feedback on this chapter. None of them, of course, is culpable for what I have made of it.

2 The General Social Survey is online at http://sda.berkeley.edu/cgi-bin/hsda?harcsda+gss08. Every one of its questions, or variables, is assigned a MNEMONIC code, which is usually easy to remember and often describes the question well. It only takes a class period to learn how to do simple correlations with what is generally acknowledged to be the most rigorously conducted and exhaustive social survey in the world of a country's beliefs and attitudes. The GSS has been administered since 1972. A useful guide is Davis and Smith (1992) and a good overview of the GSS as a resource for studying social change is provided by Davis (1997).

3 The institutions are Medicine (CONMEDIC), Science (CONSCI), the Military (CONARMY), Education (CONEDUC), the Supreme Court (CONJUDGE), Banks and Financial Institutions (CONFINAN), Big Business (CONBUS), Religion (CONCLERG), the Executive Office (CONFED), the Press (CONPRESS), the Congress (CONLEGIS), Television (CONTV), and Unions (CONLABOR).

4 Tufte's work includes *The Visual Display of Quantitative Information* (1983), *Envisioning Information* (1990), *Visual Explanations* (1997), and *Beautiful Evidence* (2006).

5 See Grady (2006) for a discussion of what Tufte offers the social sciences.

6 There are a number of very good manuals that articulate principles to guide choice of design. These include: Robert L. Harris' *Information Graphics* (1999), Stephen Few's *Show Me the Numbers* (2004), and Stephen Kosslyn's *Elements of Graph Design* (1994). Kosslyn's book is particularly illuminating because he tempers aesthetic considerations with careful attention to issues of visual perception and cognition.

7 Lists of these fonts are readily available on the Internet. In this case I used Verdana.

8 'If you cannot fit all the labels in wedges, then place all of them next to the appropriate wedges; do not put some labels in wedges, and others next to wedges' (Kosslyn, 1994: 108).

9 When color is not an option, more limited effects can be derived from shading in grayscale. To be legible, however, shading also might require increasing the size of the font, as I did in the body of the text.

10   This formal procedure is rooted in the neuropsychological process of scanning, which can be molded by experience into various scanning strategies. 'A typical scanning strategy is the one we use when reading: we start in the upper left-hand corner and move our eyes across from left to right starting at the top and progressing down' (Ware, 2008: 38). The visual inspection of an image is very much like this strategy.

11   I am indebted to Howard Wainer for bringing this flaw to my attention and to Phil Woodward for showing me how to remedy it.

12   The three questions about others' 'fairness,' 'helpfulness,' and 'trustworthiness,' are commonly referred to as measures of 'misanthropy.'

13   Stephen Few's section on small multiples in *Show Me the Numbers* (2004) is a useful guide. Also, see Tufte's seminal and imaginative discussions in *Envisioning Information* (1990: 67–80) and *Visual Explanations* (1997: 105–121).

14   To arrive at these ratios, I consulted the tabular data. What the eyes direct us to see, the mind should count!

15   The SDA software has a very user-friendly capacity for carrying out a number of sophisticated statistical analyses, including multiple regression.

16   *Science Magazine* reported in December 2003 on a number of scientific 'breakthroughs' for the previous year that could have had a countervailing effect and resulted in a boost of confidence in science. These events included finding genetic markers for mental illness, discerning climate change impacts, the role of RNA molecules in modulating gene expressions, connecting gamma ray bursts and supernovas, and the role of anti-angiogenesis in blocking the growth of cancer cells, to mention a few. Presumably any of these, singly or together, could have compensated for the discouragement by the Columbia tragedy.

17   Parenthetically, it is important that evidence of period effects be considered in a comprehensive manner. For example, once Caitlin Amos (2009) realized that CONFINAN appeared to be tracking periods of economic recession, she re-examined the evidence to see whether the trend tracked every recession since 1975 or just those that she had noticed. This sort of close reading is necessary when evaluating historic events and can improve our theoretical sensitivity as sociologists. In this regard, while it seems self-evident that there should be an increase in confidence in the military after the Gulf and Iraq wars, it is not clear why there also should have been an increase in confidence in 1984 after the Invasion of Granada, but no noticeable effect after the Invasion of Panama in 1989, which was an equally limited military engagement. Comparisons like these can contribute to a more thorough understanding of what properties of historical events influence public opinion. In short, well-designed visual displays are goldmines for new research questions, angles, and insight and should be exploited as such.

18   Bertin's major works include *Graphics and Graphic Information Processing* (1977) and *Semiology of Graphics*, which will be reissued in 2010. An accessible introduction to Bertin can be found in Wainer (2009: 193–198).

19   This is not to say, however, that further manipulation of the rows might not yield an even more elegant way of representing the data. Invariably, all analysis is provisional in this way.

20   One is in the Silent Generation (1925–1942), two in Generation X (1961–1981) and one in the Millennial Generation (1982–2002).

21   Generally speaking, those groups that tend to be more misanthropic are those with less resources and histories of discrimination—the poor, blacks, the young, the uneducated, all of which factors compound each other. Thus, for example, between 1994 and 2008, just fewer than three out of four (73 per cent) older white middle or upper class males with at least a college education asserted that other people were fair. The corresponding figure for young lower or working class black males with less than a 4-year college education was one out of five (20 per cent). Age groups were young (18–29) and old (40–60). Class was self-defined (CLASS).

22   A brief note is in order about CONFINAN and CONBUS, which together measure confidence in organized capitalism. While their organizing principle is the profit motive, they prosper by providing people access to a world of material abundance. It is thus not surprising that CONBUS is relegated to the 'Weak' institutions group. Additionally, CONFINAN is the least robust of the 'Strong' institutions, and may in time be counted as one of the 'Weak' institutions.

23   For example, I never figured out what it was about 1978 and 1993 that led to two big drops in institutional confidence. I'm still not sure why it was those years and not others. But, if we rename the years for incumbent presidents, we notice that Carter was president in 1977 and Clinton in 1993 and, with a little sleuthing, that each represented the first member of his generation to reach the Oval Office. It is possible that the public, generally, may be ambivalent and apprehensive about a decision to anoint a new generation of leaders, and that this may aggravate all of the other factors encouraging a decline in confidence.

REFERENCES

Amos, Caitlin (2009) 'Confidence in financial institutions'. Unpublished course paper. Wheaton College, MA.

Becker, Howard (1998) *Tricks of the Trade*. Chicago, IL: University of Chicago Press.

Becker, Howard (2007) *Telling about Society*. Chicago, IL: University of Chicago Press.

Bertin, Jacques (1977) *Graphics and Graphic Information Processing*. Berlin: Walter de Gruyter.

Davis, James A. (1997) 'The GSS—capturing American attitude change', *The Public Perspective*, February/March: 31–34.

Davis, James A. and Smith, Tom W. (1992) *The NORC General Social Survey: A User's Guide*. Newbury Park, CA: Sage Publications.

Few, Stephen (2004) *Show Me the Numbers: Designing Tables and Graphs to Enlighten*. Oakland, CA: Analytics Press.

Few, Stephen (2009) *Now You See It: Simple Visualization Techniques for Quantitative Analysis*. Oakland, CA: Analytics Press.

Fogel, Robert (2000) *The Fourth Great Awakening and the Future of Egalitarianism*. Chicago, IL: University of Chicago Press.

Grady, John (2006) 'Edward Tufte and the promise of a visual social science', in L. Pauwels (ed.), *Visual Cultures of Science*. Hanover, NH: University Press of New England. pp. 222–265.

Grady, John (2008) 'Visual research at the crossroads': 'Visual methods', *FSQ/Forum Qualitative Sozialforschung / Forum: Qualitative Social Research*, 9(3) [Online]. Available from: http://www.qualitative-research.net/index.php/fqs/article/view/1173 [Accessed 11 October 2010].

Harris, Robert L. (1999) *Information Graphics: A Comprehensive Illustrated Reference*. New York: Oxford University Press.

Kosslyn, Stephen (1994) *Elements of Graph Design*. New York: W. H. Freeman.

Lieberson, Stanley (1985) *Making It Count: The Improvement of Social Research and Theory*. Berkeley, CA: University of California Press.

Paxton, Pamela (2005) 'Trust in decline?' *Contexts*, 4(1): 40–46.

Putnam, Robert (2000) *Bowling Alone*. New York: Simon and Schuster.

Smith, Tom (2008) 'Trends in confidence in Institutions, 1973–2006' (Version 1.2). NORC/University of Chicago.

Strauss, William and Howe, Neil (1991) *Generations*. New York: Morrow.

Strauss, William and Howe, Neil (1997) *The Fourth Turning*. New York: Broadway Books.

Tufte, Edward (1983) *The Visual Display of Quantitative Information*. Cheshire, CN: Graphics Press.

Tufte, Edward (1990) *Envisioning Information*. Cheshire, CN: Graphics Press.

Tufte, Edward (1997) *Visual Explanations*. Cheshire, CN: Graphics Press.

Tufte, Edward (2006) *Beautiful Evidence*. Cheshire, CN: Graphics Press.

Wainer, Howard (1997) *Visual Revelations*. New York: Copernicus.

Wainer, Howard (2009) *Picturing the Uncertain World*. Princeton, NJ: Princeton University Press.

Walkenbach, John (2007) *Excel 2007 Charts*. Hoboken, NJ: Wiley Publishing.

Ware, Colin (2008) *Visual Thinking for Design*. Amsterdam: Morgan Kaufmann.

27

Visual Conceptualization Opportunities with Qualitative Data Analysis Software

Raewyn Bassett

INTRODUCTION

In the past decade, technology advances—especially the digital camera, and cell phones with photo and video features—together with decreasing costs of ownership have contributed to the renewed interest in visual studies (Sweetman, 2009). Additionally, an increasing number of qualitative software programs, or CAQDAS,[1] with the ability to import and manage visual data have made it easier for qualitative researchers to include images such as maps, photographs, scanned drawings, video, and the like in their research projects. While researchers have been slow to engage with CAQDAS (Bassett, 2004) in the past, the availability of software-compatible visual digital technologies now provides new and exciting ways to do things in qualitative research (Dicks et al., 2005).

Visual methods afford ways of looking and seeing that encourage new conceptualizations of data beyond that to be found in the text of transcribed interviews or policy or other documents (Hockey and Collinson, 2006; Sweetman, 2009). And the sensory experience of viewing an image cannot be replicated in text (Banks, 2007). Almost by accident, Collier (1957) discovered that photographs provided a means for research participants to describe their understandings of space and place, of relationships, and everyday activities that spoken questions in semi-structured interviews did not (see Chapter 11, this volume). Focusing on photographs that are meaningful to them, participants feel less the center of the researcher's attention. Photos, drawings, maps, and video can prompt memories, and/or lead participants to see the familiar in a new light (Banks, 2007). However, images are not mere illustrations or addendums to interviews (Stanczak, 2007). Details that may be overlooked, meanings not recognized at the moment of perception, information that cannot be studied closely in the field

(Frisinghelli, 2009) or tacit, embodied knowledge of which participants may be unaware (Dant, 2004; Sweetman, 2009) can be captured in images.[2]

Just as the form, meaning, and effect of an image is influenced by the technologies used in its making (Rose, 2007), so too are these influenced by the technology used to view, see, read, and interpret an image. The structure of CAQDAS programs used to analyze images and other documents encourages, but also constrains, different ways of conceptualizing visual and other data (Boden, 1994). Each CAQDAS package provides a conceptual space specific to it, based on the developer's decisions about how research is to be done. It is this conceptual space (a black box if you will) which the researcher uses to explore and manipulate data (Richards and Richards, 1994). The conceptual space referred to in this chapter is that area in a computer produced by the software program where data are read or viewed, thought about, coded, notes written, diagrams drawn, questions asked, and data retrieved and/or linked in multiple ways. How the conceptual space positions images, text, audio, and codes— that is, whether and how they are juxtaposed—affects the researcher's thinking and understanding of that data. Although the researcher can access and use only those functions the software program enables within this conceptual space, these constraints can foster creativity (Boden, 1994), as well as complacency (LaFrance, 1996). With reciprocal software–researcher engagement (O'Brien and Bassett, 2009), creative exploration and transformation of data is supported and enhanced (Boden, 1994; Richards and Richards, 1994). In the interaction between the software and the researcher, mediated spaces (Burnett, 2005) are created in which 'what we see is no longer given by our eyes but by our instruments' (Johnston, 1999: 30). Johnston (1999) has referred to this as 'machinic vision.' Perceptions of the data are decoded with the use of the different functions of the software and recoded as meaning when the researcher

'sees' them anew in software–researcher interaction. Researcher and software program work together, achieving things neither could do alone. A mediated space is created as a hybridization of the conceptual space of the software and the human user. This space exceeds, and may even overturn, the initial design, intention, and objectives of the software. It is within the boundaries of this mediated space that interactivity and creativity occur (Burnett, 2005).

Reading text and/or listening to utterances while simultaneously viewing an image in a CAQDAS space is a cognitively different experience than doing these same tasks using basic computer programs such as Microsoft Word and Windows Photo Gallery. When using several computer programs simultaneously to read text, listen to participants' dialogue, and view related images the researcher must tab between programs and screens, thus breaking thought processes as attention is redirected to each screen change. A similar case can be made for viewing photos while listening to audio and reading text on paper, without a computer. When these tasks are available simultaneously within a bounded conceptual space, cognition is not interrupted but can advance significantly without pause.

Creativity requires not merely exploration but rather a transformation of the conceptual space. By using the rules embedded in software, researchers can explore and transform the conceptual space (Boden, 1994), rearranging it by manipulating available software functions for uses other than those for which they were designed, and thereby creating new insights in the process (Richards and Richards, 1994). In this chapter, the advantages of working within the conceptual space of different CAQDAS will be explored, and the differences within the conceptual spaces offered by each of the CAQDAS packages will be noted. Most tasks related to analysis are common to all CAQDAS, but it is in their use within the conceptual space specific to a program in which analytic differences, and, I suggest, advantages, are evident. The conceptual opportunities that NVivo, ATLAS.ti, Transana, and HyperRESEARCH softwares offer to visual methods are explored in this chapter.

QUALITATIVE DATA ANALYSIS SOFTWARE REQUIREMENTS

Of the four softwares discussed in this chapter, HyperRESEARCH and Transana are available for both Macintosh and PC computers, while NVivo and ATLAS.ti are principally PC programs but can be run with PC simulation software on the Macintosh. The requirements for working with visual data using CAQDAS programs are few. Most image formats (for example, jpeg or tiff) are readily usable by most image-processing software, including CAQDAS. Upon import into NVivo software, images are converted to .jpeg files. HyperRESEARCH supports PICT files on Macintosh operating systems. Images can be imported into Transana, although the software was developed to support video rather than photographs and scanned still images. If an image is too large, image-processing software can be used to reduce its size so that it can be comfortably used within the software screen area. Video is more specific to each software program and may need to be converted to meet their requirements. In either case, the researcher may need to make decisions that consider the equipment to be used for image capture and whether to match the software choice to the equipment to be used, or vice versa.

Any number of images and video can be imported into the software. The larger the project, the more computer memory is required in order to run the software program without mishaps such as slowing of functions and crashes. This is a computer problem, however, not a software problem. In addition, the number of images and video, as well as the image quality (which affects the size of the image file) will determine the amount of data storage needed. With visual data, attention to the storage of files and ensuring sufficient RAM to run the software is necessary. Also, researchers should ensure that the data are both secure and safe. Attention should be paid to restricting access to data, in a similar manner to participant data collected in paper or audio files. In addition, backups should be planned for and maintained in order to ensure that an unexpected system crash doesn't destroy the data, and therefore the project.

Finally, user training requirements should be considered. Each program, while similar in nature, has specific tools, functions, and terminology. The flexibility, and robustness of these programs implies a complexity of use that can seem daunting. Practically, these differences may discourage users from considering a change to a different program once the investment has been made in training on the use of a particular program. However, a number of training opportunities exist, as well as user groups and help forums. The software chosen should be the one that is best suited to addressing the research questions. The time spent up-front to learn the nuances of the particular program is returned in the strength of the analysis available.

SOFTWARE SOLUTIONS FOR VISUAL STUDIES

Qualitative data analysis software has been designed to support the researcher in the interpretation and analysis of a variety of data sources, including images, text, and audio. With the import of still and moving images into CAQDAS, new options for analysis are available to researchers. The basic functions include: coding of data; searching, retrieving, and defining codes; making connections between codes and/or documents; clustering data or codes; outlining emerging understandings of the data visually; writing memos; and abstracting and exporting tables of numerical and textual data to Excel or SPSS. However, it is the arrangement of these functions in the specific software that affords the researcher distinct and very different opportunities for exploring data. To illustrate these opportunities, I shall draw upon the results of a study of qualitative researchers in Nova Scotia, Canada, in which these four software programs, HyperRESEARCH, Transana, NVivo, and ATLAS.ti were used for the analysis.

Researching Nova Scotia Researcher's use of CAQDAS programs

This pilot project set out to explore how researchers in the province used CAQDAS in their research. After receiving Dalhousie University Ethics Review Board (ERB) approval, 10 researchers were recruited to the study. Conversational interviews of 1–1.5 hours were conducted with each researcher and digitally recorded. Researchers were asked about their qualitative research experience, how they decided upon the CAQDAS program they used, which functions of the program they used and why, and what support they had in its use. At the end of the interview they were given a disposable camera and asked to take photographs that illustrated how they identify themselves as qualitative researchers. They were explicitly told, on the advice of the ERB, that they could not include people in their photographs, and that they must ensure any pictures of family, friends, and colleagues, and that any data on computers from their research projects were not visible in the photographs. Of the 10 researchers interviewed, three were research assistants or associates, two were doctoral students, and five were principal investigators. The digital audio interviews and photographs of the participants were then imported into each of the four software programs.

In this chapter, the focus is on the photographs only. The conceptual space of each software program will be described first, followed by some of the findings emerging from the use of that conceptual space to illustrate how, with user interaction, the space becomes a mediated space. Not all functions of each software program (only those used to obtain the results below) will be discussed.

Transana

Although still images such as photographs can be imported into the software program Transana, in order to utilize the full range of functions such as applying keywords to transcribed text, video, and/or audio files are required. A slide show of 36 photographs from the research study, 'Researching Nova Scotia Researchers' was made using Windows Movie Maker and imported into Transana. The juxtaposition of screens in Transana allowed for a simultaneous working back and forth by the user between photographs, transcript, keywords, and clips and collections (Figure 27.1). Time codes in the transcript link text and slide show, and a 'Notes' function enables field notes and memos to be written about the photographs and keyword searches.

Tools of the trade

Within Transana, each of the 36 photographs in the slide show was labeled using the Transcript field, and keywords applied to the text. The photographs taken by participants consisted mainly of objects, such as computers, thumb drives, journals, coffee mugs; and of places, such as offices, country roads, backyards, and flower gardens. Watching the photographs replace each other slowly as the slide show played, it was apparent that these qualitative researchers were users of technology and contemplated their data in many different places, not merely the office alone. Technologies such as digital recorders and laptops were portable, allowing the researchers to engage with their data in quiet places such as gardens or while sometimes doing

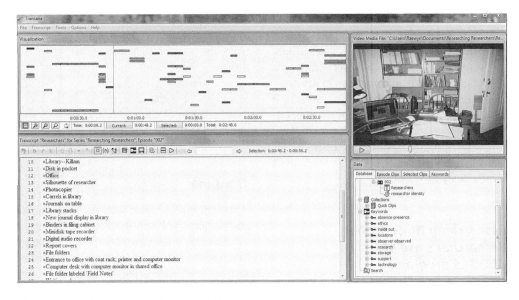

Figure 27.1   The conceptual space of Transana

other things such as driving. Using the 'Notes' function in the software, I documented my observations as I watched the photos play one by one. The Notes screen must be closed in order to use further functions in the software, so alternately the transcription space (lower left screen) can be used to record thoughts and ideas. 'Keywords' (codes) initially assigned to photographs were mere topics without conceptual depth (Sandelowski and Barroso, 2003), for example, 'shared office' and 'backyard' (lower right screen in Figure 27.1). An option in the visualization screen that allowed keywords to be viewed with the timeline of the slide show was selected (upper left screen in Figure 27.1). Simultaneously with the assignment of keywords to data, clips of the slide show, each constituting a single photo, were created.

Presence–absence

As the photos turned from one to another on screen, in some office scenes the researcher's presence could be felt, while in others not. A search using the Boolean OR to retrieve all photographs assigned the keyword 'office' enabled a closer investigation of only those photographs. They could be explored in

sequence rather than separated by other photos as they were in the slide show. A keyword for 'presence–absence' was created. One photo in particular gave a strong sense of the presence of the researcher even though she was absent from the photograph (upper right in Figure 27.1). In the Notes function in the software I wrote:

> In this clip of the office, you can imagine entering through the open door and finding the researcher there but out of sight, looking up files in a filing cabinet, or sitting in a chair for example. The photograph gives a sense for the viewer of immediately conversing with the person in the room upon entry through the open door. The researcher has a presence although absent from the photograph.

Books and a day planner open on the desk, an active computer screen in addition to the door ajar contribute to this impression. Rather than looking in on the photograph, the viewer has a sense of being able to walk into the photograph through the partly open door, thus also placing the viewer there with the researcher. Exploration of the three further photographs of offices did not provide the same strong sense of presence–absence even though in one photograph an anonymous researcher is shown at the computer keyboard, and in another, coats hanging on a coat rack imply the presence of an unseen researcher.

Temporal aspects of presence–absence

Returning to the slide show of photographs, the conceptualization of presence–absence now provided a new lens with which to 'see.' In the photograph of the office (Figure 27.1), past, present, and future are captured: in the present the viewer looks at a past scene captured by the camera and anticipates a future interaction with the out-of-sight researcher. In two other photos there was also a strong presence of the absent researcher-photographer. A temporal aspect emerged: the fusing of past (there–then) and present (here–now) (Barthes, 1977: 44), and in the photo of the office discussed above, the projection of past and present into the future.

A photo of a highway, taken by a study participant through her car windshield, implied her contemplation of research data (perhaps listening to the interviews) while she was driving. In reviewing the photograph, the viewer becomes the driver: the eyes of each combine as each looks through the car windshield down the road, the road markings giving a sense of movement. The photograph is framed in such a way that we are led out of the frame in the far distance. This scene of a 'there–then' moment captured in the photograph is also the 'here–now' as the viewer becomes the driver.

In another photograph, the fusion of past and present has an additional element: the viewer both watches the photo being taken while at the same time seeing through the eyes of the photographer. In this photo, the researcher's silhouette is caught in the flash of the camera against the glass of the window as she photographs her backyard from inside the house. The viewer sees the scene captured from the photographer's eyes while also looking in at the photographer, watching her snap the shot. The viewer is taken from her present viewing position to the past where she is also simultaneously the photographer and the viewer of the photograph as it was taken.

Moving between the various screens and functions in Transana, writing Notes, viewing the photos and visualizing keywords applied to the photographs, the researcher uses the conceptual space established by the developer. The screen where the photo is viewed can be enlarged but at the expense of the diminishing size of the windows juxtaposed with it. Data must be managed in specific ways, for example, and while photographs can be imported into Transana as single still images, they cannot be coded with keywords and the keywords then used to retrieve specific chunks of coded data. However, by manipulating the data requirements of the software and creating a slide show of the photographs, the software functions can be used to their full extent and ideas tested using Boolean searches in ways they cannot when attempted by hand. Furthermore, the positioning of photos provides ways of seeing that differ in comparison with other software, as is explained below.

NVivo

The photographs were imported into NVivo software, each as a single data source rather than as a slide show, although the latter is possible. In NVivo a photograph is displayed to the left center of the screen and adjacent to the right is an area in which notes about the content of the photographs can be written, and the pixel region assigned, linking the text to a specific area of the photograph (Figure 27.2). The photo is coded by pulling the cursor across and down, over the area of interest and assigning one or more labels (codes), called Free Nodes or Tree Nodes in NVivo (Figure 27.2). The content column can also be coded by highlighting a string of text and assigning a code. Coding 'stripes,' which visually display the codes assigned to any one photo and/or the content column, can be turned on. In Figure 27.2 , diagonally shaded stripes indicate coding to the content column while solid shaded stripes apply to the photograph. Other software functions include 'search and retrieval' tools, relationship-naming between

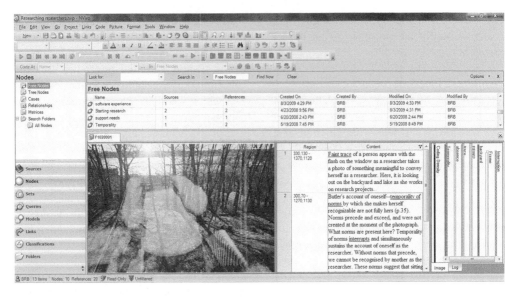

Figure 27.2   The conceptual space of NVivo 8

codes, and a tool for visually modeling ideas.

Positioning photographs

In NVivo, a content analysis of each of the photographs was conducted. Denotations of the objects in the photographs were listed in the Tree Nodes window and the photographs coded accordingly. In Transana's conceptual space this same listing was done in the transcript, which was coded to keywords or codes. In NVivo, the photographs and/or portions of them could be assigned to codes without transcription. Lost, however, was the immediate overall conceptualization of researchers as users of technology and as doers of research in various locations, as had been available in Transana. Tabbing from one photo to the next in NVivo left each photograph somewhat disconnected from the previous. Now positioned in the center of the conceptual space rather than in the upper right corner as they had been in Transana, the sense of walking into the office or of driving along the highway, as was the case previously, was absent in these same photos. In this way, however, the photos were entities in themselves; this encouraged studying each

in more depth. Interestingly, a photograph that had not had the same sense of inviting the viewer in when viewed in Transana did so in NVivo. Pursuing these conceptual differences back and forth between Transana and NVivo, it seems that where the photo is positioned in the conceptual space influences how both photo and viewer's eye meet.

The content column to the right of each photograph encouraged writing about the photos. Although much of the same work could be done in memos elsewhere in NVivo's conceptual space, the content column was in close proximity to the photograph. The content column could be used for a variety of purposes, and was not restricted to merely noting a photograph's content. It encouraged longer memos and was used to bring theoretical ideas to the photographs, and to develop those ideas next to the photograph. Thoughts about associated theories were notated (Figure 27.2), which, in turn, in an iterative back and forth movement, informed codes and memos. Memos were used to document the conceptual ideas developing as data was assigned to codes.

Cases were constructed in NVivo to cluster the photographs taken by each individual research participant. A 'case' is a data management tool, and in this study each case was an individual research participant. Attributes (variables) and the values of attributes can be assigned to cases. In this research, sociodemographic attributes and values were assigned to each case: for example, the researcher's role was assigned as an attribute, and a research associate or doctoral student was a value of that attribute. Other attributes included type of qualitative research in which the individual participant engaged, their workplaces, years of experience in research, and so on. One of the advantages of this tool is that searches of codes can be refined using cases and attributes. For instance, to answer the question, 'Does role in research influence the content of photographs taken by researchers?' the Boolean AND was used to intersect the codes which denoted the contents of the photographs (for example, printers, laptops, thumb drives, staplers, three-hole punches) with the values of the attribute 'Research role' (for example, principal investigator, research associate, doctoral student). Data to answer this question were retrieved in numerical tabular format. Clicking on any cell in the table produced the coded images and text from the associated content column. The retrieved data in answer to the above question indicated that research associates photographed the objects used in research more so than principal investigators and doctoral students. This finding made sense since research associates are more likely to use these tools than principal investigators and faculty, whose roles are more focused on coordinating and managing than doing the 'hands-on' research. Furthermore, principal investigators took more photographs of gardens and backyards where they might sit to ponder the results of the analysis than did research associates who, with doctoral students, took more photographs of offices.

Inside–outside

A zoom tool available in most CAQDAS programs enlarges details in the photograph or image. Aspects that might have been missed in normal view were made obvious. On the initial viewing in Transana of the photograph in Figure 27.2, it was the photographer's silhouette that captured the eye. Resizing the photo using the zoom tool in NVivo provided further insights. Other objects initially perceived to be outside in the yard were seen to be reflections from inside the house and vice versa. What appeared to be a slab of concrete outside was actually a table in the house, covered with an embroidered cloth trimmed with lace; a doily (a small lace mat) in the lower right-hand corner of the image had been invisible in normal view; a radiator was mistaken for a fence; what looked like the lawn outside was green carpet covering the floor of the house; and the fabric and creases of the photographer's pants were twigs, soil, and the shadows of tree branches. Such clarifications can lead to new insights in directions not previously considered, such as the social and cultural framing work of photographs (Van Eck and Winters, 2005; Rose, 2007).

Social/cultural framing

The researcher's silhouette represents her absence from the photo in accordance with the Dalhousie University ERB's instructions to exclude people in a photograph. Despite the ERB's instructions and the researcher's attempts to comply, her silhouette is captured in the flash of the camera. The researcher remains anonymous, but her presence is fully visible. The composition of any photograph organizes several aspects: (1) where the viewer looks in the image; (2) how the viewer looks at the image; and (3) the scopic regime of ocular centrism (Haraway, 1991; Jenks, 1995). The framing of the researcher's silhouette is so unexpected that it captures the viewer's attention. The photograph not only frames the present-but-absent researcher but also frames cultural thoughts and practices. Thus, the ERB's current requirements regarding photographs in social science research are framed in the photograph. The ethical concern to ensure not only the anonymity and confidentiality of the study participants but also anyone associated with them whose picture might hang on a wall or sit on a desk was included in the instructions to absent people from the photographs taken.

The specter

Moving from one photograph to another by tabbing from photo to photo after opening each in NVivo (horizontal center of Figure 27.2), the silhouette of the researcher can be traced in every other photograph. The researcher is a trace or specter (Derrida, 1994) present yet unseen, haunting the photos. Now viewers of the photographs, instead of seeing only coffee mugs and printers and office scenes can imagine the researcher in each context, tracing her through each of the photos. These insights were documented in memos in NVivo and used to construct further understandings of the code 'presence–absence.' Advantage was taken of the flexibility of NVivo's code system, where codes as 'Free Nodes' can remain standalone, unlinked to other codes as they are developed; these can later be hierarchically related to other codes and sub-codes or 'Tree Nodes.' A Tree Node of presence–absence was created with the sub-codes 'absence,' 'trace,' and 'double haunting.'

The alignment of photographs and content areas for writing in NVivo provided different ways of seeing and thinking than Transana's conceptual space. Especially potent was the positioning of images in each software program, which led to different analyses. In NVivo, the ability to write while observing the photograph and not have to open and close the writing space allowed a more continuous and immediate flow of thoughts. Coding of images in addition to coding of text provided additional advantages in the conceptual process. Constructing cases (that is, individual researchers) and grouping the photographs for each case together, as well as assigning attributes and values to each case, facilitated a more detailed retrieval of coded data to answer questions in relation to the researchers and their photographs.

This led to topical codes becoming more conceptual.

ATLAS.ti

In ATLAS.ti, the Hermeneutic Unit (HU) is the term used to refer to the research project-space. On opening the program, the default HU loads immediately and a spiraling cloud of codes, showing the most frequently used codes in correspondingly larger fonts, indicates visually which ideas in the analysis are the most prominent. Toolbars sit to the left and at the top of the screen (Figure 27.3). A large area is available for viewing data, and coding is immediately visible to the right of the document. After assigning the photographs to the HU, each photograph is opened from the Primary Document (PD) drop-down menu for exploration. Each photograph closes out when the next is opened. A photograph is viewed unencumbered by an associated writing space; however, in order to note thoughts and ideas, a memo must be opened, which is easily accessed from a drop-down menu at the top of the screen (Figure 27.3) or inserted in the right margin.

Upon import, the photographs were not grouped together in any specific order in the PD manager, although a useful numbering system there can be used for this purpose, such as keeping the documents for each participant together so they can be viewed at the same time. In this study, however, the photographs were grouped as 'Families,' a function in ATLAS.ti that allowed the photos of all participants who were research associates, for example, to be grouped in a Family of that name. Filtering by Family helps the researcher to avoid being distracted by photographs of other kinds of researchers.

Coding of photographs is undertaken in similar fashion to that in NVivo by pulling the cursor through the area of interest in the document and assigning a code. A square or rectangle is drawn around the area of interest (Figure 27.3). Coding stripes are immediately visible to the right of the photograph as

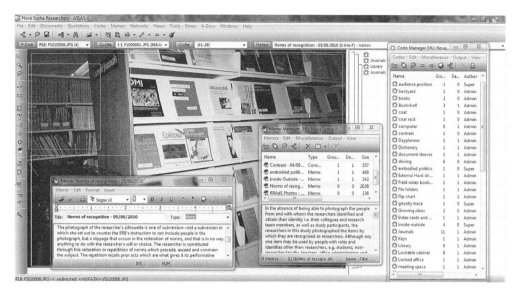

Figure 27.3 The conceptual space of ATLAS.ti

data are coded. Coding stripes are colored square brackets (]) that line up with the area of a document assigned to a code (Figure 27.3). As long as the right-hand margin is turned on, each code and bracket appears in the margin as the researcher codes. There is no limitation to the number of codes that can be displayed. In the Code Manager, codes stand alone until connected in a network. The more links between codes, the more dense the connection.

Recognizing researchers

As had been done with the two previous software programs, codes as topics, rather than concepts, were assigned to the items in each photograph. Building upon the exploration and investigation of photographs in NVivo and Transana, ways that the study participants recognize themselves as researchers took more of a focus in ATLAS.ti. A search and retrieval using the Boolean 'OR' gathered those photos assigned to 'item' codes. In ATLAS.ti, retrieved data are displayed in context, highlighted within the document of origin and in the order in which data were coded. If an image in a document was coded first, text in another document coded second,

another image third, and sound in an audio file fourth, then they are retrieved and displayed by the software in that order. If viewing and coding an image led the researcher to another document, which then led her to another image, then viewing and reading the retrieved data for a specific code in ATLAS.ti can remind the researcher of those implicit connections in the data.

After exploring the retrieval of coding for objects used in research, it became apparent that in the absence of ERB permission to include photographs of the people with and by whom they recognize themselves as researchers (that is, their research teams and the participants of research), the objects photographed by the researchers—the coffee mugs, the laptops, thumb drives, photocopiers, printers, books, and journals—took on significance as the objects by which they and others recognized a researcher. The instructions to researchers in the study from the ERB to not include people in their photographs, anchored in a history of increasing the protection of research subjects while simultaneously protecting the university from liability, excluded the very aspects by which qualitative researchers recognized themselves as researchers who interact face to face and spend time with their participants in collecting or generating data. The photographs did not differentiate qualitative researchers from those who do numerical analysis. It would be an easy conclusion to make from the results of a retrieval query using the Boolean OR to gather photos assigned to codes that suggested qualitative research might be conducted more easily in outdoor areas such as gardens or while driving. But, what could not be overlooked was that quantitative researchers, too, might contemplate their research results while in cars or gardens. The effect and power of the ERB instruction was to constitute the qualitative researcher as a researcher who is indistinguishable from any other type of researcher.

The topic codes that represented the objects in which researchers placed their recognition were brought together in a network view (Figure 27.4) for further exploration. The network view tool provides a visual space for thinking about concepts. As codes are linked to one another, the density of links between codes is recorded in ATLAS.ti (right screen in Figure 27.4). How 'grounded' a code is in data is also recorded. The 'groundedness' of a code refers to the number of times a section of a document or the full document has been assigned to a code by the researcher; hence, codes with a higher numerical value for groundedness have had data assigned to them more times than other codes. This can lead to further questions and searches of the data, such as: Do principal investigators recognize themselves through photographs that include journals more than do research associates? Codes in ATLAS.ti stand alone until linked 'symmetrically' or 'asymmetrically' in one or more network views. With linking, a hierarchical view of codes is created (center screen, Figure 27.4); however, the hierarchy is not contained within the coding structure used to code documents. In a conceptual space in which codes are not visibly accessible as hierarchies, codes can be developed more fully and are more robust; links between codes can be made later.

Tracing the specter

The specter of the researcher which emerged in NVivo could be visually traced in ATLAS.ti using hyperlinking and viewing the hyperlinks in a network view. Hyperlinking, a series of links or markers between sections of

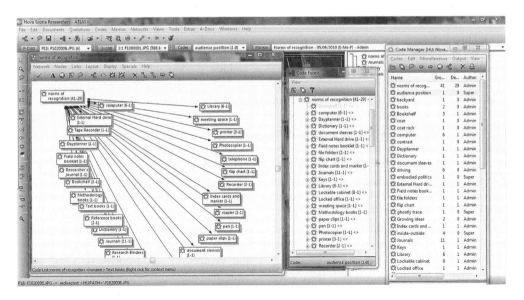

Figure 27.4   A network view in ATLAS.ti

documents (Snyder, 1996), connects one document with another in ATLAS.ti software. It is possible to retrieve the linked documents in a network view. In NVivo, the links are limited to codes, usually between two codes at a time, although workarounds are possible. Hyperlinking provides multiple rhizomatic pathways through data (Deleuze and Guattari, 1987; Mason and Dicks, 1999); pathways can be entered at any point. Two types of pathways can be constructed in ATLAS.ti: a set of linear links called a *chain*, in which sections of documents or whole documents link to each other in a straight line (Figure 27.5); and multiple pathways projecting out from a central point, called a *star*, resembling a hub (the central point, for example, a document or a code) and spokes (the links that move out from the central point to other linked items). Each provides different readings depending upon where the researcher enters the pathway. Hyperlinking, then, provides the researcher with a process other than coding to think about and helps to conceptualize the emerging analysis. Hyperlinking addresses some of the theoretical and methodological concerns expressed about fragmenting data (Coffey et al., 1996),

authorship (Barthes, 1977), representation (Denzin, 1997), and post-paradigm ethnography (Marcus and Fischer, 1986). Tracing the specter of the researcher through the hyperlinked photographs (Figure 27.5) provides an understanding in which any one image in the chain is now informed by each of the other images. In observing the hyperlinked images, for instance, the silhouette of the researcher can be traced to each photograph: about to select a book off the shelf, reading a journal in the library, present in the office or driving down the highway. In each photograph she stands before the viewer, clicking the shutter.

HyperRESEARCH

In the conceptual space of HyperRESEARCH, images and documents are positioned to the right of the screen with 'Case' and 'Code' lists juxtaposed to the left. There are three options provided by the software for positioning these three screens, based on researcher preference. In this study, I employed the option that allowed the image to be displayed as fully as possible when the cases and codes screens were selected (Figure 27.6).

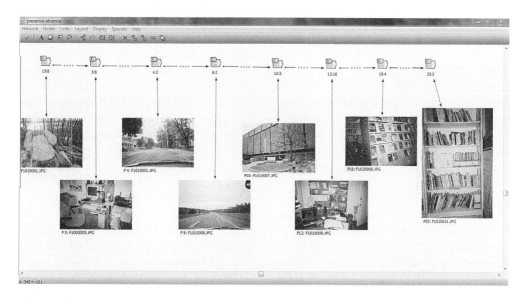

Figure 27.5 Horizontal *chain* hyperlinking in ATLAS.ti

Figure 27.6   The conceptual space of HyperRESEARCH

Boolean search and retrieval of codes, and a 'Hypothesis Tester' (a concept map in which codes can be diagrammed) are included in the conceptual space of HyperRESEARCH. A frequency report of codes provides a numerical overview of how many times data has been assigned to a code, similar to the groundedness of codes in ATLAS.ti (NVivo includes a 'percentage of document coded') and a bar chart to provide the same information visually (also included in NVivo and Transana).

Contrasting structures

In HyperRESEARCH, the photographs were displayed in much larger size and detail than in the previous software programs. Additional items were uncovered that had remained invisible until now, such as a clothesline in the upper right corner of the photo in Figure 27.2. As before, codes were applied to the photographs as they were imported into HyperRESEARCH (bottom left screen, Figure 27.6). In this software, the detail in the photographs now brought contrasts to the forefront. The most notable was the contrast in the photograph in Figure 27.6 between the hard concrete structure of the university library and the more ethereal picture of the

lone tree coming into leaf. The bent, forked branches contrasted with the straight lines of the rectangular blocks of the library, solid concrete with leaves that seem to float in space, the strength of the latter and the fragility of the former also symbolizing different versions of how knowledge is constructed.

Researchers as growers of ideas

Taking this observation back to the photographs, in one, the office in Figure 27.1, clay plant pots became visible. The pots represented growth and its absence. Two clay pots sat on the floor near the door, stacked inside each other, still with soil, perhaps awaiting a new season and new plants, or perhaps neglected, the plants now dead. On the bookshelf behind these two pots, and to the left, sits a blue plant pot out of which notepaper is bursting, symbolizing the growth of ideas (Figure 27.7). In other photographs, too, researchers had snapped green gardens and backyards upon which they looked as they pondered and reflected upon their research data and findings.

The code map in HyperRESEARCH was used to link the related codes that had been applied to these three photographs

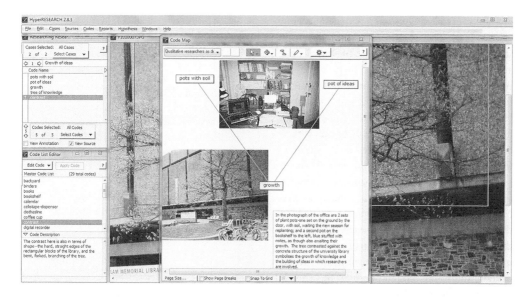

Figure 27.7   Code map linking codes, photographs, and memo in HyperRESEARCH

(growth, pots with soil, and pot of ideas). The photographs were brought into the code map and scaled to an appropriate size, and a memo written (Figure 27.7), thus visualizing hunches and ideas and encouraging their further development. The Hypothesis Tester, based on production rules (If this....Then that), was then used to think further about these ideas. In HyperRESEARCH the Hypothesis Tester is intended to test working ideas and hunches. To do so requires coding to de done directionally, unlike coding in the three previous programs. Whereas codes in the three previous software programs can include all dimensions of the code, for example, positive and negative aspects, in Hyper-RESEARCH codes must be more carefully defined with the different dimensions of a code as separate codes (Hesse-Biber and Dupuis, 2000). Using the Hypothesis Tester, the idea of researchers 'growing ideas' could be extended to their full development as knowledge in publications including journals, books, and articles on the bookcases in the many offices photographed. The use of the Hypothesis Tester was not so much out of a desire to test a hunch or hypothesis as a desire to use this tool for analysis, trying out

and making explicit different combinations of codes in the 'If this...then that' format. The Hypothesis Tester provided a very different conceptual space than ATLAS.ti, Transana, or NVivo. As with the 'Query' and 'Search' tools in the other three software programs, the results from the Hypothesis Tester are dependent upon the quality and completeness of the coding of the researcher.

As with each of the other software programs, the availability of screens for viewing and coding images in close proximity contributed to an uninterrupted conceptualization of ideas with previous ideas (that is, codes) in view. In HyperRESEARCH, the quality of the photographs in the conceptual space and the detail that was available to the eye provided new views and new insights. The positioning of images, the uncluttered screens, and the ease of use of the Hypothesis Tester provided a very different conceptual space than NVivo, ATLAS.ti, and Transana.

CONCLUSION

CAQDAS programs such as ATLAS.ti, Transana, HyperRESEARCH, and NVivo provided creative approaches to analyzing visual data. The requirements of the four software programs for the use of visual data are few: consideration should be given to the type of data produced, to equipment choices for image capture, data storage and manipulation, and user training needs, for example. Each program provides a conceptual space based on the developer's ideas about qualitative research; thus each conceptual space poses constraints as well as opportunities for analysis. Software functions can be combined in a myriad of ways not imagined by the developer. In software–user interaction, the conceptual space is transformed into a mediated space, often overturning the initial design, intention, and objectives the developer had for the use of the software in research (Burnett, 2005). For example, Transana was developed for the analysis of video. Creating a slide show of photographs manipulated the research design created by the developers, putting it to uses other than that anticipated. CAQDAS programs available for visual methods research provide opportunities not previously available to visual researchers, and push the boundaries in terms of what can be accomplished in visual analysis.

NOTES

1 Computer Assisted Qualitative Data Analysis Software is commonly referred to in its abbreviated form as CAQDAS. Specific seminar sessions devoted to the use of CAQDAS in research are often offered at conferences throughout the social sciences.

2 A number of authors in this volume have addressed ways of using photographs, maps, or video in their research, including methods such as photo-elicitation (Chapters 11 and 12), video ethnography (Chapters 5 and 31), participatory mapping (Chapter 25), rephotography (Chapters 6 and 7), and the arts (Chapter 33).

REFERENCES

Banks, M. (2007) *Using Visual Data in Qualitative Research*. London: Sage Publications.

Barthes, R. (1977) 'The death of the author', in *Image Music Text*, translated by S. Heath. New York: Hill and Wang. pp. 142–148.

Bassett, R. (2004) 'Qualitative data analysis software: Analyzing the debates', *Journal of Management Systems*, 16(4): 33–39.

Boden, M. (1994) 'Creativity and computers', in T. Dartnell (ed.), *Artificial Intelligence and Creativity*. The Netherlands: Kluwer Academic Publishers. pp. 3–26.

Burnett, R. (2005) *How Images Think*. Cambridge, MA: MIT Press.

Coffey, A., Holbrook, B. and Atkinson, P. (1996) 'Qualitative data analysis: Technologies and representations'. *Sociological Research Online*, 1(1) http://socresonline.org.uk/1/1/4.html

Collier, J. (1957) 'Photography in anthropology: A report on two experiments', *American Anthropologist*, 59: 843–859.

Dant, T. (2004) 'Recording the "Habitus"', in C. Pole (ed.), *Seeing is Believing? Approaches to Visual Research*. Oxford: Elsevier.

Deleuze, G. and Guattari, F. (1987) 'Introduction: Rhizome', in *A Thousand Plateaus: Capitalism and Schizophrenia*, translated by Brian Massumi. Minneapolis, MN: University of Minnesota Press. pp. 3–26.

Denzin, N. K. (1997) 'Lessons James Joyce teaches us', in *Interpretive Ethnography: Ethnographic practices for the 21st century*. Thousand Oaks, CA: Sage Publications.

Derrida, J. (1994) *Specters of Marx: The State of the Debt, the Work of Mourning and the New International*. New York: Routledge.

Dicks, B., Mason, B., Coffey, A. and Atkinson, P. (2005) *Qualitative Research and Hypermedia: Ethnography in the Digital Age*. London: Sage Publications.

Frisinghelli, C. (2009) 'Photographs in context: Notes on handling an archive and looking at the exhibition Pierre Bourdieu's photographic documentary Accounts in Algeria, 1957–1961', translated by M. O'Neill, *The Sociological Review*, 57(3): 512–521.

Haraway, D. (1991) 'Situated knowledges: The science question in Feminism and the privilege of partial perspective', in *Simians, Cyborgs, and Women: The Reinvention of Nature*. New York: Routledge. pp. 183–201.

Hesse-Biber, S. and Dupuis, P. (2000) 'Testing hypotheses on qualitative data: The use of HyperRESEARCH computer-assisted software', *Social Science Computer Review*, 18: 320–328.

Hockey, J. and Collinson, J. (2006) 'Seeing the way: Visual sociology and the distance runner's perspective', *Visual Studies*, 21(1): 70–81.

Jenks, C. (1995) 'The centrality of the eye in Western culture: An introduction', in C. Jenks (ed.), *Visual Culture*. London: Routledge. pp. 1–25.

Johnston, J. (1999) 'Machinic vision', *Critical Inquiry*, 26(1): 27–48.

LaFrance, M. (1996) 'Why we trust computers too much', *Technology Studies*, 3(2): 163–178.

Marcus, G. E. and Fischer, M. (1986) *Anthropology as Cultural Critique: An Experimental Moment in the Human Sciences*. Chicago, IL: University of Chicago Press.

Mason, B. and Dicks, B. (1999) 'The digital ethnographer', *Cybersociology: Research Methodology Online*, 6(1). [Online]. Available from: *www.cybersociology.com* [Accessed 25 July 2005].

O'Brien, H. and Bassett, R. (2009) 'Exploring engagement in the qualitative research process'. Poster presented at American Society for Information Science & Technology (ASIS&T) Conference, Vancouver, BC.

Richards, T. and Richards, L. (1994) 'Creativity in social sciences', in T. Dartnell (ed.), *Artificial Intelligence and Creativity*. The Netherlands: Kluwer Academic Publishers. pp. 365–383.

Rose, G. (2007) *Visual Methodologies: An Introduction to the Interpretation of Visual Materials*, 2nd edn. London: Sage Publications.

Sandelowski, M. and Barroso, J. (2003) 'Classifying the findings in qualitative studies', *Qualitative Health Research*, 13 (7): 905–923.

Snyder, I. (1996) *Hypertext: The Electronic Labyrinth*. New York: New York University Press.

Stanczak, G. C. (2007) *Visual Research Methods: Image, Society and Representation*. Los Angeles, CA: Sage Publications.

Sweetman, P. (2009) 'Revealing habitus, illuminating practice: Bourdieu, photography and visual methods', *The Sociological Review*, 57(3): 491–511.

Van Eck, C. and Winters, E. (2005) 'Introduction', in C. Van Eck and E. Winters (eds.), *Dealing with the Visual: Art History, Aesthetics, and Visual Culture*. Aldershot: Ashgate. pp. 1–13.

PART 6

Moving Beyond the Visual

28

Multimodality and Multimodal Research

Theo van Leeuwen

INTRODUCTION

The term 'multimodality' dates from the 1920s. It was a technical term in the then relatively new field of the psychology of perception, denoting the effect that different sensory perceptions may have on each other. An example of this is the so-called McGurk effect: if people are shown a video of someone articulating a particular syllable, for example, /ga/, while hearing another syllable, for example, /ba/, they perceive neither /ga/, nor /ba/, but /da/ (Stork, 1997: 239). In other words, perception is multimodal. It integrates information received by different senses.

More recently the term has broadened to denote the integrated use of different communicative resources such as language, image, sound, and music in multimodal texts and communicative events. The impetus for this came from linguistics and discourse analysis rather than from psychology. As soon as linguists began to study texts and communicative events rather than isolated sentences, they realized what they should have known all along: that communication is multimodal; that spoken language cannot be adequately understood without taking non-verbal communication into account; and that many forms of contemporary written language cannot be adequately understood unless both text and image are taken into consideration. In time this discovery led to the development of multimodality as a field of study investigating the common properties of the different modes in the multimodal mix and the way they integrate in multimodal texts and communicative events.

It is not difficult to see why such a field of study should have developed. From the 1920s onward, public communication had become increasingly multimodal. Film had changed acting, for instance, enlarging subtle aspects of non-verbal communication, and so influencing how people talk and move and smile the world over. Later, television had made non-verbal communication a decisive factor in politics, most famously in the televised election debate between Nixon and Kennedy. Writing, too, had become multimodal, as illustrations and page furniture broke up and reshaped the pages of books and magazines. Like scholars in other fields of study, linguists took notice. In the course of the twentieth century, four schools of linguistics would begin to engage with communicative modes other than language. The first was the Prague School, which, in the 1930s and 1940s, extended linguistics into the visual arts and the non-verbal aspects of the theater, and which included studies of folklore and collaborations with avant-garde artists (cf. for example, Matejka and Titunik, 1976). In the 1960s, Paris School structuralist semiotics also used concepts and methods from linguistics to understand communicative modes other than language. Largely inspired by the work of Roland Barthes, the Paris School mostly focused on the analysis of popular culture and the mass media rather than on folklore or avant-garde art (for example, Barthes, 1967, 1977, 1983). In roughly the same period, American linguists took an interest in the multimodal analysis of spoken language and non-verbal communication. Ray Birdwhistell (1973) developed an intricate set of tools for analyzing body motion, and Pittenger et al. (1960) published a highly detailed and groundbreaking multimodal analysis of the first 5 minutes of a psychiatric interview. The fourth school emerged in the 1990s. Inspired by the linguistics of M. A. K. Halliday (1979, 1985), it was this school which adopted and broadened the term 'multimodality,' and it is this school with which I will be predominantly concerned in this chapter. By the 1990s, of course, the production of multimodal texts was no longer the domain of specialists, of artists, designers, media producers, and so on, but accessible to all computer users. The study of multimodality therefore had become more urgent, and the Hallidayan-inspired approach was often applied to the development of multimodal literacy in young children and teenagers (for example, Kress, 1997; Kress et al., 2005).

Earlier work in multimodality had focused on individual communicative modes, using linguistic models to describe, for instance, visual communication as a 'language of images,' musical communication as a 'language of music,' and so on. As always, Roland Barthes was an exception here as he not only paid attention to the general principles underlying multimodal communication, devising a conceptual framework that could be applied to all communicative modes (1967), but also developed a theory of the ways text and image can integrate in multimodal texts (1977). The Hallidayan school also began its inquiries into multimodality with 'grammars' of individual communicative modes such as images (O'Toole, 1994; Kress and van Leeuwen, 1996). But Kress and van Leeuwen's theory of composition (1996: 181–230) already brought out that composition can be used to integrate, not just text and image, but also, for instance, objects in space and the elements of the built environment, and van Leeuwen's account of sound (1999), too, was multimodal, in that it paid close attention to the principles common to speech, music and other sounds as well as to the way speech, music, and other sounds integrate in multimodal texts and communicative events. In a later book, Kress and van Leeuwen (2001) sketched the outlines of a more general theory of multimodality, and in the final part of *Introducing Social Semiotics* (2005), van Leeuwen brought together his work on the integration of time- and space-based communicative modes. At roughly the same time, Baldry and Thibault (2006) published an influential and widely used method for the transcription and analysis of multimodal texts. A related approach to multimodality (for example, Norris, 2004) took up the American tradition of the micro-analysis of contextually situated communicative interactions which had begun with the already mentioned study *The First Five Minutes* (Pittenger et al., 1960). The growth of the field of multimodality studies can be tracked in the pages of the journal *Visual Communication*, and in a range of edited collections including

O'Halloran (2004), Ventola et al. (2004), Norris and Jones (2005), and Jewitt (2009).

Multimodality, then, is first of all a term for a phenomenon rather than a theory or method. It denotes a key aspect of communication: namely, that it melds a variety of communicative modes into a coherent and unified whole. As such, the term is now gaining currency beyond the narrower domain of linguistically inspired multimodality studies. But multimodality is also a term for a particular set of theoretical concepts and analytical practices, aimed at understanding how a variety of communicative resources is used in multimodal communication. Although originally inspired by linguistics, in recent years it has become more interdisciplinary, with, for instance, work on visual communication drawing both on linguistics and art theory, and work on sound drawing both on linguistics and musicology, and so on. It is with some of these concepts and methods that I will be concerned in this chapter.

TEXT AND IMAGE

Barthes' early work on the relation between text and image (1977) remains a key reference for two reasons: (1) it introduced a basic conceptual framework for understanding the integration of text and image in multimodal texts and (2) it showed that text–image relations are culturally and historically specific. This is an important point, because while there is certainly a perceptual basis for multimodality, the roles given to different communicative modes and the values attached to them vary and are motivated by the interests and preoccupations of specific socio-cultural contexts and historical periods.

Barthes introduced three distinct semantic, content-based, relations between text and image. In the first two, 'illustration' and 'anchorage,' image and text convey essentially the same content (though, of course, in different ways), but the order in which they are read and understood creates a subtle difference.

In the case of 'illustration,' the text is primary, and the image interprets it in a particular context and for a particular audience. In the Middle Ages, 'illustration' was the dominant text–image relation. The most highly valued images illustrated the key stories and key concepts of the time—stories from the Bible and Greek mythology and theological concepts, predominantly. While these stories and concepts were relatively few and relatively stable, images provided ever new illustrations of the same few stories and the same few concepts, making them attractive and accessible to audiences who could not understand Latin, and placing them in familiar, recognizable environments.

In the case of 'anchorage,' images are not understood with reference to a text but seen as naturalistic representations of the world. Therefore, they do not come already impregnated with cultural meaning, but are potentially open to a variety of readings, so that they need linguistic interpretation, linguistic closure, both in terms of their denotation, of who or what they represent, and in terms of their connotation, of their more abstract, conceptual significance. 'Anchorage' began to take over as the dominant form of image–text relation in the Renaissance, when science and exploration encouraged images that could document the world, so making it amenable to scientific labeling, classification, and interpretation.

In the case of 'relay,' Barthes' third category, there is no redundancy between text and image. Text and image do not 'say the same thing' but convey different, complementary content. In the case of 'dialogue scenes' in films and comic strips, for instance, the image shows the speakers while what they say is conveyed linguistically. Text and image therefore depend on each other to convey the whole of the content. In contemporary communication, 'relay' is extending into many other fields. In signaling it, Barthes was ahead of his time, even though it was too early to see the future significance and ramifications of the move from 'anchorage' to 'relay.' The essence of this move is that while in the case of 'anchorage' and 'illustration' text and image each convey a complete, whole message, in the case of 'relay' neither the image nor the text can convey the message on its own. In Figure 28.1, for instance, the idea of 'mortal danger' is expressed both visually, by the skull and crossbones, and linguistically, by the words *'pericolo di morte.'* Perhaps the sign-makers found the skull and crossbones icon insufficiently explicit and thought it was in need of verbal anchorage to be understood. In Figure 28.2, however, the visual and the verbal must be put together (and together with the immediate environment and placement of the sign) to understand the full message, which 'says' something like 'workmen-working (*image*) ends (*text*) here (*placement of sign*).' To put it another way, picture and text together form the equivalent of a clause ('workmen-working ends'), with the subject expressed pictorially and the predicate verbally.

The concepts of 'illustration' and 'anchorage' are closely related to the concept of 'elaboration' in Halliday's theory of conjunction (1985: 302–309), a theory which maps the possible semantic relations between clauses in a linguistic text where such relations may either be made explicit by conjunctions such as 'and,' 'but,' 'because,' etc., or remain inexplicit. In the case of 'elaboration,' one clause elaborates another, for example by rephrasing it, by making it more specific (or more general), or by providing an example of it. Nothing new is added to

Figure 28.2   Work in progress sign

the content of the first clause; it is just reiterated in some way, to clarify or strengthen it. When applied to text–image relations, this can add further detail to Barthes's conceptual framework. 'Anchoring' texts such as captions can, for instance clarify what the image shows, or generalize it, and illustrations can add specific detail to what is mentioned in the text, or exemplify it. van Leeuwen (2005: 219 ff) discusses the elaborative relations between the commentary and the images of non-fiction films and television programs in this way. The 'relay' relation, on the other hand, is not conjunctive, because while conjunction connects complete propositions (clauses and their visual equivalents), 'relay' relations connect incomplete propositions, parts of propositions (for instance, a 'subject' and a 'predicate'), or a speaker and what he or she says.

Martinec and Salway (2005) have provided the most detailed Barthes-inspired account of

Figure 28.1   Danger sign

the semantics of text–image relations. The core of their approach is a distinction between the relative *status* of text and image and their *logico-semantic relationship*. When image and text are equal in status, they say, the whole of the image connects to the whole of the text. An image may for instance show a group of people walking to a courthouse while the text says 'Janklow walks up to the courthouse with his legal team.' Image and text can be equal in both 'independent' text–image relations ('anchorage' and 'illustration' relations, as in Figure 28.1), and 'complementary' image–text relations ('relay relations,' as in Figure 28.2). In unequal image–text relations, the image relates only to part of the text, or the text only to part of the image. An image may show the Nobel Prize winning author Naipaul seated in front of his book case. The image relates only to Naipaul, not to his winning of the Nobel Prize, which is mentioned only in the caption. The status of the image can therefore be likened to that of a subordinate clause in a sentence (something like, 'Naipaul, who looks like this image, won this year's Nobel Prize').

Like van Leeuwen (2005), Martinec and Salway follow Halliday in distinguishing different types of elaboration: 'exposition,' where image and text are at the same level of generality; and 'exemplification,' where either the text is more general than the image, or the image more general than the text, as in a skull and crossbones icon accompanied by the words 'high voltage.' 'Extension' is then the addition of new, related information, as in the captions of paintings in art books, which may add details that cannot be seen, such as the year in which the painting was created, and the museum that owns it. They also introduce the possibility of 'enhancement,' where the text may add a 'circumstantial' element to the image, or vice versa—for instance, the location or timing of an event, or its reason or result. In Figure 28.3, the text adds such a circumstance, indicating the extent of the stretch of road where reindeer may cross. And, finally, they include the relation of 'projection'—the relation between

Figure 28.3   Crossing reindeer sign

the image of a speaker and his or her words (this may also include the relation between a 'thinker' and his or her thoughts, as indicated by thought bubbles in comic strips).

Following Martinec and Salway, each image should be analyzed both for the relative status of text and image and for the type of semantic relation between them. In the case of the image of Naipaul in front of his books, the status is unequal, with the image subordinate to the text, while the relation is one of elaboration (exemplification), because the relevant text ('Naipaul') is more general than the image, which shows details of Naipaul's appearance and relevant attributes (books). Figure 28.4 summarizes Martinec and Salway's account in the form of a system network. The curly bracket (brace) indicates 'both…and' (that is, text and image must be analyzed both for their relative status and for the logico-semantic relation between them), while square brackets indicate 'either…or' (for example, text and image are either equal or unequal).

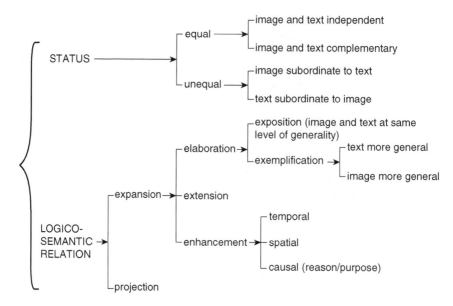

Figure 28.4   Network of text–image relations (after Martinec and Salway, 2005: 358)

The approaches I have discussed so far take their cues from the linguistics of conjunction and complex clause construction. But it is also possible to approach text–image relations from the other, visual, end, using theories of visual composition to explain the relation between text and image. These two approaches do not contradict each other. People are perfectly capable of understanding multimodal texts at two or more levels simultaneously.

COMPOSITION

Today, visual analysis must go beyond the analysis of images. Texts like Figure 28.5, a promotional poster for Amnesty International (Joan Dobkin, 1991), or Figure 28.6, a web page, hardly contain any images. Yet they are profoundly visual, full of color, line and texture. Multimodality takes a step forward here. Language itself becomes visual, and composition, color, and typography play a key role in creating structure and meaning.

Until the twentieth century, a page of printed text was a single field of dense text surrounded by margins, although there had

been exceptions such as the two-column *Gutenberg Bible* or scholarly works which had the text in the center and surrounded it with scholarly commentary. Newspapers changed this, turning the page into a modular grid of equal-sized rectangles that can be filled with either pictorial or verbal content, and in which a given text or picture might fill any number of modules, making many different page layouts possible (see Lupton, 2004). Today's websites use the same principle, with designers making creative use of the table facility provided by the designers of HTML (Hypertext Mark-up Language) in ways that have little to do with the original function of tables (see, for example, Figure 28.6).

If linear text gets its shape and structure from the progressive development of an argument or a storyline, how do such non-linear, fragmented texts cohere? Kress and van Leeuwen (1996) have attempted to answer this question by proposing that the spatial 'zones' of pictures, pages and screens (left and right; top and bottom; center and margins) interrelate textual elements by providing them with specific 'information values.' To start with left and right, if there is *Polarization* (some kind of difference or contrast) between an element placed on the left and

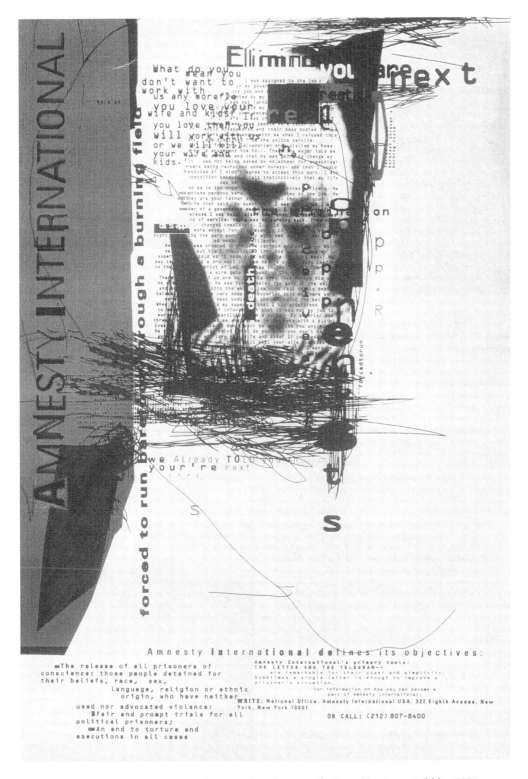

Figure 28.5   Amnesty International promotional poster designed by Joan Dobkin, 1991. Reproduced with permission

Figure 28.6   Housind.com website. (Designed by Andy Cruz, Tal Leming, Ken Barber, Rich Roat, and Bondé Prang, 2004.) © 2004 Princeton Architectural Press, Inc. Reproduced with permission

an element placed on the right, then the left element will be understood as the *Given*, as a departure point for the message that is, or should be, already familiar to the reader or viewer, while the right element will be understood as the *New*, the element that contains the information the message is trying to get across. This left–right information flow clearly corresponds to the left–right mode of writing and reading in Western culture, and is indeed reversed in cultures that write from right to left.

It is important to note that the Given–New relation applies to pictorial compositions such as the painting shown in Figure 28.7, as well as to multimodal, text-and-image compositions such as Figures 28.5 and 28.6. In Figure 28.7, a seventeenth-century painting by Guercino called 'Et in Arcadia ego' ('I am there, even in Paradise'; also known as 'The Shepherds of Arcadia' and 'The Arcadian Shepherds'), the left shows a figure who contemplates the New; the object the painting invites viewers to also meditate about is death. Examples like this illustrate that visual art has made use of Given and New composition for a long time. What is new is its introduction into the domain of modern, multimodal writing.

When there is vertical polarization—polarization between an element placed in the upper and an element placed in the lower section of a picture, page, or screen—the top element is the *Ideal,* the idealized or generalized essence of the message, and the bottom element the *Real,* contrasting with the Ideal in presenting factual details, or documentary evidence, or practical consequences. In single-page magazine advertisements, for instance, the Ideal usually depicts the

Figure 28.7   'Et in Arcadia Ego' (Guercino, 1621–1623)

'promise' of the product, the glamour or success it will bring to consumers, or of the sensual satisfaction it will give them, while the Real shows the product itself and provides factual information about it. In Figure 28.5, the name of the organization, 'Amnesty International,' appears on the left, as the Given, while the New is the typewritten story of persecution, which is to persuade readers to support Amnesty. This story is also the Ideal, the essence of Amnesty's message, and the Real provides the official version of Amnesty's objectives and methods as well as a contact address. In Figure 28.6, the Ideal contains the branding, the Given the global

navigation, while the New and Real highlight a key product.

The *Center* is another key compositional zone. Instead of polarizing the elements of the composition, the Center unifies them, providing the *Margins* that surround it with a common meaning or purpose. In Figure 28.8, for instance, the Center represents a happy, indeed overjoyous, Rank Xerox employee, and the words that surround him suggest the various ways in which Xerox makes its employees happy by 'recognizing and rewarding' their efforts.

The compositional schemas discussed here can be combined in various ways.

Figure 28.8   'Recognizing a job well done' (*Document Matters,* July 1996). © 1996 Xero28. Reproduced with permission

Figure 28.6, for instance, contains three horizontal zones—the name of the organization, Amnesty International on the left; an empty yellow zone on the right, as the New, the zone of the viewer's action ('You are next'); and the typewritten and partially obscured story in the center as the 'Mediator' (Kress and van Leeuwen, 1996: 208–211) that connects the two.

Such compositional schemas are multimodal for two reasons. They can apply to any kind of spatial configuration, whatever its mode—image, text, museum display, stage design, architectural façade—and they can integrate different kinds of element (for example, text and image) into a multimodal whole. But it is a different kind of integration from the one discussed in the previous section. The connections it establishes between elements are visual rather than verbal, informational rather than semantic, and geared toward hierarchies of importance and attention rather than to internal, logical coherence. The system network in Figure 28.9 provides a summary of the key terms.

DIAGRAMS

The pie chart in Figure 28.10 summarizes the result of a staff feedback survey. It tells us that the survey had three kinds of responses: responses with a positive attitude to change (the top segment, in yellow); responses with a negative attitude to change (the bottom left segment, in blue); and responses with a 'wait and see' attitude to change (the bottom right segment, in purple). The shading in the center indicates the amount of responses in each category. In many other contexts, a summary of this kind would have been entirely verbal, announcing the three types of response, defining and illustrating each, and then indicating the percentage of respondents in each category (which is what pie charts are normally used for). But here only the quotes are verbal. The categories are defined, not by words, but by a color (a sunny yellow for positive responses, cooler and dimmer blue and purple for the less positive ones), and the proportions are shown only visually. Composition also plays a role, centering the

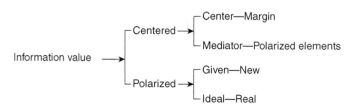

Centered	An element (the Center) is placed in the center of the composition
Polarized	There is some difference or contrast between two elements
Margin	The non-central elements in a centered composition are placed both above and to the sides of the Center and further elements may be placed in between
Mediator	The Center of a polarized composition forms a bridge between Given and New and/or Ideal and Real
Given	The left element in a horizontally polarized composition
New	The right element in a horizontally polarized composition
Ideal	The upper element in a vertically polarized composition
Real	The lower element in a vertically polarized composition

Figure 28.9 Network of information value

Where we are now

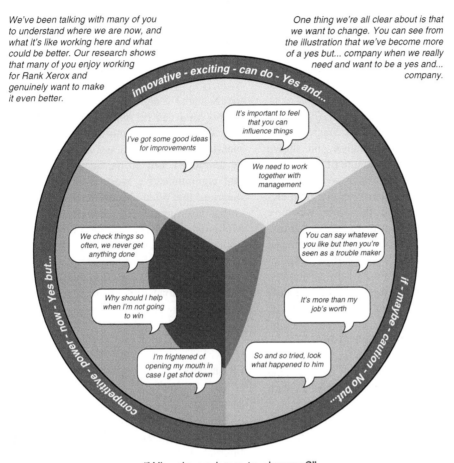

We've been talking with many of you to understand where we are now, and what it's like working here and what could be better. Our research shows that many of you enjoy working for Rank Xerox and genuinely want to make it even better.

One thing we're all clear about is that we want to change. You can see from the illustration that we've become more of a yes but... company when we really need and want to be a yes and... company.

innovative - exciting - can do - Yes and...

It's important to feel that you can influence things

I've got some good ideas for improvements

We need to work together with management

We check things so often, we never get anything done

You can say whatever you like but then you're seen as a trouble maker

Why should I help when I'm not going to win

It's more than my job's worth

I'm frightened of opening my mouth in case I get shot down

So and so tried, look what happened to him

competitive - power - now - Yes but...

if - maybe - caution - No but...

"Why do we have to change?"

Figure 28.10 'The Three Voices of XBS' (Rank Xerox, 1997). © 1997 Xero28. Reproduced with permission

distribution and making the positive responses Ideal and the less positive ones Real.

Much information is now presented in this way, diagrammatically rather than discursively. Thanks to Excel, tables are particularly popular: for instance, in corporate documents such as 'action plans,' where the horizontal dimensions will include such categories as 'action,' 'person responsible.' 'timeline,' 'success criteria,' etc. In the past, elements like 'action' and 'person responsible' would have been connected through the grammar of sentences. If I am the person

responsible and writing is my action, I write 'I write' and not as shown in Table 28.1.

Today, a new form of writing fuses language and visual communication. The elements are still linguistic, words in boxes, but they are incomplete—nominal groups rather than fully

Table 28.1 Example of language and visual fusion

Action	Person responsible
Writing	Theo van Leeuwen

formed clauses. But the 'verbs' that connect them into complete 'propositions,' the equivalent of clauses, are visual, spatial structures, diagrammatic templates. As a result, the words in the boxes can easily be replaced by pictures—for example, in the above example, a writing icon and a picture of Theo van Leeuwen.

Martinec and van Leeuwen (2008) have described a number of such diagrammatic ways of arranging information and shown how they underlie the structure of contemporary multimodal texts such as websites. The 'star' arrangement (center with marginal elements around it) and the table we have already mentioned, but there is also the taxonomy (Figure 28.11a), which links elements with a 'is a kind of' or 'is a part of' relation, and the network (Figure 28.11b), which can link elements along a variety of semantic dimensions: for example, 'a is like b,' 'a combines with b,' 'a co-occurs with b,' 'a does something to b,' and so on.

Diagrams provide only a limited vocabulary of visual 'verbs' and often use the same form for several different meanings, as with

the two examples above, or with the arrows in flowcharts, which sometimes indicate actions, sometimes transport, sometimes sequentiality and sometimes causality. What for instance is the link between 'ownership' and the 'X-team' in Figure 28.12? Does 'ownership' *relate to*, or *feed into*, or *cause* the X-team? Diagrammatic representations of this kind can be much less precise than they seem. Perhaps a more subtle and complex language of boxes and arrows needs to be developed. But, in the meantime, important communicative work is done through diagrams that often obscure or contradict the verbal information that accompanies them. Multimodal analysis can therefore make an important contribution by analyzing the communicative effectiveness of diagrams and making suggestions for their improvement, as is done, for instance, in Martinec and van Leeuwen (2008).

FRAMING

The brochure shown in Figure 28.13 was distributed to every household in Australia in 2007 to alert parents to the dangers of the Internet. Frame lines separate the zone of the Given (which shows children using the Internet) from the zone of the New (which contains advice for parents), and also separate the three areas demarcating different age groups (under 8 year olds; 8–12 year olds; 13–17 year olds). In addition, the photos on the left are all dominated by the color beige, while the text boxes on the right are in different shades of mauve. All this creates degrees of connectivity and separation between the six key elements of this page. The beige/mauve color contrast makes for a strong divide between the Given and the New (children and their parents), while the color difference between the boxes on the right is much smaller, suggesting that these three elements are more similar and present different varieties of the same kind of content.

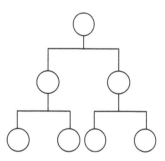

Figure 28.11a   Taxonomy

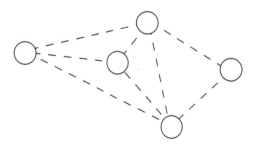

Figure 28.11b   Network

What makes an X Team...

Figure 28.12 'What makes an X-team?' (Rank Xerox, 1997). © 1997 Xero28. Reproduced with permission

I use the term 'framing' here to refer to visual devices that can create degrees of connection or disconnection between the elements of a composition—the visual equivalents of punctuation, indentation, and interlineal spacing, you might say. Disconnection devices include actual frame lines, which can of course vary in thickness, empty space between elements, and contrasts in tone or color. Connection devices include similarities in color (or other visual aspects) and connecting 'vectors'—lines that lead from one element to another. Different kinds of framing may subtly differ in meaning. Frame lines, for instance, create radically different territories for the elements they divide, while the use of empty space places them in the same textual territory, but at a distance from each other, in the way that people sitting at different tables in a café share a space and do the same kind of thing without immediately interacting.

Like composition, framing is a key multimodal device, existing, one way or another, in every communicative mode, as every communicative mode has to have resources for creating 'boundaries' between units of meaning, so creating the equivalent of sentences, paragraphs, sections, etc. van Leeuwen (2005: Chapter 1) applies the concept of framing to classrooms and offices, which, today, tend to diminish framing ('open' classrooms and

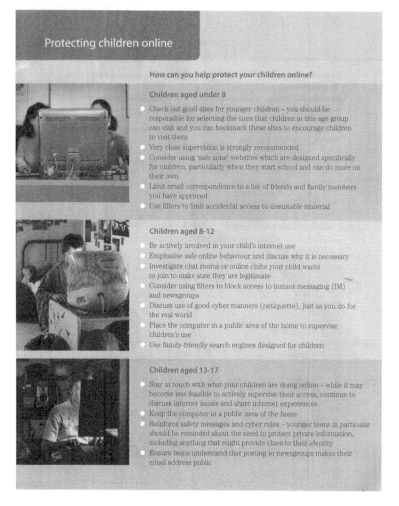

Figure 28.13   Page from Australian Government brochure (Nairn, 2007). © 2007 Commonwealth of Australia. Reproduced with permission

offices), although people often introduce ad hoc 'frames' by dragging in various kinds of partitions.

COLOR

Color is usually viewed as expressing emotive meanings. In public and commercial buildings it is said to have a direct effect: 'bright reds are energizing and good for offices in the banking or entertainment fields' (*Guardian*, 3 September 2001: 5); 'pink, properly applied, relaxes hostile and aggressive individuals

within 15 minutes' (according to the Naval Correctional Center in Seattle, as cited in Lacy, 1996: 89). In the private domain it is said to express personality traits. 'A yellow entrance hall usually indicates a person who has ideas and a wide field of interests… as this color is associated with the intellect, ideas and a searching mind' (Lacy, 1996: 29). This approach to color has been widely adopted by psychologists, with the result that color is often treated as a natural phenomenon. Yet color meanings are neither universal, nor of all times. In the Middle Ages, for instance, color denoted abstract concepts such as 'faith,' 'hope,' and 'charity,' and the rank and status of knights, and the current discourse of color as emotive and psychological originated in the Romantic era, largely inspired by Goethe's remarkable book *Theory of Colors* [1810] (1970). The changing fashions in color, too, should alert us to the fact that color preferences are not, or not just, a matter of individual personality, but are also cultural. It is therefore important not to rely too much on the decontextualized lists of emotive color meanings that can so readily be found in publications by color experts and on the Internet. Color codes do exist, but they usually apply to specific, narrow fields such as traffic and safety, or uniforms. In New South Wales, for instance, yellow traffic signs convey information ('there are pedestrians crossing here'), whereas red is used for commands such as 'Stop!' or 'No parking!'. At the University of Newcastle (NSW), Doctors of Business have the hood of their academic gown lined with 'deep Indian red' silk, Doctors of Education with jade silk, Doctors of Music with lilac silk, and so on. But in many domains of contemporary culture, color meaning is not so definite, cannot so easily be captured in a lexicon-like format, and comes about in context-specific ways, through connotation and metaphor (Kress and van Leeuwen, 2002).

In the case of connotation, a color is imported from a specific domain (for example, the Army) into a new domain (for example, street fashion), where it can then convey meanings and values linked to the domain from which the color is imported, or some fictionalized version thereof (for example, the qualities of action heroes). At my university, the Faculty of Humanities chose a brownish orange as its color because it is the color of the 'red earth' in Australia's dry and arid center, and the Faculty wanted to express its interest in practicing a form of humanities with a distinct Australian accent. This color was therefore imported from the Australian landscape into the domain of corporate identity, to signify identification with a certain kind of Australian-ness.

Hue, the aspect of color that makes us recognize colors as 'red' or 'green' is only one of the significant dimensions of color. Actual colors—for example, an actual red—are composites of a number of features: any red is either light or dark; pure or mixed in with blue or brown; intense and highly saturated or pale and diluted; and so on. These features all contribute to the communicative potential of the color, because what they literally and visibly *are* can become what they, more figuratively, *mean*. A given red may *be* 'bright' and also *mean* bright. The context will then narrow this 'brightness' down—it could, for instance, be 'brightness' in the sense of 'illumination,' as when we say that someone 'sees the light'; 'brightness' in the sense of fame, as when we say that someone is a 'shining star,' and so on. The yellow in Figure 28.13 is bright and highly saturated, and as it is here chosen to represent 'optimism,' and a 'positive outlook', the metaphoric meaning of brightness is narrowed down to 'optimism,' as when we say 'look on the bright side,' etc. The following features can all contribute to the communicative potential of a given color—or a given color scheme, because features such as 'brightness' and 'saturation' may also form the unifying factor in color schemes:

Brightness

Brightness (also known as 'value') is the scale from light to dark. I have already commented on its communicative potential.

Saturation

Saturation is the scale from full color to pale, pastel versions of the same color. Its communicative potential is based on the idea of 'fully expressed,' 'intense' versus 'toned down,' 'restrained.'

Purity

Purity is the scale from maximum purity to maximum 'mixed-ness' or 'hybridity,' or, if you like, 'impurity.' Its communicative potential flows from this characteristic.

Modulation

Modulation is the scale from a flat version of a color to maximally varied shading and nuance, and can therefore express the contrast between 'bold,' 'straightforward,' and 'subtle,' 'nuanced' (or, more negatively, 'simplistic' vs 'fussy'). Flat colors are often more 'conceptual' (green as *the* color of grass), and modulated colors more 'naturalistic' (photographs of grass will show many shades of green).

Luminosity

Luminosity is the range from 'dull,' 'matt' to 'reflective' (for example, silver and gold) and 'luminous' colors (for example, those of stained glass through which light shines from behind).

Hue

Hue, finally, is the quality of color that makes it blue, green, red, and so on. As a scale, it is also the scale from 'warm,' to 'cool', and many of its associations derive from this characteristic.

Today, colors and color schemes are also used to create textual coherence. On a page from *Cosmopolitan Magazine* which we were not allowed to reproduce here, the words 'love' and 'lust' were printed in pink, a color with a clear connotation of femininity. But metaphor played a role as well: moving from 'love' to 'lust' the color became progressively darker and more saturated: 'lust' here was a 'darker' and more 'intense' variety of 'love.' The same color was also used in the words 'how to' (the article provided readers with advice on 'Bringing Out His Romantic Side'); for the individual pieces of advice that followed ('Dish some insight,' 'Inspire a repeat performance,' 'Pay attention'), for a textbox on the left headed 'He asks for my advice but never takes it,' for the lips of the model in the accompanying photograph, and for a telephone in the drawing accompanying a short piece on 'phone sex' at the bottom of the page. Pink therefore formed a thread through the page, tying together the different elements of the page: the title, the nature of the main article as an 'advice genre' ('how to'), the actual items of advice, and the key theme that united the different articles on the page: communication, lips, a telephone.

Clearly color is communicative: it can convey ideas (for example, 'femininity' and the 'darkness' and 'intensity' of 'lust'); it can affect people emotively; and it can provide textual cohesion, linking the elements of the multimodal page together into a meaningful structure. Color is also essentially multimodal. It cannot exist on its own (color field paintings remain a relatively limited genre) and must necessarily work together with images, letter forms, clothes, interior decoration, objects, architecture and so on. It can only ever be 'multi-.'

TYPOGRAPHY

Traditionally, typography was a self-effacing craft. Legibility was its main concern, and typographers were adamant that letter forms should not draw attention to themselves. More recently, typography has become a communicative mode in its own right, and many printed texts now communicate not just through the linguistic meaning of the words but also through their *typographic meaning*.

As with color, typographic meaning can either derive from connotation or from metaphors, and always needs the context to narrow it down. In the case of connotation, the reader recognizes the context from which a letter form comes, and can therefore link that form to meanings and values associated with the context it comes from. The typewriter font used in the Amnesty poster (Figure 28.5) evokes low technology. It looks as if it has been written with an old, battered portable typewriter, by someone without access to a computer, somewhere in the Third World, and it therefore has the quality of an authentic document. But metaphor also plays a role—there is deliberate irregularity in the way the letter forms are spaced and placed on the baseline. Typographers often employ irregularity, sometimes to signify an unwillingness to produce neat, regular forms, which, in context, can become 'unconventionality,' 'playfulness,' 'rebellion,' 'lack of discipline' and so on, sometimes to signify an impossibility of producing regularity, perhaps because of surging emotions, an injury or disability, or, in this case, the battered state of an old typewriter. Metaphors like this are again based either on *what we can see in the letter forms*, on their actual visible characteristics, such as that they are round or angular, curved or straight, and so on, or on experience, on *what we know about the production of the letter forms*, for example that irregularity can be caused by poor equipment—leaking pens, or battered typewriters. As in the case of color, such features combine to form the communicative potential of letter forms (van Leeuwen, 2002). They include:

Weight

Weight is the difference between bold and less bold typefaces. Boldness increases salience and can therefore mean 'assertive,' 'solid,' 'important' (or, more negatively, 'domineering,' 'overbearing,' and so on). Lack of boldness can signify the opposite.

Expansion

Expansion is the difference between condensed, narrow letter forms and expanded, wide letter forms. Narrow typefaces make efficient use of limited space while wide typefaces 'spread themselves around.' This visible characteristic can then provide the potential for metaphoric meanings such as 'economical,' 'efficient,' or, more negatively, 'cramped,' 'overcrowded,' etc.

Slope

Slope refers to the difference between cursive, 'script'—like typefaces and upright typefaces. Cursive writing usually connotes handwriting, and the qualities we might associate with handwriting, qualities such as 'informal,' 'personal,' etc.

Curvature

A letter form can stress angularity or curvature, with all the associations that may follow from this. Curvature may also be realized by the difference between rounded ascenders and descenders (or ascenders and descenders which use loops and flicks) and straight ascenders and descenders.

Connectivity

Letter forms can be connected to each other, as in running script, or lack connection, so that they become quite separate and self-contained. This again 'means what it is'—'connectedness' and 'disconnection,' and as most forms of handwriting are 'connected,' connectivity also suggests the qualities we associate with handwriting.

Orientation

Typefaces may be oriented toward the horizontal axis by being comparatively 'flattened' or oriented toward the vertical axis. The meaning potential of horizontality and verticality derives from our experience of gravity and walking upright, so that horizontality could mean 'heaviness' or 'solidity' (but also, for example, 'inertia'), and verticality 'upward aspiration' (but also, for example, 'instability').

Regularity

Many typefaces have deliberate irregularities, through random variations in size, weight, or slope, and through irregular placement on, above, or below the baseline. As mentioned, this can signify rebelliousness, playfulness, etc., (whatever contrasts with the strict discipline of regularity) or suggest a technical or physical cause for the irregularity.

Typography is not just about letter forms. Other factors also play a role. Letter forms can be colored, textured (rough or smooth, shiny or dull, etc.); three-dimensional or flat; still or animated; abstract or semi-pictorial. The spacing between letters, words and lines plays a key role, as does the use of margins. In the example described earlier under 'Hue,' the words 'love,' 'and' and 'lust,' overlap, suggesting that, in a magazine like *Cosmopolitan*, 'love,' and 'lust,' are not distinct, but shade into each other. Examples like this bring out that typography is not just a matter of aesthetics, but makes critical contributions to the message conveyed by the multimodal text as a whole.

Decoration

In many contemporary documents, pictures are no longer discrete elements, but function as a setting, a background for written text. In ads, movie titles, book covers, etc., words have been superimposed on pictures for a long time, but today superimposition has moved into many other domains of writing. The vice-president of my university, for instance, presented his annual budget in a PowerPoint® presentation, superimposing the figures on a calm, blue ocean and a blue sky with small, wispy clouds. In doing so he perhaps sought to present himself as a visionary rather than a dry accountant (he also inserted quotes from visionary business gurus between the slides with figures). In other words, through his choice of a visual background (which, of course, remained constant throughout his presentation), he expressed his identity as a speaker. In other cases, people may use visual backgrounds to express the genre of a presentation or document, or some essential characteristic of its topic.

Traditionally, such backgrounds would have been seen as embellishment, decoration, a kind of wallpaper. But decorative motifs have always been culturally important, whether in script-based Islamic decoration, or in the nature-based motifs of nineteenth-century decoration (for example, William Morris' flowery wallpapers), and visual analysts should pay close attention to them. Figure 28.14 shows the cover of the annual report of my university's library. The background contains both words and abstract graphic motifs (lines, grids, circles), some of them illuminated by a kind of glow. The words ('access,' 'absorb,' 'resource,' 'intellect,' 'accumulate,' 'research') convey key characteristics and values of contemporary libraries. But so do the graphic elements—a rigid grid of rectangles on which larger, more strongly framed zones are superimposed, as well as points and circles that light up like the activated parts in a brain scan. The library is represented here as a rigid, rational system of classification, a grid, but within that grid, there are zones of special strength and value, and moments of illumination.

Decorative patterns have two key characteristics—they repeat themselves and they are endless—so that we can never see all of them in a single glance. This allows us to take them for granted. We know they are there, even when we do not pay attention, and we know they will continue unchanged even when we cannot see them. Thus, they provide constancy and stability to culturally salient meanings, and to the identity of speakers, text genres, and specific texts.

CONCLUSION

This chapter has moved from the analysis of text–image relations to the analysis of composition, framing, color, typography, and the use of visual backgrounds in what I have called the new writing.

Figure 28.14   Annual report. © 2005 Library, University of Technology, Sydney. Reproduced with permission

The new writing merges aspects of yesterday's text media and yesterday's image media. The screens of websites and PowerPoint® slides are far more word-oriented and far less image-oriented than the screens of film and television. At the same time, they are far more visual than the pages of books. They use the 'landscape' format familiar from film and television and they introduce visual background and filmic transitions such as fades and dissolves into written text. And they hang together, not as webs of words, but as multimodal compositions, through composition, framing, color, and typography.

As a result, the new writing can no longer be read aloud. It would not make sense, for instance, to read aloud a web page like the one shown in Figure 28.6. The link between speech and writing introduced, long ago, by the alphabet, is severed here, and alphabetic writing is mixed with an increasing range of pictographic signs.

The new writing is also read differently. Because it is no longer 'linear,' no longer organized sequentially, we no longer read it from beginning to end, gradually piecing together a sense of overall structure, gradually integrating the meaning of the parts into an overall understanding. The overall structure is now spatial, visible at a glance, and allows us to move down to more detailed levels of reading according to our interests and needs, just as we used to do with images.

Both forms of visual analysis continue to be important, because, for the time being, text and image media will continue to exist alongside the new writing. Newspapers, for instance, appear both in their traditional form and in 'new writing' form, on the Internet (Knox, 2007), and television programs, too, have their online counterparts. But the new writing is rapidly gaining importance, rapidly becoming the dominant form of multimodal communication. It is therefore a crucial task for visual analysis to develop tools for analyzing and interpreting it.

REFERENCES

Baldry, A. and Thibault, P. J. (2006) *Multimodal Transcription and Text Analysis.* London: Equinox.

Barthes, R. (1967) *Elements of Semiology.* London: Cape.

Barthes, R. (1977) *Image-Music-Text.* London: Fontana.

Barthes, R. (1983) *The System of Fashion.* New York: Hill and Wang.

Birdwhistell, R. (1973) *Kinesics in Context.* Harmondsworth: Penguin.

Goethe. J. W. von [1810] (1970) *Theory of Colors.* Cambridge, MA: MIT Press.

Halliday, M. A. K. (1979) *Language as Social Semiotic.* London: Arnold.

Halliday, M. A. K. (1985) *An Introduction to Functional Grammar.* London: Arnold.

Jewitt, C. (ed.) (2009) *The Routledge Handbook of Multimodal Analysis.* London: Routledge.

Knox, J. (2007) 'Visual–verbal communication on online newspaper home pages', *Visual Communication,* 6(1): 19–55.

Kress, G. (1997) *Before Writing—Rethinking the Paths to Literacy.* London: Routledge.

Kress, G. and van Leeuwen, T. (1996) *Reading Images: The Grammar of Visual Design.* London: Routledge.

Kress, G. and van Leeuwen, T. (2001) *Multimodal Discourse—The Modes and Media of Contemporary Communication.* London: Arnold.

Kress, G. and van Leeuwen, T. (2002) 'Color as a semiotic mode: Notes for a grammar of color', *Visual Communication,* 1(3): 343–368.

Kress, G., Jewitt, C., Bourne, J., Franks, A., Hardcastle, J., Jones, K. and Reid, E. (2005) *English in Urban Classrooms—A Multimodal Perspective on Teaching and Learning.* London: Routledge.

Lacy, M. L. (1996) *The Power of Color to Heal the Environment.* London: Rainbow Bridge Publications.

Lupton, E. (2004) *Thinking with Type—A Critical Guide for Designers, Writers, Editors & Students.* New York: Princeton Architectural Press.

Martinec, R. and Salway, A. (2005) 'A system for image-text relations in new (and old) media', *Visual Communication,* 4(3): 337–372.

Martinec, R. and van Leeuwen, T. (2008) *The Language of New Media Design.* London: Routledge.

Matejka, L. and Titunik, I. R. (eds) (1976) *Semiotics of Art: Prague School Contributions*. Cambridge, MA: MIT Press.

Nairn, G. (2007) *NetAlert—Protecting Australian Families Online*. Canberra: Department of Communications, Information Technology and the Arts. © 2007 Commonwealth of Australia.

Norris, S. (2004) *Analyzing Multimodal Interaction: A Methodological Framework*. London: Routledge.

Norris, S. and Jones, R. H. (2005) *Discourse in Action—Introducing Mediated Discourse Analysis*. London: Routledge.

O'Halloran, K. (ed.) (2004) *Multimodal Discourse Analysis: Systemic Functional Perspectives*. London: Continuum.

O'Toole, M. (1994) *The Language of Displayed Art*. London: Leicester University Press.

Pittenger, R. E., Hockett, C. F. and Danehy, J. J. (1960) *The First Five Minutes*. Ithaca, NY: P. Martineau.

Stork, D. G. (ed.) (1997) *HAL's Legacy*. Cambridge, MA: MIT Press.

van Leeuwen, T. (1999) *Speech, Music, Sound*. London: Palgrave.

van Leeuwen, T. (2002) 'Towards a semiotics of typography', *Information Design Journal*, 14(2): 139–156.

van Leeuwen, T. (2005) *Introducing Social Semiotics*. London: Routledge.

Ventola, E., Charles, C. and Kaltenbacher, N. M. (eds) (2004) *Perspectives on Multimodality*. Amsterdam: John Benjamins.

29

Researching Websites as Social and Cultural Expressions: Methodological Predicaments and a Multimodal Model for Analysis

Luc Pauwels

INTRODUCTION

The Internet is a rich resource for researchers in many respects: as a field of study, a research tool, and a means for scholarly communication. Several authors have dealt with the implications of using established research methods (survey, focus groups, content analysis, interviewing) in an online mode, or examined the question of how to take advantage of new practices of web users (for example, chatting, social networking) for studying culture (Paccagnella, 1997; Jones, 1999; Hine, 2000, 2006; Mann and Stewart, 2000; Wakeford, 2000; Weare and Lin, 2000; Lievrouw and Livingstone, 2002; Rossler, 2002; Andrews et al., 2003; Lister et al., 2003; Carter, 2005; Stewart and Williams, 2005).

Yet efforts of researchers to take advantage of the web in each of the three areas are not commensurate with the rapid expansion and impact of the online environment on several aspects of a globalizing society. Furthermore, only some of the many features and aspects of the web appear to have attracted serious attention. Paradoxically, several of the more basic characteristics of the web have been neglected. Most notably, this applies to the exploration of the visual and multimedia features of the web (as opposed to mainly verbal utterances and practices), both as a very significant source of cultural information and as an opportunity for improving the nature and depth of scholarly communications.

In this chapter, I will provide a model for analyzing the visual and multimodal nature of websites as materialized expressions of culture. The model will be preceded by a discussion of some of the methodological impediments of Internet research—and website research in particular. To illustrate the potential of multimodal website analysis the chapter also includes a separate example of decoding family websites as particularly rich exponents of material culture.

ON THE VALUE AND AUTHENTICITY OF COMPUTER-MEDIATED PHENOMENA

The current discourse about the Internet, and about computer-mediated communications (CMCs), is fortunately moving beyond technological determinism, which views technological innovation as an independent factor that subsequently produces social practices and uses. Technology is, to a large degree, what people make of it in a specific cultural context that is in constant flux and subject to endless redefinition. Each new technology does have specific features or attributes— which came about in response to cultural and social developments, for example perceived needs or institutional constraints; these features facilitate certain uses, and designers will have had specific goals in mind, but users cannot be forced to slavishly agree with these preconceptions and put them into practice. Users may adopt a technological artifact and adapt it to fit their specific needs. While the impact of new communication technologies in the media and in culture at large is still not equaled in empirical research, a growing number of empirical researchers (Springer, 1996; Bassett, 1997; Wynn and Katz, 1997; Cheung, 2000; Hine, 2000; Mann and Stewart, 2000; Miller and Slater, 2000) have gathered evidence of various kinds. This evidence seems to substantiate the conclusion that the so-called virtual world is not so virtual with respect to the majority of uses and users, and that the uses of the Internet are very much dependent on and

linked to a 'real-life' context. This conclusion was confirmed in the ESRC Virtual Society (Woolgar and Daw, 2000) study which found clear indications that virtual practices in some cases even tend to reinforce non-virtual (offline) practices (for example, more online interactions with friends may result in more frequent offline interactions with them as well). Also, these researchers noted the tendency of new technologies to 'supplement rather than substitute for existing practices and forms of organization' (Woolgar and Daw, 2000: 5). More recent research in the UK (2009) points at a marked increase in the use of the Internet by a growing and diversified section of the population for communications (primarily e-mail), but also as a central source of information, as a vehicle for social networking (to reinforce ties with family and friends and also to meet new people), as a means for more efficient shopping and banking, for expressing oneself through content production, or for entertainment needs (downloading music and video) (Dutton et al., 2009: 5). So, clearly, there are many complex interactions and connections between offline and online worlds, and both are part of the contemporary social life of an increasing number of people.

Often unmediated or direct forms of interaction are looked upon as more spontaneous, and therefore more 'truthful'— because non-verbal behavioral vocal cues are hard to control (looks, nerves, pitch, and tone of voice). However, having to cope with a number of immediate and potentially threatening forms of feedback (laughter, judgmental comments, rejection) may just as well lead to a retreat into accepted or evasive forms of behavior rather than to the display of the 'real' persona. Deliberate constructs and mediated forms of interaction are not necessarily less significant for studying culture and social life. Some studies even provide evidence for the fact that, in CMCs, the absence of real-life cues—which are so intrinsic a part of face-to-face interaction— tends to help more profound aspects of identity to emerge. Thus, people may reveal more of their identities and provide more valid information than in face-to-face situations, where their anonymity cannot be secured and where their conduct may be challenged directly (though asynchronous online communication also occasionally produces flame wars and specific forms of 'cyber bullying'). Cyber-psychologists have coined the remarkable 'openness' and freedom of reserve of people on the semi-public space of the Internet, the 'Online Disinhibition Effect' (Suler, 2004). Therefore, a 'disembodied environment' (Mann and Stewart, 2000: 210) like the Internet may have at least as much 'significance' for getting to someone's personal and cultural identity or self as meeting in person.

Identity construction, impression management, and conscious self-presentation are common practice in every communicative situation (Goffman, 1959). All forms of communication and interaction have their techniques for identity construction and impression management. None should be taken for granted or dismissed, and all—including the mediated ones—are valid for cultural research.

ISSUES OF REPRESENTATIVITY AND SAMPLING

When using the web to gain insight into cultures at large, the issue of representativeness is still a highly debated one. Some of the more optimistic authors believe that the web population is no longer predominantly male, highly educated, and based in the more affluent parts of the world. Kehoe and Pitkow (1996), for example, observed many years ago that the age of web users was becoming more diverse, that the gender imbalance of the early days was gradually diminishing, and that the web really was coming within the reach of a growing audience worldwide (Lee, 2000: 118). Others still believe that using the Internet as a 'window' on the world continues to be problematic. However, even

the more modest estimates of coverage (distribution and growth rate) note that the Internet is becoming a part of many aspects of different sorts of people's lives (see: http://www.internetworldstats.com/stats.htm and http://www.worldinternetproject.net/; Mesch and Talmud, 2006; Dutton et al., 2009), and that its technology offers many unique opportunities for research, even in its present phase of development.

Obviously, the issue of the representativeness of the population under study is closely tied to the type of research undertaken and the aims of the research project. Insofar as the research is confined to web-related phenomena—for example, corporate websites—or targets populations that are known to have an important web presence (academics, multinational companies, government agencies), there are—at least theoretically—very few problems. Nonetheless, obtaining a 'representative sample' of web-active populations or phenomena (for example, certain types of websites) is often not easy because the Internet is, for the most part, and despite sophisticated search engines and efforts to add some structure and control to it, an uncharted domain: we don't conclusively know who or what is 'out there.' Obtaining an adequate sample of web phenomena or populations is obviously far more complex than, for instance, sampling—legally registered—citizens within a community. Moreover, changes occur at an exceptional rate: new or radically overhauled sites constantly appear whereas existing websites migrate or 'die' while not being eradicated from cyberspace. The Internet is a huge data repository, but not necessarily a very permanent or predicable one. As Lee comments: 'The diffuse and democratic character of the Internet, the very attributes that make it such a valuable source for information, also make the finding of available information difficult' (2000: 119). The challenges of researching such a dynamic environment as the Internet have been vividly described by McMillan in her article, 'The microscope and the moving target' (2000). Despite all of these difficulties, web-based research does allow types of cross-national research that before were only feasible for affluent research institutions because of the high costs of travel and the time-consuming nature of such an enterprise. In some instances, an Internet-based approach allows researchers to connect with people (for example, criminals, drug users, people in combat zones or very remote places, or the politically oppressed)—and with their deeply held thoughts and convictions on sensitive issues, which are difficult or impossible to get to in offline situations. As a mainly keyboard-driven medium, the Internet allows further automation of research that is based on 'verbal' strategies, such as keyed-in responses (to questionnaires, interviews). The contents of structured questionnaires can, for the most part, be fed directly into statistical software packages, and there is no need for 'interviews' to be transcribed by research staff. Obviously, these advantages for the most part don't apply to the many non-verbal—and potentially significant—features of web content.

THE TEXTUAL BIAS IN INTERNET RESEARCH

Many years ago, Mann and Stewart proposed that one should think of CMCs as a 'new kind of discourse,' which they then further characterized as a 'hybrid showing features of both spoken and written language' (Mann and Stewart, 2000: 182). Mann and Stewart clearly considered CMC as 'a mainly text-based medium of research,' but they foresaw a future where 'miniaturized cameras' would overcome the struggles some qualitative researchers still had with the disembodied nature of this type of communication (2000: 214). This reintroduction of visual cues (web cameras indeed have now become fairly standard) will certainly, as the authors duly recognize, have an impact on the nature of the communication process itself (2000: 217). While envisioning a less purely text-based environment, Mann and Stewart again

primarily seemed to think about the visual as an 'extension' (providing some extra cues) to the mainly verbal environment (e-mail, chat rooms), as in the case of videoconferencing (talking heads in real time). But long before webcams became a fairly common feature of CMC (allowing 'mediated' face-to-face inter-actions in a previously largely disembodied environment), the Internet already had an important visual and multimedia appearance. However, to date, the complex and culturally rich visual and multimedia features of meticulously constructed websites have been largely ignored, or at least seriously underutilized, by social and cultural researchers.

Yet, websites are truly hybrid manifestations of CMCs, combining numerous visual features and cues (photographs, illustrations, typography, layout, and design features) with various types of verbal (written and spoken) and non-vocal sonic information (music, noise, sound effects). Clearly, it is not the medium that is mainly text-based, it is the researchers' focus that for long has been skewed toward written textual aspects of websites. In a sense this is not so surprising given the fact that social scientists are ill-prepared to derive valuable knowledge from sources other than verbal or numeric, and given the fact that virtually no explicit and precise tools exist to guide them in this more inclusive and integrated form of cultural analysis.

WEBSITES AS CULTURAL CONSTRUCTIONS

Whereas (multimodal aspects of) websites have definitely received far less attention in online research methodology books, they have attracted some more applied research attention. In particular, personal home pages (Chandler, 1998; Cheung, 2000; Dillon and Gushrowski, 2000; Döring, 2002) and institutional websites (Norris, 2001)—notably those of political parties or governmental bodies—have, respectively, been studied as forms and vehicles of self-presentation, or to assess their democratic or propagandistic character. But often such studies have rested on a rather limited operationalization of the phenomenon under study (for example, 'more links' means 'more democratic'), or demonstrated a preference for mainly verbal indicators and rarely ventured beyond a purely descriptive level (listing typical categories of content, such as biographies and their potential role in identity construction).

However in recent years, research has gradually become more focused on addressing the cultural dimension of websites as expressed in various aspects of their content and form (Badre and Laskowski, 2000; Barber and Badre, 2000; Luna et al., 2002; Okazaki and Rivas, 2002; Zhao et al., 2003; Cyr and Trevor-Smith, 2004; Barnett and Sung, 2005; Callahan, 2005; Singh et al., 2005; Fletcher, 2006; Würtz, 2006; Donker-Kuijer et al., 2008). However, as yet, these efforts have not produced more or less integrated models for (cultural) analysis. Moreover, the analyses of cultural dimensions in websites are very often based on Hofstede's (2001) extremely popular (Sondergaard, 1994; Kirkman et al., 2006) but contested (McSweeney, 2002) conceptualization of culture, and primarily focused on scoring websites against Hofstede's (2001) five dimensions (power distance, individualism, masculinity, uncertainty avoidance, and long-term orientation) and on developing and stimulating culturally 'appropriate' website practices, rather than on decoding websites as cultural resources.

The online environment in the form of websites uses many expressive means and calls upon many specialized decoding capabilities; it is therefore most remarkable that the textual bias is replicated even in website analysis. When researching websites, clearly one is looking at contemporary forms of 'material culture' rather than at human behavior as it unfolds in interaction (unless there are webcams to provide more fleeting and possibly unplanned visual accounts of behavior, or chat room interaction, which provides

another more or less dynamic version of (verbal) behavior). But even as relatively 'static' cultural products they provide much potentially significant material, a large part of which, in turn, is not available in 'real-life' (better: offline) situations. Therefore, the problem is not so much that web researchers are forced to work in an environment devoid of sufficient social and cultural cues, which is the old view of CMCs—namely, that it is necessarily a 'poorer' form of communication than face-to-face interaction. Given that most researchers are not trained to make sense of the hybrid features of this medium, they may feel swamped by so much promising data, so that they hardly know where and how to begin.

Furthermore, studying online phenomena should not be seen as an alternative to more direct forms of fieldwork, but as a contemporary complement to it. Whereas modes of CMC in general may be chosen because they are felt to be 'safer' than a direct confrontation with a possibly judgmental audience, this 'advantage' applies even more to websites than it does to other electronically mediated, but still more or less, 'confrontational' environments, like online discussion groups. Even when website owners allow or prompt reactions from visitors in guest books or special feedback areas, they retain the power to censor comments by making them invisible to others, or by deleting or changing parts of the feedback. These 'safety measures' may further contribute to the often amazingly high degree of disclosure one may encounter in the more personal or private types of website, such as personal home pages and family websites (Pauwels, 2008a).

'Identity play' (adopting another 'persona' or altering parts of one's persona by pretending to be of a another sex, age, culture, or profession) is much less a practical option in (private or institutional) websites than it is in purely verbal online forms of communication (MUD environments or discussion lists) where the participants enjoy (visual) anonymity. But even with respect to those electronic environments with hardly any social cues, which thus provide ample opportunity to fake or pretend, several authors have concluded that, in general, there is little evidence of what Baym rightly called the 'academic fascination with online identity play' (Baym 1998, in Hine, 2000: 119). Deliberate identity construction—trying to present a particular, most often polished, image of oneself, not by telling blatant lies but by offering a selective amount of information—is a standard practice in most forms of human exchange, only the means and degree may differ according to medium, purpose, and circumstance.

Furthermore, these 'constructions' are themselves very significant online phenomena that belong to social and cultural life in the broader sense, and for that reason are worthy of much (more) academic attention. They do not necessarily need to be fully validated by present 'real-life realities' but sometimes should be considered as reflections of the aspirations or desires of their creators (Pauwels, 2002). In general, they are not to be regarded as smokescreens or obstacles, obscuring insight into the social and cultural world of their producers.

Many books have been published about how to create and evaluate websites, including most of their multimedia features (for example, van Duyne et al., 2006; McNeil, 2008) Several of these works are a valuable resource for online researchers to learn more about the culture that is evolving around the Internet, and to learn some basic principles of good communication within this specific medium (for example, the do's and don'ts of website design). However, as most of these books were written from a business communications, commercial, or technical perspective, they offer researchers little from a cultural perspective. The crucial point for the cultural researcher is not to find out whether the websites being studied meet a number of predefined commercial or communications 'best practice' criteria, but to develop an approach that focuses on how the numerous potentially significant features of a website can be decoded as expressions of culture, thus

offering unique insights into values, norms, opinions, expectations, and aspirations of groups of people. In this respect, an amateurishly or unconventionally constructed website that seems to break all the rules of good design and communication may sometimes be much more valuable—while revealing more about the culture(s) of its producer(s)—than one that uses a predefined template and flawlessly emulates all the tricks of the trade.

Several years ago, I described the cultural decoding of websites as:

> an eclectic, multidimensional and integrated search for explicit and implicit statements on cultural issues, such as values, norms and opinions regarding gender, class, race, religion, the state, etc., as they are intentionally or unintentionally expressed and materialized in the many features of this highly hybrid medium. (Pauwels, 2005: 609)

My 'Model for Hybrid Cultural Analysis of Websites' (Pauwels, 2005) served as the basis for a new—more refined and expanded – model, which I will briefly discuss and illustrate (see the boxed insert: 'Decoding family websites as a cultural resource') in the remainder of this chapter. A more elaborate description and application of this framework will be presented in a future publication.

A MULTIMODAL MODEL FOR ANALYZING WEBSITES AS SOCIAL AND CULTURAL STATEMENTS

The revised and expanded model for analyzing websites as social and cultural data sources consists of six phases that correspond to a certain logic of discovery: from looking at rather immediately manifest features and performing straightforward measurements (phase 2) to more in-depth interpretations of the constituting elements and their intricate relations. The research thus migrates from fairly easy to quantify and code data, to more interpretative analysis focused on discovering the metaphorical and symbolic dimensions of websites or to unraveling their intended and even unintended meanings. I will briefly discuss each phase of the framework (Figure 29.1) and suggest its possible significance for disclosing websites as material expressions of culture. The literature references at the bottom of each phase do not refer to the source of the text but are intended to direct the reader to further study of the aspects covered.

1. Preservation of first impressions and reactions

This first phase precedes in fact the actual analysis. It is aimed at retaining the first general impression of the website before the researcher's initial reactions are possibly eradicated or supplanted by further, more in-depth research insights. In this initial phase researchers will try to make an instant assessment of the website in terms of 'look and feel,' their first impression with respect to genre and purpose. They should also note down their affective reactions: whether they are attracted to the web presentation, or intrigued by some features, what they immediately don't seem to like about it, what puzzles them, etc. This knowledge is important to feed a reflexive attitude: that is, the conscious reception of a website as a 'meeting of cultures' between producers, intended audiences, and researchers. Reflexivity should continue during the whole research cycle to better understand other people's reactions to it: those who, typically, have not meticulously studied the website.

2. Inventory of salient features and topics

In this phase, researchers concentrate on collecting and categorizing present and absent features and topics of the websites in their chosen sample. This involves making an inventory of website features and attributes (for example, the use of graphs and tables, the presence of webcams, feedback areas) that are present, and an inventory of main content categories and topics (for example, 'news,'

'about us,' 'photo gallery,' 'products'). These features and attributes can then be counted (or measured) and put into significant categories steered by theoretical insights or a hypothesis.

In addition to listing, counting, and clustering the salient elements that are present, it is also useful to perform a 'negative' analysis: that is to pay attention to those items, aspects, or events that are 'meaningfully absent' (that is, in a way 'expected' or forming part and parcel of the cultural reality the website refers to, or the genre the website seems to subscribe to). Absent topics and features or 'omissions' may be as culturally significant as the present ones in that they may point to cultural taboos, or implicit values and norms.

What is significant or not in this regard may require both deliberation and specific knowledge of the genre and the broader culture under study. Also, this assessment will be guided by the specific research interest. But all in all, this phase entails a rather straightforward and fairly easy-to-quantify approach yielding a first basic set of indications regarding functions, purposes, genre conformity, affiliations, and opinions, expressed in the selected websites. This phase is well-adapted for large-scale research using standardized coding sheets by different coders, since it requires minimal interpretation and is limited to a primarily denotative reading of the content and form. Even some forms of 'automated data gathering' may be possible (detection and counting of terms and words as in manifest content analysis, text analysis) (Bauer and Scharl, 2000; Bell, 2001).

3. In-depth analysis of content and formal choices

While the preceding phases yield some basic insights, the central and no doubt most encompassing third phase proposes to first look at the potential information that resides in the separate modes (intra-modal analysis) and then to look at the complex forms

THE MULTIMODAL FRAMEWORK FOR ANALYZING WEB PHENOMENA

1. Preservation of first impressions and reactions

- Categorization of 'look and feel' at a glance
- Recording of affective reactions

2. Inventory of salient features and topics

- Inventory of present website features and attributes
- Inventory of main content categories and topics
- Categorize and quantify features and topics
- Perform 'negative' analysis: significantly absent topics and features

3. In-depth analysis of content and formal choices

- Intra-modal analysis (fixed/static and moving/dynamic elements)
  - Verbal/written signifiers
  - Typographic signifiers
  - Visual representational types and signifiers
  - Sonic types and signifiers
  - Layout and Design signifiers
- Analysis of cross-modal interplay
  - Image/written text relations and typography/written text relations
  - Sound/image relations
  - Overall design/linguistic, visual, and auditory interplay
- In-depth 'negative' analysis

4. Embedded point(s) of view or 'voice' and implied audience(s) and purposes

- Analysis of POVs and constructed personae
- Analysis of intended/implied primary and secondary audience(s)
- Analysis of embedded goals and purposes

5. Analysis of information organization and spatial priming strategies

- Structural and navigational options and constraints (dynamic organization)
- Analysis of priming strategies and gate-keeping tools
- Analysis of outer-directed and/or interactive features
- Analysis of external hyperlinks

6. Contextual analysis, provenance, and inference

- Identification of sender(s) and sources
- Technological platforms and their constraints/implications
- Attribution of cultural hybridity

© Luc Pauwels

Figure 29.1 The multimodal framework for analyzing web phenomena

of interplay between the different modes (cross-modal analysis). In an actual research project these phases may be combined at some points, as meaning is often produced by the interplay of expressive systems, yet it remains useful to devote separate attention to the specific signifiers within each of the modes and sub-modes with respect to their cultural connotations.

3.1 Intra-modal analysis (fixed/static and moving/dynamic elements)

3.1.1 Verbal/written signifiers In this sub-phase, research is focused on analyzing potential culturally specific meanings that reside in the explicit and implicit content of the written utterances (for example, opinions, propositions, descriptions) as well as in the stylistic features of the written language parts and their possible meaning/effect in a broad sense (syntactic, semantic, and pragmatic aspects). The content can be analyzed in terms of topics and issues that are being dealt with and the expressed positions vis-à-vis these issues and topics: opinions, value statements (for example, politically, corporate, family oriented), forms and degree of self-disclosure, etc. With respect to style the analyst may look at such things as word register/lexicon, forms of address, use of first-person singular or plural or impersonal, temporal orientation, gendered statements, use of metaphors, rhetoric, and narrative strategies, humor, connotative meanings, use of abbreviations, redundancy, use of paralanguage (emoticons), and to numerous other language variations and choices that may potentially reveal useful information about the sender(s): social background, position, preferences, intended audience, purpose, beliefs, etc. (Wierzbicka, 1991; Foley, 1997; Crystal, 2001).

3.1.2 Typographic signifiers This sub-phase focuses on analyzing the potential culturally specific meanings that reside in the visual properties of the written texts, such as: font choice (font 'families' and their 'character'—formal, informal, authoritative,

elegant, playful, etc.); font size (importance, 'shouting' vs 'whispering'); font style and effects (for example, bold for emphasis, respect, phatic function, etc.); font direction (left to right, top to bottom, etc.) and curvature (straight or dancing); font color (cultural connotations, iconic and symbolic properties); combinations of different fonts (multiple 'voices'?); character and line spacing, legibility (font shape and size in combination with color and background); para-iconic qualities (type as image—'bloody' characters); text animations (text in motion); and intertextuality (reference to a specific type or logo, for example, Coca Cola) (Brumberger, 2003; van Leeuwen, 2005a, 2006; Stöckl, 2005; Cahalan, 2007).

3.1.3 Visual representational types and signifiers This sub-phase, of particular interest to visual researchers, is a very complex one. First, because visual representations come in many different types and shapes: graphical/conceptual representations (for example, charts); algorithmic representations (for example, photographs, scans); non-algorithmic representations (for example, drawings, paintings); abstract or non-representational forms; symbols and icons, numerical representations (tables), each involving a different analytical stance because of their very diverse referents, production processes and uses (see Pauwels, 2008b). And secondly, because visual representations have to be analyzed meticulously both for 'what they depict' ('referent' or 'content') and 'how they depict or represent' (style). The latter aspect requires very specific knowledge of each of the distinct representational processes and therefore is often overlooked (many visual studies indeed limit themselves erroneously to the depicted content). In looking at the characteristics of the depicted, the analyst should be well aware of the nature of the referent (imaginary, material, conceptual; visible/invisible, etc.?) and of the particular 'mode of representation' (Carroll, 1996: 241): for example, 'nominal' (representing a class or general example) versus 'physical' representation (depicting a particular person or thing/event). In view of space restrictions, I will limit the discussion of concrete characteristics of visual representations that might bear some cultural meaning to the ubiquitous 'photographic' image in websites.

The analysis of the 'level of the depicted' (in the case of photographs or film: the 'pre-photographic' or 'ante-filmic' level) would include scrutinizing such things as the depicted event, visual 'motives,' persons (age, sex, attributes, specific behavior, actors or real persons?, etc.), background, lighting, use of visual rhetorical figures (metaphors, metonyms), etc.

The analysis of the 'level of the depiction' (style, medium specific characteristics, post-production) includes scrutinizing:

(a) The *'material characteristics of the image'*: these characteristics are limited in this specific case, namely websites, to 'images projected on a computer screen.' They include: texture, resolution, sharpness, color spectrum, image ratio (square, panoramic, etc.), image form, image borders.

(b) The *'signifiers and codes of the static image'*: these include: composition (prominent elements, balance, planes, light contrasts, color, direction, shapes and forms); use of superimposition, reflections or double exposures; nature of lighting (intensity, direction, diffusion); camera distance (extreme close up to very long shot); focus (deep focus/selective focus, soft-focus, center focus, etc.); depth of field—broad (deep focus photography) versus narrow (shallow focus); camera angle (high/low, canted angle, etc.); focal length (wide angle to telephoto); shutter speed (frozen to blurred effect); exposure (correct or over/underexposure); special effects (filters, digital effects, etc.).

(c) The *'signifiers and codes of the shot'* (moving image): camera movements (panning, tilting, rolling, traveling, crane, handheld, steady cam, zooming, follow focus, rack focus); shutter speed (slow motion, fast motion, time lapse, freeze-frame).

(d) *Editing choices*: shot length (short, long duration); image transitions (dissolve, fade to black,..); editing style (continuity editing, propositional, dialectic, etc.).

(e) *Post-production*: digital effects, (relative) size of visuals, position on screen, sequenced or randomly changing images, live webcam images (webcam).

Each of these parameters and signifiers may express a particular culturally significant view on the depicted subject (for example, respect or superstition by avoiding a close up, high and low camera angles to express domination or subordination, shallow focus to help steer (direct or obscure) the visitors' look, etc.) (Boggs, 1991; Monaco, 2000; Giannetti, 2007).

3.1.4 Sonic types and signifiers The auditory aspect of websites is becoming increasingly varied. Sonic sources of information include:

(a) 'Spoken words or sung lyrics' with syntactic, semantic, and pragmatic features similar to written texts *plus* a set of potentially significant phonetic dimensions (tone, accent, intonation, articulation, pauses, volume, etc.).

(b) Non-verbal/vocal sound (for example, laughter, screams, sighs).

(c) Non-vocal sound/noise (for example, car breaks, train whistle, a ticking clock).

(d) Music (instrumental or vocal).

The iconic, indexical and symbolic properties of music in particular tend to provide strong cultural indications (genre, ethnic origin, ritual function, sub-cultural affiliation, iconic-indexical-symbolic), but in fact all of these different types of auditory signifiers can be analyzed for their 'content' (primarily via their iconic and indexical properties) and their more symbolic/metaphorical load.

3.1.5 Layout and design signifiers The proverb 'design is thinking made visual' (credited to the American graphic designer Saul Bass) also applies to websites. Website design and layout features are important vehicles to grab and steer the attention of visitors and to elicit a desired response from them. But, by the same token, they also reveal ideas, opinions, and aspirations of the creator and/or 'applier.'

Particular combinations of choices may, for instance, express more conservative or nostalgic feelings or conversely embody a more experimental, daring or 'avant-garde' attitude. Layout and design features will work to guide potential visitors through a web page by the use of dominant elements, iterative features, and compositional choices: themes, templates, color schemes, use of columns and frames, backgrounds, white space, spatial balance (symmetry/asymmetry, horizontal, vertical or diagonal structure), left–right, top–bottom relations and expectations, relative size and position of texts and visual representations, etc. (Kress and van Leeuwen, 2002).

These choices may result in a very rigid structure (predefined categories and spaces and pathways) or embody a more open space to wander around. They may seem to blend to a recognizable 'genre' (newsletter, family album, institutional) or exhibit a very hybrid and eclectic appearance. Again, explicit attention should be paid to cultural connotations/metaphor and intertextual references (for example, a politicians' website adopting the form of a family album).

It is important to note that the design and layout will be more revealing about the culture of the immediate sender(s) the more they are responsible for each of the constituting choices. When prefabricated templates are being used (which include content categories, for example, as with some commercially operated companies offering family website templates), researchers may be learning more about the culture (ideas, preferences) of the template developer than about its users, though the choice by the user for a particular ready-made template and graphic theme also remains significant.

3.2 Analysis of cross-modal interplay

This sub-phase pays explicit attention to the forms of interplay between linguistic, visual, auditory, spatial, and time-based elements, for, very often, meaning is constructed by an interplay of two or more elements and while the constituting parts may express a specific idea, this idea may be completely reversed in combination with other elements.

More concretely, research here will focus on:

- Relations between written parts (captions, titles, body copy) and visuals, which can be characterized by a tightly bound or a loose relation: a mere

illustrative, redundant, or highly complementary one (Garner et al., 2003; Hocks and Kendrick, 2003; Martinec and Salway, 2005; Hagan, 2007).
- Relations between sound and visuals (for example, use of off-screen comments, on-screen speakers, musical score, synchronous sound), which may be characterized by a balanced/complementary, or hierarchic (dominant/subservient), or contradictory–contrapuntist (for example, irony) stance. Sound can be used, for example, to enhance realism of the images or conversely serve a primarily expressive-symbolic function (Chion, 1994; van Leeuwen, 2007).
- And further: all possible interactions between typography; layout and design elements versus textual content, visual representations and sound which may for instance contribute to a unified view or position or reveal many incongruent ideas (for example, a retro design combined with avant-garde opinions). This includes even relations between different elements within the same mode—that is, the meaning that resides in the juxtaposition of images, or a specific combination of music or writing styles (Kress and van Leeuwen, 1996; van Leeuwen, 2005b; Knox, 2007).

3.3 In-depth 'inverted' analysis: significantly missing or incomplete content, arguments, and formal choices

This sub-phase in a way reprises phase 2, but now it involves a much more in-depth analysis of aspects, issues, and arguments that are not covered and which exactly by their absence seem to become significant (e.g. no use of close ups, no people in images, or no old people in images, absence of ethnic diversity in an ethnic diverse context, no external links, no info about a certain family member or aspects). Observing Watzlawick et al.'s (1967: 48) maxim 'one cannot not communicate,' it may further help to uncover cultural taboos or highly sensitive issues through much 'reading between the lines.'

4. Embedded point(s) of view or 'voice' and implied audience(s) and purposes

As the previous phase involved a detailed analysis of 'what' is being said or expressed through form and content, this next phase tries to further complement the inquiry into the cultural meaning of web utterances with the question: 'Who' is really saying (the earlier captured and analyzed) 'what' to 'whom' with what 'purpose'? This complex question is addressed in a meta-analytical way, combining different expressive elements that have been identified before (for example, modes of address, camera angles, personal and possessive pronouns).

The Point(s) of View (POV) and/or 'Voice(s)' of a website are the result of a combination of many features: they can be manifold and even contradictory (for example, pictures and texts originating from different people) or very consistent and unified. Obviously, POVs reside in many aspects of the website (visuals, textual, design elements like templates, etc.) and they don't easily 'add up' to one dominant or unified POV, since many websites contain materials from very different sources (for example, archive pictures, templates, journalistic texts). Yet the purpose of this phase is mainly to uncover what the dominant points of view are, as expressed in the website as a 'grand syntagma.' So a website may, for example, present itself at first sight as a family website where different family members have their say, but after closer scrutiny it may become clear that one family member is really pulling the strings and using the website as a vehicle to propagate his or her political views to an outside audience. The POVs can be very manifest (using first-person singular or plural, or a third-person voice in text or adopting subjective, half-subjective, and objective camera positions in images), but often it remains difficult to determine whose point of view in a metaphorical way is being expressed. The picture taker typically remains invisible and the expressed (or literal) standpoint is not necessarily a 'position' in a more metaphorical sense. POVs and personae as described or depicted in texts and images may even be fictitious or false (for example, in family websites parents often 'voice' the ideas and feelings of the younger children; in corporate

and commercial websites copywriters often put some words in the mouth of some real or fictitious employee or customer). The nature and variety of the POVs may add a subtextual meaning to the content (embody indicators of democracy, multi-vocality, openness, or conversely reveal autocratic traits).

Paired to the analysis of POVs is the effort to derive/determine the intended/implied primary (for example, children) and secondary (for example, their parents) audience(s) and connected to that the embedded goals and purposes, only some of which are explicitly stated (and true). This analysis will further add to an understanding of whose goals are served, whose values are propagated and who is to benefit from expressing them.

Again, purposes and audiences can be explicitly stated, but they can also more indirectly be derived from 'expected visitor/user behavior.' Website offerings, particular features (feedback areas, polls), types of address, expressed POVs, etc., may hold indications of expected behaviors such as: subscribing to views, buying a product or service, being converted? Thus, implied audiences can be identified/constructed in terms of economic status or class (for example, 'well to do' consumers), conviction (non-believers–believers), specific age groups (young children, elderly persons), other characteristics (same name bearers, nationality, hobby, health condition), etc.

This phase thus interrogates and complements 'first impressions' (phase 1) with a more in-depth analysis of manifest and latent aims. It also implies comparing explicitly stated purposes/audiences with latent/secondary ones. For example, family websites today are not limited to celebrating family events and values but often include, as secondary (or primary) goals, showing off technical or creative skills, selling products or oneself (for example, by including a résumé), or voicing political and religious opinions. As this research phase, like the preceding one usually involves a rather 'sub-textual' reading of all elements and their interplay, it consequently may involve much interpretation.

5. Analysis of dynamic information organization and spatial priming strategies

This phase focuses on analyzing the structural and navigational options and constraints (the 'dynamic' organization as opposed to static layout and design features) of websites as well as their priming strategies and outer-directed features with respect to steering preferred readings and conduct, and exercising control.

Researchers should both look at the overall information architecture/organization and at the place or position of different bits of information in that structure. The structure (menus, internal links, navigational tools) may allow for free roaming of the website or exhibit a tight order and set of rules that visitors should follow. The content, as linked with its spatial hierarchy/rhetoric (for example, items with more or less space occupied in the website, items on the homepage or buried deeper into the website, the order and flow of elements, pathways, and vectors), may express a social or cultural hierarchy as well.

For example, if in a family website the father's interests (hobbies, past, opinions) occupy more space and need fewer 'clicks' to find, this may be interpreted as a reflection of more traditional (less equal) gender roles. The numbers of layers one has to pass may sometimes be indicative of the importance or sensitivity of the item ('burying' as the counter-strategy to 'priming'). And even search engines (their options and undisclosed algorithms) may be considered potentially significant in terms of control and materialized cultural preferences (for example, when going first for commercial links, or most popular links, or blocking certain content).

Contemporary websites often use (or are being flooded by) a gamut of priming tools and strategies ('most viewed videos,' 'news,' 'eye catchers,' banners, pop-ups, internal links) of a very different nature and origin. They may also make use of numerous control mechanisms: passwords, counters, rules of conduct, forms of censorship, copyright disclaimers,

change, copying or printing blocking, privacy invading practices (cookies, or tools that capture part of the identity of the visitor). The use of each of these items can potentially tell us something about the value and belief system of its originator (trust–distrust, respect–disrespect, generous–self-serving). Other outer-directed features may include: chat rooms, bulletin boards, e-mail contacts, Wikis, blogs, guest books, forms, YouTube video links, ads, dynamic links/updates (for example, weather updates, financial info, webcam images). It may be important to study the nature and sought degree of 'interactivity' carefully. What exactly is the visitor or user of the website allowed to do, or expected to do: Just select content (menus), place an order, post a reply, add content, change content, engage in one-to-one, one-to-many, or many-to-many communication? Are they allowed to leave the website at any point? Or are connections with the rest of the Internet highly constrained?

The study of external hyperlinks, in particular, is often very rewarding as these virtual 'affiliations' are further and clear indicators and expressions of particular interests, preferences, value systems, and aspirations (political, religious, commercial, educational, etc.).

The control over the look, functionality, and contents of the website may be exercised by one person or distributed over several persons and groups (for example, social networking ites).

6. Contextual analysis, provenance, and inference

Finally, inferences with respect to possible cultural significance and meaning need to be based on a solid insight into the origin and circumstances of the different constituting elements.

But 'authorship' and 'origin,' and in this case the question of who to attribute certain choices to, is an increasingly complex matter with websites, not only because of the multi-authored nature of many sites (especially social network sites, SNS) but also because of the supporting technologies of multiple sources (which are in themselves forms of materialized culture) and the strongly intertextual and globalizing aspects of contemporary media.

When sources are mentioned or detected, one should further investigate their authority, trustworthiness, and whether they are up to date (the 'last updated on' clause referring to the whole website provides a first yardstick).

Technologies and platforms, in and by themselves (templates, browsers, programming languages, database structures, graphic tools), with (and without) certain functionalities, already embody certain cultural norms (the 'politics of technology'; Star, 1999). And the same goes for the specific application of these technologies and their interaction with the set-up and purpose of the website (enable or constrain).

The ability to construe useful information from the embedded cultural signifiers of websites rests for an important part on the assumption that one knows who or what exactly is responsible for choices and how these different choices combine to deliver intended and unintended effects. This may not be important for the user of the website, who by default will adopt a holistic view or experience, but it will be of prime importance for research to the extent that one wants to read elements as cultural expressions. Similar to the last phase in iconological research, this requires a very thorough knowledge of culture and technology.

CONCLUSIONS

Stating that the Internet (and the world wide web) form both a unique subject and tool for cultural research, I have argued in this chapter that some serious methodological problems still need to be overcome before these prospects can be realized to their fullest extent. To that aim I discussed:

- The nature and value of online expressions, with phenomena such as impression management in asynchronous environments offering a host of opportunities with respect to conscious identity construction and even identity play.
- Problems of sampling a largely unknown and very dynamic online population.
- The less than adequate knowledge of how exactly offline and online worlds are connected.
- The verbal bias in social research, both in offline and online modes, and connected to that the lack of multimodal research tools to disclose the varied multimodal nature of the web as a rich social and cultural data source.

The main part of this chapter addressed this latter challenge by providing a multimodal model as a still fairly rudimentary tool for a more culturally focused analysis of a hybrid medium such as the Internet. This model offers an overview of the multimodal signifiers and some guidance for defining cultural indicators, but, by the very nature of the enquiry (as a 'meeting of cultures' of the web producers, the researchers and the users), it cannot identify any fixed cultural meanings or interpretations.

Thus, such a model can only partly become a generic tool for cultural analysis of web phenomena. It will need to be further refined and 'customized' depending on the specific research interests and the cultural contexts involved. To be usable, the model needs to be backed up by research/literature/knowledge on different cultures (both online and offline aspects). One of the most crucial parts of the research design remains the valid operationalization of a particular research interest into observable aspects of a website as outlined in the model. At the same time, the research effort always needs to be reduced to manageable proportions. Moreover, not all dimensions of the model will yield sufficiently important data for every possible research question. If one is interested, for example, in researching changing power dynamics in the family setting (gender roles, changing relations between children, parents, grandparents), one needs to operationalize this

EXAMPLE / DECODING FAMILY WEBSITES AS A CULTURAL RESOURCE

Private or family websites are clearly among the most expressive web phenomena with regard to displaying prevailing values in a particular cultural context. Whereas paper-based family photography mainly served a 'socialization' and 'integration' function confined to next of kin and propagating mainly domestic values to a fairly secluded audience (Bourdieu,1978; Musello, 1979), the expressive means have increased dramatically once this practice moved into the semi-public realm and developed into a complex multimodal form of communication, catering for an anonymous mass of web surfers (Pauwels, 2008a). Today family self-representations on the web present a fascinating area of research into cultural change and reproduction, and into the complex role of technology in those processes at the 'grassroots' level. Many private websites contain—explicitly or more implicitly—verbal and visual statements about gender relations and role patterns, politics, religion, leisure, sports, and sexual preferences.

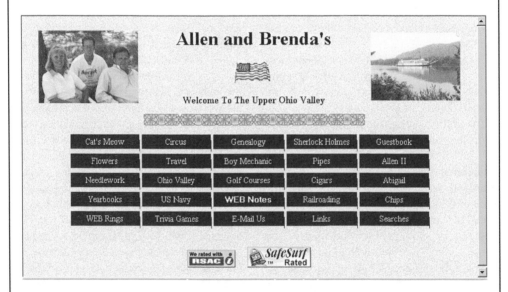

Figure 29.2   Alan and Brenda's spot on the web (used with permission)
Pictures and stories about love and caring for kin (grandparents, parents, children, and pets), material possessions (cars and houses), educational and sporting achievements, the military 'tour of duty' are typical expressions of values that are often celebrated on (American) family websites. Quite a number of website owners invest much effort in trying to entertain visitors with all sorts of games and topics of general interest to get in touch with an extended audience for a variety of purposes such as: making new friendships beyond the family sphere, voicing political and social views, and promoting skills and achievements to potential customers or employers.

Home | About Us | Family News | Resources | Links | Media | Photos | FAQ's | Contact Us |

Welcome to The Duggar Family Website!

Our prayer is that all who view this site will realize that we are ordinary people with our individual weaknesses and imperfections but we serve an extraordinary GOD who delights in demonstrating His great power!

"And He said unto me, my grace is sufficient for thee for my strength is made perfect in weakness, most gladly therefore will I rather glory in my infirmities that the power of Christ may rest upon me." (2 Corinthians 12:9)

We trust that you will find strength and encouragement from HIM who is "able to do exceeding abundantly above all that we ask..."

Grace and Peace, Jim Bob & Michelle Duggar & Family

CLICK HERE FOR MORE PHOTOS...

Figure 29.3   The Duggar Family website (used with permission)
The Duggars one of the largest families in the USA (19 kids and counting!), belong to the conservative evangelical Christian movement ('Quiverfull') which advocates procreation ('children are a gift of the Lord'), homeschooling and homesteading. Their website is very explicit about their firmly held values, norms, and beliefs and they actively seek to promote them to the outside world not only in this website but through books, magazine articles, and appearances in documentaries and TV shows. The website is both very normative in the textual parts (the words of welcome, 'Duggar Family House Guidelines' wand 'Character Qualities,' 'Parenting Advice and Practical Tips') and in the visual representation of the family's activities and physical environment (almost uniquely depicting exemplary behavior like: sense of duty, togetherness, and devoutness). The voice and point of view seem very consistent (mainly the father Jim Bob Duggar) throughout the website though there is some switching between the parents. Even when this website seems very explicit with respect to values and norms, still there are many aspects to be discovered through a more in-depth study of, for instance, the text image-relations, the content and the form of the images, the study of what is not shown or discussed (for example, there are no signs or voices of dissent, no specific interests of the individual children discussed or depicted, no pictures of friends or the depiction of the outside world is limited to beautiful scenery and family members only). This website is an extremely rich example of how cultural views (in a broad sense) can materialize in numerous features of web based artifacts.

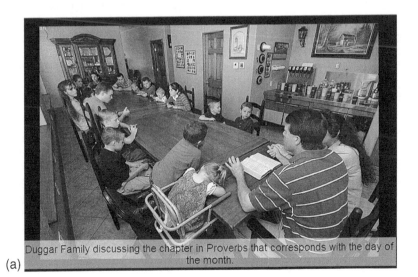

Duggar Family discussing the chapter in Proverbs that corresponds with the day of the month.

(a)

(b)

The Boy's Bedroom with 10 beds and 2 bathrooms (from left... Jeremiah top, Justin bottom, Jackson bottom, James top, Josiah, Jason bottom, Jedidiah top, Joshua bottom, Joseph top & John far right).

Figure 29.4   Two pictures from the Duggar's picture gallery (used with permission)

Most pictures from the Duggar Family website are wide angle shots to depict the whole (in physical and metaphorical terms) and the context rather than the part or the individual. They are very purposefully framed and several of the more formally posed pictures disclose a professional's touch. Apart from the clearly communicated intended meanings and the unequivocal captions to construct this 'preferred' reading, these pictures contain much information about the physical organization and the material culture of this family, and careful study of the image content and style also provides many indications of the more immaterial traits of the cultural setting.

concept or phenomenon in terms of concrete paradigmatic choices and syntagmatic effects of the website based on knowledge of cultural manifestations of this phenomenon or concept. Thus, one might benefit from looking more closely at: Who is talking in what manner for whom? What personal space (both in a literal and metaphorical sense) is every member entitled to? What view resides in the overall design and structure of the website? Who is depicted in what way and under what circumstances? etc. When researching larger samples of websites, many of such 'cultural markers' need to be translated into codebooks that stipulate the different options for each indicator. A broad cultural and multimodal literacy is required to succeed with this task. So, in the end, the meaning that can be derived from the constituting elements of the model will largely depend on the proficiency of the researcher in the various fields. Anthropological linguists will be able to extract much more useful data from looking at the textual parts and, conversely, visual scholars more from the complex layers of the visual in its multitude of appearances. The proposed model is no more than a tool for addressing the different elements and their interplay in a basic way, but it does not contend to be complete, or to supplant personal expertise. Moreover, it is only useful if the researcher has a broad and specific knowledge of the culture under study. Analyzing websites in all aspects related to their cultural expressiveness will remain a very demanding and specialized undertaking. Although one can never be equally competent in all of the discussed aspects, a basic understanding of the constituting multimodal elements of websites and their respective disciplinary frames of reference may help scholars to further disclose the Internet as a rich cultural data source. As a positive side effect it may also allow them to become more culturally savvy and expressive when using the web as a tool to communicate their insights and research findings.

REFERENCES

Andrews, D., Nonnecke, B. and Preece, J. (2003) 'Electronic survey methodology: A case study in reaching hard-to-involve Internet users', *International Journal of Human–Computer Interaction*, 16: 185–210.

Badre, A. and Laskowski, S. (2000) *The Cultural Context of Web Genres: Content vs. Style* [Online]. Available from: www.smartech.library.gatech.edu [Accessed 24 November 2008].

Barber, W. and Badre, A. (2000) 'Cultural markers and World Wide Web interface design', GVU, Georgia Tech.

Barnett, G. A. and Sung, E. (2005) 'Culture and the structure of the international hyperlink network', *Journal of Computer-Mediated Communication*, 11(1) [Online]. Available from: http://jcmc.indiana.edu/vol11/issue1/barnett.html [Accessed 14 October 2010].

Bassett, C. (1997) 'Virtually gendered: Life in an online world', in K. Gelder and S. Thornton (eds.), *The Subcultures Reader*. London: Routledge.

Bauer, C. and Scharl, A. (2000) 'Quantitative evaluation of web site content and structure', *Internet Research*, 10(1): 31–43.

Bell, P. (2001) 'Content analysis of visual images', in T. van Leeuwen and C. Jewitt (eds.), *Handbook of Visual Analysis*. London: Sage Publications.

Boggs, J. M. (1991) *The Art of Watching Films*. Mountain View, CA/London/Toronto: Mayfield Publishing Company.

Bourdieu, P. (ed.) (1978) *Un Art Moyen, essai sur les usages sociaux de la photographie*, 2nd edn. Paris: Les Editions de Minuit. (1st edn, 1965.)

Brumberger, E. R. (2003) 'The rhetoric of typography: The persona of typeface and text', *Technical Communication*, 50(2): 206–223.

Cahalan, A. (2007) 'Multitudes of interpretations: Intentions, connotations and associations of typeface designs', *Research Journal of the Australian Graphic Design Association*, 3(1): 9–18.

Callahan, E. (2005) 'Cultural similarities and differences in the design of university web sites', *Journal of Computer-Mediated Communication*, 11(1): 239–273.

Carroll, Noël (1996) 'From real to reel: Entangled in nonfiction film', in N. Carroll (ed.), *Theorizing the Moving Image*. New York: Cambridge University Press. pp. 224–251.

Carter, Denise (2005) 'Living in virtual communities: An ethnography of human relationships in cyberspace', *Information, Communication & Society*, 8(2): 148–167.

Chandler, D. (1998) *Personal Home Pages and the Construction of Identities on the Web* [Online]. Available from: http://www.aber.ac.uk/media/Documents/short/webident.html [Accessed 14 October 2010].

Cheung, C. (2000) 'A home on the web: Presentations of self on personal homepages', in D. Gauntlett (ed.), *Web Studies: Rewiring Media Studies for the Digital Age*. London: Arnold. pp. 43–51.

Chion, M. (1994) *Audio-Vision—Sound on Screen*, edited and translated by Claudia Gorbman, with foreword by Walter Murch. New York: Columbia University Press.

Crystal, D. (2001) *Language and the Internet*. Cambridge, MA: Cambridge University Press.

Cyr, D. and Trevor-Smith, H. (2004) 'Localization of Web design: An empirical comparison of German, Japanese, and United States Web site characteristics', *Journal of the American Society for Information Science and Technology*, 55(13): 1199–1208.

Dillon, A. and Gushrowski, B. A. (2000) 'Genres and the web: Is the personal home page the first uniquely digital genre?', *Journal of the American Society for Information Science*, 51(2): 202–205.

Donker-Kuijer, M. W., De Jong, M. and Lentz, L. (2008) 'Heuristic web site evaluation', *Technical Communication*, 55(4): 392–404.

Döring, N. (2002) 'Personal home pages on the web: A review of research', *Journal of Computer-Mediated Communication*, 7(3) [Online]. Available from: http://onlinelibrary.wiley.com/doi/10.1111/j.1083-6101.2002.tb00152.x/full [Accessed 14 October 2010].

Dutton, W. H., Helsper, E. J. and Gerber, M. M. (2009) 'The Internet in Britain: 2009', Oxford Internet Surveys, Oxford Internet Institute, University of Oxford.

Fletcher, R. (2006) 'The impact of culture on web site content, design and structure. An international and multicultural perspective', *Journal of Communication Management*, 10(3): 259–273.

Foley, William A. (1997) *Anthropological Linguistics: An Introduction*. Oxford: Blackwell.

Garner, R., Gillingham, M. and Zhao, Y. (2003) 'Writing photo captions for the Web', *First Monday*, 8(9) [Online]. Available from: http://firstmonday.org/htbin/cgiwrap/bin/ojs/index.php/fm/article/view/1078/998 [Accessed 12 October 2010].

Giannetti, L. (2007) *Understanding Movies*, 11th edn. Englewood Cliffs, NJ: Prentice Hall.

Goffmann, E. (1959) *The Presentation of Self in Everyday Life*. Garden City, NY: Doubleday Anchor.

Hagan, S. M. (2007) 'Visual/verbal collaboration in print: Complementary differences, necessary ties, and an untapped rhetorical opportunity', *Written Communication*, 24(1): 49–73.

Hine, Christine (2000) *Virtual Ethnography*. London/Thousand Oaks, CA/New Delhi: Sage Publications.

Hine, Christine (ed.) (2006) *Virtual Methods. Issues in Social Research on the Internet*. Oxford: Berg.

Hocks, M. E. and Kendrick, M. R. (2003) *Eloquent Images: Word and Image in the Age of New Media*. Cambridge, MA: MIT Press.

Hofstede, G. (2001) *Culture's Consequences. Comparing Values, Behaviours, Institutions, and Organizations across Nations*, 2nd edn. Thousand Oaks, CA: Sage Publications.

Jones, Steve (1999) *Doing Internet Research, Critical Issues and Methods for Examining the Net*. London, Thousand Oaks, CA and New Delhi: Sage Publications.

Kehoe, C. M. and Pitkow, J. E. (1996) 'Surveying the territory: GVU's five WWW user surveys', *The World Wide Web Journal*, 1(3): 77–84.

Kirkman, B., Lowe, K. B. and Gibson, C. B. (2006) 'A quarter century of culture's consequences: A review of empirical research incorporating Hofstede's cultural values framework', *Journal of International Business*, 37: 285–320.

Knox, J. (2007) 'Visual–verbal communication on online newspaper home pages', *Visual Communication*, 6(1): 19–53.

Kress, G. and van Leeuwen, T. (1996) *Reading Images: The Grammar of Visual Design*. London: Routledge.

Kress, G. and van Leeuwen, T. (2002) 'Colour as a semiotic mode: Notes for a grammar of colour', *Visual Communication*, 1(3): 343–368.

Lee, Raymond M. (2000) *Unobtrusive Methods in Social Research*. Buckingham/Philadelphia: Open University Press.

Lievrouw, L. and Livingstone S. (2002) *The Handbook of New Media*. London/Thousand Oaks, CA/New Delhi: Sage Publications.

Lister, M., Dovey, J., Giddings, S., Grant, I. and Kelly, K. (2003) *New Media, A Critical Introduction*. London/New York: Routledge.

Luna, D., Peracchio, L. A. and de Juan, M. D. (2002) 'Cross-cultural and cognitive aspects of Web site navigation', *Journal of the Academy of Marketing Science*, 30(4): 397–410.

McMillan, S. J. (2000). 'The microscope and the moving target, the challenge of applying content analysis to the World Wide Web', *Journalism & Mass Communication Quarterly*, 77(1): 80–98.

McNeil, P. (2008) *The Web Designer's Idea Book: The Ultimate Guide To Themes, Trends & Styles In Website Design*, F+W Media, Inc.

McSweeney, B. (2002) 'Hofstede's model of national cultural differences and their consequences: A triumph of faith—a failure of analysis', *Human Relations*, 55(1): 89–118.

Mann, Chris and Stewart, Fiona (2000) *Internet Communication and Qualitative Research: A Handbook for Researching Online*. London/Thousand Oaks, CA/New Delhi: Sage Publications.

Martinec, R. and Salway, A. (2005) 'A system for image–text relations in new (and old) media', *Visual Communication*, 4(3): 337–370.

Mesch, Gustavo and Talmud, Ilan (2006) 'The quality of online and offline relationships, the role of multiplexity and duration', *The Information Society*, 22(3): 137–148.

Miller, Daniel and Slater, Don (2000) *The Internet, An Ethnographic Approach*. Oxford: Berg.

Monaco, James (2000) *How to Read a Film. The World of Movies, Media, and Multimedia: Language, History, Theory*, 3rd edn. New York/Oxford: Oxford University Press.

Musello, C. (1979) 'Family photography', in J. Wagner (ed.), *Images of Information: Still Photography in the Social Sciences*. Beverly Hills, CA/London: Sage Publications. pp. 101–118.

Norris, P. (2001) 'Digital parties: Civil engagement and online democracy'. Paper presented at the ECPR Joint Sessions of Workshops, 6–11 April, Grenoble.

Okazaki, S. and Rivas, J. A. (2002) 'A content analysis of multinationals' Web communication strategies: Cross-cultural research framework and pre-testing', *Internet Research*, 12(5): 380–390.

Paccagnella, L. (1997) 'Getting the seats of your pants dirty: Strategies for ethnographic research on virtual communities', *Journal of Computer Mediated Communication*, 3(1) [Online]. Available from: http://jcmc.indiana.edu/vol3/issue1/paccagnella.html [Accessed 13 September 2010].

Pauwels, L. (2002) 'Communicating desired pasts: On the digital construction of private histories: What is really at stake?', *Journal of Visual Literacy*, 22(2): 161–174.

Pauwels, L. (2005) 'Websites as visual and multimodal cultural expressions: Opportunities and issues of online hybrid media research', *Media, Culture & Society*, (27)4: 604–613.

Pauwels, L. (2008a) 'A private visual practice going public? Social functions and sociological research opportunities of web-based family photography', *Visual Studies*, 23(1): 34–49.

Pauwels, L. (2008b) 'An integrated model for conceptualizing visual competence in scientific research and communications', *Visual Studies*, 23(2): 147–161.

Rossler, P. (2002) 'Content analysis in online communication: A challenge for traditional methodology', in B. Batinic, U. D. Reips and M. Bosnjak (eds.), *Online Social Sciences*. Seattle: Hofgrefe & Huber Publishers.

Singh, N., Zhao, H. and Hu, X. (2005) 'Analyzing the cultural content of web sites. A cross-national comparision of China, India, Japan, and US', *International Marketing Review* [Online]. Available from: http://goliath.ecnext.com/coms2/gi_0198-293950/Analyzing-the-cultural-content-of.html [Accessed 14 October 2010].

Sondergaard, M. (1994). 'Hofstede consequences—A study of reviews, citations and replications', *Organization Studies*, 15(3): 447–456.

Springer, C. (1996) *Electronic Eros: Bodies and Desire in the Postindustrial Age*. Austin, TX: University of Texas Press.

Star, S. L. (1999) 'The ethnography of infrastructure', *American Behavioral Scientist*, 43(3): 377–391.

Stewart, Kate and Williams, Matthew (2005) 'Researching online populations: The use of online focus groups for social research', *Qualitative Research*, 5(4): 395–416.

Stöckl, H. (2005) 'Typography: Body and dress of a text—A signing mode between language and image', *Visual Communication*, 4(2): 204–214.

Suler, John (2004) 'The online disinhibition effect', *Cyberpsychology and Behavior*, 7: 321–326.

van Duyne, D. K., Landay, J. A. and Hong, J. I. (2006) *The Design of Sites: Patterns for Creating Winning Web Sites*, 2nd edn. Upper Saddle River, NJ: Prentice Hall.

van Leeuwen, T. (2005a) *Introducing Social Semiotics*. London: Routledge.

van Leeuwen, T. (2005b) 'Typographic meaning', *Visual Communication*, 4: 137–143.

van Leeuwen, T. (2006) 'Towards a semiotics of typography', *Information Design Journal*, 14(2): 139–155.

van Leeuwen, T. (2007) 'Sound and vision', *Visual Communication*, 6(2): 136–145.

Wakeford, Nina (2000). 'New methodologies: Studying the web', in D. Gauntlett (ed.), *Web Studies: Rewiring Media Studies for the Digital Age*. London: Arnold. pp. 31–41.

Watzlawick, Paul, Bavelas, Janet Beavin and Jackson, Donald D. (1967) *Pragmatics of Human Communication: A Study of Interactional Patterns, Pathologies, and Paradoxes*. New York: W. W. Norton.

Weare, C. and Lin, W. Y. (2000) 'Content analysis of the World Wide Web—Opportunities and challenges', *Social Science Computer Review*, 18(3): 272–292.

Wierzbicka, Anna (1991) *Cross-Cultural Pragmatics. The Semantics of Human Interaction*. Berlin, New York: Mouton de Gruyter.

Woolgar, Steve (Programme Director) and Daw, Sarah (Programme Administrator) (2000) 'Virtual Society? The social science of electronic technologies, Profile 2000', ESRC Research Programme report. [Online]. Available from: http://virtualsociety.sbs.ox.ac.uk/profile.pdf [Accessed 13 September 2010].

Würtz, E. (2006) 'Intercultural communication on web sites: A cross-cultural analysis of websites from high-context cultures and low-context cultures', *Journal of Computer-Mediated Communication*, 11(1): 274–299.

Wynn, Eleanor and Katz, James T. (1997) 'Hyperbole over cyberspace: Self-presentation and social boundaries in Internet home pages and discourse', *The Information Society*, 13(4): 297–327.

Zhao, W., Massey, B. L., Murphy, J. and Fang, L. (2003) 'Cultural dimensions of website design and content', *Prometheus*: 21(1): 75–84.

30

How to 'Read' Images with Texts: The Graphic Novel Case

Jan Baetens and Steven Surdiacourt

INTRODUCTION: READING IMAGES OR LOOKING AT THEM?

In the scholarly discussion of dealing with images, the influence of semiotic thinking is still extremely important, even if semiotics is no longer the pilot science it used to be in the 1960s and 1970s. Yet even in the newer paradigms like cultural studies or medium theory, which are now trying to achieve hegemony in the field, the semiotic heritage is still visible (for the role of semiotics in cultural studies, see Hall, 1997; for its place in medium theory, more specifically in intermediality studies, see Leverette, 2003). Although the aim of this chapter is to present some tendencies within the postsemiotic approach of the image, it may be useful to recall some basic tenets of the classic semiotic school.

Visual semiotics takes as its starting point the idea that images are visual signs, that is, elements referring to something else, and that, according to the very definition of a sign as something that isn't natural but man-made (a sign is either made to function as a sign, or it is interpreted to do so—independently of a previous intention), images can never be used (that is, produced as well as interpreted correctly) without a learning process that enables the viewer to decode their symbolic meaning. The notion of 'symbol' has to be understood here in a very general sense, as defended by, among others, Nelson Goodman in *Languages of Art* (1968). As Lambert Wiesing put it:

The argument that general image theory is a sub-discipline of a general theory of symbol builds on the supposition that images necessarily are signs. Or, put differently, an object that is not a sign cannot be an image. The particularity of the image, accordingly, is exclusively intrasemiotic.... This does not mean, however, that, within this current, opinions cannot diverge. Particularly in reference to the question of what the intrasemiotic particularity of the image consists in, there is no consensus... Goodman... emphasizes the fact that images cannot be distinguished from other forms of symbolizing by means of resemblance... If we take this thought seriously, it leads us to think that images are images of the things they are images of by reason of conventions that are learned and by reason of visible resemblance. (2010: 15–16)

Yet if all semiotic schools, despite their often dramatic internal differences and conflicts, accept the idea that images are to be 'read' by the viewer, the very meaning of the word 'reading' still remains unclear. Do we understand by 'reading' a process of code deciphering that is analogous to that of natural languages, or do we give a more metaphorical sense to this word? In the recent history of semiotic thinking, the suspicion toward linguistic models of reading, which tend to see images as units of visual texts whose meaning depends on the knowledge of the codes that link a (visual) signifier to a (mental) signified, has been growing ceaselessly. More and more, there is consensus that—although their sign status is not contested—images should be analyzed in a different way from verbal signs. This, together with the awareness of an increasing importance of the visual in contemporary societies, is the paradigm shift coined by W. J. T. Mitchell as the 'visual turn':

> Whatever the pictorial turn is, then, it should be clear that it is not a return to naive mimesis, copy or correspondence theories of representation, or a renewed metaphysics of pictorial "presence": it is rather a postlinguistic, postsemiotic rediscovery of the picture as a complex interplay between visuality, apparatus, institutions, discourse, bodies, and figurality. It is the realization that spectatorship (the look, the gaze, the glance, the practices of observation, surveillance, and visual pleasure) may be as deep a problem as various forms of reading (decipherment, decoding, interpretation, etc.) and that visual experience or "visual literacy" might not be fully explicable on the model of textuality. (1994: 16).

As this quotation shows, what we have to understand exactly by terms such as 'postlinguistic' and 'postsemiotic' is still open to discussion—and the situation in 2010 is not very different from the one diagnosed by Mitchell in 1994. We all 'know' that it is necessary to go beyond what is often called

linguistic imperialism, yet in practice it is not easy to shift to completely different models of 'reading,' toward new forms, less determined by the linguistic model of the Greimasian School and, thanks to a stronger focus on the image, more sympathetic to the input of communication studies, cognitive studies, rhetoric or anthropology (for example, Groupe Mu, 1993; Fabbri, 1998; Fontanille, 2006). In spite of all these attempts, and some others that will be discussed later, one might argue—to borrow a metaphor from another field—that verbal and symbolic models of reading continue to play the role of a hidden seducer in our efforts to make sense of images.

This is undoubtedly true in a very specific field, where their presence seems to be considered both inescapable and, for that very reason, utterly dangerous: the field of intermediality or mixed media objects (for a global overview, see Rajewsky, 2005), an example of which can be found in the corpus that we will study here, the graphic novel.[1] Generally, graphic novels contain a considerable number of verbal utterances (authorial or editorial paratexts, narrator's comments or descriptions, speech balloons reproducing dialogues, written elements within the fictional universe, not to forget the too-well-known onomatopoeic expressions), and there exists a long-standing tradition of reading the medium as a combination of words and images. Of course, such an approach, which by the way is strongly criticized by more recent attempts to analyze the interaction of the verbal and the visual in terms of fusion rather than addition, does not automatically imply that the images of a graphic novel have to be read the same way as the words it contains, that is, as 'symbols.' Yet in this case the threat of linguistic imperialism hides in another corner: even if one does not interpret images as an equivalent of verbal signs, there is a widespread conviction that the very presence of these verbal signs determines the way we make sense of the image. Not only are the words said to 'anchor' the meaning of the images but also their very presence seems to induce the idea that it must be possible to convert the meaning of the images into a set of words and sentences (for a discussion of linguistic imperialism in the graphic novel, see Morgan, 2003 and Groensteen, 2007).

The reaction against the predominance of words and language in the reading of the graphic novel (and of other bimedial practices such as the photographic novel) has been twofold. On the one hand, ambitious graphic novelists have tended to avoid words within their own work. In the graphic novel genre, one may find quite a few examples of textless or wordless graphic novels, and this tendency is certainly not new. The historian David Beronå has shown convincingly that one of the actual forerunners of the modern graphic novel, in the USA as well as in Europe, has been a particular kind of wordless woodcut novel (Beronå, 2008). The very muteness of a visual narrative has always exerted a strong fascination on all those eager to defend the specificity of the graphic novel as a primarily visual medium against the harmful impact of words and texts. This attempt to 'free' the image from the word may be an illusion or a myth,[2] but that does not prevent it from playing an important role in the way contemporary graphic novelists explore their medium. On the other hand, and on a more theoretical level, scholars have tried to develop new ways of reading images that do justice to their specifically visual aspects and dimensions, without taking the utopian path of the textless image. For words and language are everywhere, even in a culture that has become massively visual, and it is more satisfying to take into account the encounter of various media and sometimes even the blurring of boundaries between these media than to pursue the impossible dream of a medium's purity. More and more, media hybridization is becoming the rule, not only within the use of each medium but also, and even more importantly, within the growing tendency of 'networking' hybrid media in the global framework that Henry Jenkins called 'convergence culture' (2006).

Visual literacy, as argued by Mitchell, should not be a copy of verbal literacy, but to follow Jenkins, various aspects of a much broader media literacy. Yet the danger of this twofold critique of traditional, that is, language-inspired, notions of literacy is that it *becomes* antiverbal *by principle*, and such an a priori antiverbalism may prove counterproductive. In the intermedial case of the graphic novel, more subtle solutions are needed to take into account the complex encounter of various kinds of literacy: verbal literacy, visual literacy, media literacy. Of course, this internal complexity grants the graphic novel a theoretical importance that is not totally in accordance with its current position in the mediascape, where other media such as film, television, or the Internet are undoubtedly more important. However, in certain cases it may be fruitful to focus on minor media to ask anew some basic questions.

ONCE AGAIN: WHAT IS AN IMAGE?

The concept 'image' is undoubtedly as multilayered, complex, and blurry as many other concepts, and its definition continues to divide the scholarly community. For this reason, it is better to use a 'tactical' definition of image, that is, a definition conceived so as to solve concrete and practical problems in specific contexts, rather than a general one. The bimedial structure of the graphic novel is a useful example of such a context, wherein our general ideas of both words and images are challenged by their specific interaction. Or, to be more precise, what is at stake in the graphic novel is the widespread perception of the fundamental otherness of words and images. This dominant-thinking paradigm has been articulated notoriously in Lessing's *Laocoon* (1984), where he distinguishes between language as a key representative of the temporal arts and the image as a premier example of the spatial arts. The renegotiation of the boundary between word and image in the context of the graphic novel will inevitably have repercussions on the definition of the image in terms of spatiality—that is, of the image as a unified field open to instantaneous perception (it is only because the image can be perceived as one single visual item that its meaning can be grasped at once)—and on the status of language in terms of temporality—that is, of the language as a string of discrete units subjected to sequential decoding.

Starting with the words, one should observe the utter importance of the visual dimension in the graphic novel.

First, language in its written form unavoidably displays a strong tendency toward 'grammatextuality'—a concept coined by the French theoretician Jean-Gérard Lapacherie (1984) and recently introduced in new media research by Terry Harpold, who writes:

> I draw here on a terminology introduced by Jean-Gérard Lapacherie, who has stressed the need for a critical vocabulary for describing aspects of written and printed texts that are autonomous with regard to the reproduction of speech. In texts in which this autonomy is in evidence, he observes, the "graphic substance" of the letter, line, and page, are foregrounded or are otherwise independent of the "phonic substance" and discursive structures they may also represent... (2009: 88–89)

Grammatextuality (the graphic equivalent of Jakobson's better-known 'literariness' or 'poetic function') is commonly associated with the typographic plays or excesses of certain literary genres, but its role in the graphic novel is no less crucial. The form of the lettering, the configuration of the words in the speech balloons and the insertions of these balloons in the panels, the presence of letters and other written symbols within the fictional world, the presence of onomatopoeias ('Wham,' 'Whoosh,' 'Whap'), the visual dialogue between words and images on the page, etc., all these elements underscore the importance of the visual form of the words in the graphic novel. A brief consideration of the translation of graphic novels makes this palpable: besides 'proper' translation issues, translators have to take into account the space of the panel and the structure of the page; letters cannot harmlessly change the writing style of the original version, and so on.

Second, the intertwining of words and images in the graphic novel helps us to understand why written language itself might be considered a form of inscribed visuality. This is the fundamental idea behind the work of Anne-Marie Christin, one of the leading French scholars in the field of the history of writing (Christin, 1995, 2002). Rejecting the logocentric, alphabetic, and Western idea of writing as a reflection of speech, she defends the idea that—seen from a historical and anthropological perspective—there is no reason to radically distinguish between writing and the image. For the image itself, which historically precedes the development of writing systems as we know them, has always been a form of writing, that is, of proposing meaningful relationships between elements that are linked by the presence of a frame. Privileged examples here are the 'reading' of the constellations in the sky or of traces left by animals. This way of communicating is not based on the alphabetic-semiotic model of autonomous signs obeying pre-existing codes, but depends on the capacity to make sense of certain relations, with the help of the notion of frame or screen and with a strong emphasis on the productive role of empty spaces or empty elements (for an application of Christin's screen-thinking to cinema, see Baetens, 2006). For Christin, the important lesson to be drawn from the original lack of distinction of image, on the one hand, and writing, on the other hand, is not only that images can now be 'read' as a form of writing (yet no longer within the framework of the Western alphabetic-semiotic systems) but also that written utterances should be analyzed as well as images (that is, as surfaces limited by screens and displaying visual relations to be interpreted by viewers in ways that are no longer linear or word-based). Christin's theory of screen-thinking proposes a more radical form of grammatextuality that can be extremely helpful when trying to cope with the presence of verbal and written elements in the graphic novel—and, more generally, in all types of intermedial encounter of visual and textual signs.

An analysis of the first pages of Art Spiegelman's (1986) famous graphic novel *Maus* may be of some help to understand Christin's screen theory. The story opens with the narrator—the son of a Holocaust survivor—recollecting a childhood memory. At the age of 10 or 11, he was roller-skating with some friends. When one of his skates came loose, his two friends left him behind, yelling: 'Last one to the schoolyard is a rotten egg' (5). This seemingly innocent event triggers the entire story. Complaining to his father that 'his friends skated away w-without [him]' (6), his father replies sarcastically: 'friends? Your friends?... If you lock them together in a room with no food for a week.../... then you could see what it is, friends!...' Then he starts to tell the story of his own youth. From a grammatextual point of view, the written elements in the panel (both the narrator's comments and the snippets of dialogue he reproduces) do not seem very interesting, at least at first sight. The reader has the impression that the text is 'leading' the visual storytelling; that the panels are merely illustrating what is being told by means of the text. The variations in the handwriting seem to refer solely to the content of the text: the harder the characters are shouting, the bigger the letters become and the more important words are capitalized. However, such a reading is superficial because the visual treatment and the montage of the handwritten captions, the dialogues and the shouts, are crucial for an in-depth comprehension of graphic storytelling. As the narrators falls, his cry '**OW!**' is emphasized by the size of the bold letters, by its position on the page (the balloon containing the word 'OW!' occupies a central position and rhymes in a visual manner with the circular panel showing a detail of the skate coming loose from the foot). A series of visual correspondences then emerge: the form of the letter O is mirrored by the more

or less round form of the caption and the perfectly circular form of the inserted image. Moreover: the form of the letter W echoes the twisting of the foot, the skate and the wheels in a V-like or W-like form. The verbal and visual correspondences, accentuated by simple montage mechanisms, remind the reader of an earlier discovery on the book's cover: the schematic representation of a Hitler-like cat, displayed on the double background of a white circle and a black swastika. The letters O and W and their figurative doubles (the form of the inserted panel and the caption and the figure composed by wheels, skate, and foot) function as a transposition of the cover background on the book's first page. This example shows that even in apparently simple images and story fragments, such as the opening scene of *Maus*, the impact of grammatextuality is tangible.

The flip side of this first renegotiation of the boundaries between words and images at the level of text and language is of course a similar operation at the level of the image. Despite the current aversion of textual anchorage and growing awareness of the danger of linguistic imperialism, images seem to be more akin to language than is generally accepted. We will not be addressing here the traditional or less traditional 'visual languages' that convert linguistic units and meanings into visual sign systems—these systems include genres and practices as diverse and well-established as, for instance, the rebus, the tradition of the 'speaking gesture' in medieval painting (see Barash, 1987), or more modern examples of sign systems: the language of the deaf, all kind of pictograms, and so on. We will consider, on the contrary, a more far-reaching interpretation of visual signs as a form of writing.

In the graphic novel, ideas similar to those advocated by Anne-Marie Christin have been recently proposed and illustrated in a book on the history of the medium by Thierry Smolderen (2009). His notion of the polygraphic diagram is a means of criticizing two basic principles proposed by Lessing (1984): first, the idea that an image is a unified field; second, the idea that the meaning of an image can be found within itself. That graphic novels disturb the notion of the image as a single field, perceivable and understandable in one glance, is not new. The sequential nature of the medium, which is not, contrary to the medium of the cartoon (in the sense of caricature), restricted to one single drawing, has been brought up by several authors to argue that Lessing's theory of the image as an example of spatial art no longer holds (see, for instance, Groensteen, 2007). What makes Smolderen's argumentation so innovative and stimulating is that he not only relies on the notion of sequentiality—nor on that of the page as 'multiframe' (Van Lier, 1988)—to articulate his view of the image as an object to be read but also that he rediscovers the internal segmentation of each individual panel. Drawing on the tradition of the eighteenth-century graphic novelists such as Hogarth and Richardson, he energetically rejected the definition of the drawing as a single field, to redefine it as a set of items and signs to be deciphered in an intertextual way. In other words, what we see when we look at a drawing is not an image but a visual field that serves as a backdrop to a multitude of signs and allusions that we have to read sequentially (this is what Smolderen calls the *diagrammatic* aspect of the image, which is the key argument in his interpretation of the image as something to be *read*), taking into account the meaning of these elements in the visual and literary culture of their time (this aspect is what Smolderen calls the *polygraphic* aspect of the drawing: each 'textual' element of the image is seen as a dialogue with an existing set of meanings and values, to which it critically answers, as in Bakhtine's intertextual theory of the novel as polyphony).

Both elements—the image as *diagram*, the image as *polyphony*—cast a new light upon the graphic novel. They enable us to see the graphic novel not only as a form of

sequential storytelling but also as a lively practice within a dynamic cultural framework. This last perspective had been abandoned gradually, since the graphic novel deserted its primal habitat: that of the newspapers and magazines, where it constituted a multifaceted means of visual communication with a readership eager to intervene in ongoing public debates. For the innovative reading of the image in a word-and-image perspective that both avoids naive linguistic imperialism (that is, the reduction of the image to a single sign obeying one or more existing codes) and naïve anti-textualism (that is, the refusal to acknowledge the textual and verbal dimension of images), Smolderen's framework is of the utmost importance.

If we summarize the renegotiations of the word-and-image frontier as sketched above, the most important conclusion might be that the graphic novel becomes once again the communicative arena it had been in the beginning. Rather than adding up a set of meanings proposed by linguistic means and a set of meanings inferred from a sequence of images, the reader of a graphic novel is confronted with a much bigger challenge. Reading the graphic novel requires the reader:

- to make sense of the 'grammatextual' layer(s) of the information, and of the 'stylistic' features of the drawing;
- to understand the textual information (inside or outside the panels);
- to scrutinize the diagrammatic and polygraphic dimension of the panels (which transforms them into reading screens);
- to interpret the sequential arrangement of the pictures (this narrativization of the visual treatment is of course a form of reading as well); and, obviously,
- to synthesize all the previous operations.

The above analysis of the first page of *Maus* followed roughly this reading trajectory. By way of clarification, we'll present it in a more systematic way. First, the reader discovers the grammatextual organization of the opening page even before he or she is aware of the story content. He or she notices the central word **'OW!'** and starts to scan the page in a concentric way, noticing the differences between the dialogues in the different panels and the narrator's voice in the upper left and bottom right corner of the page. (The captions containing the narrator's voice function in a certain sense as brackets, enclosing the page. This, of course, is discovered by the reader in a later phase of the reading process.) Second, after accommodating his or her eye to the grammatextual agitation of the page, the reader establishes links between the form and the position of the letters and the words, on the one hand, and the story content, on the other hand. This operation foregrounds the relation between the violence of the grammatextual transformations and the emotional intensity of the shown event. Third, the reader interprets the materiality of the grammatextual procedures: the letters O and W are thus linked with other visual elements: for example, the skate (the loose skate transforms the foot of the boy into a kind of 'claw,' which further 'animalizes' the character: not only his head, but also his feet are those of an animal) and the swastika on the book cover. Fourth, this formal and semantic knot is then experienced by the reader as an anticipated echo of what the story will bring.

It should be stressed that, unfortunately, the syntagmatic enumeration of this bulleted list does not really do justice to the simultaneous nature of the various aspects of the 'reading' of images, which are in practice systematically intermingled. Nevertheless, it is not totally absurd or deceiving to start the inventory with the grammatextual and stylistic dimension of the reading process. It is indeed this dimension that in a certain sense comes before the functional split between words and images. Even before the interpretation of textual and visual elements, one is invited, if not forced, to get a first global impression of what is visible on the page or in the panels. In line with this argument, authors like Marion (1993) have stressed the importance of a kind of pre-narrative or

infra-narrative layer, described as an almost instinctive reaction to what the reader detects on the page, even if he or she is not totally able to make sense of it. No less than other media, the graphic novel is a semiotic practice that we have to learn, even if the ease with which we often read graphic novels makes us forget about the efforts we had to deploy in order to get used to the singularities of its verbal and visual conventions and anti-conventions.

GRAPHIC STORYTELLING: A MATTER OF VOICES

Reading an image in the context of the bimedial structure of the graphic novel is thus a multilayered operation. The general overview hastily sketched at the end of the previous section must now be applied to the medial specificities of the graphic novel itself. More specifically, the last part of this chapter aims to specify how an image is modified into language or *speech*—and even into *narrative* speech. The question here is less 'How do images become words?' than 'How do images tell stories?' Our goal will be to rethink the notion of *narrative voice* that has been in use for many decades now in the domain of literary studies (Genette, 1983). This notion refers both to the questions 'Who tells the story?' and 'How is the story told?'

Given the importance of 'voice' in narratology, it might be tempting to simply borrow a certain number of ideas and insights from the field of literary studies and to introduce them unaltered into the discussion of the graphic novel. Such a mechanical transfer would entail a return of linguistic imperialism at another level of the analysis. Moreover, too strong an emphasis on the serial structure of the graphic novel may reduce the internal complexity of each panel and each page, resulting in a reading stance that ignores the internal diagrammaticity of each panel and gives undue preference to the narrative stream at the expense of all other types of 'visual reading,' while giving the reader also less agency in deconstructing text and image. Yet the very intermediality of the graphic novel could offer an opportunity for inventive approaches to the concept of voice, capable of offering visual re-readings of an apparently strict linguistic category.

At first sight, the difference between voice in verbal narrative and voice in the graphic novel is a difference in complexity. Certainly, both the verbal text and the graphic novel share the same possibilities of exploring a *multilayered* narrative instance, with embedded narrators and numerous possibilities of playing with symmetries and dissymmetries between the levels of author, narrator, and character's voices. But what does distinguish the graphic novel from the verbal narrative is the *multimedial* character of its voice, which always combines a verbal narrator (who tells the story with verbal means, relying or not on embedded narrators) and a visual or iconic narrator (who shows the story by drawing it—and whose function can of course always be complexified by the use of embedded graphic narrators). André Gaudreault (1999) called this visual or iconic narrator a 'monstrator,' while using the concept of 'meganarrator,' which already existed in previous forms of narrative analysis, to label the more abstract instance that gathers both the verbal and the iconic dimension of the narrative act (for an in-depth presentation of this terminology, see Baetens, 2001).

Thanks to the (relative) blurring of boundaries between the verbal and the visual, as elaborated in the previous section of this chapter, it is now possible to reinterpret these voice-related structures in a more visual sense. In this respect, three aspects should be emphasized.

The first aspect concerns the communicative features of 'graphiation,' that is, the visual part of the enunciative act of storytelling. As argued by Philippe Marion (1993), the graphiation in the graphic novel oscillates between two extreme positions: between complete transparency and complete opacity.

The former is exemplified by Hergé's Clear Line style, which can be read as an attempt to propose a narrative voice that remains as neutral and invisible as possible; the latter is illustrated by all kinds of expressive or even expressionist styles in which the 'hand' of the artist matters sometimes more than the narrative content. However, both positions are still very author-related and do not leave much space for the active communication and reader negotiation of graphic styles in a framework of the image as writing, to follow Anne-Marie Christin's line of argument. By approaching the notion of graphiation from the viewpoint of screen-thinking, a graphic style or graphiation is no longer the reflection of an artist's vision, but part of a broader network of visual elements to be read and interpreted without necessary reference to the position of the artist. Graphiation is then a criterion that helps make sense of the visual relationships on a certain surface, instead of being a short cut to a single authorial meaning.

A second aspect or mechanism deals with the traditional notion of voice-over. In contemporary graphic novels, such a voice-over, which comments verbally on the story being told by visual means, whether by an external narrator or by one of the characters of the fictional world itself, has become a stereotype (after having become almost taboo in traditional graphic storytelling, which obeyed ideals of narrative transparency and non-interventionism). However, it would be wrong to confuse the voice-over mechanism as we know it from cinema and the narrative voice in many graphic novels.[3] In the graphic novel, the overall effect of the often-dominant presence of the verbal narrator is not quite the same as that of the cinematographic voice-over. The appropriate proposition in this context is less 'over' than 'with.' In this respect, the narrator's presence is being felt as a 'voice-with' that accompanies the sequential unfolding of the images. The opposition between voice-over and voice-with may imply that both concepts are monolithic, which is not the case: just as there are various types of voice-over, according for instance to the diegetic status of the voice speaking (it may belong to a character that takes part in the action, to a protagonist or to a witness, or to a narrator who remains outside the fictional world, and so on), there are many degrees of accompaniment in the voice-with modus.

The shift from voice-over to voice-with is important for the visual reading of the images. First, a voice-over is much less intrusive, and 'anchors' therefore less the meaning of the images than a voice-over does, whose authoritative dimension is at the heart of much debate. Second, a voice-with seems also to prevent the author from making too many concessions to his or her literary superego. In the history of narrative cinema, the use of voice-over techniques has been one of the instruments, besides the use of 'authors' as scriptwriters and the recycling of existing literary material in all kinds of adaptations, of the literary turn of the movies (authors like Welles link their authorship to an intense use of narrative devices of literary storytelling). In the case of the graphic novel, the narrators seem to be much more modest, although therefore no less overwhelmingly visible throughout their stories. Since the voice does not 'cover' the image it 'accompanies,' there seems to be less craving for a rebalancing of the equilibrium between word and image, to the benefit of the former and to the expense of the latter. Words do not take the floor that is given to the image.

A third and, in our opinion, even more crucial reinterpretation of the category of voice and graphiation in a visual sense, refers to the way in which one may consider the relationship between the act of enunciation (the very act of storytelling) and the underlying model of speech production that helps understand it. What is at stake here is the fundamental difference between two ways of reproducing speech in a text. As argued by Philippe and Piat (2009), one should distinguish authors whose written text is an endeavor to imitate as faithfully as possible the oral speech of a character or a narrator

(the literary tradition sometimes uses the Russian-formalist notion of *skaz* to designate this kind of fiction) from authors who undertake to transpose in their text the very energy of oral speech to make their writing more lively and vibrant (Louis-Ferdinand Céline is the best possible example of this case: nobody speaks like him, yet no style is more oral than his).

If it is likely within graphiation to interpret certain visual styles as an attempt to reproduce the visual way of expressing someone, either a character or a narrator, it is also possible to make a more radical interpretation and to see the particular treatment of graphiation as a way of introducing the very energy of sketching and drawing into the final printed work, instead of decoding them as the direct equivalent of an individual's drawing style. As a case in point, one might take Mattotti's ballpoint-drawn graphic novel *Stigmates* (Mattotti and Piersanti, 1998) as a paradigmatic example; the singularities of the graphiation are less associated with the 'self' of a person who expresses himself through the scrawls and scratches of an idiosyncratic style than of an effort to multiply the visual effect of what happens in the story (*Stigmates* tells the story of a drunk who wakes up one morning with stigmata and starts testifying of these totally unexpected and inexplicable experiences). This brings us much closer to what Philippe and Piat call 'vocality' than any attempt whatsoever to follow some personal 'style.'

Once again, a (re)reading of the opening page of *Maus* helps to clarify some of the concepts. The extreme variability of the textual elements on this page is striking: some words are outside, others inside the frames; the size and form as well as the position of letters and balloons is shifting perpetually; because of their similar shape a confusion between balloons and inserted panels is suggested, and so on. This instability is to be seen as the graphic equivalent of the uncertainty and doubts of both the character and the narrator, as the main character doesn't yet grasp the importance of the incident he is narrating and the narrator hasn't yet found the best way to tell the story he's about to reveal. Eventually, the narrator will relate the story, based on his father's words. In this sense, graphiation hasn't a merely expressive or expressionist role. The material changes in the handwriting have an important narrative function: they reflect the differences between speakers, voices, and tones. It is a radical way of exploring a new (graphic) manner of storytelling.

These small proposals do not cover the field of possibilities in an exhaustive way. Certain meganarrators may foreground, for instance, narrative voices, in both the verbal and the iconic sense of the word, that do not aim at imitating a personal voice or an individual hand. Their ambition is rather to explore a radical formalism that cannot be reduced to questions of expression or style.[4] However, this text is not the right place to explore the subtleties of this kind of narrative voice.

To conclude, what is the relevance of the graphic novel analysis for the reading of images? If one accepts the hypotheses and methodological suggestions that have been explored in this chapter, the main conclusions are threefold.

First, it is necessary to always link the image to the intermedial field in which it is functioning (different corpuses would provide us with examples of different types of intermediality).

Second, it is not possible to define the particular features of images in contrast to those of words; even if it would be absurd to argue that words and images are one and the same category, it cannot be denied that the reading of images activates mechanisms that are typical of the reading of verbal systems and vice versa.

Third, it can prove extremely helpful to import a certain number of concepts—such as, for example, grammatextuality, diagrammaticity, or voice—that have been defined primarily in verbal contexts. If images are intermedial objects, their theory should also be open to cross-overs.

NOTES

1   We will not venture here into the debate over whether it is useful or necessary to distinguish comics from graphic novels. For this discussion has no link whatsoever with the methodological issues at stake. The differences between comics and graphic novels, if there are any, have less to do with semiotics than with aesthetics and cultural critique, and that is another story.

2   Such a myth would be comparable to the disgust inspired by old-school film scholars or aficionados who continue to believe that film as an art 'died' when the silent cinema was replaced by talking movies.

3   A simple but very telling example would be, of course, Spiegelman's (1986) *Maus*, even if one could argue that most contemporary graphic novels, whose autobiographical or semi-autobiographical tendencies are undeniable, rely on similar narrative mechanisms.

4   A good example here is the work by Francis Masse (1984), who used a very 'impersonal' drawing style and whose abundantly loquacious characters 'speak like books.'

REFERENCES

Baetens, Jan (2001) 'Revealing traces: A new theory of graphic enunciation', in R. Varnum and C. Robbins (eds.), *The Language of Comics. Word & Image in the Comics*. Jackson, MS: University of Press of Mississippi. pp. 145–155.

Baetens, Jan (2006) 'Screen narratives', *Film & Literature Quarterly*, 34(1): 2–8.

Barash, Moshe (1987) *Giotto and the Language of Gesture*. Cambridge, MA: Cambridge University Press.

Beronä, David (2008) *Wordless Books: The Original Graphic Novels*. New York: Abrams.

Christin, Anne-Marie (1995) *L'image écrite ou la déraison graphique*. Paris: Flammarion.

Christin, Anne-Marie (ed.) (2002) *History of Writing*. Paris: Flammarion.

Fabbri, Paolo (1998) *La Svolta semiotica*. Roma: Laterza.

Fontanille, Jacques (2006) *The Semiotics of Discourse*, translated by Heidi Bostic. Bern: Peter Lang.

Gaudreault, André [1988] (1999) *Du littéraire au filmique*. Paris: Colin.

Genette, Gérard (1983) *Narrative Discourse*, translated by Jane E. Lewin. Ithaca, NY: Cornell University Press.

Goodman, Nelson (1968) *Languages of Art.* Indianapolis, IN: Bobbs-Merrill.

Groensteen, Thierry (2007) *The System of Comics.* Jackson, MS: University Press of Mississippi.

Groupe Mu (1993) *Traité du signe visuel.* Paris: Seuil.

Hall, Stuart (1997) *Representation: Cultural Representations and Signifying Practices.* London: Open University and Sage Publications.

Harpold, Terry (2009) *Ex-foliations: Reading Machines and the Upgrade Path.* Minneapolis, MN: Minnesota University Press.

Jenkins, Henry (2006) *Convergence Culture: Where Old and New Media Collide.* New York: New York University Press.

Lapacherie, Jean-Gérard (1984) 'De la grammatextualité', *Poetique,* 59: 283–294.

Lessing, Gotthold Ephraim [1766] (1984) *Laocoon. An Essay on the Limits of Painting and Poetry,* translated by Edward Allen McCormick. Baltimore, MD: Johns Hopkins University Press.

Leverette, Marc (2003) 'Towards an ecology of understanding: Semiotics, medium theory, and the uses of meaning', *Image (&) Narrative* 6: [Online]. Available from: http://www.imageandnarrative.be/inarchive/mediumtheory/marcleverette.htm [Accessed 21 September 2010].

Marion, Philippe (1993) *Traces en cases.* Louvain-la-Neuve: Académia.

Masse, Francis (1984). *Les deux du balcon.* Paris: Casterman.

Mattotti, Lorenzo and Piersanti, Claudio (1998) *Stigmates.* Paris: Seuil.

Mitchell, W. J. T. (1994) *Picture Theory.* Chicago, IL: Chicago University Press.

Morgan, Harry (2003) *Principes des littératures dessinées.* Angoulême: éditions de l'An 2.

Philippe, Gilles, and Piat, Julien (2009) *La langue littéraire. Une histoire de la prose en France de Gustave Flaubert à Claude Simon.* Paris: Fayard.

Rajewsky, Irina O. (2005) 'Intermediality, intertextuality, and remediation: A literary perspective on intermediality', *Intermédialités* 6: 43–64.

Smolderen, Thierry (2009) *Naissances de la bande dessinée.* Bruxelles: Les Impressions Nouvelles.

Spiegelman, Art (1986) *Maus 1. A Survivor's Tale.* New York: Pantheon.

Van Lier, Henri (1988) 'La bande dessinée, une cosmogonie dure', in T. Groensteen (ed.), *Bande dessinée, récit et modernité.* Paris: Futuropolis-CNBDI. pp. 5–24.

Wiesing, Lambert [2005] (2010) *Artificial Presence. Philosophical Studies in Image Theory,* translated by Nils F. Schott. Stanford, CT: Stanford University Press.

31

A Multisensory Approach to Visual Methods

Sarah Pink

INTRODUCTION

While I was still contemplating this chapter, my partner arrived home with a copy of *New Scientist*. He handed it to me folded open at the review of a new book, *See What I'm Saying* by the perceptual psychologist Lawrence D. Rosenblum (2010). The very sight of and subsequent tactile encounter with *New Scientist* gave me the sense that I was about to read a popular magazine, with its glossy but floppy pages and color images. New Scientist produces both a magazine and a web site, where its readership is described as 'business decision-makers and consumers from diverse backgrounds' (http://www. newscientist.com/data/html/ns/mediacenter/ uk/intro_audience.jsp, accessed 30th March 2011) and its mission in that it 'reports, explores and interprets the results of human endeavour set in the context of society and culture' (http://www.newscientist.com/data/ html/ns/mediacenter/uk/intro.jsp, accessed 30th March 2011). I was initially drawn to

the photograph that centered the one-page review, I imagined, taken from the book and featuring a visually impaired cyclist who, the caption says, 'relies on hearing where most others use sight' (2010: 46). *New Scientist* also smells like a magazine, now it has been read and used for a while; this particular issue has a weaker scent, but still reminds me of the olfactory experience of getting too close up to a Sunday newspaper supplement in the days when I used to read real newspapers rather than reading the news online. The reviewer of *See What I'm Saying*, Richard E. Cytowic, himself a professor of neurology, describes this as an accessible book that uses examples of first-hand experiences to demonstrate how 'the five senses do not travel along separate channels, but interact to a degree few scientists would have believed only a decade ago' (Cytowic, 2010: 46). Interestingly, the idea that the senses are so interwoven and interdependent is now not only the domain of the biological and neuro-logical sciences, philosophers of perception and social scientists who seek out these fields but also is now seeping out in to the popular intellectual imagination of science magazine readers. It is likewise time for anyone who is interested in using visual methods and media as part of social research to account for the idea that neither the vision nor images can be practiced or understood without a theory, methodological appreciation, and practical awareness of multisensoriality.

How could Cytowic's review be relevant to a visual researcher? Quite apart from the points it makes about the ways that the senses are interconnected, it is a material and sensorial object in itself. Considering it in this way we might think of its visuality on two levels. As the anthropologist Tim Ingold has pointed out, the notions of the image and vision have tended to be conflated in existing literatures in visual culture studies and visual anthropology. Thus, in such works, 'it seems, vision has nothing to do with eyesight and everything to do with the perusal of images. Thus, no image, no vision' (Ingold, 2010: 15). Ingold argues that we need to recognize that visual practices go beyond looking at images. Therefore in the case of the *New Scientist* article, we might distinguish between, on the one hand, the practice of seeing the magazine as an object and evaluating and defining it based on past knowledge and experiences, which might initially be thought of as a visual practice, and, on the other hand, the practice of interpreting the visual representations that constitute the article described above—the photograph and the writing.

First, my initial experience of *seeing* it, the visual practice of evaluating it using existing experience, suggested to me it was an intellectual but popular publication. On seeing the magazine in my partner's hands, I 'knew' that the qualities of the pages would feel smooth and glossy, yet not as strong as those of, for instance, the academic journal *Visual Studies*. Such capacities for multisensory evaluation of visual/material objects are part of our everyday life practices. We see and

know '*as we go*,' as Ingold puts it (2000: 229, original italics). The everyday practice of visually evaluating a magazine involves the same principle as I have described elsewhere of learning to view and understand performances like Spanish bullfighting (Pink, 2007a). It might be conceptualized as what Cristina Grasseni calls 'skilled vision' and should be understood as not a purely visual practice but one that is situated in relation to the other senses (Grasseni, 2007).

Second, the article contains images. Its visuality in this sense works in two ways: it has a color photograph as its centerpiece, and it is full of words, which as has been pointed out for some time, are also visual representations (see Pink, 2007a). Yet the image is not purely visual. Photographs are the outcomes of multisensory contexts, encounters, and engagements. The act of taking a photograph involves the convergence of a range of different social, material, discursive, and moral elements in a multisensory environment, rather than being a solely visual process. Likewise, its presentation in a public domain involves much more than simply visual representation. The visual dimensions of the magazine should not be separated from its materiality, its smell, or its other sensory qualities. Moreover, the capacity of images to invoke experiences that we associate with other sensory categories has been recognized in existing literatures. This is especially the case for touch, which has been closely associated with vision by several scholars (for example, MacDougall, 1998; Marks, 2000), but can equally be applied to other sensory categories. Thus, when I *see* the photograph of the cyclists going over country terrain, I begin to imagine, based on my own past experiences of cycling, what it might *feel* like to engage in the same practice myself. None of these practices—of seeing, taking photographs, or viewing them—can be understood as simply visual practices. As the content of the book review tells us, neither vision nor the other senses work in isolation—'the five senses do not travel along separate channels, but interact to a degree few scientists would have believed only a decade ago' (Cytowic, 2010: 46). In fact, although a decade ago scientists might have found these ideas difficult to believe, as I elaborate below, philosophers had long suggested that the senses were interconnected in such ways.

These points have certain implications for visual researchers. If the above arguments that the senses cannot be understood in isolation from each other—as either neurological processes or within human practices—are valid, then how can we possibly continue to think that we are doing 'visual research' or using 'visual research methods.' How, in fact, can we even justify using the separate culturally constructed categories of vision, touch, smell, taste and sound? As I have argued elsewhere, these ideas need not lead to wholly dramatic changes. A field of academic practice called visual research methods can (and indeed does) continue to exist (see Pink, 2006). Moreover, the varying sets of culturally specific (and constructed) categories used by different people to understand their embodied sensory experiences have two possible roles in visual research: first, they constitute the local categories researchers seek to understand; secondly, they are useful analytical categories in research (Pink, 2009). Yet in order for us to reasonably proceed with visual research methods, a fundamental recognition of the issues raised by multisensoriality is required. Thus, visual research methods, their design, practice, and discussion, need to be informed by the following basic principles:

- Visual images are produced and consumed in multisensory environments; they stand for the multisensory configurations from which they emerge.
- Visual images are not simply visual; they are experienced through multiple and intertwined sensory channels.
- Vision itself is a culturally constructed category, as are sound, smell, taste, and touch.
- Vision involves more than just looking at images, and visual practices need to be situated as part of multisensory perception.

These propositions do not imply that scholarship around the visual should be abandoned or deconstructed. However, the 'visual' inter-disciplines (like visual studies, or visual culture studies) or visual sub-disciplines (like visual anthropology, visual sociology, visual psychology, and visual geography) need to be rethought in relation to this sensory turn. Indeed, sensory anthropologies, geographies, and sociologies have already emerged and are being consolidated. It also calls for a rethinking of the methods used in these visual sub-disciplines. If the principles of our sub-disciplines are now influenced by ideas of multisensoriality, then the question of how the methodologies that inform the production of scholarly knowledge and debate in those sub-disciplines might be subject to such theoretical shifts is equally important. In *Doing Sensory Ethnography* (Pink, 2009), I have considered how ethnographic research practices might be reconceptualized as sensory ethnography. This involved rethinking the interview, participant observation, and visual ethnography methods through a notion of multisensoriality. In this chapter, I point to three central issues when practicing visual research methods that acknowledge multisensoriality: the methodological principles that inform a multisensory approach to visual methods; the question of how, where, and why multisensory visual methods might be used; and the benefits and limitations of this approach and practice. In doing so I develop a discussion of examples of how such methods have been used in existing research and suggestions for how established visual methods, such as photo-elicitation and collaborative video, might be rethought through multisensoriality.

A MULTISENSORY METHODOLOGY

It has long been recognized that visual methods are not simply visual (for example, Pink, 2007a) and that visual images need to be understood in relation to the other senses.

Yet until recently (Pink, 2009) the question of how visual methods might be understood as multisensory had not been approached in any detail. In this section, I outline a multisensory methodology.

To understand how visual methods might be rethought through the notion of multisensoriality requires initially a distinction between research methods and methodologies. The research method refers to the actual procedure and activity that the researcher engages in—often in collaboration with a research participant and using audio-visual technologies. The method is part of a research practice in that it is usually performed in similar (although never identical) ways in different contexts. Examples of this, in the case of visual methods, include photo-elicitation, informant-directed photography, participatory video, researcher-produced video, and ethnographic filmmaking. As chapters on these methods in this book show, they are already employed in ways that are informed by methodological principles. When the approaches that are used to understand the methods are critically revised, their meanings and the types of knowledge they produce can also be understood in new ways. Yet the shifts in practice might not be radical. Even when a new methodology comes to inform research, visual research methods that are already established might continue to be used in ways that are very similar to the ways they are already practiced. However, if a new methodology is applied to understanding these practices and to interpreting the knowledge produced through them, then what on the surface might appear the same visual methods might actually be generating rather different types of research knowledge and academic meanings. They may produce new forms of empirical knowledge, and allow researchers to develop fresh arguments and engage in scholarly debate in new ways. Therefore, I do not argue *against* existing visual methodologies or methods. Rather, I examine how an acknowledgment of multisensoriality can shift the way we design and understand visual research methods, inform which methods we choose to use and influence the knowledge they produce.

A methodology thus presents a set of theoretical and/or philosophical assumptions, ideas, and principles that are applied to research methods. In this section, I will outline what a multisensory methodology entails. A methodology needs to be based on a coherent set of theoretical assumptions. The discussion of the *New Scientist* article and magazine with which I opened this chapter has already introduced some of the assumptions that inform a multisensory methodology. These assumptions originate from beyond the social sciences: from, on the one hand, philosophy in the form of the phenomenology of perception, and on the other hand, the sciences in terms of neurological understandings.

In understanding human perception as multisensory, the work of the French philosopher Maurice Merleau-Ponty has influenced the way most 'sensory' researchers have understood their work. Merleau-Ponty argued that it was impossible for 'pure sensation' ([1962] 2002: 4) to exist on its own and that actually sensations that we experience are produced when we encounter objects and their qualities—such as light, sound, and the way they feel. Yet to actually realize or be aware of sensation, it needs to be 'overlaid by a body of knowledge' ([1962] 2002: 5). As I have outlined elsewhere (Pink, 2009: 26–27), these ideas have been especially relevant to anthropologists whose work engages with questions of vision and with the production of visual representations. Thus, in discussing the relationship between sight and hearing, Ingold has quoted Merleau-Ponty's point that the body should not be understood as 'a collection of adjacent organs but a synergic system, all of the functions of which are exercised and linked together in the general action of being in the world' (Merleau-Ponty, 1962: 234, cited from Ingold, 2000: 268), thus making 'sight and hearing, to the extent that they can be distinguished at all, facets of this action' (Ingold, 2000: 268). Thus, Ingold situates sight as part of an encompassing process of perception whereby it is inseparable from other senses. The visual anthropologist and anthropological filmmaker David MacDougall has likewise used Merleau-Ponty's ideas to understand the relationship between touching and seeing with reference to film (MacDougall, 1998: 51), stressing how these senses 'overlap.' In recent years, as I indicated at the beginning of this chapter, scientific researchers are arriving at rather similar conclusions, suggesting precisely that 'the five senses do not travel along separate channels, but interact to a degree few scientists would have believed only a decade ago' (Cytowic, 2010: 46). Neurobiologists Newell, and Shams write that 'our phenomenological experience is not of disjointed sensory sensations but is instead of a coherent multisensory world, where sounds, smells, tastes, lights, and touches amalgamate' and our sensory modalities 'combine, substitute, or integrate' (2007: 1415).

These sensations are, however, given meaning by human beings (and whether or not this process in itself should be considered biological is another matter). As social scientists, one of our interests is in the question of how and which sensory categories are mobilized by people in different social and cultural contexts in order to 'make sense' of their sensory experiences. It is significant to keep in mind that the modern Western sensory categories of vision, sound, touch, smell, and taste do not automatically map onto the ways that people in other cultures categorize their sensory experiences (for example, Geurts, 2003); they are but cultural constructions. The resituating of vision as a cultural category that is used to comprehend a much more complex biological and neurological process of human perception has implications for how we understand vision and audio-visual methods and media in social research on two levels in that the visual sense is not purely visual in terms of processes of perception, and visual images are not just sources of visual content:

- Vision: vision is not just about looking at images; rather it is part of the multisensory processes through which we interpret the total environment in which we exist, as well as the specific material objects that we encounter.
- Images: if we count as images, drawings, photographs, paintings and video, etc., we can also think of images as not just visual, in that they are material, tactile, and aural too in many cases. This includes analog and digital images and their interrelations with viewing technologies.

These two principles inform how we would understand images and vision in a multisensory methodology. The task of this chapter is to consider how acknowledging these positions will have implications for visual research methods and methodologies that involve the use of visual media. In this sense, a multisensory methodology designed for visual research methods also inherits a series of principles that would inform a visual methodology (see also Pink, 2007a for an expanded discussion of the principles that inform a visual ethnography). These principles involve not only making certain commitments to understanding seeing and images in particular ways but also subscribing to principles that determine some elements of the nature of the research encounter and the researcher's own self-awareness about her or his role in this.

The key principles that inform visual research, as I have developed it elsewhere (Pink, 2007a), relate to:

- Understanding image production as emerging from relationships between people and technologies.
- Acknowledging the (varying) relationships between images and other texts (in research, analysis, and representation).
- Understanding the research encounter and thus the production of images as always collaborative and situated.
- Involving a high degree of self-reflexivity, whereby the researcher interrogates her or his role, situatedness, and subjectivity in the research encounters and the production of knowledge.
- Taking an ethical approach that is rooted in collaboration, informed consent, and continued contact.

A multisensory approach has further implications on various levels:

- Acknowledging the relationship between the visual and the other senses and the multisensoriality of the image.
- A reflexive approach would involve developing an awareness of the culturally and personally specific sensory categories that one uses as a person and as a researcher, as well as the moral values and judgments attached to these.
- Understanding the research encounter as a collaborative event that is part of a multisensory environment.
- In terms of ethics, it requires the researcher to be sensitive to the question of how sensory memories and evocations might affect the well-being of research participants. Ethics are, however, always situated.

MULTISENSORY VISUAL METHODS IN PRACTICE: TWO EXAMPLES

There is no single method or technology to be used in visual research that is informed by a multisensory approach. Although if pushed to identify one technology that is inextricable from the process of doing multisensory research (and visual research by implication) we could say that the human body itself is one of the central research tools. For the multisensory researcher—as a seeing, perceiving, knowing organism—the sensory, affective, and empathetic dimensions of being human are central to the research process. Further to this, as is demonstrated in the following examples, video recording, photography, and drawing can feature in multisensory visual research. Yet rather than being simply 'tools,' audio-visual technologies become part of the way that the researcher experiences and remembers the research encounter. In this section, I discuss the application of a multisensory approach to established visual research methods. I will attend to two ways that a multisensory approach is related to a visual one:

- *The adaptation of existing visual methods to focus on total sensory experience and multiple or*

alternative sensory categories: for example, the use of researcher-produced video recordings in ways that go beyond observation or investigating ways of 'seeing' what research participants see. Instead, the researcher would seek to immerse herself or himself more completely in the multisensory experience of the particular environment she or he is video recording and collaboratively exploring with the research participant.

- *A multisensory methodology can be applied to visual methods that already exist:* this involves rethinking established visual methods to account for the relationship between the visual and the other senses. For example, we might rethink photo-elicitation to acknowledge the multisensory qualities of images and the capacity of visual representations to evoke tactile or other sensations.

Below I elaborate examples from two methods—researcher-produced video and the use of participant-produced photographs in photo-elicitation. Readers are referred to *Doing Sensory Ethnography* (Pink, 2009) for a review of a wider range of multisensory research methods.

MAKING IMAGES AS MULTISENSORY RESEARCH ENCOUNTERS

Video observations and researcher-produced video are key methods in visual research. Their uses range from video recording ritual processes, placing of CCTV cameras in people's homes or more public institutions, to video recording people by following them as they go about their everyday lives. There is also a long history of video or film recording of people showing researchers around the places where they have lived. This method, which I have called 'the multisensory video tour' (Pink, 2009: 105) and 'Walking with Video' (Pink, 2007b) is discussed in detail elsewhere (Pink, 2007b, 2009) and originates in the techniques used by anthropological filmmakers (as well as in some genres of documentary film more widely) in the twentieth century (see also Jhala, 2007). In this section, I discuss using video in movement as a multisensory method. However, the principles might also be applied to the other methods of video research noted above.

In my own work the multisensory video tour involves the research participant showing the researcher (who holds the video camera) around her or his world. This is therefore a collaborative research method, which with particular research questions in mind, can examine peoples' relationships with their material environments, the objects, and sensory elements in this environment and their feelings and knowledge about them, and the sensory embodied experience of being and acting in and part of that environment. Between 2005 and 2007, I undertook a series of tours of a community garden project as part of research about the Slow City movement in the UK, some of which were video recorded. I have written about these video tours in detail elsewhere (Pink, 2007b, 2008, 2009). Here, I will reflect on aspects of these tours to illustrate how an audio-visual research technique actually engages all the senses. The community garden tours involved David, the chairman of the community garden committee, and also a lead gardener, showing me around the garden site, commenting on the progress that had been made in the garden, the plants and garden furniture installed, and the socialites around this. Each tour was in the 'same' garden, yet the environment in which each tour took place was unique, with different weather conditions, social encounters with different neighbors, new plants and new growth, a path and benches in place, and more. As such, the feel of the sun or rain from overhead, the affectivity of social exchanges, the material meanings and the terrain under foot were constantly shifting. This was reflected not only in what I, as the researcher, heard and saw when David 'showed' me the garden at each stage in its development, but also it formed part of the total multisensory experience of the garden, which included elements that can be categorized as tactile and olfactory. Thus, walking around the garden with a camera involved *also* experiencing the difference between the feel of the wet grass and drumming of the rain on the umbrella I was holding during the first walk, and the firm path we treaded while the hot sun was beating down on us and a dry garden with flower beds that had to be watered in the second tour. In this sense, the *experience* of the practice of researcher-produced video in this project was one through which I learnt about the research subject through all the senses. In this context, the principle of understanding vision as situated comes into play: the visual dimension of my experience of the garden can be seen as part of a multisensory experience, one in which vision is intertwined with other sensory modalities. Thus, as I simultaneously looked at and felt the wet grass underfoot, seeing and hearing the rain beating down on it, I experienced a sensation some of which would be recorded audiovisually. In the context of this particular project, I should note that although this might seem a rather mundane example, actually this was rather an important experience for the researcher to have. This is because one of the reasons that the garden was being developed was precisely because the wet grass of the field was an impediment to local people—especially the elderly—who wanted to cross the field as a short cut into the town. Thus, the experience of making the video offered me the opportunity to empathize with both the experiences of the participants in my research who were developing the site and those of people who I had never met, but for whom the development of the garden was a significant process.

Once this research experience was recorded on video, however, it could be argued that it was rendered bisensory, in that it would now just represent the sound of the rain and the image of the grass. Yet, a multisensory methodology instructs us otherwise. Above I have outlined the idea of understanding images as multisensory and acknowledging the relationships between, for example, sight and hearing (Ingold, 2000) and vision and touch (for example, MacDougall, 1998). Although when viewing the video recording of walking through the grass we cannot feel the sensation of the grass underfoot, its audio-visual representation offers opportunities to imagine it on two levels. First, for the researcher who has recorded this, the images can invoke the sensory memories of being there and the sensations and meanings these involved. Second, for the viewer who has him- or herself experienced something similar, researcher-produced video offers the opportunity to empathetically imagine her- or himself into the place occupied by the body of the researcher. As MacDougall has suggested, what he calls 'corporeal images' might be understood as 'not just the images of other bodies; they are also images of the body behind the camera and its relations with the world' (2005: 3).

While of course a video camera cannot record touch, taste or smell as it does sound and image, it nevertheless has potential to represent the multisensoriality of the research encounter. If we understand the senses as being inextricably interconnected, as suggested in the neurological and philosophical scholarship discussed at the beginning of this chapter, then we might understand that such audio-visual materials can evoke or invite the viewer to imagine an experience that involves all of the senses, rather than simply vision and sound.

IMAGE ELICITATION AS A MULTISENSORY METHOD

Photo-elicitation has been described in its basic form as inserting images into the narrative of an interview (Harper, 2002: 13). The same principle applies to using video or other images. A sensory methodology has two implications for image-elicitation methods. First, it invites us to rethink the interview itself as a multisensory process that involves not just talk (and in the case of photo-elicitation, images) but all the senses (Pink, 2009: 81–96). Second, it calls for rethinking the significance of an image when inserted into an interview narrative. Thus, the image

is reinterpreted as a multisensory artifact and the practice of viewing it as involving the interconnected senses rather than vision in isolation. I have started to explain how these processes might be conceptualized in the opening example of this chapter when discussing the *New Scientist* article. I will now elaborate through a case study from the existing literature.

Samantha Warren works within the subdiscipline of 'organizational aesthetics,' which is concerned in part with employees' feelings about their lives in organizations, through a focus on 'their sensory encounters with the world around them' (Warren, 2008: 560). Warren has used photographs as part of what she calls a 'sensual methodology' (560) to investigate employees' feelings about the environment of an organization which had been refurbished to create an environment which was more 'fun' and 'playful' (567). Warren's research process may be seen as one variation of photo-elicitation. She asked participants to produce their own photographs of these organizational environments in ways they chose themselves, thus providing a set of images that could then be discussed in interview. By understanding the contexts in which the images were produced and the research participant's experiences through a multisensory methodology, Warren's summing up of the roles played by the photographs in the interviews shows very well how photo-elicitation can go beyond the visual. Warren's discussion shows us how, in such a research process, photographs can serve various functions. First they can be seen as a prism through which to comprehend the 'aesthetic worlds' of the research participants. Second, they can be used to evoke participant's experiences of these aesthetic worlds in the context of the interviews. Finally, they can act as 'sites' for the exploration of different themes related to specific research questions or objectives—for example, in the case of Warren's research, 'to explore the socially constructed nature of participants' aesthetic judgments' (2008: 570–571). In this way, uses of the photographs in the interviews correspond with an understanding that images are produced in multisensory contexts and thus represent the experience of the body of the person holding the camera (see my discussion of MacDougall's (2005: 3) ideas, above). They also, however, acknowledge the potential of images to communicate in ways that go beyond the visual. By understanding the senses as interconnected, we can comprehend photographs as evoking the multisensory experience of the aesthetic environment represented. Yet, as Warren notes, the images could be used to interrogate the participants' socially constructed understandings. Using photographs in interviews in such a way also permits researchers to develop an understanding of the sensory categories that participants use to understand and communicate about their experiences of particular environments and activities. Yet significantly, Samantha Warren takes the discussion one step further, developing it through a reflexive discussion of her own role as researcher. By reflecting on her own experiences of the same environment, she was able to empathize with the participants' experiences, and to use her own experiences as a point of comparison with theirs (2008: 569).

As both the examples discussed in this section demonstrate, conventional techniques in visual research can be rethought through a multisensory sensory methodology. These reworkings of existing methods need not fundamentally change the ways that the methods are used. Yet they do provide us with new routes to understanding the meanings of both the images and the ways that research participants and researchers make them meaningful.

OPPORTUNITIES AND LIMITATIONS

Opportunities

New approaches to doing social research offer novel routes to knowing about other people's lives and experiences, and new types of knowledge. As such, they can clearly be seen as opportunities to go beyond existing knowledge, to make fresh contributions to academic debates and to make critical interventions 'against' established ways of working and arguments. In the qualitative methodology literature, approaches to, methods of, and technologies used for social research tend to be rethought and revised every few years. As I noted elsewhere, in the last decades this has included understanding research as reflexive, embodied, visual and, now, multisensory (Pink, 2009). Yet, considering this trajectory of the insertion of new approaches to understanding research, there is no reason why each additional 'realization' should be pitched against earlier ones. Rather, each new methodology may add to existing approaches by offering a way of further situating the ways we, as researchers, produce knowledge. It is in this spirit that I propose a multisensory approach to visual research as an opportunity rather than as a challenge to existing approaches. Therefore, we already know that social research is an embodied exercise and that we should be reflexive about the roles played in the production of knowledge. We also know that since visual images, media, and technologies play such a prevalent role in everyday life, we benefit from attending to them as the subjects of our research and may use them as routes to doing research. We might now add neurological and philosophical perspectives on the interconnectedness of the senses and thus the paradigm of multisensoriality. As I show in this chapter, an approach to research that is embodied, reflexive, and attends to visual cultures and uses visual media and methods can be usefully situated and expanded by this addition. As the examples of methods discussed in the previous section demonstrate, a multisensory approach to visual research allows one to situate the visual sense and visual methods in new ways. It makes it easier to recognize the wider environment in which visual methods are used and to understand the visual as one among a series of categories and practices.

An acknowledgment of the roles of other senses in research also affords us new opportunities to consider how *visual* research methods might be adapted for use through other sensory categories. This involves switching the use of the category of vision and the use of the image as the dominant sensory modality used in the research exercise for another. Thus, for example, to expand the methods discussed in the previous section, this might be developed in two ways. The use of video walks might be reworked in the form of sound walks or olfactory walks. Indeed, sound walks have long since been developed in arts practice. Or, instead of photo-elicitation, we might refocus on the olfactory, gustatory, tactile, or aural senses to practice scent elicitation, taste elicitation, touch elicitation, or sound elicitation. There are an increasing number of examples of such research practices in the existing literature. Next, I will focus on one from each category.

Sound walks

Above I discussed how a multisensory rendering of a research method that involved walking through and visually recording aspects of material environments could produce new types of research knowledge. Similar methods are also being developed in ways that acknowledge vision, but go beyond the use of visual media to focus on other sensory modalities. The work of Mags Adams et al. (2008), who have developed sound walk methods, is a good example. Their work is interesting from the perspective of a sensory methodology for two reasons: first, it allows one to consider the role of vision in research beyond the idea of looking at visual images; second, it shows how sound can become central to a research process, while the relationship between the senses is recognized.

Adams et al.'s (2008: 556) method involved researcher and participant together following urban sound walks along a set route,

redesigned by the researchers, in the city of Manchester (UK). Their research process entailed first a brief interview. Then, participants walked the route with the researcher, and were asked while walking it to 'concentrate on what they could hear as they walked and to look at the urban environments they passed through.' Thus, the researchers recognized the relationship between vision and hearing and indeed sought for the participants to make connections between them. Adams et al.'s discussion of this method also resonates in interesting ways with the manner in which video and photography employed in multisensory research has been conceptualized in the examples discussed above. They note that sharing the walks allowed researchers and participants to also share 'a sensory experience of the urban environment' (2008: 557), further resonating with the discussion of the video tour in the previous section. Moreover, they point out that sharing of the experience of the walk made it possible for subsequent interviews with the participants to be 'deeper and more meaningful' (2008: 557), in this sense showing some similarities with Samantha Warren's (2008) discussion of how her experiences of being in the same environment as the research participants made her more able to empathize with them during the subsequent interviews with photographs.

Sound elicitation

Above I discussed how photo-elicitation has been adapted in the work of Samantha Warren (2008) as part of a sensory methodology. Noting the history of the use of photo-elicitation in social research, the anthropologist Richard Vokes takes photo-elicitation as a starting point, but develops the method in a different direction. Vokes points to how the use of objects as a focus in interviews allows them to become 'mediators' and 'objects of translation between two perspectival domains' (2007: 292). Drawing from this, Vokes discusses how in his own work he used a method of 'radio elicitation' (2007: 292), thus using radio sound as the mediating device. Vokes developed three methods. The first method, was in a way similar to the method used by Warren (2008) of experiencing the environment that she later asked participants to photograph and discuss with her, and in other ways resonating with walking methods discussed above (Pink, 2007a, 2009; Adams et al., 2008). This involved his taking 'radio walks' around the village, resulting in him 'build[ing] up a detailed and objective, picture of the village soundscape, how this changed over time, and how radio noise was "located" within this' (Vokes, 2007: 293). The second method he calls 'unstructured radio elicitation,' whereby he stayed with people as they listened to radio programs during the course of their everyday lives, eventually asking questions and making notes during this process (2007: 293). An additional method he developed similar to photo-elicitation was 'a more formal mode of "radio elicitation" based on the classic focus-group model' (2007: 294). Vokes would play a selected prerecorded clip from a radio program to the group and then ask them questions that he had preprepared relating to this. In discussing these methods, Vokes likens 'radio elicitation' to photo-elicitation. Referring back to the work of John Collier Jr (see Collier and Collier, 1986), he suggests that both photographs and radio 'have something of a "hypnotic pull"' and 'Like Collier's photographs, radio sets also generate an intense sociality, in that they too are handled and passed round' (2007: 294).

Thus, as these examples show, attention beyond the visual allows us to recognize the merits of placing other sensory categories at the fore of our inquiries.

Limitations

It is perhaps more common for proponents of a particular method or approach to sing its benefits rather than discuss its limitations in any depth. Moreover, as I have indicated above, the purpose of a sensory methodology as proposed here is to enhance existing methods, offer new routes to knowing and provide fresh contributions to scholarly debates (and to applied research). Yet it is also important to be aware of the limits of a method for two reasons: first, so that the researcher is aware of the types of knowledge that she or he is able to produce through any one method and of the arguments that can be made based on this knowledge; and, second, because knowledge of the weaknesses and the potential points at which an approach might be criticized enables researchers to defend their use of that method against those who might take a different approach.

There remain questions and issues that sensory researchers continue to probe, explore, and develop possible responses to. It is significant here to point out that sensory social research is currently expanding and emerging as an increasingly important field of practice and theory. In terms of limitations we might best think of these on two levels: first, the *general* limitations that visual researchers working with a sensory methodology might encounter; and, second, the *project-specific* and *situated* limitations that can come into play when engaged in a particular research exercise. General limitations concern philosophical themes relating to, for instance, the impossibility of sharing or knowing another person's sensory experiences, and the subsequent practical difficulties in representing and communicating them. Related to this is the issue of how one is to articulate verbally associated sensory ways of knowing and the meanings. This applies in particular to when people show us as researchers or invite us to experience certain sensations.

I turn now to more specific instances: for example, when I was doing research about domestic cleaning practices in the home, I often experienced sensory aspects of the products and practices used by participants in the research—such as smells and textures— that they never spoke about (Pink, 2004). The researcher tends to be invited to experience such things precisely because they are not necessarily always discussed in spoken words. In this context it is important to understand video, as I outlined above, as a medium that reflects the experience of the person behind the camera. As researchers analyzing these materials, we must thus be aware that sometimes the video materials function as documents that evoke our own memories of the research context, rather than *containing* those memories as recorded knowledge.

PRACTICAL ISSUES IN VISUAL METHODS FOR THE MULTISENSORY SCHOLAR

This chapter has proposed a multisensory methodology and subsequently presented a series of examples of methods through which this can be realized. In this section, I will outline a series of practical issues that might be confronted when the methodology is applied.

Selecting the methods When designing a research project it is most important to select research methods that will best answer the questions posed. In this sense, the starting point should not be the wish to use multisensory methods. Rather, the task is to consider how a multisensory methodology and methods that perhaps focus on one or more particular sensory categories might enable the researcher to better respond to the questions that the research seeks to answer.

Remember that the research is guided by a multisensory methodology The idea of using theories of multisensoriality and the interconnected senses to guide visual research methods aims to produce new routes to knowledge through the use of audio-visual media in research. It does not necessarily involve inventing new methods especially designed to use the senses (although this

is something that could and does happen). Rather, it involves applying a particular understanding of the place of vision in relation to the other senses and of the multisensorial nature of images to the research process and the chosen methods. When applying a multisensory methodology, remember that this comes into play at all stages of the research process.

Reviewing existing texts The application of a multisensory methodology includes the ways in which researchers analyze and understand existing research texts. Therefore, for example, the same principles that have been outlined for understanding video produced in research can be applied to understanding existing documentaries or other films and photographs that are reviewed as part of the process of preparing to do practical social research.

Taking a reflexive approach Researchers who are seeking to use their senses to understand other people's worlds need to be reflexively aware of their own 'sensory subjectivities.' On the one hand, this means being aware of the sensory categories that they might use to describe the experiences, objects and activities that figure in the research. On the other hand, it requires an awareness of the moral meanings that the researcher associates with these sensory categories and experiences. Once this awareness is achieved, it may be used to reflect on how the researcher's own subjectivity influences the knowledge produced through the research process. It also offers the researcher a useful point of comparison—between her or his own sensory subjectivity and that of the research participants.

Be aware of the limits and potentials of using a multisensory methodology for understanding visual methods and media Researchers should be aware that although it would seem to make 'common sense' that photographs and video would be used for research that involves the visual sense, audio recording for the aural sense, scents for the olfactory sense and textures for the tactile sense, this might not necessarily be the case. A multisensory methodology tells us otherwise. The idea of the interconnectedness of the senses, combined with the case studies discussed above, indicates that, for instance: video research might engage seeing and hearing, but it also involves the tactile sense and can evoke smells and tastes; photographic research might not only invite participants and researchers to consider the visual dimension of the environment or activities photographed, but rather it might allow the researcher to empathize with the multisensory experiences of the persons involved in the actions or of the environments represented.

Follow ethical guidelines for visual research and discipline-specific practice Research ethics are always situated and depend on the specific configuration of personal, discipline-specific, and institutional ethical codes and procedures. It is not appropriate here to issue a set of ethical guidelines particular to the application of multisensory methodologies in visual research. Rather, researchers should take careful note of the ethical discussions available in relation to the methods discussed in this handbook, the guidelines issued by the professional associations dedicated to the disciplines in which they are working, and the institutions to which they are themselves attached. If anything, a multisensory methodology is distinguished by the collaborative approach that is taken to the encounter between researcher and participant, and this, in relation to the procedures noted above should contribute to ensuring that an ethical approach is achieved.

ACKNOWLEDGMENTS

Most ideas and examples discussed in this chapter are based on arguments and case studies presented in my two books: *Doing Visual Ethnography* (2007) and *Doing Sensory Ethnography* (2009) both published by Sage Publications.

REFERENCES

Adams, M., Bruce, N., Davies, W., et al (2008) 'Soundwalking as methodology for understanding soundscapes', in *Proceedings of the Institute of Acoustics* 30(2). [Online]. Available from: http://usir.salford.ac.uk/2461/1/Adams_etal_2008_Soundwalking_as_Methodology.pdf [Accessed 14 October 2010].

Collier, J. and Collier, M. (1986) *Visual Anthropology: Photography as a Research Method*. Albuquerque, NM: University of New Mexico Press.

Cytowic, R. (2010) 'Our hidden superpowers', *New Scientist*, 24 April: 46.

Geurts, K. L. (2003) *Culture and the Senses: Bodily Ways of Knowing in an African Community*. Berkeley, CA: University of California Press.

Grasseni, C. (2007) 'Introduction', in C. Grasseni (ed.), *Skilled Visions*. Oxford: Berghahn. pp. 1–20.

Harper, D. (2002) 'Talking about pictures: A case for photo-elicitation', *Visual Studies*, 17(1): 13–26.

Ingold, T. (2000) *The Perception of the Environment*. London: Routledge.

Ingold, T. (2010) 'Ways of mind-walking: Reading, writing, painting', *Visual Studies*, 25(1): 15–23.

Jhala, J. (2007) 'Emergency agents: A birthing of incipient applied visual anthropology in the "media invisible" villages of Western India', in S. Pink (ed.), *Visual Interventions*. Oxford: Berghahn. pp. 173–190.

MacDougall, D. (1998) *Transcultural Cinema*. Princeton, NJ: Princeton University Press.

MacDougall, D. (2005) *The Corporeal Image: Film, Ethnography, and the Senses*. Princeton, NJ: Princeton University Press.

Marks, L. (2000) *The Skin of the Film*. Durham, NC: Duke University Press.

Merleau-Ponty, M. [1962] (2002) *The Phenomenology of Perception*. London: Routledge.

Newell, F. and Shams, L. (2007) 'New insights into multisensory perception', *Perception, Special Issue on Advances in Multisensory Research*, 36: 1415–1418.

Pink, S. (2004) *Home Truths: Gender, Domestic Objects and Everyday Life*. Oxford: Berg.

Pink, S. (2006) *The Future of Visual Anthropology*. Oxford: Routledge.

Pink, S. (2007a) *Doing Visual Ethnography*. London: Sage Publications.

Pink, S. (2007b) 'Walking with video', *Visual Studies*, 22(3): 240–252.

Pink, S. (2008) 'Analysing visual experience', in M. Pickering (ed.), *Research Methods in Cultural Studies*. Edinburgh: Edinburgh University Press.

Pink, S. (2009) *Doing Sensory Ethnography*. London: Sage Publications.

Rosenblum, L. D. (2010) *See What I'm Saying: The Extraordinary Powers of our Five Senses*. New York: W.W. Norton.

Vokes, R. (2007) '(Re)constructing the field through sound: Actor-networks, ethnographic representation and "radio elicitation" in South-western Uganda', in E. Hallam and T. Ingold (eds.), *Creativity and Cultural Improvisation*. Oxford: Berg.

Warren, S. (2008) 'Empirical challenges in organizational aesthetics research: Towards a sensual methodology', *Organization Studies*, 29(4): 559–580.

PART 7

Options and Issues for Using and Presenting Visual Research

32

Interactive Media Representation

Roderick Coover

INTRODUCTION

In a paper first published in *Visual Anthropology* (Coover, 2001) and later revised in the CD-Rom *Cultures in Webs: Working in Hypermedia with the Documentary Image* (Coover, 2003), I discussed how semantic theories of metaphor, cinematic theories of montage and cognitive theories of what Goodman (1978) called 'worldmaking,' might be reconceived as strategies of ethnographic media production. Drawing examples from the films of Gardner and Östör (Forest of Bliss, 1986), Trinh (Naked spaces: living is round, 1985), and others, I looked at how approaches combining these strategies might advance ethnographic praxis.

This chapter expands these themes from the perspective of multimedia presentational practices. I will discuss ways in which digital tools might further the integration of diverse disciplinary and modal strategies in cultural research and representation, and I argue that new media tools transform how users engage with materials. The essay draws upon issues that arose when I was making multimodal interactive works, among them

Cultures in Webs (2003), *Outside/Inside* (2007a) (see Figure 32.1), and *Voyage Into The Unknown* (2008). The chapter gives special attention to ways that techniques of layering and compositing contribute to how works are made, and, in drawing parallels with Certeau's description of walking in his essay, 'Walking in the City' (1984), I will consider how digital panoramas and other scrolling environments raise possibilities for user agency.

RHETORIC AND POETICS

From note-takers to cooks, amateur photographers to telephone conversationalists, we are all medium-makers. Whether one is simply forwarding e-mails with attachments or designing complex systems, almost everyone who uses a computer is a multimedia-maker. Digital technologies shape how one imagines, constructs, and exchanges ideas. Our electronic communications are shaped by pre-existing conventions (of writing, pictorial representation, etc.), technological constraints (of the processor,

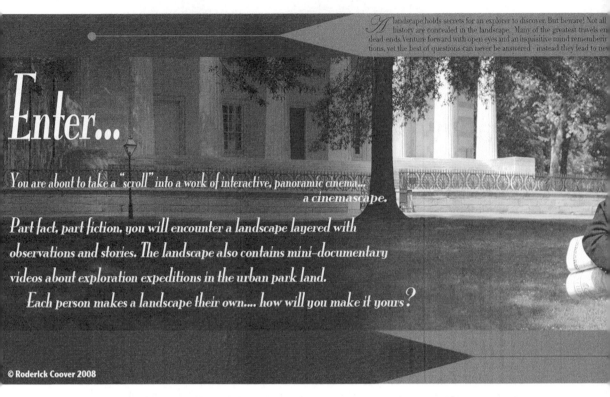

Enter...

You are about to take a "scroll" into a work of interactive, panoramic cinema...
a cinemascape.

Part fact, part fiction, you will encounter a landscape layered with
observations and stories. The landscape also contains mini-documentary
videos about exploration expeditions in the urban park land.

Each person makes a landscape their own.... how will you make it yours?

Figures 32.1–32.18 *Outside/Inside* **is an interactive scrolling panorama that was commissioned for the Museum of the American Philosophical Society, Philadelphia, and exhibited 2007–2008. © Roderick Coover 2007.**

memory, software, data transfer, etc.), interface, and use.

Digital theorist Lev Manovich has been a proponent of the argument that digital tools are giving rise to a new language, albeit a hybrid one—a way of communicating that includes both prior methods of expression and new ones (Manovich, 2001). In writing about the impact of design software like Adobe After Effects® on how images are edited and how they are used, Manovich writes,

> (T)he working method is neither animation nor graphic design nor cinematography, even though it draws from all these areas. It is a new way of making image media. Similarly, the visual language is also different from earlier languages of moving images. (2006: 5)

Layering and compositing are among the processes shaping this visual language. Layered tropes, juxtaposed paths, modally

varied arguments, and active choice-making are all devices of the digital rhetoric and poetics of the language(s) of digital media which are being incorporated by the makers of media works and are being interpreted by users, who may in turn, even directly within a work, become makers themselves. The impact on documentary production is significant.

First, hybrid spaces that combine text and video in shared environments challenge single-channel cinematic conventions of linearity and montage. The debate about these seemingly dialectical aspects of cinema— a debate characterized but never resolved by many of the great texts of film theory such as Eisenstein (1947) and Bazin (1967)—dissolves when, in digital works, long takes coexist with montage sequences. The practical result for the creators of motion media works is that much of what used to end on up on the cutting-room floor or as

In considering the study of physical phenomena... we find its noblest and most important result to be a knowledge of the chain of connections, by which all natural forces are linked together and made mutually dependent on each other.
—Alexander von Humboldt, 1811

cessful! The secrets of nature and the most exciting inquiries can arrive at answers for a person who asks no questions, in turn, will raise further ones...

The explorer setting out upon the urban landscape will discover layers that endures reveal and conceal signs of the past, fortunes built, and p about the human desires, worldviews, and the changing impression p nation. Some histories can be told by others, but mostly you must disc

little used master video tapes on the edit room bookshelves is now available. In interactive works, users may have the opportunity to access source materials and judge the maker's choice-making. This also allows one ethnographer's process to be compared with another's, and another's and another's.

Second, interactive formats enable video material to be combined with text elements such as original writing, field notes, primary documents, secondary documents, interview transcripts, and so forth. Furthermore, digital tools facilitate the inclusion of other kinds of visual materials into a project, such as maps and photographs, which can be compared with cinematic representations. Practically speaking, questions of design are not so different from those of writing or editing; the ethnographer/media-maker creates paths (arguments) via research materials. One difference for interactive works, however, is that

the research materials may be included and the processes of research and representation may be revealed. Users may be able to follow the choices and decisions that went into building an argument out of the fragments of experience and data. In the face of alternatives, the researcher encounters an increased need to present supporting evidence for how and why particular routes through the material were valuable, but may face less pressure to gel materials in narrative or expository constructs.

TROPES AND MONTAGE

Ethnographers are translators of cultural experiences. The translation occurs on-site between the researcher and those s/he meets; it also takes place between the researcher and

In 1736, the Pennsylvania Assembly decrees the lands directly behind Independence called the State House, will forever remain parkland at a time when colonial homes l and open lands reached westward. The Revolution forty years later continued the ce nature, and visitors marveled at the gardens, designed then by Samuel Vaughan.

Art or documentary?
    Concealed in the landscape are waterways, paths and the signs of explorations past....
    It is layered with the memory of the artistic interventions of the artists of the unexpected, Roderick Coover, Brett Keyser, and Winifred Lutz. And, so too, may the landscape also be layered by the memory of explorations past, and those, like yours, yet to come.

secrets. The objects of the manmade landscape and the nature is not taken. Each element of the landscape may hold stories ple held about the city and its place in a young and growing r them for yourself.

Not till we are lost, in other words not begin to find ourselves, and realize wh of our relations. — Henry D.

the intended audience(s). Classic works of ethnography such as Evans-Pritchard's *The Nuer* (1940) and Geertz's *The Interpretation of Cultures* (1973) demonstrated the necessity of developing strategies for making sense of signs and symbols in the cultural contexts in which they were encountered and then translating those to others.

The translator searches for terms of interpretation and re-presentation that might enable ideas expressed in one cultural context to be understood in another; the process is never exact. Tropes, such as metaphors, are among many tools for this kind of translation. Metaphors, for example, bridge semantic domains. A metaphor may provide a means of understanding some abstract notion through another more concrete one whose characteristics have been previously established: *love is a rose*. Semantic domains are bridged: ideas of love are expressed through

things known about roses, and perhaps, vice versa, roses acquire aspects of the idea of love—aspects which give them enhanced symbolic exchange value. However, the semantic 'bridging' also illuminates gaps between the concepts being drawn together; metaphors can both express similarities and define differences.

Evans-Pritchard's study of cultural perceptions of cows and Geertz's famous invocation of a story about knowledge and turtles demonstrated value of metaphors in the processes of sense-making and translation. Victor Turner (1974), James Fernandez (1986), and George Lakoff and Mark Johnson (1980) are among the anthropological theorists who have expanded understanding about metaphor in cultural analysis.

While tropes such as metaphor, metonym, and irony are based in language, others, as Friedrich (1983) wrote in his essay

'Polytropy,' extend beyond words. Tropes may bridge language and non-verbal kinds of knowledge—such as with images and music—and they may bridge modes. In the representation of actuality through non-fiction media, choices such as the selection of minor scale versus major scale notes, of blue-toned color palettes or film stocks versus ones with warmer tones, or of slow editing rhythms versus rapid and accelerating montage all shape interpretation. Researchers such as Taussig (1993) and Stoller (1989, 1997) have advanced understanding of how such tropes might shape practices of anthropology and cultural research.

In film, tropes are constructed through edits as well as through structural analogies and *mise-en-scène* choices (such as color palette, lighting, etc.). In his famous essay on the dialectics of montage, Soviet film director Sergei Eisenstein (1949) delineated ways that montage can be used to propose interpretations of time-based visual content, evoke tonal characteristics of actuality, and construct visual tropes. Such cinematic practices correspond to ways that tropes are used in speech. In both cases, the tropic devices point to gaps between elements (between images and/or semantic domains) that the viewer–reader is invited to bridge. The act of pointing (drawing attention to ambiguities of meaning and classifications) is something that characterizes interpretive research both in writing and in film.

However, there is no one tool or method good for all seasons. Some ideas are well expressed through a series of images, while others may be better understood via other forms of expression such as expository writing, spoken poetry, music, dance, or even a meal

gned the forking garden paths, envisioning a park for a city yet to come.
ects of history - the books, buildings, streets. They are mere fragments of
orld they imagined as well as the one that has come to be.

...It is my wish to plant in the State House Square specimens of every tree and shrub that grow in the several States on this continent... that will thrive there. — Samuel Vaughan, 1785

An order for shrubs, 1786: Trija Arbor Vitea, Red Flowering Larch, S

Coming in December
Video documentary
of the first
exploring expedition.
Join the expedition.

find means to grasp a
ar in what seems com-
en, and threatening.

Whether through distant travels or nearby adventures, the explorer makes a hypothesis and ventures out into that imagined landscape to see if indeed it holds true. The quest may require tools, and practiced methods of data collection, for who will believe your stories if you do not also gather evidence?

or a walk. The gap that is bridged by language tropes and montage is a kind of conceptual space; the bridging creates a context in which the connected elements might share that space, whether the space is imaginable in concrete terms of actuality or in abstract terms. This conceptual space frequently clarifies ways of understanding connotative aspects of experience and expression.

The linearity of film imposes constraints on poetic and rhetorical movements between images. Frames follow each other sequentially and in a temporal constant established by the presentation technology (for example, the cinema projector, the video player, the television). This temporal constant is an authority; it is an over-arching force that moderates all others. When, in Robert Flaherty's (1922) documentary *Nanook of the North* viewers watch Nanook catch a seal, they

do so in a time frame and temporal mode set by the camera which, in 1922, included time-expressions constrained by the physical length of the film reels and the temporal limits of the manual crank. The film was famously praised by Bazin (1967) for its use of inclusive shots and relatively long takes. The objectivity Bazin praised reflected the trust he gave to the mediation of the technology itself. The camera created a copy of the visual data before the lens that was translated through the medium.

This translation can be limited by a number of factors, such as light requirements or the borders of the frame. It is also constructed through the camera's shutter speed and frame rate. Although the frame rate may be altered 'for effect' in recording, in most instances (both in recording and playback), it is a controlling (and largely imperceptible!) constant.

It is small, nearly square, which I believe does not contain more than one acre...The shrubs are yet small, but most judiciously arranged... The numerous walks are well gravelled and rolled hard; they are all in a serpentine direction, which heightens the beauty, and affords constant variety. That painful sameness, commonly to be met with in garden alleys, and other works of this kind, is happily avoided here, for there are no two parts of the Mall that are alike. — Manasseh Cutler,

Visitors delighted at the marvels of the p
the park experience was so

d Fir From Scotland, English Sicermore, Snow White Mespiles, Toxicodendron Canadensis, Staphilodendron

...The walker constitutes, in relation to his position, both a near and a far, a here and a there... [The wal
fragments the space traversed... The moving about that the city multiplies and concentrates makes the c
mense social experience...broken up into countless tiny desportations (displacements and walks), compen
relationships and intersections of these exoduses that intertwine and create an urban fabric... —Miche

The single channel, linear time qualities of film and video limit switching into other modes of media reception, such as reading. Generally, single channel projection media do not allow viewers to escape the temporal constraints—or authority—of the projection mechanism. For example, viewers cannot read at their own rates or move back and forth through the text.

There are pre-digital models for combining diverse media in documentary representation. For example, in *Another Way of Telling*, Berger and Mohr (1982) developed text–image works that are part exposition, part narrative and part poetic evocation. They worked with sequences of images—often accompanied by text—that were linked both by the ideas suggested by the specific images chosen (interpretive propositions), and through visual correspondences and contrasts in the images (such as formal, compositional, or aesthetic propositions). They eloquently described the kind of viewership or image reading that such a layout provided:

> Eisenstein [1997 (1924)] once spoke of "a montage of attractions". By this he meant that what precedes the film-cut should attract what follows it, and vice a versa. The energy of this attraction could take the form of a contrast, an equivalence, a conflict, a recurrence. In each case, the cut becomes eloquent and functions like the hinge of a metaphor.... In film.... there is also a third energy in play: that of the reel, that of the film's running through time.... In a sequence of still photographs, however, the energy of attraction either side of a cut does remain equal, two-way and *mutual*.... The sequence has become a field of coexistence like the field of memory. (Berger and Mohr, 1982: 288)

A digital interface similarly allows for multidirectional movement, while adding more

Having come to the State House where the museum is located we passed through it and into a fine square... and entered the gate, held a large collection of beautiful flowers in pots, or boxes, and also a few living animals. Two great bears amused us... of the bears' house two parrots, apparently quite content chattered together; in the next cage an eagle sat right majestically perch – above his head a placard with the petition on it: "FEED ME DAILY FOR 100 YEARS." — Catherine Fritsch, 1810

Staf Tree, Prunus Canadensis, Crategus Red, Dwarf Mespibus, Calicanthus Caroling Alspice, Euonimos Lati

r) selects and itself an im- ted for by the Certeau, 1984

To give a history of disco den down. The temperate enclosing sandy deserts, possess a population ev

diverse media elements. It enables user agency. The user navigates an environment that extends beyond the limits of a printed page. By making her own choices in navigating a multimedia work, the user may become aware of the choice-making processes of the original maker(s) of the work. In some cases, the user may contribute to the work. For multitasking, 'cut-and-paste' users, elements of one work may also be incorporated into others.

To offer an example of how such opportunities in digital media can impact processes and engage translation strategies, I will reflect on my project, *The Harvest* (1999). In this multimedia documentary work, I explored ways to use simple HTML in a web-based environment to integrate research materials on-site, and then reflect on my research and refine my process. The work

built arguments through a combination of media and modes of presentation.

I developed the project using field notes, photographs and video I was gathering at a field site in a winemaking village in Burgundy, France. The research had two primary aims: to understand how synaesthetic experience translates into a sense of cultural place and to investigate how spoken use of the specific and historically rich lexicon of winemaking might provide insight into broader cultural issues. My project built upon the notion that there are 'metaphors we live by'—a concept put forward by Lakoff and Johnson (1980). This initial visit was intended to help me gather materials for a documentary film I would make later, entitled *The Language of Wine* (2005).

In the tradition of participant–observation, I worked alongside harvesters and later with

... But so were they taken aback by the construction of a prison overlooking the yard; aspirations to create an ideal image of the new state meets urban realities...

Walnut Street Jail 1799

Until the 1950s, the park was contain 6th Street, directly behind Independe mercial buildings of a working city

angea Virginiaug, Y'tea Virginiana, Ascrillas Octandrea New River Horse Chestnut, Ascrilious Pavala Sc

Coming in April
Vidtorio museum
of the third
exploring expedition.

'ving picture of the universe... On every side the barriers of prejudice were trod-
ger deemed the only habitable portion of the globe. The torrid zone, instead of
intolerable heart of a vertical sun, was found to teem with organic life, and to
an that of the temperate zones, together with a soil equally well adapted

to the support of animal and vegetable life. The frigid zones were no longer begirt with perpetu-
nature, as if to amuse herself in the loneliness of the solitude, exhibited the wildest and most fantastic fi
advanced toward the north, and found that during the partial summer, plants grew, flowers bloomed,
beings made it their permanent residence and home throughout the year.   — J. N. Reynolds, 1936

winery workers, all the time taking photos and writing. I supplemented this research with interviews, studies at other wineries, and research in libraries and museums.

As a way of sorting through the materials I was collecting, I arranged my photos and notes in a horizontally scrolling HTML (web-based) environment. This allowed me to scroll back and forth across the materials to look for correspondences, emerging themes, and motifs around which to develop my documentary film project, in a way that is similar to sorting scraps of printed materials on a tabletop. I intended to develop a cinematic storyboard; however, as I began to lay my notes and other text below the images in this format, another kind of work began to emerge. Words and images simultaneously occupied the screen space without one dominating the other. The layout allowed more of the research materials and choice-making

processes to be visible than in the pre-digital formats I had previously used for my projects. The result was a work in which three bands of text ran beneath a collection of 54 photographs. Users may discern how differing compositional approaches, conventions, and writing styles directed attention to differing details; the same images and segments of text connected multiply to other images and text elements, including side materials such as pop-up videos and slide shows. The format allowed for multiple interpretations of the same content.

Juxtaposed images draw attention to similarities and differences. Some elements that seem of little importance in a single image gain meaning through their static or changing recurrence in later images and vice versa. Photographic images of actuality generally contain a plethora of elements (objects,

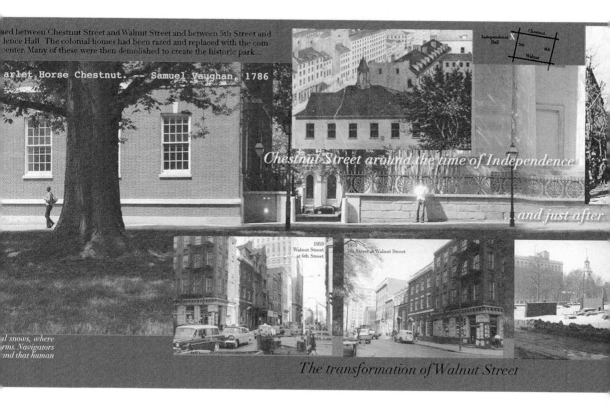

ed between Chestnut Street and Walnut Street and between 5th Street and
lence Hall. The colonial homes had been razed and replaced with the com-
enter. Many of these were then demolished to create the historic park...

arlet, Horse Chestnut. -- Samuel Vaughan, 1786

Chestnut Street around the time of Independence

...and just after

The transformation of Walnut Street

individuals, expressions, actions, light qualities, formal compositional characteristics,
etc.), all of which may gain meaning through
context. Juxtapositioning is one of the strategies that enable contextualization by provok-
ing users to see similarities and differences
between the images (or other media) of the
data set. The process of pointing to relationships allows users to draw fragmentary bits
of information together to develop a sense
of the whole, building what Berger and
Mohr called 'the context of experience'
(1982: 289). Users are given a means of
interpreting unfamiliar objects or imageries
when these are placed in relation to elements
that have already been introduced or which
are commonly understood. This is not unlike
the ways metaphors are frequently used to
characterize abstract ideas in relation to more
concrete ones. As with metaphors, which
Fernandez (1986) described as being tools

that humans use to draw the fragments of
experience into a unified sense of the whole,
so too do the multimedia processes of scrolling, juxtaposing, and linking enable users to
draw disparate elements together.

The Harvest contained at least six modes
of representation. The primary space included
a visual, sequential photo-montage (almost a
photo-roman) and three styles of writing:
diary/field notes, reflections on the visual
choice-making process, and historical-
ethnographic exposition. There were also
pop-up video clips, slide shows, and other
presentations. Each mode proposed ways to
interpret the field experience; yet, in light of
other materials, each mode alone seemed
incomplete. There is no single mode of
representation that can encompass the range
of cultural experience, knowledge, and
expression that the ethnographer engages
with; some things are simply better expressed

A creek running through this very park was buried. Its traces - the sunken trough and twisting Dock Creek Road can be followed toward the docks where sailors gathered and surely among them, explorers sought passage to distant lands seeking in the challenges of travel what other adventurers found within the American shores.

in a diary, or a painting, or a dance, etc. An interactive media approach offers some opportunities to gather together such differing modes of expression.

I found that the creative space I had developed for my own research purposes also functioned as a presentation format. The work brought forward my research process within a final product—something that rarely occurs in conventional filmmaking. Users could navigate, read, view, listen, link, and browse among the materials I had gathered and follow some of the ways that, in combination, the materials might pose questions of cultural meaning. The project suggested to me the potential for 'scrolling-environments' to contribute to solving some of the enduring challenges of documentary representation, such as those of the relations between subjects, makers, and viewers and between experiences and their interpretations.

SCROLLING THROUGH LANDSCAPES: PANORAMIC VIEWS AND VIRTUAL WALKS

The webpage may not be a page in a conventional sense that a piece of paper is a page. Although one 'scrolls' in a webpage, it may not be like a papyrus scroll either. For example, a webpage is not bound by borders; content can seem to extend limitlessly in both horizontal and vertical directions. Along with the potential for such, near endless, x-, y-axis dimensions, the page also has the potential to be layered and linked. 'Pages' and 'scrolling' are tropes that organize the

digital experience, pointing users to engage in materials in particular ways. However, each of the characteristics exploited for the production of a digital work suggests the need for an apt organizing model. For example, horizontally scrolling arrangements of materials on topographically contiguous and continuous settings more resemble a panorama than a page, and with interesting consequence for research.

Nineteenth-century circular painted and projected photographic panoramas were generally presented in rotundas. They were designed to achieve a more or less unobstructed 360° view of a location, seen from a single, central viewpoint. Such panoramas offered viewers the illusion of being able to envision places in their entirety, rather than by fragments, as through a montage of related pictures.

Although viewers of those panoramas may have had the illusion of possessing the overview, it was actually the images that encompassed the viewers, in both their exotic form (panoramic rotunda) and content (representations of foreign lands, ancients worlds, battlefields, etc). One cannot grasp such a panorama in its entirety; it offers more than one can take in at a single glance. As the viewer turns, she must try to remember what she cannot see while looking in some other direction. Both in actuality and in this medium, the impression (one might say, illusion) of unity is provided by spatial and temporal seamlessness. The illusion is authoritative—it places elements in a singular and fixed arrangement and their meanings are determined in large part by the whole in which they are, unwaveringly, contained.

However, in digital forms this is not true. The panorama can be readily combined with linked and layered materials that engage the contiguous image, whether directly or by juxtaposition. This can, potentially, offer points of disruption, encounter, and difference by creating paths into the image.

In his essay, 'Walking in the City' (1984), Michel de Certeau offered a similarly constructed description of the experience of looking down upon a city from a high-rise. From a tower, one has a panoramic view of a city, the elements of which are somewhat fixed, mappable and abstract. Certeau described the sense of authority and awe that is gained from the perch above the streets. From the top of a high-rise, looking down, a viewer possesses a sense of the whole. This sense of the whole is an abstraction,

removed from time and contact. From afar, the contiguity and continuity of the view cannot be disrupted. The viewer can hardly see the people or hear the noises from the streets below; the people and their noises are subsumed into an abstract geometric experience of structure and flow.

On the street, individual experience is different. The individual confronts—and responds to—a barrage of noises and interruptions, only some of which can be recognized. Walking offers a kind of montage—a fragmentary series of encounters, surprises, and modal shifts. In the streets, the walker makes choices. The walker selects routes and creates diversions. The walking may be interrupted by forces that the individual has no control over such the actions of other humans, creatures, natural elements, and mechanical ones. The walker responds to the

Investigations are shaped by the tools available to the explorer. Form shapes content. An investigator with access to a computer and GPS tool will render a picture under differing constraints and possibilities than those offered by sextant, mathematical compass, and/or microscope. The tools of science are also tools of art, each rendering differing views of actuality.

Letters home from the voyage of the 'EX. EX.':
Last night or rather this morning was the anniversary of the "Meteoric Shower" we had Sunday observers but the greater number observed in one hour was 71, of these I strongly suspect a large proportion were caused by the fooling of the ship, indeed when she pitches sometimes it looks as though the shoal firmament was coming down; saw what was more singular a few weeks since, which was the aurora australis, aurora from south of the line... We arrived this afternoon... The scenery of harbor is Magnificent beyond anything I have ever seen... Yours, truly, T.R. Peale.

unfolding events taking place on the street, thinking and acting spontaneously. Such events range from the mundane (a changing traffic light) to the complex (a social interaction). The differences between enjoying the overview of a place and navigating it have psychological and political dimensions: the walker acts, speaks, participates, and makes the landscape her own. The walker has agency. The walker does not have the illusion that she controls her visual field; instead, she responds to forces beyond her control and vision. The limits of her control are also reminders of her being one of a community of active agents. Certeau suggests that walking is analogous to language. The overview parallels the abstract structure like grammar, whereas walking is a kind of speaking; the choices of walking and speaking are individual, spontaneous and evolving.

The use of panorama has been particularly interesting to me in the ways that it can be used to explore prior dichotomies of seamless representation and layering (or montage), of text and image, and of still and motion imagery. Digital panoramas, and similarly constructed scrolling environments, both maximize the objective aspects of the panoramic illusion and disrupt illusions of objectivity through the inclusion of layered, composited, embedded, and linked materials. Along with other digital environments such as chat rooms, navigable games, and virtual worlds like the three-dimensional (3-D) *Second Life* (*www.Secondlife.com*), scrolling environments allow users to become virtual walkers or explorers.

In *Outside/Inside* (2007a), as well as in some of my other works such as *Something That Happened Only Once* (2007b) and

The process of collecting is both virtual and actual. It is a process of marking, unmarking, and remarking routes, weaving threads between landscapes of physical features and landscapes of ideas.

An investig
product --
of others. T

...[T]he tide was running
could not stand on the de
the sea, which was const

I am no longer in the Peacock, the poor ship has had her ribs terribly squeezed in the ice... Our voyage to this place was in the small colonial Brig, the Victorious, with every discomfort connected with a dirty and crowded vessel... We gathered all the plants, shot all the Birds, caught the fish, and got heartily sick of the natives...   Yours, truly, T.R. Peale, 1840

Voyage Into the Unknown (2008), I employed panoramas and other kinds of scrolling environments as organizing devices that explore these conditions. Such works layer and link materials to and within their virtual and seamless topographies.

OUTSIDE/INSIDE

Outside/Inside (2007a) was an installation commissioned by the Museum of the American Philosophical Society in Philadelphia for its exhibition *Undaunted: Five American Explorers 1760–2007*, which ran from 22 June 2007 to 28 December 2008. The installation kiosk in the museum presented a layered panoramic image of the park outside the museum. The materials layered upon and around the panoramic imagery included embedded videos, photographs, maps, and text.

The installation invited viewers to take a virtual stroll (or 'scroll') through a section of National Historical Independence Park, which is adjacent to the museum, with an eye to uncovering fragmentary evidence of the differing histories of the area (about four city blocks). 'Bands' of original text and quotes ran above and below a spiraling panoramic image of the park. Archival photographs and etchings of the urban landscape, taken at differing stages during its (re)development, were layered upon and around the composited panoramic photograph. The videos offered viewers mini-explorations within the park.

The structuring metaphors of walking and exploring were particularly apt. The exhibition looked at how approaches to exploration, including differing modes of representation

n is often a private and, even, lonely experience of searching for answers to a question. Turning evidence into book, the exhibit, the map – the scientist enters a social sphere where paths of inquiry criss-cross with those public works form the collective image of a landscape. Its secrets lie in the paths taken to get there.

but on the turn it was too much for the poor ship, the shocks were so heavy we
The boats cleared and one hoisted out but she was immediately stove to pieces by
y rising, and at night most had given up all hope of saving the ship or indeed our
lives... Next morning not a vestige of the ship remained. All our collections (the most valuable of any
obtained), all my knick-nacks, clothes - every thing but my rifle & the clothes on my back were -gone-
... We expect to sail from here tomorrow just where to I can't say.... Yours, truly, T.R. Peale, 1841
P.S. I heard that our collections have been sent to Washington from Philadelphia... Can't tell what to me

such as diary writing, map-making, and drawing, shaped the formation of differing kinds of knowledge. The historic park where the work was recorded is a recreation area that had been used in many different ways over the past 200 years. Independence Hall was first constructed in 1732, at which time it sat near the edge of a colonial port on the Delaware River. A small square behind the hall was established as a park to be preserved in perpetuity, and this decree endured though the US War of Independence and the subsequent growth of the city, while the lands surrounding it were transformed by industry. Tanneries and breweries lined the edge of a creek running through the city toward the Delaware River, and a prison was built overlooking the smaller park. As the city continued to grow, the creek—which had become more like an open sewer—was covered, and

the industries moved out. The industrial buildings were torn down and replaced by commercial enterprises and warehouses. Beginning in the 1950s, many of these buildings were razed for an expansion of the park. A walker would find few, discreet, signs of the land's concealed histories in the landscape's topography.

After visiting the exhibits in the historical museum, visitors are likely to walk in the park. Navigating actual or virtual terrains, an urban explorer might come upon clues to its man-made and natural histories. A number of strategies were employed in the videos embedded in *Outside/Inside* to allow users to search for concealed pasts. For example, each inset video sequence was shaped by a differing method of exploration: one video focused on measuring; another on the wildlife that made its home in that urban setting; another on the

We are surrounded by thousands of Alliga

, a boy, crouching at creekside,
in the sunlight, a handful of water
rip from my hand. The drops, they were bright!
you believe nothing, with the evidence lost.

— Robert Penn Warren, 1966

concealed waterways that ran through it; and so forth. Each video sequence was recorded in a different season, under differing weather conditions, so that tone and light vary and each draws on differing genre styles, contrasting modes of representation. The user engaged in an exploratory process not unlike that of the original researcher; the user gathered and compiled evidence from the landscape.

Modes of exposition, voices, and viewpoints mix. A multimedia environment offers the potential to present temporal continuity and uninterrupted (or contiguous) spatial representation, while at the same time allowing for montage, collage, layering, compositing, and other forms of media mixing. These media-mixing processes, which are made possible by new tools, can disrupt expectations of verisimilitude that contiguity and continuity imply; in doing so,

they can challenge the authoritative stance of objectivity that contiguous and continuous representation is often used to represent. Once dialectically opposed methods of panoramic art and cinema, such as those of continuity and montage, of close-up and long shot, or of exposition and narrative, now coexist. Historical elements can also coexist, as when nineteenth- and twentieth-century photographs of identical locations in the park were layered upon a corresponding twenty-first-century image.

The combining of modes of presentation is provocative. Cinematic and photographic viewing experiences are, equally, readerly ones. Passive 'viewers' become active 'users.' As is true with web interactivity in general, panoramic web-based works can provide bridges to critical and creative modes of representation such as writerly modes of exposition,

tors...

Nothing but sand Barrens are about and around us – When now and then an Impenetrable swamp is in sight it is hailed with the greatest pleasure for in them only Game or birds of any sort can be procured.... We are now living not "on the fat of the land" for fat there is none...

We are closely
I ever made, and
my duty altoge

The surface
If

poetry and narrative. In the same vein, differences between researcher, artist and user may also dissolve. The researcher and artist may use the same or similar programs to gather and compose their materials; similarly, users may follow, or participate in, the processes of building propositions, arguments and/or expression. There are critical and methodological shifts from product to praxis: theory and practice merge in the (potentially ongoing) process of creative activity that may serve to integrate methods of older arts such as panorama and cinema in new and hybrid environments. This integration of process and product can play an important role for makers exploring new strategies of presentation; they are vital aspects of the new rhetoric and poetics that a multimedia-maker can choose to employ.

DIGITAL CHOICE-MAKING

Choice-making is a condition that once drew me to direct cinema and ethnographic film as a student. There are many other kinds of documentary films that are tightly scripted before shooting starts, as the camera commits a preconceived text to image. However, in both direct cinema and much of ethnographic filmmaking, the researcher–maker has little control over what occurs in front of the lens. The researcher–filmmaker must make choices in filming (and with related tasks of note-taking, audio recording, etc.) that will capture impressions of an occurrence and provide sufficient evidence from which to develop later interpretations and translations. Frederick Wiseman's direct cinema works, such as *High School* (1968)

...own a few Birds as good as any and our Friend grants me all his knowledge of the Habits of these birds with which he hope to give this department of has become well acquainted as belonging to this section of the Union. – I have nearly one ...e a Bird or so every evening, hundred Drawings of Water Birds ready for Publication...
— Audubon. 1833

This interactive documentary was constructed by American Philosophical Society (APS) artist-in-residence Roderick Coover June 2007–December 2008. Special thanks go to the staff of APS for their support. Thanks also to the staffs of The Independence National Historic Park Library, The John Hay Library and The Print and Picture Collection of The Free Library of Philadelphia for their research support and for permissions granted to use of images from their archives in this work. And, thanks to friend and collaborator, Brett Keyser. © Roderick Coover 2007.

...soft and impressable by the feet of men; and so with the paths which the mind travels...
...astles in air, your work need not be lost; that is where they should be. Now put the foundation under them.
— Henry David Thoreau, 1854

and *Titicut Follies* (1974), were made without scripts or even preliminary studies. Spontaneous engagement requires differing strategies from scripted production; in Wiseman's case these included always following a perceived sequence from its beginning to its end. Robert Gardner's ethnographic films such as *Dead Birds* (1964) and *Forest of Bliss* (1986) examined how symbolic objects and actions function within cultural contexts; frequently, these meanings evolved through the course of production and post-production. Interactive and scrolling or browser environments may provide some of the same choice-making processes to users, who may in some cases also contribute to the works.

Users in these screen spaces make their paths among the data. They can see how arguments are built out of research materials and can consider what other choices might be made. A critical reader–user can also consider alternatives, which can result in the construction of arguments that contain within them a range of complementary or coexisting interpretations. This structure is ideally suited for ethnographic practices that so often weave together many points of view and that must take into account the continual evolution of cultural practices and their meanings. It allows researchers to integrate, organize, and interpret materials, to reveal their processes, and to build arguments without excluding alternatives. It allows users to engage in this process *alongside* the researcher, following a researcher's interpretive process, and comparing it with other options. The user in this way can enter into both the form and content of the work.

Like 'walking in the streets,' participation with cultures from the ground up—something that ethnographers frequently take pride in—requires continual adaptation and the incorporation of new information, interpretations, and translations. Interactive environments offer researchers 'tools' for gathering materials and building interpretations through sifting, sorting, and path-making. The production is also its presentation. The tools sustain a critical working practice that becomes part of the history of a work. For users, these environments promote re-interpretation, contextualized by agency, exploration, path-making, and choice-making.

ACKNOWLEDGMENTS

My thanks to Chris Cagle, Sarah Drury, members of the Philadelphia Cinema and Media Studies Seminar and members of the International Visual Sociology Association for their comments on this chapter.

REFERENCES

Bazin, Andre (1967) *What is Cinema?* Translated by H. Gray (ed.). Berkeley, CA: University of California Press.

Berger, John and Mohr, Jean (1982) *Another Way of Telling.* New York: Pantheon.

Certeau, Michel de (1984) *The Practice of Everyday Life.* Berkeley, CA: University of California Press.

Coover, Roderick (2001) 'Worldmaking, metaphors, and montage in the representation of cultures: cross-cultural filmmaking and the poetics of Robert Gardner's Forest of Bliss', *Visual Anthropology,* 14(4): 415–438.

Coover, Roderick (2003) [CD-ROM] *Cultures in Webs: Working in Hypermedia with the Documentary Image.* Watertown, MA: Eastgate Systems.

Dead Birds (1964) Directed by Robert Gardner. Cambridge: Documentary Educational Resources.

Eisenstein, Sergei (1949) *Film Form: Essays in Film Theory,* translated by J. Leyda (ed.). New York: Harcourt Brace Jovanovich.

Eisenstein, Sergei ([1924] 1997) 'The montage of film attractions', in P. Lehman (ed.), *Defining Cinema.* New Brunswick, NJ: Rutgers University Press. pp. 17–36.

Evans-Pritchard, E. (1940) *The Nuer, a Description of the Modes of Livelihood and Political Institutions of a Nilotic People.* Oxford: Clarendon Press.

Fernandez, James W. (1986) *Persuasions and Performances: The Play of Tropes in Culture.* Bloomington, IN: Indiana University Press.

Forest of Bliss (1985) [Film] Directed by Robert Gardner, produced with Akos Östör. Cambridge: Documentary Educational Resources.

Friedrich, Paul (1991) 'Polytropy', in J. Fernandez (ed.), *Beyond Metaphor: The Theory of Tropes in Anthropology.* Stanford, CT: Stanford University Press. pp. 17–55.

Geertz, Clifford (1973) *The Interpretation of Cultures; Selected Essays.* New York: Basic Books.

Goodman, Nelson (1978) *Ways of Worldmaking.* Indianapolis, IN: Hackett Publishing.

The Harvest (1999) [Digital Arts Installation] Directed by Roderick Coover. First exhibition at Chicago, IL: Midway Studios.

High School (1968) [Film] Directed by Frederick Wiseman. Cambridge: Zipporah Films.

Lakoff, George and Johnson, Mark (1980) *Metaphors We Live By.* Chicago, IL: University of Chicago Press.

The Language of Wine (2005) [DVD] Directed by Roderick Coover. Philadelphia, PA: Roderick Coover Productions. Available from: www.languageofwine. com.

Manovich, Lev (2001) *The Language of New Media.* Cambridge, MA: MIT Press.

Manovich, Lev (2006) 'After effects, or velvet revolution', *Millennium Film Journal,* 45/46 (Fall): 5–20.

Naked Spaces: Living is Round (1985) [Film] Directed by Trinh T. Minh-Ha. New York: Moongift Films.

Nanook of the North (1922) [Film] Directed by Robert Flaherty. USA. [Online] Available from: http://www. youtube.com/watch?v=kaDVovGjNOc. [Accessed 17 October 2010].

Outside/Inside (2007a) [Interactive Digital Media Exhibition, 22 June 2007 to 28 December 2008] Directed by Roderick Coover. Commissioned installation for the exhibition, *Undaunted: Five American Explorers 1760–2007.* Philadelphia, PA: Museum of the American Philosophical Society.

Something That Happened Only Once (2007b) [Digital Arts Installation] Directed by Roderick

Coover. First exhibition at Philadelphia, PA: Esther Klein Gallery.

Stoller, Paul (1989) *The Taste of Ethnographic Things: The Senses in Anthropology.* Philadelphia, PA: University of Pennsylvania Press.

Stoller, Paul (1997) *Sensuous Scholarship, Contemporary Ethnography.* Philadelphia, PA: University of Pennsylvania Press.

Taussig, Michael T. (1993) *Mimesis and Alterity: A Particular History of the Senses.* New York: Routledge.

Titicut Follies (1974) [Film] Directed by Frederick Wiseman. Cambridge: Zipporah Films.

Turner, Victor W. (1974) *Dramas, Fields, and Metaphors: Symbolic Action in Human Society.* Ithaca, NY: Cornell University Press.

Voyage into the Unknown (2008) [Interactive Digital Media] Directed by Roderick Coover. Philadelphia, PA: Unknown Territories, Ltd. [Online] Available from: www.unknownterritories.org/voyage.html.

33

Doing and Disseminating Visual Research: Visual Arts-Based Approaches

Dónal O'Donoghue

In his introduction to the book *What is Research in the Visual Arts*: *Obsession, Archive and Encounter*, Marquard Smith asked, 'How might other models of research from other fields and disciplines influence and shape the future of visual arts research'? (2008: xxi) With this question in mind, this chapter focuses on how models of art practice can influence and shape the future of visual research. Paying close attention to how artists work, and focusing, in particular, on the representational repertoires and scopic regimes they utilize, provides potential alternative inquiry practices, analytical frames, and dissemination possibilities for the field of visual research. The chapter is not intended as a comprehensive review of the many ways of engaging in visual research from an arts-based perspective; rather, it addresses three art forms: installation art, video art, and film.

INTRODUCTION

I begin this chapter by considering some of the more obvious connections between visual

research and the work and practices of artists who engage documentary methods in their work. I focus specifically on Tacita Dean's 2005 artwork, *Presentation Sisters*. Following that, I examine, in some detail, the work practices of Willie Doherty, an Irish conceptual artist who works mainly with photography and video. I do this to make visible the ways in which he inquires into issues of social, cultural, and political significance, and to show how he creates opportunities for specific understandings to emerge in and from his work. I focus on his installation *Same Difference* (1990) to raise questions about how meaning is produced, first in the production of an artwork and subsequently in an encounter with the work. This analysis of Doherty's installation suggests some ways that visual researchers might think about how stories are recorded and constructed, visually and spatially. I discuss how conditions for knowing, and knowing differently, are created in the form of an artwork, and show how meaning is made and empathic understandings are generated in encounters with that artwork. I demonstrate how the choice of medium is closely linked with the types of understanding that can be gleaned from an artwork.

Following the analysis of Doherty's installation, I discuss how his forms of expression used might be taken up in a visual research project. I describe how I created an installation to disseminate findings of a research study that investigated the masculinizing practices of a male single-sex residential teacher training college in Ireland during the opening decades of the twentieth century.[1] Similar to Doherty's *Same Difference*, this installation, which combined visual and textual data from the research study, disseminated the outcomes of the study to a wider and more diverse, largely non-academic, audience. It provided opportunities for relational understanding, and served a further role in the inquiry process by creating new configurations of image and text in an enclosed space while generating new questions about the topic under investigation. As an artwork, it extended and reinterpreted the narratives it depicted (Bourriaud, 2005).

Before discussing the two art installation pieces, it is important to note that during the past two decades arts-based educational researchers have identified and articulated how inquiry practices and processes in the arts can inform the research practices of educational researchers. It is their belief that the arts have the ability to contribute particular insights into, and enhance understandings of phenomena that are of interest to educators and policymakers. Elliot Eisner, the first to propose a place for the arts in educational research,[2] argued: 'the arts provide access to forms of experience that are either un-securable or much more difficult to secure through other representational forms' (2006: 11). As a way of conducting and disseminating educational research, arts-based research has become highly visible in research conferences, scholarly publications, graduate courses, theses, dissertations, websites, etc. Different methodological approaches for engaging the arts in educational research have been advanced, including a/r/tography, arts-informed research, and aesthetically

based research, to mention a few (see Cole, 2002; Cole et al., 2004; Irwin, 2004; Irwin and deCosson, 2004; Springgay et al., 2005, 2008; Bresler, 2006). Philosophical understandings and rationales for researching in, with, and through the arts have been put forward, but rarely problematized. And, in the past decade, we have witnessed a noticeable increase in the number of articles that deal with arts-based research practices that involve the visual arts (see Slattery, 2001; Sullivan, 2005, 2006; Irwin et al., 2006; O'Donoghue, 2007a, b, 2008a, b; Springgay, 2008). As I have argued elsewhere (O'Donoghue, 2009), while arts-based researchers have been active in finding ways to use artistic practices and process in educational inquiries, they have not given due attention to emerging theories and philosophies of contemporary art. Neither have they paid much attention to critical accounts of artists' practices and artists' autobiographical writings. Rather, emphasis has remained on the philosophical understandings of the role and purpose of art, even though, as Elizabeth Chaplin wrote: 'the production and reception of visual art works are social processes, and they cannot satisfactorily be explained by reference to internal aesthetic factors' (1994: 161–162). For Bourdieu, 'The work of art is an object which exists as such only by virtue of the (collective) belief which knows and acknowledges it as a work of art' (1993: 35).

In addition to arts-based educational research, in the past decade, in the UK and elsewhere, there has been a growing interest in theorizing art practice as research. Commonly referred to as practice-based research, it evolved mainly from artist practitioners working in visual and performing arts departments in universities. Moreover, it emerged at a time when the practices of art making and the production of art, broadly conceived, had shifted considerably. In the 1990s, a new generation of artists focused on knowledge production in and through art practices rather than the production of artworks as traditionally conceived. Supported by journals, conferences, and research evaluative frame-works (such as the Research Assessment Exercise in the UK), practice-based research is fast becoming institutionalized: Practice-based research doctoral degree programs are now available to students in several countries; funding for research using practice-based and practice-led methodologies is increasingly common, and conferences advancing the theory and practice of this form of research are held regularly.

Articulating the qualities of practice-based research has become a particular focus of theorizing art practice as research. For example, Henk Slager suggested that 'artistic research' is 'a mode of research not focused purposefully on generating "expert knowledge," but specifically on expressing experimental knowledge,' (2009: 2). Such knowledge, he argued, 'cannot be channeled through rigid academic-scientific guidelines of generalization, repetition and quantification, but requires full attention for the unique, the qualitative, the particular, and the local' (2009: 2). The idea that art and art making are forms of knowledge production and sites of knowledge in and of themselves underpins the theorization of art practice as research. As Karen Raney (2003) observed, ' "research" has to a large extent replaced "expression" as a model for art practice' (2003: 5). Several artists have used research methods such as interviews, questionnaires, participant obser-vation, narrative, and collaborative inquiry as a starting point or as the main body of their work. Mark Godfrey (2007) drew attention to the idea of the artist as researcher in his essay, 'The Artist as Historian.' As he observed, 'there are an increasing number of artists whose practice starts with research in archives, and others who deploy what has been termed an archival form of research' (Godfrey, 2007: 142–143). Godfrey drew his readers' atten-tion to the work of Jeremy Deller (a winner of the Turner Prize in 2004) who, in his event-based performance piece, *The Battle of Orgreave* (2001), re-enacted the clash between police and coalminers from the miners' strike in Britain in 1984 and resuscitated its memory in the minds of many former miners, politi-cians, and the general public.

Interestingly, artists' work and production practices have not informed, to any great extent, the theorizing and methodological development of visual research in the social sciences to date, even though the practice of art today is more similar than dissimilar to the project of visual research. While the project of visual research is not easily sum-marized, the chapters in this handbook dem-onstrate a general agreement that visual research is interdisciplinary and concerned with ways that culture and social relations are constituted and rendered in and through the visual, by visual means, and visual prac-tices. Considering models of artistic practice and representation is especially relevant for those visual researchers, who, influenced by work in visual culture studies, are interested in ways in which cultural practices and social relations are articulated visually, are embed-ded in visual practices, find meaning in dif-ferent forms of visuality, and are produced in and through visual processes. As an approach to inquiry, visual research is less concerned with answering predetermined questions than it is with generating new insights that are not easily available through verbal modes. This is a place where there already exists a strong connection between the work of visual researchers and artists.

PRESENTATION SISTERS

The work of the British-born artist Tacita Dean is a case in point. For example, in 2005, as part of a public art commission, she pro-duced an hour-long film called *Presentation Sisters*. Shown first at the South Presentation Convent in Cork, Ireland, as part of the Cork European City of Culture Visual Arts Program, the film traces the daily routines and lives of the last five remaining Presentation nuns in that convent. Through fixed-camera angles, close-ups, long takes, high angle shots, reaction shots, low angle shots, and forced perspective, Dean captures and emphasizes the daily rituals of the five nuns. While in the making of the artwork, Dean adopts an approach that is essentially documentary in nature, unlike a visual ethnographic or documentary study—and here I am thinking particularly of David MacDougall's visual ethnography of a boys' boarding school in northern India— *Presentation Sisters* was not made to answer specific questions. Rather, Dean is intent on recording, making sense of, and representing that which presented itself to her during her 3 days in the company of five nuns in their convent. In her arrangement of images and sounds and in the manipulation of time and space, Dean creates a work that gives material form to an invisible process: the disappearing presence of religious communities in Ireland. Much is lost in that process, and Dean's film reminds us of that which will eventually be lost, as fewer and fewer women enter the religious life.

The organic and unplanned nature of the work was explained in an interview that Dean gave Nick Coleman, published in the *Independent* on 18 March 2007 (Coleman, 2007). She explained to Coleman that she was invited to Cork to make a work for the city, but didn't quite know what she would produce. The idea came to her during a tour of the city: 'I was taken to the Titanic Centre—I'm known for my interest in sinking ships—and just by chance I saw a nuns' graveyard. The graves were like baby teeth. Tiny. And there was one grave missing.' It was that missing grave—that empty plot—which gave Dean the idea for the artwork that eventually became *Presentation Sisters*, but not before it changed due to unforeseen circumstances. She told Coleman that she had intended to make a film about the last six nuns in the Presentation Convent, 'thinking about who's going to get that last space,' and that it would be called *The Last Plot*. However, as she explained:

I arrived back in Cork to find that a nun had died in the interim period and instead of filling the last plot, they'd actually removed one of the stones and created two empty plots—they double and triple hang in these graveyards—so the whole premise of my film was dubious. I ended up filming the remaining nuns in this huge empty building they occupy because they can't get any new novices. They turned out to be amazing women. (Coleman, 2007)

While Dean's film demonstrates the similarities between the project of visual research and the project of visual art, it offers to visual researchers, especially those interested in studying specific populations and their associated cultural practices, a model for conducting research differently. In exploring the intimacy of convent life, Dean used the formal vocabularies of Dutch baroque art. She drew repeatedly on the compositional devices found in Vermeer's work of the seventeenth century. Vermeer's practices also appear to have greatly influenced the way in which she captures and represents light, and more importantly how she uses light to guide the viewer's eye. Throughout her film, Dean utilized a compositional principle of layering not only for the purpose of creating depth but also for the purpose of positioning the viewer as an observer—an observer of a world not frequently depicted or made visible to outsiders. By the very act of capturing and representing layers, Dean invites viewers to think about the many layers of meaning contained in the images that she records and presents. Dean's model of inquiry and representation is committed to paying attention; engaging in effortful observation; embracing uncertainty; courting ambiguity; being open to chance encounters; being awakened by situations and being seduced and cajoled by them; being unafraid of not knowing; being curious about knowing differently; and, being open to using representational strategies employed by others who have focused on similar qualities. This model 'restores the world to us as an experience to be lived' (Bourriaud, 2005: 32). It produces meaning, and shifts understanding by investing in the inter-human sphere. It is an approach that draws attention to the usefulness of wonderment and, particularly, to the value of wondering, especially for the type of questions or actions that it might call forth. It is a model that privileges the act of pausing.[3] Given Marcus Banks' (2007) observation that there are few if any distinctive research methods unique to visual research, Dean's artistic practice offers generative inquiry and representational possibilities. What would it mean for visual research and knowledge production in the social sciences if visual researchers adopted practices of inquiry similar to Dean's? This brings me to the case study of Willie Doherty's work *Same Difference*, in which I will, through a close reading of this installation, further elaborate opportunities for developing visual research inquiry and representational practices based on art practice.

SAME DIFFERENCE

Willie Doherty's art installation *Same Difference* is a visual and textual work that narrates an experience of living in Northern Ireland during 'The Troubles' (see Figure 33.1). The conflict in Northern Ireland that became known as 'The Troubles' has been described as an ethnic conflict, given that it was 'based on political ideologies and social/ethnic identities that happen to be divided along religious lines' (Cairns and Darby, 1998: 754). In his work, Doherty pursues two main themes, 'group loyalty' and 'maintenance of group boundaries,' both of which are considered core components of ethnic conflicts. Using narrative structures that rely on juxtaposition and decontextualization, Doherty invites his audience to consider how Donna Maguire, an alleged member of the Provisional Irish Republican Army (IRA), is perceived and essentialized by the two main religio-political communities in Northern Ireland: the Unionist/Loyalist community and the Nationalist/Republican community.

In his installation, Doherty has placed two projection screens diagonally opposite one another in a darkened room no larger than 16 × 18 ft. Onto both screens he has projected a tightly cropped image of Donna Maguire's face. He photographed Maguire's face from a TV screen following her arrest by the Dutch authorities as a suspected Provisional IRA terrorist (Mac Giolla Léith, 2002). Doherty projects words that he has gleaned from the public press onto both screens. These words come and go, always being replaced by others, but the image of Maguire's face remains. On the screen to the right of the entrance, the words being projected onto the image of Maguire's face are pejorative terms drawn from the 'anti-Nationalist popular press'—'murderer,' 'pitiless,' 'misguided,' 'evil,' etc. 'Murderer' is projected onto that screen every other time. On the screen to the left of the entrance, words of Pro-Republican sentiments are projected onto the image of Maguire's face— 'volunteer,' 'defiant,' 'honourable,' and 'committed.' The word 'volunteer' appears every second time; the term 'volunteer' is used by the Provisional IRA to describe its members. As was played out in 'The Troubles,' these two differing perspectives and articulations of Maguire are positioned in opposition to one another, and a certain tension resides in the presentation of both simultaneously and in the same place.

While addressing and giving form to the above-mentioned themes, the installation serves as a powerful means of telling a complex story of segregation and isolation in a divided and fragmented society. It succeeds in generating emphatic understanding among viewers, which leads to new and different ways of knowing about 'The Troubles' in Northern Ireland, especially for those who did not experience them at first hand. *Same Difference* holds within it the potential for understanding the conflict in Northern Ireland in new and different ways. In conceptualizing and installing the work, Doherty has set up conditions for viewers to experience what it must be like to occupy a space of conflict, one that is situated between two dominant and opposing positions.

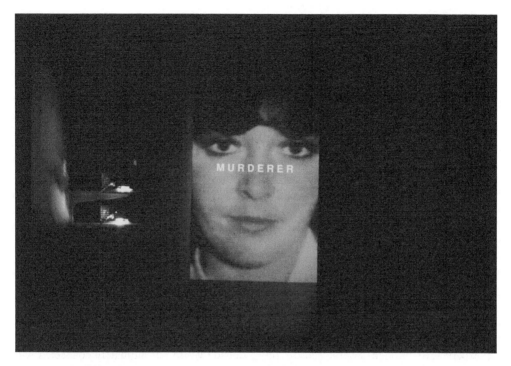

Figure 33.1 Willie Doherty, *Same Difference*, 1990. Installation with two slide-projected images and changing text

Invoking the perspectives of the two dominant communities in Northern Ireland, nationalist and unionist, and presenting them in a constructed and confined space, Doherty creates a place where viewers find themselves, through the process of interaction and attentiveness, occupying a contested terrain. Finding oneself between these positions evokes a response. Viewers tend to identify with one of the two articulations of Maguire. The installation forces viewers to do so by conveying to them that it would be impossible to remain neutral in such a place. There is no space for an alternative reading of Maguire: depending on who is doing the looking, she is either a murderer or a volunteer. Here Doherty speaks to the dangers of stereotyping as a barrier to understanding. In the installation, the physical space between the representations of Maguire is both a place of contact and a place of conflict, which closely resembles how space and territory were experienced in Northern Ireland during the period in which this work was made. While the space between both representations contributes to the polarized nature of both perspectives, it also suggests the absence of any meaningful connection or contact between these two communities. Historically, segregation (be it in the form of housing, recreation or education) played a significant role in establishing and maintaining conflict between these two communities (Hewstone et al., 2004). It serves the same purpose in this installation.

For visual researchers, the questions of importance are: How does Doherty narrate in a way that provides opportunities for meaningful engagement that create new understanding? How does Doherty create conditions for generating emphatic understanding among viewers that in turn enlarges consciousness? How does meaning unfold and become enfolded in other meanings? How does Doherty narrate a complex story using one image, several single words, and four Kodak Carousel 2050 slide projectors, two Kodak Carousel Interval Timers, two Kodak 75–120 mm zoom lenses, two Kodak 60 mm fixed lenses, two sets of 81 35 mm black-and-white text slides and two 35 mm black-and-white slides projected into two diagonally opposite corner walls in an enclosed space?[4] And, what can visual researchers learn from Doherty's narration processes?

First, he draws on the medium of installation art. Installation art is 'a term that loosely refers to the type of art into which the viewer physically enters, and which is often described as "theatrical," "immersive," or "experiential"' (Bishop, 2005: 6). It emerged in the 1960s and came into prominence in the 1970s and 1980s. As an art form, it draws from several disciplines, including architecture, cinema, performance art, sculpture, theater, and set design. Installation artworks are experienced through several senses. In *Same Difference*, Doherty creates an immersive space where the significance of territory is highlighted. In creating a bounded space and narrating the different ways in which Maguire is seen through a process of dual articulation, Doherty successfully conveys what it can be like to live in a place of conflict where surveillance is constant; segregation is promoted; neutrality is difficult; and confrontation is inevitable. Standing in this enclosed installation confronted with the image of Maguire, which can be threatening or reassuring depending on which side of the divide one stands, and witnessing how she is being perceived and described as a cold, callous, deranged murderer on the one hand, and a brave, loyal, intuitive volunteer on the other, reminds viewers of how a culture of suspicion is supported through language; how language is used to instill fear; how language is deployed to fragment and polarize a community; how practices of seeing are informed by language; and how language can inform perceptions of images. It also invites viewers to reflect on who is guilty here and who is innocent; and, how we construct and enact notions of innocence and guilt. Doherty

does not advance one cause over the other: rather, he places both together and uses one to draw attention to, and to better understand the other. As Paul O'Brien observed, 'If one query raised by the work is "which side are you on?" another possible question is "why either"?' (2003: 52). In an interview with Tim Maul in the *Journal of Contemporary Art*, Doherty explained that he tries to present 'the viewer with a number of options, so it was about making a choice where I always felt in fact there wasn't a choice but the work proposed that it was a possible to look at something from two positions simultaneously.'[5]

Second, the choices that Doherty makes in the conceptualization and creation of the installation are instrumental in setting conditions for particular understandings to emerge. His choices invite particular forms of interpretation. For example, separated from the outside world but intimately connected with its narratives, Doherty invites the viewer to make connections between what s/he sees, knows and experiences. Meaning isn't immediate. Rather, the installation requires viewers to engage in a dynamic process of meaning-making that is contingent upon searching for and making connections between what is represented, what is suggested, and what is imagined. Making meaning in the installation is a multi-sensual experience that requires a reading that extends beyond the mind to the body. In his decision to place the two screens diagonally opposite each other in the installation, Doherty not only engages in an act of segregation while drawing attention to group solidarity but also sets up particular conditions for viewing the work. *Same Difference* can never be viewed in its entirety from any single viewpoint. To view, read, and engage with the work one needs to constantly turn back and forth between screens. The viewer can never see the way in which each side of the divide perceives Maguire precisely at the same moment. Setting the conditions for reading and experiencing *Same Difference* in this way contributes to the viewer's feeling of anxiety, disorientation, uncertainty, and even fear within this confined and preplanned space, which is an intended outcome of the work. Furthermore, seeing from more than one perspective invites different interpretations. Different viewing positions allow for new configurations and formations. Because of the manner in which Doherty puts together the component parts of the installation, the viewer is urged to consider how the act of looking from a particular perspective gives us a particular viewpoint, while simultaneously closes off another. In *Same Difference*, meaning resides in, and is constructed by, this fragmented nature of viewing. In his decision to place the two screens diagonally opposite each other, Doherty also creates an in-between space between two dominant positions that eventually comes to be experienced as a place of great discomfort and unease, much like how place was experienced by denizens of Northern Ireland for the three decades of 'The Troubles.' Furthermore, the duration of the viewing is a time to be lived through.

Third, the kind of reading and understanding that the viewer secures from *Same Difference* is shaped and influenced in great part by the medium through which it was produced. The meaning of the work is constituted by, and in the form, medium, and mode of representation that Doherty has elected to use. To emphasize the fact that these readings of Maguire are ones that are projected onto her with the result that she is formed in the act of projection, Doherty uses a slide projector. Maguire is constructed outside of herself from projections that others apply to her. She has no say in the matter.

Fourth, Doherty does not offer closure in the piece: rather, the work exists in every encounter with it. It is in the encounter that the work comes into being. While the work is of 3 minutes' duration, as soon as it finishes, it starts again. It loops continuously, regardless of whether somebody is present in the installation or not. The viewer is witnessing something that is occurring over and over again, over which s/he has no control.

Labeling will continue even if s/he leaves the installation immediately.

Fifth, the form of Doherty's *Same Difference* cannot be reduced entirely to what he produced in the installation. As Bourriaud reminded us, 'form only exists in the encounter and in the dynamic relationship enjoyed by an artistic proposition with other formations, artistic or otherwise' (2002: 21). Meaning resides not only in the projected image and accompanying words but also in the space created in the installation and in the knowledge that viewers bring to the installation. Knowing something about Donna Maguire and the focus of Doherty's work more generally enables additional understandings to be secured from the installation. Knowledge about the artist, the work, and the circumstances surrounding the production of the work frames the nature of the encounter with the work and the subsequent engagement with it. The success of the work as a piece that creates opportunities for knowing more or knowing differently about 'The Troubles' in Northern Ireland is also reliant on the acrimonious relations that already existed between the two communities, one to which Maguire allegedly belonged. As Bourriaud observes, 'the artwork functions as the temporary terminal of a network of interconnected elements, like a narrative that extends and reinterprets preceding narratives' (2005: 19).

Same Difference invites visual researchers to consider how meaning is produced in place; how it is contingent on an ability to engage with singularity in order to understand plurality. The work operates as a way of creating conditions for bringing together differing histories and memories to generate meaning. It models how stories can be told using multiple modalities. As alluded to above, it is not so much 'what' Doherty tells, but the conditions he sets up provide the viewer with an experience that generates empathic understanding and invites connections and makes the installation a powerful narrative. *Same Difference* arises from, and is supported by, complex forms of engagement that require attention to that which is presented, to that which is suggested, and to that which is imagined and remembered. For visual researchers, *Same Difference* suggests new and innovative ways of disseminating findings. What if the outcomes of visual research studies were presented in the form of an installation: what new and different forms of understanding might be generated from working in and with this art form? What new and different publics might be reached by visual research disseminated in the form of an installation? How would this form of dissemination provide conditions for inquiring further into topics under investigation?

SAFE DISTANCE

The third example of a fine arts and arts-based visual research project is one that I created. Putting into practice lessons learnt from Doherty's installation *Same Difference* and influenced by the three-screen installation *Broadway/Prince Street 04-01* by the artist Beat Streuli, in 2006, I produced an installation to tell a story of how masculinities were actively produced across a range of sites in a male single-sex residential teacher training college in Ireland. Set during the opening decades of the twentieth century and given form in visual and textual articulations, my focus was on how men were made when they practiced teaching in practicing schools (see O'Donoghue, 2005, 2007c). The installation was produced from visual and textual data that I had gathered during a research study (see Figures 33.2 and 33.3).

In the installation, I created a bounded space enclosed by four floor-to-ceiling walls. Viewers entered the installation from an opening on the right side of the north wall. Using eight Kodak carousel slide projectors and interval timers, I projected photographic images that changed randomly every 10 seconds. Data consisted of four sets of 24 35 mm black-and-white text slides and four sets of 24 35 mm black-and-white image slides. They were projected onto each of the four interior

walls of the installation. I had digitally altered many of these images, but not in any significant way; some were cropped and the tonal qualities of others were changed slightly. These images were of men photographed in school classrooms or in the college environs. Life-sized, many faced the viewer, making eye contact. Others were depicted looking sideways or looking away, with their backs to the viewer. Onto these images, I projected text: extracts taken from student Teaching Practice Reports written by the Professor of Method during and after observation periods. These extracts were carefully chosen for what they suggested about how language was used to shape young male student teachers. Examples of these extracts include the following: 'A nervous and fidgety individual, very earnest but a trifle peculiar, strikes one as being old womanish'; 'Took some time to get this young man to speak and act in a manly fashion'; 'Good appearance but stands and moves rather awkwardly and speaks nervously'; 'Speaks in a manly and fairly impressive way'; and 'He has enough backbone to make a determined effort to correct his own defects.' These extracts articulate, legitimate, or make deviant particular ways of managing and experiencing the male teaching body. In the installation, these extracts come and go, always being replaced by another. These extracts sometimes appear right across and in front of the image (on the skin of the image), and other times they are written in the image (in the body of the image). The only constant is that they are constantly shifting and changing and unsettling the viewers' perceptions, and knowing.

Producing the installation provided an opportunity for me to inquire further into data that I had previously gathered. Experiencing the data as it surrounded me, enabled me to ask new and different questions that were not possible to ask when these visual and textual documents were encountered singularly in the archives during the initial research. Placing visual articulations of masculinity together with text-based ones and showing several of these combinations

AFRAID TO FACE CLASS MANFULLY

Figure 33.2   *Safe Distance*, 2006, Dónal O'Donoghue. Installation with text

simultaneously in a darkened room, I began to see how masculinities were enacted, performed, staged, and articulated in and through specific modes of representation—visual and textual—and over time. I began to make connections and notice relations between the images and texts, the images and images, and the texts and texts that I had not previously noticed, and which were not always sequential. Being surrounded by these images, in an immersive space, provided me with an opportunity to experience in new ways the manner in which the college actively engaged in constructing particular forms of masculinities as well as negotiating relations between them. In juxtaposition, images and texts presented opportunities to think further about the types of masculine roles that were available for male student teachers to inhabit, and to consider how these men took them up, moved across them, ordered them, regulated them, and defended them.

A recurring theme that emerged from the installation was relational understanding: relations between two active systems of representation—image and text—and meaning-making (re)produced in the installation. Relations between subject and object, viewer and viewed, became obvious. In the installation the viewer was presented with ways others saw, pictured, and constructed men teachers, thereby suggesting ways in which men student teachers were constructed in the gaze of others and objectified in the act of looking.

The installation provided an opportunity to rethink the nature of research texts and the relationship between such texts and their readers. Installed in the gallery of a university, it was available to a different audience in a place vastly different from scholarly conferences. Ways of engaging with the exhibition as a research text were different from how academics normally engage with research texts. In this type of work, meaning is generated through

Figure 33.3 *Safe Distance*, 2006, Dónal O'Donoghue. Installation with text

interaction and negotiation with the work. From this place, the researcher creates conditions where viewers are likely to experience the work in particular ways, although the researcher can never fully control how the work is taken up by the viewer/reader. It is based on the principle that consumption is a mode of production (Bourriaud, 2005: paraphrasing from Karl Marx). The installation also provided a different narrative structure from familiar academic research texts. It ruptured the pattern of a linear narrative, and formulated a series of discontinuous and partial stories. Instead of summary answers, it produced questions.

CONCLUSION

Artists draw attention to things that often go unnoticed. In this chapter, I have presented the idea that paying close attention to artists'

work and practices invites visual researchers to imagine other ways of conducting inquiries and of representing findings. There are a number of qualities that artists use in the production of their work; a number of commitments guide their practice. For example, in the production of *Presentation Sisters*, Tacita Dean was committed to paying attention to, and embracing chance encounters. She was committed to being awakened by situations in which she found herself. She engaged in effortful observation, embraced uncertainty, courted ambiguity, and was not unafraid of not knowing. She was curious about knowing differently. Similarly, in the production of *Same Difference*, Willie Doherty created a situation where viewers were invited to make meaning in, and through four representational forms—text, image, time, and place. This he achieved by using text and an image that were already in circulation. But the act of bringing them together for the first time in a bounded space and in ways not previously conceived created new combinations and new texts to be read and interrogated. Both artists engaged in fluid inquiries. In this chapter, I am not making the argument that visual researchers ought to take on the art practices of artists in their research inquiries. Rather, I am suggesting that visual researchers might find it helpful to identify and understand ways in which visual practitioners in the arts engage with and give visual and material form to ideas that eventually lead to new or enlarged understanding of a topic, issue, or phenomenon.

The process of paying attention to artists' work and practices suggests another way of doing collaborative inquiry in visual research. Visual researchers from a variety of disciplines can work with artists (rather than as artists) in situations that require different and multiple visual strategies for inquiring into, interpreting, and making sense of topics under investigation. I suggest collaborative inquiry for the following reason. Artists often will bring to research situations very different ways of seeing, imagining, understanding, articulating, and inquiring, which leads to better questioning and more robust inquiry practices. The ability and freedom of artists to work on an edge and between borders of the familiar and the emergent create new possibilities for knowing and working together differently. While this chapter is not intended as a comprehensive review of the many ways of engaging in visual research from an arts-based perspective, the artworks and practices considered here will, I hope, serve as an invitation to visual researchers to think further about, elaborate, and refine their inquiry and representational practices.

NOTES

1 Masculinizing practices are conceptualized as all those social, discursive, material, and institutional practices and performances that confront, challenge, form, shape, and influence male subjectivities and masculine identities.

2 In the special issue of *Studies in Art Education* devoted to arts-based research, Tom Barone (2006) claims it was in the 1970s in Stanford, when he was a doctoral student, that Elliot Eisner was imagining a place for the arts in educational research. As Eisner himself explains, in that same issue, the first Arts-Based Research Institute was offered at Stanford University to members of the American Educational Research Association in 1993.

3 Dean's practice is a practice of pause at the threshold. Her work emerges somewhere between awakening and surrender. For example, in making *Presentation Sisters*, she was awakened to the intricacies and complexities of that which presented itself to her. As she tries to make sense of that which she encounters for the purpose of giving it form, she surrenders to it—to its form, movement, quality, and so on an so forth.

4 A precise description of the technical components of the installation was taken from http://www.fineart.ac.uk/artists.php?idartlist=15 [Accessed 1 September 2009.

5 From an interview with the artist conducted by Tim Maul and published in the online journal, the *Journal of Contemporary Art*. Retrieved August 29, 2009, from http://www.jca-online.com/doherty.html. No publication date or issue number.

REFERENCES

Banks, M. (2007) *Using the Visual in Qualitative Research*. London: Sage Publications.

Barone, T. (2006) Studies in Art Education. *A Journal of Issues and Research in Art Education*, 48(1), 9–18.

Bourdieu, P. (1993) *The field of cultural production: Essays on Art and Literature*. (Randal Johnson, Intro & Ed.) Cambridge: Polity Press.

Bourriaud, N. (2002) *Relational Aesthetics*. Dijon: Les Presses du Réel.

Bourriaud, N. (2005) *Postproduction*. New York: Lukas and Sternberg.

Bresler, L. (2006) 'Toward connectedness: Aesthetically based research', *Studies in Art Education: A Journal of Issues and Research in Art Education*, 48(1): 52–69.

Cairns, E. and Darby, J. (1998) 'The conflict in Northern Ireland: Causes, consequences and controls', *American Psychologist*, 53: 754–760.

Chaplin, E. (1994) *Sociology and Visual Representation*. London: Routledge.

Cole, A. (2002) 'The art of research: Arts-informed research', *University of Toronto Bulletin*, 12(16).

Cole, A. L., Neilsen, L., Knowles, J. G. and Luciani, T. (eds.) (2004) *Provoked by Art: Theorizing Arts-informed Inquiry.* Halifax, NS: Backalong Books/ Centre for Arts-informed Research.

Coleman, N. (2007) 'Tacita Dean: In search of inspiration', The *Independent*, 18 March, [Online]. Available from: http://www.independent.co.uk/ travel/news-and-advice/tacita-dean-in-search-of-inspiration-440791.html [Accessed 8 July 2009].

Eisner, E. W. (2006) 'Does arts-based research have a future?', *Studies in Art Education: A Journal of Issues and Research in Art Education*, 48(1): 9–18.

Godfrey, M. (2007) 'The artist as historian', *October*, 120, 140–172.

Hewstone, M., Cairns, E., Voci, A., McLernon, F., Niens, U. and Noor, M. (2004) 'Intergroup forgiveness and guilt in Northern Ireland: Social psychological dimensions of "The Troubles"', in N. R. Branscombe and B. Doosje (eds.), *Collective Guilt: International Perspectives.* New York: Cambridge University Press. pp. 193–215.

Irwin, R. L. (2004) 'A/r/tography: A metonymic métissage', in R. L. Irwin and A. deCosson (eds.), *A/r/tography: Rendering Self through Arts-based Living.* Vancouver, BC: Pacific Educational Press. pp. 27–38.

Irwin, R. L. and deCosson, A. (eds.) (2004) *A/r/ tography: Rendering Self through Arts-based Living.* Vancouver, BC: Pacific Educational Press.

Irwin, R. L., Beer, R., Springgay, S., Grauer, K., Xiong, G. and Bickel, B. (2006) 'The rhizomatic relations of A/r/tography', *Studies in Art Education: A Journal of Issues and Research*, 48(1): 70–88.

Mac Giolla Léith, C. (2002) 'Troubled memories', in C.M.G. Léith and C. Christov-Bakargiev (eds.), *Willie Doherty: False Memory.* IMMA and London: Merrill. pp. 19–25.

O'Brien, P. (2003) 'Willie Doherty: Language, imagery and the real', *Circa* (104). Available from: www. recirca.com/backissues/c104/doherty.shtml [Accessed 26 August 2009].

O'Donoghue, D. (2005) '"Speak and act in a manly fashion": The role of the body in the construction of men and masculinity in primary teacher education in Ireland', *Irish Journal of Sociology*, 14(2): 231–52.

O'Donoghue, D. (2007a) 'Place-making in boys' schools: Researching with and through art practice', *Journal of Artistic and Creative Education*, 1(2): 68–101.

O'Donoghue, D (2007b) '"James always hangs out here": Making space for place in studying masculinities at school', *Visual Studies*, 22(1): 62–73.

O'Donoghue, D. (2007c) 'Teaching bodies who teach: Men's bodies and the reconstruction of male teacher identity in Ireland', in S. Springgay and D. Freedman (eds.), *Curriculum and the Cultural Body.* New York: Peter Lang. pp. 91–113.

O'Donoghue, D. (2008a) '"That stayed with me until I was an adult": Making visible the experiences of men who teach', in S. Springgay, R.L. Irwin, C. Leggo and P. Gouzouasis (eds.), *Being with A/r/tography.* Rotterdam: Sense Publishing. pp. 109–112.

O'Donoghue, D. (2008b) 'Can arts-researchers go where artists go? Questions of interpretation and practice as played out in, and through the work of the Canadian artist, Rebecca Belmore', in Vol. 5, *Working Papers in Art and Design* [Online]. Available from: http://sitem.herts.ac.uk/artdes_research/papers/ wpades/vol5/dodabs.html.

O'Donoghue, D. (2009) 'Are we asking the wrong questions in arts-based research?', *Studies in Art Education*, 50(4): 352–368.

Raney, K. (2003) *Art in Question*, London and New York: Continuum.

Slager, H. (2009) *Nameless Science* [Online]. *Art & Research: A Journal of Ideas, Contexts and Methods*, 2(2): Available from: http://www.artandresearch. org.uk/v2n2/slager.html [Accessed 24 August 2009].

Slattery, P. (2001) 'The educational researcher as artist working within', *Qualitative Inquiry*, 7(3): 370–398.

Smith, M. (2008) Introduction. In M.A. Holly and M. Smith (eds.) *What is research in the Visual Arts? Obsession, archive, and encounter.* (pp. x–xxvi) Williamstown, MA: Sterling and Francine Clark Art Institute.

Springgay, S. (2008) 'Nurse-in: Breastfeeding and a/r/tographical research', in M. Cahnmann and R. Siegesmund (eds.), *Arts-based Research in Education.* New York: Routledge. pp. 136–140.

Springgay, S., Irwin R. L. and Wilson Kind, S. (2005) 'A/r/tography as living inquiry through art and text', *Qualitative Inquiry*, 11(6): 897–912.

Springgay, S., Irwin, R., Gouzouasis, P. and Leggo, C. (eds.) (2008) *Being with A/r/tography.* Rotterdam: Sense Publishers.

Sullivan, G. (2005) *Art Practice as Research: Inquiry in the Visual Arts.* London: Sage Publications.

34

Making Arguments with Images: Visual Scholarship and Academic Publishing

Darren Newbury

Images seem to speak to the eye, but they are really addressed to the mind. They are ways of thinking, in the guise of ways of seeing. (Wilson Duff, 1975)

INTRODUCTION

In the context of this volume it seems appropriate to begin with a pedagogic story. My own visual education began, formally at least, with a vocational diploma in photography. The incident I recall took place early on in the course. I happened to be wandering along the corridor holding in my hand some 35 mm black-and-white negatives I had developed. One of my tutors, heading in the opposite direction, stopped and challenged me. Why were the negatives not in sleeves? What on earth was I doing wandering around the dusty college corridors with vulnerable negatives in my hand? Did I not care about the images? It was this last question that struck home most forcefully. Whether or not

I realized it at the time, one of the central things I was being taught was to care about, and for, images. The pedagogic implications that flow from this point will provide something of a refrain in this chapter. I want to be provocative and argue that the field of visual research has yet to fully learn how to care for images. It is not just a question of the occasional researcher taking a casual approach; rather, there is a systemic lack of care for images, despite the ostensible focus on the visual. Nowhere is this more evident than in the area of academic publishing. Ask how many volumes have been written on how to publish? Then ask how many of these specifically discuss visual forms of presentation, or the role of images as illustrations? How many even have a chapter devoted to the topic? Even books devoted to visual methods are not always a good advertisement for the use of images in the presentation of research.

I do not mean to minimize the challenges visual scholars face in the context of academic publishing practice. Doing visual publishing well involves extra work and cost, although the latter is not as significant an issue now as it was in the past. And I can tell my own stories of frustration from trying to lever attention to the careful use of visual material into a process that can seem designed to exclude such attention; sometimes, I have succeeded, sometimes I have failed. But real as these challenges are, I am not convinced that as a broad field of academic enquiry we are doing all that we should to educate the attention of scholars, students, and publishers, or even that there is a broad consensus on what is at stake. If researchers are required to argue for the value of images in the published presentation of their research, then it is important they understand precisely what they are arguing for.

In keeping with a handbook publication, this chapter is principally concerned with the practical decisions and consequences of working with images. However, underlying the discussion is a theoretical argument about images and their intellectual respectability, something that we tend to take for granted with words and numbers. I have used the quotation that heads the chapter as a point of departure for two reasons. First, the link it draws between images and thought is important to those whose academic endeavor involves grappling with visual meaning. Duff draws our attention to the complex communication and expression that takes place when images are made and viewed, and their capacity to embody ideas and theories. Second, however, it serves to alert us to a trap, one whose long history in Western thought casts doubt on the testimony of images, and which risks undermining the case for visual presentation. I am referring to the neat separation Duff makes between the eye and the mind, sensory experience and thought, and the suggestion that the appeal of images to the former is inherently deceitful, demanding vigilance on the part of the thinking viewer.[1] Little wonder that so much scholarship is devoted to visual critique, the

unveiling of images so to speak. This way of thinking has consequences for the field of visual studies. It underpins the privileging of talking/writing about images over working with them, the dominance of the intellectual over the sensory. Too much attention to images is seen as suspect, a concern with mere aesthetic matters over the serious business of research and knowledge. Ironically, the flipside of this is a degree of nervousness and caution: a fear that one will fall into the trap set by the image and be seduced, losing control of meaning. Researchers withdraw from using images, concerned that they might be misunderstood, and take refuge rather too quickly in loose arguments about their polysemic nature. These concerns do have a legitimate basis; however, this failure of nerve is both symptomatic of, and made possible by, the idea that images are less knowledge-bearing than words or numbers. Anyone who has written an academic paper or research report knows very well that words and numbers must be disciplined if they are to do what is asked of them, and even then they often elude the writer's grasp. Nevertheless, we continue to struggle with them because they are at the very core of academic work. Surely, by the same standard, it is the task of visual studies as a field to grapple with the complexities involved in working with images, not to withdraw from them.

I do not intend to pursue the philosophical arguments in any greater depth, but ask readers to keep in mind two propositions that inform my thinking. The first is the idea that the aesthetic cannot be neatly divided from the intellectual: the address to the mind is inseparable from the address to the eye. There is meaning in form, and in the form of presentation. Images are not ideas in disguise, but are themselves intellectual propositions. The second idea is that visual researchers should be attempting not just to illustrate written arguments, but to do things with images. Images have agency, as Alfred Gell (1998) has argued convincingly; and, significantly, for those arguments that suggest it is desirable to separate the information content of images from their form, the captivation of the attention of the viewer represents a 'primordial kind of artistic agency' (1998: 68–69). The point I want to make here is straightforward: if researchers recognize images as a primary means of achieving the ends they seek they will treat them with more care.

What does it mean to care about images? Of course this is not simply a matter of looking after them in any narrow sense, which at the extreme is simply to fetishize the image as object. But maybe it does start with a concern for the image in its own right. It requires us to think about where images come from, what they can tell us and how we can use them to make arguments and communicate findings. It also has an ethical dimension; we have a duty of care to images. This might seem a slightly odd claim, so an analogy with research participants is useful here. Many of the images that are of concern to researchers have lives beyond the specific research project; we might use the idea of image biographies.[2] Researchers therefore have a responsibility to consider the impact of their own uses within the life of an image. Following Gell (1998), images can be conceived of as complex distributed extensions of the agency of those who have made them or owned them or shaped them in some way. Researchers should ask how they are inflecting this agency, how they are harnessing it toward their own ends, amplifying it or even attempting to undermine it, through critique, for example. If visual studies scholars and image-based researchers are to engage with the full complexity of images *as images*, then they must, of necessity, think reflexively about what they, too, are doing with them.

There are many issues at stake here, and this chapter is only a modest contribution to a much longer debate, so it is necessary for me to set out how I intend to structure the discussion, and some of its limitations. My focus is academic publishing. I intend therefore to concentrate on how images are or can be used and the decisions researchers need to make when presenting visual material, usually alongside text. Nevertheless, I believe much of what I say here has implications that extend both forward and backward. The images I refer to are mostly still photographs, artworks, or graphic illustrations. I do not deal with film, the narrative, and rhetorical complexity of which is an object of study in its own right. Nor do I deal with the various diagrams and charts that visual researchers construct to represent their data. Readers interested in the latter should turn first to the work of Edward Tufte (see Grady, 2006). I am also concerned mainly with print publishing in journals and books. The Internet and other forms of electronic publishing offer significant new opportunities for visual researchers, which many visual scholars have embraced with enthusiasm in recent years.[3] My examples come largely from more traditional and familiar forms. Nevertheless, many of the issues that I discuss apply equally well whether one is talking about a journal paper, web-based material, or even a visual conference presentation.

The discussion is based on my experiences as editor of *Visual Studies* over the past 7 years, as well as considerations that have arisen in the publication of my own research on photography. I draw heavily on papers published in the journal to illuminate the discussion. These examples are the ones that I know best. The fact that I have played a part in shaping them has the benefit of enabling me to reflect on the thinking and decision making that made them appear the way they do. I will occasionally refer to other examples that demonstrate a thoughtful and intelligent approach to the use of images. It would no doubt be instructive to consider negative examples: those cases, of which there are not a few, where the use of images leaves a lot to be desired. However, for ethical reasons such examples are perhaps better discussed in less public contexts. Despite the limitations of my sample, I will attempt to draw out some general principles that contribute to what I am calling visual scholarship.

VISUAL SCHOLARSHIP

Visual or image-based research is a broad field encompassing a range of disciplines and forms of academic enquiry. It follows that there cannot be a single approach to the use of images in publication. However, in order to proceed we need to make some distinctions. Although the division is somewhat crude, one can think of visual images serving three different purposes: illustration, analysis, and argument. (I am talking here specifically of images in published presentations, which is distinct from methodological questions about the use of images, although there is of course a relationship between the two.)

Illustration occurs where images are used as an explanatory adjunct to an argument or discussion presented in written form. For example, they may be used to show the reader a particular cultural practice, as is common in ethnographic film or photography, or to describe a particular space or environment or object, or even to exemplify different image types. The test of whether any particular use is illustrative is to ask what happens if you take the image away. The presentation may be impoverished somewhat, but should be able to proceed, or at least one could conceive of presenting it in an alternative, albeit less satisfactory, form. In this context images are valued for the economy with which they are able to describe the world, as well as the richness that they can add to a published presentation. Words tend to dominate, but this is not essential to the definition; a descriptive ethnographic film or sequence of documentary images, for example, may be the main component of a presentation without ceasing to be illustrative of something that could be described in other ways. For practical purposes the image is treated as relatively transparent, allowing viewers access to what the re-searcher wants to show them. Of course, images are never entirely transparent in quite the way this suggests—they are always socially constructed—but there are occasions when it is legitimate to bracket out contextual arguments in order to proceed with the discussion at hand. One should of course do so carefully, otherwise alternative interpretations may disrupt what is intended. This is a very common way in which images are used in our field; and, historically, the earliest, in the form of anthropological and sociological fieldwork photographs. But if we only ever consider images as illustrations, then we are missing a great deal.

Analysis refers to instances where the image itself is the focus of attention, the object of study: for example, studies in which the content or organization of the image is examined for what it reveals about the values of a society, or studies where the history of the image is of particular relevance or interest.[4] There is a clear distinction between illustrative and analytical uses, a marked shift of attention from what the image allows the reader to see, to the nature of the image as it presents itself to the viewer, an acknowledgment that what we are looking at is an image, not the thing itself. Sartre refers to this as 'reflective consciousness' of the image (2006: 134). In this category the image is treated as having a greater degree of autonomy, and attention is drawn to its construction and effects. Even where it permits access to a world beyond, the reader is made conscious that this access is on terms set by the image. As above, it is useful to ask what happens if you take the image away. In analytical examples, the argument is in danger of collapsing, or at least becomes very difficult to sustain. The interpretation becomes instead a private act to which the reader does not have access. While one may be able to present a line of argument in analytical cases, it is unlikely to be very convincing in the absence of the visual evidence. Nevertheless, there is usually a predominance of text over images. Indeed, the analytical mode is in many respects the struggle for control of words over images.

The final category refers to those examples where the image, or more likely sequence of images, is explicitly designed to convey an argument. The paradigmatic example is the photo-essay, presented with minimal or no text. However, this is not necessary to the definition; sequences of images can be woven together with text, but nevertheless making an independent argument. It may be an argument that reinforces what is presented in text or it may not. Either way, in these cases the images have autonomy from the textual component, and if the images were taken away there would quite simply be nothing to discuss. There is no requirement that the 'author' of the visual argument needs to be the person who made the images; visual arguments can take many different forms. In a visual research context, argumentational examples are less common, though my point here is precisely that visual scholars should become more conversant with this potential. One should not forget of course that visual practitioners, photographers, filmmakers and so on, have always worked with images as their primary means of communication. Visual scholars can learn a great deal from looking at the work of those who work predominantly with pictures. Referring to the work of Robert Frank and Walker Evans, Howard Becker urges researchers to pay attention to the work of 'photographers who never pretended to be social scientists but who we would do well to claim as our own' (2004: 196). And, alongside classics such as John Berger and Jean Mohr's (1975) *A Seventh Man*, I would add Susan Meiselas's (2008) *Kurdistan: In the Shadow of History* and Susan Schwartzenberg's (2005b) *Becoming Citizens: Family Life and the Politics of Disability*, as notable examples that exist in the fertile territory between research and practice.[5]

These distinctions are intended to help think about the use of images in the publication of visual research rather than providing a definitive typology. The reader will no doubt be able to point to examples that bridge categories or that cannot easily be fitted into any particular one. That is fine; in fact, it is an important observation. The more sensitive one becomes to the complexity of images, the more one realizes they operate on multiple levels simultaneously, and in the spaces in between. Photographs that serve as descriptive illustrations in the context of an ethnography may, by virtue of their qualities as photographs and the way they are presented, also make an argument that has an ethical or humanistic dimension, seeking to expand the moral imagination of the viewer. Equally, images can migrate between categories. For example, ethnographic photographs originally understood and used principally as descriptive illustrations may later be subject to an analysis which directs attention to the form of the photograph, the way subjects are posed, and so on, in order to comment on the dynamics of cross-cultural encounters. The same photographs could be recontextualized with other images to make a visual argument about the complicity of photography with colonialism, or appropriated to construct counter narratives. In other words, the three categories—illustration, analysis, and argument—are not fixed qualities of the images themselves but relate to the way they are deployed.

The point of course is to consider these different potentialities when putting together a paper or structuring a presentation. At this point it might be useful to look at a few examples.[6]

SOME REPRESENTATIVE EXAMPLES

Danny Hoffman's (2007) paper on the environment around Freetown, Sierra Leone, is interesting for the way in which it combines two distinctly different uses of photography: one illustrative, the other offering a sophisticated visual argument. Hoffman's research in Sierra Leone was an ethnographic study of participants in the civil war, including an examination of the way the conflict had been 'inscribed on the landscape' (104). Photography was an aspect of the methodology and Hoffman made many images of his informants, ex-combatants making their living on the margins of Freetown. In the published paper, these images served an illustrative purpose, drawing on a conventional notion of documentary realism. We decided therefore to situate these images in a direct relation to the text, making them one-column width, within the two-column journal page layout, giving them short descriptive captions and including reference to them at the appropriate point as Figure 1, Figure 2, and so on. The second type of image used within the paper was, by contrast, a self-conscious attempt to find a visual form which represented 'the impact of the expansion of the urban periphery on the surrounding forest,' in a context where 'visual tropes of clear cutting and deforestation are by now so familiar that they lack any explanatory or interventionist authority' (104). In contrast to documentary realism, and drawing on West African notions of representation and aesthetics, Hoffman sought a way of representing the landscape through absence, presenting 'a vision of the disappeared that avoids the standard visual tropes of environmental degradation' (112). Readers will need to turn to the paper if they want to explore the argument more closely. For my purposes, here, the important point concerns the organization and placement of the images within the paper. Rather than placed within the text, these six photographs run parallel with it, each image centered on the page, with titles rather than descriptive captions. The reader is of course meant to switch back and forth between the images and the text, but the relationship is not one of pointing to what is *in* the image, rather it is an invitation for a more imaginative engagement *with* the image and, by extension, the environment it represents. The success of the visual strategy is something readers can judge for themselves. My main point here is to emphasize the different uses to which images may be put, and how this demands careful thinking about presentation. In the above case, the illustrative and argumentational use of images was clearly differentiated; the two sets of images serve different purposes and were presented in a way that emphasized this

point. However, the distinction is not always so clear.

Annette Kuhn's (2007) article on photography and cultural memory provides an example where these dimensions are present in relation to a single image. The paper considers as a case study a single family photograph brought to a photography and memory workshop by a Chinese man recently moved to Britain. In terms of the above categories, we would probably class this as primarily analytical in its relation to the image, though it goes beyond a simple semiotic or deconstructive reading. Kuhn's approach to the image is multi-layered and collaborative, involving what she describes as an 'interactive performative viewing' (290), paying attention not only to the people and spaces depicted but also to what is absent from the image and the memories it evoked. The way in which a single image can open onto an extended discussion about history and memory should be acknowledged, but I want to make a narrower point about presentation. With the permission of Kuhn's collaborator, the owner of the photograph, the image was reproduced in the published paper. The final reproduction involved not just the facing side of the photograph but also the reverse, with its short inscription in Chinese script and a date. Both sides of the image were shown against a black ground in order to include the patterned edge of the photographic print within the frame. The choice to present the photograph in this way was to emphasis its materiality, its qualities as an object, one that Kuhn's interlocutor had carried with him since he was a young man. The image was also presented without a caption, acknowledging that a single explanation could never be adequate to the multiple and complex narratives and emotions the photograph called forth. The careful attention to presentation in the paper proposes important methodological arguments concerning what photographs are and the complex meanings they carry.[7]

In publications from my own research I have tried to develop the use of images as a means of making arguments alongside, but nevertheless independent of, the written word. In my book on South African photography during the apartheid period (Newbury, 2009), I made a conscious decision not to make direct reference to the images in the text in the conventional form (such as Figure 1, and so on), though the images were given detailed captions. Although my study was an historical and analytical one, I wanted to deliberately undermine the certainty of a linear directional relationship from text to image. My intention was to emphasize the autonomy of the sequence of images that ran throughout the book. The aim was to have a set of images in dialog with the text, not merely providing illustrations, although they do serve as illustrations in many cases too. Images discussed specifically were on the same page or, where the practical constraints of layout did not allow this, close by the relevant text. At some points the image serves a relatively straightforward role as illustration or object of analysis, at others the images are intended to convey a point not explicitly discussed. For example, at the end of one chapter, a magazine page spread showing a photograph of the funeral that followed the Sharpeville Massacre is juxtaposed with a musician seated at a piano. The visual echo of the row of coffins in the piano keyboard was intended to summarize one of the themes of the chapter, which counter-posed the oppression of the apartheid state with culture as a form of resistance and escape.[8]

The lengthy format of a book also allows one to exploit the potential of sequences and repetition, with earlier images becoming repositioned by later ones. One of my interests was in examining the visual repertoire that developed to depict South African society during this period. Funerals were a recurring feature in this repertoire, and the book includes several images of funerals, the earliest of which is a mock funeral performed as a protest against forced removals. The point of including a number of such images was not simply to show what the images depict, but to indicate that funerals were consciously

attended to as opportunities for performative protest, with visual documentation itself an important component. I also intended that readers should recognize the history of photographic practices.

Another book-length example is Caroline Knowles and Doug Harper's (2009) collaboration on migration in Hong Kong. Harper's photographs run through the book in parallel with Knowles' text narrating the life stories of her informants. The photographs serve a variety of purposes. At times they are illustrative. The portraits, sometimes expressive, other times uncertain, give an identity to the names and voices that populate the text. The visual presence echoes the qualitative narrative approach and the focus on individual life stories. More often they go beyond illustration, bringing the reader closer to the subject matter and providing a vicarious experience of the ordinary spaces people inhabit, the views available to those who live on the high peaks, the bustling spaces where people shop and Statue Square where Filipino maids congregate on their day off.[9] Occasionally, they offer the reader glimpses of the research process, when they show Knowles engaged in interviews with her informants. The images are not captioned, something which would have interrupted their flow and placed a textual barrier between the reader and her visual engagement with the urban landscape. They operate in parallel to the text, providing an alternative means of appreciating the texture and quality of daily life, and reflexively situating the research.

Visual Studies also publishes visual essays, where the images are intended to convey an argument independently of text. In the introduction to a special issue on the visible curriculum, Eric Margolis brought together a diverse selection of historical images of school settings taken at various points in the twentieth century (Margolis, 2007). These 'visible traces' of school life were intended to prompt questions in the mind of the viewer, for example, about 'the arrangement of student and teacher bodies within the spaces of the built environment of the school' or about the 'performance of social order' (2007: 11). Presented on the page without captions (these are available at the end of the visual essay), the viewer's attention is steered toward visual and spatial concerns within the images, and to contrasts and similarities between different settings. Garvens' (2009) photo-essay offers another example. In this case the images were not found historical images, but the result of a photographic documentary project. Taken in prosthetics laboratories and clinics, the photographs represent a striking and aesthetically powerful record made during quiet moments, when the spaces were devoid of human activity. In an understated way they signify the intimate work of bodily repair that follows terrible acts of violence or occasions of human misfortune. A selection of the images were reproduced one to a page without captions, prefaced by a brief description of the project, and followed by a captions list giving title, date, and location. The space given to the images, the careful selection, the placement of textual elements and, in this case, the opportunity to reproduce the images in color are all-important to the final result. This example returns us to the idea discussed above of an expanded territory encompassing and combining research and visual practice.

SUGGESTIONS FOR AUTHORS

With these examples in mind, I now want to turn attention to some of the practical questions and decisions that need to be made in putting together a visually based submission. As is equally true when putting together any academic presentation, this is a question of both strategy and tactics. At the strategic level one should consider what individual or combination of purposes the images are intended to serve in the specific context of presentation. One must also consider how much work to ask of the reader. Howard Becker (2002) draws a contrast between analytical studies such as those by Bruno Latour,

where the text explicitly directs the attention of the reader to evidence within the image, and the strategy used in John Berger and Jean Mohr's *A Seventh Man*, where 'the authors present a lot of material and leave it to us to connect it all' (2002: 6). There is a natural inclination in academic studies toward the control offered by the former, but this can risk reducing the image to its explanation, rendering it redundant, or duplicating in text what the image does with greater elegance or economy. It may also be in the space between the images, and between images and viewer, that meaning is most productively created. This demands greater consideration of the audience and their prior knowledge than is typical of academic publishing, but perhaps that is no bad thing, especially for a field of study that crosses boundaries between theory and practice as well as between disciplines.

One may want to alert the reader in advance to the approach that has been adopted. In the now classic *Ways of Seeing*, first published nearly 40 years ago, John Berger was sufficiently uncertain about his readers' preparedness that he prefaced the book with a 'Note to the reader' (Berger, 1972). He explains that 'the form of the book is as much to do with our purpose as the arguments contained within it', and, aware that some may find the visual essays particularly challenging, comments explicitly on this strategy:

> Four of the essays use words and images, three of them use only images. These purely pictorial essays are intended to raise as many questions as the verbal essays. Sometimes in the pictorial essays no information at all is given about the images reproduced because it seemed to us that such information might distract from the points being made. (1972: 5)

It is irrelevant whether current academic audiences need this kind of prior instruction, though I think it may be more necessary than some of us would like to concede.

How many images should you include? This is rather like asking how long is a piece of string, but there are some considerations that can help set parameters. There may be practical reasons why certain images are not available to reproduce or ethical reasons why use may not be appropriate. The ubiquity of visual images in contemporary culture and the increasing ease, through the last century and into this one, with which images can be circulated and reproduced, seems like a free gift to the visual research community. No longer is it necessary to search out visual material in remote locations or dusty archives; it is all there ready and available for us to use. Except, that is, until it comes to publication. At this point our abandonment in the playground of visual culture suddenly turns sour, to be replaced by concerns about who owns the images we are looking at, and how much they might charge us to use them to illustrate a book or paper, if they allow us to use them at all.

Melinda Hinkson's (2009) article in *Visual Studies* on the removal, by police, of several of Bill Henson's artworks from a gallery in Sydney presents an interesting case. The accusation that led to the images being removed was that they constituted a form of child pornography; the article explores the cultural attitudes revealed by the debate surrounding this incident. It had been the author's intention that the article would include the image at the center of the scandal, both in its original form and in the manipulated form in which it was reproduced in the media and circulated on the Internet. However, images, as original works, are under copyright, and it was clear that we would need permission of the copyright holder, in this case the artist.[10] It could be argued that there was a second copyright in the manipulated image, if it were considered a new work in its own right (though given that the media agencies making these alterations doubtless did so without the artist's permission, this exercised me less). Unfortunately, while under normal circumstances the artist may well have granted permission, given the furor, the artist and gallery were understandably cautious. As a result the journal was unable to reproduce the image. Although the article, as published, was not able to present a key piece of evidence under discussion,

the easy availability of the image on the Internet meant that this was much less of a problem than would otherwise have been the case.

Alexander Riley's (2008) piece on narratives surrounding the crash of United Airlines Flight 93 presented a similar issue. One image, dubbed 'The End of Serenity,' taken shortly after the crash shows what might be described as a 'country postcard' scene, except for the dark cloud hovering over the landscape. Although the image was, and still is, widely available online, the woman who took the photograph was unwilling to grant formal permission to the journal. It was decided, therefore, to omit the image, provide a brief description and refer readers to where they may view the image on the Internet. In some cases it might be argued that images available on the Internet should be regarded as fair game for visual researchers. However, given the controversy around these images, we felt the circumstances weighed against such arguments.[11] Margaret Godel's (2007) study of stillbirth memorial websites raised similar issues, but in this case the additional work of contacting website creators for permission was largely successful. It is worth stating at this point that I regard the additional work of contacting image-makers and seeking permissions as an essential, and indeed informative, part of visual scholarship. One of my complaints as an editor is that many visual researchers have yet to fully grasp this point.

For quite different reasons, Jamie Joanou chose not to include any illustrations for her article on the ethics of participatory photography with young people living and working on the streets of Lima, Peru. It is worth quoting her rationale for this decision:

I have purposefully chosen not to publish the photographs discussed in this article as their publication may compromise the dignity of the participants involved. Furthermore, while it is possible to conceal participants' identities through the use of blurring techniques, it is my concern that these techniques serve to objectify and dishonor those they aim to protect. (2009: 222)

The potential impact on participants, and the perception of these images by others, has to be considered alongside the importance of images to the argument being made. In this case, the balance weighed in favor of omitting the images. In other cases, the argument may go a different way, and, furthermore, one might want to consider the role of participants in the decisions about which images to include and which to omit. Like Joanou, I find the blurring of faces an unsatisfactory approach, in most cases.[12] A key aspect of caring for images is thinking about when they should and should not be shown, and understanding the process for arriving at such decisions.[13]

One could make a strategic decision not to provide any images, as Joanou did. This might seem a somewhat perverse suggestion in the context of this chapter, but maybe it is not. Although she discussed specific photographs and photographers, Susan Sontag deliberately chose not to include any reproductions in *On Photography* (1979). The publisher had originally wanted to include images, but she was quite clear that she did not want to produce an illustrated book. One consequence of this strategy is to bring into play more of the reader's own mental stock of images, highly appropriate for Sontag's sophisticated reflections on the place of photography in modern society. My own reasons for not illustrating the examples I discuss in this chapter are twofold. First, I am asking the reader to consider the use of images in the context of published papers; extracting them from that context necessarily renders them less useful for my purposes. Second, as I am trying to encourage the reader to think critically about the uses of images in academic publications in general, rather than making a specific point about any one use, it serves my purposes better to ask readers to go and analyze these and other examples for themselves.

There may be limitations of the kind discussed above, or issues such as cost (academic authors are almost invariably responsible for permission fees), or perhaps some of the images you might want to include may simply not be available at the right quality for reproduction.[14] Assuming you are including images, from my perspective as both an author of visually based research texts, and as the editor of a journal dedicated to publishing visual studies, there are three main issues to consider.

First, determine which images will be selected: it does not follow that because you have plenty of images you should use them all. A small, but well-chosen, set of images is better than a large, unfocused selection. Images are no different than text in that respect. It is best to leave out images that, while striking or interesting in some way, do not move your discussion forward. Occam's razor is just as useful in visual research as anywhere else. For each image included, ask yourself what purpose it serves, how it develops or provides evidence for the overall argument. You might also want to reflect on how familiar your reader is likely to be with the images you are using. If they are likely to be very familiar then you can be more selective, choosing just those that are key to the discussion, leaving readers to call on their knowledge of the image world to fill in the context. If the images have not been reproduced before or are of an unusual kind, then you may want a slightly larger selection so that the reader can grasp the corpus of material you are dealing with.

Second, consider sequencing: here I am referring to internal relationships within the selected images—how they are ordered and so on. There may be a natural order suggested by the images themselves; they may be placed chronologically for example. Alternatively, you may want to consider thematic groupings. You may wish to juxtapose two images to make or reinforce a particular point, or there may be themes that recur through a longer selection of images.[15] And, of course, the sizing of images can be a way of signaling relative importance. All of these concerns will affect how you wish the images to appear in a final published version, even if some of these things may eventually be outside your control (this depends very much on the individual journal or publisher).

Third, attend to the pace of the images in relation to text, giving careful consideration to the movement of the reader's attention between the images and text. Should all images discussed in the text be included and vice versa? The answer, of course, is it depends what you are trying to do. Yes, if your text is a detailed analysis of a small number if images, or if descriptive illustrations are needed to convey to readers the social scene you are discussing. No, if you are making an argument through images. Where images are discussed in the text, it is often ideal to have them placed on the relevant pages. However, there may be instances where you want readers to see the image before they read about it, or to read before they see. Within practical constraints, authors should consider how much or how little they want to try to direct the reader's attention. There may be tension here between the desires of the author, and the practical and aesthetic considerations of importance to those finalizing the layout. Production staff are not always used to accommodating input from scholars with a visual imagination.

As discussed in a number of the examples above, there are times when one wants to make the reader look carefully at the images *as images*. In such cases conventional figure references and, sometimes, even captions are a distraction (see Becker, 2002: 5). Captions, those infamous textual anchors, are an important consideration. There is the question I have already touched upon of whether captions should be placed alongside each individual image, or, as in the photo-essay examples (and, incidentally, Berger's (1972) *Ways of Seeing*), offered for readers to consult separately from the visual presentation. Or whether they should be used at all. Elizabeth Chaplin (2006) argues provocatively that they are a positivist anachronism: an attempt, doomed to failure perhaps, to wield the power of words over images.

But, assuming one sees some value in captioning, there are still plenty of questions to

be answered. As a photographic historian, I am inclined to argue for the application of the same degree of rigor and transparency to the referencing of images as is expected in the referencing of manuscript sources or academic literature: where was the image made, when, by whom, and so on. Knowing where an image has been sourced can also give an insight into the circulation of images as objects, and may be of more than incidental interest. There are of course instances where it is appropriate to use images with little or no provenance, considering them purely in their capacity as images: for example, there is an increasing interest in photographs that have been removed from their original contexts and sold through online auction sites. Nevertheless, such information as is available can provide valuable insights for the reader. And I would endorse Susan Bielstein's (2006) plea for authors to provide greater transparency about the costs of image reproduction in their captions (160). The position of academics in the economy of images often seems absent from the discussion, and the notion of 'fair use' is often invoked as an argument for their freedom to reproduce images as they see fit (for further discussion of issues related to the 'fair use' of images, see Chapter 37 in this volume). However, it can sometimes be an excuse for laziness, a reason for not engaging with those responsible for their creation and dissemination, or with the dynamics of a complex economy of images. There is a vast difference between a young African photographer and the Reuters media empire, and academics are not always powerless players in this world, despite what they might claim. The neglect of these issues on the part of visual scholars seems curious; it is hard to believe that researchers would take a similar attitude to the provenance of textual or numeric data.

Images can acquire different kinds of captions at various stages in their lives, for example, text written on a photograph, or a descriptive catalog entry if the image is from a collection. Participants may have commented on an image during the process of research, in effect giving it a verbal caption which could serve equally well in a published context. It is important to be clear about the status of the words appended to an image. Often the least satisfactory captions are those which try to describe the image, which may simply be redundant unless the intention is to save the reader the bother of looking, or those which try and over-determine the way the image is read.[16] It can be appropriate, however, to draw the reader's attention to particular elements within the image or to aspects of its construction.

Corinne Kratz (2002) describes the careful consideration that lay behind the multi-layered captions that evolved as she created and then toured her exhibition of photographs of the Okiek people from Kenya's forested highlands.[17] Each image is accompanied by two sets of captions: the first set, in Kiswahili and English, is descriptive, naming those in the image and providing sufficient cultural context to understand what is going on; the second set, in Okiek and English, is drawn from conversations by Okiek people viewing the images, with the occasional involvement of Kratz herself. Attention was paid to tone, the use of personal names, and the impact of multiple languages on Western as well as Kenyan audiences. Kratz's reflections bring to the surface the complex decision-making process behind apparently simple captions (2002: 124–129) and provides an exemplary model for visual researchers.

In practice, there are often trade-offs between the number of images, their sequencing and how they relate to the text. It may be difficult to bring the selection of images into an ideal relationship to the written discussion. If you refer to several images within a paragraph or two, then it is likely to be impractical to have the images appear on the same page, unless they are reproduced very small. Which takes priority here, the images or the text? That has to be a decision made in relation to the specific aims of any particular presentation; but as something of a corrective, where there is doubt, I tend to give the benefit to the images. In my experience as editor of *Visual Studies*, authors do not always give sufficient thought to these issues, leaving me guessing at the author's intention, and sometimes getting it wrong.

SUMMARY DISCUSSION

My intention in this chapter has been to demonstrate that, despite its frequent reduction to narrow or technical considerations, careful attention to the use of images in published research is a fundamental component of visual scholarship, and opens onto philosophical, methodological, and ethical questions at the very heart of visual studies. Visual scholarship demands that we treat images with the same seriousness and rigor as we apply to other materials with which we work. It insists that we think carefully about what images are and how they may be used to communicate ideas and make arguments. It asks us to observe a duty of care to images, considering the ethical and political dimensions of our own uses, and our place in the image economy. Attention to these things not only makes for better research presentations, but also, I believe, contributes to a more thoughtful and reflective research practice.

I want to end with a piece of practical advice, borrowed from Howard Becker: 'The way to proceed is not to reason from methodological principles but to look at books and articles that seem to be what [you] would like to produce and work out what they have done right' (2004: 196). I hope I have given a few tools and ways of thinking that will help visual scholars to do this working out, and which will prove useful as they shape their own visual arguments.

NOTES

1 For a discussion of this idea in relation to design education, see Moore (2010).

2 For further discussion of this approach to cultural artifacts, see Appadurai (1988).

3 *Visual Studies* has recently begun to publish review essays in the area of new media to track the opportunities for visual research they provide. See also Coover (2004) and www.roderickcoover.com.

4 I include here the contextual analysis of images, which are central to sociological and anthropological accounts, not simply analyses of a semiotic or art historical kind.

5 An excerpt from Schwartzenberg's book was first published in *Visual Studies* (2005a). On Meiselas, see my review of the second edition of *Kurdistan* in *Visual Studies* 24(1).

6 The reader may find it useful to assemble some of the examples I reference here to look at alongside my discussion.

7 See Barr (2009) for another example of this approach to presentation.

8 The pianist was Dollar Brand (later Abdullah Ibrahim) who, along with many other musicians, went into exile in the 1960s in the wake of Sharpeville.

9 Within the categories I have discussed this might be considered a heightened form of illustration, rather than categorically distinct.

10 Susan Bielstein (2006) provides an excellent and very practical discussion of copyright and image permissions, although as the text mainly draws on art historical examples, it does not cover all of the territory traversed by visual studies scholars.

11 The notion of 'fair use' is often invoked in discussions of which images visual scholars can use, not always appropriately in my view. I do not have the space to develop this point here but I think this deserves greater debate within the field. One also has to be aware of the policies of publishers, some of whom regard the relatively untested legal grounds of 'fair use' with extreme caution.

12 In contrast to anonymizing participants as a default position in sociology, Paul Sweetman (2009) has proposed the idea of 'an ethics of recognition.'

13 The International Visual Sociology Association (IVSA) Code of Research Ethics includes the following advice: 'When publishing or exhibiting visual material researchers take account of research participants' interests and proceed in accordance with the consent they have been given by image creators, image owners, and subjects who are visually represented' (Papademas and IVSA, 2009: 257).

14 Images culled from the web are rarely of sufficient resolution to be reproduced in print, although there may be circumstances where the significance of the content trumps any concerns over image quality. It is not my main concern here, but technical considerations are nevertheless important. The resolution required for print reproduction is normally 300 ppi (pixels per inch), whereas the standard for screen viewing is only 72 ppi. Importantly, one also needs to bear in mind the size the image is to appear on the page: a digital image that is 300 ppi at postage stamp size will lose resolution if its size is increased. And while image software programs make it possible to resample an image at a higher resolution, this rarely helps: one cannot put back quality which is not there in the original file. The most common formats are TIFF and JPEG. TIFF is a more stable format and retains a greater degree of quality than JPEG, which compresses the image each time it is saved (making for smaller file sizes).

15 Juxtaposition is perhaps one of the most basic forms of visual argument and has a long history, with which visual researchers might wish to become better acquainted. One pleasurable starting point might be Stefan Lorant's use of images in the British illustrated magazine *Lilliput* (see Lorant, 1940).

16 In the context of image databases, descriptive captions which attempt to duplicate the visual content of the image do of course play a valuable role in enabling them to be found using keyword searches.

17 Kratz's book is an exemplary extended study of communication through the photographic exhibition form and there are many insights here that could be equally applied to the use of photographs in print or web-based publication.

REFERENCES

Appadurai, Arjun (ed.) (1988) *The Social Life of Things: Commodities in Cultural Perspective*. Cambridge, MA: Cambridge University Press.

Barr, Mary (2009) 'The alchemy of the photograph', *Visual Studies*, 24(1): 66–70.

Becker, Howard (2002) 'Visual evidence: *A Seventh Man*, the specified generalization and the work of the reader', *Visual Studies*, 17(1): 3–11.

Becker, Howard (2004) 'Photography as evidence, photographs as exposition', in C. Knowles and P. Sweetman (eds.), *Picturing the Social Landscape: Visual Methods and the Sociological Imagination*. London: Routledge. pp. 193–197.

Berger, John (1972) *Ways of Seeing*. London and Harmondsworth: The British Broadcasting Corporation and Penguin Books.

Berger, John and Jean Mohr (1975) *A Seventh Man: A Book of Images and Words about the Experience of Migrant Workers in Europe*. Harmondsworth: Penguin Books.

Bielstein, Susan (2007) *Permissions, a Survival Guide: Blunt Talk about Art as Intellectual Property*. Chicago, IL: University of Chicago Press.

Chaplin, Elizabeth (2006) 'The convention of captioning: W. G. Sebald and the release of the captive image', *Visual Studies*, 21(1): 42–53.

Coover, Roderick (2004) 'Using digital media tools in cross-cultural research, analysis and representation', *Visual Studies*, 19(1): 6–25

Duff, Wilson (1975) *Images Stone B.C.: Thirty Centuries of Northwest Coast Indian Sculpture*. Saanichton, BC: Hancock House.

Garvens, Ellen (2009) 'Making devices', *Visual Studies*, 24(3): 188–201.

Gell, Alfred (1998) *Art and Agency: An Anthropological Theory*. Oxford: Oxford University Press.

Godel, Margaret (2007) 'Images of stillbirth: memory, mourning and memorial', *Visual Studies*, 22(3): 253–269.

Grady, John (2006) 'Edward Tufte and the promise of a visual social science', in L. Pauwels (ed.), *Visual Cultures of Science*. Hanover, NE: University Press of New England. pp. 222–265.

Hinkson, Melinda (2009) 'Australia's Bill Henson scandal: Notes on the new cultural attitude to images', *Visual Studies*, 24(3): 202–213.

Hoffman, Danny (2007) 'The Disappeared: Images of the environment at Freetown's urban margins', *Visual Studies*, 22(2): 104–119.

Joanou, Jamie (2009) 'The bad and the ugly: Ethical concerns in participatory photographic methods with children living and working on the streets of Lima, Peru', *Visual Studies*, 24(3): 214–223.

Knowles, Caroline and Douglas Harper (2009) *Hong Kong: Migrant Lives, Landscapes and Journeys*. Chicago, IL: Chicago University Press.

Kratz, Corinne A (2002) *The Ones That Are Wanted: Communication and the Politics of Representation in a Photographic Exhibition*. Berkeley, CA: University of California Press.

Kuhn, Annette (2007) 'Photography and cultural memory: A methodological exploration', *Visual Studies*, 22(3): 283–292.

Lorant, Stefan (1940) *Chamberlain and the Beautiful Llama and 101 More Juxtapositions*. London: Hulton Press.

Margolis, Eric (2007) 'Guest editor's introduction (Special Issue: The Visible Curriculum)', *Visual Studies*, 22(1): 2–12.

Meiselas, Susan (2008) *Kurdistan: In the Shadow of History*. Chicago, IL: Chicago University Press.

Moore, Kathryn (2010) *Overlooking the Visual: Demystifying the Art of Design*. London: Routledge.

Newbury, Darren (2009) *Defiant Images: Photography and Apartheid South Africa*. Pretoria: University of South Africa (UNISA) Press.

Papademas, Diana and the International Visual Sociology Association (2009) 'IVSA Code of Research Ethics and Guidelines', *Visual Studies*, 24(3): 250–257.

Riley, Alexander (2008) 'On the role of images in the construction of narratives about the crash of United Airlines Flight 93', *Visual Studies*, 23(1): 4–19.

Sartre, Jean-Paul (2006) 'Description', in S. Manghani, A. Piper and J. Simons (eds.), *Images: A Reader*. London: Sage Publications. pp. 134–137.

Schwartzenberg, Susan (2005a) 'The personal archive as historical record', *Visual Studies*, 20(1): 70–82.

Schwartzenberg, Susan (2005b) *Becoming Citizens: Family Life and the Politics of Disability*. Seattle, WA: University of Washington Press.

Sontag, Susan (1979) *On Photography*. Harmondsworth: Penguin Books.

Sweetman, Paul (2009) 'Towards an ethics of recognition? Issues of ethics and anonymity in visual research'. Paper presented at the 1st International Visual Methods Conference, University of Leeds.

35

Making a 'Case': Applying Visual Sociology to Researching Eminent Domain

Brian Gran

INTRODUCTION

In Lakewood, Ohio, Jim and JoAnn Saleet stood up to City Hall in a fight against an attempt to 'take,' by *eminent domain*,[1] their family home (see Figure 35.1) (Harden, 2003; Leung, 2004). The beautiful house had been labeled 'blighted' by the city but visual evidence, including photographs in newspapers and a broadcast by the television program *60 Minutes*, was crucial in Lakewood's decision to back down, giving up the attempt to take the property.

An eminent domain application in Connecticut, on the other hand, made its way to the US Supreme Court. In an infamous decision, the court decided against the home owners. Visual evidence in this case, *Kelo v. City of New London* (2005) (herein *Kelo*) failed to prevail in establishing the right of eminent domain. Suzette Kelo's home was located in a middle-class, safe neighborhood in New London. In its decision in this case, the US Supreme Court ruled that a city government could use eminent domain law to take and sell Suzette Kelo's house to a private developer in the hopes of achieving higher tax revenue from redevelopment (see Figure 35.2). *Kelo* stands for the proposition that the government can legitimately force a family to sell their home to a private entity that promises, but cannot guarantee, economic development and tax revenue. That recent interpretation of eminent domain law was regarded as a significant departure for eminent domain law (Rutkow, 2006; cf Cohen, 2006).

Less than 5 years after the Supreme Court made the *Kelo* decision, the Pfizer Corporation (Pfizer), which had promised to build on the site where the Kelo home (and others) had been, withdrew their presence from New London. Now, the area where the Kelo home once stood can now be characterized as blighted (see Figure 35.3) (McGeehan, 2009).

In this chapter, I will show how visual evidence, as depicted by a photograph, has been important in a variety of legal cases.

Figure 35.1   Exterior of Saleet home, Lakewood, Ohio. *60 Minutes*/AP

Visual sociology can be an effective approach to showing that the *Kelo* case did not result in a watershed change in socio-legal relations. Neither *Kelo*, nor the Saleet case, resulted in a *fait accompli*.

Cases are essential to the work of lawyers and social scientists, but the definitions of what cases are differ. Lawyers must often prove a case for their client to win. A social scientist studies a case to answer a research question. But what is a 'case'? In studying what a case is, social scientists and lawyers can learn from each other, and by applying sociological notions of what a case is, visual sociology can be used effectively to document different types of cases as they move from one type to the other.

This chapter will first consider sociological case studies. It will then contrast these discussions with the ways that lawyers understand what a legal case is generally, and then focus on eminent domain cases specifically.

Applying visual sociology approaches, I will identify important changes in eminent domain over the last 150 years, with uneven results, and I will use US eminent domain laws to argue that visual sociology can contribute to discussions of what a case is in important ways.

AN OVERVIEW OF VISUAL SOCIOLOGY OF LAW

Social scientists have long made important contributions to studies of law, legal systems and structures, legal actors, and other issues of law and society (Tocqueville, 1835, 1840/2004; Weber, 1922/1978; Black, 1976; Cotterell, 1999; Deflem, 2008), as have visual sociologists more recently (Preston, 2001; Margolis, 2004). Visual sociologists, in particular, are in a unique position to help

Figure 35.2   Exterior of Kelo home, New London, Connecticut, from the New Republic. Reproduced courtesy of Institute for Justice

Figure 35.3   Former location of Kelo home, New London, Connecticut. Maria Bernier

identify the 'public use' aspects of eminent domain, an element of great social and legal contention (Rutkow, 2006).

Visual sociology can be used to document socio-legal change, including failures of law. Changes in legal practices and inconsistent applications of law have fascinated sociologists since the work of Max Weber. In his study of socio-legal change, Weber (1922/1978) wrote that modern law produces stability and calculability, important ingredients to capitalism. Since Weber's thesis, sociologists have examined whether and how a change in law will produce a change in a socio-economic system (Boyle et al., 2001; Polletta, 2001).

Visual sociology is remarkably well suited to studies of social change (Harper, 2001; Rieger, 2003). Anthropologists as well as lawyers have turned to visual evidence to study socio-legal change, notably Richard Sherwin (Sherwin, 2007; Sherwin et al., 2007). Visual sociologists have sought to understand the meaning of photos, videos, and other visual data through study of their making and distribution, their interpretation, and their impacts. One valuable approach to visual analyses is to study photographs as a means of documenting socio-legal change. In his historical study of compulsory boarding school education imposed on Native American children around the turn of the twentieth century, Margolis (2004: 75) showed how federally mandated policies were attempts to discipline and monitor the ways that Native Americans lived and were intended to produce 'changes in the soul'. Margolis, using archival photographs and other historical documents, showed how education practices and laws at that time represented formal exertions of power and control.

In her book *Moving Politics*, Gould (2009) used photos to document the importance of human emotion for the work of social activists challenging the legal status quo. In her study of ACT UP,[2] Gould presented photographic evidence of activists challenging laws by demonstrating at political conventions and in front of the US Supreme Court and the

White House. She analyzed photographs published in magazines that were intended to encourage members of a gay community to fight back against discrimination and physical violence (Gould, 2009: 411). The militancy of ACT UP activists did produce changes in law and improved understanding of people's rights to health care, but Gould's visual study also showed the importance of emotions for sustaining a social movement like ACT UP. Riis's (1890/1971) study *How the Other Class Lives* and Lorraine Hansberry's (1964) *The Movement* functioned in similar ways.[3]

In contrast to attempts to change the law, visual sociologists have also used visual data to show ways that social actors can attempt to sidestep laws. Working with photographer Ovie Carter, Duneier (2000) used photographs to show how sidewalk vendors go about their everyday work in the face of formal and informal social controls designed to prevent sidewalk vending. One picture, for instance, shows a sidewalk vendor rummaging through people's garbage, which is a Class E misdemeanor (among other municipal violations), in the hopes of finding goods to sell (Duneier, 2000: 151). While police officers and other government officials inconsistently applied laws to the vendors, the vendors developed approaches to sidestepping law, even when they sold illegal paraphernalia. While setting up their tables in illegal locations, vendors realized police officers had more pressing issues to deal with; they also knew, however, that if they did not 'respect' the officers, their tables and goods might be confiscated (Duneier, 2000: 261).

Visual sociologists have also studied how photographs and video of the laws failure can trigger social disturbances. After a jury returned 'Not Guilty' verdicts for the police officers charged with the beating of Rodney King in Los Angeles in 1992, heightened awareness through newspaper accounts, as well as repeated airings of video taken during King's beating on TV news channels, were important ingredients contributing to public outrage and played a role in the Los Angeles riots of 1992. A particularly interesting piece of visual research (Goodwin, 2002) showed how the jury was swayed by prosecutors who had trained them in applying the 'professional vision' of police officers.

In their book *The State of Sex*, Brents et al. (2009: 2) used photographs to demonstrate how laws support different structures of what many consider anti-social activities. Through analysis of photographs of prostitutes, their state-sanctioned brothels and the neighborhoods and locations in which they are based, they sought to answer the question of why prostitution is legal in 10 Nevada counties. In the process, they found that the state used laws designed to enable Nevada to build 'a tourist industry [by] turning deviance into leisure'.

There are a range of studies such as these. Mizen (2005) asked children to keep photo diaries and helped to expose illegal working conditions. Schwartzenberg (2005) asked participants to document their efforts to establish laws protecting and promoting the rights of people with developmental disabilities. Sparrman (2006) studied ways that film was used to improve the understanding of law and its objectives. These examples not only demonstrated important contributions by visual sociologists to studies of law but also showed the varieties of cases visual sociologists of law have studied. In other words, cases of law became sociological cases of study. But how does one become the other?

WHAT IS A CASE?

In their important book *What is a Case?*, Charles Ragin and Howard Becker and their contributors (Ragin, 1992) tackled this question from a variety of perspectives. Social scientists often did not confront this question head on; rather, they assumed their case was clear cut. Ragin and Becker, however, asked social scientists to think specifically about what a case is, how it is defined, and to consider the consequences of formulating a case one way versus another (Byrne, 2009).

Diane Vaughan (1992: 175) defined cases as 'organizational forms that are analyzed regarding some social event, activity, or circumstance...'. Ragin took this notion further by creating a 'conceptual map' to help determine what a case is (Ragin, 1992: 9; Harvey, 2009).

As shown in Table 35.1, cases can be seen as general concepts, or as more specific applications.

Cases are objects When a case is an object, a researcher perceives the case as a real thing in the world already bounded—that is, as given. Cases are based in research literatures; a researcher does not strive to identify a case and its empirical boundaries (Ragin, 1992: 9–10; Vaughan, 1992). The case is general and 'conventionalized' (Ragin, 1992). For instance, a piece of private property is a fundamentally important unit to understanding the organization of capitalism and its parts, including machinery, factories, homes, and other structures. Similar to social science research, a lawyer representing a plaintiff may agree with the lawyer representing the defendant on the facts of the case, but not agree on what law applies.

Cases are conventions A case can be understood as a *construct* arising from scholarly research. For this type of case, Ragin (1992: 10) argued that researchers view a case as problematic and, therefore, the subject of

Table 35.1 Conceptual map for answers to 'What is a case?'

Understanding cases	Case conception	
	Specific	General
As empirical units	1. Cases are found	2. Cases are objects
As theoretical constructs	3. Cases are made	4. Cases are conventions

scholarly interest. In this way, researchers may find that a case, as a convention, changes over time, and ask why these changes have occurred. Thus, a researcher may investigate lines separating public from private domains because they are problematic. A turn to scholarly research on the public–private dichotomy may reveal boundary changes over time in response to changes in power or other social forces, yet the public–private boundary nevertheless influences how people see the world and do things together (Gran, 2003; Gran and Béland, 2008). Similarly, a lawyer may approach an area of law as having undergone significant change over the long term. For example, in seeking to prevent application of eminent domain law to a private property, a lawyer may identify the significant legal precedents of eminent domain to demonstrate how far eminent domain law has changed from its roots to argue that current eminent domain practices are mistakenly applied.

Cases are made   When a case is *made*, a researcher sees a case as a theoretical construct. In such a situation, a case is neither empirical nor given. Instead, a case is gradually imposed on empirical evidence as it takes shape during research (Ragin, 1992), such as in theory-building using grounded theory approaches. A lawyer representing government may argue that a piece of private property is subject to eminent domain because it is blighted. Inherent in this claim is the comparison of deteriorating, uninhabitable properties to properties in which a person can safely live.

Cases are found   When cases are *found*, researchers define and establish cases. A key part of this work is identifying boundaries. A case's boundary can change, so that a case previously found can transform into another kind of case. Douglas Harper (1992) developed the concept of community through various means, including photo-elicitation. Harper allowed participants to identify their cases of community, thereby setting the community's boundaries. For lawyers, a case may be defined by a legal question such

as an injury, a contract dispute, or employer responsibilities. For instance, a lawyer may frame a situation as an accident, establish that it was caused by negligence, and contend that the boundaries extend to the negligent actor, who should be held responsible for harm.

What is a legal case?

Lawyers studying criminal law in the USA are taught to identify and prove elements of a case ('Criminal Law,' 2010). For instance, to prove the crime of murder, a lawyer needs to prove three elements: intent, act, and causation. First, the prosecutor must show beyond a reasonable doubt that the accused premeditated on the murder, that is, had given thought to committing the murder prior to the crime ('Murder,' 2010). Second, the prosecutor must show beyond a reasonable doubt that the act of murder took place. The act is the physical action taken by the defendant resulting in a person's death. Finally, causation requires the prosecutor to show beyond a reasonable doubt that the act was the actual cause of death. Some causes of action do not inherently meet the definition of murder. However, by demonstrating a cause of action, a subject may be shown to have transformed from one kind of case to another. An example is eminent domain. Once eminent domain occurs, private property transforms into public property.

Ragin's (1992) typology of cases was an important contribution to social science research. Using visual sociology, I will discuss how eminent domain law has dramatically changed over the last 135 years in the USA, and I will raise questions for contemporary practices of eminent domain law.

EMINENT DOMAIN

The act of government-taking of private property against an owner's will for specified, legitimate government purposes with an offer of just compensation is permitted under the legal concept of 'Eminent Domain' (Nedzel and Block, 2007), and is practiced in many countries (McCarthy, 2005). In the USA, eminent domain receives legal support from the Fifth Amendment to the US Constitution, which reads, in part, '...nor shall private property be taken for public use, without just compensation.' Eminent domain is often considered an inherent governmental power, even without legislation saying so. The State, however, must follow due process to appropriate the property, often by taking private property through a condemnation proceeding. The State can only take property for public uses and it must compensate the property owner(s). The courts usually defer to the legislative branch in deciding what a 'public use' is.

Contemporary controversies surrounding eminent domain revolve around what actually constitutes legitimate public uses. The concept of legitimacy has dramatically changed over time, from an idea of universal availability, to a well-defined direct public benefit, and more recently, to include potential or indirect public benefit (Kotlyarevskaya, 2006).

A VISUAL ANALYSIS OF EMINENT DOMAIN

Visual sociology can identify different kinds of cases: *object*, *found*, *made*, or *constructed*. My analysis of cases will center on the public purpose of eminent domain legal cases in the USA. Recall that the elements of eminent domain are:

- government taking;
- of private property;
- without owner's permission;
- for public purpose; and
- with just compensation.

A case can change from made to found

Visual data have played important roles in recent eminent domain cases. In one case,

photographs and video were reasons for why eminent domain failed. In another case in which eminent domain was applied, photographs demonstrate law's failure. These two cases are also examples of how a case can transition from a case that is *made* to a case that is *found*. In Lakewood, Ohio, a suburb of Cleveland, the municipal government attempted to make a case of blight apply to a home for purposes of applying eminent domain (Sartin, 2002). Lakewood is the third most populous city in Cuyahoga County, with Cleveland the first. Its proximity to Cleveland gives it an urban feel, but its middle-class population consists of young professionals, families, and residents who have raised their families in Lakewood.

For its eminent domain plans, the city government's stated goal was an indefinite public use. In 2002, the city government of Lakewood had issued a 'community development plan,' the object of which was to build new condominiums, shops, and businesses, from which the city would obtain increased tax revenues. The plan included finding that a neighborhood in the city was blighted according to Lakewood law (Sartin, 2002). This law designated a property as blighted if, among other factors, it did not have a two-car garage attached to the home; if it did not have at least two full bathrooms; if it had fewer than three bedrooms; if the home was less than 1400 square feet; and if the home's yard was smaller than 5000 square feet. According to the Institute for Justice, a libertarian organization involved in eminent domain and other public–private issues, if these characteristics were followed, a majority of Lakewood homes would have been labeled 'blighted,' including those of the then-mayor and some city council members (Institute for Justice, n.d.).

The Saleets were adamant that their home, and those of their neighbors, should not be subject to eminent domain. Many of the people there had lived in their homes for nearly 40 years when the city government started eminent domain action. Homes in the neighborhood were well-maintained, crime was not a problem, and the nearby business community was strong. A picture of the Saleet home shows a well-maintained, attractive, middle-class home (see Figure 35.4).

The city's attempt to use eminent domain to take possession of over 50 properties resulted in a powerful backlash. Articles on the Lakewood case were published in Cleveland-area newspapers, including in the *Plain Dealer*. It was pictures of the Saleets and their home in an article in the *Plain Dealer* that attracted the attention of the Institute of Justice, a libertarian interest group, to the Lakewood case ('How the West End was Won,' 2004). Their campaign against the city's eminent domain action not only consisted of legal filings but also organizing events such as picnics and candlelight vigils.

Reports of the Lakewood eminent domain effort and pictures of homes were also featured in national newspapers such as the *Washington Post*. These photos raised doubts about how the Lakewood municipal government was applying eminent domain (Harden, 2003). An important turn was when the television show *60 Minutes* featured the Lakewood story on 28 September 2003. Mike Wallace of *60 Minutes* interviewed the Saleets in their home, showing its excellent condition and beauty (Leung, 2004). Wallace then interviewed the mayor of Lakewood, Madeline Cain, who admitted that even her home did not meet Lakewood's eminent domain standards. After the *60 Minutes* story, Lakewood voters rejected the proposed development, eventually removed the 'blight' label from homes in the Saleets' neighborhood, and voted Mayor Cain out of office. According to Mrs Saleet, the *60 Minutes* publicity was the turning point in the battle against application of eminent domain in Lakewood.

Visual evidence not only can reveal abject failures of eminent domain law but also can challenge legal rationales for contemporary approaches to eminent domain law.

Figure 35.4 Interior of Saleet home, Lakewood, Ohio. Author

Around the same time as the Lakewood eminent domain case, steps were being taken in other cities in the USA to apply eminent domain to private homes. Among the most prominent eminent domain cases was one that resulted in the US Supreme Court case, *Kelo v. City of New London*, 545 US 649 (2005). Unlike the Saleet case, in *Kelo* private properties were taken by the State. The US Supreme Court decided a city could appropriate private property for a public purpose, even if that private property was to be used, at best, for an indefinite public purpose (Benedict, 2009).

Unlike the Lakewood case, blight was not part of the story in the *Kelo* case (Benedict, 2009). Instead, the private properties were characterized as standing in the way of anticipated economic development and anticipated increases in tax revenue. Figure 35.5 is a photograph of the home belonging to Susette Kelo, which was similar to the Saleets' home. While the Kelo neighborhood may not have been as affluent as the Saleet neighborhood, it was stable, and Kelo's home was attractive and well-maintained.

The *Kelo* case was controversial because the application of eminent domain was to private properties in a working-class neighborhood that, by all accounts, was not blighted. Some members of the New London neighborhood had assented to the purchase of their property by the City of New London, but other neighborhood residents had not. Yet the city government condemned the holdouts' properties, despite the owners' resistance.

Not surprisingly, hostile responses to the *Kelo* case were swift and strong (Jacoby, 2005). A series of proposed bills, including the 'Property Rights Protection Act of 2009,' were introduced in the US Congress. If it was to become law, it would prevent local governments from receiving federal economic development funds to use for eminent domain proceedings for economic development. Across the USA, more than 40 State legislatures have passed

Figure 35.5 Exterior of Kelo home, New London, Connecticut. Center for the Defense of Free Enterprise: Property Rights

legislation to prevent governments from taking private property when the primary purpose is economic development (McGeehan, 2009; 'Eminent Domain,' 2010).

The photographs of the Saleets' home and the Kelo home suggest the importance of visual sociology to case work. The properties are similar, but the outcomes are different, raising questions for inconsistent applications of eminent domain law.

Moreover, visual sociology can reveal the failure of eminent domain law as social policy, as well as raise doubts for directions in which this legal doctrine is headed. Visual evidence of the aftermath of the *Kelo* case dramatically shows how government–corporate relationships not only can fail to fulfill promises but also how these relationships destroy family homes, leaving a wasteland behind. Less than 5 years after the Supreme Court made its *Kelo* decision, the Pfizer company, which promised to build on the site of the Kelo home, withdrew from New London, Connecticut ('Pfizer,' 2009). Pfizer company leadership decided to close its research and development headquarters in New London, despite city and state government spending of $78 million on the area where Kelo and her neighbors had once lived ('Pfizer,' 2009). The empty space where the Kelo home once stood may now be characterized as blighted, with empty lots, trash, feral cats, and remnants of the homes that previously stood there (see Figure 35.6).

In Lakewood, the property was confirmed to be a private property, but not subject to eminent domain. In *Kelo*, the property was established as subject to eminent domain. These photos suggest that visual sociology can be important in case work.

A case is found

In the 1954 decision, *Berman v. Parker*, 348 US 26, the Supreme Court considered

Figure 35.6   Another View of Former Location of Kelo Home, New London, Connecticut. Maria Bernier

whether the District of Columbia Re-development Land Agency could use its powers of eminent domain to take blighted property, and non-blighted nearby, in Washington, DC. In the unanimous opinion, Justice Douglas referred to a plan developed by the National Capital Park and Planning Commission. A map of the National Capital Park and Planning Commission depicts which areas were subject to redevelopment (see Figure 35.7): the legend indicates that black areas were locations where buildings

are obsolete, as 'areas where building should be replanned and rebuilt'; gray areas were locations of blight, 'areas where some replanning and rebuilding is essential.'

The Supreme Court appeared to have readily accepted these designations of the buildings made by the National Capital Park and Planning Commission. The specific area subject to eminent domain proceedings was characterized as: '64.3 per cent of the dwellings were beyond repair, 18.4 per cent needed major repairs, only 17.3 per cent

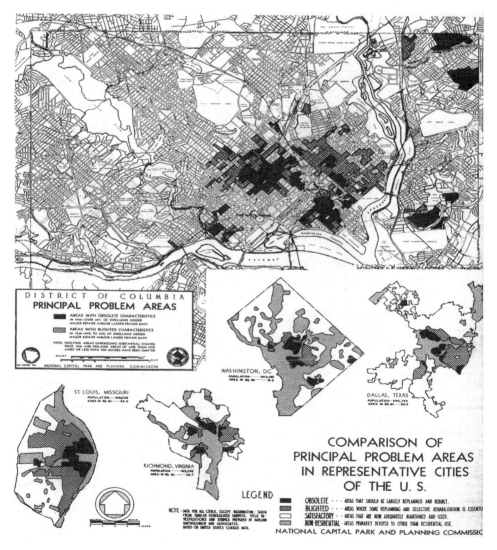

Figure 35.7   Map indicating areas subject to redevelopment, National Capital Park and Planning Commission. Comprehensive Plan for the National Capital and its Environs, 1950

were satisfactory…' and the Supreme Court noted that most had outdoor toilets, over 60 per cent did not have baths, and over 80 per cent did not have laundry facilities or central heating. In ruling that eminent domain proceedings were appropriate, the Supreme Court noted that:

> [m]iserable and disreputable housing conditions may do more than spread disease and crime and immorality….They may indeed make living an almost insufferable burden. (*Berman v. Parker*, 348 US 26)

The photograph in Figure 35.8 presents evidence of blighted properties.

Yet the Supreme Court implied that 35.7 per cent were not defined and established as blighted, implying the Supreme Court was applying a new legal standard of eminent domain. Instead, these private properties were cases that were *made*. Because their blighted character was not given, merely

their proximity to blighted properties, application of eminent domain was subject to argument. Disagreements existed over whether some properties were blighted and should be subject to eminent domain. These individual cases were neither empirical nor given. Rather than contending that destroying the property would remove blight, advocates contended the property stood in the way of redevelopment. Private properties included shops and department stores that continued to do business (see Figure 35.9).

Berman brought the case before the Supreme Court, contending that the property was not blighted. Instead, Berman maintained that the property was only to be resold to a private developer, which was an inappropriate use of eminent domain. The Supreme Court ignored the non-blighted condition of the Berman property, instead concluding that public use was a now general

Figure 35.8   Alley between B and Half Streets in March 1951, Washington, DC. Curtis Collection, DC. Archives, Washingtoniana Division, DC. Public Library

Figure 35.9   Non-blighted area subject to eminent domain, Washington, DC. National Capital Park and Planning Commission, Southwest DC, *c.* 1950

benefit to the public welfare (Nedzel and Block, 2007: 146). The decision concluded that Berman's property rights were 'satisfied... when they receive that just compensation which the Fifth Amendment exacts as the price of the taking' (348 US 36).

Similar to the *Kelo* case, visual evidence demonstrates the failure of eminent domain law. Allen (2005), writing in the *Washington Post*, subtitled her article, 'Look at how urban renewal ruined SW.' She complained, 'That's because I live in Southwest Washington, where nearly every day I contend with the wreckage—architectural, socioeconomic and cultural...' of the *Berman* case (see Figure 35.10).

Visual data can highlight significant changes in law. In the *Berman* case, visual evidence showed how the public purpose doctrine had significantly broadened from public use to general public welfare. In the process of doing research, efforts were made to define a property and establish it as subject to eminent domain. An investigator sought empirical boundaries of a case. Over time,

eminent domain practices shifted so that the focus was less on fulfilling a public function to public interests. Private properties subject to eminent domain were not simply objects; instead, qualities of private property were subject to government intentions. The change to finding a case was sometimes made on the basis of a government's police power, or that government can legitimately secure safety, health, and welfare of its citizens by maintaining public order. Police power was sometimes applied in cases of blight.

A case as an object

Visual data can reveal that the qualities of a previously private property are irrelevant to application of eminent domain. As such, visual sociology can demonstrate qualities of a case as an *object*. In the USA, it is given that a private home is personal, not government, property. When a piece of private property is an object, it is treated as real, bounded, and given. For a case as an object,

Figure 35.10   Southwest Washington, DC. Allen (2005)

its qualities are not disputed. When the qualities of that home are irrelevant to the application of eminent domain, as a case, the house is an object because researchers treat it as real, bounded, and given. State governments have exercised eminent domain since the nation's founding. One of the first federal applications of eminent domain was private property as an object. Decided in 1875, the main issues confronting the Supreme Court in *Kohl et al. v. United States*, 91 US 367, were whether the federal government has the power of eminent domain and, if it does, whether it can use eminent domain to take private property for a public function.

Once the Supreme Court decided that the federal government did have this power, the question was whether eminent domain could be used to build a federal courthouse and other federal offices. The case largely boiled down to whether the federal government could use eminent domain for a public function. In the *Kohl* case, private properties were taken by the federal government (see Figure 35.11).

The map shown in Figure 35.12, published in the *Cincinnati Commercial Tribune* (1873), shows the properties that were eventually subject to eminent domain and their market values. Kohl's tract, fifth from the left, was valued at $15,780. It was both a commercial property and a residential property; Kohl lived above his business.

Rather than situations of blight, the federal government wanted to seize private properties to build a post office, federal courthouse, and other federal buildings. Various sections of Cincinnati were considered before the decision was made to apply eminent domain to this tract and nearby properties. Initially, Kohl attempted to sell his property to the local Commission representing the federal government, but sales were unsuccessful. After the application of eminent domain was

Figure 35.11 US Custom House and Post Office, 1885, Cincinnati, Ohio. Sixth Circuit Archives. US Court of Appeals for the Sixth Circuit

announced, Kohl's estate challenged it. Figure 35.13 is a picture of the ground being broken to build the government buildings. What resulted was the building of a courthouse and other government buildings.

As a case, private property was an *object* in the *Kohl* lawsuit. The question was not whether this property was appropriately subject to eminent domain, but whether a public function was served: hearing lawsuits in a federal courthouse, delivering mail through a post office, and imposing duties via a customs house. The reason the private property was subject of the lawsuit was because the federal government wanted to take the private property to fulfill a public function. The private properties were *objects* because it was given that eminent domain could be applied to them. The federal government took the property so it could fulfill public functions; argument over the conditions of the private properties was not undertaken.

DISCUSSION AND CONCLUSION

This chapter has sought to make four contributions:

- to demonstrate the use of visual sociology in studying important socio-legal problems;
- to demonstrate types of cases of eminent domain;
- to critique Ragin's (1992) typology of cases, demonstrating that a case can transform from one type to another; and
- to critique eminent domain law.

A visual sociological analysis demonstrates the use of visual evidence in legal cases. Focusing on eminent domain cases, Ragin's (1992) typology of cases is studied to structure this discussion of eminent domain law.

I have approached eminent domain as a case that is a *convention*. Socio-legal research on eminent domain law is a collective product of scholarly research. This chapter seeks to

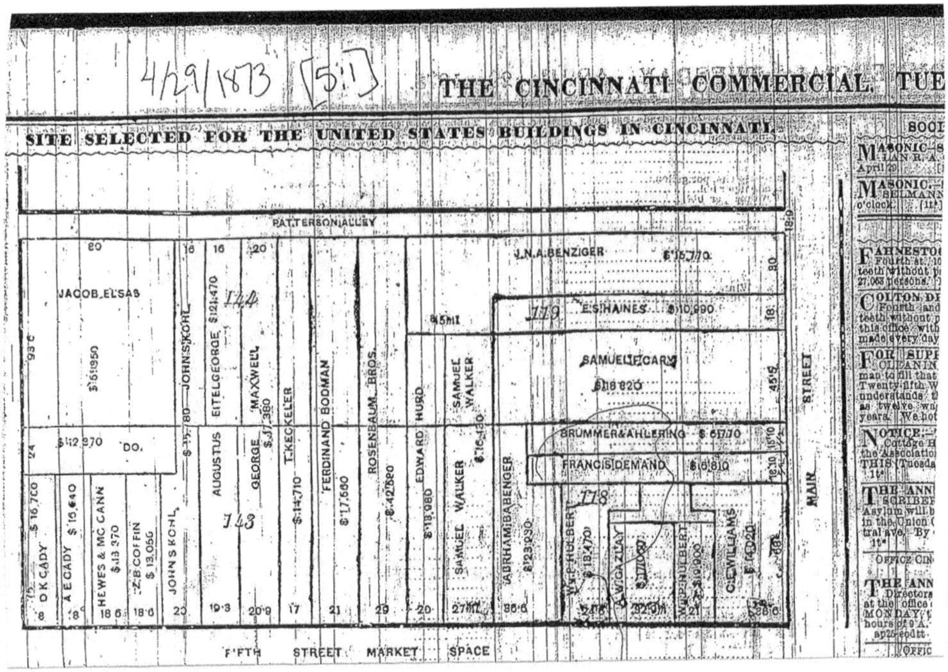

Figure 35.12   Private lots subject to eminent domain in *Kohl et al. v. United States*, the *Cincinnati Commercial Tribune* 1873. Site Selected for the United States Building in Cincinnati (29 April 1873)

Figure 35.13   Building of courthouse and other government buildings, Cincinnati, Ohio. Sixth Circuit Archives, US Court of Appeals for the Sixth Circuit

contribute to this case as a convention by demonstrating the utility of visual sociology to studies of eminent domain law. In this chapter, visual evidence was used to identify types of cases, how cases shift from one type to another, and to demonstrate the fiascos of eminent domain law.

Over the course of US history of eminent domain law, visual data have grown in importance. Prior to the *Kohl* case, the Commission established to identify the site of the new federal building considered many locations. When the process of narrowing down the final location was made public, maps of the properties and their values were published.

Prior to the *Berman* case, the National Capital Park and Planning Commission prepared maps of southwest Washington, DC. These maps identified properties to be subject to an application of eminent domain. It designated two kinds of properties, obsolete and blighted. In the *Berman* case, ultimately the Supreme Court did not distinguish between these two types of properties, deciding that the properties stood in the way of development. Indeed, the Supreme Court ignored Berman's and other parties protests that their properties were *not* blighted, but were thriving businesses that would just be sold to another private interest.

Fifty years later in Lakewood, Ohio, and New London, Connecticut, visual data played important roles in legal battles over eminent domain applications. In Lakewood, Ohio, the Saleets and their neighbors took on city hall and won. Key to their success was newspaper articles that published photographs of the Lakewood homes, mobilizing public pressure. Likely, the penultimate factor to the Saleets' successful battle was the *60 Minutes* television program that not only showed the Saleets' home to an international audience but also exposed the hypocrisy of city government officials, whose own homes should have been subject to the city's eminent domain law.

By contrast, visual data did not seem to slow down the government from applying eminent domain to the neighborhood in which Kelo lived. Instead, the US Supreme Court ruled that the city of New London could take the Kelo and nearby properties for the vague public purpose of economic development with hoped-for tax gains.

Photographs present visual evidence that those hoped-for tax gains in New London were not achieved. Instead, the visual data demonstrate the catastrophic failure of law. One beneficiary of the *Kelo* case, the Pfizer Company, has moved out of New London. The formerly middle-class neighborhood where Kelo once lived can now be considered blighted.

Visual sociology demonstrates the failure of law, and more specifically, how unevenly eminent domain can function, in both the *Berman* and *Kelo* cases. Analysts (Allen, 2005) have concluded that 50 years after the *Berman* case, southwest Washington has not reaped the benefits of redevelopment. Photographs of the area where the Kelo home was situated now starkly demonstrate a wasteland where a middle-class neighborhood once stood.

The second contribution this chapter makes is to demonstrate types of cases of eminent domain. Employing Ragin's (1992) typology of cases, this study reveals important information about eminent domain law. When a case of eminent domain was *found*, the private property was described as blighted. When a case is an *object*, private property as a case is sometimes treated as an object for eminent domain. The city government did not attempt to establish Kelo's home as blighted, but that it stood in the way of redevelopment. Private property as an object case arises in similar situations, such as taking a non-blighted property for a public use: for example, a highway. Similarly, a case is sometimes *made* for eminent domain. A struggle ensued over characterization of the Saleet home as blighted.

This chapter suggests a case can change from one type to another. I examined a case that was *found*, which changed to a case that was *made*, and subsequently changed again to a case that was *found*. In Lakewood, the municipal government attempted to find the Saleets' home as blighted. After the Lakewood government failed to characterize the property as blighted, the Saleets' home transitioned back to a found case of private property. Blight was not applied to the *Kelo* and neighboring properties, but later, after the indeterminate public use failed, it is fair to ask if these properties may now be found to be blighted.

The third contribution is a critique of Ragin's (1992) typology of cases. As noted, this study finds that a case can transform from one type to another, at which Ragin hints is possible. This study also finds that the lines separating the kinds of cases defined by Ragin can be fuzzy.

The fourth contribution is a critique of eminent domain. This chapter's analysis of eminent domain focused on the public function/public use criterion. It demonstrated how laws governing and practices of eminent domain have changed over time. Even though the Fifth Amendment has not changed, this study demonstrates that applications and practices of eminent domain have changed dramatically. This study raises questions about whether eminent domain law has moved so far from its stated goals as to be unmanageable as currently conceived.

NOTES

1 Eminent domain is government's seizure (*taking*), of private property with just compensation, for a public purpose.

2 ACT UP—**A**IDS **C**oalition **T**o **U**nleash **P**ower, an international AIDS advocacy group, based in New York City.

3 These are the kind of photographs that art historian Terry Barrett (1986) termed 'Ethically evaluative images.' They call for a judgment on the part of the viewer; photographs of the Saleets' house (discussed in this chapter) functioned in this manner. For a more complete description of Barrett's typology, see Margolis and Rowe's contribution on 'disclosing historical photographs' (Chapter 18) in this volume.

REFERENCES

Allen, Charlotte (2005) 'A wreck of a plan: Look at how urban renewal ruined SW', The *Washington Post*. [Online]. Available from: http://www.washingtonpost.com/wp-dyn/content/article/2005/07/15/AR2005071502199.html [Accessed 10 September 2010].

Barrett, Terry (1986) 'A theoretical construct for interpreting photographs', *Studies in Art Education* 27(2): 52–60.

Benedict, Jeff (2009) *Little Pink House*. New York: Grand Central Publishing.

Black, Donald (1976) *The Behavior of Law*. New York: Academic Press.

Boyle, Elizabeth H., Songora, Fortunata and Foss, Gail (2001) 'International discourse and local politics: Anti-female-genital-cutting Laws in Egypt, Tanzania, and the United States', *Social Problems*, 48(4): 524–544.

Brents, Barbara, Jackson, Crystal and Hausbeck, Kathryn (2009) *The State of Sex*. New York: Routledge.

Byrne, David (2009) 'Introduction: Case-based methods', in D. Byrne and C. C. Ragin (eds.), *The Sage Handbook of Case-Based Methods*. Los Angeles: Sage Publications. pp. 1–10.

Cohen, Charles E. (2006) 'Eminent domain after Kelo v. City of New London', *Harvard Journal of Law & Public Policy*, 29: 491–568.

Cotterell, Roger (1999) *Emile Durkheim: Law in a Moral Domain*. Edinburgh University Press/Stanford University Press.

'Criminal Law' (2010) *Cornell University Law School Legal Information Institute*, [Online]. Available at: http://topics.law.cornell.edu/wex/Criminal_law. [Accessed 5 September 2010].

Deflem, Mathieu (2008) *Sociology of Law: Visions of a Scholarly Tradition*. New York: Cambridge University Press.

Duneier, Mitchell (2000) *Sidewalk*. New York: Farrar, Straus and Giroux.

'Eminent Domain' (2010) *National Council of State Legislatures* [Online]. Available from: http://www.ncsl.org/default.aspx?tabid=13252 [Accessed: 5 September 2010].

Goodwin, C. (2002) 'Professional vision', in D. Weinberg (ed.), *Qualitative Research Methods*. Oxford: Blackwell.

Gould, Deborah B. (2009) *Moving Politics*. Chicago, IL: University of Chicago Press.

Gran, Brian (2003) 'A second opinion: Rethinking the public–private dichotomy for health insurance', *International Journal of Health Services* 33(2): 283–313.

Gran, Brian and Béland, Daniel (2008) 'Conclusion: Revisiting the public–private dichotomy', in

D. Béland and B. Gran (eds.), *Public and Private Social Policy*. Palgrave: Macmillan. pp. 269–282.

Hansberry, L. (1964) *The Movement; Documentary of a Struggle for Equality*. New York: Simon and Schuster.

Harden, Blaine (2003) 'In Ohio, a test for eminent domain rights vs. renewal at stake in case', The *Washington Post*, A03.

Harper, Douglas (1992) 'Small *N*'s and community case studies', in C. C. Ragin and H. S. Becker (eds.), *What is a Case?* New York: Cambridge University Press. pp. 139–158.

Harper, Douglas (2001) *Changing Works*. Chicago, IL: University of Chicago Press.

Harvey, David (2009) 'Complexity and case', in D. Byrne and C. C. Ragin (eds.), *The SAGE Handbook of Case-Based Methods*. Los Angeles: Sage Publications. pp. 15–38.

'How the West End was Won' (2004) *Cleveland Magazine*, Features. [Online]. Available from: http://www.clevelandmagazine.com/ME2/dirmod.asp?sid=E73ABD6180B44874871A91F6BA5C249C&nm=Arts+%26+Entertainemnt&type=Publishing&mod=Publications%3A%3AArticle&mid=1578600D80804596A222593669321019&tier=4&id=17D0F0D43A294EBA9D36CE8B3F3197AA [Accessed 11 September 2010].

Institute for Justice (n.d.) 'Ohio's 'city of homes' faces wrecking ball of eminent domain abuse'. [Online]. Available from: http://www.ij.org/index.php?option=com_content&task=view&id=1053&Itemid=165 [Accessed 5 September 2010].

Jacoby, Jeff (2005) 'Eminent injustice', The *Boston Globe*, Opinion.

Kotlyarevskaya, Olga V. (2006) '"Public use" requirement in eminent domain cases based on slum clearance, elimination of urban blight, and economic development', *Connecticut Public Interest Law Journal*, 5: 197–231.

Leung, Rebecca (2004) 'Eminent domain: Being abused?', *60 Minutes [CBS News]*. [Online]. Available from: http://www.cbsnews.com/stories/2003/09/26/60minutes/main575343.shtml [Accessed 23 October 2010].

McCarthy, Kevin E. (2005) 'Eminent domain', *OLR Research Report*, 2005-R-0321, Connecticut General Assembly, Office of Legal Research.

McGeehan, Patrick (2009) 'Pfizer to leave city that won land-use case', The *New York Times*, p. A1 (New York edn).

Margolis, Eric (2004) 'Looking at discipline, looking at labour: Photographic representations of Indian boarding schools', *Visual Studies*, 19: 72–96.

Mizen, Phillip (2005) 'Emerging into the light', *International Journal of Epidemiology*, 34(2): 257–259.

'Murder' (2010) *Cornell University Law School Legal Information Institute* [Online]. Available from: http://topics.law.cornell.edu/wex/murder. [Accessed 5 September 2010].

Nedzel, Nadia E. and Block, Walter (2007) 'Eminent domain', *University of Maryland Law Journal of Race, Religion, Gender and Class*, 7: 140–171.

'Pfizer and Kelo's ghost town: Pfizer bugs out, long after the land grab', (2009) The *Wall Street Journal*. Review & Outlook.

Polletta, Francesca (2000) 'The structural context of novel rights claims: Southern Civil Rights Organizing, 1961–1966', *Law and Society Review*, 34(2): 367–406.

Preston, Catherine L. (2001) 'Territories of images, technologies of memories', *Visual Sociology*, 16(2): 39–57.

Private Property Rights Protection Act of 2009, H.R. 1885, US House of Representatives 111th Cong. (2009).

Ragin, Charles C. (1992) 'Introduction: Cases of "What is a case?"', in C. C. Ragin and H. S. Becker (eds.), *What is a Case?* New York: Cambridge University Press. pp. 1–17.

Rieger, Jon (2003) 'A retrospective visual study of social change: The pulp-logging industry in an Upper Peninsula Michigan County', *Visual Studies* 18(2): 157–178.

Riis, J. A. (1890/1971) *How the Other Half Lives: Studies among the Tenements of New York*. New York: Dover Publications.

Rutkow, Eric (2006) 'Case comment: Kelo v. City of New London', *Harvard Environmental Law Review*, 30: 261–279.

Sartin, V. David (2002) 'Plans aim to revive neighborhoods; Lakewood targets West End for development', *The Plain Dealer*, B1.

Sartin, V. David (2002) 'Lakewood moves to revitalize', The *Plain Dealer*, B4.

Schwartzenberg, Susan (2005) *Becoming Citizens*. Seattle, WA: The University of Washington Press.

Sherwin, Richard K. (2007) 'A manifesto for visual legal realism', *Loyola of Los Angeles Law Review*, 40 (NYLS Legal Studies Research Paper No. 07/08-2). [Online]. Available from: SSRN: http://ssrn.com/abstract=1004307 [Accessed 23 October 2010].

Sherwin, Richard K., Feigenson, Neal and Spiesel, Christina (2007) 'What is visual knowledge, and what is it good for?' *Visual Anthropology*, 20: 143–178.

Site Selected for the United States Building in Cincinnati (1873) *Cincinnati Commercial Tribune*, 5: 1.

Sparrman, Anna (2006) 'Film as an educational and political device', *Visual Studies*, 21(2): 167–182.

Tocqueville, Alexis de (1835, 1840/2004) *Democracy in America*, translated by A. Goldhammer, Olivier Zunz (ed.). New York: Library of America.

Vaughan, Diane (1992) 'Theory elaboration', in C. C. Ragin and H. S. Becker (eds.), *What is a Case?* New York: Cambridge University Press. pp. 173–202.

Weber, Max (1922/1978) '*Economy and society*,' in G. Roth and C. Wittich (eds.), Berkeley, CA: University of California Press.

Legal cases cited

Berman v. Parker, 348 US 26 (1954).

Kelo v. City of New London, 545 US 469 (2005).

Kohl et al. v. United States, 91 US 367 (1875).

36

Visual Research Ethics at the Crossroads[1]

Rose Wiles, Andrew Clark and Jon Prosser

SUMMARY

This chapter provides an overview of the debates and practices that shape visual research ethics. We outline the requirements and expectations of institutional ethics review boards and legal frameworks, for example, regarding filming and photographing in public and issues of copyright. We contend that legal and institutional requirements should not be the sole determinants when making decisions about ethics, but rather must be situated within the research context and accommodated in a researcher's individual moral framework. We suggest that visual methods, and the data they produce, challenge some of the ethical practices associated with word- and number-based research, in particular around informed consent, anonymity, and confidentiality, and dissemination strategies. Overall, we argue that research ethics are contested, dynamic and contextual and, as such, are best approached through detailed understanding of the concrete, everyday situations in which they are applied. The title of this chapter 'Visual research ethics at the crossroads' is metaphorical, indicating that visual research has reached an important juncture and signifying it is timely to take stock and consider future directions in ethical practice.

INTRODUCTION

Conducting research ethically is considered the cornerstone of good practice and increasingly regarded as a professional necessity. A surge of interest in research ethics throughout Europe and North America has ensured that visual researchers need to act reflexively and critically in their ethical decision making in order to protect and enhance the reputation and integrity of visual research and protect respondents.[2] This chapter examines the widespread proposition that the majority of visual researchers endeavor to act ethically but are unsure how this is achieved. The constitution of sound ethical practice is problematic because visual methods bring into view an array of issues previously underexamined. The intention is to provide a critical overview of the forces that shape ethical policies generally and then to focus in on situated exemplars of ethical practices and decision making by visual researchers. Rather than treating ethical dilemmas as troublesome we welcome them as an opportunity for reflexivity and, we contend, to contribute to improved visual methodologies.

The rapid growths over the past two decades of visual methods and of expectations of sound ethical practice have left some visual researchers less well prepared to absorb contemporary ethical debates and practices. Word- and number-based researchers adapt and refine existing standards or absorb and apply revised ethical frameworks with relative ease compared with more visual-centric researchers. Many visual researchers, both seasoned fieldworkers and relative newcomers, are ill at ease with the daunting possibility of devising, applying, and normalizing visual ethics in their own work. As a consequence, visual ethics, in the form of statutory and legal requirements, organizational and institutional needs, and guidelines for group and personal ethical decision making, are less well developed. Visual researchers, while feeling comfortable in the belief that visual methods are of fundamental importance to qualitative research, experience apprehension when the topic of 'ethics' is raised. Our monitoring of Internet discussion groups, such as VISCOM (International Visual Sociology Association) suggests there is a general concern across the visual research community that knowledge of visual ethics needs improving, that demand for training is not always met, and that exemplars of good practice are surprisingly sparse and rarely shared. Moreover, there is an anxiety that increasingly pervasive systems of ethical regulation will place visual research at a significant disadvantage, particularly in relation to issues of confidentiality and anonymity.

This chapter is in two parts: the first part describes *current factors impacting on ethical decision making in visual research*; the second part poses the supposition that *visual ethics are at a crossroads*, requiring visual researchers to make critical decisions and

take strategic actions to improve visual ethics practiced within the social sciences. Mediating between the two parts are discussion and reflection of specific research practices that have significant bearing on how visual researchers can act in ethically appropriate ways: this includes discussion of the challenges of gaining informed consent; decisions of how, if at all, it is possible to maintain anonymity and confidentiality of research participants; and the implications of disseminating visual research data.

CURRENT FACTORS IMPACTING ON ETHICAL DECISION MAKING

In this section, we consider four factors that currently contribute to ethical decision making in research projects that incorporate visual methods (see Figure 36.1). The legal requirement of ethical practice requires compliance, yet is an aspect of visual methodology practitioners are mostly unfamiliar with. However, the *law* represents a minimalist requirement for visual researchers' ethics and more is expected from them in fieldwork situations. The *regulations* governing research ethics have increased considerably over the last decade, and include frameworks from funding bodies, professional body guidelines and institutional ethical committee practices. Visual researchers will necessarily conform to set regulations and mostly accept the moral principles they advocate. However, inevitably, the multiple methods that comprise visual methods will lead to *critical issues* around practices such as informed consent, confidentiality, and anonymity. Making sound ethical choices at times will depend, to some degree, on *individuals' moral frameworks*.

The law and visual methods[3]

Capturing visual data
Researchers are required to know the legalities of visual practices they adopt, such as

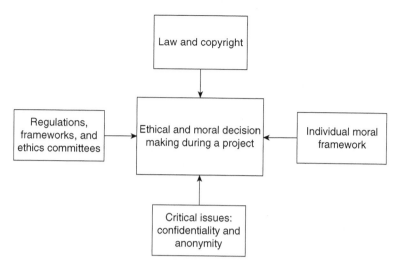

Figure 36.1 Current forces shaping ethical decision making on a research project

photographing in public places, in order to accord with notions of good practice. They find few straight answers and often wrestle with technical clarifications and subtle interpretations but these are insufficient reasons to remain ignorant. Cultural pluralism and complexity added to technical legal language make this a daunting area for the uninitiated. Visual researchers will do well to consult legal specialists but should not set the ethical and moral 'bar' too low. It will be imperative to remember that laws provide a framework of the bare minimum standards that need to be adhered to but that these, by themselves, do not necessarily equate with what the research community would consider to be acceptable ethical or moral practices. Masson notes:

There is a close relationship between law and ethics but not everything that is legal is ethical. Frequently law ... attempts only to set the minimum acceptable standard. The aspirations of ethical practice are higher .... It can never be appropriate to defend proposed practice solely on the basis that it is legal. (2004: 43)

The global upsurge in interest in visual research methods means international collaborations are becoming common, with visual researchers working across and

between cultures. However, cultural differences, along with political and socio-historical factors, ensure different nations are regulated by different laws. Whereas there are overlaps and commonalities, there will be different statutes for different situations in different countries around the world where different research disciplines are required to adhere to different laws. Warren and Karner provide a good example of this scenario in action in the USA:

If you are a journalism instructor or student interacting with or talking to "human subjects" for the media, you may ask any questions you wish, use the names of the subjects in your published research; your work is protected by the First Amendment and your notes are protected by law from subpoena. Your only obligation to your subjects is to identify yourself as a journalist. If you are a sociology student or instructor, however, you may not interact or talk to respondents unless you have received permission from your college or university's Institutional Review Board (IRB). You are not protected under the first Amendment, and your notes are not protected by law from subpoena. (2005: 29)

Warren and Karner (2005) go on to provide three US exemplars of researchers or research students involved in court cases following attempts to subpoena field notes. While we are unaware of similar cases in Europe to date, researchers should be aware that data offered in confidence do not enjoy legal privilege and they may be liable to subpoena by a court (Wiles et al., 2008a). Participatory researchers who adopt a 'photovoice' approach of giving cameras to respondents should take note of this. They should be prudent, prepared, and forearmed for those instances when collaborators present them with images that portray some form of unlawful or morally questionable activity.

Establishing common ground provides a way forward in this complex legal–cultural equation. The general rule, for example, in the USA (Krages, 2006) and the UK (McPherson, 2004), is that anyone may take photographs in public places or places where they have permission to take photographs. In the absence of specific legal prohibition, such as a statute or local ordinance, researchers are legally entitled to take photographs in public places such as streets and public parks. According to Krages (2006), the following may also be lawfully photographed from public places: accident and fire scenes, children, celebrities, bridges and other infrastructures, residential and commercial buildings, industrial facilities and public utilities, transportation facilities (for example, airports), criminal activities and law enforcement officers.

However, what constitutes a public, semi-public, and private space is not clear. Managers of shopping malls, railway stations, and public service organizations such as hospitals, leisure centers, or libraries, may not view their organizations as public places for the purposes of researchers wishing to take images. Photographing or filming military installations and nuclear facilities is prohibited in most countries, as is in some countries taking picture of bridges, ports, palaces, railway stations, non-military airports, and the police. While there is currently no privacy law in the UK, photographing someone where they might reasonably expect to be private could be considered to be against Article 8 of the European Convention on Human Rights (McPherson, 2004). Persistent or aggressive photography could also come under the legal definition of harassment (McPherson, 2004). While the law in relation to taking images in public places is explicit, what is legal and what is sanctioned in practice do not always coincide. There are numerous examples of photographers in the UK, the USA, and elsewhere being stopped from filming in public places by various state officials.[4]

Copyright and data protection

Researchers wishing to retain control of images they have created or to use images made by others by, for example, publishing them, should be aware of laws that safeguard copyright. Intellectual property rights such as data protection and copyright are convoluted and are continually modified to meet changing circumstances. The rights are analogous throughout Western countries and here we will focus on the UK for illustration purposes. However, although images are normally covered by the particular copyright law of the country in which they are made, they will automatically be protected in many other countries since most are signatories to the Berne Convention for the Protection of Literary and Artistic Works, which provides reciprocal protection.

For copyright purposes, images come under 'artistic works,' which includes, for example, paintings, cartoons, sketches, graphs, diagrams, photographs, and moving images such as films. Copyright in artistic works in the UK lasts until 70 years after the death of the artist or image-maker and is:

> an automatic right given to creators of original material that allows them to control copying, adaptation, issuance of copies to the public, performance and broadcasting. The copyright holder may be the creator, the creator's employer, their family or estate, or an authorized representative. (Jisc Digital Media, 2010)

Usually, the person who creates an image is the copyright holder. However, when the image-maker created the imagery as part of her or his work, the copyright may rest with the employer. Additionally, a creator can sell or give the copyright to another person. Researchers recording still or moving images in a public place own the copyright and can use them for a range of purposes, including archiving. However, a case could be made for respondents retaining rights over the words spoken in a video recording as the copyright for their words rests with them. In the UK, the Copyright, Designs and Patents Act 1988 introduced the concept of 'moral rights,' which are separate from property rights. Here, the owners have the right not to have their images shown in a belittling or deprecating way. Normally, researchers will typically copyright their own images by a statement— for example, 'copyright of Andrew Clark 2008' or '© Clark 2008'— which may help in any subsequent legal action. There is no bureaucratic process and no fee involved.

Visual researchers may collect, analyze, store, and reproduce 'found' images. If the images, both digital and analogue, are someone else's creation they are covered by copyright. If a researcher wishes to reproduce the work either in an article or on a website the copyright owners will need to be contacted for permission. If any 'substantial' part of an image is reproduced, copyright is still an issue, so changing a map or diagram, for example, to make it look different from the original may still infringe copyright law. If a researcher uses an image in an academic paper, and not for financial gain, permission is usually given. For images found on the Internet through Google Images™, or photographic sites such as Flickr®, it is a matter of contacting the site owner or the creator and asking for permission. Should the owner impose restrictions, such as linking to their homepage to maximize traffic or reproducing the web address, it is a sound practice to accept them.

An example of the relationship between research images and the law

As we have noted above, while it is important for researchers to know their legal rights and

obligations, they will often operate at an ethically and morally higher level. Consider, for example, the image in Figure 36.2. Initially, individual shots were taken in the street, with each individual asked for their permission to create an image based on an understanding it might be used in a public photographic exhibition. In the exhibition, two composite photographs were placed next to each other with a brief explanation, one showing multiple single head shots (on the left), and the other of multiple half-heads (on the right). The exhibition was part of a strategy to disseminate findings back to the communities in the study. The two photographs juxtaposed represented a simple notion— 'people are individuals and individuals form communities.' Yet a range of legal and ethical issues arise from this example.

The question of copyright ownership arises when an image is manipulated. It could be argued that the original images have been changed subtly, in meaning or as artifacts, by placing them in a grid (Figure 36.2, left side) but the copyright remains with the photographer. What happens legally if a graphic artist changes the original image, placing half-faces next to each other, giving a different or innovative meaning to the original images (Figure 36.2, right side)? Who owns the copyright to this new image is a matter of judgment. The image would not exist without the photographer's images; the idea is new but ideas cannot be copyrighted. However, the expression of the idea, in a physical or digital form, can be copyrighted and therefore the graphic designer would have a significant claim. The copyright in this case could be either jointly owned or there could be multiple separate copyright within the work.

Figure 36.2 also raises the question of judgment and prudence when reproducing, changing, or distributing visual data. It is both an important moral and a legal issue. The image on the right is markedly different and, possibly, more disturbing to viewers than the one on the left because some of the matched faces are purposely strongly contrasted for impact. The judgment by the

Figure 36.2   Legal issues and visual data © 2008 Jon Prosser

photographer and curator of the exhibition was that those individuals depicted would not be offended or damaged. This was a difficult decision, since there was no substantive way of rationalizing or validating that conclusion. Banks reminds us that, in visual research, researchers should be vigilant to two important issues:

> The first is legal: are they producing, reproducing or altering an image that someone else might claim to own? The second is moral, by what right (legally enforceable or otherwise) are they producing, reproducing or altering an image? (2007: 89)

Legal issues of data protection and consent also arise in relation to these images. The UK Data Protection Act 1998 affects researchers' use of photography, even in public spaces. A digital image of an individual is considered, by some administrators and bureaucrats, to be personal data for the purpose of the Act, and therefore requires consent. Yet the scenario of handing out consent forms to those individuals researchers have purposely targeted, for example in a busy street, is not viable and requires what Banks terms an

'intellectual' rather than legal resolution. He suggests that the best way to avoid problems is awareness of context:

> the researcher should know enough about the society or community through her research, both in the library and in the field, to anticipate what the likely response will be. (2007: 88)

The community where the photographs for Figure 36.2 were taken comprised a significant socio-cultural mix, but who should and should not be photographed? Asian men of the Islamic faith are represented but no women are shown. There were two reasons for this: few Islam-Asian women were in the street and photographing them required sensitivity to their religion and culture. It is important that visual researchers seeking to photograph women of Islamic faith negotiate consent *prior* to taking a photograph so that they in turn may seek their husband's approval before agreeing. In the case of Figure 36.2, consideration of the beliefs of a key section of the local community was important.

Children are shown in Figure 36.2, although attaining consent for photographing children required greater deliberation because of the particular difficulties that this poses (Alderson and Morrow, 2004; Masson, 2004; Heath et al., 2007). Parental consent is needed if a child is not viewed as having the capacity to consent (Masson, 2004). For Figure 36.2, the photographer asked both the parents and the children for their consent, regardless of the child's capacity to consent (Alderson and Morrow, 2004; Farrell, 2005). The notion of a person's 'capacity' to give consent is a judgment that relates to (so-called) 'vulnerable' members of a society: for example, the young, older people, and those with disabilities. In the UK, researchers working with children or other vulnerable groups require a Criminal Records Bureau (CRB) check conducted by the police.

Ethics regulation: committees, frameworks and professional guidance

Regulation of research ethics has increased significantly around the world during the last decade but most noticeably in North America and Europe. There was a groundswell of opinion, after the horrific biomedical experiments carried out in concentration camps during the Second World War, that some form of control was needed. In the USA, infamous cases of unethical medical research practice came to light, notably the Tuskegee syphilis study which, between 1932 and 1972, studied the long-term effect of untreated syphilis in 400 mostly poor, illiterate, African-American men, and decided not to provide them with effective treatment when it became available. The Tuskegee study was the impetus in the development of federal legislation in the USA and the production of the Belmont Report in 1979, which identified key principles for the conduct of ethical research (Macfarlane, 2009). Although legislation and regulation was developed in relation to biomedical research, their sphere of influence has spread to encompass research within the social sciences.

This development is one that many social scientists in the USA and Europe view with concern (Dingwall, 2006, 2008; Hammersley, 2009). As Warren and Karner note:

> From the 1970s onward, the federal government extended protections for human research subjects.... This step was a step that many social scientists found—and find—distressing... we agree with many of our fellow social science researchers in the twenty-first century who also feel that the restrictions on social science research have gone too far in this country. (2005: 36)

In the USA, Institutional Review Boards are charged with overseeing research on and with human subjects. The IRBs, governed by the Research Act of 1974 (Code of Federal Regulations), require all colleges, universities, and organizations that receive funding, directly or indirectly, from the Department of Health and Human Services, to screen research proposals. Their powers are considerable and their scope varied. Submission to IRBs is required for studies carried out in semi-public places such as restaurants and in private spaces such as family homes, in addition to the owner's permission. Whereas there are a few exemptions to the requirement to submit, some Boards perceive their governance as covering research in public spaces, and in particular contexts, such as hospitals and health service provision, additional or separate IRB submission is required (as in the UK[5]). Sensitive contexts and topics and research involving particularly vulnerable participants such as hospital patients, prisoners, children, and those with learning difficulties, will receive closer scrutiny from Boards.

Highly regulated systems of ethical review which originated in the USA have permeated European policy on the conduct of research (Wiles et al., 2008b). Important funding bodies in Europe—for example, the ESRC[6] in the UK and the European Commission[7]— now make a direct link between their ethical frameworks and funding since no compliance means no money. In the UK, these developments, alongside the formation of ethics committees in universities and social research organizations, mean that almost all social research must be subject to some form of ethical review by a recognized research ethics committee.

The most common principles that underpin ethical codes of practice have been referred to as:

> Respect for person and the moral requirement to respect autonomy and the requirement to protect those with diminished autonomy; Beneficence and complementary requirement to do no harm and to maximize possible benefits and minimize possible harms; Justice and the fair distribution of the benefits and burdens of research. (Papademas, 2004: 122)

Elsewhere, Wiles et al. (2008b: 8) summarize the key issues thus:

- *researchers should strive to protect the rights, privacy, dignity and well-being of those that they study;*
- *research should (as far as possible) be based on voluntary informed consent;*
- *personal information should be treated confidentially and participants anonymized unless they choose to be identified; and*
- *research participants should be informed of the extent to which anonymity and confidentiality can be assured in publication and dissemination and of the potential reuse of data.*

Guidelines and codes of practice from professional bodies—for example, the American Sociological Association (ASA, 1999), and the British Sociological Association (BSA, 2002, 2006)—are important starting points for consideration of these issues because they provide parameters and foci, enabling researchers to think through the ethical dilemmas that occur.

As we have noted, several authors observe that the regulation of social science leads to a lessening of researcher professionalism and integrity, and places inappropriate limitations (Hammersley, 2009). This is particularly apposite for visual researchers who have raised concerns that ethical regulation may render some visual research impossible and/or that limitations to their practice will be imposed that will render data meaningless

(Prosser and Loxley, 2008). Visual researchers are in a disadvantaged position because ethical frameworks and codes of practice have been drawn up by number-based and word-based researchers, and consequently anomalies, difficulties of interpretation and application, are more likely to arise in image-based researchers' applications. Visual methods frequently lend themselves to participatory and emancipatory approaches. In such contexts, participants may explicitly and voluntarily waive their rights to confidentially and anonymity, contravening one of the cornerstones of normative ethical practice in social science research. We can envisage cases arising where visual researchers will be invited to change important components of research design, in order to avoid breaking with number- and word-based conventions. Viewed positively, ethics committees will be aware of problems resulting from applying a set of broad principles to specific situations, will be astute enough to seek specialist help from experienced visual methodologists, and flexible enough to transfer their knowledge to contexts arising through the use of visual methods. The future development of ethical visual research is best served by proactive practitioners able to inform, educate, debate, and generally contribute to the effective functioning of ethical committees. Visual researchers cannot afford to sit on the sidelines when ethics are debated, but should think through and argue their ethical position.

Critical issues

In this section, we consider two issues relevant in conducting ethical research that pose particular challenges in visual research: informed consent, and anonymity and confidentiality.

Informed consent

Obtaining informed consent entails not only gaining agreement or permission to take or produce visual images but also to reproduce or display those images to different audiences and in different contexts.

In providing informed consent, participants are expected not to be deceived or coerced into taking part in research, are informed of the purpose of the research and the research process, and understand the uses to which the research will be put (Wiles et al., 2007).

The process requires careful consideration and there are a number of epistemological as well as ethical benefits of obtaining informed consent to collect and use visual images (Banks, 2007; Pink, 2007). Chief among these is the view that obtaining consent is a requisite of obtaining good-quality data. Pink (2007), among others, argues that it is through negotiation with study participants that visual data are produced that can appropriately reflect the realities and experiences of participants. The public display, publishing, or wider dissemination of visual data without the consent of individuals pictured has been described as ethically questionable (Prosser and Schwartz, 1998; Pink, 2007). Gaining consent is also important for maintaining rapport and relationships of trust between researchers and individuals in the field and as essential to ensuring the success of ongoing or subsequent research (Prosser, 2000). Like other visual researchers, Chaplin is clear in her advice to 'always ask permission before photographing someone, and always get written permission before publishing the photograph' (2004: 45).

Perhaps the most common way of obtaining consent to produce and disseminate visual material is through the use of consent forms.[8] However, their use should not be taken to mean participants have understood what it is they are consenting to or assumed that all individuals in an image have consented to their image being shown in public disseminations in the future (Pink, 2007). A consent form needs to contain information on the goals and purposes of the research, its duration, the potential use of images produced, the voluntary nature of involvement, any financial implications for the participant, disclaimers, any agreements made to provide participants with cameras, other equipment, or payment, researcher contact information, and any possible risks to the safety or well-being of participants. It is vital that researchers produce an appropriate consent form since it may be awkward to return to participants with subsequent forms requesting further permissions. However, as discussed below, the signing of a consent form does not constitute a solution to ethical dilemmas in research, nor does it mean researchers can do whatever they like with any subsequently obtained or produced data (Pink, 2007). In some cases, researchers have argued for recorded verbal consent, suggesting that consent forms would be inappropriate with some groups such as those who are suspicious of legalistic procedures or authorities, where levels of literacy are low, or in research focusing on illegal activities (Coomber, 2002; Miller and Bell, 2002).

However, while it is good ethical practice to obtain informed consent, this is not always straightforward. Below we identify six challenges to gaining informed consent in visual research.

Six challenges to gaining informed consent in visual research First, it might not always be appropriate to obtain informed consent from individuals involved in research. Arguments have been made for more clandestine research endeavors and the collection of data covertly, usually in the study of hidden or marginalized activities and groups (Humphreys, 1975; Fielding, 1982; Lauder, 2003). The use of technology such as telephoto lenses and other surreptitious techniques make covert visual research possible (Prosser, 2000). As Pink (2007) argues, the distinction between overt and covert visual research is also far from clear. For example, there are occasions when covert visual research may be considered acceptable, such as when a researcher collaborates with informants to photograph others who are not aware they are being photographed.

A second issue concerns the meaning of *informed*. It has been argued that in order to be ethical, visual research needs to be collaborative, reflexive, and represent the voices of informants (Ruby, 2000; Pink, 2007). Collaborative research requires participants to be aware of the research, and to consent to their involvement. However, whether participants can fully understand to what they are consenting is debatable (Becker, 1988; Miller and Bell, 2002; Wiles et al., 2007). Consent may mean different things in different cultures or in different relationships (Pink, 2007). Informants may be keen to collaborate in a particular piece of research without fully engaging with why a researcher is doing the research. And even if informants collaborate fully in the production of visual data, it is unlikely they will be fully aware of the researchers' intentions (Gross et al., 1988, 2003; Prosser, 2000).

A third issue concerns who is in a position to provide consent. Researchers working in institutional settings such as hospitals or schools require consent from managers or teachers before gaining consent from individuals who may be the subject of images. Research with children also requires further consideration, not least because it may require consent from parents or guardians (Mizen, 2005; Kaplan, 2008; Thomson, 2008). For example, in his study of masculinity in schools, O'Donoghue (2007) sought consent from the individual students and their parents, as well as agreeing the project plan with students, staff, and school management and securing consent for the reproduction of images during dissemination. However, asking others for proxy consent raises issues about the ability of participants to make their own decisions about taking part in research. The need to gain consent from others can also raise questions if research is focusing on sensitive issues such as drug or alcohol use or sexual behavior with young people (Valentine et al., 2001).

A fourth issue is that it may not be possible to gain consent from everyone who will be the subject of visual data. This is most notably the case when filming or photographing in public spaces or public events (Henderson, 1988). Here, Harper (2005) reports that some visual sociologists point to the precedent of photo-journalism and photo-documentary and argue that harm to subjects is unlikely to occur from 'showing normal people doing normal things' (2005: 759). However, while photographing and filming in public places may be legal in many countries, including the UK and USA, it would still be considered good practice to gain permission of those featured in the images where possible. It may well be impossible to gain consent from everyone in a crowded street or market, or at a concert or demonstration, before producing images. Nonetheless, the ethics of recording visual images of individuals in public places still warrants careful consideration. Schwartz (2002), for example, was careful to ask permission to photograph activity at anti-biotechnology and genetic engineering meetings held in public places, and documents a complicated process of gaining consent to photograph the activists. Consent is a process that also needs to be situated within local customs, as Pink (2007) suggests in her discussion of photographing a carnival in the capital city of Guinea Bissau. She was told she required permission from the head of the local office of the Minister for Culture to take the photographs. The officer consented for Pink to photograph carnival participants without their own individual consent. In practice, Pink only photographed those who gave their own permission.

A fifth challenge is that of obtaining informed consent when research participants are to produce visual data themselves (for example, Holliday, 2004; Mizen, 2005; Marquez-Zenkov, 2007), especially if images are produced that include other people and which require obtaining consent through the participant acting as a kind of ethical mediator as well as data producer. While it could be assumed that the subjects photographed consented to being photographed by the participant, it is unlikely that they will know the purposes to which the photographs could be put. It may be possible to subsequently request permission through the participant who took the image, but this is nonetheless a complex issue to manage. Similar issues are raised in relation to 'found images,' such as the use of photographs in family albums which are used for research purposes; these purposes were unlikely to have been intended when producing the image originally (for example, Schwartzenberg, 2005; Pauwels, 2008a). Albums may contain photographs taken by different individuals who are not available to give consent for the use of an image in research.

A sixth challenge concerns what participants are consenting to. There are differences between consenting to take part in research and consenting for an image to go in a book. For example, consent may be required not only to produce a photograph or film footage but also for the specific formats and contexts in which the image is displayed, such as books, conference papers, exhibitions, or for general illustrative purposes (Pink, 2007; Prosser and Loxley, 2008). While participants might give consent to having their photograph taken, they may not be consenting to subsequent display of those images. The question of what participants are consenting to becomes more complex if visual data are to be archived, resulting in unknown further reuses of data.

Consent: an illustration The Living Resemblances research project[9] required nuanced ethical decisions about the use of found images. The project investigated family resemblances and one of the methods used was a photo-elicitation method using personal and family photograph albums. The researchers negotiated who could give consent for the use of different photographs from participants' albums, and what they could be used for. The team decided on a strategy of obtaining verbal consent from the keeper of the photograph album to include the photographs in the elicitation method and to obtain signed forms for the consent to display photographs at conferences or in publications. Seeking consent from all living individuals in the photographs was determined too complex a task to complete successfully. Throughout the consent process, the researchers negotiated

the use and dissemination of the images with each participant, finding that some were keen to discuss the research with other family members before consenting to the release of photographs into the public arena. Moreover, participants preferred to provide consent on an image-by-image basis, consenting to different uses of photographs depending on their content, prompting the team to argue that participants:

> employ their own highly complex ethical systems of "consent hierarchies" to their family photo to help them make decisions about their use in [research] projects... and therefore as researchers, so should we. (Wiles et al., 2008b: 19–21)

Anonymity and confidentiality

Maintaining anonymity and confidentiality is often considered central to conducting ethical research. However, visual data present particular challenges to this, as it is often impossible or impractical to maintain the anonymity and confidentiality of individuals in images and film. Faced with this challenge, the benefits of collaborative research, where participants are encouraged to take part in the production, analysis, and dissemination of research, become clearer (Banks, 2001; Pink, 2007). The relationships established between researchers and participants in such instances can enable discussion of the implications of showing images and films, as well as enabling participants to use visual media to express their voices (Banks, 2001). There are also reports of participants questioning the need to be anonymized, and requesting to have their experiences and opinions attributed to them (Wiles et al., 2008b). If an aim of (particularly participatory) visual research is to empower and give voice to marginalized groups and individuals, but those individuals and groups are anonymized against their wishes, this raises important questions about power relationships in research and control of the research (Walker et al., 2008). Moreover, if visual data are to be shown in exhibitions or in publications, displaying anonymized images may be somewhat futile; for what is the purpose of displaying film or photographs from research in which faces have been blurred?

It has long been argued that visual methods can reveal important information that text- or word-based methods cannot. Consequently, attempting to disguise such data can remove the very point of the data. For example, there are a number of studies where visual methods are used because they enable participants to present particular aspects of their identities, anonymization of which would defeat the purpose of the method (Back, 2004; Da Silva and Pink, 2004; Harper, 2004; Holliday, 2004). In such cases, researchers tend to gain consent from participants to display their images unchanged.

Decisions also need to be made about what to anonymize in an image. Hairstyle, clothing, jewelry, tattoos, and the places where individuals are photographed can all breech confidentiality and reveal, to those who know

them, the identities of the individuals concerned. Conversely, over-anonymizing data can also be a danger. In Figure 36.3 for example, the building, the car number (license) plate, and both the adult and child would need to be anonymized, with the result that any subsequent use of the image may appear somewhat meaningless.

Anonymity problems are not restricted to photographs and video. For example, Figure 36.4 is illustrative of the complexity of maintaining 'internal confidentiality' in art-based data. The figure was produced by a child as part of a visual research project about the family. The family depicted in this drawing will be easily recognized by members of a school or neighborhood community. For example, the author's name, although hidden by a black pen, can be guessed by the size of the first and second name, and be seen when the paper on which the original is made, is

Figure 36.3   Anonymizing visual images © 2006 Andrew Clark

Figure 36.4   Anonymization in respondent-created drawings

held up to the light and the drawing shows all the information required to identify a family of four, comprising two adults and two children of different genders and a female adult with one leg (Prosser and Loxley, 2008; Clark et al., 2010).

Ways of anonymizing visual data

If participants are to be anonymized, researchers have adopted a range of strategies and techniques. Perhaps the most obvious, though perhaps less routinely used in academic outputs, are computer software packages that offer techniques such as pixilation or the blurring of faces[10] (Wiles et al., 2008b). However, it has been argued that pixelating images can dehumanize the individuals in them, and because of its widespread use on television, can invoke associations with criminality (Banks, 2001). Achieving anonymity with moving images is considerably more difficult (Wiles et al., 2008b).

Alternative approaches to anonymization can be found in the ways different types of visual data are presented. Marquez-Zenkov (2007) and Mizen (2005) adopt a more variable approach to anonymity, using pseudonyms to disguise participants' names alongside the seemingly unaltered images of those same individuals, though why names are deemed more important to hide than faces is not discussed by either author. Others do not publish images containing recognizable individuals in them. For example, Barrett's (2004) photographic essay of a needle exchange in a US city only shows photographs of hands or people with backs turned, and Moore et al.'s (2008) methodological discussion of a method in which 84 participants produced 1894 photographs of their local areas includes no images of individuals. Studies of community or 'place' also frequently show images that are absent of identifiable individuals (Crow and Wiles, 2008).

Cook and Hubbard's work with older people with dementia in care settings adopts an alternative solution to anonymity and confidentiality. One of their methods involved video recording interactions between older people in the home and with staff. One of the ways of disseminating the results of the research was through an interactive CD-ROM (Hubbard et al., 2003), in part because using still photographs or presenting transcript text was insufficient to display the often crucial non-verbal interactions they observed. The sensitivity of the recordings, and the difficulties of gaining consent from many of the participants recorded, meant that the video recordings could not be disseminated because they 'compromised the anonymity of the participants' (Cook and Hubbard, 2007: 27). Instead, the researchers worked with a film director, film crew and actors to recreate the research findings for dissemination.

Finally, there are occasions when researchers may be required to go against participants' wishes if they have consented to having their identities revealed in the dissemination of visual images. Banks (2001: 131–132) discusses the case of a documentary filmmaker working in a young offenders' institution who collected release forms from the individuals recorded to include them in the film. Some years later there was a possibility that the film would be broadcast on television. After tracing all the film's principal subjects to discuss this, one individual was unhappy with the prospect of appearing on television in this context, in part because he had gone on to live a crime-free life, concealing his past from his wife and colleagues. Consequently, despite still holding legally binding release forms, plans to screen the film were dropped. A second case is provided by Barrett's decision to publish photographs of individuals in a needle exchange. Just one female participant was willing to be photographed front-on sharing needles. However, Barrett does not show the photograph, not simply because in her 'over excitement' to be granted verbal consent to take the image she failed to get a signed consent form from the woman, but

also because, even with written consent, at a point later in time 'the young woman might feel differently about letting the world know she had a drug addiction and frequented a needle exchange' (Barrett, 2004: 149).

As the cases discussed by Banks and Barrett reveal, dissemination creates further dilemmas for the anonymity and confidentiality of visual data, particularly because researchers and participants are relinquishing control over how the data are interpreted, and possibly reused, by different audiences. The expansion of the Internet—in particular as a site to display, store, and retrieve visual images—has created further challenges (Lee, 2000; Pauwels, 2006; van Dijck, 2008), although visual researchers have always had to be careful when putting data in a public arena (Banks, 2001, 2007). Images placed on the Internet may be used in ways unintended by the original researcher or participants and, subsequently, cause distress or even damage the reputation of the participants. Placing photographs, films, and other visual data on the Internet 'intrinsically turns pictures into public property and therefore diminishes one's power over their presentational context' (van Dijck, 2008: 72). This means particular care should be taken to ensure participants understand the implications of consenting to images used in research being placed online.

Furthermore, while the Internet offers a potentially huge array of visual data for researchers to examine (Pauwels, 2008a), images found on the Internet are not simply 'there for the taking.' Rather, their appropriation for research should still 'fall within the scope of existing guidelines on ethical research practice in respect of informed consent, privacy, and confidentiality and the need to protect research participants from harm' (Lee, 2000: 135; Pauwels, 2006).

Individual moral framework

Researchers make their own ethical decisions within the context of their research.

However, the decisions they make are likely to vary. This is because researchers are aligned with different disciplines and paradigms, ask different questions, and apply different research methods. In other words, critical visual ethics are 'almost always a matter of context' (Becker, 1998: 85).

Societies are bonded by a broad agreement on ethical principles and moral behavior and it is individuals—within research communities, research groups, or acting alone—who (re)interpret those generic ethical principles to create their own interpretation of what constitutes 'right and wrong,' 'justice and injustice,' and, consequently, 'good and bad' ethical practices. There is a danger that, in striving to classify phenomena and build a systematic understanding of visual ethics that takes account of how contextual features mediate the influence of visual culture and societal norms, we lose sight of the fact that it is individuals who make ethical and moral decisions. Individuals hold a moral outlook and display a distinctive ethical orientation shaped by socialization, instilled values, and personal experiences. While there may be significant accord in terms of a collective moral compass, there is substantial disagreement about the application of ethical principles to particular research contexts. Bridging the gap between shared principles and individual's practice is imperative if visual research is to flourish.

Visual researchers need to identify their own moral positions and reflect on how this impacts on their research. We would anticipate that most readers and social scientists see themselves as being at the high end, or at the least, the 'virtuous' end, of the moral disposition spectrum, with a few acknowledging that ethics are not high on their list of methodological priorities. Most researchers will, from the outset of a study, recognize and address ethical dilemmas either before or as they arise and make decisions in accordance with their principles and beliefs. Few visual researchers knowingly place respondents in danger or unwittingly act unethically. Most researchers, we would argue,

adopt a stance close to one of three broad approaches to research ethics (Israel and Hay, 2006): namely, *consequentialist, non-consequentialist*, or *ethics of care*.

Individuals taking a *consequentialist* stance would claim that ethical decisions should be based on the consequences of specific actions, so that an action is morally right if it will produce the greatest balance of good over evil. They would weigh up a situation and choose the course of action that would result in the most beneficial outcome to society as a whole. A consequentialist might claim that it is acceptable to undertake covert visual research, for example on youth crime, if the findings of the research could be seen as benefiting wider society.

Individuals adopting *non-consequentionalist* approaches argue that priority should not be given to research ends, but, rather, that ethical decisions should be based on notions of what it is morally right to do regardless of the consequences. A non-consequentionalist approach argues that it is morally right to maintain confidence even if the consequences of that might not be beneficial or in the interests of the wider society. Non-consequentionalist approaches are akin to what Beauchamp and Childress (2001) term 'principalist,' which emphasizes principles of respect for people's autonomy, beneficence, non-malificence, and justice in making and guiding ethical decisions in research. Such value terms are commonly found in the opening paragraph of ethical guidelines and ethical advice from professional bodies and form the basis for evaluating applications to ethics committees (Israel and Hay, 2006: 37). The principles relate to issues of voluntariness, informed consent, confidentiality, anonymity, and avoidance of harm. Strict adherence to these principles may raise some difficulties for visual researchers.

In an *ethics of care* approach ethical decisions are made on the basis of care, compassion, and a desire to act in ways that benefit the individual or group who are the focus of research (Mauthner et al., 2002). This approach is used in much feminist and participatory research where researchers develop close relationships with their participants. Many established visual researchers call for the development of collaborative relationships in research which bears some relationship with an ethics of care approach (Gold, 1989; Banks 2001, 2007; Pink, 2007; Rose, 2007; Clark et al., 2010).

Key virtues such as integrity, truthfulness, and professionalism are progressively being linked to contemporary academic excellence, and reflected in the ethical standards expected by fund holders and university ethics committees (Macfarlane, 2009). Increasingly, research councils are stipulating that ethical awareness is a component of good research practice, and are requiring researchers to demonstrate that they have obtained appropriate ethical approval for their proposal. Individuals acting alone or in small groups will use their own moral compass to respond to the call for enhanced ethical practice. There are inevitable ethical gaps and anomalies resulting, for example, from ethics committee members applying principalist values and consequentially struggling to understand the ethical priorities of visual researchers working from collaborative, participatory or ethics of care perspectives. It is our contention that individuals experienced in prioritizing within an ethics of care approach (broadly understood) accentuate good practice and contribute to an informed, nuanced debate about situated visual ethics (Clark et al., 2010).

VISUAL ETHICS AT THE CROSSROADS

It is our contention that visual research methods sit uneasily within conventional social research ethical practices and regulatory mechanisms. Visual social scientists have come to a crossroads and need to be creative and constructive in their choice of direction to overcome ethical predicaments. Laws, regulations, and ethical dilemmas are omnipresent and therefore must necessarily be taken into account, but image-based researchers will need to do more. In this section, we highlight three factors: *visual culture*; further *research*; and *training*, (see Figure 36.5) which we believe need consideration in order to move visual ethics forward and maintain the integrity of visual research.

Visual culture

Researchers and the researched are neither isolated from society nor immune from its influences. The pervasive but hidden force of 'visual culture' is important to understand and take account of because it reflects powerful but implicit forces that shape everyday values, beliefs, and morals. More importantly, it influences behavior and ethical decision making by societal members, including researchers and the researched. Some elements of visual culture are global and have a significant international impact, whereas other elements are nationally, regionally, or locally felt. How does this show itself?

Being taken for granted and essentially stable, visual culture is most noticeable when changes take place. This can be seen in two examples. The first example concerns apparent innocuous indicators of change that, nonetheless, are underpinned by major shifts in government policy or public thinking which subsequently impact on empirical visual research. Take, for example, a poster produced by the Metropolitan Police in 2008 (London, UK) inviting the public to report suspicious-looking photographers, which begins with the statement '*Thousands of People Take Photos Every Day. What If One of Them Seems Different?*' and goes on to point out that '*Terrorists use surveillance to plan attacks.*' Professional and amateur photographers and researchers are increasingly being stopped from taking photographs in public spaces. In a magazine article, Delaney reports on this increasingly prevalent phenomenon:

> The Internet is home to a fast-growing, worldwide community of photographers who feel their hobby is being gradually outlawed by an increasingly

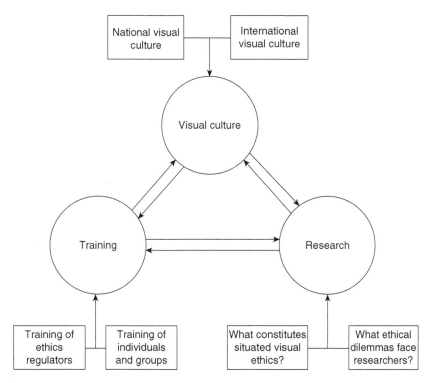

Figure 36.5 Finding a way forward—improving visual ethics practice

paranoid society. But photographers from America, Canada, Australia and beyond all seem to agree on one thing: nowhere is the situation worse than in Britain. "London Cops Declare War on Photographers," reads one headline on boingboing.net, a website at the hub of the issue. (2008: 18–19)

In the UK, photographers taking images in public spaces are experiencing reactions to the intensifying climate of fear of terrorism and pedophiles and also an intensifying climate of authoritarianism and surveillance (the UK has more CCTV cameras per head of population than any other country in the world). Heightened public sensitivity to photography in public spaces makes researcher reflexivity in such contexts especially important.

The concept of harm to others, including subjects of research, is culturally variable. The harm felt by some who believe that to take a photograph is to 'steal the soul,' transcends cultures and time. Pauwels, quoting

Grimshaw (1982), identifies loss of control as a reason why subjects in contemporary developed countries may prefer not to be photographed or filmed:

> a feeling … that some part of the self is being stolen; a sense of loss of anonymity; the non-deniability of presence on a scene when records are made a sense of concern that the features of permanence and reproducibility may make one vulnerable to ridicule or some other, unknown risk. (2008b: 245)

This point is further illustrated in the second example concerning the Internet. With no restrictions on what information can be shared, the Internet has become home to an assortment of websites containing visual data that governments have struggled to regulate (Gross et al., 2003). The ease by which a photograph or video, recorded on, for example, a mobile phone in one second can be transmitted globally in the next, has given rise to public uneasiness of visual records created of apparently inoffensive events.

Researchers are increasingly uneasy and restricted in their use of photography and video to record events and complex interactions, and unsure of legal or regulatory requirements (Sweetman, 2009). Research respondents are progressively more reticent about having their photographs taken. As described earlier, internal confidentiality is quickly undermined when respondents post images of themselves or their associates involved in a study on Facebook® or MySpace®. Administrators, legal officers, and researchers who constitute University Ethics Committees (UK) and Institutional Review Boards (USA) are increasingly uneasy with the collection and storage of visual data, often for legal reasons and out of fear of litigation. Unsurprisingly, ethics committees err on the side of caution and promote conservative visual research designs. The context in which visual research is conducted appears to be one which is increasingly restrictive and researchers need to be reflexive in identifying ways in which ethically sound research can be conducted that maintains its integrity and develops its potential. The need for further research and training for the research community is central to this.

Research

There is limited research on visual researchers' experience of ethical committees and ethics committees' experience of visual researchers, but anecdotal evidence suggests the need for further research. Pauwels notes:

> A recent conference session on ethics in visual research and in particular on the role of ethics review committees (IVSA Annual Conference, New York, August 2007) revealed the urgent need to address these (ethical) issues and also the willingness of most parties involved to improve the situation. Many participants testified about IRBs, which worked strictly by the book and were ignorant of the specific demands of visual research, and thus in good faith provided obstacles to innovative and

> well thought-through research. But there were also examples of review boards that did include people experienced in visual research, and which succeeded in making headway. (2008b: 256)

This suggests that there are important issues to be explored by consulting members of ethics review boards and applicants to those boards. Greater insight into the needs of researchers and board members, especially in terms of the ethical dilemmas they find most troublesome, would be useful. To this list of research questions we could add two more: How is ethical knowledge to be communicated to the research community? Should visual research ethics be considered differently to ethical practices and regulations covered by word- and number-centric regulations?

It is clear that many visual research dilemmas emerge only in relation to specific contexts and cannot be resolved by appeal to higher principles and codes (Birch et al., 2002; Renold et al., 2008). Visual ethics are situated in practice and the social world poses multiple ethical dilemmas. Further research in situated ethics will provide evidence that will be useful in a constructive dialogue with policymakers and allow visual researchers to think through and argue their ethical position with institutional ethics committees.

Training

Many visual researchers working within social science find devising, applying and normalizing visual ethics in their own work challenging. For them visual ethics is a minefield of statutory and legal confusion that needs to be navigated on the road to good practice. We have argued that visual research is at an ethical crossroad. Now would be an opportune moment to provide training based on prior identification of needs of those involved, including policy regulators, those charged with the task of creating and maintaining guidelines, IRB, and ethics committee members, and visual researchers.

The gap between substantive knowledge and researchers' understanding of visual ethics needs bridging. Ideally, training that filled this gap would be internationally coordinated for increased efficiency and effectiveness. At the very least, countries should look to establishing a national infrastructure of training through accessible, rigorous, and focused programs aimed at establishing visual-centric guidelines on best practice. There is a need for both face-to-face and e-learning provision, based on research evidence and focused on meeting the generic and unique needs of a broad spectrum of visual researchers, members of ethics committees and policymakers. Sitting on the ethical 'fence' is not an option for visual researchers. Being proactive is an option. Arguing for a visual perspective on research ethics requires field experience, knowledge, and a sound grasp of how to interpret and manage in situ ethical regulations and guidelines.

CONCLUSION

Researchers from a range of disciplines, paradigms, and methodological backgrounds are increasingly mandated to act ethically. Ethical reflexivity is a matter of awareness and sensitivity and is reflected in the degree of honesty and truthfulness in our dealings with others. These values are a measure of researchers' integrity and professionalism and are increasingly a requirement of all research institutions and funding bodies who aspire to excellence. To act ethically is to value integrity, inclusiveness, personal security, privacy, and dignity. For visual researchers, ethics guidelines and codes of practice cover important principles, but being 'visual' in orientation brings its own set of methodological practices and its own distinct set of ethical conundrums that require resolving. Visual methods are often collaborative and participatory, which leaves respondents at risk of being identified and misrepresented, especially on those occasions where research

has dual outcomes. Critical issues such as informed consent, confidentiality and anonymity are problematic but resolvable.

The title of this chapter 'Visual research ethics at the crossroads' is metaphorical, indicating that visual research has reached an important juncture and signifying it is timely to take stock and move in a new direction. At present, applications to conduct empirical visual research are given a label 'handle with care' by IRBs and ethics committees, who often evaluate and filter proposals through word-orientated measures based on past sound ethical practice. Visual researchers can and should meet the ethical criteria set by regulatory bodies and applied by institutional committees, but the onus is on them to make a case for consideration being given to visual methods within their specific contexts.

NOTES

1 This title is 'borrowed' from Douglas Harper (1993).

2 In this chapter, we refer to individuals and groups who take part in research as participants and respondents interchangeably.

3 This is a general guide by non-specialists and is necessarily limited in scope. This guide is not intended to be legal advice. Readers should seek legal advice from a competent lawyer if legal advice is required with regards to a specific situation.

4 An example of this in the UK context can be seen at: http://www.bakelblog.com/nobodys_business/2008/06/cops-bully-vide.html [Accessed 25 September 2010].

5 In the UK, research involving National Health Service staff or patients is subject to approval by NRES—The National Research Ethics Service: http://www.nres.npsa.nhs.uk/ [Accessed 25 September 2010].

6 Economic and Social Research Council: Framework for Research Ethics (FRE) (2010): http://www.esrcsocietytoday.ac.uk/ESRCInfoCentre/opportunities/research_ethics_framework/ [Accessed 25 September 2010].

7 European Commission (2007) Ethics for Researchers—Facilitating Research Excellence in FP7 Luxembourg: Office for Official Publications of the European Communities, ISBN 978-92-79-05474-7.

8 For examples of consent forms for the production and use of images for schools and Local

Education Authorities (UK), see http://www3.hants. gov.uk/logos/cx-logos-corporatestandards/cx-logos-imagesofpeople/cx-logos-images-sampleconsent. htm [Accessed 25 September 2010]. For an example used in social science research, see the appendices in Wiles et al. (2008b).

9 The Living Resemblances project was conducted as part of a program of work conducted by the Realities Node of the National Centre for Research Methods (UK): http://www.socialsciences. manchester.ac.uk/realities/research/resemblances/ [Accessed 25 September 2010].

10 For software to assist in anonymizing visual images, see: http//:www.yowussup.com/pixelating-images.php; and http://compression.ru/video/cartoonizer_en.html [Accessed 29 September 2010].

REFERENCES

Alderson P. and Morrow V. (2004) *Ethics, Social Research and Consulting with Children and Young People*. Barkingside: Barnardo's.

American Sociological Association (1999) *Code of Ethics and Policies and Procedures of the ASA Committee* [Online]. Available from: http://www2. asanet.org/members/ecoderev.html [Accessed 29 September 2010].

Back, L. with photographs by Evans, N., Genco, A. and Mitchell, G. (2004) 'Listening with our eyes: Portraiture as urban encounter', in C. Knowles and P. Sweetman (eds.), *Picturing the Social Landscape: Visual Methods and the Sociological Imagination*. London: Routledge. pp. 132–146.

Banks, M. (2001) *Visual Methods in Social Research*. London: Sage Publications.

Banks, M. (2007) *Using Visual Data in Qualitative Research*. London: Sage Publications.

Barrett, D. (2004) 'Photo-documenting the needle exchange: Methods and ethics', *Visual Studies*, 19(2): 145–149.

Beauchamp, T. and Childress, J. (2001) *Principles of Biomedical Ethics*, 5th edn. New York: Oxford University Press.

Becker, H. (1988) 'Forward: Images, ethics and organizations', in L. Gross, J. Katz and J. Ruby (eds.), *The Moral Rights of Subjects in Photographs, Films and Television*. New York: Oxford University Press. pp. xi–xvii.

Becker, H. (1998) 'Visual sociology, documentary photography, and photojournalism: It's (almost) all a matter of context', in J. Prosser (ed.), *Image-Based Research: A Sourcebook for Qualitative Researchers*. London: Routledge Falmer. pp. 24–41.

Birch, M., Miller, T., Mauthner, M. and Jessop, J. (2002) 'Introduction', in M. Mauthner, M. Birch, J. Jessop and T. Miller (eds.), *Ethics in Qualitative Research*. London: Sage Publications. pp. 1–13.

British Sociological Association (2002) *Statement of Ethical Practice for the BSA*. [Online]. Available from: http://www.sociology.org.uk/as4bsoce.pdf [Accessed 25 September 2010].

British Sociological Association (2006) *Visual Sociology Group's Statement of Ethical Practice* [Online]. Available from: www.visualsociology.org.uk/about/ethical_statement.php [Accessed 25 September 2010].

Chaplin, E. (2004) 'My visual diary', in C. Knowles and P. Sweetman (eds.), *Picturing the Social Landscape: Visual Methods and the Sociological Imagination*. London: Routledge. pp. 35–48.

Clark, A., Prosser, J. and Wiles, R. (2010) 'Ethical issues in image-based research', *Arts & Health*, 2(1): 81–93.

Cook, A. and Hubbard, G. (2007) 'More than meets the eye: Using video to record the interactions of older people with dementia in care settings', in A. Clark (ed.), *Making Observations: The Potential of Observation Methods for Gerontology*. London: Centre for Policy on Aging / The Open University. pp. 18–33.

Coomber, R. (2002) 'Signing your life away? Why research ethics committees (REC) shouldn't always require written confirmation that participants in research have been informed of the aims of a study and their rights—the case of criminal populations', *Sociological Research Online*, 7(1) [Online]. Available from: http://socresonline.org.uk/7/1/coomber.html [Accessed: 25 September 2010].

Crow, G. and Wiles R. (2008) 'Managing anonymity and confidentiality in social research: The case of visual data in community research', *National Centre for Research Methods Working Paper 8/08*. [Online]. Available from: http://eprints.ncrm.ac.uk/459/ [Accessed 25 September 2010].

Da Silva, O. and Pink, S. (2004) 'In the net: Anthropology and photography', in S. Pink, L. Kurti and A. Alfonso (eds.), *Working Images: Visual Representation in Ethnography*. Abingdon: Routledge. pp. 157–165.

Delaney, S. (2008) 'Framed', *Sunday Telegraph. Seven Magazine*, 18–21.

Dingwall, R. (2006) 'Confronting the anti-democrats: The unethical nature of ethical regulation in social science', *Medical Sociology Online* 1: 51–58.

Dingwall, R. (2008) 'The ethical case against ethical regulation in humanities and social science research', *21st Century Society: Journal of the Academy of Social Sciences*, 3(1): 1–12.

Farrell, A. (2005) *Ethical Research with Children.* London: Open University Press.

Fielding, N. (1982) 'Observational research on the national front', in M. Bulmer (ed.), *Social Research Ethics: An Examination of the Merits of Covert Participant Observation* New York: Holmes and Meier. pp. 80–104.

Gold, S. (1989) 'Ethical issues in visual field work', in G. Blank, J. McCartney and E. Brent (eds.), *New Technology in Sociology: Practical Applications in Research and Work.* New Brunswick, NJ: Transaction Publishers. pp. 99–112.

Gross, L., Katz, J. and Ruby, J. (1988) 'Introduction: A moral pause', in L. Gross, J. Katz and J. Ruby (eds.), *Image Ethics: The Moral Rights of Subjects in Photographs, Films and Television.* New York: Oxford University Press. pp. 3–33.

Gross, L., Katz, J. and Ruby, J. (2003) (eds.) *Image Ethics in the Digital Age.* Minneapolis, MN: University of Minnesota Press.

Hammersley, M. (2009) 'Against the ethicists: On the evils of ethical regulation', *International Journal of Social Research Methodology*, 12(3): 211–226.

Harper, D. (1993) 'On the authority of the image: Visual sociology at the crossroads', in N. Denzin and Y. Lincoln (eds.), *Handbook of Qualitative Sociology.* Beverly Hills, CA: Sage Publications. pp. 403–412.

Harper, D. (2004) 'Wednesday night bowling: Reflections on cultures of a rural working class', in C. Knowles and P. Sweetman (eds.), *Picturing the Social Landscape: Visual Methods and the Sociological Imagination.* London: Routledge. pp. 93–113.

Harper, D. (2005) 'What's new visually?', in N. Denzin and Y. Lincoln (eds.), *Handbook of Qualitative Research*, 3rd edn. Thousand Oaks, CA: Sage Publications. pp. 747–762.

Heath, S., Charles, V., Crow, G. and Wiles, R. (2007) 'Informed consent, gatekeepers and go-betweens: Negotiating consent in child- and youth-oriented institutions', *British Educational Research Journal*, 33(3): 403–417.

Henderson, L. (1988) 'Access and consent in public photography', in L. Gross, J. Katz and J. Ruby (eds.), *The Moral Rights of Subjects in Photographs, Films and Television*, New York: Oxford University Press. pp. 91–107.

Holliday, R. (2004) 'Reflecting the self', in C. Knowles and P. Sweetman (eds.), *Picturing the Social Landscape: Visual Methods and the Sociological Imagination.* London: Routledge. pp. 49–64.

Hubbard, G., Cook, A., Tester, S. and Downs, M. (2003) *Social Expression in Institutional Care Settings: A Multimedia Research Document.* CD-Rom published by the Dept. of Applied Social Science, University of Stirling.

Humphreys, L. (1975) *Tearoom Trade: Impersonal Sex in Public Places.* New York: Aldine.

Israel, M. and Hay, I. (2006) *Research Ethics for Social Scientists.* London: Sage Publications.

Jisc Digital Media (2010) [Online]. Available from: http://www.jiscdigitalmedia.ac.uk/stillimages/advice/copyright-and-digital-images/ [Accessed 29 October 2010].

Kaplan, I. (2008) 'Being "seen" being "heard": engaging with students on the margins of education through participatory photography', in P. Thomson (ed.), *Doing Visual Research with Children and Young People.* Abingdon: Routledge. pp. 175–191.

Krages, B. (2006) *Legal Handbook for Photographers.* Oregon: Amherst Media.

Lauder, M. (2003) 'Covert participant observation of a deviant community: Justifying the use of deception,' *Journal of Contemporary Religions*, 18(2): 185–196.

Lee, R. (2000) *Unobtrusive Methods in Social Research.* Buckingham: Open University Press.

Macfarlane, B. (2009) *Researching with Integrity.* Abingdon: Routledge.

McPherson, L. (2004) *Photographers' Rights in the UK* [Online]. Available from: http://www.sirimo.co.uk/2009/05/14/uk-photographers-rights-v2/ [Accessed 29 September 2010].

Marquez-Zenkov, K. (2007) 'Through city students' eyes: Urban students' beliefs about school's purposes, supports and impediments', *Visual Studies* 22(2): 138–154.

Masson, J. (2004) 'The legal context', in S. Fraser, V. Lewis, S. Ding, M. Kellett and C. Robinson (eds.), *Doing Research with Children and Young People.* London: Sage Publications. pp. 43–58.

Mauthner, M., Birch, M., Jessop, J. and Miller, T. (2002) *Ethics in Qualitative Research.* London: Sage Publications.

Miller, T. and Bell, L. (2002) 'Consenting to what? Issues of access, gate-keeping and "informed" consent', in M. Mauthner, M. Birch, J. Jessop and T. Miller (eds), *Ethics in Qualitative Research*, London: Sage Publications. pp. 53–69.

Mizen, P. (2005) 'A little "light work?" Children's images of their labor', *Visual Studies*, 20(2): 124–139.

Moore, G., Croxford, B., Adams, A., Refaee, M., Cox, T. and Sharples, S. (2008) 'The photo-survey research methods: Capturing life in the city', *Visual Studies*, 23(1): 50–62.

O'Donoghue, D. (2007) '"James always hangs out here": Making space for studying masculinities at school', *Visual Studies*, 22(1): 62–73.

Papademas, D. (2004) 'Editor's introduction: Ethics in visual research', *Visual Studies*, 19(2): 122–126.

Pauwels, L. (2006) 'Discussion: Ethical issues in online (visual) research', *Visual Anthropology*, 19(3&4): 365–369.

Pauwels, L. (2008a) 'A private visual practice going public? Social functions and sociological research opportunities of Web-based family photography', *Visual Studies*, 23(1): 34–49.

Pauwels, L. (2008b) 'Taking and using: Ethical issues of photographs for research purposes', *Visual Communication Quarterly*, 15(4): 1–16.

Pink, S. (2007) *Doing Visual Ethnography*, 2nd edn. London: Sage Publications.

Prosser J. (2000) 'The moral maze of image ethics', in H. Simons and R. Usher (eds.), *Situated Ethics in Education Research*. London: Routledge. pp. 116–132.

Prosser, J. and Loxley, A. (2008) *Introducing Visual Methods. National Centre for Research Methods Review Paper 010* [Online]. Available from: http://eprints.ncrm.ac.uk/420/ [Accessed 25 September 2010].

Prosser, J. and Schwartz, D. (1998) 'Photographs within the sociological research process', in J. Prosser (ed.), *Image-Based Research: A Sourcebook for Qualitative Researchers*, London: Falmer Press.

Renold, E., Holland, S., Ross, N. and Hillman, A. (2008) '"Becoming participant": Problematizing "informed consent" in participatory research with young people in care', *Qualitative Social Work*, 7(4): 431–451.

Rose, G. (2007) *Visual Methodologies*, 2nd edn. London: Sage Publications.

Ruby, J. (2000) *Picturing Culture: Explorations of Film and Anthropology*. Chicago, IL: University of Chicago Press.

Schwartz, D. (2002) 'Pictures at a demonstration', *Visual Studies*, 17(1): 27–36.

Schwartzenberg, D. (2005) 'The personal archive as historical record', *Visual Studies*, 20(1): 70–82.

Sweetman, P. (2009) 'Just anybody? Images, ethics and recognition', in R. Leino (ed.), *Just Anybody*. Winchester, UK: The Winchester Gallery, Winchester School of Art, University of Southampton.

Thomson, P. (ed.) (2008) *Doing Visual Research with Children and Young People*. Abingdon: Routledge.

Valentine, G., Butler, R. and Skelton, T. (2001) 'The ethical and methodological complexities of doing research with "vulnerable" young people', *Ethics, Place and Environment*, 4(2): 119–125.

van Dijck, J (2008) 'Digital photography: Communication, identity, memory', *Visual Communication* 7(1): 57–76.

Walker, R., Schratz, B., and Egg, P. (2008) 'Seeing beyond violence: Visual research applied to policy and practice', in P. Thomson (ed.), *Doing Visual Research with Children and Young People*. Abingdon: Routledge. pp. 164-174.

Warren, C. A. B. and Karner, T. X. (2005) *Discovering Qualitative Methods: Field Research, Interviews and Analysis*. Los Angeles: Roxbury.

Wiles, R. Crow, G. Charles, V. and Heath, S. (2007) 'Informed consent in the research process: Following rules or striking balances?' *Sociological Research Online*, 12(2) [Online]. Available from: http://www.socresonline.org.uk/12/2/wiles.html [Accessed 29 September 2010].

Wiles, R., Crow, G., Heath, S. and Charles, V. (2008a) 'The management of confidentiality and anonymity in social research', *International Journal of Social Research Methodology*, 11(5): 417–428.

Wiles, R., Prosser, J., Bagnoli, A., et al. (2008b) 'Visual ethics: Ethical issues in visual research', *National Centre for Research Methods Review Paper 011* [Online]. Available from: http://eprints.ncrm.ac.uk/421/ [Accessed 25 September 2010].

37

Legal Issues of Using Images in Research

Jeremy Rowe[1]

INTRODUCTION

Photographs and other visual materials have become important and essential resources for researchers. Images are drawn from many sources and are interpreted, analyzed, used to augment text, and stand on their own as portfolios and in exhibitions. Moreover, researchers create their own original visual resources as they document interviews or record events. Subjects, their relatives or communities often provide photographs to researchers. Museums, libraries, archives, and institutional collections are heavily used resources and invaluable sources for photographs. As increasing numbers of important collections are digitized, and as websites like Flickr and YouTube continue to grow, the Internet has become an important source for images of all kinds.

Regardless of the source, each image has associated contextual information, and embedded rights, which may, in fact, be very complex. This complexity increases as promises are made to subjects and sources, and as images are acquired during the course of the research. As analysis and interpretation lead to publication and dissemination, each step of these processes involves acquisition and transfer of a number of rights and permissions. Included are many associated responsibilities and liabilities that become increasingly important and complicated for both the researcher and the publisher.

Each step of the research process involves building and maintaining relationships while determining and creating the appropriate balance between diverse needs and incentives that vary across the parties involved. Commitments are made to sources of the photographs as permissions are obtained and transferred. As they write, ethnographers and other visual researchers create subtle, intricate interrelationships between text and visual materials that are highly contextual. These relationships are important to maintain as the work is published and as extracts, digests and collateral uses have the potential to deconstruct and alter the meanings and relationships embedded within the work. Understanding the process and potential implications of decisions as the process progresses can help researchers better curate these resources, minimize potential problems with subjects and image sources, and empower authors in discussing contracts with publishers.

This overview will help provide a framework for planning and making decisions about the rights and uses of photographs and other visual resources. Included will be general background discussions about copyright and ownership, permissions and rights, as images progress from original sources through collection, research, and interpretation to publication. Also included is a discussion of issues that arise in publication contracts and the implications of contract and associated ancillary rights, which are often included in such documents on the publication and subsequent uses of visual resources provided by the author.

Today, photographs permeate our lives in print, in exhibitions, in film and television, and online. Individuals are exposed to and consume thousands of images each day. The circumstances of their creation and use, their social context and cultural meaning, and the stories they convey are studied by many disciplines in the social sciences and humanities, and have generated unique languages and literacies for visual analysis. Photographs have become essential data sources for analysis and interpretation and are increasingly seen as valuable personal and cultural resources, ripe for research and analysis.

The process of acquiring and disseminating photographs has become increasingly complicated. Researchers interacting with subject populations must build and maintain relationships that can be either fostered or fractured by uses of photographs and interpretations of their subjects in print or online. As collections of photographs are assembled over time, the management and use of these materials become vital issues for both private and public collections and for the authors that access and use them.

Questions and issues related to who 'owns' the rights to use and reproduce photographs are complex and can vary significantly depending on acquisition circumstances, prior assignment of primary and ancillary

rights, age of the image, provenance, status of the previous 'owner,' and a number of other variables. Physical ownership, copyright, and reproduction rights coexist in a continually shifting legal and technological environment. As the market for, and traffic in, images continues to grow, and publishers push the envelope of digital distribution to generate a return on their investments, it is important to understand the rapidly changing environment in which researchers, collectors, curators, and publishers must work.

For years, authors and publishers have used libraries and archives as sources of images to illustrate articles and texts. Typically, the author would visit an institution, browse and select photographs, and then order copies for publication. Sometimes, researchers were permitted to bring in cameras and make their own negatives or slides; other institutions required researchers to pay the cost of creating negatives, prints, or scans.

Associated use fees were based on variables involved in the potential uses of the image, such as whether the publication was commercial or non-commercial, size of intended distribution or publication run, placement (cover, internal illustration), size of reproduction, etc.

Credit lines to acknowledge the source of the image were almost universally required. Many institutions also required a copy of the article or book after publication for verification or to help build collections. While some institutions limited image modification or cropping and required users to reproduce imaged 'full frame,' rarely was any attention paid to the context of the intended use or accuracy of presentation of the image, and few controls were in place to follow up on the proposed or future uses of the images.

Whether you are a photographic researcher seeking primary sources, a historian looking to augment textual research, collecting and interpreting visual resources, or an institution preparing an exhibition and catalog, you interact with multiple interconnected systems of laws, rights, and potential consequences.

The scope and impact of copyright laws and the interaction between these laws and academic publishing use for the web and in social media, or as a component of other outreach efforts are increasingly important for visual researchers to understand.

Today, researchers and authors face a daunting task when seeking illustrations, and must address challenging questions such as:

- What rights do you obtain when you purchase or acquire a photograph?
- What responsibilities do you have to the subject, source, or creator of the image?
- If you have a physical copy in hand (or a negative), can you copy it and use it for your own private or commercial uses?
- Can you restrict others from reproducing the image from their original copies?
- Can you permit or restrict other uses of the photograph for other purposes?
- Can you post a scanned copy of your work and the associated photographs on your web page or use them as part of an electronic publication?
- What responsibility do you have to insure that future uses comply with any agreements that you have made?
- What liability do you have for any unintended or inappropriate uses?

Copyright laws and publication contracts and their impact on the acquisition and use of visual materials such as photographs are constantly evolving. In addition, most decisions are not simply binary—there are few simple yes or no answers. Most answers involve assessing risk along a continuum from low to high risk. Incentives and priorities may vary significantly among those involved in the process. Individuals, publishers, and their attorneys each make their own determinations about potential uses and acceptable levels of risk for a given situation. The more the researcher and author know about rights and permissions, the better they can communicate and negotiate to insure that intended uses are accurately described, potential risks are moderated and the decisions made are as reasonable as possible.

Several factors are involved in ownership, permissions, and potential use of a photograph,

including copyright law, the ownership status of the seller or donor, and the permissions that are transferred as a result of sale, or transfer of rights in a publication contract. Copyright and intellectual property law has a significant potential impact, and is important to understanding ownership and use of photographs.

An exhaustive analysis and interpretation of copyright and permissions is beyond the scope of this discussion. A primary focus will be US copyright, but some references to international and non-US contexts will be made as appropriate.

COPYRIGHT OVERVIEW

The US copyright laws apply to tangible, fixed works, such as photographs, and assigns ownership to the creator, in the general tradition of *droit d'auteur*. However, in addition, copyright law in the United States also follows the Anglo-Saxon tradition of assignment of copyright to employers or to the hiring agent in specific cases defined as 'work for hire.' The US copyright protection is automatically extended when the work is created, if it meets the following four criteria. It must be:

- a work of authorship created through human effort;
- original with at least a minimal level of creativity fixed in a tangible form; and
- created by a US citizen or person living in the USA and/or published in countries that share copyright treaties with the USA.

Once a work is protected under the US copyright law, several very important rights are assigned to the copyright holder. The copyright holder may permit or restrict:

- copying or reproducing the work (such as print or electronic reproduction of a photograph);
- preparing derivative works (such as scanning to create a digital copy of a photograph);
- distributing or marketing copies of the work (such as posting digital copy on the Internet,

selling posters or postcards, or copy prints of the image); and
- publicly displaying the work (such as in a museum or gallery).

Each of these four rights is separate and the copyright holder or designee may permit or restrict others from using the material in any or all of these ways. In addition, the copyright holder may retain, assign, or license each of the rights in whole or part, to another party, such as:

- licensing a single right, such as reproduction for publication, or involve all aspects of copyright ownership for a given work;
- restricting use to a single instance, such as one print edition, or unlimited use, such as permitting unlimited print and electronic reproduction; and
- granting rights for a finite period of time, or for unrestricted use.

Researching the copyright and obtaining permissions or verifying ability to publish requires identification of the copyright holder for the work, and includes reviewing information, for example:

- type of work
- authorship (sole or joint)
- date created and potential duration of copyright protection
- creation circumstances (that is, contract service, work for hire, etc.)
- status as published or unpublished
- any transfers, assignments, or licenses that have occurred
- potential duration of copyright protection (based on creation date)
- compliance with copyright registration and renewal (for work created before 1 January 1978) to determine whether the work is now in the public domain

Determining the creation date and identifying the length of time a work is protected and whether it has passed into the public domain is an important step in deciding whether it is necessary to obtain permission for use.

The duration of ownership depends on the age of the image and the copyright laws that were in effect when the image was created.

After the time specified under copyright law, ownership control lapses, and the item enters the public domain. At this point the original creator or copyright holder has little or no legal ability to control subsequent use.

Copyright law originally assigned ownership for a finite time that has progressively expanded over time with each revision of the copyright law. Barring unusual circumstances, protection lasted for a maximum of 75 years for items created and published before the 1976 revision of the copyright law. For material originally created and published after 1 March 1978 (the effective date of the 1976 revision), copyright protection is for the life of the creator plus 50 years. Unpublished materials, such as diaries and family snapshots, were protected for the life of the creator plus 50 years.

Currently, copyright is assigned automatically at the time of creation, and © notices are no longer required for protection. Before 1986, failure to include a copyright notice, or use of an incorrect notice potentially shortened the duration of copyright protection. Materials that can be verified as meeting either of these two criteria may have fallen out of the control of the photographer or copyright holder and into the public domain.

The Digital Millennium Copyright Act (DMCA), passed in October 1998, significantly changed public domain timelines. The act (strongly supported by businesses with valuable intellectual property about to enter the public domain, such as Disney, and the estates of creative individuals such as the Gershwins) placed a 20-year moratorium on materials entering the public domain. This froze 1 January 1923 as the date for copyright protection to lapse, and for the works entered the public domain. The net effect is that no new material will automatically enter the public domain until 2018. Unfortunately, the impact on unpublished materials is unclear, as they were not specifically addressed in the act.

An interesting exclusion under copyright law is works created 'by an officer or employee of the US Government as part of that person's official duties.' This potentially simplifies the process of obtaining permissions for such resources, but it is still important to look a bit further before proceeding. The US government employs many contract workers and subcontractors that do not fall under this exclusion. The exclusion covers works created by federal employees only, not state, local, or other governmental entities. Publications by the federal government can include material from other sources licensed for specific use but with the copyright retained by the creator. Finally, it is important to note that US government publications are excluded from the US copyright protection; these works are protected by copyright in other countries.

Once copyright protection lapses, the image passes into the public domain, and the copyright holder no longer controls its use. However, it is still possible to limit access to the original image for copying and reproduction to provide some level of control for public domain images. Libraries, archives, and others collections control access to their originals and can place requirements on reproduction, and charge use fees (not copyright fees) for providing that access. Following this model, many researchers have become collectors and acquire original public domain images to simplify access and permissions for publication.

For researchers interested in images produced in the USA before 1976, it is possible to review records to help determine the level of risk in using a particular image. Prior to 1976, the US Copyright Office published semi-annual application and renewal information that can be used to begin to determine whether the original copyright was ever filed, and, if filed, was correctly renewed. Though some of these reports are being digitized, locating hard copies in a government documents collection may be required. It is interesting to note how few photographs actually appear in these listings. Even if the images do not appear in the listing, if they were published, they are potentially protected if the copyright for the publication was filed and appropriately renewed.

When photographs are protected by copyright it is usually the responsibility of the author to identify the copyright holder and obtain the appropriate permission for publication. Efforts to obtain permission for publication can be a complex and frustrating process, particularly if the copyright holder cannot be identified or located, or if any or all of the rights have been transferred to other parties. There is no central repository of information about the rights held or transferred, and in many cases significant research is required to locate the owner of the copyright. In addition, there is no requirement for the copyright holder to grant permissions or to respond to requests. A final frustration arises from the fact that once located they are not compelled to respond, and their failure to do so does not imply permission.

There is one exception to the requirement to obtain prior permission of the copyright holder for any of the four categories of uses outlined above, defined as 'fair use.' The fair use exemption permits some educational, reporting, critical uses of materials still protected under copyright law (for additional information on 'fair use,' see 17 USC Sec. 107). One of the key factors in 'fair use' is the potential impact of the use on the marketability of the item in question.

Commercial publication is seen as clearly impacting the potential market for the work, both in terms of fees for the use, and as a potential source for additional reproduction. In the digital environment, building a case for 'fair use' is troublesome for several reasons:

- the ease of duplication of digital files;
- the difficulty in controlling duplication of digital files; and
- the commercial nature of the Internet has made the market impact test of 'fair use' difficult for any materials that have been made available online.

Digitizing a photograph protected by copyright can be seen as creating a derivative work, a right not addressed under fair use that requires permission of the copyright holder under the law. Also, a compelling case can be made that any digital posting has the potential to significantly affect the market for a given image. It would be difficult to show that posting a digital copy, particularly a high-resolution digital copy, of a photograph available online would not have an effect on the potential market for the work and thereby fail that fair-use criteria.

Understanding the range of potential uses and clearly communicating to all parties throughout the process remains a vital part of preparing for print or electronic publication. Currently, the process of obtaining permissions is usually less complex for print than for electronic publication, where these processes are still evolving. Evaluation of potential uses of visual materials include a number of possible steps:

- Identify the intended uses as completely as possible. Will the material see print or electronic distribution, use an academic journal or for-profit publisher, what is the size of print run, etc.? Also, will supplemental materials such as video, DVD, or online presentation be a component of the project?
- Identify the warranties and permissions made by the source or collection. Do they provide access to the image, copyright permissions, or both? Also, for materials still protected by copyright, such as published photographs created after 1 January 1923 or unpublished images, any donor or gift stipulations that may limit use should be noted. If necessary, obtain contact information for, and permissions from, parties who may have an ownership claim to the images before publication.
- Note whether the image is from an original print or a copy print. Many collections have been built with copy prints from other collections: reproduction rights are rarely transferred along with these copy prints. Reproduction from published material may also involve the additional copyright permissions from the publisher or copyright holder. Whenever possible, for reasons of both ownership and reproduction quality, locate and work with an original print rather than a copy.
- Determine if a well-known photographer or publisher created the work. If so, the photographer, estate, or designee may retain or imply ownership of some or all rights needed for publication. Also, moral rights, potentially limiting

some uses without additional permissions, may more heavily influence materials created in other countries.

- Identify any duplication or reproduction fees that are associated with the intended use. Also, note whether copies of the publication are required by the collection. Identify necessary credits and insure that they are included throughout the reproduction and publication process and as ancillary rights are executed.
- Get all model releases, agreements, and stipulations in writing from collections and copyright holders. Many publishers now require verification of permissions, such as reproduction, display, or other rights that are involved in a given project.
- For your protection, maintain a file of correspondence related to your research, including written permissions and fees paid.

Government collections, such as the National Archives and Library of Congress, have long been popular sources of visual resources since materials produced under federal grants and contracts typically include assignment of rights to government entities. Obtaining rights for print reproduction from these sources is relatively straightforward, and other than reusing many of the same frequently reproduced images, raise few concerns as a source for older, public domain material. Recently, however, some subcontractors have begun to grant to government agency permissions for specific use only, and retain other ownership rights. This practice will necessitate obtaining permissions from the copyright holder for such material, adding a new layer of complexity for researchers and publishers, but providing additional control to the copyright holder.

Use of images in electronic government collections, such as the Library of Congress American Memory project may involve addressing the ownership claims of the subcontractors who created the digital derivative works by scanning and structuring the image collections and retain at least some ownership rights. The issue of ownership of derivative works has yet to play out in the courts, but appears to hinge on the level of creative input in digitizing projects as well as project contracts. This is yet another facet of copyright ownership and control that researchers should attend to in the future.

LICENSES

A number of online photo-hosting/posting services ebb and flow in terms of popularity: current examples include Facebook, Photobucket, YouTube, ImageShack, sites hosted by camera manufacturers like Nikon and Kodak, and many more. The contracts for many of these image-hosting/posting sites permit them to redistribute and reuse the images that have been posted to their sites. The ability to reuse the images as they see fit provides the sites with another potential source of revenue. Once posted to these sites, control of the use of the image and associated captions and source credits slips away from the researcher.

The Creative Commons is a non-profit corporation that has developed a series of licenses that can be associated with the images to indicate the potential uses intended by the creator of the image. These licenses permit the creator to openly publish permissions or restrictions to use an image commercially, to allow modification or derivative works, and define any geographic restrictions (worldwide or limited to the USA or other country only). Since the current US copyright law automatically assigns copyright to the creator with no process described to release the image to the public domain, the Creative Commons license provides for such assignment. The licenses also permit the creator to embed title, attribution, source URL, and contact information to discuss obtaining additional permissions. They offer four license conditions, which can be combined to specifically define a variety of uses, including: attribution; attribution share alike; attribution no derivatives; attribution non-commercial; attribution non-commercial share alike; and attribution non-commercial no derivatives.

The license can be embedded in individual web pages, and published to the Internet Archive (http://www.archive.org). Unlike many other image posting sites, Flickr works with the Creative Commons licenses to post, host, and associate license information with the images. Google and Yahoo also support the Creative Commons licenses and can restrict searches to identify Creative Commons licensed content.

MORAL RIGHTS

There are several definitions of moral rights that are relevant to the discussion of ownership and use of photographs and visual materials. The term moral right, derived from the French *droit morale*, typically refers to the right of authors to prevent revision, alteration, or distortion of their work, regardless of who owns the work. The application to integration of photographs and text in publication has not yet been addressed in court, but the concept is important in following the path of photographs as they are licensed for publication.

Moral rights cover three aspects of uses of photographic images, giving the author/owner/license holder the ability to:

- Have the name of the photographer/creator associated with the reproduction of the image during display or publication.
- Control changes that would impact the reputation of the creator, or that distort, mutilate, or change the intent or meaning of the photograph.
- Limit the association of the photograph with a product, service, cause, or institution without permission of the creator.

These rights, and similar issues of control, such as approval of publication venue, are critical to insuring continuity of use and to honoring the commitments made, and relationships with the subjects of the research and sources of related visual materials.

Moral rights extend beyond the life of the creator and are becoming a more important factor in use of photographs, as the USA and other countries coordinate their copyright policies under the World International Property Organization (WIPO). The concept of moral rights varies significantly across countries and cultures. In the USA, moral rights are defined in the Visual Artists Rights Act of 1990 (VARA) and apply to visual art such as photographs. In general, they transcend the assignable copyrights and address the ability of the author or creator to claim ownership and object to distortion, mutilation, modification, or derogatory action related to their honor or reputation. Some countries, such as France, include the additional right of retraction—the authority for the creator to remove the work from public view. For example, the estate of John Huston blocked a colorized version of 'Asphalt Jungle' from being shown in France, on the grounds that colorizing violated Huston's moral right of integrity by modifying the original film without his permission.

Another related issue that impacts the relationships between researchers, subjects, and publishers is the right of publicity, which addresses the use of the likeness of recognizable personalities such as Charlie Chaplin, W. C. Fields, or James Dean, as well as unauthorized pictures of private individuals. Strong lobbying, particularly by the entertainment industry and estates of prominent public figures, has led to increasing ability to control the use of photographs by individuals and their estates. Again, even though you own an original copy of a photograph, the right of publicity may limit your ability to use the image without obtaining permission from the subject or controlling estate.

An interesting example of individual control of likenesses in a cultural context has arisen in Hopi Tribal Resolution H-70-94 (adopted 23 May 1994) and policy documents from the Hopi Cultural Preservation Office. Under the Native American Graves Protection and Repatriation Act (NAGPRA), the Hopi demanded that they retain the rights to any cultural property collected through field notes, photographs, audio tapes, etc.

The Hopi people seek to limit exploitation of their culture and beliefs by controlling access to collateral materials such as photographs. The tribe has worked for years with local museums and public collections, educating archivists and assisting in identifying sensitive materials whose access and use should, in their view, be restricted. The interesting factor in this approach is the claim of a broader moral right to control access, instead of the trail of ownership upon which copyright is usually based.

In addition to the legal definition, there are moral and social responsibilities for researchers to remain consistent with the agreements made with their subjects and sources of the photographs that they acquire for research and publication.

Written agreements, such as model releases and reproduction releases from libraries, museums, and archives are essential in documenting and communicating the rights associated with, and uses permitted for visual material controlled by the author. Examples of Personal Use Agreements that can be used by researchers are available on the Stanford University Libraries site at: http://fairuse.stanford.edu/Copyright_and_Fair_Use_Overview/chapter12/12-c.html.

Reproduction releases from libraries, museums, and archives should be reviewed to insure that they accurately address all of the future potential uses of the images involved: for example single or multiple print editions, online access, etc.

The ancillary licenses, typically in publication contract boilerplate, permit a broad range of possible uses, with a variety of potential consequences. At one end of the spectrum, the publisher could license images from the work for other educational uses. Concerns for such uses typically involve potential conflicts, such as possible appearance of your images in work by other academics that may or may not be consistent with your analysis and interpretation, or are contrary to the agreements made with your subjects and sources.

Potentially more problematic are editorial use, typically involving illustration to augment a story in a newspaper or news magazine. The author and publisher have little or no control over the use, or whether it is consistent with the original commitments made by the author. Of greatest concern is licensing of images from the work for commercial use. Such uses associate the photograph with commercial products and imply relationships between the image and subjects depicted and the products or campaign.

For example, consider a case where an archive is approached by a company to license what is believed to be a unique image of a Native American prominent in local history for commercial use in the logo of a new bar. The request is declined due to issues of sensitivity regarding alcohol use by local tribes and in respect for a slowly developing and budding relationship between the tribe and the archive. The same image is then licensed to an author for use in a regional history text. The bar owner learns that the publisher has access to the image and submits a request for its use. Under the ancillary rights provisions of the contract with the author, the publisher could subsequently licenses use of the image to the bar, whose advertising campaign includes billboards and print ads that blanket the community, including the reservation. Tribal leaders become incensed at the use and hold the archive accountable. The archive explores taking legal action against the author for exceeding the use license granted for print publication of the regional history.

When making photographs in the field, there is a balance between the free-expression rights of the photographer and the privacy rights of the subject. Implicit and explicit commitments are made by the researcher about the scope of the project and potential future uses of the images produced. Obtaining written model releases can be uncomfortable and the discussion of rights and permissions can change the dynamic between researcher and subjects. It is safe to assume that most researchers focus these discussions on the use of images related to their specific project. If mentioned at all, licensing these rights to the publisher and discussion of other potential uses under the ancillary rights portions of the contract are handled delicately and often understated, since they have the greatest potential for disrupting the relationship between researcher and subject.

Contract documents frequently assign responsibility for obtaining releases and permissions and potential liability for misuse to the author. At the same time, these documents typically include permissions for the publisher to license the material for a variety of uses, including educational, editorial and commercial use. Where the uses become commercial, the shift of the burden for permissions and documentation to the author is particularly problematic. Most publishers require a written model releases that document permission of the subjects for such use, since commercial use of the likeness of an individual without permission can be seen as violating their right of publicity and lead to a claim of commercial exploitation.

Since the contract documents typically hold the publisher harmless and assign responsibility and liability to the author, the publisher is free to grant permission for virtually any type of editorial or commercial use unless specifically restricted in the contract documents. It is important that authors understand the commitments that they have made during preparation of their manuscript. It is also important for authors to understand the expectations of the publisher for ancillary uses as potential revenue streams. It is critically important to discuss and reflect in the contract documents specific permissions obtained, any limitations to potential uses, notification or prior review/approval for ancillary use and permissions obtained. The author is responsible for accurately and comprehensively conveying the potential uses to the subjects and sources of visual materials as the project evolves. Model releases and permissions obtained by the author should be consistent with the full range of potential uses permitted in the publication contract and associated documents that address ancillary uses of the work and its components.

Visual researchers create linkages between text and images that construct new meaning. The relationships are defined by the author and rely on sometimes-subtle interactions between such things as captions, tense, structure, and metaphors. The author determines the importance of maintaining these relationships for the reader. As the publication process progresses, a number of challenges arise as ancillary rights are executed. Attending to quotation, digest and other uses where the work is extracted are particularly important.

The reputations of researchers and the relationships that they build with their subjects, their peers, and source collections in libraries, archives, and museums are slow to develop and hard won. They build on a series of small successes that rely on trust and impressions. This trust can easily be eroded by misuse, misinterpretation, or misattribution. Even if successful, rebuilding it can be a long and painful process of identifying images, obtaining permissions and transferring these permissions to others, such as publishers. Loss of control or assignment of rights with unintended consequences can create awkward situations for the author and jeopardize these relationships.

In their efforts to market the work of authors and generate a return on their investment, publishers seek to minimize their overhead in terms of recordkeeping and locating and communicating with the author for permissions when opportunities arise for ancillary uses and other opportunities to generate revenue. Unless specifically stated in the contract documents, the overall assumption of rights absorbs many aspects of control, including these moral rights, giving the publisher the autonomous ability to license uses and assigning responsibility and liability to the author.

Restating the theme of this piece, the better authors understand issues of ownership, permissions, and the publication process and of the potential implications of contracts and agreements, the more effectively they can interact with others throughout the process to identify potential problems that could impact reputations and relationships.

THE DIALOG BETWEEN 'THE AUTHOR' AND 'THE PUBLISHER'

A critical part of the chain of responsibility for visual researchers is interaction with publishers through contracts and agreements. Typically identified components in contracts include Author, Publisher, and Work and specification of rights and responsibilities. 'Standard' agreements include boilerplate, which may include rights and potential uses that may not necessarily be consistent with the needs and intent of the Author. Though there are incentives that are shared by both parties, Publishers are responsible for investing in production, marketing, sales, and accounting and must generate a return on their investment to remain viable.

Authors should understand that the contract presented by the Publisher is a starting point, and typically subject to discussion and some modification. As Authors understand more about the implications of the contract and supplemental documents, they increase their ability to raise and discuss important issues with the Publisher.

An important area for discussion is the intellectual property rights associated with visual materials that are incorporated in the Work. The Author typically is responsible for providing the visual materials and assuring that the appropriate rights and permissions can be transferred to the Publisher. In assembling these materials, the Author makes commitments and signs agreements, with the primary focus on gaining access and on meeting submission deadlines. Typically, the focus is on print publication, but Publishers' contracts and agreements often include a number of other potential uses that should be understood and discussed.

Publishers seeking additional revenue sources include broader potential uses than just the print version, such as rights for database and electronic distribution, mechanical reproduction, merchandise, and commercial use. Unless specifically described or limited in the contract and associated documents, these uses can expand the possible uses of the component photographs and visual materials, often without requirements to retain captions or credit sources. Such uses potentially place publishers and sources such as libraries and archives in competition, marketing, and using the images. Unfortunately, since the Author has signed agreements with the sources, unless the agreements are aligned in terms of permissions and uses, the Author is responsible for any conflicts that arise.

The contract should also specify whether the Publisher will be solely responsible for marketing and print and electronic distribution, or if the Publisher can license these activities to third parties. If third-party licensing is to be permitted, issues related to the requisite loss of control and accountability may be moderated if the Author includes a contractual right to review and approve/deny prior to execution of these supplemental agreement.

This brief summary begins to address some of the issues and potential concerns related to the photographs and visual materials raised by a hypothetical sample contract. Authors are strongly encouraged to further research these issues to help inform their attorney and dialog with their Publisher as they review and refine the contract.

Granted rights

Publication contracts typically begin with an assignment of right to publish the work by the Author, including all photographs, illustrations, graphics, and text. To provide maximum flexibility and to create opportunities for generating additional revenue, the generic contracts sent to the Author begin with extremely broad rights. The hope is that the Author will sign as presented and not offer alternatives.

An example of the breadth might be a statement such as:

> The Author hereby grants to the Publisher the sole and exclusive right and license to print, reproduce, publish, sell, lease, display, transmit and to further license the Work, and revisions or derivative works,

in all forms, including but not limited to, digital or electronic media and any other media not yet known or recognized, in all languages within the United States and in all other countries throughout the world for the full legal term of copyright in the United States and each other applicable jurisdiction, along with the ancillary rights specified in Exhibits X...

This statement would transfer the Author's rights for that work to virtually all print and electronic content to the Publisher. It is important for the Author to read and understand the entire document, including any exhibits and supplemental documents. Each portion can refine or broaden the rights and permissions and the potential uses of the Work by the Author and Publisher.

When signed, the example of assignment of rights will require the Author to obtain permission from the publisher for any use not justifiable under the 'fair use' exemption of copyright law This would include uses such as posting extracts on websites, submitting extracts of the work for conference publication, in anthologies, etc.

If these issues are of concern, it is possible for the Author to propose a less broad license that still provides the Publisher with the opportunity to recover his investment, but provides access of interest to the Author. An example might be to limit the license to a one-time license to publish the work in printed form, but to eliminate the verbiage licensing derivative works and digital and electronic transmission. Some Publishers generate additional revenue licensing digital rights to libraries and other entities through subscription services. If so, the Author and Publisher will need to discuss implications and decide on the viability of the project under the proposed circumstances.

Non-compete clause

For Publishers to obtain a return on their investment, they often seek assurance that Author will not create other books or articles that directly compete with the ability to market the Work. For example:

> During the term of this Agreement, the Author agrees not to prepare any work, or publish or authorize the publication of any work which may be an expansion or an abridgement of or of a nature similar to the Work, or that is likely to affect prejudicially the sales of the Work or to otherwise adversely affect the value of the rights granted to the Publisher hereunder.

If the Author is actively publishing in the discipline or subject, it may be helpful to disclose and discuss with the Publisher specific limitations that meet the intent of not competing, but protect the ability of the Author to publish. Examples of possible alternative descriptions to a generic non-compete clause might include description of number of pages, style or format, price range, or specific subject and market for the Work and agreement not to compete in these specific markets.

Duties of the Author and Publisher

Contracts typically include requirements that the Author meet a defined schedule for the original manuscript, often including requirements for number of words, illustrations, etc., and response times for any revisions or corrections. Also addressed are clarification of the responsibility of the Author to produce or supply the photos, graphs, illustrations, and other collateral material associated with the Work. The Publisher needs such assurances to plan for production and promotion of the Work.

If there has been a delay by the Author or if costs are incurred for changes once the layout and proofs for the Work have been completed, the contract clarifies responsibilities, determination of costs, and reimbursal process, such as repayment to the Publisher by billing the Author, or deduction from future royalties.

The Author may also be required by the Publisher to update the Work when and as appropriate, or to permit the Publisher to do so if the Author can or will not do so.

Publishers accept responsibility for publication, registration for copyright, and inclusion of appropriate credits and also seek to limit liability for any damage to materials while in their possession, such as photographs or illustrations.

The discussion of duties and responsibilities for permissions is linked with the other sections of the contract and should be reviewed to make certain they are consistent in scope and intent throughout.

Indemnification

The Publisher needs assurance that the Author is the owner and creator of the Work, and that they have or have obtained the ability to transfer appropriate licenses and permissions to the Publisher. In addition, many contracts contain boilerplate to protect the Publisher by assigning liability for legal action against the Publisher for libelous, defamatory, or otherwise illegal content. In addition, the contract may seek protection from action by requiring the Author to indemnify and hold harmless the Publisher and its employees from legal action regarding claims or editorial changes to the Work prior to publication.

Other general contract issues

- Royalties and accounting: typically addresses verification of the royalty rate agreed upon by Author and Publisher for the original and any ancillary Works, and processes for payment and challenges of the accounting.
- Purchases and complimentary copies of the Work and any limitations to resale or distribution by the Author.
- Discontinuance of publication and remainder sales: clarification of Publisher's responsibility to keep the Work in active distribution, and how remaining copies will be dispersed if and when the publication is remaindered.
- Ability of the Author to appoint an agent for dealing with the Publisher.

- Successors and assignments: inures the benefit of the contract and binds heirs and successors to abide by the contract.
- Conditions for termination and default: clarifies triggers for action and process to be followed.
- Jurisdiction for claims and any legal action: specifies jurisdiction for any legal challenges.
- Reservation of rights by the Author: typically states that any rights not specifically stated and enumerated in the agreement (such as moral rights outlined above) revert to the Publisher.

In addition to the base contract, most agreements between Author and Publisher include additional exhibits and supplemental materials. These documents can have a significant impact on the use and distribution of not only the Work but also of the photographs, illustrations, and text from which it is composed. As a result, it is extremely important for the Author to understand and assess the potential implications of the rights and uses of the Work, and on the understanding and expectations of those depicted, or the subjects or sources of any of the component visual materials. Often these are addressed as Ancillary Rights.

In addition to print sales, many Publishers plan to augment revenue by some form of electronic distribution. Though there are hundreds of years of history of agreements for print publications, and at least a reasonable understanding of the general markets and parameters for print publication, the understanding of electronic markets is still emerging. As a result many contracts tend to be overly broad in their assertion of digital rights. Digital rights have the potential to significantly impact the use and interpretation of the visual materials within the Work, and offer the highest likelihood that they are reused and potentially reinterpreted in ways that can cause problems. These components of the contract should be carefully read and compared with other sections that address copyright and intellectual property rights.

Database and companion rights

These rights are described in a manner such as:

Electronic Storage, Retrieval, and Digital Media Rights (i.e. the right to use, produce or reproduce, distribute, perform, display, transmit or broadcast the Work or any portion thereof in which the Author has secured rights or to license such uses of the Work or any portion thereof in which the Author has secured rights by any and all methods of copying, recording, storage, retrieval, broadcast or transmission of the Work or any portion thereof, alone or in combination with other works, including in any multimedia work or electronic book, Web site or database, by any electronic, electromagnetic or other means now know or hereafter devised including, without limitation, by analog or digital signal, whether in sequential or non-sequential order, on any and all physical media now known or hereafter devised including without limitation, magnetic tape, floppy disks, interactive CD, CD-ROM, laser disk, optical disk, integrated circuit card or chip and any other human or machine readable medium, whether or not permanently affixed in such media, and the broadcast or transmission thereof by any means now known or hereafter devised, but excluding audio recording rights, video recording rights and all uses encompassed in motion picture, television, radio and allied rights).

Obviously, this wording is extremely broad and includes a tremendous range of potential uses from tangible media (CD, DVD, etc.) to online distribution to any potential future media. Included is the ability to use, and potentially repurpose, portions of the Work such as photographs and illustrations that have been included by the Author. Also included are rights to reformat into other media, and a final catch-all—'allied rights.'

It is incumbent on the Author to understand these potential uses early in the research and creative process. When obtaining rights for publication, the Author is responsible for conveying these potential uses to any contributors that are supplying visual materials. Under the contract, failure to do so places the liability with the Author.

In addition, since the exhibit outlines use of portions of the Work, there is a potential for uses that can reinterpret or change the meaning of the visual material. At best, such uses can be disconcerting for the Author; at worst, they can jeopardize the relationships with subject populations and clients.

Companion products

Companion products such as postcards, notebooks, and other merchandise are potential sources of revenue to augment print sales. Such uses can benefit both Author and Publisher. They can also compete directly with sources such as museums and archives. Unless the publication agreement with these sources includes these potential uses, and any additional fees that might be involved, the Author will be potentially liable if such competition arises. Even so, such competition can strain or destroy carefully built relationships between the Author and his sources.

An additional concern is that the Author is rarely contacted for approval of collateral uses that are frequently driven by marketing and promotion departments and emphasize marketability over intellectual accuracy.

Understanding the potential implications for these rights empower the Author to discuss with the Publisher limitations that will provide economic incentives and potential revenue, but will limit or control uses that are potentially problematic.

Unless specifically stated in the agreement with the Publisher, there is not a requirement to include captions or sources of the images. Though most Publishers do request caption or credits for ancillary uses they are rarely specifically required in the license. Also, Publishers typically do little to follow up on whether the subsequent publication accurately includes the captions or credits. When reproduction occurs without appropriate captions or credits it places an additional strain on the relationships between the Author and their sources and, as stated earlier, is a potential source of liability for the Author.

Example

The Researcher approaches a liberal activist family on the board of the Researcher's university and makes a portrait of their daughter working at her computer as an example of innovative and effective home schooling for use in a textbook. After publication, the Publisher is approached by a fundamentalist charter school looking for an image of educational computer use for an advertising campaign. Since the Author has assigned such ancillary rights to the Publisher and did not require retaining associated credits, the image is licensed for the advertising use. A local news expose on the creationist curriculum of the school is picked up by national news as a lead story and the image is used prominently as an illustration of a charter school student during discussion about the tension between creationism and evolution in school curricula. The family holds the Author personally responsible for the bad publicity and damage to their reputation and that of their minor daughter.

Ancillary rights

Publishers attempt to obtain the broadest ancillary rights to assist in marketing and to generate potential publicity and revenue. Each of these rights has potential benefits to both Author and Publisher, but each raises potential concerns that should be discussed and addressed. Examples of ancillary rights with a brief description of benefits and potential issues include:

Quotation and anthology rights
These rights address the right of the Publisher to reproduce text or visual materials from the Work in other publication venues. Concerns related to these rights involve the scope of the extracts, as well as the ability to maintain the contextual relationships between text and images, or captions and source credits if the images are reproduced separately. Such issues should be discussed and any limitations or ability for prior review by the Author should be specified in the agreement.

- Digest rights: the right to publish an abridgement of the Work in a single issue of a journal, periodical, or newspaper.

- One-shot periodical rights: the right to publish the complete Work or any extract from it in a single issue of a journal, periodical, or newspaper.
- Digest book condensation rights: the right to publish a shortened form of the Work in volume form.
- Strip cartoon book rights/picturization book rights and first serial rights, second and subsequent serial rights: the right to publish one or more extracts from the Work in successive issues of a periodical or newspaper following publication of the Work in volume form.

The ability of the Publisher to distribute digests is a significant promotional and marketing tool. Unfortunately, unless specified in the agreement, there is no:

- review by the Author for accuracy, continuity of relationships between test and images or intent prior to publication;
- requirement to include citations for the text reproduction;
- requirement to include captions and sources for visual materials;
- limitation to the scope of the extracts published; and
- limit to the number of images that can be reproduced for a given use.

Also, unless specified, there is no restriction regarding the type of venue or relationship of the publication to the Work. If these issues are a concern to the Author, or to the sources or subjects of the visual materials, they should each be discussed with the Publisher, agreed upon, and specified in the agreement.

- Mechanical reproduction rights: the right to produce or reproduce the Work or any portion thereof or to license the reproduction of the Work or any portion thereof by film micrography, reprographic reproduction, gramophone records or tapes, cassettes and compact disks, film strip, video cassettes, or by any other means or methods now or hereafter known or invented, except insofar as reproduction is for use as part of or in conjunction with a commercial cinematographic film.
- Television rights: readings from the text or showing of illustrations or photographs from the Work.

- Sound broadcasting rights: readings from the text of the Work.
- Dramatization and documentary rights: on stage, film, radio, television, or any other medium.

Unless specified in the agreement, assignment of such rights can further separate control of the component materials in the Work from the Author, sources, and subjects, and even Publisher. At best there will be discussion and coordination of the component text and visual materials as they are licensed for these ancillary uses. At the other end of the spectrum, such verbiage permits the Publisher and its assignees to use and reuse the visual materials in virtually any type of production activity that may or may not be consistent with the original Work, and with no requirement for inclusion of captions, credit, or source.

Once again, a case can be made for the potential marketing and outreach benefits to both the Author and Publisher, but if attribution and intellectual control are issues, they should be discussed and specified in the agreement.

- Merchandise and commercial rights: the right to create and sell products based upon, containing or using the text, illustrations, or photographs from the Work, other than those rights granted as digital database and companion rights.

Such boilerplate attempts to transfer any and all rights that have not been specifically included in the remaining contract or exhibits. Merchandise and Commercial activity has the potential to promote and generate revenue, but unless specifically outlined in the agreement, such uses can be overly broad and potentially problematic.

SUMMARY

For each issue related to use of visual materials in research and publication, there is a continuum of benefit and risk, from minimal at the one end to significant at the other. Publishers rightly want to minimize record-keeping and overheads that result from dozens of individual contracts with potentially varied permissions and requirements, and eliminate the need to track and obtain permission from the author for each new use. They also seek as much flexibility as possible to take advantage of new markets and distribution opportunities.

From the perspective of the Author, it is important to maintain the intellectual integrity of the work and its citations, credits, and interrelationships between images and text. The Author has responsibility to the sources and subjects that are incorporated into the Work. Releases and permissions to reproduce have been signed and the Author assures the Publisher that these rights and permissions are sufficient for the publication. It is incumbent on the Author to understand the commitments that they make during the creative process, and work with the Publisher to insure that as the contract is executed, it is done so responsibly.

NOTE

1 This chapter is based on my long experience collecting and publishing historic and current photographs. Laws governing ownership and use vary by, and within, nations and are in a constant state of flux due to changing technologies as well as changing political interpretations of those laws. It is intended as a broad overview and introduction to topics for consideration by authors; individual visual researchers should make sure they follow the laws and best practices in their individual.

Index

References such as "178–9" indicate (not necessarily continuous) discussion of a topic across a range of pages. Wherever possible in the case of topics with many references, these have either been divided into sub-topics or only the most significant discussions of the topic are listed. Because the entire work is about 'visual research methods' the use of this term (and certain others which occur constantly throughout the book) as an entry point has been minimized. Information will be found under the corresponding detailed topics.